KV-703-934

Parallel Imports

Parallel Imports

Warwick A. Rothnie

B.A., LL.B. (Hons) (Monash)
Ph.D. (London)
Barrister & Solicitor of the Supreme Court of Victoria

SOL LIBRARY

CLASS 341.758

AUTHOR ROT

BAR CODE -105386

Sweet & Maxwell
1993

AUSTRALIA
The Law Book Company Ltd
Sydney : Brisbane : Melbourne : Perth

CANADA
The Carswell Company Ltd
Agincourt, Ontario

INDIA
N.M. Tripathi Private Ltd
Calcutta and Delhi
and
M.P.P. House
Bangalore
and
Universal Book Traders
New Delhi

ISRAEL
Steimatzky's Agency Ltd
Jerusalem : Tel-Aviv : Haifa

PAKISTAN
Pakistan Law House
Karachi

© Warwick A. Rothnie 1993

All rights reserved.

No part of this publication may be reproduced or
transmitted, in any form or by any means, electronic
mechanical, photocopying, recording or otherwise,
stored in any retrieval system of any nature without
the written permission of the copyright holder
and the publisher, application for which shall be
made to the publisher.

Published in 1993 by Sweet & Maxwell
of 183 Marsh Wall, London E14 9FT
Typeset by The Midlands Book Typesetting Company, Loughborough
Printed in Great Britain by Short Run Press, Exeter

ISBN 0 421 473 606

Contents

List of Tables and Figures

Tables

Figures

ix

Table of Cases

European Court of Justice

Table of Legislation

Preface

Why 'Parallel Imports'? The first person who put that question to me directly was concerned to discover whether that label held a deliberate contrast to European usage, which refers to a doctrine of international exhaustion. I must confess that the answer is much more prosaic, at first glance: the legal system I trained and practised in only knew the issue as 'parallel imports'. Hence, I set out to examine the use of intellectual property rights to block the importation into one country of goods lawfully marketed in another.

But, did that accident of birth and education have significance? In late 1987, when I started on the research that led to this book, the Anglo-Commonwealth legal systems had reached at least three separate 'solutions' to parallel importing depending on whether copyright, patents or trade marks were the intellectual property rights at issue. (Fragmentation and diversity have increased since then!) The United States, having the 'benefits' of both the common law and doctrines of exhaustion, has fared little better. How had this happened? In contrast, the European Communities appeared to have developed a universal solution. Did 'international exhaustion' offer a simple, ready-made solution? These are two further issues this book seeks to explore.

Parallel imports also have a disturbing tendency to raise issues going to the very core of intellectual property protection. The central conflict of parallel imports – cheaper prices for consumers now *versus* incentives to invest in desirable economic and cultural activity – questions the very rationale of the intellectual property compromise. Looming fears of global 'monopolies' exploiting consumers in isolated, national markets force consideration of the apparent conflict between intellectual property and competition policies. The international system of intellectual property established in the 19th Century seems overrun by the speed of communications and the changing world trade order. In addition, as the Prices Surveillance Authority (whose reports into the effects of copyright law in Australia have stirred up such controversy) rightly recognised, simply classifying intellectual property as 'property' does not tell us much about the nature of that property. Hence, parallel imports clearly expose the possible tensions between the two functions of trade marks and force us to probe the scope and purpose of all intellectual property rights. These are exciting issues for the theoretician. But the law in the legal systems surveyed here is in such a state of flux that it is not simply enough for the practitioner to know where the latest case has brought 'the law'. The practitioner must also understand the intricacies of the theoretical issues if he or she is to serve the client's needs successfully.

In writing this book, I have been extremely fortunate to receive the support and assistance of many generous people. It is not possible to acknowledge my debt to all of them by name, indeed many offered their help only on the basis that it would remain 'off the record'. While none of them can be held responsible for the views I have expressed and many would certainly disagree with some or all of those views, I am very grateful to them all.

The book began as a Ph.D. thesis at Queen Mary and Westfield College, University of London, made possible by the grant of a Commonwealth Scholarship administered by the Association of Commonwealth Universities. Professor Gerald Dworkin, then head of the Intellectual Property Law Unit at Queen Mary, had the unenviable task of supervising and with never-ending patience endeavoured to get me to view the issue from different perspectives, to set the legal arguments in their economic context and to address the concerns of practitioners. To the extent that I have achieved any of these, the credit lies very much with him.

Not the least of my debts to Valentine Korah include introducing me to the complexities of competition policy through her famous courses at University College, London and then allowing me the priceless privilege of developing my understanding further through working with her on a number of books she was writing and taking part in many conferences she organised.

Ann Dufty and Professor Jim Lahore, with their lively commitment to practice, teaching and writing, sparked my interest in intellectual property and it is to them I owe the idea of studying parallel imports as a subject. Andrew Christie, Kirsti Rissanen, Brad Sherman and the examiners, Bill Cornish and Richard Whish, read and made thoughtful suggestions on some or all of the manuscript.

Dr Richard Nile and George Wei generously allowed me to read unpublished manuscripts of their own work and access to their primary source material on the copyright issue in, respectively, Australia and Singapore. Dr John C. Hilke, in addition to the article cited in the text, provided me with several reports generated for the US Federal Trade Commission. At a crucial stage of my research, Mr I.C. Harris, then Acting Clerk of the House of Representatives, took time from his duties to send me regular updates on the progress through Parliament of what became the Copyright Amendment Act 1991 (Cth).

Frances Thimann at Queen Mary's Intellectual Property Law Library and the library staff at the Institute of Advanced Legal Studies, London met my requests for seemingly esoteric publications with unfailing courtesy far beyond the call of duty. Leads and information which cannot be readily identified from the footnotes to the text were generously provided by Susan Blackwell of the Australian Book Publishing Association Ltd, Clive Bradley and Charles Clark at CICI, Louis-G. Brillant, Head of Circulation at the Library of Parliament Canada, Emmanuel Candi of the Australian Record Industry Association

Ltd, Gail Cork of the Australian Society of Authors Ltd, J.C. Giouw at IFPI (South East Asia) Ltd, Deborah Hurley at the OECD, Jim Keon, Director, Intellectual Property Review Branch of Consumer and Corporate Affairs Canada, Lori McDougall and Julian Rhodes at *Quill & Quire*, Penny Mountain of *The Bookseller*, Anne Murphy at the Canadian Book Publishing Council, David Payson of ADAPSO, Michael Redman at the Bill and Papers Office, Parliament House, Canberra and Derek Rossitter.

Nick Gingell at Sweet & Maxwell has been remarkably patient considering his author fled to the other side of the world. Wendy Hill, her production team and Gillian Andrews, the copy editor, have remained patient and courteous throughout.

Finally, the thesis on which this book is based was submitted in September 1991. The text as published has endeavoured to take into account developments up to June 1992 in Australia, Canada, the European Communities, the United Kingdom and the United States.

Warwick A. Rothnie
Mallesons Stephen Jaques
Melbourne, August 1992

Chapter 1: Introduction

For A$8.95, a large retail bookseller in Australia, Angus & Robertson, was offering copies of a range of cookery books for sale to the public there. At the same time, its competitors were selling at A$16.95 each. The competitors had their copies from the authorised Australian exclusive distributor. Angus & Robertson, however, had bought a shipment of 8,400 copies early in 1976 from a wholesaler in California. Five months later the books had arrived in Australia and Angus & Robertson was able to sell them at almost half price after paying for all transport costs, tariffs and other charges.[1]

That is the essence of a parallel import problem. 'Parallel imports' have two vital, distinguishing features. They are lawfully put on the market in the place of *export*, the foreign country. But, an owner of the intellectual property rights in the place of *importation*, the domestic country, opposes their importation (usually because the goods are sold in the two different countries at quite disparate prices) and, taking advantage of the lower price, some enterprising middleman buys stocks in the cheaper, foreign country and imports them into the dearer, domestic country. Hence, the imports may be described as being imported in 'parallel' to the authorised distribution network.[2]

Time-Life and two other cases usefully illustrate the nature of the problems parallel imports pose. In *Time-Life,* parallel importers could offer Australian consumers Time-Life's books at half the authorised distributor's price. But the High Court relied on copyright to bar the parallel imports and so protect Time-Life's separate, Australian property right. Despite the cheaper prices resulting from the parallel importer's activities, the act of transhipment

---

1 The facts are taken from *Interstate Parcel Express Co. Proprietary Limited v Time-Life International (Nederlands) BV* (1977) 138 CLR 534 ('the *Time-Life* case'); see Chapter 4 from Note 178 below.

2 Strictly speaking, the same person should own the intellectual property rights in both countries whether or not he exploits the market in both countries himself or does so in one or both through licensees or distributors. However, the term more generally describes situations where ownership in the domestic country and the foreign country has been split by contract between different undertakings which may or may not be linked by some form of corporate tie. American terminology introduces a third category, 're-imports', which were made by the domestic right owner and intended solely for export but have somehow found their way back on to the domestic market.

across the national frontier gave the copyright owner rights which it would not have domestically.

In *Cinzano,* a brand of vermouth was offered for sale in several different European countries under the same trade marks and trade dress.[3] In Germany, where the action was brought, the trade marks were held by a corporate subsidiary which imported, bottled and distributed 'Italian' Cinzano. In Spain, another corporate subsidiary undertook manufacture itself and an independent licensee made and sold the product in France. Although the right to use the trade mark in each country ultimately derived from the same source, the product marketed in each had different characteristics because it had been adapted to suit perceived differences in national tastes.

The Bundesgerichtshof held that a concept of international exhaustion governed German trade mark law.[4] Accordingly, from the point of view of German domestic trade mark law, the Cinzano product made and sold in Spain or France could be freely imported for sale in Germany. An unsuspecting German consumer may well have been surprised (at best) or confused when he or she sipped what was thought to be the usual 'German' product only to discover it was 'Spanish' or 'French' Cinzano. Of course, other factors may intervene to preclude the possibility of such consumer confusion. For example, German consumers may be aware, from travel abroad or long exposure on the domestic market, of the taste differences and consciously select the 'Spanish' or 'French' Cinzano ahead of 'German' Cinzano.[5] But, whether there be any confusion or deception is a question of fact. And if consumers are confused or deceived, considerable damage could be inflicted on both the value *and* function of the trade mark because consumers could not rely on it to indicate what they wanted to know.[6]

The third example extends the second. In the *Distillers Red Label* case, the European Commission condemned a dual pricing scheme which reduced the incentive for parallel imports from the United Kingdom to other Member States of the European Communities.[7] Apparently, the Commission hoped its action would force Distillers to bring its higher continental prices down to the level of the UK prices. Unfortunately, Distillers considered that the higher prices were necessary to compete effectively on the continent

---

3   Case I ZR 85/71 *Francesco Cinzano & Cie GmbH v Java Kaffeegeschäfte GmbH & Co.* [1974] 2 CMLR 21 (Bundesgerichtshof).

4   Broadly, in the trade mark context, this concept holds that where a trade mark correctly identifies the *ultimate* source of a product, its use is not misleading. See further, text at Note 18 below and following.

5   See for example *Champagne Heidsieck et cie Monopole Société Anonyme v Buxton* [1930] 1 Ch. 330 at Chapter 2, Note 35 below. As in the *Champagne Heidsieck* case, the Bundesgerichtshof does note that both French and Spanish bottles bore labels around their necks proclaiming their French or Spanish origin.

6   For a particularly potent example, see *Colgate-Palmolive Limited v Markwell Finance Limited* [1989] RPC 497 (CA), Chapter 2.2.3(b) below.

7   OJ 1978 L50/16, [1978] CMLR 400; on appeal Case 30/78 *Distillers Company Limited v Commission* [1980] ECR 2229. The provisions of the EEC Treaty affecting parallel imports are discussed in Chapters 6 and 7 below.

because special advertising and promotional efforts were essential in the face of competition from traditional products already established there, national prejudices and discriminatory tax treatment.[8] So, instead, Distillers, precluded from raising its UK prices, withdrew the product in question from the UK market altogether.[9]

These examples cast the tensions underlying the parallel import question into relief. Of prime importance, parallel imports seemingly cause two interests, those of intellectual property owners and those of consumers, to clash. As *Time-Life* shows, the presence or absence of parallel imports can have a dramatic impact. They directly affect the price consumers in the domestic market are asked to pay.[10]

While this must seemingly be in the consumers' interest, the other examples suggest that this may only be a short-term view. The *Cinzano* case suggests a link between consumer confusion (in itself against consumers' interest) and the value of trade mark rights to their holders in separate national markets. It was to protect the valuable investment made by the trade mark owner that the US Supreme Court barred parallel imports in the *Katzel* case.[11] Similar issues underlie, and are sometimes acknowledged, in both patent and copyright law.[12] The *Distillers Red Label* case also raises a potentially murkier aspect, although there the motivation seems to have been justifiable. Intellectual property owners have plenty of scope for freedom of action and are seldom forced to act completely contrary to their own interests. Parallel imports, or their threat, may lead to a product desired by consumers becoming unavailable on the market. Hence, consumers who would value it are not as well off as they could be. Where any of these considerations apply, destabilising, short-term interests may prevent desirable, long-term goals being achieved. Reconciling the apparent conflict between consumers' short-term interests and the longer term interests supporting intellectual property rights may involve complicated trade-offs.

As the three illustrations show, the issues underlying the parallel import phenomenon are economic in nature. Yet, the solutions proposed by the law

8   Ivo Van Bael, 'Heretical Reflections on the Basic Dogma of EEC Antitrust: Single Market Integration', 10 *Swiss Review of International Competition Law* 39 (1980), at 47 to 48 and 47, Note 15.

9   Following the Advocate-General's severe criticism when the case went on appeal, the Commission subsequently permitted Distillers to maintain a limited price differential for one product during a transitional period: [1983] 3 CMLR 173.

10   For more detailed consideration of the book pricing issue in Australia, see Chapter 10 below. For the tension between intellectual property and consumers' interests, see David Gladwell, 'The Exhaustion of Intellectual Property Rights', [1986] EIPR 366.

11   *A. Bourjois & Company Inc. v Katzel* 260 US 689 (1923) *revg* 275 Fed. 539 (2d Cir. 1921) *revg* 274 Fed. 856 (SDNY). See further, Chapter 2.3.3 below.

12   In copyright, see for example the *Time-Life* case and *Barson Computers (N.Z.) Ltd v John Gilbert & Co. Ltd* [1985] FSR 489, but contrast *Sebastian International Inc. v Consumer Contacts (PTY) Ltd* 7 USPQ 2d 1077(3d Cir. 1988) *revg* 664 F. Supp. 909 (DNJ 1987); in Chapter 4 from Notes 178, 149 and 408, respectively. In patents, see for example *Griffin v Keystone Mushroom Farm Inc*. 453 F. Supp. 1243 (ED Pa. 1978), Chapter 3 from Note 277.

and of many, but not all, legal commentators often seem quite divorced from such 'non-legal' considerations.[13]

As the succeeding chapters will discuss, the typical approach is to examine whether a power to block parallel imports can be found in the bundle of rights granted by the particular form of intellectual property in question. At a further level of abstraction, this approach calls into play (often unstated) contradictory assumptions which may be described as the 'principle of territoriality' and the 'principle of universality'.[14] Under the former, the circumstances of marketing in the foreign country are simply ignored. The only relevant question is whether the domestic right holder has authorised the sale of the specific goods in question within the domestic territory and no inferences at all are drawn from the fact that the domestic owner authorised their sale elsewhere.[15]

On the other hand, inferences from sale abroad are drawn under the principle of universality. The simplest step is just to imply consent to domestic marketing from the domestic owner's consent to marketing (whether directly itself or indirectly through third parties) in the foreign country.[16] The obvious difficulty with this course is that consent *implied* from such circumstances may be rebutted quite easily.[17] Long-standing recognition of the shortcomings in relying on implied consent led to the formulation of a principle or doctrine of 'international exhaustion'. In broad terms, this holds that intellectual property rights do not confer power to block imports of products embodying the intellectual property provided they were first released on to a market under the authority of the domestic intellectual property owner. As *Cinzano* shows, authority may be inferred whenever the domestic and foreign rights can be traced back to the same ultimate source by contract (whether assignment or licence) or corporate link. In other words, the territorial complication is simply ignored if the required relationship between release on the foreign and domestic markets is satisfied.[18]

---

13   For a particularly 'good' example, see the debate over the identity of the 'hypothetical manufacturer' under the UK and South African copyright legislation, Chapter 4.2.2(b) below.

14   Although both terms are taken from Friedrich-Karl Beier, 'Territoriality of Trade Mark Law and International Trade', 1 IIC 48 (1970), the interpretation offered here does not correspond to that learned author's usage.

15   Apart from the *Time-Life* case, further examples of this approach can be seen in *Pitt Pitts* (Chapter 4, Note 46), *Tilghman's* case (Chapter 3 Note 81), *Sanofi S.A. v Med-Tech Veterinarian Products Ltd* (Chapter 3 Note 280) and the *Colgate* case.

16   For examples, *Betts v Willmott* (Chapter 3 Note 76); the *Charmdale* case (Chapter 4 Note 107); and the *Champagne Heidsieck* case (Chapter 2.2.2(b)).

17   *Smith Kline & French Laboratories Ltd v Salim (Malaysia) Sdn Bhd* [1989] FSR 407, Chapter 3 Note 120.

18   There are, of course, many qualifications on the doctrine thus broadly stated. EC law, as distinct from Member States' laws, has to date applied the doctrine as a matter of principle under the EEC Treaty rather than as a manifestation of national intellectual property law. The nature of the required link between foreign and domestic markets may differ quite substantially under US law when compared to European legal systems. For the United States, see especially Chapters 3.3.2 and 4.3.3; for the European Communities and Germany, compare Beier, 'Territoriality of Trade Mark Law', at 48; Ulrich Schatz, 'The Exhaustion of Patent Rights in the Common Market', 2 IIC 1 (1971); Stephen P. Ladas, 'Exclusive Territorial Licences Under Parallel Patents', 3 IIC 335 (1972).

Although offered as solutions to the parallel import phenomenon, both the principle of territoriality and the doctrine of international exhaustion are really conclusions rather than determining premises. Each depends on underlying assumptions drawn from different views of the world and each entails important problems.

Territoriality focuses on the division of the world, in terms of law, custom, language and commerce, into nation states. However, the simple conflictual rule embodied in the principle of territoriality does not *necessarily* preclude national law from having regard to actions outside its jurisdictional scope. Indeed, intellectual property laws often have recourse to such extra-jurisdictional facts.[19]

Application of a strict principle of territoriality also seems to overlook the international character of much trade which the doctrine of international exhaustion emphasises. Sophisticated Sydney-siders have ready access to the latest magazines and television broadcasts from London or New York. Understandably, they want access to the products advertised in them. Moreover, the production and sale of many products protected by intellectual property is often carried out by large transnational conglomerates. There is more than some danger that firms engaging in international trade will seek to manipulate the isolation of national markets by intellectual property rights for their own ends rather than for purposes which intellectual property seeks to promote.

However, the doctrine of international exhaustion is also fraught with difficulty. The first hurdle lies in establishing a coherent basis for the doctrine. In German law, for example, the doctrine applies to trade marks but not other intellectual property subject-matter.[20] This difference is founded on the supposedly different nature of the various intellectual property rights. Patents, for example, are said to confer control over marketing while trade marks do not.[21] While such a conclusion may be an accurate statement of German law, it is not necessarily so of other legal systems. There is also an element of tautology in declaring that a trade mark, say, cannot be used to block parallel imports because it confers no power to control distribution when, at least in the common law world, the authority for the first proposition is often a parallel import case.[22] Moreover, if German consumers were unpleasantly surprised to discover that they had mistakenly bought 'Spanish' Cinzano for 'German' Cinzano, the consequences of

19   Beier, 'Territoriality of Trade Mark Law', at 58 to 61. For example, the act of publishing an original work in a country party to the Berne Convention confers protection in all other signatories of the Convention: see for example Stephen M. Stewart, *International Copyright and Neighbouring Rights*, Butterworths 1989 (2nd ed.), §3.27.

20   Contrast: *Cinzano* (trade mark); *Tylosin* BGH 3 June 1976 [1976] GRUR 519, 8 IIC 64 (1977) (patent); German Copyright Act section 17 noted in Friedrich-Karl Beier, 'Industrial Property and the Free Movement of Goods in the Internal European Market', 21 IIC 131, at 158, Note 74 (1990).

21   See for example Beier, 'Territoriality of Trade Mark Law', especially at 71; Ladas, 'Exclusive Territorial Licences Under Parallel Patents', at 345 to 346.

22   See for example the *Champagne Heidsieck* case and *Apollinaris v Scherer* 22 Fed. 18 (SDNY 1886), Chapter 2.2.2(b) and 2.3.2 below, respectively.

adopting a doctrine of international exhaustion for trade marks may be fundamentally at odds with the very purpose of according protection to trade marks in the first place; a point highlighted by the *Colgate* case considered in Chapter 2.

Those who contend for a doctrine of international exhaustion do not necessarily deny the validity of protecting consumers against such deceptions. They do, however, argue that it is not the function of trade marks. Instead, it has been suggested that the interests at stake should be protected by contract and laws against unfair competition and general tortious liability.[23] Whether these alternatives be adequate or suitable is a point to be considered.

An alternative theory underpinning the doctrine of international exhuastion applies more generally, perhaps, to all intellectual property rights. It argues that if the product was released in the foreign country under a parallel and equivalent right to that claimed in the domestic country, the domestic intellectual property owner will suffer no prejudice from parallel importation because the foreign rights afforded power to protect the owner's interests.[24] So, for example, if there are parallel patents, a patentee should reap the quasi-rent inherent in the patent grant whichever country is chosen.

Cinzano, where the same trade mark was used in different countries for products of different quality, offers a suggestion that the simple existence of parallel rights does not necessarily provide a solution. The *Distillers Red Label* case carries the example further since there the product was the same but the circumstances of one market entailed different consequences. The succeeding chapters will furnish further illustrations covering all intellectual property rights including quite marked differences in the content of the rights granted.[25] The real world inhabited by business and consumers does indeed show many tendencies towards internationalisation and universality. Unfortunately, it is not, like a vacuum in physics, a friction-free environment for trade. There are many real differences and 'imperfections' between national markets. It will be necessary to explore the consequences of ignoring them.

At a symposium on anti-trust law, a trial lawyer rebutted an earlier speaker's exposition of the 'new' thinking on 'vertical restraints' in distribution with the point that this science was all very well in theory, but how could anyone seriously expect him to persuade a judge and jury that paying higher prices was better for them.[26] How indeed; particularly, if the judge and jury are

23   See for example Beier, 'Territoriality of Trade Mark Law', at 63 to 65, and 72.

24   See for example Paul Demaret, *Patents, Territorial Restrictions and EEC Law*, Verlag-Chemie 1978, especially Chapters 3 and 4 and see Chapters 6 and 7 below for further consideration in the context of the European Communities.

25   Beier, although arguing for a different conclusion, indicates the considerable pitfalls in engaging on a comparison of the equivalence of the parallel rights: Beier, 'Industrial Property and the Free Movement of Goods in the Internal European Market', 21 IIC 131, at 154 to 155 (1990).

26   See John de Q. Briggs, 'Comments', *56 Antitrust LJ* 37 (1987). 'Vertical restraints' relate to the contractual dealings between different levels of the production and distribution of a good such as producer and wholesaler or wholesaler and retailer. Contrast dealings between competitors at the same level, say, rival producers or retailers of the same product which are horizontal.

popular opinion and popular opinion is persuaded that the higher prices result from exploitation by the former colonial power?[27]

The anecdote takes us back to the basic point about parallel imports revealed by the *Time-Life* case. Regardless of the intellectual property right (and its particular function) involved, parallel imports are about cheaper prices and economic issues. Opposed views of the world are in collision.

Ordinarily, making the same good available at a lower price is a highly desirable goal in a properly functioning market economy. It may signal that more producers of a good are being attracted into the industry by rents which established producers are earning.[28] As more and more producers enter the industry and seek customers, their competition should force prices lower. The rents which attracted them initially are being competed away and the quantity of the good supplied to the market is being increased in line with consumer preferences. This, in itself, is desirable because it means productive resources are being shifted from uses less highly valued by consumers to those more highly valued. A fall in prices may also reflect a fall in costs as some producers seek to increase their profits by searching for even more efficient ways to make and supply the good. Of course, if they are successful, their rents spur their rivals to strive for similar economies or attract new entrants. Thus, reductions in prices serve as a continuing discipline to producers and may free some resources for alternative uses.[29]

Hence, parallel imports appear to offer the prospect of improving the functioning of the domestic economy and intellectual property owners' attempts to block parallel imports suggest that they are trying to evade the rigorous disciplines of the market. That is the danger of excluding parallel imports.

But, there may also be welfare-enhancing justifications for blocking parallel imports. So, if parallel imports be allowed, there are also risks. The *Cinzano* example illustrates one risk particular to trade marks. A more general consideration lies in the paradox generally attributed to Telser.[30]

It should be counter-productive for a producer to seek to maintain prices much above marginal cost in a competitive market. If successful, the outcome should be reduced output as consumers switch to substitute products. Moreover, any rents accruing from the higher price would be pocketed by the distributors rather than the producer. Not only is the producer foregoing the extra revenue from selling larger quantities of its product, but any benefit of its effort goes to other businesses. In a competitive market, it is argued,

---

27 See for example the problem of book prices in Australia discussed in Chapter 10 below.

28 'Rent' here refers to the difference between the price of the good charged on the market and the marginal cost of producing the last unit of the good sold at that price.

29 For a vivid rendering, see Robert Heilbroner, *The Worldly Philosophers*, Pelican, 1983 (5th edn), Chapter 3. For a more technical exposition also surveying the complications, see F.M. Scherer and David Ross, *Industrial Market Structure and Economic Performance*, Houghton Mifflin, 1990 (3rd edn), Chapter 2.

30 Lester G. Telser, 'Why Should Manufacturers Want Fair Trade?' 3 JL&Econ. 86 (1960).

the most likely explanation for this apparently irrational behaviour is that the producer is trying to buy services from its distributors which it thinks its customers desire and which might be more costly to provide in another fashion. The *Distillers Red Label* case illustrates this.[31] Distillers' continental distributors required higher prices to fund heavier advertising and other promotional efforts. Some of its UK distributors were able to take advantage of these efforts without incurring the cost. The consequence of the free riding by UK distributors was a reduction in necessary promotional efforts by the continental distributors whose markets were being undermined.

The provision of an economic incentive for the trade mark owner to invest in competitive activity evokes a corresponding thread in patents, copyright and other exclusive rights over creative activity. Among the several explanations for patent and copyright systems, it is often argued that there is a risk that inventors, authors and other creators will be discouraged from their desirable activities through lack of sufficient incentive because it is often easier to copy something once someone else has produced it and there will also be less commercial risk involved.[32] Accordingly, intellectual property owners are granted exclusive rights to give them some measure of control over the ability of others to take advantage of their efforts. Whether providing that stimulus also requires inclusion of power to block parallel imports is the point for inquiry. Consideration of the consequences for the Australian market for books of the *Time-Life* case and the general question of domestic price levels suggests a link between these rights and justifications like that for *Distillers Red Label* and *Cinzano*.[33]

The interplay of all these forces forms the context of any attempt to study the issue of parallel imports. Overall, two general questions arise: first, can the authorised sellers in the domestic country use intellectual property rights to block parallel imports; and second, should they be able to? Of necessity, considerations affecting the second must arise in any attempt to deal with the first critically.

The existing international regime does not provide much guidance in the present context. Neither the Berne Convention nor the Paris Convention make explicit provision about parallel imports, leaving signatories largely free to determine their own national policies. This may be affected by the negotiations to include trade in products embodying intellectual property in the GATT framework. In the present state of negotiations over the Chairman's composite draft, Article 6 would allow each signatory freedom to adopt a doctrine of exhaustion or not.[34] An earlier area of controversy,

---

31   See also Chapter 7.3.2(b) below.
32   This and the other explanations are returned to in Chapters 3.1, 4.1 and 10.2.3 below.
33   Compare also *Fender Australia Pty Ltd v Bevk* (1989) 15 IPR 257 (Chapter 2 Note 142 below) and for domestic price levels, see Chapters 10 and 9 below.
34   See draft *Agreement on Trade-related Aspects of Intellectual Property Rights, Including Trade in Counterfeit Goods* (Annex III), MTN.TNC/W/FA, 20 December 1991 at 57 onward. For comment on earlier drafts, see Clive Bradley, 'Market Rights: When Does Importation Infringe?', (1991) 5 *Rights* 1, 2–3; Jörg Reinbothe and Anthony Howard, 'The State of Play in the Negotiations on Trips (GATT/Uruguay Round)',

the provisions dealing with abusive practices, has now been modified somewhat:[35] contracting parties retain the right to proscribe licensing practices or conditions which '*may in particular cases* constitute an abuse of intellectual property rights having an adverse effect on competition in the relevant market'. The non-exhaustive list of examples of such practices is: exclusive grantback conditions, no-challenge clauses and coercive package licensing.[36] Articles 40(3) and (4) provides for consultation and discussions between contracting parties where one believes that a national or domicile of the other is violating such laws. The party consulted is required to 'accord full and sympathetic consideration to' the consultations and supply to the other, at the least, publicly available non-confidential information.[37] Although there is no doubt potential for disagreement about what are 'particular cases', how they may be catered for and the practices potentially to be proscribed, the position under Article 40 now corresponds to that under Article 6 in that individual contracting parties appear to be left to determine their own national policies. At the time of writing, negotiations on the Uruguay Round have reached an impasse principally over issues relating to trade in agricultural products.

In Chapters 2 to 5, the efforts of the common law jurisdictions to cope with parallel imports are analysed. Chapters 6 and 7 turn to the rules of the European Communities. EC law forms part of the law of the United Kingdom, traditionally one of the two main bodies of the common law. EC law has also seen one of the more vigorous attempts to enforce a doctrine of international exhaustion confined to trade between the several Member States. At a period when that doctrine is becoming increasingly qualified in parts, the European Communities' experience provides a useful laboratory for assessing the doctrine's benefits and costs. An attempt to flesh out the legal analysis with consideration of some economic data and case studies is made in Chapters 8 to 11 before the threads are drawn together and conclusions essayed.

[1991] EIPR 157, 159–60. In an earlier draft, interestingly, the United States would have made 'territoriality' mandatory for *at the least* copyright in computer programs while a group of 14 so-called 'less developed countries' (LDCs) would have made international exhaustion the rule for, at least, trade-marked products: see MTN.GNG/NG11/W/70, 11 May 1990, Article 2(2)(b) and MTN.GNG/NG11/W/71, 14 May 1990, Article 7(2), respectively.

35 *Ibid.* Article 40; in an earlier guise, reportedly one of the factors precluding final agreement: see Reinbothe and Howard, 'The State of Play in the Negotiations on trips (GATT/Uruguay Round),' at 160.

36 *Ibid.* Article 40(2). Contrast the list under the text, *Status of Work in Negotiating Group*, 25 October 1990 which, at Article 42(3) included exclusive licensing and controls on imports and exports.

37 Contrast the treatment of the Brazilian law on intellectual property licensing in the *Colgate* case, Chapter 2.2.3(b), below.

Chapter 2: Trade Marks

2.1 Introduction

In 1921 Judge Hough of the US Second Circuit delivered a powerful dissent to his brothers' ruling that a trade mark symbolised production source to the exclusion of all else:

> It is not yet settled whether a trade-mark is to be primarily regarded as protecting the trade-mark owner's business from a species of unfair competition, or protecting the public from imitations.
>
> The decision in this case seems to me to lean the wrong way, because in my opinion a trade-mark is primarily a protection to the owner's business. . . . whatever rights the French manufacturer had in the United States became the rights of the plaintiff. If, therefore, the primary function of the trade-mark is to protect this plaintiff's business in his own country, it makes no difference at all that the genuine French article is the thing offered by defendant. The genuine article has become an infringement because the business of dealing in that article has become the plaintiff's business.[1]

Thus encouraged, the plaintiff successfully appealed to the Supreme Court.[2] In those pungent paragraphs Judge Hough captured the dilemma posed by parallel imports: what is the function of trade marks; what interests does the law intend them to protect?

From one point of view, a trade mark is an instrument of consumer protection. It provides information and reduces search costs. It allows consumers to identify the goods of one trader from those of another. Unscrupulous merchants cannot trick consumers into buying their bootlegged firewater under the guise of selling them 'Johnny Walker's Red Label Whisky'. From another point of view however, the trade mark may represent a valuable property right. Johnny Walker, say, may have invested considerable resources in selecting only the best quality ingredients, setting up a distillery using only state of the art practices, keeping it scrupulously clean and allowing on to the market only whisky having a consistent quality. The trade mark allows him to compete with other traders in whisky and may symbolise the value of his investment in maintaining a certain quality for his whisky. If the trade mark owner could not stop others from using the mark

---

1 *A. Bourjois & Company Inc. v Katzel* 275 Fed. 539, at 543 to 544 (1921).
2 260 US 290 (1923). The case is considered further at section 2.3.3 below.

without authorisation, there would be no incentive to invest in these kinds of activity.[3]

Ordinarily, the two interests do not conflict. Treating the domestic market in isolation, once our Johnny Walker puts his Red Label Whisky on to the market, his interest in protecting the message sent out by his trade mark and the consumers' interest in not being deceived are in harmony. But, introducing the possibility of international trade may increase the likelihood that this will not always be so. As in the *Katzel* case, the producer may not have sufficient resources to exploit the domestic market effectively from its foreign base and the goodwill may come to represent the value of the investment made by the 'agent' in developing and maintaining that market in addition to the producer's investment in making the physical good. In such circumstances, the property interest in the trade mark and the interest in consumer protection may diverge.[4] If so (and presupposing the law even recognises the difference), when trade mark rights are asserted against 'unauthorised' imports, the solution the law reaches may depend on which interest it regards as the more fundamental.[5]

In the tail end of Judge Hough's dissent lies the suspicion of a further concern. His Honour refers to 'the business of dealing in that article' as becoming 'the plaintiff's business'. In context, Judge Hough was referring to a business of dealing in a certain kind of face powder under a particular trade mark. He was not contemplating that the plaintiff there might have a monopoly over all face powders. However, long before Senator Sherman, common lawyers felt a strong antipathy towards monopolies.[6] Consequently, judges have looked askance on what appear to be traders' attempts to establish monopolies in 'articles'.

Hostility towards monopolies in domestic trade was perhaps one trait shared by both major systems of the common law world. Their laws dealing

---

3   See Nicholas Economides, 'The Economics of Trademarks', 78 TMR 523 (1988); W.R. Cornish and Jennifer Phillips, 'The Economic Function of Trade Marks: An Analysis with Special Reference to Developing Countries', (1982) 13 IIC 41; C.W.F. Baden Fuller, 'Economic Issues Relating to Property Rights in Trademarks: Export Bans, Differential Pricing, Restrictions on Resale and Repackaging', (1981) 6 ELRev. 162; W.R. Cornish, *Intellectual Property: Patents, Copyright, Trade Marks and Allied Rights*, Sweet & Maxwell, 1989 (2nd edn), ¶¶15-013–17; R.R. Officer, *Parallel Imports: An Economic Perspective*, paper presented to the First National Conference of the Intellectual and Industrial Property Society, Canberra, 24 May 1987; William M. Landes and Richard A. Posner, 'Trademark Law: An Economic Perspective', 30 JLE 265 (1987). On the tangled complications product differentiation may cause for the competitive process, see F.M. Scherer and David Ross, *Industrial Market Structure and Economic Performance*, Houghton Mifflin, 1990 (3rd edn), Chapter 16.

4   Of course, if we introduce differences between the foreign product and the domestic product (as suggested in the *Cinzano* illustration in Chapter 1), the two interests may not diverge.

5   Similar arguments have not been wanting in the case of purely domestic trade: for a seminal exploration, see Zechariah Chafee Jr, 'Equitable Servitudes on Chattels', 41 Harv. LRev. 945 (1928). However, there is much greater prospect of divergences in language, cultural and commercial conditions and the claims of commercial convenience are much less pronounced in international trade. For the supra-national EC experiment, see Chapters 6 and 7 below.

6   See for example the famous case of *Darcy v Allein* (1602) 11 Co. Rep. 84b, Moore KB 671, 74 ER 1131.

with trade marks in domestic trade may also be traced back to the case of
J.G. v Samford which exposed the ambivalence of the common law judges
to trade marks.[7] The action was brought by a clothier who had built up a
solid reputation for selling cloth of good quality under a particular mark,
the letters 'J.G.' (or 'J.S.', it is not clear) with a device called a tucker's
handle. Samford was a rival who made much inferior cloth and used the same
mark. Anderson CJ and Wyndham J considered the plaintiff should have a
remedy, but Peryam and Mead JJ thought no action lay.

Dodderidge J's comments in *Southern v How* and *Dean v Steel* suggest
that the common law judges were by then recognising a right to relief.
However, it seems that the judges proceeded on the ground that *J.G.
v Samford* was a case of deceit rather than defamation and so it was
not until 1838 that the requirement of proving some form of fraudulent
conduct on the part of the defendant was overcome.[8] The limited notion of
passing off at law in possible contrast to equity is perhaps the key to Lord
Cranworth's formulation, in a judgment which has played a crucial role in
the development of Anglo-Commonwealth trade mark law, of a trade mark
as embodying:

> . . . the right which any person designating his wares or commodities by a
> particular trade mark, as it is called, has to prevent others from selling
> wares which are not his marked with that trade mark *in order to mislead
> the public and so incidentally to injure the person who is owner of the trade
> mark. (Emphasis added)*[9]

Hence, in his Lordship's view, the dominant purpose of a trade mark was to
protect the public against deception about a branded good's source. Passing
off was subsequently extended to protect against misrepresentations about
the class or quality of goods (or services) in addition to misrepresentations
about their trade source.[10] However, the courts and commentators have for
long put off exploring the ramifications.[11]

---

7 (1584) translated in J.H. Baker and S.F.C. Milsom, *Sources of English Legal History*,
Butterworths, 1986, at 615 to 618. The case was for long known only through two
references by Dodderidge J, first, in *Southern v How* (1618) Popham 143; 79 ER 1243;
Cro. Jac. 469; 79 ER 400; 2 Rolle 5, at 26; 81 ER 621, at 635; Bridge J 125; 123
ER 1248 and, second, in *Dean v Steel* (1626) Latch 188; 82 ER 339. *Southern v How*
increased the complications since the reports differed over whether the plaintiff was the
defendant's customer or rival clothier. In *Dean v Steel*, apparently a case of defamation
which is reported in law french, Morison indicates that Dodderidge J made it plain the
plaintiff was the rival clothier, see W.L. Morison, 'Unfair Competition and "Passing
Off"', (1956) 2 Syd.LRev. 50, at 54 confirmed by Baker's translation; see also J.H.
Baker, *Introduction to British Legal History*, Butterworths, 1986 (2nd ed.), at 522.
8 See Morison, 'Unfair Competition and "Passing Off"', citing *Millington v Fox* (1838)
3 My. & Cr. 338.
9 *Farina v Silverlock* (1856) 6 De G.M. & G. 214, at 217; 43 ER 1214, at 1216.
Although a statement at common law, it was taken as describing the function of a
registered trade mark, see *Champagne Heidsieck v Buxton*, below from Note 35.
10 See in particular, *A.G. Spalding & Bros v A.W. Gamage Ltd* (1915) 32 RPC 273,
at 284 *per* Lord Parker of Waddington.
11 For a critical discussion see Morison, 'Unfair Competition and "Passing Off"', at
50 and for 'recent' extensions of the doctrine, see Suman Naresh, 'Passing-off, Goodwill
and False Advertising: New Wine in Old Bottles', [1986] CLJ 97.

But, in the United States, the legal approach would seem to have been more ready to accord significance to the trade mark owner's investment *as well as* protection of the public from deception. It was not, however, necessarily recognised that the two interests might conflict.[12]

Accordingly, apart from the competing theories of territoriality and universality canvassed in Chapter 1, any attempt to explore how the common law world copes with parallel imports under trade mark law must also involve consideration of these issues.

2.2 Anglo-Commonwealth Law

2.2.1 Introduction

Although the tension between the 'territoriality' principle and 'universality' has been readily apparent in many cases, judicial references in the jurisdictions following the Anglo-Commonwealth tradition are of comparatively recent origin.[13] Instead, the question of whether intellectual property owners, and their surrogates, could block parallel imports by relying on rights to trade marks has usually played itself out in more formal, legalistic terms. At the heart of this approach has lain the issue of the nature and function of the right asserted.

Where a trade mark or name has been relied on in an Anglo-Commonwealth jurisdiction, the two principal causes of action lie at common law in passing off or under statute for infringement of a registered trade mark. In essence, registration of a trade mark confers on the registered proprietor the exclusive right to use the trade mark for the purpose of indicating a connection in the course of trade with the goods (or services) covered by the registration.[14] In some jurisdictions, however, a registered trade mark also confers broader rights to prevent unauthorised use other than as a trade mark.[15] Hence,

---

12 See the survey in Timothy Hiebert, 'The Foundations of the Law of Parallel Importation: Duality and Universality in Nineteenth Century Trademark Law', 80 TMR 483, at 484 to 491. For the same issue in the European Communities, see *Hag II* (Chapter 6 from Note 220) and Warwick A. Rothnie, '*Hag II*: Putting the Common Origin Doctrine to Sleep', [1991] EIPR 24.

13 See, in particular, the explicit reference to territorial limitation in *Colgate-Palmolive Limited v Markwell Finance Limited* [1989] RPC 497, at 553 *per* Lloyd LJ.

14 Trade Marks Act 1938 (United Kingdom) section 4(1); Trade Marks Act 1955 (Cth) sections 58 and 62; Trade Marks Act 1953 (New Zealand) section 8(1); Trade Marks Act, 62 of 1963 (South Africa) section 44; Trade-marks Act, RSC 1985, Chapter T-13, section 19; see generally, T.A. Blanco-White and Robin Jacob, *Kerly's Law of Trade Marks and Trade Names*, Sweet and Maxwell, 1986 (2nd ed.), Chapters 2, 14 and 15; D.R. Shanahan, *Australian Trade Mark Law and Practice*, The Law Book Company, 1982, Chapter 2 at 18.

15 For example, Trade Marks Act 1938 (United Kingdom) section 4(1)(b) considered in *Bismag Ltd v Amblins (Chemists) Ltd* (1940) 57 RPC 209 (CA); the UK Government plans to amend the provision so that it restrains 'use in advertising which is contrary to honest practices in industrial or commercial mattters and would take unfair advantage of or be detrimental to the distinctive character or repute of the trade mark', see Department of Trade and Industry, *Reform of Trade Marks Law*, Cm 1203, HMSO, 1990, at ¶3.28; *Montana Wines Ltd v Villa Maria Wines Ltd* [1985] RPC 412 (CA NZ);

among other things, the exclusive right is infringed by an unauthorised use as a trade mark of the same, or a similar, trade mark which is likely to deceive or cause confusion in the course of trade.[16]

Passing off, on the other hand, arises independently of statute.[17] It provides protection for a trader's proprietary interest in the goodwill generated in a market by his business activities in association with a name, mark or get-up. The common law provides protection against damage, or the likelihood of damage, to that goodwill by another's actions which may confuse or deceive someone relying on that goodwill.[18]

Within this context, the central issue raised by parallel imports is the nature of the link indicated to the relevant (domestic) public by use of the mark on the imported products. For a registered trade mark, this resolves itself into a question of what is the connection in the course of trade indicated by the presence of the mark on the parallel imports. In Anglo-Commonwealth jurisdictions,[19] this has historically been answered by reference to the function of a trade mark as indicating 'the source' of the product which, in turn, has largely depended on early formulations of the rights conferred by an action in passing off.[20]

Initially, passing off lay against someone who suggested that his own goods, or services, were those of another by using a name, mark or get-up associated with that other. Hence, as already noted, Lord Cranworth LC spoke of:

> . . . the right which any person designating his wares or commodities by a particular trade mark, as it is called, has to prevent others from selling wares which are not his marked with that trade mark *in order to mislead the public and so incidentally to injure the person who is owner of the trade mark. (Emphasis added)*[21]

Since, at least, 1915 passing off has also protected against misrepresentations about the class or quality of goods, or services, in addition to misrepresentations about the trade source of the goods or services.[22] So

Trade Marks Act, 62 of 1963 (South Africa) section 44(1)(b) considered in *Protective Mining & Industrial Equipment Systems (Pty) Ltd v Audiolens (Cape)(Pty) Ltd* 1987(2) 961 (AD); and note the 'anti-dilution' provision in Trade-marks Act, RSC 1985, Chapter T-13, section 22.

16 See generally, *Kerly's Law of Trade Marks*, Chapter 14; Shanahan, *Australian Trade Mark Law*, Chapter 18.

17 In some jurisdictions, statutory rights similar to passing off have also been enacted; for example Trade Practices Act 1974 (Cth) section 52.

18 Staniforth Ricketson, *The Law of Intellectual Property*, Law Book Company, 1984, at 532 to 535. For a critical discussion, see Morison, 'Unfair Competition and "Passing Off" ', at 50 and Naresh, 'Passing-off, Goodwill and False Advertising', at 97.

19 A similar approach can be seen in one line of US cases, see Chapter 2.3 below and in German jurisprudence, see *Cinzano* [1974] 2 CMLR 21.

20 See *Champagne Heidsieck et Cie Monopole SA v Buxton* [1930] 1 Ch. 330; 47 RPC 28 discussed below, from Note 35.

21 *Farina v Silverlock* (1856) 6 De G.M. & G. 214 at 217; 43 ER 1214, at 1216.

22 *A.G. Spalding & Bros v A.W. Gamage Ltd* (1915) 32 RPC 273, at 284 *per* Lord Parker of Waddington. For consideration of the history of the litigation and the Court of Appeal's determination of the rehearing, see Morison, 'Unfair Competition and "Passing Off" ', at 56 to 57 and for the meaning of 'his wares' at 58 to 59.

that, it seems, the action is now broadly based on the presence of five factors: (1) a misrepresentation; (2) made by a trader in the course of trade; (3) to prospective customers of his or ultimate consumers of goods or services supplied by him; (4) which is calculated to injure the business or goodwill of another trader (in the sense that this is a reasonably foreseeable consequence); and (5) which causes actual damage to a business or goodwill of the trader by whom the action is brought or (in a *quia timet* action) will probably do so.[23]

It was following the initial development of passing off, but prior to the tort's extension in *Spalding v Gamage*, that the UK Parliament enacted the first statute for the registration of trade marks.[24]

2.2.2 Early principles

Anglo-Commonwealth courts have not adopted a simple, strictly territorial approach. Instead, they have sometimes looked to the presumed function of a trade mark as a means of ignoring territorial limitations of the trade mark grant. Three cases, two involving section 39 of the Trade Marks Act 1905 (United Kingdom), taken together expose the law's uncertain approach. None of the three, however, was the first consideration by Anglo-Commonwealth courts of the use of trade marks against parallel imports. Two earlier cases, largely overlooked since the passage of the Trade Marks Act 1938 (United Kingdom) and not referred to in any of the three later cases, are arguably central to a proper understanding of the leading case of *Champagne Heidsieck*.

(a) The 'lost' cases

In the second half of the 19th Century, the Apollinaris company had built up an aggressive business in importing and selling bottled water from continental spas in both the United Kingdom and the United States. In the United Kingdom, it had persuaded the bottlers (and owners of the various springs) to assign their UK trade mark rights to it, usually after the assignor had been using them itself for several years in the United Kingdom, and proceeded to register these rights after the passage of the 1875 Act. It had successfully used these rights against a third party infringer.[25]

Later, Snook bought bottles of 'Friedrichshall' water on the continent from someone having the right to sell them there and imported them to sell in the United Kingdom. 'Friedrichshall' water was one of the spa waters which Apollinaris had been granted exclusive rights over the UK market for

---

23   *Erven Warnink BV et al. v J. Townend & Sons (Hull) Ltd et al.* [1979] AC 731, at 742 *per* Lord Diplock; [1979] 2 All ER 929, at 932 to 933; [1979] FSR 397, at 405; [1980] RPC 31 ('the *Advocaat* case'); see generally Cornish, *Intellectual Property*, Chapter 16; *Kerly's Law of Trade Marks*, Chapter 16.
24   Trade Marks Registration Act 1875 (38 & 39 Vict. Chapter 91).
25   *Apollinaris Co. v Herrfeldt* [1887] 4 RPC 478.

and for which it had registered in the United Kingdom several trade marks. One of the trade marks, No. 48,933, was never actually used on any bottles sold by Apollinaris in the United Kingdom; it only appeared on bottles sold on the continent by Apollinaris' supplier. It was, of course, on the bottles bought by Snook and Apollinaris sued him for its infringement. The bottles bought by Snook also bore a label with a notice that they were sold subject to the condition that they were not for importation and sale in the United Kingdom, breach of which would violate legal rights there. Kekewich J held that while the mark remained on the Register, the proprietor was entitled to stop others using it. If it was not properly on the Register, the right course was for a defendant to bring a suit for rectification. Snook, however, argued that the imports were genuine and so there could be no infringement. Kekewich J dismissed this claim on the simple ground that Snook had notice of the restriction against importation into the United Kingdom and so was not at liberty to set up a claim of licence.[26]

Snook appealed. Before the appeal was heard, however, another distributor, also threatened with infringement proceedings challenged the validity of Apollinaris' trade mark registrations.[27] The Court of Appeal was clearly alarmed at Apollinaris' aggressive (to say the least) attempts to use trade mark registrations as a means to monopolise the trade in bottled water. For example, Fry LJ referred to Apollinaris' use of its registrations against importers and, apart from the mark in *Snook's* case, several registrations were dismissed as being geographical words and so not registrable; others were abandoned without argument as misleading because they identified on their face a source other than Apollinaris.[28]

The registration of trade mark No. 48,933 was simply cancelled as a mark which had never been used and, admittedly, was never intended to be used in the United Kingdom. Fry LJ considered that, if the notice against importation were to have any effect, it could only be as a matter of contract.[29]

In addition to cancelling the registration of the mark on Snook's bottles for non-use, Fry LJ also ruled in relation to some of the other registrations:

> A person who puts another's trade mark on the register cannot be a person entitled under the Act. We are not concerned here with a case in which an importer may use the mark of a manufacturer with an addition indicative of the goods having been imported by him, but *the mark of a manufacturer pure and simple cannot rightly be assumed by an importer* from that manufacturer, or by a person who buys from that manufacturer, *unless indeed where all the goods of the manufacturer go to that importer* or that dealer. If they did not, other goods of the manufacturer might reach the hands of other dealers, who might justly

---

26 *Apollinaris Co. v Snook* (1890) 7 RPC 474, at 478. For a US case by Apollinaris against a parallel importer, see *Apollinaris Co. v Scherer* 27 Fed. 18 (SDNY 1886) in section 2.3.2 below.
27 *In Re Apollinaris' Trade Marks* [1891] 2 Ch. 186; 8 RPC 137 (CA).
28 For example, *ibid.* at 232; 8 RPC at 164, 165, 158 and, respectively *per* Fry LJ for the court. See also *Saxlehner v Apollinaris Co.* [1897] 1 Ch. 893 where one of its bottlers successfully sued Apollinaris in passing off.
29 *Ibid.* at 234; 8 RPC at 165.

affix to them the manufacturer's mark. . . . *If [the bottler's] assent would justify the registration, it would follow that a manufacturer in Paris using a trade mark well known in England could allow A to register it as his trade mark, and thereby prevent B and C, who bought from the Paris maker, from selling in England. That is what has been attempted in the present case. . . . (Emphasis added)*[30]

Following that ruling, Apollinaris did not defend the appeal brought by Snook, the parallel importer.[31]

It would seem, then, that Fry LJ did not envisage circumstances where a trade mark could be used to block parallel imports, at least where the trade mark was registered by a mere importer. His Lordship would allow a registration by an importer if the mark registered included additional matter which, presumably, signified the importer's role in selection. His Lordship would also permit a mere importer to register the mark if the importer bought up *all* the manufacturer's output. But, unlike Kekewich J in *Snook*, it would seem from the second-to-last-sentence in the quotation above that Fry LJ would allow parallel imports if the trade mark owner released its wares in a foreign market.

Neither of these cases was expressly referred to in the subsequent cases which are usually considered to form the foundations for the Anglo-Commonwealth law's treatment of parallel imports. Clauson J, who decided the *Champagne Heidsieck* case, would certainly have been aware of *Apollinaris' TMs*, however, from his Lordship's ruling in the *Lacteosote* case.[32]

(b)   *The 'mainstream'*[33]

In orthodox theory, a trade mark identifies who is ultimately responsible for putting the trade-marked product on the market: a trade mark indicates source.[34] The courts have had little difficulty in finding that this function transcends national frontiers since its identity does not change simply because the company carries on business across national borders. Consequently, where the trade mark owner was the same and made the goods itself, trade mark law could not be used to block parallel imports. This was the case whether the goods were the same or not,[35] and whether distribution in the domestic market was undertaken by the trade mark owner itself or

---

30   *Ibid.* at 226; 8 RPC at 160 to 161.
31   *Apollinaris Co. v Snook* (1891) 8 RPC 166 (CA).
32   *Lacteosote Limited v Alberman* (1927) 44 RPC 211, see further section 2.2.5 below.
33   An earlier draft of the remainder of Chapter 2.2 was published as Warwick A. Rothnie, 'Gray Privateers Sink into Black Market: Parallel Imports and Trade Marks', (1990) 1 AIPJ 72.
34   *Re Powell's Trade Mark* [1893] 2 Ch. 385 (CA); *Aristoc Ltd v Rysta Ltd* [1945] AC 68 (HL); *W.D. & H.O. Wills (Australia) Limited v Rothmans Limited* (1956) 94 CLR 182; *Estex Clothing Manufacturers Pty Limited v Ellis and Goldstein Limited* (1967) 116 CLR 254.
35   The *Champagne Heidsieck* case; for the passing off issue, see text at Note 51 below.

through an exclusive distributor.[36] Clauson J set out the general principle in the *Champagne Heidsieck* case:

> . . . the use of a mark by the defendant which is relied on as an infringement must be a use upon goods which are not the genuine goods, i.e., those upon which the plaintiffs' mark is properly used, *for any one may use the plaintiffs' mark on the plaintiffs' goods, since that cannot cause the deception which is the test of infringement. (Emphasis added)*[37]

In *Champagne Heidsieck*, the parallel imports were actually of a different quality, being sweeter than those which the Heidsieck company marketed itself in the United Kingdom. The registered trade mark relied on was essentially the English bottle's label. Outwardly, three factors distinguished the parallel imports: the label was worded in French; it had superimposed on it the word 'BRUT'; and, additionally, the English bottles also bore a second label, 'Reserved for England'. Moreover, the Heidsieck company only sold its 'Brut' champagne on the continent on condition that it was not for export to the United Kingdom. In these circumstances, Clauson J refused relief for trade mark infringement because the use of the trade mark correctly identified the source of the goods. Thus, the principle of territoriality was rejected in favour of an international attribution of source.

To reach his conclusion, Clauson J relied on two key propositions. First, that the function of a trade mark was correctly identified by Lord Cranworth LC in *Farina v Silverlock*.[38] Second, that the passage of the Trade Marks Registration Act 1875 did not alter that function in any way. The Heidsieck company's counsel did not seek to distinguish *Farina v Silverlock* on the ground that it did not concern parallel imports, nor did they question whether it still adequately reflected the law of passing off after *Spalding v Gamage*.[39] Instead, they sought to argue that, on registration, the trade mark owner received a monopoly right allowing it to control the distribution of products bearing the registered mark. Clauson J ruled:

> It was, however, contended that the effect of s. 3 of the Act of 1875 (which enacted that the registration of a trade mark, prima facie, gave the registered proprietor the right to the exclusive use of such trade mark) was, not merely to give that proprietor by virtue of registration a statutory title in respect of his mark to the same rights which, before the Act, he could have obtained only by proving that the mark had become his trade mark but had the further effect of vesting in the owner of a trade mark the right to object to any person selling or dealing with goods produced by the owner of the trade mark with the trade

---

36   For the distributor, see the *Bailey's Irish Cream* case, see text at Notes 137 to 141 below; the *Diana Oil* case, see text from Note 171 below.
37   The *Champagne Heidsieck* case [1930] 1 Ch. 330, at 341 at 141. Apart from the issues discussed below, his Lordship's broad statement must be qualified to the extent that the trade mark owner has the right to choose whether or not its goods will bear its mark in the first place: *Champagne Heidsieck et Cie Monopole SA v Scotto and Bishop* (1926) 43 RPC 101; *Wellcome Foundation Ltd v Secretary of State for Social Services* [1988] 1 WLR 635, at 638 *per* Lord Ackner (HL). For a similar qualification in EC law, see the *AHPC* case, Chapter 6 from Note 116 below.
38   At Note 9, above.
39   *A.G. Spalding & Bros v A.W. Gamage Ltd* (1915) 32 RPC 273 (HL).

mark affixed, except on such terms and subject to such conditions as to resale, price, area of market, and so forth, as the owner of the trade mark might choose to impose. *It was, in effect, suggested that, whereas before 1875 a trade mark, if established as a trade mark, was a badge of the origin of the goods, the effect of s. 3 of the Act of 1875 was to make a registered trade mark a badge of control, carrying with it the right in the owner of a registered trade mark to full control over his goods, into whosesoever hands they might come, except in so far as he might expressly or by implication have released this right of control* I do not so read the section. . . . It would be astonishing, if in an Act to establish a register of trade marks, such a remarkable extension of the rights of owners of trade marks were intended to be enacted by the use of such terms as appear in the section. *The section appears to me to mean that the proprietor of a registered trade mark is to have the right exclusively to use such trade mark in the sense of preventing others from selling wares which are not his marked with the trade mark.* I do not believe that the legislature intended to say, or can fairly be held to have said, that the registration of a trade mark had the wide consequences suggested by the plaintiffs. (*Emphasis added*)[40]

So, the Heidsieck company's claim was rejected outright. The wide ambit of the proposition contended for should, however, be noticed. As reported by his Lordship, the Heidsieck company was claiming the right to control dealings in its products which it had itself released on to the market. As Buxton's counsel argued, it was an attempt to make a contractual condition run with the goods.[41] Specifically, it was not confined to the more limited proposition that domestic trade mark rights could be used to repel unauthorised imports.

The case is further complicated by the fact that 'Brut' parallel imports had been circulating freely in England for several years. Because the Heidsieck company, knowing this, had failed to take vigorous action against the imports, the public had learnt to distinguish between the 'Brut' and non-'Brut' varieties.[42] On the orthodox approach taken by his Lordship, this, however, is more relevant to passing off than an infringement action: delay and the absence of deception going rather to the question of whether the trade mark was distinctive and whether equitable relief should be granted. Still, it seems difficult to credit the Heidsieck company's claim that it never intended the 'Brut' variety of its products to be projected into the UK market

---

40 *Champagne Heidsieck* [1930] 1 Ch. at 338 to 339. Contrast the approach which seems to be developing in Canada following *Seiko Time* [1984] 10 DLR (4th) 161 (Sup. Ct, Can.) and *Nestle Enterprises Ltd v Edan Food Sales Inc.* [1991] 37 CPR (3d) 480, at 486 (FCTD); see below Chapters 2.2.3(c) and respectively.
41 *Ibid.* 335; knowledge of the contractual term was alleged, but no evidence is referred to in the report. Instead, Buxton proved knowledge that the offending variety had been on sale in England for several years to the Heidsieck company's knowledge. On the vexed question of whether restrictive covenants can run with goods, see the unresolved conflict between *National Phonograph Co. of Australia Ltd v Menck* [1911] AC 336 and *Lord Strathcona SS Co. Ltd v Dominion Coal Co. Ltd* [1926] AC 108. See further Chapter 3, especially Notes 51 to 53.
42 An earlier action had been prosecuted successfully against traders who passed off one quality of champagne as another by placing it in bottles bearing the other kind of label: *Champagne Heidsieck et Cie Monopole SA v Scotto and Bishop* (1926) 43 RPC 101.

if, as seems to have been the case, they had done nothing to stop imports from the continent for several years.[43]

Clauson J's bold rejection of the principle of territoriality lies in stark contrast to the legalistic reluctance to pierce the corporate veil in the earlier *Dunlop Tyre* case.[44] Dunlop made tyres in the United Kingdom for the domestic market and for export, charging a price 30 per cent higher on the domestic market although the tyres were the same. Both types of tyres were stamped with its UK registered trade mark. At the same time, an 'associated' company, in France, made the same tyres for the French market and owned the French trade mark. Dunlop sued Booth for infringement by importing into England tyres made in France. Tomlin J, mentioning without disapproval that Dunlop seemed to arrange its operations in various countries through a network of associated companies, enjoined only the parallel importation of the French tyres; importing the English ones was a 'perfectly legitimate trade'.[45]

His Lordship did not explain why the two types of imports were treated differently. However, applying a strict approach to legal personality, it is consistent with Clauson J's principle that 'any one may use the plaintiffs' mark on the plaintiffs' goods. . . .' The simple expedient of transferring the foreign trade mark, even to an 'associated' company for use on the *same* goods, allowed the domestic trade mark owner to block parallel imports. This seems to have been solely on the basis of the separate ownership of the trade marks in the foreign and domestic markets. If so, both *Dunlop Tyre* and *Champagne Heidsieck* seem consistent with Fry LJ's judgment in *Apollinaris' TMs*.[46]

In contrast to the treatment of registered rights in these cases, passing off presented a potentially more complicated inquiry. Typically, the scope for deception is wider and the goodwill on which the action is founded may be more amenable to 'localisation'. While orthodox belief has it that 'deception' for trade mark purposes must be deception about source, the deception actionable in passing off may arise from the quality of the product or other surrounding circumstances.[47] Success in passing off is also contingent on what goodwill the domestic public actually associates with the mark or get-up.

In *Bonnan's* case, Bonnan bought cigarettes from the manufacturer in England on condition that he not resell them there since they were 'war surplus' stocks. When he started selling them in India, the plaintiff, the local distributor and a subsidiary of the English manufacturer, unsuccessfully

43   Of course, there were the contractual bans, but we are not given any information about how actively the Heidsieck company sought to enforce them or their effectiveness.
44   *Dunlop Rubber Company Limited v A.A. Booth & Co. Limited* (1926) 43 RPC 139 (Ch. D).
45   *Ibid.* at 146, 149. Resale price maintenance was not then prohibited in the United Kingdom; see now Resale Prices Act 1976 (United Kingdom).
46   See subsection 2.2.2(a) above.
47   See for example *Spalding v Gamage* (1915) 32 RPC 273; *Imperial Tobacco Co. of India Ltd v Bonnan* [1924] AC 755 (PC); and the *Advocaat* case [1979] AC 731 (HL); see generally Morison, 'Unfair Competition and "Passing Off"', at 50; Naresh, 'Passing-off, Goodwill and False Advertising', at 97; and Cornish, *Intellectual Property*, Chapter 16.

sued him in passing off. There was some suggestion, which the plaintiff did not press, that the goods made for India were specially adapted for tropical conditions. The local subsidiary also attached a sticker to the back of most packets identifying it as the importer but, otherwise, its cigarettes were as made and packaged by its parent. The evidence before the court, however, indicated that the Indian public identified the cigarettes as coming from the parent and not the subsidiary. In dismissing the plaintiff's appeal to the Privy Council, Lord Phillimore advised:

> At the trial some evidence was given on behalf of the appellant company in order to show that it had a reputation as the sole vendor in India of Gold Flake cigarettes and that the respondents were trading upon this reputation. *It is possible* for an importer to get a valuable reputation for himself and his wares by his care in selection or his precautions as to transit and storage, or because his local character is such that the article acquires a value by his testimony to its genuineness; and if therefore goods, though of the same make, are passed off by competitors as being imported by him, he will have a right of action. (*Emphasis added*)[48]
>
> . . .
>
> The claim of the appellant company is that it can stop a trader, to whom goods have been lawfully sold under a particular description, from reselling them under that description. *Such a claim sounds extravagant. It might, however, possibly be maintained* if it could be shown that the time, place or circumstances of the resale imported some representation that the goods were other than what they were. But in this case there is no such time, place or circumstance. (*Emphasis added*)[49]

Hence, the Privy Council clearly contemplated that such a plaintiff could succeed, although only *if* it could show that the sale by the parallel importer suggested an association with the local operative by reason of some local goodwill in the mark associated with that local operative. But, on the instant facts, there was no deception because the domestic public identified the manufacturer as the source of the goods through the mark and not the distributor. Accordingly, although not expressed in such terms, *Bonnan's* case represents a truly territorial approach to the issue of parallel imports: the factual goodwill in India was decisive. It also accepts as a possibility in passing off a situation which was clearly rejected on trade mark principles in *Apollinaris' TMs*.

Tomlin J simply refused relief on the grounds of passing off in the *Dunlop Tyre* case.[50] The *Champagne Heidsieck* case also involved passing off and, in the context of goods of different quality, Clauson J once more put the principle broadly:

> I know of no case which would enable me to decide, or any principle on which I can decide, that a defendant who sells the Brut type of the plaintiffs' article

---

48 [1924] AC 755, at 760.
49 *Ibid.* at 763.
50 The reasoning is not clear. Argument and the judgment concentrate on the infringement issue. After judgment, Dunlop's counsel also sought an injunction for passing off. His Lordship stated, 'I am not prepared to grant an injunction against passing off; I do not think a passing-off injunction should be given.' 43 RPC at 149 to 150.

under the very marks which the plaintiffs themselves think proper to use to distinguish that type can be accused of deception by the plaintiffs.[51]

Two factors immediately qualify the *dictum*. *Bonnan's* case was not referred to his Lordship. Second, immediately following the quoted passage, his Lordship found no deception of the public on the evidence. The 'Brut' champagne had been available in England for several years and the Heidsieck company, although knowing this, had apparently failed to take action against its importation until suing Buxton. In addition, contrary to the position in trade mark law, the use of additional distinguishing marks, such as the 'Brut' reference, may be sufficient to avoid liability in passing off.[52]

These cases illustrate the treatment of parallel imports under laws based on the Trade Marks Act 1905 (United Kingdom). The *Champagne Heidsieck* case has been followed in Australia, Canada and South Africa;[53] the approach in *Bonnan's* case, in the United Kingdom and Canada;[54] and the *Dunlop Tyre* case in Canada.[55] Before summarising the relevant principles, the later ruling in *Juda's* case provides a link between *Dunlop Tyre* and *Apollinaris' TMs*.[56]

In *Juda's* case, a UK company, Wilkinson Sword, had registered two trade marks in Canada. It had a long history over at least 40 years of using these registrations in Canada to identify various goods made in the United Kingdom, the goods included garden tools, razor blades and swords. Until 1963, it dealt directly with a Canadian distributor. In 1963, it incorporated a Canadian subsidiary to which it sold its products for resale to the Canadian distributor. The latter provided the staff and premises of Wilkinson Sword's subsidiary. Several months after its incorporation,

---

51   [1930] 1 Ch. 330, at 336 to 337.
52   See for example *Saville Perfumery Ltd v June Perfect Ltd* (1941) 58 RPC 147, 161, 162 to 163 *per* Greene MR (CA); 174 to 175 *per* Viscount Maugham (HL).
53   *Atari Inc. v Fairstar Electronics Pty Ltd* (1982) 50 ALR 274 (Fed. C); *R & A Bailey & Co. Ltd v Boccaccio Pty Ltd* (1986) 4 NSWLR 701 (SC NSW); but *conf. Atari Inc. v Dick Smith Electronics Pty Ltd* (1980) 33 ALR 20 (Fed. C); *Mattel Canada Inc. v GTS Acquisitions Ltd* (1989) 27 CPR (3d) 358.; *Protective Mining & Industrial Equipment Systems (Pty) Ltd v Audiolens (Cape)(Pty) Ltd* 1987(2) 961 (AD).
54   See subsection 2.2.3(c) below.
55   See *Remington Rand Ltd v Transworld Metal Co. Ltd* (1960) 32 CPR 99 (Ex. Ct, Can.), domestic subsidiary acting solely as a distributor granted continuation of an interim injunction restraining parallel imports; *Wella Canada Inc. v Perlon Products Ltd* (1984) 4 CPR (3d) 287 (Ont. HC) and *Manhattan Industries Inc. v Princeton Manufacturing Ltd* (1971) 4 CPR(2d) 6, at 16 to 17 (FCTD) and *H.J. Heinz Co. of Canada Ltd v Edan Food Sales Inc.* [1991] 35 CPR (3d) 213 (FCTD). But note *Ulay (Canada) Ltd v Calstock Traders Ltd* (1969) 59 CPR 223 (Ex. Ct) where Walsh J refused an interim injunction. In circumstances very similar to *Revlon* [1980] FSR 85 (CA) (see subsection 2.2.3(a) below), his Honour considered that the *prima facie* case for infringement was less strong and the validity of the registration was also challenged. On the balance of convenience, his Honour found for the defendant. For *dicta* on the significance of the defendant credibly challenging validity, see also Strayer J's refusal to grant an interlocutory injunction in passing off to a registered user: *Nestlé Enterprises Ltd v Edan Food Sales Inc.* [1991] 37 CPR (3d) 480 (FCTD) from Note 124a below. For the strict line on *validity* which some Canadian courts have taken, see Note 56 below.
56   *Wilkinson Sword (Canada) Ltd v Juda* (1966) 51 CPR 55 (Ex. Ct); *Breck's Sporting Goods Co. Ltd v Magder* (1975) 17 CPR (2d) 201 (SC, Can.) from Note 130, below.

the subsidiary took over the final processing and packaging of the razor blades intended for distribution in Canada. They were still manufactured in the United Kingdom, and were still marked as being made in England. Subsequently, in June 1965, Wilkinson Sword assigned its Canadian trade mark registrations to its subsidiary. Nothing was done to inform the public that there had been any change in production responsibilities or ownership of the trade marks.

Meanwhile, from February 1965, Juda had been importing and selling Wilkinson Sword brand razor blades which he bought in the United Kingdom. Shortly after the assignment of the trade mark registrations, the subsidiary sued him for infringement of its trade marks and unfair competition by importing the razor blades from the United Kingdom. Juda counterclaimed for a declaration that the registrations were invalid.

Two points are of particular interest for present purposes. First, Jackett P followed the approach taken in the *Dunlop Tyre* case and roundly rejected Juda's claims that the parent and subsidiary should be treated as one single entity for trade mark purposes.[57] Second, and alarmingly for those planning to split trade mark ownership along territorial lines, his Honour found that the course of dealings in the trade mark registrations had rendered the marks non-distinctive and liable to cause deception. Accordingly, they were ordered to be removed from the register.[58] There may be some question whether his Honour's finding on the second point would be applied outside Canada, however, it does show the dangers of splitting ownership of trade marks along territorial lines without taking adequate steps to inform the public of any change.[59]

Table 2.1 presents the results of applying the principles declared in the three early rulings, showing three stylised situations and whether parallel imports would be permitted, or not, in each. Characterised like this, the trade mark's function solely to indicate source is clearly presented as the main factor in determining whether it could be used to block parallel imports. Use of the trade mark on products of differing qualities was irrelevant, except perhaps in passing off. Yet, even in this simple scheme, attempts to 'internationalise' source could be defeated by interposing the fiction of legal personality. Then, the source identified by the trade mark was restricted to the domestic owner even where the goods were to all intents and purposes identical. The consequences could potentially be unsatisfactory bearing in mind that the motive apparently underlying the *Dunlop Tyre* case was to preserve a 30 per cent margin in the domestic market.

---

57 *Ibid.* at 70 to 71. His Honour did not actually refer to *Dunlop Tyre*. However, *Remington Rand* had been referred to and was distinguished on the ground that the validity of the mark was not in question: *ibid.* at 69, Note 1.

58 *Ibid.* at 70, 72 to 91.

59 See Cornish, *Intellectual Property*, at ¶17-055. The reasoning is predicated on *Apollinaris' TMs* [1891] 2 Ch. 186, 8 RPC 137 (CA); *Bowden Wire Co. Ltd v Bowden Brake Co. Ltd* (1914) 31 RPC 385 (HL); and *Lacteosote Limited v Alberman* (1927) 44 RPC 211 (Ch. D), see further section 2.2.5. For use by an assignee which may not cause deception, see *Fender Australia v Bevk* (1989) 15 IPR 257 (Fed. C), from Note 142, below.

Table 2.1
Legal Treatment of Parallel Imports in Anglo-Commonwealth Courts
(Early Principles)

	Stylised Situation	*Trade Marks*	*Passing Off**
1.	Same trade mark owner/ Same goods	Yes	Yes
2.	Same trade mark owner/ Different goods	Yes	No
3.	Different trade mark owners/ Same goods	No	No

*This, of course, would depend on the local reputation sued on.

The incipient tension inherent between the broad, universalist approach of Clauson J in *Champagne Heidsieck* and the more formal, legalistic approach in the *Dunlop Tyre* case taken by Tomlin J has been the subject of continued dispute before the courts. A number of, sometimes contrary, factors have intervened to influence the outcomes. In line with the postulates of the principle of universality, business has increasingly adopted an international character. The incidence of international corporate groups conducting business in several countries through an interlocking network of subsidiaries has surely grown since the *Dunlop Tyre* case. The fear that they will use simple, technical devices to practise undesirable market partitioning has certainly been evident. On the other hand, many businesses too small to operate effectively on a global scale have also sought foreign markets through contractual relationships. These, and other commercial pressures such as increasingly sophisticated marketing methods, have placed greater demands on the function of trade marks.

2.2.3   International corporate groups

The area where the possible deficiencies in the *Dunlop Tyre* case first surfaced was, perhaps unsurprisingly, that of the international corporate group. It was also in this context that the narrow conception of a trade mark's function first clearly worked to the detriment of the very consumers which it was intended to protect from deception. The leading authorities are two rulings of the UK Court of Appeal, the *Revlon* and *Colgate* cases.[60] Although seemingly distinguishable on the previously irrelevant grounds of quality variation, the judgments in many respects seem irreconcilable. Thus, it seems more than likely that debate will be prolonged.

Before continuing, major change in the relevant UK legislation since the *Champagne Heidsieck* must be mentioned. The Trade Marks Act 1905 had

---

60   *Revlon Inc. v Cripps & Lee Ltd* [1980] FSR 85; *Colgate-Palmolive Limited v Markwell Finance Limited* [1989] RPC 497.

been replaced by the Trade Marks Act 1938. One of the more significant changes involved the incorporation of a definition of 'infringement' which, after the House of Lords' ruling in the *Yeast-Vite* case, extended the range of infringing acts beyond those of using the trade mark as a trade mark.[61] The new legislation also saw an attempt to specify non-infringing uses of a trade mark and section 4(3)(a), so far as relevant, now provides:

> The right to the use of a trade mark given by registration as aforesaid shall not be deemed to be infringed by the use of any such mark as aforesaid by any person—
>
> (a) in relation to goods connected in the course of trade with the proprietor or a registered user of the trade mark if, as to those goods or a bulk of which they form part, the proprietor or the registered user conforming to the permitted use has applied the trade mark and has not subsequently removed or obliterated it, or has at any time expressly or impliedly consented to the use of the trade mark; or . . .

Where the allegedly infringing use consists of use as a trade mark then, there are two alternative defences prescribed: either the trade mark was applied, and not subsequently removed, by the registered proprietor (or a registered user within the terms of its permitted use); or, alternatively, the registered proprietor (or, once again, a registered user) had consented to the defendant's use, whether expressly or impliedly.[62]

(a)   *The Revlon case*[63]

Fear that an international corporate group was using the fictions of corporate personality and the territorial limitations of trade marks to isolate national markets clearly underlay the *Revlon* case.[64] Without referring to either *Bonnan's* case or the *Dunlop Tyre* case, the decision represents a further shift away from the territorial approach towards an international concept of trade mark source by extending Clauson J's *dictum* to the international corporate group. In terms of Table 2.1, it accorded a 'Yes' answer for both passing off and infringement in the *third* stylised situation.

The parent of the group, Revlon Inc., owned the trade marks *Revlon* and *Revlon Flex* in the United States where it made and marketed the

---

61   See especially section 4(1)(b) countermanding *Irving's Yeast-Vite Ltd v Horsenail* (1934) 51 RPC 110 (HL): Board of Trade, *Report of the Departmental Committee on the Law and Practice Relating to Trade Marks*, Cmd 4568, HMSO, 1934, ¶¶184 to 185 cited in Cornish, *Intellectual Property*, at ¶17-076; Ricketson, *The Law of Intellectual Property*, at ¶36.18.

62   The legislation promised by the UK Government in response to the First Trade Mark Directive will expressly incorporate a defence largely based on the European Court of Justice's doctrine of Community exhaustion, see Department of Trade and Industry, *Reform of Trade Marks Law*, at ¶¶3.33 to 3.36; for the doctrine of Community exhaustion, see Chapter 6, below.

63   Noted by David Kitchin, 'The Revlon Case: Trade Marks and Parallel Imports (UK)', [1980] EIPR 86 with a particularly clear diagram of the corporate structure.

64   In particular, Templeman LJ caustically referred to an 'attempt to enforce price fixing by the back door. . . .' [1980] FSR 85, at 112.

Revlon Flex range of shampoos. These included an anti-dandruff product. Revlon Inc. neither owned the identical trade marks nor carried on business operations itself in England; there, operations were carried out by three of its subsidiaries. Revlon Inc. had assigned its UK trade mark registrations to 'Suisse', which was a vehicle for holding property assets. Business activity in the United Kingdom was undertaken by two registered users: 'International' arranged distribution and determined which products would be marketed, having its products made by 'Overseas'.[65] The products 'International' released in the United Kingdom included Revlon Flex shampoos identical to those Revlon Inc. put out in the United States except the anti-dandruff shampoo. International had decided not to market it in England. The anti-dandruff product was not successful in the United States and Revlon Inc. discontinued the line. At this point, the defendant somehow obtained supplies in the United States which it imported into the United Kingdom. The various Revlon companies applied for interlocutory injunctions, but failed to establish a sufficient case to answer in either passing off or infringement.

The plaintiffs failed in passing off because the parallel importation involved no misrepresentation likely to deceive the public. The anti-dandruff products carried with them a representation that they came from the international Revlon group and this was exactly what the goodwill associated with the Revlon marks in the United Kingdom indicated since, in England as in the United States, all the Revlon Flex products were simply marketed under the legend 'REVLON New York-Paris-London'.[66]

The Court of Appeal also rejected misrepresentation about the character, quality or class of the goods. The anti-dandruff products were of the same quality as the other products in the Flex range and were clearly labelled as anti-dandruff products. Since customers were already accustomed to reading labels carefully to ensure they were getting the desired variety – normal, extra dry or greasy – Buckley LJ thought it was unlikely that any 'reasonably perspicacious' member of the public would be deceived.[67] Templeman LJ agreed, but, having rejected any misrepresentation on the facts, went further:

> *In any event*, in my judgment there can be no passing off when products manufactured, named, labelled and put into circulation by a Revlon company are sold by the defendants without any alteration to the contents, name or

---

65   The registration of Overseas as a registered user was endorsed with the condition that it could only use the trade mark while it was controlled by Revlon Inc. In a remarkable tactical move, between judgment at first instance and the hearing of the appeal, Revlon Inc. replaced Overseas as the manufacturer of UK products with another subsidiary 'Manufacturing' based in Bermuda. This change, apparently, did not affect their Lordships' reasoning.

66   *Ibid*. at 102 to 103 *per* Buckley LJ (Bridge LJ agreeing); and 112 *per* Templeman LJ.

67   *Ibid*. at 104 *per* Buckley LJ; see also *Nestlé Enterprises Ltd v Edan Food Sales Inc*. [1991] 37 CPR (3d) 480, 484–5 (FCTD). Compare the abilities of the 'reasonably perspicacious' member of the public when evidence rather than judicial hypothesis supplies the point of reference: the *Colgate* case; *Reckitt & Colman plc v Borden Inc*. [1990] RPC 341 (HL).

label. The products sold by the defendants are what the defendants say they are. (*Emphasis added*)[68]

Scorning the Revlon companies' 'attempt to enforce price fixing by the back door', his Lordship continued:

> . . . the plaintiff companies form part of a multi-national group, and are not entitled by asserting the English law of passing off to prevent their own goods, put into circulation by their own group, from being exported from the United States and sold in the United Kingdom at prices determined by the importers.[69]

Templeman LJ appears to state that a 'multi-national group' could not succeed in passing off as a matter of principle. His Lordship's views are not reflected in Buckley LJ's judgment (which Bridge LJ joined). Nor, with respect, do they seem consistent with the Privy Council's advice in *Bonnan's* case which accepted that passing off would generally not lie, but further indicated that each case would depend on its own particular facts. The actual decision in *Revlon* itself, however, is consistent with *Bonnan* because the goodwill shown on the interlocutory application denoted source in the group as a whole.

Their Lordships' judgments on the infringement issue are also open to an expansive interpretation although, once again, Templeman LJ appears to go further than Buckley LJ.

Apparently, since the US products were not made by either the registered proprietor in the United Kingdom or one of its registered users, the defendant conceded its parallel importation involved use of the Revlon trade marks as trade marks. So, the only question was whether one of the special defences under the Trade Marks Act 1938 section 4(3)(a) applied. This involved two steps: establishing that:

(1) the anti-dandruff products imported were goods connected in the course of trade with Suisse, the UK registered proprietor; and
(2) Suisse had *either* applied the trade marks to the anti-dandruff products itself *or* consented to their application to the goods.[70]

The Court of Appeal was unanimous in finding the necessary connection in the course of trade and Suisse's consent to Revlon Inc. applying the trade marks to the anti-dandruff products. However, Templeman LJ only found consent in the alternative, preferring to rule that Suisse had itself applied the trade marks to the products. Both judgments stressed the role of a trade mark in indicating source and each was clearly troubled by the thought that

---

68 *Ibid.* at 112.
69 *Ibid.*
70 Proof of the necessary links to a registered user using by way of permitted use would also suffice: section 4(3)(a). Since nothing turned on the distinction between proprietor and registered users, the author will refer only to Suisse; but note the later decisions in *Diana Oil* and *Mattel*, see subsection 2.2.4(b) below.

Revlon Inc. could avoid *Champagne Heidsieck* by the simple expedient of transferring its rights to a subsidiary.[71]

For Buckley LJ, establishing a connection between Suisse and the goods made by Revlon Inc. was not 'piercing the corporate veil'. It merely recognised the legal and factual position that the UK trade marks belonged to the Revlon group as a whole and, therefore, were assets of Revlon Inc., the parent.[72] In such circumstances, the function of the trade marks was to denote goods:

> . . . which originate *from the Revlon Group*, but not from any particular part of that Group. The exploitation of the mark and of the goods to which it relates is a world-wide exercise in which all the component companies of the Group who deal in these particular products are engaged. . . . (*Emphasis added*)[73]

So, each of the trade marks had become a 'house mark of the whole group' and the necessary connection in the course of trade existed. Three factors seemed crucial. First, Revlon Inc. had not sold its products subject to an export ban (and it would be 'surprising' if its subsidiaries did use export bans). Second, even if Revlon subsidiaries were permitted a substantial degree of autonomy, Revlon Inc. could at any time impose its will on them. Third, in fact, the subsidiaries were readily pursuing a policy of acting worldwide as 'the Revlon Group'.[74] Templeman LJ similarly relied on the function of the trade marks to denote source in the Revlon group or one of its companies. In his Lordship's view, however, the connection in the course of trade existed 'because all the companies are members of a group headed by Revlon Inc. and they are all engaged in exploiting and using the' trade marks.[75]

Hence, despite Buckley LJ's protestations to the contrary, it would seem that the trade source indicated when a member of a corporate group uses a trade mark is not the particular person entered on the register, but each and every member of the whole corporate group. That broad proposition is highly redolent of the exhaustion approach illustrated by *Cinzano*, based on a broader 'economic', rather than a strictly legal, view of the firm. Under the UK statute, however, an additional step was required: proof that the registered proprietor had applied, or consented to the application, of the trade mark to the parallel imports.

As to consent, Buckley LJ was at first reluctant. The territorial limitations of UK trade mark rights meant that use of the Revlon trade marks in the US could not infringe the UK registrations. Hence, Suisse's consent to use the

---

71 [1980] FSR 85, at 106 *per* Buckley LJ; at 114 *per* Templeman LJ; *Champagne Heidsieck* being referred to favourably by Buckley LJ at 108 and treated as accurately stating the law by Templeman LJ at 113 and 115.
72 *Ibid.* at 105. Contrast the *Dunlop Tyre* case.
73 *Ibid.* at 106.
74 *Ibid.* On the absence of an export ban, contrast the *Champagne Heidsieck* case.
75 *Ibid.* at 114.

trade marks in the United States was not required and there was no reason to give it. However, his Lordship continued:

> Upon further consideration I have changed my mind. Revlon [Inc.] deals with wholesalers in the United States to whom it sells its products without any condition against export. By so doing Revlon [Inc.] puts the purchasers of its products in the position of being able to export those goods with the mark upon them to the United Kingdom without any possibility of Revlon [Inc.] objecting. If Revlon [Inc.] were itself to export the United States products in question to the United Kingdom marked with the [Revlon trade marks], none of the subsidiary companies could, in my opinion, object (a) because for the reasons already stated they have, in my view, consented to Revlon [Inc.]'s use of the mark to designate appropriate products of Revlon [Inc.]'s manufacture; and (b) because Revlon [Inc.] has the power by virtue of its control over the subsidiaries to overrule any objection by any of them.[76]

There is more than a little difficulty in following the chain of reasoning. It seems, in effect, to reproduce the reasoning used to establish the necessary connection in the course of trade. Hence, although his Lordship refers to two factors, they seem to boil down to three.[77] First, despite *Champagne Heidsieck*, Revlon Inc. had sold the goods without an export restriction. Second, the trade mark was used as the 'house mark of the whole group'. Third, the subsidiaries were ultimately 'mere instruments' of Revlon Inc.[78]

On the question of whether Suisse had applied the trade mark, views diverged. Buckley LJ refused to extend Cross LJ's *dictum* in *GE Trade Mark*.[79] While it was feasible to attribute the act of a subsidiary to its controlling parent, the subsidiary's inability to control its parent precluded attributing the parent's act to its subsidiary.[80] Templeman LJ, alone on this point, refused to be impeded by logical nicety and denied that it was possible to substitute 'the monkey for the organ-grinder'.[81] His Lordship noted that the trade marks were ultimately assets of Revlon Inc. which could control their disposition at whim. Accordingly:

> In these circumstances Revlon Inc. are in no better position than Heidsieck, who held the British trade marks in their own name. In a group such as the Revlon group, the legal ownership of the trade marks and the registration of users are mere instruments. Revlon Inc. orchestrates the business of the group through Revlon Inc. subsidiaries for the benefit of Revlon Inc.

---

76 *Ibid.* at 107. See also *per* Templeman LJ at 117.
77 Cornish reduces the considerations to (1) the mark was a 'house mark' and (2) Revlon Inc.'s power over its subsidiaries: Cornish, *Intellectual Property*, at ¶18-002. The first is itself a conclusion based on a number of factors (of which the second is one). The circularity is reinforced by Buckley LJ's subsequent explanation of the *Revlon* ruling:

> This court held that the marks, or get up, in that case had been developed as a house mark distinctive of the whole group and that every company in the group must be taken to have consented to the mark's being used by every other company of the group to designate the products so marked as products of the group as a whole.
> *Chanel Ltd v F.W. Woolworth & Co. Ltd* [1981] 1 WLR 485, at 491.

78 The phrase is from Templeman LJ, see *ibid.* at 115 (quoted at Note 82 below); Buckley LJ is strongly influenced by the lack of export bans.
79 [1970] RPC 339, at 395.
80 [1980] FSR 85, at 107.
81 *Ibid.* at 116

In my judgment *where a parent company chooses to manufacture and sell wholly or partly through a group of subsidiary companies in different parts of the world, products which bear the same trade mark and attract an international reputation, neither the parent nor any subsidiary can complain in the United Kingdom if those products are used, sold and re-sold under that trade mark.* A purchaser of a Revlon product from a Revlon company in the United States or the United Kingdom or in any other part of the world, whether a Revlon company operates in that part of the world or not, is at least entitled to assume that he will not be sued by a Revlon company in the United Kingdom, or in Delaware or Venezuela or New York or anywhere else, merely because of the place of manufacture of the product which he has acquired under the name of REVLON. (*Emphasis added*)[82]

This passage, referring as it does to 'international reputation', quite strongly suggests views underlying the principle of universality. The first paragraph of the extract also stresses Templeman LJ's view that territorial rights were being manipulated by international corporate groups. By the end of the second paragraph, the vigour of the rhetoric carries his Lordship away from what the trade mark signifies at the point of sale to manipulations based on place of manufacture.

Buckley LJ's judgment is not pitched in terms as sweeping as the forceful language used by Templeman LJ. In particular, whatever the substance of his Lordship's meaning, absent are the categoric denials of relief in passing off or for trade mark infringement to an international corporate group engaged in a 'uniform' business worldwide. However, there are strong points of similarity. Both judgments are clearly impressed with Clauson J's reasoning in *Champagne Heidsieck*. Both are also much concerned to prevent legal technicalities circumventing what each clearly saw as the result achieved in that case. By ignoring the legal separation of trade mark ownership, previously crucial, both roundly rejected the principle of territoriality in favour of the source function of a trade mark and accommodation of the law to business reality as perceived under the principle of universality.

Apart from Templeman LJ's sweeping views, *Revlon*'s extension of preceding case law can be seen in two main factors. First, 'export bans' had not previously assisted the trade mark owner (although they might also be thought irrelevant under the principle of territoriality). This factor, however, would seem to weaken the universal character of source. Second, the concept of a 'house mark' was extended. If the ties of corporate control are exercised, attributing a connection in the course of trade to the controller must be at least as sound as attribution through a contractual licence. However, just as in licensing, control must actually be maintained.[83] *Revlon* goes further by

---

82   *Ibid.* at 115 to 116. Although Templeman LJ's views are made about the 'application' point and are put in more forceful terms, the first paragraph is very similar to the reasoning which persuaded Buckley LJ to find the necessary connection between Suisse and the trade marks used on the anti-dandruff products: compare *ibid.* at 106.

83   The Australian High Court has required more substantial evidence than just a corporate relationship: *Farmer & Co. Ltd v Anthony Hordern & Sons Ltd* (1964) 112 CLR 163, at 167 to 168. For licensing, see for example *McGregor TM* [1979] RPC 36 (Ch. D).

allowing the *potential* for corporate control to override the actual discretion exercised by the subsidiaries. Hence, in Table 2.1's third stylised situation, *Revlon* moved the law to yield 'Yes' answers. Despite Buckley LJ's reluctance to extend the *GE Trade Mark* case to the facts in *Revlon*, both judgments extended the general understanding of a registered trade mark as signifying the goods of the proprietor by emphasising that the trade mark denoted products originating *from the group*. In contrast to the emphasis on the absent export bans, it signals a shift away from the strict definition of parallel imports to embrace the concept of an economic rather than a legal undertaking.[84]

Between *Revlon* and *Colgate*, judicial opinion equivocated. The approach taken in *Champagne Heidsieck* and *Revlon* has commended itself to the High Courts of Malaysia and New Zealand.[85] Young J, in the New South Wales Supreme Court, thought it inappropriate to overturn such long-standing authority at first instance.[86] *Revlon* has also been distinguished, however, in two cases before the High Court in England, which seized on the Court of Appeal's emphasis of the absence of export bans and the goods' identical quality. In *Wilkinson Sword*, Falconer J allowed the plaintiff to proceed with its passing off action on the basis of an alleged deception about quality.[87] More significantly, where the parallel imports were different in quality (and apparently unsuitable for use on the domestic market), the plaintiff has succeeded in an infringement action. In *Castrol GTX*, the trade mark owner in both the foreign and domestic markets was the same. However, its consent to export from the foreign market was expressly countermanded in the licence agreements and by notice endorsed on the product.[88] Returning to the simple, stylised situations of Table 2.1, *Castrol GTX*, at least, represented a retreat not only from the high-water mark of *Revlon*, but even the long-standing *Champagne Heidsieck* case, supplying the answer 'No' to the second row. The judge found consent and territoriality the dominant considerations, thus allowing trade mark law to block parallel imports in the second situation. In this state of the law, the Colgate-Palmolive group took action against Markwell.

---

84   Indeed, at least one defendant on similar facts appears to have assumed its only defence lay in the rules of the EEC Treaty: *Chanel Ltd v F.W. Woolworth and Co. Ltd* [1981] FSR 196 (CA).

85   *Winthrop Products Inc. v Sun Ocean (M) Sdn Bhd* [1988] FSR 430, at 436 to 438 (applying Templeman LJ's views); and *Tamiya Plastic Model Co. v Toy Warehouse Ltd* cited in Brendan Brown, 'Parallel Importation: A New Zealand Perspective', [1989] EIPR 274, and 277, respectively.

86   The *Bailey's Irish Cream* case (1986) 4 NSWLR 701, at 709 to 710 and see also the interlocutory applications involving Atari, *Atari v Dick Smith Electronics Pty Ltd* (1980) 33 ALR 20; and *Atari v Fairstar* (1982) 50 ALR 274, below from Note 133.

87   *Wilkinson Sword Ltd v Cripps & Lee Ltd* [1982] FSR 16, at 19 to 21, and 28 (Ch. D), an interlocutory application to strike out the Statement of Claim.

88   *Castrol Ltd v Automotive Oil Supplies Ltd* [1983] RPC 315 (Vivian Price QC, sitting as a deputy judge), considered in John Drysdale, 'Castrol Limited v Automative Supplies Limited: Parallel Imports - Revlon Revisited', [1983] EIPR 224.

(b)   *The Colgate case*[89]

The *Colgate* case concerned the international manufacturing and distribution arrangements of the Colgate-Palmolive group. Genuine 'Colgate' products marketed in Brazil were imported into the United Kingdom. Members of the Colgate-Palmolive group successfully sued the importer, Markwell, in passing off and for trade mark infringement.

Colgate-Palmolive Company ('Colgate-US'), the parent, operated through subsidiaries in over 50 countries throughout the world. Like Revlon Inc., it often permitted its subsidiaries a considerable degree of local independence particularly over the products they market, the new products they launch, the formulation of those products and their marketing and promotional programmes. However, among the matters it circumscribed are what products the subsidiary may export and to whom they may be exported.

In both the United Kingdom and Brazil, Colgate-US owned the Colgate trade marks;[90] having licensed the use of those in the United Kingdom to 'Colgate-UK' (which was the sole registered user of the trade marks in that country), and the use of those in Brazil to its Brazilian subsidiary, 'Colgate-Brazil'.

In both countries the packaging and get-up for Colgate products was virtually identical, featuring a predominantly red package on which the word 'Colgate' was written in white script.[91] The brand type was indicated by a 'flash' to the right of the word Colgate. In the United Kingdom, this flash identified the product as one of 'Great Regular Flavour' (the largest selling product), 'Blue Minty Gel' or 'Junior'; Great Regular Flavour being further differentiated from Blue Minty Gel by the colour of the flash, dark blue and a lighter blue, respectively; Junior was also only sold in tubes of 25ml size made from aluminium. The Brazilian toothpastes were 'Com Fluor', with the words 'Com Fluor MFP' in a dark blue flash, and 'Menta Natural' in a green flash. In addition, each of the Brazilian products was otherwise worded in Portuguese.

Apart from the differences in packaging, there was a marked difference in quality between the products from the two countries, the Brazilian products being inferior in composition and therapeutic benefit. These differences were explained on the basis of both economic circumstances and climate.

Markwell arranged to import seven shipments of the Brazilian toothpastes into the United Kingdom where it placed them for retail sale in outlets as diverse as local corner shops and the widespread, national Tesco chain. The parallel imports were offered at cheaper prices and, often, were displayed

---

89   Discussed briefly in Daniel Alexander, 'Colgate-Palmolive v Markwell Finance–The Carving Knife Sharpened', [1989] EIPR 456.

90   So far as trade mark law was concerned, the UK action was based on six registrations of two basic variants: the word 'COLGATE' and the word 'Colgate' in white script marked on a red carton.

91   Colgate-UK had been using this get-up since 1955. But, one of the four types on the market since 1981, Colgate Tartar Control featured instead a gold packet with red lettering.

alongside Colgate-UK's products. The shipments were obtained through the agency of a Brazilian import/export business which bought the first shipment on the open market in Brazil but obtained the others directly from Colgate-Brazil using the stratagem of a stated intention of exporting them to Nigeria.

At the heart of Markwell's defence, in both passing off and trade mark infringement, lay the vexed issue of legal policy towards international corporate groups carrying on business in more than one country. Markwell argued that the principle of universality, and not that of territoriality, applied. In Markwell's submission, the Colgate-Palmolive group deliberately set out to adopt a uniform presentation of its products worldwide, clearly seeking to claim the advantages of an international goodwill without adequately differentiating products of different quality. Therefore, it had adopted the world as its market and could not rely on trade mark or passing off rights to insulate national markets. This argument, tailored to the needs of each form of action, was forcefully supported by reliance on the *Champagne Heidsieck* and the *Revlon* cases, which Markwell claimed held that no-one infringed by selling the plaintiff's goods in the marks and trade dress the plaintiff itself saw fit to sell the very goods in.[92]

The Court of Appeal in *Colgate* rejected Markwell's reliance on these *dicta*. Instead, it distinguished both cases on the ground that neither dealt with deception of the public by use of a trade mark on goods of different quality and reasserted the territorial limitations of trade marks and passing off.

On appeal from Falconer J, Markwell left unchallenged two crucial findings of fact: first, that the Brazilian imports were markedly inferior in quality to those Colgate-UK itself put out; and second, that customers in the United Kingdom expected products in the Colgate get-up to have a particular quality. These findings had been supported by a considerable body of evidence showing actual confusion and deception of the trade and consumers. Hence, in passing off, *Revlon* and *Champagne Heidsieck* were distinguished because neither actually involved a misrepresentation about quality. *Revlon* did not involve products of different quality. Although *Champagne Heidsieck* did, because of the plaintiff's delay, consumers were not deceived.

Instead, Markwell supported its appeal by an argument on the facts and the policy argument derived from *Champagne Heidsieck* and *Revlon*. First, it relied on the distinctive flashes used on the toothpaste packaging arguing that UK customers were accustomed to distinguish 'Great Regular Flavour' from 'Blue Minty Gel' solely by reference to the flashes used on the get-up

---

92 In passing off, see the *Champagne Heidsieck* case [1930] 1 Ch. at 336 to 337, quoted at Note 51 above. Neither judgment discusses *Champagne Heidsieck* on infringement, but see *ibid.* at 341, text at Notes 35 to 43 above. For the *Revlon* case, see [1980] FSR 85, at 112 *per* Templeman LJ on passing off, and at 115 for infringement. Buckley LJ (Bridge LJ agreeing) formulates the principles more narrowly. See subsection 2.2.3(a) above.

to the right of the Colgate brand name. Hence, the customers would necessarily readily notice that they were buying 'Com Fluor' or 'Menta Natural' instead of the usual product. Unfortunately, hypotheses about the capacities of 'reasonably perspicacious' consumers were constrained by the overwhelming body of evidence establishing trade and consumer confusion.[93] Even assuming consumers realised that they were buying 'Com Fluor' or 'Menta Natural', deception would not necessarily be avoided. In the *Revlon* case, consumers might well consciously have chosen to buy anti-dandruff shampoo instead of the non-medicated products offered by the UK subsidiaries. But, leaving aside the therapeutic benefits, they would still get products of the same standard. The consumer's bargain in the *Colgate* case may have been of an entirely different order since the Brazilian imports were undisputedly inferior.

Second, Markwell argued that the imports were Colgate goods in their original state marked as Colgate saw fit. Hence, the Colgate-Palmolive group, by choosing a common house livery for products of differing quality, was the author of any deception. This argument was defeated by the confusing difference in quality together with the localised, territorial nature of goodwill in a passing off action.[94]

At first instance, Falconer J had found passing off on the grounds of misrepresentation about both the *origin* and the *quality* of the Brazilian imports.[95] The Court of Appeal upheld passing off only on the ground of *quality*. In doing so, there may be an important difference in approach between the judgments of Slade and Lloyd LJJ.

Slade LJ considered that reputation for quality was local but would not have restricted any representation about source territorially. Had the domestic and imported products been comparable in quality, Slade LJ would have applied Clauson J's ruling as extended in *Revlon*. Use of the uniform Colgate marks and get-up conveyed the same message about source in Brazil as it did in the United Kingdom: the products were the products of the international Colgate-Palmolive group controlled by Colgate-US. This was the significance in passing off of the adoption of an international corporate livery.[96]

Lloyd LJ, however, met Markwell's argument head on. Goodwill was a

---

93 [1989] RPC at 510 *per* Slade LJ. The evidence is summarised in greater detail by Falconer J at [1988] RPC 305 to 306. The test is that proposed by Buckley LJ in *Revlon* [1980] FSR 85, at 104. The use of distinguishing marks has also been advocated by the West German Federal Supreme Court, see Case I ZR 85/71 *Francesco Cinzano & Cie GmbH v Java Kaffeegeschäfte GmbH & Co.* [1974] 2 CMLR 21.

94 Both Slade and Lloyd LJJ cited with approval Lord Diplock's *dictum* in *Star Industrial Co. Ltd v Yap Kwee Kor* [1976] FSR 256, at 269: [1989] RPC at 508 to 509 *per* Slade LJ, 531 *per* Lloyd LJ. Hence, the goodwill associated with the Colgate marks and get-up in the United Kingdom was local in character and separate from that attaching to the Colgate businesses in other countries.

95 [1988] RPC 286, especially at 305.

96 [1989] RPC at 513, at 515 to 516 *per* Slade LJ.

territorial concept and manufacturers ought to be allowed to choose for themselves what goods of theirs were released onto the local market.[97]

The blunt force of this statement seems to conflict with Slade LJ's acceptance of the transnational nature of messages about source. If goodwill is local and divisible, why is the message about source not limited territorially like that about quality? Admittedly, Lloyd LJ does not go so far as to rule that representations about source are territorially limited like those about quality may be. His Lordship's judgment is confined to the question of quality. Moreover, such an assertion conflicts directly with the *Champagne Heidsieck* and *Revlon* cases and a recent ruling in the Canadian Supreme Court.[98] It is, however, consistent with the sceptical view expressed in *Bonnan*.

On the trade marks issue, their Lordships' ruling also significantly narrowed the impact of the *Revlon* case. Before rejecting Markwell's arguments in terms of the legislation, Lloyd LJ rejected Markwell's broader claim based on the corporate relationships of the Colgate-Palmolive group and the identical appearance of the Brazilian and UK trade marks in the following terms:

> But however sensible that reply might seem in an era of multinational companies possessing a network of registered trademarks and a worldwide presentation, it does not accord with the present, as yet perhaps under-developed system of trade mark protection. [Markwell]'s response may well represent the law of the future. The present reality is that each country grants trademark protection within its own territorial limits.[99]

Like the defendant in *Revlon*, Markwell conceded that its sale of the Brazilian product constituted use of Colgate trade marks condemned by section 4(1) of the Trade Marks Act 1938 (United Kingdom) unless saved by section 4(3)(a).[100]

The first part of the section 4(3)(a) defence was satisfied because Colgate-Brazil was Colgate-US' subsidiary and had used the trade marks under a licence agreement with the usual obligation to conform to Colgate-US' quality controls. Accordingly, Colgate-US had the necessary connection in the course of trade with the Brazilian imports.[101]

However, Slade and Lloyd LJJ destroyed Markwell's reliance on *Revlon* by ruling, first, that the trade marks on the Brazilian imports were Brazilian trade marks, not UK ones, and second, refusing to infer consent from the corporate relationship of the group members. Reaching these conclusions

---

97 *Ibid.* at 531. The third member of the bench, Sir George Waller, agreed with the judgments of both his brother judges.

98 The *Seiko Time* case, see subsection 2.2.3(c) below.

99 [1989] RPC 497, at 533.

100 If *Champagne Heidsieck* has any force, the concession is much more questionable here. The trade marks concededly used were the UK registrations of which Colgate-US was the proprietor and, as the Court of Appeal found, the imports were goods connected in the course of trade with Colgate-US. For the latter point, see [1989] RPC 497, at 519 *per* Slade LJ.

101 [1989] RPC 497, at 519 *per* Slade LJ citing *Aristoc v Rysta* [1945] AC 68 (HL).

involved reasserting the principle of territoriality and reviving fictions of legal personality denied in *Revlon*.

Independently of any relationship of agency, Slade and Lloyd LJJ held that Colgate-US had not applied the relevant trade marks to the Brazilian imports. The Trade Marks Act required a distinction between Brazilian trade marks and UK trade marks because a trade mark was a mark used, or proposed to be used, *in the United Kingdom* as a trade mark. Since trade marks are territorial and national in character, section 4(3)(a) was concerned only with dealings in the UK trade marks. At the time Colgate-Brazil applied the Colgate marks to the Brazilian imports, there was no question of those products being intended for use in the United Kingdom. So, Colgate-US had only authorised Colgate-Brazil to apply the Brazilian, not the UK, trade marks to the Brazilian imports.[102]

In Lloyd LJ's view, this would have been obvious if the Brazilian and UK trade marks had been visually different and the fact that they outwardly appeared the same did not change matters. But, with respect, it was the very fact that the trade marks were the same which had previously changed matters. In both *Revlon* and *Champagne Heidsieck*, trade mark infringement was denied because the trade mark conveyed the same message wherever it was used: *origin* in the *same* source.

Determining which trade marks had been applied was a subjective test dependent on the trade mark owner's intentions in Lloyd LJ's opinion.[103] However, whether a subjective or objective test were used, it was 'obvious' to his Lordship that Colgate-US had only applied the Brazilian trade marks. Factors which presumably led to that conclusion were the sale of the Brazilian imports expressly for export to the Nigerian market, the corporate group's policy of restricting exports to countries where there was no other member of the group and the different quality of the goods intended for the Brazilian and UK markets. Significantly, the Brazilian law which forbade export restrictions did not affect this conclusion.[104]

The principle in the *GE* case, imputing a subsidiary's acts to its parent, was also curbed. For Slade LJ, the *Revlon* case did not establish that every authorised application of a trade mark to goods by a subsidiary must necessarily be an application by the parent and attributing the act of the subsidiary to its parent in the absence of a true agency relationship would involve piercing the corporate veil. This his Lordship was plainly reluctant to

---

102 *Ibid.* at 521 to 522, 523 to 524 *per* Slade LJ; 533 to 534 *per* Lloyd LJ.

103 [1989] RPC at 534. Slade LJ would seem consistent with this preference. At 522, his Lordship concluded that, in using the Brazilian marks on the Brazilian products, the marks so used could not be described as marks 'proposed to be used' in the United Kingdom and this is a subjective test: *Imperial Group Ltd v Philip Morris & Co. Ltd* [1982] FSR 72 (CA).

104 Brazilian law number 5772, Article 90 was given effect in the trade mark licence agreement by clause 6 which stated that the licence did not contain 'restrictions to the industrialization or marketing, including exportation of the goods covered by the same trademarks to any country.'

do. As the agency point had not been raised in the court below, the Court of Appeal expressed no concluded view.[105]

Markwell, despite its stratagem to obtain the Brazilian imports in the first place, argued consent in two ways. First, it sought to infer consent from the clause in the trade marks licence which excluded any export bans. Second, it relied on *Revlon's* inference of consent from the corporate structure and use of a uniform 'house' trade dress.

The Court of Appeal did not use the distinction between Brazilian and UK trade marks to dismiss the claims based on consent. Instead, the court noted that Colgate-Brazil had agreed with another Colgate subsidiary, Global Export, not to export Brazilian products to any other country where another Colgate subsidiary operated. Then, severely limiting the effect of clause 6 (and the Brazilian law it implemented), the court ruled that the absence of restrictions on a particular activity did not amount to consent to undertake that activity.[106] Indeed, a court at first instance has ordered Customs to disclose to the domestic registered proprietor of trade marks the identity of an importer of *identical* goods made and marked abroad by a subsidiary of that registered proprietor.[106a] In contrast, the Revlon subsidiaries were found to consent to their parent's actions because they could not object.[107]

The *Revlon* argument led to a difference of opinion, although both Slade and Lloyd LJJ rejected it. Lloyd LJ, like Falconer J at first instance, simply distinguished *Revlon* because Colgate-Brazil sold the goods on condition that they be exported to Nigeria.[108] This had not, of course, saved the Heidsieck company in *Champagne Heidsieck*. Nor did it apply to the first of the seven shipments procured for Markwell which had been acquired on the open market in Brazil.

As in passing off, Slade LJ would have considered *Revlon* controlling if use of a trade mark only made a representation about the *origin* of the trade-marked goods. In his Lordship's opinion, however, a *registered* trade mark, in addition to its primary function of denoting source, also had a secondary function of denoting *quality*. Therefore, *Revlon* was distinguishable because

---

105   *Ibid.* at 523; see *ibid.* at 533 *per* Lloyd LJ. See also *Farmer & Co. Ltd v Anthony Hordern & Sons Ltd* (1964) 112 CLR 163, at 167 to 168; and the *Fender* case discussed below, see text from Note 142.

106   *Ibid.* at 525 *per* Slade LJ, at 534 *per* Lloyd LJ. Slade LJ further considered that clause 6 was intended to comply with Brazilian law and was to be construed strictly. It meant only that Colgate-US could not rely on the trade mark licence agreement to impose export bans. The implications of this analysis for 'technology transfer agreements' and the present Uruguay Round negotiations in GATT could be profound.

106a See *Wellcome Foundation Ltd v Attorney-General*, Kaplan J (HC Hong Kong), 4 March 1992 reported [1992] 7 EIPR D-137 and Paul Rawlinson, 'Parallel Imports: A Welcome Decision for Asia,' [1992] 7 EIPR 239. The ground for the decision would seem to be that importation constituted infringement of the local trade mark registration because the foreign manufacturer applied only the foreign trade mark to the goods, notwithstanding that they were of the same quality as the local goods.

107   See especially [1980] FSR 85, at 117 *per* Templeman LJ.

108   [1989] RPC 497, at 535 *per* Lloyd LJ citing Falconer J at [1988] RPC at 318.

of the difference in quality between the imported products and the locally produced products:

> . . . a trader by applying a U.K. registered trade mark to goods and thereby indicating their origin gives an assurance to consumers in this country that the goods are of the quality which they have come to expect from products bearing that trade mark. I accept Mr Hobbs' submission that there is nothing incongruous in holding that a U.K. registered trade mark is infringed in relation to goods which do not conform to an identifiable quality which purchasing members of the public in this country ordinarily receive by reference to that trade mark.[109]

Accordingly, his Lordship concluded there was no compelling reason to imply consent since, in the circumstances, it would sanction improper use of the UK trade marks and practise a deception on the public in the United Kingdom.

There is much common sense in Slade LJ's recognition that a registered trade mark serves a dual function, indicating both source *and* quality. But, with respect, it must be considered controversial. Orthodoxy tends to regard the function of a registered trade mark as indicating source. The quality indication is secured only indirectly by relying on the trade mark owner's self-interest. As it seems to be a rare decision involving goods from the same 'origin' but of different quality, the *Champagne Heidsieck* case lies very much at the foundation of this approach.[110]

Although the *Revlon* and *Colgate* cases concerned a very particular form of legislation, there are good reasons for considering them to be of wider application in Anglo-Commonwealth jurisdictions. For present purposes, sections 4(1) and 4(3)(a) were largely intended to codify the law declared in the case law up to *Champagne Heidsieck* which itself proceeded from perceived first principles.[111] Those principles, and the concepts which have sprung from them are the very foundations of trade mark theory in all the Anglo-Commonwealth jurisdictions; in particular, 'use as a trade

---

109   *Ibid.* at 527.

110   See also *Television Radio Centre (Pty) Ltd v Sony KK* 1987(2) 994 SA (AD) ('Sony'). For the more general case where adopting a narrow conception of the function of a trade mark did not raise a conflict between the source and quality roles, see *Aristoc v Rysta* [1945] AC 68 and *Estex Clothing Manufacturers Pty Limited v Ellis and Goldstein Limited* (1967) 116 CLR 254 and generally D.R. Shanahan, *Australian Trade Marks Law and Practice*, Law Book Company, 1982 at 21 to 26; but note the author's cogent arguments for recognition of a wider function at 244 to 255. Interestingly, although the broader function of a trade mark as denoting quality is recognised, confining the legal function to source is justified on grounds of permitting parallel imports: Friedrich-Karl Beier, 'Territoriality of Trademark Law and International Trade', 1 IIC 48, at 63 to 64, and 66 to 67 (1970); Cornish, *Intellectual Property*, at ¶¶15-013 to 15-017 and 18-001 to 18-005.

111   *Aristoc v Rysta* [1945] AC 68 and compare the Court of Appeal's reasoning in *Revlon* with that of Dillon J at first instance; see especially *per* Templeman LJ at [1980] FSR 85, 114. See also Blanco-White and Jacob, *Kerly's Law of Trade Marks*, at ¶14-29. (Ignoring as not relevant to parallel import questions the 'new' remedy of 'importing a reference', see for example Cornish, *Intellectual Property*, at ¶¶17-063 to 17-077.)

mark', 'connection in the course of trade', the 'house mark' principle and consent.[112]

For a number of reasons, the *Colgate* case must be considered a startling about-face on much of the previous case law dealing with parallel imports. In terms of the stylised situations of Table 2.1, it affirmed the tide's retreat, allowing trade marks to block parallel imports in the second situation. It reasserted the territorial limitation of trade marks and the significance of the fictions of legal personality. In passing off, however, it seems a reaffirmation of previously declared principles; the result depending largely on the facts proved.

The contrasts with *Revlon* are striking. In *Colgate*, the excluded goods were directly connected in the course of trade with the registered proprietor of the trade marks in the United Kingdom, being both made and marketed under its authority. The domestic trade marks in *Revlon* were owned and licensed to legal persons quite distinct from the owner of the foreign trade marks. Further, these distinct legal persons actually exercised independent judgment, refusing to market the foreign product domestically. Yet, the Revlon group could not exclude the parallel imports. In contrast, the *Colgate* court was extremely reluctant to go behind such legal distinctions. Further, even without separating ownership, the territorial limitations of trade mark law applied in *Colgate* would permit Revlon to exclude from the domestic market goods which it had applied only the foreign trade marks to.

Colgate's reliance on quality differences and the 'presence' of export bans also has powerful implications for previous case law. Each had previously been treated as largely irrelevant to infringement questions. Of the two, the suggestion that trade marks have a function of indicating quality may prove the more far-reaching, suggesting that the whole concept of a trade mark's function requires reconsideration. However, as far as parallel imports are concerned, the potential for export bans or, which may not be the same thing, territorially limited licences has significant practical effect (where 'anti-trust' laws do not condemn such restraints). Admittedly, Slade and Lloyd LJJ distinguished *Revlon* because of the quality differences. However, as Lloyd LJ's judgment suggests, the territorial *situs* of registered trade mark rights could apply equally where the parallel imports are not different in quality to the domestic goods. Certainly, where the imports are inferior in quality, the shortcomings of the principle of universality underlying *Revlon* and *Cinzano* are obvious. Broader justification, along the lines of *Distiller's Red Label*, for denying parallel imports where there are no 'quality' differences may be seen in the cases discussed in section 2.2.4 below.

---

112 See the *Diana Oil* case (1987) 8 IPR 545 (SC, Vic.) and *Fender Australia Pty Limited v Bevk and Sullivan* (1989) 15 IPR 257 (Fed. C), see text at Notes 171 and 142 below, respectively.

(c)   *Some problems of passing off*

Champagne Heidsieck, *Revlon* and *Colgate* had all involved issues of passing off as well as infringement. As argued above, the judgment in each on the issue of passing off seems to reflect the underlying preferences for either the principle of territoriality or of universality betrayed in the parts of the judgments dealing with the infringement question. (Indeed, one could almost go so far as to say that the view each judge took on the likelihood of deception in passing off coloured the conclusion about the infringement question.) During the 1980s, there were also a number of attempts to block parallel imports by relying on rights arising in passing off alone. Unsurprisingly, these also reflect a considerable tension about the appropriate standard.

Perhaps most interestingly, they raise a crucial difference in the nature of the remedies available under the two forms of action. Where registered trade marks are concerned, the choice has been between no injunction at all (because no infringement) or an absolute bar on importing products marked with the infringed trade mark. However, since it cures only the misrepresentation made by use of the mark rather than just use of the mark, much greater flexibility is possible in passing off. Preventing the misrepresentation may not necessarily entail an injunction barring all parallel importing activity.

The *Seiko Time* case is particularly interesting because the judgment clearly states the dangers which the common law seeks to avoid by allowing parallel imports.[113] Seiko-Time was the exclusive distributor in Canada of watches bearing the 'Seiko' brand name. It was a wholly owned subsidiary of the watches' Japanese manufacturer. The manufacturer had registered the word 'Seiko' as a trade mark in Canada, but Seiko-Time was not a registered user of the registered trade mark. In the five years of its operations Seiko-Time had, solely through its own efforts, considerably improved sales of Seiko watches in Canada. As a result of these activities, the public and dealers associated the brand name 'Seiko' with a product which was of high quality, sold by sales staff who were informed about the product and its qualities and who could provide important point-of-sales service such as advice and on-the-spot adjustments, supported by the manufacturer's warranty and after-sales service. Seiko-Time had spent considerable effort and money in providing the facilities and training the staff necessary to make this scheme a success and in promoting the Seiko watch, together with its associated customer services, to dealers and the public.

Consumers Distributing Co. was a catalogue sales chain in the United States and Canada. It was not an authorised 'Seiko' dealer. It offered for sale in Canada watches made by Seiko-Time's parent bearing the 'Seiko' brand name. These were identical in manufacture to those offered by

---

113 *Consumers Distributing Co. Ltd v Seiko Time Canada Ltd* (1984) 10 DLR (4th) 161 (Sup. Ct, Can.) overruling (1983) 128 DLR (3d) 767, 60 CPR (2d) 222, 34 OR (2d) 481 (CA, Ont.); (1980) 112 DLR (3d) 500 (HCJ Ont.).

Seiko-Time. However, it did not offer the full range of 'Seiko' watches. Nor did it provide the point-of-sales service required by Seiko-Time of authorised dealers, nor any after-sales service. When asked by purchasers, it did stamp the Seiko warranty although it was not an authorised dealer and, accordingly, could not, contrary to the expectations of its customers, bind Seiko-Time to provide the warranty service to them.

Seiko-Time proved that Consumers Distributing Co.'s activities damaged its goodwill with evidence of complaints from the consuming public and from its authorised dealers. However, that confusion was not shown to have continued after an interlocutory injunction was granted enjoining Consumers Distributing Co. from holding itself out as an authorised 'Seiko' dealer.

At first instance, Seiko-Time successfully sued Consumers Distributing Co. in passing off. Holland J held that Consumers Distributing Co. was not selling the same product as Seiko-Time because the product associated by Canadian consumers with the brand was a composite product of (1) the watch itself boxed with an instructional booklet, (2) the point-of-sale service, (3) the warranty properly filled out by an authorised dealer, and (4) the after-sale service.[114]

Since the reputation and goodwill in the Seiko brand name was associated with Seiko-Time's product, and not just the watches sold by Consumers Distributing Co., Consumers Distributing Co. was, by selling watches bearing that brand name, misrepresenting its product as that of Seiko-Time and accordingly was liable in passing off.[115] The interlocutory injunction was made permanent and, further, Consumers Distributing Co. was permanently enjoined from advertising and selling 'Seiko' watches in Canada.

Having been summarily rejected by the Ontario Court of Appeal, Consumers Distributing Co. successfully appealed to the Supreme Court of Canada.

The Supreme Court unanimously overruled the grant of the further injunction because, once Consumers Distributing Co. was prevented from holding itself out as an authorised Seiko dealer, there was no evidence of any confusion of the public or injury to Seiko-Time's reputation. Accordingly, there was no basis for the injunction.[116]

Estey J considered that the consequences of Seiko-Time succeeding were 'startling'. His Honour found three compelling arguments against such success.[117] First, success would grant Seiko-Time a 'monopoly' on the sale in Canada of a product as if it were subject to a patent. Second, it meant that the common law would be recognising 'a right to entail and control the sale of personal property, however legitimately acquired' when someone else was also marketing the identical product. This could happen when the manufacturer had already released the product into the distribution stream and received its profits from the first sale. Third, such a result was

---

114 112 DLR (3d) 500, at 509.
115 *Ibid*. at 518.
116 10 DLR (4th) 161, at 175 to 176. Estey J gave the court's opinion.
117 *Ibid*. at 174.

fundamentally in conflict with the common law doctrine of restraint of trade and free competition. That is, his Honour was clearly concerned about the monopolistic tendencies of using the passing off right for such ends and the implications for unencumbered commercial dealings in the goods.

However, Estey J recognised two important qualifications. First, his Honour did not reject outright the possibility that such a 'startling' injunction would be justified if the record had shown evidence of confusion continuing after the grant of the first, interlocutory injunction.[118] Second, Estey J made it quite plain that the question of trade mark infringement was not before the court and, hence, unconsidered.[119]

The court in *Seiko Time* was not referred to the English Court of Appeal's earlier decision to grant an interlocutory injunction, *Sony v Saray*.[120] Apart from the parties and the brand at issue, the facts in *Saray* were very similar to those in *Seiko Time*. In particular, the benefits of dealing with Sony's carefully selected authorised dealers were heavily promoted to the public as was the fact that Sony's own guarantee was only available from the authorised dealers. The most significant factual difference with *Seiko Time* was the defendant's very poor reputation. Saray's business practices had been the subject of media attention on two occasions. It had also been prosecuted for violation of consumer protection laws and had given a number of undertakings in that regard. However, the undertakings do not appear to have effected any change in Saray's business practices and it continued holding itself out as able to sell 'authorised' Sony products complete with Sony's own guarantee. Moreover, it had continued to do so after giving further undertakings at an interlocutory stage of the passing off proceedings.

In those circumstances, the Court of Appeal amended the interlocutory injunction granted at first instance to prevent Saray from selling Sony equipment *unless* each item of equipment sold bore a sticker (which could be easily seen by the customer) stating that Saray was not an authorised Sony dealer and the guarantee would be honoured by Saray, not Sony.[121] Even with such a recalcitrant defendant, the Court of Appeal, unlike the judge at first instance in *Seiko Time*, was extremely reluctant to forbid Saray dealing in any of Sony's branded products.

A further step has been taken with the grant of interlocutory injunctions

118 *Ibid.* at 174 to 175.
119 *Ibid.* at 179, 184. See also Note 55, above.
120 [1983] FSR 302. The decision at first instance in *Seiko Time* was referred to their Lordships but not cited in the judgment. For an Australian case in which the plaintiff was granted final judgment, see *Star Micronics Pty Ltd v Five Star Computers Pty Ltd* [1990] 18 IPR 225 (Fed. C) at Note 124c below. Note also the curious case of *Yardley v Higson* [1984] FSR 304 (CA) where interlocutory injunctions were granted in passing off and for copyright infringement, the discussion focusing on whether the plaintiff had misused the court's equitable jurisdiction.
121 *Ibid.* at 307 to 308. In fact, there was a second labelling requirement where Saray had modified the item to conform to UK technical requirements. A further factual difference which did not seem to play on their Lordships' decision was that Sony did have a sizeable manufacturing operation in the United Kingdom.

in *Sharp Electronics of Canada Ltd v Continental Electronic Info. Inc.*[122] The imports concerned 'Sharp' branded fax machines; otherwise, the fact situation largely corresponded to that in the two earlier cases. However, Sharp Electronics sold its products conforming to the requirements of the British Columbia Electrical Standards Board (ESB), the Canadian Standards Association (CSA) and the federal Department of Communications (DOC). With few exceptions, Continental's imports did not comply with these standards, although they did comply with the corresponding US standards (where they had been bought). At the interlocutory stage, however, Sharp Electronics only proved that it was unlawful to sell fax machines in British Columbia without ESB approval. The CSA standards were not proved to be mandatory, and the nature of the DOC standards was left open for a subsequent hearing or trial.

Continental was enjoined from holding itself out as an authorised distributor in accordance with *Seiko Time*. However, Melnick LJSC went further and restrained Continental from selling any fax machines bearing the Sharp brand which did not have ESB approval. According to his Honour:

> This is not a case, as in [*Seiko Time*], where an appropriate disclaimer will allow consumers to make an informed choice as to how much risk they wish to assume. British Columbia consumers, although they may not actively search for evidence of government safety approval when they purchase such electrical devices, are entitled to rely upon the government's diligence in serving as a watchdog. Selling some Sharp Fax machines without safety approval could, therefore, create confusion in the minds of consumers in that they may well expect all Sharp Fax machines to be safety approved. Further, any association in the minds of the public of 'Sharp' with non-safety approved equipment, especially if any of the non-approved machines were to be involved in or cause accident or mishap, could conceivably damage Sharp Electronics' reputation. Therefore, in advertising, offering for sale and selling Fax machines not approved according to the applicable safety laws and regulations of the province, I find that Sharp Electronics has established a fair question to be tried . . .[123]

It is not entirely clear how far this line of cases reflects the current position when injunctions are sought on the basis of passing off. Continental, in *Sharp Electronics*, had demonstrated that it could get ESB approval for some of the machines it imported. On the other hand, Melnick LJSC considered that the closest analogy was to the *Castrol GTX* case.[124] There and in *Colgate*, where there were clear physical differences between the domestic and foreign products, the court had no compunction about granting a general injunction against the parallel importing.

In contrast, Strayer J refused an interlocutory injunction in passing off to the Canadian registered user of two Nestle marks which was trying to prevent imports purchased in the United States from a sister subsidiary.[124a] The first

---

122   (1988) 23 CPR (3d) 330 (SC, British Columbia).
123   *Ibid*. at 337.
124   For *Castrol GTX* [1983] RPC 315, see above at Note 88.
124a *Nestlé Enterprises Ltd v Edan Food Sales Inc*. [1991] 37 CPR (3d) 480 (FCTD).

ground of refusal was the plaintiff's delay in seeking relief. Strayer J further considered that the potential for consumer confusion was insufficiently proved because purchasers of the plaintiff's range of coffee products would be in the habit of carefully scrutinising the branding and get up of coffee jars before making their selection. There were substantial differences in the labelling and get up among the local product range as well as between that range and the imports; the imports were also clearly branded as 'Mountain Blend' a brand not otherwise available in Canada; they were clearly marked as being derived from chicory, not coffee and their US manufacturing source was clearly stated.[124b] Apart from the issue of delay, conclusive in itself on an application for an interlocutory injunction, the state of the evidence before his Honour leaves the territorial principle noticed in *Bonnan's* case intact. Final judgment on liability was granted in Australia where the unauthorised dealer was wrongly holding out that the products complied with Australian technical standards and were covered by the manufacturer's warranty.[124c]

One point which is very clear, however, is that where the action is founded on passing off, scrupulous attention must be paid to proving the relevant facts. The plaintiff in *Seiko Time* 'failed' because it did not prove continuing confusion after the grant of the initial injunction. Contrast *Saray*. It also seems important to establish clearly that the defendant is holding itself out as part of the 'authorised' network.[125]

2.2.4 Independent distributors

The *Colgate* case raised parallel import issues in the context of an international corporate group. Other recent cases have been concerned with foreign producers operating in the domestic market through exclusive

---

124b *Ibid.* at 483–4 and 484–5, respectively. The action being in passing off and not infringement, the plaintiff's status as a registered user and the defendant's attack on the validity of that status were further considerations: ibid. at 486, 485 and 486, respectively. In referring to Edan's challenge to validity, Strayer J derived support from *Syntex Inc. v Novopharm Ltd* [1991] 36 CPR (3d) 129 (FCCA) where Heald JA was heavily influenced to refuse an interlocutory injunction because of Canadian requirements on pharmacists to substitute 'generic' products for 'branded' products when filling prescriptions (see Chapter 8 from Note 78). Strayer J, however, thought it appropriate to stand over the potential impact of the Canada-United States Free Trade Agreement until full trial: *ibid.* at 487. For a successful infringement action brought by a registered user, see *Mattel v GTS Acquisitions* [1989] 27 CPR (3d) 358 below from Note 177.
124c *Star Micronics Pty Ltd v Five Star Computers Pty Ltd* [1990] 18 IPR 225 (Fed. C). Star Micronics succeeded on copyright infringement, breach of sections 52 and 53 of the Trade Practices Act 1974 (Cth) and passing off. However, it is not clear what form of relief would have been granted as, in view of the 'small' number of infringing sales (71 printers), at 239 of the report Davies J sent the parties away with the admonition that '[a] commercial solution to the litigation, rather than a legal judgment, would seem to be more appropriate.'
125 Contrast *Saray* where the defendant's salesman actually named Sony, [1983] FSR at 307 and *Star Micronics*, with the strict view taken by Grosskopf JA in *Pentax*, where the proof was lacking: 1987(2) SA 961, at 977. In *Pentax*, however, the plaintiff was bound to honour the guarantee on all Pentax products, not just those it sold itself: *ibid.* 973 to 977.

distributors. Once again, the reasoning used in these decisions signals a shift. As in *Colgate*, the territorial limitation of trade mark rights to national jurisdictions is promoted to the fore and there is evidence of a reworking of other trade mark concepts.

The position of distributors under trade mark law generally, so far as marks for goods are concerned, has historically been at best uncertain. Except in special cases where the seller took special pains to select only goods of a certain quality and offered them on the market under his mark as having a certain standard,[126] a seller's association with goods was for long thought too transitory and insubstantial to amount to a connection with their preparation and production for the market qualifying for protection as a trade mark for goods. Hence, in the *Estex* case,[127] the connection denoted by a mark on goods was to its foreign manufacturer rather than the domestic wholesalers and retailers which imported them.

In the context of parallel imports, the concern has once more been market partitioning which, where the distributor was a licensee, has been dealt with by resort to the source function. It has been held, on an interlocutory application, that where the distributor is a validly registered proprietor of the trade mark, the source function of a trade mark does not preclude barring the parallel imports. This apparently depended on the territorial limitations of the trade mark in conjunction with the fiction of legal personality since the *Dunlop Tyre* case was cited in support of the ruling.[128]

However, that decision was subsequently distinguished in *Juda's* case on the ground that the validity of the trade mark's registration had not been challenged. There, the trade mark had become deceptive because it now (correctly) denoted source in the assignee but nothing had been done to inform the public of the change in source.[129] The Supreme Court of Canada endorsed *Juda's* hostility to assignments aimed at defeating parallel importers in *Magder's* case.[130]

Gibson J, at first instance, found the registered trade mark of Breck's

---

126 For example, *Major Brothers v Franklin & Sons* [1908] 1 KB 712. See also *Wilkinson Sword (Canada) Ltd v Juda* (1966) 51 CPR 55 (Ex. Ct), above from Note 56.
127 *Estex Clothing Manufacturers Pty Limited v Ellis & Goldstein Limited* (1966) 116 CLR 254. See also *Breck's Sporting Goods Co. Ltd v Magder* (1975) 17 CPR (2d) 201 (SC Can.) discussed below, see text from Note 130. However, in *dicta*, Aickin J has expressed the view that a retailer which merely imports goods and sells them also uses the trade mark as a trade mark: *Pioneer K.K. v Registrar of Trade Marks* (1977) 137 CLR 670, at 688. In that case, Pioneer had done much more including assembling the products, servicing and repairing them and undertaking advertising and promotional activities all in association with the trade marks: see Shanahan, *Australian Trade Marks Law*, at 21 to 26.
128 *Remington Rand Ltd v Transworld Metal Co. Ltd* (1960) 32 CPR 99 (Ex. Ct), for *Dunlop Tyre*, see text from Note 44, above. Contrast *Breck's Sporting Goods Co. Ltd v Magder* (1975) 17 CPR (2d) 201 (SC Can.) discussed below, see text from Note 130.
129 *Wilkinson Sword (Canada) Ltd v Juda* (1966) 51 CPR 55 (Ex. Ct), Note 56 above.
130 *Breck's Sporting Goods Co. Ltd v Magder* (1975) 17 CPR (2d) 201 (SC Can.) upholding (1973) 10 CPR (2d) 28 (CA Fed.) overruling (1971) 1 CPR (2d) 177 (Ex. Ct).

infringed by parallel imports of French fishing gear and granted injunctions against further importation. The fishing gear was all made in France by the one manufacturer under the brand 'Mepps', all products being stamped 'Made in France'. Breck's had become the manufacturer's exclusive distributor in Canada and, some years later, the *Mepps* trade mark in Canada was assigned to it. Breck's had also come to assemble and package the product for the Canadian market. Subsequently, Magder bought *Mepps* fishing gear in France and also began importing it directly into Canada where Breck's sued for trade mark infringement. Gibson J found that the trade mark symbolised goods sold in Canada by Breck's, although ultimately deriving from France. Magder's imports could not denote goods sold in Canada by Breck's and so infringed.[131]

However, this decision was overturned on appeal. Both the Federal Court of Appeals and the Supreme Court rejected Gibson J's conclusion that the trade mark was distinctive of Breck's' goods in Canada and instead found its registration was invalid. In Canada, the trade mark had originally indicated goods made in France by the French manufacturer and, despite the subsequent dealings in the mark, it still indicated that source to the public. Once again, as in *Juda's* case, at no time had anything been done to inform the public of any change in the connection signified by the trade mark.[132]

Initial consideration by Australian courts also suggested that, at least at first instance, the approach declared in *Champagne Heidsieck* and *Revlon* was too deeply entrenched to be rejected.[133]

The *Dick Smith* and *Fairstar* cases were both applications for interlocutory injunctions; the first successful, the second not. The facts were essentially the same. Atari Inc. manufactured 'Video Computer Systems'. It distributed these products worldwide through a network of exclusive distributors. To each of its products, it affixed two trade marks which were registered in Australia in Atari's name. The exclusive distributor in Australia does not appear to have been a registered user or licensee of the trade marks. The defendants each bought Atari's products abroad, imported them into Australia and sold them with Atari's trade marks affixed. Fairstar showed further enterprise by offering its own limited form of warranty to its customers. Neither defendant had Atari's, nor its exclusive distributor's, permission to sell Atari trade-marked products in Australia.

131   1 CPR (2d) at 183 to 184.
132   17 CPR (2d) at 207, 210 *per* Laskin CJC; 10 CPR (2d) at 31 to 33 *per* Jackett CJ. Contrast *Fender* (1989) 15 IPR 257, from Note 142 below, Fender-Australia had endorsed all products sold by it with a notice stating that it was the registered proprietor of the Fender marks in Australia.
133   *Atari Inc. v Dick Smith Electronics Pty Ltd* (1980) 33 ALR 20 ('the *Dick Smith* case') (SC Vic.) and *Atari Inc. and Another v Fairstar Electronics Pty Ltd* (1982) 50 ALR 274 ('the *Fairstar* case') (Fed. C); for both, see John Hockley, 'Parallel Importation of Trade Marked Goods into Australia', 16 IIC 549 (1985). *R. & A. Bailey & Co. Ltd v Boccaccio Pty Ltd* (1986) 4 NSWLR 701 (SC NSW) ('*Bailey's Irish Cream* case'), see further Julie Dodds, 'Intellectual Property', in R. Baxt and G. Kewley, *An Annual Survey of Australian Law 1986*, The Law Book Company Limited, 1987, at 294 to 297.

Starke J considered that the *Champagne Heidsieck* case might not be followed in Australia because the definition of a trade mark on which it was decided was different to that in the Australian Act. His Honour did not think it appropriate that such an issue should be decided on an interlocutory application and granted the injunction.[134]

In contrast, Smithers J found that *Champagne Heidsieck* was not subject to such an attack and considered that undesirable consequences for ordinary commerce would follow if Atari were to succeed.[135] His Honour expressed his opinion in terms as broad as Clauson J's earlier rejection of the Heidsieck company's argument:

> . . . there would be serious consequences in ordinary commerce in relation to cases where people buy on the ordinary market goods which are sold with trade marks affixed to them . . .
>
> . . . once a manufacturer puts a trade mark on his goods and sends them into the course of trade on the billowing ocean of trade, wherever people bona fide deal with those goods under that name and by reference to that trade mark, *not telling any lies or misleading anyone in any way at all*, they are simply not infringing the trade mark. They are not 'using' the mark in the relevant sense. The Act is to be read by considerations such as these and these must be the considerations which ultimately support the *Champagne [Heidsieck]* case. (*Emphasis added*)[136]

The broad and colourful language used by his Honour may, perhaps, conceal that it is possible for 'genuine' goods to tell lies or mislead when international trade is involved as *Cinzano* and *Colgate* show.

Bailey's Irish Cream case was a final judgment and concerned the efforts of the producer of a liqueur, Bailey's Original Irish Cream, to protect its exclusive distributor in Australia against imports from the Netherlands. The plaintiff produced, bottled and labelled this liqueur in Ireland. It distributed the liqueur throughout the world through a network of exclusive distributors. The liqueur was sold in bottles of a distinctive shape and these bore labels comprised of words and an artistic work, any copyright in which was owned by the plaintiff. The plaintiff had registered an Australian trade mark substantially in the form of the label, its Australian distributor being the registered user. The defendant's bottles (and liqueur), bought in the Netherlands, were identical to those offered on the Australian market through the plaintiff's authorised distributor. There were only minor differences in the labels. One difference was the name and address of the exclusive distributor for the country in which the plaintiff intended the bottle to be sold. The plaintiff succeeded on infringement of its copyright but failed under its trade mark.[137]

---

134 33 ALR 20, at 23 to 24.
135 50 ALR 274, at 276 to 277.
136 *Ibid.* at 277. The same result was reached by South African courts in similar fact situations: *Pentax* 1987(2) SA 961 (AD); *Frank & Hirsch (Pty) Ltd v Roopnand Brothers* 1987(3) SA 165 (D&CLD) ('*TDK*').
137 For consideration of parallel imports involving copyright, see Chapter 4 at Note 207.

On the trade mark issue, the plaintiff's argument anticipated the view successful in *Colgate* by arguing that the territorial nature of trade mark rights required the court to have regard only to those bottles which the plaintiff had attached the Australian trade mark to. These were defined as the bottles which the plaintiff had selected for the Australian market – that is, those affixed with a label bearing the Australian distributor's name and address.[138] The defendant relied on the course of authority establishing that a trade mark is a badge of origin, not control and asserted that it was unreal to split a worldwide market and a worldwide trade mark into national components.

Young J felt that there were points of attractiveness in the plaintiff's argument that the *Champagne Heidsieck* and *Revlon* cases were inconsistent with High Court authority. The plaintiff argued that these established that the trade mark proprietor must, at least, have a commercial understanding that its products marked with its trade mark would be projected into trade in Australia before they could be considered 'genuine' goods.[139] However, his Honour considered that it would be 'too bold a step' to accept the argument since it involved rejecting the line of authority based on *Champagne Heidsieck* by relying on cases which were concerned with entirely different issues.[140] Accordingly, Young J, like Smithers J, adopted *Champagne Heidsieck*.[141]

To this point, the decisions show considerable determination to enforce the role of a trade mark as an indicator of source and to ensure that, once a trade mark owner released its product on to the 'billowing oceans of trade', those goods would pass wherever the gales of competition might blow them. Arguments that distributors required protection from 'free riders' received short shrift. However, like the Advocate-General in the *Distillers' Red Label* case, courts have been increasingly responding to demands to protect distributors from such inroads and have been developing trade mark principles to achieve their ends.

---

138   The *Castrol GTX* case was referred to his Honour but not cited in the judgment. The plaintiff ran a second argument that its consent to use of the mark on the Dutch bottles had ceased once those bottles had reached the final purchaser in the Netherlands: 4 NSWLR 701, at 705 to 706. The second argument, while ingenious, would appear flawed since it claimed that the trade mark owner alone can determine whether or not the goods were in the course of trade. But, this issue should also involve what the purchaser did, or intended to do, with the goods. Otherwise, it seems difficult to assess when the goods have reached their final purchaser. See for example *W.D. & H.O. Wills (Australia) Ltd v Rothmans Ltd* (1956) 94 CLR 182.

139   *Ibid.* at 709 referring to *Re Registered Trade Mark 'Yanx'* (1951) 82 CLR 199, *Rothmans* case (1956) 94 CLR 182; and the *Estex* case (1967) 116 CLR 254.

140   *Ibid.* In an ironic twist, Young J felt the force of Aickin J's warnings in the *Pioneer* case (1977) 137 CLR 670, at 688 on this danger although, in *Pioneer*, Aickin J overturned a decision of the Registrar seeking to impose a condition on a registered user which would have prevented it using its rights against parallel importers.

141   *Ibid.* at 709 to 710, expressing his ruling in quite general terms:

> . . . the right of exclusive use conferred by the Trade Marks Act 1955 (Cth), s 58, upon the registered proprietor to the exclusive use for the trade mark in relation to goods only operates to prevent the sale in Australia of goods which are not the proprietor's but which are marked with the proprietor's mark.

The discussion which follows divides the issue into cases where the distributor received an assignment of the domestic rights and those where it was a licensee. The different form of the distributor's relationship to the trade mark necessitates some difference in the minutiae of legal analysis. But, fundamentally, the underlying concerns are the same. The courts have been increasingly impressed by the valuable investments made by the distributor in developing the market and are seeking ways to allow them the fruits of that success.

(a) *Assignee distributors*

In 1987, Fender-Australia was appointed the exclusive distributor for Australia of *Fender* trade-marked guitars and accessories, formalising a relationship dating from 1978. Its products were made for it in the United States by Fender-US, the original owner of the Australian trade mark registrations. Fender-Australia was owned independently of Fender-US and had received the Australian trade marks by assignment from Fender-US several months after its appointment as exclusive distributor. Its rights to use the trade marks would end with the distributorship. It was also only permitted to use the Fender name and marks in association with Fender-US' products.

Sullivan and Bevk each owned music stores. They had separately imported Fender products from the US where they had been made, marked and sold by Fender-US. Sullivan and Bevk had both imported second-hand guitars which they were offering for sale as second-hand. Some of Bevk's imports, however, were new, bought at retail. Fender-Australia sued them both for trade mark infringement over the sales of all the imports.[142]

Under the terms of its appointment, Fender-Australia was responsible at its own expense for advertising and promoting Fender products in Australia. Its responsibilities included running an efficient repair and maintenance service and stocking adequate quantities of repair and replacement parts. It had established a network of over 200 authorised dealers throughout Australia with service facilities in each state. Its promotional activities included a network of sales representatives regularly visiting its authorised outlets, product information bulletins, exhibitions, seminars and clinics. It also undertook substantial advertising. It further assumed some responsibility for quality control: inspecting each product, changing electrical parts unsuitable for Australia and overseeing the expertise of its authorised dealers and repairers, sometimes restricting the lines supplied to dealers whose expertise was insufficient. Since its assumption of exclusive distribution rights, sales figures showed 'a story of continuous and rapid expansion'.

Burchett J started with a strong affirmation of the territoriality principle.

---

142 *Fender Australia Pty Limited v Bevk & Sullivan* (1989) 15 IPR 257 (Fed. C). Bevk's challenge to the validity of Fender-Australia's registration as owner was reserved for a subsequent hearing.

His Honour noted that even where a product was made overseas and sold around the world it was possible for an independent *Australian* goodwill to develop around the Australian trade mark.[143] On the facts, Burchett J concluded:

> . . . members of that section of the Australian public having an interest in acoustic and electric guitars would be likely to understand the trade marks in question as indicating products acquired from their American producer, *and* distributed in Australia by [Fender-Australia]. The marks are badges of a commercial origin in Australia, *as well as* of an anterior source overseas. (*Emphasis added*)[144]

Burchett J then proceeded to find that Fender-Australia could use its Australian trade mark rights to bar parallel imports of new Fender products but not of the secondhand goods.

In finding that the parallel imports of the new goods infringed Fender-Australia's registered trade mark, Burchett J did not rely on the *Dunlop Tyre* case which does not appear to have been cited to his Honour.[145] Instead, Burchett J relied on the independent, valuable goodwill in the trade mark Fender-Australia had built up in Australia and on the territorial limitation of trade mark rights, ruling that:

> . . . [Fender-Australia] is not a subsidiary of the United States corporation. The tie between them is contractual. As an entity independently controlled, [Fender-Australia] has built up its own goodwill, and it has been permitted to attain by assignment the position of registered proprietor of the trade mark. Protection of its rights under the mark would carry out the statutory purpose, for that purpose is to make effective the use of the mark by the registered proprietor to identify and distinguish goods connected in trade with it, and with its goodwill.[146]

Fender-Australia had not itself affixed the trade mark to the parallel imports and there was no ground to infer its consent to that affixation. *Revlon* did not apply because the 'house mark' concept was limited to very special circumstances not present in this case.[147] *Champagne Heidsieck* and

---

143   *Ibid*. at 261.
144   *Ibid*. Compare Gibson J's conclusion in *Magder*'s case; see text at Note 131 above.
145   The authorities which provided most support were a decision of the US Supreme Court, *Bourjois v Katzel* 260 US 689 (1923) *revg* 275 Fed. 539 (2d Cir. 1921) *revg* 274 Fed. 856 (SDNY 1920) and the Exchequer Court's ruling in *Breck's Sporting Goods Co. Ltd v Magder* (1971) 1 CPR (2d) 177. On the difficulties with the *Katzel* case, see section 2.3.3 below; for the latter, see text at Notes 130 to 132 above.
146   15 IPR 257, at 270.
147   His Honour considered that in the majority judgment the finding of consent did not depend just on sale by the overseas manufacturer without a limitation on export. That factor was combined with sale by a member of a corporate group of a very special nature. The mere fact of corporate interrelationship was itself insufficient. The relevant factors seem to have been: (a) the registered proprietor (Suisse) carried on no other business; (b) its rights to use the Revlon marks existed only as long as it was controlled by the parent of the Revlon group (so also Fender-Australia's rights to use the Fender marks were restricted to products made by Fender-US); (c) use of the trade marks in conjunction with the endorsement: 'REVLON New York, Paris, London.'; (d) the products sold

the *Bailey's Irish Cream* case were also distinguished because they only concerned the situation where the registered proprietor was the same in both countries and itself made and sold the goods in both countries.[148] Applying the territorial approach taken in *Colgate*, Burchett J concluded that the trade mark on the parallel imports was not the Australian trade mark:

> Here, the mark affixed to the guitars purchased by Mr Bevk in the United States was affixed, not as a trade mark under the Trade Marks Act 1955 with which the United States manufacturer had no concern, but as a trade mark in the United States under United States law.[149]

Fender illustrates one particular difficulty in conceptualising the same trade mark as being either Australian or foreign. In *Colgate*, the goods were made by different manufacturers and intended for different markets. Here, however, the manufacturer was the same. If Fender-US did not designate part of its production for Fender-Australia but merely supplied from its general production, it seems ludicrous to speak of applying the US trade mark or the Australian trade mark.[150] However, with respect, in *Fender* the distinction is accurate. The evidence before Burchett J showed that Fender-Australia undertook some work to adapt the products to the Australian market as well as providing the comprehensive pre- and post-sales services associated by the relevant public with the mark. In such circumstances, it must be correct to identify Fender-Australia as the source of the goods in Australia.

Burchett J's reasoning mixes two otherwise conflicting approaches. On one hand, taken in isolation, his Honour's distinction between the US and Australian trade marks suggests a purely territorial solution: the trade marks were owned by different legal persons in the different territories, therefore it infringed the rights of one to import the goods of the other.[151] Indeed, as in the *Colgate* case, the trade marks need not even be owned by different persons. On the other hand, Burchett J stressed Fender-Australia's independent goodwill. Thus, denotation of source did not depend only on registration, the trade mark also had to distinguish the goods as being

---

domestically were not identified as coming from the registered users; and (e) there was no creation of any separate goodwill such as that built up by Fender-Australia: *Ibid*. at 267 to 268.

148   *Ibid*. at 266.

149   *Ibid*. at 271; this, of course, was the very point which had troubled Buckley LJ in *Revlon*, above at section 2.2.3(a). The *Colgate* case relied on was the decision at first instance.

150   Compare *Mattel Canada Inc. v GTS Acquisitions Ltd and Nintendo of America Inc.* (1989) 27 CPR (3d) 358, see text from Note 177 below.

151   On this aspect, note his Honour's distinction of *Champagne Heidsieck* and the *Bailey's Irish Cream* case referred to above at Notes 35 and 137 above respectively, together with the reference to the copyright cases which refused to imply consent from the mere fact of marketing by the copyright owner in another country: *ibid*. at 269 referring to *Interstate Parcel Express Co. Pty Ltd v Time-Life International (Nederlands) BV* (1977) 138 CLR 534 among others. If as has been argued (see among others Ladas, 'Exclusive Territorial Licences Under Patents', 3 IIC 335 at 345 to 346 (1972)), a trade mark does not serve a marketing function, the analogy to these copyright cases would seem apt; for the *Time-Life* case, see Chapter 4.2.2(c) below.

the registered proprietor's in fact. This second approach is more akin to *Champagne Heidsieck* and *Revlon* which both disregarded territorial limitations and, in *Revlon*, legal fictions.

His Honour's reliance on Fender-Australia's independent goodwill is not without its difficulties. 'Goodwill' is a concept of passing off rather than the law of trade marks.[152] Admittedly, in the *Champagne Heidsieck* case, Clauson J considered that the creation of registered trade mark rights did not enlarge rights existing at common law. But, the context was different.[153] His Lordship's opinion did not address the question of the relationship of trade marks and passing off in a wider context and there is ample authority concluding that the two actions are not co-extensive.[154] Indeed, it has been authoritatively laid down that one of the main objects in introducing the registration of trade marks was to obviate the need of proving goodwill.[155] Accordingly, with respect, in trade marks the critical question is whether the defendants' use of the trade mark makes an incorrect connection in the course of trade.

This criticism does not necessarily mean, however, that the conclusion of infringement against the 'new' parallel imports is wrong. As the registered proprietor, absent a challenge to validity, the Trade Marks Act postulates that the connection indicated is to Fender-Australia and, since the parallel imports had never been connected with Fender-Australia, the postulated connection would be incorrect.[156] If the Fender marks in Australia actually reflected a connection in the course of trade with someone other than Fender-Australia, the appropriate course would be to challenge Fender-Australia's registration as proprietor.[157]

The distinction between passing off and registered trade marks may often not matter. However, in this case, the failure to recognise it helped mislead his Honour on the issue of the second-hand goods. Moreover, as a practical

---

152 That his Honour was indeed applying the passing off concept is confirmed in part by the reference to *Bourjois v Katzel* 260 US 689 (1923) section 2.3.3 below and the treatment of the second-hand imports, below from Note 159.

153 His Lordship was addressing an argument that the mere fact of registration afforded the proprietor an absolute right to stop anyone selling the proprietor's own goods to which the proprietor itself had affixed the trade mark; Clauson J finding that such a right existed neither in passing off or infringement. Clauson J thought it would be surprising that an Act to introduce a registration system would have introduced such far-reaching changes, but *then* went on to conclude that the defendant's use complained of was not actually use as a trade mark because the only connection indicated was with the trade mark owner, which (on the narrow view of the relevant connection taken by his Lordship) was true: [1930] 1 Ch. 330, at 338 to 339, see above from Note 35.

154 For example, *Saville Perfumery Ltd v June Perfect Ltd* (1941) 58 RPC 147.

155 See *GE Trade Mark* [1973] RPC 297, at 327 *per* Lord Diplock.

156 For example, *Irving's Yeast-Vite Ltd v Horsenail* (1934) 51 RPC 110 (HL); *Mark Foy's Ltd v Davies Coop and Co. Ltd* (1956) 95 CLR 190.

157 For examples, see *Juda's* case (1966) 51 CPR 55 (Ex. Ct); *Magder's* case (1975) 17 CPR (2d) 201 (SC Can.); see text at Notes 56 to 58 and 130 to 132, respectively. This was, of course, the point postponed. But, *Fender* would seem distinguishable in that (a) the advertising promoted Fender-Australia's corporate name as well as the trade marks; and (b) the products were sold bearing a label identifying Fender-Australia as the trade mark owner: 15 IPR at 261.

matter, it means that trade mark owners must prove the goodwill which it was one part of the Act's intention to abandon. Further, the form of liability may drastically affect the remedy.[158]

On the second-hand goods, Burchett J held:

> A person who sells used goods, though by reference to a name they bore as a mark when sold new, does not by doing so represent that there is any connexion in trade between him and the manufacturer or original distributor of the goods, nor that any goods so marked are wearing his badge: cf. *Shell* case at 425. Nor does he represent that there is any connexion in trade between the goods, in their character of used goods, and the registered proprietor of the mark: cf. *Champagne Heidsieck* case, where Clauson J said that 'the exclusive right to use the mark conferred on the registered proprietor . . . is the right to use the mark as a trade mark – i.e., as indicating that the goods upon which it is placed are his goods and to exclude others from selling under the mark wares which are not his'. It would be an unwarranted extension of the protection offered by the *Trade Marks Act*, and an undue restriction of the freedom of trade, to construe s. 62 as concerned with an importation and sale of used guitars.[159]

Hence, his Honour denied infringement for two reasons: first, selling second-hand goods by reference to the trade mark on them did not indicate any trade connection between the seller and the trade mark owner; and, second, it also did not indicate any trade connection between the trade mark owner and the *second-hand* goods.

The reference to the *Shell* case appears to refer to the passage where Kitto J pointed out that whether a trade mark was being used to indicate a connection in the course of trade depended on the particular context of the usage. To Burchett J, the singular feature of the context under his consideration was that the goods were second-hand, being sold as such by a second-hand business. From this, a number of alternative solutions led to the same conclusion: no infringement.

First, his Honour reviewed the authorities to conclude that once goods were bought for consumption they were no longer in the course of trade. The rights conferred by registration did not extend beyond the point of retail sale and use by the consumer.[160] However, immunity followed not just from this conclusion but in combination with the 'fundamental nature' of trade marks 'as an aspect of the goodwill of a particular business'. In his Honour's view:

> The goodwill of a business producing or marketing goods is connected with the sale of the goods it supplies, not with a market in what those goods will become after they have been used for some time. The goodwill with which the mark of Holden cars is connected is that of a business manufacturing and selling

---

158 See the *Seiko Time* case (1984) 10 DLR (4th) 161 (SC Can.) and the other cases discussed in subsection 2.2.3(c) above.

159 15 IPR at 265. The reference to the *Shell* case is a reference to *The Shell Co. of Australia Ltd v Esso Standard Oil (Australia) Ltd* (1963) 109 CLR 407 ('the *Oil Drop* case').

160 *Ibid.* at 262 to 264, the case law review including *Aristoc v Rysta* [1945] AC 68, *W.D. & H.O. Wills (Australia) Ltd v Rothmans* (1956) 94 CLR 182 and the *Estex* case (1966) 116 CLR 254.

new cars. A business selling used cars may also have a goodwill, and a mark associated with it, but that goodwill is not to be confused with the goodwill of General Motors, however much the reputation of Holden cars may assist a particular sale. Generally, a second-hand business will deal in a number of different makes of goods, as indeed is the case here . . .[161]

Alternatively, the retail sale and subsequent use of the goods broke the connection between the goods and the trade mark owner and a new connection was imposed: between the second-hand dealer and the goods. The latter connection was the relevant one for trade mark purposes.[162]

Finally, since Burchett J considered it would be very inconvenient in practice to distinguish between goods sold second-hand in Australia and those sold second-hand overseas, his Honour concluded: 'The sale of imported second-hand Fender guitars, together with other makes of second-hand guitars, is not deceptive and does not impinge on the goodwill to which [Fender-Australia]'s trade mark is related.'[163]

There are, with respect, a number of difficulties with his Honour's reasoning. Taking the 'interposition of a new origin' theory first, it leads to a result fundamentally at odds with trade mark law. A trade mark registration gives the trader the *exclusive* right to distinguish its goods from those of other traders. Except in special circumstances of concurrent use, no other trader may use the mark for that purpose on goods of the class covered by the registration. Otherwise, the function of the trade mark would be undermined because to permit such use would practise deception on the public. Yet, the 'interposition of a new origin' theory posits exactly that deception.

The alternative 'fundamental nature' argument is also suspect. It turns on 'principles which predate legislative intervention in the area of trade marks.'[164] As the subsequent references to 'goodwill' indicate (six times in the same paragraph), Burchett J introduces considerations of passing off where they were not previously appropriate. As already discussed, under the Trade Marks Act the issue is whether the defendant is using the registered trade mark without permission as a trade mark. But, as discussed in connection with 'new' goods, this is a different test, not dependent on questions of goodwill.

Accordingly, the question of the respective business goodwills involved is irrelevant in an infringement action. The real issue is whether the defendant is using the registered trade mark *as a trade mark* inconsistently with the registered proprietor's exclusive rights. So understood, Burchett J's example of General Motors and the car dealer needs to be re-examined. What connection in the course of trade does the dealer's employment of the *Holden* trade mark denote? It seems unlikely that any reputation the dealer may have for offering 'good quality' second-hand cars attaches to the *Holden* mark rather than the dealer's own trade name and get-up. In

---

161   *Ibid*. at 264.
162   *Ibid*. for the interposition of a new origin.
163   *Ibid*. at 265.
164   *Ibid*.

using the *Holden* mark, what the dealer tells the public is that he is offering cars made and prepared for the market by General Motors and, so long as they are not being presented as anything other than second-hand vehicles, the trade connection indicated is true. This is different to the situation in *Fender*, however, because in *Fender* the imported, second-hand goods, had never been connected in the course of trade with the registered proprietor in *Australia*.[164a]

The authorities referred to by Burchett J on this part of the case were not particularly helpful, dealing for the most part with the issue of whether second-hand goods were being passed off as new. However, there are cases inconsistent with his Honour's views.

In *Hoover v Air-Way*, Bennett J granted an interlocutory injunction for infringement, but not passing off, against a defendant selling reconditioned products of the plaintiff.[165] In the *Shell* case referred to by Burchett J, Kitto J, discussing the introduction into the Act of the words 'in the course of trade', says at one point:

> . . . but presumably the purpose was to ensure that (to take an example) anyone who put petrol not being 'Shell' petrol into a can marked 'Shell', but without any intention of supplying it to anyone else, should not be held to infringe the trade mark 'Shell' . . .[166]

This passage, at the least, suggests that the trade-marked bottle (or, more accurately, the bottle and its contents) could well pass into and out of the course of trade – a conclusion Burchett J was not well-disposed towards. The *dictum* could be read more broadly so that even a consumer may infringe the registration if, after using the contents, he were to refill the bottle and attempt to deal with it commercially. Two days before Burchett J delivered judgment, Fraser J in the New Zealand High Court granted interlocutory injunctions for trade mark infringement against an importer of second-hand tyres from Japan. On the strength of the plaintiffs' case, Fraser J considered that the relevant question was whether or not the defendant importer's actions amounted to use of the mark on the second-hand goods as a trade mark or as likely to be taken as importing a reference to the plaintiffs or their tyres. He held:

> Although there is no evidence of any actual confusion on the part of any consumer, I infer that persons buying from the defendants second-hand tyres which bear the trade mark and device of the plaintiffs *would naturally assume* that the tyres had been made *by or with the authority of the plaintiffs*, the proprietors and users of the marks. Such an assumption may well carry with it a further assumption as to quality (eg on the basis of previous usage of the plaintiffs' tyres) and the risk in the future that the quality of the Japanese tyres

---

164a See *South Pacific Tyres NZ Ltd v David Craw Cars* [1992] 24 IPR 99 (HC NZ) at Notes 167–8 below.

165 (1936) 53 RPC 399 (Ch. D). The unchallenged evidence before his Lordship was that the defendant had replaced the three essential parts of the vacuum cleaner; bag, motor and brush. See generally, Cornish, *Intellectual Property*, at ¶¶17-001 to 17-002.

166 109 CLR at 424.

will be attributed to the plaintiffs' tyres. I think that confusion must inevitably follow from the fact that the tyres are being sold in the way of trade with a trade mark and device identical to that of the plaintiffs.[167] (*Emphasis added*)

As the quotation makes clear, the fact that the defendants made it clear they were selling second-hand goods was irrelevant to the trade mark issue. Accordingly, Fraser J held that the plaintiffs had established a strong *prima facie* case to relief.

In *David Craw Cars*, the plaintiffs apparently had no interest in or arrangement with the Japanese manufacturer of the imports and Fraser J distinguished the *Fairstar* case from the instant facts on the basis of a possible quality difference between the foreign and domestic goods *and* the fact that the foreign tyres were not marked by or with the authority of the plaintiffs.[167a] With respect, Fraser J's conclusion, although only a decision at an interlocutory stage, is persuasive and equally applicable to the facts in *Fender*: the imports in *Fender* did not indicate a connexion in the course of trade with the registered proprietor.

The inconsistency between Burchett J's ruling on second-hand and new goods draws out the fallacy underpinning the principle of universality. Had Burchett J adopted the approach suggested above, it may well have been necessary to bar the second-hand parallel imports as well as the new products. Moreover, his Honour's refusal to distinguish between second-hand goods sold in Australia and those sold overseas must be questioned. If Fender-Australia had first sold the second-hand goods new in Australia, it is arguable that their subsequent sale second-hand would not have infringed its rights because the connection in the course of trade indicated would have been a connection with it.[168] In this hypothetical case, the situation would seem appropriate to apply Clauson J's conclusion against infringement in the *Champagne Heidsieck* case because territorial limitations like those found compelling in *Colgate* and by Burchett J on the issue of new parallel imports would not arise. But, for used goods originally sold outside Australia, the position would be quite different. Applying the conclusion reached by Burchett J for new goods, parallel imports should be blocked because the trade connection, as in *Dunlop Tyre*, would be to someone other than the registered proprietor.

---

167 *South Pacific Tyres NZ Ltd v David Craw Cars Ltd* [1992] 24 IPR 99, 104–5, judgment 24 July 1989. Immediately before stating his conclusion, his Honour made it plain that he considered the defendant's use *both* use as a trade mark *and* use likely to be taken as importing a reference to the plaintiffs or their goods: *ibid.* at 103. For comment, see Barbara Sullivan, 'Trade Mark Infringement Decisions in Australia and New Zealand: Second-hand Goods,' (1991) 2 AIPJ 44 and my further comment (1991) 2 AIPJ 157.

167a *Ibid.* 101 and 103, respectively.

168 The *Estex* case (1966) 116 CLR 254, at 271 to 272 holding that the 'manufacturer' responsible for projecting the goods into the course of trade in Australia, rather than a 'mere' distributor or retailer, is the connection indicated by the use of the trade mark. But, note Aickin J's *dicta* in *Pioneer K.K. v Registrar of Trade Marks* (1977) 137 CLR 670, at 688 that such use may also indicate a connection with subsequent users which Burchett J recognises when finding that the Fender mark in Australia designated a dual source; one proximate, the other anterior.

Burchett J considered such a distinction 'inconvenient in practice' since a second-hand dealer would never know whether he was infringing or not.[169] That was not a problem before his Honour. The goods giving rise to the action were all bought overseas. Further, Fender-Australia's goods were all sold with labels identifying it as the exclusive distributor. If the defendant could not work out whether the second-hand goods infringed, why was he in any better position *vis-à-vis* the new guitars he also imported?

Overall, *Fender* presents some intriguing issues. Of prime concern, Burchett J accepted the argument rejected in the *Bailey's Irish Cream* case based on the inconsistency between *Champagne Heidsieck* and the more modern approach taken in more recent Australian High Court authority. This was mainly to protect a valuable commercial investment. It is not clear, however, that his Honour did so because he recognised the fundamental territorial limits to trade mark rights or required actual, independent goodwill to be proved.

(b)   *Licensee distributors*

In its *Seiko Time* decision, the Supreme Court of Canada refused to grant an injunction in passing off against a discount house's sales of 'genuine', imported Seiko products. However, referring to *Remington Rand*, the court distinguished the position under trade mark law and commented that Seiko-Time may have had standing to sue for infringement if it had been a registered user.[170] Since then, further cases have raised the issue and the registered user successfully repelled the parallel imports in one of those, *Mattel*, on the basis of infringement of *its* trade mark rights.

In Australia, McGarvie J, faced with the situation, refused to grant relief under the Trade Marks Act. A business in Greece, Calogeropoulos & Sons, was registered in Australia as the proprietor of the trade mark *Diana* for olive oil which it produced in Greece for sale throughout the world. Calogeropoulos had appointed an exclusive distributor for Australia, Delphic, which had been registered as a registered user. However, although the product was good in quality, sales were poor because of the high price demanded by Calogeropoulos from Delphic. Relations between the two were not the best and Calogeropoulos was persuaded by Elco to supply it with stocks to sell in Australia. When Elco started selling in Australia under the *Diana* mark, Delphic sued after Calogeropoulos refused to act. Delphic succeeded on the tort of inducing breach of contract but not for infringement.

McGarvie J found no infringement of Calogeropoulos' rights as registered proprietor. On this point, his Honour agreed with and applied Young J's decision in the *Bailey's Irish Cream* case.[171]

---

169   15 IPR at 265.

170   (1984) 10 DLR (4th) 161, at 184 *per* Estey J, see text at Note 119 above.

171   The *Diana Oil* case (1987) 8 IPR 545, at 555 (SC Vic.). His Honour saw that part of the case as a straightforward application of *Champagne Heidsieck*.

However, McGarvie J went on to consider whether any rights of the registered user had been infringed. McGarvie J assumed that the rights in a registered trade mark prevented anyone using the trade mark inconsistently with its use to indicate a connection in the course of trade with *either* the proprietor *or* the registered user. That is, infringement proceedings also lay to protect an indication of source in the registered user.[172] Delphic would have succeeded, but for Calogeropoulos' direct consent to Elco's actions; in such circumstances, a registered user could not sue where its proprietor could not.[173]

McGarvie J *assumed* that a trade mark may denote two different sources: one being the registered proprietor, the other its registered user. Some support for the assumption may be derived from the *Pioneer* case. There Aickin J was confronted by an argument from the Registrar that to be valid under the Act, use by a registered user had to be a use indicating source only in the registered user. In rebutting that proposition, Aickin J said only that:

> The references [in the definition of 'trade mark'] to the registered proprietor or the registered user are not mutually exclusive alterantives [*sic*]. The use by a registered user may properly indicate a connexion both with the registered user and the registered proprietor, including a connexion which does not distinguish between them. This must follow from the fact that the use need not indicate the identity of either the registered proprietor or the registered user.[174]

In this passage, his Honour did not directly rebut the proposition that the use could refer to the registered user alone. However, earlier in his judgment, Aickin J stated:

> These cases demonstrate that the *essential requirement* for the maintenance of the *validity* of a trade mark is that *it must indicate a connexion in the course of trade with the registered proprietor*, even though the connexion may be slight, such as selection or quality control or control of the user in the sense in which a parent company controls a subsidiary. Use by either the registered proprietor or a licensee (whether registered or otherwise) will protect the mark from attack on the ground of non-user, but *it is essential both that the user maintains the connexion of the registered proprietor* with the goods and that the use of the mark does not become otherwise deceptive. Conversely *registration of a registered user will not save the mark if there ceases to be*

---

172   *Ibid.* at 556.

173   *Ibid.* relying on *Levi Strauss v The French Connection* [1982] FSR 443. The argument that consent to marketing in a foreign country is no consent to marketing in the domestic country (see the copyright case, *Pitt Pitts* discussed at subsection 4.2.2(a) below) could not apply here as Calogeropoulos sold to Elco for the very purpose of Elco selling in Australia, see 8 IPR at 549 to 550.

174   137 CLR at 686. Perhaps, drawing on this has led to the suggestion that the source indicated by a trade mark may have a composite nature, being to the registered proprietor and the registered user together, if both are identified in connection with the trade mark's use, see Anthony Muratore and Donald Robertson, 'The Trade Marks Act 1955 and Parallel Imports', (1984) 7 UNSWLJ 117, at 131 to 133.

the relevant connexion in the course of trade with the proprietor or the mark otherwise becomes deceptive.[174a] (*Emphasis added*)

While his Honour's views about relying on use by an unregistered licensee to defeat an application for expungement on grounds of non-use seem to conflict with the express statutory provisions, Aickin J clearly contemplated that the relevant connection in the course of trade was to the registered proprietor *alone* and it is in that context that his Honour's subsequent remarks must be read.

Furthermore, in a successful application to strike out a registered user joined as a plaintiff with the registered proprietor, Falconer J said:

> That [section] seems to me to be a complete code of the rights of the registered user, certainly in so far as the bringing of actions for infringement is concerned, and it seems to me quite clear that the only circumstance that the statute provides for in which the registered user may be a plaintiff is where he has called upon the proprietor to take proceedings in respect of the infringement in question and the proprietor after the stipulated period of two months has either refused to do so or has neglected to do so. In those circumstances, the registered user may himself bring proceedings in his own name and, it goes on to say, 'as if he were the proprietor.' That gives him the right to bring not only the proceedings but to sue as if he were the proprietor, with all the rights there, so it seems to me, of the proprietor.[175]

The question, then, is what is meant by a registered user suing 'as the proprietor'. The Trade Marks Act 1955 (Cth) section 78(1), subject to any agreement to the contrary, gives a registered user the right to sue for infringement in its own name in specified circumstances and section 6(1) provides that the connection in the course of trade to be indicated may be one *either* to the proprietor *or* the registered user in its definition of 'trade mark'. But, section 77(1) provides that 'permitted use' 'shall be deemed to be use by the registered proprietor' and section 62(1) only exempts from infringement a registered user using by way of permitted use. Moreover, the Act tolerates a registered user's permitted use for the same rationale that unregistered licensing is now permitted: the use by the registered user is ultimately subject to the registered proprietor's control and so denotes source in the registered proprietor.[176] Hence, from the context and role of registered users in the scheme of the Act, the role of the registered user

---

174a   *Ibid.* at 683 referring to *Re Bostitch TM* [1963] RPC 183; *British Petroleum Co. Ltd v European Petroleum Distributors Ltd* [1968] RPC 54; *GE Trade Mark* [1969] RPC 418, [1970] RPC 339 (CA); and *Heublein Inc. v Continental Liqueurs Pty Ltd* [1960] 103 CLR 435.

175   *Levi Strauss* [1982] FSR 443, at 444 to 445 discussing Trade Marks Act 1938, section 28. Section 28(2) actually states that permitted use 'shall be deemed to be use by the proprietor thereof, and shall be deemed not to be use by a person other than the proprietor . . .' which is materially the same as Trade Marks Act 1955 (Cth) section 77(1) discussed below.

176   See *McGregor's TM* [1979] RPC 36, Shanahan, *Australian Trade Marks Law and Practice*, at 25 to 26, and 244 to 255 and Cornish, *Intellectual Property*, at ¶¶17-058 to 17-062. See also, Lahore *et al.*, *Intellectual Property in Australia: Patents, Designs and Trade Marks*, Butterworths, 1981, Service 33, §4.4.015(c).

suing 'as the proprietor' should be limited to insuring that the trade mark is only used to indicate a connection in the course of trade to the registered proprietor. A registered user's rights to sue for infringement must be limited accordingly.

Subsequently, however, a registered user has successfully obtained an interlocutory injunction against a parallel importer for infringement of its trade mark rights and for unfair competition.[177] 'Nintendo USA' was the registered proprietor in Canada of the trade mark *Nintendo* for video games. It was the exclusive distributor of Nintendo games for North America but had appointed 'Mattel' as its exclusive distributor in Canada; Mattel becoming the registered user. GTS was buying Nintendo games in the United States and importing them into Canada for sale.

The products for sale by both Nintendo USA and Mattel were made in Japan by Nintendo USA's parent company. For Mattel, the manufacturer included in its games instruction booklets in both French and English while English instructions alone were included in Nintendo USA's games. In addition, all games and literature intended for Mattel was stamped by the manufacturer with Mattel's own logo and trade mark. Among other things, Mattel provided a warranty, repair service and an advice 'hot line' for customers with problems. In the three years of Mattel's appointment, it had spent over C$20 million in advertising and had increased sales from C$5 million to C$68 million. Under the terms of the distributorship, Mattel also had to achieve minimum sales in the forthcoming year of C$50 million.

Joyal J first distinguished *Champagne Heidsieck* from the instant case since it was not the registered proprietor but the registered user seeking relief.[178] Then, after referring to the *Seiko Time, Remington Rand* and *Dunlop Tyre* cases, his Honour continued:

> This review of case law indicates to me that *the lack of any deception on the public* by the sale of any trademark owner's own goods *is not conclusive* of the kind of issue before me. The *Seiko* [*Time*] case to which I have referred not only leaves the door open to other considerations if a registered trademark owner or a registered user is involved, but also opens wider that same door to other tests whenever some kind of unfair competition is raised. (*Emphasis added*)[179]

In this context, Joyal J considered that Mattel's status as a registered user entitled it to some protection and, in conjunction with the Act's general prohibition on unfair competition, concluded that the *Nintendo* trade mark had been converted into Mattel's trade mark thereby more than satisfying the threshold test of a serious question to be tried on an interlocutory application: 'As in the *Dunlop* [*Tyre*] case and the *Remington Rand* case

---

177   *Mattel Canada Inc. v GTS Acquisitions Ltd and Nintendo of America Inc.* (1989) 27 CPR (3d) 358. For subsequent proceedings, see 28 CPR (3d) 534. Followed in *H.J. Heinz Co. of Canada Ltd v Edan Food Sales Inc.* [1991] 35 CPR (3d) 213 (FCTD). Contrast *Nestlé Enterprises v Edan Food Sales Inc.* [1991] 37 CPR (3d) 480 (FCTD), a registered user suing in passing off; see Note 124a above.
178   *Ibid.* at 362.
179   *Ibid.* at 365.

the defendant is selling a product under the plaintiff's trademark for which neither leave nor licence has been obtained.'[180]

Apart from Joyal J's recognition that deception of the public is not the true test under trade mark law (in contrast to *Fender*), the case is significant because his Honour found that Mattel's status as a registered user gave it rights independently of the registered proprietor. Indeed, those rights were greater than the registered proprietor's because Nintendo USA was unlikely to succeed before his Honour.

In light of Burchett J's decision in *Fender*, it should also be noted that Mattel had also developed factually independent goodwill. However, Joyal J did not formally base his infringement ruling on that goodwill. Rather, it depended on Mattel's rights as a registered user. The provision which deemed a registered user's permitted use 'use by the proprietor' transmuted the trade mark into 'the plaintiff's trade mark'. That the licensor could confer on its licensee greater rights than it possessed itself might be thought surprising.[181] It also, in effect, meant that the trade mark could potentially denote two different 'sources', thus becoming deceptive or lacking in distinctiveness.[182]

In summary then, the *Mattel* case (although, as the author has argued, built on doubtful foundations) shows a significant shift from the treatment of the stylised situations shown in Table 2.1. Under *Mattel*, trade mark law was used to block parallel imports in the second situation even though the trade mark owner in the domestic and foreign markets was the same. *Diana Oil* might support that shift if it be explicable on the ground that the proprietor had *expressly* consented to the parallel importer's actions. In addition, both *Fender* and *Mattel* show considerable attention to the domestic distributor's development of 'independent goodwill' and are concerned to afford protection to valuable commercial investment. Such an approach may counteract the straightforward application of *Champagne Heidsieck*, *Revlon* and the *Bailey's Irish Cream* case.

2.2.5 Champagne Heidsieck still rules?

Since 1986 or 1987, if not earlier, the approach of courts in the Anglo-Commonwealth jurisdictions considering parallel imports and trade marks appears to have undergone a marked shift. *Champagne Heidsieck* and, even more so, the principle of universality have seemed increasingly marginalised.

180 *Ibid.* at 366, applying the *American Cyanamid* rules (citations omitted). His Honour's conclusion that the registered user was entitled to 'some protection' followed from the fact that 'the permitted use of a trademark by a registered user has the same effect for all purposes of the Act as the use thereof by a registered owner' under Trade Marks Act section 49(3): *ibid.* at 365 (compare Trade Marks Act 1938 (United Kingdom) section 28 and Trade Marks Act 1955 (Cth) section 77).

181 But, for copyright, see Copyright Designs and Patents Act 1988 (United Kingdom) section 27(3).

182 Notwithstanding this, the approach seems sanctioned by the Supreme Court of Canada: *S.C. Johnson and Son Ltd v Marketing International Ltd* (1975) 105 DLR (3d) 423, at 427 to 428 *per* Pigeon J; and, possibly, *Pioneer* (1977) 137 CLR 670.

The danger of consumer confusion like that ignored in *Cinzano* and the risk of undermining valuable investment as in the *Distillers' Red Label* case have increasingly brought to the fore approaches based on the principle of territoriality. There have been exceptions. Also, most cases have drawn careful distinctions between the instant facts and the situations in *Champagne Heidsieck* and *Revlon*. However, they must raise questions about the continuing validity of the ruling in *Champagne Heidsieck*.

Returning to the stylised situations in Table 2.1, the first major development of the early principles reviewed in subsection 2.2.2(b) above took place in row 3. *Revlon*, alarmed at the use of legal fictions to circumvent *Champagne Heidsieck*, appeared to convert the power afforded by the uncited *Dunlop Tyre* to block parallel imports, a 'No' answer in terms of Table 2.1, into a 'Yes' answer; parallel imports were permitted.[183] Since then, however, its ambit has been increasingly narrowed.

In *Fender*, arguably distinguishable on the grounds that 'different' goods were involved and that there was no corporate relationship, parallel imports of new products were blocked. *Revlon* was described as depending on the very special nature of the corporate group involved. Both cases, however, share a marked concern with what the trade mark in the domestic country actually signified to the relevant public; that is, in terms of *Fender*, with the question of independent goodwill in the domestic territory.[184]

Colgate seems even more fatal. There, ownership of the domestic and foreign trade marks was not even split. The same member of the corporate group, the parent, retained ownership of the trade mark rights in both the foreign and domestic countries. Thus, row 2 of Table 2.1 changed from the 'Yes' dictated by *Champagne Heidsieck* to 'No', parallel imports are not permitted. A number of elements combined to achieve this result: acknowledgement of the territorial limitation of registered trade marks, the risk of consumer confusion and the explicit rebuttal of any express or implied consent to the parallel importing. The third and, possibly, the second of these factors find a place in the reasoning of *Revlon*. Note also the protection afforded, or contemplated for, a registered user in both *Mattel* and *Diana Oil*. The latter turning on the proprietor's express consent; the former, like *Fender*, showing a strong concern for valuable business investment in creating and maintaining a market.

The transmutation of row 2 is highlighted by the decision of the South African courts in *Sony*.[185] In *Pentax*, a judgment delivered contemporaneously

---

183 For *Revlon*, see subsection 2.2.3(a). See also *Winthrop Products Inc. v Sun Ocean (Malaysia) Sdn Bhd* [1988] FSR 430 and *Tamiya Plastic Model Co. v Toy Warehouse Ltd* cited in Brown, 'Parallel Importation: A New Zealand Perspective', [1989] EIPR 274, at 277.

184 For *Fender*, see text at Notes 142 and following above. This characterisation of *Fender* is also supported by Burchett J's reliance on Muratore and Robertson, 'The Trade Marks Act 1955 and Parallel Imports', (1984) 7 UNSWLJ 117, especially at 130 to 133.

185 *Sony* 1987(2) SA 994 (AD). For the otherwise vigorous enforcement of *Champagne Heidsieck*, see *Pentax* 1987(2) SA 961 (AD) and *TDK* 1987(3) SA 165 (D & CLD); in the latter case, extending to copyright: 1991(3) SA 240 (D & CLD); see Chapter 4 at Note 213a.

with *Sony*, the Appellate Division refused to block parallel imports on the basis that they were the genuine goods of the trade mark owner which it had freely released into commerce. Arguably, the trade mark proprietor could be taken to have consented to the goods' importation since they were released on to the market without any conditions and, indeed, were accompanied by a guarantee valid anywhere in the world. In reaching the conclusion, the central authority relied on was *Champagne Heidsieck*. But, in *Sony*, although marked and released into trade by the trade mark owner, the goods were considered non-genuine and so their parallel importation was blocked. The goods were videocassette recorders which required important modification before they could receive television signals in South Africa. Since the parallel importer carried out the modifications on its imports (apparently, less than expertly), the use of the trade mark on the parallel imports no longer correctly indicated the right connection in the course of trade.[186]

The apparent divergence from the irrelevance of the differences in quality in *Champagne Heidsieck* is explicable in the court's eyes by the fact that the difference in quality in *Sony* resulted not from the act of any person under the control of the registered proprietor but by some remote third party. Through that tampering with the goods, they ceased to be 'parallel' imports.[187] So, the uncharacteristic (in South Africa) success against parallel importers does not seem to lie in any adoption of the principle of territoriality. The third party's interference with the goods and *Pentax* seem also to preclude any general argument in South Africa that the trade mark proprietor must specifically intend to release its goods in the domestic country.

Still, the judgment contains the seeds of recognition of territorial limitations. The result in *Sony* leads to the suggestion that the registered proprietor could also sue a parallel importer which imported unmodified (and unsuitable) goods into South Africa for infringement. While the plaintiffs' success in *Sony* is not all that far removed from the plaintiffs' success in *Fender*, *Sharp Electronics* and *Mattel*, success against an importer of unmodified (and unsuitable) goods would destroy any remaining difference.

What of *Champagne Heidsieck*'s ruling on row 1 endorsed by the Court of Appeal in *Revlon*? The qualifications on the early cases made by the more recent raise four factors which alone, or in some combination with each other, could reasonably cast doubt on the result reached in *Champagne Heidsieck*: the territorial limitation of trade mark rights, a change in the trade mark principles implemented by the legislation, consent, and different goods.

Significant differences in quality have certainly loomed large in all of *Castrol GTX*, *Colgate*, *Fender*, *Mattel*, *Sharp Electronics* and, in somewhat different fashion, *Sony*.[188] Still, by itself, this factor seems neither necessary

---

186. *Ibid.* at 1012 to 1013 *per* Grosskopf JA.
187   Compare Case 102/77 *Hoffmann-La Roche v Centrafarm* [1978] ECR 1139, Chapter 6 from Note 110.
188   For 'difference in quality', see further Chapter 2.4 below.

nor sufficient to permit the blocking of parallel imports. The fact that the parallel imports in *Champagne Heidsieck* were different in quality to those released locally had been considered irrelevant by Clauson J and, in *Diana Oil*, the goods seem to have been of the same quality but McGarvie J contemplated the registered user's success.[189]

Consent, express or implied, has been of increasing importance since *Revlon*. In *Castrol GTX* and *Colgate*, it was expressly precluded by limitation on the foreign licensee confining its rights to use the trade mark in the foreign territory. In *Castrol GTX*, the products themselves were also endorsed with a notice to this effect. In *Fender*, in the absence of the very special corporate relationship found in *Revlon*, the domestic registered proprietor never had anything to do with the release of the goods on the foreign market and so could not be taken to have ever consented to their entry into commerce. But, the registered proprietor explicitly consented to importation in *Diana Oil*. In contrast to all these cases, the goods were sold subject to an express prohibition on their export in *Champagne Heidsieck*.[190]

Once again, 'consent' does not stand on its own. The essence of parallel imports is that they have been placed on the market under the aegis of the domestic right owner *somewhere*. In the *Champagne Heidsieck* formulation, the location of release 'on to the market' is irrelevant because the function of the trade mark is to denote source in the mark owner and, there, the owner was the same. The owner was the same in *Diana Oil, Castrol GTX, Colgate, Sharp Electronics* and *Mattel* too. But, in these cases, consent was considered relevant because of the territorial limitation of trade mark rights. The trade mark rights in the two separate countries were recognised to be distinct entities. In effect, these cases endorse the argument, rejected in the *Bailey's Irish Cream* case, that the owner must have some intention that the goods released be projected into trade in the domestic country.

In terms of trade mark theory, this result is reached in either of two ways. In *Diana Oil* and *Mattel*, as in *Fender* and *Dunlop Tyre*, it is achieved by regarding the domestic trade mark as indicating a different source to that of the mark in the foreign country. That is, the connection in the course of trade indicated by the trade mark in the domestic country was a connection with the registered user as well as, or instead of, the registered proprietor. But, *Colgate*, particularly in Slade LJ's judgment, goes further. The trade mark's function includes not just indications about source but also about quality. The connection in the course of trade indicated by the trade mark is not just associated with a particular person but also with a particular product. *Sony* lies somewhere in between. The importer's interference destroyed the attribution of source – the connection in the course of trade – but, the decision must raise some possibility to exclude 'unsuitable' imports even where the attribution of source has not been undermined.

Champagne Heidsieck lies at the root of the rejection of any role for the

189   The 'Brut' variety had in fact been in circulation for a number of years.
190   There the fact that imports had been continuing for several years to the plaintiff's own knowledge could arguably impute tacit consent.

function of a trade mark in indicating quality, at least where the question arises in the context of parallel imports. There are a number of reasons for regarding its theoretical interpretation of the 1905 Act as no longer representing good law.

First, even at the time Clauson J handed down his decision, the narrow conception of a trade mark's role at common law proclaimed in *Farina v Silverlock* was no longer entirely accurate. In *Spalding v Gamage*, the House of Lords had extended passing off to cover not just deception about trade source but also deception about quality.[191] Admittedly, that was a case in passing off rather than under the Act and, on that part of the case, Clauson J must certainly have had the possibility of confusion in mind when he found, as a fact, that the public was not deceived by use of the brand on the imports.

But, trade mark law itself has moved on. At the time of his Lordship's ruling in *Champagne Heidsieck*, there is more than a hint of the idea that a trade mark identified manufacturing source, that it designated goods from a particular 'manufactory'.[192] Hence, the law took a strict line on assignments and forbade licensing. This concern with manufacturing source is particularly evident in Clauson J's decision in *Lacteosote Ltd v Alberman*, denying the validity of a trade mark assignment along with the domestic distribution business it was associated with:

> If it were not so, the result would be that a mark distinctive of goods produced and sold in the business carried on by Famel would become by the assignment distinctive, not of goods produced and sold in that business by Famel, or his successors, but of goods sold in a newly separated and, therefore, different business by persons who succeeded Famel *as vendors in Great Britain of the goods but not as producers of them.* Such a position seems to me to be inconsistent with the principle that a trade mark is distinctive of goods with which a particular business (whether carried on by the original trader or his successors) is concerned. If the identity of the business is destroyed, the mark is destroyed with it. (*Emphasis added*)[193]

The assignment in *Lacteosote*, as in *Juda's* case later, was motivated by an attempt to block parallel imports. Nearly 40 years earlier, the Court of Appeal had roundly rejected such a scheme in *Apollinaris' TMs*.[194] There, Fry LJ refused to allow a mere importer to register in the United Kingdom a known trade mark of its foreign supplier. The authorised importer might register the trade mark with additional distinguishing material to indicate its role in selection. Alternatively, the authorised importer might be allowed to register the trade mark if it bought up all the foreign manufacturer's output. To hold otherwise, in Fry LJ's opinion, would enable the mere importer to

---

191 (1915) 32 RPC 273.
192 Even then, there were exceptions for dealers whose brand came to indicate the 'selection' role: for example *Major Bros v Franklin and Sons* (1908) 25 RPC 406; but, they were exceptions rather than the rule: See generally, Shanahan, *Australian Trade Mark Law*, 23, at 40 to 42.
193 (1927) 44 RPC at 233 to 234.
194 [1891] 2 Ch. 186; 8 RPC 137 (CA) expressly relied on by Clauson J at 44 RPC 211, at 224.

prevent its rivals from buying up some of the manufacturer's goods and also importing them.[195]

Apollinaris' TMs was clearly hostile to the idea that a manufacturer which has used a trade mark to identify its goods could simply assign that mark to a mere importer, partly from fear of deceiving the consuming public and partly from fears of monopolising trade. Hence, in *Pinto v Badman*, Fry LJ subsequently denied the validity of assigning a trade mark 'in gross' because a trade mark was the badge of 'the manufactory of the goods in which the mark has been used to be affixed' which his Lordship derived from Lord Cranworth's ruling in the *Leather Cloth* case.[196] As discussed in subsection 2.2.2(b) above, Lord Cranworth's views on the function of a trade mark were also adopted by Clauson J in *Champagne Heidsieck*. The rationale of the approach underlying Clauson J's earlier ruling in *Lacteosote* has also been described as:

> The reason would appear to be that the making and vending of goods are so closely related that severance of the goodwill would almost by necessity create public confusion. If the right to the trade mark was assigned solely in conjunction with the right to sell the goods to which the mark attached, the effect would be to sell the trade mark alone.[197]

Whatever may be the position at common law, the extremely narrow, legalistic conception of the role of a trade mark on which these cases are based has long since been found unacceptable. After the shortcomings revealed by decisions based on the approach taken in *Apollinaris' TMs*, the trade marks legislation was amended to permit assignments without goodwill.[198] The express reason given for the amendment was the case law's unsuitability to 'modern conditions of trading'.[199] As a result of the

---

195   *Ibid.* at 226; 8 RPC at 160 to 161, see text at Note 30, above. Contrast *Bonnan's* case in passing off, see text at Notes 48 to 49 above. Fry LJ did not expressly deal with the case of an *unknown* trade mark (which was intended to be used) for which, arguably, the feared dangers of public deception would not arise, but, on the other hand, the denial of competition from other importers still would. On the question of 'monopoly', inter-brand and intra-brand competition, see the discussion of *Guerlain* in subsection 2.3.4(a) and *Sylvania* in Chapter 3 from Note 215, respectively, below.
196   (1891) 8 RPC 181, at 194 to 195 (CA) citing *The Leather Cloth Co. Ltd v The American Leather Cloth Co. Ltd* (1865) 11 HLC 523, at 534 to 535 *per* Lord Cranworth LC. See generally Shanahan, *Australian Trade Mark Law*, at 223 to 228.
197   Shelley Lane, *The Status of Licensing Common Law Marks* (forthcoming), text at the end of §E(i)(b).
198   See Board of Trade, *Report of the Departmental Committee on the Law and Practice Relating to Trade Marks*, at ¶¶102 to 123 cited in Ricketson, *The Law of Intellectual Property*, at ¶¶38.3 to 38.4 and Cornish, *Intellectual Property*, at ¶17-056; the immediate spur being *Re Sinclair's TM* (1932) 49 RPC 123 which did not involve parallel imports. See now for example Trade Marks Act 1938 (United Kingdom) section 22; Trade Marks Act 1955 (Cth) sections 82, 118; Trade Marks Act RSC 1985, Chapter T-13, sections 48, 49.
199   *Ibid.* at ¶107 quoted in Ricketson, *The Law of Intellectual Property*, at ¶38.4. Modern practices have developed to such an extent that the UK Government now feels justified in removing most of the remaining restrictions on licensing and 'trafficking', see Department of Trade and Industry, *Reform of Trade Marks Law*, at ¶¶4.34 to 4.43, especially at ¶4.36 on the public's increased sophistication.

amendments, *Lacteosote* was held to be no longer good law in the *4711* case, where Sir Raymond Evershed MR indicated in *dicta* that a manufacturer could now validly assign its mark to an importer/distributor.[200]

Magder's case is arguably in line with *Apollinaris' TMs* since the legislative change.[201] Laskin CJC, however, clearly placed the plaintiff's claim that the mark there had come to distinguish its function as a distributor in the same category as the plaintiff's claims in *Juda's* case.[202] In *Juda's* case, the plaintiff was not expressly denied because it was an importer seeking to maintain rights to a manufacturer's trade mark. Rather, it failed because nothing had been done to inform the public of either the registration's assignment or the plaintiff's processing activities.[203] Even so, the approach is thought unlikely to apply outside Canada.[204]

Similarly, the previously inflexible attitude to licensing derived from the same principles no longer applies under the Act or, seemingly, at common law.[205] Moreover, Fry LJ's statement that other dealers could justly affix a mark to goods even if the producer had elected not to place the mark on them seems controverted by subsequent authority.[206]

Accordingly, notwithstanding the rejection of Starke J's doubts in the *Dick Smith* case by the *Fairstar* and *Bailey's Irish Cream* cases, it seems more than arguable on other grounds that the principles underpinning *Champagne Heidsieck* have undergone substantial modification. Hence, there seems ample justification for the view that the marked shift in judicial attitudes towards parallel imports since at least the second half of the 1980s represents a rejection, rather than just distinguishing, of that case.

In terms of Table 2.1, this could be thought of as reversing the answer in row 1 from permitting parallel imports to exclude them. However, with the possible exceptions of *Mattel* (which was an interlocutory application) and *Diana Oil*, none of the cases has permitted the blocking of parallel imports where the local representative merely acted as a distributor. In the other cases, the local representative undertook some processing functions. Arguably, like *Mattel*, this places them in row 2 rather than row 1.[207]

---

200 *R.J. Reuter Coy Ltd v Muhlens* (1953) 70 RPC 235, at 250 and onward, for the *dicta*, see *ibid.* at 251 to 252.

201 See for example the possible reservation made in *Muhlens* for marks plainly deceptive on their face: *ibid.* at 251.

202 17 CPR (2d) at 207.

203 51 CPR 55. Contrast *Fender* 15 IPR 257 at Notes 142 and following, above and see also, the comments of Aickin J in *Pioneer* (1977) 137 CLR 670, see Notes 127, 168 and 174 above.

204 Cornish, *Intellectual Property*, at ¶17-055.

205 On the 'explanation' of *Bowden Wire Ltd v Bowden Brake Company Ltd* (1914) 31 RPC 385 (HL), see Shanahan, *Australian Trade Mark Law*, Chapter 17; Cornish, *Intellectual Property*, at ¶¶17-060 to 17-062 and see the UK Government's position referred to in Note 199 above.

206 *Wellcome Foundation Ltd v Secretary of State for Social Services* [1988] 1 WLR 635, at 638 *per* Lord Ackner; *Champagne Heidsieck v Bishop and Scotto* (1926) 43 RPC 101. At *Apollinaris TMs* [1891] 2 Ch. 186, at 226; 8 RPC 137, at 160 to 161, Fry LJ said: '. . . other goods of the manufacturer might reach the hands of other dealers, who might justly affix to them the manufacturer's mark'.

207 On the question of what are 'genuine goods', see Chapter 2.4, below.

2.3   United States of America

2.3.1   Introduction

Reference to the US treatment of 'gray' market goods, despite the bewildering array of legislation and litigation, proves illuminating.[208] The nature of the competing claims is exposed nakedly. As is the seeming intractability of reconciling them; with all branches of the government, executive, legislature and judiciary divided.[209] In particular, there is explicit concern that trade mark owners (especially transnational corporate groups) will use their trade mark rights to practise monopolistic manipulation of the market; there is an ongoing debate about the source of consumer confusion which reflects the different approaches taken in *Revlon* and *Colgate*; and, further, there is explicit concern like that recently recognised in *Fender* and *Mattel* about the dangers of free riding on desirable market making investments.

Presently, there appear to be five federal legislative provisions directly relevant to parallel importing of trade-marked goods. It would also appear that the various states have some legislation affecting the issue. In addition, the US courts also recognise a form of common law trade mark generically described as the tort of unfair competition. Unless otherwise indicated, the discussion concentrates on the federal legislation.

The Lanham Act contains three relevant sections; the Tariff Act, two. Section 32(1) of the Lanham Act provides the general remedy for infringement. It proscribes the use in commerce of any reproduction, counterfeit, copy or colourable imitation of a registered trade mark which is likely to cause confusion.[210] In 1962, the section was amended to make it plain that

---

208   'Gray' market being the US term for parallel imports of trade-marked products: Brian D. Coggio, Jennifer Gordon and Laura A. Coruzzi, 'The History and Present Status of Gray Goods', 75 TMR 433 (1985); John A. Young Jr, 'The Gray Market Case: Trademark Rights v. Consumer Interests', 61 Notre Dame LRev. 838 (1986); Yvon O. Hecksher, 'Parallel Imports Furore: A Case of Smoke Exhalation?' 15 *International Business Lawyer* 32 (1987).

209   For the executive, see the discussion of section 337 of the Tariff Act of 1930 and the history of *US v Guerlain Inc.* 155 F. Supp. 77 (SDNY 1957) *vacated* 357 US 924 (1958) and *dismissed* 172 F. Supp. 107 (SDNY 1959), see subsection 2.3.4(a) below. For the legislature, see the recurrent introduction of opposing Bills – usually one to bar parallel imports, the other to permit them – none of which has so far passed either House: for example, Trademark Protection Act of 1991, section 894, Cong. Rec. 23/4/91, page S4863 reported in Legislation, 'Hatch Bill Revives Effort to Curb Gray market Imports', 41 PTCJ 546 (1991).

210   15 USC §1114(1) provides:

> Any person who shall, without the consent of the registrant:
> (a) use in commerce any reproduction, counterfeit, copy, or colorable imitation of a registered mark in connection with the sale, offering for sale, distribution, or advertising of any goods or services on or in connection with which such use is likely to cause confusion, or to cause mistake, or to deceive; or
> (b) reproduce, counterfeit, copy or colorably imitate a registered mark and apply such reproduction, counterfeit, copy, or colorable imitation to labels, signs, prints, packages, wrappers, receptacles or advertisements in connection with the sale, offering for sale, distribution, or advertising of goods or services on or in connection with which such use is likely to cause confusion, or to cause mistake, or to deceive,
> shall be liable in a civil action by the registrant for the remedies hereinafter provided.

Among other things, the remedies include damages and injunctions, 15 USC §§1116 and 1117, respectively.

its purpose was 'to outlaw the use of trademarks which are likely to cause confusion, mistake or deception of any kind, not merely of purchasers, nor simply as to source of origin'.[211]

Section 42 of the Lanham Act makes special provision for importation of products bearing marks which 'copy or simulate' registered trade marks, enabling the registered owner of the trade mark to have the products seized by Customs at the border.[212]

The reference to 'section 1526 of title 19' (see Note 212 below) is to section 526 of the Tariff Act. This was enacted to close an apparent loophole in the protection offered to registered owners under the statutory predecessor of section 42 of the Lanham Act after the Second Circuit's decision in *Bourjois v Katzel*.[213] Unlike section 42 of the Lanham Act, it applies only to domestic, not foreign, registered owners and is not expressly limited to 'copies' or 'simulations' or such like. It provides:

> Except as provided in subsection (d) of this section, it shall be unlawful to import into the United States any merchandise of foreign manufacture if such merchandise, or the label, sign, print, package, wrapper, or receptacle, bears a trademark owned by a citizen of, or by a corporation or association created or organized within, the United States, . . . unless written consent of the owner of such trademark is produced at the time of making entry.[214]

Section 43 of the Lanham Act is a general catch-all provision, applying to both registered and unregistered trade marks. Section 43(b) prohibits importing products which would breach section 43(a). Section 43(a) provides civil liability against making false advertisements or representations, including about origin, in connection with goods.[215]

---

211   *Syntex Laboratories Inc. v Norwich Pharmacal Company* 437 F. 2d 566, 568 (2d Cir. 1971) a case concerning product, not source, confusion. The amendment deleted the words 'purchasers as to the source of origin of such goods or services' after the word 'deceive' at the end of section 32(a).
212   15 USC §1124 provides:

> Except as provided in subsection (d) of section 1526 of title 19, no article of imported merchandise which shall copy or simulate the name of the [*sic*] any domestic manufacture, or manufacturer, or trader, or of any manufacturer or trader located in any foreign country which, by treaty, convention, or law affords similar privileges to citizens of the United States, or which shall copy or simulate a trademark registered in accordance with the provisions of this chapter or shall bear a name or mark calculated to induce the public to believe that the article is manufactured in the United States, or that it is manufactured in any foreign country or locality other than the country or locality in which it is in fact manufactured, shall be admitted to entry at any customhouse of the United States; . . .

The remainder of the section provides the registration machinery necessary to enable Customs to enforce the prohibition.
213   274 Fed. 856 (SDNY 1920) *revd* 275 Fed. 539 (2d Cir. 1921) *revd* 260 US 689 (1923), see section 2.3.3 below. The Supreme Court's decision overruling the Court of Appeals was made without reference to the amending statute, Tariff Act of 1922, Pub. L. No. 67–318, tit. III section 526, 42 Stat. 858, at 975 (1922).
214   19 USC §1526. The omissions relate to the administrative procedures of registering the trade mark with Customs. Subsection (d) exempts goods imported only for personal consumption from the prohibition.
215   15 USC §1125. The cases under this section correspond generally to those in passing off discussed at subsection 2.2.3(c) above. Typically, as in the passing off cases, the relief granted tends to be limited to the conduct which actually causes the false

Finally, section 337 of the Tariff Act provides a form of relief to domestic complainants against unfair methods of competition or unfair acts in the importation of articles into the United States.[216] 'Unfair acts' have been interpreted to include violations of the provisions already outlined.[217] Parallel imports have been found to violate section 337 at the administrative level. But, findings at that level are subject to executive veto and this decision was quashed on the ground that it clashed with long-standing regulatory policy and should not be allowed to prejudice the policy review then being undertaken.[218] As yet, there does not seem to have been any change in that policy, the legislation is liable to GATT challenge and, in any case, the infringement issues raised are the same as under the other provisions.

The main issue before the courts appears to be whether *Bourjois v Katzel* and section 526 of the Tariff Act express a broad principle against parallel imports or should be confined to the narrow fact situation considered in *Katzel*. This issue presents itself in two ways.

First, the trade mark owner seeking to exclude parallel imports must convince a court that using the trade mark on genuine goods is a 'copy' or 'simulation' likely to cause the confusion forbidden by the Lanham Act. The second form of the problem is whether section 526 of the Tariff Act should be interpreted literally (and broadly) to exclude all unauthorised importations of trade-marked goods or should be limited to the narrow fact situation which provoked its passage. Subsidiary (although vital in practice) issues involve the extent to which a complainant denied relief under section 526 by Customs may assert it, or the other rights, in the federal courts and how much Customs' interpretation of section 526 affects the interpretation of rights under the Lanham Act.[219]

---

representation. So, if the defendant can continue the importation without making the false representation, the plaintiff may be unable to block the parallel imports: *Norman M. Morris Corp. v Weinstein* 466 F. 2d 137 (5th Cir. 1972), *Seiko Time Corporation v Alexander's Inc.* 218 USPQ 560 (SDNY 1982) and *Société des Produits Nestlé SA v Casa Helvetica Inc.* 777 F. Supp. 161 (D. Puerto Rico 1991).

216　19 USC §1337(a) as amended by The Omnibus Trade and Competitiveness Act of 1988 Pub. L. No. 100–418, §1342, 102 Stat. 1107, at 1212 (1988). The amendments made it substantially easier for domestic complainants to succeed, but did not affect the test of intellectual property infringement, see the summary review in Mark R. Joelson, John C. Lindsay and Joe Griffin, 'US Omnibus Trade and Competitiveness Act of 1988', 16 *International Business Lawyer* 408 (1988).

217　*In re Certain Alkaline Batteries* 225 USPQ 823 (ITC 1984), further proceedings denying power to review Presidential veto *sub. nom. Duracell Inc. v US International Trade Commission* 778 F. 2d 1578 (Fed. Cir. 1985) discussed in Coggio *et al.*, 'The History and Present Status of Gray Goods', at 475 to 486.

218　*Ibid*. The Commission split 3–2 on the reasoning, the majority relying on the separate legal existence of trade mark rights in each jurisdiction having the primary function of protecting the domestic business goodwill of the trade mark owner. In contrast, the minority found exclusion necessary to prevent consumer confusion. For section 337's contravention of GATT in a case of patent infringement under the pre-1988 legislation, see John W. Rogers III, 'The Demise of Section 337's GATT-legality', [1990] EIPR 275 and Elizabeth M. Saltzer, 'The Future of Section 337 of the Tariff Act of 1930: The Response of the United States Trade Representative to the GATT Panel Report', (1992) 23 IIC 350.

219　See sections 2.3.5 and 2.3.6 below.

Like *Cinzano* and *Champagne Heidsieck*, the vexing question is how goods marked and freely sold by the producer could cause deception or confusion. Hence, there has been much anxious attention to whether the imports are 'genuine'. The fear that corporate groups might use formal assignment of domestic rights to practise international price discrimination is the other recurring concern as in *Revlon*.

2.3.2 Identifying source: a universal approach

The Apollinaris company presented the District Court with its first opportunity to rule on parallel imports and trade marks in 1886.[220] Apollinaris was the exclusive distributor in the United Kingdom and the United States of mineral water from a European spring discovered and owned by one Saxlehner, identified by the trade mark *Hunyadi Janos*. Apollinaris owned this mark, both by registration and at common law, in the United States. The labels on Apollinaris' bottles identified it as 'Sole Exporter for England and the United States' while Saxlehner's bottles sold in Europe bore a label stating that they were not for export and were not intended for sale in England and the United States. The report does not reveal whether Apollinaris was more than a mere importer and seller. But, it seems likely that Apollinaris received the water already bottled.[221]

Scherer tried to buy water from Saxlehner for importation into the United States but was refused. Undeterred, he then bought bottles from a German distributor, labelled in Saxlehner's continental style, and imported them into the United States, selling at a cheaper price than Apollinaris.

The case was decided on common law principles.[222] Judge Wallace refused relief on the grounds that:

> *Defendant is selling genuine water, and therefore the trade-mark is not infringed.* There is no exclusive right to the use of a name or symbol or emblematic device except to denote the authenticity of the article with which it has become identified by association. The name has no office except to vouch for the genuineness of the thing which it distinguishes from all counterfeits . . . . (*Emphasis added*)[223]

---

220 *Apollinaris Co. Ltd v Scherer* 27 Fed. 18 (SDNY 1886) *per* Judge Wallace. See Hiebert, 'Foundations of the Law of Parallel Importation', at 497 to 502 and Coggio *et al.* 'The History and Present Status of Gray Goods', at 445 to 447.
221 Apollinaris seized a ship carrying bottled *Hunyadi Janos* from the Continent to the United States in an English port: *Apollinaris Co. v Wilson* (1886) 55 LJ(Ch.) 665. See also the nature of the UK business relationship described later in *Saxlehner v Apollinaris Co.* [1897] 1 Ch. 893. For cases involving UK trade marks and Apollinaris, see from Note 25 to 31 and 194 to 206, above.
222 The first federal statute regulating trade marks, enacted in 1870, was ruled unconstitutional and invalid in the *Trade Mark Cases* 100 US 82 (1879). The Act of 1881 was more limited in nature and it was not until the Trade Marks Act of 1905 that Congress provided a substantive remedy for infringement by statute: for example Beverly W. Pattishall, 'Two Hundred Years of American Trademark Law', in American Bar Association, *Two Hundred Years of English and American Patent, Trademark and Copyright Law*, American Bar Center, 1977, at 61 to 62.
223 *Ibid.* at 20.

His Honour's first impression was that equity should intervene to stop a purchaser from Saxlehner doing something which Saxlehner could not himself do, but, as the goods were genuine and there was no deception of the public such as to divert custom from one business to a rival's, there was nothing to found relief on.[224] In essence, Judge Wallace found that Scherer's imported waters came from the same spring and so had the same source as the trade mark designated. The fact that the US trade mark belonged, both by registration and at common law, to Apollinaris was simply ignored. Judge Wallace did not deny the validity of Apollinaris' trade mark ownership. Instead, he denied that trade marks could be used like patents to divide up territories because, unlike patents, trade marks were not statutory creatures. Once the trade-marked product was put on the market, trade mark rights could not be used to control its further destination.[225]

The approach taken by Judge Wallace was subsequently applied to permit parallel imports under the Trade Marks Act of 1905.[226] Schoening, by agreement with the German manufacturer, was the exclusive importer into the United States of violin strings made in Germany under the trade mark *Eternelle* and, as owner, had registered the trade mark under the 1905 Act. The plaintiff bought *Eternelle* violin strings in Germany from Schoening's supplier and sought to import them into the United States. Schoening invoked the Customs procedure and had the strings excluded.[227] The plaintiff sued for their release. The court ruled that the plaintiff could legitimately import the goods into the United States without Schoening's consent. As in *Apollinaris v Scherer*, since the goods were genuine, the possibility of deception was rejected and therefore their importation could not be blocked.[228]

The result in these two cases is the same as in *Champagne Heidsieck*, but there are important differences in the method used to reach it. In *Apollinaris v Scherer* and *Fred Gretsch*, importation was allowed by resort to a doctrine of exhaustion. The 'universal' nature of brand identity also played a role in *Champagne Heidsieck*. But, as *Dunlop Tyre* shows, Anglo-Commonwealth law would not disregard the vesting of title to the domestic trade mark in hands different to the source on the foreign market.[229]

---

224   *Ibid.* at 22. His Honour thought the circumstances would be different if Saxlehner and Scherer had conspired to import the offending bottles into the United States. Then there would be something in Scherer's conscience for equity to attach.

225   *Ibid.* at 21.

226   *Fred Gretsch Manufacturing Co. v Schoening* 238 Fed. 780 (2d Cir. 1916), expressly endorsing *Apollinaris v Scherer* and a decision of the Second Circuit which did not involve parallel imports, *Russia Cement Co. v Frauenhar and Others* 133 Fed. 518 (2d Cir. 1904) (Judge Wallace presiding member). Both Second Circuit rulings are discussed in Hiebert, 'Foundations of the Law of Parallel Importation', at 503 to 505.

227   Then section 27, now section 42 of the Lanham Act.

228   238 Fed. 780, at 782.

229   Arguably, Fry LJ's judgment in *Apollinaris' TMs* [1891] 2 Ch. 186; 8 RPC 137 (CA) would limit the scope available for trade mark assignments, contrast Kekewich J's ruling at first instance in *Snook* (1890) 7 RPC 474.

2.3.3 Identifying source: Bourjois v Katzel

The broad principle that genuine (in the widest sense of having the same ultimate source of manufacture or production) goods did not cause deception and, therefore, were not infringements of common law or statutory trade mark rights survived only until 1923. Meanwhile, the federal courts were developing a broader concept of the role of a trade mark in domestic trade.[230] The potential for parallel importing, premised on a theory of universal manufacturing source, to undermine valuable property rights and cause consumer deception came into sharp relief in the *Katzel* case.[231]

An independently owned US company took an assignment at considerable expense of a foreign manufacturer's cosmetic business in the United States together with the trade mark registered in the United States for that business. The company continued to obtain its supplies of *Java* powder from the foreign vendor but did the packaging itself. Through its efforts, the public in fact came to identify it, and not the foreign manufacturer, as the source of the product in the United States. Mrs Katzel, however, taking advantage of currency fluctuations obtained the same product from the French manufacturer and imported it in its original markings into the United States. The US company sued her for infringing its registered trade mark.

At first instance, an injunction was granted, relying on the US company's goodwill which meant that deception would result from Mrs Katzel's imports. On appeal, the Second Circuit quashed the injunction. The majority, relying on *Fred Gretsch*, held that a trade mark protected the public against deception about the source of the product. Since the trade mark on Mrs Katzel's imports accurately identified the source of the product as the French manufacturer, there was no infringement. Judge Hough, however, dissented in terms already considered.[232]

The case was appealed further. Before the Supreme Court delivered its verdict, however, there was a large outcry and Congress hurriedly passed what is now section 526 of the Tariff Act of 1930.[233]

Without referring to the new statutory provision, the Supreme Court unanimously reversed the Second Circuit's decision. Holmes J, for the court, relied on three factors to block the parallel imports. First, his Honour noted that the foreign manufacturer could not sell its products directly into the United States. That would be inconsistent with the assignment. Accordingly,

---

230 The US courts began increasingly to stress the role of a trade mark as protecting goodwill, see *Hanover Star Milling Co. v Metcalf* 240 US 403, at 412 (1916) which was itself an action brought by the producer and did *not* involve parallel imports; and *Scandinavia Belting Co. v Asbestos & Rubber Works of America* 257 Fed. 937 (2d Cir. 1919) *cert. dend* 250 US 644.

231 *A. Bourjois & Company Inc. v Katzel* 274 Fed. 856 (SDNY 1920) *revd* 275 Fed. 539 (2d Cir. 1921) *revd* 260 US 689 (1923). See Coggio *et al.* 'The History and Present Status of Gray Goods', at 448 to 450. For the European Communities' handling of a similar situation, see the *Hag* cases, Chapter 6 from Notes 88 and 220 below.

232 See Note 1 above. The lower courts' rulings are dealt with in more detail in Hiebert, 'Foundations of the Law of Parallel Importation', at 505 to 510.

233 19 USC §1526(a) (1988), above at section 2.3.1.

it could not defeat its bargain by conveying its goods to others for importation. Second, mere ownership of goods did not necessarily convey the right to sell them under a specific trade mark. In this connection, unlike Judge Wallace, Holmes J could see no reason why the rights granted by a registered trade mark should be treated differently to those conferred by a patent.[234] Then, his Honour concluded:

> It is said that the trade mark here is that of the French house and truly indicates the origin of the goods. But that is not accurate. It is the trade mark of the plaintiff only in the United States and indicates *in law and it is found by public understanding* that the goods come from the plaintiff although not made by him. (*Emphasis added*)[235]

The judgment identifies a broad range of factors to support the conclusion that the trade mark in fact denoted the US company's goods and not the foreign producer's: the purchase of the business and trade mark for a large sum; the plaintiff's role in packaging the product, admittedly in a fashion similar to the original producer; its careful selection of colours appropriate to the US market; its maintenance of quality standards; its energetic advertising and promotion of the product; and the clear identification of its responsibility for the product.[236]

Katzel did not involve the same statutory provision as *Fred Gretsch*; but, shortly after, the actual decision in *Fred Gretsch* was effectively overruled by *Aldridge*.[237] Accordingly, if the trade mark owner did not consent to their importation, Customs was obliged to bar entry to so-called 'genuine' goods since the use of the registered trade mark on those goods copied or simulated the registered mark.

Under the approach taken in *Katzel*, however, the trade mark owner's rights did not extend to blocking imports of the product on which there was no use of a trade mark as a trade mark.[238] Coty sold toilet powders and perfumes in the United States under the trade marks *Coty* and *L'Origan*. Prestonettes bought the genuine powder, pressurised it, added a binder and sold the resulting mixture in a metal case. It also bought genuine perfume essence in bottles, rebottled it in smaller bottles and sold it. Both products were sold under Coty's registered trade marks. The District Court granted injunctions for infringement, but permitted Prestonettes to continue

---

234   Referring to *Boesch v Gräff* 133 US 697, Chapter 3.3.4 below: 260 US 689, at 692.
235   *Ibid.* For the earlier point, see *ibid.* at 691.
236   'Made in France–Packed in the USA by A.Bourjois & Co. Inc. of New York . . .' The plaintiff also claimed that Mrs Katzel's imports undermined quality by advertising her wares as 'Poudre de Riz de Java' instead of 'Poudre Java', the former being said to conjure negative associations with rice powder in the United States.
237   *A. Bourjois & Company Inc. v Aldridge* 263 US 675 (1923) *per curiam*; extending *Katzel* to section 27, the statutory precursor to Lanham Act section 42 and in identical terms. In *Katzel*, Holmes J referred to the action as being brought under sections 17 and 19 which have been replaced by sections 33 and 34 of the Lanham Act; and the District Court referred to the action as being a suit in equity.
238   *Prestonettes Inc. v Coty* 264 US 350 (1924).

its activities with packaging using the following labels 'Prestonettes Inc. not connected with Coty, states that the contents are Coty's . . . independently rebottled in New York.'[239] The Second Circuit rejected the labelling permission, considering that the delicate nature of the perfumes meant there was too great a danger of quality deterioration which imposed an intolerable burden of vigilance on Coty.

The Supreme Court restored the District Court's decision, Holmes J considering it consistent with *Katzel*. Coty could not stop Prestonettes from buying the product, modifying it and selling the modified product under a notice stating accurately what its component parts were and where they derived from. The proposed usage was not use as a trade mark and could not deceive the public about the source of the product.[240]

It is not entirely clear whether the Supreme Court's reasoning in these cases was based on protecting the trade mark owner's property or of protecting the public from deception. Judge Hough, dissenting in the Second Circuit, had justified the injunction against parallel imports on the grounds that they violated the plaintiff's property. But, the third of Holmes J's considerations entwines the two interests.[241] Because the trade mark, both in law and in fact, indicated that the US company was the source of the goods, the US company had a valuable property right which required protection. If that right was not protected, the public would be deceived because goods bearing the trade mark would come before it from two different sources instead of one. There is some suggestion in the first two of his Honour's considerations that the protection of the property right was foremost. But, in *Katzel*, the two interests were not in conflict: protecting the trade mark owner's property right coincided with protecting the public from deception.

Whichever of the two factors be foremost, Holmes J's opinion was a clear rejection of the exhaustion doctrine and an affirmation of the principle of territoriality. The court looked at what the trade mark actually represented in the United States. The territorial nature of the plaintiff's trade mark rights meant that confusion must result if the imports were allowed.[242]

---

239 *Ibid.* at 367. For powder, the label was similar, referring to 'compounded' and not 'rebottled'. For both, the whole label was to be in lettering of the same size, style and colouring.

240 *Ibid.* at 368. The reasoning would appear to be similar to that adopted by the House of Lords in *Irving's Yeast Vite Ltd v Horsenail* (1934) 51 RPC 110 and provides an alternative, and consistent, explanation for the decision in the *Russia Cement* case 133 Fed. 518, at 520 (2d Cir. 1904). The New York legislature subsequently outlawed the sale of products in this manner unless contained in the original package and under the labels affixed by the person entitled to do so: see *Lanvin Perfume Inc. v Le Dans Ltd* 9 NY 2d 516; *cert dend* 368 US 834 (1961). For repackaging cases in the European Communities, see 102/77 *Valium* [1978] ECR 1139 and 1/81 *Pfizer* [1981] ECR 2913 in Chapter 6 Note 113 below.

241 See Hiebert, 'Foundations of the Law of Parallel Importation', at 510 to 511.

242 In addition, *Katzel* confirmed that US law, unlike the approach taken by the UK courts in *In re Apollinaris* and *Lacteosote Ltd v Alberman*, recognised that trade marks could designate source in someone other than the manufacturer. See subsection 2.2.2(a) and section 2.2.5 above.

2.3.4   Monopoly, property or deception – territoriality unravelling

Following *Katzel*, the lower courts applied both the Lanham and Tariff Acts stringently to exclude parallel imports until 1957. This seems to have been done largely on the basis of protecting the domestic trade mark owner's property rights.

In *Sturges v Clark D. Pease Inc.*[243] the exclusive distributor in the United States of Hispano-Suiza brand cars, who had registered the *Hispano-Suiza* trade mark in the United States, relied on section 526 of the Tariff Act to bar importation of a car bearing the registered trade mark even though the car was intended only for the importer's personal use. The court did not examine whether the trade mark owner possessed domestic goodwill. Presumably this was assumed from the registration. Under the statute, the importer had a perfect right to import the car but had no right to import the car bearing the foreign trade mark:

> The object of this drastic statute is to protect the owner of a foreign trade-mark from competition in relation to goods bearing the mark. . . . A mark betokening the origin of a car is an important element in its value, and the American owner of the mark is entitled to have the benefit of such sales as are effected by it. Buyers are likely to purchase Hispano-Suiza cars from Clark D. Pease Inc. in order to secure the mark if they cannot otherwise obtain that advantage. If they are allowed to import for personal use without its consent, Clark D. Pease Inc. may certainly lose customers who would be willing to buy from them rather than possess cars bearing no trade-mark. To obtain such advantages the local owner of the foreign mark is given control of the importation of all cars bearing it.[244]

Subsequently, the Eighth Circuit allowed an exclusive distributor of German denture blanks to restrain parallel imports under the common law principles of unfair competition.[245] The distributor failed under the Lanham and Tariff Acts because it was not the owner of the registered trade marks. But, the distributor had so used the marks that the public had come to identify it, and not the foreign manufacturer, as the source of the goods. Hence, the exclusive distributor could exclude even the foreign manufacturer, and purchasers from that manufacturer, from competition with it in the domestic market.[246]

---

243   48 F. 2d 1035 (2d Cir. 1931) *per* Augustus N. Hand J with Learned Hand and Swan JJ.
244   *Ibid.* at 1037. See also *Coty Inc. v Le Blume Import Co. Inc.* 292 Fed. 264 (SDNY 1923) *per* Judge Learned Hand *affd* 293 Fed. 344 (2d Cir. 1923). These cases were decided before the statutory provisions for importation for personal use were passed.
245   *Perry v American Hecolite Denture Corp.* 78 F. 2d 556 (8th Cir. 1935). Contrast other cases under section 43(a) Lanham Act, at Note 215 above.
246   *Ibid.* at 560 to 561. Interestingly, in deciding what acts may constitute sufficient use, the court relied on *Bonnan's* case. The relevant acts generating the necessary goodwill included selecting an anglicised version of the denture blanks' trade name, selecting the particular brand of denture blanks from the wide range of denture blanks and materials available, packaging the product itself in distinctive 'little green boxes', maintaining a quality control policy and replacement scheme and conducting advertising and a demonstration scheme.

The first judicial questioning of the strict territorial approach taken in *Katzel* occurred after some 24 years in 1957. However, it was not until the spate of cases in the 1980s (beginning another 25 years later) that courts at the appellate level began seriously to question *Katzel*. This questioning has taken a number of forms. Underlying all of them is a re-assertion of the argument in *Apollinaris v Scherer* that the imports are 'genuine'. The judicial source of the modern 'revival' can be traced to the extraordinary case of *US v Guerlain Inc*.[247]

(a)   *Guerlain*

In *Guerlain*, the government prosecuted Guerlain under section 2 of the Sherman Act for monopolising, or attempting to monopolise, trade in its branded goods.[248] Guerlain was using its status as registered owner of the trade mark *Guerlain* to bar trade competitors from importing *Guerlain* perfumes into the United States. The facts resemble those considered by the UK Court of Appeal in *Revlon*. Guerlain was closely associated with a French company which originated the trade mark, first marketed products under the trade mark and supplied the product or its essential ingredients, manufactured under secret formulae, to Guerlain in the United States for packaging and sale to the public in the United States. Guerlain itself blended the essential ingredients before packaging some of the products. The French associate was also carrying out similar activities in other countries through other associates. In the United States, Guerlain heavily promoted its products to emphasise their French origin.

In these circumstances, the government argued, first, that a domestic trade mark owner which formed part of a 'single international enterprise' was not entitled to use section 526 to block imports, and second, that in doing so Guerlain was breaching section 2 of the Sherman Act.

Judge Edelstein found as a fact 'beyond any gnawing doubt' that Guerlain and the associated companies in the group were all part of a single international enterprise.[249] First, the French associate controlled Guerlain by contracts which allowed Guerlain to use the trade mark only as permitted by the French associate on Guerlain products; which further required Guerlain

---

247   155 F. Supp. 77 (SDNY 1957) *vacated and remanded* 357 US 924 (1958) *dismissed* 172 F. Supp. 107 (SDNY 1959). Apart from the still unresolved judicial controversy, *Guerlain* sparked a fierce academic debate, see in particular Milton Handler, 'Trademarks – Assets or Liabilities', 48 TMR 661 (1958), Walter J. Derenberg, 'Current Trademark Problems in Foreign Travel and the Import Trade', 49 TMR 674 (1959), E.C. Vandenburgh, 'The Problems of Importation of Genuinely Marked Goods is not a Trademark Problem', 49 TMR 707 (1959), Robert A. Bicks, 'Antitrust and Trademark Protection Concepts in the Import Field', 49 TMR 1255 (1959).

248   15 USC §2. There were actually three actions against three different groups of perfume companies; Guerlain, Parfums Corday Inc. and Lanvins Parfums Inc. As the facts were essentially the same in each case, except as indicated, the author refers only to the action against Guerlain.

249   155 F. Supp. 77, at 80.

to reassign the trade marks if it ceased to sell Guerlain products; and which gave the French associate the unfettered right to stop supplying Guerlain at the end of any year. Second, Guerlain acted according to the desires of the French associate. Third, the two companies were 'component parts of a single international business enterprise engaged in manufacturing and marketing Guerlain toilet goods'.[250]

Judge Edelstein then considered whether Guerlain could rely on section 526 of the Tariff Act to bar imports emanating from within the group and held that the section could only be used by an American trade mark owner which was independent of the foreign manufacturer. The judgment suggested two alternative grounds for the conclusion. First, Judge Edelstein distinguished *Katzel* because the Guerlain marks did not denote to the American public that the US distributor was the source of the goods:

> It can hardly be claimed by the defendants in the cases at bar that the trade-marks indicate an origin with them in the United States, *inasmuch as the whole burden of their advertising is to emphasize French origin.* A competing importer's identical toilet goods coming from the French part of the international enterprise could in no way harm a defendant's good will and reputation, as was stated to be possible in the Katzel case. (*Emphasis added*)[251]

However, Judge Edelstein went on in somewhat broader terms to dismiss Guerlain's claim that its trade marks were a property right entitling it to protection from free riding whether or not consumers were deceived about source:

> The exclusive right to sell in the American market on the part of an international concern exploiting world markets is not an element of good will except in so far as it may be made so artificially by import prohibitions. A competing importer selling identical merchandise under the same trade-mark would not be a 'pirate' or 'cheat'. The public would not be deceived about the authenticity or origin of the product and the reputation of the trade-mark owner could not suffer from the marketing of inferior merchandise under his mark.[252]

The second sentence in this quotation is arguably consistent with the earlier holding that there was no factually distinct goodwill indicating a separate US source of the perfumes. But the third sentence suggests a wider meaning for the first sentence's reference to an 'international concern exploiting world markets'. In the third sentence, Judge Edelstein seems to state that the domestic trade mark owner could not succeed even if the imports were of inferior quality. Hence, it seems, in his Honour's view, an 'international concern' could not block imports whatever quality the domestic public associated with the trade mark. This is in marked contrast to Holmes J's reasoning in *Katzel*.

---

250   *Ibid.* at 89. In the actions against the other two defendants, the unity arose from similar contractual controls together with stock ownership and control of the board of directors: *ibid.* at 93, 96, respectively.
251   *Ibid.* at 81 to 82.
252   *Ibid.* at 82.

It is also inconsistent with Circuit Court opinion at the time overruling the Commissioner of Patents' refusal to register trade mark assignments to exclusive distributors and/or subsidiaries of foreign manufacturers. In *Roger & Gallet*, the court ruled that a trade mark did not just designate manufacturing source and considered that *Katzel* required a showing of factual goodwill only in the alternative to legal title.[253] Similarly, in *Watson v E. Leitz Inc.*, the Commissioner's refusal to register a subsidiary as the owner by assignment from the parent because the subsidiary would then be able to exclude imports even by its parent was overruled.[254]

Judge Edelstein then found that Guerlain's use of its trade mark rights to block imports violated section 2 of the Sherman Act. As the government argued, his Honour found that the relevant market was 'the trade-marked toilet goods of each defendant' and, as there could hardly be, there was no doubt that each had a monopoly in the market so defined. This power was misused, contrary to the Sherman Act, by the use of trade mark rights to prevent competition from third-party importers.[255] Judge Edelstein also rejected Guerlain's argument that it needed to block the imports to protect its expenditure on advertising and promoting its products because price differentials resulting from an illegal monopoly could not be justified.[256]

The finding of market power was crucial. Attempting to assess market power is often a complicated and difficult task. But, with respect, the formulation of the relevant product market in *Guerlain* seems singularly narrow.[257] In principle, it involves attempting to identify which products are substitutes in both consumption and production. That is, a product market is defined by looking at what consumers consider to be alternative ways of satisfying their needs *and* also by looking at what alternative sources of supply those needs could be met from. In theory, if the producer of a particular product could raise its price significantly without either customers switching to other products or new producers being attracted into the market to compete for those customers, the producer would have market power.[258]

---

253   *Roger & Gallet v Janmarie Inc.* 245 F. 2d 505 (CCPA 1957). In fact, factual goodwill was shown since the exclusive distributor's products were labelled, 'Roger & Gallet, New York, Distributors.'

254   254 F. 2d 777 (CADC, 1958). The Second Circuit agreed with both the *Roger* and *Leitz* courts: *Avedis Zildjian Co. v Fred Gretsch Mfg Co.* 251 F. 2d 530 (2d Cir. 1958). For a similar case in Australia involving a licence rather than assignment, see *Pioneer* (1977) 137 CLR 670.

255   155 F. Supp. 77, especially at 87. There are repeated references to the intention of excluding import competition at 86 to 87.

256   *Ibid.*

257   Markets tend to be defined in two main dimensions: the relevant products and the geographical area. For present purposes, the controversy is about the definition of the relevant products. A third dimension is the timescale over which the assessment should be carried out.

258   Even within these principles, there is plenty of scope for argument over how large a price rise is significant and how long the time frame allowed for all these changes to occur should be. See F.M. Scherer and David Ross, *Industrial Market Structure and Economic Performance*, Houghton Mifflin, 1990 (3rd ed.), especially at 74 to 78, 351 to 356; Valentine Korah, *An Introductory Guide to EEC Competition Law and Practice*, ESC Publishing, 1990 (4th ed.), §§4.2.1 to 4.2.5; Richard Whish,

The importance of the definition of the relevant product market is that too wide a definition will underestimate the producer's market share while one too narrow will exaggerate it. *Guerlain* is a good example. If the market be narrowly defined as Guerlain's trade-marked toilet goods, Guerlain of course has a monopoly. On the other hand, if the market be defined more broadly, it seems that there were about 90 different manufacturers competing in the United States with 408 different brands. Even if the market be limited to those perfumes in the same price range and of similar quality to Guerlain's, its market share was estimated at 2.9 per cent of an annual market valued at US$120 million in retail sales.[259] This was split among several different fragrances identified by different brand names. It seems very difficult to support a finding of market power for such a small share.[260]

To counter the government, Guerlain placed considerable reliance on Supreme Court recognition that neither the 'natural' monopoly every manufacturer had over its own products nor the power conferred by a trade mark created an illegal monopoly for the purposes of the Sherman Act.[261] Judge Edelstein rebutted this reliance on two grounds. First, the products in *Cellophane* were bought by industrial concerns which compared the alternative products on the basis of objective factors. However, consumers often could not tell the difference between perfume fragrances and there was evidence that the same fragrance would hardly sell at all without a strongly promoted brand name. Hence,

> . . the most important element in the appeal of a perfume is a highly exploited trade-mark. There seems to be agreement that no quality perfume can be successfully marketed without a famous name. It would appear that, to a highly significant degree, it is the name that is bought rather than the perfume itself. This fact gives the market a rigidity not found in the cellophane case.[262]

Since consumers did not compare rival perfumes on objective grounds, *Cellophane* did not apply.

A second distinction lay in Guerlain's intention to exclude rival importers

Competition Law, Butterworths, 1989 (2nd ed.), at 278 to 302 and Richard A. Posner, *Antitrust Law: An Economic Perspective*, The University of Chicago Press, 1976, at 125 to 134. An excellent, short overview of the considerations and complexities may be found in Ernerst Gellhorn, *Antitrust Law and Economics*, West Publishing Co., 1986 (3rd ed.), at 97 to 108.

259   The figures are provided by Handler, 'Trademarks – Assets or Liabilities', at 667.

260   It is, of course, necessary to have regard to the particular characteristics of the market in question and if there be high barriers to entry, such as a strong pharmaceutical patent, a narrower sub-market may be appropriate: Scherer and Ross, *Industrial Market Structure and Economic Performance*, at 76. The question is certainly one of degree. In the United States, for example, two distributors each having about 20 per cent of the market for dental X-ray machines were found not to have market power: *H.L. Hayden Co. of New York Inc. v Siemens Medical Systems Inc.* 879 F. 2d 1005 (2d Cir. 1989). There, seven producers had 95 per cent of the market which was described as 'very competitive'. The European Commission has applied a more stringent test, see for example *Davidson Rubber* [1972] CMLR D72, see subsection 7.3.1(b) below; but contrast, *Odin* OJ 1990 L209/15.

261   *US v E.I. du Pont de Nemours & Co.* 351 US 377, especially at 393 (1956) ('the *Cellophane* case').

262   155 F. Supp. at 84 to 85.

from the market. Thus, it was not seeking to exploit the natural monopoly every manufacturer had in its own product. Similarly, Guerlain's power under the trade mark was not being attacked, but rather:

> What is under attack is, in effect, an attempt (successfully executed) by each defendant, as a part of a single international business enterprise, to limit the resale of its products for the express purpose of excluding competition and controlling prices.[263]

The first ground of distinction raises what can only be described as the vexed role of advertising and image in the competitive process.[264] Judge Edelstein's approach can be described as both shallow and rather paternalistic. Image is a form of product differentiation and, where tastes are different, helps to increase consumer welfare. Like trade marks, it also helps to promote competition over quality. Advertising also promotes competition by providing information and reducing search costs. It is possible, however, that product differentiation and advertising could be carried too far. Judge Edelstein's approach accepts the view that advertising and image create barriers to entry. This could certainly be possible. But, the judgment does not explain why existing rival brands or new entrants are unable to compete for consumers' loyalty. The small share of the market actually held by Guerlain does not suggest that it could stifle either form of competition. Guerlain would have difficulty exploiting consumers since they had available to them a wide range of alternative products, some of which competed in terms of quality and image, others on the basis of price. In such circumstances, it might be wondered whether there were sound grounds for the courts or government to intervene with the public's choices about image.

The validity of the approach taken in *Guerlain* is questionable on another ground. The case went on appeal to the Supreme Court where the government, which had succeeded at first instance, applied to have the action dismissed. The government apparently thought that the issue should be resolved by legislation rather than through anti-trust litigation.[265] In the event, the action was dismissed but Congress did not pass the legislation.

(b) Circuit Court qualifications

The first half of the 1980s saw a marked upsurge in litigation in the United States over gray market goods.[266] The recurrent issue which the courts

---

263 *Ibid.* at 87, for the earlier point, see *ibid.* at 86.
264 For a survey of the complexities, see Scherer and Ross, *Industrial Market Structure and Economic Performance*, at 405 to 407 and c. 16; and see further Chapters 8 and 10 below.
265 Bicks, 'Antitrust and Trademark Protection Concepts in the Import Field', at 1259, then Acting Assistant Attorney-General, Antitrust Division of the US Justice Department.
266 Some of the causes of this are explored in John C. Hilke, 'Free Trading or Free-Riding: An Examination of the Theories and Available Empirical Evidence on Gray Market Imports', 32 *World Competition* 75 (1988), see Chapter 11 below.

wrestled with was whether the parallel imports were 'genuine'. In seeking to answer this, many of the decisions, like *Guerlain*, made much of whether the domestic trade mark owner was a corporate affiliate of the foreign source.

Although its facts raised the question of a 'single international enterprise' prominently, the first reopening of the gray market issue was based simply on a large scepticism that consumers could be confused by the use of trade marks on 'genuine' goods.

Mamiya Camera Co. ('Mamiya') was a Japanese company which manufactured, among other things, medium format photographic equipment in Asia. This equipment was manufactured with *Mamiya* trade marks affixed to it. It sold the equipment to its worldwide distributor, J Osawa & Co. Ltd ('Osawa'). Osawa in turn appointed Bell & Howell: Mamiya Co. ('BHMC') as its exclusive distributor in the United States. BHMC was the registered owner in the United States of the *Mamiya* trade marks. Almost all of its issued capital was owned by Osawa through one of Osawa's wholly owned subsidiaries while Mamiya owned the remainder. Osawa itself owned 30 per cent of Mamiya, the next four largest shareholders owning a combined total of 18 per cent.

Masel Supply Co. bought Mamiya equipment in Hong Kong and imported it into the United States, selling it in its original packaging. The equipment was identical to that imported by BHMC and bore the trade marks owned by BHMC in the United States. BHMC sued Masel for infringement of its trade mark rights and was granted a preliminary injunction by the District Court. The Second Circuit quashed the preliminary injunction.[267]

Judge Neaher rejected the defendant's reliance on the identical manufacturing source of its goods because the theory underlying the submission ignored the potential for independent goodwill to exist in different territories. The trade mark itself indicated more than the mere physical origin of the goods. It could indicate the company which took responsibility for the quality of the goods.[268] His Honour also rejected reliance on the single international enterprise theory. On trade marks, the facts in *Guerlain* did not raise the question of independent goodwill and the wider statements were inconsistent with *Katzel* and subsequent authority.[269]

---

267   *Bell & Howell: Mamiya Co. v Masel Supply Co.* 548 F. Supp. 1063 (EDNY 1982) *revd* 719 F. 2d 42 (2d Cir. 1983) ('the *BHMC* case'). The same plaintiff, having changed its name, subsequently obtained preliminary injunctions against two other importers: *Osawa & Co. v B & H Photo* 589 F. Supp. 1163, at 1170 (SDNY 1984), below from Note 271.

268   548 F. Supp. at 1069 to 1071.

269   *Ibid.* at 1075 to 1077. (Judge Neaher's statements about section 526 require reconsideration in light of *K-Mart*, see section 2.3.5 below.) The anti-trust arguments were also dismissed as inconsistent with *Cellophane* as criticised by Handler, 'Trademarks – Assets or Liabilities', at 661. The criticism of *Guerlain* and the Customs regulation on anti-trust grounds was sustained in *Olympus* 792 F. 2d 315, at 319 (2d Cir. 1986). But, there were only four other manufacturers competing in this market segment (medium format cameras), suggesting that closer examination might be warranted: Seth E. Lipner, 'The Legality of Parallel Imports: Trademarks, Antitrust or Equity', 19 *Texas International Law Journal* 553, at 561 and 574 (1984).

The Second Circuit vacated the decision because there was insufficient evidence to support the finding of a likelihood of confusion. In doing so, the court ruled:

> On the basis of the present record, irreparable injury may well not be present herein since there would appear to be little confusion, if any, as to the origin of the goods and no significant likelihood of damage to BHMC's reputation since thus far it has not been shown that Masel's goods, which have a common origin of manufacture with BHMC's goods, are inferior to those sold by BHMC and are injuring BHMC's reputation. Further, it does not appear that the lack of warranties accompanying MAMIYA cameras sold by Masel amounts to irreparable injury, since the consumer can be made aware by, among other things, labels on the camera boxes or notices in advertisements as to whether the cameras are sold with or without warranties. Thus, less drastic means would appear to be available to avoid the claimed confusion . . . . On the facts of the present case, BHMC has not shown that the sale of the subject camera equipment by another distributor is likely to cause any consumer to be misled about the product he or she purchases.[270]

The Second Circuit rounded off its opinion by warning that a trial court was not bound by findings on an application for preliminary injunctions.

The Second Circuit stressed the importance of the trade mark as an indicator of manufacturing source. It did also refer to the issue of BHMC's reputation. But, where the goods had a common origin, it seems the court considered reputation would only be damaged if the physical goods were of inferior quality, considering that alternative means were available to protect against confusion over warranty availability. The court, in effect, applied the test first adopted in the *Apollinaris v Scherer* and rejected by the Supreme Court in *Katzel*.

Subsequent litigation involving the same trade mark and the same plaintiff found the District Court for the Southern District of New York respectfully suggesting that the Second Circuit's approach was misdirected. Judge Leval considered that the doubts expressed by the Second Circuit in the *BHMC* case, about whether an infringement action could lie against goods genuinely marked abroad would be resolved in favour of the *Katzel* and *Aldridge* cases.

In a detailed opinion, his Honour concluded that the acceptance of the territorial nature of the trade mark right by the Supreme Court meant that the principle of exhaustion could not apply when the domestic trade mark owner developed a separate, factually independent goodwill from that of the foreign manufacturer. In such a case, any exhaustion occurring by the release into commerce of the product on a foreign market by the foreign manufacturer was the exhaustion of a legally distinct and factually different trade mark.[271]

His Honour carefully reviewed the factors giving rise to the plaintiff's

---

270   719 F. 2d at 46. For a strong criticism of the test applied by the Second Circuit, see Lipner, 'The Legality of Parallel Imports', at 567 to 574.
271   589 F. Supp. 1163, at 1174. The issues raised by *Guerlain* were dealt with in similar fashion to Judge Neaher in *BHMC: ibid.* at 1176 to 1178.

independent, domestic goodwill. These included maintaining a wide stock of peripheral equipment for prompt supply to demanding customers; incurring substantial advertising and promotional expenditures including organising seminars to educate users, dealers and potential customers about the capabilities of the equipment; offering sales rebates; maintaining an authorised dealer network capable of providing full after-sales support; devoting considerable care in handling merchandise including quality inspections and providing free warranty repairs even to purchasers of gray market equipment to prevent any dissatisfied consumer backlash.[272]

Based on this domestic goodwill, the tangible costs to the plaintiff, together with the intangible damage to the trade mark's reputation resulting from reduced opportunity to advertise and the risk of disparagement by dissatisfied dealers and customers, meant that there was a compelling case of likelihood of confusion causing irreparable harm. Further, with the advent of gray market competition, the plaintiff had suffered a 'drastic decline' in sales. This led to laying off a large part of its personnel, causing delays in providing the warranty service. The plaintiff had 'severely slashed' its advertising budget. The advertising it maintained was largely benefiting its gray market competitors. Its dealers had become demoralised, 40 per cent of them dropping the Mamiya line. It also incurred uncompensated costs in providing free warranty service to purchasers from gray market outlets. The gray marketers' lack of quality controls also meant more defective goods were getting on to the market. The very submission of gray market goods to the plaintiff for warranty repair was compelling evidence of consumer confusion.[273]

In *BHMC*, the Second Circuit had suggested that consumers could be protected against confusion about the warranty coverage for parallel imports by less restrictive means than total exclusion. The means it suggested were the use of labels on the packaging and notices in the advertising.[274] The suggestion is like that made in the Anglo-Commonwealth cases, *Seiko Time* and *Saray*, considered at subsection 2.2.3(c) above. It is also similar to part of the reasoning used by the European Court of Justice in denying power to block imports from another Member State marketed by a firm totally independent of the trade mark owner.[275]

---

272   *Ibid.* at 1165 to 1166. In contrast, Judge Neaher at first instance in *BHMC* had relied on (1) Masel's failure to supply any evidence backing up its claim that the public associated the trade marks with the Japanese manufacturer only; and (2) BHMC's role in (a) determining the terms and conditions of the US warranties (although these were printed and packed by Mamiya in Japan); (b) providing the repair services to support the warranty (although receiving partial remuneration from Mamiya for those services); (c) incurring substantial expenditure in advertising the product range and establishing and maintaining a nationwide dealer network: 548 F. Supp. at 1079.
273   *Ibid.* at 1168 to 1169.
274   719 F. 2d 42, at 46. There is evidence of this happening to some extent in the United States, see Hecksher, 'Parallel Imports Furore: A Case of Smoke Exhalation', 15 IBL 32 (1987).
275   192/73 *Hag I* [1974] ECR 731, at ¶14; for that case and the subsequent rejection of the so-called doctrine of 'common origin', see Chapter 6 from Note 88 below.

In *Osawa*, Judge Leval denied that using labels or advertising by the plaintiff would reduce the likelihood of damage. First, his Honour did not readily see why the plaintiff should be driven to this extra cost when it was not responsible for the confusion. Second, many consumers might not discover the difference until it was too late and the resultant hostility would still damage the plaintiff's goodwill.[276]

The European Court of Justice did not express an opinion on the use of additional, distinguishing matter when it overruled *Hag I* in *Hag II*. Advocate-General Jacobs, however, did. He considered that the effectiveness of such techniques was likely to be a question of fact and there were likely to be situations where such devices would be inadequate, especially where the marks were identical.[277]

The *Hag* cases, of course, concerned imports from a completely independent source, rather than parallel imports. But, with respect, Judge Leval's and Advocate-General Jacobs' rejection of the use of additional material is sound. The basic point of the Advocate-General's reasoning is that the trade mark's use on the imports means something different to what domestic consumers expect. As a result, the trade mark owner potentially loses the incentives which the grant of the exclusive rights are intended to supply. These are precisely the problems which parallel imports threaten to cause (and which are ignored by the extremely narrow definition of the trade mark's function proposed in *Champagne Heidsieck*, *Cinzano* and *Apollinaris v Scherer*). Professor Beier has made a similar point in the context of imports sourced from an independent producer where he considered that additional distinguishing matter should only be resorted to in the most exceptional circumstances. He is, however, on record as expressly favouring parallel imports.[278] The question which then arises is what is it about parallel imports which makes them so exceptional? Notwithstanding the consent to marketing in the foreign country, the risk of confusion and the damage to goodwill is potentially the same. That leaves the fear that the trade mark will be used as

---

276   589 F. Supp. 1163, at 1168 and 1169 respectively.

277   C-10/89 *Hag II* [1990] 3 CMLR 571, at 593 to 595. Judge Joliet has expressed his Honour's agreement with the Advocate-General's opinion, René Joliet and David T. Keeling, 'Trade Mark Law and the Free Movement of Goods: The Overruling of the Judgment in Hag I', 22 IIC 303 (1991), text at Note 29. In Anglo-Commonwealth law, the additional distinguishing matter would not preclude infringement, see *Saville Perfumery Ltd v June Perfect Ltd* (1941) 58 RPC 147. See also Friedrich-Karl Beier, 'Trademark Conflicts in the Common Market: Can They be Solved by Means of Distinguishing Additions?', 9 IIC 221 (1978).

278   See Beier, 'Trademark Conflicts in the Common Market: Can They be Solved by Means of Distinguishing Additions?', at ¶10:

> The creation of a risk of confusion is the oldest and most important act of *unfair competition*, whose prevention serves the interests of the trade mark owner in preserving his goodwill as well as the interests of the consumer in being protected against deception. (*Emphasis added*)

For use of additional distinguishing matter only where there is absolutely no other solution, see *ibid.* at ¶35. For his most recent defence of parallel imports, see Friedrich-Karl Beier, 'Industrial Property and the Free Movement of Goods in the Internal European Market', 21 IIC 131 (1990).

an instrument of monopoly which can only really be examined after a proper analysis of the market circumstances.

Prior to the Second Circuit's ruling in *BHMC*, *Guerlain* was followed in an application for interlocutory injunctions against a number of parallel importers.[279] The Parfums Stern group owned the trade mark rights to *Oscar de la Renta* throughout the world and was engaged in producing and distributing fragrance products under that mark throughout the world. The group was described as owning the registered trade marks in the United States and throughout the world. It, and its affiliated or related companies, had spent considerable money promoting the mark in the United States and elsewhere and it stood 'behind its product' and had 'developed goodwill in conducting its business'. Parallel imports of the sort in question had existed for several years.

In refusing relief, the District Court ruled that Parfums Stern had failed to establish a substantial likelihood of success on the merits because trade mark rights under the Lanham Act were not infringed by importation of products produced by a single international enterprise bearing the marks affixed by that single international enterprise.[280] Parfums Stern also failed to satisfy that court that the other factors necessary for preliminary relief were in its favour.[281]

Like the marginalisation of *Revlon* by *Colgate*, *Fender* and other cases, however, other District Courts have been quick to distinguish *Parfums Stern* where the parallel imports were not made by a 'cog or entity' in a 'single international enterprise' and where there have been differences in product quality.[282] But, the issue is still undecided at the Circuit Court level.

Subsequently, in circumstances where the relationship between foreign manufacturer and domestic exclusive distributor was purely contractual, two Circuit Courts refused to follow the approach suggested by the Second Circuit in *BHMC*. Both, like *BHMC*, were applications for preliminary injunctions.

---

279 *Parfums Stern Inc. v United States Customs Service* 575 F. Supp. 416 (SD Fla. 1983).

280 *Ibid.* at 419 to 420; at 418 describing the group as:

> . . . a cog or entity in what appears to be a single international enterprise operating through an amoeba-like structure consisting of members of Milton Stern's family, various parent and subsidiary corporate enterprises, both foreign and domestic, interrelated, each to the other or to the Sterns.

281 In particular, as in *Champagne Heidsieck*, parallel imports had existed for several years, so it could not prove irreparable harm if the imports continued: *ibid.* at 420. The judgment did not discuss what the goodwill represented in detail. But, the delay and the distinguishing of *Katzel* and the *BHMC* case 548 F. Supp. 1063 (EDNY 1982) suggest that the trade mark did *not* represent an independent US source. Moreover, there is some suggestion that the products were all made in the United States in any case.

282 See *Dial Corp. v Encina Corp.* 643 F. Supp. 951 (SD Fla. 1986); *Selchow & Righter Co. v Goldex Corp.* 225 USPQ 815 (SD Fla. 1985) (domestic trade mark owner manufactured its own goods too); *Dial Corp. v Manghnani Investment Corp.* 659 F. Supp. 1230 (DConn. 1987); *Epocha Distributors Inc. v Quality King Distributors Inc.* 2 USPQ 2d 805 (EDNY 1987); *Bambu Sales Inc. v Sultana Crackers Inc.* 683 F. Supp. 899 (EDNY 1988) (rejecting mere assertion of corporate affiliation without proof); *PepsiCo Inc. v Giraud* 7 USPQ 2d 1371 (DPuerto Rico 1988).

In *Model Rectifier*, the plaintiff imported plastic kits for radio-controlled, automobile models under the *Tamiya* trade mark. Before selling, it inspected each kit and replaced any broken and missing parts and labelled the ends of each box with its own name. It maintained a spare parts inventory and spent over US$100,000 each year on advertising and promotion. It had been a distributor for 17 years, but had only been granted exclusivity since 1981 when the *Tamiya* trade mark was also assigned to it. Among other things, it alleged that the defendants' imports had been sold with broken or missing parts and that customers had looked to the plaintiff to make good the defects, mistakenly believing it to be the source of the parallel imports. The Ninth Circuit held that there was 'ample evidence of the likelihood of confusion' and agreed that the plaintiff was likely to succeed on the merits. It further noted the 'heavy burden' for a successful allegation of anti-trust violation on the ground of exercising trade mark rights and found that the defendants' allegations had not even made a colourable showing on this part of the case.[283]

The exclusive distributor's relationship to the foreign producer was also contractual in *Premier Dental*.[284] Although its appointment dated from 1974, the trade mark had only been assigned to it recently, its use of the trade mark was closely circumscribed and, as in *Guerlain*, it was obliged to reassign once the exclusive distributorship ended. The Third Circuit held that the decisive issue was what the goodwill associated with the mark symbolised. It expressly rejected the Second Circuit's finding in the *BHMC* case that there must be confusion about the *origin* of the gray market goods or of injury to the domestic distributor's reputation by the sale of *inferior* gray market goods under the trade mark. Instead, the court believed: 'that [*Katzel*] and Section 526 make it clear that an American distributor's goodwill can be harmed even by the sale of gray market goods that are identical to those sold by the distributor'.[285] However, earlier in the opinion, when confronted with the single international enterprise argument from *Guerlain* and suggestions that it be extended even to situations where there was no corporate affiliation between the two firms exploiting the foreign and domestic markets, the court had expressed itself in careful terms *about the effect of section 526*:

> . . . we conclude that where a trademark is owned and registered in this country by an exclusive distributor who is independent of the foreign manufacturer and who has separate goodwill in the product, the distributor is entitled under

---

283 *Model Rectifier Corporation v Takachiho International Inc.* 221 USPQ 502 (9th Cir. 1983) *affg* 220 USPQ 508 (CD Cal. 1982), delivery of judgment noted but not reported 509 F. 2d 1517.

284 *Premier Dental Products v Darby Dental Supply Co.* 794 F. 2d 850 (3d Cir. 1986) *cert. dend* 479 US 950, 93 L Ed 2d 385 (1987).

285 794 F. 2d 850, at 859. Here, although the goods were physically identical, the packaging was different; the US version being worded in English only and not English and German, the producer's name was more prominent and the exclusive distributor for the United States was also identified. The instructions in each product for the United States had been composed by the US distributor and were in English only, not English, German, French, Italian and Spanish as in the imports.

Section 526 to prevent the importation even of genuine merchandise obtained from the same foreign manufacturer.[286]

In further contrast to the *BHMC* case, the Third Circuit held the plaintiff's reputation in the *Impregum* mark would inevitably be injured by the mere existence of an alternative source of supply, regardless of the standard of service and financial guarantees offered by that competing source. Since the relevant issue was the existence of the plaintiff's domestic reputation, disclaimers would not be effective to prevent the damage threatened by the rival source.[287]

The next Circuit Courts to consider the issue, however, reasserted the inability of domestic subsidiaries to use trade mark rights to block imports of 'genuine' goods. *Guerlain* was not cited, but the underlying fear of monopolising the trade is present. In *Olympus*, primarily concerned with the validity of Customs' regulations implementing sections 526 and 42, the majority was not prepared to rule that *Katzel* and *Aldridge* applied to situations outside the 'special equities'. Hence, they were not prepared to allow the domestic distributor, a wholly-owned subsidiary of the foreign manufacturer, to exclude 'genuine' goods.[288]

The rationale of this approach was elaborated by the Ninth Circuit in *CAL Circuit Abco*.[289] NEC Corporation, a Japanese company, manufactured computer chips. It operated in the United States through a wholly owned subsidiary, NEC-USA, of which NEC's directors constituted a majority of the board of directors. NEC-USA manufactured some chips for itself but imported 90 per cent from NEC. The assignment of the domestic mark to NEC-USA took place in 1983. NEC remained the owner of the trade mark outside the United States and continued marketing its computer chips under the trade mark outside the United States. CAL Circuit bought identical NEC computer chips abroad and imported and sold them in the United States. In motions for summary judgment on the ensuing infringement action, both parties stipulated that the imports were 'genuine' but there was evidence that some purchasers from CAL Circuit thought their computer chips were covered by NEC-USA's warranty.

The Ninth Circuit held that trade mark law did not generally consider the sale of genuine goods bearing a true trade mark an infringement. It found

---

286   *Ibid*. at 858. Premier had asserted violation of Lanham Act sections 32, 42 and 43 as well. The Third Circuit seems to have treated the appeal as being from the District Court's grant of a preliminary injunction enforcing the assertion of rights under section 526: *ibid*. at 852.

287   *Ibid*. The factors expressly mentioned by the court as developing the independent domestic goodwill included Premier's long tenure as exclusive distributor, its considerable expenditure of time and money on advertising and promotional expenditure including providing seminars and instructions about the product and running a toll-free telephone advice line: *ibid*. at 854 to 855.

288   *Olympus Corporation v US* 792 F. 2d 315, at 321 *per* Oakes and Pratt JJ (2d Cir. 1986) *affg* 627 F. Supp. 911 (EDNY 1985). For the issues of the Customs regulations, see section 2.3.5 below.

289   *NEC Electronics v CAL Circuit Abco* 810 F. 2d 1506 (9th Cir. 1987) *cert. denied*. 108 S. Ct 152 (1987).

that *Katzel* provided a limited exception to the general principle where the domestic trade mark owner had real independence from the foreign manufacturer.[290] That independence was lacking here because NEC could compel NEC-USA, its wholly-owned and controlled subsidiary, either to consent to NEC selling its products in the United States or to reassign the trade mark to NEC.[291] In addition, because of the common control, NEC-USA was in no danger of being unable to ensure the quality of its products.

The court went so far as to state 'Nor is it inaccurate to say that the mark 'NEC' on [CAL Circuit]'s products truly designates the chips as having been manufactured under the control of [NEC], even if the mark has become associated here with NEC-USA.'[292]

Finally, the court concluded that trade mark law could not be used to establish a worldwide discriminatory pricing scheme. If the plaintiff had a remedy under section 526 of the Tariff Act, it should proceed under that Act, not trade mark law.[293]

CAL Circuit Abco provides direct appellate court approval for a single international enterprise theory. However, it goes much further than that, as the quotation shows. The court was prepared to disregard the plaintiff's domestic goodwill to maintain the view that a trade mark indicated manufacturing origin, a position largely rejected since *Katzel*. The court's reliance on its earlier decision in *Monte Carlo Shirt* to support this conclusion seems problematic. There, the court had ruled that the function of a trade mark was to protect the public from deception about source, but it had also noted that a 'showing of likely buyer confusion as to the source, origin *or sponsorship* of goods is part of a cause of action for infringement of a registered trade mark . . . (*Emphasis added*)'.[294] Whether the test of source or sponsorship be applied in *Monte Carlo Shirt*, the same result is achieved since the imports had been made for Monte Carlo's own exploitation in the United States according to Monte Carlo's own specification and had only been rejected for late delivery. Monte Carlo was both the trade mark owner and the person seeking to exploit it by distribution in the United States. In *CAL Circuit Abco*, however, a domestic exclusive distributor had been

---

290   *Ibid.* at 1509. *Katzel* involved an arm's-length assignment between foreign producer and domestic purchaser, the latter having complete control and responsibility for the goods being sold under the mark.
291   *Ibid.* at 1510.
292   *Ibid.*
293   Ibid. at Note 4. For 'worldwide discriminatory pricing', see *ibid.* at 1511.
294   *Monte Carlo Shirt Inc. v Daewoo International (America) Corporation* 707 F. 2d 1054, at 1058 (9th Cir. 1983). Assumption of 'responsibility' rather than sponsorship is used in *Premier Dental* 794 F. 2d 850 (3d Cir. 1986); for a discussion of 'sponsorship' meaning responsibility of quality control, albeit by a licensor, see *Original Appalachian Artworks Inc. v Granada Electronics Inc.* 816 F. 2d 68, at 75 *per* Cardamone J concurring (2d Cir. 1987). Both these cases, of course, did not involve international corporate groups.

interposed which had built up a distinct goodwill as sponsor of products under the mark.[295]

The only factor distinguishing *CAL Circuit Abco* from the earlier cases is the fact that the domestic distributor was a wholly-owned subsidiary of the foreign producer. However, in *Monte Carlo Shirt*, the Ninth Circuit had earlier recognised that a trade mark could signify the sponsor of the product in the domestic market. The primary motivation for the result in *CAL Circuit Abco* seems to be a desire to avoid allowing trade mark owners to enforce a discriminatory pricing scheme by means of their trade marks, although in *Model Rectifier*, a judgment not referred to in *CAL Circuit Abco*, the Ninth Circuit itself had earlier largely scorned the anti-trust prospects of such a claim.

As yet, there remains considerable doubt about domestic exclusive distributors' power to block parallel imports. The Third Circuit has approved the theory that a domestic trade mark owner can block parallel imports under the Lanham or Tariff Acts if it is not a corporate affiliate of the foreign marketer but only contractually associated.[296] The Second Circuit has chosen to distinguish *Olympus* on another ground, although in circumstances where the *CAL Circuit Abco* distinction still remains open.[297] The DC Circuit has attacked the distinction head on.[298]

(c)   *Authorised application abroad*

While the courts were grappling with the problems posed by domestic exclusive distributors asserting trade mark registrations against parallel imports, another stream of cases raised the question of 'genuine' goods in a slightly different way. In these cases, the domestic trade mark owner has expressly authorised affixation of the mark to the goods which it is trying to exclude. Two variations have surfaced so far. In one, the domestic trade mark owner has subcontracted the goods' production abroad with the intention of selling them, once ready, in the United States but, for one reason or another, the domestic company has refused to take delivery of the goods and it has tried to block the subsequent importation of the products into the United States. Although there have been allegations of inferior quality goods in each case to date, this allegation has not been sustained at trial. The Ninth and Second Circuits have reached apparently inconsistent

---

295   The *CAL Circuit Abco* court's reliance on *Diamond Supply Co. v Prudential Paper Products Co.* 599 F. Supp. 470 (SDNY 1984) also needs consideration in light of the Second Circuit's opinion in *El Greco Leather Products Co. Inc. v Shoe World Inc.* 1 USPQ 2d 1016 (2d Cir. 1986) *revg* 599 F. Supp. 1380 (EDNY 1984). For both cases, see subsection 2.3.4(c) below.
296   *Weil Ceramics and Glass Inc. v Dash* 878 F. 2d 659 *revg* 618 F. Supp. 700 (DNJ 1985), see section 2.3.6, below.
297   *Original Appalachian Artworks Inc. v Granada Electronics Inc.* 816 F. 2d 68 (2d Cir. 1987) *affg* 640 F. Supp. 928 (SDNY 1986), below from Note 300.
298   *Lever Bros Co. v US* 877 F. 2d 101 (DC Cir. 1989), see section 2.3.6 below.

conclusions.[299] In another variation, the goods were produced abroad under a licence which clearly limited the licensee's rights to use the trade mark to the foreign territory somewhat like *Castrol GTX* and *Colgate*.[300]

In *Monte Carlo Shirt*, the Ninth Circuit was concerned with a claim of unfair competition at common law (akin to passing off). The imported shirts had actually been made up for Monte Carlo according to its own specifications and had been intended for sale by it in the United States but were rejected for late delivery. The manufacturer had sold the shirts to one of its US affiliates which was selling them as made and prepared for Monte Carlo. The court distinguished the *Katzel* and *Prestonettes* cases because they did not address the central issue of the instant case:

> . . . whether the unauthorized sale of a genuine, unaltered product initially manufactured for the plaintiff can form the subject of a trade mark claim. In such a case there can be no deception as to the nature of the product. Buyers of the product, although perhaps mistaken about how the product came into the retailer's hands, get precisely what they bargain for.[301]

The court considered that the same test of infringement applied whether at common law or under statute for infringement. Thus, the plaintiff needed to show 'likely buyer confusion as to the source, origin or sponsorship of goods'. It concluded:

> No such confusion was possible in this case. The goods sold by [defendant] were not imitations of Monte Carlo shirts; they were the genuine product, planned and sponsored by Monte Carlo and produced for it on contract for future sale. The shirts were not altered or changed from the date of their manufacture to the date of their sale.[302]

The absence of plaintiff's consent to market the shirt was irrelevant to the trade mark issue, although the plaintiff did sue successfully for breach of contract.

The Ninth Circuit had found support for its conclusions in *dicta* from the Second Circuit that it seemed 'anomalous in any event that a trade mark infringement action would lie here when the soap sold by Interstate is in fact genuine and not spurious'.[303]

The Second Circuit had simply refused the plaintiff relief under the

---

299 *Monte Carlo Shirt Co. Inc. v Daewoo International (America) Corp.* 548 F. Supp. 1063 *vacd* 707 F. 2d 1054 (9th Cir. 1983) common law; followed in *Dombicare USA Inc. v Toys 'R' Us Inc.* 21 USPQ 2d 1711 (DN. Cal. 1991); *El Greco Leather Products Co. Inc. v Shoe World Inc.* 599 F. Supp. 1380 (EDNY 1984) *revd* 1 USPQ 2d 1016 (2d Cir. 1986) statute and common law.
300 *Original Appalachian Artworks Inc. v Granada Electronics Inc.* 816 F. Supp. 68 (2d Cir. 1987) *affg* 640 F. Supp. 928 (SDNY 1986) ('the *Artworks* case'); see also *J. Atkins Holdings Ltd v English Discounts Inc.* 729 F. Supp. 945 (SDNY 1990); *Dial Corp. v Encina Corp.* 643 F. Supp. 951 (SD Fla. 1986); *Selchow & Righter Co. v Goldex Corp.* 225 USPQ 815 (SD Fla. 1985); *Dial Corp. v Manghnani Investment Corp.* 659 F. Supp. 1230 (DConn. 1987); *PepsiCo Inc. v Giraud* 7 USPQ 2d 1371 (DPuerto Rico 1988).
301 707 F. 2d 1054, at 1057, Note 3.
302 *Ibid.* at 1058.
303 *DEP Corporation v Interstate Cigar Company Inc.* 622 F. 2d 621, at 622 Note 1 (2d Cir. 1980).

Lanham Act because it had no rights in the trade mark it based its infringement action on. Hence, the plaintiff had no standing to sue. The court expressly refrained from dealing with the effect of *Katzel* on the perceived anomaly.

The Second Circuit directly confronted the issue in the *El Greco* case. El Greco had a policy of strictly controlling the quality of shoes sold under its *Candies* mark. It ordered a stock from a Brazilian producer, but cancelled the order before it was delivered. It was unclear whether the order was cancelled for poor quality or production delays. The shoes, however, were produced and were being sold in the United States under the *Candies* mark. The District Court had followed the *Monte Carlo Shirt* and *DEP Corp.* cases in denying the plaintiff relief for infringement of its registered trade mark under the Lanham and Tariff Acts. In a split decision, the Second Circuit refused to follow both cases and found that the plaintiff's rights were infringed. The majority found that the Lanham Act entitled a trade mark owner to control the quality of the goods distributed under that trade mark. Accordingly, goods could not be considered 'genuine' until the trade mark owner had authorised their distribution and the mere act of ordering them did not authorise distribution without prior inspection.[304] In this case, unlike *Diamond Supply v Prudential Paper Products*,[305] the plaintiff had not waived its rights to control quality.

Unless the plaintiff in *Monte Carlo Shirt* be taken to have certified the quality of Daewoo's imports or to have authorised their disposal anywhere, the two Circuit Court decisions are not reconcilable. The Second Circuit itself has suggested an alternative basis for the *Diamond Supply* case: that the goods had been intended for sale in the United States.[306] However, the shoes in *El Greco* had also been ordered (and so, were intended) for the US market. It was only the fact that they had not met El Greco's standards which precluded their importation as the *Artworks* court later noted.[307]

With respect the *El Greco* case is the better view. In principle, a trade mark can hardly serve its function if its owner does not have the power to choose which goods will bear the mark in the first place. While it may not matter to purchasers of shirts how the goods came into the retailer's hands, the history of many kinds of goods could be very important when trying to assess their quality. Further, denying the trade mark owner power to control rejects which come into the hands of parties outside the contractual

---

304   1 USPQ 2d 1016, at 1017 to 1018 *per* Pratt J. Altimari J dissented on the grounds that '[i]t is not necessary to a finding of genuineness that the goods be distributed with the trademark holder's express authorization': *ibid.* at 1020.

305   589 F. Supp. 470 (SDNY 1984) where the trade mark owner instructed the manufacturer that he 'did not care' how the rejected goods were disposed of.

306   See *Artworks* 816 F. 2d 68, at 72 (2d Cir. 1987), also explaining *Sasson Jeans Inc. v Sasson Jeans LA Inc.* 632 F. Supp. 1525 (SDNY 1986) on the same basis. But, earlier in *El Greco*, the Second Circuit had explained *Diamond Supply* on the ground of quality control (see text at Note 304, above): 1 USPQ 2d 1016, at 1018.

307   *Ibid.*

relationship could undermine its incentives to invest in quality and such like.[308]

The second type of situation, where the domestic trade mark owner has authorised a foreign licensee to exploit the mark in a limited territory, confronted the Second Circuit in *Artworks*.

The plaintiff (OAA) made and sold 'soft sculpture' dolls on the US market under the brand *Cabbage Patch* which it had registered as a trade mark. It had also licensed Coleco to market a slightly smaller and inferior quality range of Cabbage Patch dolls in the United States. Both ranges were marketed in the United States under the *Cabbage Patch* trade mark identifying OAA's association with the product. Coleco had invested millions of dollars in promoting the mark, becoming recognised in the public's eyes as the source of its range of Cabbage Patch dolls and achieving 'tremendous' sales in the United States. OAA had also licensed Jesmar to make and sell dolls similar to the Coleco range. But, Jesmar's licence permitted it to use the trade mark only in Spain. Jesmar agreed not to sell outside Spain and also agreed to sell only to buyers which themselves agreed not to resell outside Spain. Granada, of course, managed to buy Jesmar dolls in Spain and was selling them in the United States where OAA brought its infringement action.

As far as the Second Circuit was concerned, the only material difference between the Jesmar imports and the US products was the language of the 'adoption papers'. All US dolls came with 'birth certificates', 'adoption papers' and instructions in the English language. If the relevant paper was returned to OAA, the owner of the doll would receive a 'birthday card' one year after purchase. These papers were proved to be 'an important element of the mystique' of the dolls.[309] Unfortunately, Jesmar's papers were all in Spanish and OAA refused to process them. OAA proved in evidence 'numerous letters' from dissatisfied US purchasers of Jesmar imports who thought they had been buying Coleco dolls.

The Second Circuit confined *Olympus* to the question of whether Customs could permit imports as an exercise of agency enforcement discretion. It did not bar the trade mark owner from pursuing private remedies against the importer either under section 526 of the Tariff Act or section 32 of the Lanham Act.[310] Next, noting the confusion in the market-place, the court

---

308 See for example the UK *Colgate* case; the care in the blending and bottling process of perfumes acknowledged in the *Prestonettes* case; even the shelf-life of batteries: *Duracell Inc. v Global Imports Inc.* 12 USPQ 2d (SDNY 1989).

309 816 F. 2d 68, at 70 (2d Cir. 1987) citing 640 F. Supp. 928, at 930. Jesmar boxes also featured the *Cabbage Patch* trade mark and OAA's name and US address in English, but were otherwise worded in Spanish. For similar cases, see *Dial Corp. v Encina Corp.* 643 F. Supp. 951 (SD Fla. 1986); *Dial Corp. v Manghnani Investment Corp.* 659 F. Supp. 1230 (DConn. 1987); *PepsiCo Inc. v Giraud* 7 USPQ 2d 1371 (DPuerto Rico 1988) but contrast *Société des Produits Nestlé SA v Casa Helvetica Inc.* 777 F. Supp. 161 (D Puerto Rico 1991) see Note 338a, below; *PepsiCo. Inc. v Nostalgia Products Corp.* 18 USPQ 2d 1414 (DIll. 1990) (consent judgment).

310 *Ibid.* at 71 *per* Oakes J (Winter J, joining, had dissented in *Olympus*). For Customs' regulation, see section 2.3.5, below.

rejected Granada's claim that there could be no trade mark infringement where the impugned goods were the trade mark owner's 'own goods':

> Although this argument has *some* force in cases where the imported goods are identical to the domestic goods and are intended for sale in the United States, as in *Sasson Jeans* or *Monte Carlo Shirt*, for example, in a case such as this where the goods are confusingly different, the argument ignores the fact that [section 32] was intended to prevent any consumer confusion over similar goods. In light of this statutory purpose, the fact that *a single entity owns the trademark world-wide is not dispositive*. (*Emphasis added*)[311]

Hence, OAA succeeded because it showed that, first, there was consumer confusion in the US market resulting from the material differences in the imports and, second, the imports were never intended for the US market. Judge Cardamone concurred; preferring to find for OAA simply on the ground that it had a right to relief 'from potential consumer confusion as to whether it sponsored the importation of these genuine but "inferior" dolls'.[312]

It is possible to read *Artworks* as consistent with *CAL Circuit Abco*, since the factual situation in *Artworks* did not involve a US distributor which was a corporate affiliate (let alone subsidiary) of the foreign manufacturer *and* there was found to be a material difference between the domestic and foreign products. However, on every other consideration, the opinions seem totally opposed. Indeed, the suggested distinctions hardly seem likely to have received the *Artworks* court's approval. *CAL Circuit Abco* ignored evidence of consumer confusion which played a large part in the *Artworks* opinions. Note also the qualification of the identical goods argument as having *some* force. Moreover, in the face of consumer confusion, the majority opinion in *Artworks* explicitly rejected the theory underpinning *Guerlain*, *Parfums Stern* and *CAL Circuit Abco*, that ownership of the trade mark in both markets is vested in a single entity.[313]

Artworks is not without its difficulties, however. The majority's argument that the foreign goods must be intended for the domestic market by the domestic mark holder is similar to the claim first put in the Anglo-Commonwealth cases in *Bailey's Irish Cream*. The *El Greco* and *Monte Carlo Shirt* cases illustrate one problem with the argument. The majority in *Artworks* does suggest a way out of this difficulty, but one more complicated and fraught with danger than the simple test of consumer confusion proposed by Judge Cardamone in his concurring opinion.

---

311 *Ibid*. at 73, having earlier distinguished *DEP Corp.*, *El Greco*, *Sasson Jeans*, *Monte Carlo Shirt* and *Diamond Supply*.
312 *Ibid*. at 76.
313 The difference is reinforced by (a) the brusque dismissal of Granada's feeble anti-trust claim for want of standing: *ibid*. at 74, and (b) the complete absence of any negative comment on OAA's refusal to process Spanish language papers in the United States at all.

2.3.5   K Mart and the meaning of §526

Some 64 years after *Prestonettes*, the Supreme Court delivered its next reasoned judgment on the relationship of parallel imports and trade marks. The judgment in the *K Mart* case, however, unfortunately does not provide clear principles for the resolution of the substantive issues, being confined instead to largely procedural matters and revealing a heavily divided bench.[314] The case concerned the validity of Customs regulations made under section 526 of the Tariff Act. These implemented the statutory ban but introduced three exceptions permitting imports when:

(1) Both the foreign and the US trade mark or trade name are owned by the same person or business entity ('the same owner exception') (This exception would cover both *Champagne Heidsieck* and *Colgate*);
(2) The foreign and the domestic trade mark or trade name owners are parent and subsidiary companies or are otherwise subject to common ownership or control ('the corporate affiliate exception') (This exception would cover *Revlon per* Templeman LJ and the *Dunlop Tyre* case); or
(3) The articles of foreign manufacture bear a recorded trade mark or trade name applied under authorisation of the US owner ('the authorised use exception') (This exception would cover *Revlon per* Buckley and Bridge LJJ).[315]

An association of trade mark owners (COPIAT) and several individual trade mark owners, seeking to bar parallel imports without recourse to expensive and uncertain infringement actions, argued that the regulation was inconsistent with the plain meaning of the words in section 526 and sought a declaration that it was invalid. The Court of Appeals for the District of Columbia agreed, overruling the District Court.[316]

K Mart Corp., a parallel importer, and the US Government appealed. They argued that the cases and legislative background to section 526's enactment established that the section was solely intended to reverse the Second Circuit's decision in *Katzel*. Its meaning was limited by that purpose. In addition, this interpretation was supported by Customs' long-standing,

---

314   *K Mart Corporation v Cartier Inc.* 6 USPQ 2d 1897 (1988) *revg Coalition to Preserve the Integrity of American Trademarks ('COPIAT') v U.S.* 790 F. 2d 903 (DC Cir. 1986) *rev'g* 598 F. Supp. 844 (DCDC 1984).
315   19 CFR §133.21(c) ('the regulation'). The same owner exception had been introduced in 1936; the corporate affiliate exception first saw the light of day between 1953 and 1959 and was revived in 1972; the authorised use exception also dated from 1972: see Young, 'The Gray Market Case: Trademark Rights v. Consumer Interests', at 842 to 843.
316   *COPIAT* 790 F. 2d 903 (DC Cir. 1986). For a review of the DC Circuit's decision and the conflicting judgments in *Vivitar Corporation v U.S. et al.* 761 F. 2d 1552, at 1555 to 1556 (Fed. Cir. 1985) *affg* 593 F. Supp. 420 (CIT 1984); *cert. denied* 474 US 1055 (1986) and *Olympus Corporation v U.S.* 792 F. 2d 315, at 320 to 321 (2d Cir. 1986) *affg* 627 F. Supp. 911 (EDNY 1985), see Seth E. Lipner, 'Gray Market Goulash: The Problem of At-the-Border Restrictions on Importation of Genuine Trademarked Goods', 77 TMR 77 (1987) and Coggio *et al.*, at 468 to 475; briefly summarised in Warwick A. Rothnie, 'Gray Privateers Sink into Black Market: Parallel Imports and Trade Marks', (1990) 1 AIPJ 72, at 92 to 93.

consistent interpretation which Congress was said to have acquiesced in. K
Mart's purposive arguments ultimately rested on its contention that a trade
mark indicated source alone. Thus, it harks back to *Apollinaris v Scherer*.
COPIAT, on the other hand, saw a trade mark as a property right protecting
goodwill and argued that section 526 had a more sweeping effect than merely
overriding the Second Circuit's ruling in *Katzel*. Hence, it argued for a broad,
literal interpretation.

The Supreme Court upheld the validity of the same owner and corporate
affiliate exceptions by a five-four majority. By a different five-four majority,
it found the authorised use exception invalid.

The only member of both majorities was Kennedy J. Kennedy J did
not have occasion to consider the policy underlying section 526 or trade
mark infringement generally. Instead, his Honour upheld the validity of
the same owner and corporate affiliate exceptions on a narrow principle
of statutory interpretation under US administrative law. Kennedy J focused
on two apparent ambiguities in the wording of section 526.[317] In light
of these ambiguities, Customs, as the agency charged with the section's
administration, was entitled to adopt any reasonable definition of the
provision which did not conflict with Congress' clearly expressed intent.
Having done so, the courts would defer to the agency's interpretation.
However, the ambiguities did not extend to 'authorised use' situations and
so his Honour found Customs' third exception invalid.[318]

The remaining members of the bench delved into the underlying policy
arguments. However, they were profoundly divided, agreeing only that
(1) situations corresponding to *Katzel* were caught by the statute, and (2)
Customs could permit imports where the domestic trade mark owner was
a subsidiary of the foreign source. The reasoning used to reach the second
point, in particular, shows marked variance. Four justices considered that
section 526, and *Katzel*, were broad statements of principle; effectively these
judges favoured interpreting trade mark rights as strong property rights
territorially limited.[319] Three justices, however, considered that section 526
was properly confined to the narrow fact situation in *Katzel*, adopting the
parallel importers' arguments in favour of the Customs' exceptions.[320]

---

317   One ambiguity lay in the words 'of foreign manufacture'; the other, 'owned by'.
It was not clear whether ownership meant merely legal title or required a search into
ultimate beneficial ownership. Similarly, it was not clear whether foreign manufacture
described the place of manufacture or the nationality of the person performing the
manufacture: 6 USPQ 2d 1897, at 1902.

318   *Ibid*. at 1902 to 1903. White J agreed with Kennedy J's reasons for upholding
the validity of the first two exceptions but joined with Brennan J in upholding also
the authorised use exception disallowed by Kennedy J. For a succinct analysis of the
competing coalitions on each point, see N. David Palmeter, 'Gray Market Imports: No
Black and White Answer', 12(1) *World Competition* 49 (1988).

319   Scalia J joined by Rehnquist CJ, Blackmun and O'Connor JJ. These justices refused
to endorse the same owner and corporate affiliate exceptions because the exceptions
went further than the case of a mere subsidiary acting as a distributor. They also would
have permitted an exception for a domestic subsidiary/distributor only as an element of
agency enforcement discretion: 6 USPQ 2d 1897, at 1913 to 1915 *per* Scalia J, noting
that Customs had not even argued for the case he was prepared to accept.

320   Brennan J joined by Marshall and Stevens JJ; White J also joining in part.

The ramifications of *K Mart* are still largely unclear. The question it raises is to what extent domestic trade mark owners can still block parallel imports. The question further subdivides into the use of section 526 itself and whether *K Mart* affects the interpretation of the Lanham Act.

The actual situation in *Katzel* remains unaffected under both Acts. All justices agreed that section 526 required exclusion of unauthorised imports where there was a domestic trade mark owner which had developed domestic goodwill *and* the imports had been made and marked by an independently owned foreign producer. On the further questions, the outcome can only be described as uncertain.

2.3.6 After K Mart

The second area of unanimity in *K Mart* was that Customs may validly interpret section 526 to permit imports where the US trade mark owner is a wholly-owned subsidiary of the foreign producer. Whether this means that rights of enforcement under either the Tariff or Lanham Acts are precluded is a different question.

To the extent that it depends on the regulation being a valid exercise of agency discretion, domestic trade mark owners might still bring private actions for an order that Customs exclude the imports.[321] Presumably, the same might follow under section 42 of the Lanham Act whether the trade mark was in domestic or foreign hands.[322] The prospect of private actions might also arise for the broader aspects of the corporate affiliate exception.[323]

The lower courts are as divided as the Supreme Court bench. So far, two Circuit Courts have delivered opinions, each diametrically opposed on the significance of corporate affiliation, physical identity and domestic goodwill.

In a majority judgment heavily larded with references to Brennan J's opinion in *K Mart*, the Third Circuit adopted the Customs interpretation as defining infringement by parallel importation under the Lanham and Tariff Acts in *Weil Ceramics*.[324] Weil was the exclusive distributor for the United

---

321 *Vivitar Corporation v U.S. et al.* 761 F. 2d 1552 (Fed. Cir. 1985), see also *Dial Corp. v Encina Corp.* 643 F. Supp. 951 (SD Fla. 1986) and *De Pasquale v Rolex Watch USA Inc.* 632 F. Supp. 1525 (SDNY 1986); but *contra Weil Ceramics and Glass Inc. v Dash* 878 F. 2d 659, at 666 (3d Cir. 1989) *revg* 618 F. Supp. 700 (DNJ 1985) below from Note 324.

322 See *Lever Bros Co. v US* 877 F. 2d 101 (DC Cir. 1989), below from Note 334, but *contra Olympus* 792 F. 2d 315 (2d Cir. 1986) and *Weil* 878 F. 2d 659, at 666 (3d Cir. 1989). *Olympus*, in turn, may not affect other Lanham Act rights: *Artworks* 816 F. 2d 68 (2d Cir. 1987).

323 But here the splintering of the bench makes predictions even more tenuous.

324 *Weil Ceramics and Glass Inc. v Dash* 878 F. 2d 659 (3d Cir. 1989) *revg* 616 F. Supp. 700 (DCNJ 1985); see also *Yamaha Corp. of America v ABC International Traders* 703 F. Supp. 1938 (CD Cal. 1988); *Yamaha Corp. of America v US* 745 F. Supp. 734 (DDC 1990). Although not as sweeping in the opinion, the majority appears to overstate the extent of the agreement by Rehnquist CJ, Blackmun, O'Connor and Scalia JJ to the

States of Lladro porcelain made in Spain. Dash's company, Jalyn, bought Lladro porcelain from the manufacturer in Spain and was importing it for sale in the United States without Weil's permission. When Weil's actions for trade mark infringement and violation of section 526 came on for summary judgment, both parties stipulated that Dash's imports were 'genuine'. The District Court, however, granted Weil injunctions on the basis of its proved, separate and independent goodwill in the Lladro mark.[325]

There were complications. Both Weil and the Spanish manufacturer were wholly-owned subsidiaries of the same holding company. The Spanish manufacturer had not imposed any restrictions on Jalyn about where the goods could be resold; there is even a suggestion in Judge Becker's concurrence that the manufacturer knew Jalyn intended to sell them in the United States. Weil had initially owned the mark in the United States when it was independently owned. But, when ownership of Weil had been acquired by the holding company, the US trade mark had been assigned to another subsidiary, being reassigned to Weil in 1983 after the parallel imports started. On the other hand, although the imports were stipulated to be genuine, Weil distributed in the United States only premium quality Lladro goods while some of Jalyn's imports were of lesser quality.[326]

Two points were crucial to the majority's opinion. First, unlike the US trade mark owner in *Katzel* and *Premier Dental*, Weil was not owned independently of the foreign manufacturer but shared corporate links.[327] The fact that Dash's imports were genuine (in the majority's view, identical) was the second.[328] On sections 32 and 42, the majority ruled:

> Consumers who purchase Jalyn imported LLADRO porcelain get precisely what they believed that they were purchasing. For that same reason, Weil's investment in and sponsorship of its trademark is not adversely affected because the goodwill that stands behind its product is not diminished by an *association with goods of a lesser quality*.[329] (*Emphasis added*)

This conclusion is heavily influenced by the majority's reading of *K Mart* as ruling that Customs' corporate affiliate exception is an *absolute* exception to

court's ruling on the corporate affiliate exception: see 878 F. 2d 659, 665 Note 5 and contrast 6 USPQ 2d 1897, at 1913 to 1915.
325   618 F. Supp. 700, at 711 to 714, 715 to 718. The factors explicitly relied on included the use of Weil's name and efforts as an important factor in developing the US market, its quality controls over the merchandise (inspection and replacement of imperfects), selection of appropriate retail outlets, spending 10 per cent of its budget on advertising (under its own name), other promotional efforts through showrooms, trade and gift shows, leaflets, posters and running a Lladro Collectors' Society, and importing its own line of French crystal under the Lladro brand. Compare *Disenos Artisticos E Industriales SA v Work* 676 F. Supp. 1254 (EDNY 1987).
326   Compare 878 F. 2d 659, at 682 to 683 *per* Judge Becker concurring; 668 at Note 11 *per* Judge Higginbotham.
327   *Katzel* as a special exception to the general rule is the connecting thread through the whole opinion, *Premier Dental* is explained at *ibid.* at 666 Note 7.
328   If the imports had not been identical, *Artworks* might have applied: *ibid.* at 668 Note 11; but contrast the quotation Note 329 below.
329   *Ibid.* at 672 (*emphasis added*), contrast the broad rejection of *BHMC* in *Premier Dental*, above at Note 285.

section 526 and the dangers of establishing an undesirable monopoly in the domestic market inherent in a corporate grouping.[330]

In a fascinating opinion, Judge Becker concurred. His Honour believed, 'in contrast to the majority, that under current trademark law, genuine goods with genuine marks can serve as the basis for an infringement suit'.[331] In Judge Becker's opinion, the majority read *K Mart* too broadly and *Katzel* too narrowly. *Katzel* did not mandate relief to all independent owners of US trade marks, nor did it preclude relief to domestic trade mark owners which were corporate affiliates.[332] The crucial question was what goodwill the trade mark represented in the United States. However, his Honour also refused relief to Weil. First, the source of any confusion was not Jalyn but the Lladro group. The latter caused any confusion in the United States by releasing goods of different quality on to the market under the same mark. It could have used different marks or refused to sell to Jalyn in the first place. Second, and extraordinarily given the grounds for his Honour's concurrence, Weil as a subsidiary of the Lladro group had a unity of interest with the group such that it 'would have an extremely difficult if not impossible time proving a separate and independent good will'.[333] On this part of the case, Judge Becker rejected the adequacy of the evidence produced to the District Court on advertising and inspection.

Judge Becker's reasons for refusing Weil relief stand in marked contrast to the bulk of his opinion. The first part proceeds on a theory heavily based on the principle of territoriality; the last part on a strong theory of universality. Indeed, Judge Becker's rejection of the possibility that Weil could establish a separate and independent goodwill because of its unity of interest with its parent leaves little room for difference with the majority's approach. Hence, the Third Circuit clearly considered a corporate relationship between the domestic mark owner and the foreign manufacturer a crucial determinant of success based on trade mark rights. In addition, at least two members of the *Weil Ceramics* court regarded *K Mart*, and the Customs regulation, as conclusive.

In contrast, the DC Circuit of the Court of Appeals refused to apply Customs' interpretation to section 42 of the Lanham Act, which, in its pre-Lanham Act form, had caused the *Katzel* controversy and the passage of section 526. In both the United States and the United Kingdom, the *Shield* and *Sunlight* trade marks were used on soap and dishwashing liquid. The trade mark registrations were owned by members of the same corporate group, Lever-US for the United States and Lever-UK for the United

---

330 See *ibid.* at 666, the emphasis is Judge Higginbotham's.
331 *Ibid.* at 676.
332 See especially *ibid.* at 678, 680. *Premier Dental* receives much greater prominence in Judge Becker's opinion.
333 *Ibid.* at 684, relying on *Copperweld Corp. v Independence Tube Corp.* 467 US 752 (1984) for the 'unity of interest' theory. Judge Becker thought much greater difficulty would attend on cases where the 'parent' only held '20, 40 or even 60 percent of the subsidiary': *ibid.* at Note 13.

Kingdom, each also making its own products for its market. Despite these links, the products were different in composition; the differences arising because of different water qualities and consumer preferences in the two countries. Lever-US sought an order against Customs to exclude imports from the United Kingdom under section 42, submitting in evidence letters from customers 'expressing their rage or disappointment with what they had believed, at the time of purchase, to be a discounted version of the familiar US product'.[334] The DC Circuit provisionally upheld Lever-US' claims to exclude parallel imports of Lever-UK's products and remanded to the District Court for detailed consideration of the legislative history and administrative practice.[334a]

In its resolution of the case, the DC Circuit pronounced:

> We think the natural, virtually inevitable reading of §42 is that it bars foreign goods bearing a trademark identical to a valid US trademark but physically different, regardless of the trademarks' [*sic*] genuine character abroad or affiliation between the producing firms. On its face the section appears to aim at deceit and consumer confusion; when identical trademarks have acquired different meanings in different countries, one who imports the foreign version to sell it under that trademark will (in the absence of some specially differentiating feature) cause the confusion Congress sought to avoid. The fact of affiliation between the producers in no way reduces the probability of that confusion; it is certainly not a constructive consent to the importation.[335]

As the court acknowledged, the facts before it did not involve imports of identical goods. Hence, that ground remains open to distinguish it from a simple statement of territoriality. However, in the context of US courts' approach following *K Mart*, the court directed a broadside against the notion that affiliation with the foreign manufacturer was sufficient to justify parallel importing:

> Customs' central thesis, that affiliation between the foreign producer and domestic markholder automatically defines the foreign goods as genuine, draws on an important truth – that a trademark holder cannot infringe its own mark. To the extent that the affiliate exception extends this principle to goods imported into the US by companies affiliated with the US markholder, it does nothing more than treat the two companies as being constructively one for infringement purposes. As such it seems unobjectionable.
>
> But the exception contained in 19 CFR § 133.21.(c)(2) does more. Merely on the basis of affiliation between the US markholder and the foreign *producer*, it extends the non-violation that is implicit in importation by the markholder or with its consent to a radically different matter, imports *by third parties*. Inferring non-violation from that relation seems no more plausible than an inference of

---

334   *Lever Bros Co. v US* 877 F. 2d 101, at 103 *per* Williams J (DC Cir. 1989). See also *Ferrerro USA Inc. v Ozak Trading Inc.* 18 USPQ 2d 1052 (DNJ 1991) (plaintiff affiliated to foreign source but goods materially different physically and imports violated labelling laws).

334a   Lever-US succeeded on remand to the District Court: 24 USPQ 2d 1297 (DDC 1992).

335   *Ibid.* at 111.

consent to import from the US markholder's licensing production abroad, which the *Artworks* and *Dial* courts obviously rejected.[336] (*Emphasis added*)

In reaching this position, the court rejected Customs alarm about the consequences for administrative efficiency and roundly scorned Customs' policy claims based on breaking down international price discrimination and greater ease of corporate groups in controlling the destination of their products.[337]

Apart from its position as one of two Circuit Court opinions dealing with parallel imports in the post-*K Mart* world, *Lever* is significant as the first Circuit Court since *BHMC* to contemplate blocking parallel imports where the domestic owner was a corporate affiliate of the foreign source. That contemplation would have been withdrawn, however, if Lever-UK had been shown to have consented to the export of its goods from the United Kingdom to the United States.[338] Notwithstanding that questionable qualification *Lever* should be endorsed for its recognition of a fundamental truth – that the confusion in the domestic market undermines the function of the trade mark regardless of the relationship between the trade mark owners in the foreign and domestic markets.[338a]

2.3.7 A review

With the trilogy of Supreme Court cases in the 1920s, it might have been thought that the crucial point in blocking parallel imports under US law would be either legal title to the trade mark or factually distinct goodwill from the foreign source. After a period when it was necessary to show only legal title, factually distinct goodwill no longer proves necessarily sufficient.

Pending legislative invention or the forging of a new majority on the Supreme Court, two things (apart from uncertainty) seem clear. First, where the domestic trade mark owner proves factually distinct goodwill *and* is owned independently of the foreign source, *Katzel* and *K Mart* establish entitlement to block parallel imports. Second, regardless of local goodwill, if the domestic registrant is a corporate affiliate of the foreign source, Customs will not automatically exclude imports from that foreign source under section 526. The same rule probably applies under section 42 of the Lanham Act.

Whether the domestic registrant can obtain a court order compelling Customs to exclude such imports is another question. The Federal Circuit (pre-*K Mart*), the DC Circuit and, perhaps, the Second Circuit may contemplate such an order. If the imports were not physically identical

---

336 *Ibid*. at 109 to 110. Contrast *Weil Ceramics* 878 F. 2d 659, at 666, 668 and 673 *per* Higginbotham J.
337 *Ibid*. at 110.
338 *Ibid*. at 103 Note 3.
338a *Société des Produits Nestlé SA v Casa Helvetica Inc*. 777 F. Supp. 161 (D Puerto Rico 1991) is arguably consistent. Although based on *Weil Ceramics*, *CAL Circuit Abco* and *Olympus*, Judge Cerezo expressly found that there was no evidence of deception or consumer dissatisfaction: *ibid*. at 165, 166–7.

to the domestic product, the prospects of such an order are much improved. It may also be necessary in the Second Circuit to show that the imports were never intended for the domestic market. It would certainly be necessary to show that the domestic registrant held factually distinct goodwill. On the other hand, where corporate affiliation exists, the Ninth and Third Circuits will not contemplate such an order even if factually distinct goodwill exists *unless*, possibly, the imports are physically different to the domestic goods.

What will suffice for factually distinct goodwill is also a difficult question. In *CAL Circuit Abco*, the Ninth Circuit ignored the domestic subsidiary's independent goodwill in the absence of any physical difference between the goods. The Third Circuit seems to have taken the same approach in fact in *Weil Ceramics*. Hence, trade mark owners should treat any stipulation that the goods are genuine with extreme disfavour. In *Lever* and *Ferrero*, the physical differences were partly in response to consumer preference and partly dictated by necessity – the different chemical properties of the two countries' water and different modes of washing in *Lever*; smaller size (cosmetic) and inclusion of banned substances in *Ferrero*, the labelling in *Ferrero* may also have violated federal law.[339] The language difference in *Artworks* and *Premier Dental* may also have constituted a physical difference, but not so in *Casa Helvetica*. Presumably, as in the Anglo-Commonwealth cases such as *Sony* and *Sharp Electronics*, differences resulting from technical standards (if not falling within *Lever*) would also suffice.

It does, however, seem extraordinary that the trade mark owner could succeed in *Artworks* on the basis of, admittedly powerful, language variations in 'adoption papers', while purchasers who may have got 'B' quality Lladro porcelain rather than 'A' could not be protected in *Weil Ceramics*.

Assuming the identical goods obstacle has been hurdled, a number of steps are routine in establishing domestic goodwill. Heavy advertising and promotional expenditure; preferably in association with the domestic trade mark owner's own name or brand, but at least so that the relevant trade recognises it as the source and not some foreign producer. The domestic trade mark owner should also adopt an active role in quality control and, if the goods are suited, maintain a replacement service, and careful selection of appropriately skilled retail outlets. It should not venture into court without bundles of testimonials from angry dealers and deceived (and disappointed) purchasers of the parallel imports. Evidence of dramatic impact on sales, employment and advertising expenditure as in *Osawa* would be advisable. As in *Model Rectifier*, evidence of a comparatively small market share in the relevant market may counter fears of monopolistic exploitation, even if an anti-trust suit is not alleged.

Outside the corporate affiliate minefield, it is possible for a domestic trade mark owner which also authorises the application of the trade mark in the foreign market to bar parallel imports. Showing factually distinct

---

339   See also *Dial Corp. v Encina Corp.* 643 F. Supp. 951 (SD Fla. 1986) and *PepsiCo Inc. v Giraud* 7 USPQ 2d 1371 (DPuerto Rico 1988).

goodwill may suffice. But, as in *Artworks*, it will be necessary to rebut any presumption that the goods were intended for domestic use. A licence clearly limited to the foreign territory may be sufficient, but a material difference in the goods would help to put the matter beyond dispute. If the goods are initially intended for the domestic market, their release should be conditional on the owner's right to certify quality and any rejection should make it clear that they can only be released into the domestic market (if at all) as unbranded rejects.

2.4 Conclusion

If Judge Hough could say in 1921 that it was not then clear whether the law protected trade marks as a species of business property or as a means of preventing consumer deception, it is not altogether clear that either branch of the common law world has yet resolved the matter. This results, in large part, from the contentious nature of the, often unstated, issues underlying parallel import situations.

In the United States, there have certainly been parallel import cases which can be argued as having viewed a trade mark as a species of property. *Katzel* and *Premier Dental* are two prime candidates. Both (and the other cases in similar vein) can be viewed as more qualified. On the facts of each, the trade mark represented a source in the domestic market other than the foreign producer alone. Hence, the property right and the interest in preventing consumer deception can be portrayed as in harmony. In any case, these cases treat a trade mark and the message it conveys as having a discrete territorial aspect. There is, however, another vigorous line of cases betraying symptoms of the theories of universality and exhaustion. The most recent include the *CAL Circuit Abco* and *Weil Ceramics* cases. Arguing that consumers are not deceived about the production source of branded goods, they have scorned claims that trade marks confer property rights. In *CAL Circuit Abco*, if not in *Weil Ceramics*, reaching this conclusion ironically involved ignoring evidence of real consumer confusion.

Three other factors characteristic of the *CAL Circuit Abco* line of cases bear mention. Since the first check inflicted by *Katzel*, all have involved national courts in wrestling with the ramifications of transnational corporate groups. All have prominently featured fears that a business enterprise is seeking to maintain an unjustified monopoly over trade in the article. (Such fears, when raised, usually receive short shrift in the rival stream.) None has suggested that the interests the trade mark owner is seeking to protect are undeserving. Rather, they have indicated that other means of protection are more appropriate.

A similar debate can be discovered in the Anglo-Commonwealth jurisdictions. Compare *Revlon* with *CAL Circuit Abco* and *Weil Ceramics*. But, the arrival (at least in the field of registered trade marks) of broader concerns has been much more recent. *Castrol GTX* and *Colgate* have proceeded on a theory of the trade mark as a territorial property right; but did so in circumstances where considerable consumer deception would have resulted if the parallel imports were not excluded. Arguably, the same can be said of *Fender* and *Mattel*. But, in the latter two cases, the court was also clearly impressed by the prejudice parallel imports would cause to investment in promoting the trade mark undertaken by the domestic 'agent'.

Such explicit reference to the value of the local investment has been the exception rather than the rule in the Anglo-Commonwealth cases. Perhaps doubtful about conceding monopolies in the commerce of articles, the courts have felt more comfortable referring to the policy objective of preventing consumer deception.[340] Hence, they have focused on whether the parallel imports are 'genuine'. Even this has provoked a considerable array of opinion. In *CAL Circuit Abco*, the goods were genuine because the goods released in both markets were the same physically; in *Weil Ceramics*, there appear to have been qualitative differences, but these were by the producer's own act; in *Revlon*, the quality was apparently the same, but the therapeutic properties were different. In this line of cases, the court in *Sony* was forced to concede that major (and defective) tampering with the goods destroyed their pristine character. In the cases approaching the issue from a territoriality perspective, *Colgate* involved significant quality difference; the courts in *Artworks* and *Mattel* were content to find 'material differences' in the presence of language differences in documentary inserts.[341] Other courts have been prepared to take their cue from *Katzel* and have recognised that, even where goods are physically identical, the investment of the local 'agent' in promoting the product and developing the brand's goodwill means that goods are only genuine if they come through the local 'source'.[342]

In both traditions, the emphasis lies heavily on legalistic formalism. The US cases of the past decade could (almost) be said to depend on the accident of whether or not the domestic trade mark owner was a corporate subsidiary of the foreign producer. While the *Revlon* court in the United Kingdom was worrying about attempts to substitute 'the monkey for the organ grinder', some US courts pressed on with catching 'the monkey' and others, as in *Artworks*, were letting 'the organ grinder' free. Although, apart from *Revlon*, Anglo-Commonwealth courts have largely not been caught up in the tentacles of transnational corporate groups, careful attention to legal nicety has been essential. In *Juda's* case, failure to advertise the

340 Hiebert claims that the equal ranking of the property and consumer deception rationales in the United States is directly traceable to the need of avoiding fears that trade marks were injurious restraints on freedom of trade: Hiebert, 'Foundations of the Law of Parallel Importation', at 494 to 497. In fact, his quotations from Justice Duer's opinion in *Amoskeag Mfg Co. v Spear* 2 Sand Super Ct 599, at 605 (NY City Super. Ct 1849) read remarkably like a modern economic defence of trade marks as a property right, encouraging investment and so promoting competition: *ibid*. at especially 495.
341 Of course, language is a major political and cultural issue in Canada; and no one would want to be responsible for spoiling a child's enjoyment of its Cabbage Patch doll.
342 See *Premier Dental's* rejection of *BHMC*, contrast *CAL Circuit Abco* and *Weil Ceramics*; in the Anglo-Commonwealth world support is more limited, *Mattel, Sharp Electronics* and, perhaps, *Fender*.

reassignment of ownership and processing responsibility invalidated the trade mark registration.[343] Careful drafting of the terms on which the foreign producer may use its trade mark rights is necessary in both traditions.[344]

The approach taken in *CAL Circuit Abco* and *Weil Ceramics*, founded on a theory of universality or exhaustion, has the not inconsiderable virtue of avoiding much of this technicality and legal formalism. It would also ensure that a producer or its domestic 'agent' did not secure a monopoly over the trade in the particular article in question. But, both theories fail to achieve the object which they claim to be founded on, protection of consumers from deception. Further, none of these courts has convincingly explained where that undesirable monopoly is to be found. Moreover, none of these courts has really tackled the question of how to secure the investments in promoting goodwill which made the market attractive to free riders in the first place. On the other hand, the cases supporting a theory of territoriality, in addition to emphasising legal formality, may fail to address valid concerns about anti-competitive market manipulation adequately.[345]

Much of the common law's complexity over parallel imports and their continuing controversy can be attributed to its failure to acknowledge that Judge Hough's problem even exists, let alone attempting to resolve it. Having recognised it, any solution needs to address the three, not necessarily consistent, concerns: the need to protect consumers from deception, the need to protect the market from anti-competitive practices and the need to encourage desirable investment.

---

343 Contrast *Fender*. For a US counter-example, see the even more convoluted circumstances in *J. Atkins Holdings Ltd v English Discounts Inc.* 729 F. Supp. 945 (SDNY 1990) where an English producer sold its US distribution business to an independent Canadian firm and some months later assigned the trade mark rights to a US company formed for that purpose by the owners of the Canadian firm and Judge Leval (presiding earlier in *Osawa*) approached a parallel importer with marked disfavour.

344 Compare *Artworks* and *Colgate*; in *Castrol GTX*, there was also a notice on the foreign goods.

345 The *BHMC* and *Osawa* cases seem like situations warranting closer inspection.

Chapter 3: Patents

3.1 Introduction

Doubt about the interests served by trade marks has obscured the conflict between competing contentions based on universalist (or exhaustion) or territorial views when parallel imports are sought to be blocked using trade marks. That problem has not beset the interpretation of patent law, patents are quite clearly 'property' rights. The classification, as has been pointed out in another context however, does not prescribe a solution to the problem.[1] Where patents have been used in attempts to block parallel imports, the proxy in the struggle between the competing philosophies has been 'consent' – does the act of foreign marketing, whether under a corresponding patent or not, lead to an implication of consent to importation, use or sale of the patented article in the domestic market.

In both of the main streams of the common law, 'universalists' have won the day where the foreign marketing was initiated by someone having authority to sell there and in the domestic market as well. If foreign marketing was by someone without domestic authority, 'territorialists' have largely prevailed and consent is not usually implied. The partial victory of the universality approach has been further limited by the fairly willing acceptance in both common law streams of a power to rebut the presumed consent.

Sir Arnold Plant, one of the more vigorous critics of the patent system, reports that David Hume identified property rights as a function of scarcity. In a world of scarce resources, property rights allowed property owners to ensure that the scarce means they owned were directed towards the ends they most valued. If there were no scarcity, there would be no need for property. Plant then went on to point out a paradox of patents (and copyright); in his view, patents did not arise out of scarcity, instead they set out to create a scarcity in their subject-matter, inventions, to enable the 'owners' to restrict their use and raise their price.[2]

1 Prices Surveillance Authority, *Inquiry into Book Prices: Interim Report*, Prices Surveillance Authority, Report No. 24, 1989, at 4, 9 to 10; see further Chapter 10 below.
2 Arnold Plant, 'The Economic Theory Concerning Patents for Inventions', (1934) 1 *Economica* reprinted in Arnold Plant, *Selected Economic Essays and Addresses*, Routledge & Kegan Paul, 1974, Chapter 3 at 35. A controversial elaboration of Hume's

The existence of such a paradoxical situation has been justified on a number of grounds. There are four main explanations. First, 'natural rights': the product of a person's mind is as much their property as the products of their manual toil; second, 'reward': justice requires that society should reward those who advance its welfare; third, 'investment incentive': imperfections in the market's operation require that an incentive be provided inventors and their financial backers to invest in creating and developing new inventions; and fourth, 'social contract': in exchange for the inventor publicly disclosing the secrets of the invention, society grants a limited monopoly.[3]

In the common law world, the most likely explanation for the patent system lies largely in either the incentive to investment or reward a patent is thought to provide.[4] Simply stated, the incentive theory posits that a rational business will not invest in the highly risky and costly business of developing a new product (or process) unless it believes, *before it starts*, that it will reap the benefits of success. The danger perceived is that rival firms may well be able to copy the innovation once it is made more cheaply because they will not incur all the risks associated with 'trail-blazing' and it may be much easier to 'reverse engineer' an existing product than to explore the unknown. If it is, or usually proves, cheaper to imitate, then the rational business will wait for someone else to develop the innovation and copy it. Hence, the development of new products and processes must be seen as a dynamic process, taking into account *before* the commitment to invest is made perceptions about the prospective earnings after the invention is made. That is, the paradoxical scarcity which provoked Plant may arise only once the invention has been made in the first place.[5]

Fearing that the *ex ante* incentives will be insufficient, the patent system intervenes to create the seeming paradox observed by Plant. It holds out the promise of an exclusive right to practise the invention for a limited term of years, so enabling the patentee some power to raise price above the marginal costs of production and recoup the initial investment in development. How great that power is depends on a large number of complicated factors including the extent of the advance on existing technology made by the invention (whether it is a drastic breakthrough or a minor embellishment); the range of substitute products to perform the function of the invention; and the ease with which others may invent around what is claimed in the patent.

thesis is the so-called 'Coase Theorem', see R.H. Coase, 'The Problem of Social Cost', 3 *JL. and Econ.* 1 (1960) reprinted in R.H. Coase, *The Firm, The Market and The Law*, The University of Chicago Press, 1988, Chapter 5.

3 The seminal study is Fritz Machlup, *An Economic Review of the Patent System*, Study No. 15, US Senate Sub-Committee on Patents, Copyrights and Trademarks of the Committee on the Judiciary, 85th Cong. 2d Sess., 1958. The theories are outlined at 21 to 22 before an extensive review.

4 Paul Demaret, *Patents, Territorial Restrictions and EEC Law*, Verlag-Chemie, 1978, Chapter 1; W. R. Cornish, *Intellectual Property*, Sweet & Maxwell, 1989 (2nd ed.), ¶¶3-023 to 3-035 allowing some role to the contract theory.

5 The literature on the theory and the practice is voluminous, a good overview is F.M. Scherer and David Ross, *Industrial Market Structure and Economic Performance*, Houghton Mifflin, Boston, 1990 (3rd ed.), Chapter 17.

The patent system is not the only means which could be used to overcome the perceived problem. At least as long as the modern system has existed, if not longer, alternative proposals have included the provision of governmental subsidies or contracts to fund research or the award of prizes and bonuses to the successful rather than relying on the market system.[6] For most kinds of commercial activity, however, the drawbacks of the alternatives probably exceed those of patents.[7] The disadvantage of a patent system depends significantly on precisely how much social cost it imposes, which may vary quite substantially from product to product. The advantages of government contracts depend on the government having better information about what is desired and the likely outcome of success than private parties. Government contracts and prizes are also subject to significant costs in the real world.[8] It is difficult to imagine a bureaucracy being established to process efficiently the complicated choices between what projects to fund, to what extent and to ensure that researchers keep within cost constraints. If a system of prizes were instituted, there is the additional danger that governments might not be prepared to pay a suitable award once the innovation has been made.[9]

The patent system would not be controversial if it only conferred benefits on society. Unfortunately, it also involves costs. The power to raise price above the marginal cost introduces static inefficiencies. Some consumers pay more for the product than they would if it were priced 'competitively' at marginal cost, others are denied the product altogether although they would value it more highly than alternative uses of their resources. Rival firms are forced to continue using less efficient methods of production, thereby introducing a further distortion of the economy. In addition, people may be arbitrarily diverted from other, more productive activities by the mere existence of a patent system. For example, the types of invention covered by the patent system are arbitrarily defined, so inventors of things potentially not protected by patents may be induced to divert their attentions away to areas covered by the patent system.

While these costs are certainly endured, economists are not all certain about the benefits. Some economists argue that inventions will be made and technology advance without a patent system at all, arguing that the remorseless pressure of competition in an open economy will force firms continually to invest in improving their products and the ways of producing

---

6   For a model, see Brian D. Wright, 'The Economics of Invention Incentives: Patents, Prizes and Research Contracts', 73 Am. Econ. Rev 691 (1983).

7   Defence and space exploration contracting in the US are areas where government contracts have been used extensively although not without problems of moral hazard and often permitting exclusive rights for non-government exploitation, see F.M. Scherer, *The Economic Effects of Compulsory Licensing*, New York University, Monograph 77-2, 1977, at 78 to 85 and Scherer and Ross, *Industrial Market Structure and Economic Performance*, at 146 to 148. On the multiplicity of EC programmes, see for example William Wallace, *The Dynamics of European Integration*, Pinter Publishers, 1990, Chapters 2 and 3.

8   See especially Demaret, *Patents, Territorial Restrictions and the EEC*, at 9 to 12.

9   *Ibid.* Wright, referring to two examples of prizes being used, notes a similar problem in 'The Economics of Invention Incentives', at 703 to 704.

them. Plant has put this view most forcefully. His belief that inventors would invent anyway is the reason that he perceived the patent system as contrary to the role of property rights perceived by Hume. Most economists acknowledge that some form of incentive may be necessary, but some of these have pointed out that firms have a whole range of methods at their disposal to ensure that they, and not their rivals, appropriate the benefits of their investment in new technology.[10]

The economic evidence, although making considerable strides in the past decade, is still quite incomplete. One of the more ambitious attempts is a survey by Richard Levin and associates.[11] Levin *et al.* surveyed 650 'high-level' R & D managers in the United States representing some 130 different lines of business as defined by the US Federal Trade Commission. The companies surveyed were restricted to those with publicly traded securities. Of the five alternatives listed as preferred means to appropriate the benefits of investment in R & D, patents scored quite poorly, particularly for innovations relating to processes rather than products. Generally, lead time, learning curves and sales and service efforts were regarded as more effective devices than patent protection.[12]

Three important qualifications must be made. First, the survey was confined to firms with publicly traded securities. These tend to be larger firms more readily able to exploit alternative means of reaping the benefits of investment such as reliance on product differentiation, advertising and effective sales forces. Equally important, smaller, non-listed firms often play a significant role in the initiation of innovation, but may need to collaborate with larger, established firms to bring the development to fruition or penetrate a market successfully.[13] As Scherer notes, even with patents small

10 For an overview, see Scherer and Ross, *Industrial Market Structure and Economic Performance* at 626 to 630. See also Chapters 8 to 10 below.

11 Richard C. Levin, Alvin K. Klevorick, Richard R. Nelson and Sidney G. Winter, 'Appropriating the Returns from Industrial Research and Development', [1987] 3 *Brookings Papers on Economic Activity* 783. Other major empirical studies include Edwin Mansfield, 'R & D and Innovation: Some Empirical Findings', Chapter 6 in Zvi Griliches (ed.), *R & D, Patents and Productivity*, NBER/Chicago University Press, 1984. For a UK study also reporting similar results, see Christopher T. Taylor and Z.A. Silberston, *The Economic Impact of the Patent System: A Study of the British Experience*, Cambridge University Press, 1973, its consistency being confirmed by Richard Gilbert [1987] 3 *Brookings Papers on Economic Activity* 821 and Scherer and Ross, *Industrial Market Structure and Economic Performance*, at 629 Note 46.

12 Apart from lines of business with only one response, 23 business lines rated patents higher than five on a seven point scale, including drugs, pesticides, industrial organic chemicals, other chemical products, relatively uncomplicated mechanical equipment, roasted coffee and products of steel rolling and finishing mills: *ibid.* at 795 to 796. For pharmaceuticals, see Chapter 8 below.

13 *Ibid.* at 797, and 831. Economists have now well documented that 'invention' is often a relatively quick and cheap step while development to commercialisation consumes the bulk of investment in R & D, see for example 'Invention and Innovation in the Watt-Boton Steam Engine Venture', Chapter 2 in F.M. Scherer, *Innovation and Growth*, The MIT Press, 1984; more generally Scherer and Ross, *Industrial Market Structure and Economic Performance*, at 616 to 620; on the rather inconclusive evidence about firm size and innovation, see Scherer and Ross, *Industrial Market Structure and Economic Performance*, at 645 to 660.

firms face large difficulties trying to enforce their rights against large firms, but their task would be even greater, given the difficulties with licensing, if they did not have relatively clear, secure property rights to bargain with.[14]

Second, Levin *et al.* found quite substantial variation between industries about the effectiveness of protection. Perhaps more significantly, they also found quite substantial variation within individual industries (lines of business). Even in the same industry, some firms were much more likely to regard patents as a useful means of recouping their investment in innovation than others, and further, as relatively more effective than other forms of 'protection'.[15] This is consistent with a view of an industry as a heterogeneous continuum of firms, competing in the market with different levels of technology and different competitive strategies, rather than all competing at the technological frontier with similar strategies.[16] It does not, however, necessarily mean that those firms competing most fiercely by innovation rely on patents the most. For example, a firm which relies more on patents may do so because it is less effective (for whatever reason) in its efforts to compete by sales and service efforts.

The reasons offered for why patents were considered ineffective are also instructive. Where the invention related to a process rather than a product, patents were not highly regarded precisely because they required public disclosure.[17] On a seven-point scale, 60 per cent of respondents, however, rated at five or higher as the weakness of patents, the ability of competitors to 'invent around' them.[18] Lack of ready patentability for new processes was the only other constraint rated this highly by more than 20 per cent of respondents. While there is little doubt that the patent system is more than somewhat arbitrary in the types of innovation which it accords protection to, the importance of the lack of ready patentability may suggest that a significant amount of firms' R & D may be directed to areas not sufficiently important to warrant the costs of patent protection. Interestingly, the authors considered the most probable explanation of the effectiveness of patents in industries such as the chemical industries was the existence of 'comparatively

14   Scherer and Ross, *Industrial Market Structure and Economic Performance*, at 629 to 630; on the unattractiveness of licensing, see Levin *et al.*, 'Appropriating the Returns from Industrial Research and Development', at 795; William Kingston, *Innovation, Creativity and the Law*, Kluwer Academic Publishers, 1990, at 73 Note 39.

15   Levin *et al.*, 'Appropriating the Returns from Industrial Research and Development', at 794 Table 1; and note the comments of Richard Gilbert at *ibid.* at 821 and Zvi Griliches at *ibid.* at 825 to 826.

16   See for example Dosi *et al.*, *The Economics of Technical Change and International Trade*, Chapters 4, and 5.

17   Levin *et al.*, 'Appropriating the Returns from Industrial Research and Development', at 795 but note the comments at 805.

18   *Ibid.* at 802 to 803. For a much smaller sample, Mansfield reports that 60 per cent of innovations are legally imitated within four years: 'R & D and Innovation: Some Empirical Findings', in Griliches (ed.), *R & D, Patents and Productivity*, at 143. The cost and time taken to invent around may vary quite substantially from industry to industry: Levin *et al.*, 'Appropriating the Returns from Industrial Research and Development', at 807 to 812.

clear standards' in assessing the patent's validity and enforcing it against infringers.[19]

Scherer's investigation of the effects of compulsory licensing decrees under US anti-trust laws emphasises some of the contradictions. As with Levin *et al.*, his sample is composed of firms sufficiently important to attract anti-trust scrutiny. In summary, first, he found that exposure to compulsory licensing decrees did in fact cause the firm concerned to reduce its patenting activity. Patenting declined on average by 15 per cent or 21 per cent 'if a patent-weighted average is taken'. The impact of the compulsory licensing decrees was found to vary according to their severity. For decrees characterised as having 'little' effect, there was little change or a small increase; for the 26 firms assessed as suffering decrees of 'moderate' or 'great' impact, patenting fell by 24 and 22 per cent respectively; for the six firms required also to license future patents, the reduction was 33.3 per cent.[20] Second, the firms did not, however, correspondingly reduce their commitment to investing in R & D. That is, it would seem the effect of the decrees was to drive firms into relying to a greater extent on know-how and secrecy at the expense of using the patent system.[21]

Finally, Scherer's third main conclusion was that the compulsory licensing decrees did not have the effect of reducing concentration in the industries concerned. Any decline in concentration observed might have been expected in any event.[22]

Two further fragments of empirical evidence add to the ambivalent findings about the use and effects of the patent system. A survey of 196 US *Fortune 500* firms on the effects of know-how licensing obtained 71 responses of which 53 were detailed. Some 78 per cent of these firms considered that the time it took competitors to 'reverse engineer' their technology was not a sufficient period in which to recoup their investments.[23] This may raise questions about Levin *et al.*'s finding that firms found secrecy a more effective method of protection than patents, particularly as there seems likely to have been some degree of overlap between the two studies' participants. One point is that secrecy may not be a terribly effective method of securing the investment from the firm's point of view. This is further supported by the numerous findings that secrecy is much preferred where the invention relates to a process and not a product.

---

19 *Ibid.* at 798; which might surprise those in the industry, see for example R.D. Satchell, 'Chemical Product Patent Practice in the United Kingdom', 1 IIC 179 (1970) and Volker Schmied-Kowarzik, 'Chemical Inventions According to the New German Patent Act', 1 IIC 190, especially at 217 to 223 (1970) and Cornish, *Intellectual Property*, at ¶¶4-032 and 4-033 and 4-036 to 4-039.
20 Scherer, *Innovation and Growth*, at 207 to 208. The full survey is part of Scherer, *The Economic Effects of Compulsory Patent Licensing*.
21 *Ibid.* at 208 to 216.
22 *Ibid.* at 217 to 220. This finding is consistent with Levin *et al.* and Mansfield's findings that patents do not usually create lasting barriers to competition.
23 Joel A. Bleeke and James A. Rahl, 'The Value of Territorial and Field of Use Restrictions in the International Licensing of Unpatented Know-How: An Empirical Study', 1 *Northwestern Journal of International Law and Business* 450, at 464 (1979).

A further piece of evidence is the very tentative finding that the more significant the invention, the more likely it is that the inventor will not secure anything like the full value of the gains from the breakthrough.[24] This study found that the *median* difference between the social rate of return and the private rate (to the innovator) was roughly two to one. That is, in crude terms, society gained roughly twice as much from the innovation as did the innovator. The study, however, was limited to only 17 innovations and even within this group, Mansfield and associates found significant variation. For six of the innovations, the private returns were under 10 per cent of the innovation's value; while private returns exceeded 40 per cent for five innovations. From the range of possible explanations, Mansfield and associates considered that the most likely predictor was whether the innovation was significant or not. The more important the innovation, the more likely that it would attract vigorous imitation.

Despite its longevity, the patent system is regarded by many economists with a considerable degree of scepticism. There remains a lot to explore, however, and there are also quite large problems with the alternatives proposed to a patent system. There is increasing evidence that larger firms do not rely just on patents to induce their innovative efforts. The function of patents, however, varies quite significantly from industry to industry and, noticeably, within any given industry. Moreover, there does not appear to be systematic evidence, at least in these surveys of US industry, of patents constituting effective barriers to competition. Indeed, compulsory licensing decrees do not seem to have caused any marked increase in deconcentration. In addition, firms' hostility to public disclosure may indicate that the patent system serves a valuable role on the theory of the 'social contract'. Finally, although individual inventors and smaller firms undoubtedly experience considerable difficulty in using the patent system, they are also often likely to be less able to exploit the alternative means of appropriating the benefits of investing in innovation used by larger firms. Their ability to exploit the fruits of their investment effectively therefore may well depend on the availability of sound property rights.

3.2 Anglo-Commonwealth Law

3.2.1 The nature of the patentee's right

A patent under the laws of the Anglo-Commonwealth jurisdictions is a territorial right. The rights conferred by the patent are limited to the territory of the jurisdiction granting the patent. A patent conferred in one jurisdiction does not confer rights outside that jurisdiction.[25]

24 Edwin Mansfield, John Rapoport, Anthony Romero, Samuel Wagner and George Beardsley, 'Social and Private Rates of Return from Industrial Innovations', 91 QJEcon. 221.
25 Under the Paris Convention and the Patent Co-operation Treaty, an applicant for a patent in the United Kingdom receives the right to claim priority for that application in foreign jurisdictions. However, the applicant only acquires enforceable

In the Anglo-Commonwealth jurisdictions, the state confers on the holder of the patent the right to exclude others from doing certain specified acts. Since 1 June 1978, the rights conferred on a patentee in the United Kingdom have been expressly identified in the Patents Act 1977 (United Kingdom) ('the 1977 Act'). The 1977 Act expressly limits the patentee's right to sue for infringement to acts done in the United Kingdom.[26] In section 60 it makes specific provision for what constitutes infringement and what does not:

(1) Subject to the provisions of this section, a person infringes a patent for an invention if, but only if, while the patent is in force, he does any of the following things in the United Kingdom in relation to the invention without the consent of the proprietor of the patent, that is to say:

(a) where the invention is a product, he makes, disposes of, offers to dispose of, uses or imports the product or keeps it whether for disposal or otherwise;

(b) where the invention is a process, he uses the process or he offers it for use in the United Kingdom when he knows, or it is obvious to a reasonable person in the circumstances, that its use there without the consent of the proprietor would be an infringement of the patent;

(c) where the invention is a process, he disposes of, offers to dispose of, uses or imports any product obtained directly by means of that process or keeps any such product whether for disposal or otherwise.

Subsection 60(2) is not relevant for present purposes.

Subject to the impact of Community law, subsection 60(1)'s identification of importation as an infringing act codifies the prior law. Prior to the 1977 Act, the right to control importation was not expressly conferred on the patentee, nor was importation expressly identified as an infringing act.[27] The form of grant emphasised the territorial nature of the monopoly a patent conferred. As already indicated, patents granted under the Patents Act 1949 had 'effect throughout the United Kingdom and the Isle of Man'.[28]

rights against others in those jurisdictions by applying for and obtaining the grant of a patent in that jurisdiction. Similarly, until the Community Patent Convention comes into force, applications under the European Patent Convention must designate the signatory countries for which grant is sought and any resulting patent(s) are separate grants made by each country. Patents in some countries may only be granted following grant under the UK Act. These patents, however, have force not by virtue of the grant under the UK Act, but by virtue of the domestic legislation, see for example Malaysian and Singaporean patents.

26 Section 60. Previous legislation declared that patents had 'effect throughout the United Kingdom and the Isle of Man'. See Patents Act 1949 (United Kingdom) section 21 ('the 1949 Act').

27 The legislation does not appear to have defined either aspect of the patentee's rights: see for example the 1949 Act. Instead, the patentee's exclusive rights to 'make, use, exercise and vend' the invention and the prohibition on others doing so without the patentee's consent had to be found in the grant in the Letters Patent, see Patents Rules 1968, Schedule 4. The Acts of other Commonwealth countries expressly included positive grants in similar terms: see for example Patents Act 1952 (Cth) section 69; Patents Act RSC 1970 section 46 (both now replaced with legislation in similar form to the 1977 Act section 60(1): Patents Act 1990 (Cth) section 13 and definition of 'exploit' in Schedule 1; Patents Act RSC 1985, Chapter P-4, section 42).

28 The 1949 Act section 21. This provision does not have a counterpart in the the 1977 Act. However, it is clear that the law is not changed: for example section 60 which confines acts of infringement to acts done in the United Kingdom.

Accordingly, it was not infringement of a UK patent to sell and deliver outside the United Kingdom a product which was covered by the claims of a UK patent.[29] This was so even where the parties to the contract were situated in the United Kingdom and carried out the negotiations relating to the transaction there.[30]

However, bringing a patented product into the United Kingdom for use or sale would infringe a UK patent.[31] The law also went further. The importation into the United Kingdom of products resulting from the use abroad of a process, or method, which was patented in the United Kingdom could also infringe the UK patent. It did not matter at what stage of the course of manufacture the process, or method, was used provided that the process, or method, did not play only a trivial part in the manufacture of the product.[32]

These cases depended on the proposition that the patent confers on the patentee the exclusive right to do certain acts within the United Kingdom and is infringed by doing any of those acts within the jurisdiction without the UK patentee's permission. *Caldwell v Vanvlissengen* demonstrates the determination of the rule against importing without the patentee's consent. There, the Dutch owners of a ship using a screw-propeller patented in the United Kingdom infringed the plaintiff's rights when their ship entered UK waters. The screw-propeller had been lawfully attached to the ship in the Kingdom of Holland where such devices were not patented and had been known for several years. Sir G. Turner VC held that:

> ... but it must be remembered that British ships certainly cannot use this invention without the license of the patentees, and the burthens incident to such a license; and foreigners cannot, I think, justly complain that their ships are not permitted to enjoy, without license and without payment, advantages which the ships of this country cannot enjoy otherwise than under license and upon payment. It must be remembered that foreigners may take out patents in this country, and thus secure to themselves the exclusive use of their inventions within Her Majesty's dominions; and that, if they neglect to do so, they, to this extent withhold their invention from the subjects of this country. It is to be observed also that the enforcement of an exclusive right under a patent does not take away from foreigners any privilege which they ever enjoyed in

---

29 *Badische Anilin und Soda Fabrik v Basle Chemical Works, Bindschedler* [1898] AC 200 (HL).
30 *Badische Anilin und Soda Fabrik v Hickson* [1906] AC 419 (HL).
31 *Universities of Cambridge and Oxford v Richardson* (1802) 6 Ves. Jun. 689, at 708 to 709; 31 ER 1260, at 1269 to 1270; *Betts v Nielson* (1868) LR 3 Ch. App. 429; *Pfizer Corporation v Ministry of Health* [1965] AC 512 (HL).
32 *Elmslie v Boursier* (1869) LR 9 Eq. 217; *Wright v Hitchcock* (1870) LR Ex. 37; *Von Heyden v von Neustadt* (1880) 14 Ch. D 230; *Saccharin Corporation Limited v Anglo-Chemical Works Limited* (1899) 17 RPC 307; *Wilderman v F. W. Berk & Co.* (1925) 42 RPC 79; *Beecham Group Limited v International Products Limited* [1968] RPC 129 (HC, Kenya); *Beecham Group Limited v Shewan Tomes (Traders) Limited* [1968] RPC 268 (SC, App. Jur., Hong Kong); *Beecham Group Limited v Bristol Laboratories Pty Limited* (1968) 118 CLR 618, [1968] RPC 301(HCA, FC); *Beecham Group Limited v Bristol Laboratories Limited* [1978] RPC 153.

this country; for, if the invention was used by them in this country before the granting of the patent, the patent, I apprehend, would be invalid.[33]

Accordingly, under subsection 60(1) it is an infringement of the patent to import into the United Kingdom, without the patentee's consent, a patented product, or a product obtained directly by means of a patented process.[34] Therefore, when considering parallel imports, the crucial question becomes how far the patentee's consent to importation (and subsequent use) can be inferred from some association between the domestic patentee and the marketing abroad of a product made according to the patent.

In considering this question, in the United Kingdom it is now necessary to distinguish between marketing in the European Communities and marketing outside the European Communities. If the product is marketed with the patentee's consent in a Member State of the European Communities, the rules relating to the free movement of goods and competition under the EEC Treaty require consideration. Similarly, subsection 60(4) of the 1977 Act applies the Community Patent Convention's provisions about exhaustion to patents under the 1977 Act. The Community Patent Convention, however, is not yet in force. Moreover, neither it nor the EEC Treaty extend to imports from countries which are not members of the European Communities.[35] Accordingly, it is necessary to look to the general law to discover when the patentee's consent will be inferred in such circumstances.

The courts in the United Kingdom have not as yet considered the meaning of the phrase 'without the consent of the proprietor of the patent' in the context of parallel imports. When they come to do so, they are directed by subsection 130(7) of the 1977 Act to interpret this phrase, as nearly as practicable, in accordance with any uniform interpretation which may emerge under the Community Patent Convention. Obviously, such an interpretation cannot emerge until the Convention comes into force. Furthermore, the signatory nations themselves have different approaches to the issue of 'international exhaustion'.[36] In addition, as specific provision for exhaustion has been made in the Convention, the traditional approach of the common law would probably regard that provision as conclusive of the changes intended to the previously existing law. Accordingly, it is likely that the UK courts could be expected to apply the principles developed under the old law to decide whether the patentee has consented to the importation.

Unlike many systems, Anglo-Commonwealth law has steadfastly turned its

---

33   (1851) 9 Hare 415, at 430; 61 ER 570, at 577. But see now the 1977 Act section 60(5)(d) and (7).
34   Subject to the impact of EC law, the 1977 Act, in effect, codifies the pre-existing law. For present purposes and disregarding the effects of EC law, the law of other British Commonwealth jurisdictions corresponds to subsection 60(1), see for example Patents Act 1990 (Cth) section 13(1) and 'exploit' in Schedule 1; Patents Act RSC 1985, Chapter P-4, section 42.
35   For EC law, see Chapters 6 and 7 below. For the current status of the Community Patent Convention, see Chapter 6.5.
36   For an overview as at 1978, see Demaret, *Patents, Territorial Restrictions and EEC Law*, at 59 to 62.

back on a general doctrine of exhaustion once a patentee releases a patented article on to the domestic market.[37] Instead, spurning economic arguments, it has focused on questions of 'consent' and, in some situations, allows a patentee to control dealings in a patented article after it has been sold. This focus in domestic trade, which crystalised in tandem with the forming of the main approaches to parallel imports, must be considered before analysing the parallel import question. Partly, it explains some of the concerns raised by the judges in some of the cases. More significantly, it helps to show that the contradictions in the two leading cases, *Betts v Willmott* and *Tilghman's* case, represent not just the common law's eccentricity but, rather, fundamental differences in philosophy.[38]

3.2.2   The policy of commercial convenience: domestic rules

A number of issues present themselves when considering a patentee's attempts to restrict domestic trade in patented articles. The first issue is the extent to which a patentee can place conditions on subsequent dealings in the patented article. A subsidiary issue is whether an exclusive licensee may impose such restraints, especially if the exclusive licensee has an unlimited licence. Second, the basis of the restriction, patent or contract, must be determined. The third issue involves whether the purchaser must be notified of the restraint to be bound by it and, if so, when notice must be effected and how.

The first case of interest is *Thomas v Hunt*. Thomas held a patent in England for improvements in the manufacture of soap. He licensed a firm to use the invention 'in the manufacture of soap, and respectively to have, enjoy, and sell the said soap so manufactured as aforesaid for their own use and benefit absolutely upon payment of a royalty'. The firm, having made the soap and paid the royalty, sold some to Hunt who, in turn, resold it. Thomas sued him for infringement. Williams J, giving the judgment of the court, tersely held 'The defendant is clearly entitled to judgment on this demurrer. The vendee of the licensee has all the privileges of a vendee including that of selling again. The very object of the licence would be frustrated if this were not so.'[39]

The firm's licence under the patent was unconditional (apart from payment of the royalty) being for their 'own use and benefit absolutely'. In turn, the firm did not place any restriction on Hunt. Accordingly, like any purchaser of goods, Hunt was free to deal with them in whatever manner he saw fit.

---

37   South Africa is an exception, see *Stauffer Chemical Co. v Agricura Ltd* 1979 BP 168 (CP) and Timothy Donald Burrell, *South African Patent Law and Practice*, Butterworths, 1986 (2nd ed.). For some other approaches, see Demaret, *Patents, Territorial Restrictions and EEC Law*, at 59 to 60, Note 1; for the United States, section 3.3.2 below.

38   *Betts v Willmott* (1871) LR 6 Ch. App. 239; *Société Anonyme des Manufactures de Glaces v Tilghman's Patent Sand Blast Company* (1883) 25 Ch. D 1 (CA), see section 3.2.3 below.

39   (1864) 17 CB(NS) 183, at 187 to 188; 144 ER 74, at 76.

Counsel for Hunt was not even called on. It is, however, interesting to note the approaches counsel proposed to adopt:

> (1) That an article manufactured under a licence from the owner of a patent, and in respect of which a royalty has been paid to the owner of a patent, may be freely sold and re-sold by all the world:
>
> (2) That otherwise the owner of a patent would be paid many times over in respect of the same article manufactured under a licence from the owner of the patent:
>
> (3) That the price of the article is increased by the royalty paid in the first instance by the licensee; and therefore the defendant, who paid such increased price to the licensee, has virtually paid the royalty for the article:
>
> (4) That the licence given to the licensees to manufacture, enjoy and sell, includes a licence to purchasers from licensees to re-sell the article purchased by them.[40]

The first three arguments form an interesting contrast to the fourth. The fourth argument depends on analysing the contractual arrangements between the various parties. It starts from a presumption that commercial convenience requires goods to circulate free from restrictive conditions. Then one looks to see whether the arrangements between the parties countermand that presumption. This is the approach the court chose to adopt. In contrast, the first three arguments depend on what is almost an economic analysis of the nature of a patentee's rights under a patent. Counsel, in effect, seems to have been prepared to argue that the purpose of a patent was to secure to a patentee the right of putting articles made according to the patent into circulation first so that the patentee could secure sales on the best possible terms. Having put the article into circulation, however, the patentee should not be allowed to keep on extracting 'monopoly' profits for the same article. This is essentially the doctrine of exhaustion.[41]

There are two particularly striking aspects about counsel's arguments. First, he was prepared to raise them in 1864.[42] Second, and of greater moment, prior to the United Kingdom's entry into the European Communities, English courts have resolutely refused to adopt such reasoning.

The leading case on attempts by patentees to impose restrictions in domestic trade is *National Phonograph Company of Australia Limited v Menck*.[43] The plaintiff was the manufacturer and distributor of electrical

---

40 *Ibid.* outlined in footnote (b) to the report.

41 See, for example, the approach in the United States, section 3.3.2 below.

42 Similar arguments may be traced at least to 1846, see the quotation from *Hindmarch*, 493 in *National Phonograph Co. of Australia Ltd v Menck* (1908) 7 CLR 481, at 524 *per* Barton J:

> Indeed, when an article has once been sold by the patentee, or his licensee, the object of the law has been attained; the patentee has obtained (or had the means of obtaining) the profit which it was intended he should receive, and any subsequent sale of the article is not within the meaning of the prohibition contained in the patent.

Sir R. Webster apparently drew the same conclusion from Lord Tindal CJ's judgment in *Crane v Price, Webster's Patent Reports*, 393, see his comment in *Webster's Patent Reports* at 413, Note (p) cited by Isaacs J in *Menck* (1908) 7 CLR at 540.

43 [1911] AC 336; 12 CLR 15 (PC).

equipment such as phonographs and of sound records and blanks. It owned three patents in Australia for a phonograph, sound records and blanks and the production of sound records and blanks. It had established a two-tiered distribution system: it sold to jobbers who, in turn, sold to dealers. Jobbers contracted with the plaintiff to sell only to dealers on the plaintiff's list of approved dealers. Although buying from jobbers, 'approved' dealers also contracted directly with the plaintiff. These contracts imposed a number of constraints on the business methods the dealer might employ. In particular, the minimum price at which dealers could sell to other dealers and the public was fixed and, in various circumstances, dealers were also forbidden to deal in the products of the plaintiff's trade competitors.[44]

The plaintiff alleged that Menck had violated these conditions and purported to remove him from its list of approved dealers. Menck elected to treat the plaintiff's conduct as a repudiation of their contract and proceeded to deal with the plaintiff's goods as if he were an ordinary purchaser, not subject to the contractual restraints. In consequence, the plaintiff sued him for breach of contract and patent infringement.

The High Court of Australia denied the plaintiff relief on both grounds. The Privy Council upheld the High Court's finding on breach of contract but found that Menck had infringed the plaintiff's rights under the patents.

On the infringement issue, the plaintiff argued that, as a patentee, it could sell its patented articles on terms and conditions which conferred only a limited right to deal with the patented article. Such terms and conditions would run with the goods regardless of notice. In contrast, Menck argued, successfully before the High Court, that the patentee could only impose restrictions on dealings in patented articles on the first sale of the article. Once the patented article had been sold, the power of the restrictions to bind ended and, thereafter, a purchaser could deal with the goods as he pleased.[45]

In the Privy Council, Lord Shaw of Dunfermline first considered the general principle:

> To begin with, the *general principle*, that is to say, the principle applicable to *ordinary goods* bought and sold, is not here in question. The owner may use and dispose of these as he thinks fit. He may have made a certain contract with the person from whom he bought, and to such a contract he must answer. Simply, however, in his capacity as owner, he is not bound by any restrictions in regard to the use or sale of the goods, and it is out of the question to suggest that restrictive conditions run with the goods. . . . It would be contrary to the public interest and to the security of trade, as well as to the familiar rights attaching to ordinary ownership, if any other principle applied. (*Emphasis added*)[46]

---

44   The resale price maintenance clause would now be illegal under Trade Practices Act 1974 (Cth) section 48 which is not affected by the exception for intellectual property rights in section 51(3).

45   (1908) 7 CLR 481 *per* Griffith CJ, Barton and O'Connor JJ relying heavily on US authority; Isaacs and Higgins JJ dissenting. For the US case law, see section 3.3.2 below.

46   [1911] AC at 347; see also *Taddy v Sterious* [1904] 1 Ch. 354 (Ch. D) and *McGruther v Pitcher* [1904] 2 Ch. 306 (CA).

Where the articles in question were made under a patent, however, the general principle required some modification so that it did not conflict with 'the right of property conferred by the State' giving the patentee a monopoly 'to make, use, exercise, and vend the invention . . . in such manner as to him seems meet'. In the Privy Council's view, the principles could be reconciled; but not on the terms of the two competing contentions before it:

> There is no doubt that, if the doctrine contended for by the appellants and affirmed by the dissentient judges in the Court below were to be given effect to, namely, that the conditions imposed by the patentee run with the goods, a radical change in the law of personal property would have been made. But if that latter view be an extreme view, and if the restriction upon alienation, use or otherwise of the chattel purchased be a restriction arising from the fact that the person who has become owner has done so with the knowledge brought home to him of the limitation of his rights of alienation or otherwise, then there seems to be no radical change whatever. All that is affirmed is that the general doctrine of absolute freedom of disposal of chattels of an ordinary kind is, in the case of patented chattels, subject to the restriction that the person purchasing them, and in the knowledge of the conditions attached by the patentee, which knowledge is clearly brought home to himself at the time of sale, shall be bound by that knowledge and accept the situation of ownership subject to the limitations. These limitations are merely the respect paid and the effect given to those conditions of transfer of the patented article which the law, laid down by statute, gave the original patentee a power to impose. . . . It may be added that where a patented article has been acquired by sale, much, if not all, may be implied as to the consent of the licensee to an undisturbed and unrestricted use thereof. In short, such a sale negatives in the ordinary case the imposition of conditions and the bringing home to the knowledge of the owner of the patented goods that restrictions are laid upon him.
>
> These principles harmonize the rights of the patentee with the rights of the owner.[47]

Having considered the matter in principle, Lord Shaw reviewed the relevant English case law and concluded:

> In their Lordships' opinion, it is thus demonstrated by a clear course of authority, *first*, that it is open to a licensee, by virtue of his statutory monopoly, to make a sale sub modo, or accompanied by restrictive conditions which would not apply in the case of ordinary chattels; *secondly*, that the imposition of these conditions in the case of a sale is not presumed, but, on the contrary, a sale having occurred, the presumption is that the full right of ownership was meant to be vested in the purchaser; while *thirdly*, the owner's rights in a patented chattel will be limited if there is brought home to him the knowledge of conditions imposed, by the patentee or those representing the patentee, upon him at the time of sale. . . . *On the one hand*, the patented goods are not, simply because of their nature as chattels, sold free from restriction. Whether that restriction affects the purchaser is in most cases assumed in the negative from the fact of sale, but depends upon whether it entered the conditions upon which the owner acquired the goods. *On the other hand*, restrictive conditions do not, in the extreme sense put, run with the goods, because the goods are patented. (*Emphasis added*)[48]

47   *Ibid.* at 348 to 349.
48   *Ibid.* at 353.

Accordingly, Menck, having notice of the conditions by reason of his contract with the plaintiff, was bound by the conditions and had infringed the plaintiff's patents.

The first important aspect of the *Menck* case is the Privy Council's clear rejection of the doctrine of exhaustion. The majority in the High Court had accepted Menck's argument that a patent only entitled the patentee to reap his profit by being the first to put the patented article into the course of trade. Instead, Lord Shaw chose to resolve the issue by reference to the rules of the passing of title and the incidents thereto, an approach which began emerging with *Thomas v Hunt* and *Betts v Willmott*.[49]

Second, the *Menck* case makes it clear beyond doubt that it is the patent which excepts the articles from the general rule of commercial convenience applying to ordinary goods. The common law rule does not apply because of the statutory monopoly conferred by the patent. The dictates of trade are such, however, that the rule is presumed to operate unless the patentee expressly countermands it.

Third, the *Menck* case is clear authority that a purchaser of a patented article will not be bound by restrictions on its use unless the restrictions be brought home to the purchaser before the purchase is completed.[50]

The *Menck* case has been followed on a number of occasions by the courts.[51] A qualification must, however, be noted. The rule that conditions do not run with goods unless the goods embody a patented invention or, perhaps copyright,[52] is certainly the general rule; but has never been conclusively decided. In particular, Lord Shaw himself, once again speaking for the Privy Council, failed to apply it in a highly controversial case involving the charterparty of a ship.[53]

---

49   Sometimes referred to as a 'doctrine of leave and licence', see *Betts v Willmott* (1871) LR 6 Ch. App. 239, section 3.2.3 below, which their Lordships regarded as having settled the law on the two main points for 'at least a quarter of a century': [1911] AC at 354; *Heap v Hartley* (1888) 5 RPC 603 (Ch. County Palatine), on appeal (1889) 42 Ch. D 461 (CA).

50   See also, the *Gas Light* cases – *The Incandescent Gas Light Company Limited v Cantelo* (1895) 12 RPC 262 (QBD); *The Incandescent Gas Light Company Limited v Brogden* (1899) 16 RPC 177; *Wellsbach Incandescent Co. v Doyle* (1899) 16 RPC 391. In *Cantelo*, the condition failed even though it was endorsed on the goods by label. The buyer paid for the goods which were then handed to him over the counter packaged so that the notice was concealed. It was not otherwise brought to his attention.

51   See 35 Halsbury (4th ed.), at ¶411. It must, however, now be read in light of statutory changes such as the ban on tying introduced in the Patents Act in 1907, now section 44 of the 1977 Act; the ban on resale price maintenance, see for example Resale Prices Act 1976 (United Kingdom) section 9; and territorial restraints affected by the EEC Treaty, see Chapters 6 and 7 below.

52   But see *Barker v Stickney* [1919] 1 KB 121, at 132 *per* Scrutton LJ. On the effect of licence restrictions in copyright, see the *Time-Life* case, Chapter 4.2.2(c) below.

53   See *Lord Strathcona SS Co. Ltd v Dominion Coal Co. Ltd* [1926] AC 108; contrast *Howie v New South Wales Lawn Tennis Ground Ltd* (1956) 95 CLR 132, at 156 *per* Dixon CJ, McTiernan and Fullagar JJ and *Port Line Ltd v Ben Line Steamers Ltd* [1958] 2 QB 146, at 166 *per* Diplock J, the latter not finding favour in *Swiss Bank Corporation v Lloyd's Bank Ltd* [1982] AC 584 (HL). On the point generally, Zechariah Chafee Jr, 'Equitable Servitudes on Chattels', 41 Harv. LRev. 945 (1928); Zechariah Chafee Jr, 'The Music Goes Round and Round: Equitable Servitudes and Chattels', 69 Harv. LRev. 1250 (1956); E.C.S. Wade, 'Restrictions on User', (1928) 44 LQR 51.

Three further questions require consideration: whether 'the chain of notice' from the patentee to the person against whom the restriction is sought to be enforced must be unbroken; whether restrictions may be imposed by licensees or only the patentee; and what degree of knowledge must be shown.

In *Menck*, Lord Shaw referred to restrictions binding the purchaser of a patented article if knowledge of the restriction has been brought home to the purchaser at the time of sale. This suggests that the restriction might be enforceable against someone who bought with knowledge of it, but bought from someone who was not themselves bound by the condition for want of notice.[54] There, however, the goods passed down the chain of distribution from the plaintiff to Menck, the dealer, by way of intermediary jobbers (and, it seems, possibly other dealers). Each jobber and dealer, apparently, also contracted directly with the plaintiff. As a result of their contracts, each link in the chain had full knowledge of the restrictions before they bought the goods.

The situation may have arisen in *British Mutoscope and Biograph Company Limited v Homer*.[55] The plaintiffs held a patent for a particular kind of machine and had leased ten of them to one Maynard on condition that he pay for the maintenance of the machines and a royalty of 25 per cent of the takings. He kept the machines at leased premises. When he fell behind in the rent, the landlord distrained; seizing the machines and putting them up for auction. One was sold to Homer. Homer refused to pay any royalty to the plaintiffs for use of the machine, claiming that he had bought it outright and, with the passing of title, the right to use it was inseparably attached to it. The plaintiffs relied on notice of their rights and the principle that one who has no title to sell cannot confer good title by sale. The plaintiffs had notified the landlord and the auctioneers of their conditions of use, both before and at the sale.

As Homer admitted notice of the conditions, Farwell J found infringement along the lines approved in *Menck*. It is not clear from the report, however, whether the landlord had notice of the conditions before distraining. There must be a strong possibility that he did not. If he did not, Farwell J may have been suggesting that the conditions can still run although the chain of notice has been broken. Another explanation is that a distrainor does not sell in his personal capacity, selling instead as some sort of agent or trustee for the person whose property has been distrained.

Of greater difficulty is *Badische Anilin und Soda Fabrik v Isler*.[56] The plaintiff held several patents in connection with its dye-making business. It licensed these to the Society for Chemical Industry in Basle on condition that the Society could only sell to consumers and not to dealers. Subsequently, the plaintiff acquired a new patent for Rhodamine 6G dye which was always sold in tins clearly labelled to the effect that purchasers were not licensed

54 For example, suppose a buyer from Cantelo who bought after noticing the label: for *Cantelo*, see Note 50 above.
55 [1901] 1 Ch. 671.
56 [1906] 1 Ch. 605; [1906] 2 Ch. 443 (CA).

to resell the tin except in the unopened, original package in an unchanged condition with the labels intact. The label also expressly stated that agents and dealers were not empowered to vary the terms of the licence. For several years, the Society had been selling dyes to Isler, a dealer. In line with the terms of the licence, this was stopped. However, he arranged to get supplies through a firm who were both dealers and consumers. Both the firm and Isler denied any knowledge that the Society's licence was limited and claimed they believed the Society had a 'full and free' licence.

In an action for patent infringement, Isler escaped liability at first instance solely because Rhodamine 6G dye was not covered by the licence. Both the plaintiff and the Society had assumed the Rhodamine 6G dye came under the licence. It was not and a licence for it had never been executed between the two. The Court of Appeal refused to consider 'the other issues' and decided the case simply on the ground that the only restriction on the sale of the dye proved was that on the labels which Isler had complied with.[57]

For present purposes, interest in the case lies in Buckley J's opinion that Isler would have been liable if Rhodamine 6G had been covered by the terms of the licence from the plaintiff to the Society. In that case, it would have made no difference that Isler did not have notice because the licensee, having only limited title, could not confer powers greater than that title. The earlier decision in *Cantelo*, requiring notice brought home to the purchaser himself, was distinguished on the ground that the vendor there was an agent, not a licensee. As an agent, the law regarded the sale as a sale by the patentee.[58]

Buckley J's analysis of the consequences of a sale by a limited licensee is certainly one logical result of the decision in *Heap v Hartley* and reliance on patent rights to control dealings in goods. If the licensee has no power to do the act complained of, allowing a purchaser from the limited licensee to do the act would violate the fundamental principle, *nemo dat quod non habet*. But, it is difficult to imagine a decision less in accord with the policy of commercial convenience generally underlying Lord Shaw's opinion in the *Menck* case. As already indicated, the Court of Appeal preferred not to go into this issue and Buckley J's view must be considered doubtful in view of *Lissen* and *Bernstein*.[59]

In *Lissen*, the then Simonds J meted out quite brusque treatment to the plaintiff's claims of patent infringement by violation of restrictions imposed on a licensee. Lissen, the defendant, proved that it had bought the offending radio from Hazeltine's licensee for the United Kingdom. Hazeltine, however, claimed that the radio was nonetheless an infringing article because the licensee had failed to pay the royalty on the radio due under the licence and, further, because a nameplate required to be affixed to the radio under the licence was not attached.

Simonds J dismissed the point about non-payment of royalty for want of

---

57   [1906] 2 Ch. 443, at 444.
58   [1906] 1 Ch. 605, at 610 to 611.
59   *Hazeltine Corporation v Lissen Limited* (1938) 56 RPC 62; *Gillette Industries Limited v Bernstein* [1942] Ch. 45 (CA).

evidence, but also considered that failure to pay a royalty was no ground for regarding the radio as an infringing article.[60] His Lordship then considered the allegation about the nameplate. Since Lissen was not proved to have notice of the condition, it was free to deal with the radio as it liked. The fact that Lissen had purchased from a licensee and not the patentee did not prevent application of the principles set down in *Menck*:

> Buying patented goods without any notice of any restriction affecting them, [Lissen] could use them and sell them in any way [it] liked and it would not be competent for the patentee to rely on a penalty which the licence sought to impose for breach of the restriction.
>
> I see no distinction in principle between such a case as this, where the condition or qualification of a licence is the affixing of a plate, and such cases as [*Cantelo*] where the condition limited the user or [*Menck*] where the condition under review affected the selling price. To affect a purchaser of a patented article, it must be established that the condition has been brought to his notice at the time of purchase. If it is not, he can deal with it as he will.[61]

Isler's case was not cited or considered in the *Lissen* case. But, apart from Simonds J's *dicta* about the effect of sale without payment of the royalty, *Lissen* simply applies the decision in *Menck* and continues the judicial policy of promoting commercial convenience.[62] Hence, at least in domestic trade, the better view seems to be that notice of any restriction on dealing in a patented article must be brought home to the defendant before the defendant acquired the article.

The authority for the view that only a patentee, and not an exclusive licensee, can impose restrictions is rather tenuous. On a special case, Warrington J (as his Lordship then was) held that an otherwise unconstrained, exclusive licensee could not impose post-sales restraints on its purchasers. His Lordship's order was subsequently overturned on appeal. The Court of Appeal found that the special case did not state the facts sufficiently to enable it to deal properly with the matter between the parties.[63]

The facts, as they appeared before Warrington J, involved a patentee who had given an unrestricted, exclusive licence to the plaintiff company under a patent for the manufacture of razors. These were made and sold in boxes, each box labelled as giving the purchaser, or any person into whose hands it may come, 'a limited licence to use or sell the same' on condition that the boxes not be resold by retailers below a set price, 1 guinea. The plaintiff sold boxes to a wholesaler who, in turn, sold some to the defendant. The defendant sold boxes retail below the minimum price. The plaintiff sued for infringement.

---

60 *Ibid.* at 66 to 67.
61 *Ibid.* at 68.
62 See also *Gillette Industries Limited v Bernstein* [1942] Ch. 45, where the Court of Appeal refused to find against a retailer of razor blades undercutting the fixed price because his knowledge of the price clause before he bought them was not proved.
63 *Gillette Safety Razor Company Limited v A.W. Gamage Limited* (1908) 25 RPC 492; *ibid.* at 782 (CA).

The defendant argued that the plaintiff, as an exclusive licensee, had no property in the patent and so could not impose conditions on the use of patented articles. Such conditions could only be imposed by the patentee. On the basis of some contracts, the plaintiff argued that it was the owner of the patent in equity.

In the absence of any contractual relationship, Warrington J appeared to find that the defendant did not infringe the letters patent because the plaintiff had an unrestricted right to deal with the patented articles as it pleased. As the plaintiff had an unrestricted right to deal with the patented articles, so too did the defendant. The label was, therefore, ineffective.[64]

If this part of the ruling be right, it seems that only a patentee, or perhaps someone with a licence in the patent coupled with a grant, can impose restrictions on subsequent dealings with patented products. Unless it represents an outright rejection of any further qualification on the policy of commercial convenience, it seems somewhat peculiar to make the suggested distinction. Such an outright rejection seems rather doubtful given the whole-hearted endorsement of the qualification, when the restraint is imposed by the patentee, in *Menck* some three years after Warrington J's decision.[65] His Lordship's view, with respect, seems open to question on a number of grounds. The Court of Appeal refused to go into the question. The facts were particularly unclear; indeed, on the evidence at that stage of the proceedings, there was considerable doubt that notice of the condition had been brought home to the defendant before purchase. Further, his Lordship may have considered that an exclusive licensee did not hold a proprietary interest since, at the time, the common law did not allow an exclusive licensee to sue for infringement of the licensed patent.[66] The statutory right of an exclusive licensee to sue may require alteration of that approach.[67]

There has not been much consideration of the degree of knowledge which must be shown since most of the cases have turned on whether there was any notice at the relevant time at all. It does not, however, seem that the defendant must know the condition is imposed under a patent.[68] The notice

64   *Ibid.* at 499 to 500.
65   In summing up the principles, Lord Shaw did actually refer to conditions imposed by a 'licensee' at [1911] AC 353 at Note 48 above. Too much should probably not be made of this, since his Lordship was there dealing with a condition imposed on a direct 'licensee' by the patentee and, in the context, seems to have been using the term to refer generally to any person authorised to deal in patented articles.
66   *Heap v Hartley* (1889) 42 Ch. D 461 (CA).
67   The Court of Appeal was prepared in strong terms to protect an exclusive licensee's proprietary interest, as against the licensor: *British Nylon Spinners v Imperial Chemical Industries Ltd* (1952) 69 RPC 288, at 294; [1952] 2 All ER 780, at 783; see also *Roussel-Uclaf v GD Searle & Co. Ltd* [1977] FSR 125, at 130 *per* Graham J, at Note 121 below. But see the qualification as against third parties relying on Warrington J's opinion in 35 Halsbury (4th ed.), at ¶407, Notes 3 and 4. An exclusive licensee of copyright may have a right enforceable against third parties, a view not necessary to the decision: *British Actors Film Company v Glover* [1918] 1 KB 299, at 309. But note, statutory intervention was necessary to protect an exclusive licensee's 'proprietary interest' against the copyright owner's 'consent', see Chapter 4.2.2(b) below.
68   *Dunlop Rubber Company Limited v Longlife Battery Depot* [1958] RPC 473, at 476 to 477 *per* Lloyd-Jacob J on the theory that an innocent infringer is still an infringer. But

need not be contractual. In the *Longlife Battery* case, the defendant's own general knowledge that the condition existed sufficed, as communication by correspondence would have done if it could have been established that the offending article had been acquired after the correspondence was received.[69] It has also been argued that any restrictions must be clear (since any ambiguities will be read against the person seeking to enforce them) and that if actual knowledge be not proved, the lesser standard of wilful and reckless disregard must at least be shown.[70]

3.2.3 Parallel imports[71]

As already indicated in section 3.2.1 above, when the use of patents to block parallel imports falls to be considered, the result turns on consent: whether the domestic patentee's consent can be inferred from the simple fact of lawful release on the foreign market. Although purporting to apply a uniform approach to the issue, the two leading cases in fact stand at the head of two substantially different philosophical approaches. *Tilghman's* case turned on the territorial nature of patent rights; the earlier decision of *Betts v Willmott* disregarded that consideration and treated the question as it would have done if the patented articles had been marketed domestically.[72]

Before either case, however, the Court of Common Pleas was confronted with an assignor's attempt to undermine the assignment. In *Walton v Lavater*, there was a patent for a particular kind of peg which could adhere mechanically to solid surfaces such as glass, walls, panels and furniture.[73] Walton had acquired the patent in the United Kingdom by assignment from Lavater. Lavater, however, was importing and selling such pegs in the United Kingdom having manufactured them abroad under patents he owned in the country of manufacture. Walton's infringement action succeeded.

The territorial nature of the patent may explain that success or it may simply be put on the basis that the patentee, having once parted with the

note, similar reasoning was used by Buckley J in *Isler's* case to reach the conclusion that a defendant without notice of the condition at all was bound: [1906] 1 Ch. 605.

69   For correspondence having a similar effect in a parallel import case, see *Smith Kline & French Laboratories Ltd v Salim (Malaysia) Sdn Bhd* [1989] FSR 407, 15 IPR 677 (HC Kuala Lumpur).

70   George Wei, 'Parallel Imports and Intellectual Property Rights in Singapore', unpublished manuscript text at Notes 47 to 49 published in full: (1990) 2 S. Ac. L. J. 286; portion on parallel imports and copyright: [1992] EIPR 139.

71   See 35 Halsbury (4th ed.), at ¶584; Wei, 'Parallel Imports and Intellectual Property Rights in Singapore', unpublished manuscript text, at §III; Cornish, *Intellectual Property*, at ¶6-011; W. Aldous *et al.*, *Terrell on the Law of Patents*, Sweet & Maxwell, 1982 (2nd ed.), ¶6.33; Harold G. Fox, *The Canadian Law and Practice Relating to Letters Patent for Inventions*, The Carswell Company Ltd, 1969 (4th ed.), at 301 to 302; Mary Vitoria *et al.*, *Encyclopaedia of United Kingdom and European Patent Law*, Sweet & Maxwell, 1977, at ¶¶4-303 to 4-304; and A.M. Walton *et al.*, *Patent Laws of Europe and the United Kingdom*, Butterworths, 1983, at ¶¶941 to 950.

72   *Société Anonyme des Manufactures de Glaces v Tilghman's Patent Sand Blast Company* (1883) 25 Ch. D 1 (CA); *Betts v Willmott* (1871) LR 6 Ch. App. 239, see text at Notes 81 to 88 and 76 to 80 below, respectively.

73   8 CB(NS) 162; 141 ER 1127.

right, cannot confer further powers under it.[74] The argument put forward by Lavater to support his conduct casts some obscurity on the matter. Somewhat speculatively, he sought to defend himself on the ground that the mere act of sale in the United Kingdom was not infringement; infringement required manufacture as well as sale in the United Kingdom. Erle CJ held:

> . . . but it appears to me to be clearly the intention of the Crown in granting letters-patent for a new invention, to prohibit and prevent third persons from using the patented article for the purpose of profit by selling. The object is, to give to the inventor the profit of his invention; and the most effectual way of defeating that object would be the permitting others to derive from the sale of the patented article the profit which it was intended to secure to the patentee. It seems to me, therefore, that proof that a party has sold the patented article, without proof of his having made it or procured it to be made, would be good evidence to warrant a jury in finding that he has been guilty of an infringement.[75]

This object of the patent was derived from the words expressed in the form of the grant in the letters patent. The 'inventor' here was understood, not as the one who brought the new teaching into the United Kingdom, but as his assignee.

Although the court's focus on the profit to be derived from a patent suggests an approach based on an exhaustion theory, it must be understood in the context of the defendant's argument. Their Lordships' opinions were directed at explaining why manufacture in the United Kingdom was not a necessary element of infringement. Since the inventor had assigned his exclusive right to practise the patent within the jurisdiction, he too was precluded from practising it within the jurisdiction.

This analysis is supported by *dicta* of Lord Hatherley LC in *Betts v Willmott*.[76] Betts held patents in England and France for metallic capsules of tin and lead compressed together which were used to seal corks into bottles. Under the patents, he manufactured the capsules in England himself and in France through an agent. The agent had been instructed not to sell any capsules for export to England since Betts intended to reserve England for domestic production. The term of the patent in England had been extended for a further period of five years. In France, however, the patent had expired.

Betts discovered Willmott using the capsules in England; the latter having acquired them from a wholesaler who did not buy the capsules from Betts in England. In answer to the infringement charge, Willmott raised the

---

74   See *Betts v Willmott* LR 6 Ch. App. 239, at 245 at Note 79 below. But, in a similar US case involving a trade mark, Holmes J considered such conduct unthinkable *and* was heavily influenced by the territorial nature of the right: *Bourjois v Katzel* 260 US 689 (1923), Chapter 2.3.3 above.

75   8 CB(NS) 162, at 185 to 186; 141 ER at 1136 and *per* Keating J at 188; 141 ER at 1137.

76   (1871) LR 6 Ch. App. 239. Compare *Holiday v Mattheson* 24 Fed. 185 (CCSDNY, 1885) in the United States, section 3.3.4 below; and 187/80 *Merck & Co. Inc. v Stephar BV* [1981] ECR 2063 in the European Communities, Chapter 6.3.1 below.

possibility that the capsules had been made by Betts' French agent and lawfully acquired on the market in France. Betts was unable to disprove that possibility. Instead, he relied on the territorial nature of the patent. In the words of his counsel, '. . . if it was made by the Plaintiff's agent abroad, that fact would not legalize its sale in this country, in violation of the English patent'.[77]

Lord Hatherley LC rejected Betts' contention without calling on counsel for Willmott. His Lordship held that, while there had been use, or sale, of Betts' patented invention in England, Betts had failed to prove that the use, or sale, was unauthorised. His Lordship declared:

> . . . where a man carries on the two manufactories himself, and himself disposes of the article abroad, unless it can be shewn, not that there is some clear injunction to his agents, but that there is some clear communication to the party to whom the article is sold, I apprehend that, inasmuch as he has the right of vending the goods in France or Belgium or England, or in any other quarter of the globe, he transfers with the goods necessarily the licence to use them wherever the purchaser pleases. When a man has purchased an article he expects to have the control of it, and there must be some clear and explicit agreement to the contrary to justify the vendor in saying that he has not given the purchaser his licence to sell the article, or to use it wherever he pleases as against himself. He cannot use it against a previous assignee of the patent, but he can use it against the person who himself is proprietor of the patent, and has the power of conferring a complete right on him by the sale of the article.[78]

The first point to notice is Lord Hatherley's clear rejection of any argument based on the territorial nature of the rights conferred by a patent. Where the patentee himself is making and selling the product, it makes no difference whether he sells the product 'in France or Belgium or England, or in any other quarter of the globe'.

Second, the fact that the patentee himself had sold the article in the foreign country was conclusive. Further confirmation of this lies in his Lordship's earlier consideration of situations where either the domestic or foreign patent had been assigned, while ownership of the other was retained. In either situation, sale by the patentee in one jurisdiction could not defeat the rights of the assignee in the other:

> . . . the importer would be restrained, because the licence to sell, which belonged originally to the patentee, would then be vested in his assignee; and therefore no licence in England given by the original patentee after he had sold the patent could authorize the use of the article, so as to defeat the right of the assignees in England. And, of course, in exactly the same way, if the original patentee assigned his patent in France, no sale by him in England would be allowed to defeat the rights of the assignee in France. In other words, it comes within the doctrine of leave and licence, and there could be no leave and licence in such a case.[79]

---

77 *Ibid.* at 242 and see the report of Betts' evidence under cross-examination at 241.
78 *Ibid.* at 245. Earlier, at 243, Lord Hatherley considered the case identical to the situation where the plaintiff manufactured in different parts of England.
79 *Ibid.* at 244 to 245.

Third, arising from the second, Lord Hatherley did not base his rejection of Betts' territorial argument on an explicit theory of patent exhaustion. Betts' powers over the patented article were, in effect, 'exhausted'. But, that was not the basis for his Lordship's conclusion. Instead, Lord Hatherley rejected the territorial argument on the ground of Betts' consent coupled with general commercial convenience.[80] His Lordship did recognise that a patentee could impose constraints on the free dealing in his patented product. Even at this early stage, however, general commercial convenience required that the restraint had to be brought home to the purchaser of the product. It was not enough for the patentee merely to forbid his *agents* to sell their produce into the import trade.

Betts v Willmott was governed by the principles which would have operated if the transaction took place in the domestic market. General commercial convenience, or the usual expectations on purchasing goods, led to the implication of consent where there was no *explicit* agreement to the contrary. No such implication was drawn when the importer was a licensee of the foreign patent. Here the territorial nature of a patent predominated.

This was *Tilghman's* case. The respondent, Tilghman, owned corresponding patents in Belgium and England for a process of cutting and grinding hard substances which was particularly useful for obscuring and ornamenting glass lamp globes and similar articles. The appellant was based in Belgium and Tilghman granted it 'full and entire liberty, power and authority during the continuance of the patent for the term of 20 years to employ said invention and to put it into practice for all articles of glassware . . . at its manufactory of Vel St-Lambert, and not elsewhere . . . .' The licence was subject to certain other conditions not presently material and payment of royalties.

The appellant used the process to make large quantities of glassware articles and sold them in Belgium and England. Tilghman sent out circulars in England threatening to sue purchasers of the articles made in Belgium for infringement of its English patent. The appellant sought to have the issue arbitrated and applied for an injunction restraining the circulars pending the outcome of the arbitration.

Pearson J held that the facts before him were too unclear to warrant granting the injunction.[81] But, his Lordship also expressed doubts that a licence under a Belgian patent could confer rights to import patented articles into England in defiance of an English patent.[82] With its position undermined, the appellant appealed.

The crucial point was the Court of Appeal's finding that the licence was purely a licence under the Belgian patent which did not confer rights under the English patent. Accordingly, the appellant was forced to argue that the

---

80   'When a man has purchased an article he expects to have the control of it . . .'. See also *Taddy v Sterious* [1904] 1 Ch. 354 (Ch. D); *McGruther v Pitcher* [1904] 2 Ch. 306 (CA).
81   (1883) 25 Ch. D 1, at 3.
82   *Ibid.* at 4 to 5.

grant of a licence under the Belgian patent necessarily implied a licence to sell in England. This argument was roundly rejected. Cotton LJ considered that:

> In my opinion there is a fallacy there. This grant was simply a grant to the [appellant] of a license to exercise the invention in Belgium, notwithstanding the existence there of a patent which would otherwise have precluded them from manufacturing the article or dealing with the invention in Belgium. That was the grant.[83]

Consequently:

> . . . they can sell anywhere where the law of the country does not prevent them selling. But there is no grant there of a right to sell in England. . . . the mere fact that the grantors of the license had a monopoly in England would not, in my opinion, import as a matter of construction into this instrument the grant of a right to interfere with that monopoly when there had been no express grant of a right to sell in England.[84]

Lindley LJ, too, laid heavy emphasis on the separate, territorial nature of each patent in rejecting the appellant's arguments:

> The Belgian patent would have no force or effect outside Belgium. It is not by reason of the Belgian patent that the Belgian patentee can make or sell in England. A man may make or sell things in England whether he has a Belgian patent or not. . . . By means of that patent he becomes the owner of certain things in Belgium, and as owner of them he can sell them anywhere where he is not restrained. Now if I could find in this agreement any reference whatever to England or any indication that the grantor conveyed or purported to convey any right whatever to make or do anything in England, I should then feel the full force of the appellant's contention that the Defendants were derogating from their own grant. But I cannot find anything of the kind.[85]

His Lordship summed up bluntly:

> . . . the case stands simply in this way: [Tilghman] have two patents, they grant one of them and they say nothing about the other. They reserve, therefore, to themselves whatever rights they may have under the other, unless there was some fraudulent concealment or misrepresentation. This strikes at the root of the whole thing.[86]

There is some difficulty in reconciling Cotton and Lindley LJJ's reliance on the territorial nature of patents and their clear refusal to imply consent with Lord Hatherley's earlier willingness to imply consent and ignore the territorial issue. Cotton LJ simply stated that a licensee stood in a very different situation to that of a purchaser:

> When an article is sold without any restriction on the buyer, whether it is manufactured under one or the other patent, that, in my opinion, as against

---

83 *Ibid.* at 8.
84 *Ibid.* The point is unclear in the European Communities, see 19/84 *Pharmon v Hoechst* [1985] ECR 2281, Chapter 6.4 below and *GEMA Custom Pressing*, Chapter 7.3.1(g) below.
85 *Ibid.* at 10. Only these two Lord Justices sat on the bench for this case.
86 *Ibid.* at 11, Cotton LJ made a similar reservation for fraudulent conduct: *ibid.* at 8.

the vendor gives the purchaser an absolute right to deal with that which he so buys in any way he thinks fit, and *of course* that includes selling in any country where there is a patent in the possession of and owned by the vendor.[87]

Why 'of course'? A licence, as his Lordship had already pointed out, merely gave permission to do an act otherwise unlawful while a sale, without more, gave the purchaser absolute title. But, with respect, this hides a significant philosophical shift because the starting point is a premise that the licence was one to sell in Belgium alone and the principle of territoriality played a powerful role in interpreting the appellant's licence as one to make and sell in Belgium alone. In fact, the terms described in the judgment specified only the place of manufacture. Cotton and Lindley LJJ simply assumed – it might be thought a fairly natural assumption – that that meant sale also in Belgium only. Similarly, it was open to Lord Hatherley, like Lindley LJ (who refrained from any comment on *Betts v Willmott*), to consider that consent given under the foreign patent said nothing about the other.[88]

The conflict in underlying philosophies is reinforced by the shift away from the approach favoured by Lord Hatherley in a series of cases involving purchasers from licensees under the foreign patent.

In 1891, a New Zealand merchant, 'Briscoe', found itself being sued for infringement by importing into New Zealand rolls of wire from the United States. It had bought the rolls in the United States from a wholesaler which had, in turn, bought them from the United States licensee of the American company, 'Washburn', which owned process patents in both countries for the wire's manufacture. Each roll imported bore a stamp:

LICENSE STAMP
No. 842769
IOWA BARB WIRE Co.
ALLENTOWN P.A.

Parties dealing in or using barb wire not bearing our license
stamp are liable to suit for infringement.

Issued by
WASHBURN & MOEN M'F'G CO.[89]

The New Zealand Court of Appeal, and Williams J at first instance, were unanimous in the view that this stamp did not give Briscoe any licence to import the rolls into New Zealand nor could such a licence be implied from the fact of purchase from the American licensee. *Tilghman's* case controlled, although the grounds for Washburn's success admit interpretation. The case is further complicated by the form of proceeding which was a legal argument on the pleadings before trial of the facts.

---

87   *Ibid.* at 9. (*Emphasis added*)
88   The 'illogicality' of the implication in *Betts v Willmott* is subject to vigorous attack in Walton *et al.*, *Patent Laws of Europe and the United Kingdom*, ¶¶948 to 950.
89   *Briscoe & Co. v Washburn and Moen Manufacturing Company* (1891) 10 NZLR 85, at 88.

Williams J put the case on a combination of the territorial nature of patents and the doctrine of leave and licence. Having referred to *Tilghman's* case, his Honour stated: 'The license to manufacture and sell in America is a license in respect of rights granted by American law, and is independent of the rights the plaintiffs have acquired here by virtue of the law of New Zealand.'[90] *Thomas v Hunt* was distinguished. It showed that 'the rights of the vendee to resell arise from the original license'. But:

> In the present case the license to manufacture and sell had no reference to the patent right granted in New Zealand. The right of the vendee therefore to sell in New Zealand cannot be given by the licensee, nor does the absence of such right in the least interfere with the object of the license, which was to authorise the manufacture and sale in America notwithstanding the American patent.[91]

Like Cotton LJ in *Tilghman's* case, Williams J seems to consider that *Betts v Willmott* was consistent with this interpretation because it showed that a vendor transferred the rights in the article which the vendor itself had and, here, the US licensee had no rights in New Zealand to transfer.[92]

That is, Williams J attempted a synthesis. The principle of territoriality was crucial but not determinative on its own. If the US licensee had held rights under the New Zealand patent, it might have conveyed them to Briscoe by the sale but, as the two patents were separate territorial rights, the US licensee did not have any such rights to pass on because Williams J refused to imply them. The accident of whether the vendor held rights in both markets proved vital in determining whether the purchaser could reasonably expect to have unfettered control over the purchase.

On appeal, Prendergast CJ agreed with Williams J's finding, but may have intended a broader ruling:

> The sale, or offering for sale, or even the having in New Zealand barbed wire manufactured by the patented process in America under a license which I assume to have been granted under the United States patent, confers no rights within New Zealand by the licensor who grants the license under the United States patent, but holds also a New Zealand patent. This question is concluded by authority.[93]

The authority his Honour had in mind is not identified. Hence, it is not clear how far his Honour was concurring in Williams J's synthesis of *Betts v Willmot* and *Tilghman's* case. One of his brothers on the Court of Appeal stated that Williams J's decision on this point was not challenged on appeal.[94] The third member of the bench, Conolly J, focused on Briscoe's admission

---

90   *Ibid*. at 91.
91   *Ibid*.
92   *Ibid*. at 92.
93   *Ibid*. at 100.
94   *Ibid*. at 103 *per* Denniston J who subsequently, in dealing with an argument c estoppel, delivered himself of the view that, if Briscoe chose to assume the licence w; absolute and universal, it did so at its own risk.

that it knew Washburn had a patent in New Zealand when it bought the wire in the United States:

> This being the case, the defendants knew that the purchase for sale in New Zealand of wire purchased from the Iowa Barb Wire Company would not be lawful, and they cannot protect themselves by having purchased the same wire for the same purpose at second hand. Messrs Peabody and Co. could not convey greater rights than the Iowa Barb Wire Company possessed, and the last-named company could not make or sell wire for sale in New Zealand: [*Tilghman's* case].[95]

The first part of this passage suggests quite a broad rule: knowledge of the New Zealand patent imputed knowledge that no licence was granted under it by purchase abroad. (Any further extent of Briscoe's admission is not elaborated on in the report.) The second sentence, which *Tilghman's* case is cited as authority for, is more limited; bringing the ruling back within the maxim *nemo dat quod non habet*.

Even the narrower ruling indicates a shift; first, from *Tilghman's* case which did not directly hold this; and second, potentially, from the rule applying to sales made wholly within the domestic market which Lord Hatherley considered decisive. Lord Hatherley required express agreement to the contrary to negative the implication of consent. That may be thought consistent with the subsequent development of the rule for sales in the domestic market which, apart from *Isler's* case, required that notice be brought home to the defendant before purchase.[96] Subject to the question of notice, which two members of the New Zealand Court of Appeal did not see fit to comment on, *Briscoe's* case suggests that cases involving parallel imports were developing on lines separate from that of purely domestic cases.

The factual problems, judicial pronouncements and even the state of domestic law at the time baffle further speculation about the implications of *Briscoe's* case. Although *Briscoe* was not referred to, a later series of cases involving the patents for ampicillin confirm the existence of a train of judicial opinion at odds with Lord Hatherley's initial approach.

The Beecham and Bristol pharmaceutical groups occupied a number of courts from the late 1960s to the early 1980s over Beecham's patents for the production of ampicillin. Parallel importing by purchasers from the foreign licensee was an issue in several cases.

During the 1950s, Beecham discovered and took out three sets of patents in various countries of the world for penicillin products and the processes of manufacturing them. First, Beecham discovered and patented 6–amino penicillanic acid ('6–APA') and various processes for producing it. 6–APA was capable of combining with a vast number of organic

---

95 *Ibid.* at 106, Peabody being the wholesaler Briscoe had bought from in the United States.

96 That clarification of the rule in cases of domestic sale, of course, came after *Briscoe*'s case, see section 3.2.2 above. There is also the possible interpretation that Briscoe actually had knowledge.

compounds and proved to be a major discovery because it opened the way to the preparation of semi-synthetic penicillins. Subsequently, Beecham discovered that particularly good therapeutic results were obtained by combining 6–APA with alpha-amino-acyl groups. In particular, Beecham discovered that 6–APA reacted with the carboxylic acid of alpha-amino-benzene to produce alpha-amino-benzyl penicillin. Beecham also patented the combination of 6–APA with the alpha-amino-acyl group, the product alpha-amino-benzyl penicillin and various processes for the manufacture of these products. Alpha-amino-benzyl penicillin features an asymmetric carbon atom. This meant that alpha-amino-benzyl-penicillin could be produced in two forms: a *dextro* and a *laevo* epimer. After further research, Beecham discovered that the *dextro* epimer possessed antibiotic qualities of exceptionally high therapeutic value substantially greater than those of the *laevo* epimer. Beecham obtained yet another patent for the *dextro* epimer, which it called ampicillin, and two processes for separating the two epimers.

The demand for the products of Beecham's patents worldwide and the potential avenues for further research were such that Beecham entered into a number of licensing arrangements with the Bristol group. Of main concern to the present inquiry were two agreements, one made at New York and the other in Panama. The overall effect of these agreements was to appoint Bristol Beecham's exclusive licensee for North America and certain other named territories. Beecham reserved for itself a territory comprised substantially of the British Commonwealth.

Then, Bristol discovered that ampicillin combined with acetone to form a product which it called hetacillin. The singular feature of hetacillin was that the reaction was reversible. When combined with water, hetacillin reverted almost entirely to acetone and ampicillin. The reaction was quite simple, and quick, to induce. It could be effected by combining the hetacillin with water in a syringe or by ingesting hetacillin and letting it react with the moisture in the stomach. Accordingly, hetacillin had all the therapeutic advantages of ampicillin. Bristol also claimed it had additional advantages. The Bristol group began producing hetacillin in the United States and, among other places, distributed it in the United Kingdom, Singapore, Kenya, Hong Kong and Australia.

In the United Kingdom, Bristol did not seek to rely on its licence to produce ampicillin as a defence.[97] Therefore, the case depended solely on whether hetacillin infringed any of the Beecham patents. At first instance, in the Court of Appeal and the House of Lords, Bristol was unanimously held to have infringed the product and process claims relating to ampicillin

---

97 *Beecham Group Limited v Bristol Laboratories Limited* [1978] RPC 153; for interlocutory proceedings see [1967] RPC 406 (CA). Apart from the cases discussed below, other litigation on the infringement and validity questions occurred in New Zealand and South Africa. For New Zealand, matters culminated in a Court of Appeal decision: *Beecham Group Ltd v Bristol-Myers Co.* [1981] 2 NZLR 600 (CA); for South Africa, see *Beecham Group Ltd v B-M Group (Pty) Ltd* 1977(1) SA 50 (TPD, FC); [1977] RPC 220 and the further cases referred to in Burrell, *South African Patent Law and Practice.*

and alpha-amino-benzyl penicillin.[98] D.W. Falconer QC Esq., sitting as a deputy judge, and the Court of Appeal also found the product claims for 6–APA infringed. However, the House of Lords reserved its opinion on this point.[99]

Three of the Commonwealth cases clearly arose out of the same situation and all involved applications for interlocutory injunctions.[100] Beecham had licensed Bristol-Myers to make and sell ampicillin in North America under a licence governed by the law of the State of New York. Under a licence made in Panama, it had also licensed a Bristol subsidiary to make and sell ampicillin in certain named countries largely in Central and South America. This licence was governed by English law. Bristol-Myers had made the hetacillin in the United States and sold it to the Panamanian subsidiary there. The Panamanian subsidiary then sold it, in Panama, to a number of different companies. At this point, the facts reported and the arguments made begin to vary.

In the Kenyan action, the Panamanian subsidiary sold directly to International Products which imported the hetacillin into Kenya for sale. The only evidence about the licences was that the Kenyan patents were not patents expressly licensed to the Bristol group in the New York or Panamanian licences.

The defendants argued that *Tilghman's* case was distinguishable because International Products was a purchaser from the licensee and not the licensee. As a purchaser, it acquired good title to the drugs free from all restrictions under Beecham's patents anywhere in the world. The *Isler* and *Hazeltine* cases were not referred to the court, nor was *Briscoe's* case.

In Rudd J's opinion there were two central points. Neither of the licences in question expressly licensed any rights under the Kenyan patents and the Kenyan patents were rights separate to and independent of those which had been licensed.

Rudd J distinguished between sales by a licensee in the country of the licensed patent and sales outside that country. If the sale was in the country

98 The process claims were infringed by the importation of hetacillin under the 'Saccharin' doctrine because the process of manufacturing hetacillin relied on the production of ampicillin and alpha-amino-benzyl penicillin (under the licensed processes) as essential steps. The product claims were infringed under the 'pith and marrow' test since, to all intents and purposes, hetacillin in use was ampicillin. Its form as hetacillin was 'evanescent and reversible'. For 'Saccharin', see Cornish, *Intellectual Property Law*, at ¶6-010; for 'pith and marrow', *ibid.* at ¶¶6-002 to 6-006.

99 Having already found against Bristol on the other points, it was unnecessary to consider the point. Their Lordships, accordingly, did not wish to consider the potential ramifications for the pharmaceuticals industry of ruling that an antibiotic of which one of the constituents lawfully used in its production abroad could infringe a patent for that constituent in the United Kingdom. But see now Patents Act 1977 (United Kingdom) paragraph 60(1)(c), which requires the product to be produced directly from the patented process.

100   Kenya: *Beecham Group Limited v International Products Limited* [1968] RPC 129 (HC); Hong Kong: *Beecham Group Limited v Shewan Tomes (Traders) Limited* [1968] RPC 268; Singapore: *Sime Darby Singapore Ltd v Beecham Group Ltd* [1968] 2 MLJ 161 (Fed. Ct); at first instance in the High Court, [1968] 1 MLJ 86. It seems likely that the other cases involved the same agreements.

of the licensed patent, the sale by a licensee for that country could release the patented article from all further restrictions in that country if there was nothing to the contrary contained in the agreement. But, his Honour continued:

> I, however, respectfully do not agree that on such a sale in one country by a bare licensee the article is necessarily freed from the licensor's monopoly under unlicensed patents in other countries. . . .
>
> In the case of a sale by a licensee the matter must depend on the extent of the authority conferred on the licensee by the licensor under the licence or other agreements between them. In this case the American and Panamanian patents are not the same as the patents registered in Kenya, and it follows that a release or discharge from the monopoly of the United States or Panamanian patents does not necessarily imply a release from the Kenya patent. Whether there is such a release from the Kenya patent must depend upon the contract. The mere ownership of the patented articles does not imply a discharge from foreign patents. See *Boesch v Graff* in America and the *Tilghman's* case in England. In order to obtain freedom from the Kenya patent there must be a sale with the authority of the patentee in Kenya, and I would say that that authority must amount to an authority to discharge the patented articles from the operation of the Kenya patent.[101]

An argument appears to have been made to his Honour that under American law, the sale by the patentee would convey to the purchaser full and free title to deal in the patented article.[102] Rudd J distinguished two of the US cases referred to support this argument on the grounds that they involved dealings with a patent in one country alone.[103] A further case, *Curtiss Aeroplane*, involved greater difficulty; however, it was distinguishable from the instant facts because Rudd J considered it involved a licensee with full power to sell anywhere in the world not just in the territory of the licensed patent. His Honour was fortified in this distinction by the US court's own interpretation of *Tilghman's* case, the result of which the US court respectfully concurred in.[104]

His Honour concluded by rejecting any necessity to imply an authority to sell in Kenya:

> Even if one could imply additional terms into the contract there is no necessity to do so. There was ample scope for use under the licensed patents covering the world, with the exception of Kenya and other Commonwealth countries. There is no necessity to imply an extension involving use by a purchaser in Kenya free from the monopoly of patents registered in Kenya.[105]

101 *Ibid.* at 134 to 135. For *Boesch v Gräff* 133 US 697 (1890), see section 3.3.4 below.
102 The report does not put it exactly this way, but the same argument was run in the Singapore case and that is how the court interpreted it: see [1968] 2 MLJ 161, at 166.
103 [1968] RPC 129, at 132; referring to *Adams v Burke* 84 US 453 (1874) and *Keeler v Standard Folding Bed Co.* 157 US 659 (1894) and deriving some support for his conclusion from *Boesch v Gräff*, see section 3.3.4 below.
104 *Ibid.* at 133 to 134. Rudd J considered that UK law would reach the same result albeit by different reasoning to the Second Circuit on the facts in *Curtiss Aeroplane*. For *Curtiss Aeroplane and Motor Corporation v United Aircraft Engineering Corporation* 266 Fed. 71 (2d Cir. 1920), see section 3.3.4 below.
105 *Ibid.* at 136.

The licensees had 'ample scope' to exercise the rights they had bargained for without intervention from the courts.

The action in Hong Kong related only to Beecham's first two patents. The Hong Kong Supreme Court in its Appellate Jurisdiction found that hetacillin was an infringement and the defendants claimed Beecham's consent to their acts by its licences. The court considered that the New York licence was expressly limited to granting rights in the United States and Canada. The terms of the Panamanian licence proved to the court also expressly excluded Hong Kong and Kowloon from the terms of the grant and, in addition, the court referred in the report to a further term of the licence which expressly denied any right to sell where 'prevented by letters patent not licensed hereunder'.[106]

In these circumstances, the court accepted the plaintiff's analysis of the effect of a licence as simply an immunity, entitling the licensee to do something which would otherwise be unlawful. Accordingly, it was necessary to investigate the terms of the licence to ascertain the extent of the immunity conferred. All that was conferred here was immunity from action in the US courts for infringement of the patents in the United States.[107]

Later in the judgment, the court explained its understanding of *Tilghman's* case:

> The basis of this decision is that when the patentee issues his licence he relieves his licensee of the liability to actions for infringement within the same territorial limits as is covered by the patent; and that is all. *Consequently, the licence, by reference to the patent, carries its own inherent territorial limitation without any express words to that effect*, unless it can be extended expressly, or by necessary implication, beyond those territorial limits. *(Emphasis added)*[108]

In view of the court's findings about the express terms of the licences, this passage is *obiter*. Nevertheless, as argued earlier, it corresponds with the judicial approach in *Tilghman's* case in contrast to *Betts v Willmott* and makes explicit the *inherent* limitation of the licence to the jurisdiction of the patent concerned.

A further variation of the facts with similar emphasis on the territorial limits of patent rights arose in Singapore. Here, 'Sime Darby' had bought in Panama from the Panamanian subsidiary and was importing the hetacillin into Singapore and offering it for sale. The technical questions on whether hetacillin infringed Beecham's patents were resolved in Beecham's favour and the issue turned on consent. Since both the Bristol companies had made and sold the hetacillin in countries where they were expressly licensed to do so, they were exonerated.[109]

---

106   [1968] RPC 268, at 284 and 285 for the New York and Panamanian licences, respectively.
107   *Ibid*. at 284 to 285. Compare *Heap v Hartley* (1888) 5 RPC 603 (Ch. County Palatine), on appeal (1889) 42 Ch. D 461 (CA).
108   *Ibid*. at 286.
109   [1968] 2 MLJ 161, at 166. The court noted that the injunction was granted only against International Products in the Kenyan action and not Bristol itself.

Sime Darby was in a different position. Wee Chong Jin CJ, for the court, held that:

> A licensee's rights depend on his grant and prima facie a grant of a licence to sell in one country gives no rights to sell elsewhere. Bristol's licence agreements in our view do not extend these prima facie rights and clause H of the sixth article, which we have earlier set out, clearly indicates that Bristol cannot sell where Beecham or any one else for that matter has any patent which can prevent Bristol from so selling.[110]

Betts v Willmott was distinguished, as a case of vendor and purchaser, along the lines taken by Cotton LJ in *Tilghman's* case which 'clearly' applied.[111] Hence, as the Bristol group had no rights over Singapore to confer, Beecham had not consented to Sime Darby's actions and it was an infringer. Finally, the Chief Justice rejected Sime Darby's arguments that American law, which governed the licence to Bristol-Myers, would lead to a different result, agreeing with Rudd J's opinion in the Kenyan case.[112]

Brief mention only need be made of the Full High Court's ruling in Australia.[113] As it was also an application for an interlocutory injunction, the court was anxious not to preclude proper investigation of the facts at trial. The competing legal arguments were alluded to shortly and the court resolved the case into two legal questions: whether infringement under the *Saccharin* doctrine was made out and which of *Betts v Willmott* and *Tilghman's* case, if either, applied. The court, however, took the comparatively rare step of granting the interlocutory injunction preventing Bristol selling hetacillin in Australia because:

> All that can be said without danger of prejudicing the ultimate decision is that upon the material at present before the Court the plaintiff has shown, in our opinion, so substantial a probability of succeeding in the action that it is entitled to have the status quo preserved.[114]

Accordingly, *at least* three separate courts, Rudd J in Kenya, the Appellate Jurisdiction in Hong Kong and the Federal Court in Singapore, have placed heavy emphasis on the territorial nature of patent rights.[115] All

---

110 *Ibid*. Clause H as set out at 165 provided:

> Nothing contained in this agreement shall be construed as preventing either party hereto from manufacturing, using or selling any product or from using any process or apparatus in any area of the world, except in so far as said party may be prevented from so doing by Letters Patent not licensed hereunder.

111 For Cotton LJ's distinction of *Betts v Willmott* in *Tilghman*, see Note 87 above.

112 *Ibid*. The context presumably indicates that his Honour interpreted this to be the effect of American law. There does in fact appear to be authority for this view, see *Canadian Filters (Harwich) Limited v Lear-Siegler Inc*. 412 F. 2d 577 (1st Cir. 1969), but this was not dealing expressly with the effect of any exhaustion doctrine, as to which see section 3.3.2. below.

113 *Beecham Group Limited v Bristol Laboratories Pty Limited* (1968) 118 CLR 618; [1968] RPC 301.

114 *Ibid*. at 625; 304.

115 Indeed, the approach in the Kenyan case together with *Tilghman*, has led some commentators to argue that consent is *always* rebutted wherever all that is granted in the foreign market is a right to use the foreign patent: Walton *et al., Patent Laws of Europe and the United Kingdom*, at ¶949.

clearly thought that the separate territorial existence of the different patents was sufficient justification not to imply authority to sell in the country of importation. A licensee in one country had sufficient business opportunity in that country to preclude any need to imply a further licence. Notably, it was not necessary in any of the cases to show that the purchaser had any knowledge of the limits to its title which was considered so crucial by Lord Hatherley in *Betts v Willmott* and in almost all of the cases on domestic sales. The underlying assumption, which can be traced back to Lindley LJ in *Tilghman's* case and made explicit in the Hong Kong court's *dictum*, is that a grant of rights under one patent does not convey rights under another. The fact that foreign trade was involved, not domestic trade, was considered to introduce significant qualifications on the rules governing domestic trade.

The approach taken in the litigation over ampicillin continued in *Minnesota Mining and Manufacturing Company v Geerpres Europe Limited*.[116] The plaintiff owned patents in the United States and the United Kingdom for an abrasive cleaning and scouring material. It had licensed its US patent to Union Carbide. The evidence before the court indicated that this licence did not include a licence under the UK patent. Union Carbide sold patented abrasive to a company in the United States which, in turn, sold it to Geerpres in the Netherlands. Geerpres then sought to import it from the Netherlands into the United Kingdom. The plaintiff sued for infringement of its UK patent and applied for an interlocutory injunction.

Graham J rejected Geerpres' argument that the plaintiff's patent rights were exhausted by the sale under licence in the United States. His Lordship found that the instant case came within the principle of *Tilghman's* case rather than *Betts v Willmott*:

> [Geerpres] are not, as in *Betts v Willmott*, purchasers from the patentees without notice of any restrictions on their rights: nor is this a case where, contrary to the decision in *Deutsche Grammophon*, the patentee himself has sold the goods in question in one country and then tried to stop their import into another such country by virtue of his patent in that second jurisdiction. . . . It seems to me that, on the contrary, [Geerpres] here are basically in the same position as the licensees in the *Tilghman* case, namely, that they have no greater right in the articles which they bought from James H. Rhodes & Co. in New York than the latter could give them. Rhodes, it is clear, bought the articles from Union Carbide, who were not the patentees, but were licensees of the [plaintiff] under their United States patent only. . . . no right by that agreement [was] given to Union Carbide to license anyone under the [plaintiff's] English patent here in question. This being the position, Union Carbide cannot pass on to Rhodes any rights which they themselves have not got, and Rhodes equally cannot pass on any such rights to [Geerpres]. The latter, therefore, though they could presumably use or sell the goods in question in the U.S.A., cannot import them into this country without running foul of the [plaintiff's] English letters patent.[117]

---

116   [1974] RPC 35.
117   *Ibid.* at 40 to 41. For consideration of the issues raised by the United Kingdom's membership of the European Communities, see Chapters 6 and 7 below.

Subsequently, the UK Court of Appeal granted the UK assignee of a patent an interlocutory injunction against the assignors/inventors who were importing and offering for sale a product covered by the patent.[118] The reasoning presumably proceeded from the separate, territorial nature of the patent as in the case of a purchaser from an assignee envisaged by Lord Hatherley. The court, however, did not discuss the point, simply referring to the fact that the assignee held the patent.[119]

Since *Betts v Willmott* there has been, then, an unbroken chain of cases stressing the territorial independence of patent rights and the domestic patentee's power to block parallel imports under the patent without positive restrictions of the sort envisaged by Lord Hatherley, and which are essential for domestic sales under a patent. That chain has now been broken in Malaysia.

VC George J appears to have treated the case as an unencumbered sale in the foreign market governed by *Betts v Willmott*.[120] 'SKF' held patents for a drug, cimetideine (widely known as 'Tagamet'), in many parts of the world including the United Kingdom and West Malaysia. A UK and a Belgian 'associated' company made and sold the drug for SKF in the United Kingdom and Belgium, respectively. A further associated company also made and sold the drug in Australia. The UK producer only sold to specified wholesalers in the United Kingdom and only on condition that they not export it, or sell for export, from the European Communities. The goods were not, however, labelled to indicate that limitation. Nor was similar evidence proved about sales by either the Belgian or the Australian producer.

SKF appointed 'Zuellig' as the sole importer and distributor of the drug for West Malaysia. Zuellig was, however, further restricted to buying its needs from the Australian producer.[121] 'Salim' was a druggist in West Malaysia and had been buying cimetideine from Zuellig. It also arranged to buy quantities from a wholesaler in the United Kingdom, Stainweld, and was importing them into West Malaysia. Stainweld was not an authorised distributor of SKF's in the United Kingdom. VC George J found as a fact that Salim had no notice of any restrictions on the sale of the supplies it bought in

118 *Netlon v Bridport-Gundry Ltd* [1979] FSR 530 (CA).

119 The 'assignee', although not the inventor, was in fact the original patentee in both the United Kingdom and Italy, the invention having been communicated to it along with the right to patent. The court refused to go into the EC issues, for which see Chapters 6 and 7 below.

120 *Smith Kline & French Laboratories Ltd v Salim (Malaysia) Sdn Bhd* (1989) 15 IPR 677; [1989] FSR 407 (HC, Kuala Lumpur).

121 Zuellig's rights as sole, rather than 'exclusive', importer presumably precluded the possibility that it might itself prevent the importation: see *Roussel-Uclaf v GD Searle & Co. Ltd* [1977] FSR 125, at 130; where, on an interlocutory application, Graham J considered an exclusive licensee could sue its licensor and another licensee for infringement by importation, but refused an interlocutory injunction on the balance of convenience. But see the qualification ooon an exclusive licensee's powers as against third parties in 35 Halsbury (4th ed.) at ¶407, Note 4., relying on Warrington J's opinion in *Gillette Safety Razor Company Limited v A.W. Gamage Limited* (1908) 25 RPC 492, appeal upheld 25 RPC 782 (CA), at Note 63 to 67 above.

the United Kingdom from Stainweld. His Honour also considered it highly likely that Stainweld had also bought the drug free of any restrictions since there was evidence before his Honour that the 'Belgian' drug was on sale in the United Kingdom and its sale could not be restricted under EC law.[122]

Having been notified by solicitor's letter of the restrictions, Salim discontinued its imports from the United Kingdom. The litigation continued over the imports made before notification.

In these circumstances, VC George J held:

> In a situation where the drug manufactured in the United Kingdom and in Belgium is sold in the open market in the United Kingdom without notice of restrictions in respect of resale given to the purchaser, any complaint of breach of such restrictions cannot be heard.[123]

His Honour then referred to the *Menck* case and *Time-Life* which explained that the implication of unencumbered sale was necessary as a matter of business efficacy under a patent because the patent grant conferred an absolute power to block any dealings in the article protected.[124] He then concluded:

> . . . where the plaintiffs by themselves or by their associated company sell their patented product in, say, the United Kingdom, without giving effective notice of any restrictions in respect of the resale and the produce is purchased by a Malaysian merchant by way of import, that the plaintiffs or some associated company of the plaintiffs happen to have patent rights in West Malaysia that gives them exclusive rights to import the product into West Malaysia will be of no avail to them vis-à-vis such an innocent importer of the product.[125]

Treated simply as a case where the domestic patentee had sold the product on the foreign market without restriction, his Honour's decision stands alongside *Betts v Willmott* and, if it be too late in the day to overturn that authority, is unexceptionable. VC George J's ruling, however, goes much further than that and is, with respect, questionable on a number of grounds.

First, his Honour extended the principle in *Betts v Willmott* to cover sales abroad by 'associated' companies. (Indeed, in the first quotation above from his Honour's judgment at page 283, VC George J refers only to purchase 'in the open market' and does not qualify the principle to sale by the domestic patentee.) This appears to be the first time in a patents

---

122 For some reason this interpretation of EC law did not affect the UK company. With respect, the interpretation may be perfectly accurate for intra-EC trade, but whether it governs trade outside the European Communities requires further consideration, see Chapter 6 below. Note also the possibility that exhaustion of the UK patent under EC law could also operate to exhaust the patent extension in Hong Kong: *The Wellcome Foundation Ltd v Attorney General*, unreported, Kaplan J, 4 March 1992, [1992] EIPR D-137 as discussed in Paul Rawlinson, 'Parallel Imports: A Welcome Decision for Asia', [1992] EIPR 239, 241.
123 15 IPR 677, at 683.
124 *Ibid*. at 683 to 684; for *Interstate Parcel Express Co. v Time-Life International (Nederlands) BV* (1977) 138 CLR 534, see Chapter 4.2.2(c) below.
125 *Ibid*. at 684.

case that an Anglo-Commonwealth court has so willingly disregarded the separate legal personality of corporate bodies.[126]

Second, his Honour's approach stands in marked contrast to the chain of authority since *Tilghman's* case. Neither it nor the subsequent cases applying it appear to have been referred to his Honour.

The sales in the foreign market, in *Salim*, seem to have been by 'associated' companies which must be considered in the position of licensees on the usual principles governing legal personality. In such cases, from *Tilghman's* case onwards, the crucial question has been what authority did the licensee in the foreign market possess and the territorial nature of patent rights precluded *any* assumption of authority to sell under the domestic patent. SKF's failure to prove the terms of its Belgian associate's licence may seem like a vital omission.

In particular, the cases involving Beecham's patents relating to ampicillin steadfastly refused to draw an implied consent to importation as a matter of business necessity because the foreign licensee had ample scope to exploit its rights in the foreign market. In drawing the implication, on the other hand, VC George J relied in part on the *Time-Life* case which involved copyright and was primarily concerned with distinguishing copyright from patents rather than any distinction under patent law between domestic sales and sale in a foreign market.[127] The cases on Beecham's ampicillin patents, which did recognise that distinction, were also not considered in the *Time-Life* case.

Further, where the foreign sale has been made by a licensee, it has not generally been necessary to show that the defendant had notice of the restrictions. The fact that the licensee did not have authority to sell in the domestic market has precluded it from conferring authority on the defendant. VC George J, however, made such notice brought home to the defendant crucial as in *Betts v Willmott* and the cases on domestic sales. His Honour considered it 'inexplicable' that SKF had not caused the packaging and labelling of its drug to bear the appropriate notice.[128]

In summary, then, *Salim* represents a shift away from the territorial approach predominant for over a century back to a more universalist view like that of Lord Hatherley in *Betts v Willmott*. How widely that shift will gain acceptance remains to be seen. Certainly, there is some reason to believe VC George J's opinion is representative of Malaysian policy and, potentially, other countries similarly placed.[129]

126　A similar approach has been suggested in New Zealand on the doubtful authority of *Betts v Willmott*, see Andrew Brown and Anthony Grant, *The Law of Intellectual Property in New Zealand*, Butterworths, 1989, at ¶6.74. Even in trade marks, the proposition has not received much enthusiasm apart from the *Revlon* case, see Chapter 2.2 above.

127　For *Time-Life*, see Chapter 4.2.2(c) below.

128　At 15 IPR 677, at 684, his Honour goes so far as to suggest that this may have been a deliberate omission on SKF's part to take advantage of innocent purchasers buying in good faith in 'one of the great market places of the world'.

129　Malaysia has, for example, recently amended its copyright law to allow parallel imports, see Khaw Lake Tee, 'The 1990 Amendments to the Malaysian Copyright Act

Even so, *Salim* demonstrates one further powerful point about the use of patents to block parallel imports. Once Salim was notified of SKF's position it was precluded from further parallel importing. Anglo-Commonwealth law has steadfastly refused to adopt a doctrine of exhaustion and, perhaps unlike the corresponding position under trade mark law, patents can be used quite effectively to block parallel imports.[130]

3.3 The United States of America

3.3.1 The Patent Code

Broadly speaking, US patent law will allow patents to block parallel imports in similar circumstances to Anglo-Commonwealth law. However, while US law shares many basic propositions in common with Anglo-Commonwealth law, the reasoning adopted by the US courts may be somewhat different.

Under the Patent Code, the patentee is granted the right to exclude others from making, using or selling the patented invention within the United States during the term of the patent.[131]

Like its Anglo-Commonwealth counterparts, a US patent is a territorial right. It confers exclusive rights within the 'United States'. Accordingly, it is not an infringement of a US patent to make, use or sell outside the United States an invention patented in the United States. Infringement of a US patent requires the doing of an act comprised in the patent monopoly within the territory of the United States.[132]

It follows, then, that unauthorised importation into the United States and use or sale of an article patented in the United States infringes the US patent.[133] But, the patentee does not have an action based on its US patent until a patented article enters the United States.[134]

1987', [1991] EIPR 132, at 135 to 137. Contrast Kaplan J's ruling in *The Wellcome Foundation Ltd v Attorney General* [1992] EIPR D-137 and [1992] EIPR 239.

130   For trade marks, see Chapter 2.2 above.

131   35 USC §§154, 271(a) (1982) under US Constitution, Article 1, §8. §154 provides the positive grant of the exclusive right to the patentee:

> Every patent shall contain . . . a grant to the patentee, his heirs or assigns, for the term of seventeen years, of the right to exclude others from making, using, or selling the invention throughout the US . . .

§271 confers the right to sue for infringement providing under the heading 'Infringement of Patents':

> Except as otherwise provided in this title, whoever without authority makes, uses or sells any patented invention, within the United States during the term of the patent therefor, infringes the patent.

For convenience, the title of the US Code is referred to as 'the Patent Code'.

132   35 USC §154 (1985); *Deepsouth Packing Co. v Laitram Corporation* 406 US 518 (1972); the decision in this case is now affected by 35 USC §271(g), introduced in 1984. See Donald S. Chisum, 4 *Patents: A Treatise on the Law of Patentability, Validity and Infringement*, Matthew Bender & Co. Inc., 1987, 1991, at §16.05; E.B. Lipscomb III, *Lipscomb's Walker on Patents*, The Lawyer's Co-operative Publishing Co., 1987 (3rd ed.), at §22.12.

133   *Boesch v Gräff* 133 US 697 (1890), section 3.3.4 below.

134   *Re Northern Pigment Company* 71 F. 2d 447, at 454, 458 (CCPA 1934); *In re Orion Co.* 71 F. 2d 458 (CCPA 1934).

Prior to 23 February 1989, however, it was not an infringement of a US patent to import into the United States a product made abroad according to a process which was patented in the United States.[135] The patentee did have, and continues to have, a right to seek administrative relief under section 337 of the Tariff Act of 1930.[136] On 23 February 1989, the Process Patent Amendments Act of 1988 came into force, conferring on US patentees of processes power to sue for the importation of products made abroad according to the patent.[137] The new legislation has not been tested by a parallel import case yet.

Accordingly, the central question now is whether the importation takes place with the authority of the US patentee. As in the Anglo-Commonwealth cases, this in turn becomes a question of what authority may be inferred from the fact of authorised sale abroad. Also, a tension similar to that in the Anglo-Commonwealth cases over the significance of the separate, independent nature of patent rights exists. That tension is exacerbated by the adoption of a doctrine of domestic exhaustion by the US courts.

3.3.2 Domestic exhaustion

The courts were compelled to allow market division within the United States by the terms of the Patent Code itself.[138] The extent to which the patentee could divide its markets territorially was substantially curtailed, however, by a theory of exhaustion of the patent grant. Once the patentee had put the patented article onto the market and received the price for it, the patentee was *deemed* to have received the benefit of the exclusive right. The article

---

135 *Merrill v Yeomans* 94 US 568, at 572 to 574 (1876); *American Ball Co. v Federal Cartridge Corporation* 70 F. 2d 579, at 582 (8th Cir. 1934); *In re Orion Co.* 71 F. 2d 458 (CCPA 1934); *Smith v Snow* 294 US 1 (1935); *Sutton v Gulf Smokeless Coal Co.* 77 F. 2d 439 (4th Cir. 1935); *In re Amtorg Trading Corp.* 75 F. 2d 826 (CCPA, 1935); *B.B. Chemical Co. v Ellis* 117 F. 2d 829 (1st Cir. 1941) *affd* 314 US 495; *John Mohr & Sons v Vacudyne Corporation* 354 F. Supp. 113 (ND Ill. 1973); *Astra-Sjuco AB v ITC* 207 USPQ 1, at 8 (CCPA 1980).

136 Note, however, that the use of section 337 in its unamended form against patents is the subject of a GATT panel condemnation, John W. Rogers III, 'The Demise of Section 337's GATT-legality', [1990] EIPR 275. Before that, section 337 was substantially amended by the Omnibus Trade and Competitiveness Act of 1988, Pub. L. No. 100–418, 102 Stat. 1563. For analysis of attempts to rely on the unamended procedure in the context of patents, see Keith E. George, 'Importation of Articles Produced by Patented Processes: Unfair Trade Practices or Infringement?', 18 *George Washington Journal of International Law and Economics* 129 (1984); James Matthew Gould, 'Protecting Owners of US Process Patents from the Importation of Pharmaceuticals Made Abroad by Use of the Patented Process: Current Options, Proposed Legislation and a GATT Solution', 42 *Food Drug Cosmetic Law Journal* 346 (1987) and generally, Chisum, 4 *Patents*, at §16.05[3] Note 13. For reform options proposed to date, see Elizabeth M. Saltzer, 'The Future of Section 337 of the Tariff Act of 1930: The Response of the United States Trade Representative to the GATT Panel Report', (1992) 23 IIC 350.

137 35 USC §271(g) also part of the Omnibus Trade and Competitiveness Act; Chisum, 4 *Patents*, §16.02[6] at Notes 8 and 9. For a successful action under the new legislation, see *Bristol-Myers Co. v Erbamont Inc.* 723 F. Supp. 1038 (DDel. 1989).

138 35 USC §261.

was said to pass outside the scope of the 'monopoly'. The effectiveness of any conditions on subsequent dealings in the article then fell to be determined according to the general law.

This rule was conclusively established by the Supreme Court in *Keeler v Standard Folding Bed Company*.[139] The patent in question related to a type of folding bedstead. It had been assigned for the state of Massachusetts to the respondent, Standard, where Keeler ran a furniture business. Knowing of Standard's rights, Keeler bought a carload of the patented beds in Michigan from Welch, which owned the patent rights there, to sell them in Massachusetts. When he commenced selling them in Massachusetts, Standard sued for infringement. The Circuit Court granted an injunction and Keeler appealed. The question presented to the court was:

> . . . whether a dealer in patented articles, doing business in Massachusetts, and knowing that the right to manufacture, use and sell such articles within that State belongs to another, may purchase such articles of the patentee in Michigan, in the ordinary course of trade, for the purpose of resale in Massachusetts, and may sell them there in defiance of the rights of the licensee.

Shiras J, speaking for the majority, summarised the previous decisions of the court as establishing the principle that:

> . . . a person who buys patented articles from a person who has the right to sell, though within a restricted territory, has a right to use and sell such articles in all and any part of the United States; that when the royalty has once been paid to a party entitled to receive it, that patented article becomes the absolute, unrestricted property of the purchaser, with the right to sell it as an essential incident of such ownership.[140]

Payment of the royalty (or other price) released the article from the exclusive right conferred by the patent. The patent was, in effect, exhausted as far as that article was concerned because the patentee had received the benefit intended by statute.

In his Honour's view, the court was balancing two competing interests. The first interest was the patentee's interest, conferred by statute, in securing the reward for the invention made available to the public. The public's interest in being able to deal in goods unfettered by restrictions, the policy of commercial convenience, was the second interest. The resulting rule appropriately balanced the conflicting claims:

> The conclusion reached does not deprive a patentee of his just rights, because no article can be unfettered from the claim of his monopoly without paying

---

139   157 US 659 (1895). In addition to this and the other cases noted below, the Supreme Court also considered the question in *Rubber Co. v Goodyear* 76 US (9 Wall.) 788 (1869); the *Paper Bag Cases* 105 US 766 (1881). For copyright, see *Bobbs-Merrill Co. v Strauss* 210 US 339 (1908), see Chapter 4.3.3(a) below; for a similar approach involving trade marks, see *The Parkway Baking Co. Inc. v Freihofer Baking Company Inc.* 255 F. 2d 641 (2d Cir. 1958). For EC law and patents, see 15/74 *Sterling Drug* [1974] ECR 1147, Chapter 6.3.1 below.
140   *Ibid.* at 664, see also 666.

its tribute. The inconvenience and annoyance to the public that an opposite conclusion would entail are too obvious to require illustration.[141]

Shiras J was prepared, however, to leave open the possibility of one qualification: he reserved the question of the effect of a special contract brought home against the purchaser:

> . . . we think it follows that one who buys patented articles of manufacture from one authorised to sell them becomes possessed of an absolute property in such articles, unrestricted in time or place. Whether a patentee may protect himself and his assignees by special contracts brought home to the purchasers is not a question before us, and upon which we express no opinion. It is, however, obvious that such a question would arise as a question of contract, and not as one under the inherent meaning and effect of the patent laws.[142]

There are a number of differences between Shiras J's approach and that of the Anglo-Commonwealth cases. In the United States, the payment of the price demanded released the patented article from 'tribute'. This ground had been repeatedly overlooked in favour of examination of the patentee's consent in the Anglo-Commonwealth cases. In consequence, Anglo-Commonwealth courts had readily acknowledged the power of special notice, brought home to the purchaser, to bind the purchaser as a matter of *patent law*.[143] The majority in the US Supreme Court, however, refused to accord any weight to notice, requiring a special *contract*; that contract being valid, *if at all*, not under the patent but in contract law.

Brown J, with Fuller CJ and Field J concurring, dissented. His Honour clearly felt anxious about allowing a buyer to act in violation of the patent right when that buyer was fully aware of the patentee's rights. Brown J felt that the course of authority bound him to accept the general rule of exhaustion when all that was in issue was a right to use the patented article. He was not, however, prepared to extend that rule to a case where the buyer bought the articles for resale.[144] Some of the earlier cases did concern only the right to use;[145] and some clearly rested on the purported distinction between the right to use and the right to sell.[146] *Adams v Burke* on its facts, however, did not involve such a distinction. Moreover, as the dissent in *Adams v Burke* argued, the distinction appears purely arbitrary. But, in

---

141 *Ibid.* at 666 to 667. The main inconveniences in his Honour's mind were identified at 662 in series of rhetorical questions which included whether a person, having bought a patented article, could subsequently remove with it to another part of the country and whether it should be treated like any other item of personal property passing on death to the estate's legal representatives. See also at 672 *per* Brown J in dissent.

142 *Ibid.* at 666.

143 The Anglo-Commonwealth courts presumed that no limitation was intended and imposed some stringency on how and when notice would be effected, see the *Menck* case in section 3.2.2 above.

144 157 US 659, at 671 to 672.

145 *Wilson v Rousseau* 4. How. 646 (1846); *Bloomer v McQuewan* 55 US (14 How.) 539; *Bloomer v Millinger* 68 US (1 Wall.) 340, see Notes 160 to 163 below.

146 See especially *Adams v Burke* 84 US (17 Wall.) 453, at 455, 456 *per* Miller J (1873), see text at Note 153 and following below.

fairness to Brown J, his Honour appears to accept the rule for the right to use only on the ground that it is too late in the day for change.

Wilson v Rousseau, Bloomer v McQuewan and *Bloomer v Millinger* all concerned the right to continue using a patented invention in a defined area after the term of the initial patent expired and was renewed. The defendant in each case was allowed to continue use, the patentee being 'entitled to but one royalty for a patented machine'.[147]

A patentee had, however, successfully sued a 'user' in *Mitchell v Hawley*, apparently on the theory that the rights granted under the licence were expressly limited in time.[148] Hawley owned a patent for improved machinery in felting hats. He granted one Bayley the exclusive right to exercise the rights under the patent for the states of Massachusetts and New Hampshire. The licence was expressed to be made for the duration of 'the remainder of the original term of the said letters patent'. The licence also enjoined Bayley not in any way or form to dispose of, sell, or grant any licence to use the machines beyond the third day of May 1867, the date the initial term would expire. (Bayley also had the right to renew his licence on payment of a fair and reasonable compensation if the patent was renewed.) Bayley licensed Mitchell to run and use two sets of the machines at a town in Massachusetts. This licence does not appear to have been subject to any conditions. When the patent was renewed for a further term, Hawley sued Mitchell for infringement.

According to a unanimous Supreme Court, a purchaser of a patented article did not acquire any interest in the patent but did acquire title to the actual article which, *to the extent of the sale*, ceased to be within the limits of the patent monopoly. The exhaustion principle *only* applied to unconditional sales of patented articles.[149] Here, the general rule did not apply because Hawley had not given Bayley an unlimited title. Accordingly, Bayley could not confer on Mitchell rights which he did not himself possess. Notice to Mitchell of that limitation was not essential because the law put the onus on the purchaser to check whether the seller had authority to convey good title.[150]

Mitchell v Hawley must be considered of singularly doubtful authority. Shiras J in *Keeler* referred to it only for the proposition that, by sale, a patentee parts with his exclusive right in the article.[151] Admittedly, *Mitchell v Hawley* involved a licence (in fact, a sub-licence) of a right to use and not sale. But, it is difficult to see why a sub-licensee without notice of any conditions should be denied protection under a policy of commercial

---

147   *Bloomer v Millinger* 68 US (1 Wall.) 340, at 350; see also *Chaffee v Boston Belting Company* 63 US (22 How.) 217, at 223 *per* Clifford J (1859) where the defendant's reliance on an assignment during the first term of the patent failed because its assignor had granted a full, exclusive licence to another *before* the assignment and the defendant held no authority from the exclusive licensee.

148   83 US (16 Wall.) 544 (1872); see Ward S. Bowman Jr, *Patent and Antitrust: A Legal and Economic Appraisal*, The University of Chicago Press, 1973, 143 to 145.

149   *Ibid.* at 547 to 548 *per* Clifford J.

150   *Ibid.* at 550.

151   157 US 659, at 663.

convenience when that same policy intervenes to 'protect' a purchaser with notice.

The case has also been described as 'one of those cases the Court is disposed quietly to forget'.[152] Nowhere is this better demonstrated than by the Supreme Court's decision one year later in *Adams v Burke*.[153] At least for territorial, rather than time, restrictions, the majority refused to apply the principle of *nemo dat quod non habet* in favour of a theory of exhaustion.

A patent had been granted for an improved form of coffin lid. The patentee assigned all its right, title and interest in the patent 'for, to and in a circle whose radius is ten miles, having the city of Boston as a centre'. Somewhat later, the patentee assigned the rest of its interest to Adams. The Boston assignees sold several coffin lids in Boston to Burke, an undertaker who carried on his business at Natick which was about 17 miles from Boston. He intended to use the coffin lids at Natick and did so. Adams, of course, sued Burke for patent infringement, and failed.[154]

By majority, the Supreme Court held that Burke could use the coffin lids outside the territory in which the sellers' rights extended. In other words, the sellers could authorise Burke to use the patented article outside their territory even though they could not themselves use the patented articles there. This resulted from the nature of the article and the right in question. Miller J held that the sole value of the coffin lid was in its use and the implications to be drawn from a transfer of the right to use were different to those of a transfer of the rights to make or sell. His Honour acknowledged that each of the rights conferred by a patent was a separate, substantive right capable of being dealt with independently of the others. But, this general principle required some qualification when the sole value of the article was in its use and the right concerned was the right to use alone:

> But, in the essential nature of things, when the patentee, or the person having his rights, sells a machine or instrument whose sole value is in its use, he receives the consideration for its use and he parts with the right to restrict that use. The article, in the language of the court, passes without the limit of the monopoly. . . . That is to say, the patentee or the assignee having in the act of sale received all the royalty or consideration which he claims for the use of his invention in that particular machine or instrument, it is open to the use of the purchaser without further restriction on account of the monopoly of the patentees.[155]

This was particularly the case for coffin lids, which were capable of use once and only once. His Honour concluded by reiterating the vital distinction between the rights conferred by a patent:

> Whatever, therefore, may be the rule when patentees subdivide territorially their patents, as to the exclusive right *to make* or *to sell* within a limited

152 Bowman, *Patent and Antitrust Law*, at 143 Note 9.
153 *Adams v Burke* 84 US (17 Wall.) 453 (1873).
154 For a corresponding unsuccessful case against the vendor rather than the purchaser, see *Hobbie v Jennison* 149 US 355 (1893). (Sale completed in the vendor's designated territory, vendor knew the articles were intended for use in another's territory.)
155 *Ibid.* at 456.

territory, we hold that in the class of machines or implements we have described, when they are once lawfully made and sold, there is no restriction on their *use* to be implied for the benefit of the patentee or his assignee or licensees.[156]

Bradley, Swayne and Strong JJ dissented in an opinion delivered by Bradley J. Bradley J expressed concern about allowing territorial division of domestic markets but found that the patents statute itself precluded judicial attack on this policy. His Honour advanced three reasons for rejecting the arguments adopted by the majority.[157] First, the words of grant to the assignees were the same for each right. According a different meaning to the words granting the right to use would, therefore, defeat the intention of the parties. The assignees could take more than they had bargained and paid for, rendering the balance of the rights remaining to the patentee valueless or a patentee could extract large sums from an assignee for an assignment, then effectively defeat the assignment.[158] Second, it was questionable how the assignees could confer greater rights than they possessed themselves. Third, Bradley J considered that the cases relied on by Miller J were distinguishable because they were concerned with restrictions on the time during which a right could be exercised rather than the territory. It is not immediately apparent, however, why territorial restraints should be treated more liberally than time limitations. Moreover, his Honour's opinion does not take into account *Mitchell v Hawley*, which might otherwise be thought to support the main thrust of the dissent.[159]

The key factor in Miller J's reasoning was that the court was concerned with articles whose sole value was in their use. That was the class of goods which his Honour had described. For such articles, the law *deemed* that purchasers could deal with them once the patentee had received the price the patentee claimed for their use. Having received that price, the patent was exhausted as far as that particular article was concerned because the advantage intended by statute had been gained. This distinction is, with respect, open to criticism.

The coffin lids in *Adams v Burke* themselves hardly seem to fit the proposed category. The lids themselves were to undergo further 'processing' by being incorporated with a base to make a whole. Burke did not intend to bury himself 'several' times, he intended to sell them to purchasers from him of coffins. Burke was not an end-user, but a 'middleman'.

In any event, the concept of an article whose sole value lies in its use does not appear to define a distinct class. The whole point of producing an article is that someone will use it in some way for some purpose. The steps of production and sale are simply the means by which that article

---

156   *Ibid.* at 456 to 457 (*Miller J's emphasis*).
157   *Ibid.* at 458 to 460.
158   In *Keeler*, Shiras J agreed with this point, although to different ends, asking, 'And is there any solid distinction to be made, in such a case, between the right to use and the right to sell?': 157 US 659, at 662.
159   Bowman notes that neither Miller nor Bradley JJ referred to *Mitchell v Hawley: Patent and Antitrust Law*, at 144.

reaches its user. Moreover, any article can be sold provided a willing buyer can be found.

The concept of an article whose sole value lies in its use can be traced back to *Bloomer v McQuewan*. The patent there was for a planing machine which proved so successful that Congress had extended the term of the patent twice. The machine seems to have been fairly substantial, being 'set up' at workshops and factories. In the first case under the patent, *Wilson v Rousseau*, an assignee for a certain territory was permitted to sue an invader of his territory during the first renewal because the Act extending the term expressly preserved the rights of those using the machines at the date of the renewal.[160] Then *Bloomer v McQuewan* arose. Barnet had bought from the original patentee the right to make and use 50 machines at Pittsburgh during 'the said term' of the patent. McQuewan bought two of these from Barnet and used them there. Later, under the second renewal, Bloomer took an assignment of the exclusive right to build and use planing machines under the patent for an area which included Pittsburgh and sought to stop McQuewan using the machines without a new licence.

For the majority, Taney CJ held that Bloomer failed under the exhaustion doctrine. The machine's purchaser, having bought it for the purposes of 'using it in the ordinary pursuits of life', acquired it free of the patent monopoly. His Honour concluded:

> The right to construct and use these machines had been purchased and paid for without any limitation as to the time for which they could be used. They were the property of the respondents. *Their only value consists in their use.* (*Emphasis added*)[161]

So, Taney CJ drew a distinction between the rights to make and sell and the right to use. The reason for this is that the 'only value' of the machines 'consists in their use'. According to Taney CJ:

> . . . the value of the implement or machine in the hands of the purchaser for use, does not in any degree depend on the time for which the exclusive privilege is granted to the patentee; nor upon the exclusion of others from its use. . . . He does not look to the duration of the exclusive privilege, but to the usefulness of the thing he buys, and the advantages he will derive from its use. He buys that article for the purpose of using it as long as it is fit for use and found to be profitable.[162]

But, with respect, as Bradley J pointed out in *Adams v Burke*, the price claimed by the patentee might well vary depending on the extent of the rights sold. Taney CJ's views may represent a perception in the early 19th Century

---

160 *Wilson v Rousseau* 4. How. 646 (1846).
161 55 US (14 How.) 539, at 553. For the exhaustion doctrine, see *ibid.* at 549 to 550. The dissent was based on the ground that Barnet had not bought the right to the machines for the duration of their life, but for 9 years and 6 months (the unexpired part of the first term): *ibid.* at 558 *per* McLean J. It is unclear from the report whether Taney CJ's finding that the machines had been bought 'without any limitation as to the time for which they could be used' depended on a different interpretation of the contract, principle or failure to affect McQuewan with special notice.
162 14 How. 539, at 550.

that articles had a single, objective value which did not change according to circumstances. It was only with the growth of commerce during that century that judges came to recognise that the 'value' of an article was its value in exchange in the 'market'.[163] Taney CJ and, after him, Miller J did not seem to recognise this commercial fact.[164]

Professor Bowman has sought to explain *Adams v Burke* 'as an *implied* contract case in which the implication is insufficient', noting that the effect of any special contracts brought home to purchasers was undecided.[165] That question was also reserved in *Keeler* where, however, Shiras J indicated that any condition could only take effect as a question of contract and not under patent law.

The basic ruling in *Keeler*, that an unrestricted sale by the patentee exhausts the exclusive right over the article once and for all, has not been successfully challenged. Subsequent benches, with varying degrees of success, have considered that a patentee can effect a conditional transfer and continue to enforce the patent against those acting outside the condition. Equally, however, other benches have delivered themselves of sweeping opinions that any transfer by the patentee frees the protected article from all further restraint. Stripped of the protective power of the patent, then, the conditions have been struck down under the anti-trust laws. The process depends quite significantly on the type of restraint imposed; but, arguably and more importantly, it reflects shifting, almost cyclical, judicial views about what is permissible under a patent.

3.3.3   Anti-trust

At first glance, there is an unresolved tension between patent law and anti-trust or competition policy: the patent has the express purpose of conferring a 'monopoly' while anti-trust is directed to the elimination of

---

163   See George M. Armstrong Jr, 'From the Fetishism of Commodities to the Regulated Market: The Rise and Decline of Property', 82 Northwestern University LRev. 79 (1988).

164   Contrast Miller J's approach to that of Idlington J's in *Hatton v The Chatterton-Copeland Co.* (1906) 37 SCR 651, at 653 under Canadian law, quickly finding that Hatton had not paid a reasonable price to buy the unrestricted right to use the patented article because:

> The rights to make, use or sell a patented article are daily subject matter of limitation in regard to time and place and *mode of user thereof*. So infinitely varied are these that no fixed price or terms can be attached uniformly to all of these modes of licensing the use of a patent right.
>   The patentee and those claiming under him arrange these various rights of use between themselves, and it is not our province to do more than determine whether or not the use has been within or beyond the intention of the parties (*Idlington J's emphasis*).

165   *Patent and Antitrust Law*, at 144. Contrast the failure of express notice, at least for tie-ins and price fixing, in *Straus v Victor Talking Machine Co.* 243 US 490 (1917) and *Motion Picture Patents Co. v Universal Film Manufacturing Co.* 243 US 502 (1917), subsection 3.3.3(a) below. It might, however, be wondered what an express stipulation against use outside the territory would achieve if a grant of the right to make, use and vend only within a designated territory was insufficient.

monopoly.[166] It has long been recognised that rights under a patent do not confer absolute immunity from the anti-trust laws. Indeed, *Keeler* indicates that once the patented article has been sold with the patentee's authority, any subsequent legal questions fall to be considered under the general law. The courts have not, however, always applied this interpretation, particularly when there have been attempts to stipulate express limitations on the rights transferred. Nor was *Keeler* concerned with how authorised release on a foreign market affected rights in the United States. More generally, *Keeler* says nothing about what limitations a patentee may impose directly on a licensee.

(a)   Generally

Some seven years after *Keeler*, the Supreme Court upheld the terms of a patent licence which imposed a minimum resale price and a non-competition obligation on the licensee.[167] The defendant licensee claimed that the licence was void for violation of the Sherman Act. The court, however, held that the patentee could deny anyone the right to exploit the invention at all and so could impose these particular conditions under its patents.[168] Hence, to the extent that the court recognised a patentee's power to reserve rights *under the patent* after parting with the patented article, albeit to a direct 'purchaser', *Bement* conforms to the approach taken in *Mitchell v Hawley*.

Mitchell v Hawley, described as 'the leading case', was prominently referred to in the next case when the court narrowly upheld a patentee's infringement action against an attempt to breach a tie-in.[169] Significantly, the action was against someone who neither owned nor used the patented article. The patent concerned a stencil duplicating machine and had been

---

166 This crude summary requires modification in the light of increasing attention to dynamic, or longer-run, competition under US anti-trust law: see *Continental TV Inc. v GTE Sylvania Inc.* 433 US 36 (1977). For a thought-provoking view, see Richard M. Buxbaum, 'Restrictions in the Patent Monopoly: A Comparative Critique', 113 UPenn.LRev. 633 (1965). The primary source, from a laissez-faire, neo-classical perspective, is Bowman, *Patent and Antitrust Law*; alternative views: William F. Baxter, 'Legal Restrictions on Exploitation of the Patent Monopoly: An Economic Analysis', 76 Yale LJ 267, (1966); Louis Kaplow, 'The Patent-Antitrust Intersection: A Reappraisal', 97 Harv.LRev. 1813 (1984). Succinct, fairly recent summaries by a lawyer and economist, respectively: Donald F. Turner, 'Basic Principles in Formulating Antitrust and Misuse Constraints on the Exploitation of Intellectual Property Rights', 53 Antitrust LJ 485, at 491 to 492 (1984) and Janusz A. Ordover, 'Economic Foundations and Considerations in Protecting Industrial and Intellectual Property', 53 Antitrust LJ 503, at 513 to 514 (1984).

167 *Bement v National Harrow Company* 186 US 70 (1902), Shiras J joined in the opinion of the court. See generally Bowman, *Patent and Antitrust Law*, at 124 to 125, 149 to 151.

168 *Ibid.* at 93 to 94; the court did, however, read down the extent of the non-competition obligation to preserve the defendant's rights to use other patents which it might legally obtain.

169 *Henry v A.B. Dick Co.* 224 US 1 (1911). The court split 4–3 and occasioned considerable bad blood on the bench: see Holmes' letter to Pollock, 21 March 1912 reprinted in Mark De Wolfe Howe (ed.), *The Holmes-Pollock Letters*, Cambridge University Press, 1942, 189 to 190.

sold by the patentee, the Dick Co., subject to the restriction that it be used only with ink supplied by the Dick Co., although ink was not covered by the patent. Henry, knowing of the restriction, sold ink to the purchaser for use in the duplicator and was found liable for patent infringement. Lurton J, for the majority, acknowledged the exhaustion rule for unfettered sales, but characterised this case as a sale subject to conditions. Henry, having notice of the restriction, was bound by it; and violating it, infringed the patent.[170] White CJ, in dissent, argued that the article escaped the patent monopoly on being sold and so the restriction was an attempt to extend the patent monopoly by contract.[171]

The particular form of the proceedings in *Bement* seems to have played a large part in its disposition.[172] When the evidence clearly established that a similar licence scheme was being used as a market-sharing cloak between competitors to fix prices and interfere with unlicensed rivals, it passed beyond the patent's protection and was struck down.[173] Hence, some limit to the patentee's powers were set by anti-trust law.

In the next five years followed a quick succession of decisions striking down attempts to impose resale price maintenance and tie-ins.[174] In each of these cases, the patentee had sold the patented article and was attempting to enforce the condition against a sub-purchaser who had notice of the restraint.[175] The essential proposition in each was that the patentee had sold the article for the price claimed thereby exhausting the exclusive right. Accordingly, the condition fell to be assessed under the general law.

---

170   For acknowledgement of the exhaustion rule, *ibid.* at 23 to 24; for power to impose 'lesser' restrictions than complete denial of use, *ibid.* at 24 to 25; note also extensive citation of the UK cases, *ibid.* at 40 to 43.
171   *Ibid.* at 53 for a succinct statement of his Honour's view.
172   Peckham J's opinion refers repeatedly to the defendant's failure to prove 'prior contracts of a like nature including other parties' and so did not investigate the defendant's claims that the licence was really part of a patent pool between horizontal competitors, see for example *ibid.* at 83, 84, 87, 94 to 95; on the likely validity of defendant's claims, see Bowman, *Patent and Antitrust Law*, at 125 Note 9.
173   *Standard Sanitary Manufacturing Co. v US* 226 US 20 (1912); see Edwin P. Grosvenor, 'The "Rule of Reason" as Applied by the United States Supreme Court to Commerce in Patented Articles', 17 Columbia LR 208, at 212 to 213 (1917) and a somewhat different interpretation in Bowman, *Patent and Antitrust Law*, at 158 to 161.
174   For resale price maintenance ('rpm'), see *Bauer v O'Donnell* 229 US 1 (1913); *Straus v Victor Talking Machine Co.* 243 US 490 (1917); *Boston Store v American Graphophone Co.* 246 US 8 (1918). For tie-ins, see *Motion Picture Patents Co. v Universal Film Manufacturing Co.* 243 US 502 (1917).
175   The patentee's attempt to clothe the scheme as a licence in *Straus* was readily dismissed by Clarke J for the majority 'Courts would be perversely blind if they failed to look through such an attempt as this 'License Notice' thus plainly is to sell property for a full price, and yet to place restraints upon its further alienation, such as have been hateful to the law from Lord Coke's day to ours . . . .' 243 US at 500 to 501.
Factors assisting in this conclusion included that (1) the patentee received payment on sale although purporting to restrict future use; (2) there was no scheme for registering the qualified title in any public register; (3) the patentee in fact did not maintain close supervision over the 'licensed' machines; and (4) even if the patentee did nothing to reclaim a machine sold in violation of the 'licence', an 'infringer' gained title to it only some 16 years later on the patent's expiration 'long after it has been worn out or become obsolete'. McKenna, Holmes and Van Devanter JJ dissented in all these cases. Lurton J was no longer on the bench.

The *Dick Co.* case was expressly overruled in the *Motion Picture Patents* case. The plaintiff patented a device for feeding film through a projector and licensed the right to make and sell the projectors on condition that they only be used with film also designated by the plaintiff. The film had itself been the subject of an expired patent. The defendants, all with notice, were purchasers using unauthorised film in the projectors and the suppliers of that film. Clarke J, for the majority, characterised the restriction as one on an unpatented product, not one on the use of a patented article; and held that the patentee's right was:

> . . . to use the mechanism to produce the result with any appropriate material, and the materials with which the machine is operated are no part of the patented machine. . . . The difference is clear and vital between the exclusive right to use the machine which the law gives to the inventor and the right to use it exclusively with prescribed materials to which such a license notice as we have here seeks to restrict it.[176]

Professor Powell has lucidly pointed out the logical fallacy in this: 'If A is married to B, then B is married to A.'[177] He has suggested that, as a matter of policy, Clarke J's opinion can logically be defended as holding that the patentee's right to exclude others from using is confined only to prohibiting all use and not just some use.[178] But, the opposite policy conclusion is equally open as Holmes J, provoked to written dissent, chose:

> I suppose that a patentee has no less property in his patented machine than any other owner, and that in addition to keeping the machine to himself the patent gives him the further right to forbid the rest of the world from making others like it. In short, for whatever motive, he may keep his device wholly out of use. . . . So much being undisputed, I cannot understand why he may not keep it out of use unless the licensee, or, for the matter of that, the buyer, will use some unpatented thing in connection with it. Generally speaking the measure of a condition is the consequence of a breach, and if that consequence is one that the owner may impose unconditionally, he may impose it conditionally upon a certain event.[179]

Holmes J was prepared to recognise some policy limits to the patentee's power, but this was not such a case:

> But there is no predominant public interest to prevent a patented tea pot or film feeder from being kept from the public, because, as I have said, the patentee may keep them tied up at will while his patent lasts. Neither is there any such interest to prevent the purchase of the tea or films, that is made the condition of

176   243 US 502, at 512.
177   T.R. Powell, 'The Nature of a Patent Right', 17 Columbia LRev. 663, at 675 to 676 (1917), see also 243 US 502, to 520 *per* Holmes J, quotation at Note 180 below. Notwithstanding this, see *Mercoid Corp. v Mid-Continent Investment Co.* 320 US 661, at 666 (1944) cited in *US v Crown Zellerbach Corporation* 141 F. Supp. 118 (NDIll. 1956). For tying now, *Jefferson Parish Hospital District No. 2 v Hyde* 466 US 2 (1984).
178   *Ibid.* at 675 to 679.
179   243 US 502, at 519. Note, although *Menck* adopted a similar course, US law differs from Anglo-Commonwealth law in that the Patent Code has never recognised a power of compulsory licensing for non-use. Anti-trust powers may be used to this end.

the use of the machine. The supposed contravention of public interest sometimes is stated as an attempt to extend the patent law to unpatented articles, *which of course it is not*, and *more accurately* as a possible domination to be established by such means. But the domination is one only to the extent of the desire for the tea pot or film feeder, and if the owner prefers to keep the pot or the feeder unless you will buy his tea or films, I cannot see in allowing him the right to do so anything more than an ordinary incident of ownership. . . . (*Emphasis added*)[180]

For Professor Powell, neither the majority nor minority opinions provided a convincing basis for their underlying policy assumptions.[181] The majority did not explain why a patentee might prohibit totally, but not partially.[182] On the other hand, Holmes J's approach has been criticised for allowing the patentee too great a latitude; for example, potentially allowing the patent to cloak a cartel.[183] Unlike the *Dick Co.* case, it has been cogently argued that *Motion Picture Patents* was a clear case of an illegal cartel.[184] Indeed, the whole series of cases needs to be seen in the context of a decade of heightened concern about cartelising practices. Shortly before *Bauer v O'Donnell*, the Supreme Court had condemned price fixing on unpatented articles as illegal *per se*, in circumstances highly redolent of cartelising.[185]

---

180 *Ibid.* at 520. See also the Patent Misuse Reform Act of 1988 at Note 238a below. The rejection of the 'domination' argument is an early rejection of what has come to be known as the 'leverage' theory: Bowman, *Patent and Antitrust Law*, at 157 to 158; Richard A. Posner, *Antitrust Law: An Economic Perspective*, The University of Chicago Press, 1976, at 172 to 174; for a critical view, Scherer and Ross, *Industrial Market Structure and Economic Performance*, at 565 to 567.

181 A recent summary of the fallacies in the 'scope of the patent' debate is Louis Kaplow, 'The Patent-Antitrust Intersection: A Reappraisal', 97 Harv.LRev. 1813, at 1845 to 1849 (1984). His counter-proposal has not escaped economic criticism on the grounds of unsoundness and practical unworkability: Ordover, 'Economic Foundations and Considerations in Protecting Industrial and Intellectual Property', at 513 to 514.

182 17 Columbia LRev. 663, especially at 679. For the mirror criticism of the majority's view in the *Dick Co.* case, see Buxbaum, 'Restrictions in the Patent Monopoly: A Comparative Critique', 113 UPenn.LRev. 633, at 645 to 647 (1965). Bowman notes that *Motion Picture Patents* at least has the merit of being consistent with the approach on price maintenance initiated in *Bauer v O'Donnell*: Bowman, *Patent and Antitrust Law*, at 157.

183 Turner, 'Basic Principles in Formulating Antitrust and Misuse Constraints on the Exploitation of Intellectual Property Rights', 53 Antitrust LJ 485, at 491 to 492 (1984); William F. Baxter, 'Legal Restrictions on Exploitation of the Patent Monopoly: An Economic Analysis', 76 Yale LJ 267, at 276 to 278 (1966).

184 See especially, Grosvenor, 'The "Rule of Reason"', at 221 to 229 and for the *Dick Co.* case, see *ibid.* at 210 to 212 and compare Posner, *Antitrust Law*, at 172 to 173. In *Motion Picture Patents*, however, Holmes J himself, perhaps echoing *Bement*, specifically excluded the question of 'a combination of patents such as to be contrary to the policy that I am bound to accept from the Congress . . .': 243 US at 521.

185 *Dr Miles Medical Company v John D. Park & Sons Company* 220 US 373 (1911), Holmes J dissented. The case has attracted considerable comment: Lester G. Telser, 'Why Should Manufacturers Want Fair Trade?', 3 JL &Econ. 86 (1962); Posner, *Antitrust Law*, at 151, 66; William S. Comanor, 'Vertical Price Fixing, Vertical Market Restrictions and the New Antitrust Policy', 98 Harv. LRev. 983, at 984 (1985); Ernest Gellhorn, *Antitrust Law and Economics*, West Publishing Co., 1986 (3rd ed.), at 282 to 289. For the cartelising context, see William F. Baxter, 'Vertical Practices – Half Slave Half Free', 52 Antitrust LJ 743, at 743 to 744 (1983).

Public, or Congressional, concern had reached such levels that in 1914 Congress passed the Clayton Act and the Federal Trade Commission Act, the former specifically outlawing tying whether unpatented or patented articles were involved.[186]

Bauer, Straus and *Boston Store* involved attempts to make price stipulations run with the goods, they were restrictions on purchasers from purchasers of the patentee; the refinement is difficult to support in *Motion Picture Patents*, however – the purchaser bought from the licensee and not the patentee.[187] Price restrictions arose again in the context of a licence between patentee and manufacturing licensee.[188] As in the *Bement* case, the Supreme Court unanimously upheld the agreement. Taft CJ did so, however, not on the ground that the patentee, having the power of absolute prohibition, could impose lesser restrictions, rather:

> One of the valuable elements of the exclusive right of a patentee is to acquire profit by the price at which the article is sold. The higher the price, the greater the profit, unless it is prohibitory. When the patentee licences another to make and vend, and retains the right to make and vend on his own account, the price at which his licensee will sell will necessarily affect the price at which he can sell his own patented goods. It would seem entirely reasonable that he should say to his licensee, Yes, you may make and sell articles under my patent, but not so as to destroy the profit that I wish to obtain by making them and selling them myself.[189]

The patentee (General Electric) having a lawful monopoly, it was 'entirely reasonable' that steps were taken to reap the profits of it. In this case, the steps included a licence to Westinghouse – the next largest competitor in the light bulb market – which fixed the price Westinghouse could sell at and obliged Westinghouse to sell only through consignment agents.[190]

The difficulty with this case, as with Holmes J's dissent in *Motion Picture Patents*, is the extremely wide latitude allowed to the patentee. As with *Motion Picture Patents*, economists have not been slow to suspect that

---

186 Clayton Act section 2; in addition to the jurisdictional requirement of interstate commerce, the practice also had to be shown to have the effect of substantially lessening competition. The political context was Woodrow Wilson's presidential campaign promising 'The New Freedom': Eleanor M. Fox, 'The Modernization of Antitrust: A New Equilibrium', 66 Cornell LRev. 1140, at 1148 (1981).

187 Powell even characterises it as a case of patentee and purchaser: 17 Columbia LRev. 663. In fact, one of the successful defendants was a licensee of the purchaser, the other supplied the offending film.

188 *US v General Electric Co.* 272 US 476 (1926).

189 *Ibid.* at 490.

190 Bowman addresses the difficulty of reconciling this approach with the majority's in *Bauer v O'Donnell: Patent and Antitrust Law*, at 127. GE's own sales system through consignment agents escaped liability also, subsequently overruled in *Simpson v Union Oil Co.* 377 US 13 (1964) but note *US v Arnold, Schwinn & Co.* 388 US 365; 18 L. Ed. 2d 1249 (1967) at Note 211 below. For the consignment system, see Posner, *Antitrust Law*, at 153 to 157, Phillip E. Areeda, 8 *Antitrust Law: An Analysis of Antitrust Principles and Their Application*, Little, Brown & Co., 1989 at ¶¶1621, 1473.

General Electric and Westinghouse were really engaging in a conspiracy to divide the market, raise price and restrict output.[191]

Of course, it would be possible to operate a system of law where a patentee was exempt from anti-trust laws altogether, but this is not a view which has commended itself to US courts. Before moving on to consider restraints involving territorial division, it is necessary to note that the *General Electric* view of what is 'entirely reasonable' has not found widespread acceptance.

The US courts have distinguished the initial holding so much that commentators have argued that it only operates if the patentee licenses only a single licensee.[192] Twice, the Supreme Court itself has divided 4–4 on whether to overrule *General Electric*.[193] More typical is the *Univis* case.[194] The District Court found that the finishing of spectacle lens blanks by retailers fell within the scope of the patent and on the authority of *General Electric* upheld the patentee's right to enforce a resale price maintenance clause against finishers. The Supreme Court dismissed this consideration and focused on the fact that the patentee had sold the lens blanks to the finishers:

> . . . where one has sold an uncompleted article which, because it embodies essential features of his patented invention is within the protection of his patent, and has destined the article to be finished by the purchaser in conformity to the patent, he has sold his invention so far as it is or may be embodied in that particular article. The reward he has demanded and received is for the article and the invention which it embodies and which his vendee is to practice upon it. He has thus parted with his right to assert the patent monopoly with respect to it and is no longer free to control the price at which it may be sold either in its unfinished or finished form. No one would doubt that if the [patentee] had sold the blanks to a wholesaler or finishing retailer, without more, the purchaser would not infringe by grinding and selling them. *The added stipulation by the patentee fixing resale prices derives no support from the patent* and must stand on the same footing under the Sherman Act as like stipulations with respect to patented commodities. (*Emphasis added*)[195]

Hence, using language much redolent of Miller J's reasoning in *Adams v Burke*, the Supreme Court restated a patentee's prospects of imposing price restrictions in much the same terms as territorial restrictions had been treated

---

191 Lester Telser, who restarted the debate over 'vertical' restraints in 1962, has recently claimed that his initial article was written to demonstrate that *General Electric* was an unjustified use of rpm: Lester G. Telser, 'Why Should Manufacturers Want Fair Trade II?', 33 J L & Econ. 409, at 410 (1990); Gellhorn, *Antitrust Law and Economics*, at 393 to 394; Scherer and Ross, *Industrial Market Structure*, at 550 Note 24; but contrast Bowman, *Patent and Antitrust Law*, at 128 to 132.

192 Bowman, *Patent and Antitrust Law*, at 197 citing *Newburgh Moire Co. v Superior Moire Co.* 237 F. 2d 282 (3d Cir. 1956). For other qualifications, see *ibid.* at Chapter 9 generally.

193 See *US v Studiengesellschaft Kohle mbH* 670 F. 2d 1122 (DC Cir. 1981) (below from Note 230) citing *US v Line Material Co.* 333 US 287 (1948) and the *per curiam* approval of *US v Huck Manufacturing Co.* 382 US 197 (1965) *affg* 277 F. Supp. 791 (ED Mich. 1964).

194 *US v Univis Lens Company Inc.* 316 US 241; 86 L. Ed. 1408 (1942).

195 *Ibid.* at 251; 86 L. Ed. 1418. In fact, similar to *Motion Picture Patents*, the patentee had granted an exclusive licence under the patent to a subsidiary which made the blanks and sold them to the various classes of reseller.

in *Keeler*. While Shiras J had left open the effect of contractual clauses imposed under the general law, the attempted resale price maintenance in *Univis* was illegal *per se* except to the extent that state 'fair' trade laws operated.[196]

As yet, under the 'new' liberality ushered in by *Continental v Sylvania*, the Supreme Court has not overturned the basic illegality of resale price maintenance.[197] It has, however, been more flexible in refusing to characterise agreements as involving price fixing.[198] Accordingly, under this dispensation, there is some likelihood that attempts to impose restrictions under a patent would be viewed more favourably along the lines of *Bement* and, perhaps, *General Electric*.

(b) Territorial restrictions

Adams v Burke and *Keeler* involved attempts to stop the flow of goods from one geographic area within the United States to another. Proceeding from the inconvenience to a purchaser of an article if they could not carry it throughout the country as their business dictated, these cases ruled that the power of the patent over the article was exhausted once the patentee authorised its sale. Any further control over it fell to be considered under the general law. In the 19th Century, nothing remiss was seen in the patentee's division of the patent rights along territorial lines by assignment. The Patent Code now provides in section 261:

> . . . patents, or any interest therein, shall be assignable in law by an instrument in writing. The . . . patentee, or his assigns or legal representatives may in like manner grant and convey an exclusive right under his . . . patents to the whole or *any specified part of the United States*. (*Emphasis added*)[199]

Section 261 appears to grant the patentee power to transfer exclusive rights to specified parts of the United States. Hence, controversy of the sort arising in *Motion Picture Patents* for tie-ins (and presumably price restrictions) seems to be forestalled where the restriction is territorial. Chisum notes that this has been questioned; in 1966, Professor Baxter was able to argue that

---

196 The court did indicate earlier that Univis had increased its market share from 20 per cent to 50 per cent of local retailers while the scheme was in operation: *ibid.* at 246; 86 L. Ed. 1416. That was not relevant given the finding of *per se* illegality. For the 'fair trade' laws, see Scherer and Ross, *Industrial Market Structure and Economic Performance*, at 548 to 550.

197 *Continental TV Inc. v GTE Sylvania Inc.* 433 US 36 (1977), patented articles were not involved and the ruling expressly excluded price conditions. The ramifications of this ruling are considered below from Note 215.

198 *Monsanto Co. v Spray-Rite Service Corp.* 465 US 752 (1984); termination of price cutting dealer on complaints from other dealers was not necessarily an anti-trust violation, but the court has failed to take up the Justice Department's invitation to overturn the rule that price fixing is illegal *per se; Business Electronics Corp. v Sharp Electronics Corp.* 108 S. Ct 1515 (1988). See generally, John J. Flynn, 'The "Is" and "Ought" of Vertical Restraints After Monsanto Co. v Spray-Rite Service Corp.', 71 Cornell LRev. 1095 (1986).

199 35 USC §261. The deletions make provision for applications for a patent.

anti-trust law should compel the patentee to grant identical licences for a given territory to all qualified applicants *once* the patentee granted any assignment or licence for that territory. The learned professor fully intended the consequences of this proposal, since he stated: 'The patentee's power *to auction off exclusive positions will thus be destroyed* without impairing significantly his ability to capture through royalties the economic value of his innovative contribution.'[200] (*Emphasis added*)

The genesis of this startling conclusion lies in a remarkable piece of historical conjuring as a result of which Professor Baxter demonstrates that the section has been solely concerned with the legal formalities attendant on assignments and goes on to conclude: 'On its face the section leaves untouched the validity of territorial restrictions in licenses; *it should be construed as irrelevant to the substantive validity of similar restrictions in* assignments.'[201] (*Emphasis added*)

With respect, Professor Baxter seems to stand matters on their head. The first part of the quotation may follow from the history of the section which, on his analysis, indicates that the 'exclusive right' referred to is a right arising by assignment and not a 'mere' licence, exclusive or otherwise. The second, emphasised part, however, flies directly in the face of that survey. Even if economists regard *legal* distinctions between assignments and licences as arbitrary, that is no warrant for disregarding section 261's authorisation of assignments for a 'specified part of the United States'.[202] Buxbaum's questioning has greater force. His position is that simply because the patent may permit a particular practice does not confer immunity under the anti-trust laws. Whether or not the practice is immune depends on the market context.[203]

The courts, however, have tended to regard even exclusive licensing for parts of the United States as a proper exercise of a patentee's powers and accorded wide latitude under the anti-trust laws. In a case involving an alleged abuse of the anti-trust laws by the grant of an exclusive licence for the whole of the United States, the Sixth Circuit indicated:

> In granting a license the patentee may limit the licensee's right to sell. He may grant a license to make and use the patented articles, but withhold the right to

---

200   Baxter, 'Legal Restrictions on Exploitation of the Patent Monopoly: An Economic Analysis', 76 Yale LJ 267, at 347 (1966). See Chisum, *5 Patents*, at §19.04[3](h) Note 83, also referring to Gibbons, 'Domestic Territorial Restrictions in Patent Transactions and the Antitrust Laws', 34 Geo. Washington LRev. 893 (1966).

201   *Ibid.* at 352. The historical survey runs from 349 to 351.

202   US courts have tended in the opposite direction, recognising that exclusive licensees may sue their grantors for patent infringement: for example *Security Materials Co. v Mixermobile* 72 F. Supp. 450 (SDCal. 1947) and in anti-trust cases '[f]rom a competition-oriented perspective, there is little difference between an assignment and a license of patents rights': *Miller Insituform Inc. v Insituform of North America Inc.* 605 F. Supp. 1125, at 1131 (MD Tenn. 1985) *affd* 830 F. 2d 606 (6th Cir. 1987) cited in Chisum, *5 Patents*, at §19.04[3](h) Note 85 ((1991) Supp.).

203   Buxbaum, 'Restrictions in the Patent Monopoly: A Comparative Critique', at 659. Both he and Baxter start from the proposition that not everything a patentee does with the patent is automatically immune from the anti-trust laws.

sell them. He may license one to make, another to vend, and still another to use, and he may confine each to a specified part of the United States.[204]

The Sixth Circuit also saw nothing questionable under the anti-trust laws in the grant of an exclusive licence for the whole United States which was used to deny the plaintiff any supplies of the patented article at all.

On this approach, the exclusive licensee for California of the right to use, operate and sell a patent relating to mobile mixers successfully sued an exclusive licensee for another part of the United States who began using a licensed machine in California without authorisation.[205]

A more sophisticated analysis was undertaken in *Crown Zellerbach*. The patent was for a dispensing mechanism used in towel-dispensing cabinets. Prior to the action, the agreement had been through a number of variations. The patentee, ALSCO, granted Crown exclusive rights over use of the patent for the supply of paper towelling in the eastern half of the United States, reserving the western half and rights over cloth towelling in the East for itself. Judge Hoffman refused to grant Crown and ALSCO's motion to dismiss for want of cause because:

> The complaint sets up a situation where patent licences have been utilized to support a system of pervasive control in the paper towel cabinet and paper towel industry. Regardless of the possible legality of each of the agreements and practices standing alone, their total effect, qualified by the alleged unlawful purpose to restrain trade, will suffice to support the complaint against a motion to dismiss.[206]

Considering the exclusive licence for paper towelling customers in the East, Judge Hoffman went on, however, to state that '[v]iewed simply as a territorial limitation upon Crown's license, this agreement is a valid exercise of ALSCO's patent rights' because territorial licences, 'without more, were a reasonable means for the patentee to secure the reward granted to him'.[207] The 'without more' that his Honour had in mind on this part of the case was ALSCO's agreement to provide Crown with protection against competition. The presumption of validity in the licensor's reservation of its own exclusive territory has been attacked as too generous on the ground that such protection could be used to foreclose desirable competition;[208]

---

204 *Beckton, Dickinson & Co. v Eisele & Co.* 86 F. 2d 267, at 269 (6th Cir, 1936) described as '[p]erhaps the leading case': Chisum, 5 *Patents*, at §19.04[3](h) text at Notes 91 to 92. See also *Brownell v Ketcham Wire & Manufacturing Co.* 211 F. 2d 121 (9th Cir. 1954).

205 *Security Materials Co. v Mixermobile* 72 F. Supp. 450 (SD Cal. 1947) cited in Chisum, 5 *Patents*, at §19.04[3](h) text at Notes 88 to 89. The cases, if not the principle, of *Adams v Burke* and *Keeler* are distinguishable since the defendant was a direct licensee and not a sub-purchaser. (In *Hobbie v Jennison*, the defendant grantee sold within the terms of the grant, albeit knowing of the sub-purchaser's purpose.) Contrast, however, *Motion Picture Patents* for tie-ins.

206 *US v Crown Zellerbach Corporation* 141 F. Supp. 118, at 126 (ND Ill. 1956).

207 *Ibid.* at 127 citing §261, *General Electric* and *General Talking Pictures Corp. v Western Electric Co.* 305 US 124 (1938). Judge Hoffman went on to express doubts about the legality of the 'customer allocation' restriction: *ibid.* at 128.

208 Buxbaum, 'Restrictions in the Patent Monopoly: A Comparative Critique', at 660 to 661.

the doubts about the promise of exclusivity to the licensee, on the ground that it is in the nature of the exclusivity promise anyway.[209] On the other hand, one might argue that licensee protection could be justifiable in some circumstances.[210]

The benign approach to territorial restrictions under patents received a check in 1967. In the *Arnold, Schwinn* case, there was a dual system of distribution for unpatented articles, bicycles. Schwinn distributed a portion of its bicycles through consignment agents, the rest by sales to independent wholesalers and retailers; both systems involved territorial and customer restraints. As in *Dr Miles*, the Supreme Court held the system where the bicycles were actually sold to the wholesalers illegal *per se*.[211] Corresponding restraints imposed on Schwinn's genuine consignment agents were not struck down. Schwinn responded to the judgment by replacing the independent wholesalers with a distribution subsidiary.[212]

Arnold, Schwinn expressly reserved consideration on the treatment of patented articles.[213] Some lower courts, however, relied on the ruling and the exhaustion doctrine to strike down territorial restrictions, at least at the sub-purchaser level.[214]

Ten years later, *Arnold, Schwinn* was expressly overruled.[215] Once again, the case did not concern patents. Sylvania was a producer of television sets whose market share had declined to 1 or 2 per cent. After a policy review, it decided to try and attract the most aggressive and competitive retailers as its distributors by conferring on them a limited degree of territorial protection. Sylvania phased out its wholesalers and would directly supply only approved resellers. Additional dealers to a territory would be appointed only if Sylvania thought local demand warranted it or the local dealer was not performing to expectations. Approved dealers were obliged to sell Sylvania products only from designated locations and risked losing their appointment for non-compliance. Under this scheme, Sylvania's market share increased to 5 per cent in the space of three years.

---

209   *Ibid.* at 659.
210   See the discussion of *Sylvania* from Note 215 below (distributors) and in the EC context, see 258/78 *Maize Seed* [1982] 2015 and *Davidson Rubber* [1972] CMLR D52 at chapter 7.2.1 and 7.3.1(b), respectively, below.
211   *US v Arnold, Schwinn & Co.* 388 US 365; 18 L. Ed. 2d 1249 (1967) overruled *Continental T.V. Inc. v GTE Sylvania Inc.* 433 US 36, 56 L Ed 2d 568 (1977), below from Note 215. Interestingly, Posner, who has condemned this ruling caustically in *Antitrust Law*, at 163 to 164, was government counsel and argued for violation on a rule of reason test.
212   Scherer and Ross, *Industrial Performance and Economic Structure*, at 563 Note 65.
213   *Ibid.* at 379 Note 6. The footnote has been described as 'strange' since the cases it cites to justify the reservation all relate to price restraints: Chisum, 5 *Patents*, at §19.04[3](h) text at Notes 97 to 99.
214   See Jerry R. Selinger, 'Patent Licensing in the Afterglow of Sylvania: Practicalities of Life Under the Rule of Reason', 63 JPat.Off. Soc. 353, at 367 to 370; Chisum, 5 *Patents*, at §19.04[3] Note 100.
215   *Continental T.V. Inc. v GTE Sylvania Inc.* 433 US 36; 56 L Ed 2d 568 (1977), rehearing on remand 694 F. 2d 1132 (9th Cir. 1982).

Continental was one of Sylvania's most successful dealers in San Francisco. Against Continental's wishes, Sylvania proposed opening a rival retailer near to a Continental outlet. Sylvania was also resisting Continental's demands for rights to sell in Sacramento and Continental decided to start selling in Sacramento anyway.

Sylvania, in ambiguous circumstances, drastically reduced Continental's credit line from $300,000 to $50,000; Continental withheld repayments on Sylvania's credit finance; Sylvania terminated Continental's appointment and sued to recover the outstanding moneys. Continental cross-claimed for violation of the anti-trust laws.

Powell J refused to distinguish *Arnold, Schwinn* on the ground that 'location clauses' gave rise to different considerations to territorial and customer restrictions.[216] Instead, Powell J expressly rejected the distinction between sale and non-sale transactions and considered that there was no justification for applying a rule of *per se* illegality to non-price, vertical restrictions. Instead, non-price, vertical restrictions should be assessed under the 'rule of reason' standard.[217]

In a side-note, Powell J indicated that the 'ancient rule against restraints on alienation' was outmoded and irrelevant to the regulation of vertical restraints on distributors under the anti-trust laws.[218]

The reasoning used to reach this conclusion signalled a major shift in the Supreme Court's approach to anti-trust questions.[219] Powell J accepted that vertical restraints presented complicated issues because they held out the prospect of increased inter-brand competition at the simultaneous cost of intra-brand competition. Inter-brand competition is rivalry between different producers of the same generic product, in *Sylvania* the rival brands of television sets such as RCA, Phillips and Sylvania. Competition between sellers of the same brand is intra-brand competition.[220] The restraints are 'vertical' because they operate between different levels of the chain of production and distribution; between, say, producer and reseller as here rather than between rivals at the same level ('horizontal' competition).

---

216 *Ibid.* at 46; 578, Burger CJ, Stewart, Blackmun and Stevens JJ joining. Contrast White J concurring; Brennan and Marshall JJ dissenting.

217 *Ibid.* at 57 to 59; 584 to 585. The exclusion of price restrictions is at *ibid.* at 51 Note 18; 581. The 'rule of reason' requires an assessment of whether, in the particular market circumstances in question, the pro-competitive gains from the conduct outweigh the anti-competitive costs: for the seminal, compendious statement, see *Chicago Board of Trade v US* 246 US 231, at 238 (1918) *per* Brandeis J.

218 *Ibid.* at 53 Note 21; 56 L Ed 2d 568, at 582.

219 Eleanor M. Fox and Laurence M. Sullivan, 'Antitrust – Retrospective and Prospective: Where Are We Coming From? Where Are We Going?', 62 NYULRev. 936, at 954 (1987) ('a landmark opinion'); Gellhorn, *Antitrust Law and Economics*, at 426 ('[c]learly the most significant decision'); see also Eleanor M. Fox, 'The Modernization of Antitrust: A New Equilibrium', 66 Cornell LRev. 1140, at 1152 (1981).

220 433 US 36, at 51; 56 L Ed 2d at 568, at 581. Powell J considered that the two types of competition are independent; it was possible for fierce competition between the distributors of a monopolist to exist just as it was possible for there to be fierce competition in the market-place if many producers only used one distributor each. But, contrast, Robert L. Steiner, 'The Nature of Vertical Restraints', 30 *Antitrust Bulletin* 143 (1985).

Non-price vertical restraints reduced intra-brand competition because they limited 'the number of sellers of a particular product competing for the business of a given group of buyers'. On the other hand, inter-brand competition was promoted by enabling the producer to achieve efficiencies in distribution. The efficiencies Powell J had in mind were those associated with 'the so-called "free rider" effect':

> . . . new manufacturers and manufacturers entering new markets can use the restrictions in order to induce competent and aggressive retailers to make the kind of investment of capital and labor that is often required in the distribution of products unknown to the consumer. Established manufacturers can use them to induce retailers to engage in promotional activities or to provide service and repair facilities necessary to the efficient marketing of their products. Service and repair are vital for many products, such as automobiles and major household appliances. The availability of such services affect a manufacturer's goodwill and the competitiveness of his product.[221]

Sylvania presents a contrast to Judge Hoffman's analysis in *Crown Zeller-bach*. Judge Hoffman had expressed some doubts about the anti-trust validity of granting the licensee protection. Powell J, however, recognised that 'mere' distributors may have a valid interest requiring protection. Moreover, it is a dual interest; the distributors' investment inured to the benefit of the producer, enhancing inter-brand competition. A further important aspect is Powell J's recognition that 'established manufacturers' may well have need of such techniques.

Powell J did not hold that one type of competition was more important than the other; hence, his direction for trial under a rule of reason. There are, however, some indications that he favoured a preference for inter-brand competition. The impact of the injury to intra-brand competition was reduced by buyers' ability to travel 'and, *perhaps more importantly*, to purchase the competing products of other manufacturers.'[222] (*Emphasis added*) His opinion also lent some credence to the claims of then Professors, and subsequently Circuit Judges, Bork and Posner that manufacturers had no interest in restraining intra-brand competition unless the restraint promoted increased sales.

Arguably, if consumers have the choice of rival brands using different methods of distribution which they can switch to, the anti-competitive dangers of a restraint on intra-brand competition may be reduced. Both Bork and Posner have gone further and argued that vertical restraints should be regarded as pro-competitive and *per se* legal.[223] Their views can be traced back to 'the discovery' that it seems counter-productive for a producer to

---

221   *Ibid*. at 55; 583. Powell J's approach should be borne in mind when considering a number of EC cases: in distribution, *Consten & Grundig* and the *Metro* cases; for technology licensing, *Maize Seed* and *Davidson Rubber*, for the EC competition rules, see Chapter 7 below.
222   *Ibid*. at 54; 583.
223   Robert Bork, *The Antitrust Paradox*, Basic Books, Inc., 1978, at 297 and Appendix; Richard A. Posner, 'The Next Step in the Antitrust Treatment of Restricted Distribution: *Per Se* Legality', 48 UChic.LRev. 6, at 22 to 26 (1981).

impose vertical restraints. The initial effect, at least, of vertical restraints is to raise price which, in turn, will reduce the quantity sold. Unless the producer be a monopolist at the resale level, this reduces overall revenue from the product at the additional cost of affording the distributor an unearned profit. Three explanations of this seemingly irrational behaviour have been suggested: reinforcement of a cartel at the producers' level; a cartel at the resale level; or an attempt to induce desirable distribution services vulnerable to free riding.[224]

To a considerable degree, Bork (in particular) assumes away the cartel problem and both he and Posner argue cartels should be attacked as such rather than indirectly. This, of course, assumes it is always possible and easy to detect cartels. Bork then makes a crucial gloss in asserting that what is in the interests of the producer is always desirable in the sense of increasing total welfare because, in the absence of market power, the (economically) rational producer will only impose price-raising restrictions if they will increase output.

The pressure for a rule of *per se* legality is resisted on a number of fronts. Both Comanor and Scherer have demonstrated that Bork's claim is possible but depends crucially on the special case where *all* consumers value the services equally. If marginal consumers value the services more than other consumers, total output may be increased but total welfare may be decreased.[225] Other economic concerns include scepticism over the prevalence of free riding and concern about the potential for inefficient rigidities to develop.[226] Others challenge the central role accorded to 'efficiency' in anti-trust interpretation by Bork and Posner.[227]

At the least, the conflicts of opinion and the complexities of the factual considerations dictate a need for caution. *Sylvania* in the context of distribution, but seemingly of application generally for non-price vertical restraints,

---

224 The seminal article is Lester G. Telser, 'Why Should Manufacturers Want Fair Trade?', 3 *JL &Econ.* 86 (1962). Before developing his thoughts further, Posner provided a succinct summary of the view Powell J seems to have endorsed in Posner, *Antitrust Law*, at 147 to 151.

225 The initial criticisms, F.M. Scherer, 'The Economics of Vertical Restraints', 52 Antitrust LJ 687 (1982); William S. Comanor, 'Vertical Price Fixing, Vertical Market Restrictions and the New Antitrust Policy', 98 Harv. LRev. 983, at 984 (1985); now conveniently along with other criticisms in Scherer and Ross, *Industrial Market Structure and Economic Performance*, Chapter 15.

226 Scherer and Ross, *Industrial Market Structure and Economic Performance*, Chapter 15, noting for example pre-sales charges in the very automobile sales showroom situation colourfully relied on by Posner (*Antitrust Law*, at 149), *ibid.* at 555. No doubt, the retort is that their existence does not prove they are necessarily always 'efficient'.

227 See Fox and Sullivan, 'Antitrust – Retrospective and Prospective' at 936; John J. Flynn and James F. Ponsoldt, 'Legal Reasoning and the Jurisprudence of Vertical Restraints: The Limitations of Neoclassical Economic Analysis in the Resolution of Antitrust Disputes', 62 NYULRev. 1125 (1987); Fox, 'The Modernization of Antitrust: A New Equilibrium', at 1140. For a critique of the meaning of 'efficiency', see Jules L. Coleman, *Markets, Morals and the Law*, Cambridge University Press, 1988, Chapters 3 to 5. For an EC view, see Luc Gyselen, 'Vertical Restraints in the Distribution Process: Strength and Weakness of the Free Rider Rationale under EEC Competition Law', (1984) 21 CMLRev. 647.

points out the need, if not importance, of taking into account the impact of the practice on inter-brand competition.[228]

The courts in the United States were not slow to react to the *Sylvania* reasoning.[229] The leading example, with heavy emphasis on the dynamic, *ex ante* approach to competition underpinning the patent system, is *Studiengesellschaft Kohle*. In 1953 a Dr Ziegler had discovered and patented a process for producing aluminum trialkyls ('ATAs'). These had no previous commercial use, but with the new process could be made at 5 per cent of the previous cost. No other processes were commercially competitive. He granted 'Hercules' the exclusive right to sell ATAs using his process in the United States. Hercules was also granted a non-exclusive licence to use the process for producing ATAs; Dr Ziegler reserving the right to license others in the United States to use the process to make ATAs for their own use. Hercules exploited its rights by forming a production and sales joint venture company with 'Stauffer'. Dr Ziegler in fact granted a number of 'use' licences in the United States, including one to Ethyl Corp. Ethyl Corp., however, pressed for sales rights and, after losing an anti-trust action, was granted a special licence on condition of paying an additional 2 per cent royalty to Hercules. There were no constraints on the price or other terms affecting Ethyl Corp.'s sales. In 1970, the government sued the parties for anti-trust violation. It argued, by analogy to *Univis*, that the process patent was exhausted once the product was made under the licence; hence, any restrictions on dealing in those products exceeded the scope of the patent and was illegal. The DC Circuit reversed the District Court's ruling that the restrictions were illegal *per se*. Judge Oberdorfer considered that a formalistic approach based on *per se* rules unsupported by demonstrable economic effect was precluded by *Sylvania*.[230]

The District Court's criticised formalism lay in two matters. It had analysed the anti-trust effect of the licences by first determining what restrictions were outside the scope of the monopoly and then tested them under the anti-trust law. This failed to pay due regard to the fact that patents by definition restrained trade and so, inevitably, led to finding an anti-trust violation.[231] Moreover, the approach treated licences of process patents differently to those of product patents without showing any 'functional difference' between the two. That a patentee of a process had no power over products made by a means other than that covered by the patent did not compel the

---

228 Scherer's 'tentative' conclusion suggested reduced concern where inter-brand competition is vigorous and consumers have a range of distribution methods to choose from: 'The Economics of Vertical Restraints', 52 Antitrust LJ 687, at 707 (1982).

229 The Justice Department under a 'reformed' William F. Baxter as Assistant Attorney-General adopted enforcement standards at least as benign for patent licensing: see for example Abbot B. Lipsky Jr, 'Current Antitrust Division Views on Patent Licensing Practices', 50 Antitrust LJ 515 (1981).

230 *US v Studiengesellschaft Kohle mbH* 670 F. 2d 1122, at 1126, 1129 to 1130 (DC Cir. 1981). The ruling was made 'even assuming *arguendo* that ATAs constitute a relevant market and that the agreements are not defensible as quantity restrictions . . .': *ibid.* at 1126.

231 *Ibid.* at 1128.

conclusion that the patentee also had no power over products made using the process. Hence, although not explained that way, Judge Oberdorfer implicitly rejected the logical fallacy pointed out by Professor Powell in commenting on *Motion Picture Patents*.[232]

Instead of the two-step process taken in the District Court, Judge Oberdorfer proposed a qualified test based on *General Electric*:

> . . . the protection of the patent laws and the coverage of the antitrust laws are not separate issues. Rather, the conduct at issue is illegal if it threatens competition in areas other than those protected by the patent, and is otherwise legal. *The patentee is entitled to exact the full value of his invention but is not entitled to endanger competition in other areas by manipulating his patent monopoly.* It was thus error to consider the scope of the patent protection irrespective of any competitive effects in the first phase of the case, and then rule separately on the anticompetitive effects of the arrangement without consideration of the protection of the patent.[233] (*Emphasis added*)

In Judge Oberdorfer's view, the licensing arrangements satisfied the standard of the rule of reason and the District Court had failed to give adequate consideration to a number of important factors: the patentee could lawfully have licensed no one or granted only an exclusive licence; the process commanded the market because of its inherent superiority and not any 'side arrangement' such as a price-fixing cartel; the licences did not purport to affect products not made by the patented process; the profits from the process were at risk from the competition of anyone who invented around it and, indeed, acted as strong incentives to attract potential competitors; and the Supreme Court's ruling in *Sylvania*.[234]

Although finding more favour than the broad interpretation of *General Electric*, Judge Oberdorfer's test has been criticised for assuming that the patentee's own practising of the invention or the grant of a fully exclusive licence would not breach the anti-trust laws.[235] Certainly, Judge Oberdorfer placed strong reliance on his interpretation of what the scope of the patent authorised and the presumed legitimacy of either self-practice or an exclusive licence under the patent:

> None of these restraints go beyond what the patent itself authorizes. Such an exclusion of competitors and charging of supra-competitive prices are at the core of the patentee's rights, and are legitimate rewards of the patent monopoly.[236]

But, it is not an unqualified reliance. Judge Oberdorfer expressly acknowledged that simply because the patentee could refuse to license at all did not

232 *Ibid.* at 1133 to 1134, see Note 177 above.
233 *Ibid.* at 1128 (footnote omitted).
234 *Ibid.* at 1138. Earlier he also mentioned the valuable role of some protection for licensees in inducing their investment in the technology: *ibid.* at 1135.
235 Turner, 'Basic Principles in Formulating Antitrust and Misuse Constraints on the Exploitation of Intellectual Property Rights', 53 Antitrust LJ 485, at 490.
236 670 F. 2d at 1128; the restraints referred to being the effects of the agreements condemned by the District Court, (1) the exclusion from the market of other potential sellers of ATA made by Ziegler's process; (2) prices above competitive levels; (3) retarded development of new uses of ATAs because of their high price; and (4) consequential restrictions on trade in aluminum alkyls other than ATAs.

mean power to license on any condition.[237] Having referred to the fact that the anti-competitive effects identified by the District Court did not exceed those 'authorised' by the patent, he stated: 'There is no basis in the record for a finding of other anticompetitive effects.'[238] The judgment also makes careful reference to the many Supreme Court rulings striking down attempts to use patents as a cloak for price fixing, market division and attempts to monopolise products not subject to the patent; footnote citations also point to the dangers feared by, among others, Baxter and Buxbaum. But, the evidence under consideration did not suggest the presence of any of these dangers. Further, the licences did not control licencees' rights to deal in ATAs produced by means other than the licensed process (although no economically competitive process was yet available) nor was there any requirement to assign or license back any improved processes they might develop. Judge Oberdorfer was also certainly aware that the judgment allowed a *de facto* monopoly over ATAs but, taking a dynamic view, this was itself a spur to others to find new ways of making ATAs.

Hence, *Studiengesellschaft Kohle* affords a considerable degree of latitude to the patentee and licensing of the patent.[238a] Particularly noticeable is the rejection of the argument that a patent apparently so dominating should be licensed to all comers.[239] Given the government's failure to delineate a market, it is not possible to conclude that ATAs were a discrete market. Nor is it possible to speculate on the relationship of Ethyl Corp. and the joint venture between Hercules and Stauffer. Perhaps, for example, oligopolistic interdependence made any explicit price fixing unnecessary. This, however, ignores the availability of 'use' licences granted presumably to major users. Judge Oberdorfer gave primacy to the goals of the patent system in this case. But, his Honour was aware that patents could be used unacceptably in the light of anti-trust goals. Any failure to investigate assumed anti-trust abuses seems to stem from the limited evidence proved in the case. In reaching his conclusions, Judge Oberdorfer derived further support from the Ninth Circuit's earlier rejection of the government's claim that patent licensing should be viewed as inherently anti-competitive.[240]

---

237   *Ibid.* at 1131.

238   *Ibid.* at 1135, in the next paragraph noting that 'Exclusive licences are tolerated because they *normally* threaten competition to no greater extent than is threatened by the patent itself.' (*Emphasis added*)

238a   The approach has been extended by legislation to relax the application of the 'patent misuse' doctrine to practices such as 'tie-ins': see Patent Misuse Reform Act of 1988, 17 USC §271(d)(4) and (5) and Donald A. Gregory and James J. Trumell, 'Tie-outs – Misuse of Patents', [1992] EIPR 317.

239   This finding might also be justifiable on the principle that exercise of superior skill and forethought and even luck does not found a charge of monopolising: *US v Alcoa* 148 F. 2d 416 (2d Cir. 1945); *Berkey Photo Inc. v Eastman Kodak Co.* 603 F. 2d 263 (2d Cir. 1979).

240   670 F. 2d 1122, at 1137 referring to *US v Westinghouse Electric Corp.* 648 F. 2d 642 (9th Cir. 1981) *affg* 471 F. Supp. 532 (ND Cal. 1978), text at Note 244 and following below. For an interesting case distinguishing *Studiengesellschaft Kohle*, see *International Wood Processors v Power Dry Inc.* 792 F. 2d 416 (4th Cir. 1986). In a bid to refinance exploitation of a patent, some sub-licensees joined together to acquire the patent and

(c)   Foreign trade

The anti-trust laws strike not only at interferences with interstate commerce but also trade between the United States and foreign countries.[241] In 1897, du Pont, ICI and their main German rival agreed to divide up the world into a number of exclusive territories and 'free' territories. Du Pont was left to exploit a territory centred on the United States and ICI, on the British Empire. Each party agreed not to compete directly or indirectly in the designated area of the others. This agreement was ended in 1906, a year prior to du Pont's first prosecution for violation of the anti-trust laws. In its place, the parties set up an arrangement in which each granted exclusive rights under its patents to the others in their respective foreign territories. By the time of this action, the agreement had expanded to include a wide range of chemical products and many major producers in different parts of the world. Judge Ryan agreed with the government that the patent licensing arrangements were primarily a cloak to prevent competition between the various parties.[242]

The question was next briefly considered in *Dunlop v Kelsey-Hayes*. Dunlop held two patents for automobile disc brakes in several countries. It had granted exclusive licences under the patents to different companies in Japan, Italy, Germany and Australia, expressly forbidding them to export their patented articles to the United States. In the course of an unsuccessful infringement action against Kelsey-Hayes, Kelsey-Hayes alleged that the export bans constituted an anti-trust violation as 'an illegal division of world markets'. The Sixth Circuit dismissed the claim shortly:

> Dunlop's agreements with its licensees in Japan, Italy, Germany and Australia cannot be characterized as true horizontal agreements dividing markets. They are merely territorial licences granted by a patentee such as are permitted by 35 USC§261. If one who received a patent from the United States may so restrict his licences without violating the domestic antitrust laws, it would seem clear that a patentee could do the same thing with foreign licences without violating the antitrust laws of this country.[243]

terminate another sub-licensee which they had earlier unsuccessfully attempted to buy out. The horizontal element would seem conclusive, contrast *Miller Insituform Inc. v Insituform of North America Inc.* 830 F. 2d 606 (6th Cir. 1987).
241   For the European Communities' similar approach, see Valentine Korah, *EEC Competition Law and Practice*, ESC Publishing Ltd, 1990 (4th ed.), at ¶2.5.
242   *US v Imperial Chemical Industries Ltd* 100 F. Supp. 504 (SDNY 1951). His Honour's order that ICI not use its patents in the United Kingdom to block imports from the United States under the compulsory licences which he ordered sparked considerable controversy: see 105 F. Supp. 215 (SDNY 1952) and *British Nylon Spinners Ltd v Imperial Chemical Industries Ltd* [1953] 1 Ch. 19 (CA). The UK Court of Appeal granted Spinners, owned 50 per cent by ICI, an injunction preventing ICI complying with the US order in contravention of an exclusive licence ICI had granted Spinners after the initial orders: Areeda and Turner, 1 *Antitrust Law*, at ¶238.
243   *The Dunlop Company Limited v Kelsey-Hayes Company* 484 F. 2d 407, at 417 (6th Cir. 1973). Kelsey-Hayes had supported its claim with the Supreme Court's *per se* condemnation of horizontal market sharing under a trade mark in *US v Topco Associates Inc.* 405 US 596 (1976). That case, and the companion *Sealy* case 388 US 350, have been fiercely attacked by Professors Bork and Posner, see Bork, *The Antitrust Paradox*, at 271, Posner, *Antitrust Law*, at 165 to 166 and Gellhorn, *Antitrust Law and Economics*, at 205

In this passage, the Sixth Circuit appears to hold that, as a patentee may grant territorial licences within the United States, it may do so with impunity in foreign trade. If so, the court appears to be adopting an approach which harks back to the *Dick Co.* and *General Electric* cases. It would also seem inconsistent with what seems an otherwise unobjectionable opinion in the *ICI* case and fails to recognise the limits on a patentee's powers accepted in *Studiengesellschaft Kohle*. It is not, however, very clear from the report what, if any, evidence Kelsey-Hayes led to support its allegation.

The relationship of the anti-trust laws to licensing under foreign patents was the central issue in *Westinghouse*.[244] Westinghouse had technology-sharing agreements relating to heavy industrial electrical products with members of the Mitsubishi group going back to 1923. In 1966–7, it had granted two Mitsubishi companies licences under all its foreign patents except those in Canada. The agreements did not expressly forbid Mitsubishi using or selling the invention in either the United States or Canada, but, when Mitsubishi had approached Westinghouse for permission to operate in the United States, it had always been refused. Stern also indicates that the market in the United States was heavily concentrated, in some cases being a duopoly, and barricaded by high entry barriers. The nature of the entry barriers and the basis for the market definition is not otherwise elaborated, presumably depending in part on Westinghouse's patents. Neither point was raised in Judge Duniway's opinion for the Ninth Circuit. His Honour did, however, indicate that Westinghouse benefited from licences of Mitsubishi's patents and know-how as well as royalties. The US Government sought an order that Westinghouse license Mitsubishi to use the US patents as well.

The appeal was confined to two points. First, the government argued that the Mitsubishi companies had been Westinghouse's licensees for so long that they had become wedded to Westinghouse's technology and could not develop their own without infringing Westinghouse's patents. The second argument was that the licence agreements masked a horizontal conspiracy to keep out of each other's territory. This argument failed on the facts; the first, as a matter of law.

The central point of Judge Duniway's opinion is that Westinghouse only did what the patent authorised and so there could be no anti-trust violation. Judge Duniway found support for this in *Dunlop v Kelsey-Hayes* which also showed that the rule for foreign patents was not different to that for domestic trade. His Honour considered it a 'rule that a holder of a United States patents has a right to refuse to license them'. Further: '. . . no court has held that patentee must grant further licences to potential competitors merely because he has granted them some.'[245] To find otherwise 'would

to 211. Unfortunately, their claims appear somewhat embarrassed by fact, see Scherer and Ross, *Industrial Market Structure and Economic Performance*, at 560 to 561.

244   *US v Westinghouse Electric Corporation* 648 F. 2d 642 (9th Cir. 1981) *affg* 471 F. Supp. 532 (ND Cal. 1978); see the comment by the government's chief trial attorney, Richard H. Stern, 'US v. Westinghouse Electric Corp.: Division of International Markets Permitted', [1983] EIPR 20.

245   *Ibid.* at 648. See also *ibid.* at 647.

severely limit the protection extended by Congress in the laws under which Westinghouse's United States patents were granted'. The anti-trust laws did not go so far.

In conjunction with this claim, the government also argued that, even if the agreements were lawful at the outset, they had reached a point where they were no longer justified. This was flatly rejected: '. . . so too would the patent system be undermined if a licensing agreement, perfectly legal when signed, might later form the basis of an antitrust violation because the licensee had flourished under the agreement.'[246]

The second claim, of a conspiracy to isolate the markets, was brushed aside for want of evidence. The fact that Mitsubishi had sought permission to sell in the United States, had been refused and then had not entered the US market for fear of patent infringement was not the result of agreement but rather of the patents themselves. Mitsubishi's desire to avoid patent infringement: '. . . undoubtedly has an effect on competition, but this is an effect which results from the monopoly granted by the patent laws and does not establish an antitrust violation.'[247]

Judge Duniway's opinion, then, is a very strong endorsement of a very broad immunity for the patentee from the anti-trust laws. There are few, if any, signs of the qualifications which Judge Oberdorfer explicitly referred to in *Studiengesellschaft Kohle* shortly after. From Judge Duniway's opinion, it does not seem that any greater latitude resulted from a perceived difference between domestic and international trade. *Westinghouse*, like *Dunlop v Kelsey-Hayes* before it, assimilated the treatment of foreign licences to that of domestic.

There are, with respect, a number of concerns with Judge Duniway's approach. In so far as his Honour suggested that an agreement which was lawful when signed could not become unlawful at a later date, there must be some doubt.[248] Stern, for example, suggests that a vendor's non-competition obligation on the sale of a business, while reasonable for an initial period, must become unreasonable after the passage of time when the buyer has had a chance to build up goodwill.[249] The difficulty with this example is that the law may require the duration of the restraint to be fixed in advance (itself no easy task). Still, the point remains, circumstances may change and so affect the anti-trust considerations. Perhaps, the fear of prejudicing the patentee's incentive to license can be harmonised with the danger of circumstances changing by permitting the initial licences for the term of the patents (or any lesser period agreed), but then requiring the licensee to face the world independently at the licence's expiry.

The need for any harmonisation on the *Sylvania* approach assumes that the market was in fact as Stern alleged, a barricaded oligopoly. That was

---

246 *Ibid.*
247 *Ibid.* at 649.
248 Judge Duniway's words are more limited than that. For a contrary view, see *US v Jerrold Electronics Corp.* 187 F. Supp. 545, 557 (1960) *aff'd per curiam* 363 US 567 (1961).
249 [1981] EIPR at 22 to 23.

not a view which received any support in Judge Duniway's opinion. But, where it has been proved, the courts have forbidden co-operation between an incumbent and the most likely new entrant.[250]

Stern also attacked the Ninth Circuit's rejection of the concealed market-sharing arrangement. He does not, however, appear to be advancing a theory of even a tacit understanding between the parties – one which would seem rebutted by Mitsubishi's requests to enter the US market anyway. Rather, he argues that, the licences having been entered into, 'it is eminently foreseeable that a licensee will refrain from patent infringement'.[251] Does this show agreement? The difficulty with his argument lies partly in its foundation on the unlikelihood of a licensee's ever risking its own protection from non-licensees for success in an action of infringement or challenge to the patent's validity. There does not seem much fairness in allowing the licensee to take more than it bargained for while still protecting itself from others by means of the patents.[252] Stern would, presumably, confine this sort of intervention to special cases of the sort he claimed *Westinghouse* was. While the claims he makes of the facts do raise cause for doubt, they are not how the court saw the situation. Indeed, both the District Court and the Ninth Circuit interpreted the government's claims much more broadly and independent of the fact situation:

> What the government is really proposing is this: Since all monopolies undesirably limit competition, every patent licensing contract should, if at all possible, be viewed as a 'combination in restraint of trade.' Taken to its logical limits, this argument would find almost every patent licensing agreement to be illegal. . . . This is a demand calculated to alter and substantially reduce the scope of the patent monopoly. It should be addressed to Congress, not to the courts.[253]

3.3.4 Parallel imports

Turning to parallel imports and US patent law, the policy tensions reviewed when only domestic trade is involved need to be kept in mind. In domestic trade, once the patentee had sold an article protected by the patent, the power of the patent was said to be exhausted. Any further controls on dealings in the article need to be considered under general law. Where the patentee's action lay directly against a licensee, different considerations *might* operate. In particular, considerable latitude has been accorded to patentees seeking to restrict the territory in which a licensee could make,

---

250   *Yamaha Motor Co. v FTC* 657 F. 2d 971 (8th Cir. 1981).
251   [1981] EIPR 23.
252   Even the European Commission would permit the licensor to terminate the licence if the licensee attacks the licensed technology: see for example Know-how group exemption, Regulation 556/89, Article 3(4).
253   *Westinghouse* 471 F. Supp. 532 at 542 *per* Judge Weigel, see also *Studiengesellschaft Kohle* 670 F. 2d 1122, at 1137 to 1138 (DC Cir. 1981). Contrast Baxter, 'Legal Restrictions on Exploitation of the Patent Monopoly: An Economic Analysis', 76 Yale LJ 267, at 347 (1966).

use or sell articles covered by the patent. Licences under foreign patents have been treated at least as generously as domestic licences. Attempts to dress up 'sales' as restricted licences might, however, meet with considerable suspicion. But, since the *Sylvania* ruling, even the general law is likely to look benignly on territorial restraints imposed on sub-purchasers, especially in unconcentrated markets. Anti-trust concerns, however, have played little role to date in the parallel import cases.

A case like *Betts v Willmott* in Anglo-Commonwealth law begins the study of US treatment, *Holiday v Mattheson*.[254] The result was the same. Holiday owned patents for the same product in the United States and the United Kingdom. Mattheson bought the patented product in the United Kingdom from a purchaser of Holiday without any express restrictions or conditions. He imported the product into the United States with the intention of using or selling it and was sued for infringing the US patent.

Judge Wallace in the Circuit Court dismissed the action on the general rule of property in goods passing on sale. His Honour held:

> When the owner sells an article without any reservation respecting its use, or the title which is to pass, the purchaser acquires the whole right of the vendor in the thing sold: the right to use it, to repair it, and to sell it to others; and second purchasers acquire the rights of the seller, and may do with the article whatever the first purchaser could lawfully have done if he had not parted with it. The *presumption* arising from such a sale is that the vendor intends to part with all his rights in the thing sold, and that the purchaser is to acquire an unqualified property in it; and it would be inconsistent with the presumed understanding of the parties to permit the vendor to retain the power of restricting the purchaser to using the thing bought in a particular way, or in a particular place, for a limited period of time, or from selling his rights to others. It is quite immaterial whether the thing sold is a patented article or not; or whether the vendor is the owner of a patent which gives him a monopoly of its use and sale. If these circumstances happen to concur the legal effect of the transaction is not changed, *unless by the conditions of the bargain the monopoly right is impressed on the thing purchased*; and if the vendor sells without reservation or restriction, he parts with his monopoly so far as it can in any way qualify the rights of the purchaser.
>
> The purchaser does not acquire any rights in the monopoly, but he does acquire the right of unrestricted ownership in the article he buys as against the vendor, including, as an inseparable incident, the right to use and enjoy it, and to transfer his title to others.[255] (*Emphasis added*)

The striking aspect of this case is its similarity to the approach taken by Lord Hatherley in *Betts v Willmott*. Judge Wallace did not refer at all to the territorial nature of the patents in the United States and the United Kingdom. To all intents and purposes, he treated the sale in the United Kingdom as if it had been a sale in the United States and, accordingly, applied the domestic principle of exhaustion. As in *Betts v Willmott* but

---

254   24 Fed. 185 (SDNY, 1885).
255   *Ibid.* at 185 to 186; Judge Wallace, it will be remembered, presided in *Apollinaris Co. v Scherer*, see Chapter 2.3.2 above.

unlike the approach subsequently declared by Shiras J in *Keeler*, Judge Wallace did consider that rights under the patent could be preserved by appropriate contractual terms.

The territorial nature of the patent was, however, crucial in *Boesch v Gräff*.[256] Gräff and others owned a patent in the United States for mitrailleuse lamp burners. Boesch had bought the burners from one Hecht, in Germany. Some of Gräff's co-owners owned patents for the identical invention in Germany. But, under German patent law, Hecht could sell the burners without the patent owners' permission.[257] Gräff and his co-owners sued for infringement of the US patent.

Fuller CJ, for the court, posed the question for resolution as:

> . . . whether a dealer residing in the United States can purchase in another country articles patented there, from a person authorized to sell them, and import them to and sell them in the United States, without the license or consent of the owners of the United States patent.[258]

This form of the question squarely presented the separate territorial nature of the patent grant for consideration. The independent territorial nature of the patent right proved decisive:

> The right which Hecht had to make and sell the burners in Germany was allowed him under the laws of that country, and purchasers from him could not be thereby authorized to sell the articles in the United States in defiance of the rights of patentees under a United States patent. A prior foreign patent operates under our law to limit the duration of the subsequent patent here, but that is all. The sale of articles in the United States under a United States patent cannot be controlled by foreign laws.[259]

Three factors suggest that Fuller CJ intended making a general statement of principle that acts done outside the United States did not affect the patentee's rights within the United States. First, there is the form in which he phrased the issue before the court. Second, he stated that foreign laws cannot control the sale of patented articles in the United States. The third lies in a key element of the rebuttal of the principle of territoriality by its characterisation as 'conflictual rule'. Fuller CJ considered that the function of a foreign patent had a very limited role in US law: it served only to fix the term of a domestic patent founded on a foreign invention.

However, the instant facts did not call for such a broad principle. The articles bought by Boesch had not been put on the market by Gräff or with his consent. Accordingly, *Boesch v Gräff* left the courts with considerable

---

256   133 US 697 (1890).
257   Section 5 of the Imperial patent law of Germany provided that: '. . . the patent does not affect persons who, at the time of the patentee's application, have already commenced to make use of the invention in the country, or made the preparations requisite for such use': 133 US at 701. The German courts had upheld Hecht's rights to rely on this section.
258   *Ibid.* at 702.
259   *Ibid.* at 703.

scope for continuing the policy battle.[260] In cases not involving parallel imports, however, the courts have steadfastly pointed to the territorial independence of separate national patents.[261]

The next cases involved separate ownership created by assignments of the rights in corresponding patents in different countries. In *Featherstone v Ormond Cycle Co.*,[262] the patentee in the United Kingdom had assigned his corresponding patent in the United States to the complainant, Featherstone. The Ormond Cycle Co. was the patentee's licensee in the United Kingdom and imported pneumatic tyres made according to the patent into the United States. Circuit Judge Townsend held that the US patent had been infringed. The owner of the UK patent could not authorise sales in the United States in conflict with the US patent. Accordingly, the UK patentee could not empower its licensee to sell the patented article in the United States.[263] The separate ownership of the patents provided a clear basis for adopting the territorial approach taken in *Boesch v Gräff*.

Dickerson v Matheson was the first in a series of cases about the patent ownership regime established by a major chemicals and dye manufacturer.[264] 'Bayer', retaining its patent in Germany, assigned its US patent for benzo-purpurine to Dickerson. Before the assignment it had licensed both patents to 'Aniline' of Berlin.

Matheson, well aware that Bayer consistently blocked exports to the United States, sought to buy one ton of the benzo-purpurine in Europe free from any restriction preventing importation into the United States. He had approached Bayer directly, but had been informed that restrictions on its import into the United States would be imposed. Therefore, he arranged for an agent to place an order with Aniline 'strong for export'. The agent went to Aniline's London offices and, before paying for the goods and taking delivery of them, was given an invoice on which was printed a condition prohibiting export to the United States. A similar condition was printed on the packaging of the goods.

The Second Circuit distinguished between sales by a patentee, or a licensee, with rights in both a foreign country and the United States and a sale by a licensee in only the foreign country. In the former case, if the purchaser bought without restrictions, the purchaser would acquire unrestricted title and could import into the United States freely. In the latter case, the licensee could not authorise importation into the United States as it did not have the authority of the US patentee. Accordingly, if Matheson's agent had bought without restrictions, he would have been free to import the benzo-purpurine. However, the printing of the condition on the invoice was

---

260 To similar effect, Chisum, 4 *Patents*, at §16.05[3]. A further point worth noting is Fuller CJ's subsequent dissent in *Keeler*.
261 See *Goodyear Tire & Rubber Co. v Rubber Tire Co.* 164 Fed. 869 (CC SD Ohio 1908) *per* Circuit Judge Lurton; *Canadian Filters (Harwich) Limited v Lear-Siegler Inc.* 412 F. 2d 577 (1st Cir. 1969).
262 53 Fed. 110 (SDNY 1892).
263 *Ibid.* at 111. Compare Lord Hatherley's *dicta* in *Betts v Willmott*, Note 79 above.
264 57 Fed. 524 (2d Cir. 1893).

held to incorporate it into the terms of the sale. Hence, restrictions had been imposed and Matheson received no authority to import.[265]

The Second Circuit, therefore, both approved the reasoning in *Holiday v Mattheson* and followed *Boesch v Gräff*. Within the same judgment, it reached the same position as the Anglo-Commonwealth law in *Betts v Willmott* and in *Tilghman*. Like those cases, however, it did not explain why the territorial nature of the patent was unimportant in the *Holiday v Mattheson* situation.

In *Tinling's* case, the product was phenacetine and once again Bayer's US patent had been assigned to Dickerson.[266] There was no patent in Germany, however. Bayer produced the phenacetine in Germany and sold it there in boxes bearing notices prohibiting its importation into and sale in the United States. Tinling bought up boxes in Germany and imported them into the United States where he was sued by Dickerson. The matter came before the courts on Dickerson's application for a temporary injunction.

Tinling argued that Dickerson was really only Bayer's agent. Since the phenacetine was bought from Bayer, it could be brought into the United States free from the patent.

The Eighth Circuit held that Tinling did not have authority to import the phenacetine into the United States and so had infringed the patent because the express condition against importation meant that the phenacetine was not freed from the patent monopoly. In so deciding, the court made several assumptions in favour of Tinling. First, for the sake of argument, it assumed that Bayer owned the US patent. Second, it conceded, without deciding, that the principle in *Holiday v Mattheson* was correct.

The court then found that, just as a patentee could sell without restrictions, so it could sell its patented articles subject to restrictions on future dealings with the article. From this it followed that:

> If the corporation sold the patented article subject to such a restriction, the purchasers, with notice of this limitation, whether immediate or remote, could acquire no better right than strangers to infringe upon the monopoly secured by the patent. That monopoly would still remain intact, and purchasers of the phenacetine which had been sold under the restriction must be liable for its use and sale in the United States to the same extent as those who made it or bought it of strangers within their limits.[267]

It is not entirely clear from the report how Tinling became affected with notice. The Eighth Circuit stated that the notice to the purchaser could be 'immediate or remote'. This suggests that the purchaser need not be bound by contract with the patentee and that it may suffice if the notice is brought to the purchaser's attention by some other means. The court also stated that the patent monopoly 'would still remain intact'. Tinling would be treated as any other person acting without the patentee's authority, in other words, as

---

265 *Ibid*. at 527 to 528.
266 *Dickerson v Tinling* 84 Fed. 192 (8th Cir. 1897).
267 *Ibid*. at 195.

an infringer. As in *Holiday v Mattheson*, this suggests that liability rested on patent law, not contract. It also supports the conclusion that the notice need not be brought home to the purchaser by contract. On this analysis, the Eighth Circuit's approach corresponds to the Anglo-Commonwealth treatment of domestic sales but applies a different rule for foreign trade to that indicated for domestic trade by *Keeler*.

Sheldon's case also involved the phenacetine patent. The goods had been seized in an abortive smuggling attempt and Sheldon had bought the product at a Customs' sale of condemned goods. Before buying, Sheldon had notice of Dickerson's patent and his objection to importation but argued that sale by the Customs validated his dealings with the product in the United States. The Second Circuit tersely noted that there was no authority for this proposition and found the patent infringed.[268]

Although the court in *Sheldon* did not discuss the grounds of liability in detail, its decision is certainly consistent with the earlier holding in *Matheson* as Sheldon had clear notice before his purchase. Hence, where the foreign seller also had power to sell in the domestic market, the presence or absence of notice was determinative. One Circuit Court, however, only assumed, without deciding, this for the purposes of an interlocutory proceeding. If the foreign seller did not also have domestic authority, the Second Circuit's *dictum* proposed a rule based on territoriality.

That proposal was upheld by the Second Circuit in *Daimler Manufacturing Co. v Conklin*.[269] Conklin, on holiday in Europe, bought a Daimler motor car in Germany from Daimler Motoren Gesellschaft which had authority to sell such vehicles in Germany. No limitations about the use of the car were imposed on Conklin at the time of the sale. At the end of his holiday, Conklin returned to the United States taking his car which he intended to use, not sell. In the United States, however, Daimler Manufacturing Co. owned patents for the car and various components incorporated into it by assignment from the German inventor. In the ensuing infringement action, it was not clear from the facts before the court whether the car and components were covered by equivalent patents in Germany. Conklin claimed that they were not but, the court seems to have assumed they were.

Conklin, relying on the authorities from *Wilson v Rousseau* to *Keeler*, argued that the cases distinguished between the patentee's right to sell and the right to use. In the latter case, the sale of the article took the article outside the scope of the patent and the purchaser could deal with the article free from constraint. At first instance, this argument was accepted.

On appeal, the Second Circuit rejected Conklin's contentions:

> We think this does not follow. The use of articles covered by a United States patent within the United States can no more be controlled by foreign law than the sale can. The sale by a German patentee of a patented article may take it out of the monopoly of the German patent, but how can it take it out of the

268 *Dickerson v Sheldon* 98 Fed. 621, at 622 (2d Cir. 1899).
269 170 Fed. 70 (2d Cir. 1909) *cert. denied* 216 US 621 (1910).

monopoly of the American patentee who has not sold. The purchaser abroad could not get any greater rights than the patentee has from whom he buys.[270]

As in *Boesch v Gräff*, the court ignored the sale in Germany because of the separate territorial nature of the two patents. In *Conklin's* case, the patents had originally been owned by the same patentee and, at least in the United States, assigned to a different legal person. However, it was not just the separate ownership of the patents which was decisive. The patents themselves were independent rights. If they had not been territorially independent, the rule confirmed in *Keeler* would have operated. The Second Circuit distinguished these cases because they did not deal with acts outside the United States where US laws had no effect:

> The language of the court in these cases . . . as to the right to use or sell, must be understood to mean use or sell within the United States, the territory which the letters patent cover. It cannot be supposed that the court was speaking of a right to use or sell in other countries, where our laws have no force.[271]

Hence, the exhaustion theory seemed to be confined to acts within the United States.

However, parallel imports were allowed on the exhaustion theory in *Curtiss Aeroplane*.[272] During World War I Curtiss sold a large number of its JN-4 aeroplanes and spare parts to the British Government's Imperial Munitions Board in Canada. The aeroplanes and the additional engines were covered by patents which Curtiss owned in both the United States and Canada. Curtiss also granted the Board the exclusive right and licence under its Canadian patents:

> . . . to manufacture such aeroplanes and/or engines within the Dominion of Canada, for sale to or use by the British government or the governments of any of its possessions, but not for manufacture, use, or sale otherwise.

The agreements between Curtiss and the Board also contained clauses that the aeroplanes and engines would 'become and be the absolute property of the British government'.

At the end of the war, the Board was disbanded and its assets sold off. 'United', having been rebuffed once, bought a large number of the JN-4 aeroplanes and engines through an intermediary. It intended to sell them in the United States and had informed the Board of its intention before the sale was complete. The Board did not impose any restrictions on United's ability to deal with the aeroplanes and engines. When United began selling them in the United States, Curtiss sued for infringement of its US patents.

Circuit Judge Rogers, for the court, viewed it as highly significant that Curtiss had given its permission to the making of the products, had aided in their manufacture by providing technical assistance and had been compensated for every one. In addition, knowing of United's intended use,

---

270 *Ibid.* at 72.
271 *Ibid.*, references omitted.
272 *Curtiss Aeroplane and Motor Corporation v United Aircraft Engineering Corporation* 266 Fed. 71 (2d Cir. 1920).

the UK Government had sold the aeroplanes without any restraint about their use or sale in the United States. The parties understood and intended that the aeroplanes and engines were to become the absolute property of the British Government. And, having 'searched in vain for any restriction or condition as to the right to use or to vend', the British Government obtained 'a full and unqualified right to use and sell the planes and engines' which it could pass on to subsequent purchasers. Furthermore, the very nature of the products in question and the reason for their purchase indicated that they were intended to be used anywhere throughout the world, including the United States. Indeed, if they had been used in the United States during the war as part of the training of Canadian pilots, Curtiss could hardly have claimed its US patents were infringed.[273]

His Honour distinguished the cases in which parallel imports had been barred. They fell into either of two categories. Either the purchaser's ability to deal in the products was explicitly and unequivocally restricted or the products had been put onto the market abroad without any participation by the patentee in the United States.[274] Here, the patentee had participated in the sale of the products, reaping the reward for that sale, and had sold them unconditionally. Accordingly, Judge Rogers found that the case fell within the rule developed in *Adams v Burke* and *Keeler*:

> If a patentee or his assignee sells a patented article, that article is freed from the monopoly of *any* patents which the vendor may possess. If the thing sold contains inventions of several United States patents owned by the vendor, the article is freed from each and all of them; and if the vendor has divided his monopoly into different territorial monopolies, his sale frees the article from them all. *If the vendor's patent monopoly consists of foreign and domestic patents, the sale frees the article from the monopoly of both his foreign and his domestic patents*, and where there is no restriction in the contract of sale the purchaser acquired the complete title and full right to use and sell the article in any and every country.[275] (*Emphasis added*)

Although these cases were all concerned with domestic market division under a single US patent, Judge Rogers also relied on *Holiday v Mattheson* to extend the exhaustion theory to market division based on foreign and domestic patents. As in *Holiday v Mattheson*, payment in full to Curtiss of the price demanded was crucial. It meant that Curtiss could no longer be concerned with the price charged for the product. Its monopoly was exhausted.

No doubt, the UK Government would have been put to considerable commercial inconvenience if its aeroplanes could not be bought in Canada for use in the United States. But, it might be wondered why the express terms of the agreement limited its powers of sale and use explicitly to itself

---

273 *Ibid*. at 75, 77, 79. These facts have been relied on to suggest that the contract of sale between the parties expressly contemplated the Board acquiring unfettered title to the aeroplanes and parts: see *Beecham Group Limited v International Products Limited* [1968] RPC 129, at 133, 135 *per* Rudd J, text at Note 104 above.
274 *Ibid*. at 77.
275 *Ibid*. at 78.

and the governments of its possessions if commercial sale and use in the United States were contemplated. Nor did Judge Rogers explain why the UK Government needed to impose restraints about use under US patents which it did not own. Instead, relying on factual distinctions, he avoided analysing why the territorial nature of patent rights did not prevent acts under the Canadian patent from exhausting the US rights. His Honour was not assailed by the doubts the Eighth Circuit felt about *Holiday v Mattheson*. Nor did he find anything inconsistent in the Second Circuit's own earlier decision in *Conklin's* case.

Subsequently, the importer of a machine bought from the foreign patentee of a foreign patent infringed the legally separate owner's rights under the corresponding domestic patent in *T.C. Weygandt Co. v Van Emden*. The principles underlying this finding were not discussed.[276]

However, *Griffin v Keystone Mushroom Farm Inc.* raised the choice between the exhaustion theory and the independent territorial nature of foreign and domestic patents directly.[277] Griffin owned patents in both the United States and Italy for a composting machine and its components. He had appointed 'Longwood' as his exclusive licensee in the United States and another person, Carminati, as his exclusive licensee in Italy. 'Keystone' ran a mushroom farming business in the United States. It bought three of Griffin's composting machines f.o.b. Genoa from Carminati. It imported them into the United States, using one on its own farm and selling the other two. When Griffin sued for infringement of his US patent, Keystone applied for summary judgment dismissing the action. Chief Judge Lord in the District Court refused the application.

Keystone relied on two overlapping arguments. First, it argued that the exhaustion theory based on *Adams v Burke* applied to articles sold outside the territorial limits of the United States as well as to those sold within the United States. Second, if Griffin could stop importation into the United States, Keystone argued that the licensing arrangements between Griffin and Carminati would give Griffin a windfall 'double recovery' which was not intended by the Patent Code.

Chief Judge Lord rejected the first argument as inconsistent with *Boesch v Gräff* and *Conklin's* case. These cases showed that the source of the alleged infringer's authority under the foreign law was irrelevant to the issue of infringement of a US patent. His Honour expressly rejected Keystone's argument that *Boesch v Gräff* did not apply because Hecht, the seller in Germany, did not derive his rights from the patentees by referring to the form of the question posed by Fuller CJ.[278]

His Honour also rejected Keystone's second argument as misconceived. It did not acknowledge that the US patent was a separate right existing independently of the Italian patent. As it was a separate right, Griffin was

---

276   40 F. 2d 938, at 940 (SDNY 1930).
277   453 F. Supp. 1243 (ED Pa. 1978) compare *Tilghman's* case, from Note 81, above.
278   *Ibid.* at 1285, see Note 258 above.

entitled to charge a fee for its use in addition to that charged for use of the Italian right. Furthermore, the contrary approach could involve the court in invidious comparisons of the extent of protection afforded under the foreign and domestic patents and, also, under the two licensing agreements. In his Honour's words:

> The 'double recovery' theory advanced by defendant fails principally in that it misconceives the underlying theory of patent infringement under the United States Patent laws . . . .
>
> The plaintiff's action is premised in the final analysis not on wrongs done to three composting machines covered by United States patents but rather on invasion of his rights under those patents. These machines were the mere instruments of that alleged tortious activity. The sale or use of each machine in both countries represents potentially two separate torts against the plaintiff and infringes potentially on two separate sets of right held by him (assuming the conceptual underpinning of the Italian patent law to conform to our own). The non-tortiousness of defendant's conduct in Italy cannot enter into an adjudication of the plaintiff's rights in this country. That the plaintiff has been or can be compensated by Carminati, thereby making the sale and the defendant's acts in Italy non-tortious, therefore cannot compromise his discrete right to exclusive practise of the patented article in the United States.[279]

Chief Judge Lord's reasoning clearly adopts the broad interpretation of *Boesch v Gräff*, even though it was open to his Honour to take the distinctions accepted in *Holiday v Mattheson* and the *Curtiss* case. Furthermore, the terms of the opinion do not suggest that his Honour intended to rely on the more limited distinction drawn in *Dickerson v Mattheson* between a licensee for one jurisdiction and a licensee for both jurisdictions.

The District Courts of New Jersey and Kansas were subsequently unable to agree on the correct approach to resolving the issue. Judge Sarokin in New Jersey applied the exhaustion theory to deny the patentee a remedy and then the territoriality principle to find the defendant, Med-Tech, an infringer.[280] In Kansas, Chief Judge O'Connor refused to endorse Judge Sarokin's approach.[281]

Sanofi owned patents in the United States for a drug, acepromazine maleate. It had appointed American Home Products Corporation (AHPC) as its exclusive licensee for the sale of this drug for veterinary purposes in the United States which was the only use for which the drug was approved in the United States. Med-Tech had not obtained the drug from AHPC. Med-Tech, or its parent, had placed two orders for the drug with a broker. The broker had arranged to buy the drug in France, where the drug was not patented, from one of Sanofi's subsidiaries. The subsidiary had sold the drug to the broker on condition that it not be imported into the United States and on the fraudulent understanding that the drugs were intended for South America.

---

279 *Ibid.* For the problems of comparing the two patents and the two licences see 1286 to 1287.
280 *Sanofi SA v Med-Tech Veterinarian Products Inc.* 565 F. Supp. 931 (DNJ 1983).
281 *Sanofi SA v Med-Tech Veterinarian Products Inc.* 222 USPQ 143 (DKan. 1983).

Med-Tech did not know of the condition nor did it participate in the fraud. Apparently, Sanofi's subsidiary did not publicise its condition in the United States although it did advertise its products there. When Med-Tech began selling the drug in the United States, Sanofi and AHPC sued for infringement of the US patent.

Sanofi and AHPC argued that, as a matter of law, a sale of a patented article abroad by the patent holder did not waive its rights under the patent. Alternatively, they argued that any waiver of the patentee's rights could not affect the position of the exclusive licensee. A third argument based on fraud was dismissed because Med-Tech was not a party to it and had bought the drugs without notice of the fraud.

Judge Sarokin rejected the plaintiffs' first contention but accepted the alternative argument. In rejecting the first claim, his Honour applied *Holiday v Mattheson* and distinguished the cases based on *Boesch v Gräff* because:

> Here, however, it was the patentee that made and profited from the initial sale abroad, and, despite having had the opportunity to do so, it placed no restrictions in the sales contract upon further disposition of the product by the purchaser.[282]

That is, two factors defeated Sanofi's contention. First, the patentee itself had sold the drug, thereby receiving full compensation under the monopoly. Second, it had sold without placing restrictions on subsequent dealings in the drugs.

The decision may mean that it is necessary to distinguish between sales by (independent) licensees and subsidiaries since the first factor ignores the separate legal personality of Sanofi and the subsidiary which actually made and sold the drugs. Only in *Tinling's* case had a court previously contemplated overlooking distinct legal personality and there it was an assumption made for the purposes of the interlocutory proceedings when, even on the assumption, the court found clear grounds for rejecting the defendant's argument. Furthermore, both the *Conklin* and *Griffin* cases appear inconsistent with Judge Sarokin's view. Accordingly, some doubt must attach to this aspect of his Honour's ruling.[283]

The second factor is also difficult. The subsidiary had sold the drugs to the broker on condition that they could not be imported into the United States and on the understanding that the drugs would be imported into South America. However, Judge Sarokin held that Sanofi had waived its rights because it did not impose *written* conditions on the purchaser at the time of sale.[284] Accordingly, the presumption that the seller intended to pass

---

282   565 F. Supp. 931, at 938.
283   In related proceedings against other members of the Med-Tech Group, Chief Judge O'Connor observed that the French subsidiary was not the patentee and could not licence anyone under the patent. Moreover, the evidence before his Honour did not justify disregarding the separate corporate personality of Sanofi and its subsidiary: 222 USPQ 143, at 148 to 149 (DKan. 1983) at Note 286 below.
284   565 F. Supp. at 938.

all its title in the goods applied and, as against Sanofi, Med-Tech got full, unrestrained title.

His Honour does not explain why the conditions must be in writing to be effective. The requirement appears to be a device to limit the patentee's ability to disrupt the operation of ordinary commercial policy for dealings in goods. It is also worthy of note that Judge Sarokin chose to base the decision on this ground rather than absence of notice to Med-Tech.

Judge Sarokin found Med-Tech liable for infringement, however, on the plaintiffs' second contention. The rule that the sale of a patented article, whether abroad or domestically, exhausts the patentee's monopoly only applied where the seller had authority to sell in the United States. Since AHPC was Sanofi's exclusive licensee for sale of the drug in the United States for veterinary uses, Sanofi itself had no authority to sell the drug in the United States for that purpose. Accordingly, Sanofi could not confer on another, here Med-Tech, a right which it did not itself possess.[285]

Yet again, the decision does not explain why the territorial nature of patent rights is presumed not to apply in one case but does in the other.

Judge Sarokin's opinion must be contrasted to that of Chief Judge O'Connor's in the District Court for Kansas. After successfully enjoining the defendants in the New Jersey action, Sanofi and AHPC brought an action in Kansas against other members of the Med-Tech group. The relief sought, however, was only an injunction protecting AHPC's exclusive licence and, as in New Jersey, was granted because Sanofi could not defeat its earlier licence by a later licence.[286]

In doing so, Chief Judge O'Connor advised that he had reservations about Judge Sarokin's approach: 'This court is not bound by, nor do we necessarily accept, the New Jersey court's conclusion that plaintiff Sanofi should be barred from receiving a preliminary injunction in this case.'[287]

First, Chief Judge O'Connor was not as ready as Judge Sarokin to pierce the corporate veil and disregard the 'corporate separateness' of Sanofi and its French subsidiary. More significantly, Chief Judge O'Connor's doubts stemmed from concerns in line with *Griffin* and a broad interpretation of *Boesch v Gräff*:

> . . . were we to hold as [Med-Tech] suggest, we would throw the current licensing system into a state of chaos. Anytime someone acquired a patented product from a seller in privity with the patentee, they would have an implied license. A licensing agreement in international patent situations such as this, however, requires more than just the possession of the patented article. See Griffin v Keystone Mushroom Farm Inc. Words and conduct sufficient to indicate a contractual relationship are required to form a licensor-licensee relationship. In this case, for example, if the defendants had bought the acepromazine maleate from a European licensee of Sanofi, defendants contend

---

285 *Ibid.* at 939 to 940. The *Curtiss Aeroplane* case was expressly distinguished as a case where the foreign seller was granted power to sell anywhere, including the United States, and Judge Sarokin found that the correct analogy was to *Conklin, ibid.* at 941 to 942.
286 222 USPQ 143, at 149 (DKan. 1983).
287 *Ibid.* at 148.

that they would have an implied license to sell the drug in the United States. This situation would make the United States licensing agreement worthless.[288]

Chief Judge O'Connor did not reject the cases on actual sale abroad by a domestic patentee. But, as in *Griffin* and like the Anglo-Commonwealth courts in *Tilghman*, *Briscoe* and the *Beecham* cases, he clearly placed considerable importance on the international context and the territorial limitations of patents. He was not prepared to imply a licence for the United States from mere sale abroad because the economic consequences for international licensing and, particularly, the domestic licensee would be catastrophic.

The facts of *Hattori* do not advance the debate much further, although parts of Judge Cedarbaum's ruling indicate sympathy for the application of the domestic exhaustion rule to foreign trade.[289] 'Refac' held a number of patents in the United States and elsewhere relating to timepieces. It had sued a member of the Seiko group for infringement of its US patents as a result of which it had granted Hattori a non-exclusive licence under all its US patents, any patents owned by other members of the Refac group and all 'non-US counterparts' of those patents.[290] Refac also promised not to sue Hattori or any purchaser from it under any of its existing or future patents. Hattori had made watches and components protected by Refac's patents and sold them abroad. Some of these were bought up by third parties and imported into the United States. When Refac started suing the importers for patent infringement, Hattori sought a declaration that the terms of the licence precluded Refac from such actions.

Judge Cedarbaum resolved the issues by reference to whether the licence granted Hattori the right to sell abroad as well as in the United States. As a matter of construction, his Honour found that Hattori was licensed to sell within the United States and abroad, there being no geographical restriction on the right of sale granted. Refac's attempt to infer one by relying on the grant of a right to make and sell products 'coming within the scope of US Patents' was rejected because in long-standing patent usage 'scope' defined the invention protected not the geographical area of protection. Further, even if the right to sell was limited to sale within the United States, as a matter of law a sale abroad for resale in the United States was the exercise of a right to sell *in the United States*.

In reaching his conclusion, Judge Cedarbaum restated his understanding of the exhaustion doctrine:

> In general, the first sale of a product by a patentee or licensee exhausts the patent monopoly, and deprives the holder of patent rights of any further control over resale of the product. This principle applies to an *authorized first sale abroad* by a patentee or licensee *who also has the right to sell in* the United

288   *Ibid.* at 149, references omitted.
289   *Kabushiki Kaisha Hattori Seiko v Refac Technology Development Corporation* 690 F. Supp. 1339 (SDNY 1988).
290   This phrase was understood by the parties to grant rights in the United States to practise the teaching in the foreign patent: *ibid.* at 1343 Note 3.

States. Following such a sale, the holder of United States patent rights *is barred from preventing resale in the United States* or from collecting a royalty when the foreign customer resells the article here.[291]

As expressed, his Honour's views could be seen as a marked shift in favour of international exhaustion. There is, for example, no qualification limiting the exhaustion for notice brought home to the purchaser. His Honour's reliance on *Univis* might well support such an extensive view of the effect of exhaustion. However, that sort of issue was not under consideration and would be inconsistent even with the parallel import cases relied on. Furthermore, the opinion does not refer to the quite substantial body of contrary judicial opinion. *Hattori*, then, is perhaps best seen as Judge Sarokin viewed *Curtiss Aeroplane*; a case in which the parties expressly contemplated the licensee having full and free rights in both the foreign and domestic markets.

3.4 Conclusion

In both the United States and the Anglo-Commonwealth jurisdictions, the first and key issue is whether the person who made the first sale in the foreign market also had authority to sell in the domestic market. If so, the (rebuttable) presumption is that the territorial nature of patents will be disregarded. It will not usually matter whether the foreign marketing is initiated by the domestic patentee or a licensee provided the person has authority to sell in both markets. The nature of patents as discrete, territorially limited rights will prevail, however, if the first sale in the foreign market is by someone not also authorised to sell in the domestic market.

Although reaching essentially similar results, it is important to bear in mind that the two bodies of law rely on different means. In the United States, the presumption arises under a form of the exhaustion doctrine, while it depends solely on implied consent in the Anglo-Commonwealth countries.

In the case of a foreign sale where the seller has authority also to sell in the domestic jurisdiction, both bodies of law recognise that the presumption of authority to import may be rebutted. This requires clear notice to the importer that importation into the domestic market is not authorised. Notice must be effected before the importer makes the purchase of the goods in question.

In the Anglo-Commonwealth jurisdictions, it is clear that effective notice operates as a matter of patent law rather than contract. So, it is probably not necessary that the notice be contractually binding. Hence, a letter of warning or even the importer's own prior knowledge may be sufficient to rebut the general presumption. In at least one case, *Salim*, 'inexplicable' failure to

---

291 *Ibid.* at 1342, citations omitted are to *Univis Lens Co.*, *Holiday v Mattheson*, *Curtiss Aeroplane* and Judge Sarokin's ruling in *Sanofi v Med-Tech*.

endorse the patented articles themselves with an appropriate notice was viewed with considerable disfavour.

In the United States, it is not entirely clear whether notice rebutting the general presumption takes effect under the patent or as a matter of contract. It may well be that the treatment of parallel imports departs from the US courts' treatment of domestic exhaustion issues in this respect. However, the courts' approach before *Sylvania*, and perhaps again in the recent case of *Hattori*, suggests that a court which regards the condition as taking effect under contract rather than the patent would probably also find the condition contrary to the anti-trust laws. Apart from *Hattori*, that approach has not received much acceptance by the courts in cases of parallel imports.

Where the foreign sale is initiated by a licensee or assignee limited to the foreign market, most Anglo-Commonwealth and US courts have relied on the contrary presumption: a licence to import will not be implied. In these cases, the territorial limitations of patents have predominated. There are at least two areas of danger for patentees seeking to block parallel imports. First, recently, a court in each of the two bodies of law has indicated willingness to penetrate the corporate veil of 'corporate separateness'; another court has declined to follow.[292] The theory of this approach has not been thoroughly articulated but seems to rest on treating all members of the corporate group effectively as one person. As in trade marks, the proposition should be regarded as dubious, particularly in circumstances where anti-trust-type laws would not intervene. If it were to gain credence, however, it would be necessary to apply the same measures as govern the first situation, where the foreign seller has power of sale in both markets.

The second danger has primarily arisen in the United States (although *Salim* is arguably an example also) and involves a domestic patentee which licenses the foreign sale in circumstances where it has been argued that the domestic patentee reaped the reward claimed for the patent. The approach has not received widespread acceptance in either stream.[293] Moreover, arguably, it has only operated where the domestic patentee has given the foreign seller unfettered power of sale.[294] There must be some doubt about the one exception, where the rule did not operate anyway as it would have undermined the domestic licensee.[295]

In the Anglo-Commonwealth jurisdictions, it is unclear whether an exclusive licensee can assert the domestic patent to block imports by its licensor or against third-party purchasers from the licensor in the foreign market. On a theory of encouraging investment, the better view is that the exclusive licensee has rights in the patent which it could assert against both the licensor and third-party purchasers. In copyright, however, the UK courts

---

292 *Sanofi v Med-tech* (DNJ) and *Salim*; contrast *Sanofi v Med-tech* (DKan.).
293 Cases against it include *Tilghman*, *Briscoe*, the *Beecham Group* cases, the *Dickerson* cases, *Conklin*, *Griffin* and *Sanofi* (DKan.).
294 *Curtiss Aeroplane* and *Hattori*.
295 *Sanofi* (DNJ), contrast *Sanofi* (DKan.).

forced the legislature to intervene to ensure this result.[296] It is clear that an exclusive licensee in the United States has this power.

Where the highest degree of certainty is required and (as will usually happen) it is not possible to contract directly with the prospective importer, the clearest course is to ensure that the patented articles and their packaging are clearly labelled to indicate the limits of any 'licence'. The labelling would need to pay careful regard to the requirements of domestic competition and similar laws.[297]

In both streams of law, there is a fundamental contradiction. For one class of cases, the discrete territorial existence of patents is presumed irrelevant; while for the other, it is presumed overriding. No adequate explanation has been offered in either system about why the general policy of commercial convenience dictates contrary results. The contradiction is deepened by the realisation that, as a matter of practice, the presumption of free circulation hardly ever operates if the patentee wishes to defeat it and is properly advised.

---

296 See Chapter 4.2.2(b) below.
297 For example, the circumstances when a product sold in a Member State of the European Communities may be sold subject to the condition that it not be used or sold in another Member State are very limited. This does not necessarily mean, however, that circulation outside the European Communities is also obligatory.

Chapter 4: Copyright

4.1 Introduction

The treatment of parallel imports under copyright is, in some ways, more like patents than trade marks. Copyright, like patents, is quite clearly regarded as a property right, so the obscuring issues about function like those seen for trade marks have not occurred. There have, however, been other distractions; not least, the particular form of the Anglo-Commonwealth legislation, particularly the introduction of a 'hypothetical manufacturing test'.[1] The gymnastics of statutory interpretation associated with that test apart, however, considerations of territoriality seem to have played the main role in the copyright laws of the Anglo-Commonwealth countries. In the United States, the marked split between exhaustion and territoriality seen for patents and trade marks divides the copyright cases too.

The justifications and criticisms of copyright are much like those for patents.[2] The justifications fall into two broad camps: those which spring from the natural rights of the creator; and those which tend to promote society's well-being. The economic argument, encouraging investment in creating and publishing, has been the lodestone of the common law's approach.[3] In summary, creators in theory will not turn their efforts to creating copyright works if they see no prospect of remuneration for their efforts and, once again in theory, the prospects for that remuneration are

---

1   See subsection 4.2.2(b) below.
2   See Chapter 3.1 above. A concise review of the arguments, adverse to copyright, is Robert M. Hurt and Robert M. Schuchman, 'The Economic Rationale of Copyright', 56 Am. Econ. Rev. (Supp.) 421, at 421 to 425 (1966) based on Arnold Plant, 'The Economic Aspects of Copyright in Books', (1934) 1 *Economica* 167 and *The New Commerce in Ideas and Intellectual Property*, Athlone Press, 1953, both reprinted in Arnold Plant, *Selected Essays and Addresses*, Routledge & Kegan Paul, 1974, Chapters 4 and 5. See generally, W. R. Cornish, *Intellectual Property*, Sweet & Maxwell, 1989 (2nd ed.), at ¶¶9–023 to 9–026. For an algebraic explication, see William M. Landes and Richard A. Posner, 'An Economic Analysis of Copyright Law', 18 JLS 325 (1989).
3   See especially Zechariah Chafee Jr, 'Reflections on the Law of Copyright', 45 Columbia LRev. 503, at 506 to 510, 719 to 721 (1945). So-called 'moral rights', arising from the natural rights view, only received explicit statutory recognition (albeit in a qualified way) in the United Kingdom with the passage of the Copyright, Designs and Patents Act 1988.

drastically diminished without copyright because copyright works can often be copied quite easily and more cheaply, both as a matter of production costs (for example, because editing, typesetting and even many advertising costs can be avoided) and as a matter of risk.

The introduction of intermediaries between the creator and the public, such as a publisher, record company or 'movie studio', affects the theoretical analysis in two situations.[4] In theory, the price the intermediary will be prepared to pay the creator for the right to exploit the creator's work will reflect the expected profit from exploitation. Provided the intermediaries bid competitively (or new intermediaries can enter to compete for any rents), the creator should be able to buy the intermediary's services at cost and so indirectly secure the intended rent.[5] The second qualification lies in the conflict of interest between author and publisher perceived by Sir Arnold Plant when the publishing intermediary alone bears the cost of exploitation.[6]

4.2 Anglo-Commonwealth Law

4.2.1 Context

Copyright in the United Kingdom is now governed by the provisions of the Copyright, Designs and Patents Act (CDPA) 1988.[7] Prior to that, the statutory sources of UK law had been the Copyright Act 1911 which was replaced by the Copyright Act 1956.[8] In large part, the various members of the Commonwealth have copyright statutes derived from the 1911 or 1956 Acts. Prior to the CDPA 1988, some formal concession towards the civil law concepts of *droit d'auteur* and *neighbouring rights* was made by dividing copyright subject-matter into 'works' and 'other subject matter'.[9] In practice, the division did not represent the philosophical concerns recognised by the civil law and, apart from being found in different parts of the relevant Act, the main differences lay in the specific rights conferred on the copyright owner and the term of copyright. The distinction is no longer maintained in

---

4　Chafee explained it with his customary elegance, *ibid.* at 508 to 510.

5　Of course, in the real world, the rational course of action for either creator or publisher is attended with much more uncertainty, see for example Alchian's rueful discussion, in response to the Hurt/Schuchman paper, of his disagreement with his publisher over the price of one of his texts: Armen A. Alchian 'Discussion', 56 Am. Econ. Rev. (Supp.) 421, at 438 (1966). On the question of competition in book publishing, see Chapter 10 below.

6　See 'The Economic Aspects of Copyright in Books', in *Selected Essays and Addresses*, at 74 to 75; see further Chapter 10 below.

7　For present purposes, its commencement may be taken as 1 August 1989; but a number of provisions came into force on other dates: CDPA 1988 section 305 and SI 1989/816 and 955.

8　The 1911 Act and the 1956 Act, respectively.

9　On the concepts of 'author's right' and 'neighbouring right', see Stephen M. Stewart, *International Copyright and Neighbouring Rights*, Butterworths, 1989 (2nd ed.), at ¶¶7.11 to 7.14.

the United Kingdom under the CDPA 1988.[10] But, the CDPA 1988 has seen the introduction into the UK copyright statute of explicit 'moral rights'.[11]

For economic rights, however, the approach of the legislation has remained largely unchanged in many respects. Copyright confers on the owner the exclusive right to perform certain enumerated acts. In broad terms, the enumerated acts are the right to publish the work first, to reproduce it in a material form, to perform (or otherwise show) the work publicly, to transmit the work by some means of broadcasting or other diffusion, and to make adaptations of the work.[12] These are the primary rights of the copyright owner. Each may be dealt with separately and independently of the others.[13] Moreover, each separate copyright may be dealt with on a limited territorial basis in either of two forms – intra-national or international.

Under the so-called principle of national treatment, the bundle of rights comprising copyright are independent national rights, limited to the jurisdiction of the country under whose laws it subsists.[14] Once a right to copyright exists under a nation's laws, the copyright so created is separate from and independent of 'corresponding' copyrights subsisting under other nations' laws. Therefore, an owner of copyright may deal with corresponding copyrights subsisting under different countries' laws separately. In addition to the ability to treat 'corresponding' national copyrights separately and independently, a copyright owner may subdivide the territorial rights within the jurisdiction creating the copyright.[15]

Following from the territorial independence of copyright, acts which would infringe a copyright subsisting within one country if done within that country do not infringe the laws of that country when performed outside its jurisdiction.[16] Infringement requires the doing of a forbidden act within the jurisdiction.[17]

Unlike some other jurisdictions, the Anglo-Commonwealth laws have not

---

10   CDPA 1988 section 1.

11   See Gerald Dworkin's chapter on the United Kingdom in Stewart, *International Copyright and Neighbouring Rights*, at ¶¶18.75 to 18.85 and Cornish, *Intellectual Property*, at ¶¶11–047 to 11–059.

12   The precise form of the right varies depending on the legislation, see for example CDPA 1988 section 16(1) as explained in subsequent sections; and the 1956 Act sections 2(5), 12(5), 13(5), 14(4) and 15(3).

13   For example the CDPA 1988 section 90; the 1956 Act sections 36(2)(a), 49(5) and (6).

14   Copyright under the CDPA 1988 extends to England, Wales, Scotland and Northern Ireland with provision to extend to offshore territories and colonies: sections 157 to 158 and see Dworkin in Stewart, *International Copyright and Neighbouring Rights*, at ¶18.11. For national treatment under the international conventions affecting the existence of copyright, see Stewart, *ibid.* at ¶¶3.16 to 3.23.

15   *British Actors Film Co. v Glover* [1918] 1 KB 299 which concerned the letting of the professional, not amateur, rights for the 'provinces' for a limited period.

16   On bringing an action in country A for a wrong committed in country B, see Richard Arnold, 'Can One Sue in England for Infringement of Foreign Intellectual Property Rights?' [1990] EIPR 254.

17   *'Morocco Bound' Syndicate v Harris* [1895] 1 Ch. 534, Kekewich J refused to grant an injunction *quia timet* to restrain the threatened performance of a dramatic work in Berlin because the performance would take place outside the jurisdiction of the Crown.

expressly conferred on the copyright owner a right to control distribution, whether directly by the grant of a 'distribution right',[18] or indirectly by a *droit de destination* derived from the right of reproduction.[19] Accordingly, in the Anglo-Commonwealth jurisdictions, it is not infringement of a copyright owner's exclusive right of reproduction to copy (or reproduce) the copyright work in another country and import the resulting copy into the first country because the act of reproduction, the infringing act, does not take place in the jurisdiction. Therefore, the copyright owner must show that some other right has been infringed by importing or dealing with the foreign-made work in the domestic market.

That power may be sought in one of three potential sources. Anglo-Commonwealth legislation confers a power to control certain kinds of imports (and dealings in them once imported).[20] In some jurisdictions, imported copies may be liable to the copyright owner's remedies in conversion and detinue.[21] It has also been argued (largely unsuccessfully) that parallel imports may infringe the 'primary' right conferring the exclusive right to publish a work.[22]

4.2.2 'Secondary' infringement

For parallel imports, the prohibition on importing and selling 'hypothetically infringing copies' is the most important. Plainly, a copyright owner's exclusive rights would not be of much value if an infringer could evade the copyright simply by doing the infringing act outside the jurisdiction and then bringing the fruits of that 'infringing' act into the jurisdiction.[23] Accordingly, copyright owners have been granted indirect protection of their interests by rights to prevent dealings in articles embodying the copyright.

Control of imports, in fact, predates the adoption of copyright in its modern form with the Statute of Anne 1709.[24] Copyright Acts and their precursors were long intended to 'seal off' the domestic market from

18 See for example 17 USC §§106(3) and 109(a) in the United States (see section 4.3.1 below) and in Germany, Eugen Ulmer and Hans Hugo von Rauscher auf Weeg in Stewart, *International Copyright and Neighbouring Rights*, at ¶15.06. On the extent of the Anglo-Commonwealth right of publication, see subsection 4.2.3(a) below.
19 As in France and Belgium, the subject of a study session by the Association Litteraire et Artistique Internationale, 5 to 8 October 1988, Munich. See Frank Gotzen, 'Distribution and Exhaustion in the EC Proposal for a Council Directive on the Legal Protection of Computer Programs', [1990] EIPR 299.
20 CDPA 1988 sections 22, 23 and 27, see section 4.2.2 below. In the CDPA 1988, aspects of so-called 'secondary' infringement because the infringement does not involve exercising one of the primary acts comprised in the copyright, but a dealing in an article embodying the copyright: see Cornish, *Intellectual Property*, at ¶11–022; Dworkin in Stewart, *International Copyright and Neighbouring Rights*, at ¶18.46.
21 See subsection 4.2.3(b) below.
22 See subsection 4.2.3(a) below.
23 The infringer's act outside the jurisdiction may not necessarily infringe any copyright law governing the jurisdiction where the act is performed. The law in question may not confer copyright protection for that particular act. The 'infringer' may be the owner of the copyright in that particular jurisdiction or otherwise entitled to do the act through some form of compulsory licence.
24 8 Anne Chapter 19.

the foreign. This insularity grew from two commingled purposes. The forerunners of copyright law were used as an economic tool to encourage the development of industry and the dissemination of culture throughout the realm. In addition, they were used as a political tool to control what was disseminated, a tool of censorship.[25]

To a considerable extent, these two objects tended to isolate England as a market. The laws, in effect, imposed an absolute ban on importing into England works written in English printed abroad.[26] Moreover, until the 1840s, English law only recognised exclusive rights in writings which had been published first in England by an English subject or foreign resident of England.[27] It was only with the extension of copyright recognition throughout the Empire and various foreign countries, and acknowledgement that copyright could subsist in works first published abroad, that problems akin to parallel importing could arise.[28]

With the introduction of the printing press into England in 1471, exploitation of written materials became possible on a substantial, commercial scale. There being only four printers in the realm, the first statutory intervention in the field sought to encourage greater dissemination of printed materials and printing and so permitted importation of printing materials on a fairly liberal basis compared to other forms of commerce undertaken by foreigners.[29] It was not long, however, before domestic commercial interests developed sufficiently to challenge the concessions to foreign printers and booksellers, with the latter losing their favourable trading terms during the 1520s.[30] In 1533, The Printers and Binders Act repealed the Act of Richard III and banned the importation and sale of books printed abroad on the basis of protecting domestic industry from foreign competition.[31]

---

25 Generally, James, Murray and James, *Copinger & Skone James on Copyright*, Sweet & Maxwell, 1980 (12th ed.), at c. 2; Stanisforth Ricketson, *The Law of Intellectual Property*, Law Book Company, 1984, at c. 4; Gavin McFarlane, *Copyright: The Development and Exercise of the Performing Right*, John Offord (Publications) Ltd, 1980; A. Birrell, *Seven Lectures on The Law and History of Copyright in Books*, Cassell and Company Ltd, 1899; Cornish, *Intellectual Property*, at ¶¶9–001 to 9–022; Copyright Law Review Committee, *The Importation Provisions of the Copyright Act 1968*, AGPS, 1988, App. D, at 279 to 369 including a full list of legislation.

26 The US 'manufacturing clause' introduced in 1891 on the recognition of copyright in foreign authors only expired on 1 July 1986, see Barbara Ringer and Hamish Sandison, 'United States of America', in Stewart, *International Copyright and Neighbouring Rights*, at ¶21.61. For the economics of the clause, see Craig K. Morris, 'The Manufacturing Clause: Death-Defying Provision of the US Copyright Law', [1982] *ASCAP Studies in Copyright* 185.

27 Ricketson, *The Law of Intellectual Property*, at ¶4.42.

28 See the International Copyright Acts of 1837, 1844, 1852 and 1875 and the Colonial Copyright Act 1847.

29 Importation of Books by Aliens Act 1483, 1 Ric. III, Chapter 9: *Copinger & Skone James on Copyright*, at ¶21; Ricketson, *The Law of Intellectual Property*, at 58.

30 Ricketson, *The Law of Intellectual Property*, at 58, citing 14 & 15 Hen. VIII, Chapter 2, 21 Hen. VIII, Chapter 16.

31 25 Hen. VIII, Chapter 15. The Act's preamble referred to the 'marvellous number of printed books' being imported into the realm to prejudice the interests of the 'King's natural subjects' and noted that bookbinders were in such a state that 'having no other faculty wherewith to get their living, be destitute of work and likely to be undone, except some reformation herein be had': *Copinger & Skone James on Copyright*, at ¶21.

Beginning around the same time, the political and religious struggles associated with the Reformation and then the Tudor and the Stuart periods led to a series of Proclamations on censorship. As well as forbidding the printing of books in England without prior examination and licence from the Crown, these complemented the protection of commercial interests by banning importation of books printed abroad.

The political and commercial were linked when Mary I incorporated the Stationers' Company to administer the censorship laws.[32] As the guild representing the trades associated with printing and bookselling, it also regulated, among its members, the ownership of rights in writings. Its powers lapsed briefly in 1640 with Parliament's triumph over the prerogative courts. However, by 1643 political concerns coalesced with economic interest to reinstate the powers of the Stationers' Company. On one hand, Parliament wished to resume control over what it saw as the licentiousness of the libels resulting from an unrestrained and multitudinous press. On the other, the trade, through the Stationers' Company, considered it was suffering economic hardship from the excesses of unrestricted competition.[33]

The Restoration separated enforcement of the censorship and commercial interests, but continued the prohibitions of both on imports of books printed abroad.[34] Following the Revolution of 1689, attacks on the vested interests of the Stationers' Company led to non-renewal of its powers in 1694.

Failing to retrieve its position by pressing the censorship arguments, the Stationers' Company skilfully exploited concerns about the economic plight of authors (and their families) to persuade Parliament to confer on authors *and their assigns* exclusive rights to print and reprint written works.[35] The 18th Century also saw the introduction of a further, direct government interest in controlling imports – the collection of customs duties.[36]

The ban on imports continued until the 1840s, when expanding commercial interests in foreign trade forced some relaxation of protectionist policies. The subsistence of copyright was extended to the United Kingdom and throughout the British Empire, to works first published in the British Empire and, finally, on a reciprocal, bilateral basis with 'foreign' countries.[37] To secure foreign protection for the works of British authors, British law found it necessary to recognise the existence of copyright-like rights in foreign

---

32 *Copinger & Skone James on Copyright*, at ¶¶22 to 23; Ricketson, *The Law of Intellectual Property*, at 59.

33 *Copinger & Skone James on Copyright*, at ¶¶24 to 26; McFarlane, *Copyright: The Development and Exercise of the Performing Right*, at 29; Ricketson, *The Law of Intellectual Property*, at 61 to 62.

34 *Ibid.*

35 The Statute of Anne, 8 Anne, Chapter 19. The preamble declared that the practice of printing, reprinting and republishing books 'without the consent of the Authors or the Proprietors of such Books and Writings' acted 'to their very great Detriment, and too often to the Ruin of them and their Families' and so set out to prevent such practices for the future.

36 Copyright Law Review Committee, *The Importation Provisions of the Copyright Act 1968*, at 285 to 286, 292 to 294.

37 See the International Copyright Acts of 1837, 1844, 1852 and 1875 and the Colonial Copyright Act 1847.

countries and accord protection to such rights in the United Kingdom as if they had arisen under UK law.

Hence, the territorial and divisible nature of copyright developed partly from the halting acknowledgment of rights outside the domestic jurisdiction and partly from a desire to ensure that copyright could be exploited for its full economic value. No doubt, it is much easier to administer the local law in domestic courts. But, it also seems likely that no country in the 19th Century was prepared to surrender control over legal rights in its territory any more than was absolutely necessary to secure adequate protection of its own interests abroad. This policy may have coincided with commercial need. Publishers have long recognised that a 'title' sells better when someone in the market undertakes to 'publish' it there, rather than act as a 'mere' distributor and perhaps few, if any, authors or publishers in the 19th Century possessed the resources, know-how or inclination to undertake publishing in a foreign country.

Anglo-Commonwealth legislation now provides that copyright is infringed by importing articles embodying the copyright ('copyrighted articles') into the jurisdiction unless the owner of the relevant copyright in that jurisdiction has consented to the importation. A further prohibition affects commercial dealings in such copyright works once they have been imported.

The CDPA 1988 defines the copyright owner's rights in the following terms:

22. The copyright in a work is infringed by a person who, without the licence of the copyright owner, imports into the United Kingdom, otherwise than for his private and domestic use, an article which is, and which he knows or has reason to believe is, an infringing copy of the work.
23. The copyright in a work is infringed by a person who, without the licence of the copyright owner–
     (a) possesses in the course of a business,
     (b) sells or lets for hire, or offers or exposes for sale or hire,
     (c) in the course of a business exhibits in public or distributes, or
     (d) distributes otherwise than in the course of a business to such an extent as to affect prejudicially the owner of the copyright,
     an article which is, and which he knows or has reason to believe is, an infringing copy of the work.

Section 27 then defines the term 'infringing copy':

(2) An article is an infringing copy if its making constituted an infringement of the copyright in the work in question.
(3) An article is also an infringing copy if–
     (a) it has been or is proposed to be imported into the United Kingdom, and
     (b) its making in the United Kingdom would have constituted an infringement of the copyright in the work in question, or a breach of an exclusive licence agreement relating to that work.
(4) . . .
(5) Nothing in subsection (3) shall be construed as applying to an article which may lawfully be imported into the United Kingdom by virtue of any enforceable Community right within the meaning of section 2(1) of the European Communities Act 1972.

There are some important changes, but the combined effect of these provisions appears to be substantially the same as that of the corresponding provisions under the 1956 Act.[38] In turn, the 1956 Act reproduced the effect of the 1911 Act. As already indicated, the legislation in force in much of the Commonwealth derives from, and substantially reproduces, these two Acts. In terms, the 1956 Act provided:

5(2) The copyright in a literary, dramatic, musical or artistic work is infringed by any person who, without the licence of the owner of the copyright, imports an article (otherwise than for his private and domestic use) into the United Kingdom . . . if to his knowledge the making of that article constituted an infringement of that copyright, or would have constituted such an infringement if the article had been made in the place into which it is so imported.

5(3) The copyright in a literary, dramatic, musical or artistic work is infringed by any person who, in the United Kingdom . . . and without the licence of the owner of the copyright:
(a) sells, lets for hire, or by way of trade offers or exposes for sale or hire any article, or
(b) by way of trade exhibits any article in public,
if to his knowledge the making of the article constituted an infringement of that copyright, or (in the case of an imported article) would have constituted an infringement of that copyright if the article had been made in the place into which it was imported.

5(4) The last preceding subsection shall apply in relation to the distribution of any articles either–
(a) for the purposes of trade, or
(b) for other purposes, but to such an extent as to affect prejudicially the owner of the copyright in question,
as it applies in relation to the sale of an article.[39]

These provisions were expressed to apply 'without prejudice' to the operation of the primary, direct infringement provisions.[40]

---

38 Apart from changing the structure of the provisions, the more significant changes will be discussed in greater detail below. They principally relate to the requirement of knowledge, the effect of exclusive licence agreements and the introduction of section 27(5). While section 27(5) is new, it appears to express the law as presently stated in Case 270/80 *Polydor Limited v Harlequin Record Shop* [1982] ECR 329; [1982] 1 CMLR 677, see Chapter 6.3.2 below.

39 The 1956 Act section 5. The same protection is conferred on Part II subject-matter in section 16(2) to (4). The legislation in Canada, New Zealand and South Africa is in virtually identical terms: see Copyright Act, RSC 1985, Chapter C-42, section 27(4) previously RSC 1970 Chapter C-30, section 17(4) (Canada); Copyright Act 1962 (New Zealand) section 10(2); Copyright Act, No. 98 of 1978 (South Africa) section 23(2). The provisions of the Indian Copyright Act 1957 while more closely based on the 1911 Act have substantially the same effect: see the *India Book Distributors'* case, see text at Notes 203 to 206 below. The Australian legislation has one marked difference in that it specifies the importer as the person assumed to have made the article when determining whether an article would have infringed if made in Australia: see Copyright Act 1968 (Cth) sections 37 to 38, quoted at Note 64 below. For recent changes to, or proposals to change, this legislation, see section 4.2.4, below.

40 The 1956 Act sections 5(1), 16(5). The primary, direct provisions provide that it is an infringement of copyright to do, or to authorise the doing of, an act comprised in the copyright in a work without the permission of the copyright owner: for example the 1956 Act section 1(2) for literary, artistic, dramatic and musical works.

The gist of an action under these provisions requires the plaintiff to prove that the defendant has (1) imported into the domestic jurisdiction;[41] (2) without the licence of the copyright owner in the domestic jurisdiction; (3) an article the making of which (a) infringed copyright, or (b) would have infringed copyright if it had been made in the domestic jurisdiction; (4) with knowledge that the article so infringed, or would have infringed, the copyright subsisting in the domestic jurisdiction.

Of these, three issues are relevant in the context of parallel imports. First, what is the meaning of the test 'or would have constituted an infringement of the copyright if the article had been made in' the domestic market ('the hypothetical manufacturing requirement'). Second, what acts of the domestic copyright owner will confer its licence on the importation. Third, what knowledge must the defendant have. The act of importation may be assumed.[42] It may not, however, always be possible to fix the defendant with the necessary knowledge at the time of importation.[43] But, the provisions relating to sale and commercial dealing are separate wrongs, so infringement also occurs if the defendant has the necessary knowledge when these subsequent acts take place if it was unlawful to import the articles in question.[44] Furthermore, parallel imports have, by definition, been made lawfully in the place of manufacture. So, the actual making of the imported articles did not infringe copyright. The imported articles are not 'pirate' copies. Parallel imports are concerned only with 'hypothetically' infringing copies.[45]

(a)   *First principles: a principle of territoriality*

In the *Pitt Pitts* case, the original owner of copyright in a musical work, '*La Fileuse*', had assigned the rights for 'England and Colonies' to Pitts while retaining ownership in Germany and Belgium.[46] George & Co. bought copies of the work in Brussels and imported them for sale into England. Pitts sued George & Co. for infringement of his English copyright. The

---

41   (Or selling, letting for hire or by way of trade exhibiting, exposing or offering for sale or hire after such importation.) In the UK legislation, the domestic jurisdiction also includes various external territories in addition to the United Kingdom itself.

42   A threatened or impending importation may, of course, provide grounds for an injunction *quia timet*.

43   For an example, see *The Who Group Limited and Polydor Limited v Stage One (Records) Limited* [1980] FSR 268 [1980] 2 CMLR 429 (Ch. D), see text at Notes 103 to 106 below. Apparently, the articles in question, sound recordings, were shipped in bulk containers. Not all the contents were infringing copies and it was questionable whether the defendant even knew what the containers held prior to taking delivery and unpacking them.

44   For a case where a defendant claimed to be the agent of the importer and was considered liable for selling and so forth after importation even if not the importer and probably as a joint tortfeasor in the importation, see *Lotus Development v Vacolan* (1990) 16 IPR 143 (Fed. C) (application for interlocutory injunction).

45   9 Halsbury (4th ed.) at ¶920 Note 9 citing the *Pitt Pitts* and *Hoffnung* cases, see text from Notes 46 and 58, respectively, below.

46   *Pitt Pitts v George & Co.* [1896] 2 Ch. 866 (CA).

owner of the German and Belgian copyrights had produced the copies which George & Co. bought and had sold them to a distributor who, in turn, sold them to George & Co. in Brussels.

Kekewich J dismissed the action with costs at first instance. Lindley and Rigby LJJ upheld Pitts' appeal, Lopes LJ dissenting.

The case turned on the construction of the involved provisions of the International Copyright Act 1844 ('the International Act') and the Copyright Act 1842 ('the 1842 Act').[47] The majority clearly adopted the principle of territoriality and, consequently, the independence of corresponding national copyrights at the expense of a literal interpretation of the statutory provisions. This step was taken after a considered analysis of the history of copyright regulation in England and the legislative object of the provisions.

The 1842 Act dealt only with copyright subsisting in books first published in the United Kingdom. By section 15, it infringed copyright to print such books in any part of the British Empire without the written consent of the copyright proprietor. The section further provided that importing books printed contrary to section 15 was an infringement, as was selling, publishing, or exposing for sale or hire any book known to have been so printed or imported. This section, then, dealt only with printing or publishing books within the British Empire. It did not address the printing or publishing of books outside the British Empire.

However, subject to the copyright owner's authorisation, section 17 absolutely prohibited importing into any part of the British Empire copies of a book first composed, written, printed or published in the United Kingdom if the imported copies were made outside the Empire. Once again, sale and similar acts were penalised if done knowingly.

These provisions only concerned protection of copyright in books first published in the United Kingdom while the copies imported by George & Co. related to a work which had been first published in Germany. The existence of copyright protection in the United Kingdom for such a work depended on the International Act. Section 2 empowered the Crown, by ordinance, to confer copyright on the authors of books first published in foreign countries. Section 3 entitled authors on whom the Crown had conferred copyright under section 2 to the benefit of the 1842 Act as if their books had been published first in the United Kingdom. However, the literal terms of section 10 denied relief against the importation of copies made in the country where the work was first published.[48]

George & Co. argued that sections 2, 3 and 10 of the International Act comprised a complete code for the protection of copyright in works first published abroad. Accordingly, as the imported copies had been printed in the foreign country of first publication, there was no infringement. The plain, literal interpretation of section 10 exactly covered the case.

---

47 7 & 8 Vict., Chapter 12, 5 & 6 Vict. Chapter 45, respectively.
48 Section 10 begins by prohibiting importing into the British Empire books 'printed or reprinted in any foreign country except that in which such books were first published . . .'.

The Court of Appeal accepted that George & Co.'s arguments were correct if section 10 were read literally.[49] But, neither Lindley nor Rigby LJJ were prepared to accept George & Co.'s contention because such a construction would seriously undermine the UK assignee's position, exposing the assignee to direct and indirect competition from the assignor and rendering the assignment valueless.

Lindley LJ considered that such a construction was against all common sense and legal principle. It would defeat the object of the Act – to confer on foreigners copyright interests in the British Empire co-extensive with those of British subjects. It would enable any assignor to compete with his assignee unless there was express agreement to the contrary.[50] His Lordship then based himself squarely on the separate and independent territorial nature of national copyrights in rejecting George & Co.'s alternative contention that the lawful purchase of the copies from the copyright owner abroad entitled the purchaser to dispose of the copies as it pleased:

> The defendant is the purchaser of the books he has imported, and it is contended that he has a right to dispose of those books as he likes without any interference from the owner of the foreign copyright or the plaintiff, who claims under him. The right, however, of the defendant to use in this country the books which he bought abroad depends on the law of this country and not on the law of the place of sale. The copyright in this country confers upon the plaintiff rights here which no contract of sale abroad by other persons can deprive him of. Even if the defendant had bought his copies direct from the proprietor of the foreign copyright, the defendant would be in no better position as against the plaintiff than such proprietor himself; and for reasons already given he could not justify what the defendant claims the right to do.[51]

Rigby LJ reviewed the historical development of copyright laws in the United Kingdom and concluded that the International Act was intended to make the protection of 'foreign' copyrights (that is, copyrights subsisting in the United Kingdom by virtue of first publication in a foreign country) as effective as 'home' copyrights (where copyright subsisted because the work had been published first in the United Kingdom). In Rigby LJ's opinion, construing section 10 of the International Act in the manner suggested by George & Co. would defeat this intention because it would render the

---

49   *Ibid.* at 874 *per* Lindley LJ; at 877 to 878 *per* Lopes LJ; 881 to 882, 886 *per* Rigby LJ.

50   *Ibid.* at 876:

> Is it to be inferred that the foreigner entitled to copyright in this country is liable to have that copyright infringed by any importer of books printed in his own country, or is the inference to be that as regards such books he is entitled to the same protection as a British author would have under [the 1842 Act]? The latter inference is most in accordance with legal principles and good sense, and is the only inference consistent with the preamble and s. 3 of [the International Act].

51   *Ibid.* (Compare his Lordship's similar treatment of patents in *Tilghman's* case, see Chapter 3.2.3 above.) For a demonstration of the point, see *Anglo-Canadian Music Publishers' Association Ltd v J. Suckling & Sons* (1889) 17 OR 239 ('the *Suckling* case') as discussed in the *Clarke, Irwin* case (1960) 22 DLR 2d 183, at 185 to 186, see text from Note 71 below.

assignee of a foreign copyright the owner of a completely different and less effective right than the proprietor of a home copyright:

> An assignee would have the comparatively unimportant advantage of being able to stop all imports for private use except from the country of origin while at the same time being exposed to the threat of imports for commercial purposes from the country of origin by the assignor or any other person who could get hold of books lawfully printed in Germany.[52]

When trade conditions favoured imports from Germany, the object of the Act would be 'entirely frustrated'.

Nor was his Lordship persuaded by arguments that the assignee could protect its interest with appropriate covenants. This assumed that copyright law itself was not adequate. Moreover, the effectiveness of such covenants was not clear as they could not bind purchasers from the assignor.[53]

The significance of the majority's decision is underlined by Lopes LJ's dissent. Lopes LJ was compelled to accept the literal meaning of the sections. The International Act could be given effect on such an interpretation and there was a reasonable explanation for such a policy, although his Lordship thought the reason 'by no means clear'. The place of first publication was the most likely place where travellers would buy copies for their personal use. Such people would be protected by the literal interpretation. Accordingly, there was no justification for refusing to apply the literal meaning of section 10.[54]

Moreover, the alternative approach favoured by the majority involved considerable difficulties of its own. In particular, it caused considerable violence to the wording of the 1842 Act in sections 15 and 17. In terms, both of these sections only applied to protect books which had been first published in the United Kingdom.[55] Lindley LJ accepted this argument as it applied to section 15 but was not prepared to do so for section 17. His Lordship felt that the latter section was of wider import than section 15 and any other interpretation would render section 3 of the International Act 'absolutely nugatory'.[56] Rigby LJ disagreed about both sections; for him, the

---

52 *Ibid.* at 882.
53 *Ibid.* Lindley LJ considered that a law allowing the assignor to compete with its assignee, unless prevented by express agreement 'would not be very creditable'. *Ibid.* at 876.
54 *Ibid.* at 881. Contrast Copyright Law Review Committee, *The Importation Provisions of the Copyright Act 1968*, at 297 to 299, 334 to 335 for an argument that Parliament actually intended the result pursued by George & Co. as 'a straightforward recognition' that the copyright owner in the place of first publication would have reaped the intended reward. The argument is flawed in its foundation on Lord St Leonards' antipathy to the divisibility of copyright expressed in *Jefferys v Boosey* (1854) 4 HLC 184; 10 ER 681 since his Lordship expressly distinguished between an assignment of the copyright for the whole jurisdiction and a purported one for a geographical part of the jurisdiction, the latter alone being specifically condemned: 4 HLC at 993 to 994; 10 ER at 751. See also 3 *Nimmer on Copyright*, at §10.01[B], text at Notes 18 to 21. Moreover, Lord St Leonards certainly never envisaged that the existence of copyright, or any acts done under it, in a foreign country could affect the existence of, or rights under, a copyright in the United Kingdom (and dominions): 4 HLC at 991; 10 ER at 750.
55 *Ibid.* at 877 to 878.
56 *Ibid.* at 875.

important factor was not the place of printing but the absence of consent to the importation.[57]

Two central features stand out in the *Pitt Pitts* case. First, the principle of territoriality was clearly adopted. It operated to insulate copyright under one country's laws from any corresponding copyright under another's. Therefore, lawfully producing and selling copyrighted articles outside the jurisdiction did not stop their subsequent importation into the jurisdiction from constituting indirect infringement of the copyright in that jurisdiction.

Second, the principle of territoriality was adopted as a result of the application of both legal principle and an economic or business view. The prospective devaluation of the economic value of the assignee's rights was as significant a factor in the adoption of the principle as juristic considerations of national sovereignty. The majority clearly rejected contractually barring the assignor's competition against its assignee as both inadequate and unnecessary.

Harvey J, in the Supreme Court of New South Wales, also endorsed the adoption of the principle of territoriality to protect economic interests like that espoused by the *Pitt Pitts* case in *Albert* v *S. Hoffnung & Company Limited*.[58]

Albert took an assignment of the copyright for Australia in a musical work, *My Own Iona*, from the owner of the copyright for the British Empire. Hoffnung bought sound recordings of the musical work in England and imported them into Australia and Albert successfully sued him for copyright infringement by importation and sale.

Hoffnung had purchased the sound recordings from British Zonophone Co. (BZC), their manufacturer. BZC was not the owner of the copyright in the United Kingdom. However, it had acquired a compulsory licence to make and sell the sound recordings in the United Kingdom by giving the notice and paying the specified royalty to the UK copyright owner required under section 19 of the 1911 Act. Hoffnung argued that section 19 was a special defence which permitted sale of the resulting sound recordings throughout the Empire. It further denied having the knowledge required by the section. Harvey J rejected both contentions.[59]

His Honour considered that the assignment created a separate, local copyright which itself required notice and royalty payments under section 19. As this requirement had not been met, BZC did not have the right to make the sound recordings in Australia although, in making them in the United Kingdom, it had not infringed any copyright.[60] His Honour then turned to the question of whether Hoffnung's import and sale of the sound recordings in Australia infringed Albert's copyright:

---

57 *Ibid.* at 883, 884 to 886.
58 (1921) 22 SR (NSW) 75 (Sup. Ct, NSW). This case arose under the 1911 Act as applied in Australia by the Copyright Act 1912 (Cth).
59 On the knowledge factor, see subsection 4.2.2(d) below. For a corresponding US case, see *T.B. Harms Company v JEM Records Inc.* 655 F. Supp. 1575 (DNJ 1987), section 4.3.4 below and, in the European Communities, compare Case 19/84 *Pharmon v Hoechst* [1985] ECR 2281, a compulsory licence of a patent, Chapter 6.4 below.
60 22 SR (NSW) 75, at 80.

The making of these records in Australia would, in my opinion, be an infringement unless notice had been given to the plaintiff and royalties paid to him. I see no indication in the Act whatever of any intention that provided records are lawfully made in any part of the British Empire they can be sold in the way of trade or imported for sale into every part of the Empire which has adopted the Copyright Act. Although the defendant company might quite lawfully purchase these records in England because of notice and payment to [the United Kingdom copyright owner] it by no means follows that they can bring them into Australia; any more than it would follow that because they might legally acquire records made in a foreign country they could import them into Australia. In my opinion the importation of these records into Australia is not protected by s. 19 from being a breach of copyright.[61]

In this context, the main interest in the *Hoffnung* case lies in application of the principle of territoriality to foreign sales authorised by compulsory licence. As the right to make and sell derived from a compulsory licence, it is difficult to argue that the UK copyright owner had consciously consented to dealings in the copyright. However, the payment of a royalty, at whatever level, lends some support to the economic arguments underlying a doctrine of exhaustion. *Pitt Pitts* and *Hoffnung*, therefore, clearly applied the principle of territoriality to imports where copyright was held by different persons (albeit by assignment) in both the foreign and domestic jurisdictions. Arguably, this is consistent with *Betts v Willmott's* treatment of patents; but, if so, neither *Pitt Pitts* nor *Hoffnung* gives any indication why consent should be inferred in one case and not in the other.

(b) *The hypothetical manufacturing requirement*

The test of infringement posed by the hypothetical manufacturing requirement provokes a difficult question of interpretation in several Anglo-Commonwealth jurisdictions. The *Pitt Pitts* and *Hoffnung* cases had established that lawful manufacture in the place where the article was actually made was irrelevant and did so on an approach squarely based on the principle of territoriality. But, in both cases, the actual maker did not have authority or a legal right to make the articles in the place of importation. In Australia, booksellers reported to the Prices Surveillance Authority that they were in fact allowed to import copies from the United Kingdom where the owners of the UK and Australian copyright were the same *until* the Copyright Act 1968 identified the 'hypothetical manufacturer' as the importer.[62] The publishers, through the UK-based Publishers' Association, dispute this claim.

The difficulty in interpreting the hypothetical manufacturing requirement in many Anglo-Commonwealth laws arises when the actual maker of the article has authority to make the article in the place of importation as well

---

61 *Ibid.* at 80 to 81.
62 Prices Surveillance Authority, *Inquiry into Book Prices: Interim Report*, PSA, Report No. 24, 1989, at 9.

as the place where the article was made.[63] In the legislation enacted by most countries, the hypothetical manufacturing requirement does not identify the circumstances of the hypothetical manufacture apart from specifying the place of manufacture – the domestic market. In particular, the test does not specify the assumed manufacturer's identity.[64]

Three main alternatives have been suggested for the interpretation of the hypothetical manufacturing requirement. First, some courts have held that the test requires the maker to be none other than the person who actually made the article in question ('the actual maker theory'). Second, as specified in the Australian legislation, the test might posit the importer as the hypothetical maker ('the importer theory'). Third, it has been suggested that the test requires the maker to be anyone but the holder of the right to make the article in the domestic jurisdiction ('the public theory'). The details and effects of these competing tests will be developed below.

The issue has arisen with varying degrees of analysis and conflicting results

---

63   For an argument on further complications under the UK Acts arising from their application by extension to countries other than the United Kingdom, see J.A.L. Sterling and M.C.L. Carpenter, *Copyright Law in the United Kingdom*, Legal Books Pty Ltd, 1986, at ¶¶547 and onward.

64   Under the 1956 Act a person infringed copyright by importing into the United Kingdom, without consent, an article 'if to his knowledge the making of that article . . . would have constituted such an infringement if the article had been made in the [United Kingdom]': sections 5(2), 16(2). The same problem arises in Canada, New Zealand, South Africa and India. In contrast, the Australian provisions identify the hypothetical manufacturer as the importer of the article. Subject to the exception introduced by the 1991 amendments and section 24(2) of the Circuit Layouts Act 1989 (Cth), the Copyright Act 1968 (Cth) section 37 provides:

> . . . the copyright in a literary . . . work is infringed by a person who, without the licence of the owner of the copyright, imports an article into Australia . . . if the importer knew, or ought reasonably to have known, that the making of the article would, if the article had been made in Australia *by the importer*, have constituted an infringement of the copyright. (*Emphasis added*)

For circuit layouts, see *Avel Pty Ltd v Wells* (1992) 23 IPR 353 (Fed. C, FC) at Note 214, below; for the 1991 amendments, see section 4.2.4, below introduced expressly to remove the ambiguity at the heart of the 1956 Act section 5, see *Report of the Committee appointed by the Attorney-General of the Commonwealth to Consider What Alterations are Desirable in the Copyright Law of the Commonwealth*, Commonwealth of Australia, 1959, at ¶98 ('the Spicer Committee'). Contrast Board of Trade, *Report of the Copyright Committee*, HMSO, Cmd 8662, 1952, at ¶¶277 to 281 ('Gregory Committee') which refers to the fact that copyright might be owned by different people in different countries, but goes on to state that copyright owners or licensees would have an interest in blocking imports which would compete with 'material lawfully made in this country', especially at ¶280.

Singapore and Malaysia both have Acts modeled on the Australian. However, at a late stage, the Singaporean legislation was altered to remove the references to 'by the importer', apparently to ensure the possibility of parallel imports. Contrast Copyright Bill 1986, cll. 31 and 32 to Copyright Act, No. 2 of 1987, sections 32 and 33 and see *Television Broadcasts Ltd v Golden Line Video and Marketing Pte Ltd* [1989] 1 MLJ 201, at 205, see text at Notes 163 to 170 below. The author is very grateful to Mr George Wei of National University of Singapore for providing him with materials from the *Report of the Select Committee on the Copyright Bill*, 1986, A82–91, B34–7 and 70 to 73. The Copyright Act 1987 (Malaysia), 36(2) has also recently been similarly amended by the Copyright Amendment Act 1990, see Khaw Lake Tee, 'The 1990 Amendments to the Malaysian Copyright Act 1987', [1991] EIPR 132, at 135 to 137.

in Canada, New Zealand, South Africa, the United Kingdom, India and, by way of *dicta*, in Singapore.

It has been suggested that the case of *Quillet* posits adoption of the actual maker theory and is representative of the Canadian courts' approach to the issue.[65] *Quillet* concerned an attempt by the exclusive distributor for Canada to block imports from France of a dictionary which had been bought there from the French copyright owner. The French copyright owner had appointed the plaintiff as its exclusive *agent* to import and sell the dictionary in Canada. Although the contract, had accorded the plaintiff the right to register itself as the owner of copyright in Canada, Lesage J refused to grant the plaintiff an interlocutory injunction on the ground that it had not established an interest in the copyright entitling it to relief. He appears to have regarded the transaction as a sham with the plaintiff being a mere distributor.[66] On that ground, *Quillet* is consistent with other authority around the Commonwealth and has little to say about the hypothetical manufacturing test.[67] Further, as a final consideration in refusing to grant the interlocutory injunction sought, his Honour considered:

> . . . the broad principle of freedom of trade favours the defendant and it is reasonable that he should be capable of pursuing his business freely until such time as it is established that he does not have the right to do so. Freedom is to be regarded as the general rule while restriction should be the exception. It is advisable to let the parties remain in the general *statu quo* until the restriction is established.[68]

This passage does not itself bear directly on the interpretation of the hypothetical manufacturing test. It may, however, suggest a disposition towards a restrictive interpretation of the test. But Lesage J had earlier acknowledged that copyright may be divided territorially and had indicated that the plaintiff would have succeeded in some circumstances:

> Had the petitioner actually held the copyright, he could have said works printed in Canada and, having published it, would have been the only one to be in a position to sell it.[69]

Hence, it seems Lesage J may well have contemplated applying the test on the actual maker theory. There are, however, considerable doubts that

---

65   *Maison du Livre Française de Montréal Inc. v Institut Littéraire du Québec Ltée* (1959) 31 CPR 69 (Que. Superior Ct), cited by Duncan C. Card, 'Parallel Importation of Copyright Property: A Proposal to Amend the Canadian *Copyright Act*', (1990) 6 IPJ 97, at 105. Arguing that Canadian law requires amendment to block parallel imports Mr Card refers to the preponderance of case law supporting this view set out in Copyright Law Review Committee, *The Importation Provisions of the Copyright Act 1968*, at 316 to 364; the Canadian cases at 344 to 351: 6 IPJ at 101 to 102.

66   *Ibid.* at 73 to 74; describing the plaintiff's methods as 'contrived' and 'devious'.

67   See for example *Avel Pty Ltd v Multicoin Amusements Pty Ltd* (1990) 65 ALJR 179 (HCA, FC), see subsection 4.2.3(a) below, but note *Les Dictionnaires Robert Canada SCC et al. v Librairie du Nomade Inc. et al.* (1987) 16 CPR (3d) 319 (FTD), at Note 92 below.

68   *Ibid.* at 77.

69   *Ibid.* at 74.

subsequent rulings by Canadian courts (which do not refer to the case) are consistent with his Honour's restricted interpretation.

In *Clarke, Irwin,* the author of a literary work, *The Land of the Long Day,* granted Clarke, Irwin 'the sole and exclusive world rights to copyright, produce and publish' the work.[70] Under these rights, Clarke, Irwin was distributing the work in Canada at C$4.00 per copy. Clarke, Irwin had also granted a US company the 'sole and exclusive rights to publish the work in the United States'. The US company sold some copies to a wholesaler from whom the defendant bought 100. The defendant imported these into Canada where it was selling them at C$1. 98 per copy and Clarke, Irwin successfully sued it for infringement of its Canadian rights.

The defendant argued that Clarke, Irwin was the owner of the copyright in both Canada and the United States, hence the *Pitt Pitts* case (and the *Suckling* and *Hoffnung* cases) was distinguishable. Spence J rejected the distinction and instead based himself squarely on the territoriality principle established by the *Pitt Pitts, Suckling* and *Hoffnung* cases.[71]

Some support for the defendant's argument was found in an opinion given by the then deputy Attorney-General for Canada to a Canadian Royal Commission into copyright.[72] However, Spence J considered that that opinion was directed to the case of a US owner of both the US and Canadian copyrights who appointed a sole sales representative in Canada which was not the case before his Honour. The instant facts did not involve a mere Canadian sales agency, but a Canadian copyright owner and a publisher in its own right.[73]

Instead, his Honour attributed 'considerable interest' to the Royal Commission's conclusion that the hypothetical maker under the Canadian Act should be the person who actually made the articles.[74] However, Spence J concluded:

> In this case I am of the opinion that the words 'would infringe copyright if it had been made within Canada' mean *when applied to the present situation* that the work would infringe copyright *if it had been made within Canada by others than the plaintiff including [the United States grantee].* (*Emphasis added*)[75]

---

70   *Clarke, Irwin & Co. Ltd v C. Cole & Co. Ltd.* (1960) 22 DLR (2d) 183 (Ont. HC) interpreting section 27 of the Copyright Act of 1952.

71   *Ibid.* at 185 to 186. The *Suckling* case is referred to at Note 51 above.

72   The opinion is that of Mr F. P. Varcoe QC in *Report of the Royal Commission on Copyright 1957* at 91 to 92 cited in 22 DLR (2d) 183, at 187 to 188. Mr Varcoe also recommended that the law should be amended to allow exclusion of the parallel imports in that situation: *Report of the Royal Commission* at 199 cited in Card, 'Parallel Importation of Copyright Property: A Proposal to Amend the Canadian *Copyright Act*', (1990) 6 IPJ 97, at 100.

73   22 DLR (2d) 183, at 187. It is not precisely clear what Spence J understood by the term 'sole sales representative', although it may well mean the situation in *Quillet* where Lesage J also seemed to limit the power to block parallel imports to copyright owners in Canada who printed and published the work there, see text at Notes 65 to 69 above.

74   *Ibid.* at 187 to 188. The Royal Commission also considered that an importer would infringe if it bought from a foreign licensee not authorised to sell in Canada.

75   *Ibid.* at 188. Later his Honour concluded that the US grantee was not a mere agent for Clarke Irwin in the United States: at 189 to 190.

Writing in 1967 Professor Fox considered that the *Clarke, Irwin* case decided that 'the words "if made in Canada" are to be construed as meaning "if made in Canada by the person who made them" '.[76] This was certainly the view taken by the Royal Commission which Spence J cited with 'considerable interest'. However, Spence J did not purport to define the phrase conclusively. His Honour carefully confined his decision to the instant facts with the words 'when applied to the present situation'. On the facts before his Honour, it was not necessary to go further. The case only concerned manufacture abroad by someone without authority to make the articles in Canada. Any wider statement would have been *obiter*.

Additionally, the actual terms of Spence J's ruling are broader than the limited interpretation favoured by the Royal Commission and Professor Fox. The words 'if it had been made within Canada by others than the plaintiff *including* [the United States grantee]' do not suggest a test limited solely to the actual maker of the articles in question.

Subsequent Canadian case law does not seem to support the narrow interpretation suggested by Professor Fox for the *Clarke, Irwin* case. The reported judgments do not devote much consideration to the issue. Most of them also concern imports of articles actually made by persons lacking authority to make the articles in Canada. However, there are indications from some cases that a wider interpretation is correct.

The correct interpretation of the test confronted Callon J in the *Godfrey, MacSkimming* case.[77] The plaintiffs were the holders of the exclusive world rights to the copyright in four literary works. They had granted Follett Publishing Co. the exclusive rights to publish and print the works in the United States. Under the terms of that grant the works were actually printed in Canada for Follett by the plaintiffs. Follett sold copies to a wholesaler in the United States. Coles bought copies from this wholesaler and imported and sold them in Canada. The plaintiffs obtained an injunction for infringement of their Canadian copyright.

Callon J first rejected Coles' argument that it did not have the knowledge necessary to infringe. His Honour then dealt with the argument based on printing of the copies in Canada by the plaintiffs:

> I cannot agree with the defendant's submission that the mere printing of the American or Follett edition of the works in Canada entitles the defendant to import for sale or hire into Canada those works when the defendant is seized with the knowledge that such importation is without the consent of New Press. By s. 3 of the *Copyright Act*, the sole right to publish, to produce or to reproduce a work is in the owner of the copyright and he is the only person who can authorize others to do the things that the Act gives him the sole right to do. Where, as in this case, the defendant is impressed with the knowledge that the sale or the distribution of the American or Follett edition had not been authorized by the owner of the copyright, the importation for sale into Canada

---

76 Harold G. Fox, *The Canadian Law of Copyright and Industrial Designs*, Carswell Coy Ltd, 1967 (2nd ed.), at 492.
77 *Godfrey, MacSkimming & Baque Ltd et al. v Coles Book Stores Ltd* (1973) 40 DLR (3d) 346 (Ont. HC) interpreting Copyright Act, RSC 1970, Chapter C-30, section 17(4).

of the work that to his knowledge infringes copyright is within the scope of s. 17(4) of the *Copyright Act*.[78]

In some respects, the case is not particularly helpful. Callon J focused more on two facts which do not address the meaning of the hypothetical manufacturing requirement. His Honour emphasised that Coles knew the Canadian copyright owners objected to the importation and concentrated on Coles', and Follett's, lack of authority to deal with the copyright in Canada. His Honour simply rejected that 'mere printing' in Canada by the Canadian copyright owners was a defence. The basis of that rejection is not explained. It may have been arguable that the plaintiffs were acting as Follett's agent to print the copies. On that basis, perhaps, Follett should be regarded as the maker. Callon J did not so express himself, however. Nor did his Honour analyse the precise form of the relationship through which the plaintiffs printed the books for Follett.

Accordingly, the *Godfrey, MacSkimming* case found infringement by importation even though the actual maker of the infringing articles would not have infringed copyright (and, indeed, did not) by making the books in Canada.

The next two cases involved applications for interim injunctions in which Weatherston J delivered judgment orally. In the *McClelland and Stewart* case, his Honour denied relief to an exclusive licensee for the Canadian rights which was seeking to bar imports originating from the exclusive licensee of the US rights.[79] The actual maker of the imported articles, the US exclusive licensee, did not have authority to make the articles in Canada.

His Honour did not discuss the meaning of the hypothetical manufacturing requirement. Instead, Weatherston J dismissed the motion for delay and because of substantial doubts that the plaintiff was entitled to relief. On the evidence, it was questionable whether Coles had the necessary knowledge.[80] In addition, section 28 of the Copyright Act RSC 1970 Chapter C-30 appeared to provide a complete defence.[81]

---

78   *Ibid.* at 348. Contrast the US cases, *Sebastian International Inc. v Consumer Contacts (PTY) Ltd* 7 USPQ 2d 1077 (3d Cir. 1988) and *Cosmair Inc. v Dynamite Enterprise Inc.* 226 USPQ 344 (SD Fla. 1985), see section 4.3.4 below.

79   *McClelland and Stewart Ltd v Coles Book Stores Ltd* (1974) 55 DLR (3d) 362 (HC Ont.).

80   *Ibid.* at 364.

81   *Ibid.* at 365. Section 28(3) provided:

Notwithstanding anything within this Act it shall be lawful for any person –

. . .

(d)   to import any book lawfully printed in Great Britain or in a foreign country that has adhered to the Convention and the Additional Protocol . . . and published for circulation among, and sale to the public within either . . .

The United States did not adhere to the Convention at the relevant time but was deemed to do so by reason of section 4(2). Weatherston J did not refer to section 28(4) which provided that –

This section does not apply to any work the author of which is a British Subject, other that a Canadian citizen, or the subject or citizen of a country that has adhered to the Convention and the Additional Protocol.

But, the authors of at least some of the titles may well have been Canadian citizens, see the *Simon & Schuster* case below.

The brief nature of the judgment in the *Simon & Schuster* case does not carry the Canadian interpretation of the hypothetical manufacturing requirement much further.[82] The plaintiffs included the author, who appears to have been a US citizen, who owned copyright in both the United States and Canada. She had 'given' the publishing rights to the other plaintiffs. Coles bought copies of the work lawfully in the United States and imported them for sale into Canada. The plaintiffs successfully obtained an interim injunction to restrain further sales.

Weatherston J found that subsection 28(4) deprived Coles of the benefit of sub-section 28(3) this time. Thus, it seems, subsection 28(3) only authorised imports in defiance of sub-section 17(4) when the author was a Canadian citizen.[83] His Honour explained his decision in the *McClelland and Stewart* case as resting on the absurdity of denying a right to sell if a right to import existed. Further important differences lay in proof of ownership of the copyright, notice to Coles that copyright subsisted and the promptitude with which the plaintiffs acted against Coles.[84]

The subsequent cases all concerned manufacturers abroad which did not have authority to make the articles in question in Canada. Infringement was found in all.

In *Record Wherehouse*, the plaintiffs assigned the exclusive right in the United States to manufacture and distribute certain musical works to a US corporation, granting an exclusive licence for Canada to a Canadian company.[85] The defendant bought sound recordings of the work in the United States from a discount wholesaler which in turn had bought the copies from the owner of the US rights. Mahoney J followed Harvey J's reasoning in the *Hoffnung* case to find infringement.[86]

Muldoon J extended this reasoning to a situation where the market division appeared to be effected by exclusive licences and not assignment.[87] The plaintiffs were the owner of the copyright in various musical works throughout the world and its Canadian subsidiary. The subsidiary was the exclusive licensee for Canada. The defendants imported and sold records bought in Mexico from the exclusive licensee of the rights for Mexico, CBS Records International.

His Honour first commented that-

> The plaintiffs' posture in this action may seem to be somewhat odd, in that they are complaining about the defendants' importing, distributing and selling the

---

82   *Simon & Schuster Inc. et al. v Coles Book Stores Ltd* (1975) 61 DLR (3d) 590, 23 CPR (2d) 43 (HC Ont.).
83   *Ibid.* at 591 to 592. See also *Benjamin Distribution Ltd v Les Editions Flammarion Ltée* (1982) 68 CPR (2d) 251, at 255 *per* McCarthy JA (CA Quebec).
84   *Ibid.* at 592.
85   *Fly By Nite Music Co. Ltd et al. v Record Wherehouse Ltd* (1975) 20 CPR (2d) 263 (FTD).
86   *Ibid.* at 270 to 271, see text from Note 58 above.
87   *A & M Records of Canada Ltd et al. v Millbank Music Corp. Ltd et al.* (1984) 1 CPR (3d) 354 (FTD).

Californian plaintiff's own goods, which, the plaintiffs incidentally allege, are of inferior quality in comparison with their goods which are sold in Canada.[88]

After remarking on the instant case's similarity to the *Hoffnung* and *Record Wherehouse* cases, his Honour adopted Spence J's interpretation of the hypothetical manufacturing requirement and found infringement. In Muldoon J's words, 'Spence J went on to hold "would infringe" means if made in Canada by others than the plaintiff.'[89] Accordingly, his Honour granted an interim injunction.

Factually, the case was similar to the earlier authorities in that the actual maker of the imported articles did not have authority to make them in Canada; although it did in Mexico. However, it is worthy of note that his Honour treated the offending articles as the copyright owner's. On this part of the case, Muldoon J appeared willing to disregard the licensing arrangements, perhaps, suggesting further support for a broad interpretation of Spence J's ruling.

The remaining two cases concerned imports of books made in France by the French copyright owner. Unlike *Quillet*, the copyright for Canada had been assigned by the French copyright owner to the respective Canadian plaintiffs. In each case, injunctions were granted against importation and sale.[90] Accordingly, these cases correspond to the *Suckling* and *Hoffnung* cases. In neither did the court explain the theory underlying the hypothetical manufacturer requirement.

In the *Benjamin* case, the court did not draw adverse inferences from the close corporate affiliation between the assignor and assignee.[91] Nor, in the *Dictionnaires Robert* case, was any concern expressed about the apparently technical, formalistic insertion of the assignee into the authorised distribution chain.

The *Dictionnaires Robert* case is of some further interest because Denault J appears to find infringement under both section 17(4) and 17(1); which provided for 'primary' infringement. Hence, Denault J seems to have found infringement by producing or reproducing the work.[92]

The Canadian cases reviewed do not really explore the meaning of the hypothetical manufacturing requirement in a detailed manner. However, despite fairly strong opinions expressed to the contrary, the cases tend to

---

88   *Ibid.* at 357.
89   *Ibid.* at 358.
90   *Benjamin Distribution Ltd v Les Editions Flammarion Ltée* (1982) 68 CPR (2d) 251 (CA Quebec); *Les Dictionnaires Robert Canada SCC et al. v Librairie du Nomade Inc. et al.* (1987) 16 CPR (3d) 319 (FTD). In the *Dictionnaires Robert* case, the French copyright owner initially distributed its products in Canada through an exclusive distributor. Following the assignment, the new owner continued with the same exclusive distributor.
91   68 CPR (2d) 251, at 254 for the fact of affiliation.
92   16 CPR (3d) 319, at 328 to 329. Section 17(1) deemed infringement by any person who did, without the consent of the copyright owner, anything that only the owner of the copyright had the right to do. The copyright owner's exclusive rights were specified in section 3(1). Apart from the right to produce or reproduce, the other rights specified do not appear applicable. See now RSC 1985, Chapter C-42, section 27(1).

suggest that Canadian courts follow a broader test than the actual maker theory. In fact, the words used by (but not the circumstances before) Spence J in the *Clarke, Irwin* case seem sufficiently broad to encompass the public theory applied in New Zealand. Much closer attention to the test has been forced on the courts in the other jurisdictions. In any event, notwithstanding the case law, parallel imports from the United States have proved a continuing practical problem for the publishing industry since at least the mid-1980s and have led to a government announcement that it will amend the legislation to strengthen copyright owners' rights against parallel importers.[93]

Returning to 1973, a South African case, *Music Machine*, did not advance matters further than the *Hoffnung* case.[94] The Gramophone Co. owned the copyright in South Africa in two sound recordings, The Beatles – 'Let It Be' – and George Harrison – 'All Things Must Pass'. Music Machine bought copies of these from a wholesaler in the United States and imported them for sale into South Africa. These copies had been made in the United States but not by the Gramophone Co. or the US copyright owner and did not infringe US law because the US law then in force apparently did not recognise copyright in sound recordings.

Moll J found infringement, ruling that:

> Even if, therefore, a copy may lawfully have been made in the place where it was made, its importation into the Republic without the licence of the owner of the copyright could constitute an infringement of the copyright in this country. See Halsbury, *Laws of England*, 3 ed., vol. 8, para. 782, pp. 431, 432, which goes so far as to suggest that, even if the copy were made with the permission of the copyright owner in the place where it was made, it would constitute an infringement to import such copy without the permission of the owner of the copyright in the place where they were so imported.[95]

As the manufacturer of the sound recordings in the United States did not have authority to make them in South Africa, *Music Machine* is consistent with the most restricted test, the actual maker theory.

The next case, the *Fletcher Construction* case, has provoked considerable difficulty, although, on its facts, it was arguably no different than the *Hoffnung* case.[96] The case concerned a system for providing recorded music over a diffusion service in buildings. A US corporation, Muzak, had developed this system and franchised it throughout the world. In New Zealand, one of its franchisees was Fletcher Construction. Muzak provided its prerecorded tapes to Fletcher Construction for transmission over the latter's diffusion service and, after an interval, the tapes were

---

93   See Chapter 10.3 below.
94   *Gramophone Co. Ltd v Music Machine (Pty) Ltd* 1973(3) SA 188 (WLD) involving *Copyright Act*, No. 63 of 1965, sections 17(2) and (3). This, and the subsequent South African cases are reviewed in O. Dean and C. Puckrin, 'Case Comment: Infringement of Copyright by Parallel Importation', [1983] EIPR 190.
95   *Ibid.* at 198.
96   *J. Albert & Sons Pty Ltd v Fletcher Construction Co. Ltd* [1974] 2 NZLR 107.

returned to Muzak in the United States. A collecting society owned the exclusive rights in New Zealand to broadcast or transmit via a diffusion service the musical works in question and Fletcher Construction had the necessary licence from it. Albert, however, was the exclusive licensee for New Zealand of the right to reproduce the musical works in any material form and Fletcher Construction did not have a licence from Albert.

Arguing that the imported tape reproduced the musical works in a material form, Albert sued Fletcher Construction for infringement by importing the tape without Albert's licence. Since making and transmitting were distinct rights requiring separate authority, Albert argued that making the tape in New Zealand without its licence would be an infringement and so it claimed that the hypothetical manufacturing requirement was met 'if the article had been made by any person, not being a person who had specific authority from the copyright owner to make it, in New Zealand'.

Fletcher Construction countered that its right to transmit necessarily included the right to make or import sound recordings embodying the musical works. In support of this proposition, it relied on section 19 of the Copyright Act 1962 (New Zealand).[97]

Quilliam J accepted Albert's contentions. His Honour appeared to decide against Fletcher Construction for either of two reasons. His Honour found that section 19 did not have the effect contended for by Fletcher Construction.[98] In any case, if it did, the acts of making and importing were distinct rights requiring separate authority and section 19 only authorised making, not importing. In the course of so holding, his Honour said:

> The correct interpretation of the words in s 10(2) is indeed troublesome but I have come to the conclusion that the plaintiffs' argument must be preferred. The reason I have set out earlier at such length the scheme of the Act is to show the way in which it establishes a separation of rights at every level from the moment of composition of a work. Every form of transaction with regard to a work is a separate one, and is given separate protection, and is capable of being dealt with separately on an economic basis. It is in this way that the making of an article (that is, the reproduction of the work in any material form – s 7(3)(a)) and the importing of an article (as contemplated s 10) become entirely separate matters. Section 10(2) prescribes when the importing of a work is infringed, and it chooses as the test for determining infringement the fulfilment of the two conditions set out. Those conditions are, first, the absence of a licence from the owner of the copyright, and secondly, the knowledge that the making of the article constituted an infringement, or, alternatively, that it would have constituted an infringement if the article had been made in New Zealand. To read s 10(2) in such a way as to mean that a person who has the right to 'make' is automatically to have also a licence to 'import' is to depart from the very basis upon which the statute proceeds. The implications of that interpretation go further. It would only be necessary to show that the owner of the copyright has given to someone in New Zealand authority to make a record.

---

97 Compare the 1956 Act sections 6(7) and (9).
98 [1974] 2 NZLR 107, at 115. Quilliam J also rejected Fletcher Construction's argument that the tapes were ephemeral recordings for the purpose of broadcasting under section 19(11): *ibid.*

Thereupon anyone else could import the work because the making of the record with authority would have meant that there was no infringement. This cannot be the way in which the section should be interpreted unless that is plain that that is meant. I do not think that is the case. The proper construction, in my view, is that proposed on behalf of the plaintiffs, namely, that *it is an infringement to import a record if the making of that record in New Zealand would, in general terms, constitute an infringement, that is, by anyone who did not have specific authority to make it* (*Emphasis added*).[99]

Quilliam J concluded that the public theory correctly defined the hypothetical manufacturing requirement. Importation will infringe if the making of the article in the jurisdiction would require a licence to be lawful.[100] His Honour, in effect, ruled that the hypothetical manufacturing requirement is met if the article embodies a copyright subsisting in the jurisdiction. In that case, whether the importer infringes depends on the separate elements of licence and knowledge. If the importer has the necessary knowledge but no licence from the copyright owner in the jurisdiction, the importer infringes.

Quilliam J offered two reasons for this conclusion. The first was the separation of rights 'at every level' effected by the copyright system which entailed that: 'Every form of transaction with regard to a work is a separate one, and is given separate protection, and is capable of being dealt with separately on an economic basis.' This led his Honour to conclude that importing and making are separate rights requiring separate consents.

The separation of rights perceived by Quilliam J is not controversial, either at the national or international level. His Honour's further conclusion about the separate nature of the rights to import and to make requires closer scrutiny. At the practical level, it seems hard to justify such a distinction. From the right owner's point of view, there may be little difference whether the grantee makes the articles in the jurisdiction or imports them. Considerations of public policy favouring domestic production over imports are not likely to concern private, commercial parties. However, the value of the right conferred on a grantee of the right to reproduce the copyright in the jurisdiction would be substantially undercut if a right of importation could be dealt with separately.[101]

At the level of logic, whether a right to import exists separately from the right to make (reproduce) depends on whether the Act creates such a separate right. The basis for such a right lies in the indirect infringement provisions. Yet, these in turn depend on whether the making of the imported article would infringe. So, it seems, the legislation itself does not necessarily contemplate separate rights to import and to reproduce.

The second reason underlying his Honour's conclusion is, with respect,

---

99 *Ibid.* at 114.
100 See Laddie, Prescott and Vitoria, *The Modern Law of Copyright*, Butterworths, 1980, at 388.
101 Contrast *Briscoe & Co. v Washburn* (1891) 10 NZLR 85, see Chapter 3.2.3 above.

also subject to criticism. His Honour considered that the implications of including a right to import in a right to make meant that:

> It would only be necessary to show that the owner of the copyright has given to someone in New Zealand authority to make a record. Thereupon anyone else could import the work because the making of the record with authority would have meant that there was no infringement.

It is difficult to understand why permitting one person a right to make an article generally licenses anyone else to import (even putting to one side the distinction Quilliam J had drawn between the rights to make and import). If the copyright owner had power to block importation before licensing someone to make copies, there does not seem to be any reason or principle suggesting that the grant of rights to 'A' passes any rights to 'B' and 'C' which they did not already have.

The element which so plainly struck Quilliam J, and drew his Honour on to the further, more questionable conclusions, however, may itself justify his Honour's overall conclusion that Fletcher Construction had infringed Albert's rights. His Honour was plainly impressed by the separate and distinct nature of each aspect of a copyright. This division was intended to allow the copyright owner to exploit its rights for their full economic value and extended to the territorial exploitation of the right throughout the world.[102] On this ground, arguably, Quilliam J was in accord with the clear adoption of the principle of territoriality in *Pitt Pitts* and *Hoffnung*.

The *Fletcher Construction* case has been subjected to critical consideration by three cases in the United Kingdom. In the first, *Stage One (Records)*, Goulding J enjoined parallel importing of a named sound recording but refused to grant an interlocutory injunction against the parallel importer generally.[103]

'The Who' owned copyright throughout the world in various sound recordings, Polydor was the exclusive licensee of those copyrights for the United Kingdom. A third corporation was the exclusive licensee for Canada and the United States. Stage One bought records in bulk in the Netherlands and imported them into the United Kingdom. Some of these included records made in the United States under the exclusive licence from 'The Who'. A number of threats were made to Stage One which gave undertakings not to import specified titles. However, negotiations over the general problem broke down and the plaintiffs issued proceedings.

The facts were sufficient to meet the actual maker theory and the plaintiffs had argued the case before his Lordship on the actual maker theory,

---

102   Although, territorial distinctness at the international level more probably arises from the separate, national treatment underlying the recognition of copyright across national borders.

103   *The Who Group Limited and Polydor Limited v Stage One (Records) Limited* [1980] FSR 268; [1980] 2 CMLR 429 (Ch. D). This case, the *Charmdale* and *Harlequin* cases are the subject of a comment: Michael Hicks, 'The Harlequin, Who and Charmdale Cases: Parallel Imports – UK and EEC Law', [1980] EIPR 237.

reserving the right to argue the importer theory at trial.[104] It was on this basis that Goulding J enjoined imports of the named titles. His Lordship rejected Stage One's contentions that sections 5 and 16 were intended to ban imports only of pirate copies or from countries which did not provide 'relevant protection' to copyright:

> I do not accept the foregoing argument. It seems to me to restrict without due cause the actual meaning of the words employed in sections 5 and 16 of the Act of 1956. It is also contrary to an opinion expressed in successive editions of *Copinger on Copyright* now to be found in paragraph 477 of the 11th edition.[105]

Goulding J refused the general injunction, however, largely on procedural grounds. The plaintiffs' delay for a number of years in enforcing their rights had allowed Stage One to build up a substantial business which would be seriously prejudiced by the grant of a broad injunction. Moreover, his Lordship saw considerable difficulties in formulating an injunction because it would need to be framed to allow for imports made in the United States by the owner of the UK copyright and cope with the rules for the free movement of goods between Member States of the European Communities.[106]

Goulding J was not required to decide conclusively between the competing theories in *Stage One (Records)*, but the differences between the tests proved decisive in the *Charmdale* case.[107] The question came before Browne-Wilkinson J on a preliminary question of law. 'CBS' produced sound recordings in the United States. It owned, or was the exclusive licensee of, the copyright in those sound recordings in both the United States and the United Kingdom and had appointed its wholly owned subsidiary, CBS UK, as its exclusive licensee of the rights for the United Kingdom. Charmdale distributed records throughout the United Kingdom and imported from the United States some of records bought on the open market which had been made by CBS. CBS UK sought injunctions to stop the importing. Nothing turned on whether CBS was the owner or the exclusive licensee of the rights passed on to CBS UK.[108]

CBS UK supported its claim on two grounds. First, it argued that the hypothetical manufacturing requirement should be tested by the public or importer theories, not the actual maker theory. Alternatively, if the actual maker theory applied, it argued that manufacture by CBS would infringe because CBS UK, as the exclusive licensee, was the only person entitled to exercise the copyright in the United Kingdom and so should be regarded as the owner there. Charmdale simply countered that CBS, as the owner of the copyright, could not infringe its own copyright under section 1(2).

---

104 [1980] FSR at 275; 2 CMLR at 436.
105 *Ibid.* See now the 12th edition ¶532 amended in light of the *Charmdale* case, see text from Note 107 below.
106 [1980] FSR at 275, at 276 to 278; 2 CMLR at 435, at 437 to 438 respectively. For the EC rules on free movement, see Chapter 6 below.
107 *CBS United Kingdom Ltd v Charmdale Record Distributors Ltd* [1980] FSR 289; but see now CDPA 1988 section 27(3)(b), see text at Notes 38 and 173, this chapter.
108 *Ibid.* at 295.

Browne-Wilkinson J rejected CBS UK's contention that it should be regarded as the 'owner' of the copyright within the United Kingdom.[109] Under the general law a licensee did not enjoy proprietary rights; its rights were contractual only and section 19 merely granted exclusive licensees a procedural right to sue.[110] Section 19 was drafted on the basis that there were two separate persons, the owner and the exclusive licensee, which enjoyed concurrent rights under the 1956 Act and so did not intend exclusive licensees to replace the owner completely.[111] Further, the words 'or otherwise' in section 49(5) could take effect without applying to exclusive licences since, for example, title to some rights could pass by operation of law.[112]

To rebut the actual maker theory, CBS UK placed great reliance on the fact that 'the whole system of licensing will break down' if exclusive licensees did not have exclusive rights. Browne-Wilkinson J described this as 'a formidable argument of convenience which I would find compelling were it not for one factor'. As his Lordship interpreted the 1956 Act, section 19 did not empower an exclusive licensee to sue the copyright owner for copyright infringement. It may have a remedy in contract, but not copyright.[113] His Lordship considered that there was no reason to grant the exclusive licensee greater protection against reproductions from its copyright owner originating abroad. This left his Lordship free to consider the actual maker, importer and public theories on their respective merits.

Browne-Wilkinson J first dealt with the public theory. His Lordship distinguished the *Fletcher Construction* case on its facts since, there, the actual maker of the tapes would have been an infringer if it made the tapes in New Zealand.[114] However, his Lordship did not address the issue why

---

109   The basis for this contention rested on the wording of section 49(5) of the Act:

> In the case of any copyright to which (whether in consequence of a partial assignment *or otherwise*) different persons are entitled in respect of the application of the copyright –
> (a)   to the doing of different acts or classes of acts, or
> (b)   to the doing of one or more acts or classes of acts in different countries or at different times,
> the owner of the copyright, for any purpose of this Act, shall be taken to be the person who is entitled to the copyright in respect of its application to the doing of the particular act or class of acts, or, as the case may be, to the doing thereof in the particular country or at the particular time, which is relevant to the purpose in question. . . . (*Emphasis added*)

CBS UK argued that the words 'or otherwise' covered exclusive licences.
110   [1980] FSR 289, at 295. See also *Video Parktown North (Pty) Ltd v Paramount Pictures Corporation* 1986(2) SA 623, at 632 to 633 (AD), especially text at Notes 147 to 148 below. Browne-Wilkinson J did not cite authority. The proposition is consistent with *Heap v Hartley* (1889) 42 Ch. D 461. Lush J, however, was prepared to consider, but did not decide, that an exclusive licensee may well have a licence coupled with a grant: *British Actors' Film Company v Glover* [1918] 1 KB 299, at 309. Note, however, the limited terms of section 19(2)(a), see Note 113 below.
111   *Ibid*. See also *Video Parktown North (Pty) Ltd v Paramount Pictures Corporation* 1986(2) SA 623, at 632 to 633 (AD), especially text at Notes 147 to 148 below.
112   *Ibid*. at 295 to 296.
113   *Ibid* at 296. Section 19(2)(a) provides 'The exclusive licensee shall (except as against the owner of the copyright) have the same rights of action, and be entitled to the same remedies, under section seventeen of this Act as if the licence had been an assignment . . . .'
114   *Ibid*. at 297, 298. At 298, his Lordship states, 'it was not, and could not be, argued that the actual maker of the tapes in the United States could have lawfully made the tapes in New Zealand . . . .'

the harm caused to an exclusive licensee by imports made by the copyright owner was not as detrimental as that caused by imports made by a foreign licensee; presumably because of his views about the effect of a licence under the general law.[115]

His Lordship then turned to Quilliam J's reasoning. Having quoted the passage extracted above from his Honour's judgment, Browne-Wilkinson J confessed that he was not sure that he 'fully understood how Quilliam J did in fact construe the section.' His Lordship singled out three specific difficulties.[116] First, it was logically difficult to conceive someone granting a specific authority to a hypothetical manufacture. Second, it was not any importation of a copyright article which would infringe; only those which would infringe if made in the jurisdiction. Accordingly, the section itself required 'one to find out whether the hypothetical maker would have been authorised to make' the imported article in the domestic jurisdiction.[117] Third, his Lordship was not persuaded that the grant to a specific person of a right to make inherently licensed the public at large to import copyright articles at will. In any event, his Lordship concluded that: '. . . because Quilliam J's test excepts any person specifically authorised by the copyright owner; manufacture by the copyright owner must be an *a fortiori* case.'[118]

Having dismissed the public maker theory, Browne-Wilkinson J rejected the importer theory. Although it was desirable to preserve uniformity of national laws relating to an international subject like copyright, two factors compelled rejection of the approach taken in Australia. His Lordship considered that the hypothetical manufacturing requirement must be interpreted in the same way in the provision against *selling* the banned imports as in the provision banning imports.[119] Here considerations based on a policy of commercial convenience intervened. Traders who bought the imported articles from the actual importer would be severely prejudiced by adopting the importer theory. In many cases, they would not know, and have no reasonable means of ascertaining the identity of, the importer. Whereas the identity of the original manufacturer could usually be found on the article. Therefore, there was no 'obvious reason' for adopting the importer theory.[120]

While his Lordship's proposition that the test for infringement by importation and by commercial dealings in imports is the same must be correct, the second, with respect, is not compelling. An on-seller's liability under the provision is not dependent just on the 'unlawful' nature of the

---

115 The issue is still controversial under the EC's competition rules, see for example 258/78 *Maize Seed* [1982] ECR 2015 and *GEMA-Custom Pressing*, at Chapter 7.2.1 and Chapter 7.3.1(g), respectively, below.

116 [1980] FSR 289, at 298.

117 Since the copyright owner could well consent to imports which had been made by someone not having authority to make within the jurisdiction, this construction raises a different question to whether the copyright owner has consented to the importation.

118 [1980] FSR 289, at 298.

119 For example the 1956 Act sections 5(2) and (3).

120 [1980] FSR 289, at 299.

article in question. The seller must also be shown to know that the article has that unlawful nature since knowledge is a separate element of the wrong independent of the hypothetical manufacturing requirement.[121]

The second reason for rejecting the importer theory offered by Browne-Wilkinson J was that 'the state of knowledge and intentions of the assumed maker may be of decisive importance'. His Lordship appears to have had two types of problem in mind here: whether the production of the article in the first place involved copying in the sense of derivation from the copyright source; and whether the statutory defences of fair dealing may render infringement dependent on the purpose for which the copy was made. His Lordship concluded:

> In these types of case the answer to the question 'Would the hypothetical making of the article in the United Kingdom have been an infringement?' may differ according to whether the alleged copy was made by the actual maker or by an importer. It seems to me a wayward construction of the Act to hold that the importation of a book consciously copied by the actual maker was not an infringement under section 5(2) because the importer could show that he was not aware of the original.[122]

To some extent, this reasoning seems to contradict the first ground on which his Lordship rejected the importer theory. On one hand, his Lordship feared that on-sellers may be liable although they do not have 'guilty' knowledge; yet, on the other, importers may escape liability because they also lack that knowledge. Surely, the defendant's state of knowledge should have the same effect. Moreover, as already indicated, to construe the hypothetical manufacturing requirement by reference to the effects of knowledge is misplaced.

Browne-Wilkinson J's reasoning must be questioned further. It is not really necessary to delve into the copying issue. With parallel imports, by definition, there has been copying. It is one of the circumstances of the imported article's making. There is no need to question its presence.

The other factor suggested by Browne-Wilkinson J was the statutory defences of fair dealing. Most of these situations may well be *de minimis*. However, if the law were to provide consistent protection, it would be the purpose of the importer which determined whether such a defence were available, not the purpose of the actual maker in another jurisdiction. The fact that the actual maker made the copy for, say, the purposes of a judicial proceeding in another country should not assist an importer who intended to exploit the copy commercially in the country of importation.

Finally, the extract quoted from Browne-Wilkinson J's judgment suggests that his Lordship's motivation in part for rejecting the importer theory was a concern that importers could evade the provision too easily. It is ironic that his Lordship's favoured interpretation promotes, rather than prevents, that possibility.

---

121 See for example the *Barson Computers* case [1985] FSR 489, at 503 *per* Pritchard J, see text at Notes 155 to 156 below.
122 [1980] FSR 289, at 299.

Browne-Wilkinson J then explained his reasons for adopting the actual maker theory:

> First, once one assumes any maker other than the actual maker the difficulties I have just mentioned as to the state of knowledge and motives of the hypothetical maker are thrown up. If one can look at the true facts, that is to say at the state of knowledge and the motives of the actual maker abroad, these difficulties disappear. Next, the statute, in terms, only requires one to hypothesise a single alteration from the true facts, namely, the local situation in which the work was made. Unless this hypothesis necessarily involves further hypotheses I do not think it is a sound application of the principles of construction to introduce by implication such further hypotheses. It seems to me probable that the alternative of hypothetical making in the United Kingdom was introduced to exclude any argument that because the copying was done outside the jurisdiction of the United Kingdom it could not constitute an infringement of a United Kingdom copyright. In assuming the making in the United Kingdom, the legislature was concerned only to change the geographical location and nothing more.[123]

His Lordship found support for these conclusions in two cases, other than the *Fletcher Construction* case, cited to his Lordship. However, *Stage One (Records)*, already considered, did not involve facts necessary for consideration of this issue. Moreover, it was an interlocutory hearing and counsel conceded, for the purposes of the hearing only, that the provision should be interpreted on the actual maker theory. Accordingly, with respect, its authority is limited. The *Clarke, Irwin* case was the second. As has already been indicated, there are considerable doubts that this case adopted the actual maker theory. Certainly, it is putting the matters too highly to say, as Browne-Wilkinson J did, that:

> Spence J cited with approval two other authorities, not judicial decisions, which clearly stated that the importation of articles made outside Canada by the owner of the Canadian copyright would not be an infringement, since the hypothetical maker is to be taken to be the actual maker, and making by the Canadian copyright owner would not be an infringement.[124]

Spence J did not derive assistance from one of those authorities, the opinion of Mr Varcoe QC. Moreover, while his Honour found assistance from the other, the terms of his expressed conclusion were broader than the Royal Commission's apparent adoption of the actual maker theory and subsequent Canadian cases, apparently not cited to Browne-Wilkinson J, bear out this difference.

Browne-Wilkinson J's approach is in striking contrast to that of Quilliam J. Quilliam J was plainly motivated by the scheme of the Act which his Honour saw as founding an elaborate system for the economic exploitation of the asset created. His Honour refused to interpret the specific terms of the legislation in a way which would substantially reduce the economic value of the copyright asset. In contrast, Browne-Wilkinson J focused on

---

123 *Ibid.* at 300.
124 *Ibid.* at 301. For *Clarke, Irwin*, see text from Note 71 above.

the specific terms of the legislation and discounted arguments based on economic implications.

In the third UK case, *Harlequin*, Megarry VC also adopted the actual maker theory. It is not so clear that the Court of Appeal did.[125] Polydor was the exclusive licensee for the United Kingdom of copyright in a sound recording by the Bee Gees, 'Spirits Having Flown'. Two companies related to Polydor were the licensees for Portugal. Harlequin bought copies of the sound recordings from the related companies in Portugal and imported them for sale into the United Kingdom. Polydor sought an interlocutory injunction against Harlequin pending resolution of an infringement action. Megarry VC granted the injunction, the Court of Appeal discharged it on grounds of a Free Trade Agreement between the European Economic Community and Portugal.[126]

For Harlequin, it was argued that the indirect infringement provisions should be interpreted to catch imports of articles made abroad in infringing circumstances but to allow imports of articles made abroad which did not infringe a copyright in the place of making.

Megarry VC rejected this submission. His Lordship noted that the provision referred to importation without licence and not manufacture without licence and turned to the meaning of the hypothetical manufacturing requirement:

> What seems plain is that this second alternative necessarily postulates a making of the article that constitutes no actual infringement of copyright. If there is an actual infringement of copyright in the making of the article, it is covered by the first alternative, and so there is no need for the second alternative. Only if the making escapes the first alternative can there be work to do for the second alternative. In considering the second alternative, one starts, therefore, with a making which did not in fact constitute an infringement of copyright. *The second alternative then continues by requiring a single hypothesis to be made, namely, that instead of the article being made where it was in fact made, it was made in the country into which it was imported. That is all. The statutory hypothesis is geographical, nothing more. There is nothing to require any hypothetical alteration in the article, the owner of the copyright, the making, or anything else. (Emphasis added)*[127]

His Lordship accepted that it would be valid to make a hypothesis which was the inevitable consequence of any hypothesis required by the statute. However:

> Accept that to the full, and still I can see no reason why the word 'inevitably' should be softened into 'probably'. The hypothetical must not be allowed to oust the real further than obedience to the statute compels. In my judgment, there is no reason why, in applying the second alternative, it should be assumed or accepted that there is any alteration in the person who in fact made the article.

125 *Polydor Limited and Another v Harlequin Record Shop and Another* [1980] FSR 194, [1980] 1 CMLR 669 (Ch. D); [1980] FSR 362 (CA).
126 But, see *270/80 Polydor Limited and RSO Records Inc. v Harlequin Record Shops Limited and Simsons Records Limited* [1982] ECR 329, see Chapter 6.3.2 below.
127 [1980] FSR at 199; 1 CMLR at 673.

The sole hypothetical change is in the place in which the article is made; there is nothing to change the person who made it.

Construed in that way, section 16(2) seems perfectly rational. Put in simple language, the rule is that an importer into this country must refrain from importing articles which he knows either were in fact made in breach of copyright or, if they had been made here, would have been made in breach of copyright. The second limb is needed to prevent articles manufactured abroad without any breach of copyright from being knowingly imported so as to impair the rights of the owner of the copyright here. The manufacture and circulation of those articles abroad is not a matter which Parliament could regulate, even if the rights of the copyright owner were prejudiced: but once the articles are imported, Parliament could effectively protect the owner of the copyright here, and in my judgment has done so. I cannot see any rational ground for assuming, contrary to the facts, that when the articles so imported were hypothetically manufactured here, this was done *by the owner of the copyright here* instead of by the actual manufacturer, against the import of whose articles the owner of the copyright here needs protection.[128] (*Emphasis added*)

His Lordship then found that this conclusion happily agreed with that in the *Charmdale* case, although, as his Lordship noted, that case had proceeded on different arguments.

Three matters call for comment. First, Megarry VC clearly accepted that the interests of the domestic copyright owner required protection against unauthorised imports. As the copyright owner in both Portugal and the United Kingdom was the same, his Lordship's judgment recognises that that protection extends to protecting the interests of exclusive licensees. This does not seem to be 'in consonance' with the views of Browne-Wilkinson J in the *Charmdale* case.

Second, Megarry VC's opinion was given in the context of an argument that the hypothetical maker should be assumed to be the domestic copyright owner. The judgment was directed to rejecting that argument. Neither the public nor the importer theories were before his Lordship. Allied to this, the facts of the *Harlequin* case did not require consideration of either of these theories. These factors must be borne in mind when considering his Lordship's conclusion that:

. . . there is no reason why, in applying the second alternative, it should be assumed or accepted that there is any alteration in the person who in fact made the article. The sole hypothetical change is in the place in which the article is made; there is nothing to change the person who made it.

But, this passage clearly reflects the very broad terms of the passage emphasised in the earlier quotation.

Third, as in the *Charmdale* case, Megarry VC concluded that the hypothetical manufacturing requirement warranted making only a single assumption contrary to fact. This must be taken in the context of the specific argument put to his Lordship – that it should be assumed the hypothetical maker was the domestic copyright owner which, as his Lordship noted, would

128   *Ibid.* at 200; 673 to 674.

have the consequence of denuding the domestic copyright of protection. Arguably, making only the single assumption in *Charmdale* would have the very consequence which Megarry VC in *Harlequin* sought to avoid.

Harlequin successfully appealed to the Court of Appeal. It did not succeed on the interpretation of copyright law but on a point of EC law subsequently overturned by the European Court of Justice.[129]

In the Court of Appeal argument concentrated on whether a licence to import into the United Kingdom could be implied from sale by a licensee in Portugal. Subject to the issues of implied consent and the effects of EC law, however, Templeman LJ found Polydor's rights infringed in terms which throw some doubt on the validity of Browne-Wilkinson J's judgment in the *Charmdale* case. Templeman LJ first found that subsection 49(5): '. . . makes a geographical distinction between the licensee of the copyright in Portugal, and the licensee of the copyright in the United Kingdom'.[130] His Lordship referred to subsection 49(6) and concluded:

> It follows that under section 16(2) it is no defence for the defendants to say that the records in question were manufactured by the Portuguese licensees. For the purposes of importing those records into the United Kingdom the defendants require the consent of the plaintiffs, and if they have not obtained the consent of the plaintiffs, (as they have not) they are, in my judgment, guilty of an infringement of copyright under section 16(2). As a matter of domestic law, the plaintiffs are entitled to enforce that section against the defendants, unless the fact that the United Kingdom licensee, namely the first plaintiffs, and the Portuguese licensees are members of the same group of companies makes any difference, or unless the domestic laws give way to a contrary provision of community law.[131]

His Lordship appears to regard subsections 49(5) and (6) as treating an exclusive licensee as the 'owner' of the copyright for the purposes of infringement by importing. If so, a broad reading of Templeman LJ's opinion seems to conflict with Browne-Wilkinson J's approach in the *Charmdale* case since the importer required Polydor's consent.

But, the two cases are technically distinguishable. In both *Charmdale* and *Harlequin*, the same person owned the copyright in the jurisdictions of export and import. However, in *Harlequin*, the imported articles were not made by the copyright owner, they were made under licence from the copyright owner and the Portuguese licensees' authority would not constitute a defence as against the copyright owner because the authority to make was limited to Portugal.[132] As a matter of substance, however, it cannot make any difference to the domestic exclusive licensee whether it faces competition from a parallel licensee or the copyright owner.[133]

129   Case 270/80 *Polydor Limited and RSO Records Inc. v Harlequin Record Shops Limited and Simsons Records Limited* [1982] ECR 329, see Chapter 6.3.2 below.
130   [1980] FSR 362, at 365.
131   *Ibid.*
132   This distinction is also recognised in patent law: *Tilghman's* case (1883) 25 Ch. D 1 (CA), see Chapter 3.2.3 above.
133   The CDPA 1988 has been amended to remove the anomaly, see text to Note 38 above.

The courts in South Africa have followed the UK courts in adopting the actual maker theory to interpret the hypothetical manufacturing requirement. As in the United Kingdom, arguments about the effect of parallel importing on the economic value of the copyrights were given short shrift.

Like *Music Machine*, *Videorent Parkmore* did not really explain the South African interpretation of the hypothetical manufacturing requirement.[134] Nor do the reported facts disclose the relationship, if any, between the copyright owner in South Africa and the maker of the offending imports. The applicant failed to obtain an interim interdict against the respondent because it did not prove the respondent had the necessary knowledge.[135] In the context of holding that the changes to the copyright legislation did not affect the law, Goldstone J noted that the indirect infringement provisions still applied only to 'spurious or infringing' copies.[136] His Honour did not explain whether the copies in question were, or were not, infringing copies, although it would seem that the applicant did not even allege that they were.[137]

Goldstone J returned to the issue in *Anthony Black Films*.[138] The respondent bought videocassettes in the United Kingdom where they had been made by the second applicant which was the non-exclusive licensee throughout the world, including South Africa, of the first applicant's copyright in various cinematograph films. The applicants sought to justify their attempt to stop this activity because it was destroying a large part of the potential income they expected to derive from exploiting the rights in South Africa. Determining the issue as a preliminary question of law, Goldstone J followed Browne-Wilkinson J and Megarry VC in adopting the actual maker theory:

> If the interpretation contended for by the applicants is correct, one consequence would be that whether or not an article is an 'infringing copy' in the Republic would be determined in a case such as the present not upon who made it in fact, but upon the identity of the person who imported it, or possibly on the purpose of the person who imported it. If imported by the respondent, it would be an infringing copy, whereas, if imported by the first applicant, the owner of the copyright, or by the second applicant, the non-exclusive licensee in South Africa, it would not be an infringing copy. This consequence appears to me to lead to a situation out of keeping with the general approach and intention of the Act and introduces more anomalies than does the interpretation adopted by the English Courts.

134 *Columbia Pictures Industries Incorporated v Videorent Parkmore* 1982(1) SA 49 (WLD).
135 *Ibid.* at 52.
136 Since the *Music Machine* case, the Copyright Act, No. 98 of 1978, had replaced the Copyright Act, No. 63 of 1965. The new Act no longer confined the hypothetical manufacturing requirement to manufacture '(in the case of an imported article)'. Goldstone J found that this did not change the existing interpretation of the statute since the hypothetical manufacturing requirement applied only to imports: *ibid.* at 51.
137 *Ibid.* For the applicant's omission, see *ibid.* at 52.
138 *Twentieth Century Fox Film Corporation and Another v Anthony Black Films (Pty) Ltd* 1982(3) SA 582 (WLD). Compare 158/86 *Warner Bros v Christiansen* [1988] ECR 2605, see Chapter 6.4 below.

All of the aforegoing demonstrates that 'the argument of convenience' is not quite as convenient as it appears at first blush. Quite apart from the aforegoing, like the English Judges, I too am of the opinion that the plain words of the opinion lead inevitably to the same conclusion.
. . .

It is plain that the 'article' referred to is the article which is imported. It is the making of that article in the Republic which is the hypothesis. Why should one introduce into that hypothesis a maker other than the actual maker? To do so would be to do something not embraced by the provision in question As MEGARRY V.-C. pointed out, there is no necessity to extend the hypothesis further than the words used by the legislature necessarily require.[139]

His Honour approved Browne-Wilkinson J's criticisms of the *Fletcher Construction* case and rejected the purpose test proposed in Laddie, Prescott and Vitoria as usurping the role of the legislature.[140]

Goldstone J, then, adopted the actual maker theory for three reasons. His Honour considered that an alternative theory (it is not clear which) would involve more anomalies than it solved. It would also be 'out of keeping with the general approach and intention of the Act'. Furthermore, like Megarry VC but in different circumstances, his Honour considered that there was no necessity to make any assumptions about the hypothetical making than that of geographical translation.

With all due respect, the rejection of Twentieth Century Fox's arguments because they made infringement depend on the identity of the importer or the importer's purpose cannot be right. The identity of the relevant actor is crucial. This applies whichever test is used, the difference lies in the time at which the relevant identity is assessed. Under the importer test, the identity of the actor is determined at the time of importation; the relevant time is earlier, at the time of reproduction, under the actual maker test. Nor can it be right to reject questions of purpose since the legislation itself makes importation only for certain purposes an infringement, obviously necessitating some inquiry into purpose.

His Honour's reasoning appears directed to rejecting the 'formidable argument of convenience'. As in the *Charmdale* case, the applicants had argued that the actual maker theory would undermine the position of exclusive licensees. Goldstone J noted:

I do not agree. The point is that the objection based upon the 'argument of convenience' cannot be wholly met by an extended interpretation of s. 23(2).

---

139   *Ibid*. at 592 to 593.
140   *Ibid*. at 593, 594 respectively. For the purpose test see Laddie, Prescott and Vitoria, *The Modern Law of Copyright*, at ¶11.7. The learned authors rejected the actual maker test because it could undermine an exclusive licence. They next rejected the importer theory because it would mean an authorised importer would be liable for a criminal prosecution under section 21 of the 1956 Act, although not liable for infringement. Thirdly, the learned authors rejected the public theory adopted in New Zealand because it was inconsistent with the existence and wording of the 'fair use' defences to infringement. See ¶11.6. The rejection of the actual and public theories is compelling. However, the rejection of the importer theory may be answered by the courts' refusal to extend liability for conversion against a defendant who escaped liability under the primary and secondary infringement provisions. see Chapter 4.2.3(b) below.

For this reason it seems to me it loses much of its force. This line of reasoning can be taken further. As MEGARRY V.-C. points out in the *Polydor* case the second limb of the provision 'is needed to prevent articles manufactured abroad without any breach of copyright from being knowingly imported so as to *impair the rights of the owner of the* copyright here.' Save for an exclusive licensee, who is to be treated in terms of s. 25 as if he had an assignment, it is only the owner of the copyright who is protected against infringement (*Goldstone J's emphasis*).[141]

As already discussed, given the different nature of the arguments before Megarry VC, Goldstone J's reliance on his Lordship's reasoning may be open to question. Moreover, his Honour did not discuss the effect, if any, of Templeman LJ's judgment on the validity of Megarry VC's reasoning.

Goldstone J appears to deny relief because the second applicant is only a non-exclusive licensee and the Act confers protection only on owners and exclusive licensees.[142] This does not, however, explain why the first applicant, the owner, should not be entitled to protection. Nor does it explain why a copyright owner's interests are not harmed by unauthorised imports of articles made and sold abroad by itself but are injured if the articles were made and sold abroad under its authority by a licensee as was the case in *Harlequin* and in the next South African case, *Video Parktown North.*[143]

The parallel importer was enjoined in *Video Parktown North* at first instance by McCreath J. Simplifying the convoluted dealings in the title to the copyright subsisting in the films, Video Parktown had bought the videocassettes in question abroad where they were made by the sub-licensee which did not have authority to make or sell in South Africa.[144] The judgment does not discuss the meaning of the hypothetical manufacturing requirement, but on this interpretation of the facts the case would be consistent with the actual maker theory.

So far as relevant, the appeal concentrated on whether Paramount had standing to sue. Slomowitz AJ, for the court, held that it did; either as owner or through some form of power of attorney from the copyright owner.[145] Two aspects of his Honour's opinion bear consideration.

---

141   *Ibid.* at 591 (references omitted).
142   It should also be noted that Goldstone J appears inconsistent with Browne-Wilkinson J by ruling that an exclusive licensee should be treated 'as if he had an assignment'. See now, *Video Parktown North (Pty) Ltd v Paramount Pictures Corporation* 1986 (2) 623, at 632 to 633 (AD), especially text at Notes 147 to 148 below.
143   *Video Parktown North (Pty) Ltd v Paramount Pictures Corporation* 1986(2) SA 623, at 632 to 633 (AD), at first instance, *sub nom. Paramount Pictures Corporation v Video Parktown North (Pty) Ltd* 1983(2) SA 251 (TPD).
144   This point is not clear at first instance, but see on appeal 1986(2) SA 623, at 628 *per* Slomowitz AJ and Dean and Puckrin, 'Case Comment: Infringement of Copyright by Parallel Importation', at 192 (Puckrin was one of Paramount's counsel).
145   *Ibid.* at 635 to 636. The further aspects were Paramount's unsuccessful appeal for an account of profits and McCreath J's rejection for want of standing of Video Parktown's application to expunge the copyright registration. The rejection was upheld, but not for want of standing.

First, his Honour may have endorsed the application in South Africa of the actual maker test, although this is by no means clear. Early in the judgment, Slomowitz AJ indicated that the appeal would have been resolved quite simply if the only transactions in the copyright had been the conferral on Paramount of exclusive rights worldwide.[146] Out of context, this could be taken to suggest that Paramount could not have succeeded against Video Parktown but for the intervention of the sub-licensee limited to the United Kingdom. Given the care with which the opinion is drafted, however, it seems more likely that his Honour was referring to Video Parktown's appeal on the issue of Paramount's standing to sue. It is not possible to advance the matter further; in any case, the facts were such that Paramount could succeed even on the actual maker theory.

The second matter bears on the nature of an exclusive licence. One part of Video Parktown's argument was that Paramount lost any rights to sue by its appointment of another party as the exclusive licensee of the copyright throughout the world. Slomowitz AJ rejected this argument on the ground that an exclusive licence did not extinguish the rights of the owner. Instead, as Browne-Wilkinson J had held, the statutory power for an exclusive licensee to sue was merely procedural and did not confer substantive rights. The owner alone possessed a proprietary interest in the copyright and could intervene to protect that interest even after the grant of an exclusive licence.[147] Some caution needs to be taken with Slomowitz AJ's opinion since he derives it from an analysis of copyright as a positive right of property and not just a negative right to exclude others from doing acts otherwise lawful.[148] This may be specific to South African law, since it seems inconsistent with the UK Court of Appeal's approach in *Pitt Pitts*, and, on the nature of a patent, in *Tilghman's* case.

Despite almost unequivocal rejection by the courts of the United Kingdom and South Africa, those in New Zealand have remained unrepentant; Pritchard J adhered to the public theory in *Barson Computer*.[149]

Acorn Computers Ltd made and distributed computers and associated technology throughout the world. It claimed copyright in both the United Kingdom and New Zealand in drawings and prototypes of components of its products and in the working programs, manuals and brochures which it created. Barson was its exclusive distributor in New Zealand. Gilbert bought Acorn products lawfully in the United Kingdom and imported and sold them in New Zealand. Acorn and Barson sued for copyright infringement and passing off. Gilbert undertook to stop passing off its merchandise as Acorn

---

146 *Ibid.* at 628: 'Had the matter rested there *caedit quaestio.*'
147 *Ibid.* at 633. See text at Notes 109 to 113 above. The Copyright Act of 1978 section 25 did not, like the corresponding UK provision, limit the exclusive licensee's powers to all the world *except* the owner. Instead, it entitled the exclusive licensee to the same rights of action and remedies 'as if the licence had been an assignment'.
148 *Ibid.* at 631 at 632.
149 *Barson Computer (N.Z.) Ltd and Others v John Gilbert & Co. Ltd* [1985] FSR 489 (HC NZ).

products sold by authorised dealers, but the plaintiffs sought an interlocutory injunction for copyright infringement. The issue came before Pritchard J as a preliminary point of law on the basis of an agreed set of facts which assumed copyright subsistence and the plaintiffs' ownership.

Pritchard J considered the earlier cases in detail and concluded that the public theory was the correct interpretation of the hypothetical manufacturing requirement. His Honour relied on two key factors. First, the international division of copyright interests which gave copyright owners in different jurisdictions distinct property rights deserving of protection against unauthorised competition. The anomaly which would arise by adopting the actual maker theory was the second.

On the first point, his Honour considered:

> It is generally true that a purchaser of articles made under copyright by or with the licence of the owner of the copyright, can make any use he likes of his purchases and will not thereby infringe copyright. But it is otherwise when copies are taken across an international frontier for purposes of trade without the consent of the person who owns the copyright in the country of importation. This principle has international recognition. It is implemented by a system whereby each nation provides in its own legislation that such importation is a separate species of secondary infringement.
>
> The object is to protect the interests of persons who own copyright in the country of importation. If, for example, a copyright owner licenses the making of copies of the original work in a foreign country and has no protection against importation of those copies into other countries where he owns the copyright the value of his copyright in the country of importation will be diminished. Foreign made copies could then be imported into the country where the copyright owner is domiciled and where he owns the copyright – possibly flooding the market with copies manufactured abroad far more cheaply than they can be made in the 'home' country. Or the foreign made copies might be imported into another overseas country to the detriment of an exclusive distributor or licensee appointed in that country by the copyright owner – and to the ultimate detriment of the copyright owner.
>
> Similarly, the unauthorised importation for resale of copies made, not by a licensee, but by the person who owns the copyright in the country of importation will have an adverse effect on the business of any exclusive licensee or distributor in the country into which the copies are imported – and so deplete the royalties or other payments which the owner of the copyright can expect to receive.[150]

That is, in addition to protecting the copyright owner's interest, Pritchard J also considered that an exclusive licensee has a valid interest to protect. In his Honour's view, injury to this interest ultimately harmed the copyright owner too.

After critically reviewing the preceding cases, his Honour concluded:

> This much is clear: section 10(2) is intended to afford the owner of the New Zealand copyright protection against the importation of copies from overseas. That can only be because such importations will be injurious to the value of

---

150 *Ibid*. at 493 to 494.

the copyright and to the interests of the copyright owner. If the importation of copies is permitted, the injury will occur irrespective of the source from which the importer obtains his supplies. I can see no reason to discriminate between copies made by the owner of the copyright and copies made by anyone else – the importation of either will adversely affect the value of the copyright in the country of importation. In short, the identity of the actual maker is immaterial.[151]

Pritchard J considered that allowing imports of one sort of lawfully manufactured articles (that is, those made by the owner) but not of another (those made under licence) was anomalous. Each was equally damaging to the domestic owner's exploitation of the rights in the domestic jurisdiction. The division of copyright into national rights justified such partitioning. This led his Honour to adopt the public theory which was explained in the following terms:

> . . . infringement by importation occurs whenever articles are brought into New Zealand for purposes other than private or domestic use, without the consent of the person holding the exclusive right to manufacture those articles in this country if the articles are such that anyone who did manufacture them here would infringe copyright (unless, of course, he first obtained consent to manufacture in New Zealand from the person holding the exclusive manufacturing rights in this country). Or to put it another way, *if an article is such that nobody could legitimately manufacture it in New Zealand without the consent of the person owning the exclusive manufacturing rights, then its importation without consent is a secondary infringement of copyright.* Quilliam J. was at pains to make it clear that *the person whose consent is required to importation – and whose consent would be required if the articles were made in New Zealand – is the person who holds the particular facet of the copyright which relates to manufacture in New Zealand, whether that facet is retained as an incident of the original copyright or was acquired by virtue of assignment.* When the rule is enunciated in that way, it is clear that it is unnecessary to fix the person who is the hypothetical maker with any particular identity. His identity is irrelevant. The question is simply whether anybody could legitimately manufacture the imported article in New Zealand without the consent of the person owning, by virtue of copyright, the sole manufacturing rights in New Zealand. (*Emphasis added*)[152]

Put in this way, Pritchard J made the test of infringement whether the holder of the relevant copyright interest in New Zealand had authorised the importer to bring in the imported articles. His Honour acknowledged that the practical effect of his test was the same as the importer theory.[153]

After explaining his Honour's understanding of the *Fletcher Construction* case, Pritchard J considered the *Charmdale* case. Pritchard J first dealt with Browne-Wilkinson J's rejection of the 'formidable argument of convenience'. In his Honour's view this rejection was misplaced because it did not take into account the harm to the copyright owner's interest and:

---

151   *Ibid.* at 508.
152   *Ibid.* at 499 to 500.
153   *Ibid.* at 509.

. . . there is no obstacle to the copyright owner asserting the copyright in protection of his own commercial interests in the country of importation – no reason in principle why he should be precluded from asserting his proprietary rights just because that assertion might benefit his licensee as well as himself.[154]

Pritchard J also disagreed with Browne-Wilkinson J.'s rejection of the importer theory. That rejection confused the requirement of knowledge with the requirement of hypothetical manufacture.[155] The perceived problems of copying and fair dealing were more apparent than real and, in any event, the hypothetical manufacturing requirement did not preclude inquiries about either because they were separate issues irrespective of who was the hypothetical maker.[156]

Pritchard J then examined the *Harlequin* case. In his Honour's opinion, the actual maker theory did not just involve a single hypothesis as claimed by Megarry VC. It also required a second hypothesis: not only did the theory require geographical transfer of the place of manufacture, it also required the actual maker to be transplanted into a new and unaccustomed environment. Moreover, Pritchard J considered that some doubt attached to Megarry VC's views in the Court of Appeal:

Templeman L.J. did not seem to be concerned with the identity of the actual maker; rather he rested his judgment on the fact that anyone wishing to make copies in England would require the consent of the licensee for England. . . . at least . . . there is nothing expressed in his judgment which conflicts with the decision in [the *Fletcher Construction* case].[157]

Then, Pritchard J rejected Gilbert's claim that, as a matter of grammar, the section required the actual maker theory. In his Honour's view, the section referred to the article, not its making so that the reference was 'if *to make* that article' not, as Gilbert argued, 'if *that making*'.[158]

Finally, his Honour rejected Gilbert's claim that the copyright owner would derive a double benefit from the copyright if the actual maker theory was not adopted. This would not happen because by barring imports the copyright owner was depriving itself of royalties on sales of articles intended for resale in the country of import. More fundamentally, however:

Section 10 is concerned with the distribution of copies of copyright material for purposes of trade. It is designed, in my view, to give the owner of the copyright control of the exploitation of the copyright in those countries to which his copyright extends. There is no reason, in principle, why the copyright owner should not use this control as he thinks fit, nor any reason why the transfer of title to copies of the protected work should have the effect of extinguishing

154 *Ibid.* at 501 to 502.
155 *Ibid.* at 503.
156 *Ibid.* at 497 to 498, 503.
157 *Ibid.* at 506, but see text at Notes 131 to 132 above; the criticism of Megarry VC's opinion is at 505.
158 *Ibid.* at 506 to 507. (Original emphasis)

any of the copyright owner's rights – any more than the transfer of title to the original work effects a transfer of the copyright in that work.[159]

In the author's respectful opinion, there is a lot to recommend Pritchard J's approach, at least insofar as it is consistent with the importer theory. The approach is squarely based on the territorial nature of copyright established by the international conventions and it focuses attention on what must surely be the central question in a provision designed to control imports – the act of importation. As *Pitt Pitts* and the *Hoffnung* cases had long established, the fact that something was done lawfully in a foreign market has very little, if anything, to do with whether copyright in the domestic market has been exercised. And if, as none of these cases questioned, it be right that a copyright owner may protect itself or its domestic licensees against imports from a licensee limited to a foreign market, it is anomalous to deny protection on the actual maker theory where, as will be the case, the economic injury is the same; or, in the case of a domestic exclusive licensee, aggravated. The anomaly is confirmed by the same courts' acceptance of the principle of territoriality when the issue is not the identity of the hypothetical manufacturer, but implied consent.[160] The approach may, however, lead to some potential danger of international price discrimination or market sharing; an issue which must be considered.[161]

The force of the anomaly has provoked two kinds of response. In enacting the CDPA 1988, the UK Parliament has overridden the UK courts' refusal to protect exclusive licensees; further entrenching the territorial concept. The Singaporean and Malaysian Parliaments have sought to remove the anomaly by undermining the principle of territoriality.[162]

The Singaporean position has been explored by way of *dicta* in *Television Broadcasts*.[163] Television Broadcast held the copyright in certain films and had granted to a second company the exclusive right to exploit the copyright throughout the world excluding Hong Kong. The second company had sub-licensed Crown Video the exclusive rights for Singapore to reproduce the film as a video and to exhibit the resulting videos by way of private let or hire for home use. Crown Video's rights included the power to authorise others to make videos from the film and to exhibit the videos by way of private rental. All videos made under Crown Video's licence bore a label notifying that the copyright was only licensed for private rental and that such rental by persons without Crown Video's permission would constitute

---

159   *Ibid.* at 507.
160   See subsection 4.2.2(c) below.
161   The argument lies at the heart of Chapter 10 below.
162   For the legislative positions, see text at Notes 38 and 173, this chapter. For Canadian and South African proposals at Notes 174a and 174b and an Australian move to undermine the principle of territoriality, although not in the context of the hypothetical manufacturing requirement, see section 4.2.4.
163   *Television Broadcasts Ltd & Others v Golden Line Video & Marketing Pte Ltd* [1989] 1 MLJ 201 (HC Sing.) discussed in Wei, 'Parallel Imports and the Law of Copyright in Singapore', [1992] EIPR 139, 140–3 an adaption of Wei, 'Parallel Imports and Intellectual Property Rights in Singapore', (1990) 2 S. Ac. L. J. 286.

an infringement. Golden Line bought videos made by Crown Video in Singapore and was hiring them out by way of private rental. It was not, however, one of Crown Video's authorised distributors and the plaintiffs sued it for copyright infringement. Golden Line successfully struck out the Statement of Claim for want of a cause of action because Singaporean law did not recognise a right of rental.[164]

It seems that Golden Line's counsel only discovered that the videos were made in Singapore at the hearing before Chan Sek Keong J and had sought to rely on the *Charmdale* case; Television Broadcasts countering with *Barson Computers*. Chan J rejected the relevance of either case. First and, with respect, correctly, Chan J pointed out that the videos in question were not imported. Chan J also advanced a second reason for rejecting the authority of both cases which depended on the particular wording of the Singaporean Act. Unlike the legislation surveyed in the other Anglo-Commonwealth jurisdictions, the Singaporean Act does not posit a hypothetical manufacture. Instead, it specifies that an unlicensed importation or commercial dealing in an imported article infringes: 'in the case of an imported article, [if] *the making of the article was carried out without the consent of the owner of the copyright'*.[165] (*Emphasis added*)

Of this provision, Chan J said:

> These words, as a matter of grammatical construction, are a clear reference to the actual making of the article before it is imported into Singapore. An actual making must imply an actual maker and that maker must also be abroad. . . . It would therefore appear that in the area of copyright protection our legislature has adopted a mercantile policy of allowing in Singapore a free market where copyright articles, whether parallel imports or made under licence in Singapore, may be sold or dealt with in competition with one another.[166]

The passage was not necessary to the decision, but it is difficult to fault Chan J's grammatical construction. Hence, in testing infringement by imported articles, the Singaporean and Malaysian Acts look to the authority of the actual maker of the imported article.

If the actual maker made the article with the consent of the domestic copyright owner, importation into Singapore or Malaysia would seem to be warranted under the legislation. This would necessarily include the situation where the domestic copyright owner itself made the article abroad. Further, it does not seem to depend on whether copyright protection subsisted in the place of foreign manufacture.[167] Matters may be more complicated if

---

164 *Ibid.* at 204. The alternative argument based on public exhibition of the videos in Golden Line's premises was rejected because it was not pleaded. Contrast 158/86 *Warner Bros v Christiansen* [1988] ECR 2605 where a right of rental existed, see Chapter 6.4 below.

165 Copyright Act 1987 (Sing.) sections 32, 33, 104, 105 and compare Copyright Act 1987 (Malaysia) section 36(2) as amended by the Copyright Amendment Act 1990.

166 [1989] 1 MLJ 201, at 205; the words referred to being those emphasised in the preceding quotation.

167 Compare 187/80 *Merck v Stephar* [1981] ECR 2063 (patents), see Chapter 6.3.1 below.

the domestic and foreign copyright owners are different persons or, with greater qualification, if the domestic copyright owner only authorised foreign manufacture for sale in the foreign market.

In the second situation, Mr Wei has interpreted Chan J's judgment as contemplating importation if the manufacture took place under a limitation to reproduce and sell in the foreign market only since Chan J considered that the issue was whether the actual manufacture of the article was performed with consent.[168] The proposed interpretation is certainly consistent with Chan J's *dicta* and the mercantile policy Chan J perceived in the Singaporean Act (a perception supported by the legislative history of the provision).[169]

The first situation, where the owner, if any, of the foreign copyright is different to the domestic owner, raises greater difficulties. Ordinarily, one would expect that the owner of the copyright referred to in the legislation should be the owner of the domestic copyright.[170] But, in the case of reproduction in the foreign market, the consent of the owner of the domestic copyright is irrelevant to the actual maker. This analysis, however, depends on the principle of territoriality which seems inconsistent with the mercantile policy perceived in the Singaporean Act. The inconsistencies would be exacerbated if the two owners were members of the same corporate group.[171] Mr Wei acknowledges that, where the domestic owner be a subsidiary of the foreign owner, the only plausible line of reasoning is based on implied consent. But, unless the legislation entails acceptance of an exhaustion doctrine, Anglo-Commonwealth courts usually permit implied consent to be rebutted.[172]

It is necessarily hazardous to speculate on future judicial attitudes. It seems clear, however, that under the policy perceived in the Singaporean Act (and probably the Malaysian), where the actual maker has authority from the owner of the domestic copyright to sell the imported articles in the domestic market, the imports will be allowed whether the importer is licensed or not. It remains to be seen whether that policy will be strong enough to overwhelm more long-standing approaches based on territoriality in other cases.

As previously discussed, in the United Kingdom, sections 22 and 23 of the CDPA 1988 now provide that importing, or commercially dealing with, infringing copies infringes copyright. Section 27(3)(b) defines 'infringing copy' to include an article if 'its making in the United Kingdom would have constituted an infringement of the copyright in the work in question,

---

168   Wei, 'Parallel Imports and the Law of Copyright in Singapore', at 140 to 141.

169   For the Singaporean and Malaysian histories, see text at Note 64 above.

170   See for example in the case of trade marks *Colgate-Palmolive Ltd v Markwell Finance Ltd*, see Chapter 2.2.3(b) above.

171   See for example *Smith Kline & French Laboratories Ltd v Salim (Malaysia) Sdn Bhd* (1989) 15 IPR 677 (HC Kuala Lumpur), see Chapter 3.2.3, text from Note 121 above.

172   Even *ibid*.

or a breach of an exclusive licence agreement relating to that work.' (*Emphasis added*) The powers of an exclusive licensee to sue have not been altered.[173]

The new definition does not, in terms, reject the actual maker theory as in the corresponding Australian legislation. However, it removes the ground on which Browne-Wilkinson J based his Lordship's adoption of that theory. An imported article will infringe if, among other things, making it in the United Kingdom would breach an exclusive licence agreement. The new definition does not affect *Charmdale* insofar as it is consistent with *Harlequin* and the foreign maker also has authority to make the article in the domestic jurisdiction.

Even at the first stage of the inquiry into whether copyright can be used to block parallel imports in the Anglo-Commonwealth countries, courts and legislatures have been unable to reach agreement. Some have clearly relied on the principle of territoriality to resolve the issue; others have not. New Zealand courts and Australian (by the terms of its legislation) have applied the principle.[174] Although the factual situations in Canada tend to fit the actual maker theory, the reasoning applied is more in line with recognition of the principle of territoriality.[174a] The courts in South Africa and the United Kingdom have fallen into the second category when the actual maker had authority also in the domestic market; but, otherwise, have relied on the territorial nature of copyright to block imports. The UK Parliament has intervened to strengthen the territorial protection of exclusive licensees. At the other extreme, Singapore and Malaysia have recently amended their laws with the intention of undermining the territorial nature of copyright and promoting parallel imports. Perhaps the greatest puzzle attaches to the approach of the South African and UK courts, the latter before the CDPA 1988. They have readily accepted that the territorial nature of copyright may be used to block parallel imports where the foreign maker did not have authority to make and sell in the domestic market. Yet, in adopting the actual maker theory, they have refused to accord protection where the economic injury to the copyright owner is the same as in the other cases and have rejected the alternative approaches on grounds which, with respect, do not seem convincing. Indeed, the UK courts' approach provoked legislative intervention and, apparently, the South African government plans to amend its Act to make it clear the hypothetical manufacturer is the importer.[174b].

---

173 Compare and contrast Templeman LJ's unconcern in the context of copyright in *Harlequin* at Notes 130 to 133, above and 201, below, the 1956 Act section 19 and CDPA 1988 section 101.
174 For the Australian amendments introduced by the Copyright Amendment Act 1991 (Cth), section 4.2.4 below.
174a For plans to strengthen the legislation against parallel imports, see Chapter 10.3, below.
174b Owen H. Dean, 'The Implications for the Entertainment Industry of Proposed Amendments to the South African Copyright Act', [1991] Ent. LR 197, 198.

(c)   *Implying licence from sale abroad*

The second element that the copyright owner must show is that the importation occurred without its licence.[175] In this context, 'licence' simply means 'consent'. It need not be given formally, an oral or implied licence will suffice.[176] The central issue is how consent may be implied. The problem here is to find when, if ever, a sale abroad of a copyright article may imply a licence to import that article into the domestic jurisdiction.

Those Anglo-Commonwealth courts which have considered the issue have unanimously distinguished copyright law from the approach in both trade marks and patents law. This is usually put as the inevitable consequence of the separate national treatment of copyright interests.

The early ruling that importing an article lawfully made abroad infringed the domestic copyright set the pattern. However, the proposition is not conclusive. An article may be made and sold lawfully abroad in a number of different situations. The domestic owner of the copyright may have marketed the article abroad itself. It may have done so in circumstances where it kept the rights to market the article in the domestic market for itself or it may have licensed the domestic rights to another, exclusively or otherwise. Alternatively, the foreign marketing may have been through a licensee. That licensee may also have had rights to market the article domestically. Again, the foreign copyright might be owned by a person different to the domestic owner. The foreign owner may, or may not, be affiliated with the domestic owner in some way. Finally, the marketing abroad may take place independently of the copyright owner under some form of compulsory licensing. The question is whether these differences affect the outcome.

When the sale abroad took place through an independent owner of the foreign copyright even though the two rights derived from the same source initially, the *Pitt Pitts* and *Suckling* cases denied any implied right in the purchaser to sell domestically. Lindley LJ held:

> The copyright in this country confers upon the plaintiff [the domestic copyright owner] rights here which no contract of sale abroad *by other persons* can deprive him of. Even if the defendant had bought his copies direct from the proprietor of the foreign copyright, the defendant would be in no better position as against the plaintiff than such proprietor himself. . . . (*Emphasis added*)[177]

The owner of the domestic copyright there had taken it by assignment from the owner of the foreign copyright. The result in the *Hoffnung* case reached

---

175   The onus is on the plaintiff in an infringement action to prove the absence of the copyright owner's consent: *Avel Pty Ltd v Multicoin Amusements Pty Ltd* (1990) 65 ALJR 179 (HCA, FC) (correspondence between copyright owner and distributor obtained in discovery admissible on issue of 'licence'). But, note, given the difficulties in proving a negative absolutely, a credible denial of licence seems to oblige the defendant to raise circumstances from which consent may be inferred: *Computermate Products (Aust) Pty Ltd v Ozi-Soft Pty Ltd & Others* (1988) 83 ALR 492, at 498 (Fed. C, FC).
176   *Interstate Parcel Express Co. Proprietary Limited v Time-Life International (Nederlands) BV* (1977) 138 CLR 534, at 539, 544 to 545 *per* Gibbs J; 556 to 557 *per* Jacobs J ('the *Time-Life* case'), citing with approval *Copinger & Skone James on Copyright*, 11th ed., at paragraph 404.
177   [1896] 2 Ch. 866, at 876 (CA).

the same conclusion where the imported articles are made abroad under compulsory licence.

The full High Court of Australia carefully considered the meaning of 'licence of the copyright owner' and the circumstances in which such licences would be implied in the *Time-Life* case, the facts of which were briefly raised in Chapter 1.[178]

To recapitulate, 'Time-Life' was a wholly owned subsidiary of Time Inc. Time Inc. had appointed Time-Life as the exclusive licensee throughout the world, excluding the United States and Canada, for its copyrights in various literary works. These rights included a series of books dealing with cookery called *Foods of the World* which Time-Life was distributing throughout Australia at a price supporting a recommended retail price of $A16.95. Experiencing difficulties in obtaining supplies from Time-Life, IPEC, which ran a chain of retail bookshops, Angus & Robertson, procured shipments of the books in the United States and was selling the books in Australia at $A8.95 retail.

The books had been printed in the United States by Time Inc. IPEC bought the books in the United States from a wholesaler, Raymar Inc. In turn, Raymar had the books from Little, Brown & Company, Time Inc.'s distributor in the United States. Raymar did not impose any restrictions at the sale to IPEC. Nor had Time Inc. or Little, Brown imposed any on their sale to Raymar.

Time Inc. and Time-Life sued IPEC for infringement of the Australian copyright in the books by importing and sale. Fearing that its participation would involve it in breach of the US anti-trust laws, Time Inc. sought and was granted leave to discontinue. It was joined as a defendant. Delivering final judgment, Bowen CJ in Eq. held that IPEC had infringed Time-Life's copyright interest as exclusive licensee. IPEC appealed to the High Court.

The arguments at first instance and before the High Court concentrated on the fact that all sales of the books in the United States had been without restrictions. Indeed, at the time such restrictions violated US anti-trust law.[179] From this, IPEC developed two arguments: first, that it had the right to import the books as an implied term of the contract of sale; alternatively, by analogy with patents, that an unrestricted sale carried with it the right to import the books into Australia. The High Court unanimously upheld Bowen CJ in Eq.'s rejection of both arguments.[180]

---

178 (1977) 138 CLR 534. At first instance *sub. nom. Time-Life International (Nederlands) BV v Interstate Parcel Express Co. Proprietary Limited* (1976) 12 ALR 1 (SC NSW) *per* Bowen CJ in Eq. See James Lahore, *Intellectual Property Law in Australia: Copyright*, Butterworths, 1988 (2nd ed.), at ¶4.11.455; Ricketson, *The Law of Intellectual Property*, at ¶9.170. For parallel imports into Australia of books, see now Copyright Amendment Act 1991 (Cth) discussed at section 4.2.4.

179 See *US v Addison-Wesley Publishing Co.* 1976–2 CCH Trade Cases, ¶61,225 at §V, see section 4.2.4 below.

180 The High Court rejected IPEC's further argument based on an implied warranty of quiet possession as irrelevant. Gibbs J held that a warranty of quiet possession did not warrant that the buyer had the right to import the books into Australia or that the warrantor consented to such importing: *ibid.* at 544; 554 *per* Stephen J, with whom

The implied term argument failed because it was not necessary to give the contract of sale business efficacy. Nor could it be considered 'as one that would go without saying.'[181]

Bowen CJ in Eq. rejected the second argument because it would seriously undermine the value of exclusive licences and subvert the vertical and horizontal partitioning of rights set up by the international copyright system. An unrestricted sale generally carried the right to deal freely in the purchased article. However, a sale in one country could not affect the operation of laws in another country which the articles might be taken to. In Australia, one of those laws was copyright law which did not imply a licence of the sort arising in patent law under *Betts v Willmott* and the *Menck* case because:

> In my view they are of little assistance in dealing with the problem with which I am faced. It does not appear to me that the mere sale in the ordinary course of trade without restrictions should be treated as having the effect of removing from the shoulders of the purchaser the obligation of complying with the municipal laws of other countries, including the copyright laws in force in those countries. Nor does it appear to me that the mere sale of goods in the ordinary course of trade should, for the purposes of copyright law, be treated as importing a 'licence' to import for the purposes of sale or a 'licence' to sell. I am not aware of any case dealing with copyright law where it has been decided that it would do so, and it cannot be altogether put on one side that if the principle contended for by [IPEC] be correct then not only will the procedure of granting exclusive licences for particular areas of copyright be seriously undermined, but the national division of copyright set up under the system of International Copyright Conventions in so far as it provides for partial assignments and exclusive licences, both vertical and horizontal, would to a significant degree be subverted.[182]

With respect, his Honour's opinion appears equally applicable to patents. The patent acts do not include statutory prohibitions like the copyright prohibition on imports of hypothetically infringing copies. However, this difference may be more apparent than real since the patent monopoly also precludes importation for sale.[183] Indeed, the case for patents may seem stronger. In many countries copyright is granted simply by the act of creation. For patents, however, formal grant by the awarding jurisdiction is

---

Barwick CJ and Jacobs J agreed. Stephen J also questioned how a warranty given by Time Inc. to Little, Brown could benefit IPEC. For infringement by publication, subsection 4.2.3(a) below.

181 12 ALR 1, at 10 *per* Bowen CJ in Eq. The long-standing exclusive distributorship arrangements meant that the vendor(s) would have been most unlikely to consent to such a term. Perhaps, as in Beecham's patent cases involving ampicillin (see Chapter 3.2.3 above), the contract could be given business efficacy simply by dealing with the books in the United States. IPEC did not press this argument on appeal. See also the rejection of a similar term in *Lorenzo v Roland* (1992) 23 IPR 376, 382 (Fed. C, FC).

182 *Ibid.* at 13. His Honour plainly felt difficulty acceding to IPEC's argument when, in his Honour's view, IPEC knew all along Time Inc. and Time-Life objected to IPEC's activities and would not have granted the licence if requested: *ibid.* at 14. Citation to *Menck* [1911] AC 336 (PC) omitted.

183 See for example *Pfizer Corporation v Minister of Health* [1965] AC 512 and the comments of Gibbs J in the *Time-Life* case 138 CLR 534, at 542.

necessary. Bowen CJ in Eq. did not explain how the different conclusion arose. It was to this difference that the High Court addressed itself.

Stephen J, with whom Barwick CJ and Jacobs J agreed, rebutted the analogy with patent law by relying on the difference in the nature of the rights conferred by copyright. Referring to the patent cases, his Honour said:

> They [*Betts v Willmott* and the *Tilghman* case] should, I think, be seen as confined to the quite special case of the sale by a patentee of patented goods and as turning upon the unique ability which the law confers upon patentees of imposing restrictions upon what use may after sale be made of those goods. If the patentee, having this ability, chooses not to exercise it and sells without imposing any such restrictions, the purchaser and any successors in title may then do as they will with the goods, for they are then in no different position from any purchaser of unpatented goods. But, to ensure that consequence despite the existence, albeit in the instance unexercised, of this power on the patentee's part, the law treats the sale without express restriction as involving the grant of a licence from the patentee authorizing such future use of the goods as the owner for the time being sees fit. The law does this because, without such a licence, any use or dealing with the goods would constitute an infringement of the patentee's monopoly in respect of the use, exercise and vending of the patent. A sale of goods manufactured under patent is thus a transaction of a unique kind because of the special nature of the monopoly accorded to a patentee; the licence, whether absolute or qualified, which arises upon such a sale is attributable to the existence and character of that monopoly. Absent that monopoly, peculiar to patents, there is no occasion for any licence. The buyer of monopoly-free goods, goods not the subject of patent rights, obtains by his purchase title to and possession of the goods and with it, of course, goes the ability, subject to the relevant laws of the jurisdiction in question, to use and deal with the goods as he sees fit. But this is only the consequence of chattel ownership and nothing in the nature of a licence is involved. The buyer of a book in which copyright exists is just such a buyer; the book, once bought by him, is not thereafter subject to any monopoly rights of the copyright owner but may be dealt with by the buyer entirely as he chooses. The copyright in the literary work of course remains with the copyright owner; the buyer has bought no part of it and remains as he was before his purchase, unable lawfully to enjoy any of those exclusive rights, reproduction, adaption or the like, which ownership of the copyright preserves exclusively for the copyright owner.
>
> Because a copyright owner, unlike a patentee, has no monopoly in the use of or dealing in a book which he sells, there exists no general prohibition of such use or dealing calling for modification, as in the case of patented articles, by any implied grant of a licence. Instead the buyer of such a book obtains just such rights, no more and no less, as does the buyer of any other chattel and those rights, which flow from his acquisition of ownership and possession, do not involve any licence.[184]

After considering the *Menck* and other cases of domestic sale, his Honour concluded:

> The origin of and reason for the existence of the concept of the grant of an implied licence to use patented goods, arising upon a sale of those goods

---

184 *Ibid.* at 549 to 550. *Tilghman*'s case (1883) 25 Ch. D. 1 (C4) omitted.

unaccompanied by any express restriction as to their future use, lies in the patentee's monopoly which otherwise would extend to the use to which the patented goods are put after he has disposed of them by sale. Without such a licence, implied or express, a purchaser might not lawfully put those goods to use; hence the need for a licence and, on a sale by the patentee without express restriction, for the law's implication of a licence. In the case of literary work which is subject to copyright no such need arises, the concept is entirely foreign to it. The sale of a copy of the work involves no retention by the copyright owner of any power over that copy regarding the use to which it is put or any dealings in it; his copyright he retains and, in consequence, the congeries of exclusive rights specified in s. 31(1)(a) of the Act, but no right whatever in relation to the subsequent use of the particular copy of the work which he has sold.[185]

Gibbs J took a similar line in rejecting IPEC's analogy to patent law. He did, however, introduce a qualification not expressed by Stephen J. Having noted that importation also infringed the rights under a patent and having explained the business need for an implication on the sale of a patented article, Gibbs J continued:

However no similar necessity exists to imply a term of this kind upon the sale of a book the subject of copyright. The owner of copyright has not the exclusive right to use or sell the work in which copyright subsists.... The buyer of a book in which copyright subsists does not need the consent of the owner of the copyright to read, or *speaking generally* to resell, the book. The necessity to imply a term in the contract which exists when a patented article is sold does not arise on the sale of a book the subject of copyright. It was not, and could not be, suggested that the sale of a copy of a book is a licence to do the acts comprised in the copyright and set out in s. 31 of the Act.

An owner of copyright who sells a book in which copyright subsists passes to the buyer all the rights of ownership. He does not however consent to any particular uses of the book – generally speaking his consent is irrelevant. For the reasons given, the cases on patent law are distinguishable.[186] (*Emphasis added*)

Gibbs J concluded:

The 'licence of the owner of the copyright', of which the sections speak, means the consent of the owner to the importation of the articles into Australia for the purposes of selling them, or to their sale after importation, and such a licence cannot in my opinion be inferred from the mere fact that the owner of the copyright has sold the goods without any express restriction on their subsequent disposal.[187]

The court did not rule that the copyright statute required an express licence as some of the judges acknowledged that a licence may be implied in some circumstances; for example, sale of a large quantity of books for delivery in Australia to a person known to be a bookseller.[188] Hence,

---

185   *Ibid*. at 552 to 553.
186   *Ibid*. at 542 to 543 (references omitted).
187   *Ibid*. at 544 to 545.
188   *Ibid*. at 543 *per* Gibbs J. See also Jacobs J at 557, who at 556 indicated that 'licence' should be 'positive' licence. Jacobs J also thought that implication might follow

the court simply denied that a licence could be implied merely from an unrestricted sale by the copyright owner abroad – circumstances in which a licence would be implied under patent law. With respect, the author does not disagree with that conclusion, but the chain of reasoning raises questions of policy and theory.

Both Gibbs and Stephen JJ considered that the need for the implication found in patent law did not exist in copyright law because the exclusive rights conferred on a patentee included power to control, and forbid, dealing in the article embodying the invention, even after its sale. Copyright did not grant such power. Rather, it was necessary to distinguish between ownership of the article and of the copyright embodied in it. Hence, sale of the article passed rights in it but not to the copyright. Therefore, in the importation of copyright articles, the element of licence from the copyright owner required a positive grant. The analysis raises a number of difficulties, particularly with the perceived difference between patented articles and copyright articles. The crux of the matter is the need to imply licence in one case but not in the other, which was said to depend on the different nature of the rights in question.

The first difficulty with the theory is that, even in patent law where foreign trade is concerned, the need to imply the licence is only found in the specific fact situation of *Betts v Willmott*. In virtually every other situation, the courts have been unable to discover an overriding business need for implication. *Betts v Willmott* was the nearest patent case to the facts of *Time-Life*, and both Gibbs and Stephen JJ referred to *Tilghman's* case, but not those involving Beecham and Bristol-Myers. Neither of the learned judges specifically adverted to the apparent inconsistency between the later cases and *Betts v Willmott*. Instead, they both placed heavy reliance on the *Menck* case involving domestic trade.

The next problem is whether the proposed distinction between patented and copyright articles is sustainable.[189] Certainly, there are cases in domestic trade in which the distinction between copyright and the article embodying it has been made.[190] The *Cooper* and *Marshall* cases are instructive. In each, the producer of engraving blocks sold them to another for a specific purpose, the blocks and the drawings they were based on being the subject of copyright owned by the producer. The buyer subsequently sold the blocks to the defendant. The defendants did not have notice of the restriction and

---

for individual works of art at 556 although if consent were to be implied, presumably, the copyright owner would need to know that the buyer was an art dealer who intended to operate in Australia.

189 One commentator has dismissed it, see Lahore, *Intellectual Property Law in Australia: Copyright*, at ¶4.11.460; but not so, Cornish, *Intellectual Property*, at ¶12–009 and Ricketson, *The Law of Intellectual Property*, at ¶9.170.

190 *Murray v Heath* (1831) 1 Barn. & Adol. 804; 109 ER 985; *Pollard v Photographic Company* (1888) 40 Ch. D 345; *Cooper v Stephens* [1895] 1 Ch. 567; *W. Marshall and Co. Limited v A. H. Bull Limited* (1901) 85 LT(NS) 77 (CA).

then set about using them for purposes other than that which the producer had authorised.[191]

Romer J denied that the sale of the blocks included an assignment of any copyright. The authority to take copies from the blocks was limited to the specified purpose and was personal only. It did not confer rights beyond its terms.

Subsequently, the Court of Appeal endorsed *Cooper* in *Marshall*. Romer LJ, as his Lordship had become, once again relying on the two grounds: first, of the difference between ownership of the chattel and of the copyright and secondly, of the power to enforce limitations against innocent third parties as a matter of copyright law. His Lordship ruled:

> The sale of the [blocks] in themselves to the persons from whom the defendants obtained them, with liberty to these persons to print and publish for a particular purpose, would clearly not deprive the plaintiffs of their original copyright in the work as against the world, nor could the defendants as purchasers of the [blocks] from the original purchasers from the plaintiffs get a better right to print and publish copies from those [blocks] than the persons from whom they bought them.[192]

These cases show two interesting contrasts with those in patent law such as the *Menck* case. First, when the patentee sold the article embodying the patented invention, the patentee could only enforce restrictions against subsequent purchasers by proving that the purchaser had notice of the restriction; but, in copyright, the rule expressed by the maxim *nemo quod non habet* applied. Second, the sale of a patented article exhausted all the patent rights for that particular article unless a restriction was explicitly imposed. In copyright, if sale carried any rights in the copyright, these were strictly limited to the purpose of the transaction.

Similarly, Anglo-Commonwealth courts have held that sale of a sound recording did not convey any right to use the record for the purposes of broadcasting or public performance.[193] Although the recording in *Cawardine* bore a notice, relief was not made contingent on it.

There does not seem any difference in principle between these situations and the case in patents when, say, the patent relates to a process or a machine and the buyer is intended to be restricted to use only for its own purposes and not resale. In such a case, the difference cannot lie in the distinction between the right and the article embodying the right. Nor is

---

191   In *Cooper's* case, Cooper sold to Lilley for use solely in Lilley's advertising sheets. Lilley then sold to Stephens who used them for other purposes. In *Marshall v Bull*, Marshall sold to Rowe on condition that Rowe only use them to print reproductions for Marshall's books. After Rowe sold to Bull, Bull published designs printed from the blocks in its own books.

192   85 LT(NS) 77, at 82 to 83. Rigby and Cotton LJJ agreeing. Some of the authorities cited in Eaton S. Drone, *A Treatise on the Law of Property in Intellectual Productions*, Little, Brown & Co., 1879, at 374 Notes 2 and 3, would enforce such covenants against third parties without notice in England.

193   *APRA v 3DB Broadcasting Co. Pty Ltd* [1929] VLR 107; *Gramophone Company Limited v Stephen Cawardine & Company* [1934] Ch. 450.

it arguable that copyright is different because each aspect of copyright is separate and divisible, since the same is true of a patent. It is only the means of imposing the restriction which is different. Certainly, a lot can be said of the rule in patents for commercial convenience. But, on the other hand, it could as easily be said that someone who intended to engage in resale rather than use of a patented article could have specifically contracted for the right. The point, for present purposes, is the difficulty with the supposed distinction between patented and copyright articles made in *Time-Life* by the High Court.

Stephen J seems to have derived the distinction between ownership of copyright and the chattel embodying it at least in part from the US law dealing with domestic sales.[194] One problem with this is that in this respect US law largely treats patented articles the same.[195] One potential difference between US and Anglo-Commonwealth law is that US law does expressly accord the copyright owner the power to control the 'first sale' of the article embodying the copyright. But, it does not seem likely that Anglo-Commonwealth law would permit someone to deal in copyright articles until the copyright owner had authorised their release on to the market.

Gibbs J was somewhat more qualified in his opinion, although, unfortunately, he did not explain the impact of the qualification on resale introduced by: 'The buyer of a book in which copyright subsists does not need the consent of the owner of the copyright to read, or *speaking generally* to resell, the book.'[196] Later, his Honour did indicate that the copyright owner did not need to consent to any particular use of the book by the purchaser since, 'generally speaking' that consent was irrelevant. So, the initial qualification may simply refer to the posited distinction between the copyright and the article it was embodied in, despite its attachment to the verb 'to resell'.

The problem remains, particularly with Stephen J's broad formulation which suggests that the buyer of a book, like any other purchaser of a

194 138 CLR at 553 referring to *Harrison v Maynard, Merrill & Co.* 61 Fed. 689 (2d Cir. 1894); *Independent News Co. v Williams* 293 F. 2d 510 (3rd Cir. 1961). Gibbs J refers to the latter at *ibid.* at 544, see subsections 4.3.3(a) and (b), respectively, below.

195 Compare *Bobbs-Merrill v Straus* with *Bauer v O'Donnell* 229 US 1 (1913) where Day J drew a distinction between patent and copyright over the power to control use, but applied the same rule to the right to 'vend' which US law recognised for each subject-matter. But, for the US position corresponding to *3DB* and *Cawardine*, see *Irving Berlin Inc. v Daigle* 31 F. 2d 832 (5th Cir. 1929); *Buck v Jewell-LaSalle Realty Company* 283 US 191, at 197; 75 L. Ed. 971, at 975 (1931); *Jewell-LaSalle Realty Company v Buck* 283 US 202, at 204; 75 L.Ed. 978, at 980 (1931); *Buck v Swanson* 33 F. Supp. 377, at 387 to 388 (DNebr. 1939); *Interstate Hotel Co. of Nebraska v Remick Music Corporation* 157 F. 2d 44 (8th Cir. 1947); *Chappell & Co. Inc. v Middletown Farmers Market & Auction Co.* 334 F. 2d 303 (3d Cir. 1964); *Red Baron-Franklin Park Inc. v Taito Corp.* 883 F. 2d 275 (4th Cir. 1989); Melville B. Nimmer and David Nimmer, 2 *Nimmer on Copyright*, Matthew Bender & Co. Inc., 1990, at §8.14. Indeed, the conception of the distinction between the article and the right embodied in it seems to have arisen in US patent law, see *Bloomer v McQuewan*, see Chapter 3.3.2 above.

196 138 CLR at 543 (*Emphasis added*).

chattel, may deal with it as he sees fit. But, subject to the laws of fair dealing, the buyer of the book may not for example recite it as part of a performance to the public or broadcast. Where works other than 'books' are involved, the range of restrictions may be even greater. Of course, these may be described as exercises of the copyright or as actions subject to the relevant laws of the jurisdiction. But, it does suggest that the perceived difference between copyright and patents is less than obvious.

The perceived difference cannot lie in the separation of copyright interests, horizontally and vertically, permitted by the international copyright system since a similar regime exists under patent law. Nor can the difference arise from the inclusion of a statutory power to block imports under copyright. As Gibbs J pointed out, despite his brother's statements to the contrary, patent law confers a power corresponding to the statutory prohibition on imports in copyright.[197]

Furthermore, it is no more necessary for the business efficacy of a contract for the sale of a patented article that a licence for importation be implied than in a contract for the sale of a copyright article. Without circumstances such as those suggested in the case of copyright by Gibbs and Jacobs JJ, the purchaser can readily benefit from the contract by using the patented article in the jurisdiction where it was sold.[198] The objections suggested by Jacobs J do not, with respect, really meet the point. His Honour said:

> Importation is forbidden unless a licence has been given. If s. 37 were construed as the appellant contends, it would be unnecessary. If on a sale outside Australia an express positive restriction were imposed on import into Australia for purposes of sale, there would be no liberty to sell in Australia quite apart from s. 37. The purpose of the section is to deal with the case where no positive licence has been given and its purpose would be defeated if mere absence of restriction were held to import a licence.

Hence, Jacobs J considered that the secondary infringement provisions would be completely defeated by accepting IPEC's argument.[199] However, with respect, it is not clear how an express stipulation against importation could bind anyone other than in contract if the statute did not include a power to control imports since the court's unanimous ruling was that copyright is not infringed by simply using, or reselling, an article embodying the copyright. The secondary infringement provisions are necessary to give the copyright owner any power to control such actions as a matter of copyright law. If copyright law were consistent with the policy ruling patent law, the provision would still be necessary even if it required the copyright owner expressly to ban importation. Moreover, in the absence of an express stipulation the provision would still exclude imports of articles made lawfully abroad without the domestic copyright owner's consent, for example, under

---

197   See *ibid.* at 542 referring to *Pfizer Corporation v Minister of Health* [1965] AC 512.
198   See for example the cases involving Beecham's ampicillin patents in Chapter 3.2.3 above.
199   138 CLR at 556 to 557.

a compulsory licence provision or because the foreign jurisdiction does not confer the appropriate copyright protection.

Accordingly, with respect, the judgments do not really explain why a copyright article is treated differently to a patented article in international trade. The distinction perceived between use of a copyright article and a patented article seems highly questionable even in domestic trade. When the article is imported, the *Time-Life* case is consistent with the patent cases involving sale abroad by a limited licensee. But, that result in *Time-Life* itself highlights the anomaly of the corresponding patent situation in *Betts v Willmott*.

The UK Court of Appeal approved the reasoning of the *Time-Life* case in *Harlequin*. Templeman LJ held that Harlequin had infringed Polydor's rights as exclusive licensee in the United Kingdom of copyright in certain sound recordings. It required Polydor's consent and did not have it. Moreover, consent could not be implied from the unrestricted sale of the sound recordings in Portugal by the Portuguese licensees, corporate affiliates of the plaintiff.

In rejecting Harlequin's claims, Templeman LJ did not rely on the patent law principle that sale by a limited licensee could not confer rights outside the territory conferred on that licensee. Rather his Lordship based his decision on the absence of positive consent to importation by either Polydor or any other member of the group. His Lordship relied on the *Time-Life* case to support his conclusion that:

> In the present case section 16(2) forbids import without the necessary consent and no member of the group of companies consented to the import of records from Portugal to the United Kingdom. The Portuguese companies did not forbid export from Portugal, but they did not authorise, and no one authorised, the import of the records into the United Kingdom and, therefore, section 16(2) applies. The purchasers in Portugal can do as they please with the records, but if they choose to bring the records into the United Kingdom they bump into United Kingdom law and must comply with the Copyright Act 1956 and there is nothing in the terms of trade between them and the Portuguese companies which in my judgment implied any licence by the Portuguese companies or anyone else for the import of the records into the United Kingdom.
>
> Thus, in the present case, the sale of records by the Portuguese licensees conferred ownership and possession on the defendants, but did not constitute a licence from anyone to import those records into the United Kingdom.[200]

The *Harlequin* case is a stark contrast to the *Revlon* case which Harlequin based its defence on.[201] The *Revlon* case concerned alleged trade mark infringement by parallel importing. The successful defence was that the domestic trade mark owner had impliedly consented to the otherwise infringing use. This consent was implied from the interlocking corporate structure of the Revlon group and that group's uniform adoption as a 'house mark' of an identical trade mark on goods of comparable quality. The trade

---

200 The *Harlequin* case [1980] FSR 362, at 365 to 366.
201 See Chapter 2.2.3(a) above.

mark in question was owned by different legal entities in the foreign and domestic markets, but the owner in the latter was a wholly owned subsidiary of the owner in the former. Templeman LJ's minority opinion placed even greater importance on the intercorporate relationship. In *Harlequin* too, the respective copyrights were under the same ownership and were, no doubt, being exploited through a co-ordinated plan. In the *Revlon* case, consent was inferred from silence since the foreign manufacturer had not expressly forbidden its purchasers to import the goods into the United Kingdom. Therefore, consent could be, and was, implied. In *Harlequin* also, the Portuguese manufacturers did not expressly forbid export to the United Kingdom. However, silence implied the absence of consent. Hence, unlike trade marks, a licence to import could not be inferred merely from sale outside the jurisdiction without restriction on where or how the article may be dealt with.

A further aspect of the *Harlequin* case is that Templeman LJ appears to contemplate that the Portuguese licensees, or someone other than Polydor, could have authorised importing the records into the United Kingdom. Perhaps, Templeman LJ had in mind that the copyright owner's rights in the copyright, but not contract, might override the exclusive licensee's powers.[202] But, even then, it would seem something more than merely authorising sale in the foreign market would be required to imply consent to importation.

This aspect of his Lordship's decision should be contrasted to the opinion of the High Court of Delhi, Division Bench in *Penguin Books Limited v Indian Book Distributors et al.*[203] Penguin was the exclusive licensee in India of the copyright in some 23 book titles. IBD was importing and selling them in India without Penguin's authority, having bought the books in the United States from Penguin's wholly owned subsidiary, Penguin Inc., the exclusive licensee for the United States.

Penguin sought an interlocutory injunction for infringement of its rights. The High Court refused the application and Penguin appealed successfully. IBD had relied on the illegality under then US law of resale restrictions. Avadh Behari Rohattgi J based the Division Bench's decision squarely on the separate and independent nature of national copyrights under the international copyright system. His Honour held:

> Copyright law is a territorial concept; each nation has its own copyright laws. In America it may not be possible to place restrictions on the resale of books. But sale within the United States obviously cannot abrogate the effect of the laws of the particular place into which they are imported. It appears to me that an importer would be subject to the law of the particular country into which he happens to take the books. The importer cannot disregard the laws of other countries. . . . American books cannot be sold into India so as to defeat the rights of the exclusive licensee.[204]

---

202 See for example *Charmdale*, see text at Notes 109 to 113 above.
203 [1985] FSR 120. The *Barson Computers* case is consistent with this case.
204 *Ibid.* at 125 to 126 *per* Avadh Behari Rohattgi J, G.C. Jain J agreeing.

And subsequently:

> In importation it is the locale that matters. Territorial division and geographical area are of importance. Outside a defined territory the sale of a copyright work may constitute a sale of an 'infringing copy', because there is infringement of territorial restrictions.[205]

His Honour clearly relied on the territorial nature of copyrights and the limited authority conferred by the copyright in the United States. In fact, the decision is even stronger on the territorial aspect because, for the purposes of the action, Penguin conceded that it was identical to Penguin Inc.[206]

In the *Bailey's Irish Cream* case, already considered in the context of trade marks, the plaintiffs were the owner and its Australian exclusive licensee of a registered trade mark and the copyright subsisting in the appearance of the trade mark. The defendants were importing bottles of a liqueur into Australia for sale bearing the trade mark on a label, having bought the labelled bottles in the Netherlands from the copyright owner's operative there. Accordingly, as well as using the trade mark, the labels embodied the first plaintiff's copyright. Neither the first plaintiff nor its licensees expressly authorised the defendants' use of the copyright work in Australia. The trade mark action failed because its use on the imported bottles was held accurately to identify the source of the product. However, following the *Time-Life* case, Young J found copyright infringement.[207]

The defendants tried to distinguish the *Time-Life* case on three grounds related to the copyright work's use as a trade mark. First, they argued that a copyright work specially created for use as a trade mark was an exception to the rule in the *Time-Life* case. Second, they argued that creation of a work for use as a trade mark impliedly surrenders any copyright protection inconsistent with the work's use as a trade mark. Third, the defendants argued that every subsequent commercial dealing in a trade mark involved its use. Therefore, they said, the copyright owner must impliedly consent to any activity which was permitted by trade mark law. In essence, these arguments relied on the defendants' right to deal in products bearing the trade mark as giving a corresponding right to use the copyright work.

Young J rejected the first argument as not being necessary to give the contract for the sale of the bottles business efficacy.[208] Presumably, the defendants could have dealt with their purchases in the Netherlands.

His Honour rejected the second argument because the owner of concurrent copyright and trade mark rights was generally entitled to protection of both.[209] His Honour considered that the *British Leyland* case was directed to

---

205 *Ibid.* at 128 to 129.
206 *Ibid.* at 126.
207 R. & A. Bailey & Co. Ltd v Boccaccio Pty Ltd and Others (1986) 4 NSWLR 701, see Chapter 2 at Notes 137 to 141 above; see Lahore, *Intellectual Property in Australia: Copyright*, at ¶4.11.465. The Australian government has announced plans to reverse this result by legislative amendment: Attorney General's *Press Release*, 18 March 1992.
208 4 NSWLR 701, at 712.
209 *Ibid.* at 713, citing *Taverner Rutledge Ltd v Specters Ltd* [1959] RPC 83; 355 (CA); and *Ogden Industries Pty Ltd v Kis (Aust.) Pty Ltd* [1982] 2 NSWLR 283, at 300.

a special case rather than setting down a general proposition.[210] Furthermore, to the extent that it relied on the doctrine of non-derogation from grant, it was inconsistent, in this field, with the *Time-Life* case's rejection of the implied warranty of quiet possession.

Also following the *Time-Life* case, Young J rejected the third argument:

> It seems to me that in essence what I have to do is to consider the whole of the factual material and say whether the law implies a licence in those circumstances. Apart from the mere fact of sale by the first plaintiff to its Netherlands' distributors and the fact that for the reasons that I have set out earlier in this judgment the first plaintiff cannot object to use of its trade mark of [*sic*] those bottles, there are no other facts which could lead to the inference of an implied term. In my view the case is not really any different to the bare facts considered in [the *Time-Life* case]. . . .[211]

The conclusion that use of a copyright work as a trade mark did not extinguish the copyright is consistent with the distinct existence of the two rights.[212] But, it does lead to the perhaps surprising result that the same facts may result in different outcomes depending on the rights asserted. In similar circumstances, the Third Circuit in the United States refused to allow copyright protection in what it regarded as essentially a claim based on trade mark, although the court considered that the legislature should intervene.[213] In *TDK (No. 2)*, a court at first instance in South Africa also refused to block parallel imports on the basis of copyright infringement. Having failed on the basis of its trade mark rights, TDK redesigned the cardboard backing placed in the cases of its blank cassettes and assigned the resulting copyright to Frank & Hirsch for South Africa. Although this would result in infringement under the actual maker theory, Booysen J held that copyright in the 'accessory part' could not be relied on to block importation of the product which that accessory part had been merged in.[213a]

In the *Ozi-Soft* case, the plaintiffs were the copyright owners in various computer programs and their Australian licensee. The copyright owners had made and sold diskettes embodying their computer programs abroad

---

210   *British Leyland Motor Corporation Ltd v Armstrong Patents Co. Ltd* [1986] 2 WLR 400; [1986] 1 All ER 850.

211   *Ibid.* at 714.

212   Note *Catnic Components Ltd v Hill & Smith Ltd* [1978] FSR 405, at 427 to 428 where Whitford J considered that copyright in drawings in a patent specification might be abandoned on its publication. But, the suggestion has not received much support, see the cases referred to in Lahore, *Intellectual Property Law in Australia: Copyright*, at ¶¶3.9.340–3.9.355.

213   See the *Sebastian* case discussed in section 4.3.4 below.

213a   *Frank & Hirsch (Pty) Ltd v A Roopnand Brothers (Pty) Ltd* 1991 (3) SA 240 (D & CLD); his Honour also had some difficulty with the practicalities of calculating any damages or the profits on an accounting – points not usually acknowledged as considerations justifying refusal of relief in contract or tort cases where the relevant tests of sufficient proximity are otherwise met. For the trade mark issue, see Chapter 2 from Note 185. With respect, the reasoning of Young J would seem to be borne out by the express disapplication of the copyright provisions where the copyright was embodied in a computer chip protected under the Circuit Layouts Act 1989 (Cth), see Note 214, below.

where the defendants had bought them on the open market. The defendants imported the diskettes into Australia for the purposes of trade. They did not have the express consent of the plaintiffs for their activities. But, the diskettes had not been sold to them abroad under any express condition about resale.

At first instance, Einfeld J refused to distinguish the *Time-Life* case on the ground that the copyright owner there was under a legal prohibition against imposing express restrictions on resale. On appeal, the defendants focused on the absence of any exclusive licence granted for Australia and the sale abroad without restriction. After noting that the plaintiff bore the onus of proving the absence of consent, the Full Court held:

> Silence as to the imposition of a restriction is not, in our view, necessarily indicative of a grant of freedom from restriction. . . . Counsel for the respondents submitted that whilst a bare consent or permission might constitute a licence for the purposes of s 37 of the Copyright Act, nevertheless there must be evidence of the necessary facts from which one can properly infer the giving of that consent or permission by the copyright owner. We agree. Taking into account all the circumstances relied upon by the appellant, they fall well short of laying the necessary foundation from which the court might properly infer that in this case the copyright owners gave consent or permission to the importation of the diskettes into Australia for the purpose of sale . . .[214]

Contrast the South African case *Anthony Black Films* where one factor in persuading Goldstone J to reject the 'formidable argument of convenience' was that the plaintiffs were the copyright owner (in both jurisdictions) and its non-exclusive licensee (in both jurisdictions). On similar facts, diametrically opposed results were achieved.

Summarising then, when the issue raised is whether the importation has taken place with the copyright owner's consent, the courts have adopted an approach based on the territorial nature of copyright. Mere sale abroad of the copyright article does not imply authority to import it into the domestic

---

[214] *Computermate Products (Aust) Pty Ltd v Ozi-Soft Pty Ltd & Others* (1988) 83 ALR 492, at 498 (Fed. C, FC) (reference to *Time-Life* (1977) 138 CLR 534, at 556 to 557 *per* Jacobs J omitted). See Lahore, *Intellectual Property in Australia: Copyright*, at ¶4.11.456. In examining whether there were sufficient circumstances to infer consent, a failure to object and even, perhaps, an intention not to take any action to object may not necessarily constitute a licence: *Avel v Multicoin* (1990) 171 CLR 88, 123 *per* McHugh J. Other courts have felt confirmed in their conclusion that sale abroad did not imply consent to importation where the copyright owner had appointed an exclusive distributor: *Lorenzo v Roland* (1992) 23 IPR 376, 383 (Fed. C, FC), *Star Micronics* (1990) 18 IPR 225, 230 (Fed. C) and *Broderbund Software v Computermate* (1991) 22 IPR 215, 228; technical differences between products or adaptation to the local market: *Lorenzo v Roland* and *Star Micronics*. To the extent that *Star Micronics* involved copyright subsisting in a computer chip, it must now be read in light of the Circuit Layouts Act 1989 (Cth) which expressly permits, among other things, parallel importation of layouts and circuits sold abroad by, or with the consent of, the owner of the EL rights. That permission extends to any copyright lawfully embodied in the layout or chip. See sections 24(1) and 24(2) and *Avel Pty Ltd v Wells* (1992) 23 IPR 353 (Fed. C, FC). How these provisions will be interpreted where the owner of the *EL rights* in Australia is different to the owner in the foreign market gives rise to the same issues as the *Television Broadcasts* case discussed above at Notes 163 to 172.

jurisdiction. This does not seem to depend on whether the foreign seller also had authority to sell in the domestic market. Rather, it is put on the absence of any need for business efficacy to imply a licence to import. This puts the copyright cases on implied consent on the same footing as the patent cases where the foreign sale was effected by someone without authority to sell in the domestic market. As in those cases, the explanation for the underlying principle does not really seem to justify the different treatment of patent cases where the foreign seller also has power to sell in the domestic market.

(d)　*The knowledge element*[215]

Having successfully negotiated the requirements of 'hypothetical' manufacture and licence, the copyright owner must prove that the defendant knew the article was an 'infringing copy'. The defendant must have *knowledge* that making the article in the jurisdiction would have infringed the plaintiff's copyright.[216]

As with the other elements, the plaintiff bears the onus of proving the defendant had the necessary knowledge.[217] Moreover, the plaintiff must prove the defendant had the necessary knowledge at the time of the act subject to complaint.[218] As this can be difficult at the time of importing, it is important to remember that subsequent commercial dealing in imported 'infringing copies' also constitutes infringement.

The real difficulty, however, lies in what constitutes knowledge; what facts must be proved to show that the defendant knows the copies being imported are 'infringing copies'. If too stringent a test were adopted, a defendant could readily escape liability on the ground that actual knowledge cannot subsist until the court has ruled that copyright subsists and is being infringed. This is all the more so, given the obscurity of the hypothetical manufacturing test.

To date, the courts have suggested two alternative tests. The CDPA 1988 may introduce a third. The most widely adopted test is that proposed by Harvey J in the *Hoffnung* case. His Honour ruled that the defendant had the necessary knowledge because it had 'notice of facts such as would suggest to a reasonable man that a breach of copyright law was being

---

215　See generally, Lahore, *Intellectual Property in Australia: Copyright*, at ¶¶4.11.475–4.11.485; Sterling and Carpenter, *Copyright Law in the United Kingdom*, at ¶546.

216　But, note that the requirement in CDPA 1988 sections 22 and 23 is knowledge or reason to believe, quoted in the text at Note 38 above.

217　See for example *Sillitoe v MacGraw-Hill Book Co. (UK) Ltd* [1983] FSR 545; *Infabrics v Jaytex* [1978] FSR 451, at 463.

218　The terms of the indirect infringement provisions are quite clear on this point. For example, in the *Time-Life* case IPEC imported two shipments of the offending cookery books. Notice was only proved for the second shipment and liability was determined for that shipment alone. Acquisition of knowledge between issue of the writ and the date of trial will not suffice: *Arrowin Ltd v Trimguard (UK) Ltd* [1984] RPC 581.

committed . . .'[219] Hence, the plaintiff's written notice to the defendant claiming copyright in the material subject-matter sufficed to infect the defendant with 'knowledge'.[220]

Apart from a letter of demand at least five other ways of infecting the defendant with knowledge have been approved by the courts under Harvey J's test: personal attendance on the defendant to inform orally;[221] advertisements in trade and public press and circulars to the trade;[222] copyright notice in book or on record;[223] defendant having been a former distributor;[224] and ignoring the potential peril or closing the defendant's eyes to the danger.[225]

Despite the widespread currency of Harvey J's test, the New South Wales Court of Appeal formulated a second approach in 1978.[226] It sought to shift the emphasis from an objective test based on the 'reasonable man' to a test more closely based on the individual circumstances before the court. The Court of Appeal considered that the question was what reasonable inferences could be drawn from the whole evidence before the court:

> It seems to us that the principle is more accurately put by saying that a court is entitled to infer knowledge on the part of a particular person on the assumption that such a person has the ordinary understanding expected of persons in his line of business, unless by his or other evidence it is convinced otherwise. In other words, the true position is that the court is not concerned with the knowledge

219 (1921) 22 SR (NSW) 75, at 81. In an earlier case, not involving parallel imports, his Honour had ruled that:

> . . . knowledge of the material facts is all that this section requires the plaintiff to prove, and that it is also sufficient to show that there were within the knowledge of the defendant such facts as would give rise to a reasonable suspicion that copyright existed, and was being infringed.

> *Meccano Ltd v Anthony Hordern & Sons Ltd* (1918) 18 SR (NSW) 606, at 611.

In addition to the cases cited below, Harvey J's test was also approved in *Video Rent* 1981(3) SA 42, at 51 and would appear to have been applied in *Star Micronics* (1990) 18 IPR 225, 235 to 236.

220 See *Hoffnung* 22 SR (NSW) at 81. Such written notice from the plaintiff to the defendant claiming copyright has sufficed in the *Meccano* case 18 SR (NSW) at 614; *Time-Life* case 12 ALR 1, at 12 to 13; *Music Machine* case 1973(3) SA 188, at 208 (in conjunction with other factors); *Video Parktown North* 1983(2) SA 251, at 262 (in conjunction with other factors).

221 *Time-Life* 12 ALR 1, at 12 to 13 (followed by letter from solicitor); *Music Machine* 1973(3) SA 188, at 208 (followed by letter and in association with 'closed eyes' test).

222 *Fly By Nite* 20 CPR (2d) 263.

223 *Clarke, Irwin* 22 DLR (2d) 183, at 189; *Godfrey, MacSkimming* 40 DLR (2d) 346, at 348 (together with warning letter); *Simon & Schuster* 61 DLR (3d) 590, at 592 (together with 'closed eyes'); *A & M Records* 1 CPR (3d) 354, at 357; *Video Parktown North* 1983(2) SA 251, at 262 (together with warning letter).

224 *Benjamin Distribution* 68 CPR (2d) 251.

225 *Simon & Schuster* 61 DLR (3d) 590, at 592 (together with copyright notice in book); *Music Machine* 1973(3) SA 188, at 207. Moll J considered that no reasonable man could believe that Beatles' records were not subject to copyright (followed by letter and personal visit).

226 *RCA Corporation v Custom Cleared Sales Pty Ltd* (1978) 19 ALR 123. Approved in *Sillitoe v McGraw-Hill Book Co. (UK) Ltd* [1983] FSR 545 (Ch. D) (counsel's advice that there was no infringement rejected as foundation for lack of knowledge); *International Business Machines Corporation v Computer Imports Ltd* [1989] 2 NZLR 395 (pirated copies).

of a reasonable man but is concerned with reasonable inferences to be drawn from a concrete situation as disclosed in the evidence as it affects the particular person whose knowledge is in issue.[227]

The Court of Appeal went on to explain:

> In inferring knowledge, a court is entitled to approach the matter in two stages; where opportunities for knowledge on the part of the particular person are proved and there is nothing to indicate that there are obstacles to the particular person acquiring the relevant knowledge, there is some evidence from which the court can conclude that such a person has the knowledge. However, this conclusion may be easily overturned by a denial on his part of the knowledge which the court accepts, or by a demonstration that he is properly excused from giving evidence of his actual knowledge.[228]

Hence, the test emphasises that what must be proved is the defendant's actual knowledge, allowing for reasonable inferences from the circumstances. It may be questioned whether the NSW Court of Appeal's test results in significant change; certainly not in those cases where the defendant is directly notified of the plaintiff's claims. Furthermore, it is arguable that some Canadian and South African cases applying Harvey J's test have actually applied a test similar to that proposed in the *RCA* case.[229]

Under the CDPA 1988, sections 22 and 23 replace the test of 'knowledge'; in its place a defendant will be liable for importing an article 'which he knows or has reason to believe is' an infringing copy. A similar change has been introduced into the importation provisions of the Australian Act by section 3 of the Copyright Amendment Act 1991. (The article must also in fact be an infringing copy.) This change in wording may be thought to release the court from the strait-jacket of finding, or inferring, actual knowledge, thus giving statutory effect to the test proposed by Harvey J in *Hoffnung*. However, as the test of knowledge has been interpreted, particularly in Canada, it may be doubted whether it causes significant change.[230]

4.2.3   Other forms of liability

Legislation derived from the 1911 and 1956 Acts provides copyright owners with two further potential avenues for civil relief against parallel imports. It has been argued that distributing parallel imports to the public infringes the copyright owner's exclusive right to publish the work. In addition, a parallel importer may be liable under the statute for conversion.

---

227   *Ibid.* at 126.
228   *Ibid.*
229   For example the *Simon & Schuster, Fly By Nite* and *Music Machine* cases almost proceed on the court's view of what someone in the defendant's position and experience would be likely to know.
230   See Cornish, *Intellectual Property*, at ¶11–022.

(a) *Publication right*

Prior to the CDPA 1988, the copyright owner was granted the exclusive right to publish the work.[231] 'Publish' was further expanded to mean 'issue copies of the work to the public.'[232] Unlike the common law and the 1911 Act, the statutory language did not expressly limit the right to a right of first publication. Accordingly, in view of the wide definition of 'publish', it had been argued that the right to publish was infringed by acts of distribution without authority from the copyright owner.[233]

In the United Kingdom, the problem was resolved in favour of confining the right to a right of first publication.[234] One factor in persuading the House of Lords to this view was the anomaly created by the alternative. If the right of publication were not confined to a right of first publication, two separate sets of provisions could apply to unauthorised distributions. Hence, reliance on the publication right would render the 'secondary' infringement provisions substantially ineffective. As already discussed, the 'secondary' infringement provisions apply only to 'infringing copies' and are conditional on the defendant knowingly acting contrary to the copyright owner's interests. Neither condition is a requirement of enforcing the exclusive right to publish. Accordingly, it was considered unlikely that Parliament intended the right to publish to control such acts.

However, an Australian court at first instance found a parallel importer engaged in offering for sale and selling the imported articles liable for infringement of the right to publish.[235] Some support for this approach was found in the terms of the Australian Act which in places refers expressly to 'first publication'.[236] Bowen CJ in Eq.'s ruling has been approved in India.[237] It has, however, been conclusively rejected by the High Court of Australia for the policy reasons accepted by the House of Lords in *Infabrics v Jaytex*. Hence, a mere exclusive distributor, with authority only to import and sell copyright articles, was found to have no interest in the copyright and so no standing to sue for its alleged infringement.[238]

---

231 For example 1956 Act sections 2(5)(b), 3(5)(b); Copyright Act 1968 (Cth) sections 31(1)(a)(ii), 31(1)(b)(ii).
232 1956 Act section 49(2)(c); but see Copyright Act 1968 (Cth) section 29(1)(a), which refers to 'supply' not 'issue'.
233 See for example *British Northrop Ltd v Texteam Blackburn Ltd* [1974] RPC 57 *per* Megarry J, offering reproductions of an artistic work to the public for sale was publishing; *Infabrics Ltd v Jaytex* [1978] FSR 451, *per* Whitford J, offering and exposing for sale was not publishing; [1980] FSR 161 *per* Buckley LJ, offering and exposing for sale was not publishing but selling was publishing.
234 *Infabrics Ltd v Jaytex Ltd* [1982] AC 1, at 15 to 17 *per* Lord Wilberforce, at 21 to 25 *per* Lord Scarman (HL).
235 The *Time-Life* case (1978) 12 ALR 1, at 15 *per* Bowen CJ in Eq.
236 See generally, Ricketson, *The Law of Intellectual Property*, at ¶¶9.125 to 9.126.
237 *Penguin v India Book Distributors* [1985] FSR 120, at 129 to 131. Note also the brief views of Denault J in the *Dictionnaires Robert* case, see text at Note 92 above.
238 *Avel Pty Ltd v Multicoin Amusements Pty Ltd* (1990) 171 CLR 88; 18 IPR 443; 65 ALJR 179, at 180 *per* Mason CJ, Deane and Gaudron JJ, at 184 to 185 *per* Dawson J, and 190 to 191 *per* McHugh J.

The CDPA 1988 changes the terminology slightly, but, at least insofar as parallel imports are concerned, not the application. By section 16(1)(b), the copyright owner is granted the exclusive right 'to issue copies of the work to the public'. The expression 'issue to the public copies of a work' has been further defined in section 18(1) to mean 'the act of putting into circulation copies not previously put into circulation, in the United Kingdom or elsewhere'. Paragraph 18(1)(b) goes on expressly to exclude importation of copies marketed elsewhere from the definition. Hence, the position established by *Infabrics v Jaytex* has been preserved.[239]

(b)   *Conversion and detinue*

Prior to the CDPA 1988, the copyright owner was accorded all rights and remedies in conversion and detinue over 'infringing copies' as if the copyright owner owned them.[240] Given the definition of 'infringing copy', a similar problem to that arising under a wide definition of 'publish' could arise. The House of Lords has, however, now ruled on two occasions that the conversion remedy is ancillary to the infringement provisions.[241] Hence, in those jurisdictions preserving a remedy in conversion, a defendant is probably only exposed if first found to be in breach of the primary or secondary infringement provisions. Delivery up and seizure have been preserved in the United Kingdom, but conversion damages were repealed as too draconian.[242]

4.2.4   Re-engineering the works

Since 1987, three Anglo-Commonwealth countries have legislated to undermine the application of the principle of territoriality as it affects parallel imports of copyright articles; at the same time, the United Kingdom took steps to strengthen the principle.[243] While the steps in Singapore, Malaysia and the

---

239   The somewhat unhappy wording of the section which also creates a rental right for sound recordings, films and computer programs has led to an argument that the right is no longer a right of first publication but some form of distribution right, see J. A. L. Sterling, 'Copyright, Designs and Patents Act 1988: The New Issuing Right', [1989] EIPR 283; the view has not received widespread acceptance: Cornish, *Intellectual Property*, at ¶11–021.

240   See for example 1956 Act section 18, Copyright Act 1968 (Cth) section 116.

241   *Infabrics Ltd v Jaytex Ltd* [1982] AC 1, at 17 to 18 *per* Lord Wilberforce, 26 *per* Lord Scarman; *Caxton Publishing Co. Ltd v Sutherland Publishing Co. Ltd* [1939] AC 178, at 184 *per* Lord Thankerton, 188 *per* Lord Russell of Killowen, 201 *per* Lord Porter. See also Laddie, Prescott and Vitoria, *The Modern Law of Copyright*, at ¶¶12.38 to 12.39; Ricketson, *The Law of Intellectual Property*, at ¶¶12.16 to 12.18.

242   CDPA 1988, Schedule 1, section 31(2) and see Department of Trade and Industry, *Intellectual Property and Innovation*, HMSO, Cmnd 9712, 1986, at ¶12.2. The remedy seems to have been unknown in South African law, see *Video Parktown North* 1986(2) SA 623, at 640 *per* Slomowitz AJ.

243   The measures in the United Kingdom, Singapore and Malaysia related to the general application of the hypothetical manufacturing test, see text at Notes 38, 64, 162 to 173, above. Apart from the Australian measures to be considered here, a similar issue

United Kingdom apply to copyright subject-matter generally, the Australian legislation so far has been directed specifically at copyright in certain kinds of 'books'.[244] The sensitive nature of the issues raised by copyright in books – particularly about their price and availability – has a long history in Australia.[245] The seeds of the Copyright Amendment Act 1991 (Cth), however, can be traced to the early 1970s.

Apparently at the instigation of then Commonwealth Attorney-General Murphy, the US Justice Department filed an anti-trust action in November 1974 against a large number of US publishers alleging breach of the Sherman Act, section 1; the conspiracy alleged an agreement between the major US and UK publishers known as the Traditional Markets Agreement.[246] The Traditional Markets Agreement had been operating since the end of World War II. Under it the world market for English language publishing was effectively divided into three territories: the British market (which covered 70 countries, present and former members of the British Commonwealth and so included Australia), the US market and a free area. Simplifying, the US publishers had agreed with the UK Publishers' Association not to compete in the other's reserved territory and to exchange copyright interests on a reciprocal basis for the respective territories. As a result of the consent decree in *Addison-Wesley*, the US publishers undertook not to operate the Traditional Markets Agreement and not to enter into any similar agreement. The rights of individual publishers to contract with one another on a non-reciprocal basis, however, were preserved. Hence, there was nothing to stop any individual US publisher assigning its rights to a particular title for the traditional British market to an individual UK publisher provided it was not done on the understanding that the UK publisher would reciprocate with its rights for the US market.

Attorney-General Murphy had become Murphy J of the Australian High Court when the *Time-Life* case was heard. His Honour agreed in dismissing IPEC's argument that it had an implied licence to import the books in

is under consideration in Canada, Chapter 10.3 below and the South African government is reportedly proposing to amend the legislation so that the importer is the hypothetical manufacturer, see Dean, 'The Implications for the Entertainment Industry of Proposed Amendments to the South African Copyright Act', at 198.

244 Following the Prices Surveillance Authority's *Inquiry into the Price of Sound Recordings*, Report No. 35, 1990, the government has also announced plans to make similar provision for copyright in sound recordings: Joint Press Statement by Treasurer John Dawkins and Attorney-General Michael Duffy, *Prices Report on Records Finalised*, 10 June 1992. The PSA has also recommended that the importation provisions be amended to permit parallel importing of computer software: *Inquiry into Prices of Computer Software: Interim Report*, Report No. 44, 12 October 1992. The government has also announced that it plans to reverse the result in the *Bailey's Irish Cream* case insofar as it applies to copyright in labels: see Attorney General's *Press Release*, 18 March 1992. For an outline, see [1992] 12 EIPR D-258.

245 For a historical review of some of the questions, see Richard Nile, 'Cartels, Capitalism and the Australian Book Trade', (1990) 4(1) *Continuum* 71.

246 15 USC §1. For the background, see Robert Haupt, 'Bound for Botany Bay', *Sydney Morning Herald*, 5 November 1988, at 86 to 87; for the eventual settlement of the action, see *US v Addison-Wesley Publishing Co*. 1976–2 CCH Trade Cases at ¶61,225.

question into Australia.[247] However, he considered that the facts of the case suggested that the Time companies were abusing copyright to double the price of the cookery books in Australia and that the trial court should have required the Time companies to prove that their conduct did not breach the Australian competition laws before granting relief:

> Neither [IPEC] nor [the Time companies] chose to expose the full facts. The evidence is scanty, but suggests that the Australian public will suffer if the respondents succeed, that the copyright is being used to manipulate the Australian market, and that [the Time companies] will control the outlets and the price to the public will be almost doubled, and the Australian public will have delayed access to publications freely available in the United States.[248]

None of the other judges was attracted to this opinion and Murphy J in the end recommended that IPEC's appeal be dismissed too.

There are considerable difficulties with Murphy J's approach. Generally, the provisions of Part IV of the Trade Practices Act 1974 (Cth) only affect exercises of copyright where it is used to establish resale price maintenance under section 48 or a misuse of market power under section 46. It is unlikely that the Time companies' actions involved a breach of either provision unless the relevant market be defined as Time Inc.'s cookery books, a position which, although attractive to Murphy J, has not attracted much support.[249]

Subsequently, the Copyright Law Review Committee (CLRC) spent five years investigating the use of copyright to block parallel imports.[250] After a careful inquiry, its main recommendation was amendment of the law to permit parallel imports if the copyright article, or one 'substantially similar' to it, was unavailable in Australia and could not be made available in Australia within a reasonable time having regard to the nature of the industry. The CLRC was aware of the imprecision of the standards proposed, but considered that further discussion with the various interest groups was necessary given the wide range of industries potentially affected. On the evidence before it, the CLRC did not find that widespread, unjustified price discrimination was being practised against Australian consumers. The CLRC did acknowledge, however, that its powers in this area were limited.[251]

---

247   138 CLR at 558 to 559.
248   *Ibid*. at 560. See *ibid*. at 561 for the suggestion that Time-Life should disprove breach of the competition law before being entitled to relief in copyright.
249   See *Broderbund Software Inc. v Computermate Products (Australia) Pty Ltd* (1991) 22 IPR 215 (Fed. C) where the copyright owner was found to have only 10–17% of the market for software for educational purposes or for entertainment purposes. For the criticism of Murphy J's view, see W. R. Cornish and Peter G. McGonigal, 'Copyright and Anti-trust Aspects of Parallel Imports under Australian Law', 11 IIC 731 (1980); Copyright Law Review Committee, *The Importation Provisions of the Copyright Act 1968*, at 44 to 63; PSA, *Inquiry into Book Prices: Final Report*, PSA, Report No. 25, 1989, at 14. The point is returned to in Chapter 10.2.1 below.
250   CLRC, *The Importation Provisions of the Copyright Act 1968*. For further recommendations, see Lahore, *Intellectual Property in Australia: Copyright*, at ¶4.11.457 to 4.11.458.
251   *Ibid*. at ¶¶79, 88.

The debate did not die,[252] and the Commonwealth Government authorised the Prices Surveillance Authority (PSA) with the objective of obtaining a fuller economic analysis. The PSA's report is the subject of more detailed consideration in Chapter 10 below. Here, it suffices to note that the PSA found widespread price discrimination and considerable delays in the publication of books in Australia. It, therefore, recommended repeal of copyright owner's powers to block imports subject to two exceptions, imports of 'pirate' copies and, on a transitional basis as an 'infant industry', parallel imports of books first published in Australia by resident Australian authors.[253]

The Commonwealth Government announced that it proposed to implement the recommendations of the two inquiries and has now done so, in somewhat modified form, in the Copyright Amendment Act 1991.[254]

The 1991 Act, in effect, repeals the right to block imports of copies of a 'non-infringing book'.[255] A 'non-infringing book' is defined to mean a book made in certain specified countries in circumstances which did not infringe any copyright subsisting in a work or published edition in that country; books made under a compulsory licence are expressly excluded from this definition.[256] The 1991 Act's explanatory memorandum indicates that the countries to be specified are those signatory to at least one of the international conventions which Australia has joined or which otherwise give reciprocal protection to Australian authors. The term 'book' itself was not previously defined, and is now done so by exclusion – for the purposes of the new importation provisions, 'book' does not include a periodical; a manual sold with computer software for use with that software; or a book whose main content is one or more musical works.[257]

Section 44A then provides that any copyright subsisting in a 'non-infringing book' is not infringed by importing copies of it into Australia in four situations. The first situation is where the work was not published in Australia either first or within 30 days of first publication elsewhere. In this situation, the power to block imports (and commercial dealings

252   See for example Robert Haupt, 'Bound for Botany Bay', *Sydney Morning Herald*, 5 November 1988, at 86 to 87.

253   PSA, *Inquiry into Book Prices: Final Report*, at 7, 39. The PSA has reached similar conclusions for copyright in sound recordings and computer software, see PSA, *Inquiry into the Prices of Sound Recordings*, Report No. 35 and PSA, *Inquiry into the Prices of Computer Software: Interim Report*, Report No. 44, respectively.

254   The following account is based on Warwick A. Rothnie, 'Parallel Imports and Books in Australia: Copyright Amendment Act 1991; [1992] Ent. LR 39.

255   The 1991 Act sections 5 and 8 inserting new sections 44A and 112A into the Copyright Act 1968 ('the 1968 Act'). Section 44A affects sections 37 and 38 dealing with works and section 112A affects sections 102 and 103 insofar as they provide for published editions. Since the amendments for published editions introduced by section 112A correspond to those for works introduced by section 44A, for brevity the author will refer to section 44A only.

256   The 1991 Act section 2(b); with consequential amendment of the definition of 'infringing copy' in section 10(1) of the 1968 Act.

257   Sections 44A(7), 112A(7). The PSA, in its report on software prices, has recommended repeal of the exclusion for computer software manuals.

in imports) of copies of non-infringing books is repealed entirely. This provision only affects works first published on or after 23 December, the date the amendments made by the 1991 Act came into force.[258]

The second situation applies to all books where a power to prevent imports still exists.[259] In this situation, copyright is not infringed by importing copies of the non-infringing book if the copyright owner is unable to meet demand within 90 days of receiving a written order for copies. Only the person who has placed (and not withdrawn) the unsatisfied written order gains the right to bring in the imports and may do so in either of two situations; first, if the copyright owner does not provide written confirmation within 7 days of receiving the order that it will supply the order within 90 days; or second, if the order is not in fact satisfied within 90 days. The copies imported may not be 'second-hand copies'. This power, like the first, permits importation for commercial dealing.

The third situation is an extension of the individual's right to import a copy for personal use and was originally recommended by the CLRC. Under it, a single copy of a non-infringing book may be imported at any time provided the importation is to fulfil a written or verifiable telephone order from a customer of the importer and the customer has undertaken that the copy is not intended to be dealt with in a commercial manner.[260]

The fourth situation entitles a bookseller to import two or more copies of a work (or edition) to satisfy a written or telephone order from a library which (a) is not conducted for profit and (b) does not intend to sell or otherwise deal commercially in the imported copies. This provision was introduced at a late stage following pressure from the Australian Booksellers' Association and corresponds to the bulk of parallel imports which occur in Canada.[260a]

A number of further issues require comment. Since the extent of copyright protection against imports is made contingent on the place of first publication and not on the nationality of the author or other copyright owner, the government considers that the principle of national treatment embodied in Article 5(1) of the Berne Convention is not violated.

Unlike the Singaporean and Malaysian Acts, the amendments do not affect the traditional test of hypothetical manufacture, they simply remove the need for the copyright owner's licence to importation in the specified situations.

Copyright owners who wish to retain any power to block parallel imports in works first published on or after 23 December 1991 will need to co-ordinate the date of publication in Australia with the date of any prior first publication elsewhere so that copies are made available to the Australian public within 30 days of the date of first publication. The requirement of simultaneous publication under the 1911 Act was once held satisfied by the supply of six copies having regard to anticipated demand and the publisher's

---

258 Sections 44A(1), 112A(1).
259 Sections 44A(2), 112A(2).
260 Sections 44A(3), 112A(3). Sections 44A(5) and 112A(5) provide some guidance on verification.
260a Sections 44A(4), 112A(4). For Canada, see Chapter 10.3, below.

intention to meet demand as and when it arose.[261] The copyright owner must still also bear in mind the importation rights conferred under section 44A(2). The amendments do not, however, affect the price which may be charged and this presumably may reflect the costs of special transport arrangements a review by the PSA of the amendments after some 18 months of operation has been foreshadowed.

It is probably necessary for a copyright owner which receives an order under section 44A(2) to reply in writing within seven days if it intends supplying the order and forestalling the parallel imports since the two time periods are expressed in the alternative.[262] Further, to forestall parallel imports, the complete order must be filled within the 90-day period.[263] This creates one difficulty in that the copyright owner's obligation under section 44A(2) is only to satisfy the 'reasonable requirements' of the person placing the order.[264] No guidance is given about how these two provisions are to be reconciled. Nor is there any indication about how the concept of reasonableness is to be assessed. Presumably the only reasonable quantity to a copyright owner which did not want parallel imports, none, can hardly be intended. A large book chain would perhaps be expected to want more copies than a small corner shop, but what about a business which intended starting up a wholesale operation? Having precluded the concept of reasonableness from the copyright owner's point of view, the only concept applicable can be that of the person placing the order.

Sections 44A(6) and 112A(6) preclude the powers under section 44A(2) and 112A(2) if the order is placed for copies of a hardback version and the copyright owner can 'supply in Australia enough copies of a paperback version of the book to fill any reasonable order'. What is more interesting is the opposite situation – where hardback copies are available but the order relates to paperback copies.

The wording of sections 44A(2) and 112A(2) seems broad enough to include an order for a paperback edition even when the work has not been released in Australia in paperback. The Explanatory Memorandum does not state this explicitly and only refers to a situation where there are two different paperback editions of the book.[265] It does not, however, state that either of the two editions must have been released in Australia. Moreover, when the Commonwealth Government first announced its intention to amend the 1968 Act, the then Attorney-General indicated that parallel importing of paperback editions not already released in Australia was intended.[266] That intention is also consistent with the findings of the PSA.[267]

---

261 *Francis, Day & Hunter v Feldman & Co.* [1914] 2 Ch. 728 (CA).
262 See sections 44A(2)(d) and 112A(2)(d) and note also Explanatory Memorandum, dated 29 May 1991, at ¶10.
263 Sections 44A(6), 112A(6).
264 Sections 44A(2)(c), 112A(2)(c).
265 Explanatory Memorandum, 26904/91, at ¶9, first indent.
266 News Release by Lionel Bowen, Deputy Prime Minister and Attorney-General, 'Government Moves on Book Prices', 21 and 22 December 1989, at 2.
267 See Chapter 10 below.

Accordingly, when acquiring publishing rights for a book in Australia it will be highly advisable to investigate the plans of foreign publishers to issue paperback versions.

4.3   The United States of America

4.3.1   Introduction

As in the Anglo-Commonwealth jurisdictions, US law also provides the copyright owner with some power to control imports. However, in the United States, copyright law, like both patents and trade mark law, must be considered in light of an exhaustion policy, the 'first sale' doctrine.[268]

As yet, the precise relationship of the power to control imports with the 'first sale' doctrine in the field of parallel imports is unclear. Cases involving copyright and parallel imports seem to have arisen only quite recently and are only few in number.[269] To date, the courts have suggested three competing approaches to the issue. Two have received the considered backing of an appeal court.[270]

The statutory provisions relevant are sections 106, 109(a) and 602(a) of the Copyright Act of 1976.[271] In addition, the potential application of section 337(a) of the Tariff Act may be applicable if it is possible to show

268   Neither the statute nor the original cases actually refer to the 'first sale' doctrine. It derives from the fact that the copyright owner loses its ability under copyright law to control subsequent dealings in a copyright article once the owner has first parted with ownership of the article.

269   One explanation is that copyright owners did not have rights to control imports until the passage of the Copyright Act of 1976 §602: for example Stephen W. Feingold, 'Parallel Importing under the Copyright Act of 1976', 32 J. Copr. Soc'y 211 (1984) reprinted from NYU Jnl Int'l Law and Pol. 113, at 211 (1984). But contrast the terms of Copyright Act of 1790 (1 Stat. 124) section 2 and Revised Statutes §4965, which forbade importing articles subject to US copyright without the consent of the copyright owner. There are some suggestions that US copyright law may have barred parallel imports in earlier case law. However, in these cases the copyright owner sued the defendants not for parallel importing but for printing and selling their own piratical copies of the work: see for example *United Dictionary Company v G & C Merriam Company* 208 US 260 (1908) *affg* 146 Fed. 354 (7th Cir. 1906) *revg* 140 Fed. 768 (ND Ill. 1905); *Harper & Bros. v M. A. Donoghue & Co.* 144 Fed. 491 (ND Ill. 1905) *affd* without opinion 146 Fed. 1023 (7th Cir. 1906); *Bentley v Tibbals* 223 Fed. 247 (2d Cir. 1915). But note *United Film Manufacturing Co. v Copperman* 218 Fed. 577 (2d Cir. 1914), apparently allowing parallel imports. Other explanations lie in the ban on imports of English language books not printed in the United States: 17 USC §601, see 2 *Nimmer on Copyright*, at §7.22[C][1] and [2] and the frustrations and expense associated with trying to bar imports by other means.

270   *Sebastian International Inc. v Consumer Contacts (PTY) Ltd* 847 F. 2d 1093 (3d Cir. 1988) *revg* 66 F. Supp. 909 (DNJ 1987) text from Note 408 below *BMG Music v Perez* 952 F. 2d 318 (9th Cir. 1991) text from Note 431, below.

271   17 USC §§106, 109(a) and 602(a), respectively (1988); but, in the case works and semiconductor chip products, see 17 USC §§109(b)(1)(c), 905(2) and 906(b) (1991) discussed at 3 *Nimmer on Copyright* §18.06[E].

that parallel imports infringe copyright.[272] The right to control imports is conferred by section 602(a):

> Importation into the United States, without the authority of the owner of the copyright under this title, of copies or phonorecords of a work that have been acquired outside the United States is an infringement of the exclusive right to distribute copies or phonorecords under section 106, actionable under section 501 . . .

The subsection goes on to permit some imports in a number of specified circumstances without the copyright owner's authority, such as for specified governmental purposes and an individual's private use.

Section 106 identifies the exclusive rights granted to the copyright owner and, in relevant part, provides:

> Subject to sections 107 through 120, the owner of copyright under this title has the exclusive right to do and to authorize any of the following:
> (1)   to reproduce the copyrighted work in copies or phonorecords;
> (2)   to prepare derivative works based on the copyrighted work;
> (3)   to distribute copies or phonorecords of the copyrighted work to the public by sale or other transfer of ownership, or by rental, lease or lending;
> (4)   . . . to perform the copyrighted work publicly; and
> (5)   . . . to display the copyrighted work publicly.

Hence, unlike the Anglo-Commonwealth laws, the US Copyright Act expressly grants the copyright owner the exclusive right to distribute reproductions to the public in subsection 106(3). This right is, however, subject to the qualifications introduced by sections 107 to 118. For present purposes, section 109(a) is immediately relevant:

> Notwithstanding the provisions of section 106(3), the owner of a particular copy or phonorecord lawfully made under this title, or any person authorized by such owner, is entitled, without the authority of the copyright owner, to sell or otherwise dispose of the possession of that copy or phonorecord.

Section 109(a) itself only refers to section 106. However, section 602(a) makes importation without authority an infringement of the exclusive distribution right conferred by section 106. The position is further complicated by the terms of section 501:

> Anyone who violates any of the exclusive rights of the copyright owner as provided by sections 106 through 118, . . . or who imports copies or phonorecords into the United States in violation of section 602, is an infringer of the copyright. . . .[273]

Hence, section 501 seems to treat the right of distribution under section 106 as distinct and independent of the right to control imports provided by

272   For a summary of the terms of section 337, see Chapter 2.3.1 above. For copyright cases involving section 337(a), see *Warner Bros Inc. v US ITC* 229 USPQ 126 (Fed. Cir. 1986); *Bally/Midway Mfg Co. v USITC* 219 USPQ 97 (Fed. Cir. 1983) and *In re Certain Audio Visual Games* 214 USPQ 217 (ITC 1981). The latter two cases are unlikely to have been parallel import cases. The industry requirement has been relaxed since the *Warner Bros* case.
273   17 USC §501 (1992).

section 602(a). In view of the concatenation of cross-references, therefore, parallel imports require discussion of whether section 109(a) governs the importation right conferred by section 602(a).

Before examining this relationship, one further aspect of the legislative scheme requires notice. Section 109(b)(1)(c) provides that section 109 does not affect the provisions of chapter 9, dealing with mask works and semiconductor chip products. Section 905(2) grants the owner of a mask work the right to import and distribute semiconductor chips products. That right is subject to section 906(b), however, which provides:

> . . . the owner of a particular semiconductor chip product made by the owner of the mask work, or by any person authorised by the owner of the mask work, may import, distribute, or otherwise dispose of or use, but not reproduce, that particular semiconductor chip product without the authority of the owner of the mask work.[273a]

Apart from expressly authorising importation, section 906(b) is apparently intended to apply the 'first sale' doctrine to semiconductor chip products made, or authorised to be made, by the owner of the relevant mask work.[273b]

In its various reports on the Copyright Bills, Congress did not refer to the relationship of section 109(a) to section 602(a). The final House Report stated that:

> Section 109(a) restates and confirms the principle that, where the copyright owner has transferred ownership of a particular copy or phonorecord of a work, the person to whom the particular copy or phonorecord is transferred is entitled to dispose of it by sale, rental, or any other means. Under this principle, which has been established by the court decisions and section 27 of the present law, the copyright owner's exclusive right of public distribution would have no effect upon any one who owns 'a particular copy or phonorecord lawfully made under this title' and who wishes to transfer it to someone else or to destroy it.[274]

As a subsidiary point, it is worth noting that under the 'first sale' doctrine exhaustion prevents the copyright owner placing restrictions on dealing in the article by way of rental.[275]

273a   17 USC §906(b) (1990).

273b   Except for the express authorisation to import, the House Report on the Semiconductor Chip Protection Act expressly adopted the case law on the copyright provisions: 3 *Nimmer on Copyright* §18.06[E]. For the corresponding Australian provision see Note 214, above. For the question of 'authorisation', see Chapter 4.3.4, below and compare *Television Broadcasts* discussed at Notes 163 to 172, above.

274   *The House Report on the Copyright Act of 1976*, House Report 94–1476, 94th Cong. 2d Sess., at 79, reprinted in 4 *Nimmer on Copyright*, App. 4, at 4–41 and 17 USC §109 at 38. See also, Richard Colby, 'The First Sale Doctrine – The Defence that Never Was?', 32 J. Copr. Soc'y 77 (1984) and Feingold, 'Parallel Importing under the Copyright Act of 1976', at 211.

275   Subsequently, Congress amended the Copyright Act to accord a rental right in both phonorecords and computer programs. See now 17 USC §109(b)(1)(a) (1990) as amended by Record Rental Amendment Act of 1984, Pub. L. No. 98–450, 98 Stat. 1727 and Computer Software Rental Amendments Act of 1990, Pub. L. 101–650, 104 Stat. 5134. A similar right for 'films' has failed to be accepted, see 2 *Nimmer on*

Referring to section 602(a), the House Report noted that the section was intended to deal with two distinct situations:

> . . . importation of *'piratical'* articles (that is, copies or phonorecords *made without* any authorization of the copyright owner), and unauthorized importation of copies or phonorecords *that were lawfully made.* The general approach of section 602 is to make unauthorized importation an act of infringement in both cases, but to permit the United States Customs Service to prohibit importation only of 'piratical' articles. (*Emphasis added*)[276]

4.3.2 Parallel imports and 'literary property'

The earliest US case involving parallel imports in the context of US copyright seems to have been the *Copperman* case.[277] Copperman was publicly exhibiting a motion picture film, *The Great Circus Catastrophe*, in the United States for an entry fee. He had bought his print in the United Kingdom from the authorised distributors of Nordisk Film Company which had written the screenplay and produced the film. Statutory copyright could subsist in films but, at the time Copperman bought his print, the film had not been registered for copyright in either the United Kingdom or the United States. Even so, Nordisk was selling it through a distribution network in Europe and its distributors were authorised to sell each print only on condition that the buyer did not export, sell for export or use the print outside the country of purchase. Somehow, Copperman obtained his copy without notice of the condition. Further, he only bought after checking that the film was not subject to copyright in the United States. Sometime after Copperman bought his print, Nordisk registered the film for copyright in the United States and assigned its rights to Universal which sued Copperman when he started exhibiting the print in the United States.

In these circumstances, Judge Ward, for the Second Circuit, upheld the District Court's dismissal of Universal's suit. First, Judge Ward considered that, even though Nordisk's common law rights in its play remained after distribution of positive prints of the film, Nordisk could not use those rights to stop public performances of the film by exhibition to the public. The plain sale of the print carried the right of performing it. Citing the *Straus* case and the *Dr Miles Medical* case, his Honour ruled:

Copyright, at §8.12[B][7], Note 81. For a Singaporean rejection of a rental right, see *Television Broadcasts*, see subsection 4.2.2(b) above. Contrast the CDPA 1988 section 18 and in the European Communities, see Case 158/86 *Warner Bros* [1988] ECR 2605 and the proposed directive on rental and distribution rights in copyright, Chapters 6.4 and 6.5, respectively, below.

276 The *House Report*, at 169 reproduced in 4 *Nimmer on Copyright*, App. 4, at 4–144; 17 USC §602, at 116.

277 *Universal Film Manufacturing Co. v Copperman* 218 Fed. 577 (2d Cir. 1914). Contrast the 'literary property' case, *Capital Records Inc. v Mercury Records Corporation* 221 F. 2d 657 (2d Cir. 1955), Learned Hand J dissenting; itself inconsistent with *RCA Manufacturing Company Inc. v Whiteman et al.* 114 F. 2d 86 (2d Cir. 1940) *cert. dend* 61 S. Ct 393. See also 2 *Nimmer on Copyright*, at §4.06[B].

But exercise of the performing right by one or by many purchasers of positive [copies] would be entirely consistent with the Nordisk company's common-law property in the play itself. The attempt, however, to annex a condition as to the use of the [copies] after it was absolutely sold, was vain. Such conditions cannot be made to accompany an article throughout its changes of ownership.[278]

Second: '. . . neither [Nordisk] nor its assigns [Universal] as the owner of statutory copyright in this country could repudiate the license it had given before copyright to the purchaser of the film in England. . . .'[279]

Copperman could be taken as authority for the proposition that the US doctrine of 'first sale' applies equally to sales first made outside the United States as well as within. There are, however, a number of difficulties with the case. Judge Ward did not address the implications of denying statutory protection in the United States because of a purchase in the United Kingdom. Instead, Copperman had been given a licence when he bought the film print in the United Kingdom and it was too late in the day to repudiate it.

The second point in his Honour's reasoning may be somewhat inconsistent with the first, since, if the right be exhausted, it may seem strange to refer to a licence at all. But, the point cannot be taken too far since there is more than some ambiguity about the effect of conditions imposed on a purchaser in a foreign market of an article protected in the United States by an intellectual property right.[280] Judge Ward was presumably strongly influenced by the fact that Copperman had actually checked to see whether a copyright was registered and had no notice of any restraint when he bought the print at a time when it was not subject to copyright claims in either country. The case is further complicated by the uncertain nature of an owner's powers over 'literary property', that is, unpublished copyright in the United States.[281] Moreover, if Judge Ward held that the right to perform the work publicly was exhausted on the first sale, that approach has not found favour in subsequent cases even in purely domestic trade.[282]

Although the *Sebastian* case is consistent with a broad reading of *Copperman, Copperman* itself has not played a part in any of the cases

---

278   218 Fed. 577, at 579; the Supreme Court authorities cited were *Bobbs-Merrill Co. v Straus* 210 US 339 (1908) from Note 288, below and *Dr Miles Medical Co. v John D. Park & Sons Co.* 220 US 373 (1911), Chapter 3, Note 185, above.

279   *Ibid.* at 580.

280   For example in patents, in *Holiday v Mattheson* 24 Fed. 185 (SDNY 1885), the condition was said to take effect under the patent. Subseqently in domestic trade such a condition could only operate in contract, see *Keeler v Standard Folding Bed Co.* 157 US 659 (1894); but there is also the uncertain effect of *Boesch v Gräff* 133 US 697 (1890). See Chapter 3.3.

281   Contrast *RCA Manufacturing Company Inc. v Whiteman et al.* 114 F. 2d 86 (2d Cir. 1940) *cert. dend* 61 S. Ct 393 and *Capital Records Inc. v Mercury Records Corporation* 221 F. 2d 657 (2d Cir. 1955). See also 2 *Nimmer on Copyright*, at §4.06[B].

282   See for example *Red Baron-Franklin Park Inc. v Taito Corp.* 883 F. 2d 275 (4th Cir. 1989), text from Note 426 below, and the decisions there cited. It has been suggested that Judge Ward's ruling was a factual finding of the scope of the licence rather than a legal conclusion based on sale: 2 *Nimmer on Copyright*, at §8.12[D], Note 120.

interpreting section 602(a).[283] *Copperman* also did not involve consideration of a statutory power to control imports. If nothing else, *Copperman* shows the potential of the 'first sale' doctrine in copyright to affect the outcome of copyright owners' attempts to use copyright in blocking parallel imports even if the statutory adoption of the doctrine arguably did not embrace the distribution right.

4.3.3 The first sale doctrine

In the *Sebastian* case, the Third Circuit relied on the history and philosophy of the 'first sale' doctrine, in addition to section 109(a)'s wording, to conclude that the 'first sale' doctrine limited the right to bar imports provided by section 602(a) after admitting that the express wording of the provisions did not permit definite conclusions.[284] Accordingly, the Third Circuit appears to support a theory of international exhaustion as a result of its understanding of the history and philosophy of the 'first sale' doctrine. Conversely, the Australian High Court found support for adopting the principle of territoriality, and so rejecting international exhaustion arguments, partly in the 'first sale' doctrine as expounded in the United States.[285] As in patents, some consideration of the doctrine is necessary.[286]

Neither case reviews the development of the 'first sale' doctrine exhaustively. Such a review, however, does not afford a conclusive answer because, apart from the problematic ruling in *Copperman*, the 'first sale' doctrine really only arose in the context of domestic sales prior to the *Scorpio* case. A review of the 'first sale' doctrine shows that the contradictory approaches of the *Sebastian* and *Time-Life* cases results from different judicial policies rather than different legal provisions.

In patents, notwithstanding the 'false' start of the distinction between the right to use and the rights to make and sell, the courts repeatedly justified the exhaustion theory on economic grounds. The patented article escaped the patentee's monopoly because the patentee had received the special compensation intended by Congress.[287]

Copyright law too explained the 'first sale' doctrine on economic grounds and, like patents, first developed a distinction between ownership of copyright and ownership of the article embodying the copyright. On this

---

283 See *Sebastian International Inc. v Consumer Contacts (PTY) Ltd* 847 F. 2d 1093 (3d Cir. 1988) *revg* 664 F. Supp. 909 (DNJ 1987), text from Note 408 below.

284 *Ibid.*

285 The *Time-Life* case (1977) 138 CLR 534, at 544 *per* Gibbs J, 553 *per* Stephen J. Note also the UK Court of Appeal's approval of the overall conclusion reached in the *Time-Life* case: the *Harlequin* case [1980] FSR 362, at 366 *per* Templeman LJ. See section 4.2.2(c), above.

286 See generally, 2 *Nimmer on Copyright*, at §8.12; J. M. Kernochan, 'The US' First Sale Doctrine', paper delivered at Association Litteraire et Artistique Internationale, Study Session, 5–8 October 1988, Munich; Colby, 'The First Sale Doctrine – The Defence that Never Was?', 32 J. Copr. Soc'y 77 (1984).

287 Chapter 3.3.2 above.

distinction, copyright law used three arguments to build the 'first sale' doctrine. One argument was the economic theory; the second, reliance on the policy against restraints on alienation; and third, the courts brought to bear their antagonism to monopolies and attempts to perpetuate them. It was not always clear which, if any, was crucial.

(a)   *Before statutory adoption of the 'first sale' doctrine*

The leading case on the 'first sale' doctrine is the Supreme Court's ruling in the *Straus* case.[288] Bobbs-Merrill was a publisher owning copyright in a book the retail price of which it was trying to fix at one dollar. It purported to do this by printing a notice on the book's title page: 'The price of this book at retail is One Dollar net. No dealer is licensed to sell it at a less price, and a sale at a less price will be treated as an infringement of the copyright.' Straus was selling copies of the book for 89¢ each. Both he and the wholesaler whom he bought the copies from knew the book was subject to copyright and that Bobbs-Merrill sought to fix the retail price at one dollar. The wholesaler, apparently, had bought some of the copies directly from Bobbs-Merrill but was not under a positive contractual obligation to enforce the price stipulation.

Bobbs-Merrill did not challenge the validity of the 'first sale' doctrine. Instead, it argued that the notice restricting price acted to qualify the title transferred to the buyer and so the 'first sale' doctrine did not apply because title to the copies in question had not been transferred absolutely. Hence, Bobbs-Merrill argued, Straus was in the position of a licensee who, by disregarding the terms of his licence, became an infringer.

The argument was rejected. Day J first distinguished the series of patent cases which shortly after led to the short-lived ruling in the *Dick* case on the grounds of the differences between patents and copyright.[289] Then, his Honour ruled:

> In our view the copyright statutes, while protecting the owner of the copyright in his right to multiply and sell his production, do not create the right to impose, by notice, such as is disclosed in this case, a limitation at which the book shall be sold at retail by future purchasers, with whom there is no privity of contract. This conclusion is reached in view of the language of the statute, read in the light of its main purpose to secure the right of multiplying copies of the work, a right which is the special creation of the statute. True, the statute also secured, to make this right of multiplication effectual, the sole right to vend copies of the book, the production of the author's thought and conception. The owner of the copyright in this case did sell copies of the book in quantities and at a price satisfactory to it. It has exercised the right to vend. What the complainant

---

288   *Bobbs-Merrill Co. v Straus* 210 US 339 (1908) *affg* 147 Fed. 15 (2d Cir. 1906). For an explanation of the derivation of the right to 'multiply copies', see Colby, 'The First Sale Doctrine – The Defence that Never Was?', at 92 to 93. For an earlier defeat involving almost the same facts, see *Bobbs-Merrill Co. v Snellenburg* 131 Fed. 530 (ED Pa. 1904).
289   *Ibid*. at 345. For the *Dick* case, see Chapter 3, from Note 169.

contends for embraces not only the right to sell copies, but to qualify the title of a future purchaser by reservation of a right to have the remedies of the statute against an infringer because of the printed notice of its purpose so to do unless the purchaser sells at a price fixed in the notice. To add to the right of exclusive sale the authority to control all future retail sales, by a notice that all future retail sales must be made at a fixed sum, would give a right not included in the terms of the statute, and, in our view, extend its operation, by construction, beyond its meaning, when interpreted with a view to ascertaining the legislative intent in its enactment.[290]

Bobbs-Merrill failed because it had sold the copies in question and could not rely on contract to enforce its price clause against Straus. There being no contractual relation, the court did not need to determine the validity of any contractual clause.

In Day J's view, the notice restricting price was an ineffective attempt to extend the statutory monopoly beyond what the legislature had intended. The legislature's main purpose was 'to secure the right of multiplying copies' to the copyright owner. The sole right of vending was just a corollary of the right of multiplying necessary to ensure that the right of multiplying was effective. That right became exhausted once Bobbs-Merrill sold those copies in quantity at a price satisfactory to it. Thereby, it gained any special remuneration which was the purpose of conferring copyright. There is also a suggestion of the policy of commercial convenience underlying the rule against restraints on alienation in the alarm about allowing the copyright owner to control all future retail sales.[291]

The following year, Congress incorporated the 'first sale' doctrine into the copyright legislation.[292] The *Straus* case, however, could be read as leaving open a number of issues – the contractual validity of such restrictions; what of attempts to restrict the copyright on matters other than resale prices, long subjected to judicial disapproval;[293] how important was the satisfactory nature of the price received.

---

290 *Ibid.* at 350 to 351. Compare *Bauer v O'Donnell* 229 US 1 (1913) subsequently applying the same rule to patents, see Chapter 3.3.3(a) above. *Straus* is sometimes seen simply a ruling that copyright law does not justify the anti-trust breach involved in resale price maintenance: for example *Waltham Watch Co. v Keene* 202 Fed. 225 (SDNY 1913) nonetheless deriving in both patent and copyright law a general policy against post-sales restraints, *RCA Manufacturing Company Inc. v Whiteman* 114 F. 2d 86 (2d Cir. 1940).
291 This is even more explicit in Judge Holland's decision in the *Snellenburg* case 131 Fed. 530, at 533 (ED Pa. 1904).
292 17 USC §27:

> The copyright is distinct from the property in the material object copyrighted, and the sale or conveyance, by gift or otherwise, of the material object shall not of itself constitute a transfer of the copyright, nor shall the assignment of the copyright constitute a transfer of the title to the material object; *but nothing in this title shall be deemed to forbid, prevent or restrict the transfer of any copy of a copyrighted work the possession of which has been lawfully obtained.*

> Reproduced from 4 *Nimmer on Copyright*, App. G. (*Emphasis added*).

The provision also formally sanctioned the distinction between the copyright and the article it was embodied in, now found in 17 USC §202.
293 For example, five years later the Supreme Court condemned a horizontal agreement between major publishers to enforce resale price maintenance, see *Straus v American Publishing Association* 231 US 222 (1913).

Prior to the *Straus* case, the *Henry Bill* case had allowed the copyright owner, 'HBP', to stop a bookseller selling its books in contravention of a stipulation that they only be sold to consumers by subscription.[294] Judge Hammond appeared to base his decision on the grounds of a transfer of less than absolute title to the copy and the copyright owner's right to receive value for the use of its work in addition to the murky circumstances by which the defendant came into possession of the copy.

HBP held copyright in a book which it sold only by subscription directly to the public. HBP solicited orders through agents operating in exclusive territories. The canvassing agents merely supplied the subscribers' orders to HBP and delivered the ordered books to the subscribers on HBP's behalf. The contracts of sale were always between HBP and the subscribing purchaser. On receipt of a subscription, HBP supplied copies to an agent for delivery to the specified subscriber. At no stage did the agent ever own the copies which it received from HBP to deliver to a subscriber. Smythe was a bookseller who had placed six copies of HBP's book on sale in his bookshop. The copies had been obtained from the canvassing agent in another district who had 'surreptitiously' diverted them from their designated subscribers. When the agent for Smythe's district complained, HBP successfully sought injunctions for infringement of its copyright. HBP was unable to prove positively that Smythe knew the book was only available for sale by subscription and Smythe had said he believed it could be got for retail sale. However, HBP had made it widely known through advertising that the book would only be available for sale through subscription and HBP had rigidly adhered to that policy. So, Judge Hammond seems to have inclined to the view that, if Smythe did not know about the restriction, he should have.

In granting the injunction, Judge Hammond seems to have regarded Smythe as a licensee acting in breach of a restriction placed in his licence. The crucial point seems to have been that the agents who passed on the books to Smythe never themselves had title to the copies.[295]

Subsequent cases, although endorsing Judge Hammond's approach and the distinction between *Henry Bill* and the *Clements* and *Baldwin* cases, begin to suggest a hardening of attitudes. In *Maynard, Merrill,* the publisher Maynard, Merrill stored unbound, printed pages of its works at its bookbinders, Alexander's, which sometimes bound up lots of Maynard, Merrill's books in anticipation of orders. There was a fire at Alexander's which was thought to have reduced Maynard, Merrill's stocks to waste. Thinking its stocks were unrecoverable, Maynard, Merrill authorised Alexander's to sell them off. Alexander's sold the materials to Fitzgerald. Fitzgerald, in turn, sold to some wastepaper dealers on condition that they only use the paper for waste paper

---

294 *Henry Bill Publishing Co. v Smythe* 27 Fed. 914 (CC SD Oh. 1886).
295 Contrast the copyright owners' failures in similar schemes where the agents actually acquired title to the copies before distributing them to subscribers: *Clements v Estes* 22 Fed. 899 (CC DMass. 1885); *Baldwin v Baird* 25 Fed. 293.

purposes. Harrison came into possession of undamaged copies, or sheets, which he bound together and was selling to the public. He denied having any knowledge of any conditions on the use which the 'wastepaper' stocks could be put to. Maynard, Merrill sued him for copyright infringement and obtained a preliminary injunction. Harrison successfully appealed. Having sold the copies outright, even with an agreement restricting their subsequent use, copyright was exhausted:

> But the right to restrain the sale of a particular copy of the book by virtue of the copyright statutes has gone when the owner of the copyright and of that copy has parted with his title to it, and has conferred an absolute title to the copy upon a purchaser, although with an agreement for a restricted use. The exclusive right to vend the particular copy no longer remains in the owner of the copyright by the copyright statutes. The new purchaser cannot reprint the copy. He cannot print or publish a new edition of the book; but, the copy having been absolutely sold to him, the ordinary incidents of ownership in personal property, among which is the right of alienation, attach to it. If he has agreed that he will not sell it for certain purposes or to certain persons, and violates his agreement, and sells to an innocent purchaser, he can be punished for his violation of his agreement; but neither is guilty, under the copyright statutes of an infringement.[296]

Of interest is the type of 'sale' which will cause this exhaustion of the power to control sale. It will suffice if the buyer gets an 'absolute title to the copy . . . although with an agreement for a restricted use'. In the context of Judge Hammond's opinion in the *Henry Bill* case, Judge Shipman was probably focusing on the effect of transferring title to the copy. If so and the copyright owner confers title on the recipient of the copy, the recipient may confer full and free title in the copy on any other good faith purchaser. However, the copyright owner does not appear to have imposed the restriction in the *Maynard, Merrill* case. The express condition was imposed by Fitzgerald, somewhat further down the distribution chain. Maynard, Merrill, not realising the true state of affairs, seems simply to have sold the sheets without condition.

The Seventh Circuit applied *Maynard, Merrill* in *Doan*.[297] Doan bought second-hand copies of American Book Co.'s books, repaired them and was reselling them. The acts of repair included trimming and cleaning pages, recovering and rebinding the copies. American Book Co. sued him for copyright infringement and unfair competition. Liability in copyright was avoided because American Book Co. had itself sold the books and this sale carried with it the right of alienation. Following the *Maynard, Merrill* case, the right of alienation included the right to repair and renew.[298] To negate any unfair competition, however, Doan was enjoined to include a notice on each copy stating that he had repaired it.[299]

---

[296] *Harrison v Maynard, Merrill & Co.* 61 Fed. 689, at 691 *per* Shipman J (2d Cir. 1890).
[297] *Doan v American Book Co.* 105 Fed. 772 (7th Cir. 1901).
[298] *Ibid.* at 776 to 777 *per* Circuit Judge Jenkins.
[299] *Ibid.* at 778. Circuit Judge Woods concurred in the copyright result only, considering it obvious that Doan was selling second-hand copies. Hence, there was no risk of unfair competition.

The power to rebind and resell seems to have been carried further by the Second Circuit in *Kipling*.[300] Putnam bought from Kipling's authorised publisher unbound printed sheets of Kipling's copyright works. Apparently, Kipling received a royalty of 10 per cent on this sale to Putnam. Putnam bound these together with some of Kipling's public domain works and materials produced by another author. It was selling the resulting volumes to the public when Kipling sued for copyright infringement. Judge Coxe, for the court, found that copyright was not infringed by a purchaser binding and reselling the copies in this way. His Honour then discussed whether Kipling's claim that his publishers were not authorised to sell unbound sheets defeated Putnam's right to deal with the copies as they pleased:

> It is not quite apparent how the intent or purpose of the copyright act can be limited by a private agreement between the author and his publisher. There is nothing in the law, surely, which prohibits the owner of a copyright from selling unbound books, if he desires to do so, and what he may do, his agent or his licensee may do also. If Mr Kipling had personally sold the unbound volumes to defendants it probably would not be contended that he could recover damages under the statute because they were bound and resold. He stands in no more favourable condition because the sale was conducted by his agents.[301]

His Honour was impressed by the absence of any express stipulation between Kipling and his publisher forbidding such sales. But, if there had been one, it could only take effect in contract, not copyright.

With respect, this seems to go much further than the *Henry Bill* and *Maynard, Merrill* cases since both stressed that the copyright owner's power to control sale under copyright law was not lost unless the selling agent had authority from the copyright owner to make the sale or had, at least, acquired title to the copy in question. On the facts, it may have been possible to infer that Kipling's publisher had authority to transfer title to the unbound copies.[302] But, that was not Judge Coxe's ground for the decision. An alternative explanation may lie in Putnam's presumed lack of knowledge of any restrictions on Kipling's publisher since, in *Henry Bill*, Judge Hammond inclined to protect the copyright owner because Smythe probably should have known HBP would not countenance sales to him. It may be argued that the apparent authority of Kipling's publisher would be much broader than that of HBP's canvassing agent.[303]

---

300   *Kipling v G. P. Putnam's Sons et al.* 120 Fed. 631 (2d Cir. 1903).
301   *Ibid*. at 634.
302   Relying on the bare fact that Kipling received royalty payments from the sale seems questionable. For acquiescence in the publisher's conduct, it should be at least necessary to show that Kipling knew, or had notice of, what the payment was for.
303   Both these grounds are distinctions accepted in the difficult case, *National Geographic Society v Classified Geographic Inc.* 27 F. Supp. 655 (DMass. 1939). Plaintiff successfully sued defendant in copyright for making compilations from plaintiff's magazines which defendant resold as separate volumes. District Judge Brewster considered that *Kipling's* case depended on the copyright proprietor's consent to the compilation. Moreover, the defendant at bar had approached plaintiff for its permission and had been refused. 27 F. Supp. at 660.

Hence, the *Kipling* case showed a significant hardening from the more sympathetic approach taken by Judge Hammond to copyright owners' attempts to control subsequent dealings in copies of their work.

In *Snellenburg*, as already mentioned, Judge Holland refused to treat a notice purporting to fix a retail price as anything other than transfer of 'absolute title to the copy'.[304]

(b) *Statutory adoption*

After the statutory adoption of the 'first sale' doctrine, the courts generally continued to uphold a purchaser's right to rebind and resell copies once they had initially been sold.[305] Similarly, in *Scarves by Vera*, Judge Cashin refused to stop the defendant from making and selling handbags from the plaintiff's scarves and towels on the basis of copyright infringement. The defendant knew of the plaintiff's objections. However, it had lawfully bought the products on the market without any restrictions on its title. To ensure there was no unfair competition, the defendant was, however, required to adopt a form of labelling dictated by the court designed to clarify the manufacturing source of the bags.[306]

In addition to the civil action, the 'first sale' doctrine has fallen for consideration in criminal cases as copyright infringement also gives rise to liability as a misdemeanour.[307] In a criminal action, the prosecution must prove five elements beyond a reasonable doubt: first, infringement of a copyright; second, in a work the relevant copies of which had not been the subject of a 'first sale'; third, done wilfully; fourth, with knowledge that the copy has not been the subject of a 'first sale'; and fifth, for profit.[308]

304　*Bobbs-Merrill Co. v Snellenburg* 131 Fed. 530 (ED Pa. 1904).
305　*Ginn & Co. v Appollo Pub. Co.* 215 Fed. 772; and *Fawcett Publications Inc. v Elliot Publishing Co. Inc.* 46 F. Supp. 717 (SDNY 1942) upholding Elliot's right to sell Fawcett's magazines in Elliot's own covers and containing the first use of the words 'first sale':

> It is conceded here that the defendant has not multiplied copies but merely resold the plaintiff's under a different cover. The exclusive right to vend is limited. It is confined to the first sale of any one copy and exerts no restriction on the future sale of that copy. The defendant is not charged with copying, reprinting or rearranging the copyrighted material of the plaintiff or any of its component parts nor has it removed the plaintiff's copyright notice.
>
> 46 F. Supp. 717, at 718 (citations omitted).

See also *Lantern Press Inc. v American Publishers Co.* 419 F. Supp. 1267 (EDNY 1976) where defendant was allowed to continue selling plaintiff's paperback copies, rebound as hardbacks, for a price below the plaintiff's authorised hardback publisher. But note, *Bureau of National Literature v Sells* 211 Fed. 379 (WD Wash. 1914) in which selling second-hand books as new constituted unfair competition, not copyright infringement; and *National Geographic Society v Classified Geographic Inc.* 27 F. Supp. 655 (D. Mass. 1939), above at Note 303.
306　*Scarves by Vera Inc. v American Handbags Inc.* 188 F. Supp. 255 (SDNY 1960).
307　'Any person who wilfully and for profit shall infringe any copyright secured by this title . . . shall be deemed guilty of a misdemeanour . . .': 17 USC §104 (1948).
308　*US v Atherton* 561 F. 2d 747, at 749 (9th Cir. 1977).

The criminal actions are complicated somewhat by the prosecution's burden of positively proving each element beyond a reasonable doubt.[309] But, they shed further light on what will amount to a valid reservation of title rather than a mere restriction on use and the extent to which the copyright owner must receive value for the 'first sale'.

Compared to the subsequent decisions in the *Hampton, Wise, Drebin* and *Atherton* cases, some aspects of the *Wells* case seem controversial.[310] Tobin owned copyright in aerial survey maps. He licensed 107 of his customers to reproduce his maps for their own use. Each customer was allowed to use the negatives Tobin supplied, and the resulting maps, 'for such time as it deems fit'. The licences further provided that the licensee received '[n]o right of sale or transfer of either this license, negative or maps reproduced therefrom . . . except as to the foregoing license'. The rights to use or reproduce, or authorise others to use or reproduce, the maps was expressly reserved to Tobin. Wells was not one of Tobin's customers, but he was found selling copies of Tobin's maps without Tobin's permission. The prosecution failed to disprove a 'first sale' of the relevant copies beyond reasonable doubt. Instead, it proved that Tobin had not made the copies sold by Wells, but it was possible the copies were made by Tobin's licensees.

To meet this possibility, the prosecution argued that anyone who sold copies made by a lawful, but restricted, licensee infringed the copyright where the copyright owner had reserved the sole right of selling or transferring title to copies produced under the licence. Wells defended by arguing that a transfer of copies made and belonging to a lawful licensee ended the copyright owner's power to control distribution of those copies.

In Judge Ingraham's opinion, the crucial question was whether Tobin had retained title to the copies in issue since the 'first sale' doctrine turned on this issue. His Honour found that the licensees owned title to the copies on either of two grounds. Either the licensees owned the copies they produced by presumption of law from Tobin's failure expressly to reserve title to each copy. Alternatively, Tobin had actually sold title in the copies to the licensees. His Honour reasoned from the failure expressly to reserve title as follows:

> A copyright license is a grant of the right to make, use, or sell the copyrighted work; it is an assignment of rights less in degree than the copyright itself. In the present case the right to *reproduce* the copyrighted work for his own use has been granted and sold to the licensee. The publishing of copies under that

---

309 See now 17 USC §109(c) (1988). Whether the onus of disproving a 'first sale' falls on the plaintiff in civil cases or is an affirmative defence seems still undecided: see *American International Pictures Inc. v Foreman* 576 F. 2d 661, at 663 (5th Cir. 1978) and the *House Report* at 17 USC 109(c) (1988), at 39.

310 *US v Wells* 176 F. Supp. 630 (SD Tex. 1959), *US v Wise* 550 F. 2d 1180 (9th Cir. 1977), *US v Drebin* 557 F. 2d 1316 (9th Cir. 1977), *US v Atherton* 561 F. 2d 747 (9th Cir. 1977), *US v Sachs* 801 F. 2d 839 (6th Cir. 1986). See also *US v Bily* 406 F. Supp. 726 (ED Pa. 1975). To the extent that *Atherton* ruled that 'interstate transportation' of infringing (but genuine) copies was a criminal offence, it has been disapproved: *Dowling v US* 473 US 207, 87 L. Ed. 2d 152 (1984).

license is lawful because the licensee is exercising a property right that has been granted to him.[311] (*Emphasis added*)

As the licensee owned the right to *publish*, Judge Ingraham refused to assume that the licensee did not own the copies which it produced under its licence:

> Such a limitation on the grant of a right cannot be presumed and must appear on the face of the grant itself. Since the Tobin license does not specify that all copies published thereunder remain the property of the copyright proprietor, it follows that title to all copies published under the license belongs to the licensee and not to the copyright proprietor.[312]

Alternatively, Judge Ingraham thought Tobin may have sold his rights in the negatives and maps because he had granted a right to use the negatives and maps indefinitely.[313]

Accordingly, Judge Ingraham concluded:

> If the copy was lawfully published by and belongs to a licensee, the copyright proprietor no longer has an exclusive right to vend it, and such a copy can hardly be deemed piratical. Furthermore, it can be argued that the copyright proprietor exhausted his right to vend such copies by granting and selling to the licensee the right to publish them. Thus he would have had the opportunity to exercise one time his exclusive right to vend over such copies by the act of granting the license and receiving a consideration therefor.[314]

Judge Ingraham's treatment seems inconsistent with the terms of the licence. His Honour's emphasis on the mere fact of ownership seems consistent with the approach in *Maynard, Merrill,* but contrasts with the *dicta* in the later *Hampton* case where the Ninth Circuit ruled that even if the instant agreement was an assignment of rights, the assignment was for a limited purpose – non-theatrical exhibitions – and Kodascope could not grant rights inconsistent with that limitation.[315] Judge Ingraham's references to rights of reproduction and rights of publishing introduce considerable ambiguity, especially as it is not entirely clear what is meant by the term 'publish'. From the context, it seems to mean more than a right to make and use which is all the terms of the agreement seemed to contemplate.

The implication Judge Ingraham refused to draw is in marked contrast to that rejected in the *Time-Life* case. In *Time-Life,* the Australian High Court refused to imply a licence to use. In contrast, the implication refused in *Wells* meant that there were no restrictions on use by a purchaser. Hence, the terms of Judge Ingraham's opinion, especially his Honour's emphatic

---

311 *Ibid.* at 634.
312 *Ibid.*
313 *Ibid.*
314 *Ibid.* at 635. Contrast the result when a *civil* action was brought against the *licensee*: *Creative Arts Inc. v Abady & Sultan Inc.* 134 USPQ 388 (SD Fla. 1961), the defendants were the exclusive licensees to sell the plaintiff's artistic works in several states excluding Florida. Their sales in Florida constituted infringement.
315 See below from Note 316.

requirement of an express reservation of title, suggest a strong policy preference against any restrictions on dealings with material, commercial objects. Put baldly, his Honour ruled that the grant of a right to make and use carried with it the right to sell unless expressly denied.

Hampton, a civil action, was the first of a number of cases dealing with cinematograph films; it recalled the approach in *Henry Bill* and contrasts to that in *Kipling* and *Wells.*[316] Paramount's predecessor in title had licensed Kodascope to make prints of a silent movie, The Covered Wagon, for non-theatrical exhibitions. Kodascope sold a print to Hampton who was showing it to the public. The Ninth Circuit found that Paramount, the copyright owner, had successfully reserved title in the contentious print instead of merely imposing restrictions on its use. Hence, the 'first sale' doctrine did not protect Hampton's use of the copy for theatrical purposes.

Hampton's argument that Kodascope's licence was in substance an assignment of the right to exhibit the film was rebutted because the agreement clearly stated it was a licence and, furthermore, the parties' intention was only to allow Kodascope to make prints of the film for licensing to 'non-theatrical' users. It was never intended to allow Kodascope to sell the prints it produced. Therefore, Hampton could not get unrestricted title to use the copies from Kodascope because Kodascope did not have unrestricted title itself.[317] Judge Hanley found further reason to deny Hampton relief because Hampton had not made all reasonable inquiries to check Kodascope's title to pass on the rights it claimed.[318] Arguably, since Hampton was exhibiting the film in public, it would now be considered that the 'first sale' doctrine did not affect the right of public performance.[319]

However, *Independent News,* another rebinding case, rejected arguments based on the transfer of less than 'absolute title' to the copy and the inadequacy of the payment received by the copyright owner.[320] Independent News published, and owned copyright in, the Superman comics. It sold them to wholesalers on condition that they were offered to retailers for sale only during a specified period. At the end of that period, the retailers were required to return all unsold copies to the wholesaler. The wholesaler was then obliged to mutilate the copy but was permitted to sell it as waste paper. Mutilating the copies merely took the form of removing the covers. These

---

316　*Hampton v Paramount Pictures Corporation* 279 F. 2d 100 (9th Cir. 1960) *cert. dend* 364 US 882.

317　*Ibid.* at 103. The licence was for an unlimited term; the consideration was a flat lump sum; there was no obligation to return outstanding prints or negatives; Kodascope could adapt the film in whatever way it liked and Kodascope was granted exclusive territorial rights over Paramount's whole territory. *Hampton* was distinguished from the much earlier *Copperman* case because in *Hampton* the copyright owner had not (1) sold a copy of the copyright work, or (2) authorised the actual seller, Kodascope, to make such sales.

318　*Ibid.* at 104 to 105.

319　*Red Baron-Franklin Park Inc. v Taito Corp.* 883 F. 2d 275 (4th Cir. 1989) and the decisions there cited, see section 4.3.4 below.

320　*Independent News Co. Inc. v Williams* 293 F. 2d 510 (3d Cir. 1961), the second case relied on by Stephen J in the *Time-Life* case.

were returned to Independent News to gain the credit. Bearing in mind the *Straus* case, Independent News' contracts with its wholesalers bound the wholesalers to obtain undertakings from purchasers that the purchaser would only use the paper as waste paper. But, in fact, the wholesalers never obtained such undertakings. Both the retailer and the wholesaler received full credit for the returns. Williams bought mutilated copies from wastepaper merchants, covered them with his own covers and then sold them. He did not know that the materials he bought were restricted to use only as waste paper.

Independent News unsuccessfully sued him for conversion, unfair competition and infringement of its copyright and trade marks. It argued that it had not received the full price for the recovered copies, they had been sold as waste paper not as literary works and so the 'first sale' doctrine did not apply.

The court rejected this argument on the authority of the *Maynard, Merrill* case. Williams' position was even stronger since the wastepaper sellers were not themselves subject to a contractual restriction. Judge McLaughlin did not directly address the economic argument advanced by Independent News. Instead, his Honour concentrated on the fact that Independent News had transferred ownership of the copies. Transfer of ownership carried with it all the normal incidents of title:

> Under [section 27], once there is lawful ownership transferred to a first purchaser, the copyright holder's power of control in the sale of the copy ceases. This aptly fits the present situation.
>
> . . .
>
> These provisions are considered to mean that the copyright proprietor is not empowered, merely by virtue of his copyright, to control the sales of published copies after they have come into the lawful ownership of the first purchaser. Whenever the copyright proprietor parts with title to a particular copy, the incident of his statutory monopoly having been exhausted by the exercise of the power of sale, is extinguished; the ordinary incidents of alienation belonging alike to all property attach to the material object in the hands of the new owner; and that copy is no longer under the copyright law insofar as the purchaser's right is concerned.[321]

Judge McLaughlin considered that Independent News had a legitimate interest to protect, but also the power to protect it. It had not, however, taken appropriate steps for its own protection. It could have destroyed the copies. Instead, it had chosen to sell them as waste paper.

The *Platt & Munck* case revived the argument about the economic function of copyright.[322] It also examined the earlier references to lawful ownership in the light of section 27's wording applying the 'first sale' doctrine to copies 'the *possession* of which has been lawfully obtained'. (*Emphasis added*)

---

321 *Ibid*. at 517 citing *US v Wells* 176 F. Supp. 630, at 633 to 634 (SD Tex. 1959) and Horace G. Ball, *The Law of Copyright and Literary Property*, 1944 at 437 and onward.
322 *Platt & Munck Co. Inc. v Republic Graphics Inc.* 315 F. 2d 847 (2d Cir. 1963) discussed in 2 *Nimmer on Copyright*, at 8-123, 8-124-7. Contrast 58/80 *Dansk Supermarked* [1981] ECR 187, see Chapter 6.3.1 below.

Platt & Munck contracted the manufacture of its copyright jigsaw puzzles and books to Republic. After their manufacture, it refused to accept delivery or pay for them because of alleged quality shortcomings. Republic then sold the products off to various distributors which were selling them to the public. When Platt & Munck sued Republic and the distributors for copyright infringement, Republic claimed its actions were justified under a manufacturer's lien granted by state law and its *lawful* possession of the copies in accordance with section 27.

Judge Friendly rejected the literal interpretation of section 27 proposed by Republic as inconsistent with the section's history and interpretation:

> Such a literal reading of the 'but nothing' clause is unacceptable. If lawful possession by another sufficed to deprive the copyright proprietor of his right to control the transfer of the copyrighted objects, any bailee of such objects could sell them without infringing the copyright, whatever his liability for conversion might be. In view of the necessary role played by manufacturers, shippers and others in producing and distributing copies of copyrighted works, the result in many cases would be that a copyright proprietor could not present his work to the public without risking the loss of part of his copyright protection. True, only the right to vend is involved; the copyright proprietor could still prevent possessors and even owners of the objects from making copies of them. *** But 'the author is just as much injured by being deprived of the price of a genuine copy as by having a piratical copy substituted for it.' *** A literal reading of the clause would mean, moreover, that an innocent purchaser of a copy from a conceded pirate would be free to resell it without liability for infringement. Yet the cases to the contrary are legion.[323]

Citing the House Report on the 1909 Act, Judge Friendly concluded that Congress had 'not intended to change in any way' the existing law. Congress had been concerned about the undesirability of allowing copyright owners to control dealings in copyright objects once the copyright owner had first sold it.[324] Accordingly, in his Honour's opinion, transfer of possession only, without ownership, did not deprive the copyright owner of its right to control the first sale of copies and the *Independent News* case showed that 'lawful ownership' in the copyright article must have been 'transferred to a first purchaser'. The *Straus* case further indicated that the person acquiring title must have paid 'a satisfactory price for it'.[325]

But, the 'first sale' doctrine did not require a voluntary first sale by the copyright owner in all cases:

> . . . the 'first sale' which terminates the exclusive right to vend patented or copyrighted objects need not be a truly voluntary one, but can consist of some reasonable and recognized form of compulsory transfer, such as a judicial sale or a court-compelled assignment. In such cases the ultimate question embodied in the 'first sale' doctrine – 'whether or not there has been such a disposition of

---

323 *Ibid.* at 851.
324 *Ibid.* at 852 referring to House Report No. 2222, 60th Cong. 2d Sess. See 4 *Nimmer on Copyright*, App. 13, App. 13-25 under section 41, the number of 17 USC §27 prior to the Copyright Act of 1909's codification as part of the United States Code in 1948.
325 *Ibid.*

the article that it may fairly be said that the patentee [or copyright proprietor] has received his reward for the use of the article,' *** – is answered in the affirmative, since the proprietor or patentee has received from his creditor some value for which the copyrighted or patented article is now demanded unless the debt is paid.[326]

Although state law permitted the manufacturer to exercise its lien without prior adjudication, federal law would compel prior adjudication where the subject-matter was a federally created right, copyright.[327] Accordingly, if the manufacturer showed that the copyright owner had unjustifiably refused to pay the price agreed for the work done, the court would infer that the copyright owner had received value for the use of its copyright and, presumably, title would pass.

Judge Friendly sought to balance the needs of copyright owners against those of persons dealing commercially with articles embodying copyright material. In his Honour's opinion, the economic function of copyright held the key. Copyright owners would be deprived of modern methods of mass production and distribution if mere bailees could defeat the right of first putting copies into circulation. The copyright owner was just as much injured by losing 'the price of a genuine copy as by having a piratical copy substituted for it'. On the other hand, the community could not be subjected unreasonably to the copyright owner's monopoly. Once the copyright owner received value for the copy, 'a satisfactory price', it was freed from the monopoly. The copyright monopoly over sale was exhausted.

If Republic proved that Platt & Munck had refused to honour the contract without justification, Republic could sell off the copies without Platt & Munck's permission to recover the value of the work done.[328]

Circuit Judge Freedman, acting by designation, applied Judge Friendly's economic function approach to deny relief in *Burke & Van Heusen*. Burke & Van Heusen owned copyright in various musical works. It licensed Beecham Products to incorporate the works in records restricted for sale packaged with one of Beecham's shampoo products. Beecham sold the package to Arrow Drug which, knowing of the restriction on Beecham's right to use the copyright, separated the two products and sold them individually. Arrow Drug obtained summary dismissal of the resulting infringement action. The authorised sale of copies embodying the copyright work triggered the application of the 'first sale' doctrine because the copyright owner received the price it had demanded for use of its right and so the economic function of copyright was served. As in the *Scarves by Vera* case, the

---

326 *Ibid*. at 854 (citation omitted).
327 *Ibid*. at 855.
328 Although Judge Friendly derived his conclusions as much from patent law as copyright, trade mark law has not conclusively resolved this question, contrast *Monte Carlo Shirt Co. Inc. v Daewoo International (America) Corp.* 548 F. Supp.1063 *vacd* 707 F. 2d 1054 (9th Cir. 1983) to *El Greco Leather Products Co. Inc. v Shoe World Inc.* 599 F. Supp. 1380 (EDNY 1984) *revd* 1 USPQ 2d 1016 (2d Cir. 1986), see Chapter 2.3.4(c) above.

defendant's knowledge of the copyright owner's opposition to its conduct was immaterial.[329]

Subsequently, District Judge Tenney linked the economic function of copyright and the judicial policies against restraints of trade and on alienation.[330] Both Blazon and De Luxe were trade competitors, each making and selling children's hobby horses and ancillary equipment. De Luxe bought one of Blazon's models, painted it over to obscure the copyright notice and affixed its own trade marks to the hobby horse. De Luxe claimed it was using the Blazon product to illustrate how its own would work, having not yet produced units of its product for commercial sale. Among other things, Blazon alleged this infringed copyright in its hobby horse, but Judge Tenney dismissed its claim for a preliminary injunction.

His Honour cited an earlier edition of *Nimmer on Copyright* and the *Burke & Van Heusen* case to explain why the copyright owner needed only a limited right to put copies in public circulation first:

> The statute included the right to vend and publish as a protected right, as a complement to the preservation of the right to copy, since 'it would be anomalous indeed if the copyright owner could prohibit public distribution of his work when this occurred through unauthorized copying but were powerless to prevent the same result if the owner's own copies (or copies authorized by him) were stolen or otherwise wrongfully obtained and thereafter sold or published.'
>
> However, '[t]his rationale becomes inapplicable in the situation where the copyright owner first consents to sale or other disposition of his work. . . . [A]t this point the policy favouring a copyright monopoly for authors gives way to the policy opposing restraints of trade and restraints on alienation.' The same rationale, policy considerations and rule of law apply to the right to publish as well.
>
> Accordingly, once the item has been lawfully obtained, as in the case at bar, the 'first sale' doctrine ... would apply and the proprietor thereafter loses his right to control its subsequent vending and/or publication.[331]

Paula is similar to *Scarves by Vera*, although it applied the *Burke & Van Heusen* and *Blazon* cases. The plaintiff made and sold greeting cards, post cards and stationery on which it had printed its original, copyright designs. The defendant bought the plaintiff's products, lifted the designs from their card backing and applied them to his own ceramic products which he then sold. For each of the plaintiff's designs that he used, he first bought a copy of the copyright work from the plaintiff. Judge Mahon dismissed the plaintiff's copyright infringement action but compelled the defendant to identify the copyright source of the designs on his products.[332]

---

329 *Burke & Van Heusen Inc. v Arrow Drug Inc.* 233 F. Supp. 881 (ED Pa. 1964).
330 *Blazon Inc. v De Luxe Game Corp.* 268 F. Supp. 416 (SDNY 1965).
331 *Ibid.* at 434 (citations omitted). In the last paragraph quoted, Judge Tenney refers to items having been 'lawfully obtained'. However, in the context of the previous and succeeding paragraphs, this does not seem intended to contradict the ruling in the *Platt & Munck* case. The passages from *Nimmer on Copyright* now cite *Blazon* as authority for the propositions.
332 *C.M. Paula Company v Logan* 355 F. Supp. 189 (ND Tex. 1973).

Similarly, the defendant escaped liability for copyright infringement in *Lantern Press*. Lantern Press had granted exclusive hardcover rights to one publisher on condition that the copies be sold for a minimum price of US$4.08. It also granted exclusive paperback rights to Pocket Books with a minimum price condition of US 50¢. American Publishers bought copies of the paperback edition on the open market, rebound them as hardbacks and was selling them retail for US$1.96–2.11. Lantern Press had received the price which it had asked for the paperback copies and title had passed with its authority. Accordingly, a straightforward application of the *Straus* case and the 'enhancement cases' exonerated American Publishers.[333]

The *Wise, Drebin* and *Atherton* cases, like the *Hampton* case, involved the film industry.[334] Like *Wells,* they were also criminal prosecutions, but the decisions show greater affinities for the approach taken in *Hampton*. The respective defendants had all been convicted of multiple counts of criminal infringement by selling and hiring out copies of motion picture films. They appealed, primarily arguing that the prosecution had not disproved the possibility of a 'first sale' beyond reasonable doubt. As in the *Wells* case, the prosecution did not try to prove where the defendants had obtained the copies from. Instead, it relied on evidence that the copyright owners did not sell the copies, they only licensed them for limited purposes for limited periods of time. Factual differences between the cases led to the convictions of Wise and Drebin being upheld but Atherton was acquitted.

Apart from material sold for salvage, the film studios in *Wise* and *Drebin* provided comprehensive evidence that they had not sold copies of the films in question at all. The films were released to exhibitors under licence. The licences only included the right to exhibit the film for a limited period. Most of the licences expressly reserved title in the copy to the film studio. However, this was not fatal in the few cases where title was not expressly reserved because the general tenor of the whole agreement was found to be inconsistent with interpretation as a sale.[335] As the 'first sale' doctrine ended the right to control sale of particular copies only, evidence that the studios had previously sold copies of other films, not the subject of charges, was irrelevant.[336] Accordingly, following the *Hampton* case, such transactions were not 'first sales'. Hence, the exhibition agreements, 'on their face and by their terms' were found to be restricted licences.

However, the prosecution's case broke down for some film titles. In these cases, copies had been subject to network courtesy arrangements, VIP contracts or sales for salvage.

333 *Lantern Press Inc. v American Publishers Co.* 419 F. Supp. 1267 (EDNY 1976).
334 *US v Wise* 550 F. 2d 1180 (9th Cir. 1977); *US v Drebin* 557 F. 2d 1316 (9th Cir. 1977); *US v Atherton* 561 F. 2d 747 (9th Cir. 1977). To the extent that *Atherton* ruled that 'interstate transportation' of infringing (but genuine) copies was a criminal offence, it has been disapproved: *Dowling v US* 473 US 207, 87 L. Ed. 2d 152 (1984).
335 See *Wise* 550 F. 2d at 1190 to 1191; *Drebin* 557 F. 2d 1316, at 1326 *per* Judge Jameson. In the *Drebin* case, most of the licences also expressly forbade copying, duplicating or further lending of the copy licensed by the licensee.
336 *Drebin* 557 F. 2d 1316, at 1326; See also *American International Pictures v Foreman* 576 F. 2d 661, at 665 to 666.

For films shown on television, the network often sought rights to retain a copy for file, reference and audition purposes. If the film studio expressly reserved title to the print and paid the network only for the network's out-of-pocket expenses in producing the print, a 'first sale' had not occurred.[337] VIP contracts involved provision of a print for the personal use of important celebrities. Payment for the cost of making the print would not be fatal if the terms of the licence clearly indicated a loan.[338]

The sale of old, worn-out copies for 'salvage' posed a problem of a different nature. In *Wise,* the defendant relied on the *Maynard, Merrill* and *Independent News* cases to argue that any sale at all activated the 'first sale' doctrine. The prosecution countered with two arguments. First, the sale had been only of the film and not of the copyright photoplay embodied on it. Second, it argued that no prints had been sold for salvage. It was unnecessary for Judge Jameson to address these arguments because the prosecution's evidence showed that it was impossible for Wise's copies to have been copies sold for salvage. If, however, they had been 'salvage', the defendant would have succeeded on the authority of *Maynard, Merrill* and *Independent News.*[339]

The point was necessary, however, in the *Atherton* case. Judge Hufstedler rejected the approach taken by Judge Friendly in the *Platt & Munck* case and the cases following it. Judge Hufstedler considered that the civil actions were divided over whether a sale in breach of restrictions imposed on the seller by the copyright owner amounted to a 'first sale'. However, the *Maynard, Merrill, Straus* and *Independent News* cases clearly established that a 'first sale' could take place even where the copyright owner did not receive a reward for use of its copyright. The crucial factor was that the copyright owner had chosen to transfer title absolutely. Accordingly, Judge Hufstedler concluded that the 'just reward theory' should not be imported into criminal cases.[340] Since the prosecution had not proved that the copies sold for salvage, or the courtesy copies owned by the networks, could not be the copies obtained by Atherton, Atherton's convictions were quashed.

The *Wells, Wise, Drebin* and *Atherton* cases are examples of the dangers facing the prosecution when it does not, or cannot, prove how the defendant acquired the copies which form the subject-matter of the infringement action.[341]

Judge Jameson, in *Wise,* distinguished *Wells* on its facts suggesting that the

---

337 *Wise* 550 F. 2d at 1191, the NBC's *Camelot* print. Contrast the effect of failing to reserve title to the ABC's *Funny Girl* print; although Judge Jameson found that the contract granted ABC an option to buy the print. This together with the failure to trace the history of this particular copy proved fatal: see also *Atherton* 561 F. 2d at 750 Note 4.

338 *Ibid.* at 1192. Apart from expressly granting a licence, reservation of title, provision for return of the copy and, perhaps, prohibiting copying or lending (*Drebin* 557 F. 2d at 1327) would seem necessary.

339 *Ibid.* at 1193. The evidence was to similar effect in *Drebin* 557 F. 2d at 1327.

340 *Ibid.* at 751.

341 The ways in which the Government can seek to meet its burden of proof are further discussed in *US v Sachs* 801 F. 2d 839, at 842 to 845 (6th Cir. 1986).

copyright owner in *Wells* had actually sold the copies.[342] But, in *Wells*, Judge Ingraham also stressed that a licensee was presumed to be the full owner of copies made by it. In contrast, the Ninth Circuit, following the *Hampton* case, engaged in a much more discriminating analysis of the arrangements entered into by the copyright-owning film studios. Admittedly, most of the agreements considered by the Ninth Circuit seem to show drafting with a much more careful eye to reserving title. However, the Ninth Circuit was prepared to review the arrangements. Judge Ingraham, with respect, seemed to apply a general policy conclusion almost without regard to the factual situation. To the extent that there was any conflict between *Wells* and the *Hampton* case, the Ninth Circuit preferred to follow the *Hampton* case.[343]

The Ninth Circuit agreed with the parallel civil cases that the use of the word 'possession' in section 27 did not detract from the need for a sale or transfer of title by the copyright owner. However, it questioned Judge Friendly's reliance on the 'just reward' theory and Judge Hufstedler refused to import it into the criminal context.

With respect, Judge Hufstedler's concentration on the issue of whether the copyright owner had transferred title and rejection of a just reward theory is supported by a long line of authorities. Although the *Straus* case first introduced the idea of a fair reward for use of the copyright, the courts did not actually examine whether the copyright owner had received 'fair' value for use of its copyright.[344] Rather, the issue was always whether the copyright owner had exercised its option to introduce the copy into circulation. The courts spoke in terms of a reward, or economic function, theory because the copyright monopoly was seen as introduced to empower the copyright owner to select the terms on which the copyright article was first offered to the public; that reward being seen as the incentive to publish. Only with such control could the copyright owner secure any reward which it claimed. However, the courts did not actually examine whether the copyright owner had received fair and adequate remuneration. The copyright owner was left to decide such matters for itself.[345]

In *Wise,* Judge Jameson had been constrained to distinguish and limit the civil case, *Foreman,* on grounds similar to the *Wells* case.[346] The *Foreman* case involved a civil action by seven major film distributors against Foreman for conducting a business of selling and hiring out copies of films in which they owned copyright. The Fifth Circuit considered that the plaintiffs' unrebutted evidence conclusively established that Foreman could not have

---

342 550 F. 2d at 1191 Note 18.
343 *Ibid.* at 1190 to 1191 Note 17.
344 The *Platt & Munck* case may, perhaps, be seen as an attempt to find grounds on which the copyright owner's 'consent' to the first circulation of the contentious copies can be implied or inferred.
345 For a similar issue in the European Communities, see Cases 55 & 57/80 *Musik-Vertrieb Membran GmbH v GEMA* [1981] ECR 147 and Case 187/80 *Merck v Stephar* [1981] ECR 2063, see Chapter 6.3.1 below.
346 *American International Pictures Inc. v Foreman* 400 F. Supp. 928 (SD Ala. 1975), after *Wise,* reversed 576 F. 2d 661 (5th Cir. 1978).

acquired any copies which the plaintiffs had sold. Accordingly, the Fifth Circuit found Foreman liable for substantially the same reasons applied in the *Hampton, Wise* and *Drebin* cases.

Judge Godbold's opinion for the Fifth Circuit also suggests a policy approach at odds with Judge Ingraham's in the *Wells* case. Where the District Court in *Foreman* had relied on a common law presumption that possession was lawful to dismiss the plaintiffs' case, Judge Godbold found that the policy of the law was clearly to favour the rights of the copyright owner. His Honour considered that the copyright certificate was *prima facie* evidence that the copyright holder had retained all rights granted by the copyright, the right to vend being one of these rights. This coupled with the plaintiffs' assertions that Foreman could not have acquired copies which the plaintiffs had sold, sufficed to condemn Foreman.[347] Judge Godbold, although applying the law under the 1909 Act, noted that Congress had expressly rejected the decision at first instance by enacting section 109(c).[348]

(c)   *The 1976 Act*

Subject to two limited exceptions, the adoption of section 109, with its clarified wording, in the 1976 Act is not seen as altering the law developed by the courts under section 27 of the 1909 Act.[349]

Following the express wording of section 109(a), the Western District of Texas rejected an argument that the 'first sale' doctrine applied in a case of mere lawful possession.[350] Similarly, unauthorised retention of copies by a former distributor could not support a 'first sale' under section 109(a).[351] But, a mere gift of materials intended for destruction sufficed to constitute a 'first sale'.[352]

The first qualification was introduced to protect the viability of the music industry. In 1983, Congress concluded that the new copying technology seriously prejudiced the sound recording industry. The proliferation of 'home taping' and shops hiring out records compelled special measures.[353] Accordingly, Congress passed the Record Rental Amendment Act of

---

347   576 F. 2d 661, at 665. Judge Godbold expressly refused to rely on presumptions 'foreign to and in conflict with copyright law'. The approach in this case of domestic trade seems similar to that underlying *Time-Life*, *but*, it was in a context where the copies had *not* been sold.

348   *Ibid*. at 663, Note 1.

349   See for example 2 *Nimmer on Copyright* at §8.12 and note the comments in the *House Report* 79 reprinted in 4 *Nimmer on Copyright*, App. 4–41.

350   *Schuchart & Assoc. v Solo Serve Corp.* [1983] CCH Copyright Law Decisions at ¶25,593 (WD Tex. 1983) cited in 2 *Nimmer on Copyright* at 8–125.

351   *Wildlife International Inc. v Clements* 591 F. Supp. 1542 (SD Oh. 1984).

352   *Walt Disney Productions v Basmajian* 600 F. Supp. 439, at 442 (SDNY 1984). Judge Carter applied *Atherton* in ruling that section 109 simply required the copyright owner to part with title to the particular copy.

353   See House Report No. 98–987, 98th Cong. 2d Sess. (1984) cited in 2 *Nimmer on Copyright*, at §8.12[B][7] and referred to in Colby, 'The First Sale Doctrine – The Defence that Never Was?'.

1984.[354] Applying only to phonorecords, not copies, the Act amended section 109(b)(3) to preserve the 'first sale' doctrine as it applied to sales. However, the mere sale of a *phonorecord* would not carry with it the right to rent, lease or lend the phonorecord.[355] A similar amendment has also been introduced for computer programs,[355a] but failed for videotapes.[356]

Section 117 has also been suggested as introducing a second potential qualification.[357] This section was apparently introduced to ensure that purchasers of copyright programs could 'input' and adapt for use their programs on their machines and to ensure that they could make 'back up' copies.[358] However, the section appears to have restricted rights to lease, sell or otherwise transfer such copies only to situations in conjunction with a sale, lease or other transfer of the program and machine which the copy was made on. It has been held to render the 'first sale' doctrine totally inapplicable.[359]

(d) *Summary*

The 'first sale' doctrine developed as part of domestic trade. As in the corresponding patent cases, it purports to depend on the distinction between ownership of the copyright on one hand and ownership of the copy on the other. It simply holds that once a copyright owner parts with ownership of an article embodying the copyright, the copyright owner's ability to control the distribution of that copy in copyright law is gone. At this stage, it is not clear

---

354   Pub. L. No. 98–450, 98 Stat. 1727.
355   But see Colby, 'The First Sale Doctrine – The Defence that Never Was?', arguing that the previous law did not confer these rights either.
355a   For both phonorecords and computer programs, see 17 USC §109(b)(1)(A) (1990).
356   2 *Nimmer on Copyright*, at §8.12[B][7], Note 81, suggesting that different considerations apply because it was technologically more difficult to copy tapes and viewers usually only viewed the tape once unlike the multiple uses made by home tapers of sound recordings. It has been suggested that the real basis may be in the absence of powerful pro-home taping lobby groups for sound recordings at an early stage in the 'industry's' development: Kernochan, 'The US' First Sale Doctrine', ALAI Study Session, Munich 1988. For EC developments, see Case 158/86 *Warner Bros* [1988] ECR 2605 and the proposed directive on rental and distribution rights for copyright, at Chapters 6.4 and 6.5, respectively, below.
357   2 *Nimmer on Copyright*, at §8.08.
358   The National Commission on New Technological Uses of Copyrighted Works feared that copyright owners could stop buyers from using the programs:

> It is easy to imagine, however, a situation in which the copyright owner might desire, for good reason or none at all, to force a lawful owner or possessor of a copy to stop using a particular program. One who rightfully possesses a copy of a program, therefore, should be provided with a legal right to copy it to that extent which will permit its use by that possessor.

> *Final Report of the National Commission on New Technological Uses of Copyrighted Works*, 31 July 1978, at 12 cited in 2 *Nimmer on Copyright* at 8-105.

359   *Midway Manufacturing Co. v Strohon* 564 F. Supp. 741, at 744 to 745 especially Note 2 (ND Ill. 1983). The thrust of this decision concentrates on the fact that the modifications the defendant made to the program involved substituting duplicate parts which the defendant made by infringing the plaintiff's copyright. Contrast the position in the EC's Software Directive, Article 4(a) and 5(1).

whether the plaintiff must disprove a 'first sale' or whether it is an affirmative defence in civil cases.[360]

The doctrine is confined solely to the right to vend (or distribute) copies. It does not affect the other rights comprised in the copyright. For example, sale of a reproduction of a musical composition does not automatically carry with it the right to perform the composition in public, although the buyer may resell the copy.[361] This follows from the separate and distinct nature of each aspect of the copyright.

The central aspect of the 'first sale' doctrine is that ownership of the copy in question must pass from the copyright owner. It is not until the copyright owner transfers, or authorises the transfer, of title in the copy that the 'first sale' doctrine arises to extinguish the right of controlling distribution of that copy in copyright law. It does not matter what form the transfer takes or that the copyright owner was compelled to make the transfer.[362] The courts have sometimes distinguished between a transfer of less than absolute title and a transfer of absolute title coupled with restrictions on subsequent use. It would seem, however, that most attempted qualifications on title amount to restrictions on subsequent use. The courts have accepted only a mere passing of possession while retaining full ownership,[363] rental,[364] and unlawful retention of copies[365] as valid situations in which title did not pass. As in patents, use (or attempted sale) by a licensee outside the terms of its licence may also constitute infringement.[366]

Three reasons have been advanced to support the development of the 'first sale' doctrine. First, copyright is seen as 'moneyed' interest. It is intended to encourage authors with the lure of monopoly profits. The second reason is the policy of commercial convenience expressed by the rule against restraints on alienation.[367] The third factor is the law's abhorrence of monopolies in general, especially perpetual ones. In the interests of free trade and of society, the copyright owner's monopoly is strictly controlled. Hence, once the copyright owner has had a chance to secure the benefit of the exclusive

---

360   The *Foreman* case, see text at Notes 346 to 348 above.

361   *Red Baron-Franklin Park Inc. v Taito Corp.* 883 F. 2d 275 (4th Cir. 1989), see text from Note 426 below.

362   For examples of sale, compare the *Henry Bill* case and *Clements v Estes* above at Notes 294 to 295; for transfer by gift, *Walt Disney v Basmajian* and *Wildlife International v Clements* above at Notes 352 and 351, respectively; for compulsory transfer, see the *Platt & Munck* case, above at Notes 322 to 328; for the inadequacy of possession alone, see the *Platt & Munck* case, above at Notes 322 to 328; and of leasing, see *Hampton*, above at Notes 316 to 318.

363   The *Henry Bill* case, the *Platt & Munck* case, above at Notes 294 to 295 and 322 to 328, respectively.

364   *Hampton, Wise, Drebin, Atherton* and *Foreman*, above at Notes 316 to 318, 334 to 345 and 346 to 348.

365   The *Platt & Munck* case and *Wildlife International v Clements*, above at Notes 322 to 328 and 351, respectively.

366   *Creative Arts Inc. v Abady & Sultan Inc.* 134 USPQ 388 (SD Fla. 1961), above at Note 314.

367   Of perhaps doubtful strength in the United States following *Sylvania* 433 US 36 (1977), Chapter 3 above, Note 215.

right by exercising its choice over the terms on which it parts title to the copy in the United States, it has been considered that the object of copyright law has been met and exhaustion takes effect. The view of copyright as a 'moneyed' interest has sometimes led courts to speak of the copyright owner's right to receive a satisfactory price for the copy. This has been expressly rejected in the criminal context.[368] The better view in civil cases would also seem to be that this is not necessary, except, perhaps, in cases where the court has been seeking to imply the copyright owner's consent to the transfer of title.[369]

With the exception of the conflicting *Copperman* and *Mercury* cases, parallel imports were not an issue in the cases on the 'first sale' doctrine. The *Copperman* case simply assumed that the sale abroad without restrictions licensed the article for use within the jurisdiction. It adopted, in effect, a concept of international exhaustion. But, it did not explain why; nor does its actual result seem likely to be followed today.[370] Moreover, at the time of the sale abroad, statutory copyright did not subsist in the United States. The *Mercury* case, on the other hand, acknowledged the territorial independence of each national jurisdiction inconsistently with international exhaustion. However, it did not refer to *Copperman* and Judge Learned Hand dissented.

Recently, the 'first sale' cases have been developing attention to the doctrine's inapplicability to the other rights comprised in the copyright, proceeding from the separate and distinct nature of each aspect of the copyright.

4.3.4 Parallel imports

To date the US courts have suggested three approaches to the parallel import problem in the copyright field. First, the courts focused on whether the goods in question were originally made and sold in the United States. The second concentrated on copyright as a tool to control the number of copies in circulation within the jurisdiction and denied application of the 'first sale' doctrine to parallel imports. The ascendancy of the 'first sale' doctrine is affirmed by the third approach.

The first attempts at reconciling sections 109 and 602(a) suggested that the courts would allow the 'first sale' doctrine free rein where the imported articles had actually been made and sold first in the United States by the copyright owner. If the goods were first made and sold outside the United States, however, it appeared that the 'first sale' doctrine would not apply.

In the *Nintendo* case, District Judge Freeman granted a preliminary

---

368   The *Atherton* case, above at Notes 334 to 345.
369   See the 'scrap' cases, *Maynard, Merrill, Independent News*, above at Notes 296 and 320 to 321, respectively; the 'enhancement' cases such as *Scarves by Vera*, above at Note 306; for an implication of consent, see *Platt & Munck*, above at Notes 322 to 328.
370   *Red Baron-Franklin Park Inc. v Taito Corp.* 883 F. 2d 275 (4th Cir. 1989), see text from Note 426 below.

injunction restraining the importation and sale of computer circuit boards for use in an audio-visual game, 'Donkey Kong' or 'Crazy Kong'.[371] At the time, 'Donkey Kong' was one of the most popular of these sorts of games available in the United States. Nintendo Co. Ltd of Japan had developed the game and the circuit board and had assigned its copyright for the United States in the circuit board's program to its wholly owned US subsidiary, Nintendo of America Inc. ('Nintendo'). Nintendo, as the exclusive distributor of the games in the United States, was both manufacturing circuit boards and importing them for incorporation into the product.

Meanwhile, Nintendo Co. Ltd had licensed another Japanese company, Falcon Inc., to make and sell circuit boards for 'Crazy Kong' in Japan. 'Crazy Kong' circuit boards were virtually identical to 'Donkey Kong' circuit boards, although only the latter were available through authorised channels in the United States. By the terms of Falcon's licence, Falcon was expressly forbidden to deal in the games, or the circuit boards, outside the territories of Japan. Nor was it allowed to license other parties to make and sell the circuit boards or games. On each board made by it, Falcon placed a notice identifying the board as made under licence from Nintendo Co. Ltd, but this notice did not indicate that Falcon's licence was limited.

The defendant Elcon was buying circuit boards made by Falcon from another US corporation and making them up into the 'Crazy Kong' games for sale throughout the United States.

In granting the preliminary injunction for both copyright infringement and unfair competition under state law, Judge Freeman was evidently impressed by four factors. Nintendo had gone to great expense and considerable efforts to advertise and promote the 'Donkey Kong' game. Second, it was an extremely expensive and painstaking business to develop a new circuit board. The risks associated with such an enterprise were large. But, it was relatively easy and cheap to copy the circuit board once developed. Third, Elcon's activities were making substantial inroads into Nintendo's market share and, finally, audio-visual games of this sort had a relatively short commercial life. The first three in particular are the classic factors in any parallel importing situation.

On the copyright issue, his Honour found that Elcon had infringed Nintendo's exclusive distribution rights under section 106(3) and also its importation rights under section 602(a). Judge Freeman ruled that importing Falcon circuit boards infringed Nintendo's copyright because neither Nintendo nor its parent had authorised the importation. His Honour rejected an argument that the sale by Falcon carried a licence by Nintendo Co. Ltd because:

> . . . the licensing agreement clearly prohibited Falcon Inc. from importing or exporting 'Donkey Kong' or 'Crazy Kong' circuit boards into the United States.

371   *Nintendo of America Inc. v Elcon Industries Inc.* 564 F. Supp. 937 (ED Mich. 1982). See also *Microsoft Inc. v Very Competitive Computer Products* 671 F. Supp. 1250 (ND Cal. 1987) at Notes 406 to 407 below.

There is no evidence to show that either plaintiff or Nintendo Co. Ltd ever authorized anyone to import 'Crazy Kong' games into the United States.[372]

Although Elcon does not appear to have argued section 109(a), the argument of consent seems based on a crude version of the 'first sale' doctrine. The express terms of Nintendo Co. Ltd's licence to Falcon, however, precluded such consent being implied. But, given the terms of the notice Falcon attached to the circuit board, it might be wondered how an innocent third party could ascertain that its right to deal in the circuit boards was limited. The more so as Elcon had bought through another company which actually imported the circuit boards. While Judge Freeman's attention to commercial considerations contrasts to that of the English and South African cases based on the *Charmdale* case and all the Anglo-Commonwealth cases concerned to prevent goods' owners imposing hidden restraints on the alienation of chattels by private agreement, his Honour's approach is consistent with the *Harlequin* case and, in both the Anglo-Commonwealth countries and the United States, the patent cases on sales abroad by limited licensees.

A further interesting aspect of the judgment is his Honour's repeated reliance on the absence of consent from both Nintendo and Nintendo Co. Ltd. Since Nintendo was the copyright owner in the United States, Nintendo Co. Ltd's consent would not seem relevant. This may reflect a concern that the US right owner be independent of the foreign right owner, or own rights independently of the foreign producer, concerns which have arisen in US patent and trade marks law particularly as a result of anti-trust considerations.[373]

This aspect aside, however, *Nintendo* indicates an approach based on the principle of territoriality. The product imported by Elcon was only very slightly different to that made and sold in the United States by Nintendo; it was made and sold abroad by a legally separate person; and that person's authority to make and sell was expressly limited to a defined territory outside the United States and excluding the United States.

More detailed treatment of the interplay between the 'first sale' doctrine and the importation right was required in *Scorpio*.[374] 'CBS' owned the US copyright in six sound recordings. The defendant 'Scorpio' imported phonorecords embodying the sound recordings into the United States from

---

372 *Ibid*. at 944.
373 Compare *US v Guerlain Inc*. 155 F. Supp. 77 (SDNY 1957) *vac. and rem*. 357 US 924 (1958) *dis*. 172 F. Supp. 107 (SDNY 1959) (trade mark); *Sanofi SA v Med-Tech Veterinarian Products Inc*. 565 F. Supp. 931 (DNJ 1983), but see also 222 USPQ 143 (DKan. 1983) (patent); and, in the United Kingdom, contrast *Harlequin* [1980] FSR 194 (CA) (copyright) and *Revlon* [1980] FSR 84 (CA) (trade mark).
374 *Columbia Broadcasting System Inc. v Scorpio Music Distributors Inc*. 569 F. Supp. 47 (ED Pa. 1983) *affd without opinion* 738 F. 2d 424 (3d Cir. 1984). This case is critically examined in Richard H. Stern, 'Case Comment: Nintendo of America Inc. v. Elcon Industries Inc. and CBS Inc. v. Scorpio Music Distributors Inc. Parallel Imports in the U.S. – The Exercise of Copyright', [1984] EIPR 203, at 204 to 205 and Feingold, 'Parallel Importing under the Copyright Act of 1976', at 218 to 227.

the Philippines. A Philippines corporation, Vicor Music Corporation, had
made the phonorecords in the Philippines under a licence to do so granted
by a Japanese company, CBS-Sony. CBS had consented to the agreement
between Vicor and CBS-Sony. When CBS-Sony terminated the licence,
Vicor had 60 days to liquidate its stock. It sold some to another Philippino
business, Rainbow Music Inc. which, in turn, sold them to a US corporation,
International Traders Inc. The latter had supplied the phonorecords to
Scorpio under an order placed by Scorpio.

CBS sued for infringement, relying on section 602(a). The matter came
before District Judge Green on an application for summary judgment.
Granting the application, his Honour rejected Scorpio's reliance on the
'first sale' doctrine as expressed in section 109(a) and the case law:

> [Scorpio's] contentions would be more persuasive were it not for the phrase –
> 'lawfully made under this title' – in §109(a). I conclude that the section grants
> first sale protection to the third party buyer of copies which have been legally
> manufactured and sold within the United States and not to purchasers of imports
> such as are involved here. The protection afforded by the United States Code
> does not extend beyond the borders of this country unless the Code expressly
> states. Absent a clearly expressed legislative intent to the contrary, statutory
> language must be recognized as conclusive. Thus, I cannot honor Scorpio's
> request that the court 'decide the breadth and meaning of §602 [by taking
> §109(a) into consideration] perhaps *in a manner that circumscribes the apparent
> intent of Congress as reflected by the express language of section 602 and its
> legislative history.*
>
> Construing §109(a) as superseding the prohibition on importation set forth
> in the more recently enacted §602 would render §602 virtually meaningless.
> Third party purchasers who import phonorecords could thereby circumvent the
> statute, in every instance, by simply buying the records indirectly. Moreover,
> declaring legal the act of purchasing from a U.S. importer who does not
> deal directly with a foreign manufacturer, but who buys recordings which
> have been liquidated overseas, would undermine the purpose of the statute.
> The copyright owner would be unable to exercise control over copies of the
> work which entered the American market in competition with copies lawfully
> manufactured and distributed under this title. This court cannot construe the
> statute so as to alter the intent of Congress, which has set restrictions on the
> importation of phonorecords in order that the rights of United States copyright
> owners can be preserved.[375] (*Original emphasis*)

His Honour, in effect, treated the rights of the copyright owner under
one country's laws as independent of and separate to rights under another
country's laws.[376] The crucial point is Judge Green's finding that the 'first
sale' doctrine only operated on goods lawfully made and sold within the
United States. It did not apply to goods made and sold abroad. In reaching

---

375 *Ibid*. at 49 to 50 (citation omitted).
376 The report does not clarify who owned the copyright in the Philippines or the
precise relationship between CBS-Sony and CBS. It may be that, if CBS was not
the owner of the Philippines copyright or the ultimate beneficiary of it, the fact
of CBS' consent to the Philippines licence would be irrelevant in an exhaustion of
rights analysis.

that conclusion, he had regard to the express words of sections 109 and 602 and the legislative history of section 602.[377]

In reaching his conclusion, Judge Green relied on four factors – first, the terms of section 109(a), 'lawfully made under this title'; second, the principle that one country's laws did not operate extraterritorially; third, the contrary interpretation would render section 602 'virtually meaningless'; fourth, the purpose of the statute or Congress' intent. With respect, these factors are open to some questioning.

While it might be expected that something made and sold outside the United States – whether under a copyright or not – was not 'lawfully made' under a US statute,[378] it is not clear why the 'first sale' doctrine is dependent on both manufacture and sale in the United States. In relying on this factor, Judge Green appears to have been influenced by Scorpio's concession that adopting its arguments would be inconsistent with the actual wording of section 109(a) and so did not subject the clause 'lawfully made under this title' to a searching technical analysis.[379]

There is some doubt that Congress expressed any concluded view. The *House Report* does indicate briefly what the clause is intended to convey:

> To come within the scope of section 109(a), a copy or phonorecord must have been 'lawfully made under this title,' though not necessarily with the copyright owner's authorization. For example, any resale of an illegally 'pirated' phonorecord would be an infringement, but the disposition of a phonorecord legally made under the compulsory licensing provisions of section 115 would not.[380]

The specific example of an article 'lawfully made under this title' although 'not necessarily with the owner's consent' is one of a domestic nature. However, it hardly seems conclusive and is given only as an example, not as a definition.

By interpreting section 109(a) as applying only to copies and phonorecords made and sold in the United States, his Honour drew a conclusion from the other factors. The central factor underlying Judge Green's analysis is that the Copyright Act, and section 109(a), does not operate extraterritorially. But, this in turn is a conclusion based on other considerations.

In the United States, the general rule for determining whether a statute has extraterritorial effect has been explained by Judge Friendly in the following terms: 'Absent a clearly expressed statutory intent to the contrary, the judicial presumption is that the Code does not apply to actions not occurring in, or *having an effect in,* the United States. (*Emphasis added*)'[381]

---

377 Contrast 2 *Nimmer on Copyright*, at §8.12[B][6], text at Note 62 and see Note 67.

378 *Beechwood Music Corp. v Vee Jay Records* 328 F. 2d 728 (2d Cir. 1964) *affg* 226 F. Supp. 8 (SDNY) below at Note 381.

379 This point is elaborated in Feingold, 'Parallel Importing under the Copyright Act of 1976', at 225.

380 The *House Report*, at 79 reproduced in 4 *Nimmer on Copyright*, App. 4, 4-41-42.

381 *Beechwood Music Corp. v Vee Jay Records* 328 F. 2d 728, at 729 *per* Judge Friendly (2d Cir. 1964) *affg* 226 F. Supp. 8 (SDNY).

To state that section 109(a) does not have extraterritorial effect because the 'first sale' abroad does not occur in the United States *or have an effect there* seems circular when the question to be determined is whether that 'first sale' abroad has an effect on rights in the United States.[382] Judge Green's finding, however, may be regarded as consistent with one view of *Beechwood Music*. In *Beechwood Music,* the copyright owner successfully sought a preliminary injunction against the sale of certain records embodying songs and performances by the Beatles. The defendant had argued that the production and sale of such records in the United Kingdom entitled it to make such records in the United States under the compulsory licensing provisions then in force. This contention was roundly rejected.

Judge Green's third factor was that section 602 would be rendered 'virtually meaningless' by a ruling which did not confine the 'first sale' doctrine to domestic sales. Such a ruling would also 'undermine the purpose of the statute'. However, an alternative interpretation is conceivable which would leave some scope for section 602 to operate and satisfy the policy underlying the 'first sale' or exhaustion doctrine. Arguably, a copy or phonorecord could lawfully be made abroad without any authority or involvement of the US copyright owner in circumstances which did not trigger the economic basis for the 'first sale' doctrine. Examples could be where a completely independent party made the copy or phonorecord in a country where the relevant copyright was not recognised or could be used under a compulsory licence.[383] Such an approach may not please domestic copyright owners. But, the point here is that it does not leave section 602 'virtually meaningless'.

The terms of his Honour's opinion show that he considered the purpose of the statute was to allow the domestic right owner to control foreign copies entering the market in competition with the 'authorised' product. Arguably, this is consistent with the historical development of the principle of territoriality, but his Honour does not explain the derivation or why Scorpio's actions are incompatible with it. For example, one aspect of the transaction which would bear further inquiry is the grounds on which CBS consented to the licence between CBS-Sony and Vicor. The judgment does not deal with the most controversial point about parallel imports by failing to explain why the policy of the statute requires, or permits, protection for CBS' domestic products against competition from foreign products which CBS itself had allowed to be released abroad.[384]

---

382   See the *Sebastian* case 664 F. Supp. 909, at 917 to 918 *per* Judge Barry (DNJ 1987) *revd on other grounds* 847 F. 2d 1093 (3d Cir. 1988).

383   For example, the *Beechwood Music* case, *T.B. Harms Company v JEM Records Inc.* 655 F. Supp. 1575 (DNJ 1987), below at Notes 403 to 404 and, under EC law, see Case 19/84 *Pharmon v Hoechst* [1985] ECR 2281 (patents), at Chapter 6.4 below.

384   The issue may be considered even more pressing if, as has been suggested, CBS was receiving, or had a right to receive, royalties from Vicor: see Feingold, 'Parallel Importing under the Copyright Act of 1976', at 222. But, compare *Time-Life* (1976) 12 ALR 1, at 11 to 13 *per* Bowen CJ in Eq., *Barson Computers* [1985] FSR 489 and, in patents, *Griffin v Keystone Mushroom Farm Inc.* 453 F. Supp. 1243 (ED Pa. 1978), at subsection 4.2.2(c) and Chapter 3.3.4 above.

Instead, his Honour focused on the implications of allowing 'indirect' purchasing which 'would undermine the purpose of the statute'. If the importer had purchased directly from the foreign manufacturer and was aware of the importer's intentions, that may supply grounds for inferring consent to the importation. But, if the manufacturer was not aware of the importer's intentions, inferring consent is logically difficult. The 'first sale' doctrine as it operates domestically, however, applies without distinction between direct and indirect sales.[385] Even then, copyright still operates domestically to allow the copyright owner control over competition with the copyright work.

Judge Green's concentration on the indirect nature of the transaction no doubt lies in the facts before his Honour. Scorpio was not the actual importer. Nor had the actual importer, International Traders, bought directly from Vicor. But these questions go to whether Scorpio should be liable as an importer or under some other right such as the distribution right. They do not relate to whether Scorpio was the owner of phonorecords 'lawfully made under this title'. That is a separate issue, not dependent on the identity of the owner but on facts about the manufacture of the phonorecord in question.[386]

Accordingly, the *Scorpio* case represents a policy decision that section 109(a) does not affect the right granted by section 602 where the copy or phonorecord in question was made and sold outside the United States. Why that policy decision was made remained to be explained. Four District Courts have resiled from the distinction drawn in *Scorpio* in varying degrees and the Third Circuit, which affirmed Judge Green's ruling without opinion, has subsequently indicated 'some uneasiness' with the approach, although it did so in a case where the facts did not raise the question and the judgment specifically did not 'pass on' the validity of *Scorpio*.[387] The Ninth Circuit, however, has adopted it.[387a]

The *Cosmair* case continued the distinction between manufacture and sale abroad and domestically.[388] It, however, involved manufacture and sale in the United States and the 'first sale' doctrine was found to apply. Cosmair owned copyright in a design for a trade mark *The Polo Player*. It manufactured and sold CIF in the United States a shipment of its products bearing the trade mark to Dynamite; the parties understanding that the goods were for export only. Dynamite actually exported the goods, but then reimported them.

---

385 Section 4.3.3 above.
386 Indeed, his Honour resolved this issue separately by finding Scorpio liable as a vicarious or contributory importer: 569 F. Supp. 47, at 48.
387 *Sebastian International Inc. v Consumer Contract (PTY) Ltd* 847 F. 2d 1093, at 1098 Note 1 (3d Cir. 1988) *revg* 664 F. Supp. 909 (DNJ 1987), text from Note 408 below.
387a *BMG Music v Perez* 952 F. 2d 318 (9th Cir. 1991).
388 *Cosmair Inc. et al. v Dynamite Enterprises Inc. et al.* 226 USPQ 344 (SD Fla. 1985).; see also *Neutrogena Corp. v US* CCH Copyright Law Decisions (DSC 1988) in 2 *Nimmer on Copyright*, at §8.12[B][6] Notes 66 to 67.

While the goods were held up in Customs, Cosmair applied for a preliminary injunction for infringement of its copyright in the trade mark design.
District Judge Hoeveler refused the application because Cosmair had failed
to establish a substantial likelihood of success on the merits. His Honour
distinguished the *Nintendo* and *Scorpio* cases because the copies of the work
had been made and sold in the United States by the US copyright owner.
Accordingly, section 109(a) denied Cosmair the right to rely on section
602.[389] Cosmair also had difficulty convincing the court that it had a valid
copyright to protect. Two other aspects of the case are of interest.

Having some doubt about the reasoning in the *Scorpio* case, Judge
Hoeveler questioned the relationship between sections 109(a) and 602(a)
which it established. His Honour thought that the legislative history of
section 602(a) showed that it was intended to apply to copies or phonorecords
'lawfully made' – the same phrase used in section 109(a). This suggested
that the two sections should apply to the same categories of copies and
phonorecords and Judge Hoeveler referred to an example given by the
Register of Copyrights in her *Supplementary Report on the 1965 Revision
of United States Copyright Law* in support of the proposition that section
602(a) would apply 'where the copyright owner had authorized the making
of copies in a foreign country for distribution only in that country'. From
this, Judge Hoeveler considered that situations not falling within the example
would probably be subject to the 'first sale' doctrine.[390] In the end, however,
it was sufficient to distinguish *Scorpio* and *Nintendo* on their facts.

The second point of interest is that Judge Hoeveler considered the case
was probably not one in which the public interest would be served by
granting a preliminary injunction. His Honour drew on a trade mark case
in commenting that:

> There has been no showing that the products are not genuine. There is evidence
> that the public would be able to acquire the products at lower prices than
> offered by authorized distributors. That factor can be considered in determining
> the effect on the public interest.[391]

His Honour clearly favoured the consumer welfare benefits the parallel
imports apparently conferred.

The doubts expressed by Judge Hoeveler in *Cosmair* and the *Parfums
Stern* case were not pursued in a subsequent case heard in the Southern

---

389 *Ibid*. at 346 to 347. His Honour was not sure whether the actual passing of title
or the parties' intention should govern whether there had been a 'first sale'. But see 2
Nimmer on Copyright, at §8.12[B][6] Note 66.
390 *Ibid*. at 347. District Judge Barry criticised reliance on such an isolated example
amid such a vast and confusing legislative history in *Sebastian International Inc. v
Consumer Contract (PTY) Ltd* 664 F. Supp. 909, at 916 to 917 (DNJ 1987) *revd* 847
F. 2d 1093 (3d Cir. 1988).
391 226 USPQ 344, at 348, citing *Parfums Stern Inc. v US Customs Service* 575 F.
Supp. 416, at 421 (SD Fla. 1983), see Chapter 2.3.4(b) at Notes 279 to 282 above.
'Public interest' was a factor for consideration in deciding whether to issue a preliminary
injunction.

District of Florida. But the facts in *Selchow & Righter* are distinguishable in that the parallel imports were made abroad by the copyright owner in the foreign market and the domestic copyright had been assigned to an independent company. Hence, the case fits within the scheme established by *Scorpio*.[392]

Criticism of *Scorpio* was revived in *Stark*.[393] *Stark* involved unauthorised imports of books printed in the United Kingdom and, on its facts, is essentially indistinguishable from the *Scorpio* and *Nintendo* cases. District Judge Legge, however, seemed uncomfortable with the reasoning in the *Scorpio* case and suggested a new view of why section 109 might not limit section 602. In addition, Judge Legge offered an explanation of why the Copyright Act should seek to bar parallel imports.

The plaintiffs were the owners in the United States of copyright in some 18 literary works. Stark imported wholesale quantities of these works into the United States from the United Kingdom. The UK publishers were not the owners of the rights in the United States although the owners in each country derived title from the same source, the respective authors. Stark tried to resist summary judgment on a number of grounds. For present purposes, its arguments about the 'first sale' doctrine, the First Amendment and the effect of the consent decree in *Addison-Wesley* are relevant.[394] Although finding difficulty with the *Scorpio* case, Judge Legge granted the plaintiffs summary judgment.

In his Honour's view, the consent decree and section 602 did not conflict. Section 602 allowed the copyright owner to prevent others importing copyright materials while the consent decree was directed against horizontal agreements to divide territories and expressly preserved individual copyright owners' rights to exercise their rights under the copyright laws of any country. This case was just an individual copyright owner's exercise of its powers. Hence, in this respect, copyright was treated no differently to patents.[395]

Judge Legge also considered that section 109 did not affect rights under section 602. His Honour considered that, although it did refer to section 106,

---

392 *Selchow & Righter Co. v Goldex Corp.* 612 F. Supp. 19 (SD Fla. 1985), the imports were simply described as unauthorised at 25. See also *CBS Inc. v Casino Record Distributors of Florida Inc.* 654 F. Supp. 677 (SD Fla. 1987), Note 402 below.
393 *Hearst Corporation et al. v Stark* 639 F. Supp. 970 (ND Cal. 1986); but see also *Microsoft Inc. v Very Competitive Computer Products* 671 F. Supp. 1250 (ND Cal. 1987) at Notes 406 to 407 below and *BMG Music v Perez* 952 F. 2d 318 (9th Cir. 1991) from Note 431 below.
394 *US v Addison-Wesley Publishing Co.* 1976-2 CCH Trade Cases at ¶61,225 (SDNY 1976), see section 4.2.4 above.
395 639 F. Supp. 970, at 981. See also Mark R. Joelson, 'Parallel Imports into the United States: Copyright and Anti-Trust', [1980] EIPR 281, at 282 to 283 and note the similarly relaxed anti-trust treatment of copyright after *Sylvania* 433 US 36 (1977) in *W. Goebel Porzellanfabrik v Action Industries Inc.* 589 F. Supp. 763 (SDNY 1984). For patents, contrast *ICI* 100 F. Supp. 504 (SDNY 1951) to *Dunlop v Kelsey-Hayes* 484 F. 2d 407, at 417 (6th Cir. 1973) and *Westinghouse* 648 F. 2d 642 (9th Cir. 1981), see Chapter 3.3.3(c) above. Moreover, Judge Legge thought that a subsequent statute, the 1976 Act, would override a consent decree if there were conflict.

section 602 was a later enactment creating additional, independent rights to those given by section 106.[396]

Even if section 109 did limit section 602, however, Judge Legge considered that it did not authorise 'wholesale importations into the US of copyrighted materials manufactured outside this country'. Section 109 referred to 'copy or phonorecord' in the singular in contrast to the use of the plural in section 602. Accordingly, section 109 only applied to imports of single copies, not wholesale quantities.[397]

With respect, this distinction does not seem supportable. The Copyright Act does recognise a difference between imports for commercial purposes and those for private purposes. That recognition, however, is afforded by section 602.[398] Moreover, it is unlikely that section 109 was intended to be confined to single copies or phonorecords since it 'restate[d] and confirm[ed]' the 'first sale' principles developed by the courts and under section 27 where it had always applied to goods bought in quantity for commercial purposes.[399]

The more intriguing aspect of the case arose under Stark's allegation that the plaintiffs' action violated First Amendment rights. Stark claimed that the books imported were out of print in the United States or otherwise not available there. Hence, he was doing the public a service and to enjoin his actions would stifle the free dissemination of ideas which the First Amendment to the US Constitution sought to protect. As the power to make laws for copyright itself stemmed from the US Constitution,[400] Judge Legge found it necessary to balance the rights arising under the First Amendment and the Copyright Act. Barring Stark's imports did not offend that balance because section 602 was part of a scheme which encouraged creative activity and dissemination of its results to the public. The Copyright Act gave the author a monopoly to derive a special reward from the fruits of the author's creative activity during the limited term of the monopoly. During the term of the monopoly, the author could derive that special reward by controlling the

---

396   *Ibid.* at 976. It is not entirely clear why section 602(a) is a 'later' enactment to sections 106(3) and 109: see 2 *Nimmer on Copyright*, at §8.12[B][6] Note 75. The view seems to have been first expressed by Judge Green in *Scorpio* 569 F. Supp. 47 at 49 to 50, see quotation at Note 375 above.

397   *Ibid.*

398   The second exception to the general prohibition on imports provided by paragraph 602(a)(2) is in the following terms:

> This subsection does not apply to –
>
> . . .
>
> (2)   importation, for the private use of the importer and not for distribution, by any person with respect to no more than one copy or phonorecord of any one work at any one time, or by any person arriving from outside the US with respect to copies or phonorecords forming part of such person's personal baggage; or . . . .

399   See for example *Bobbs-Merrill Co. v Straus* 210 US 339 (1908); *Independent News Co. Inc. v Williams* 293 F. 2d 510 (3rd Cir. 1961), see subsection 4.3.3(a) and (b), respectively, above. Note also the criticisms of the *Stark* case in *Sebastian* 664 F. Supp. 909, at 918 Note 13 (DNJ 1987) *revd on other grounds* 847 F. 2d 1093 (3d Cir. 1988). See too 2 *Nimmer on Copyright* at §8.12[B][6] at Notes 72 to 76.

400   Article I, section 8, clause 8.

terms on which the work was made available to the public. In his Honour's opinion:

> By prohibiting the unauthorized importation of works, section 602 preserves the copyright owners' right to control their copyrighted works. Congress and the Supreme Court have given the copyright owner the prerogative to determine when or whether a particular work will be published, re-released or removed from print.
>
> . . .
>
> While the Court in *Harper* was discussing the 'fair use' doctrine and the right of first publication, the same reasoning applies here. Defendants' unauthorized importations have an undermining effect on the copyright owners' control over the public dissemination of the copyrighted works. By prohibiting the unauthorized importation, section 602 enhances the owners' rights to retain creative control.[401]

Judge Legge then, although adopting reasons different to those in *Scorpio,* still recognised the territorial nature of copyright interests in his attempts to explain why section 109 did not override the copyright owner's powers under section 602. While the distinction he sought to make in the terminology of the sections seems difficult to maintain, Judge Legge based himself squarely on the view that the power to control all imports for economic reasons was part of the scheme intended by Congress for the exploitation of copyright.

In a trial on the issue of damages, parallel imports had been found to infringe US copyright. The imported phonorecords had been made and sold in Mexico by the US copyright owners under a notice that they were for sale in Mexico only. Since the imports were made and sold outside the United States, the judgment is consistent with *Scorpio* although the reasoning is not stated.[402]

Scorpio was applied without criticism in the *Harms* case.[403] JEM imported into the United States phonorecords featuring the song 'Ol' Man River' which had been made in New Zealand under that country's compulsory licensing provisions. It had the approval of the US owner of the copyright in the sound recording for the importation, but not of Harms, the owner in

---

401   639 F. Supp. 970, at 978; see also *BMG Music v Perez* 952 F. 2d 318, 320 (9th Cir. 1991) at Note 431 below. Compare *Time-Life* (1976) 12 ALR 1, at 11 to 13 *per* Bowen CJ in Eq., *Barson Computers* [1985] FSR 489 and, in patents, *Griffin v Keystone Mushroom Farm Inc.* 453 F. Supp. 1243 (ED Pa. 1978), see subsection 4.2.2(c) and Chapter 3.3.4, respectively, above. The reference to *Harper* was to *Harper & Row Publishers Inc. v Nation Enterprises Inc.* 471 US 539 (1985). Publication of excerpts from former President Ford's unpublished memoirs was not a 'fair use' within the meaning of the Copyright Act because the Act was '. . . intended to motivate the creative activities of authors and inventors by the provision of a special reward, and to allow the public access to the products of their genius after the limited period of exclusive control has expired.' Accordingly, the copyright owner was entitled to choose when and how it published the work.

402   *CBS Inc. v Casino Record Distributors of Florida Inc.* 654 F. Supp. 677 (SD Fla. 1987). From the report it appears that there had been an earlier hearing where liability was determined on 22 September 1986.

403   *T.B. Harms Company v JEM Records Inc.* 655 F. Supp. 1575 (DNJ 1987). This case is in some respects analogous to the *Hoffnung* and *Fletcher Construction* cases at sections 4.2.2(a) and (b) above, respectively.

the United States of copyright in the musical work, 'Ol' Man River'. Nor had JEM complied with the compulsory licensing requirements under US law. Harms sued JEM for infringement of its copyright.

District Judge Bissell rejected JEM's argument that the exclusive right of distribution was lost for a work available for compulsory licensing and found for Harms. Judge Bissell adopted the reasoning in the *Scorpio* case based on the words 'lawfully made under this title' and the effect adopting the defendant's arguments would have on section 602(a) – rendering it meaningless:

> Here, as in that case, to allow the defendant to rely on a limitation of the owner's exclusive rights to circumvent the prohibition on importation would tie the hands of the copyright holder who seeks to exercise his rights to control copies of the work which enter the American market. Thus, in order to construe the Copyright Act so as to fulfill Congress' intent to set restrictions on the importation of phonorecords in order to preserve the rights of these owners, the court finds that the exclusive rights of a copyright owner to enforce section 602 are not limited by the compulsory licensing provisions of the Act.[404]

Judge Bissell clearly saw a copyright subsisting under US law as a territorial right, independent of corresponding rights existing under other countries' laws. Hence, his Honour adopted as US law principles like those affirmed in the *Hoffnung* and *Fletcher Construction* cases in Anglo-Commonwealth jurisdictions.

Senior Judge Troutman applied *Scorpio* without comment in another case arising out of the parallel importing of Cabbage Patch dolls from Europe.[405] The doubts about *Scorpio* held by Judge Legge in the *Stark* case do not seem to have assailed Judge Jensen also sitting in the Northern District for California in *Very Competitive Computer Products*.[406] The defendants were licensed by Microsoft to make and sell the software in question in Taiwan, among other places, but were also exporting to California when Microsoft obtained a preliminary injunction protecting its US copyright. The report relates to a number of interlocutory motions; in the course of one of which, Judge Jensen indicated that any sub-licence to the defendants did not extend to the United States and so their sales activity there infringed Microsoft's US copyright.[407] The infringement theory is not discussed, but the facts are consistent with *Nintendo* and *Scorpio*.

Building on the concept of copyright as a tool to control undesirable competition in the *Stark* case, the District Court in the *Sebastian* case rejected the reasoning adopted in *Scorpio* and *Cosmair*.[408] Judge Barry

---

404   *Ibid.* at 1583.
405   *Original Appalachian Artwork Inc. v J.F. Reichart Inc.* 658 F. Supp. 458, at 463 (ED Pa. 1987). For the factual context, see the *Artworks* case at Chapter 2.3.4(c) above.
406   *Microsoft Inc. v Very Competitive Computer Products* 671 F. Supp. 1250 (ND Cal. 1987).
407   *Ibid.* at 1258.
408   *Sebastian International Inc. v Consumer Contacts (PTY) Ltd* 664 F. Supp. 909 (DNJ 1987) *revd* 847 F. 2d 1093 (3d Cir. 1988). Compare the US trade mark cases on so-called 're-imports', at Chapter 2.3.4(c) above.

granted a preliminary injunction against imports of goods first made and sold lawfully in the United States. On appeal, however, the Third Circuit reversed, casting considerable doubt on the *Scorpio* case in the process.

Sebastian made and sold a range of 'personal care beauty supplies'. It had registered copyrights for the labels on two of its products, Shpritz Forte and Wet. At its base in California, it orally agreed to sell stocks of its range to Consumer Contact 'for sale in South Africa but not elsewhere'. On receiving the shipment in South Africa, Consumer Contact promptly reshipped them to Fabric Inc. in the United States. Fabric had arranged a number of outlets for public distribution. When Sebastian discovered that Fabric, rather than Consumer Contact, was running the US end of this scheme, it sought to justify continuance of a preliminary injunction under copyright law instead of contract.

In the District Court, Judge Barry held that section 602 created a separate right independent of the distribution right in section 106. Hence rights under section 602 were not qualified by section 109. In doing so, however, her Honour rejected the reasoning adopted in *Scorpio* and relied, instead, on a control theory like that suggested in *Stark*.

Judge Barry could find no convincing reasons to read in the territorial distinction suggested by the *Scorpio* case. Crucially, Judge Barry rejected the *Scorpio* case's reliance on the words 'lawfully made under this title' for the conclusion that the 'first sale' doctrine did not apply extraterritorially. A number of reasons were advanced for this rejection.[409] In her opinion, the words 'lawfully made' in section 109(a) were not decisive. The same words were used in the *House Report* in referring to section 602, suggesting that they were intended to refer to the same thing. Similarly, the phrase 'under this title' offered little guidance. It simply meant made in accordance with the Copyright Act with the copyright owner's consent or statutory authority. Section 602(a) itself did not refer to the place of manufacture. It spoke generally of copies 'acquired outside the United States'. The *Scorpio* case's reliance on the presumption against extraterritorial operation of statutes was circular. Moreover, its interpretation of section 109(a) meant that section 602 would be unnecessary since importation for commercial purposes would infringe the distribution right in any case if the 'first sale' doctrine did not apply to copies first made and sold abroad. Yet Judge Barry considered that Congress had certainly intended to remedy some shortcoming by section 602(a) as its inclusion resulted from responses to a draft bill lacking an equivalent provision.

Judge Barry also rejected the reasoning of the *Cosmair* case as logically flawed. It depended on only one example of the many considered and was not based on the wording of section 602(a). That is, section 602(a) did not depend on the place of manufacture.

Instead, Judge Barry ruled that the importation right granted by section 602 was independent of both sections 106 and 109 and was a distribution

---

409   664 F. Supp. 909, at 916 to 918.

right separate to that granted in section 106. The rationale underlying each distribution right was the same. But, in her Honour's opinion, the limitation introduced by section 109 was necessary for and applicable to the section 106 right only:

> Importation is an 'act of copying' because it increases the number of copies or phonorecords of that work available in this country. From the viewpoint of the United States copyright owner, importation of works acquired outside the United States interferes with his fundamental right to control the number of copies or phonorecords available of his work in this country no less than the mass copying of his work which might occur at the local copy shop.
>
> . . .
>
> It would make no sense if the copyright owner could prevent unauthorized reproduction but not unauthorized distribution. Similarly, it would make no sense if a copyright owner could prevent the making of unauthorized copies or phonorecords by mechanical photocopying or recording but not prevent the saturation of the market with unauthorized parallel imports. The importation right does no more than ensure the copyright owner's ability to control the maximum number of copies or phonorecords of his work available in this country.
>
> . . .
>
> In sum, the 1976 Act creates two types of distribution rights: one involving the act of vending, which is limited by the first sale doctrine, and one involving the act of importation, which is not.[410]

Crucially, Judge Barry reasoned that the copyright owner may control the number of copies of the copyrighted work in circulation in the jurisdiction.[411] By means of this control, the copyright owner is enabled to reap the reward which Congress intended. Unauthorised parallel imports would undermine that reward just as effectively as 'piratical' copying. Accordingly, where previously only a contractual remedy, if any, was available, Congress had enacted a speedy remedy in copyright to overcome the complexities of a contract action.

Judge Barry's decision in the District Court attracted two criticisms from the learned authors of *Nimmer on Copyright*.[412] The first was that section 602(a) requires 'copies . . . acquired outside the United States'. On appeal, the Third Circuit did not simply find section 602 inapplicable on this ground. One of the defendants to the case, Fabric, may well have acquired the goods in question outside the United States. But, arguably, if the 'first sale' exhausts the power to control distribution, the distribution right was spent by the time Fabric acquired the goods. The second criticism was that Judge Barry interpolated the words 'lawfully made' into section 602 although they are not part of the statutory language. But, Judge Barry derived the interpolation from the legislative history and not the statute's

---

410 *Ibid*. at 919 to 920.
411 For similar recognition in a patent case involving domestic licensing, see *Studiengesellschaft Kohle* 670 F. 2d 1122 (DC Cir. 1981), text at Chapter 3.3.3(b) from Note 230 above.
412 At §8.12[B][6] Note 67.

express words. Further, Third Circuit also found that the statutory language itself not conclusive either way.

The Third Circuit reversed, although acknowledging the inadequacies of contract. It subordinated section 602 to section 109 and, consequently, quashed the preliminary injunction. Questioning the validity of the reasoning adopted in the *Scorpio* and *Harms* cases too,[413] Judge Weis seemingly characterised the case as one where the copyright owner itself had made and sold the goods in the United States, and held:

> Section 602(a) does not purport to create a right in addition to those conferred by section 106(3), but states that unauthorized importation is an infringement of the 'exclusive [section 106(3)] right to distribute copies.' Because that exclusive right is specifically limited by the first sale provisions of section 109(a), it necessarily follows that once transfer of ownership has cancelled the distribution right to a copy, the right does not survive so as to be infringed by importation.[414]

The categorical terms in which Judge Weis expressed this conclusion forms an interesting contrast with his Honour's admission that neither his interpretation nor that suggested by Judge Barry was conclusively supported by the statutory language.[415] The reason lies in his Honour's perception of the function of section 109(a) and its interaction with section 602(a). Judge Weis considered that the 'first sale' doctrine developed because, in selling the copy, the copyright owner received its reward for future distributions of that copy. His Honour continued:

> Nothing in the wording of section 109(a), its history or philosophy, suggests that the owner of copies who sells them abroad does not receive a 'reward for his work'. Nor does the language of section 602(a) intimate that a copyright owner who elects to sell copies abroad should receive 'a more adequate reward' than those who sell domestically. That result would occur if the holder were to receive not only the purchase price, but a right to limit importation as well.[416]

Judge Weis expressed some concern for the harshness of the result. His Honour first noted that, although the matter had been dealt with in copyright law, the real issues underlying the case were those raised by gray market goods or parallel imports. In his Honour's view, it was an 'anomalous situation' for the dispute to be 'superficially targetted' at the product label when it was really about the whole product. In this situation, the court was confronted with a conflict between the interests of manufacturers and those of consumers. Consumers wanted access to identical goods at lower prices. Manufacturers sought better protection to ensure they received a fair return. Judge Weis thought this battle should be resolved elsewhere: 'We think that the controversy over "gray market" goods, or "parallel importing", should

---

413   847 F. 2d 1093, at 1098.
414   *Ibid.* at 1099.
415   *Ibid.* at 1097.
416   *Ibid.* at 1099.

be resolved directly on its merits by Congress, not by judicial extension of the Copyright Act's limited monopoly.'[417]

Pinning a dispute on the copyright subsisting in a product's label does seem artificial if the dispute can properly be characterised as one about the product itself. However, the characterisation also raises problems; there would have been little interest in importing the physical product if it did not bear the copyright label. Moreover, as the instant facts illustrated and Judge Weis himself admitted, contract was inadequate to meet the problems posed by parallel importing.[418] Right owners had turned to copyright because of the vagaries and expense associated with actions under trade marks law and section 602 of the Copyright Act had been introduced in response to heavy lobbying about unfair import competition.[419]

Questions, with respect, clamour. Resort to the history of section 109(a) and the 'first sale' doctrine might seem questionable because, until section 602(a) was passed, the 'first sale' doctrine concerned only the exhaustion, within the United States, of a US copyright. Except for the isolated and questionable *Copperman* case, the effect of a sale exercising a copyright subsisting outside the United States under another country's laws had not arisen prior to the passage of section 602(a).

Did Judge Weis intend to make a broad statement or one limited to the instant facts? The broad terms in which the two quotations from Judge Weis' opinion set out above are expressed hardly seem directed only to a sale by the copyright owner within the United States. The difficulty is compounded by his Honour's reservation of the validity of *Scorpio* and *Harms*.[420]

Despite the broad language used by Judge Weis and the reservation of the validity of *Scorpio* and *Harms,* it is arguable that Judge Weis considered Sebastian's sale to Consumer Contacts as an exercise of the US copyright. For example, in describing the instant facts, his Honour said, 'instead, this case centers on actual copies of labels printed in this country by the copyright owner'.[421] There are considerable difficulties in so describing the judgment, however. Later, Judge Weis agreed with Judge Barry's criticism of *Scorpio* in making the critical factor under section 602(a) the place of sale and explained the Third Circuit's disagreement with Judge Barry as follows: '. . . in our view, a first sale by the copyright owner extinguishes *any* right later to control importation of those copies'.[422] (*Emphasis added*) Arguably, that statement should be read in light of the context, domestic reproduction and

---

417   847 F. 2d 1093, at 1099. Contrast the *Bailey's Irish Cream* case (1986) 4 NSWLR 701 at Chapter 2.2.4 and section 4.2.2(c) above.
418   *Ibid.* referring to *Johnson & Johnson v DAL* 798 F. 2d 100 (3d Cir. 1986).
419   The first draft of the Bill did not include an importation right. This right was introduced in the first Revision in response to pressure from influential lobby groups such as publishers and the record industry: see the sources cited in Feingold, 'Parallel Importing under the Copyright Act of 1976', at 229 to 230.
420   *Ibid.* at 1098 (including Note 1). For recognition of the difficulty of supporting *Scorpio* and *Harms*, notwithstanding the reservation, see 2 *Nimmer on Copyright*, at §8.12[B][6], Note 67 to 69.
421   *Ibid.*
422   *Ibid.* at 1099.

sale by the domestic copyright owner. But, that still leaves the problem of the reservations about the validity of *Scorpio* and *Harms*. Although the Third Circuit 'specifically [did] not pass' on *Scorpio's* interpretation of the phrase 'lawfully made' in section 109, it confessed 'some uneasiness' with the interpretation. Some indication of a possible interpretation lies, perhaps, in the factual differences Judge Weis perceived between *Scorpio* and *Harms* and those of the instant case:

> *Scorpio* and *Harms*, although not binding on us, demonstrate a significant difference from the factual situation presented here. In those district court cases, the copies were produced abroad and the sales occurred overseas. The courts reasoned that the foreign origin of both manufacture and sale made the first sale doctrine inapplicable. However valid that interpretation of the 'lawfully made under this title' language of section 109(a) – and we specifically do not pass upon it in this case – it does not affect our decision here.

> II

> The facts, seen here in the context of the first sale doctrine, are not complex. We do not confront a license agreement or copies produced in a foreign country under that agreement by someone other than the owner; instead, this case centers on actual copies of labels printed in this country by the copyright owner. Sebastian produced and sold the same copies which it now seeks to control.[423]

The references to foreign licences pick up Judge Weis' earlier view that the extension of section 602(a) from 'piratical' copies to include those lawfully made was specifically to catch imports of articles lawfully made abroad by licensees.[424] Hence, perhaps, Judge Weis contemplated reconciling the statutory provisions along the following lines. The 'first sale' doctrine, as expressed by section 109, is a fundamental condition governing the exercise of distribution rights in copyright. When the domestic copyright owner itself sold an article embodying the copyright the copyright owner's rights to control importation and other distribution would be exhausted. It would not matter where that article was made or sold. On the other hand, if the article were made abroad under licence (which did not include the right to import and sell in the United States), the 'first sale' doctrine yielded to the power to control imports.

That, of course, is only speculation. If so, however, it is difficult to see why the nature of the injury is different when the domestic copyright owner itself sells the goods expressly subject to a condition that they only be marketed abroad. The copyright owner receives some form of compensation for the licensee's activity abroad and the dangers to consumers from any fetters on alienation are just the same. Judge Weis, with respect, does not explain why the territorial approach is consistent with the objects of the Copyright Act in one situation, but not in the other. Given the acknowledged ambiguity in the

---

423 *Ibid.* at 1098. Note 1, omitted, contains the confession to 'some uneasiness'. That arose because Congress clearly expressed itself when the place of manufacture was important and it had not done so in section 602(a). There was also caution about importing concepts of source of origin from trade mark law into copyright.
424 *Ibid.* at 1097.

statutory language, it could hardly be argued that the Act compelled such a result. Instead, his Honour takes an approach which even his Honour admits leaves the law in an unsatisfactory state.

At the policy level, it might be wondered whether denying Sebastian the right to block these imports would do much to encourage companies to engage in the export trade. Perhaps, the dangers of the disincentive are limited, since the right owner has various measures of self-help available, from the terms on which it contracts in the first place (although admitted by Judge Weis to be inadequate) and refusing to supply further a firm so blatantly in breach of its contracts. The need for such technicality might itself be thought undesirable. Judge Weis offered a different rebuttal: domestic producers selling abroad were not entitled to *greater* rewards than those selling in the domestic market. The Third Circuit was concerned that copyright owners would be 'double dipping', being paid twice for the one copyright. It may well be true to say that a copyright owner which sells its product abroad receives 'a reward for his work'. But, as Judge Barry made clear in the District Court, the essential question should be whether the copyright owner has received a reward for the exercise of the copyright in the United States. Under the territorial approach, sale abroad does not imply a reward for use of the domestic right.[425]

At least one District Court has now refused to bar parallel imports in the *Scorpio* situation, apparently relying on *Sebastian*; the Fourth Circuit reversed its ruling on other grounds.[426] The imports were circuit boards for video games which Taito, the US copyright owner, had licensed for manufacture, sale and use only in Japan. Red Baron bought the boards in Japan, imported them into the United States, assembled them in video game cabinets and was using them in its games parlours which were open to the public. The District Court found that, on the lawful sale of the circuit boards in Japan, the 'first sale' doctrine exhausted Taito's rights to control distribution and public performance.[427] For the purposes of the appeal, Taito conceded that its power to control importation and sale was exhausted and successfully argued that the 'first sale' doctrine did not exhaust its right to control public performance.[428] Judge Winter, for the court, held that the 'first sale' doctrine did not affect the right of public performance even though the only practical use of the circuit boards was in games parlours open to the public.[429] His Honour did so because:

> By its very terms, the statute codifying the first sale doctrine, 17 USC §109(a), is limited in its effect to the *distribution* of the copyright work. It prohibits the

---

425 Compare *Time-Life* (1976) 12 ALR 1, at 11 to 13 *per* Bowen CJ in Eq., *Barson Computers* [1985] FSR 489 and, in patents, *Griffin v Keystone Mushroom Farm Inc.* 453 F. Supp. 1243 (ED Pa. 1978), Chapter 3, Note 277 above.

426 *Red Baron-Franklin Park Inc. v Taito Corp.* 1989 CCH Copyright Law Decisions at ¶26,353 (ED Va. 1988) *revd on other grounds* 883 F. 2d 275 (4th Cir. 1989). See also 2 *Nimmer on Copyright*, at §8.12[B][6], Note 69.

427 883 F. 2d 275 at 277 to 278.

428 *Ibid.* at 278 for the concession.

429 *Ibid.* at 279.

owner of the copyright in a work who has sold a copy of the work to another from preventing or restricting the transferee from a further sale or disposition of the possession of the copy. Thus, by its terms, §109(a) has no application to the other four rights of a copyright owner . . . .[430] (*Original emphasis*)

Arguably, if it were regarded as distinct from the distribution right granted by section 106(3), similar reasoning could apply to the right to control importation. That, however, would seem to be reading too much into Judge Winter's opinion in the light of the second and third sentences in the quotation show. Judge Winter carefully refrained from commenting on Taito's concession.

In contrast, the Ninth Circuit in *Perez* limited the Third Circuit's ruling in *Sebastian* to its specific facts.[431] BMG and others owned copyright in the United States in various phonorecords. Perez was importing into the United States copies of the phonorecords made abroad. It is not entirely clear from the report whether the plaintiffs had themselves made the copies which Perez imported, although the suggestion is that the plaintiffs had at least authorised manufacture and sale. In those circumstances, Judge Beezer approved the distinction drawn in *Scorpio* between copies made and sold in the United States and copies not so made and sold. If the 'first sale' doctrine were permitted to override the power to control imports in the latter situation:

> . . . [c]opyright owners would no longer have an exclusive right to distribute copies or phonorecords of works manufactured abroad, an interest clearly protected by §602. *Scorpio*'s concern over the possibility of rendering meaningless §602 is justified and, for that reason, so is its result.[432]

In so holding, Judge Beezer distinguished *Sebastian* as dealing only with the case of copies made and sold in the United States.[433]

Hence, the Ninth Circuit, like District Judges Legge and Barry, appears to have considered that the function of section 602 is to allow the copyright owner to control the number of copies of the protected work in circulation in the United States. Possibly, that rationale would not apply where the copyright owner itself released, or authorised the release of, the copies into the United States. Therefore, if the copyright owner intends the copies to be released only on a market outside the United States, it should be careful to ensure that the sale of the copies actually takes place outside the United States.

---

430 *Ibid*. at 280.
431 *BMG Music v Perez* 952 F. 2d 318 (9th Cir. 1991).
432 *Ibid*. at 319, citing favourably 2 *Nimmer on Copyright* §8.12[B] at 8-143 (1991). At 952 F. 2d 420, Judge Beezer also dismissed Perez' defence under the First Amendment of the US *Constitution* based on the unavailability of the works in the United States.
433 *Ibid*. at Note 3. The Ninth Circuit 'specifically decline[d] to pass on' the facts of *Sebastian* as they were not the facts before it.

4.4   Conclusion

In copyright, the niceties of statutory interpretation have seemingly played a far more important role than in either trade marks or patents. In some jurisdictions, this has led to some surprising inconsistencies in the principles to be applied. In four jurisdictions – Australia, India, New Zealand and, perhaps more tentatively, Canada – copyright law clearly bars parallel imports. In doing so, each of these jurisdictions has squarely based its laws on the territorially independent nature of copyright established by the international regime regulating the subsistence of copyright. Singapore and Malaysia, on the other hand, have opted for a form of international exhaustion. The approach of the United States, the United Kingdom and South Africa is less clear. In the United Kingdom and South Africa the courts' interpretation of the hypothetical manufacturing test seems to conflict with that of the requirement of the owner's licence. The statutory adoption of a right of distribution subject to the 'first sale' doctrine may provide the basis for a theory of international exhaustion in the United States.

In the Anglo-Commonwealth countries, the copyright owner must turn to the 'secondary' infringement provisions for relief against imports. These do not provide relief where the imported article is imported solely for the private and domestic purposes of the importer. Apart from that limitation, in the field of parallel imports, the copyright owner must show that (1) there has been an importation of a hypothetically infringing article (2) without the licence of the copyright owner (3) which the defendant knows is a hypothetically infringing article.[434] These provisions apply against not only the importer but also persons who sell, or otherwise deal by way of trade in, the imported article.

The main difficulty lies in establishing what is a hypothetically infringing article. In Australia, New Zealand and India, there has been a clear adoption of the principle of territoriality. Accordingly, any article imported without the consent of the holder of the exclusive rights in the jurisdiction, if made outside the jurisdiction, will be a hypothetically infringing article. In these jurisdictions, even articles made by the copyright owner, if imported by another without the owner's consent, will be hypothetically infringing copies. The position is probably the same in Canada, although the case law is by no means as clear.

In the United Kingdom and South Africa, it is necessary to identify the actual maker of the article imported. If the actual maker possesses authority to make in the domestic market, the article will not be a hypothetically infringing article. This is particularly important where the maker is the owner of the copyright. In this situation, the grant of an exclusive licence in the domestic market has been held not to derogate from the owner's power *under copyright law* to make the article in the domestic market. Hence, in South Africa, articles can be imported to the detriment of

---

434   Singapore and Malaysia no longer apply a test based on hypothetical manufacture, see section 4.2.2(b) above.

exclusive licensees. In the United Kingdom, this test may be qualified by Templeman LJ's decision in the *Harlequin* case. In any case, the CDPA 1988 has extended the definition of an 'infringing copy' to include a copy imported in derogation of an exclusive licence agreement.

On the requirement of licence, copyright law in the Anglo-Commonwealth countries has clearly adopted the principle of territoriality. Mere sale abroad does not imply, of itself, a licence to import. Something much more specific must be shown.

Interestingly, while the United Kingdom strengthened recognition of the principle of territoriality in the CDPA 1988 by increasing protection for exclusive licensees, three other jurisdictions have taken policy decisions to undermine the acceptance of the principle in their copyright laws. All have done so by modifying the need for the domestic copyright owner's consent. In Singapore and Malaysia, the modification applies generally to all articles embodying copyright. The modification is confined to the importation of books in Australia.[435]

Almost as striking is the contrast between patent and copyright law in the Anglo-Commonwealth jurisdictions. In particular, the courts have not really explained why copyright law treats parallel imports differently to the patent law solution when the issue is implying the owner's consent to importation. The solution accepted for copyright could also be applied for patents; the reverse is equally true.

Until the 1980s, the US counterpart to the European exhaustion of rights doctrine, the 'first sale' doctrine, was concerned virtually exclusively with the exhaustion of copyright by a domestic sale. The US copyright owner's power to control subsequent distribution of copies of the work was gone once the copyright owner had transferred title in the copy to another in the United States. The effect of transfers of title outside the jurisdiction was largely unconsidered.

Under the Copyright Act of 1976, the US courts have suggested three approaches to balance the rights given by section 602(a) against the effect of section 109(a). One considered decision at an appellate level, the *Sebastian* case, appears to have rejected one conclusively: that based broadly on the territorial nature of copyright. This approach saw copyright as being intended to allow the copyright owner to control the number of copies of its work in circulation within the jurisdiction (reasoning consistent with the other main appellate consideration, *Perez*). Accordingly, section 602(a) was seen as a right independent of the distribution right granted by section 106(3). Therefore, section 602(a) was not affected by the 'first sale' limitation imposed by section 109(a). Section 109(a)'s proper role was to preserve the rights of owners of copies once the copyright owner had released the copy into circulation. This is consistent with a narrow view of the effect of the 'first sale' doctrine as it operated before the 1976 Act was passed.

---

435 Imports of sound recordings are presently also under consideration, see section 4.2.4 above.

The second approach: that suggested in the *Scorpio* case. It too was questioned in the *Sebastian* case, but endorsed by the Ninth Circuit in *Perez*. *Scorpio* drew a distinction between imports of copies according to where they were first made and sold. If the copies were first made and sold abroad lawfully, the 'first sale' doctrine did not apply. It did apply if they were first made and sold in the United States. The facts in *Sebastian* were probably consistent with the latter situation.

The third approach was that taken by the Third Circuit in *Sebastian*. Although the facts concerned copies first made and sold domestically, the doubts Judge Weis cast on the *Scorpio* and *Harms* cases and the broad terms in which his Honour's opinion was expressed suggest that the court sought to state a principle of general application. *Sebastian* held that section 602(a) was an adjunct to section 106(3) and, as such, was subject to section 109(a). Accordingly, on a broad reading, any sale anywhere by the US copyright owner would exhaust the US rights to control distribution of that copy. Indeed, one district court has gone so far as apply the 'first sale' doctrine to sales abroad by a licensee limited to sales in the foreign market. However, the facts in *Sebastian* did not call for such a wide statement. Moreover, Judge Weis was careful to distinguish the instant facts from a situation where the imports were legally made and sold abroad by a licensee (or someone else) not authorised to sell in the United States, a distinction also drawn in *Perez*.

One problem with the *Sebastian* case is that neither section 109(a) nor 602(a) expressly depend on the place where the copies were first made and sold. Section 602(a) itself only refers to imports of articles acquired outside the United States. The place where the copies are first made and sold is largely a random factor, dependent on the complexities of contract and sales of goods laws. Perhaps, more significantly, Judge Weis also did not explain why the copyright owner was 'double dipping' if it sold the goods itself, but was not where the foreign sale took place through a licensee. From the copyright owner's point of view, the difference does not seem significant since, subject to a doctrine of exhaustion, the impact of the copies is on the value of the copyright in the foreign market. Moreover, as Judge Weis appeared to concede, the decision does not adequately balance manufacturers' demand for a fair return against consumer interest in lower prices for identical products. There seems ample room to distinguish the decision. Nor is it binding on co-ordinate appellate courts. Indeed, the Ninth Circuit in *Perez* specifically refrained from passing on *Sebastian*. Accordingly, it is too early to predict the final approach of US copyright law to parallel imports.

Summarising, speaking in very broad terms, there are signs that the important factor in some jurisdictions is whether the imports result from foreign marketing initiated by someone empowered to sell in both the foreign and domestic markets. However, the characterisation is not applied in copyright with anything approaching a significant degree of consistency yet. It seems that the uncertainty reflects unresolved judicial tension about the appropriate response. Apart from the different policies seemingly pursued by the UK courts when considering the hypothetical manufacturing requirement and implied consent, this policy conflict is seen most markedly in a comparison of the *Sebastian* case on one hand and the *Time-Life* case on the other. *Sebastian* relied on the 'first sale' doctrine to permit parallel imports; the same doctrine helped the Australian High Court to arrive at the opposite conclusion.

Chapter 5: The Common Law: In Review

In Chapter 1, it was suggested that parallel imports bring into conflict two competing policies: what the author has for convenience referred to as 'the principle of territoriality' and as 'the principle of universality' (of which the doctrine of exhaustion is a manifestation). After surveying the common law world's treatment of parallel imports under the laws relating to copyright, patents and trade marks, it might be more accurate to speak of the courts as having developed three distinct approaches to parallel imports.

First, some courts have interpreted the relevant legislation as clear adoptions of the principle of territoriality. The most straightforward examples are the rules developed by the courts in Australia, New Zealand and India in copyright law.[1] Second, at the other extreme, some courts seem to have advocated adoption of an approach based on a principle of universality. Examples of this are to be found particularly in trade marks.[2] The third approach is a hybrid of the first two: some situations dictate the application of the principle of universality, while others are treated under an approach based on territoriality. Hence, in patents, we find a ruling that a sale abroad by a licensee under a foreign patent implies no consent to importation into the domestic market because the foreign patent does not grant rights of exploitation in the domestic market while, apparently, if the same sale had been made abroad by the domestic licensee, business necessity requires the implication of consent to importation.[3] It might be thought rather surprising that, as a matter of intellectual property law, some attempts to block parallel imports are subject to a principle of universality while others are governed by a principle of territoriality.

As a result, the legal treatment of parallel imports by the 'common law' results in a legalistic, complicated and confused body of law. There is no consistency in approach across the different categories of intellectual

---

1   *Time-Life* (1937) 138 CLR 534, *Barson Computers* [1985] FSR 489 and *Indian Book Distributors* [1985] FSR 120, see Chapter 4, text from Notes 178, 149 and 203 respectively.

2   Especially, *Revlon Inc. v Cripps and Lee Ltd* [1980] FSR 85 (CA) *per* Templeman LJ and *Apollinaris v Scherer* 27 Fed. 18 (SDNY 1886), Chapter 2.2.3(a) and 2.3.2 respectively.

3   The illustration is taken from the *Tilghman's* case (1883) 25 Ch. D 1, at 9 *per* Cotton LJ, contrast Lindley LJ's opinion; see Chapter 3, text from Note 81.

property, nor is there much coherence in the treatment of parallel imports involving the same subject-matter. Different countries purporting to apply the same legal principles also often arrive at completely contradictory results.

The simplest situation in which parallel imports can occur is where the same person makes and markets the product in both the foreign (export) and domestic (import) countries and also owns the relevant intellectual property rights in each. Prior to the *Colgate* case, it could confidently be said that a trade mark could not be used to block parallel imports in the Anglo-Commonwealth countries. That would seem also to be the case in the United States. However, the 'territoriality' theory endorsed in *Colgate* must throw considerable doubt on the earlier Anglo-Commonwealth cases.[4] In theory, the patent laws of the Anglo-Commonwealth countries also permit parallel imports. However, in practice this is readily circumvented by giving the necessary notice and only the most ill-advised patentee is defeated by this condition.[5] The position under US law is more complicated. There is authority to the same effect as *Betts v Willmott* and also for the use of notices excluding importation.[6] But, these cases arguably conflict with a number of others, not directly binding, which rely on the territorial limitations of the US patent grant.[7] In copyright, although its rationale in common law countries is much like that of patents, it is not possible to generalise at this level. South African law certainly permits parallel imports; the United States and the United Kingdom probably do as well.[8] Australia, India, New Zealand and, perhaps, Canada do not. The position in the United Kingdom and South Africa is complicated by the nature of the legislation; the courts do not imply the copyright owner's consent to importation, but the copyright owner cannot establish the precondition under the hypothetical manufacturing requirement.[9]

Matters get more complicated when the intellectual property rights are exploited through a licence. Considerations perhaps relevant include whether the licensee be appointed for the foreign or domestic country, whether owned independently or related to the right owner and whether exclusive

---

4 *Colgate-Palmolive Ltd v Markwell Finance Limited* [1989] RPC 497 (CA) and *Wellcome Foundation Ltd v A.-G.* [1992] EIPR D-137 (at Chapter 2, Note 106a) an application for a Norwich Pharmacal order; for the earlier approach, see *Champagne Heidsieck v Buxton* [1930] 1 Ch. 330, Chapter 2.2.3(b) and 2.2.2(b) respectively.

5 *Betts v Willmott* (1871) LR 6 Ch. App. 239; *Smith Kline & French Laboratories Ltd v Salim (Malaysia) Sdn Bhd* (1989) 15 IPR 677; see Chapter 3, text from Notes 76 and 120 respectively. See also Chapter 8, text at Note 6.

6 *Holiday v Mattheson* 24 Fed. 185 (SDNY 1885); for notice, see *Dickerson v Mattheson* 57 Fed. 532 (2d Cir. 1893) and *Sanofi v Med-Tech Veterinarian Products Inc.* 565 F. Supp. 931 (DNJ 1983); see Chapter 3, text from Notes 254, 264 and 280 respectively.

7 *Boesch v Gräff* 133 US 697 (1890), see Chapter 3 from Note 256.

8 Depending on the facts for the United States, see *Sebastian International Inc. v Consumer Contacts (PTY) Ltd* 847 F. 2d 1093 (3d Cir. 1988). Contrast *BMG Music v Perez* 952 F. 2d 318 (9th Cir. 1991); see Chapter 4, text from Notes 408 and 431 respectively.

9 There is some doubt about the position in UK law following the *Harlequin* case [1980] FSR 397 (CA), see Chapter 4, from Note 125.

rights have been granted or not (this assumes, which need not necessarily be the case, that the same person owns the rights in both countries).

Assuming a foreign licensee not expressly licensed also for the domestic market, it is no longer possible to state with any certainty what legal presumption is made in trade marks in the Anglo-Commonwealth countries. *Revlon* would suggest that the presumption lies in favour of parallel imports unless expressly rebutted. On this approach, two rebuttals have been identified so far: exclusion of a grant of the domestic rights and a difference in the quality of the foreign and domestic goods. The way the Court of Appeal in *Colgate*, however, inferred that rights under the domestic trade mark were not granted suggests that the presumption lies against importation. There, the court was impressed by the territorial nature of trade mark rights and considered that the absence of an express prohibition did not imply consent to importation. Once again, there is room for qualification since the court referred to the fact that Colgate-US never intended the Brazilian products to enter the United Kingdom; this intention was supported by long-standing corporate policy and the clear difference in quality of the imports.[10] In the United States, on the other hand, the most important criterion seems to be whether the licensee is an independent entity or related to the domestic right owner as part of the same corporate group. In the latter case, many courts will permit parallel imports, but this is not yet established conclusively.[11]

In patents, the Anglo-Commonwealth courts clearly presume against parallel importing when the sale abroad is by a licensee simply granted rights under a foreign patent.[12] The position is somewhat more complicated in the United States. There is authority for a strict territorial approach; there is also authority for exhaustion, unless either the territorial restriction was notified to the defendant in writing or importation would derogate from the grant of a domestic, exclusive licence.[13] The nature of the imports in question may also be relevant.[14]

In this context, copyright in the Anglo-Commonwealth countries is treated more like patents. In the United Kingdom and South Africa, reproduction and sale abroad by a licensee simply granted rights under a foreign copyright will not, of itself, lead to permitting parallel imports under the hypothetical manufacturing requirement. In this situation, parallel imports will also not be allowed in Australia, India, New Zealand and, probably Canada. In all

---

10   Even the South African courts may have recognised that quality differences may introduce different considerations: *Sony* 1987(2) SA 994 (AD), see Chapter 2, from Note 185.

11   Contrast *Weil Ceramics and Glass Inc. v Dash* 878 F. 2d 659 (3d Cir. 1989) to *Lever Bros Co. v US* 877 F. 2d 101 (DC Cir. 1989) and note also the importance of quality differences, for example *Original Appalachian Artworks Inc. v Granada Electronics Inc.* 816 F. 2d 68 (2d Cir. 1987); see Chapter 2, from Notes 324, 334 and 300 respectively.

12   A possible exception is the *Salim* case, see Chapter 3, from Note 120.

13   Contrast *Griffin v Keystone Mushroom Farm Inc.* 453 F. Supp. 1243 (EDNY 1978) to the *Sanofi* case 565 F. Supp. 931 (DNJ 1983), but note also the co-ordinate ruling in *Sanofi* 222 USPQ 143 (DKan. 1983); see Chapter 3, text from Notes 277 and 280.

14   *Curtiss Aeroplane and Motor Corporation v United Aircraft Engineering Corporation* 266 Fed. 71 (2d Cir. 1920), see Chapter 3, from Note 272.

jurisdictions, moreover, authorisation of the sale abroad does not lead to the implication of authority to import. 'Positive' consent, which may arise by implication in some circumstances, is required.[15] The US position is far from clear. There is District Court authority applying either territoriality or exhaustion; one appellate decision carefully distinguished its facts from this situation. The Third Circuit's ruling in *Sebastian* is expressed in places in terms broad enough to indicate that the doctrine of exhaustion would apply. However, other parts of the judgment suggest that the principle of territoriality would operate where the foreign sale was by a licensee limited to make and sell abroad; this would conform to the same Circuit's earlier decision to allow the result, if not the reasoning, in *Scorpio* to stand and has been endorsed by the Ninth Circuit in *Perez*.[16]

If a licence to exploit the domestic market be granted, two further elements may assume importance: the identity of the person initiating foreign marketing – the owner of the domestic right, a licensee or someone else; and the scope of the domestic licence – especially, whether or not it be exclusive. In all jurisdictions, only an exclusive licensee has standing to sue for infringement; in the United States, this is by analogy to a partial assignment.[17] The exclusive licensee of trade mark rights in the United States must demonstrate in addition that use of the trade mark in the United States designates a source different to that denoted by the use in the foreign market. Circumstances need to be established leading to an inference that the US exclusive licensee is understood by its public to be the sole source of the product so marked in the United States. Once again, if the exclusive licensee in the United States is associated with the foreign source by corporate ties and not just contract, some courts will ignore the principle of territoriality and even evidence of actual consumer confusion.[18]

In the Anglo-Commonwealth countries, there is authority that an exclusive licensee cannot prevent imports of goods first sold abroad by the domestic right owner by asserting either trade mark, copyright or patents.[19] The Australian case on trade marks, however, arose in circumstances where the domestic right owner expressly consented to the importation. Importation

---

15 For some suggested instances of implication, see the *Time-Life* case (1977) 137 CLR 534, Chapter 4, from Note 178.

16 *Columbia Broadcasting System Inc. v Scorpio Music Distributors Inc.* 569 F. Supp. 47 (ED Pa. 1983) *affd without opinion* 738 F. 2d 424 (3d Cir. 1984) and *BMG Music v Perez* 952 F. 2d 318 (9th Cir. 1991), but see *Red Baron-Franklin Park Inc. v Taito Corp.* 1989 CCH Copyright Law Decisions at ¶26,353 (ED Va. 1988) *revd on other grounds* 883 F. 2d 275 (4th Cir. 1989), see Chapter 4, from Notes 374, 431 and 426 respectively.

17 *Premier Dental Products v Darby Dental Supply Co.* 794 F. 2d 850 (3d Cir. 1986) (trade mark); the *Sanofi* cases (patent), see Chapter 2 from Note 284 and Chapter 3 from 280 respectively. In the Anglo-Commonwealth countries, the power is conferred by statute and may be much more limited, see Chapter 4, from Note 109.

18 *NEC Electronics v CAL Circuit Abco* 810 F. 2d 1506 (9th Cir. 1987); *Weil Ceramics*; contrast *Lever Bros* and the *Artworks* case; see Chapter 2, text from Notes 289, 324, 334 and 300 respectively.

19 See *Delphic Wholesalers Pty Ltd v Elco Food Co. Pty Ltd* (1987) 8 IPR 545 ('the *Diana Oil* case'); *CBS United Kingdom Ltd v Charmdale Record Distributors Ltd* [1980] FSR 289; and, perhaps, *Salim*; see Chapter 2, from Note 171, Chapter 4, from Note 107, and Chapter 3, from Note 120, respectively.

may well have been denied if the foreign sale had been initiated in other circumstances, certainly if by someone other than the domestic right owner.[20] In the United Kingdom, a statutory amendment was introduced to provide that importations of copyright articles in breach of an exclusive licence are barred.[21] In Australia, India, New Zealand and, probably, Canada the grant of an exclusive licence in copyright is not so important because the domestic right owner may still block imports which it sold abroad itself simply on the question of consent. Since it was the nature of a licence which led to the result in *Charmdale*, similar reasoning could well be applied in patent cases where the domestic patent owner has not clearly precluded importation by notice affecting the importer.

Separating the ownership of the intellectual property rights in the foreign and domestic markets by assignment usually leads to parallel imports being blocked. Where the foreign marketing was made by an assignee, Anglo-Commonwealth and US courts have blocked parallel imports on the ground that the assignee had no powers under the domestic rights.[22] Similar reasoning has been used when foreign marketing is initiated by the assignor. The same interpretation is applied for copyright in the Anglo-Commonwealth countries; the US position is far from clear in light of the *Sebastian* case, however, *Perez* supports exclusion. US case law requires a qualification in trade marks where the assignment is between members of the same corporate group.[23] A similar qualification has been suggested in Anglo-Commonwealth trade mark law in what has subsequently proved to be the narrow circumstances of a 'house mark for the whole group'.[24]

The strongest (in a very tentative sense) generalisation which can be drawn from reviewing the common law world's approach to parallel imports is that parallel imports may be blocked when the initial foreign sale is effected by someone without clear authority to exploit the intellectual property right in the domestic market. The most common examples of this are where ownership of the rights in the two markets has been divided or exploitation is through a licensee. The explanation of this approach is the separate and distinct territorial nature of intellectual property rights. Indeed, in deciding whether a domestic right owner has consented to a foreign licensee (or assignee) operating in the domestic market, the courts usually

---

20 *Ibid.*; other cases have blocked parallel imports where there have been quality differences, at least once when the right owner would not have succeeded: *Mattel Canada Inc. v GTS Acquisitions Ltd* (1989) 27 CPR (3d) 358, see Chapter 2, from Note 177.

21 *CBS UK Ltd v Charmdale Record Distributors Ltd* [1980] FSR 289 and see the *Video Parktown North* case; but note *British Actors' Film Company v Glover* [1918] 1 KB 299, at 309; see Chapter 4, from Note 109.

22 For patents, see *Betts v Willmott*; *Daimler Manufacturing Co. v Conklin* 170 Fed. 70 (2d Cir. 1909) *cert. dend* 216 US 621 (1910), but note *Curtiss Aeroplane* where the assignment was held to contemplate use and sale anywhere in the world and the assignor received full compensation for each aircraft sold. See Chapter 3, from Notes 76, 269 and 272 respectively.

23 Contrast *CAL Circuit Abco* to *Lever Bros*, see Chapter 2 from Notes 289 and 334 respectively.

24 Contrast *Revlon* and *Colgate*, Chapter 2.2.3(a) and (b) respectively.

operate from an assumption founded on the principle of territoriality: the absence of an express prohibition does not imply permission. Similarly, the US courts have consistently refused to permit parallel imports which would undermine a domestic, exclusive licence.[25]

The next generalisation which can be offered is that, where rights of exploitation are conferred on the same person in both the foreign and domestic markets, parallel imports of that person's products may be allowable. This generalisation is not as widely accepted as the preceding one. First, it has not received anything approaching unqualified support in copyright. In the United States, there are rulings against it including *Perez* by the Ninth Circuit, although these are questioned by the Third Circuit's ruling in *Sebastian*. Australia, India, New Zealand and, probably, Canada have not applied it; the United Kingdom and South Africa have. However, in the United Kingdom and South Africa the result was achieved by an interpretation of the 'hypothetical manufacturing requirement' and a very different rule based on territoriality applied when the focus was on the issue of consent to importation. The approach in the United Kingdom and South Africa has largely depended on whether an exclusive licensee has a property right which it can assert against its licensor. The CDPA 1988 section 27(3)(b) has markedly improved the exclusive licensee's position in the United Kingdom, a similar strengthening would occur under plans announced for South Africa. Second, particularly in patents, the proposition is very easily defeated by the use of a simple notice.

The explanation of this second generalisation is usually put on the basis of consent. For example, in both the Anglo-Commonwealth and US jurisdictions, a domestic patentee which sold on a foreign market is presumed to have impliedly consented to use in the domestic market as well. Being implied, the consent to importation may be rebutted by clear notice to the prospective defendant before the purchase.[26] The approach in trade mark law is not so clear. There is Anglo-Commonwealth authority for the view that consent to importation is implied unless rebutted.[27] There is also (perhaps, now questionable) authority for the view that the power to engage in parallel importing derives from the function of a trade mark as denoting source and so cannot be rebutted.[28] The US cases which permit parallel imports of trade-marked products proceed from the function of the

---

25 The Copyright, Designs and Patents Act 1988 (United Kingdom), section 27(3)(b) achieves a similar result in copyright and there are some suggestions that it might also apply in Canadian trade mark law. In US trade mark law, the proposition may depend on the presence or absence of a corporate relationship.

26 The US cases have not really confronted the reconciliation of this rebuttable implication and the domestic exhaustion doctrine. A similar problem arises in US copyright law, although one appellate decision appears to suggest that the exhaustion rule is not rebuttable: the *Sebastian* case but contrast *Perez* see Chapter 4 from Notes 408 and 431.

27 *Revlon* introduced the issue of consent, since acted on in *Castrol GTX* [1983] RPC 315, the *Colgate* case, the *Diana Oil* case and *Mattel*, see Chapter 2.

28 The *Champagne Heidsieck* case, the *Bailey's Irish Cream* case (1986) 4 NSWLR 701 (SC NSW), Chapter 2 Notes 35 and 137 respectively.

trade mark theory. Hence, there, the debate over whether parallel imports are permissible depends on what 'source' the trade mark use in the United States identifies.[29]

A further point which often arises relates to how a limitation against parallel importing is effected. Here, two situations must be distinguished: one, where the person selling in the foreign market also sells the same product in the domestic market; the other, where different people exploit the two markets. In the second situation, where, say a licensee (or assignee) exploits one market and the licensor (or assignor) the other, the limitation against parallel importing may be said to be 'inherent' in that no special notice prohibiting parallel imports is usually required. Hence, a purchaser from a licensee limited to the foreign market alone need not know that the licensee's powers were limited for an attempt to block parallel imports to succeed.[30]

On the other hand, where the person selling in the foreign market also has power to sell in the domestic market, any prospective parallel importer must have notice of the restriction against parallel imports before the specific goods in question are purchased.[31] Such notice need not be contractually binding; it is usually sufficient if the defendant can be shown to know of the right owner's objections before purchase.[32] A clear notice on the goods or their packaging indicating that they were made under intellectual property rights granted by country 'A' and excluding rights under other countries' laws would be the most effective way of ensuring notice.[33]

Sometimes, the permissibility of parallel imports has been made to depend on whether the foreign and domestic markets are exploited by members of the same corporate group. This has been particularly the case in the United States in the field of trade marks, but has not been established conclusively.[34]

29   *CAL Circuit Abco*, *Weil Ceramics*, *Lever Bros* and the *Artworks* case see Chapter 2, text from Notes 289, 324, 334 and 300 respectively.
30   The notice of limitation to sale and use in Canada partly relied on in *Castrol GTX* may well be superseded by *Colgate*, although, in *Colgate*, the defendants could hardly argue that they did not know of the policy against importing into the United Kingdom from Brazil; Chapter 2 Note 88 and section 2.2.3(b) respectively.
31   In the copyright laws of the Anglo-Commonwealth countries, dealing commercially with the goods after importation is also an infringement. So, subject to satisfying the hypothetical manufacturing requirement, if the knowledge element is not proved at the importation stage, the defect may still be remedied at the subsequent stage(s).
32   One US court has suggested that the notice must be in writing to be effective, see *Sanofi* 565 F. Supp. 931 (DNJ 1983), but contrast the earlier cases such as *Dickerson v Matheson* 57 Fed. 532 (2 nd Cir. 1893); see Chapter 3 Notes 280 and 264 respectively.
33   For examples of notices held effective, see the *Castrol GTX* case and *CBS Inc. v Casino Records*. See Chapter 3, Note 120, Chapter 2, Note 88 and Chapter 4, Note 402 respectively. Any notice under UK law would need to take into account the effects of EC law and only limit circulation within the European Communities as permitted by the Court of Justice's case law. On the complexities of this, see *Bayer Dental* OJ 1990 L351/46, 15 December 1990, see Chapter 7 from Note 204.
34   *CAL Circuit Abco*, *Weil Ceramics*, *Lever Bros* and the *Artworks* case see Chapter 2, text from Notes 289, 324, 334 and 300 respectively. The US Customs may, however, automatically refuse to exclude imports from a corporate affiliate under section 526 of the Tariff Act as an exercise of administrative discretion: *K Mart Corp. v Cartier Inc.* 6 USPQ 2d 1897 (1988) *revg COPIAT v US* 790 F. 2d 903 (DC Cir. 1986) *revg* 598 F. Supp. 844 (DCDC 1984), see Chapter 2.3.5.

The possibility has been raised once in the context of patents, but has not received much enthusiasm in the only other case to consider the point.[35] *Revlon* appeared to herald the acceptance of a similar qualification in Anglo-Commonwealth trade mark law, but has since been held to define a very limited exception.[36] *Salim* alone has suggested that the existence of a corporate relationship should affect the outcome in patent law. But, Templeman LJ, who took the broadest view in *Revlon*, specifically rejected an attempt to incorporate the approach into copyright law in the *Harlequin* case.

Three questions are thrown up for further consideration. Why should the power to block parallel imports be treated differently depending on the intellectual property right being asserted? What difference does it make if the product was marketed abroad by the owner of the domestic right (or someone else empowered to exploit the domestic market) on the one hand or, on the other, a licensee (or assignee of the foreign right or assignor of the domestic right, as the case may be)? Further, what difference does the existence of a corporate relationship between the persons exploiting the foreign and domestic markets make?

The most common explanation for the different results according to the intellectual property subject-matter is the different function of each right. Hence, the Australian High Court in *Time-Life*, with the apparent concurrence of the UK Court of Appeal in *Harlequin*, has suggested that the distinction between patents and copyright lies in the nature of the monopoly conferred. Copyright, it is said, does not include a power to prohibit use, while patents do. It is, of course, true that a book or a sound recording may be put to some use without infringing copyright. But neither may be put to every use which takes its owner's fancy. Neither, for example, may be performed in public without the copyright owner's consent. Moreover, what is true of books does not necessarily hold for all forms of copyright article. Any use of a computer program in which copyright subsists and which is embodied on a disk or tape necessitates an exercise of the right to reproduce the underlying work.[37] Nor can the difference lie in the separate and distinct nature of each aspect of the bundle of rights comprising copyright, since the same is true of patents. Hence, with respect, the supposed distinction between copyright and patents is at best tenuous.

A second objection to the *Time-Life* dichotomy between copyright and patents is that exactly the same implication refused there in copyright is also refused in patent law when the sale abroad is by a limited licensee. Hence,

---

35 Contrast the two *Sanofi* cases; 565 F. Supp. 931 (DNJ 1983) and 222 USPQ 143 (DKan. 1983), see Chapter 3 from Note 280.
36 See *Colgate* and *Fender Australia v Bevk* (1989) 15 IPR 257. Note also the much earlier case of *Dunlop Rubber Company Limited v A.A. Booth & Co. Limited* (1926) 43 RPC 139 (Ch. D) not referred to in *Revlon*, see Chapter 2.2.3(b) and Chapter 2 Notes 142 and 44.
37 Indeed the Fourth Circuit refused to imply a right of public performance for a computer program in circumstances where it acknowledged that the only functional use of the program would involve public performance: *Red Baron* 883 F. 2d 275 (4th Cir. 1989), see Chapter 4 from Note 426.

the consent implied to importation when the foreign sale is by a domestic patentee (or, perhaps, trade mark owner) appears to be the anomaly.[38]

The treatment of trade marks is similarly based on the different function of trade marks: to indicate 'source'. In Anglo-Commonwealth law, it might be thought that the emphasis on consent in the *Revlon* case belied this justification. In any case, those courts which use this justification to permit parallel importing do so on a singularly narrow definition of 'source' which may well lead to the deception and confusion of consumers which it is one of the functions of a trade mark to prevent.[39] Recognition that such dangers do exist has led Anglo-Commonwealth courts to a more discriminating conception of the 'source', if not the function, of a trade mark.[40]

The function of a trade mark can also be put on an economic ground like that long accepted by the common law for patents and copyright. As a property right, a trade mark encourages investment in promoting and sustaining the reputation the public associates with the mark. Hence, in theory, a trade mark provides an incentive to invest in the quality of the product sold under the trade mark. The Anglo-Commonwealth courts historically have not viewed trade marks in this way. But, more recently, the importance of a trade mark in protecting valuable investments against free riding has been referred to in Australia and Canada.[41] From this point of view, *Colgate* can also be seen as a decision to protect the domestic investment in quality from free riding by foreign imports of inferior quality. Although acceptance is certainly not unanimous, US courts have long recognised this 'property' aspect of a trade mark.

From this perspective, parallel imports raise the same issues whatever the subject-matter of intellectual property being asserted. There is a risk that some, if not all, of the incentive to invest in desirable ends encouraged by the granting of the property right will be undermined.

Why, then, does the common law treat sales abroad by someone having rights to exploit the domestic market differently to sales by someone not expressly so empowered? There are two 'classic' situations: sales abroad by the domestic right owner compared to sales by a foreign licensee; and foreign sales by an assignor (or an assignee).

The explanation offered in the common law world is that the licensee limited to a foreign territory (or an assignor or assignee) has no powers

---

38 In Anglo-Commonwealth trade mark law, the *Champagne Heidsieck* case must be subject to some question since *Colgate*. Since the 1980s, the position in the United States can at best be described as uncertain.

39 Contrast *Colgate* and *Lever Bros* to *CAL Circuit Abco* and *Weil Ceramics*. A case where deception or confusion would not seem to have been a factor as a result of the plaintiff's delay is *Champagne Heidsieck*.

40 *Colgate* recognises that a trade mark makes a representation about quality; the United States has long recognised this and adapted the concept of 'source' accordingly: *Bourjois v Katzel* 260 US 290 (1923), Chapter 2.3.3; *Premier Dental*, and *Artworks*, Chapter 2 from Notes 284 and 300 respectively.

41 *Fender* and *Mattel*; Chapter 2 Notes 142 and 177 respectively. For the United States, recognition can be traced back to *Katzel*.

under the separate and distinct rights in the domestic territory and so cannot confer greater powers than it holds itself. As a general proposition, it may seem unobjectionable. Certainly, for example, the unfairness in allowing a foreign assignor to sell the domestic rights for considerable value and then undermine its grant by direct or indirect parallel importing was readily apparent to Congress and received short shrift from Holmes J.[42]

Further examination may raise questions about some of the situations, however. It could, for instance, be argued that the domestic right owner which assigned the foreign rights receives compensation for the ensuing foreign sales by the assignee. If the domestic assignor does not receive a royalty for every foreign sale by the assignee, the value of the rights exercised may still be reflected in any lump sum or other consideration paid.[43] This argument does not apply to the case of importation into a domestic assignee's territory following sale abroad by the assignor, but could apply in the case of a foreign sale by a licensee. The argument also presupposes that the right owner is not entitled to separate fees for each use of territorially independent rights. This rebuttal, however, can hardly be called in aid if the issue is whether the principle of territoriality or a doctrine of exhaustion applies.

The next complication with the basic proposition is that in characterising the foreign licence as a licence limited to the foreign market, the courts usually apply a presumption based on the principle of territoriality.[44] There is no reason why the presumption made for sales by licensees could not also be made where the sale abroad was by the domestic right owner.[45] Indeed, the unknowing purchaser in the foreign market is just as inconvenienced whether it buys from the domestic right owner or a limited licensee. Yet, in one case, the purchaser gets the protection of a notice requirement, while not in the other. The argument that the domestic right owner has consented to unrestricted use in one case, but not the other, does not withstand examination since in both cases the consent (or lack of it) is usually implied.

Accordingly, the different treatment of foreign sales by domestic right owners (or someone else authorised to sell in both markets) to that of sales by a limited licensee, assignee or assignor reflects preference for a different policy choice. In one case, the common law world has opted for a principle of universality or exhaustion, while in the other, territoriality.

The third issue is whether it makes a difference that the two markets are being exploited by members of the same corporate group or independent

---

42 See the *Katzel* case. Lindley LJ considered that a legal system which allowed such a result would defy common sense and would not be very creditable: *Pitt Pitts* [1896] 2 Ch. 866, at 876.

43 This sort of argument played some role in *Curtiss Aeroplane*, Chapter 3 from Note 272. The argument is that any rents will be transferred to the assignor in a competitive auction of the rights.

44 See for example the *Tilghman* case (1883) 25 Ch. D 1 (CA), Chapter 3 from Note 81.

45 The *Colgate* case comes very close to recognising this.

firms. The origin of the proposition lies partly in trade mark law and partly in anti-trust.[46] Based on the function of a trade mark to denote source, the theory can have little application to other intellectual property rights. Under this approach, imports would be permitted even if they resulted in deception or confusion of the domestic public simply because the corporate relationship meant the imports had the same source and so did not violate the function of the trade mark. The crucial role posited for the corporate relationship does not seem convincing. It has not found universal acceptance in the United States.[47] It has been rejected in the Anglo-Commonwealth countries.[48] European exhaustion doctrines apply to both corporate and contractual links, hence they have also rejected the distinction.[49]

In the *K Mart* case on section 526 of the US Tariff Act, Brennan J indicated that the approach towards an independent, domestic assignee should not apply in cases involving corporate affiliates because of the different 'equities'. In his Honour's view, there were two main differences.[50] First, the corporate affiliate did not risk 'the same sort of investment' as an independent assignee. In any event, the corporate group had a whole 'panoply of options' for preventing import competition unavailable to the independent, domestic assignee.

Brennan J gave three examples of the 'panoply of options' available to the corporate group. The corporate affiliates could simply agree that the group would not import directly into the domestic market except through the domestic affiliate. This seems to be nothing more than simply granting the domestic affiliate exclusive rights under the intellectual property. It is not entirely clear why this raises different considerations to a contract between independent firms granting one exclusive rights to the domestic market, whether as assignee or exclusive licensee. His Honour's second example was that the domestic affiliate could (where legal) oblige the foreign affiliate to impose restrictions on resale of the product or at least its export to the domestic market. Once again, there does not seem to be any reason why an independent firm could not contractually bind the foreign licensor or assignor to the same effect. The third example was that the corporate group should stop selling abroad entirely. This may be a practical consideration if the domestic market accounts for by far the overwhelming bulk of the market for the product in question. But, it must be questionable whether a legal system should provide incentives for such conduct. Further, in the realms of pure theory, there is arguably nothing to stop an independent, domestic assignee from buying the rights to the foreign market and then refraining from selling there also.

---

46 *US v Guerlain Inc.* 155 F. Supp. 77 (SDNY 1957) *vacated and remanded* 357 US 924 (1958) *dismissed* 172 F. Supp. 107 (SDNY 1959), Chapter 2.3.4(a).
47 *Lever Bros*, the *Artworks* case.
48 *Colgate*; *dicta* in *Fender*; and *Mattel*.
49 See *Cinzano v Java Kaffeegeschäfte* [1974] 2 CMLR 21 (BGH) in Chapter 1; 16/74 *Centrafarm v Winthrop* [1974] ECR 1183, see Chapter 6 from Note 106; Friedrich-Karl Beier, 'Territoriality of Trademark Law and International Trade', 1 IIC 48 (1970).
50 6 USPQ 2d 1897, at 1907 (1988).

Hence, with respect, as options to prevent parallel imports, there does not seem to be anything which poses a vital distinction between corporate affiliates and independent firms. Furthermore, the first two examples are likely to prove equally ineffective in either case. If costs associated with transport, duties and technical differences are not prohibitive, both examples are likely to prove ineffective to the extent that they depend on contract regardless of whether exploitation be through a corporate group or an independent firm.[51]

Brennan J's first difference, based on the investment perceived to be at stake, threatens to overlook that it will cost the corporate group (even if it be characterised as an amorphous entity) at least as much to establish and maintain its presence in the domestic market as an independent firm.

A more likely explanation is that Brennan J perceived the corporate group as a single entity which derived the benefit of the intellectual property right from the initial exercise in the foreign market and so was not entitled to charge a further fee in the domestic market. Hence, his Honour could be taken as supporting an approach based on universality and exhaustion rather than territoriality. In turn, this raises the question already discussed, of why intellectual property law should treat foreign marketing by the domestic right owner (or other person authorised to sell in the domestic market) differently to a sale abroad by, say, a limited licensee.

Despite the reluctance of most Anglo-Commonwealth courts to embrace the treatment of a corporate group as a single entity, some policy support for Brennan J's approach may be seen in his Honour's earlier references to the so-called '*Copperweld*' doctrine. That is, US anti-trust and EC competition law do not generally regard arrangements between corporate affiliates as subject to the prohibitions on anti-competitive agreements.[52] This still does not avoid the intellectual property issue of why a domestic right owner selling abroad should be treated differently to a foreign sale initiated by a limited licensee. Furthermore, it does not automatically lead to a finding of anti-competitive behaviour where a corporate affiliate seeks to block parallel imports. The question then becomes one of whether the corporate affiliate's exercise of its intellectual property rights raises the prospect of monopolisation or abuse of a dominant position proscribed by laws seeking to control unilateral exercises of market power.[53] This in turn requires a finding that the person seeking to exercise the intellectual property right possesses the necessary degree of economic power in a properly defined market, a condition which may often be lacking.

The existence of a corporate relationship between those exploiting the

---

51 Even the Third Circuit in *Sebastian* recognised that contract was a poor defence, see Chapter 4 from Note 408.

52 See *Copperweld Corp. v Independence Tube Corp.* 467 US 752 (1984). For the EC, see case 15/74 *Centrafarm BV v Sterling Drug Inc.* [1974] ECR 1147, see Chapter 6 from Note 93.

53 For example, section 2 of the Sherman Act, 15 USC §2 (1988) and EEC Treaty, Article 86.

foreign and domestic rights, then, may raise questions of anti-trust or competition policy. It does not, however, seem to dictate different solutions for parallel imports as a matter of intellectual property law. There is no compelling reason why intellectual property law should apply an approach based on a principle of universality (or exhaustion) to one case and one based on a principle of territoriality in the other.

Consumers suffer the same loss if parallel imports be denied. Purchasers of goods are threatened with the same commercial inconvenience, if any, if their dealings in the articles be restricted. Correspondingly, if parallel imports be allowed, right owners risk the same threats to invest in innovation and exploiting the fruits of that innovation; consumers also risk reduced, or delayed, access to products which they might otherwise derive some advantage from. Hence, arguably, parallel imports should be subject to the same treatment − exhaustion or territorial independence − regardless of subject-matter, identity of the person responsible for initiating foreign marketing or the presence of corporate links.

Some European jurisprudence, as already indicated, avoids the anomaly by treating parallel imports in the same way whether they arise through corporate links or some form of bargain. But, apart from the special case of EC law, international exhaustion is usually confined to trade marks. Moreover, in the 'common law' world, an approach based on the principle of territoriality predominates. There have been moves in Singapore and Malaysia, particularly in copyright law, to shift to an approach based on exhaustion; also in Australia. Conversely, the principle of territoriality has been strengthened by the legislature for copyright law in the United Kingdom and increased protection has also been proposed in Canada and South Africa.[54]

The adoption of an exhaustion-type rule, following experience in the European Communities, has sometimes been suggested as the appropriate policy solution.[55] Before accepting or rejecting such a policy, an examination of how it works and its consequences is necessary. Some examination of 'exhaustion', mainly in the context of domestic trade in the United States, has already been made. The EC's rules, however, make evident the most concerted attempt to apply a doctrine of exhaustion in something like an international context. An examination of the EC rules is also necessary to complete an understanding of UK law. Moreover, it may also demonstrate to what degree the rule has been successful and what steps must be taken if it is to be effective from the points of view of both the goals intellectual property seeks to promote and the 'interests' of consumers.

---

54 The piecemeal approach in Australia towards copyright is examined further in Chapter 4.2.4 and 10. Canadian experience is the subject of Chapter 10.3.
55 See for example Staniforth Ricketson, *The Law of Intellectual Property*, The Law Book Co., 1984, at ¶¶54.19 to 54.20.

Chapter 6: Driving to Integrate the Market

6.1 Introduction

There is growing recognition that the European Court of Justice (ECJ) has markedly changed how it treats parallel imports in its efforts to integrate the internal market under the EEC Treaty; there is not, however, much agreement about what the 'new' approach is.[1] Some argue that efforts to use national intellectual property laws to block parallel imports will only be struck down where they discriminate against imports solely because they are imports;[2] others seem to indicate that the explanation lies in the changing nature of the subject-matter under consideration;[3] still others argue that the modification is less radical and identify 'consent to marketing' as the litmus test.[4]

There are difficulties in accepting any of the individual theories as a complete explanation of the change observed by all. A test based solely on consent does not seem to account for the increasing number of situations where parallel imports have been blocked *although* marketed in the 'foreign' Member State with the 'domestic' right owner's consent;[5] similarly, a theory based on the changing nature of the subject-matter does not account for

---

1 This may be thought hardly surprising since the rulings of the ECJ, consisting of up to 13 judges who deliver a single judgment from which there are neither concurring opinions nor dissents take on a singularly Delphic character: see for example T.C. Hartley, *The Foundations of European Community Law*, Clarendon Press, 1988 (2nd ed.), Chapter 2.

2 See now Giuliano Marenco and Karen Banks, 'Intellectual Property and the Community Rules on Free Movement: Discrimination Unearthed', (1990) 15 ELRev. 224 and, in places, Georges Friden, 'Recent Developments in EEC Intellectual Property Law: The Distinction Between Existence and Exercise Revisited', (1989) 26 CMLRev. 193.

3 Lucette Defalque, 'Copyright – Free Movement of Goods and Territoriality: Recent Developments', [1989] EIPR 435 seems to suggest, in part, that the treatment of copyright lies in a sensitivity to cultural aspirations and the particular dictates of 'the performing right'.

4 Friedrich-Karl Beier, 'Industrial Property and the Free Movement of Goods in the Internal European Market', 21 IIC 131 (1990). For still another, early, recognition that change is afoot, see Martijn Van Empel, 'EEC Law and Intellectual Property: Free Movement and Positive Integration', (1991) 29 *Bar European News* 1.

5 For example, 158/86, *Warner Bros Inc. v Christiansen* [1988] ECR 2605, from Note 184 below.

the emergence of qualifications across subject-matters;[6] if discrimination be the test, it would seem to mandate a much greater revision than its proposers concede.[7] A further difficulty is that these arguments concentrate on developments in only one field; seemingly overlooking an almost parallel train of developments in the ECJ's interpretation of the EEC Treaty's competition rules.

In the present context, the aim is to unfold how what was a fairly clear and strong doctrine of exhaustion applying to trade between the European Communities' (EC's) Member States has developed and to attempt to identify the reasons which have led to the modifications. Perhaps the main point which emerges is that, however desirable freeing up trade may be in the interests of passing on the benefits of lower prices to consumers, trade across international frontiers (even within a 'common' market) exposes a wide range of legal and policy differences which may prove particularly prejudicial to the goals intellectual property laws seek to encourage. A complicating factor, on the other hand, is that business may seize on obstacles to market integration only to resist the pressures for change which the establishment of the internal market seeks to encourage.[8]

Parallel imports confront the EC with a complication not faced in other jurisdictions. The basic object of the EC is market integration: to create a unified market out of the several national markets of the Member States.[9] But, within the internal market, intellectual property rights have largely remained regulated by the individual Member States.[10] Hence, if the national law allows an intellectual property owner to block parallel imports, intellectual property rights could be used to disrupt integration of the market.

The EEC Treaty has two independent sets of rules which have been used to regulate the use of national intellectual property rights in blocking parallel imports: the 'free movement rules' and the 'competition rules'. For present purposes, Title 1 of Part II, 'Foundations of the Community', deals with the abolition of customs duties, quotas and like measures between the Member

---

6   For example, see the discussion of C-10/89 *SA CNL-Sucal NV v HAG GF AG* [1990] 3 CMLR 571, from Note 220 below.

7   Compare 78/70 *Deutsche Grammophon GmbH v Metro-SB-Grossmärkte GmbH & Co. KG* [1971] ECR 487 and 15/74 *Centrafarm BV v Sterling Drug Inc.* [1974] ECR 1147 to 55 & 57/80 *Musik-Vertrieb Membran v GEMA* [1981] ECR 147 and 187/80 *Merck & Co. v Stephar* [1981] ECR 2063; at Notes 70, 93, 134 and 141, respectively.

8   On practical difficulties in drawing the line within the EC, see further Chapters 8 and 9 below.

9   The tasks of the EC are prominently stated to be achieved 'by establishing a common market': EEC Treaty, Article 2. Article 3 then sets out the activities of the EC which may be broadly paraphrased as removing institutional barriers to the common market and trade between the Member States. On the role of Articles 2 and 3 in the interpretation of the competition rules, see Korah, *EEC Competition Law and Practice*, at §1.2.3.

10   Belgium, the Netherlands and Luxembourg have formed a regional association for certain purposes; adopting for example common trade mark and designs laws. On the singular nature of the EC as a *sui generis* form of association having some of the characteristics of an international organisation and some of the characteristics of a 'national' federation, see Hartley, *Foundations of European Community Law*, especially at Part II.

States, replacing them with a common customs tariff for the EC's dealings with third countries and a free trade area within the customs union. (The further work of the common market and, now, the single market being to convert that free trade area into a truly unified market.) In particular, Articles 30 and 34 prohibit governmental restrictions on imports and exports, respectively, within the EC. Article 36, however, qualifies the prohibition with an exception in favour of 'industrial and commercial property':

> The provisions of Arts. 30 to 34 shall not preclude prohibitions or restrictions on imports, exports or goods in transit justified on grounds of . . . the protection of industrial and commercial property. Such prohibitions or restrictions shall not, however, constitute a means of arbitrary discrimination or a disguised restriction on trade between Member States.

Chapter 3 of Title 2, 'Free Movement of Persons, Services and Capital', makes provision for services similar to that made by Articles 30 and 34 for goods. While it does not, in terms, include an exception corresponding to Article 36, a similar limitation has been read in.[11]

The 'competition rules' are found in Part III of the EEC Treaty, 'Policy of the Community'. For present purposes, Article 85(1) prohibits arrangements between undertakings which: '. . . may affect trade between member states *and* which have as their object or effect the prevention restriction or distortion of competition with the common market. . . .' (*Emphasis added*). Then follows a list of examples of potentially anti-competitive practices. Under Article 85(3), however, the Commission has power to exempt arrangements from the prohibition. Further, Article 86 proscribes the abuse of a dominant position in the common market, or a substantial part of it, where the abuse may affect trade between Member States.[12]

Both sets of rules are subject to the 'guarantee' of Member States' property systems provided by Article 222. Although it has played a role in the form taken by the ECJ's reasoning, the broad terms of Article 222 have limited its application in EC law.[13]

Since 1966, the ECJ has identified four alternative situations in which these provisions of the EEC Treaty override an intellectual property owner's attempts to use its domestic rights under the laws of one Member State to

---

11 For exceptions to the principle of freedom to provide services throughout the EC, see further 62/79 *Coditel v Ciné Vog Films* [1980] ECR 881 ('*Coditel I*') from Note 125 below. For detailed consideration of the free movement rules, see L.W. Gormley, *Prohibiting Restrictions on Trade within the EEC*, T.M.C. Asser Instituut, 1985; P. Oliver, *Free Movement of Goods in the EEC*, London Law Centre Limited, 1988 (2nd ed.) and Derek Wyatt and Alan Dashwood, *The Substantive Law of the EEC*, Sweet & Maxwell Ltd, 1987 (2nd ed.), Part III.

12 For detailed consideration, see Valentine Korah, *EEC Competition Law and Practice*, ESC Publishing, 1990 (4th ed.); Richard Whish, *Competition Law*, Butterworths, 1989 (2nd ed.); Wyatt and Dashwood, *The Substantive Law of the EEC*, at Part VII; and Christopher Bellamy and Graham D. Child, *Common Market Law of Competition*, 1987 (3rd ed.).

13 See 56 & 58/64 *Consten & Grundig v Commission* [1966] ECR 299 at section 6.2 below. Article 222 provides that 'This Treaty shall in no way prejudice the rules in Member States governing the system of property ownership.'

repel parallel imports. One arises when the intellectual property rights are used against parallel imports as a result of an agreement with another party contrary to Article 85.[14] A second is the possible use of intellectual property rights in the abuse of a dominant position contrary to Article 86.[15] A third is the so-called exhaustion rule under which EC law prevailed over national intellectual property rights if the imports had been marketed in another Member State by the domestic right owner or with its consent.[16] Finally, the fourth situation so far identified has been the situation where the intellectual property right in question is owned in the two Member States by different, unrelated persons *but* the rights in both Member States were originally owned by the same person – the so-called common origin doctrine.[17] A crucial distinction exists between the first two situations and the second pair based on the different parts of the EEC Treaty they derive from. The third and fourth situations only ever apply to trade between Member States of the EC; it is possible for the first and second situations to arise in trade between the EC and a third country.[18]

Using the competition rules, the ECJ quickly established the overriding importance of market integration in EC law. Private parties could not be allowed, by private agreements to split ownership of their intellectual property on national lines, to partition off national markets. The Achilles' heel inherent in this approach was shortly exposed since it depended on collusive action between undertakings. When collusion was lacking and the threat to market integration remained obvious, the ECJ translated its philosophy of integrating the market to the free movement rules. However, the narrow foundation on which the ECJ's approach has been based has not provided adequate solutions. The failure to deal with the underlying issues is reflected in the continual stream of cases referred to the ECJ for opinion. More recently, and more spectacularly, it has seen the demise of the 'common origin' doctrine, fairly considerable qualifications in the ECJ's basic rule of exhaustion and what is, arguably, a more discriminating approach under the competition rules.

6.2   The Overriding Object: Market Integration

Contrasting two of the ECJ's major competition rulings in 1966 highlights the vigour of the ECJ's assault on agreements which sought to partition the common market to establish the overriding importance of the goal of

---

14   *Ibid.*

15   24/67 *Parke, Davis & Co. v Probel* [1968] ECR 55; 402/85 *Basset v SACEM* [1987] ECR 1747, see Chapter 7.4 below.

16   78/70 *Deutsche Grammophon GmbH v Metro-SB-Grossmärkte GmbH & Co. KG* [1971] ECR 487 from Note 70 below.

17   This doctrine is primarily identified with trade marks, see 192/73 *Van Zuylen Frères v Hag AG (Hag I)* [1974] ECR 731, from Note 88 below.

18   See section 6.3.2 and Chapter 7.5 below.

integrating the internal market motivating EC law.[19] Subsequent decisions, however, showed the shortcomings of relying on the competition rules.

The *STM* and *Consten & Grundig* cases both concerned exclusive distribution arrangements in France organised by German manufacturers.[20] In each, the manufacturer promised not to appoint another distributor in France and the distributor agreed not to take on competing products.[21] The distributors further agreed to undertake the publicity of the products in France and to carry out guarantee and after-sales service and related activities. The crucial difference lay in the arrangements to block parallel imports found in *Consten & Grundig* but not present in the *STM* case.

The arrangements made between Grundig and Consten in 1957 involved several layers of restraints on conduct. Grundig, a German manufacturer of various lines of electrical goods, appointed Consten as its exclusive distribution agent for France and Consten agreed not to sell or act for Grundig's competitors. Consten also agreed not to sell Grundig products, directly or indirectly, outside its contract territory with Grundig similarly undertaking to prevent imports into Consten's territory. To bolster Consten's protection, Grundig had also licensed Consten to use its registered trade mark, *Grundig*, in France and permitted Consten to register a second trade mark, *GINT*, which was subject to an international registration in favour of Grundig. Consten agreed to use it only on Grundig products and to reassign the mark if it ceased to represent Grundig in France. Grundig's goods bore both trade marks.

Grundig's agreement with Consten was one of a network of agreements with exclusive agents in other European countries, all on similar terms. In Germany, Grundig sold directly to the wholesale industry which it obliged not to sell Grundig products outside Germany.

In 1962, Consten sued another French company, UNEF, under French law for unfair competition and for infringement of the trade mark *GINT*.[22]

---

19 For similar arguments that the two cases are reconcilable on the basis of the market integration philosophy, see René Joliet, *The Rule of Reason in Antitrust Law*, Martinus Nijhoff, 1967, at 155 to 173; Valentine Korah, 'The Rise and Fall of Provisional Validity – The Need for a Rule of Reason in EEC Antitrust', 3 *Northwestern Journal of International Law & Business* 320, at 344 to 348 (1981); and Bellamy and Child, *Common Market Law of Competition*, at ¶¶2.058 to 2.064.

20 56/65 *Société Technique Minière v Maschinenbau Ulm* [1966] ECR 235; 56 & 58/64 *Consten & Grundig v Commission* [1966] ECR 299; before the Commission: *Re Grundig's Agreement* [1964] CMLR 489.

21 In EC jargon, the obligation accepted by the manufacturer is described as an 'exclusive dealing' obligation while that accepted by the distributor is an 'exclusive purchasing' obligation. For the current acceptance of these characterisations, see Commission Regulations 1983/83 and 1984/83. For the EC approach of separating exclusivity arrangements into their component parts, see Joliet, *The Rule of Reason in Antitrust Law*, at 160 and onward, using different terminology; René Joliet, 'Trademark Licensing Agreements Under the EEC Law of Competition', 5 *Northwestern Journal of International Law & Business* 755 (1983) – an abridged version appears at 15 IIC 21 (1984).

22 The form of the unfair competition appears to have been UNEF's attempts to undermine the exclusive distribution contract, the provisions of which were generally known, so violating its duty to respect the contractual relations between Consten and Grundig. See *Re Grundig's Agreement* [1964] CMLR 489, at 492. Professor Korah

UNEF complained to the Commission that Grundig's arrangements with Consten were in breach of Article 85 of the EEC Treaty and the French courts suspended Consten's actions pending the Commission's ruling.

UNEF had been buying Grundig products from German wholesalers and importing them into France since 1961 when it had discovered that it could buy Grundig products in Germany at prices between 14 to 23 per cent cheaper than in France, although, with the establishment of the common market, the price differences were falling. UNEF was so successful that its sales accounted for 10 per cent of all Grundig products sold in France.

The Commission condemned the whole of the arrangements under Article 85(1) of the EEC Treaty and refused to exempt under Article 85(3).[23] In the Commission's view, the arrangements were intended to stifle competition in Grundig products at the wholesale level in France and, given the complicated nature of the products, intra-brand competition in the products was of 'particular importance'.[24] Exemption was denied because the absolute territorial protection effected by the arrangements was not indispensably necessary to achieve the improvements in production and distribution of Grundig products in France claimed for the products.[25] Moreover, the price differences between France and Germany at the retail level showed that consumers were not receiving a fair share of the benefits deriving from any improvements in production and distribution.[26] Finally, the Commission declared that absolute territorial protection was 'particularly noxious to the realisation of the Common Market'.[27]

On appeal, the ECJ, apparently overriding the Advocate-General's detailed criticism of the legal and factual basis of the Commission's decision, upheld the Commission insofar as it had condemned the arrangements conferring absolute territorial protection on Consten. However, the ECJ quashed the decision insofar as it did not relate to absolute territorial protection.

Three elements reveal the strength of the ECJ's attack: the categorical language which the ECJ used to condemn Consten and Grundig's arrangements; the factual circumstances of the case – leaving aside the market insulation, the facts do not seem to present a strong case on anti-competitive grounds; and the far more lenient treatment accorded exclusive distribution in the *STM* case.

Ruling that Article 85 applied to vertical agreements as well as to horizontal ones, the ECJ first declared:

> . . . an agreement between producer and distributor which might tend to restore the national divisions in trade between Member States might be such as to

---

also suggests that Consten's action was based on UNEF's inducement of the German wholesalers to breach their contracts with Grundig: Korah, *EEC Competition Law and Practice*, at §2.2.1.

23   Grundig had notified the exclusive distribution agreement in 1963 after Regulation 17 of 1962 came into force: *Re Grundig's Agreement* [1964] CMLR 489, at 494.

24   *Ibid.* at 495 to 496.

25   *Ibid.* at 501 to 502.

26   *Ibid.* at 499 to 500.

27   *Ibid.* at 504.

frustrate the most fundamental objections [sic] of the Community. The Treaty, whose preamble and content aim at abolishing the barriers between States, and which in several provisions gives evidence of a stern attitude with regard to their reappearance, could not allow undertakings to reconstruct such barriers. Article 85(1) is designed to pursue this aim, even in the case of agreements between undertakings placed at different levels in the economic process.[28]

The ECJ then examined whether Consten and Grundig's arrangements 'restricted' competition. The necessary restriction lay in an agreement between Consten and Grundig to use French law to give Consten absolute territorial protection: it sought to block completely all parallel imports of Grundig products from entering France.[29] The agreement was evidenced by several factors. First, there was Grundig's promise not to supply third parties which might even indirectly deliver products onto the French market. Second, there was Consten's reciprocal promises not to export Grundig products from France or knowingly sell to third parties which might export. This was particularly outrageous as part of a network of distribution agreements similarly banning exports. Third, there was Consten's registration in France of the *GINT* mark; the international entitlement of which belonged to Grundig, which Consten agreed to use only on Grundig products and which Consten undertook to reassign to Grundig if it ceased to be Grundig's distributor in France. It was also a mark which had been brought into existence as a result of Grundig's failure to use its *Grundig* mark (also carried on the goods supplied to Consten) successfully to block parallel imports into the Netherlands in 1956. Of such an agreement, the ECJ ruled:

> Since the agreement thus aims at isolating the French market for Grundig's products and maintaining artificially, for products of a very well-known brand, separate national markets within the Community, it is therefore such as to distort competition in the Common Market.[30]

In its final ruling on the Commission's finding that the exclusive distribution arrangements were a restriction on competition contrary to Article 85(1), the ECJ pronounced:

> The state of affairs found to be incompatible with Article 85(1) stems from certain specific clauses of the contract of 1 April 1957 concerning absolute territorial protection and from the additional agreement on the GINT trade mark rather than from the combined operation of all the clauses of the agreement, that is to say, from the aggregate of its effects.[31]

---

28 [1966] ECR at 340. The distinction being to Germany's *Gesetz gegen Wettbewerbsbeschränkungen* ('Statute Against Restraints of Competition') which adopts a much stricter stance against horizontal agreements (those between competitors at the same level of production or distribution) than it does against vertical agreements, compare for example section 1 and section 18. See Joliet, *The Rule of Reason in Antitrust Law*, Chapter 2 and Strobl, Killius and Vorbrugg, *Business Law Guide to Germany*, CCH Editions, 1988 (2nd ed.), Chapter 10.

29 *Ibid.* at 342 to 343. For a similar argument that the ECJ condemned a market partitioning agreement based on analysis of the French and German texts of the judgment, see Hans Ulrich, 'The Impact of the "Sirena" Decision on National Trademark Rights', 3 IIC 193, at 208 to 210 (1972).

30 *Ibid.* at 343.

31 *Ibid.* at 344.

Immediately before that passage, the ECJ noted that the 'Commission did not adequately state the reasons why it was necessary to render the whole of the agreement void'. Hence, the ECJ did not endorse the Commission's view that the whole agreement between Grundig and Consten was void.

Moreover, according to the ECJ, this type of restriction was so pernicious that it could never be justified under Article 85(1). No amount of economic data showing the pro-competitive tendencies of the arrangement or proof of factual error on the Commission's part would invalidate the conclusion that the agreement was a prohibited restriction on competition. If such an agreement were to be permitted under EC law, it would have to be under Article 85(3): '. . . no possible favourable effects of the agreement in other respects, can in any way lead, in the face of abovementioned restrictions, to a different solution under Article 85(1)'.[32] In fact, it seemed that the ECJ did not envisage even exemption under Article 85(3) for absolute territorial protection since it appears to reject an argument that the absolute territorial protection was necessary to induce Consten to undertake the risks of launching what it described as a well-known, but previously unknown *to the French*, brand on the French market as having 'no connexion with the improvements in distribution referred to in Article 85(3)'.[33]

For present purposes, two more points of legal significance remain. Consten argued that the Commission's decision violated its rights under Article 36 and Article 222. The ECJ noted that condemning the collusion to split the common market would be defeated if Consten could use its trade mark rights unilaterally for the same end. It then ruled that Article 36, being a limitation on Articles 30 to 34, had no effect on the competition rules.[34] In addition, Article 222, guaranteeing the system of property ownership set up in each Member State, was not undermined by action under the competition rules since the Commission's order to refrain from using rights under national trade mark law to block parallel imports did 'not affect *the grant* of those rights but only limit[ed] *their exercise* to the extent necessary to give effect to the prohibition under Article 85(1)[35]' (*Emphasis added*). Consten could not misuse its rights under French trade mark law to defeat the objectives of the EEC Treaty's competition rules.

Consideration of the factual circumstances of the case serves to highlight the strength of the ECJ's ruling on the goal of integrating the internal market since the facts claimed by Consten and Grundig provide a sound base for speculating that the arrangements may have been pro-competitive rather than anti-competitive or, at least, required further investigation.[36]

These must themselves be set against two other matters. Trade between

---

32   *Ibid.*
33   *Ibid.* at 349 to 350.
34   But see 40/70 *Sirena Srl v Eda Srl* [1971] ECR 69 at ¶5, from Note 64 below.
35   *Ibid.* at 345. See now René Joliet and David T. Keeling, 'Trade Mark Law and the Free Movement of Goods: The Overruling of the Judgment in Hag I', 22 IIC 303 (1991) at §IX.1.
36   In fact, this conclusion is the substance and tenor of the Advocate-General's long and detailed opinion.

France and Germany had only just been liberalised following the establishment of the common market and the lowering of customs barriers when Grundig's arrangements with Consten fell for consideration by the Commission and much of the ECJ's deliberations over the case took place against the background of the crisis leading to the Luxembourg Accords.[37]

Consten and Grundig relied on the increased penetration of the French market against a range of competing brand names and claimed that their arrangements were necessary to allow the brand to break into the 'new' market. Both the Commission's and the ECJ's decisions are remarkable for their apparent failure to consider the impact of the arrangements on inter-brand competition.[38] This failure is all the more noteworthy since the importance of inter-brand competition lay at the heart of Advocate-General Roemer's opinion and was a significant factor under the test enunciated by the ECJ in the *STM* case.[39]

Instead, the Commission found the existence of a restriction on intra-brand competition sufficient to condemn Consten and Grundig's arrangements under Article 85(1). It went further and stated that it considered intra-brand competition for these types of products was more important than inter-brand competition; inter-brand competition only being relevant for simple, mass-produced goods. For any sort of complicated product, such as the televisions, radios and other products at issue, inter-brand competition was unhelpful because the consumer could not adequately compare the rival products.[40] Contrast the approach advocated by the US Supreme Court in the *Sylvania* case where the Supreme Court noted the complexity of assessing the impact of vertical restraints under anti-trust law and directed examination of competition both between rival brands and between sellers of the same brand. Strikingly, the Supreme Court considered that inter-brand competition was the primary concern for products such as televisions.[41] This is not to say that the US approach should be adopted *ipso facto* in the EC.[42]

---

37 See for example Korah, 'The Rise and Fall of Provisional Validity', at 344.

38 *Consten & Grundig*, of course, predated the US Supreme Court's *per se* condemnation of vertical restraints in *US v Arnold Schwinn & Co*. 388 US 365 (1968) subsequently overruled in *Continental T.V. Inc. v GTE Sylvania Inc*. 433 US 36 (1977) which restored the 'rule of reason' analysis, see Chapter 3, from Note 215. However, rule of reason analysis underlay *White Motor Co. v US* 372 US 253 (1963) and seems to form the basis of Germany's Statute Against Restraints of Competition, on which see for example Joliet, *The Rule of Reason in Antitrust Law*, Chapter 2 and Strobl, Killius and Vorbrugg, *Business Law Guide to Germany*, Chapter 10.

39 See [1966] ECR at 357, 358, 359 to 360, 369 to 370, 371 to 372.

40 [1964] CMLR at 495 to 496. For similar analysis by the ECJ, see [1966] ECR at 343.

41 See 433 US at 581, especially Note 19.

42 For one view that EC circumstances may warrant a more stringent approach to vertical restraints, see Michel Waelbroek, 'Vertical Agreements: Is the Commission Right not to Follow the Current US Policy?', 25 *Swiss Review of International Competition Law* 45 (1985); note also the evidence referred to in F.M. Scherer and David Ross, *Industrial Market Structure and Economic Performance*, Houghton Mifflin, 1990 (3rd ed.), 553, text at Note 32. It has also been convincingly argued that freeing up restraints on intra-brand competition may promote inter-brand competition when the restraints are imposed by an entrenched 'leading brand', see Robert L. Steiner, 'The Nature of Vertical Restraints', 30 *Antitrust Bulletin* 143, especially 178 to 183 (1985).

Rather, as Advocate-General Roemer was at pains to stress, the Commission did not consider one important aspect of competition at all and, in this case, the ECJ was prepared to support that failure.

In denying exemption, the Commission stated that Consten would not need absolute territorial protection if it sold at profit margins roughly equal to those of other Grundig wholesalers throughout the market.[43] It did not really consider the parties' arguments in favour of absolute territorial protection: the need for a higher return to undertake a more risky investment in opening up a new market and the greater costs incurred by Consten compared to the German wholesalers which did not have national publicity costs or costs associated with providing a guarantee and after-sales service. Rather, the Commission stated that Consten need not undertake the publicity functions for France since they could easily have been performed by Grundig. As Advocate-General Roemer pointed out, the Commission substituted its own opinion for that of the businessmen whose livelihood was at stake without even investigating whether Grundig had sufficient resources to fund such activities in France and all the other countries it exported products to under similar arrangements.[44] The ECJ did, at least, refer to Grundig products as those of a 'very well-known brand'.

Much of the Commission's attention focused on the significant price differences between France and Germany for Grundig products. However, at the time of its decision, it relied on retail prices at least two years old; that is, dating from, at or before the lowering of customs barriers between the Member States. In the time elapsed, there was apparently evidence of continual retail price falls in France reducing the price differences with Germany which took place even on products not subject to parallel importing.[45] In addition to relying on figures current before, or just after, the common market lowered customs barriers between France and Germany, the Commission's figures apparently related to a small proportion only of the Grundig products sold in France by Consten.[46]

Hence, the ECJ clearly indicated that collusion to insulate national markets by means of 'absolute territorial protection' was automatically caught by Article 85(1) and would be treated with, at the very least, considerable scepticism under Article 85(3). Apart from rejecting the Commission's condemnation of the whole arrangement, however, *Consten & Grundig* is not entirely clear on what actually constituted 'absolute territorial protection'. On this point, comparison with the immediately preceding *STM* case suggests a reduced scope for *Consten & Grundig*'s seemingly categorical, *per se* language.

---

43 [1964] CMLR at 500 to 501. (Contrast STM's problems in the *STM* case, text after Note 47 below.) In fact, the Advocate-General argued that, on the figures before him, the profit margins were similar taking into account the greater burdens assumed by Consten compared to the German wholesalers, see [1966] ECR at 372.
44 For example [1966] ECR at 370, 376.
45 *Ibid.* at 373 to 374.
46 *Ibid.* at 373.

As already indicated, the significant difference between the two cases was that parallel imports were possible. Although Maschinenbau Ulm appointed STM its sole distributor for France, it did not promise to prevent indirect shipments of its products into France. Nor did it require STM to refrain from exporting Maschinenbau Ulm's products to other parts of the EC. In such circumstances, the ECJ instructed the national court to assess the actual impact of the agreement on the market.[47]

The agreement between the two parties dated from 1961. It had not been notified to the Commission, even with a request for 'negative clearance'. By 1962 difficulties had arisen. Bills of exchange used by STM in payment for deliveries of Maschinenbau Ulm's products were not honoured and Maschinenbau Ulm sued for its money in the French courts. It seems STM experienced considerable difficulty persuading French customers to buy Maschinenbau Ulm's products. On appeal, STM raised issues of EC competition law and the Cour d'Appel, Paris sought the ECJ's guidance through a preliminary reference under Article 177 of the EEC Treaty.

The question before the ECJ was, in effect, whether an agreement granting an 'exclusive right of sale' was a restriction of competition contrary to Article 85(1) even though it did not restrict parallel imports or preclude the concessionaire from selling competing goods.[48] The ECJ was faced with three competing arguments.

STM claimed that prohibitions on re-exports and on parallel imports were inherent in exclusive dealerships. Accordingly, exclusive dealing agreements would restrict competition of their very nature and, as the agreement had not been notified, it was void under EC law.[49]

The Commission, adopting a formalistic approach, also relied on the failure to notify to condemn the agreement. It argued that there was a restriction of competition because the exclusive dealing agreement, even though not absolute, limited the contracting parties' freedom of action and adversely affected the position of third parties on the market. Moreover, the possibility of parallel imports was purely theoretical and, in reality, the only source of supplies would be the exclusive dealer.[50]

Maschinenbau Ulm, on the other hand, argued that Article 85(1) required a 'rule of reason' approach and, in this case, such an approach would

---

47 In US terminology, this seems to correspond to directing a 'rule of reason' inquiry; but, see further Chapter 7.

48 For the precise wording of the question, see [1966] ECR at 247. STM was effectively precluded from selling competing goods under its agreement because the right was conditional on Maschinenbau Ulm's consent: *ibid.* at 237.

49 *Ibid.* at 243 to 244.

50 *Ibid.* at 240. The Report does not expand on the Commission's argument. However, it seems to mean that because the parties have contracted with each other, they are precluded from contracting with other parties. Hence, they have limited their own freedom of action and restricted the competitive opportunities of third parties which are also precluded from contracting with the parties. See for example the *Blondel*, *Hummel* and *Jallate* decisions discussed in Joliet, *The Rule of Reason in Antitrust Law*, at 146 to 152. Similar reasoning pervades Commission decisions through the 1970s and 1980s even after the ECJ's rejection of the theory in *STM* and 258/78 *Maize Seed* [1982] ECR 2015, Chapter 7.2.1 below.

conclude that the agreement was not restrictive because it promoted competition.[51] First, it pointed out that inter-brand competition in the market-place was intense, so the dealership arrangement could only have limited effect on competition. Then, it stressed that the dealership agreement did not inhibit parallel imports and so did not partition the common market. Third, it emphasised that such agreements were widely used to open up new markets and to rationalise production and, for small and medium-sized enterprises, might prove the only means of engaging in export trade. It argued that if the supplier did not have sufficient resources and capability to set up in the new market itself (or was otherwise precluded from doing so), it would need a distributor which often would not risk investing in making a market for the new product and seeking new customers without being guaranteed that it would appropriate any benefit of its investment through some protection from 'free riders'. Correspondingly, it argued that the supplier could justifiably expect some surety that the distributor would actually attempt to exploit the advantages conferred.

The ECJ ruled that a clause 'granting an exclusive right of sale' did not of its very nature conflict with the prohibition in Article 85(1). But, depending on the factual circumstances, such a clause could do so.[52] It held:

> The competition in question must be understood within the actual context in which it would occur in the absence of the agreement in dispute. In particular, it may be doubted whether there is an interference with competition if the said agreement seems really necessary for the penetration of a new area by an undertaking. Therefore, in order to decide whether an agreement containing a clause 'granting an exclusive right of sale' is to be considered as prohibited by reason of its object or of its effect, it is appropriate to take into account in particular the nature and quantity, limited or otherwise, of the products covered by the agreement, the position and importance of the grantor and the concessionnaire on the market for the products concerned, the isolated nature of the disputed agreement or, alternatively, its position in a series of agreements, the severity of the clauses intended to protect the exclusive dealership or, alternatively, the opportunities allowed for other commercial competitors in the same products by way of parallel re-exportation and importation.[53]

Note that the ECJ extended its inquiry into the factual situation whether the restrictive nature of the arrangement was sought in the parties' object or arose from the effect.

Joliet and Korah have suggested that the ECJ's judgment in *Consten & Grundig* is a *per se* condemnation of market partitioning.[54] This may be right once the object of market partitioning is found. But, even in *Consten & Grundig*, the ECJ found that object by analysing the distributorship arrangements in their context. The ECJ looked beyond the formal terms

---

51   *Ibid.* at 241 to 242.
52   See the ECJ's reply to the first question, stressing that particular attention should be paid to whether the agreement led to partitioning of the market. *Ibid.* at 251.
53   *Ibid.* at 250. This is consistent with the ECJ's classification of Grundig as a 'very well-known brand': [1966] ECR 299 at 343.
54   Joliet, *The Rule of Reason in Antitrust Law*, at 164 to 165; Korah, 'The Rise and Fall of Provisional Validity', at 347.

of the exclusive distribution arrangement to find the market partitioning intention at least in part from the Grundig distribution network which created a web of sealed distribution compartments.[55]

Hence, two important principles seem to have been established. The main object of the EEC Treaty was to integrate the internal market. But, the goal of market integration may require reconciliation with the potentially conflicting needs of sound competition policy. Some qualification on trade between Member States may be permitted, even under Article 85(1), in the interests of encouraging desirable investment. The line was drawn, however, at 'absolute territorial protection' – collusion to prevent any cross-frontier trade at all – and a strict approach to such arrangements under Article 85(3) was foreshadowed.

The role of competition rules in achieving market integration is in important respects limited since they are predicated on the presence of concertation, or of an abuse of a dominant position, and in *Parke, Davis* there was neither.[56] Hence, the owner of a patent could use it to block parallel imports from another Member State where the product was not protected.

Parke, Davis held patents for a pharmaceutical, chloramphenicol, in the Netherlands and used them to block imports of the drug from Italy where it was not patented.[57] Accordingly, to allow the imports would have rendered the patents of little value in the Netherlands.[58] The ECJ baldly made three rulings. First, the mere use of a patent to exclude imports did not of itself amount to an agreement or concerted action liable to the prohibition of Article 85(1). Second, the mere existence of a patent did not necessarily mean that its owner held a dominant position on the market subject to Article 86. Third, a higher price for a patented product compared to the price of the product elsewhere where it was not protected by a patent was not necessarily an abuse of a dominant position.[59] Therefore, on the information before the ECJ, Parke, Davis could use its patents to block trade in goods lawfully on the market in another Member State.

Unlike *Consten & Grundig*, the ECJ seems to have regarded Parke, Davis' use of its patent rights as a unilateral exercise. However, not mentioned, Parke, Davis had a licensee in the Netherlands which it was obliged to exercise its rights to protect.[60] As the ECJ does not deal with the licence, it is unclear why it thought Parke, Davis' use of its patent rights was a unilateral action not giving rise to the concertation element required by Article 85(1).

---

55 [1966] ECR at 343. This was reinforced by the trade mark arrangements.
56 24/67 *Parke, Davis & Co. v Probel* [1968] ECR 55.
57 At the time, pharmaceuticals and their manufacturing processes were not patentable under Italian law.
58 [1968] ECR 55, at 77 to 78 *per* Advocate-General Roemer.
59 *Ibid.* at 71 to 72. The same three points were reiterated in 40/70 *Sirena Srl v Eda SrL* [1971] ECR 69, at ¶¶9, 16 and 17. For corresponding treatment of a trade mark under Article 86, see also 102/77 *Valium* [1978] ECR 1139, at ¶16.
60 *Ibid.* at 76 to 77, Advocate-General Roemer's opinion. It is not clear on what basis Parke, Davis was obliged to exercise its patent rights to protect its Dutch licensee: whether of agreement, Dutch law or just self-interest.

One explanation, which could be thought compelling, is that the products imported did not originate from Parke, Davis. On the facts before the ECJ, they were not parallel imports but would have been counterfeit if a patent had existed in Italy.[61] In contrast, Consten had sought to block 'genuine' Grundig goods. Even in those cases where the ECJ adopted a ruling most at odds with the economic function of a patent, it did not go so far as to deny the patentee the right to bar imports from other Member States which it did not originate.[62]

An alternative is to contrast the nature of the agreement found in *Consten & Grundig* to that in *Parke, Davis*. On the facts before the ECJ, *Parke, Davis* may not have had the same collusive nature since Parke, Davis and its Dutch licensee may not have so obviously sat down and set out to arrange matters, for whatever reason, to insulate a part of the common market against imports of genuine products from other sources at the wholesale level. This may be the ground on which Advocate-General Roemer excluded the licence.[63]

It would be tempting to speculate that the ECJ's ruling would have been the same had it been aware of the state of affairs described by Dr. Johannes. As will become apparent, however, from the cases under the free movement rules, this seems unlikely. Certainly, until the 1980s, the ECJ was not much moved by arguments about the economic function of intellectual property rights.

Although provoking alarm at the time, the *Sirena* case probably should not be seen as altering EC law drastically.[64] Sirena, relying on its registered trade mark in Italy, *Prep*, sued Eda for infringement by importing the same product, shaving cream, bearing the trade mark into Italy. Eda obtained the products in Germany from the owner of the registered trade mark there. Both Sirena and the German trade mark owner had acquired their rights to the trade mark by assignment from the original owner, Mark Allen, a US company, Sirena doing so as long ago as 1937. While there was no evidence of a transfer of manufacturing or production technology from Mark Allen at the same time, Mark Allen, as late as 1969, clearly regarded the individual owners of the *Prep* trade mark in each of the Member States as its exclusive distributors and licensees. Following *Consten & Grundig*, the ECJ advised the Italian court making the reference that such a combination

---

61 Johannes states that, unknown to the ECJ, the Italian manufacturer of the drug, Carlo Erba, made the drug under a valuable know-how licence from Parke, Davis and that the territory it was entitled to exploit included the Netherlands: Hartmut Johannes, *Industrial Property and Copyright Law in the European Community Law*, Sijthoff, 1976, at 67 to 69. This is not, however, what the Commission argued before the ECJ: see [1968] ECR 55, at 76 *per* Advocate-General Roemer.
62 See 15/74 *Centrafarm BV v Sterling Drug Inc.* [1974] ECR 1147 and 187/80 *Merck v Stephar* [1981] ECR 2063, see Notes 93 and 141 respectively, below.
63 [1968] ECR at 77.
64 40/70 *Sirena Srl v Eda Srl* [1971] ECR 69. Two aspects of the ruling excited alarm: first, the apparent disparagement of trade mark rights compared to patents, see in particular ¶7 and contrast C-10/87 *Hag II* [1990] ECR I-3717 [1990] 3 CMLR 571; second, retrospectively, the implications of the 'common origin' doctrine, see Notes 88 and following.

of assignments could be subject to the prohibition in Article 85(1) provided that the restrictive effects of the agreements arising before the EEC Treaty commenced were still continuing.[65]

Later in the year, the ECJ stated that an exclusive distributorship would be incompatible with Article 85(1) of the EEC Treaty:

> . . . when, *de jure* or *de facto*, it prevents the distributor from re-exporting the products in question to other Member States or prevents the products from being imported from other Member States into the protected area and from being distributed therein by persons other than the exclusive dealer or his customers.[66]

This ruling, however, was directed at a distributorship agreement which included a prohibition on exports and does not seem to have been directed at exclusive distributorships of the kind considered in the *STM* case.[67]

Hence by 1971, the ECJ had adopted a seemingly definitive and enduring approach to parallel imports under the competition rules which stressed the overriding importance of the goal of integrating the internal market in EC law and considered arrangements involving absolute territorial protection beyond the pale. It did not, however, condemn all arrangements involving exclusivity *per se*.

6.3   The Free Movement Rules

The cases under the EEC Treaty's competition rules clearly established two principles: integrating the market as the basic goal of EC law and, consequently, that EC rules took precedence over merely national laws governing intellectual property. But, *Parke*, *Davis* and, perhaps, *Sirena* had also revealed the limitations of relying on the competition rules. A more potent means of controlling the use of intellectual property rights to block trade between the Member States lay in the rules establishing free movement.

The ECJ has given the phrase 'measures having equivalent effect' in Articles 30 and 34 a wide interpretation. Broadly speaking, a quantitative

---

65   *Ibid.* at ¶¶9 to 12 and see also Advocate-General Dutheillet de Lamothe's opinion at 88 to 91 where his Honour analyses the trade mark assignment in terms of whether there was an ongoing arrangement to partition the market. The significance of the continuing agreement was emphasised by Advocate-General Mayras discussing *Sirena* in *Hag I* [1974] ECR 731 at 750. See also 51, 86 & 96/75 *EMI Records Ltd v CBS United Kingdom Ltd* [1976] ECR 811, at 864 to 865 *per* Advocate-General Warner. The ECJ, perhaps due to the uncertain facts before it, was more than usually inscrutable: appearing to say both that the national court must find concertation to partition the market and that the effect of such multiple assignments was automatically caught by Article 85(1): [1971] ECR 69 at ¶¶9 to 12.

66   22/71 *Béguelin Import Co. v G.L. Import Export SA* [1971] ECR 949, at ¶12. It went on to say that agreements and national laws on unfair competition could be used to block imports *only if* the attack did not depend on the fact that the imports were parallel imports: ¶¶14 to 15.

67   The facts are not entirely clear, but see *ibid.* at 967 *per* Advocate-General Dutheillet de Lamothe.

restriction is some form of national measure other than a customs duty
or similar pecuniary charge which amounts 'to a total or partial restraint
of, according to the circumstances, imports, exports, or goods in transit'.[68]
Measures having equivalent effect, then, are forms of national measure
'which are capable of hindering, directly or indirectly, actually or potentially,
intra-Community trade'.[69]

As in the cases under the competition rules already discussed, much of
the case law under the free movement rules shows an overriding concern
with attempts to partition the market and preserve price differences between
Member States. For the most part, these cases do not concern themselves
with why these price differences arose.

The free movement rules have been used in two ways to defeat attempts
by intellectual property owners to use their rights to block parallel imports.
First, the ECJ has developed a rule of Community exhaustion. This has
alternatively been based on its distinction between the existence and the
exercise of the intellectual property right, on the specific subject-matter
of the right and the consent of the right owner to release of the product
embodying the right onto the market. The shifting basis at the foundation
of the Community exhaustion doctrine may well help to explain the change
in the ECJ's application of the rules observable in the 1980s. The common
origin doctrine, now largely rejected, was the second method.

6.3.1   The drive to integrate the internal market

Deutsche Grammophon manufactured and sold 30cm long-playing records
in Germany under the Polydor label for a price of DM19 or 20 retail.[70]
It obliged its retailers in Germany not to sell below this price and refused
to allow imports unless they were sold at the prevailing retail price. It had
also promised its distributors that it would vigorously oppose any attempts to
undermine the retail price system. All these arrangements were valid under
Germany's copyright and competition rules.

Metro, denied supplies by Deutsche Grammophon for refusing to abide by
the system of price maintenance, obtained supplies of Polydor records from
France and was selling them retail at DM11.95 to 12.95 plus VAT. These
records had been produced by Deutsche Grammophon, sold in France by

---

68   2/73 *Geddo v Ente Nazionale Risi* [1973] ECR 865 at ¶¶5 and 7. See further Wyatt
and Dashwood, *The Substantive Law of the EEC*, at 124 to 125; Gormley, *Prohibiting
Restrictions on Trade within the EEC*, Chapters 2 and 3; and Oliver, *Free Movement of
Goods in the EEC*, Chapter 5.
69   8/74 *Dassonville* [1974] ECR 837, at ¶5. See further Wyatt and Dashwood, *The
Substantive Law of the EEC*, at 127 and onward; Gormley, *Prohibiting Restrictions on
Trade within the EEC*, Chapter 3; Oliver, *Free Movement of Goods in the EEC*, Chapter
6. It is the power given by national law to block parallel imports which is attacked by the
free movement rules, see Joliet and Keeling, 'Trade Mark Law and the Free Movement
of Goods', at §IV.
70   78/70 *Deutsche Grammophon GmbH v Metro-SB-Grossmärkte GmbH & Co. KG*
[1971] ECR 487, at 490.

its wholly owned subsidiary, Polydor Paris, and had made their way to Metro via a wholesaler in Strasbourg and Swiss import-export firms.

Before the German courts, Deutsche Grammophon successfully relied on its rights, akin to copyright, in sound recordings to block the parallel importing by Metro and other price cutters. Metro, arguing violation of Article 85, forced a preliminary reference to the ECJ. As is by now well-known, the ECJ found Deutsche Grammophon's use of German copyright law to block parallel imports incompatible with the rules on the free movement of goods.

Apparently finding that Deutsche Grammophon's use of its rights were not 'the subject, the means or the result of an agreement' banned by Article 85(1),[71] the ECJ ruled that Article 36 did not justify using the exclusive right to distribute sound recordings to block imports of the sound recording marketed in another Member State by the right owner, or with its consent because such an exercise of the right would lead to isolation of national markets 'repugnant to the essential purpose of the Treaty':

> 11. . . . it is nevertheless clear from [Article 36] that, although the Treaty *does not affect the existence of rights* recognized by the legislation of a Member State with regard to industrial and commercial property, *the exercise of such rights* may nevertheless fall within the prohibitions laid down by the Treaty. Although it permits prohibitions or restrictions on the free movement of products, which are justified for the purpose of protecting industrial and commercial property, Article 36 only admits derogations from that freedom to the extent to which they are *justified for the purpose of safeguarding rights which constitute the specific subject-matter* of such property.
>
> 12. If a right related to copyright is relied upon to prevent the marketing in a Member State of products distributed by the holder of the right or with his consent on the territory of another Member State on the sole ground that such distribution did not take place on the national territory, such a prohibition, which would legitimize the isolation of national markets, would be repugnant to the essential purpose of the Treaty, which is to unite national markets into a single market.
>
> That purpose could not be attained if, under the various legal systems of the Member States, nationals of those States were able to partition the market and bring about arbitrary discrimination or disguised restrictions on trade between Member States.
>
> 13. Consequently, it would be in conflict with the provisions prescribing the free movement of products within the common market for a manufacturer of sound recordings *to exercise the exclusive right to distribute* the protected articles, conferred upon him by the legislation of a Member State, *in such a way as to prohibit the sale in that State of products placed on the market by him or with his consent in another* Member State *solely* because such distribution did not occur within the territory of the first Member State. (*Emphasis added*)

---

71 The ECJ did not expressly deny that the necessary agreement existed. It simply stated the principle under the competition rules and said that it would be necessary to examine the impact of the rules on the free movement of goods if such an agreement was not found: [1971] ECR 487, at ¶¶6 and 7. The relevant, formal answer was solely in terms of the free movement rules.

Two points are overwhelmingly clear from the judgment. First, as in *Consten & Grundig*, the factor motivating the ECJ's ruling is fear that intellectual property rights could be used to isolate national markets within the common market contrary to the essential purpose of the EEC Treaty. Deutsche Grammophon's only explanation for blocking the parallel imports was that the product had not been marketed on the domestic territory. Second, the owner of the exclusive right to distribute sound recordings in one Member State could not use that right to block imports into that Member State of copies which had been marketed in another Member State by the owner or with the owner's consent. This is the so-called 'exhaustion' rule.

What is not so clear is how the ECJ deduced its exhaustion rule from its determination to stop market partitioning. In point 11, the ECJ seems to offer two possibly inconsistent links: one based on a distinction between the existence and the exercise of an intellectual property right; the second, the specific subject-matter of the right. On one hand, the ECJ considered that the rules on the free movement of goods, qualified by Article 36, did not affect the *existence* of intellectual property rights but could affect the way in which the rights were *exercised*. Perhaps alternatively, Article 36 could justify restrictions which had the purpose of safeguarding rights constituting *the specific subject-matter* of the intellectual property. The need for the second articulation points up the circularity of the first: if a right cannot be exercised, it is difficult to regard it as existing.[72]

The dichotomy between existence and exercise goes back to *Consten & Grundig* where the ECJ spoke of the grant of a right and its exercise. Alexander has argued that the German phrase (the language of the case), 'den Bestand dieser Rechte', may be better translated as 'rights inherent in the intellectual property'.[73] This would accord with the ECJ's reference to 'safeguarding the specific subject-matter' of the intellectual property in *Deutsche Grammophon* and is in line with the Advocate-General's references to 'the essence and substance' of the rights.[74] It may also describe the effect of the ECJ's ruling in *Consten & Grundig* since the Commission and the ECJ were careful not to make an order affecting the registration of the trade mark rights. Rather, as the ECJ stated, it was controlling one particular

---

72   For this criticism, see Valentine Korah, 'Dividing the Common Market through National Industrial Property Rights', (1972) 35 MLR 634, at 636 (also at Korah, *EEC Competition Law and Practice*, Chapter 9.2) suggesting that the use of such a tool gives the final arbiter considerable discretion to control *undesired* uses of an intellectual property right. See also the *Nancy Kean* case, from Note 158 below.

73   Willy Alexander, 'Industrial Property Rights and the Establishment of the European Common Market', (1972) 9 CMLRev. 35, at 40.

74   24/67 *Parke, Davis* [1968] ECR 55 at 77 to 78, 78/70 *Deutsche Grammophon* [1971] ECR 487, at 507 where, as well as reasserting his reliance on the 'substance and essence' of the rights, Advocate-General Roemer refers to 'the *existence* and substance'. In *Consten & Grundig*, Advocate-General Roemer treats Consten's use of the trade mark *GINT* as an abuse of trade mark rights: [1966] ECR at 366, the approach preferred by Alexander, 'Industrial Property Rights and the Establishment of the European Common Market', at 40.

way in which those rights could be used to prevent Article 85(1) being circumvented.[75]

Reliance on the 'specific subject-matter' of the property is also not without difficulty.[76] In *Deutsche Grammophon*, the ECJ did not explain how the specific subject-matter of an intellectual property right was to be determined or whether it would be determined by national law or under EC law.[77] Nor did it define the specific subject-matter of the right under consideration. Limiting itself to sound recordings, it spoke of exercising 'the exclusive right to distribute the protected articles'.[78] The ECJ did not identify where it derived this 'definition' from. In this case, at least, the nature of the right seems to have been found in the factual context and the relevant German law.[79]

The ECJ concentrated the main part of its decision on the impact of the free movement rules, treating Article 85 almost in passing. Before the ECJ, however, much of the argument centred on Article 85 and whether it could apply to arrangements between parent and subsidiary. Subsequently, in the *Sterling Drug* case, the ECJ explained that Article 85 did not affect such arrangements.[80] This does not explain why the arrangements between Deutsche Grammophon and its distributors in Germany were not caught by Article 85.[81]

---

75 See especially [1966] ECR at 345:

> The injunction contained in article 3 of the operative part of the contested decision to refrain from using rights under national trade-mark law in order to set an obstacle in the way of parallel imports does not affect the grant of those rights but only limits their exercise to the extent necessary to give effect to the prohibition under Article 85(1).

For a similar point, see René Joliet, 'Patented Articles and the Free Movement of Goods within the EEC', (1975) 28 *Current Legal Problems* 15, at 23 and *Hag II* [1990] CMLR 571 from Note 220 below.

76 See W.R. Cornish, *Intellectual Property*, Sweet & Maxwell, 1989 (2nd ed.), at 21; (but, contrary to his references to 'legal obscurantism' there, he subsequently notes that potentially justifiable reasons for blocking parallel imports may exist: at 200 to 201); W.R. Cornish, 'The Definitional Stop Aids the Flow of Patented Goods', [1975] JBL 50; Beier, 'Industrial Property and the Free Movement of Goods in the Internal European Market', at 148 to 149. For a contrary view see René Joliet, 'Patented Articles and the Free Movement of Goods within the EEC', (1975) 28 CLP 15, at 19.

77 As Johannes argued, if definition were left to national law, uniformity would be lost and the achievement of a truly common market would be denied: Johannes, *Industrial Property and Copyright Law in the European Community Law*, at 12 to 15.

78 [1971] ECR 487 at ¶13.

79 Article 85 of the Law on Copyright as set out in Advocate-General Roemer's opinion accords the manufacturer of a sound recording 'the exclusive right of reproducing and distributing the recording'. See [1971] ECR at 504. Moreover, it seems that within the EC at that date only German and Italian law recognised the right in issue: *ibid*.

80 15/74 *Centrafarm BV v Sterling Drug Inc.* [1974] ECR 1147, at ¶41 because 'if the undertakings form an economic unit within which the subsidiary has no real freedom to determine its course of action' the arrangements 'are concerned merely with the internal allocation of tasks as between the undertakings'. See also *Béguelin* [1971] ECR 949 at ¶8.

81 The case law shows that the restrictive nature of agreements can be determined from the existence of a network of agreements within the Member State: 23/67 *Brasserie de Haecht v Wilkin (No. 1)* [1967] ECR 407 and subsequent cases leave little scope for truly 'unilateral' action by the right owner: see for example 107/82 *AEG v Commission* [1983] ECR 3151. In *Parke, Davis*, Advocate-General Roemer seems to suggest that

If the EC were assumed to be a unified market, the ECJ's ruling would compare favourably with the laws affecting goods distributed domestically in Germany and the United States.[82]

At the relevant date, however, it seems that copyright-like protection for sound recordings was granted only in Germany and Italy. In other Member States, if any protection were to be found, it lay in laws on unfair competition. Although there have been suggestions that the unfair competition laws in France gave the 'right owner' at least as strong protection, it would also seem that sound recordings were consistently cheaper in France.[83] The difference in the basis of protection and the apparently persistent price differences suggest that market conditions were not uniform throughout the common market. Furthermore, it seems likely that Deutsche Grammophon did not have the chance to reap the special reward in France which the German legislature had felt necessary to encourage the desired 'technical quality' and 'considerable economic expenditure' associated with making sound recordings.[84] Focusing on the right owner's consent to marketing, even where it apparently did not own a right, the ECJ avoided considering the economic reasons for the price discrimination.[85] As in *Consten & Grundig*, the principle was applied without regard for why the price differences arose.

The Commission also regarded *Deutsche Grammophon* as an important landmark. Following the case, the retail price of sound recordings in Germany apparently fell by at least 25 per cent and, even 11 years later, had still not reached previous levels, fluctuating around DM16 to 18.[86] In Johannes' view, this meant that the consumer had benefited from the common market, since the German consumer could now get five records for the price of four previously.[87] He did not, however, venture an opinion on whether the quality of the recordings had changed or whether any reduced

such agreements were not caught because the right owner could achieve the same result unilaterally: [1968] ECR at 77. With respect, this objection is hardly to the point where there is collusion.

82 For Germany, see *Gesetz uber Urheberrecht und verwandte Schutzsrechte* (Law on Copyright and Related Protection Rights), section 17 cited in Advocate-General Roemer's opinion, [1971] ECR at 504; for the United States, see Chapter 4.3.3 above. See also Hartmut Johannes, 'Technology Transfer Under EEC Law – Europe Between the Divergent Opinions of the Past and the New Administrations: A Comparative Law Approach', [1982] *Fordham Corporate Law Institute* 65, at 67 to 68. He, however, argues that the lack of uniformity within the internal market demands even stricter treatment of attempts to block parallel imports.

83 Johannes, *Industrial Property and Copyright Law in the European Community Law*, at 23.

84 From the official explanatory notes on section 85 of the Law on 'Copyright' (*Bundesratsdrucksache* 1/62, at 95) cited in Johannes, *Industrial Property and Copyright Law in the European Community Law*, at 30 and 47 to 48; see also Joliet, 'Patented Articles and the Free Movement of Goods within the EEC', at 20.

85 See Joliet, 'Patented Articles and the Free Movement of Goods within the EEC', at 19 to 20; Johannes, *Industrial Property and Copyright Law in the European Community Law*, at 40, Note 116.

86 Johannes, 'Technology Transfer Under EEC Law – Europe Between the Divergent Opinions of the Past and the New Administrations: A Comparative Law Approach', at 80.

87 *Ibid.*

profit margins had led Deutsche Grammophon to a more cautious approach in selecting and releasing new material.

With what has turned out to be the minor exception of a diversion for trade marks, the 'common origin' principle, *Deutsche Grammophon* fixed the EC's legal approach to parallel imports under the rules governing free movement of goods until well into the 1980s. Three questions remained: whether the approach espoused applied to other forms of intellectual property; if so, what was their specific subject-matter, or, what went to their exercise rather than their existence; and the content and significance of consent. The full implications of basing the doctrine on 'consent' were brought home forcefully and, perhaps, surprisingly.

The ECJ did not apply the rule of Community exhaustion in the next case where intellectual property rights were used against imports from another Member State. Instead, in *Hag I*, in circumstances where the domestic right owner had not been associated at all with the 'foreign' marketing, the ECJ developed a doctrine of common origin to deny a trade mark owner the power to block imports under the same trade mark first marketed in another Member State by an independent company.[88] The considerable controversy generated by the ruling has now been ended by the ECJ expressly overruling the decision.[89] It remains, however, as a potent example of just how determined the ECJ was to force integration of the internal market as far as possible in this period.

The facts may be briefly stated.[90] In Western Europe, the Café Hag name and trade mark is virtually synonymous with decaffeinated coffee. It dated back almost to the turn of the century in Germany when Hag AG of Bremen procured its first patents for decaffeinating raw coffee. Shortly after starting in Germany, it commenced operations under the mark in Belgium and Luxembourg. By 1935, a wholly owned subsidiary was making the product in Belgium where, together with the Luxembourg rights, it owned the trade mark registrations. At the end of the Second World War, the Belgian authorities sequestered the business as enemy property and sold it off with the trade mark to a Belgian concern, the Van Oevelens, who subsequently sold the Benelux rights to Van Zuylen Frères. Neither Belgian business had any connection with Hag AG.

Hag AG continued to sell decaffeinated coffee under the *Café Hag* trade mark in Germany and, having failed in its attempts to penetrate the Belgian

88   192/73 *Hag I* [1974] ECR 731.
89   *Hag II* [1990] ECR J-3717; [1990] 3 CMLR 571 from Note 220 below. For some of the commentaries, see F.A. Mann, 'Industrial Property and the EEC Treaty', (1975) 24 ICLQ 31; W.R. Cornish, 'Trade Marks, Customer Confusion and the Common Market', (1975) 38 MLR 329; Cornish, *Intellectual Property*, at ¶18–008; Michel Waelbroeck, 'The Effect of the Rome Treaty on the Exercise of National Industrial Property Rights', 21 *Antitrust Bulletin* 99 (1976) and contrast F.G. Jacobs, 'Industrial Property Rights and the EEC Treaty: A Reply', (1975) 24 ICLQ 643 who, as Advocate-General in *Hag II*, subsequently advised the ECJ to overrule the earlier case; Gormley, *Prohibiting Restrictions on Trade within the EEC*, at 190 to 191.
90   For a more expanded statement, see Warwick A. Rothnie, 'Hag II: Putting the Common Origin Doctrine to Sleep', [1991] EIPR 24 and Joliet and Keeling, 'Trade Mark Law and the Free Movement of Goods'.

and Luxembourg markets under the label, 'Decofa', began introducing decaffeinated coffee into Luxembourg under the *Café Hag* trade mark. Van Zuylen brought infringement proceedings as a result of which the Tribunal d'Arrondissement of Luxembourg made preliminary reference to the ECJ.

Quickly dismissing the relevance of Article 85 in the absence of any concerted action between Hag AG and either of the Belgian businesses, the ECJ restated its dichotomy between the existence and the exercise of an intellectual property right and the role of Article 36 in safeguarding the specific subject-matter of such rights. It then ruled:

> 10. Thus the application of the legislation relating to the protection of trade marks at any rate protects the legitimate holder of the trade mark against infringement on the part of persons who lack any legal title.

In terms reminiscent of *Sirena*,[91] the ECJ noted the danger of market partitioning particularly as trade mark rights were of indefinite duration, and continued:

> 12. Accordingly, one cannot allow the holder of a trade mark to rely upon the exclusiveness of a trade mark right – which may be the consequence of the territorial limitation of national legislations – with a view to prohibiting the marketing in a Member State of goods legally produced in another Member State *under an identical trade mark having the same origin*.
> 13. Such a prohibition, which would legitimize the isolation of national markets, would collide with one of the essential objects of the Treaty, which is to unite national markets in a single market. (*Emphasis added*)

The ECJ did recognise that allowing similar products from different sources to circulate in the same market would lead to consumer confusion but suggested that:

> 14. Whilst in such a market the indication of origin of a product covered by a trade mark is useful, information to consumers on this point may be ensured by means other than such as would affect the free movement of goods.

As the ECJ has now recognised, if the function of a trade mark be to indicate the origin of the goods or services marketed under it, the *Hag I* ruling clearly negates that function.[92] Until consumers in Belgium and Luxembourg had been educated, perhaps at considerable expense, to ignore the *Café Hag* mark and look for an indication of German or Belgian origin, the ECJ's ruling sanctioned consumer deception.

Four months later, the ECJ confirmed the vitality of its exhaustion doctrine for both patents and trade marks in the companion cases *Sterling Drug* and *Winthrop*, respectively.[93]

A US company, Sterling Drug, owned patents for a pharmaceutical, 'Negram', in several Member States of the EC including the United Kingdom

---

91 See [1970] ECR 69 at ¶7.
92 See *Hag II* [1990] ECR I-3717; [1990] 3 CMLR 571 below from Note 220.
93 15/74 *Centrafarm BV v Sterling Drug Inc.* [1974] ECR 1147 and 16/74 *Centrafarm BV v Winthrop BV* [1974] ECR 1183. For the inapplicability of Article 85, see Note 80 above.

and the Netherlands. It sold the drug in each Member State through separate marketing subsidiaries, although it does not seem that the drug was made in each Member State. The drug was produced in the United Kingdom having a price about half that in the Netherlands. *Negram* was the trade mark registered for the drug in each Member State where it was owned not by Sterling Drug but by the local marketing subsidiary. Buying the drug in the United Kingdom where it had been lawfully marketed by Sterling Drug's UK subsidiary, Centrafarm imported it into the Netherlands and sold it. Sterling Drug sued Centrafarm for infringement of the Dutch patent, Sterling's Dutch subsidiary, Winthrop, taking action on the basis of the trade mark. The Dutch Supreme Court, considering that Dutch law would treat Centrafarm's actions as infringement of the patent and the trade mark, referred several questions to the ECJ.

In the *Sterling Drug* case, the ECJ ruled that a patentee could not use its rights in a Member State to block imports of a product which had been marketed by it or with its consent in another Member State.[94] The ECJ clearly rejected any reliance on economic justifications for the attempted discrimination between the Member States' markets, focusing on the patentee's consent to the marketing as the determining criterion.

Having restated its dichotomy between the existence and the exercise of intellectual property rights and the limitation of Article 36 to protecting the specific subject-matter of the right, the ECJ described the specific subject-matter of a patent as:

> 9. . . . the guarantee that the patentee, to reward the creative effort of the inventor, has the exclusive right to use an invention with a view to manufacturing industrial products and putting them into circulation for the first time, either directly or by the grant of licences to third parties, as well as the right to oppose infringements.[95]

Two aspects of the 'definition' bear comment: whence it derived and its dual nature.

As in *Deutsche Grammophon*, it is not entirely clear where the definition of the specific subject-matter derives from.[96] The reference to 'the right to

---

94   *Ibid.* at ¶15. Compare *Winthrop* [1974] ECR 1183 at ¶10.
95   *Ibid.* at ¶9. The Advocate-General, with respect, was more careful in describing the rights of manufacture and first marketing as 'an essential constituent of a patent right'. His Honour then limited the use of this right to opposing the marketing in the jurisdiction of products which had been made by third parties or which had been put on sale without the patentee's consent: [1974] ECR at 1173 to 1174.
96   The formulation bears some resemblance to the doctrine of *domestic* exhaustion accepted by the German *Reichsgericht* in 1902:

> The effect of the patent resides in the fact that domestically no-one, except for the patentee (and those persons authorized by him), may produce the product or place it on the market. Thereby, however, the effect of patent protection *is exhausted*. If the patentee produces the product and places it on the market within his right to preclude the competition of others, he has thereby enjoyed the advantages which the patent grants him and has thus expended his rights. A patent does not grant to its holder the right to prescribe the conditions under which trade with his product is to take place.

51 RGZ 139, cited in Ulrich Schatz, 'The Exhaustion of Patent Rights in the Common Market,' 2 IIC 1, at 4 (1971)   (*The emphasis is from the Schatz quotation*).

oppose infringements' is singularly unhelpful since the Dutch Supreme Court seems to have ruled that parallel importing was an infringement under Dutch law. The Advocate-General could not 'countenance' allowing the patentee to block imports of products which it had itself marketed or consented to for two reasons. It was simply 'not compatible with the basic principle of the EC system governing the circulation of goods'.[97] Moreover, a patent related to an industrial product and so could not be divorced from manufacturing activity which was an essential element of the patent. Without manufacturing activity in the country of import, there was no need for the restriction on imports and such a restriction was revealed in its true character as simply an attempt to obstruct trade between Member States.[98] This second reason is, at least, an attempt to ground the Community exhaustion rule in the function and purpose of a patent. But, with respect, unless the national law made manufacture within the jurisdiction a condition of the grant, it seems difficult to make the 'essence' of the right depend on manufacture in the jurisdiction.

The ECJ included in its definition of the specific subject-matter both the purpose of the patent and the way that purpose was intended to be achieved: its function and its essence.[99] According to the ECJ, a patent existed 'to reward the creative effort of the inventor'. It did so by guaranteeing the patentee 'the exclusive right to use an invention with a view to manufacturing industrial products and putting them into circulation for the first time' or licensing others to do so. The inclusion of the patent's object in the definition of its specific subject-matter is noteworthy as the ECJ was not so explicit in *Winthrop*.[100]

Moreover, the reference to 'the reward' of the patentee was misleading. By speaking of the role of a patent as rewarding the creative endeavour of an inventor, the ECJ appears to opt for one of several competing rationales for the patent system.[101] But, as the judgment subsequently goes on to show, it did not accept the implications of that adoption. Instead, as in *Deutsche Grammophon*, it focused solely on the act of marketing within the EC by the right owner or with its consent to determine the point at which the patent became 'exhausted'.

Sterling Drug had argued that the depressed prices of Negram in the United Kingdom should entitle it to block imports into the Netherlands

---

German law, however, did not extend exhaustion to international trade: see *Voran*, BGH 29 February 1968 [1971] CMLR 592 and Beier, 'Industrial Property and the Free Movement of Goods in the Internal European Market', at 158 Note 74.

97   [1974] ECR at 1173 to 1174. At 1175, his Honour advised that exhaustion was a doctrine of national, domestic law having no bearing on EC law.

98   *Ibid.* at 1175.

99   The latter phrase is used by Valentine Korah, 'National Patents and the Free Movement of Goods Within the Common Market', (1975) 38 MLR 333, at 335.

100   [1974] ECR 1183 at ¶8, see Notes 106 to 107 below.

101   For example, the theory of 'natural rights', the 'reward' theory, or the 'incentive' theory, see Fritz Machlup, *An Economic Review of the Patent System* (Study of the Sub-Committee on Patents, Trademarks and Copyrights of the Committee on the Judiciary, US Senate, 85th Congress, Study 15, Washington, 1958). Whether this rationale be accepted in all the Member States is far from clear.

with its Dutch patent. A large part of the price difference between the two countries arose because in the United Kingdom the National Health Service was able to use monopsony bargaining power to extract lower prices for its product. This commercial power was further enhanced by the compulsory licensing provisions for pharmaceuticals enacted in UK patent law at the time. In addition, it appears that almost half the price difference was due to a collapse in the value of the pound sterling against the Dutch guilder. Sterling Drug plausibly argued that its right to exploit its Dutch patent monopoly to the full ought not to be undermined by the United Kingdom's social policies.[102] However, the ECJ rejected this:

> 24. The existence of factors such as [governmental measures adopted in the exporting country with a view to controlling the price of that product] in a Member State, however, cannot justify the maintenance or introduction by another Member State of measures which are incompatible with the rules concerning the free movement of goods, in particular in the field of industrial and commercial property.

Further explanation was delayed until the *Merck* case.[103] Although, the issue of varying protection in Member States underlay *Deutsche Grammophon*, it was only in *Sterling Drug* that the ECJ first identified two situations where intellectual property may be used to block the free movement of goods:

> 11. Whereas an obstacle to the free movement of goods of this kind *may be justified* on the ground of protection of industrial property *where* such protection is invoked against a product coming from a Member State where it is not patentable and has been manufactured by third parties without the consent of the patentee *and* in cases *where* there exist patents, the original proprietors of which are legally and economically independent, a derogation from the principle of the free movement of goods *is not, however, justified where* the product has been put onto the market in a legal manner, *by the patentee himself or with his consent, in the Member State from which it has been imported*, in particular in the case of a proprietor of parallel patents. (*Emphasis added*)[104]

In this carefully formulated paragraph, the ECJ clearly stressed how important the patentee's consent to marketing in a Member State was to

---

102 See the similar arguments in Alexander, 'Industrial Property Rights and the Establishment of the European Common Market', at 50 to 51; Joliet, 'Patented Articles and the Free Movement of Goods within the EEC', at 33 to 35; Paul Demaret, *Patents, Territorial Restrictions and EEC Law*, IIC Studies, Verlag-Chemie, 1978. In EC usage, the 'reward' theory may be much more limited than the 'incentive' theory: see Joliet, 'Patented Articles and the Free Movement of Goods within the EEC', at 15 and 434/85 *Allen & Hanburys Limited v Generics (UK) Limited* [1988] ECR 1245 at ¶31. Even so, similar reasoning should apply under both theories where the patentee has been deprived of a chance to derive its reward in the place of first sale.
103 187/80 *Merck v Stephar* [1981] ECR 263; discussed at Note 134, below. See also, in the field of copyright, 55 & 57/80 *Musik-Vertrieb Membran v GEMA* [1981] ECR 147; discussed at Note 141, below.
104 Advocate-General Trabucchi's formulation was not so precise, referring to the right to block imports 'manufactured by third parties or put on sale without the consent of the patent-owner'. [1974] ECR 1147 at 1175.

successful reliance on Article 36 to justify blocking the free movement of goods. The patentee could use its rights to block imports where it had not consented to the first marketing in two situations: one, where another owned the patent and, seemingly, the common origin doctrine would not apply; the other, where the product was not patentable and had been made by unlicensed third parties. Two other situations were not expressly dealt with: first, where the goods came from a Member State which had granted a patent for them but they had been sold by someone without the patentee's consent; second, where the imports were sold in that Member State with the patentee's consent but there was no patent protection.[105]

The result in *Winthrop* was the same; the ECJ was not deflected by niceties of legal personality. The paragraphs of the ECJ's opinion setting out the dichotomy between the existence and the exercise of an intellectual property right are virtually identical in both *Hag I* and *Winthrop*.[106] From this point, the judgments diverge and the ECJ provides a first definition of the specific subject-matter of a trade mark:

> 8.   In relation to trade marks, the specific subject-matter of the industrial property is the guarantee that the owner of the trade mark has the exclusive right to use that trade mark, for the purpose of putting products protected by the trade mark into circulation for the first time, and is therefore intended to protect him against competitors wishing to take advantage of the status and reputation of the trade mark by selling products illegally bearing that trade mark.

Then, in point 10, the ECJ concluded that the trade mark owner could not use its rights in one Member State to oppose imports from another Member State where the product had been marketed in that other Member State by the trade mark owner or with its consent because 'there can be no question of abuse or infringement of the trade mark'. Ground 11 explained that such an obstacle to market integration was not necessary 'to guarantee the essence of the exclusive right flowing from the trade mark'.

Unlike *Sterling Drug*, there was no express exception for cases which would not be caught by a doctrine of common origin. Further, in *Winthrop*, rather than a reward for creative effort, it is arguable that the ECJ identified the purpose of the trade mark as being to protect its owner against competitors wishing to take advantage of the status and reputation of the trade mark by selling products *illegally* bearing it.[107] This was achieved, as in patents, by giving the right owner an exclusive right to put marked products into circulation for the first time.

A final point. The corporate relationship between Sterling Drug and its

---

105   For one possibility, see 19/84 *Pharmon v Hoechst* [1985] ECR 2281; for the second, see *Merck*; Notes 167 and 141 below respectively.

106   Compare 16/74 *Winthrop* [1974] ECR 1183 at ¶¶4 to 7 and 192/73 *Hag I* [1974] ECR 731 at ¶¶6 to 9. The formula is repeated in 119/75 *Terrapin* [1976] ECR 1039, at ¶5; 102/77 *Valium* [1978] ECR 1139, at ¶6; 3/78 *American Home Products Corporation* [1978] ECR 1823 at ¶¶7 to 10; 1/81 *Pfizer* [1981] ECR 2913 restates the principles without material variation in ¶6.

107   See *ibid*. at ¶8; whether or not this was intended then, it seems to be the role now attributed to trade marks, see *Hag II* [1990] 3 CMLR 571 below from Note 220.

subsidiaries in the United Kingdom and the Netherlands protected the arrangements from scrutiny under Article 85. The economic dependence from which that immunity sprang, however, meant that the right owner's consent to the first marketing in the other Member State could be readily inferred under the free movement rules.

The nature of trade marks was not to be corralled so easily as patents, however. In *Terrapin*, the integrationists' nightmare confronted the ECJ – two conflicting trade marks of wholly independent provenance. When a UK company sought to expand its business under the trade mark *Terrapin* into Germany, it came into conflict with a series of prior registrations based on 'Terra' and 'Terranova' owned by a completely unrelated German business. The ECJ allowed Terranova to use its German trade marks to block imports of Terrapin's products from the United Kingdom and other Member States.[108]

Having stated its formula setting out the dichotomy between the existence and the exercise of an intellectual property right and the role of Article 36 in safeguarding the specific subject-matter of such rights in point 5, the ECJ continued:

> 6.   It follows from the above that the proprietor of an industrial or commercial property right protected by the law of a Member State cannot rely on that law to prevent the importation of a product which has lawfully been marketed in another Member State by the proprietor himself or with his consent. It is the same when the right relied on is the result of the subdivision, either by voluntary act or as a result of public constraint, of a trade-mark right which originally belonged to one and the same proprietor. In these cases *the basic function of the trade-mark to guarantee to consumers that the product has the same origin is already undermined by the subdivision of the original right.* Even where the rights in question belong to different proprietors the protection given to industrial and commercial property by national law may not be relied on when the exercise of those rights is the purpose, the means or the result of an agreement prohibited by the Treaty. In all these cases the effect of invoking the territorial nature of national laws protecting industrial and commercial property is to legitimize the insulation of national markets without this partitioning within the common market being justified by the protection of a legitimate interest on the part of the proprietor of the trade-mark or business name.
>
> 7.   On the other hand in the present state of Community law an industrial or commercial property right legally acquired in a Member State may legally be used to prevent under the first sentence of Article 36 of the Treaty the import of products marketed under a name giving rise to confusion where the rights in question have been *acquired by different and independent proprietors under different national laws.* If in such a case the principle of the free movement of goods were to prevail over the protection given by the respective national laws, *the specific objective* of industrial and commercial property rights would be undermined. (*Emphasis added*)

Terranova could stop Terrapin selling the latter's products in Germany under a confusing mark, otherwise trade mark rights would be completely negated.

---

108   119/75 *Terrapin (Overseas) Ltd v Terranova Industrie C.A. Kapferer & Co.* [1976] ECR 1039.

The emphasis on the goal of integrating the internal market remained. The ECJ identified three situations where it would operate. But, as *Terrapin* was not a case of parallel importing, exhaustion by the right owner's consent to first marketing could not apply. Nor was there evidence of collusion to partition the market. What is new is the explanation of the common origin doctrine. The ECJ explained *Hag I* on the ground that splitting ownership of the trade mark rights throughout the EC destroyed the 'specific objective' of a trade mark. Hence, the ECJ refused to extend the doctrine of common origin into one based on concurrent user.

As a proposition of national trade marks law, the explanation is certainly questionable. Taken to its extreme, it should mean that trade mark rights are not assignable. That it reflects a policy choice to require trade mark rights to be dealt with on an EC-wide basis rather than as national units seems supported by the earlier ruling in *EMI v CBS*, where the ECJ denied application of the common origin doctrine on the *additional* ground that 'the same proprietor holds the trade-mark right in respect of the same product in all the Member States' and consequently there were no opportunities for partitioning the common market.[109]

The confusion inherent in the shadowy dichotomy between the existence and the exercise of a right and the vague concept of a specific subject-matter wrought a need for a third peg. The 'specific objective' of the trade mark is not identified in point 7, but seems to refer back to the 'basic function' identified in point 6. Neither had found expression in the earlier formulations of existence and exercise or the specific subject-matter. Perhaps, with hindsight, it lies implicit in the references to protecting the 'status and reputation' of a trade mark in *Winthrop*. The cases following *Terrapin* confirm the addition of this new element(s).

Terrapin set one limit to the precedence of the goal of market integration over national intellectual property rights; it did not warrant risking consumer confusion where similar trade marks sprang up independently in different parts of the EC. The next two cases revealed further qualifications, even where the same person was responsible for marketing in both Member States. One line of cases concerned how far parallel importers could repackage genuine goods and reapply the original trade mark. Whether the parallel importer could swap the trade mark owner's trade marks was the second.

In *Valium*, the ECJ repeated its formula about the dichotomy between the existence and the exercise of an intellectual property right and the role of Article 36 in safeguarding the specific subject-matter of the right.[110] But, it was forced to go further:

> 7. In relation to trade-marks, the specific subject-matter is in particular to guarantee to the proprietor of the trade-mark that he has the exclusive right

---

109   51, 86 & 96/75 *EMI Records Ltd v CBS United Kingdom Ltd* [1976] ECR 811 at ¶12, see section 6.3.2 and Chapter 7.5 below.
110   102/77 *Hoffmann-La Roche v Centrafarm GmbH* (the case is referred to simply as '*Valium*') [1978] ECR 1139 at ¶6.

to use that trade-mark for the purpose of putting a product into circulation for the first time and therefore to protect him against competitors wishing to take advantage of the status and reputation of the trade-mark by selling products illegally bearing that trade-mark. [This, of course, is the definition from *Winthrop* ¶8.]

In order to answer the question whether that exclusive right involves the right to prevent the trade-mark being affixed by a third person after the product has been repackaged, regard must be had to the *essential function* of the trade-mark, *which is to guarantee the identity of the origin of the trade-marked product to the consumer* or ultimate user, by enabling him without any possibility of confusion to distinguish that product from products which have another origin. This guarantee of origin means that the consumer or ultimate user can be certain that a trade-marked product which is sold to him has not been subject at a previous stage of marketing to interference by a third person, without the authorization of the proprietor of the trade-mark, such as to affect the original condition of the product. [Compare *Terrapin* ¶6.]

The right attributed to the proprietor of preventing any use of the trade-mark which is likely to impair the guarantee of origin so understood is therefore part of the specific subject-matter of the trade-mark right. (*Emphasis and subdivision added*)

The facts giving rise to the enhanced definition of trade mark rights under EC law involved further attempts at market integration by Centrafarm. It obtained Hoffmann-La Roche's Valium tablets in the United Kingdom where they were sold in packages of 100 or 500 tablets. It then repackaged the tablets in bottles of 1,000, applied the trade marks *Valium* and *Roche* to the bottles together with the legend 'Marketed by Centrafarm GmbH' and sold the bottles in Germany where Hoffmann-La Roche only sold the tablets in packages of 20 and 50 through chemists and 250 (consisting of five packages of 50) to hospitals. Centrafarm's repackaging was apparently carried out in the Netherlands under the supervision of a pharmacist and in accordance with the Dutch laws on health and safety. Centrafarm also announced its intention to sell tablets bought in the United Kingdom in smaller packages through chemists but had not yet done so.

The ECJ considered that such repackaging might interfere with the integrity of the goods, thereby undermining the origin guaranteed by the trade mark. Accordingly, it concluded that trade mark laws *might* justifiably be used to block import and sale of repackaged goods. But, concerned that such a power could be used as a disguised restriction on trade and so to partition the common market artificially, the ECJ ruled that justification would only lie where the repackaging would 'adversely affect the original condition of the product'.

Determining how the facts required these principles to be applied fell to the national court. But, in reaching its conclusions, the ECJ emphatically did not rely on the treatment of trade mark rights under national law. In point 4 of the judgment, it noted that the laws of the Member States had been discussed, but no clear answer provided. Similarly, Advocate-General Capotorti stressed that national law treatment of 'ancillary functions' was not relevant. The real issue, under EC law, was how much protection would not conflict 'with the full observance of the principle of the free movement of goods'.[111]

To assist the national court, the ECJ gave two examples where it considered interference with the condition of the product was unlikely. This would depend, however, on the nature of the product and any other relevant circumstances.[112] First, repackaging might be allowed if the trade mark owner sold its product in a double packaging and the repackaging affected only the external packaging.[113] Second, inspection of the repackaging by a public authority to ensure that the product was not adversely affected might also suffice. However, to protect the consumer against deception, any would-be repackager would also be required to notify the trade mark owner of its intentions and also state on the new packaging that it had carried out the repackaging.[114]

The national court subsequently rejected Centrafarm's repackaging under a chemist's supervision, despite the Oberlandesgericht Karlsruhe's earlier acceptance that all national requirements had been satisfied.[115]

A further limitation on Community exhaustion developed in the *AHPC* case.[116] For apparently legitimate reasons, AHPC sold the same drug in different Member States under different trade marks. In the case in question, it sold the drug in the United Kingdom under the name 'Serenid' and in the Netherlands as 'Seresta'. As marketed in each Member State, the drugs were not identical; although they had the same therapeutic effect, their taste was different.[117] Centrafarm bought Serenid in the United Kingdom, relabelled it 'Seresta' and offered it for sale in the Netherlands. Noticeably, AHPC did not dispute Centrafarm's right to import and sell Serenid in the Netherlands. But, for obvious reasons, this was unattractive to Centrafarm.

The boldness of this attack on the substance of trade mark rights is demonstrated by Centrafarm's main argument: the right to choose which of two names a trade mark owner might use to market its products under did not form part of the essential function of the trade mark right; rather, it served 'solely to defend the goodwill of the trade-mark' on the Dutch market, merely protecting the 'commercial and publicity function of the trade-mark itself to the exclusive benefit of' AHPC.[118]

---

111   *Ibid.* at for example 1175, 1176 to 1177.
112   For these points, see *ibid.* ¶10.
113   The hint was taken, and subsequently endorsed, in 1/81 *Pfizer v Eurim-Pharm* [1981] ECR 2913. Note, however, that Eurim-Pharm cleverly did not itself apply Pfizer's trade mark. The trade mark Pfizer put on its internal packaging was visible through transparent material forming the new packaging Eurim-Pharm used.
114   [1978] ECR 1139, at ¶12.
115   For the referring court's acceptance, see [1978] ECR at 1178 *per* Advocate-General Capotorti; for the proceedings' outcome, see *Valium-Roche*, BGH, 10 November 1983, [1984] GRUR 530, at 533 cited in Hans-Christian Kersten, 'EEC Anti-trust Policy on "Grey Market" Exports and Imports Within the Common Market', (1988) 16 IBL 134, at 138 at Note 30.
116   3/78 *Centrafarm BV v American Home Products Corporation* [1978] ECR 1823.
117   Adhering to the Germanic view that a trade mark only denotes source and has nothing to say about quality (see Friedrich-Karl Beier, 'Territoriality of Trade Mark Law and International Trade', 1 IIC 48 (1970)), the ECJ regarded the products as identical.
118   [1978] ECR 1823 at 1846 *per* Advocate-General Capotorti.

The ECJ was not prepared to allow Centrafarm so much. EC law would permit trade mark rights to stop imports in these circumstances so long as they were not being used to disguise an ulterior purpose of partitioning the internal market. Having stated the now three-tiered formula from *Valium*, the ECJ turned to the implications of the guarantee of origin and found that an essential part of the trade mark owner's rights was to identify its product by placing the mark of its choice on the product. It would usurp those rights to allow another to place, or change, the trade marks on the product. This was so, even where the product was only distinguishable by the Member State in which it was first released.[119] In the view of the ECJ, the essential function of a trade mark, to guarantee the product's origin, 'meant that only the proprietor may confer an identity upon the product by affixing the mark'.[120] The concept itself appears to derive from Advocate-General Capotorti's opinion. His Honour, with respect, correctly pointed out that it was impossible to separate the trade mark's function of identifying a product from its role of guaranteeing the origin or authenticity of the product. To achieve the latter, it must do the former.[121]

Neither the *AHPC* case or *Valium* seem to sit comfortably with the earlier case law, particularly the mercifully isolated *Hag I* case where competing producers, using the same trade mark, were advised to distinguish their products by other means. Both the Advocate-General and the ECJ recognised that allowing AHPC's claim could afford considerable scope for trade mark owners to partition the internal market artificially. Accordingly, the ECJ indicated in points 21 and 22 that the use of different, national trade mark rights to block relabelling would not be justified under Article 36 where it formed 'part of a system of marketing *intended* to partition the markets artificially (*Emphasis added*)'.

This part of the ruling has excited considerable controversy because its seemingly subjective nature appears to conflict with the objective criteria specified in *Valium* at point 10.[122] The ECJ's reference to an intention to partition the market artificially seems to derive from the Advocate-General's opinion. Advocate-General Capotorti, however, proposed resort to the trade mark owner's subjective intentions only as a second step. First, he considered that a national court should investigate whether the use of different trade marks in different Member States was objectively justifiable; for example by the existence of a prior conflicting registration in one. But, his Honour clearly recognised that an astute trade mark owner could exploit such opportunities to partition the internal market by deliberately choosing in

---

119 *Ibid.* at ¶¶13 to 16.
120 *Ibid.* at ¶13.
121 *Ibid.* at 1846 to 1847.
122 Marenco and Banks, 'Intellectual Property and the Community Rules on Free Movement: Discrimination Unearthed', (1990) 15 ELRev. 224, at 253 to 254; John Handoll, 'Pfizer Inc. v. Eurim-Pharm: Repackaging of Drugs in Transparent Holders', [1982] EIPR 83; Martin Röttger, 'Article 36 – More Subjective Views on Objectivity', [1982] EIPR 215; Martin Röttger and Hugh Brett, 'The Hoffmann La Roche Ruling Repackaged by the National Court', [1979] EIPR 283.

one Member State a trade mark blocked in another. In this, he was fortified by Centrafarm's evidence that AHPC's trade marks consistently differed between Member States, particularly between those where prices were high and those where they were low.[123] Further, after referring to the objective factors in *Valium*, the ECJ concluded:

> 10. . . . Where the essential function of the trade-mark to guarantee the origin of the product is thus protected, the exercise of his rights by the proprietor of the trade-mark in order to fetter the free movement of goods between Member States may constitute a disguised restriction within the meaning of the second sentence of Article 36 of the Treaty if it is established *that the use of the trade-mark right by the proprietor, having regard to the marketing system which he has adopted, will contribute to the artificial partitioning of the markets* between Member States. (*Emphasis added*)

Arguably, then, the ECJ in *Valium* would not have ignored evidence of a subjective nature that a power to control repackaging was being manipulated to partition the internal market.[124]

If trade marks are a complex subject-matter and little understood, copyright is no less involved. *Coditel I* raised issues of television and cable broadcast.[125] La Boétie produced a film, *Le Boucher*, in France. It granted Ciné Vog exclusive distribution rights for Belgium although, to maximise revenues from the film, it restricted Ciné Vog's rights to permit television or cable broadcast until 40 months after the first cinema release of the film in Belgium. La Boétie also granted exclusive rights in the film for Germany to a German company; but without a restriction on television or cable release date.

Le Boucher was broadcast in German on German television. Coditel picked up the broadcast in Belgium and retransmitted it to subscribers of its cable network. All this took place before the restriction on Ciné Vog's television broadcasting had expired. Ciné Vog sued and the Belgian courts found Coditel in breach of Belgian copyright laws. The first question was whether or not EC rules prevented Ciné Vog from relying on its rights under Belgian copyright law.

The ECJ found two matters salient. First, films could be presented to the public by performances which could be repeated an infinite number of times and Coditel's retransmission of the film was a new act of public performance under Belgian law. In this respect, films differed from articles, like books or records, which were made available to the public by a single act of distribution. Hence, the 'essential function' of copyright in broadcasting

---

123 [1978] ECR at 1850 to 1852. For an inquiry into the problems of adopting uniform trade marks throughout the EC, see Jeremy Phillips, 'Do National Brands Have a Future in the European Market?', [1991] EIPR 191.
124 See also the discussion in Röttger, 'Article 36 – More Subjective Views on Objectivity', at 215.
125 62/79 *Coditel I* [1980] ECR 881. For comment, see Cornish, *Intellectual Property*, at §12–032; Korah, *EEC Competition Law and Practice*, 164; Gormley, *Prohibiting Restrictions on Trade within the EEC*, at 205, 225 to 226. For the second case on the competition rules, see Chapter 7.2.2.

(or performing) films entitled the copyright owner to demand fees for any performance of the film.[126]

Second, it was not possible to exploit the copyright in films without regard for the prospect of television broadcast. That prospect could severely affect the returns from cinema distribution.[127]

Accordingly, the ECJ found it necessary to tolerate restrictions on the provision of services arising from national laws for the protection of intellectual property which did not amount to either 'a means of arbitrary discrimination' or 'a disguised restriction on trade between Member States'.[128]

The ECJ considered that an assignment of copyright 'to create artificial barriers to trade between Member States' might be contrary to the free movement rules. That was not the case here, however, because there was a compelling practical reason for splitting the rights along national lines. In many Member States, television was organised along national lines through legal broadcasting monopolies.[129]

The ECJ did not investigate why the German film rights were not restricted for television rights in the same way as in Belgium. It could have been through the superior bargaining power of the German broadcasting monopoly or as a result of German laws against restrictive practices. Either possibility presents an interesting contrast. An eminently practical way of dealing with the NHS' virtual monopsony over drug purchasing in the United Kingdom, for example, would be to separate exploitation rights to the United Kingdom from those of other Member States. That argument, however, had been given short shrift in *Sterling Drug* and would be for copyrighted articles in *Musik-Vertrieb*.[130]

Even more surprising is the reasoning at point 13. Advocate-General Warner had been prepared to rest his opinion supporting Ciné Vog's action simply on the ground that the 'essence' of a performing right was the owner's ability 'to authorize or forbid each and every performance of the work'.[131]

---

126 *Ibid.* at ¶¶12, 14. At ¶12, the ECJ ruled:

> A cinematographic film belongs to the category of literary and artistic works made available to the public by performances which may be infinitely repeated. In this respect the problems involved in the observance of copyright in relation to the requirements of the Treaty are not the same as those which arise in connexion with literary and artistic works the placing of which at the disposal of the public is inseparable from the material form of the works, as in the case of books or records.

Records and films (in the form of videocassettes) developed a disturbing tendency of refusing to obey this classification, see Notes 174 and 184 below.

127 *Ibid.* at ¶14.

128 *Ibid.* at ¶15. It is not entirely clear how this derogation is read into the rules on the free movement of services. Advocate-General Warner favoured interpolating a provision like Article 36 to fill a lacuna in the EEC Treaty: *ibid.* at 878. Gormley suggests that a better basis may be by analogy with *Dassonville* under Article 30: see Gormley, *Prohibiting Restrictions on Trade within the EEC*, at 226.

129 *Ibid.* at ¶¶15 to 16. On the frustration so far of the Commission's efforts to introduce a compulsory licensing scheme for cross-border transmissions, see Edward Orff, 'Television Without Frontiers – Myth or Reality?', [1990] EIPR 270.

130 See from Note 134 below.

131 [1980] ECR at 879; compare *Red Baron-Franklin Park Inc. v Taito Corp.* 883 F. 2d 275 (4th Cir. 1989) at Chapter 4 Note 426 above.

The ECJ did not stop there. Rather, distinguishing between the performing right and the right to distribute an article, it ruled:

> . . . the owner of the copyright in a film and his assigns have a legitimate interest in calculating the fees due in respect of the authorization to exhibit the film on the basis of the actual or probable number of performances and in authorizing a television broadcast of the film only after it has been exhibited in cinemas for a certain period of time.

For the first time, then, the ECJ explicitly took into account the economic impact of its ruling.

The proposition is scarcely challengeable. But, with respect, why does the reasoning not apply to articles? A producer of a sound recording is unlikely to embark on that expensive and, perhaps, risky business without first calculating the anticipated fees from distribution. So too, a book publisher or the patentee of a drug.[132] The fact that products may be imported from a Member State where prices are depressed by, say, governmental action seems just as relevant as the impact of alternative forms of distributing films – cinema release, television broadcast or videocassette hire or sale. If Gormley be right and the derogation from Article 59 permitted intellectual property derives from some 'rule of reason' justifiable in the general interest, it would seem that those 'benefiting' from derogations expressed in the EEC Treaty are in a less advantageous position than those for whom the EEC Treaty framers failed to provide.

Coditel I also suggests limitation of the common origin doctrine since exploitation of the rights clearly derived from the same source. The ECJ, however, did not take up the possible point.

If the preceding three cases started suggestions of some qualification to the doctrine of Community exhaustion, the next three could, if anything, be described as the high point so far of the priority of integrating the internal market over national intellectual property rights.

Musik-Vertrieb discovered a profitable trade in buying gramophone records in various Member States, including the United Kingdom, and importing them for sale into Germany. GEMA, a copyright collecting agency for music composers, sued it for infringement of the copyrights it held. It wanted a royalty or licence fee for the right to reproduce its composers' works on Germany's market. But, it sought only the difference between the fee it would have charged for sound recordings reproduced in Germany less the amount of any royalty already paid in the Member State where the record was made.[133] Finding that German copyright law would permit GEMA's action, the Bundesgerichtshof sought directions on the impact of EC law from the ECJ.[134]

---

132 For example, the economic considerations are lumped together in Cornish, *Intellectual Property*, at ¶9–024.

133 Allowance for royalties paid the composer in the Member State of reproduction followed action by the Commission under Article 86: *GEMA* OJ 1971 L134/15, 20 June 1971.

134 55 & 57/80 *Musik-Vertrieb Membran v GEMA* [1981] ECR 147. Contrast *Warner Bros*, from Note 184 below.

The ECJ first rejected a distinction between patents, trade marks and record manufacturers' rights on the one hand and composers', or authors', rights on the other. In this action, it was concerned with rights of commercialisation, not moral rights, and so the free movement rules governing distribution of goods would apply. Expressly rejecting a principle of territoriality in the absence of copyright harmonisation, the ECJ found that copyright posed a vital threat to the integration of markets if it could be used to prevent or restrict imports of copyright works 'lawfully marketed in another Member State by the owner himself or with his consent'.[135] GEMA argued that it was not trying to prohibit the imports, just to levy a royalty. Noting that GEMA's rights to do this stemmed solely from the right of exclusive exploitation in conflict with the free movement rules, the ECJ condemned GEMA's attempt in strong terms:

> 18. . . . *no provision of national legislation* may permit an undertaking which is responsible for the management of copyrights and has a monopoly on the territory of a Member State by virtue of that management *to charge a levy on products imported from another Member State where they were put into circulation by or with the consent of the copyright owner* and thereby cause the Common Market to be partitioned. *Such a practice would amount to allowing a private undertaking to impose a charge on the importation of sound recordings which are already in free circulation in the Common Market on account of their crossing a frontier*; it would therefore have the effect of entrenching the isolation of national markets which the Treaty seeks to abolish. (*Emphasis added*)

The references to a monopoly by virtue of copyright management seem, with respect, curious. If the real evil in GEMA's practice lay in the aggregation of exclusive rights it had assembled, Article 86 rather than the free movement rules would seem a more appropriate vehicle to condemn GEMA's activities.[136]

GEMA further pleaded the statutory licence provisions in the United Kingdom which effectively set a royalty ceiling of 6.25 per cent and so deprived the copyright owner of the chance to exploit its exclusive right fully. The ECJ rejected this out of hand. In doing so, the ECJ overrode Advocate-General Warner's acceptance of these arguments. It was precisely because of the economic consequences of the statutory licence that the learned Advocate-General, distinguishing *Sterling Drug* on perhaps tenuous grounds, would have permitted GEMA to charge an additional royalty for records sourced from there. But, the ECJ could not tolerate disparities between national laws being used to allow individuals to defeat the market integration object. Hence, having chosen to release the goods into the internal market with all the advantages that should entail, the right owner should also bear the consequences of a 'unified' market. As in *Deutsche*

---

135 *Ibid.* at ¶¶12 to 15. Interestingly, the judgment identified *Terrapin* as the *most recent* statement of its 'well-established case-law': *ibid.* at ¶10.

136 But, see *Tournier* [1991] 4 CMLR 248 at section 6.4, and Chapter 7.4 and 7.5 below.

Grammophon and *Sterling Drug*, any other result would lead to artificial partitioning of the internal market.[137]

Two days later, the ECJ bluntly confirmed that goods embodying copyright did not warrant treatment different to other intellectual property rights. Imerco tried to stop Dansk Supermarked selling 'seconds' dinner sets in Denmark imported from the United Kingdom. Of the attempts to rely on artistic copyright or trade marks, the ECJ simply stated:

> The exclusive right guaranteed by the legislation on industrial and commercial property is exhausted when a product has been lawfully distributed on the market in another Member State by the actual proprietor of the right or with his consent.[138]

As Advocate-General Capotorti made clear, '[t]he decisive factor is that the product has been duly placed on the market in another Member State'.[139]

Imerco had commissioned the dinner sets for sale as part of its fiftieth anniversary celebrations, and wanted them to meet a suitably high quality. About 1,000 of the sets failed to meet its requirements on quality and Imerco permitted the manufacturer to sell them in the United Kingdom on condition that they would not be exported to Scandinavia. Dansk Supermarked had obtained the sets from the United Kingdom and was selling them without any indication that they were seconds; it seems that the indications were removed before the sets came into Dansk Supermarked's hands. In those circumstances, the ECJ was prepared to sanction the use of the Danish laws on unfair competition against deceptive marketing practices provided, as in *Béguelin*, that:

> 16. . . . the actual fact of the importation of goods which have been lawfully marketed in another Member State cannot be considered as an improper or unfair act since that description may be attached only to offer or exposure for sale on the basis of circumstances *distinct from the importation itself.* (*Emphasis added*)[140]

The third case in this series was *Merck*[141]. It resuscitated the dispute in *Musik-Vertrieb* in even more compelling form because the first marketing took place where there was no intellectual property protection. As in the *Parke, Davis* case, Merck tried to stop imports into the Netherlands of pharmaceuticals marketed in Italy; the drug in question, Moduretic, not being patented or patentable there. However, Merck had itself sold the drugs in Italy.

Merck's argument was simple: within the terms of *Sterling Drug*, it had been deprived of any chance to gain the reward for its creative (inventive)

---

137   [1981] ECR 147 at ¶¶24 to 25; for the Advocate-General, see *ibid*. at 178.
138   58/80 *Dansk Supermarked A/s v Imerco A/s* [1981] ECR 187 at ¶11. See Karen Dyekjaer-Hansen, 'Imerco v. Dansk Supermarked: Parallel Importation of Branded Seconds', [1982] EIPR 85.
139   *Ibid*. at 199.
140   For further consideration of the use of unfair competition laws against imports, see Michael Rose, 'Passing Off, Unfair Competition and Community Law', [1990] EIPR 123.
141   187/80 *Merck & Co. v Stephar* [1981] ECR 2063.

effort because, in the absence of patent protection in Italy, such a chance did not exist. But, from the viewpoint espoused by the ECJ's case law, it did not seem logical to differentiate between importers from low-priced Member States where there was patent protection, such as France and the United Kingdom, and a low-priced Member State where there was not, Italy. Accordingly, Merck could not use its Dutch patent rights to block imports of its drug from Italy.[142] After quoting its definition of the specific subject-matter of a patent from *Sterling Drug* the ECJ stated:

9. . . . the *substance* of a patent right lies essentially in according the inventor an exclusive right of first placing the product on the market.

10. That right of first placing a product on the market enables the inventor, by allowing him a monopoly in exploiting his product, to obtain the reward for his creative effort without, however, guaranteeing that he will obtain such a reward in all circumstances.

11. It is for the proprietor of the patent to decide, in the light of all the circumstances, under what conditions he will market his product, including the possibility of marketing it in a Member State where the law does not provide patent protection for the product in question. If he decides to do so he must then accept the consequences of his choice as regards the free movement of the product within the Common Market, which is a fundamental principle forming part of the legal and economic circumstances which must be taken into account by the proprietor of the patent in determining the manner in which his exclusive right will be exercised. (*Emphasis added*)

As in *Deutsche Grammophon*, *Sterling Drug* and *Musik-Vertrieb*, the intellectual property owner's consent to the first marketing was crucial because of the primacy of the goal of integrating the internal market first identified in *Consten & Grundig*.

The ECJ justified its ruling by relying on two entwined factors: the fact that a patent does not *guarantee* a monopoly reward; and the patentee's act of choice in marketing its product where it was not protected by a patent.[143] In doing so, it jettisoned any significance for the function (or purpose) of a patent by introducing a concept of 'the substance of a patent'. With respect, neither is necessarily compelling.

Advocate-General Reischl correctly observed that a patent is not a guarantee of a reward, it only offers a prospect. Many factors influence the patentee's ultimate return: the usefulness of the invention and the availability of substitute products to name but two.[144] Such factors, and even legislative devices such as compulsory licences, can only properly be used to limit the

---

142 The argument is one strongly pressed by Advocate-General Reischl who considered that any result other than denial of Merck's right to block the imports could only be brought about by reconsidering the existing cases, a move which he did not think justified: *ibid*. at 2092.

143 See also Korah, *EEC Competition Law and Practice*, at §9.4.1; see §9.4.2 on the problem of 'reward' or 'incentive'. Compare *Merck* at ¶11 with *Musik-Vertrieb* at ¶25.

144 [1981] ECR at 2090 to 2091. However, these are the consequence of choosing the market as the mechanism for assessing the value of any given invention instead of some other method such as tax subsidy or governmental grant, see Demaret, *Patents, Territorial Restrictions, and EEC Law*, at 9 to 12.

patentee's return on its invention in the context of a functioning patent system. To slide from limitations on a patentee's return within the patent system, as the Advocate-General and ECJ did, to limitations imposed in the absence of a patent destroys the purpose of a patent system since, if a patent be a means of rewarding the creativity of the inventor, the purpose requires a monopoly, albeit only temporarily. If there be no monopoly, the patentee cannot derive the special reward for its creativity and is left competing in the market-place like any other commercial concern without the encouragement to invent the adoption of a patent system deems necessary.[145]

To declare that the patentee had its choice and must accept the consequences is also, with respect, too simplistic. First, in many national systems, the grant of a patent is subject to a working requirement, leading to some form of compulsory licence for failure to exploit the patent. In such a situation, the patentee is effectively deprived of its right to choose.[146] Second, exposing the patentee to the risk of 'exhaustion' by marketing in a non-patented jurisdiction may prove counterproductive. Rather than promoting integration, it may have the effect of quarantining the unpatented Member State from the rest of the market. One possible reaction of a patentee would be to stop marketing its products directly in the unpatented territory.[147] Another, reported, consequence of *Merck* was that pharmaceutical companies successfully lobbied the French Government to raise the maximum price it fixed for pharmaceuticals. So, as in the *Distillers Red Label* case, rather than the lowest prices flowing uniformly through the internal market, some consumers were deprived of some of the advantage of cheaper prices without, at the same time, necessarily compensating the patent owners effectively.[148]

Hence, in *Merck* and *Musik-Vertrieb* the conclusion that the right owner had 'consented' to the exhaustion of its power over distribution by choosing to release its product on to the internal market seems to be dictated by the policy priority accorded to the goal of integrating the internal market rather than the justifications which purported to lead to the conclusion. *Dansk Supermarked* comes nearest to explicitly admitting this. The crucial point, then, was the policy priority of the goal of integrating the internal market. Therefore, to the extent that *Valium*, *AHPC* or *Coditel I* appeared to represent qualifications to the basic doctrine declared in *Deutsche Grammophon*, the ECJ seemed to have turned its back on them; particularly the significance of economic considerations first admitted in *Coditel I*.

On this point, it is interesting to notice that *Musik-Vertrieb* and *Dansk Supermarked* seem to overlook the existence of the three preceding cases.[149]

---

145   Demaret, *Patents, Territorial Restrictions and EEC Law*, at 1 to 2.
146   For example, *ibid.* at 6, Note 12; at 14, Note 45. This is not relevant where the marketing takes place in a country without patent protection, but is relevant in the *Sterling Drug* situation. For EC action on this issue, see Note 198 below.
147   But, see further Chapter 8.
148   Korah, *EEC Competition Law and Practice*, at 161.
149   Both judgments refer to *Terrapin* as the most recently decided case in point: *Musik-Vertrieb* [1981] ECR 147 at ¶10; *Dansk Supermarked* [1981] ECR 187 at ¶11.

If nothing else, this enabled the ECJ to avoid having to explain any differences between the cases. Apart from possible differences in the legal issues (which the ECJ did not expressly rely on),[150] another possible difference lies in the personnel of the ECJ. The changes in personnel cannot be used to signify much because of the extreme uncertainties which must attend any speculation about how a particular case was decided. However, the suggestion of an abrupt break between *Coditel I* and *Musik-Vertrieb* indicated, perhaps, by the latter's outright dismissal of any relevance for the economic considerations and territorial limitations found compelling in *Coditel I*, in particular, may be supported by the changing composition of the bench.[151]

Table 6.1 sets out which judges sat in each free movement case down to and including *Nancy Kean*.[152] In the period between *Nancy Kean* and *Deutsche Grammophon*, there were three presidents of the ECJ; Judges Lecourt, Kutscher and Mertens de Wilmars. Judge Kutscher's term as president coincided with the rulings in *Valium*, *AHPC* and *Coditel I*. He succeeded to the presidency after Judge Lecourt who last sat in a free movement case in *Terrapin*. The presidency passed from Judge Kutscher to Judge Mertens de Wilmars and Judge Kutscher's last free movement case was *Coditel I*.

Of the judges from the free movement cases during the Lecourt presidency, four took part in decisions during both the Kutscher and Mertens de Wilmars presidencies – Judges Mertens de Wilmars, Pescatore, Mackenzie Stuart and O'Keeffe; a further three, Judges Kutscher, Donner and Sørensen did not take part in free movement cases after the Kutscher presidency. Comparing the nine-member bench in *AHPC* to the seven members of *Musik-Vertrieb*, three in the former did not sit in the latter. Two of these three also did not take part in *Coditel I*. Two of the nine-judge panel in *Coditel I* did not take part in *Musik-Vertrieb*. One of these two also did not sit in *Merck* when two more judges who had not previously taken part in a free movement case sat. Further, one other judge who took part in *Valium*, *AHPC* and *Coditel I* did not sit in *Merck* (although he did in *Musik-Vertrieb*). In all, three of the nine judges in *AHPC* did not sit on the seven-member panel in *Musik-Vertrieb*, a fourth did not take part in *Merck* as well; two judges in *Coditel I* did not sit in *Musik-Vertrieb* and two also did not sit in *Merck*. Hence, bearing in mind that *AHPC*, *Coditel I* and, later, *Merck* were decided by nine judges and that *Musik-Vertrieb* was a panel of seven judges, it may be that the majority in favour of the result in the three cases during the Kutscher presidency was extremely narrow; perhaps, correspondingly, the majority in *Musik-Vertrieb* and *Merck* was also slender.

---

150 Noticeably, *Terrapin* itself did not involve issues like those in *Musik-Vertrieb* or *Merck* since it was not a case of parallel importing; also, being concerned with trade marks (if that were the relevant distinction), it raised the subject-matter of *Valium*, *AHPC* and one part of *Dansk Supermarked*.
151 On the secrecy attending the ECJ's decision-making, see further Hartley, *The Foundations of European Community Law*, Chapter 2.
152   144/81 *Keurkoop BV v Nancy Kean Gifts BV* [1982] ECR 2853.

Table 6.1
Judges Sitting in Free Movement Cases 1971–82

Judge/Case	DG	H	SD/W	EMI	Ter	V	AH	Cod	MV	DS	Mer	Pf	Pol	NK
Lecourt	X	X	X	X	X									
Donner	X	X	X	X										
Trabbucchi	X	X	X				X							
Monaco	X	X	X											
Mertens	X	X	X	X	X	X	X	X	X		X		X	X
Pescatore	X	X	X		X	X	X	X	X	X	X		X	X
Kutscher	X	X	X	X	X	X	X	X						
Sørensen		X	X	X		X	X							
O Dálaigh		X	X											
Mackenzie Stuart		X	X			X	X	X	X		X		X	X
O'Keeffe				X	X	X	X	X	X		X		X	X
Capotorti				X	X							X		
Bosco						X	X	X	X		X		X	X
Touffait						X	X	X	X	X	X	X	X	X
Due								X		X	X		X	X
Koopmans								X	X			X	X	X
Everling											X		X	X
Chloros											X		X	X
Grévisse													X	X

X	= Judge sat in the case	Ter	= *Terrapin v Terraware*
DG	= *Deutsche Grammophon*	V	= *Valium*
H	= *Hag I*	AH	= *AHPC*
SD/W	= *Sterling Drug and Winthrop*	Cod	= *Coditel I*
EMI	= *EMI v CBS*	MV	= *Musik-Vertreib*

DS	= *Dansk Supermarked*
Mer	= *Merck v Stephan*
Pf	= *Pfizer v Eurim-Pharm*
Pol	= *Polydor v Harlequin*
NK	= *Keurkoop v Nancy Kean*

In any case, after *Merck* and *Pfizer*, the ECJ seemed to have taken a strong stance in favour of integrating the internal market where the imports sought to be blocked had been marketed within the EC by the domestic right owner or with its consent. Some sort of qualification had been recognised in cases involving trade marks and repackaging or relabelling; but, as the *Pfizer* case confirmed, it was limited. A further qualification had been recognised for broadcasts (diffusion) of films. If anything, that qualification seems to have been more limited than the one accepted for trade marks because its bases, economic considerations and territorial limitations, were categorically rejected in *Musik-Vertrieb* and *Merck*.

6.3.2 Imports from outside the EC

A further factor highlighting the policy nature of the Community exhaustion doctrine is its non-application to trade between a Member State and countries outside the EC (so-called 'third countries'). While for the most part the priority of integrating the internal market over the goals of national intellectual property rights was clear in trade between the Member States, a different rule applied where the goods were being imported from outside the EC. In terms which seem generally applicable to all intellectual property rights, the ECJ has expressly refused to apply the doctrine of common origin to imports of trade-marked products from a third country and the doctrine of exhaustion in *Deutsche Grammophon* to imports embodying either copyright or industrial designs.

The question first arose for consideration in *EMI v CBS*.[153] The EMI group owned the trade mark *Columbia* in all the Member States of the EC and some other parts of the world; the same trade mark was owned by the CBS group in the United States and elsewhere. Each group operated in the other's market under a different trade mark. CBS, however, was importing into the United Kingdom, Denmark and Germany some of its records made in the United States bearing the *Columbia* trade mark. It had recently stopped a US firm from importing EMI products into the United States under the *Columbia* mark. The national courts found that EMI could repel CBS in the EC too, subject to the operation of the free movement rules.

CBS relied mainly on the *Hag I* case to immunise the national laws. The Columbia mark had been developed in 1894 by a US company which operated throughout the world including most of the future Member States of the EC. In the 1920s, the American company had assigned its European assets, including the trade marks, to an independently owned UK business and, after further changes in share ownership, from 1931 the US and European trade marks had been owned by completely independent businesses. There had, however, been a number of commercial arrangements between the two businesses including agreements not to use the conflicting

---

153   51, 86 & 96/75 *EMI Records Ltd v CBS United Kingdom Ltd* [1976] ECR 811.

marks in each other's territory and for the exchange of repertoire; prior to 1956, the exchange was done on a systematic basis and, between 1962 and 1971, EMI claimed that agreements were short-lived and for the exploitation of 'specific repertoire'. It was common ground that all agreements had ceased operating by 1974.

The ECJ, taking its lead from Advocate-General Warner, distinguished between the application of the free movement rules and the competition rules to the case. The competition rules might apply to any continuing arrangements between EMI and CBS which had effect within the EC. On the other hand, no application could be found for the free movement rules.

First, the ECJ negated the application of the free movement rules:

> 10. . . . the exercise of a trade-mark right in order to prevent the marketing of products coming from a third country under an identical mark, even if this constitutes a measure having an effect equivalent to a quantitative restriction, does not affect the free movement of goods between Member States and thus does not come under the prohibitions set out in Article 30 et seq. of the Treaty.
>
> 11. In such circumstances the exercise of a trade-mark right *does not in fact jeopardize the unity of the common market* which Article 30 et seq. are intended to ensure.
>
> 12. *Furthermore* if the same proprietor holds the trade-mark right in respect of the same product *in all the Member States* there are no grounds for examining whether those marks have a common origin with an identical mark recognized in a third country, *since that question is relevant only* in relation to considering whether *within the Community there are opportunities for partitioning the market.* (*Emphasis added*)

The ECJ also rejected CBS' arguments based on the common commercial policy and the free circulation within the EC of products from third countries which had lawfully passed the customs frontier.

Hence, the ECJ clearly stated that the free movement rules only apply to trade between the several Member States because of the role of those rules in integrating the internal market. The same reasoning applied to the doctrine of common origin although, somewhat problematically, point 12 seems to proceed on the basis that this doctrine existed independently of the free movement rules.

In contrast, the ECJ considered that an agreement to use trade mark rights to isolate the EC from third countries might breach Article 85 or that use of trade mark rights in this way might, possibly, breach Article 86.[154]

The second consideration of the role of the free movement rules where the imports came from outside the EC involved the use of copyright in sound recordings to block imports into the United Kingdom from Portugal.[155] This time, there was a free trade agreement between Portugal and the EC which included provisions worded very similarly to Articles 30 and 36 of the EEC

---

154   On the competition rules, see Chapter 7.5.

155   270/80 *Polydor Limited v Harlequin Record Shops Limited* [1982] ECR 329. For the facts and UK Court of Appeal's judgment, see Chapter 4 from Notes 125 and 200.

Treaty. At the time, Portugal was negotiating with the EC for its admission to the EC. The ECJ bluntly rejected the importers' argument:

> 18. The considerations which led to that interpretation of Articles 30 and 36 of the Treaty do not apply in the context of the relations between the Community and Portugal as defined by the Agreement. It is apparent from an examination of the Agreement that although it makes provision for the unconditional abolition of certain restrictions on trade between the Community and Portugal, such as quantitative restrictions and measures having equivalent effect, *it does not have the same purpose as the EEC Treaty*, inasmuch as the latter, as has been stated above, *seeks to create a single market reproducing as closely as possible the conditions of a domestic market.*
> 19. It follows that in the context of the Agreement restrictions on trade in goods may be considered justified on the ground of the protection of industrial and commercial property in a situation *in which their justification would not be possible within the Community.* (*Emphasis added*)

That is, the free trade agreement did not impose the same overriding priority to the goal of integrating the separate markets. In point 20, the ECJ indicated that its conclusion was all the more necessary because the free trade agreement did not include the necessary tools to ensure proper integration of the market such as the uniform application of EC law and the progressive abolition of legislative disparities within the common market.

The ECJ's ruling in *Polydor* may require some reconsideration if the EEA Treaty comes into force following the ECJ's Opinion in *Second EEA Treaty Opinion*.[155a] The EEA Treaty includes a number of provisions which are 'textually identical' to the provisions of the EEC Treaty. These include articles 11, 12, and 13 of the EEA Treaty corresponding to articles 30, 34 and 36, respectively, of the EEC Treaty and articles 53 and 54 of the EEA Treaty corresponding to articles 85 and 86, respectively, of the EEC Treaty. (The power to grant exemptions under article 53(3) of the EEA Treaty is to be exercised in accordance with articles 55 and 56.) In adopting these provisions in this form, the intention of the contracting parties was:

> to arrive at and maintain a uniform interpretation and application of [the EEA Treaty] and those provisions of the Community legislation which are substantially reproduced in [the EEA Treaty] *and* to arrive at an equal treatment of individuals and economic operators as regards the four freedoms and the conditions of competition . . . .[155b] (*Emphasis added*)

To this end, Article 6, without prejudice to the future development of case law, adopts the case law of the ECJ given prior to the date of signature of the EEA Treaty for the relevant provisions. In addition, Articles 105 and 111 provide for the EEA Joint Committee to keep the case law of the ECJ and the EFTA Court (established pursuant to Article 108(2)) under constant

155a   Opinion 1/92 *Re the Draft Treaty on a European Economic Area (No. 2)* [1992] 2 CMLR 217. For the first Opinion, see Opinion 1/91 *Re the Draft Treaty on a European Economic Area* [1992] 1 CMLR 245. In both Opinions, the ECJ was called on to opine only about the compatibility with the EEC Treaty of the system of judicial supervision to be set up by the EEA Treaty.
155b   EEA Treaty, penultimate recital as reproduced in [1992] 1 CMLR 921. See also Art. 1(1).

review and to seek to resolve any discrepancies which may arise between the two.[155c]

Accordingly, it might be thought that the distinction between the EEC Treaty and corresponding provisions in an EFTA agreement drawn by the ECJ at points 18 to 20 of *Polydor* will no longer apply. However, *Polydor* itself forms part of the ECJ's case law in force prior to the date of signature of the EEA Treaty and the EEA Treaty, while a significant advance on an EFTA agreement, does not abolish the difference between EC Member States and EFTA countries. Indeed, the third last recital expressly preserves the possibility of any EFTA country acceding to the EC. Moreover, the ECJ has already opined that there are 'divergences between the aims and context of the [EEA Treaty] and those of Community law' which stand 'in the way of the achievement of the objective of homogeneity in the interpretation and application of the law in the EEA'.[155d] Therefore, the possibility of different rules applying to the free movement of goods within the EC compared to between the EC and an EFTA country may well still remain.

The third situation in which the issue might fall for consideration is where the goods are first imported into one Member State and then an attempt is made to import them into another Member State where the right owner seeks to block them. Where the goods were able to enter the first Member State because there was no corresponding intellectual property right, the answer is clear. The ECJ has held that the intellectual property right in the second Member State may be used to block the imports provided that the goods were not marketed in the first Member State by the owner of the right in the second Member State or with that person's consent.[156] A reservation had been made for the case where there was an intellectual property right in the first Member State which had not been created independently of the one

---

155c   Note in particular art. 111(3) entitling a contracting party to request the ECJ 'to give a ruling on the interpretation of the relevant rules.' In addition, under the '*procès-verbal agréé ad article 105*', decisions of the EEA Joint Committee will not affect the case law of the ECJ. The operation of these provisions is substantially the subject matter of *Second EEA Treaty Opinion* and, as they undermined neither the binding nature of the ECJ's rulings nor the Community legal order, were found to be compatible with the EEC Treaty.

155d   *First EEA Treaty Opinion* [1992] 1 CMLR 245 ¶¶14–29; *Second EEA Treaty Opinion* [1992] 2 CMLR at ¶17, ¶18 confirming that those divergences remain after amendment. In particular, the ECJ found that the EEA Treaty will not establish throughout the EEA the essential characteristics of the Community legal order: the primacy of EC law over that of individual Member States and the direct effects 'of a whole series of provisions': especially at ¶¶20 and 21. Article 6 read with Protocol 35 (apparently unchanged: see *Second Draft EEA Treaty Opinion* at ¶5) was insufficient in itself to secure the objective of homogeneity: *First EEA Treaty Opinion* at ¶¶26 to 28. Therefore, in the ECJ's opinion, it seems that at least one of the essential requirements for the doctrine of Community exhaustion is missing.

156   144/81 *Keurkoop BV v Nancy Kean BV* [1982] ECR 2853 at ¶29, a case involving industrial design, see from Note 158 below. As always, 'consent' includes the case of marketing by a member of the same corporate group. Exercise of the right would also be subject to any constraints imposed by the competition rules. For rulings of national courts to the same effect, see *Re Patented Bandages* [1988] 2 CMLR 359; *Re Patented Feedingstuffs* [1989] 2 CMLR 902; *Minnesota Mining and Manufacturing Company v Geerpres Europe Ltd* [1974] RPC 35.

subsisting in the second Member State. But, the rejection of the doctrine of common origin would seem to remove that reservation, subject to the operation of the competition rules.[157]

6.4 Qualification

The drawing of any line must prove arbitrary in many respects. Unfortunately, the 'real' world refuses to be categorised and pigeon-holed as theory would hope. It might, perhaps, be argued that the *Coditel I, Valium* and *AHPC* cases represent the start of the break with the past. Certainly, aspects of each suggest precursors for some of the approaches the ECJ has attempted in the cases from *Nancy Kean* onwards.

However, these cases are separated from the future by the imposing trilogy of *Musik-Vertrieb, Dansk Supermarked* and *Merck*. These three later cases clearly belong in the line of jurisprudence established with *Deutsche Grammophon*. All the hallmarks are there in striking language: the overriding importance of market integration; the consequent touchstone of the right owner's consent to marketing of the imported product; the elaboration of the concept of the specific subject-matter of intellectual property as an almost abstract emanation of EC law without regard to national law and a blind eye to economic considerations and differences between the legal regimes of different Member States.

After these cases comes a questioning, long overdue, of the basic dichotomy between existence and exercise culminating in the ECJ's sanction of the ban on parallel imports in *Warner Bros v Christiansen*, specifically taking into account the *economic* implications of a contrary ruling on the value of the national intellectual property right, and in the rejection of the common origin doctrine.

Some of the cases in this new period can fit within the earlier jurisprudence without much violence especially as many of them do not involve attempts to block imports first marketed in another Member State by the domestic right owner. Most of these cases, however, share marked differences to the formula built on *Deutsche Grammophon*. In particular, the dichotomy between the existence and the exercise of a right all but disappears; the ECJ becomes increasingly sensitive to differences between national laws and, in some cases, considerations of an economic nature play an increasingly important role.

The design appearance of ladies' handbags provided the first point of departure.[158] Nancy Kean held a registered design in the Benelux for a ladies' handbag. It was not the author of the design which appeared to be based on a US design patent registered in someone else's name.

---

157 *Ibid.* For rejection of the common origin doctrine, see below from Note 220.
158 144/81 *Keurkoop BV v Nancy Kean Gifts BV* [1982] ECR 2853. See Valentine Korah, *Know-how Licensing and the EEC Competition Rules Regulation 556/89*, at 27 to 28.

Its supplies of bags made according to the design were obtained from a producer in Taiwan. Keurkoop, also not the author of the design, had also procured virtually identical handbags from Taiwan, but, apparently from different manufacturers. When Keurkoop put its bags on the market in the Netherlands, it was successfully sued by Nancy Kean.

During the litigation, Keurkoop claimed that the action breached the EC rules on the free movement of goods in two respects. First, it claimed that by allowing someone other than the author to register the design *and* permitting only the author to challenge such a registration, the Benelux law was itself contrary to Articles 30 to 36. Second, it relied on the obstacle to intra-EC trade posed by Nancy Kean's possible exercise of the right to stop imports of the handbags from other Member States where they were in free circulation. Apparently, Nancy Kean only held rights for the design in the Benelux, Denmark and the United Kingdom. A different party held a design right in France and the design was not protected in Germany at all. A German business, Otto GmbH, was importing identical handbags from Taiwan into Germany and some of these were finding their way on to the Dutch market.

The ECJ dismissed both contentions. Interestingly, in doing so, it appeared to abandon its cherished concepts formalised as the dichotomy between the existence and the exercise of an intellectual property right and the specific subject-matter of the right; but not the test of consent to marketing nor the doctrine of common origin.

In answering the second question, the ECJ ruled that Article 36 justified use of intellectual property rights to block imports from another Member State which had been marketed there *without* the consent of the intellectual property owner or 'a person legally or economically dependent on him'.[159] It did, however, note an exception to this general principle where the exercise of the right was the purpose, means or result of some agreement contrary to Article 85(1).[160]

To that extent, the judgment is consistent with the earlier case law such as *Sterling Drug*, *Terrapin*, *Musik-Vertrieb* and *Merck*. However, there was a significant change in the ECJ's reasoning linking the absence of consent to the role of Article 36. The ECJ did not repeat its formulas about the dichotomy between the existence and the exercise of the right or its specific subject-matter. Rather, it admitted that its function was to fix the boundary between uses of intellectual property rights which EC law would tolerate and those which it would not:

> 24.   Article 36 is thus intended to emphasize that the reconciliation between the requirements of the free movement of goods and the respect to which

---

159   *Ibid*. at ¶25.
160   *Ibid*. at ¶¶26 to 28. The facts surrounding the French registration in particular gave rise to some suspicions since it and the Benelux registrations were almost simultaneous and the form of the Benelux law, allowing registration by the first applicant rather than the author, could lend itself to exploitation by those intent on partitioning the common market. As in *Valium* and *AHPC*, this was for the national court to investigate.

industrial and commercial property rights are entitled must be achieved in such a way that protection is ensured *for the legitimate exercise*, in the form of prohibitions on imports which are 'justified' within the meaning of that article, of the rights conferred by national legislation, but is refused, on the other hand, in respect *of any improper exercise* of the same rights which is of such a nature as to maintain or establish artificial partitions within the common market. The exercise of industrial and commercial property rights conferred by national legislation must consequently be restricted as far as is necessary for that reconciliation.[161] (*Emphasis added*)

In the author's opinion, the change is to be commended. At the least, it makes the policy choice confronting the ECJ explicit rather than hiding it behind an obscure distinction between the existence and the exercise of intellectual property rights. Admittedly, it does not establish objective criteria allowing the application of the rule to be predicted with any degree of certainty. But, 'objective' criteria are only a means to an end and cannot themselves be fixed until the policy objective has itself been properly identified. In terms of *Nancy Kean*, such objective criteria would relate to identifying what is an artificial partitioning of the internal market.[162]

The ECJ's answer to the first question suggests why it was necessary to change the formulation. The peculiarity of the Benelux law which Keurkoop had hoped to seize on was that it granted design rights to the first applicant rather than the author. While any person could challenge the registration for lack of novelty,[163] only the author could challenge for want of authorship within a limited period.

The ECJ did not simply rule that industrial designs were subject-matter embraced in the phrase, 'industrial and commercial property'. Nor did it limit itself as in the field of copyright to considerations of the economic function of designs law in commercial distribution. Instead, it examined the very law itself and found it justifiable within the purposes of Article 36. After noting in point 14 that a design was like a patent, trade mark and copyright 'inasmuch as its aim is to define exclusive rights which are characteristic of that property', the ECJ ruled:

> 15. . . . According to Article 3 the exclusive right to a design is acquired by the first person to file it without it being necessary to inquire whether that person is also the author of the design or a person entitled under him. *The reason for the rule is to be found in the function of the right to the design in economic life and in a concern for simplicity and efficacy.* Finally, by virtue of the detailed rules laid down in Article 5 of the law the author of the design may, during a period of five years, claim the right to its registration and may at any time claim to have the registration annulled.
> 16. Those features, which are neither exhaustive nor limitative, nevertheless allow it to be said that *legislation having characteristics of the kind of* [sic]

---

161 Contrast Advocate-General Lenz' more orthodox approach at *ibid.* at 2882.
162 For the objection, note Joliet and Keeling, 'Trade Mark Law and the Free Movement of Goods', text at their Note 28.
163 In the so-called 'relative' sense and not the 'absolute' sense: see Friden, 'Recent Developments in EEC Intellectual Property Law', at 193; *Thetford Corp. v Fiamma SpA* [1988] ECR 3585 from Note 199 below.

> *those which have just been described constitutes legislation for the protection of industrial and commercial property for the purposes of Article 36 of the Treaty. (Emphasis added)*

If the test of the dichotomy between the existence and the exercise of an intellectual property right had any substance, the ECJ's reasoning can only go to the existence of the intellectual property right.[164] Hence, the ECJ could hardly restate its dichotomy between the existence and the exercise of intellectual property rights in answering to the second question.

The ECJ's reasoning led to one more breach with the old orthodoxy. In *Nancy Kean*, the 'conditions and procedures' governing the protection of designs was a matter for national law 'in the present state of Community law and in the absence of Community standardization or of a harmonization of laws' about these matters.[165] Admittedly, if one were to accept the dichotomy between existence and exercise as valid, such conditions and procedures would presumably fall within the existence of the right. But, this characterisation does not explain why the ECJ felt it necessary to justify such matters under Article 36. It had not previously paid so much respect to differences between national laws because allowing such differences would affect the role of the free movement rules and could lead to artificial partitioning of the common market.[166]

The ECJ's tampering with the *existence* of intellectual property was resumed in the following cases which reflect a new respect for the content of national laws on intellectual property. However, in *Nancy Kean*, the intellectual property right owner's interests could be protected without violence to the requirement of consent since the imports had not been marketed with the right owner's consent or by someone legally or economically dependent on the right owner. The ECJ was next called on to repulse an attempt to do away with even that degree of protection for intellectual property owners. Once again, however, it was able to avoid the issue.

Differences in philosophy between the Dutch and British patent laws, persisting despite the ECJ's edicts establishing a common market in drugs, returned to the forefront.[167] Pharmon contracted to buy a shipment of frusemide from DDSA. Frusemide was protected in both the Netherlands

---

164 For a thought-provoking argument to this effect in the context of the post-*Pharmon* cases, see Friden, 'Recent Developments in EEC Intellectual Property Law', at 193 and note the Advocate-General's valiant attempts to fit the case within the orthodox formula forcing him to layer the law further with categories for proprietorship, 'the structure of the right' and 'the content of the right': [1982] ECR at 2880 to 2881.

165 [1982] ECR 2853 at ¶18.

166 See for example *Musik-Vertrieb*, *Merck*, *Valium* and *Sterling Drug*. The ECJ subsequently rejected an argument that patent law was more uniform than designs law: *Thetford* from Note 199 below. On the significance of these changes, compare Korah, *EEC Competition Law and Practice*, 161 and Marenco and Banks, 'Intellectual Property and the Community Rules on Free Movement: Discrimination Unearthed', at 232.

167 19/84 *Pharmon v Hoechst* [1985] ECR 2281. Compare the *Hoffnung* case and *T.B. Harms Company v JEM Records Inc.*, see Chapter 4 Notes 58 and 403 respectively. On the qualified nature of the 'common' market for pharmaceuticals, see Chapter 8 below.

and the United Kingdom by patents owned by Hoechst. DDSA, however, had a compulsory licence under the Patents Act 1949 (United Kingdom) section 41 to make and sell the drug in the United Kingdom.[168] Before Pharmon could take delivery of its shipment, Hoechst obtained an injunction from the Dutch courts preventing its importation into the Netherlands.

The main issue referred to the ECJ was whether the free movement rules, either where the patented product was marketed by the patentee or with its consent or by analogy with the *Hag I* case, prevented the use of a Dutch patent to block imports of a product made abroad under a compulsory licence. In particular, Pharmon cunningly argued that Hoechst's decision to seek patent protection in the United Kingdom, knowing that the patent would be subject to compulsory licences *on demand*, was a sufficient act of choice to bring the case within the consent doctrine decreed in *Merck*.

Without discussing the doctrine of common origin, the ECJ brusquely rejected Pharmon's claim:

> 25. It is necessary to point out that where, as in this instance, the competent authorities of a Member State grant a third party a compulsory licence which allows him to carry out manufacturing and marketing operations which the patentee would normally have the right to prevent, *the patentee cannot be deemed to have consented to the operation of that third party*. Such a measure deprives the patent proprietor of his right to determine freely the conditions under which he markets his products.
>
> 26. As the Court held most recently in [*Merck*], the substance of a patent right lies essentially in according the inventor an exclusive right of first placing the product on the market so as to allow him to obtain the reward for his creative effort. It is therefore necessary to allow the patent proprietor to prevent the importation and marketing of products manufactured under a compulsory licence in order to protect the substance of his exclusive rights under his patent. (*Emphasis added*)

At point 29, the ECJ also expressly stated that the outcome in no way depended on any conditions against export imposed by the terms of the compulsory licence or the payment of royalties under it to the patentee. Unlike the Advocate-General, the ECJ did not refer to the issue of whether DDSA's sale had been made directly to Pharmon in the Netherlands or Pharmon's purchase had taken place on the open market in the United Kingdom.[169]

---

168 Section 41(1), since repealed, provided in part:

> Without prejudice to the foregoing provisions of this Act, where a patent is in force in respect of (a) a substance capable of being used as food or medicine . . .; or (b) a process for producing such a substance or in the production of food or medicine; . . . the comptroller shall, on application made to him by any person interested, order the grant to the applicant of a licence under the patent on such terms as he thinks fit unless it appears to him that there are good reasons for refusing the application.

Subsection 2 made it plain that the provision's object was to secure the lowest prices for food and medicine consistent with the patentee deriving a 'reasonable' advantage from its patent. The licence actually granted DDSA included a prohibition on export, but this was ignored.

169 See Korah, *Know-how Licensing Agreements and the EEC Competition Rules*, at 93 Note 6, 104 Note 5.

The result has been accorded solid support and, with respect, is welcome.[170] But, despite the reference to conformity with *Merck*, the ruling leads to absurdity. The patentee whose rights are exercised under a compulsory licence can still prevent imports into other Member States to protect its opportunity to claim a reward for its creative effort *despite* receiving a 'reasonable' royalty from the compulsory licensee which may well take the price above a competitive market equilibrium. In contrast, if a patentee markets the product in an unprotected market where above-competitive returns cannot be captured as in *Merck*, it cannot claim the right to seek the same reward. Moreover, if the right owner makes the mistake of granting licences freely where they would otherwise be compulsorily available, *Musik-Vertrieb* would indicate that the consensual act disables it from relying on its intellectual property rights.

This has led Demaret to argue that *Pharmon* must force reconsideration of the earlier cases built on *Deutsche Grammophon*. In his view, the economic impact on the copyright owner or patentee is identical whether the product is actually made under a compulsory licence or the right owner's freedom of action is constrained by a ceiling set by the availability of compulsory licences. The argument is even stronger if there is no parallel protection available in the Member State of first marketing.[171]

Since the ECJ did not even refer to the 'common origin' doctrine, it seems this principle does not now apply to patents.[172] Hence, it would seem that the qualification for 'independent' patents made in point 11 of *Sterling Drug* may now be limited to cases where ownership has been divided by an agreement which has 'continuing effects'.[173]

Basset continued the qualifications. It could simply be seen as an extension of *Coditel I*'s special rule for the right of public performance but, as

---

170   See for example Paul Demaret, 'Industrial Property Rights, Compulsory Licences and the Free Movement of Goods under Community Law', 18 IIC 161 (1987); Beier, 'Industrial Property and the Free Movement of Goods in the Internal European Market', at 153 to 154; for analyses in terms of the *Deutsche Grammophon* jurisprudence, see Guy J. Pevtchin and Leslie Williams, '*Pharmon v. Hoechst* – The Limits on the Community Exhaustion Principle in Respect of Compulsory Licenses', [1986] *Fordham Corporate Law Institute* 287, at 296 to 304; Norbert Koch, 'Article 30 and the Exercise of Industrial Property Rights to Block Imports', [1986] *Fordham Corporate Law Institute* 605. The Advocate-General endorsed the Commission's fears that a ruling in favour of Pharmon would have the contrary effect of fragmenting the market by making the Member State with the most liberal compulsory licensing provisions the rule throughout the EC and so further and potentially acting as a disincentive for Member States to adhere to the Community Patent Convention: [1985] ECR at 2287.

171   *Ibid.* at 175 to 177, distinguishing trade marks. Beier, however, rejects any balancing approach, see Beier, 'Industrial Property and the Free Movement of Goods in the Internal European Market', at 153 to 155.

172   Gormley is driven reluctantly to this conclusion: Laurence Gormley, 'Current Survey: The Common Market', (1985) 10 ELRev. 447, at 449. See also Demaret, 'Industrial Property Rights, Compulsory Licences and the Free Movement of Goods under Community Law', at 174 to 175.

173   This would seem to be confirmed by *Hag II* [1990] 3 CMLR 571 from Note 220 below. For *Sterling Drug*, see text from Note 93 above and note the similar proviso to *Nancy Kean* at ¶25.

previously discussed, aspects of *Coditel I* seem to represent a departure from the 'general' rule.[174] Furthermore, *Coditel I* itself seemed to have precluded its application to records.

SACEM, the French copyright collecting agency for composers, demanded that Basset, a discotheque owner, pay it a fixed fee of 8.25 per cent of Basset's receipts for a licence to play copyright music in the discotheque. The 8.25 per cent figure was the sum of two separate aspects of copyright subsisting in a work under French law: the right of performance and the severable right of reproduction; in effect, a fee for use of the performing right, 6.6 per cent, and a supplementary mechanical reproduction fee (based on the right of reproduction) of 1.65 per cent.[175]

Ordinarily, under French law, the transfer of one aspect of the copyright, say, the performance right, does not entail the transfer of the other. Moreover, to be valid an assignment must specify the extent and purpose of the use which the assignee may put the work to. Hence, under French law, it seems that a record is usually produced by assigning the reproduction right to the producer expressly limited to use of the record for private purposes in return for a reproduction fee. If the record is subsequently played in public, such as in a discotheque, the performance is liable both to a fee for exercise of the performing right *and* the 'reproduction' of the work to the public. The latter is described as the supplementary mechanical reproduction fee.

Basset argued that the supplementary mechanical reproduction fee was a restriction on trade between the Member States condemned by Article 30 presumably because it was characterised as part of the reproduction right rather than the performing right and the records he imported had already been subjected to a levy for the right of reproduction. As such, *under French law*, the supplementary mechanical reproduction fee constituted an additional levy on the article, the record, rather than on the performance. In his argument, the restriction arose because French law would allow a further levy on goods already in circulation in another Member State with the copyright owner's consent. In other words, he claimed that the supplementary mechanical reproduction fee was like the additional royalty GEMA had sought on the import of records from the United Kingdom in *Musik-Vertrieb*.

He also raised a claim under Article 86 which was perfunctorily dismissed for want of evidence, the referring court having found the fee to be reasonable.[176]

---

174 402/85 *Basset v SACEM* [1987] ECR 1747. See also 395/87 *Ministère Public v Tournier* [1991] 4 CMLR 248 at ¶¶11 to 13 and generally, Defalque, 'Copyright – Free Movement of Goods and Territoriality: Recent Developments', at 435. See also *Coditel I*, especially at ¶12 at Note 126 above.

175 This outline is based on Advocate-General Lenz' opinion, particularly at 1754 to 1755 and Gillian Davies and Hans Hugo von Rauscher auf Weeg, *Challenges to Copyright and Related Rights in the European Community*, ESC Publishing Limited, 1983, at 139 to 142.

176 [1987] ECR 1747 at ¶18 to 21. For the subsequent consideration of the issues in *Tournier* and *Lucazeau* [1991] 4 CMLR 248, see text from Note 218 below.

The ECJ, having pointed out that SACEM charged the same fees whether the record was first made and sold in France or another Member State, ruled:

> 15. . . . disregarding the concepts used by French legislation and practice, the supplementary mechanical reproduction fee may thus be analysed as constituting part of the payment for an author's rights over the public performance of a recorded musical work. Moreover, the amount of that royalty, like that of the performance fee strictly so called, is calculated on the basis of the discotheque's turnover and not the number of records bought or played.
> 16. It follows that, even if the charging of the fee in question were to be capable of having a restrictive effect on imports, it does not constitute a measure having equivalent effect prohibited under Article 30 of the Treaty inasmuch as it *must be regarded as a normal exploitation of copyright* and does not constitute a means of arbitrary discrimination or a disguised restriction on trade between Member States for the purposes of Article 36 of the Treaty.[177]
> (*Emphasis added*)

That is, the fee was part of the right owner's power to charge for each and every performance of the work to the public.

Viewed in this way, the result seems to accord with the approach of intellectual property and, even, the ideology of the free movement rules.[178] *Musik-Vertrieb* was concerned with the right of reproduction (strictly speaking, distribution) and *Basset* with the right of performance. The former was exhausted on first sale; the latter was not since it entitles the owner to a separate fee for each and every performance. But, the reasoning used to reach that conclusion is surprising.

The judgment does not refer to either of the earlier touchstones, the dichotomy between the existence and the exercise of a right or its specific subject-matter. Instead, it described the supplementary mechanical fee as 'a normal exploitation of copyright'.[179] Moreover, as in *Nancy Kean*, there is a strong deference to the approach and provisions of the national law. Indeed, the combination of these factors seems to have led the ECJ to conclude that the supplementary mechanical fee did not conflict with Article 30 at all.[180]

The phrase 'normal exploitation' is surprising in itself. Prior to *Deutsche Grammophon* and *Musik-Vertrieb*, it was probably a 'normal' use of

---

177 For the Advocate-General, see 1758 to 1759, who also reached the perhaps startling conclusion in light of the cases from *Deutsche Grammophon* to *Merck* that, insofar as international treaty obligations bound French law to treat foreign copyright works like domestic works, any restriction on intra-EC trade resulting must be tolerated.

178 For a similar US case involving copyright in software, see *Red Baron-Franklin Park Inc. v Taito Corp.* 883 F. 2d 275 (4th Cir. 1989), see Chapter 4 from Note 426.

179 This has been taken to mean that the practice formed part of the specific object of copyright: Defalque, 'Copyright – Free Movement of Goods and Territoriality: Recent Developments', at 435; Advocate-General Jacobs has described it as part of the essential function, see *Tournier* [1991] 4 CMLR 248, at 259, 261. In *Basset*, Advocate-General Lenz described it as an aspect of the specific subject-matter of the copyright at [1987] ECR 1759 at ¶27.

180 *Ibid.* at 436 and see *Tournier* [1991] 4 CMLR 248, at 259, 261 *per* Advocate-General Jacobs. *Basset* at ¶16 does, however, refer to Article 36 as well; see also Marenco and Banks, 'Intellectual Property and the Community Rules on Free Movement: Discrimination Unearthed', at 228 to 229.

copyright-like rights to block imports which had been first sold in a foreign, rather than the domestic, market. The 'normality' of that practice did not save it from the overriding priority of integrating the internal market. Earlier, in point 14, the ECJ does note that SACEM's practice is in accordance with the normal practices of copyright management in that it charges separate fees for performance regardless of the origin of the recording in question. So, it could be argued that part of the 'normality' was that the fee was levied regardless of whether the record was an import or not. The main thrust of points 14 and 15, however, seems to be that, the peculiarities of French (and Belgian) law aside, what SACEM did corresponded to practice in other Member States.

The fact that the ECJ disregarded the French law's characterisation of the fee as a payment for use of the right of reproduction is also worthy of comment. In reaching this conclusion, the ECJ noted that the fee was calculated in the same way as the performance fee proper; that is, as a flat rate levy on turnover rather than on the basis of each record played.[181]

Advocate-General Lenz had also adverted to this point as one of the reasons for rejecting the application of Article 30 to the supplementary mechanical fee. Having rejected as too narrow SACEM's contentions that Article 30 did not apply because the fee was charged for the provision of services or because it was levied on domestic records and imports without distinction, he listed a number of factors which might persuade the ECJ that Article 30 did not apply at all.[182] First, he referred favourably to the Commission's view that nothing would be gained by condemning the supplementary mechanical fee. SACEM's bargaining power was such that it would simply raise the level of the fee for use of the performing right. Second, the Advocate-General thought that the fee probably did not affect imports. Under French law, fees charged by copyright management societies had to be levied on a flat-rate basis which, although it is not clear, he seems to take as meaning that different levels of fee could not be charged to different discotheques. So, all that would happen would be a reduction in royalty remittances to other management societies without *necessarily* influencing individual purchasing decisions by discotheque operators. Further, according to the Advocate-General, discotheques would buy their music according to the public demand and not the price. The final reason, added 'for the sake of completeness', was the inapplicability of *Musik-Vertrieb* to the present situation which involved a right 'similar to the right of performance'.[183]

181 This is the method usually employed by management agencies, see Michael Freeguard, 'Collective Administration of Rights', at ¶A18 in Stephen M. Stewart, *International Copyright and Neighbouring Rights*, Butterworths, 1989 (2nd ed.), Annex.
182 For the rejection of the 'narrow' factors, see [1987] ECR 1747, at 1755 to 1756. In the end, although he favoured the view that Article 30 did not apply, he was also prepared to admit a role for Article 36 and the international conventions: *ibid.* at 1760, ¶29.
183 *Ibid.* from 1756; for the first point, see ¶15; for the flat-rate basis, see ¶17 also seeming to reject the claim that administration of a composite fee would be too difficult and note the different levels of fees charged discotheque operators in *Tournier* [1991] 4 CMLR 248; and the public preference, see ¶18.

The ECJ's reasoning in points 14 to 16 seems to be an acceptance of the Advocate-General's final reason. Its reference to the flat-rate calculation may, arguably, only be a factor confirming its classification of the fee as in the nature of an exercise of the performing right. Interestingly, however, in *Warner Bros*, where the right of performance was also relied on, the Danish law there in question was justified *only* under Article 36. So, as the confirmation of *Basset* in *Tournier* suggests, the ECJ would seem to have accorded some weight to the earlier considerations referred to by the Advocate-General.

If so, it lies in marked contrast to all the cases preceding *Nancy Kean* (except, perhaps, *Coditel I*) that a right to block imports could arise in part because French law dictated the calculation of royalties on a flat-rate basis. From the point of view of that earlier case law, whether or not the same result could be achieved by another means, it must also seem surprising that the ECJ did not insist on those other means being used – particularly in view of the long-running nature of the dispute between SACEM and some discotheque operators with their insistent claims that it was charging unfair and discriminatory fees.

If it were possible to overlook the ECJ's sleight of hand in *Basset*, the magician's art is exposed in *Warner Bros*.[184] Christiansen ran a business hiring out films on videocassettes ('videos') in Denmark. While in the United Kingdom, he bought a copy of the video *Never Say Never Again*. This he took back to Denmark and included in his stock of videos for hire. Not yet having been released onto the Danish market, it was highly sought after by local 007 fans.

The copyright owner, Warner Bros, and its Danish outpost, Metronome, quickly brought suit under Danish copyright law which granted the right owner power to control video rental. Warner Bros itself had freely put the video on the market in the United Kingdom where there was no similar right to control hire.[185] Warner Bros did not deny Christiansen's claim that the UK sale price took into account the possibility that the video could be used for hire.

The ECJ upheld Warner Bros' right to use Danish copyright law to extract a further charge for the right to hire out the video or even to forbid any hiring out at all. It was not swayed by Christiansen's argument based on *Musik-Vertrieb* and *Merck*. He pointed to Warner Bros' consent to the sale and, as in those two cases, argued that Warner Bros had made its choice,

---

184   158/86 *Warner Bros Inc. v Christiansen* [1988] ECR 2605. See generally, Defalque, 'Copyright – Free Movement of Goods and Territoriality: Recent Developments', at 435.
185   But, see now Copyright, Designs and Patents Act, 1988 section 18(2). At the time however, UK law, in company with Eire, the Netherlands and Germany, did not recognise a rental right. Germany did guarantee the right owner fair compensation. Only France and Denmark had specifically accorded the right owner a rental right. Case law or commentators had recognised rental rights in phonograms in the remaining Member States. See *ibid.* at 2621 *per* Advocate-General Mancini.

having regard to its own interests, and must accept the consequences of the internal market. Instead, the ECJ ruled:

18. That objection cannot be upheld. It follows from the foregoing considerations that, where national legislation confers on authors a specific right to hire out video-cassettes, that right would be rendered worthless if its owner were not in a position to authorize the operations for doing so. It cannot therefore be accepted that the marketing by a film-maker of a video-cassette containing one of his works, in a Member State which does not provide specific protection for the right to hire it out, should have repercussions on the right conferred on that same film-maker by the legislation of another Member State to restrain, in that State, the hiring-out of that video-cassette.

So, the fact that Warner Bros did not have a right of rental in the United Kingdom, where it had sold the video, could not affect its rights to stop the hiring out of that video in Denmark.

The ECJ's conclusion should be applauded. As, too, should its recognition of the economic functions of the exclusive rights comprised in a copyright. But, the ruling opens up gaping questions about its previous decisions based on *Deutsche Grammophon*. The difficulty of reconciling *Warner Bros* with the earlier case law based on *Deutsche Grammophon* is heavily underlined by Advocate-General Mancini's opinion finding the use of Danish law in this way clearly inconsistent with the 'consistent case law of the Court'.[186] It might well be asked why Merck's Dutch patent was not rendered worthless by imports it had marketed in Italy where there was no patent protection. An examination of 'the foregoing considerations' is necessary.

At points 9 and 10, the ECJ noted that the rental right applied without distinction to both imports and domestic videos. But, in contrast to *Basset*, there was likely to be an effect on intra-EC trade caught by Article 30 because of the potential for imports to satisfy the demand for videos to rent. Although finding in point 12 that the universal application of the rental power did not *of itself* amount to arbitrary discrimination, it was still necessary to consider whether the Danish law (not just the right owner's exercise of it) was justified. It was. According to the ECJ:

13. It should further be pointed out that literary and artistic works may be the subject of commercial exploitation, whether by way of public performance or of the reproduction and marketing of the recordings made of them, and this is true in particular of cinematographic works. *The two essential rights of the author, namely the exclusive right of performance and the exclusive right of reproduction, are not called in question by the rules of the Treaty.*
14. Lastly, consideration must be given to the emergence, demonstrated by the Commission, of a specific market for the hiring-out of such recordings, as distinct from their sale. The existence of that market was made possible by various factors such as the improvement of manufacturing methods for video-cassettes which they have bought and, lastly their relatively high purchase price. The market for the hiring-out of video-cassettes reaches a wider public than the market for their sale and, at present, offers great potential as a source of revenue for makers of films.

186   [1988] ECR 2605, at 2623 to 2624.

15. However, it is apparent that, *by authorizing the collection of royalties only on sales* to private individuals and to persons hiring out video-cassettes, *it is impossible to guarantee to makers of films a remuneration which reflects the number of occasions on which the video-cassettes are actually hired out and which secures for them a satisfactory share of the rental market.* That explains why, as the Commission points out in its observations, certain national laws have recently provided specific protection of the right to hire out video-cassettes. (*Emphasis added*)

Point 16 simply states that, therefore, laws conferring the power to control rental are justified under Article 36.

The considerations operating on the ECJ seem to be three. First, the law applied to all videos without regard to where they were made and sold. The rental right is then assimilated to one of the two *essential* rights of the copyright owner, the rights of reproduction and of performance, which are not questioned by the EEC Treaty. Finally, copyright owners could not reap their economic return from hire without a rental right.

The justifications raise at least as many questions as they purport to answer. The Danish law did not discriminate between imports and domestic goods (although it was still necessary to test the law for justification). The same could also be said of *Musik-Vertrieb*, however. GEMA sought to charge the same level of royalty on all sound recordings whether they were made domestically or imported. But, the ECJ disallowed this because the right of reproduction had been exhausted by the first sale in the internal market.

Although it does not expressly say so, the ECJ seems to assimilate the Danish rental right to the right of authorising (public) performance.[187] While it is clear that playing a sound recording in a discotheque open to the public would be a public performance, there is much greater difficulty claiming the same about the hiring out of videos, particularly if the video is only replayed by the borrower among the close circle of family and friends.[188] It is for this reason that it has been found necessary to amend copyright laws to confer a rental right where it is felt desirable to allow the right owner to share in the proceeds of the commercial activity.

Which brings us to the third justification. One salient economic fact confronted the ECJ. According to the Commission, about 90 per cent of video sales in the EC were for the purposes of rental. As in *Coditel I*, this was plainly a sobering antidote to the principled application of the market integration policy. But even here questions remain. Since they are not reported, it is not possible to consider the Commission's estimates. Perhaps worthy of some comment, Advocate-General Mancini reported a vast boom in the sales of videos in the United Kingdom during the preceding four years while the situation had not changed much in Denmark.[189] The policy of opening up market possibilities which was felt to underlie *Deutsche*

187   See also the earlier 60 & 61/84 *Cinéthèque* [1985] ECR 2605.
188   See for example *Television Broadcasts*, see Chapter 4 from Note 163.
189   [1988] ECR 2605, at 2624.

Grammophon could arguably just as readily be called in aid of allowing Danish consumers the benefits available to UK purchasers of video.

Further, the ECJ concluded that the only way a copyright owner could participate in the rental market was through a rental right. Christiansen had levied the unanswered charge that the price of Warner Bros' videos included an element for prospective rental. At the time Christiansen engaged his entrepreneurial flair, however, it was far from clear that even a majority of Member States considered that a rental right for videos was necessary.[190] Moreover, even where similar rights were conferred, the anomalies introduced by differences in national legislation had almost always been rejected as a justification for blocking imports.

To repeat, with all due respect, the author does not find the result in *Warner Bros* objectionable. What is striking is the contrast between it and much of the ECJ's earlier case law. As in *Nancy Kean*, the ECJ appears to have abandoned the purported dichotomy between the existence and the exercise of the right (although it does offer a definition of the two *essential rights* of the copyright owner). Instead, it embarked on a consideration of whether the law in question was itself justified. Further, as in *Nancy Kean*, the ECJ seems to accord considerable latitude to the several national legislators in determining the role of the free movement rules. Finally, as in *Coditel I* and *Basset* – although perhaps more questionably in theory if not on practical grounds, the ECJ accorded great importance to the economic consequences of its ruling. The fact that its rental right under Danish law would be rendered worthless meant that Warner Bros could still use its Danish rights to control dealings in the video which it had voluntarily sold in the United Kingdom without restriction.

But, the fact that Merck's patent in the Netherlands could be rendered worthless by the import of its drug from Italy where it was not protected did not mean that Merck could control dealings in the imported drug. So too in *Musik-Vertrieb*; which also concerned copyright. There the right owner also derived some reward from its exclusive rights and, somewhat like *Warner Bros*, GEMA was not attempting to exclude imports absolutely. Much the same could be said of *Sterling Drug* and *Deutsche Grammophon*. In all these cases, the ECJ dismissed out of hand the right owners' claims that the economic purpose of their right was being undermined. Instead, it stood on the goal of integrating the internal market which would be obstructed if the right owners' arguments were accepted. The economic argument which the ECJ found so forceful in *Warner Bros* is, or should be, equally compelling in each of the other cases.[191]

---

190 The incorporation of a rental right in CDPA 1988 (United Kingdom), section 18 was only a last-minute change of policy by the government which had steadfastly resisted the necessity in both its Green and White Papers, see David Gladwell, 'The Exhaustion of Intellectual Property Rights', [1986] EIPR 366, at 367. The United States too had expressly rejected a rental right for videos, see Chapter 4, Note 356.

191 For similar arguments, see Demaret, 'Industrial Property Rights, Compulsory Licences and the Free Movement of Goods under Community Law', at 161; Marenco and Banks, 'Intellectual Property and the Community Rules on Free Movement: Discrimination Unearthed', at 224.

Allen & Hanburys dealt with an issue similar to that not reached in *Pharmon*: restrictions on trade between Member States imposed through statutory licences.[192] Generics imported a drug, Salbutamol, into the United Kingdom from Italy where it was not patentable.[193] In the United Kingdom, Allen & Hanburys held a patent for the drug which had been endorsed with a licence of right under section 46 following the enactment of the Patents Act 1977. This meant any domestic producer was entitled to make and sell the drug subject to agreeing terms with the patentee or, in default, as set by the Comptroller. Even if no licence had been taken out, the domestic producer could gain immunity from an injunction by undertaking to take out a licence. These rights did not extend to importers of the drug. The issue was whether failure to extend the licence of right provisions to importers of the drug made elsewhere in the EC, even without the UK patentee's consent, conflicted with the rules on the free movement of goods.

The ECJ ruled this discrimination against imports from other Member States contrary to Article 30 and not justified under Article 36. Once a patent was subjected to a licence of right, its specific subject-matter was altered. The patentee was no longer entitled to control the granting of licences but was only entitled to a 'fair return' from its patent.[194]

There were no reasons justifying discrimination against importers from other Member States. In a common market, the problems of guaranteeing actual payment of licence fees and of checking the origins and quantities of the drug sold under the licence were the same whether imported from another Member State or made domestically.[195] As in *Sterling Drug*, the problem of guaranteeing the drug's quality could only be justified under the need to protect public health.[196] Finally, the ECJ dismissed an argument that the importer had an unfair cost advantage due to the free rider effect; the goods being unpatented in Italy. But, instead of pointing out that this may be a factor in determining the level of the royalty due the patentee, the ECJ held at point 31 that the patentee's right to 'a fair return' is intended 'precisely to afford the proprietor recompense for the research costs he has incurred'. Therefore, it did not matter whether the licensee had the product made domestically or in another Member State.

One implication of this case, read with *Pharmon* and *Musik-Vertrieb*, is that a prudent intellectual property owner should always ensure that terms for the exploitation of its intellectual property under a form of statutory licence are fixed by the statutory licensing authority rather than private agreement.[197]

---

192   434/85 *Allen & Hanburys Limited v Generics (UK) Limited* [1988] ECR 1245. See Friden, 'Recent Developments in EEC Intellectual Property Law', at 202 to 204.
193   Advocate-General Mancini states that it was patented but third parties could also make the drug without the patentee's consent: *ibid.* at 705.
194   *Ibid.* at ¶¶12 to 14.
195   *Ibid.* at ¶¶17, 19.
196   *Ibid.* at ¶21.
197   For a contrary view, see Robert Strivens, '*EMI Electrola GmbH v. Firma Patricia*', [1989] EIPR 297, at 299. The intellectual property owner will need to be careful, however, that it does not potentially involve itself in an abuse of a dominant position: T-30/89 *Hilti AG v Commission* [1992] 4 CMLR 16 at ¶99.

Following this ruling, the Commission has successfully challenged under Article 169 the laws of Italy and the United Kingdom which subject a patent to compulsory licensing if the resulting product is not manufactured in the jurisdiction on the basis that this requirement discriminates against manufacture elsewhere in the EC and so is a disguised restriction on trade contrary to Article 30.[198]

Thetford may be thought of as simply an extension of *Nancy Kean* to the field of patents.[199] Fiamma, like Keurkoop in *Nancy Kean*, imported goods, here portable toilets, from one Member State where they did not have intellectual property protection, Italy, into another, the United Kingdom. In the United Kingdom, they were covered by a patent in Thetford's name. The imports had not been made or sold in Italy with any participation by Thetford. Needless to say, Fiamma did not have Thetford's consent for the importation.

In fact, of the Member States, Thetford's portable toilets were probably only patentable in the United Kingdom because of a peculiarity of UK law at the time. Under the Patents Act 1949, section 50, inventions were deemed not to lack novelty by reason of publication in a specification dating back more than 50 years. A similar provision operated in *Nancy Kean*, but had not been considered.

The ECJ applied its decision in *Nancy Kean*.[200] But, following Advocate-General Mischo, it appeared to revive its dichotomy between the existence and the exercise of a right:

> 15. It follows that, as the Court held in [*Parke, Davis*], since the *existence* of patent rights is at present a matter solely of national law, a member-State's patents legislation, such as the legislation at issue, is covered *in principle* by the derogations from Article 30 which are provided for in Article 36.[201] (*Emphasis added*)

Thus, it would also seem that the ECJ interprets *Nancy Kean* the same way.

But, it is necessary to look closer. The ECJ considered that the United Kingdom's patent legislation is protected by Article 36 *in principle*. Then, it continued on to examine whether or not the legislation itself was 'a means of arbitrary discrimination or a disguised restriction on trade between member states'. The United Kingdom's adoption of 'relative novelty' was not a means of arbitrary discrimination because it applied wherever the specification was filed and whether the applicant was foreign or not.[202] Moreover, it was not

---

198 C-235/89 *Commission v Italy* and C-30/90 *Commission v United Kingdom* [1992] 2 CMLR 701. The Commission's position is now adopted by the Community Patent Convention, Article 46, see Chapter 6.5 below.

199 35/87 *Thetford Corp. v Fiamma SpA* [1988] ECR 3585 noted Richard Eccles, 'Patentee's Rights to Prevent Imports', [1989] EIPR 26.

200 Fiamma seems to have relied mainly on a greater degree of harmonisation in the field of patents than designs which the ECJ rejected at *ibid*. at ¶14.

201 For the Advocate-General, *ibid*. at 552 to 554.

202 *Ibid*. at ¶17.

a disguised restriction on trade because it pursued a reasonable object: the 'rediscovery' and utilisation of 'old' inventions otherwise lost.[203]

That is, the ECJ proceeded to examine whether the law itself was justified.[204] Such an approach hardly fits with treating the existence of the right as inviolate and seeking only to regulate its exercise. Hence, the ECJ's own analysis does not support the dichotomy between existence and exercise and confirms the lack of substance to that dichotomy.

In addition to inviting the ECJ to set minimum criteria for the grant of a patent in the EC, Fiamma also claimed that Thetford's remedy should be confined to a royalty rather than the injunction which UK law would permit. The United Kingdom apparently argued that the form of remedy should be left to national law.[205] As in answering the first question, the ECJ only partially accepted Fiamma's invitation. It noted that the grant of an injunction was consistent with the substance of a patent right under EC law.[206]

The defendants in *Renault* were manufacturers of spare parts and components for cars and their trade association.[207] When Renault sued them for infringing its Italian design registrations for various body panels, they argued that the Italian law of registered designs breached the free movement rules because it allowed Renault, among others, to charge enhanced prices for individual components. In their argument, this was not justified under EC law because the right owner secured all necessary benefit of the right through sales of the cars, embodying the components, as a whole.

The ECJ bluntly rejected the challenge to the Italian law. Expressly referring to *Nancy Kean* in point 10, it stated that the determination of the conditions and procedures for design protection was a matter of national law in the absence of EC standardisation or harmonisation. In point 11, as in *Thetford*, it went on to note that the power to prevent manufacture by third parties and to prevent imports made without its consent 'constitutes the substance' of the right owner's exclusive right: 'To prevent the application of the national legislation in such circumstances would therefore be tantamount to challenging the very existence of that right.' Finally, in point 12, it examined whether or not the law was justified in a somewhat more cursory fashion to either *Nancy Kean* or *Thetford*. The

---

203 *Ibid.* at ¶19. The ECJ did not mention Fiamma's allegation that the rule was only one of administrative convenience: Eccles, 'Patentee's Rights to Prevent Imports', at 27. But, note the apparent acceptance of similar considerations in *Nancy Kean* at [1982] ECR 2853 at ¶15.

204 Once again, the ECJ followed the Advocate-General in this approach. That the subject of scrutiny was the law itself rather than any purported exercise is confirmed by the football example the Advocate-General quotes: *ibid.* 554 to 555. See also Friden, 'Recent Developments in EEC Intellectual Property Law', at 198 to 201.

205 Eccles, 'Patentee's Rights to Prevent Imports', at 27.

206 [1988] ECR 3585 at ¶24. Advocate-General Mischo, citing *Allen & Hanburys*, noted that the position would be different if domestic infringers were not subject to injunctions: *ibid.* at 557 to 558.

207 53/87 *Consorzio Italiano della Componentistica di Recambio per Autoveicoli and Maxicar v Régie Nationale des Usines Renault* [1990] 4 CMLR 265. For the issue under Article 86, see Chapter 7.4 below.

law was not caught by Article 36 because it was enforceable alike against imports and domestic manufactures and did not otherwise discriminate in favour of national production.[208]

Patricia, like *Nancy Kean*, could have been decided by a straightforward application of the dichotomy between existence and exercise and the consent doctrine.[209] Significantly, the ECJ decided the case on the simple lack of consent.

The rights of reproduction and distribution of certain musical works by Cliff Richard had expired in Denmark but not in Germany. Patricia and Lüne-ton made recordings of those works in Germany and sold them to a distributor in Denmark unconnected with the former copyright owner there. Perhaps being a bit too clever, the Danish distributor sold them back to Patricia and Lüne-ton. They commenced selling the records in Germany and were sued by EMI Electrola, the local copyright owner. Subject to any impact of the free movement rules, EMI's action was successful before the German court.

Both Advocate-General Darmon and the ECJ dismissed a role for the doctrine of Community exhaustion. Advocate-General Darmon, however, appeared to do so by relying on *Deutsche Grammophon* while the ECJ's reasoning has more in common with *Nancy Kean*; expressly referring in point 8 to the formulation based on determining what was a *lawful* and what an *improper* exercise of the right. Certainly, however, the crucial factor was EMI's lack of consent to the marketing in Denmark.[210] But, that was important for two reasons. As in *Nancy Kean*, Article 36 required the ECJ to distinguish between 'lawful' and 'improper' exercises of the right to forestall artificial partitioning of the common market.[211] Then, given the diversity between national laws, it was for national law to sort out 'the terms and conditions' of copyright protection.[212] Since there were 'good' reasons for the differences in terms of protection, Germany's laws imposed *justified* restrictions on trade between Member States.[213]

The ECJ resumed consideration of the impact of the free movement rules on parallel imports in *API*.[214] As discussed in Chapter 8 below, parallel imports of pharmaceuticals into the United Kingdom grew at an ever

---

208   Advocate-General Mishco also pointed out that the law allowed the same powers to foreign and domestic right owners: *ibid*. at 274. For an argument that the cursory nature of the ECJ's inspection of the law's justification involves some departure from *Warner Bros* based on a narrower interpretation of *Thetford*, see Friden, 'Recent Developments in EEC Intellectual Property Law', at 206.
209   341/87 *EMI Electrola GmbH v Patricia Im-und Export Verwaltungsgesellschaft mbH* [1989] ECR 79.
210   *Ibid*. at ¶10.
211   *Ibid*. at ¶8.
212   *Ibid*. at ¶11.
213   *Ibid*. at ¶13. It seems the term was the same in both countries but calculated from different dates. In Germany, the term ran from the date of the legislation which had reduced the term from life plus 50 years: *ibid*. at 421 *per* Advocate-General Darmon.
214   266–7/87 *R. v Pharmaceutical Society of Great Britain; ex parte the Association of Pharmaceutical Importers* [1989] ECR 1295, see generally Leigh Hancher, 'The European Pharmaceutical Market: Problems of Partial Harmonisation', (1990) 15 ELR 9, at 27 to 30.

increasing rate during the 1980s facilitated in part by abbreviated procedures for marketing authorisation of parallel imports. Of the 220 product licences issued for parallel imports, about 50 were for drugs sold in other Member States under a different name. In mid-1986, the Pharmaceutical Society issued a statement reminding its members, pharmacists dispensing prescriptions to the public, that it was a breach of their ethical code to substitute a generic product for a branded product specified in a prescription. The volume of parallel imports into the United Kingdom declined markedly. The Association of Pharmaceutical Importers engaged in legal action aimed at forcing the Pharmaceutical Society to rescind the rule.[215]

The ECJ first ruled at points 14 to 16 that the Pharmaceutical Society's rule was subject to the operation of Articles 30 and 36. The Society was a professional body which, among other things, was entrusted by statute with power to discipline its members for misconduct. That power included the sanction of dismissal for breach of the ethical code. Hence, although neither the society nor its ethical code were strictly speaking organs of the state, the statutory backing for its disciplinary powers sufficed for the rule to constitute a 'measure' under Article 30.

Next, in contrast to Advocate-General Darmon, the ECJ held that the rule could have the effect on trade between Member States condemned by Article 30. Confronted with the remarkable falling off in parallel imports following the Society's statement, although causation was disputed, the ECJ accepted that the possibility of the rule affecting imports in particular cases could not be excluded.[216]

The ECJ then considered in points 21 to 23 that such a rule could be justified under Article 36. In the absence of EC legislation on the subject, it was a matter for regulation by the Member States and the ECJ found no evidence that either the rule went beyond the desirable objective in view of its use as a means of arbitrary discrimination or a disguised restriction. Significantly, however, the justification for the rule lay in the exception in Article 36 for the protection of health:

> 20.   In that regard, it should be noted that among the grounds of public interest set out in Article 36, *only the protection of health could be relevant.* A rule prohibiting a trader from substituting, even with the consumer's consent, another product for the brand ordered would *go beyond* what could be necessary for the protection of industrial and commercial property. (*Emphasis added*)

The reference to 'the consumer' has been accused of some ambiguity: is the consumer the prescribing doctor or the patient?[217] But, since the rule obliged the dispensing chemist to comply with the expressly stated intentions of the prescribing doctor, it would seem difficult for the doctor's wishes to be overridden on this point. Point 20 continued by confirming that the right

---

215   The second case involved the corresponding rule in the terms of service of chemists employed by the NHS.
216   [1989] ECR 1295 at ¶19; contrast the Advocate-General at 757 to 760.
217   Hancher, 'The European Pharmaceutical Market: Problems of Partial Harmonisation', at 29.

to prevent relabelling recognised by *AHPC* cannot be relied on where 'the practice of using different marks for the same product is for the purpose of artificially partitioning the markets'. Hence, having been invited by the Commission to 'clarify' the earlier ruling, the ECJ reaffirmed the subjective element of the reservation.

The ruling in *Tournier* may be dealt with briefly.[218] Parallel imports were at issue; the facts involved the continuing dispute between SACEM and the discotheque owners, although here one of the discotheque owners instituted a criminal prosecution of SACEM's Director-General for attempting to impose excessive, unfair or undue royalty payments on the use of records in discotheques. The result confirmed *Basset*. Three points are worthy of comment. First, in point 14, accepting Advocate-General Jacobs' advice, the ECJ ruled that any abusive or discriminatory nature of the royalty payments *was not* a matter for consideration under the free movement rules. It was relevant *only* under the competition rules. Second, before confirming *Basset*'s ruling that the performing right was not covered by the Community exhaustion rule in points 12 and 13, in point 11 the ECJ also confirmed the continuing validity of *Musik-Vertrieb*. Third, Advocate-General Jacobs seemed to confirm the interpretation of *Basset* as not even involving a contravention of Article 30 since he had some difficulty in envisioning what the necessary interference with trade between Member States might be.[219]

After the ruling in *Hag I*, Van Zuylen was acquired by Jacobs Suchard, the leading supplier of coffee on the German market, in 1979. Following a reorganisation, the decaffeinated-coffee-making business and the Benelux registrations for the *Café Hag* trade mark associated with it were spun off into a wholly-owned subsidiary, Sucal. Sucal determined to launch a counter-attack on Hag AG in Germany. For this campaign, however, it apparently decided to use a new get-up unlike that used in the Benelux countries and resembling Hag AG's. At some point in the mid-1980s, the campaign was launched. But, Hag AG persuaded the German courts to grant it an injunction for infringement of its German trade mark registrations. On appeal, the Bundesgerichtshof requested guidance from the ECJ, essentially about whether the doctrine of common origin applied to this 'situation in reverse' or could be distinguished. The ECJ took neither approach. Instead, accepting Advocate-General Jacob's detailed and cogent advice, it overruled its ruling in the *Hag I* case and abandoned the doctrine of common origin.[220]

According to the ECJ, it has consistently held since *Deutsche Grammophon*

218 395/87 *Ministère Public v Tournier* [1991] 4 CMLR 248; for the aspects dealing with the competition rules, see Chapters 7.4 and 7.5. See also C-270/86 *Cholay v SACEM*, unpublished, McKenna and Co., *European Community Law Bulletin*, January/February 1991, at 9; the operative part only is published at [1990] ECR I-4607.

219 *Ibid.* at 259. The ECJ simply stated that Articles 30 and 59 did not prevent SACEM's efforts to charge the supplementary mechanical fee.

220 C-10/87 *SA CNL-Sucal NV v Hag GF AG* (otherwise referred to as '*Hag II*') [1990] ECR I-3717, [1990] 3 CMLR 571. See Warwick A. Rothnie, '*Hag II*: Putting the Common Origin Doctrine to Sleep', [1991] EIPR 24 and Joliet and Keeling, 'Trade Mark Law and the Free Movement of Goods', 22 IIC 303 (1991).

established that Article 36 permitted derogations from the fundamental principle of the free movement within the internal market only where those derogations were required to safeguard the specific subject-matter of the intellectual property in question. Therefore, the owner of an intellectual property right in one Member State could not invoke that right to block imports lawfully sold in another Member State by that owner himself, with his consent or by a person legally or economically dependent on him.[221]

Then the ECJ, once again adopting the Advocate-General's view, laid to rest any doubts lingering from *Sirena* about the importance of trade marks under EC law:

> 13.   Trade mark rights are, it should be noted, an essential element in the system of undistorted competition which the Treaty seeks to establish and maintain. Under such a system, an undertaking must be in a position to keep its customers by virtue of the quality of its products and services, something which is possible only if there are distinctive marks which enable customers to identify those products and services. For the trade mark to be able to fulfil this role, it must offer a guarantee that all goods bearing it have been produced under the control of a single undertaking which is accountable for their quality.[222]

The ECJ did not, however, then simply rule that allowing Belgian Hag to use the Hag trade marks in Germany would destroy the function of the trade marks in Germany.

Following the approach largely settled since *Terrapin*, in point 14 the ECJ referred to both the trade mark's specific subject-matter and its essential function. Unlike the broad statement of principle, there is nothing new in either of these definitions, the wording for each being virtually identical to earlier cases.[223] Hence, the specific subject-matter allowed the trade mark owner the right of putting products bearing the trade mark onto the market for the first time and so to stop free riding on the reputation and goodwill associated with the trade mark. But, to determine the exact scope of this exclusive right, it was necessary to take into account the essential function of the trade mark which was to guarantee the source of the marked product to consumers or end-users by permitting them to distinguish it, without possibility of confusion, from those having a different source. Then the ECJ applied these principles to the preliminary reference:

> 15.   . . . the determinant factor is the absence of any consent on the part of the proprietor of the trade mark protected by national legislation to the putting into circulation in another Member State of similar products bearing an identical trade mark or one liable to lead to confusion, which are manufactured and marketed by an undertaking which is economically and legally independent of the aforesaid trade mark proprietor.
>
> 16.   In such circumstances, *the essential function of the trade mark would be jeopardised* if the proprietor of the trade mark could not exercise the right

---

221   *Ibid.* at ¶12.
222   For the more detailed explanation of Advocate-General Jacobs, see [1990] 3 CMLR at 582 to 583, citing Cornish, *Intellectual Property*, at ¶15–002.
223   Compare *Valium* [1978] ECR 1139, at ¶7; *AHPC* [1978] ECR 1823, at ¶¶11 and 12, above from Notes 110 and 116 respectively.

conferred on him by national legislation to oppose the importation of similar goods bearing a designation liable to be confused with his own trade mark, because, in such a situation, consumers would no longer be able to identify for certain the origin of the marked goods and the proprietor of the trade mark could be held responsible for the poor quality of goods for which he was in no way accountable. (*Emphasis added*)

Hag AG had not consented to Sucal's activities and Sucal was not legally or economically dependent on Hag AG. So, the essential function of the trade mark would be undermined if German Hag could not use its German trade mark rights to block imports of Belgian Hag's products. Otherwise, consumers and end-users would not be able to identify the source of the product with any degree of certainty and the trade mark owner could be blamed for the quality of products over which it had no control.

The following three points of the judgment interred *Hag I* and its doctrine of common origin. The ECJ stated that its analysis was not affected by the fact that one person had initially owned the trade mark rights in question and had subsequently lost control of some of the rights by an act of sequestration prior to the creation of the Community. Provided the trade mark rights fulfilled an independent role in the two Member States, both owners could rely on their rights against the other to block imports which they had not consented to the other marking. Hence, not only could Hag AG stop Sucal using the *Café Hag* mark in Germany, but, in the circumstances of *Hag I*, Van Zuylen could have blocked Hag AG in the Benelux.

Much like the German national courts, the ECJ rejected the doctrine of common origin by focusing on the doctrine of Community exhaustion, going back to first principles and applying them to the situation afresh. Despite the reference in point 12 to its consistent approach since *Deutsche Grammophon*, the ECJ did not refer to the dichotomy between the existence and the exercise of intellectual property rights. This accords with its repeated rejection, or overlooking, of the concept since *Nancy Kean*.[224]

Perhaps more important is the interplay between the newly declared role of trade marks in a market economy and the concepts of the specific subject-matter and essential function. In its definition of the role of trade marks in point 13, the ECJ seems to identify two separate aspects. The first is the function of the trade mark in signalling to consumers the quality or source of the branded goods. In terms of Chapter 1 above, this is (at least partly) the aspect recognised in *Cinzano*. The second aspect, however, is an economic definition. The trade mark performs its function by encouraging the brand owner to invest in improving and maintaining the quality of the branded goods. This is more like the role of a trade mark pressed in *Distillers Red Label*. Arguably, this corresponds to the view of a trade mark as a property right. These two aspects may not always be in harmony, as Chapter 2 in particular explored. Moreover, it seems the ECJ in *Hag II* does not accord these separate aspects equal weight.

---

224 See also Joliet and Keeling, 'Trade Mark Law and the Free Movement of Goods', at §V. In the CMLR report, ¶12 refers to the 'settled case law'.

In reaching its conclusion, the ECJ referred to at least four considerations in points 14 to 16 to reach its conclusion: consent, legal and economic ties, the specific subject-matter, and the essential function of the trade mark. It seems fairly clear that consent and a relationship of legal or economic dependence are alternatives. Both amount to ways of imputing the right owner's agreement to the activities in the other Member State.

Furthermore, it seems that 'consent' in this dual sense is the primary factor in the ECJ's considerations. In point 15 of *Hag II*, the ECJ described the absence of 'consent' as determinative. Point 16 explained why. If independent producers could use confusingly similar trade marks on similar products, end-users could not rely on the trade mark to identify source accurately and the trade mark owner could be (wrongly) held responsible for quality variations which it could not control. So, 'consent' was linked to the role of the trade mark in a system of undistorted competition. If the trade mark owner exercised its prerogative of consent, it assumed responsibility for the characteristics of the product marketed under the trade mark. If confusion resulted from its own conduct, it would be its own fault.

The link between 'consent' and the trade mark's role indicates a further consideration. Despite accurately identifying the duality in the role of trade marks, 'consent' was decisive because of only one aspect. 'Consent' determined whether use of a trade mark to block consumer confusion over the source of the product was justified. This aspect of the role of trade marks appears to correspond to the essential function of the trade mark identified by the ECJ in point 14. The second concept referred to in point 14 is the specific subject-matter of the trade mark. This takes on the appearance of a property right, allowing the trade mark owner the choice of putting products on the market with or without the trade mark and empowering the owner to stop free riding on the goodwill and reputation symbolised by the trade mark. In this sense, the specific subject-matter of a trade mark seems to correspond to (or derive from) the other aspect of a trade mark's role. It would further seem, in view of the interaction of 'consent' and the essential function of a trade mark described in point 16 of *Hag II*, that the specific subject-matter of the trade mark is of less importance than its essential function. If so, using the property right to block imports would only be justified under EC law where it was necessary to protect the trade mark's essential function.

One further comment should be made about *Hag II* at this point. The terms of the judgment are quite carefully expressed to reject the doctrine of common origin insofar as the trade mark division was caused by an act of expropriation. The judgment does not expressly deal with the case where the same trade mark is owned in two Member States by different persons. Advocate-General Jacobs did address the question somewhat ambivalently in his opinion and recognised that division by voluntary assignment could potentially attract scrutiny under either the consent element of the free movement rules or some form of concertation caught by Article 85.[225]

---

225   For example, [1990] 3 CMLR 571, at 588, 601 to 602.

The ECJ itself has expressed a view, albeit one not expressly raised by the facts. In *Terrapin* at point 6, which the judgment in *Hag II* did not even refer to, the doctrine of common origin was expressed to apply to subdivisions 'either by voluntary act or as a result of public constraint'. However, the Advocate-General's criticism that *Terrapin* confused 'historical origin' with 'commercial origin' applies with almost equal force to voluntary assignments, particularly where the subdivision took place in the far distant past.[226] In *Coditel I*, moreover, under Article 59, the ECJ allowed a territorial subdivision of copyright where the subdivision could be justified, at least in part, by objective circumstances.

If the two businesses were genuinely operated independently, it would certainly be extremely difficult to argue that applying a theory of exhaustion by consent to marketing was at all consistent with the essential function of a trade mark as defined by the ECJ. This would be particularly so where the subdivision took place many years ago. With the increasing integration of the common market and, particularly, increasing awareness of the programme for a Single Market in 1992, it would, however, be easier to make a policy decision against new or recent subdivisions; especially in the absence of 'objective' justifications for the division. Whether such a policy should be adopted is highly debatable. At least one judge has expressed his view that the only means to strike voluntary divisions down lies in the competition rules.[227]

Subsequently, the ECJ has confirmed the continuing vitality of the exception to a trade mark owner's power to block imports of repackaged products which the trade mark owner had sold in another Member State.[228]

6.5   Harmonisation at the EC Level

Before attempting a review of the principles developed by the ECJ under the free movement rules, it is necessary to survey a secondary body of EC law affecting the control of parallel imports. Many, but by no means all, of the problems within the EC caused by parallel imports can be seen to arise from the separate and differing treatment of intellectual property rights under national laws. Trying to achieve a genuine, EC-wide internal market dictates treating intellectual property on an EC-wide rather than a national basis. For example, the problems of varying levels of protection or inconsistent compulsory licence schemes as in *Merck* or *Musik-Vertrieb* are avoided and the likelihood of conflicts between the two aspects of a trade mark identified in point 13 of *Hag II* is much reduced in a genuinely integrated market.

---

226   *Ibid.* at 586 to 587.
227   Joliet and Keeling, 'Trade Mark Law and the Free Movement of Goods', at §V. For the application of the competition rules to this problem, see Chapter 7.5.
228   C-347/89 *Freistaat Bayern v Eurim-Pharm GmbH*, unreported, 16 April 1991, see McKenna and Co., *European Community Law Bulletin*, May/June 1991, at 5. The information available at the time of writing is too brief to permit further comment.

While the point has been obvious for a long time, giving it practical expression has proved quite difficult.[229] The campaign has been waged on two fronts: attempts to create a single right for the whole EC; and harmonisation by directive specifying minimum requirements to be enacted by the several Member States.

An as yet unsuccessful attempt in the field of patents is the Community Patent Convention ('the Convention'). If it comes into effect in its present form, the Convention envisages two types of patent: Community patents and national patents.[230] The Community patent would largely be effective throughout the whole of the EC.[231] Giving effect to the ECJ's judgment in *Sterling Drug*, marketing of a product covered by the Community patent by the patentee or with its express consent within the EC would exhaust the patentee's rights to control further distribution of that product.[232] This 'exhaustion' is expressly subject to any developments of EC law which may permit restriction of parallel imports. Exhaustion is also expressly restricted in two other situations. First, the exhaustion rule would not apply to a product marketed by someone other than the patentee under a compulsory licence.[233] Second, if a product has been marketed in a Member State under the national prior use rights, its right to circulate is confined to the territory of that Member State.[234]

Similar rules apply to national patents once the Convention comes into force.[235] Hence, the Convention effectively applies a doctrine of EC-wide exhaustion to patents which are confined to the territory of one, or selected Member States.

The first Council Directive on trade marks may be more limited in

229   For a review, see Beier, 'Industrial Property and the Free Movement of Goods in the Internal European Market', 132 to 141.

230   Originally adopted in 1975, it has been republished with amendments and additional Protocols at OJ 1989 L401/10, 30 December 1989. It had not been ratified by all Member States by 31 December 1991. A special conference was convened at Lisbon on 4–5 May 1992, empowered to amend, unanimously, the number of ratifications necessary to bring into force: Fourth Protocol, OJ 1989 L401/51. At the time of writing, Denmark and Eire have failed to ratify. The failure of the conference to reach agreement means that the CPC is not expected to enter into force until at least 1993. See 'Community Patent Convention's Problems Remain Unresolved', 6 World Intellectual Property Report 158 (1992); Irwin M. Krittman, 'European National Patents Versus EPC and CPC Patents', 158 World Intellectual Property Report 252 (1992. For a review of the history of the Convention's adoption from a perspective favourable to exhaustion, see A. Benyami, 'Infringement of the Rights Conferred by a European Community Patent: Substantive Community Law', Ph. D. Thesis, University of London, 1990, especially at §12.3.

231   Articles 2(2) and 3. There are, however, several exceptions to the unitary effect. For example, the Community patent may not take effect in a Member State where there is a prior unpublished national patent application, Article 78.

232   Article 28.

233   Article 45(1). This is now the position reached by EC law under the EEC Treaty: 19/84 *Pharmon v Hoechst* [1985] ECR 2281.

234   Article 78(1).

235   Article 76. Exhaustion is expressly extended to marketing in another Member State under a national patent by a person having economic connections with the national patentee in the 'domestic' Member State.

the exceptions it permits to EC-wide exhaustion when compared to the Convention. It provides that a trade mark does not permit '. . . the proprietor to prohibit its further use in relation to goods which have been put on the market in the Community under that trade mark by the proprietor or with his consent. . . .' and then only allows the proprietor 'to oppose further commercialization of' goods marketed by the proprietor, or with consent, only 'for legitimate reasons' and gives an express example of a change or impairment of the goods' condition after they have been marketed. Arguably, this covers only the situation in *Valium* and not *AHPC*.[236]

Subject to power to continue control over the rental of a computer program, the software directive also requires Member States' laws to provide that 'The first sale in the Community of a copy of a program by the rightholder or with his consent shall exhaust the distribution right within the Community of that copy, with the exception of the right to control further rental of the program or a copy thereof.'[237] Noticeably, this provision does not include any form of exception. Once the copy of the computer program has been *sold* in the EC, power to control its distribution (other than by rental) is exhausted. Whether the software owner would be able to control commercial exploitation along the lines discovered by the US Fourth Circuit in *Red Baron* may then prove debatable if the program is sold rather than let.[238]

A similar provision has been included in the Commission's draft proposal for the establishment of Community plant variety rights. Once again, disposal in the EC by the right holder, or with its consent, would end the power to control the acts comprised in the right with the exception of use as 'propagating material for the production of further individuals' when the disposal was not for that purpose.[239] There is also a draft proposal for a directive on the protection of biotechnological inventions.[240]

Following the problems revealed in *Warner Bros*, the Commission has proposed a draft directive on rental rights, lending rights and certain rights

---

236 89/104/EEC, Article 7, OJ 1989 L40/1, 11 February 1989. Relabelling, however, should properly be characterised as an (unauthorised) use of a right which has not been exercised. Similar wording is used in the Draft Regulation, Articles 16 and 17. The Commission's initial intention was to adopt universal exhaustion, but the Member States and industry forced alteration, see Beier, 'Industrial Property and the Free Movement of Goods in the Internal European Market', at 159 to 160.

237 Article 4(c) OJ 1990 L122/42, 17 May 1991.

238 For *Red Baron-Franklin Park Inc. v Taito Corp.* 883 F. 2d 275 (4th Cir. 1989), see Chapter 4 from Note 426. Arguably, the performance right is not exhausted (for example *Tournier*), but the reproduction would presumably be authorised under Article 5(1) of the Directive. The earlier draft of the directive was not even limited just to sale in the EC, see OJ 1989 C91/4, 12 April 1989 and Frank Gotzen, 'Distribution and Exhaustion in the EC Proposal for a Council Directive on the Legal Protection of Computer Programs', [1990] EIPR 299.

239 Article 15, OJ 1990 C244/1, 28 September 1990. For the rights of the holder, see Article 13. But contrast the rulings under the competition rules, in *Erauw Jacquery* [1988] ECR 1919 and *Comasso*, see Chapter 7.2.4 and 7.3.2(a) respectively.

240 Beier, 'Industrial Property and the Free Movement of Goods in the Internal European Market', at 139.

related to copyright. In addition to requiring Member States to provide for both rental and lending rights for copyright and related rights, the draft directive also proposes to introduce a distribution right for performing artists, phonogram producers, producers of cinematographic works, and broadcasting organisations. The proposed right is subject to a ban on prohibiting importation into another Member State of 'subject matter' which 'has been put into circulation within the Community by the right owner or with his consent'.[241]

6.6   Overview

It was recognised quite early that the continuation of national intellectual property rights in the EC could pose obstacles to the goal of integrating the internal market simply because they are national, and not EC-wide, in scope. But, including intellectual property in Article 36's list of derogations from the rules on the free movement of goods made it plain that intellectual property, even regulated on a national basis, served desirable ends in an integrated market and could not simply be overridden. The challenge is to work out where the dividing line between justified ('legitimate') and unjustified ('improper') uses falls.

The first division is between trade within the internal market and trade between third countries and the EC. The free movement rules enshrined in the EEC Treaty only apply to trade between Member States of the EC; trade between third countries and the EC is not affected.[242]

For trade in the internal market, the ECJ developed two rules of interpretation to apply the free movement rules; the doctrine of Community exhaustion and the doctrine of common origin. The latter has proved of extremely limited application and seems to have been largely rejected.[243] The doctrine of Community exhaustion may be broadly summarised as holding that an intellectual property right may not be used to block imports from another Member State where they have been marketed by the 'domestic' right owner, with their consent or by someone having legal or economic connections to the 'domestic' right owner. Hence, sale in the other Member State by a licensee or another member of the same corporate group is clearly covered by the rule. Marketing in the other Member State by a completely

---

241   Article 7; for the rental and lending rights, see Article 1. The draft directive is discussed in Silke von Lewinski, 'Rental Right, Lending Right and Certain Neighbouring Rights: The EC Commission's proposal for a Council Directive', [1991] EIPR 117. For the draft Directive on term of copyright, see COM(92)33 final – SYN 395 [1992] 2 CMLR 104.
242   *EMI v CBS*; *Polydor*; and *Nancy Kean*, see section 6.3.2; but question the effect of the EEA Treaty, especially Articles 11 to 13, 53 and 54 read in light of Articles 6, 105 and 111.
243   *Hag II*, from Note 220 above.

independent person which is not part of some arrangement reached with the 'domestic' right owner does not result in exhaustion.[244]

The search for a simple rule has proved vain. It has not proved possible to state one single rule which may be applied in all situations. It has proved necessary to create exceptions; the number of which seems to be increasing.

Qualifications have been recognised for trade marks. A trade mark owner could use its rights to prevent the repackaging or relabelling of goods which it had sold in another Member State. Both were based on the need to preserve the integrity of goods offered to consumers under the mark. The ECJ also incorporated reservations on the qualifications. Neither could be used as a means of arbitrary discrimination or to impose disguised restriction on trade within the internal market. In particular, in the case of repackaging, if it could be carried out without prejudicing the condition of the marked goods, the trade mark owner's power to block imports would not arise.[245]

Increasingly, qualifications are also recognised for copyright-like rights. The first empowered the copyright owner to control dissemination of films in different Member States by broadcast or cable diffusion. This was extended by analogy to public performances of sound recordings. A further extension of the analogy covered the hiring out of videos. All of these qualifications purported to be based on a distinction between the right of reproduction and that of performance. However dubious assimilation of the right in question to either category, they did have one thing in common. Denying the right owner the power to control the activity in question severely prejudiced its prospects of participating in highly lucrative returns. Certainly, exploitation of the rights to a film could have been severely affected by retransmission of a broadcast in a neighbouring state. Whether that was necessarily so in the case of the rental market in the state of the law then prevailing might have been more questionable.

Arguably, the creation of these exceptions is consistent with the general doctrine of Community exhaustion. None of the cases refusing to regard the right owner's power as exhausted has involved the simple situation which first confronted the ECJ – attempts to block the importation for sale of goods sold by the 'domestic' right owner in the other Member State. The more complicated nature of the challenges could be seen as provoking more sophisticated treatment depending on the nature of the particular right being asserted.

A number of difficulties lie in the path of this course. There are three main ones. First, the reasoning used by the ECJ to reach the results in any given case has undergone a marked change. Second, the results reached are increasingly contradictory; particularly of earlier cases. Third,

---

244 It would not seem that a sale by an independent right owner in another Member State under a genuine delimitation agreement triggers the exhaustion rule: see for example under the competition rules, 35/83 *BAT Cigaretten-Fabriken GmbH v Commission* [1985] ECR 363.
245 *Pfizer v Eurim-Pharm*, at Note 113 above.

the justification for the qualifications accepted in copyright is of general application.

The substantial shift in the ECJ's reasoning, particularly since *Nancy Kean*, has been increasingly recognised.[246] Table 6.2 attempts to summarise the concepts applied in the free movement cases involving intellectual property from *Deutsche Grammophon* to *Hag II* and the outcome of each case.

The outcome of each case is indicated by the column headed 'Exhaustion', here a 'Yes' indicates that the ECJ ruled in favour of exhaustion so that the owner could not use its domestic intellectual property rights against the activity in question. The column headed 'Consent' indicates whether the marketing of the imports took place in the 'foreign' Member State through the right owner, with its consent or through someone legally or economically dependent on it. The columns, 'Existence/exercise', 'Specific subject-matter' and 'Essential function' identify whether or not the particular concept was referred to in the case in question. The column 'Economic impact' indicates whether or not the ECJ took into account or rejected what effect its ruling would have on the right owner's position, and the column 'National law' indicates the extent to which the ECJ deferred to the national law and territorial limitations.

Hence, in *Deutsche Grammophon*, the ECJ relied on both concepts of the dichotomy between existence and exercise and of the right's specific subject-matter; did not refer to (or rejected) the relevance of the right's essential function, the economic impact of its ruling and any role for national law or territorial limitations; the right owner, however, consented to the marketing in the 'foreign' Member State and the doctrine of Community exhaustion applied. In contrast, in *Coditel I*, the ECJ relied on the right's essential function, the economic consequences of its ruling, the role of national law and territorial limitations; it ignored or did not refer to the dichotomy between existence and exercise and the specific subject-matter; there was consent, but the Community exhaustion rule was not applied.

Perhaps, the most noticeable fact is the preponderance of cases in the lower half of Table 6.2 in which the Community doctrine of exhaustion was not applied. This could be partly explained by the increasing number of cases brought where the right owner had not consented to the marketing in the 'foreign' Member State. That, however, does not account for the cases where there was consent.

The second striking factor is that, apart from *Coditel I*, the significance of each concept generally reverses when comparing the cases from *Nancy Kean* onwards to those before it. This is particularly pronounced in the columns for 'Existence/exercise', 'National law' and 'Economic impact'. In the later cases, even where the existence of the right is referred to, the ECJ engages in some form of analysing the justification for the provision.

---

246 In addition to the commentators cited at Notes 2 to 4, above, see also Demaret, 'Industrial Property Rights, Compulsory Licences and the Free Movement of Goods under Community Law', at 161; Joliet and Keeling, 'Trade Mark Law and the Free Movement of Goods'; and Rothnie, '*Hag II*: Putting the Common Origin Doctrine to Sleep'.

Table 6.2
Analysis of Concepts and Results in Free Movement Cases

	Intellectual property right	Existence/ exercise	Specific subject-matter	Essential function	Economic impact	National law	Consent	Exhaustion
Deutsche-Grammophon	Copyright	●	●	X	X	X	●	●
Hag I	Trade mark	●	●	X	X	X	X	●
Sterling Drug	Patent	●	●	?	X	X	●	●
Winthrop	Trade mark	●	●	X	X	X	X	●
Terrapin	Trade mark	●	●	●	X	X	●	X
Valium	Trade mark	●	●	●	X	X	●	X
AHPC	Trade mark	●	●	●	X	X	●	X
Coditel I	Copyright	X	X	X	●	●	●	●
Musik-Vertrieb	Copyright	X	X	?	X	X	●	
Dansk-Supermarked	Copyright/ Trade mark	●	●	X	X	X	●	●
Merck	Patent	X	●	X	X	X	●	●
Pfizer	Trade mark	X	●	?	X	X	●	●
Nancy Kean	Design	X/J	X	X	●	●	X	X
Pharmon	Patent	X	?	?	?	●	X	X
Basset	Copyright	X	?	?	●	●	●	X
Warner Bros	Copyright	J	●	?	●	●	●	X
Allen & Hanburys	Patent	J	?	X	X	–	X	●
Thetford	Patent	J	X	X	●	●	X	X
Renault	Design	X	X	X	●	●	X	X
Patricia	Copyright	X	?	X	●	●	●	X
API*	—	X	X	?	–	–	●	●
Tournier	Copyright	X	?	?	●	●	●	X
Hag II	Trade mark	X	●	●	X	●	X	X

Notes: X indicates 'No'
● indicates 'Yes'
J national law examined for justification
? arguable
– not applicable
* In *API*, consideration is confined to the ECJ's comments on the derogation for industrial or commercial property, not for public health.

This change is less pronounced for the concepts 'Specific subject-matter' and 'Essential function'. After *Terrapin*, both are always referred to where the right is a trade mark. But, as *Hag II* seems to indicate, the trade mark's essential function has become the main factor and specific subject-matter is waning. For cases involving patents, the ECJ seems to have shifted to a somewhat different concept, the substance of the right. This actually arose in *Merck* and coincided with the even further reduced importance (if not outright rejection) of the purpose of the patent. For copyright, the situation is even more complicated. In the later cases, the ECJ chose to talk of the *two* essential rights of the copyright owner although, arguably, in *Warner Bros* it defined a third and also referred to the normal exploitation of copyright. The essential rights have been taken to refer to either the specific subject-matter or the essential functions of copyright. Furthermore, in *Coditel I* and, with a very high degree of probability, *Basset*, *Warner Bros* and *Tournier*, the ECJ seems to have regarded the object of conferring the essential rights as being to secure the copyright owner's participation in the profits of the activity. Hence, for copyright in particular and patents, the concepts of specific subject-matter and essential function seem either not to have proved useful or are still in the process of resolution.

Since *Nancy Kean*, the ECJ seems to have abandoned the concept of the dichotomy between the existence and the exercise of intellectual property rights and, at the least, to have significantly reduced the role of a right's specific subject-matter. On the other hand, it has markedly increased the roles of differences between national laws, territorial limitations and consideration of the economic consequences. Furthermore, it has largely abandoned its former doctrine of common origin.

At the end of section 6.3.1 above, a number of possible contrasts between *Coditel I*, *Valium* and *AHPC* on the one hand, and, on the other, *Musik-Vertrieb*, *Dansk Supermarked* and *Merck*, were discussed. Table 6.1 also drew attention to the shifting composition of the bench during that period. By way of completeness, as Table 6.3 shows, the composition of the ECJ had undergone considerable transformation from the panel which decided *Musik-Vertrieb* and *Merck*. Four judges from the Lecourt presidency remained on the bench until *Nancy Kean*. After, only Lord Mackenzie Stuart continued. Three of the four judges who first sat in free movement cases during the Kutscher presidency continued after *Nancy Kean*, as did two of the three who first sat during the Mertens de Wilmars presidency. A further 12 judges first sat in free movement cases after *Nancy Kean*. After *Nancy Kean*, four of the seven judges in *Musik-Vertrieb* or five of the nine in *Merck* did not take further part in cases involving intellectual property and the free movement rules.

Professor Beier has forcefully argued that the ECJ has effectively abandoned much of its former reasoning to concentrate solely on the test of consent.[247]

---

247 Beier, 'Industrial Property and the Free Movement of Goods in the Internal European Market', at 153 to 156.

Table 6.3
Judges Sitting in Free Movement Cases 1981–90

Judge/Case	MV	DS	Mer	Pf	Pol	NK	Pha	Bas	War	A&H	Th	Pat	Ren	API	SAC	H II
Mertens	X		X		X	X										
Pescatore	X	X	X		X	X										
Mackenzie Stuart	X		X		X	X	X	X			X		X			
O'Keeffe	X		X	X	X	X										
Bosco	X		X	X	X	X	X	X	X	X	X		X			
Touffait	X	X	X			X								X		X
Due			X		X	X	X	X	X	X	X		X	X		
Koopmans	X		X	X	X	X	X	X	X	X	X	X	X		X	
Everling			X		X	X	X		X		X		X			
Chloros			X		X	X										
Grévisse					X	X								X		X
Bahlmann							X	X	X		X		X	X		X
Galmot							X		X	X	X		X	X		X
O'Higgins								X	X		X	X	X	X		X
Schockweiler								X	X	X	X	X	X	X	X	X
Joliet								X		X				X		X
Rodríguez								X	X	X		X		X	X	X
Moitinho									X	X	X		X	X	X	X
Mancini											X	X	X		X	
Kakouris										X	X			X	X	X
Díez												X			X	X
Zuleeg															X	X
Slynn														X		X

X   = Judge sat in the case
MV = *Musik-Vertreib*
DS = *Dansk Supermarked*
Mer = *Merck v Stephan*
Pf = *Pfizer v Eurim-Farm*
Pol = *Polydor v Harlequin*

NK   = *Nancy Kean*
Pha = *Pharmon*
Bas = *Bassett*
War = *Warner Brothers*
A & H = *Allen & Hanburys*
Th   = *Thetford v Fianna*

Pat = *EMI Electrola v Patricia*
Ren = *Renault*
API = *API*
SAC = *Tournier*
H II = *HAG II*

The contention has a deceptive simplicity and strong support for it can be found in the case law. As Table 6.2 shows, the right owner had not consented to the marketing in the 'foreign' Member State in seven of the 13 cases where the ECJ has not applied the doctrine of Community exhaustion. In *Pharmon*, the fact that the patentee had not consented to the compulsory licensee's actions was decisive. So too in *Hag II*, where the vital role of consent was placed on the ground that, if the trade mark owner voluntarily chose to undermine the trade mark's essential function, the owner had only itself to blame. There are difficulties, however.

If consent be the true criterion, why was it necessary to engage in an exploration of whether the national law in question was justified? Moreover, the test leads to absurdity. In *Pharmon*, Hoechst was allowed to block imports into the Netherlands because it had not consented to their marketing under the compulsory licence in the United Kingdom. The Dutch patentee in *Merck* could not block imports (which it had sold) from Italy where there was no patent. So, in *Merck*, the patentee did not have the chance to reap the reward for its creative effort which a patent, according to the ECJ, is intended to offer. But the patentee received at least some compensation in *Pharmon*. The contrast is compounded by part of the explanation offered for rejecting exhaustion in *Pharmon* – the prospect of obtaining that very reward for creative endeavour was diminished.[248]

Then, there are the cases where the right owner did consent to the marketing in the 'foreign' Member State and exhaustion did not prevail. This highlights the problem of defining what the consent must relate to. For trade marks, the answer appears to be that consent to distribution by a first sale does not include consent to subsequent interference with the goods in such a way as may compromise their quality or to remark the goods. In copyright, consent to reproduction or distribution does not include consent to performance. But, at the time of the *Warner Bros* action, how was rental determined to be more like performance than an exercise of distribution? Member States' law had not yet arrived at a uniform solution and, historically, the 'first sale' doctrine in the United States allowed rental activities to be unrestricted. As the Advocate-General in *Warner Bros* did, it could just as easily be argued that a copyright owner which sold its video in a Member State where there was no rental right lost the power to control its rental in another Member State where such a power existed as to deny the patentee protection in *Merck*.[249] As in the common law world, the ECJ has not really explained why the individual elements of the bundle of rights comprised in copyright are not affected by the exhaustion doctrine while the otherwise equally divisible rights in a patent are.[250]

---

248   See *Pharmon* [1985] ECR 2281, at ¶26 and also Demaret, 'Industrial Property Rights, Compulsory Licences and the Free Movement of Goods under Community Law', at 161.
249   Note also the UK Government's late change of mind, above at Note 190.
250   Even in 60–61/84 *Cinéthèque* [1985] ECR 2605, the ECJ did not explicitly adopt the argument based on the need to promote culture and, in the parallel import cases, emphasises that it is dealing with commercial exploitation.

An alternative explanation has been offered by Marenco and Banks. They argue that the free movement rules are solely concerned with striking down 'protectionist' measures. Laws which discriminate between 'domestic' production and 'foreign' production are condemned while those that apply with equal effect regardless of the Member State where the goods were first sold are not affected.[251]

As with the test based solely on consent, quite a few cases can be found where the ECJ explicitly referred to the absence of discrimination against imports in its reasons for upholding the right owner's action.[252] Indeed, the approach taken in *Nancy Kean* to assess the justification of the Benelux designs law bears comparison to the analysis taken in at least two cases under the *Cassis de Dijon* exception justifying the use of unfair competition laws against imports.[253] But, as the authors themselves acknowledge, the ECJ has not relied exclusively on the absence of discrimination against imports from other Member States.[254] In *Nancy Kean*, *Thetford* and *Renault*, the fact that the right owner had not consented to the production and sale of the imports was also important. In those cases and *Basset*, *Warner Bros* and *Tournier* (where there was consent), the economic consequences of denying the right owner were also prominent.

Marenco and Banks identify four cases which they consider cannot be explained on the basis of their theory and suggest that they have been wrongly decided: *AHPC*, *Musik-Vertrieb*, *Merck* and *Hag I*.[255] *AHPC* creates a difficulty for their theory. The ECJ has expressly confirmed it, including its purposive test, despite the Commission submission requesting 'clarification'.[256] Furthermore, the difference between its subjective nature and the objective nature they perceive in *Valium* is arguable.[257] Even so, it seems difficult to envisage the ECJ allowing a right owner to use national differences consciously as part of a scheme to partition the internal market if the intention could be proved and were not otherwise 'justified' as in *Warner Bros*.

Marenco and Banks regard *Musik-Vertrieb* and *Merck* as unsupportable because the right owner in each was denied the opportunity to exploit its

---

251 Marenco and Banks, 'Intellectual Property and the Community Rules on Free Movement: Discrimination Unearthed', at 224.
252 See for example *Nancy Kean*, *Basset*, *Thetford*, *Renault*, above from Notes 158, 174, 199 and 207 respectively.
253 See 6/81 *BV Industrie Diensten Groep v JA Beele Handelmaatschappij BV* [1982] ECR 707 and 177/83 *Kohl v Ringelhan & Rennet* [1984] ECR 3651. For *Cassis de Dijon*, see 120/78 *Rewe v Bundesmonopolverwaltung fur Branntwein* [1979] ECR 649. Generally, see Gormley, *Prohibiting Restrictions on Trade within the EEC*, 206 to 210; Rose, 'Passing Off, Unfair Competition and Community Law', at 123.
254 They acknowledge that the ECJ had not adopted their approach, but point to the inconsistent body of decision developed in consequence: Marenco and Banks, 'Intellectual Property and the Community Rules on Free Movement: Discrimination Unearthed', at 241.
255 *Ibid*. at 254; they are qualified about *AHPC* and the ECJ itself has abandoned *Hag I*.
256 See *API* [1989] ECR 1295 at ¶20.
257 See Note 122 above.

right to its fullest potential in the 'foreign' Member State. The author certainly does not disagree with that criticism. But, it is a very precise definition of 'discrimination' which is at work here. It is possible to argue that the imported records in *Musik-Vertrieb*, for example, were only being subjected to a levy corresponding to that applied to domestic production. Hence, there was no discrimination. But, the only reason the imports had not been subjected to the full levy in the first place was because they were marketed outside Germany. In this sense, they were only subject to the further levy because they were imports – which is the kind of discrimination the ECJ decided to condemn.[258] One aspect arises because of the other. That is the problem *national* regulation of intellectual property causes in the EC.

Marenco and Banks' criticism of *Musik-Vertrieb* and *Merck* is based on the economic consequences to the right owner of denying it protection where the imports were marketed in another Member State where the right owner could not properly exploit the intellectual property right. This could be because there was no corresponding right as in *Deutsche Grammophon*, *Merck* and *Warner Bros* or because the right was subject to some form of statutory control such as a compulsory licence provision as in *Pharmon* or *Musik-Vertrieb*. It should also be recognised that other governmental policies such as price controls can have the same effect.

If *Musik-Vertrieb* and *Merck* should be reconsidered, what protects the three cases lying at the root of the Community exhaustion doctrine, *Deutsche Grammophon*, *Sterling Drug* and *Winthrop*? The parallel imports in these cases also arose in part because of different legal regimes, different governmental policies and different economic conditions. The economic considerations which lead Marenco and Banks to accept that *Musik-Vertrieb* and *Merck* need reconsideration apply equally to these cases also.[259]

The argument based on the economic consequences to the right owner is of general application. In the context of the free movement rules, the ECJ, however, has only ever accepted it for copyright cases which it has characterised as not involving the exercise of an 'exhaustable' aspect of the right; that is, by analogy to the (infinitely repeatable) performing right: see *Coditel I*, *Basset*, *Warner Bros* and *Tournier*. It has expressly refused to apply the concept to mere rights of distribution or reproduction in *Deutsche Grammophon*, *Musik-Vertrieb* and, in patents, *Sterling Drug* and *Merck*. Since *Nancy Kean*, it has also expressly reaffirmed the continuing validity of *Musik-Vertrieb*, although not applying it, in *Patricia* and *Tournier*.[260] The primacy of the essential function of a trade mark over its economic rationale clarified in *Hag II* confirms that the ECJ also does not consider the economic argument applicable to trade marks.[261]

---

258   Compare *Beguelin* and *Dansk Supermarked* for unfair competition.
259   See for example Demaret, *Patents, Territorial Restrictions and EEC Law*, at 87, 91.
260   [1989] ECR 79 at ¶9; [1991] 4 CMLR 248 at ¶¶11 to 13.
261   Demaret considers it does not apply to trade marks, see Demaret, 'Industrial Property Rights, Compulsory Licences and the Free Movement of Goods under Community Law', at 176 to 177.

The emphasis on the trade mark's essential function in *Hag II*, however, opens up an interesting line of argument. The essential function of a trade mark according to the ECJ is to indicate the source of the marked product to consumers. That is, the essential function of a trade mark is its purpose. The ECJ has not defined an essential function of either patents or copyright, at least not in so many terms. In defining the specific subject-matter of a patent in *Sterling Drug*, however, it also indicated what the patent's purpose was: to reward the creative effort of the inventor.[262] The purpose of the two essential rights conferred by copyright would also seem to be the same since the qualifications on the Community exhaustion doctrine have been largely motivated by the need to ensure adequate recompense for the copyright creator.[263] So, a possible path to rationalise some of the more problematical rulings in this field lies potentially open.

The ECJ, however, has certainly not taken this course as a matter for general application. The confirmation of *Musik-Vertrieb* in both *Tournier* and *Patricia* does not suggest that it is presently ready to do so for transactions simply involving the importation and sale of patented or copyright articles. *Hag II*, despite recognising the economic role of trade marks in point 13, also does not indicate any change for trade-marked goods. In these situations, right owners seem condemned to await fruition of the moves towards uniform, Community rights. The limited role of the economic argument so far accepted under the free movement rules contrasts with its much greater acceptance by the ECJ in the context of the competition rules.

---

262 [1974] ECR 1143 at ¶9. In *Merck*, after referring to this purpose, the ECJ redefined the argument in terms of 'the substance of the right': [1981] ECR 2063 at ¶¶4, 9. In *Pharmon*, however, 'substance' and purpose were reunited: [1985] ECR 2281 at ¶26.
263 Compare *Coditel I*, *Basset*, *Warner Bros* and *Tournier*.

Chapter 7: Competition Policy in the EC

7.1 Introduction

The importance of encouraging investment – in contrast to its more limited role in qualifying the goal of integrating the internal market under the free movement rules – has played a far wider role under the competition rules. Both the ECJ and the Commission have relied on it in varying degrees to limit the goal of integrating the internal market for all kinds of intellectual property. While there are important differences in how both institutions have recognised the need to encourage investment, its widespread application under the competition rules highlights its as yet limited role under the doctrine of Community exhaustion. That failure is exposed all the more starkly with the Commission's announcement in *Comasso*,[1] effectively sanctioning 'absolute territorial protection' and positing contractual obligations which seem contrary to the exhaustion doctrine under the free movement rules.

Parallel import issues may arise under the competition rules in three broad ways. In colluding to block parallel imports, two parties may agree to split the ownership of intellectual property rights along national lines so that rights under national law may be used against third-party parallel importers. Alternatively, in an agreement, say, licensing intellectual property rights, the two parties may fetter their own ability to engage in trade across frontiers. These two types of agreement may well form part of the same overall arrangement. In the context of distribution agreements, a good example of the 'layered' analysis required under the competition rules is *Consten & Grundig*.[2] The third method, illustrated by *Tournier*, is a refusal to deal with a prospective licensee in potential abuse of a dominant position.[3]

Consten & Grundig involved several layers of restraints on conduct which the Commission found restricted competition contrary to Article 85(1). First, Grundig appointed Consten its exclusive distributor for France, thus depriving itself of the ability to appoint others to distribute its

---

1 OJ 1990 C6/3; [1990] 4 CMLR 259 (19(3) Notice), see text from Note 181 below.
2 56 & 58/64 *Consten & Grundig v Commission* [1966] ECR 299, see Chapter 6.2 above.
3 395/87 *Ministère Public v Tournier* [1991] 4 CMLR 248, see section 7.4 below.

products. Second, Grundig required Consten to promise not to export Grundig products out of France. In return, Grundig promised it would not itself sell into Consten's territory. Nor would it permit others to do so. Third, Grundig transferred to Consten the *GINT* mark for Consten to use in infringement actions against parallel importers. All this, of course, took place in the context of a network of similar agreements intended to seal off each Member State from the others at a time when the implementation of the common market had just removed legislative barriers such as tariffs and quotas.

The ECJ appeared to uphold the Commission's decision condemning 'absolute territorial protection', the arrangements to use the trade mark to repel all 'unauthorised' imports and the interlocking network with its reciprocal promises not to export genuine Grundig products into other members' territories. The contemporaneous ruling in the *STM* case,[4] however, suggests that *Consten & Grundig* did not automatically condemn the exclusive distributorship insofar as exclusive distribution rights were not coupled with export bans. Although it is arguable, it seems the better view is that it was the combination of all these elements as part of a continuing arrangement which led to the restriction contrary to Article 85.

At the time of *Consten & Grundig* and the *STM* case, the application of the rules on free movement to prevent splitting intellectual property rights to create barriers against parallel imports was not clear.[5] Even after the Community exhaustion doctrine was developed under the free movement rules, however, the ECJ confirmed that it was part of the function of EC competition policy to control such collusion.[6] Moreover, with the development of exceptions to the Community exhaustion doctrine under the free movement rules, further scope for the competition rules will arise.

In determining which of the onion-skin-like layers are permissible under the EC's competition policy, two observations stand out. The most striking is the apparently divergent approaches taken by the ECJ and the Commission.[7] Second is the extent to which obstructions of parallel importing are permitted under the competition rules even by the Commission.

Underlying the approaches taken by both the ECJ and the Commission, however, is a common theme: the need to encourage investment in pro-competitive activity by ensuring that those making the investment can appropriate the benefits accruing from the investment. Adoption of this explanation under the competition rules for all forms of intellectual property contrasts with its so far more limited acknowledgement under the free

---

4   56/65 *Société Technique Minière v Maschinenbau Ulm* [1966] ECR 235, see Chapter 6.2 above.

5   The key rulings in *Deutsche Grammophon* and *Sterling Drug* were still some years away, see Chapter 6, Notes 70 and 93 respectively.

6   258/78 *Nungesser KG and Eisele v Commission* [1982] ECR 2015, especially at ¶¶62 to 63 at section 7.2.1 below. The facts in that case involved a successful use of plant breeders' rights to block parallel imports before *Sterling Drug* had been decided.

7   See Valentine Korah, *EEC Competition Law and Practice*, ESC Publishing, 1990 (4th ed.), Chapter 14 but contrast Richard Whish, *Competition Law*, Butterworths, 1989 (2nd ed.), at 232 to 238.

movement rules. That acknowledgement is in many respects quite recent, although broadening. The greater resort to the need to encourage investment under both sets of rules points to shortcomings in the Community exhaustion doctrine and also suggests that the rationale should have wider application under the free movement rules.

The long-standing practice of the Commission – which can be traced back to distribution cases before *Consten & Grundig* and which does not seem to have undergone much alteration since then – regards almost all, if not all, contractual layers affecting parallel imports as restrictions on competition caught by EEC Treaty Article 85(1).[8] However, applying a variant of the need to encourage investment, it will exempt many such 'restrictions' under Article 85(3). This process has now reached the stage that many restrictions are *'per se* legal', qualifying for automatic exemption on compliance with the terms of one of the various group exemptions adopted by the Commission.[9]

In contrast, particularly in the 1980s, the ECJ has resorted to a more dynamic analysis under Article 85(1).[10] The ECJ's approach has several aspects. In contrast to many of the Commission's decisions, the ECJ has largely treated distribution and licensing agreements as vertical relationships, rather than horizontal ones, and so less likely to lead to anti-competitive concerns. At the same time, the ECJ has tended to analyse an agreement's impact on the market *ex ante*, at the time the agreement was entered into, and not *ex post*, after the event. These two factors seem to have led the ECJ to take into account a far wider range of factors when assessing whether an agreement restricts competition under Article 85(1) than does the Commission. Moreover, its cases have led it to clear ever more 'restrictive' obligations under Article 85(1).

How far the ECJ's approach extends is controversial. Its decisions are few in number and often appear to be internally contradictory; what could be broad statements of principle often sit uncomfortably amid hedging qualifications. Those who argue for a wide interpretation point to the ECJ's increasing reliance on the need to encourage incentives to invest and its general applicability to all forms of intellectual property subject-matter. On the other hand, the proponents of the narrow view point to the qualifications built into the ECJ's opinions, the need to focus on integrating the internal market and the perhaps unfortunate bifurcation of Article 85.[11]

---

8   Chapter 7.3. For the seminal analysis of the Commission's approach in the distribution context, see René Joliet, *The Rule of Reason in Antitrust Law: American, German and Common Market Laws in Comparative Perspective*, Martinus Nijhof, 1967.

9   The phrase is from Joliet, *The Rule of Reason in Antitrust Law*, at 151.

10   Chapter 7.2, for 'dynamic analysis' see Korah, *EEC Competition Law and Practice*, especially Chapters 10 and 14. The process can also be traced back to the foundations of the ECJ's jurisprudence: see especially the *STM* case.

11   Contrast Valentine Korah, *Know-how Licensing Agreements and the EEC Competition Rules: Regulation 556/89*, ESC Publishing, 1989, at 30 to 36 and Mario Siragusa, 'Technology Transfers Under EEC Law: A Private View', [1982] *Fordham Corporate Law Institute* 95 to Helmut R.B. Schröter, 'Antitrust Analysis under Article 85(1) and (3)', [1987] *Fordham Corporate Law Institute* 645 and, more qualified, Whish, *Competition Law*, at 232 to 238; Michel Waelbroeck, 'Antitrust Analysis under Article 85(1) and (3)', [1987] *Fordham Corporate Law Institute* 693.

The difference of approach between the two institutions has important practical implications. Under the Commission's approach almost all agreements tending to affect the flow of parallel imports are caught by Article 85(1) and so are invalid unless exempted. Unless the agreement is structured to comply with the requirements of a group exemption, there is very little chance of it ever receiving individual exemption. Too many agreements must be notified and the Commission, which has exclusive power to grant exemptions, has too few resources to deal with them individually. This has two dangers for the creation and dissemination of innovation.[12] The licensing and distribution process may become rigid and static: agreements may be structured to suit formalistic legal requirements rather than the demands of the parties and the market context. Second, the uncertainty surrounding the legal enforceability of contracts may have a chilling effect on investment in innovation and its dissemination. Before parties commit their resources, they must be sure that they can appropriate the profits deriving from the investment. If the licensor cannot get the royalties due for use of its technology, it is unlikely to license. Similarly, a licensee is unlikely to risk its capital in creating a new market if someone else can 'free ride' on the investment to cream off the profits.

A related problem is that most competition policy enforcement in the EC is undertaken by the Commission. In applying its interpretation of the competition rules, it will often seek to force the parties to renegotiate parts of their bargain to conform more closely to the patterns fixed in its group exemptions. This may well happen when the negotiating strength of the parties has changed, yet another factor which may magnify disincentives to invest.[13]

7.2 The ECJ's Rulings

7.2.1 Maize Seed

The central case is the ECJ's ruling in *Maize Seed*.[14] The ECJ quashed the Commission's decision finding 'open exclusivity' a *per se* restriction on competition contrary to Article 85(1) but upheld the Commission's condemnation of 'absolute territorial protection'; thus confirming the more limited interpretation of *Consten & Grundig* suggested at the time by the virtually contemporaneous *STM* case. The reasoning for quashing part of the Commission's decision is crucial as subsequent cases seem to have adopted it

---

12   See also Korah, *EEC Competition Law and Practice*, Chapter 14.
13   For an example, see *German Television Stations Film Purchases* OJ 1989 L284/36 ('the *ARD* case') under appeal T-157 & 168/89 OJ 1990 C14 and 23 where the licensee was forced to renegotiate after it had identified all the suitable films at its own expense and had lost the element of surprise over its competitors, see text from Note 162 below. See Warwick A. Rothnie, 'Commission Re-runs same Old Bill (Film Purchasing by German Television Stations)', [1990] EIPR 72.
14   258/78 *Nungesser KG & Eisele v Commission* [1982] ECR 2015.

in extending market analysis under Article 85(1) to obligations outside 'open exclusivity'.

By 1980, the EC's production of maize was still in shortfall by some 12 million tonnes a year despite cultivating more than an additional 3 million hectares (yielding 50 quintals per hectare) over 20 years by introducing hybrid maize.[15] Natural varieties of maize apparently do not grow well in the colder climates of northern Europe. Hence, considerable effort went into developing strains better adapted to the northern climate. The French Government, in particular, devoted considerable resources to research in this area and one of its public administrative bodies, INRA, had considerable success through hybridisation techniques. After many years of development, INRA registered two varieties of hybrid maize seed in the official French catalogue for seed varieties – in 1957 (INRA 200) and 1958 (INRA 258). More than 20 years later, 90 per cent of hybrid maize seeds exploited commercially in the EC still used lines originally developed by INRA. However, while varieties owned by INRA had accounted for virtually all maize sold in France during the early 1960s, by the 1980s they accounted for only 10 per cent.

As a public administrative body, INRA could not exploit the fruits of its researches itself so a company was set up to organise propagation, conservation and marketing of basic and certified seed of its varieties. This function eventually devolved onto Frasema, membership of which was open to any seed breeder licensed under French law which applied to join. Both in France and in other countries granting protection to 'plant breeders' rights', Frasema enjoyed exclusive production and marketing rights of INRA stock.

In 1960 to 1961 and 1965 INRA contracted with Eisele, among other things, to assign its rights in several varieties (including INRA 200 and INRA 258) to him and he undertook to prosecute and maintain the registration of those varieties under German laws on seed varieties. (The contract anticipated the common organisation of the seed market and Germany's accession to the UPOV Convention on plant breeders' rights. At the time, German law only granted plant breeders' rights to nationals of Germany.) A number of other obligations were entered into. Eisele undertook to deal only in INRA seeds and agreed to buy two-thirds of his requirements in France with the balance to be produced by him, or on his behalf, in Germany. INRA promised that it, and those claiming through it, would do everything in their power to stop sales from France directly into Germany.[16] In Germany, Eisele operated through his company, Nungesser.

Some 13 years after the original notification, the Commission, treating the arrangements as an exclusive licence, found that the arrangements restricted competition contrary to Article 85(1) and denied exemption under Article

---

15　*Ibid.* at 2084 *per* Advocate-General Rozès.

16　There were other obligations found by the Commission to restrict competition, for example a requirement for Eisele to co-ordinate prices with INRA/Frasema but these were not all appealed.

85(3).[17] The appeal to the ECJ focused on whether the Commission was right in finding the exclusive licence restricted competition and in refusing to exempt.

(a) *The ruling*

According to the ECJ, the Commission's conclusion that the exclusive licence restricted competition depended on two sets of circumstances whose implications for competition policy were not necessarily the same:

> 53. . . . . The *first* case concerns a so-called *open exclusive licence* or assignment and the exclusivitiy [*sic*] of the licence relates solely to the contractual relationship between the owner of the right and the licensee, whereby the owner merely undertakes not to grant other licences in respect of the same territory and not to compete himself with the licensee on that territory. On the other hand, the *second* case involves an exclusive licence or assignment with *absolute territorial protection*, under which the parties to the contract propose, as regards the products and the territory in question, to eliminate all competition from third parties, such as parallel importers or licensees for other territories. (*Emphasis added*)

The ECJ first dealt with the potential implications of an open exclusive licence:

> 56.   The exclusive licence which forms the subject-matter of the contested decision concerns the cultivation and marketing of hybrid maize seeds which were developed by INRA after years of research and experimentation and were unknown to German farmers at the time when the cooperation between INRA and the applicants was taking shape. For that reason the concern shown by the interveners as regards the protection of new technology is justified.
> 57.   In fact, in the case of a licence of breeders' rights over hybrid maize seeds newly developed in one Member State, an undertaking established in another Member State which was not certain that it would not encounter competition from other licensees for the territory granted to it, or from the owner of the right himself, might be deterred from accepting the risk of cultivating and marketing that product; such a result would be damaging to the dissemination of a new technology and would prejudice competition in the Community between the new product and similar existing products.
> 58.   Having regard to the specific nature of the products in question, the Court concludes that, in a case such as the present, the grant of an open exclusive licence, that is to say a licence which does not affect the position of third parties such as parallel importers and licensees for other territories, is not in itself incompatible with Article 85(1) of the Treaty.

Turning to absolute territorial protection, the ECJ stated that collusion to block parallel imports had consistently been held to restrict competition in the common market since *Consten & Grundig* because it resulted in 'artificial maintenance of separate national markets, contrary to the Treaty'.[18]

17   [1978] 3 CMLR 434.
18   [1982] ECR 2015, at ¶61. For the conclusion on this part of the case, see ¶¶66 to 67.

Moreover, at least insofar as it related to exclusive selling rights for maize seed, it could *never* be exempted since it was not indispensable:

> 77.   As it is a question of seeds intended to be used by a large number of farmers for the production of maize, which is an important product for human and animal foodstuffs, absolute territorial protection *manifestly* goes beyond what is indispensable for the improvement of production or distribution or the promotion of technical progress, as is demonstrated in particular in the present case by the prohibition, agreed to by both parties to the agreement of any parallel imports of INRA maize seeds into Germany even if those seeds were bred by INRA itself and marketed in France. (*Emphasis added*)

So, the ECJ rejected the Commission's *per se* condemnation of any exclusive licences but confirmed and, indeed, strengthened the proscription of absolute territorial protection.

The ECJ's ruling raises many important issues for the treatment of parallel imports under EC competition policy; some positive, others less so. The most positive is the ECJ's endorsement of the need to take into account incentives to invest *and* its application under Article 85(1). The problems include identifying when the ECJ's approach applies; drawing the line between open exclusivity and absolute territorial protection; and the ECJ's flat rejection of any possibility for absolute territorial protection.

(b)   *The crucial factors underpinning the reasoning*

The reasoning at points 56 to 58 of *Maize Seed* offers five elements which led to the conclusion clearing open exclusivity:

(a) the specific nature of the products in question;
(b) the fact that the licence concerned new technology;
(c) the years of research and experimentation invested by INRA in developing that technology;
(d) the risk that the licensee would not invest if it were subject to competition; and
(e) the consequent damage to the dissemination of new technology prejudicial to inter-brand competition if the licence did not go ahead.

The judgment did not explain why the nature of the products is important. Indeed, earlier in its judgment it had refused to distinguish plant breeders' rights from other forms of intellectual property, particularly patents.[19] However, the criterion is reiterated in subsequent rulings and the Commission analyses the competitive impact of agreements by categories according to their intellectual property subject-matter. Furthermore, the subject-matter of the licence played a role in condemning any prospect of exemption for

---

19   *Ibid.* at ¶¶33 to 43, although, having reached that conclusion, it affirmed that it would still be necessary to take into account the specific nature of the products forming the subject-matter of the plant breeders' rights: *ibid.* at ¶43. Note also the consideration in ¶61 of absolute territorial protection by reference to *Consten & Grundig*, a case of distribution and trade mark licensing.

absolute territorial protection under Article 85(3). Hence, the reference may have a limiting effect on the general application of the ECJ's clearance of open exclusivity.

The remaining four factors relate to encouraging investment under the competition rules. That is, an open exclusive licence was not in itself a restriction on competition caught by Article 85(1) because of the desirability of encouraging investment in innovation.[20] This reasoning is much the same as that used by the ECJ to qualify the goal of integrating the internal market in interpreting the 'free movement' rules where, anomalously, it has only been accepted for some aspects of copyright.

The ECJ seems to consider investment from two angles. The German Government, intervening, argued that totally prohibiting any exclusive licence under Article 85(1) would undermine the incentive to innovate by reducing the attractiveness of licensing.[21] The ECJ referred to INRA's years of research and experimentation in developing a product which, at the time of its negotiations with Eisele, was unknown to German farmers and concluded that the concerns of the German Government regarding 'the protection of new technology' were justified.[22] The subsequent conclusion that an open exclusive licence does not of itself restrict competition contrary to Article 85(1) is not directly linked to this point. But, the context leads to the inference that INRA (and others) would not license their 'new technology' unless it (and they) could appropriate the benefits of their investment.[23] The second aspect, more fully reasoned than the first, was that a licensee might not accept the risks of cultivating and marketing the product if it were not protected from competition by other licensees or the licensor itself. Hence, dissemination of the new technology throughout the EC might be impeded and inter-brand competition between the new product and similar, existing products might be prejudiced.

It has been suggested that the justification of the prejudice to disseminating new technology may apply almost automatically since there was no showing of either particular investment costs or risks.[24] As Advocate-General Rozès' opinion makes clear, however, the judgment was given in the context of a manufacturing licensee for a new market, where the product needed adaptation to meet local conditions and where, even for imported products, the licensee undertook special marketing functions (such as labelling and quality control), bore the costs of maintaining the register and also had to create demand for the new product.

Relying on both economic principle and subsequent case law, it has

---

20 For distribution, see the *STM* case, Chapter 6.2 above.
21 [1982] ECR 2015, at ¶55.
22 *Ibid.* at ¶56, quoted above.
23 Korah considers that the ECJ's reference to the licensor's investment shows that the ECJ was taking the need to protect it into account: Korah, *Know-how Licensing Agreements and the EEC Competition Rules*, at 32; see also Jens Fejø, *Monopoly Law and Market*, Kluwer, 1990, at 338. Siragusa, on the other hand, focuses on the prospective licensee's investment: Siragusa, 'Technology Transfers Under EEC Law: A Private View', at 120 to 123.
24 Siragusa, 'Technology Transfers Under EEC Law: A Private View', at 121.

also been argued that the crucial aspects of *Maize Seed* are the need to encourage technology transfer and the consequent enhancement of inter-brand competition.[25] However, both *Coditel II* and *Pronuptia* are closely tied to the specific nature of the subject-matter in issue and *Pronuptia*, harking back to *Consten & Grundig*, turned on whether the trade mark was new or well-known.[26] Hence, while arguably the need to encourage investment and the enhancement of inter-brand competition *ought* to be the overriding considerations, the actual reasons given by the ECJ include potential for qualification.

The ECJ's ruling stands in marked contrast to the reasons published by the Commission. For example, in *Maize Seed* itself, the Commission merely referred to the possibility of exemption:

> In principle, just as in the case of a patent, where exclusive propagation rights are granted by the holder of breeder's rights to a licensee within the Common Market, as is the case [here], the exclusivity *is capable of being considered* to have satisfied all the tests *for exemption* under Article 85(3). There are even circumstances in which exclusive selling rights linked with prohibitions against exporting *could also be exempted*.[27] (*Emphasis added*)

That is, either form of arrangement could qualify for exemption, not clearance. The Commission indicated that an exemption might be forthcoming if it were necessary to protect a small or medium-sized enterprise attempting to penetrate a new market or promote a new product provided that parallel imports were possible. In point 55 of the Commission's decision, however, the possibility of an exemption in *Maize Seed* was rejected. There was 'no question of a new market being penetrated or a new product being launched'. Even at the date of the licence, the licence included absolute territorial protection which could not be exempted.

That ruling springs directly out of the Commission's policy on patent licensing.[28] Its subsequent decisions on know-how are not much different and the same rules seem to apply for copyright. The Commission's approach can be traced back to the distribution cases. But, in the case of franchising and plant breeders' rights, the Commission's reasoning has been more constrained by the ECJ's rulings.[29]

While the Commission has also accepted the need to encourage investment as qualifying the goal of integrating the internal market under the competition rules, it did so virtually exclusively under Article 85(3). Moreover, differing with the ECJ further, the Commission in many cases refers only to the fact

---

25   See especially *ibid.* at 121 to 123; more qualified is Korah, *Know-how Licensing Agreements and the EEC Competition Rules*, at 30 to 36.

26   262/81 *Coditel SA v Ciné Vog Films (No. 2)* [1982] ECR 3381, section 7.2.2 below; 161/84 *Pronuptia de Paris GmbH v Schillgalis* [1986] ECR 353, section 7.2.3 below.

27   [1978] 3 CMLR 434, at ¶54.

28   See subsection 7.3.1(b) below. The Commission applied exactly the same reasoning in *Maize Seed* and gave as its published reason for the delay in adopting the group exemption for patents the long wait for the ECJ's ruling on the appeal, see *10th Report on Competition Policy*, at ¶6, EC Commission, 1981.

29   For the different subject-matters, see section 7.3.1 below.

that the prospective licensee requires protection from competition for its investment. Sometimes the Commission accepts exclusivity is in the licensor's interest where the licensor was not otherwise big enough to break into the new market effectively and that, coupled with a non-competition obligation, it may ensure that the licensee exerts itself to exploit the licence successfully. Hence, rather than protecting the licensor's investment, the Commission tends to focus on the role of exclusivity in allowing licensors, otherwise too small to expand, to penetrate more of the common market more quickly.

(c)   *Other unresolved issues*

Before moving on to examine how the ECJ applied its *Maize Seed* reasoning in subsequent cases, it remains to consider some further unresolved issues in *Maize Seed* itself.

(i)   Open exclusivity or absolute territorial protection

The ECJ cleared open exclusivity in the circumstances of *Maize Seed* but found absolute territorial protection a *per se* restriction on competition and even refused to exempt it in terms tantamount to *per se* condemnation. It is therefore important to be clear about what is an open exclusive licence and what will turn an exclusive licence into one involving absolute territorial protection. Unfortunately, there is considerable ambiguity particularly as the two definitions are not mutually exclusive.

The ECJ itself defines an open exclusive licence as one where:

> 53. . . . the exclusivity of the licence relates solely to the contractual relationship between the owner of the right and the licensee, whereby the owner merely undertakes not to grant other licences in respect of the same territory and not to compete himself with the licensee on that territory.

One omission from this definition, particularly in the light of the ECJ's subsequent references to the importance of the licensor's investment, is the reciprocal obligation on the licensee not to compete in the territory reserved for the licensor. However, the shortfall in supplies and the higher prices in Germany made it unlikely the problem would arise in *Maize Seed*.

Although such an obligation is not expressly mentioned by the ECJ, it would fall within the general words of the definition as relating solely to the contractual relationship between the licensor and the licensee.[30] Neither of the potential qualifying factors, nature of the product or the novelty of the technology, necessarily detracts from this view.

The omission lends some weight to the Commission's apparent view in decisions under Article 85(3) that the investment requiring protection is only the licensee's investment. It is also supported by claims that a licensor or

---

30   See also the corresponding definition of 'absolute territorial protection' referring to the elimination of 'all competition from third parties' at [1982] ECR 2015, at ¶53.

an assignor cannot justifiably claim protection against competition from its licensee or assignee. These may be based on either or both of two bases. First, the licensor (or assignor) receives compensation for the use of its right by the licensee (or assignee), and second, the licensor (or assignor) should get all the protection necessary through the cost advantages of not having to incur transport costs or licence (or assignment) fees.[31]

The first proposition is undeniable, although for reasons explored particularly in Chapters 6 and 8 it does not necessarily follow that the right owner is 'double dipping' even where a corresponding right exists in the 'foreign' market. The second proposition rests on the view that the right owner's interest is properly limited to ensuring solely that the product is produced by the most efficient producer, which may or may not be the case.

In the author's view, *Maize Seed* recognises the need to encourage the dissemination of technology through licensing. This requires both the licensor's and the licensee's willingness to participate in the transaction. If so, failing to take into account the licensor's desire to protect its 'own' market is unrealistic. Both of the propositions set out above depend to a considerable extent on the theoretical world of perfect knowledge in which information is discoverable instantaneously and costlessly. Whether the conduct of licensors and licensees in the real world of uncertain and imperfect information can be guided by this assumption is not just an abstract issue. First, in practice, licensors are often extremely reluctant to pass on technology where they perceive a credible threat to their 'own' (domestic) market.[32] Second, there are credible claims that the returns from licensing when contrasted to self-practice are 'trivial'.[33] Both points take on

31   For the first, see René Joliet, 'Patented Articles and the Free Movement of Goods Within the EEC', (1975) 28 *Current Legal Problems* 15, at 36 and the reasoning in *Curtiss Aeroplane v United Aircraft Engineering* 266 Fed. 71 (2d Cir. 1920), see Chapter 3 from Note 272. For the second argument, see William F. Baxter, 'Legal Restrictions on Exploitation of the Patent Monopoly: An Economic Analysis', 76 Yale LJ 267, especially at 316 to 317 (1966) and Paul Demaret, *Patents, Territorial Restrictions and EEC Law*, Verlag-Chemie, 1978, at 19 to 35, 44 to 53. The latter does not necessarily deny that there will ever be justifications for such protection, but proceeds on the basis that they will be extremely rare and takes a very narrow view of the investment in development which should be fostered, a single licensee to work the idea up to commercialisation.

32   See Joel A. Bleeke and James A. Rahl, 'The Value of Territorial and Field of Use Restrictions in the International Licensing of Unpatented Know-How: An Empirical Survey', 1 *Northwestern Journal of International Law & Business* 450, at 463, 471 and 473 (1979), emphasising the key role played in US licensors' decisions on whether they could block imports into the US market especially through reliance on US patent rights and note the recognition of this point in *US v Crown Zellerbach* 141 F. Supp. 118 (ND Ill. 1956). See also the concerns about control, especially for process technology, revealed in Edwin Mansfield, Anthony Romero and Samuel Wagner, 'Foreign Trade and US Research and Development', 61 Rev.Econ. & Stat. 49 (1979).

33   See William Kingston, *Innovation, Creativity and the Law*, Kluwer Academic Publishers, 1990, at 73 especially text at Note 39. A survey of 30 US firms indicated that by far the preferred method of exploiting foreign markets was through a subsidiary although, where the innovation related to processes, the role of direct exports greatly increased. As the technology matured, however, firms became increasingly likely to license rather than export, see Mansfield, Romero and Wagner, 'Foreign Trade and US Research and Development', at 54 to 56 and note Scherer's speculations arising thereon in Robert B. Helms (ed.), *Drugs and Health*, American Enterprise Institute, 1981, at 48.

particular importance if the licensor has ambitions of continuing to compete in the market especially where production techniques and the ability to generate further innovations depend on cumulative knowledge.[34] Further, as Demaret's analysis clearly reveals, the conclusion against licensor protection depends on a heavy policy preference for the perceived goals of competition over intellectual property.[35] Whether that policy preference is correct is certainly arguable.[36] Even within the EC, the Commission does not accept the arguments for denying the licensor protection since it accords licensees' promises not to invade their licensor's territory group exemption.[37]

The definition of 'absolute territorial protection' in the ECJ's judgment at point 53 covered the elimination of 'all competition from third parties, such as parallel importers or licensees for other territories'. The inclusion of 'licensees for other territories' raises problems of its own. As it has been put colourfully, 'A bucket in which four holes have been mended will still not hold water if a fifth hole remains'.[38] In addition, the licensor in a vertical relationship arguably has no interest in granting any licensee more protection than is necessary to induce its investment particularly in the presence of strong inter-brand competition. The ECJ does not explain why a licensee may be protected from competition by the licensor or by licensees for the same territory but not licensees for another territory. Perhaps, there are elements of the debate about whether licensors should be able to claim protection against licensees at work although the reference to parallel importers suggests that the primary consideration is the policy goal of integrating the internal market.[39] Whatever the merits of this view under the free movement rules, the limitation on licensee competition is not necessarily a restriction on competition.

---

34 Especially for smaller firms competing against larger rivals: see for example *Velcro/Aplix* [1989] 4 CMLR 157 in the EC and for claims about US firms' attempts to break into the Japanese market, Donald M. Spero, 'Patent Protection or Piracy – A CEO Views Japan', [September-October 1990] *Harvard Business Review* 58. The argument may be of considerably broader application however, see Giovanni Dosi, Keith Pavitt and Luc Soete, *The Economics of Technical Change and International Trade*, Harvester Wheatsheaf, 1990. Intellectual property theory is also worked up from the same theories of costless information, for further consideration of the use of market imperfections to appropriate the benefits of investments, see Chapters 8 to 11 below.

35 At one point, he even goes so far as to express the view that the 'general' policy should prevail over the 'particular' which might be thought alien to the common law: for his view see Demaret, *Patents, Territorial Restrictions and EEC Law*, at 35.

36 Contrast, for example *US v Studiengesellschaft Kohle mbH* 670 F. 2d 1122 (DC Cir. 1981), Chapter 3 above from Note 230.

37 Regulation 2349/84, Article 1(1)(3); Regulation 4087/88, Article 3(1)(c); Regulation 556/89, Article 1(1)(3). For further discussion of the Commission's approach, see Chapter 7.3, below.

38 Korah, *Know-how Licensing Agreements and the EEC Competition Rules*, Chapter 3.3 Note 8 at 106. See also René Joliet, 'Trademark Licensing Agreements Under the EEC Law of Competition', 5 *Northwestern Journal of International Law and Business* 755, at 802 to 804 (1983). But, see further *Maize Seed*'s apparent rejection of this point in ¶77 discussed at subsection 7.2.1(c)(ii) below.

39 This is an adaptation of the arguments put in Hartmut Johannes, *Industrial Property and Copyright in European Community Law*, Sijthoff, 1976, at 66 to 67, 70 to 75. But, note that a licensee for the same territory has at least the licence fees and the licensor has at least the transport costs.

Despite expressly referring to licensees for other territories in its definition of absolute territorial protection, in the later parts of its judgment the ECJ focused its attention on INRA and Eisele's co-operation to block parallel importers. This is more in line with the case law on the free movement rules where the ECJ has not expressly dealt with the question of a direct sale by one licensee into another's territory.

The Commission has interpreted the case law to mean that a right is exhausted on the grant of a licence for some part of the EC without the need for actual sale and carried this view through to the competition rules.[40] Under the free movement rules, Advocate-General Mancini agreed with the Commission's interpretation in *Pharmon*, but the ECJ resolved the reference on the question of consent and did not consider the further question.[41] Subsequently, a three-judge chamber accepted the Commission's view that a manufacturing location clause under a patent restricted competition because it denied the licensee the option of manufacturing elsewhere, even in Member States where no patent had been granted.[42] Since then, the Fifth Chamber seems to have retreated somewhat since it cleared a direct export ban.[43]

Moreover, if the terms of a group exemption can be complied with, the Commission does exempt bans on licensees manufacturing or using the licensed technology in other licensees' territories;[44] actively seeking sales in the other licensees' territories; and, in some cases, sales to unsolicited customers.[45]

(ii)   Absolute territorial protection: never exempted

In *Maize Seed*, the ECJ apparently rejected any possibility of exempting absolute territorial protection out of hand.[46] The ECJ did not explore why INRA and Eisele had sought to block parallel imports; rather the fact of agreement to block parallel imports was sufficient to preclude any prospect of exemption. This followed from the nature of the products in question, they were important foodstuffs. Yet, the specific nature of the products was one of

---

40   See *GEMA-Custom Pressing* in *15th Report on Competition Policy*, EC Commission, 1986, ¶81, see Note 159 below. See further James S. Venit, 'In the Wake of Windsurfing: Patent Licensing in the Common Market', [1986] *Fordham Corporate Law Institute* 517, at 523 to 528.

41   19/84 *Pharmon v Hoechst* [1985] ECR 2281, at 2285 for the Advocate-General; see Chapter 6 from Note 167.

42   The court appears to have treated the contract as expressly banning manufacture outside the patent territory: 193/83 *Windsurfing v Commission* [1986] ECR 611, at ¶¶82–5 and see Advocate-General Lenz at *ibid.* 633 to 634.

43   27/87 *Erauw Jacquery* [1988] ECR 1919, section 7.2.4 below.

44   Regulation 556/89, Article 1(1)(4); Regulation 2349/89, Article 1(1)(4). Under the franchise regulation, the obligation permitted is not to engage in business in competition with the licensee: Regulation 4087/88, Article 3(1)(c).

45   *Ibid.* at Article 1(1)(6).

46   [1982] ECR 2015, at ¶77.

the factors in the ECJ adopting a *flexible* approach under Article 85(1), not a *per se* condemnation.[47]

Perhaps, as the second half of point 77 in *Maize Seed* suggests, the fact uppermost in the ECJ's mind was INRA and Eisele's successful co-operation to exclude parallel imports. Before *Sterling Drug* had been decided, Eisele had successfully sued a parallel importer and both INRA and Eisele had successfully intimidated another would-be parallel importer. The ECJ rejected an argument that the confirmation of the doctrine of Community exhaustion in *Sterling Drug* and *Winthrop* was sufficient to deal with this problem. In line with the primacy of market integration established in *Consten & Grundig*, the ECJ ruled that enforcing integration of the internal market was a function of the competition rules too.[48]

In Eisele's case there may well have been good reasons why he should have been allowed to stop the parallel importers in question and require absolute protection generally.[49] The failure of INRA's attempt to penetrate the Belgian market, where its concessionaire was subjected to direct competition from French producers, adds indirect support to the argument that Eisele needed the protection to secure his investment. One parallel importer, Louis David KG, had apparently bought seeds over two and a half years old for which there could have been considerable doubts about performance and quality.[50] One or the other parallel importer may also have obtained its supplies at 'bargain basement' prices in France after the sowing season was over.[51] Eisele had to pay registration fees for the plant breeders' rights,[52] establish his own production plant and special, refrigerated storage facilities. In addition, Eisele selected seed sizes to conform to the machinery specifications and climatic conditions in Germany (as a result of which he set more stringent standards than applied (or were necessary) in the more benign French climate). Moreover, the Commission relied on price differentials of 70 per cent, between the two countries, but Advocate-General Rozès favoured the appellants' claims that the differences were between 15 and 25 per cent.[53]

Subsequently, both the ECJ and the Commission have adopted a less strict position. It is not clear how much this represents acceptance of the fact that even absolute territorial protection may be necessary to induce desirable

---

47 On the seeming inconsistency of relying on the same factor to justify a flexible approach under Article 85(1) and a *per se* condemnation under Article 85(3), see for example Korah, *Know-how Licensing Agreements and the EEC Competition Rules*, at 35.
48 The ECJ rejected the UK Government's arguments to this effect since market integration was also a goal of the competition rules: [1982] ECR 2015, at ¶¶62 to 63. Presumably, if matters stood at this point, applying the competition rules to achieve integration would need to reflect qualifications on the exhaustion rule adopted under the free movement rules.
49 For a cogent, concise argument on general principles, see Eleanor M. Fox, 'Maize Seed: A Comparative Comment', [1982] *Fordham Corporate Law Institute* 151.
50 [1980] ECR 2015, at 2097 to 2098, 2122 *per* Advocate-General Rozès.
51 *Ibid.* at 2120.
52 The amount quoted by the Advocate-General was DM80,000: *ibid.* at 2113.
53 *Ibid.* at 2019 to 2021.

investment in some cases or depends on other factors: a perceived increase in the effectiveness of the rules on the free movement of goods; greater sophistication in the definition of 'absolute territorial protection'; or, even, the demands of the specific products in question.

7.2.2 Coditel II

Coditel II confirmed the application of the need to encourage investment in the context of copyright for the broadcast of films.[54] It did not draw a distinction between open exclusivity or absolute territorial protection although it permitted *de facto* absolute territorial protection under Article 85(1). In addition, the ECJ went beyond *Maize Seed* in attempting some consideration of when an exclusive licence might offend against Article 85(1).

The case was a second reference at a further stage of appeal against the finding that *Coditel* had infringed Ciné Vog's exclusive rights in the film *Le Boucher* by capturing a German television broadcast and retransmitting it in Belgium over a cable network. Ciné Vog had acquired those rights by exclusive licence from the French owner which had also authorised the German broadcast.

The ECJ reiterated that the Treaty's implications for film producer's rights were not the same as for 'literary and artistic works the placing of which at the disposal of the public is inseparable from the circulation of the material form of the works . . . ' and interpreted *Coditel I* as establishing that the right to require fees for each and every showing of the film was an essential function of the copyright.[55] Despite this, the ECJ then noted in points 13 and 14 that some aspects of the copyright's exercise could be contrary to Article 85 if they serve to give effect to an agreement restricting competition in the common market.[56] But, like the open exclusive licence in *Maize Seed*:

> 15. . . . the mere fact that the owner of the copyright in a film has granted to a sole licensee the exclusive right to exhibit that film in the territory of a Member State and, consequently, to prohibit, during a specified period, its showing by others, is not sufficient to justify the finding that such a contract must be regarded as the purpose, the means or the result of an agreement, decision or concerted practice prohibited by the Treaty.

That is, the grant of an exclusive licence to broadcast a film in one Member State only was not necessarily a restriction on competition. In the ECJ's view, this followed very much from the nature of the 'product'. An exclusive licence for film exhibition did not of itself restrict competition because of:

> 16. [t]he characteristics of the cinematographic industry and of its markets in the Community, especially those relating to dubbing and subtitling for the

---

54 262/81 *Coditel SA v Ciné-Vog Films SA (No. 2)* [1982] ECR 3361. For the Commission's first interpretation (described by one commentator as 'disingenuous'), see *12th Report on Competition Policy*, EC Commission, 1983, at ¶48. For *Coditel I* involving the free movement rules, see Chapter 6 above from Note 125.
55 *Ibid.* at ¶¶ 11 to 12.
56 *Ibid.* at ¶¶13 to 14.

benefit of different language groups, to the possibilities of television broadcasts, and to the system of financing cinematographic production in Europe.

The nature of films was considered to be such that they will not be produced unless investors are guaranteed the chance to reap the profits using exclusive licences if necessary.[57]

Extending its analysis further than *Maize Seed*, the ECJ then looked at when an exclusive licence might fall foul of Article 85(1). A broad investigation of the licence's impact was required:

> 17. . . . the exercise of those rights may, none the less, come within the said prohibitions where there are economic or legal circumstances the effect of which is to restrict film distribution to an appreciable degree or distort competition on the cinematographic market, regard being had to the specific characteristics of that market.

It might seem difficult, however, to work out when the qualification would operate if the scheme organised for *Le Boucher* did not offend because the licensee could effectively stop any other broadcast in the interests of charging fees.

Advocate-General Reischl was concerned that the need to charge fees did not in itself justify exclusivity.[58] He concluded that the real justification lay in the likelihood that returns would be higher with just one licensee but noted that the ECJ could limit the generality of his conclusion by holding it only applied to *new* films. For these, there was an obvious need to ensure security of investment. The case of old films known to the public and which had covered their costs was not thought as compelling. His more general explanation accords with the need to encourage investment propounded by the ECJ in *Maize Seed*. The narrower proposition may too, but seems to be predicated on a 'fair reward' theory.[59]

The ECJ avoided the problem by noting its information was insufficient and directing the national court to investigate further, directing it to establish in particular:

> 19. . . . whether or not the exercise of the exclusive right to exhibit a cinematographic film creates (1) barriers which are artificial and unjustifiable in terms of the needs of the cinematographic industry, or (2) the possibility of charging fees which exceed a fair return on investment or (3) an exclusivity the duration of which is disproportionate to those requirements, and (4) whether or not, from a general point of view, such exercise within a given geographic

---

57   On film financing generally see *per* Advocate-General Reischl at *ibid.* at 3412. On the impact of television broadcasts, see *Coditel I*, Chapter 6 above from Note 125; on video rental, see *Cinétheque* [1985] ECR 2605 and *Warner Bros*, Chapter 6 above from Note 184.

58   *Ibid.* at 3411 to 3412.

59   The difference can be important. As Advocate-General Reischl's opinion shows, the 'reward' theory can be limited by *ex post* notions of what is necessary to recover costs while an 'incentive' theory, believing that mere recovery of costs might be insufficient spur, would allow the right owner to reap as much of the returns as it could capture, see Joliet, 'Patented Articles and the Free Movement of Goods Within the EEC', at 30 to 31. On the ECJ's perhaps inconsistent case law, see Korah, *Know-how Licensing Agreements and the EEC Competition Rules*, at 28 to 30, 35 to 36.

area is such as to prevent, restrict or distort competition within the common market. (*Author's numbering*)

In the first of the four factors, the ECJ directed the national court to investigate whether artificial and unjustifiable barriers in terms of the film industry's needs were created. If exclusive licences in the film industry were necessary to attract investment funds, the consequent market partitioning would seem to be neither artificial nor unjustifiable.[60] Like *Maize Seed*, then, *Coditel II* appears to refer to the need to encourage investment. This factor has also been seen as an instruction to assess the competitive impact of the licence at the level of the market as a whole.[61] The ECJ's phrase 'in terms of the needs of the cinematographic industry' supports that view although point 17 may also direct attention to the intra-brand effect.

Even where exclusive rights were justifiable in terms of the needs of the film industry, it seems that it may still be found to restrict competition if any of the remaining three factors be found. The fourth seems like a catch-all phrase, restating the general test it is supposed to illustrate.[62] The second permits intervention if more than a 'fair return on investment' is being earned. The ECJ does not clarify how a fair return on an exclusive right is to be calculated, but there must be some danger it is applying a perhaps misplaced notion of the 'reward theory' of the sort suggested in the narrower explanation offered by Advocate-General Reischl.[63] The third factor, 'an exclusivity the duration of which is disproportionate to those requirements', has occasioned the Commission's first and only interpretation of *Coditel II* in a formal decision.[64]

7.2.3 Pronuptia

Pronuptia continues the chain of references to a liberal application of Article 85(1) in the context of 'distribution franchising'.[65] Clauses conferring exclusive licences were cleared because of the need to encourage investment,

---

60   See the factors enumerated at ¶16 and also *ibid.* at 3411 to 3412 *per* Advocate-General Reischl, at Note 57 above.

61   Barry E. Hawk, 2 *United States, Common Market and International Antitrust: A Comparative Guide*, Prentice Hall Law & Business, 2nd ed. (1990 Supp.), at 728.

62   *Ibid.*

63   In the case of ornamental and industrial designs, the ECJ has suggested a similar approach to determine whether the right holder is abusing its industrial property right: 53/87 *Consorzio Italiano della componentistica di Ricambio per Autoveicoli e Maxicar v Régie Nationale des Usines Renault* [1990] 4 CMLR 265, at ¶16 and 238/87 *Volvo AB v Eric Veng (UK) Limited* [1989] 4 CMLR 122.

64   *German Television Stations Film Purchases* OJ 1989 L284/36 ('the *ARD* case'); exemption granted but under appeal T-157 & 168/89 OJ 1990 C14 and 23, see Note 162, below. Although the considerations mentioned by the ECJ in *Coditel II* seem broad enough to include the importance attributed to the existence of national broadcasting monopolies in point 16 of *Coditel I*, the Commission did not attempt the point and so, perhaps, confirmed the emphasis in *Coditel II* on the impact of all forms of exploitation on the right owner's ability to capture returns on its investment rather than the existing institutional barriers noted in the earlier ruling.

65   161/84 *Pronuptia* [1986] ECR 353.

this time explicitly extended to both the franchisor and its franchisees. As in both *Maize Seed* and *Coditel II*, however, the ECJ's reasoning is very much qualified by the characteristics of distribution franchising and also reiterates the thread distinguishing between new products and old. *Pronuptia*, with a more limited parallel to *Coditel II*, is also an advance on *Maize Seed*; acknowledging that absolute territorial protection may benefit from exemption.

The franchisor was the West German subsidiary of the well-known French vendor of wedding dresses and accessories and operated in Germany through its own outlets as well as franchisees. It sued one of its franchisees, Mrs Schillgalis, for unpaid royalties. It succeeded at first instance, but lost the appeal when the Oberlandesgericht (Frankfurt am Main) considered that the exclusive territory accorded the franchisee was a restriction on competition caught by Article 85(1) since the franchisor was deprived of the ability to license or supply other dealers in the territory.[66] The further appeal to the Bundesgerichtshof led to the preliminary reference on which the ECJ ruled.

According to the ECJ at point 15, distribution franchises were not in themselves anti-competitive. They permitted businesses which had established themselves on one market to profit from their success by expanding into another without risking their own capital and, at the same time, generating additional revenue from fees. Moreover, the franchisees benefited from access to the franchisor's experience which otherwise would have required considerable effort to reduplicate and also from the franchisor's successful reputation. Taking into account the specific nature of distribution franchises, two conditions were necessary to make such a desirable system work and clauses implementing these conditions were outside the ban in Article 85(1):

> 16. First, the franchisor must be able to communicate his know-how to the franchisees and provide them with the necessary assistance in order to enable them to apply his methods, without running the risk that the know-how and assistance might benefit competitors, even indirectly . . .

From this, among other things, the franchisor could forbid the franchisee selling the business without the franchisor's prior approval and could even forbid the franchisee during the contract and for a reasonable period after its expiry from opening another shop of a similar nature in an area where it might compete with other members of the network.[67] Thus, under the guise of encouraging the franchisor to disclose its know-how, the ECJ went a step further than *Maize Seed* and expressly acknowledged that members of the network are entitled to some protection against competition from each other.

---

66 *Ibid.* at ¶7. The agreements had not been notified and exemption depended on whether the exclusive dealing group exemption, then Regulation 67/67, applied.
67 The ECJ does not explain why the ban on unauthorised use of the know-how is limited to uses in direct competition with other members of the network: see Michel Waelbroeck, 'The *Pronuptia* Judgment – A Critical Appraisal', [1986] *Fordham Corporate Law Institute* 211, at 216.

17. Secondly, the franchisor must be able to take the measures necessary for maintaining the identity and reputation of the network bearing his business name or symbol . . .

So, as points 18 to 22 went on to identify, the franchisor could force the franchisee to use the franchisor's know-how and business methods; to conform to the network's uniform methods of presentation concerning layout, decoration and location of the contract premises; not to assign the franchise without the franchisor's approval; to use goods conforming to quality specifications or even supplied from designated sources where policing quality controls was impractical; and to submit advertising to the franchisor's approval about its nature (but not prices).

The ECJ then examined the agreement for clauses which it considered would restrict competition contrary to Article 85(1): those which tended to share markets between the franchisor and franchisees or between franchisees or which affected price competition between members of the network. Despite having *cleared* both the franchisee's obligation not to open up a shop of a similar nature where it might compete with another member of the network *and*, separately, the franchisee's obligation to operate the franchise only from the location designated in the franchise, the ECJ found these two clauses *in conjunction* restricted competition:

24. [The location clause's] real effect becomes clear if it is examined in conjunction with the franchisor's undertaking to ensure that the franchisee has the exclusive use of his business name or symbol in a given territory. In order to comply with that undertaking the franchisor must not only refrain from establishing himself within that territory but also require other franchisees to give an undertaking not to open a second shop outside their own territory. A combination of provisions of that kind results in a sharing of markets between the franchisor and the franchisees or between franchisees and thus restricts competition with the network. As is clear from [*Consten & Grundig*], a restriction of that kind constitutes a limitation of competition for the purposes of Article 85(1) if it concerns a business name or symbol which is already well-known . . . (*citation omitted*)

Perhaps, the ECJ considered that unless the franchisee was told it must operate the franchise *only* from the designated site the franchisor was not *necessarily* bound to take action against a franchisee which chose to operate out of its territory.[68] But, it seems hardly likely that the Commission and even the ECJ would have much trouble rejecting a claim that the franchisor's action was purely unilateral if a franchisor subsequently acted against a franchisee for opening an outlet outside its territory – especially in competition with another member of the network.[69]

If the brand was already well-known, the ECJ considered that the need

---

68 This notion of the effect of exclusivity promises runs through Joliet, 'Trademark Licensing Agreements Under the EEC Law of Competition', at 755.
69 See for example 107/82 *AEG Telefunken v Commission* [1983] ECR 3151 (selective distribution); 277/87 *Sandoz Prodotti Farmaceutici SpA v Commission*, unreported judgment 11 January 1990, the operative part is at [1990] ECR I-45 (6th Chamber).

to encourage investment was relevant only under Article 85(3). Point 24
continued:

> It is of course possible that a prospective franchisee would not take the risk of
> becoming part of the chain, investing his own money, paying a relatively high
> entry fee and undertaking to pay a substantial annual royalty, unless he could
> hope, thanks to a degree of protection against competition on the part of the
> franchisor and other franchisees, that his business would be profitable. That
> consideration, however, is relevant only to an examination of the agreement in
> the light of the conditions laid down in Article 85(3).[70]

Exemption was not forthcoming, however. The franchise agreements had
not been notified. Nor could they benefit from the group exemption for
exclusive dealing since franchising was a transaction essentially different to
distribution.[71]

The reconciliation between point 24 and points 15 to 17 of the judgment,
and with *Maize Seed*, seems difficult. The ECJ, in the earlier parts of its
judgment, appears to be saying that conditions necessary to induce the
franchisor to enter the contract are not restrictions on competition. But, in
the later part, a condition necessary to get the franchisee in was a restriction
and could only be exempted. This leads to the absurdity that the franchisor
may protect itself and other members of the network but the other party to
the agreement cannot have the same protection!

The analogy made in point 24 to *Consten & Grundig* also appears
misplaced. In *Consten & Grundig*, the relegation of well-known brands
to Article 85(3) reflected a policy choice that intra-brand competition was
at least as important as inter-brand competition.[72] But, in *Pronuptia* there
was nothing to stop the franchisee from selling to customers from outside its
territory while in *Consten & Grundig* there were cumulative export bans and
apparent concertation to block any parallel imports.

Pronuptia, therefore, seems to have the contradictory effect of emphasising
the fact that *Maize Seed* depended on new technology, but reducing the
apparent endorsement of inter-brand competition.[73]

---

70 Unlike *Maize Seed*, there is no reference to the resources devoted by the franchisor,
but compare the earlier discussion of [1986] ECR 353 ¶16.
71 *Ibid.* at ¶15; for the same view, see Joliet, 'Trademark Licensing Agreements Under
the EEC Law of Competition', at 763 to 766. For a cogent critique, see Waelbroeck,
'The *Pronuptia* Judgment – A Critical Appraisal', at 224 to 225 and Valentine Korah,
Franchising and the EEC Competition Rules: Regulation 4087/88, ESC Publishing Ltd,
1989), at 22 to 23, 119.
72 Contrast *Consten & Grundig* to *Continental TV Inc. v GTE Sylvania Inc.* 433 US
36, 53 L Ed 2d 568 (1977), see Chapter 6, Notes 38 to 42.
73 If the brand's 'well-known' status corresponded to it also being an entrenched,
leading brand, vertical restraints might well constitute an anti-competitive danger: *see*
for example Robert L. Steiner, 'The Nature of Vertical Restraints', 30 *Antitrust Bulletin*
143 (1985) and, more generally, F.M. Scherer and David Ross, *Industrial Market
Structure and Economic Performance*, Houghton Mifflin, 1990 (3rd ed.), Chapter 15.
It has been argued that a more accurate translation of the French rendered here as
'well-known', *répandu*, is 'widespread', see Korah, *Franchising and the EEC Competition
Rules: Regulation 4087/88*, at 4 Note 5.

7.2.4   Erauw Jacquery

In *Erauw Jacquery*, two things are clear. The judgment concerned plant breeders' rights in basic seeds and, in relation to basic seeds, found that an export ban imposed on the licensee did not restrict competition contrary to Article 85(1).[74] After that, things are less clear. The Fifth Chamber may have justified the export ban on grounds either, or both, of the need to encourage investment or the specific nature of the plant breeders' rights in question. In any case, it seems reasonably certain that the export ban approved in *Erauw Jacquery* would have been caught by a wide interpretation of the definition of 'absolute territorial protection' in *Maize Seed*.

In Erauw Jacquery, the exclusive agent for Belgium of plant breeders' rights in E3 seeds of Gerbel multi-row barley licensed propagation and sales rights to a number of multipliers which produced basic and certified seed for sale to farmers for cereal crops.[75] Among other terms, the standard form contracts required the multiplier to abide by minimum prices fixed by the agent and forbade the multiplier either exporting basic seeds or exporting, directly or indirectly, the certified seed. One of the multipliers did not honour the fixed price and when sued pleaded Article 85 in its defence. In answer to the preliminary reference, the ECJ cleared the export bans but considered the price-fixing clause would be anti-competitive if it perceptibly affected trade between Member States. The national court was left to investigate whether the clause had this effect.

In clearing the export bans, the ECJ simply ruled:

> 10.   In this respect, it must be pointed out that, as the Court acknowledged in [*Maize Seed*] the development of the basic lines may involve considerable financial sacrifices. *Consequently*, a person who has made considerable efforts to develop varieties of basic seeds which may be the subject of plant breeders' rights must be allowed to protect himself against any improper handling of those varieties of seeds. To that end, the breeder must be entitled to restrict propagation to the growers which he has selected as licensees. To that extent, the provision prohibiting the licensee from selling and exporting basic seeds falls outside the prohibition contained in Article 85(1) of the Treaty.

> 11.   Therefore . . . a provision of an agreement concerning the propagation and sale of seed, in respect of which one of the parties is the holder or the agent of the holder of certain plant breeders' rights, which prohibits the licensee from selling and exporting basic seed, is compatible with Article 85(1) of the Treaty in so far as it is necessary in order to enable the breeder to select the growers who are to be licensees. (*Emphasis added*)

The Fifth Chamber's reasons seem to blend competing theories. The conclusion is almost a rule of *per se legality*, or at best an extremely

---

74   27/87 *Erauw Jacquery SprL v La Hesbignonne Société Co-opérative* [1988] ECR 1919 (5th Chamber). In fact, a third matter not relevant here is also clear: an obligation on the licensee to observe fixed prices is a restriction on competition caught by Article 85(1).

75   In very broad terms, 'basic' seed is seed engineered for the generation of 'certified' seed and, generally, must be generated anew each year. 'Certified' seed may be used either for the generation of more 'certified' seed or for sale, ultimately, to farmers for crop-sowing purposes.

truncated inquiry into the legal and economic context of the agreement. If the clause be necessary, it is not contrary to Article 85(1). There appears to be no need to investigate the state of inter-brand competition, whether there were barriers to entry or the possibility of parallel imports. The absence of inquiry into these factors is highlighted by two others. The Fifth Chamber, unlike the Advocate-General, did not distinguish between direct and indirect export bans.[76] The national court not having seen fit to refer a question about certified seeds, the Fifth Chamber seems to have ignored the export bans affecting those seeds. Second, once again unlike the Advocate-General, the Fifth Chamber considered the agreement constituted a horizontal relationship.[77]

Thus far relatively straightforward. Complications set in when trying to establish why the export ban was necessary. According to the ECJ in point 11, the export ban is permissible if it is necessary 'to enable the breeder to select the growers who are to be licensees'. Earlier, in point 10, it had said the breeder *must* have the right to limit production to the licensees chosen by it. This approach has overtones of the 'specific subject matter' approach taken in *Coditel II* and, indeed, the ECJ at point 9 reports the Commission as arguing that the ban on exporting basic seeds arose from the very *existence* of plant breeders' rights. The conclusion and process of reasoning used by the ECJ *identified so far* supports that thesis. But, it is not why the Fifth Chamber said the breeder must have the right to reserve production to its chosen licensees. Instead, at point 10, the right arose because of the breeder's considerable investment which, accordingly, gave it the right to protection against improper handling of its seeds. In the English, 'improper' here is ambiguous. Referring back to the breeder's considerable investment in development, it may mean simply 'unauthorised'. But, it could also anticipate what seem to be references to the specific subject-matter of plant breeders' rights and so may be referring to actions which would prejudice that specific subject-matter; in terms of *Maize Seed*, referring to 'the specific nature of the products in question'. The competition policy implications of the second meaning, which the Commission seems to favour, are potentially much narrower than of the first.[78]

Even if the second meaning be correct and *Erauw Jacquery* be confined to plant breeders' rights, the case does, however, represent a further advance on *Maize Seed* since it expressly permitted some export bans under Article 85(1).[79]

---

76 [1988] ECR 1919, at 1931 *per* Advocate-General Mischo, requiring a rule of reason analysis for the ban on direct exports but condemning the ban on indirect exports outright as tantamount to absolute territorial protection.

77 *Ibid.* at ¶15 on the price-fixing clause. Contrast Advocate-General Mischo at *ibid.* at 1930, 1932, showing also that the classification as horizontal was unnecessary to the conclusion that the price-fixing clause was illegal.

78 This seems to follow from its argument that the clause went to the existence of the right: *ibid.* at ¶9 and see further *Comasso*, see Note 181 below.

79 But note, unlike *Maize Seed* there was potential for intra-brand competition, at least within Belgium, since the multipliers' rights were not exclusive. This possibility would, however, have been chimerical if price fixing were allowed. Compare the US rule where the rule of reason treatment of vertical restraints is confined to non-price

7.2.5 Stergios Delimitis

The ECJ's ruling in the *Stergios Delimitis* case requires brief mention.[80] *Stergios Delimitis* did not concern the grant of an exclusive territory or export bans. It was a dispute between a café owner in Germany, Delimitis, and the brewer from which it had undertaken exclusively to buy its alcoholic and non-alcoholic drinks. When Delimitis terminated the arrangement, Henninger Bräu deducted some DM6,000 from the lease guarantee which it repaid him. He sued to recover the money, arguing that the agreement was in breach of Article 85 and not qualified for exemption.

The ECJ ruled that the agreement could not benefit from the special provision for beer supply agreements in Regulation 1984/83. First, the drinks covered by the agreement were only specified in a price list which Henninger Bräu could unilaterally alter. Hence, the drinks covered were not specified in the agreement as required by Article 6 of that regulation. Second, the agreement did not comply with the requirements of Article 8(2) since it did not expressly allow Delimitis to buy non-alcoholic drinks from third parties which offered them on more advantageous terms than Henninger Bräu.[81] Accordingly, if parts of the agreement were found to restrict competition contrary to Article 85(1), they would be void as the agreement had not been notified to the Commission.

For present purposes, interest in *Stergios Delimitis* lies in the guidance the ECJ gave the national court for determining whether or not the agreement in question, or part of it, restricted competition contrary to Article 85(1). The ECJ summarised its conclusions on this point in the following terms:

> 27. . . . a contract for the supply of beer is prohibited under Article 85, paragraph 1, of the EEC Treaty if it satisfies *two cumulative conditions*. In the *first* place it is necessary, taking account of the economic and legal context of the contract in dispute, for the national market for the distribution of beer in bars to be difficult to gain access to for competitors which might become established in this market or increase their share of this market. The fact that the contract in dispute is dependent, in this market, on a group of similar contracts which produce a cumulative effect on the interplay of the competition *only constitutes one factor* amongst others in assessing whether such a market is in fact difficult to gain access to. In the *second* place, it is necessary for the contract in dispute to contribute significantly to the blocking effect produced by all these contracts in their economic and legal context. The significance of the contribution of the individual contract is dependent on the position of the contracting parties in the market in question and on the duration of the contract. (*Emphasis added*)

That is, a contract for the supply of beer contravened Article 85(1) if two conditions were satisfied. First, the agreement, in the context of

---

restraints: *Continental TV Inc. v GTE Sylvania Inc.* 433 US 36 (1977) (although there is considerable debate over what is, and what is not, a price restraint).
80 C-234/89 *Stergios Delimitis v Henninger Bräu AG*, unreported, 28 February 1991. References are to an unofficial translation of the ruling provided by the ECJ.
81 For these points, see *ibid.* at ¶¶34 to 37 and 38 to 42 respectively. For beer agreements generally, see Valentine Korah and Warwick A. Rothnie, *Exclusive Distribution and the EEC Competition Rules*, Sweet & Maxwell, London, 1992 (2nd edn).

the cumulative effect of all such agreements in the Member State and that state's licensing requirements, must contribute to foreclosing entry into the market of rival brewers. But, second, even if rival brewers were foreclosed, the agreement in question itself must contribute to that foreclosure significantly. In the absence of both elements, the agreement would not restrict competition contrary to Article 85.[82]

Stergios Delimitis at best refers to the need to encourage incentives in investment only tangentially.[83] It primarily concerned an exclusive purchasing obligation rather than the creation of exclusive territories for which, arguably, greater concern might exist given the goal of integrating the internal market. Furthermore, there is a case for arguing that the rules applying to 'tied houses' under brewery contracts are less stringent than for other agreements.[84] *Stergios Delimitis* may, however, potentially have relevance for its confirmation of *Brasserie de Haecht (No. 1)* and the similarities in reasoning between that case and the *STM* case.[85] Although *Brasserie de Haecht (No. 1)* and *Stergios Delimitis* were not concerned with disseminating new technology, in common with *STM* and *Maize Seed* they also emphasise the role of inter-brand competition. All these cases instruct the relevant tribunal of fact to examine the impact of the agreement in its market context.

7.2.6 Summary

Since *Maize Seed*, the ECJ has shown an increasing willingness to permit agreements obstructing parallel imports under Article 85(1). The common justification in each case has been the need to encourage investment and its consequent spur to the dissemination of technology and the enhancement of inter-brand competition. In each case, however the ECJ also limited the general applicability of that justification by reference to at least one of two qualifications.

The broad principle is qualified by being tied to the specific needs of the subject-matter in question. Moreover, in at least two cases, the ECJ has purported to limit recognition under Article 85(1) of the need to encourage investment to 'new' rights. But, only in *Pronuptia* in the context of franchising, did the ECJ explicitly limit 'new' technology to a term shorter than the protection under the applicable intellectual property regime. These qualifications are consistent with arguments that the ECJ has not adopted

---

82 On determining whether the individual contract made a 'significant' contribution, see *ibid*. at ¶¶25 to 26.

83 *Ibid*. at ¶¶10 to 11 and compare Regulation 1984/83, recitals 13, 15 and 6.

84 See for example Zechariah Chafee Jr, 'The Music Goes Round and Round: Equitable Servitudes and Chattels', 69 Harv. LRev. 1250, at 1256, 1261 (1956) and compare Regulation 1984/83, Article 8(2).

85 23/67 *Brasserie De Haecht SA v Wilkin (No. 1)* [1967] ECR 407. See generally, Whish, *Competition Law*, at 230 to 232, 580 to 581.

a general rule.[86] Despite the ECJ's repeated reference to the nature of the specific subject-matter in issue before it, two other trends are observable.

The ECJ has not failed to accept the relevance of the need to encourage investment under Article 85(1) for *any* category of intellectual property it has considered since *Maize Seed*. In *Pronuptia*, the shortcoming in the agreement under consideration lay in the fact that the brand was well-known (the technology was not new) rather than the nature of franchising. Second, each case successively extended the justification to what within the EC has been regarded as ever more restrictive conduct. Once again, *Pronuptia* only failed to permit what was described as absolute territorial protection under Article 85(1) because the brand was well-known and, contrary to what seemed to have been the position in *Maize Seed*, the possibility of exempting absolute territorial protection in such circumstances was at least considered. Both of these trends are consistent with the argument that the need to encourage investment is of general application. This is hardly surprising since it is the rationale underlying intellectual property.

Notwithstanding this, the ECJ has not stated expressly that the principle is of general application. Its judgments are few in number and there are sufficient ambiguities and qualifications in them to leave ample scope for different views. Moreover, by far the majority of competition cases are determined by the Commission.

7.3   The Commission's Approach

Turning to the Commission, a number of characteristics stand out. It has accepted the need to encourage investment as qualifying the goal of integrating the internal market across the spectrum of intellectual property. But, it has almost invariably done so under Article 85(3) and not 85(1). Particularly under Article 85(1), its decisions seem to be expressed legalistically and formalistically. Taking its cue from *Consten & Grundig*, it does not view agreements broadly according to whether they are largely horizontal or vertical. Instead, it defines legal categories such as distribution (in which there are a number of subcategories), franchising, patent licensing and so on. This means that sometimes agreements having similar characteristics may well receive different treatment under EC competition policy depending on which category they are consigned to. Formalistically, the Commission often treats almost any fetter on the parties' freedom of action as a restriction of competition contrary to Article 85(1). This emphasises the significance of intra-brand competition at the expense

---

86 See for example Barry E. Hawk, 'The American (Antitrust) Revolution', [1988] ECLR 53, especially at 70 to 73 suggesting that the ECJ has at times applied approaches based on what is 'inherent' in the transaction and also accepted restraints which are 'ancillary' to a lawful transaction; Nicholas Green, 'Article 85 in Perspective: Stretching Jurisdiction, Narrowing the Concept of a Restriction and Plugging a Few Gaps', [1988] ECLR 190, at 195 to 201 suggesting three different approaches; 'inherency', 'ancillary' and 'dissemination of new technology'.

of analysing the agreement's impact on the market. Its analysis also stresses competition *ex post* and often seems predicated on an assumption that technology licences, in particular, are horizontal in nature. At times, this has led the Commission to adopt what seem to be strained interpretations of the ECJ's judgments.

7.3.1 Exclusivity as between the parties to the agreement

(a) *The Commission and distribution*

The Commission's treatment of attempts to restrain parallel trade within the EC by means of distribution agreements has formed the model on which its approach to licences of intellectual property is based. EC competition policy differentiates between forms of distribution quite rigidly: so far the main categories recognised include exclusive distribution, exclusive purchasing, selective distribution and various types of franchising. Selective distribution is further subdivided into 'simple' systems, and 'complex' systems where the obligations on the participants are more onerous and require exemption.

Anticipating *Maize Seed*, the ECJ in the *STM* case had earlier indicated that distribution agreements involving 'open exclusivity' (although, this phrase was not used) should be assessed by an approach like a 'rule of reason'.[87] But, in selective distribution systems the grant of exclusive territories automatically renders the agreement restrictive of competition.[88]

Exclusive distribution has two main components.[89] First and centrally, the supplier *must* agree to supply goods for resale to the reseller alone in a defined territory. Second, the reseller *may* agree to obtain its supplies of the goods in question only from the supplier.[90] Additional obligations may be included; in particular, relating to trade marks and get-up,[91] provision of customer support services, promotion of sales and stocking of complete ranges or minimum quantities.[92] Provided the reseller is only forbidden to engage in an active sales policy outside its territory and the agreement is not between competing manufacturers or does not otherwise lead to obstructing

---

87 See Chapter 6.2 above.
88 26/76 *Metro SB-Grossmärkte GmbH v Commission* [1977] ECR 1875, at ¶20 ('*Metro I*'); 86/82 *Hasselblad (UK) Limited v Commission* [1984] ECR 883 at ¶¶38 to 53.
89 Regulation 1983/83 (OJ 1983 L173/1 amended L281/24) now provides a group exemption for exclusive distribution, its counterpart for exclusive purchasing being Regulation 1984/83 (OJ 1983 L173/5 amended L281/24). See generally, Korah and Rothnie, *Exclusive Distribution and the EEC Competition Rules*; Whish, *Competition Law*, Chapters 17 to 18; Hawk, 2 *United States, Common Market and International Antitrust: A Comparative Guide*, Chapter 10.
90 In exclusive purchasing, the second obligation is compulsory and the supplier may not grant the reseller an exclusive territory: Regulation 1984/83, Articles 1 and 2.
91 170/83 *Hydrotherm v Andreoli* [1984] ECR 2999, see Note 147 below.
92 Notwithstanding these additional obligations, EC competition policy regards distribution and franchising as distinct and in several important respects treats them differently, see Note 71 above.

parallel imports, such agreements between only two undertakings in general qualify for group exemption.[93]

In an exclusive distribution system, the supplier may not control whom the reseller may sell to in its exclusive territory. The arrangements for distribution in the territory are left to the reseller.[94] But, in a selective distribution system, the distribution network is 'closed'. Effectively, each level of distribution may sell only to other authorised dealers or, ultimately, end-users.

Prior to the *STM* case, the Commission regarded 'open exclusivity' in distribution as a restriction on competition caught by Article 85(1) because it denied third parties the chance to act as distributors of the product on level terms with the exclusive distributor.[95] That the third parties could buy direct from the supplier (but outside the exclusive territory) and ship the goods in themselves was irrelevant under Article 85(1) as was the fact that there were many rival brands on the market. In these circumstances, exemption was forthcoming. But, unlike other types of agreement involving intellectual property licences, the need to encourage investment was not directly referred to. Instead, exclusivity was simply the price of the benefits which warranted exemption: the exclusive tie led to a rationalisation of distribution costs and intensification of sales effort in the contract territory while parallel import potential and competition from other brands restrained the dangers of price elevation above costs.[96]

These benefits, although ultimately expected to flow through to the consumer, are primarily savings on transaction costs which accrue to the supplier's advantage. The gains to the dealer in the form of encouragement to exploit the territory more intensively are seen indirectly, more as incidental to the supplier's advantage. The Commission did not place much weight on any interest the dealer might have in protecting its investment in making the market.[97] The Commission's limited view of why exclusivity might be sought

---

93 Since exclusive purchasing does not accord the reseller an exclusive territory, it may not ban an active sales policy by the reseller. For export bans, see section 7.3.2 and for absolute territorial protection, see section 7.3.3.

94 Regulation 1983/83, recital 8; Regulation 1984/83, recital 8. See also *Omega* [1970] CMLR 182, at 197; an old case. It is unclear, but the obligation on the exclusive distributor to use a selective distribution system took the agreement outside the forerunner of the present group exemptions, Regulation 67/67, probably because the selective distribution was coupled with quantitative limits on the number of resellers which could be appointed.

95 See *Blondel* [1965] CMLR 180, at 181 to 182; *Isbecque/Hummel* [1965] CMLR 242, at 244 and *Maison Jallatte/Voss-Vandeputte* [1966] CMLR D1, at D3 discussed in Joliet, *The Rule of Reason in Antitrust Law*, at 146 to 152. See also Note 112, below.

96 *Ibid.* at 182 to 183; 244 to 246 and D4 to 5, respectively. The exclusive distribution regulation is similarly limited. The reference under Article 85(3) to the competitive factors keeping price down shows that the Commission, even at this early stage, viewed competition under Article 85(1) as a very narrow intra-brand concept (not even taking into account the potential for parallel imports).

97 On transaction costs, see R.H. Coase, 'The Nature of the Firm', (1937) 4 *Economica* reprinted in R.H. Coase, *The Firm, the Market and the Law*, University of Chicago Press, 1988, Chapter 2; Oliver E. Williamson, *Markets and Hierarchies*, Free Press, 1975, both accounts emphasising incentives to invest.

and given in these distribution cases contrasts with its equally one-sided view of the role of the need to encourage investment in other areas and even in some later cases where exclusive distribution is combined with selective distribution. Even where it does recognise the need to encourage investment, the Commission often fails to recognise, or does not expressly admit, that the licensor/supplier may have a valid investment in its own market to protect. The ECJ, on the other hand, in cases like *Maize Seed*, *Coditel II*, *Pronuptia* and *Erauw Jacquery*, appears to recognise the licensor/supplier's interest.

Whether the *STM* case led to much change in the Commission's approach is debatable. In later distribution cases involving exclusivity the Commission adopted the same narrow interpretation of 'competition' under Article 85(1) and the Commission's subsequent treatment of exclusivity in other areas such as patents, franchising, plant breeders' rights and know-how mirrors that taken in *Maison Jallatte/Voss-Vandeputte*. But, many distribution agreements will include more obligations than mere 'open' exclusivity, providing ample scope for the Commission to find a 'restriction'.[98]

The treatment of selective distribution has a number of similarities to the Commission's approach to exclusive distribution. The central concept of selective distribution systems under EC competition policy is that the distribution network is closed.[99] Distributors within the network can generally only sell to other distributors within the network or to end-users. The permissible object of such restraints is to ensure that goods of a particular nature receive the high-quality treatment the supplier believes consumers require to get the benefit of the product. Examples include complex consumer goods where consumers are likely to require a broad range to choose from and extensive advice from trained sales staff perhaps backed up by after-sales services such as installation assistance, technical advice, sufficient range of spare parts and guarantee service;[100] motor vehicles;[101] watches;[102] and high-quality porcelain dinner sets and ornaments.[103] If, first, the standards set are objective and not applied in a discriminatory manner (that is, anyone who meets the standards can gain admission to the network) and second, members are free to sell at their own prices to customers anywhere in the common market and provide their

---

98 It has also been suggested that conditions in the EC may not warrant the same degree of liberality as in the United States, see Michel Waelbroeck, 'Vertical Agreements: Is the Commission Right not to Follow the Current US Policy?', 25 *Swiss Review of International Competition Law* 45 (1985). This would certainly be a relevant consideration, but it is not the reasoning the Commission publishes. Nor does it explain why many of the additional restrictions also benefit from automatic exemption under the group exemptions.

99 On selective distribution, see Paul Demaret, 'Selective Distribution and EEC Law After *Ford*, *Pronuptia* and *Metro II*', [1986] *Fordham Corporate Law Institute* 149; R.J. Goebel, 'Metro II's Continuation of the Selective Distribution Rules: Is this the end of the Road?', (1987) 24 CMLRev. 605 and generally Whish, *Competition Law*, at 613 to 624; Hawk, 2 *United States, Common Market and International Antitrust: A Comparative Guide*, at 483 to 525.

100 *Metro I* and 75/84 *Metro v Commission (No. 2)* [1986] 1 CMLR 118 ('*Metro II*').

101 Regulation 123/85, OJ 1985 L15/16.

102 *Omega* [1970] CMLR 189.

103 *Villeroy & Boch* [1988] 4 CMLR 461.

after-sales services to all consumers regardless of where in the common market the customer bought the product,[104] the selective distribution system is 'simple' and not caught by Article 85(1).

Why selective distribution systems established according to 'qualitative' criteria only do not restrict competition is not clearly explained. Certainly, they may lead to a rationalisation of distribution and a more intensive sales effort. But, the explanation must in part also lie in some form of free rider phenomenon. Although it will not always be the case, distributors may refuse to assume the extra burdens of the selective network if at the same time they will face competition from dealers able to sell at cheaper prices since they do not have to provide the additional services. Advocate-General Slynn implicitly acknowledged as much in *Hasselblad* by recognising that *quantitative* requirements may be justifiable under Article 85(3).[105] Further support can be found in the Commission's earlier exemption of the Omega selective distribution system which did not admit all qualified dealers but limited entry according to the perceived size of the market. There, the Commission recognised that the advantages of more intensive sales efforts and customer service would not be forthcoming unless each retailer could achieve a certain level of turnover. Hence, limiting the number of retailers who met the necessary standards admitted to the network was indispensable.[106] However, in the context of selective distribution systems, the Commission is reluctant to exempt obligations which confer some degree of territorial protection on dealers.[107]

(b)   *The Commission and patents*

For patent and know-how licences, the Commission's approach may be traced back to *Davidson Rubber*.[108] There, Davidson, a US company, held patents and secret know-how for the production of upholstered items used in motor vehicles such as elbow rests and seat cushions. To exploit its technology in the EC where it did not operate, it granted three exclusive manufacturing and sales licences in 1959, one for each of France, Germany and Italy. The sales exclusivity was limited since each licensee was permitted

---

104   *Metro I*, at ¶20; 86/82 *Hasselblad (UK) Limited v Commission* [1984] ECR 883, at ¶¶34 to 35, 46; *Bayo-n-ox* OJ 1990 L21/71 [1990] 4 CMLR 930, at ¶56 (under appeal T-12/90 OJ 1990 C92/14).
105   *Ibid.* at 921 to 923.
106   *Omega* [1970] CMLR 182, at 199.
107   Compare *Hasselblad* [1984] ECR 883; the Commission also apparently required Omega to remove its quantitative limits at a later date because of 'changed conditions': see D. G. Goyder, *EEC Competition Law*, Clarendon Press, 1988, at 218. Motor vehicles, however, appear to be a special (but increasingly questioned) case where exemption is the rule: Regulation 123/85, OJ 1985 L15/16. For the possibilities of mixed systems to co-exist even for intra-brand competitors, see Yvon O. Heckscher, 'Parallel Imports Furore: A Case of Smoke Exhalation?', 15 *International Business Lawyer* 32 (1987); Scherer and Ross, *Industrial Market Structure and Economic Performance*, Chapter 15.
108   [1972] CMLR D52.

to sell to a car manufacturer based in its territory for supply to subsidiaries outside the territory.

The evidence indicated that Davidson's licensees had achieved a 20 per cent market share in Germany, 40 per cent in France and only 8 per cent in Italy where the licensee used a process of its own, developed after it took the licence. According to the Commission, Davidson's process was the most important in the EC for making elbow rests, being the only one patented. But, there were a number of alternative methods available, some older and some newer. Indeed, Davidson's process was almost solely used for producing elbow rests since competing processes were often considered more suitable for other applications. Apart from Davidson's licensees, there were 12 other main manufacturers spread through the territories. These accounted for about one-third of car manufacturers' requirements since the car manufacturers also made their own supplies using the various competing processes (including Davidson's).

Having forced Davidson and its licensees to drop, among other things, the requirement of sales exclusivity,[109] the Commission still found the licence agreements *noticeably* restricted competition:

> 35. . . . [Davidson] undertook to each of those undertakings to authorise no-one else to exploit its patents and its know-how concerning elbow-rests and cushions for cars in a defined part of the territory of the Common Market.
> 36. A patent confers on its holder the exclusive right to exploit the invention covered by it. The holder may cede, by licences, for a given territory, the use of the rights derived from its patent. However, if it undertakes to limit the exploitation of its exclusive right to a single undertaking in a territory and thus confers on that single undertaking the right to exploit the invention and to prevent other undertakings from using it, it thus loses the power to contract with other applicants for a licence. In certain cases such exclusive character of a licence relating to industrial property rights may restrict competition and be covered by the prohibition set out in Article 85(1).
> 37. In the present case, as set out above, the Davidson process is the most important process for manufacture of elbow-rests for cars. The number of competing processes, like the number of manufacturers using them, is limited and the Davidson licensees hold a considerable share of the market in those articles in the EEC, if account is taken of the fact that the car manufacturers themselves manufacture large quantities for their own needs. In those circumstances, although mitigated by the provision that the sale of the contract articles can be freely made between member-states of the EEC, the exclusivity conferred by [Davidson] to each of its licensees has the consequence, apart from the restriction of liberty on [Davidson], that the position of third parties, particularly the manufacturers of interior fitments for cars, who may wish to use the process in question is noticeably altered since they are prevented from exploiting this process within the Common Market.[110]

109 The parties effectively had the benefit of sales exclusivity for 11 years since the Commission did not force the change until October 1970: *ibid.* at ¶13.
110 Contrast the Commission's earlier position in the non-binding *Official Notice on Patent Licensing Agreements*, JO 1962 No. 139/2922, item I. E (24 December 1962) reproduced in an unofficial translation CCH, *Common Market Reports* at ¶2698. The Notice cleared such restraints as unlikely to affect trade between the Member States and because they were more akin to 'unobjectionable' assignments, see Part III of the Notice.

But, after exploring the economic impact of the licences under Article 85(3), the Commission exempted the amended agreements. They were desirable because a more efficient manufacturing process was introduced and exploited in the EC and this would not have happened without the exclusivity accorded the licensees which was necessary to enable them to appropriate the benefits of their investments:

> 47. . . . [Davidson] would not have succeeded in having its new process used in Europe by third parties if it had not agreed to limit its licensees in that part of the world to a small number of undertakings by giving them an assurance that in the territories assigned to them it would not cause them to have competition from new licensees. Indeed, in the present case, without exclusivity the licensees would not have agreed to make the investments necessary to develop the process and adapt it to the requirements of the European market.

That is, the Commission under Article 85(3) accepted for patents and know-how the rationale of protecting investment which has subsequently been adopted by the ECJ under the competition rules and, more limitedly, under the 'free movement' rules. But, as point 47 of *Davidson Rubber* makes plain, the Commission regarded the incentive worthy of protection as the licensee's, not the foreign licensor's. Once the sales exclusivity was removed so that the licences conferred open exclusivity, contrast the more extensive consideration made by the ECJ in *Maize Seed*.

The Commission found Davidson's licences were caught by Article 85(1) because in *certain cases*, the grant of exclusivity under an industrial property licence *may* restrict competition and, in the specific circumstances of *Davidson Rubber*, manufacturing exclusivity (and even more so sales exclusivity) did so *noticeably*.[111] This was because Davidson lost its freedom to license other manufacturers and (which seems to be the reverse side of the same coin):

> . . . the position of third parties, particularly the manufacturers of interior fitments for cars, who may wish to use the process in question is noticeably altered since they are prevented from exploiting this process within the Common Market.[112]

---

111 The emphasis is the present author's. Although the agreements related to both patents and know-how, it seems likely that the Commission is referring only to the patents in the phrase 'industrial property licence'. It is not until the mid-1980s that the Commission began treating know-how as technology capable of being licensed like a patent rather than as information to be communicated once and for all, see Korah, *Know-how Licensing Agreements and the EEC Competition Rules*, at 10 to 11, 53. As discussed in 7.3.1(c) below, however, very similar principles evolved.

112 [1972] CMLR D52 at ¶37. Point 39 goes on to explain the impact of manufacturing exclusivity on parallel imports. Since rivals cannot exploit the technology, they are denied any opportunity to export to other parts of the common market and so trade between Member States is potentially affected. There is more than some degree of irony in finding that an agreement voluntarily entered into by Davidson deprived it of its liberty. The agreement did, of course, prevent third parties contracting with it, but that is the effect of any contract. The two-sided formulation, taken from the distribution cases, bears considerable similarity to *Klor's Inc. v Broadway-Hale Stores* 359 US 207, at 213 (1959), the reasoning of which, if not the result, is criticised in Thomas G. Krattenmaker and Steven C. Salop, 'Anticompetitive Exclusion: Raising Rivals' Costs to Achieve Power Over Price', 96 Yale LJ 209, at 220, 222 Note 56 and 268 to 272 (1986).

These factors suggest that the Commission had not yet concluded that exclusive licences automatically restricted competition contrary to Article 85(1) as the German government feared in *Maize Seed*.[113] The restriction on third parties was noticeable because Davidson's process was the most important. Although there were competing processes in the market, they were limited in number as was the number of rival manufacturers and the Davidson process accordingly held 'a considerable share of the market'.[114] Strangely, this last finding depended on including the market shares of the car manufacturers which made some of their own requirements in competition with the independent licensees and only some of whom used Davidson's process on a royalty-free basis.

The reasoning bears many of the hallmarks later rejected by *Maize Seed* for new technology: it assessed the state of the market *ex post*; the analysis is more appropriate to horizontal agreements and seems incomplete. Unlike the ECJ in *Maize Seed*, the Commission did not consider under Article 85(1) the licensees' refusal to invest without the promised exclusivity. Nor could any of the licensees use its patents without Davidson's permission. After the licences had been granted, competition in the market would be increased by allowing the licensees to sell against each other and even by allowing third parties access to the technology. However, as *Maize Seed* shows, looking at the situation after the licences have been granted – analysing *ex post* – is the wrong time to assess competitive impact. Before any licences were granted – analysing *ex ante* – there was no competition to restrain since no-one was prepared to risk investing in the new technology and creating a new market without protection. On the Commission's approach, there is a danger that the incentive to invest in such technology licences in the future may be chilled as parties realise they will not keep the protection they need. For this reason, in *Maize Seed*, the ECJ specifically mentioned that INRA's hybrid maize seeds were unknown to German farmers at the time INRA and Eisele embarked on their co-operation and that the desirable investment would not have been made without the promised exclusivity. Hence, the ECJ treated such licences as vertical and analysed competitive impact *ex ante*.

Moreover, assuming that the licensees' market shares be considerable, two further points need to be considered. The very point of intellectual property rights is to confer some degree of market power.[115] Then, competition in the

113 [1982] ECR 2015, at ¶55. Compare also *Burroughs/Delplanque* [1972] CMLR D67 and *Burroughs/GEHA* [1972] CMLR D72 where the licence agreements received negative clearance (not exemption) because (1) market share was only 10 per cent, (2) there were no barriers to imports from other parts of the EC and (3) the sales licences were non-exclusive: see ¶6 of each report. ¶5 of each report is in identical terms to ¶36 of *Davidson Rubber*.

114 The Italian licensee had an 8 per cent share, although it was in the process of switching to a new process of its own, the German licensee had captured 20 per cent of its market and the French, 40 per cent. In addition there were at least 12 other manufacturers: [1972] CMLR D52, at ¶¶31 to 32. In the statement of facts, the importance of Davidson's process appears to rest in large part on its status as the only one accorded patent protection: *ibid.* at ¶31.

115 Contrast the approach taken in the United States in *Studiengesellschaft Kohle mbH* 670 F. 2d 1122 (DC Cir. 1981), see Chapter 3 from Note 230.

market-place (as distinct from opportunities to use a particular process or product) is only inhibited if third parties' opportunities to enter the market are foreclosed. This requires that there be significant barriers to entry which *Davidson Rubber* does not really explore.[116] From the reported information, however, there seem considerable doubts that any barriers would have been substantial. Davidson did hold two patents. But, in themselves they did not block market access since there were competing processes. In addition, royalty payments to Davidson from its licensees were falling, suggesting perhaps that their use of Davidson's process or its value was declining. Moreover, one of the licensees had developed its own unpatented process which it was using more and more. The Commission also seems to overlook the nature of the product and the end-user. Car manufacturers are not such shrinking violets that they could be intimidated and exploited by the suppliers of mere elbow rests, especially as they had production capacity of their own.

The subsequent treatment of patents and of exclusivity in other areas reinforces concern that the Commission was not really assessing market impact under Article 85(1), or did so only for a short-lived period.

In *Kabelmetal/Luchaire*, Kabelmetal in Germany licensed its patents and know-how for a cold steel extrusion process exclusively to Luchaire in France. After the Commission forced removal of a ban on exports to other parts of the EC, an exemption was granted because the licensee would not otherwise have invested. The analysis followed *Davidson Rubber* closely. Luchaire was estimated to have captured only 20 per cent of the French market and faced direct competition from six rivals using different cold extrusion processes. In addition, there was a range of other manufacturing processes available such as deep drawing and machining, casting, and forging and sintering.[117] The Commission, having described the licensed process as important, described 'the number of strictly competing and comparable processes' and the number of rival manufacturers as 'relatively small'. That end-users also made their own products and Kabelmetal had 'a considerable turnover in Germany' also aggravated the anti-competitive impact. Once more, Kabelmetal lost its own freedom and the position of third-party potential licensees was 'seriously' affected.[118]

---

116 Contrast the ECJ's directions in *Stergios Delimitis*, section 7.2.5 above, a case of exclusive purchasing. There is no clear agreement on what constitutes a barrier to entry and when it will be significant. Government regulation controlling access, such as licensing requirements or, in some cases, patents, is a fairly clear example as is a minimum efficient scale large in relation to the size of the market. But, an intellectual property right does not in itself create a dominant position: 24/67 *Parke, Davis & Co. v Probel* [1968] ECR 55; 238/87 *Volvo AB v Eric Veng (UK) Limited* [1989] 4 CMLR 122 and 53/87 *Consorzio Italiano della componentistica di Ricambio per Autoveicoli e Maxicar v Regie Nationale des Usines Renault* [1990] 4 CMLR 265, see further section 7.4 below. Beyond these examples, much depends on the time scale (the longer the assessment period, the lower barriers are likely to be) and belief about who should be permitted access – all comers or only those potentially as efficient as the incumbents.
117 [1975] 2 CMLR D40, at ¶¶17 to 18.
118 *Ibid.* at ¶25; compare *Davidson Rubber* [1972] CMLR D52 at ¶37. Describing the number of rival processes and producers as 'relatively small' signals an unrealistically atomistic conception of the market. The size of Kabelmetal's turnover in Germany

Next, the Commission denied exemption for an exclusive licence to make and sell coupled with a partial export ban in view of the other restrictions on competition in the agreement.[119] For the first time, the Commission alluded to the dichotomy between the existence and the exercise of the right: neither exclusivity nor the export ban went to the existence of the patent right and, accordingly, exclusivity was simply '. . . an appreciable restriction of competition in view of the size of the licensee's turnover in respect of the patented devices, and of its market share in France and in certain other member-States of the EEC.'[120] Why the size of the licensee's turnover in the licensed products hindered third parties' ability to compete is not explained since the licensee held a mere 6.98 per cent of the French market in face of competition from 'a number of other types'.[121]

The decision advised that an exclusive licence and even some forms of export ban could be exempted if it provided 'a stimulus for the licensee to penetrate a territorial, or product, market not yet exploited by the licensor'.[122] However, as in its own *Maize Seed* decision, it was unnecessary to consider exemption for these aspects as other 'restrictions' precluded an exemption anyway.[123]

After *Maize Seed*, the Commission adopted its group exemption for patent licences.[124] In addition to permitting some forms of export ban, this provided automatic exemption to a licensor's promise not to compete for sales in its licensees' territory and also a licensee's promise not to invade the licensor's territory provided the other conditions of the group exemption were met. Having set out its interpretation of *Maize Seed* in recital 11 and stating that

suggests the Commission thought Kabelmetal was capable of expanding into France (and all the other EC markets) itself, thus rendering the agreement horizontal: compare Hartmut Johannes, 'Technology Transfer Under EEC Law – Europe between the Divergent Opinions of the Past and the New Administration: A Comparative Law Approach', [1982] *Fordham Corporate Law Institute* 65, at 83 to 84 (although speaking in his personal capacity, then Head of Division for Industrial Property Rights, Commission's Competition Directorate-General). For criticism of the Commission's assumption (in a distribution context), see 56 & 58 *Consten & Grundig* [1966] ECR 299, at 370 to 371 *per* Advocate-General Roemer.

119 *AOIP v Beyrard* [1976] 1 CMLR D14. The intervening decision, *Zuid-Nederlandische Bronbemaling en brond-Boringen BV v Heidemaatschappij Beheer NV* [1975] CMLR D67, did not involve exclusivity and was clearly a horizontal cartel entrenched by high entry barriers; for a horizontal conspiracy condemned in the United States, see *International Wood Processors v Power Dry Inc.* 792 F. 2d 416 (4th Cir. 1986).

120 *Ibid.* at ¶21. But see ¶37 for the rubric about restricting third parties' access to the technology.

121 *Ibid.* at ¶¶14 to 15. Less helpfully, we are also told the licensee had 17.63 per cent of French exports to other parts of the Common Market. The proportion of the licensee's turnover devoted to the products was FF8 million out of FF190 million.

122 [1976] 1 CMLR D14, at ¶39. The export ban which might have been approved was permitted to have as its object the mutual protection of the parties or other licensees.

123 *Ibid.* at ¶40. These included agreement not to challenge the validity of the licensed patents, a non-competition obligation and royalty payments continuing past the expiry of the patent most recent at the date of the contract: *ibid.* at ¶41.

124 Regulation 2349/84, OJ 1984 L219/15. See generally, Valentine Korah, *Patent Licensing and the EEC Competition Rules: Regulation 2349/84*, ESC Publishing, 1985.

agreements not within the definition should be accorded similar treatment, the Commission explained in recital 12 that exclusivity obligations should be *exempted* because they:

> generally contribute to improving the production of goods and to promoting technical progress; they make patentees more willing to grant licences and licensees more inclined to undertake the investment required to manufacture, use and put on the market a new product or to use a new process, so that undertakings other than the patentee acquire the possibility of manufacturing their products with the aid of the latest techniques and of developing those techniques further. The result is that the number of production facilities and the quantity and quality of goods produced in the common market are increased.

Thus, in the context of Article 85(3) *not* 85(1), the Commission accepted the need to encourage investment to help disseminate new technology and almost treated patent licences as vertical relationships. As in *AOIP/Beyrard*, however, the investment explicitly acknowledged is that to be undertaken by the licensee.[125] The difference in meaning attributed to 'competition' for the purposes of Article 85(1) and (3) is not explained.

As with the other obligations relating to territorial protection under the patent regulation, exclusivity as between licensor and licensee may last only 'in so far and as long as one of the licensed patents remains in force'.[126] Hence, if the licensor or licensee were to promise the other not to compete with it for sales in a territory where a patent either was no longer in force or had never been granted, the group exemption would be lost.[127]

(c)   *The Commission and know-how*

The Commission now treats know-how much the same as patents, although this was not always the case.[128] In the know-how group exemption, recitals 6 and 7 (first half) correspond to recitals 11 and 12 in the patent group exemption,[129] as do Articles 1(1)(1) to 1(1)(3) in each. Since know-how

---

125   In *AOIP v Beyrard* [1976] 1 CMLR D14, the Commission did, however, refer to the mutual protection of both licensor and licensee at ¶39, a rare hint that the licensor is entitled to protection against competition from its own licensee, perhaps picked up in the group exemption by the reference to improving the patentee's willingness to license and leading to exemption for reciprocal promises of exclusivity between licensor and licensee.

126   Regulation 2349/84, Article 1(1)(1) to 1(1)(3).

127   *Boussois/Interpane* [1988] 4 CMLR 124 discussed in Korah, *Know-how Licensing Agreements and the EEC Competition Rules*, at 8, 41 to 43. On the problem of exclusive licences to undertakings holding a dominant position on the market, see *Tetra Pak* [1990] 4 CMLR 47, below from Note 239.

128   See generally, Korah, *Know-how Licensing Agreements and the EEC Competition Rules*, Chapter 1; Siragusa, 'Technology Transfers Under EEC Law: A Private View', [1982] *Fordham Corporate Law Institute* 95, at 104 to 111. The know-how regulation even suggests that in some respects know-how may need greater protection since it is not a proprietary right: Regulation 556/89, OJ 1989 L61/1, recital 2.

129   The concept of 'competition' is, however, introduced into know-how regulation, recital 6: Korah, *Know-how Licensing Agreements and the EEC Competition Rules*, at 56. The individual decisions setting out the encouragement of the licensee's investment

does not have a fixed term, the know-how regulation limits the benefit of the group exemption to a period of ten years for the first licence affecting the territory.[130] This may be extended for the life of any patents included in the technology package if this be longer although it is unclear whether the patents need to be in force in the territories of both the licensor and the licensee.[131]

The know-how regulation in many respects treats technology transfers more liberally than the patent regulation. In particular, it does not require the patents to be the 'dominant' component of the package,[132] nor need patents exist in all Member States provided some secret, substantial and identified know-how exists in each.[133] However, the technology licence must still be the main purpose of the agreement and if the main purpose is rather the licensing of some other intellectual property, such as a trade mark or copyright, the know-how regulation will not apply.[134]

(d)   *The Commission and plant breeders' rights*

Maize Seed, of course, concerned plant breeders' rights and there the Commission treated the 'open exclusive' aspect of the agreement in the same way as it treated open exclusivity in the patent cases.[135] The ECJ, as already discussed, did not uphold this aspect of the decision. The most recent consideration by the Commission is *Comasso*, after the ECJ's ruling in *Erauw Jacquery*, and is more directly concerned with the treatment of export bans and absolute territorial protection.[136]

(e)   *The Commission and franchising*

In *Pronuptia*, the ECJ distinguished between three types of franchise: production, distribution and service franchises. Broadly speaking, the difference appears to be that, in the first, the franchisor provides know-how and a brand image to the franchisee so that the latter can make the product which it sells under the franchise while, in the second case, the franchisor

---

are *Campari* [1978] 2 CMLR 397, at ¶68; *Mitchell Cotts/Sofiltra* [1988] 4 CMLR 111, at ¶25; *Boussois/Interpane* [1988] 4 CMLR 124, at ¶20; *Rich Products/Jus-rol* OJ 1988 L69/21, ¶¶41, 43; *Delta Chemie/DDD* OJ 1988 L309/34, at ¶¶41, 43.
130   Regulation 556/89, Article 1(2).
131   Regulation 556/89, Article 1(4), and see Korah, *Know-how Licensing Agreements and the EEC Competition Rules*, at 117 to 119.
132   *Boussois/Interpane* [1988] 4 CMLR 124, at ¶19.
133   Contrast *ibid*. for patent licensing.
134   *Moosehead/Whitbread* OJ 1990 L100/32; [1991] 4 CMLR 391, at ¶16. The know-how regulation does not expressly require that the patents be ancillary, rather it extends to patent and know-how agreements (where the licensee manufactures) which do not qualify under the patent regulation: Regulation 556/89, Article 1(7)(6) and see Korah, *Know-how Licensing Agreements and the EEC Competition Rules*, at 88 to 90, 100.
135   [1978] 3 CMLR 434, at ¶36 (449 to 450).
136   See Note 181 below.

also supplies the product so that the franchisee largely acts as a reseller. In a service franchise, the 'product' is the provision of some service by the franchisee under the franchise.[137] It is unclear how these different categories will be treated since the ECJ has considered only distribution franchises. The Commission, however, has signalled its intention to treat distribution and service franchises virtually identically.[138]

The ECJ has not considered production franchises. In two cases, the Commission has relied on reasoning similar to that in the distribution and technology licensing cases to find the exclusive rights under a trade mark accorded to the franchisee/licensee restrictive of competition but granted exemptions.[139]

For distribution and service franchises, the Commission has applied the ECJ's ruling in *Pronuptia* virtually without deviation.[140] It goes even further and accords automatic exemption to such agreements which include open exclusivity and location clauses.[141] So one might question the need to find them restrictive of competition in the first place. This becomes particularly apparent from the way the Commission applied the ECJ's ruling in *Pronuptia* in the individual decisions preceding the adoption of the group exemption.[142]

In none of the cases considered by the Commission was either franchisor or its network dominant or otherwise able to prejudice competition by denying market access to rival brands since competition was vigorous and entry at the retail level was easy. In two, the franchise brand at most accounted for 1 to 2 per cent;[143] and in others market share did not exceed 5 per cent throughout

---

137   For example, cleaning services as in *Service Master* [1989] 4 CMLR 581.

138   *Service Master* [1989] 4 CMLR 581; the franchise regulation, Regulation 4087/88, recital 4.

139   *Campari* [1978] 2 CMLR 397; *Moosehead/Whitbread* OJ 1990 L100/32; [1991] 4 CMLR 391; from Note 148 below.

140   For the restrictive effect and franchisee incentive, see *Pronuptia* [1989] 4 CMLR 355 at ¶28; *Yves Rocher* [1988] 4 CMLR 592, at ¶¶54, 63; *Computerland* [1989] 4 CMLR 259, at ¶¶25, 33; *Charles Jourdan* [1989] 4 CMLR 591, at ¶¶32, 39; and *Service Master* [1989] 4 CMLR 581, at ¶¶32, 39 (services).

141   Regulation 4087/88, recitals 7, 9 and 10, Articles 2(a), (c), 3(1)(c) and 3(2)(i). The agreement must, of course, comply with the other requirements of the regulation to benefit from its group exemption, on these see Korah, *Franchising and the EEC Rules Competition Rules*. Provided there are only two parties to the agreement the main exclusions are agreements between competing producers, agreements instituting absolute territorial protection or resale price maintenance and a limitation on the permissible post term use restraint to a period of one year.

142   Korah hopes that this was because of the jurisdictional requirement to acquire experience before promulgating a group exemption under Regulation 19/65, see Korah, *Franchising and the EEC Rules Competition Rules*, at 6 to 7. But, the practice is almost as old as the Commission's competition policy (see for example Joliet, *The Rule of Reason in Antitrust Law*, at 150 to 151, 174 to 176) and the adoption of a group exemption does not seem to lead to a change in practice. *Velcro/Aplix* [1989] 4 CMLR 157, where the Commission confined its decision to the period after the expiry of the last of the patents initially licensed, might suggest a different approach, but contrast T-30/89 *Hilti AG v Commission* [1992] 4 CMLR 16.

143   *Charles Jourdan* [1989] 4 CMLR 591, at ¶5, where the Commission defined the market narrowly as 'medium to high quality shoes' rather than shoes to reach even this level and *Computerland* [1989] 4 CMLR 259, at ¶3, but market share assessed by sales value soared to 4 per cent and the Commission relied on the network's plans to expand.

most of the EC.[144] Moreover, the restriction of intra-brand competition (on which the ECJ's ruling in *Pronuptia*, point 24 turned) appeared negligible in many cases. Yves Rocher started off as a mail order business and had 10 million mail order customers as well as about 1,000 franchise outlets whose average annual turnover was less than ECU300,000 each. Charles Jourdan sold its products through franchise outlets, 'franchise corners' in major department stores and through general shoe retailers. Only one franchisee was appointed for each territory, but franchise corners and general retailers could be (and were) appointed within franchise territories. Computerland franchisees were not so much given exclusive territories as promised that a competing outlet would not be set up within a one-kilometre radius (two kilometres for the first year of operation) and they were permitted to sell to and advertise for customers outside that area.

(f) *The Commission and trade marks*

As the franchising cases show, obligations relating to trade marks often occur in agreements dealing with other forms of distribution and licensing. They are often treated benignly. But, EC competition policy's layered approach usually requires them to be analysed as separate agreements which must also conform to the competition rules. The most famous instance is, of course, the first: in *Consten & Grundig* the assignment of the trade mark *GINT* was used to reinforce the system of absolute territorial protection created in the distribution agreement.[145]

If the trade mark obligations do not implement or reinforce a closed territory, the ECJ has indicated a fairly benign approach in the few instances where it has considered the issue. For example, in *Pronuptia* in the context of franchising, a location clause alone was cleared on the ground of protecting the brand's reputation. But, in combination with territorial exclusivity – itself permitted on grounds of protecting the franchisor's interest in its know-how – the well-known brand became an instrument of territorial partition.[146] Similarly, in *Hydrotherm*, the ECJ upheld the application of the group exemption to a plainly 'open' exclusive dealership coupled with the assignment of a trade mark unless the parties actually used the trade mark assignment to obstruct parallel imports.[147]

However, in what amount to 'production franchises', the Commission has applied the same formalistic approach to exclusive licences as it adopted for licences of patents, know-how and plant breeders' rights and in the

---

144 *Service Master* had 6 per cent in the United Kingdom, but like *Computerland* planned to expand. *Yves Rocher* [1988] 4 CMLR 592 had 15 per cent for some products in France, but even there averaged only 7.5 per cent.
145 See also 28/77 *Tepea v Commission* [1978] ECR 1391; 279/87 *Tipp-Ex GmbH & Co. KG v Commission*, unreported judgment of 8 February 1990, the operative part is at [1990] ECR I-261 (5th Chamber); but contrast 170/83 *Hydrotherm v Andreoli* [1984] ECR 2999, Note 147 below.
146 *Pronuptia* [1986] ECR 353, at ¶¶19, 24; above at section 7.2.3.
147 170/83 *Hydrotherm v Andreoli* [1984] ECR 2999, at ¶¶20 to 22.

pre-*STM* distribution cases. In *Campari*, Campari-Milano communicated its know-how for the production of Campari bitters to national licensees, granted them exclusive licences of its trade mark, subjected them to a non-competition requirement and also forbade actively selling outside the allotted territory. Campari-Milano also prescribed quality standards for the product and manufacturing plant and supplied each licensee with the special Campari ingredient. Although the network was partially closed, the Commission granted exemption by analogy to the distribution cases. It analysed the exclusive trade mark rights as a restriction on competition separate to the ban on active sales because the licence deprived Campari-Milano of the chance to compete in the territory itself and to license third parties.[148] Exemption followed because of the more intensive exploitation in a vigorously competitive market. Exclusivity was indispensable because:

> 77. . . . none of the licensees and in all probability no other undertaking in the spirituous liquors industry would have been prepared to make the investment necessary for a significant increase in sales of Bitter if it were not sure of being protected from competition from other licensees or Campari-Milano itself.

By the time the exemption expired, Campari-Milano had integrated forward: in some cases replacing its exclusive licensees with wholly-owned subsidiaries, in others turning them into exclusive distributors.[149]

The decision in *Moosehead/Whitbread* suggests that the Commission's approach has not changed markedly.[150] However, on the broader market analysis which the author has argued for under Article 85(1), the oligopolistic state of the UK brewing and retail market indicate that the dangers of foreclosure seem much greater than in many of the earlier decisions.[151] Curiously, the Commission examined the impact of exclusivity under Article 85(1) *ex post*, while assessing other potential restraints, such as the agreement not to challenge the validity of Moosehead's trade mark, *ex ante*. Since the Commission was there prepared to concede that the trade mark was not well-known,[152] one might have expected the need to encourage investment also to have been considered under Article 85(1).[153]

So, at this stage, the Commission's approach requires each case to seek individual exemption which will be of limited duration and thus require renegotiation on expiry. There may be considerable disincentives in this

---

148 [1978] 2 CMLR 397, at ¶¶51 to 52.

149 *18th Report on Competition Policy*, EC Commission, 1989, at ¶69.

150 OJ 1990 L100/32; [1991] 4 CMLR 391. See Warwick A. Rothnie, 'EC Competition Policy, the Commission and Trade Marks', (1991) 19 *International Business Lawyer* 495.

151 Monopolies and Mergers Commission, *The Supply of Beer*, Cm 651, HMSO, 1989. From Moosehead's point of view, not Whitbread's, a production and distribution agreement with Whitbread or one of the other 'big six' brewers was probably the only way Moosehead could build up a significant presence in the market.

152 OJ 1990 L100/ 32; [1991] 4 CMLR 391, at ¶15.4(b).

153 Compare *Pronuptia* [1986] ECR 353 at ¶24.

process.[154] Other implications are less clear. It is plain from *Moosehead* that the know-how regulation will not apply if the Commission believes the main object of the agreement is the trade mark licence.[155] Furthermore, from *Campari*, it seems that the location clause permissible may not ban a change in premises absolutely. Although the Commission cleared a clause limiting the franchisee's power to shift manufacturing premises in its territory to plant meeting the franchisor's objective, technical standards relating to quality,[156] such franchisees are not the 'small' businessmen envisaged by the ECJ in *Pronuptia*. Nor, subject to any need to ensure the quality of production, does there seem to be the same need to control the location and layout of manufacturing premises as for customer outlets.

(g)   The Commission and copyright

The Commission, as in its patent licensing decisions, distinguishes between the existence of copyright and its exercise. Obligations which go to the existence of copyright are untouched by the competition rules while those which relate merely to its exercise must conform to the requirements of the competition rules.[157]

Most of the Commission's reported comments on agreements involving copyright have focused on contractual export bans affecting goods embodying copyright works.[158] But, in *GEMA-Custom Pressing*, the Commission suggested that anything other than a non-exclusive licence for the whole EC is a restriction on competition. Apparently, some record labels arranged to have their discs intended for sale in other parts of the EC pressed in Germany and GEMA

---

154 As Omega found out for its selective distribution system, continuing exemption of exclusivity is not necessarily a matter of form (although where circumstances have changed careful scrutiny is certainly warranted): see D.G. Goyder, *EEC Competition Law*, Clarendon Press, 1988, at 218. When Campari's exemption came up for renewal, the Commission found its modes of distribution had substantially changed. In some Member States, Campari had integrated into production itself and in others had replaced its franchisees with exclusive distributors: *18th Report on Competition Policy*, EC Commission, 1989, at ¶69.

155 OJ 1990 L100/32; [1991] 4 CMLR 391, at ¶16.1.

156 [1978] 2 CMLR 397, at ¶61.

157 See for example the Commission's explanatory memorandum accompanying its proposal for a Council directive on the legal protection of computer programs OJ 1989 C91/16; reiterated in the *18th Report on Competition Policy*, EC Commission, 1989, at ¶42 as demonstrating the Commission's 'conclusions about the relationship of copyright and the competition rules'. For criticism of this approach, in the context of patents, see Richard M. Buxbaum, 'Restrictions in the Patent Monopoly: A Comparative Critique', 113 UPenn.LRev. 633 (1965); Louis Kaplow, 'The Patent-Antitrust Interface: A reappraisal', 97 Harv. LRev. 1813, at 1845 to 1849 (1984); Willy Alexander, 'The Horizontal Effects of Licensing a Technology as Dealt with by the EEC Competition Law', [1988] *Fordham Corporate Law Institute* Chapter 11.

158 *Knoll/Hille-Form* in *13th Report on Competition Policy*, EC Commission, 1984, at ¶144; *Nielsen-Hordell/Richmark* in *12th Report on Competition Policy*, EC Commission, 1983, at ¶88; *STEMRA* in *11th Report on Competition Policy*, EC Commission, 1982, at ¶90; *Ernest Benn Ltd* in *9th Report on Competition Policy*, EC Commission, 1979, at ¶118; and *Dutch Publishers' Association* in *6th Report on Competition Policy*, EC Commission, 1976, at ¶153.

sought a royalty from the custom presser. According to the brief details published by the Commission, 'standard practice' in the industry only charged the supplier at the place of supply and not the presser in the place of production. The Commission declared:

> ... a licence granted by a Community copyright protection society is valid throughout the Community, and authorizes manufacture, even by way of custom pressing, in any Member State. In that event, however, it is in principle for the supplier alone, and not for the pressing firm, to obtain a licence to manufacture sound recordings and pay royalties. A separate requirement to pay royalties to the national copyright protection society having jurisdiction over the place of manufacture according to the rates applicable there would in practice mean the re-erection of national barriers by contractual means between Member States. The Court of Justice in 1981 [Cases 55 & 57 *Musik-Vertreib Membran v GEMA*] decided that this is not permitted under Community law, even if the royalty fees differ from one Member State to another.[159]

The decision highlights the complexity caused by the national regulation of intellectual property in the internal market. Arguing from the free movement cases, the rights to control reproduction and, under German law, distribution are assimilated into one; consent to one action includes consent to the other. But, *GEMA-Custom Pressing* goes further than *Musik-Vertrieb*. In *Musik-Vertrieb*, the right owner was still allowed to choose which products it would release on to the market, and, having done so, bore the consequences of free movement. *GEMA-Custom Pressing* could be seen as undermining that power of choice in that, having elected to release some goods into the market, the power to select which ones is removed. The difference is largely one of degree. But, the ECJ has not expressly gone so far under the free movement rules.[160] Moreover, despite the Commission's analogy to the rules governing patent licensing, the Community Patent Convention would permit infringement actions against a licensee exercising the patent outside its appointed territory.[161] The shift is disclosed further by consideration of the competition rules. The condemnation of the royalty charge on the custom presser corresponds to the finding in *Davidson Rubber* that manufacturing exclusivity restricted competition which the ECJ rejected for new technology in *Maize Seed*.

In the *ARD* case, the Commission, relying on the grant of exclusivity disproportionate in duration to the needs of the film and television industries,

---

159 *15th Report on Competition Policy*, EC Commission, 1986, at ¶81. For earlier applications of the same principle, see *BIEM-IFPI* in *13th Report on Competition Policy*, EC Commission, 1984, at ¶150 and *The Old Man and the Sea* in *6th Report on Competition Policy*, at ¶164.
160 The point was avoided in *Pharmon*, see Chapter 6 from Note 167, and note the problems under the competition rules in *Maize Seed*.
161 CPC, Article 42(2) OJ 1989 L401/10, 30 December 1989. There is, of course, the question of how far the CPC reflects the EEC Treaty. For the Commission's view that copyright licensing is subject to the same principles as patent licensing, see *6th Report on Competition Policy*, at ¶162; *Nielsen-Hordell/Richmark* in *12th Report on Competition Policy*, at ¶88.

distinguished *Coditel II*, but exempted exclusive rights to broadcast feature films on television.[162]

Simplifying, ARD, one of four television networks broadcasting nationally in Germany, entered into three agreements with the copyright owners of the MGM and United Artists' film library. Under the most important agreement, ARD bought the exclusive right to broadcast 1,350 of MGM and United Artists' films in the German language for a large part of German-speaking Europe (including Germany, Luxembourg and Province Alto Adige). ARD had to broadcast the films for a first time at some stage between 1984 and 1998 and, from the date of that first broadcast, retained its exclusive rights over the film (including, usually, the right to an unlimited number of repeats) for 15 years. The agreement covered existing films and films to be produced in the future. Although it included the James Bond films, it did not include MGM's seven most popular films such as *Gone With The Wind* and *Ben Hur*. Under the agreement, ARD's exclusivity was subject to two 'licensing windows' by which MGM and United Artists could license third parties broadcast rights on pay-TV for up to 25 per cent of ARD's films for one year.

The second agreement gave ARD an exclusive right to go through MGM and United Artists' film library during a three-year selection period to choose which of the 3,000 existing films it wanted. During this period, MGM and United Artists could not grant broadcast rights for the library to other television stations in the contract area. ARD also bought a right of first negotiation which required MGM and United Artists to give ARD the option of licensing rights in the remaining films on the same terms as any third party MGM and United Artists proposed to license. This right ran from late 1983 until the end of 1996.

Applying its familiar approach with an alarming twist, the Commission found that the agreements restricted competition because they restricted third parties' access to the films, but, after forcing some changes, granted an exemption. More films than previously were made available to German consumers at cheaper rates and there was sufficient competition both at the film production level and the television broadcast level to ensure that the benefits were passed on.

The changes the Commission forced during negotiations included permitting MGM and United Artists to license non-German-language broadcasts for the territory and a greater number of 'licensing windows'. Under these additional windows, ARD agreed to pay up to half the dubbing and print costs of any licensee if prints did not already exist.

On its face, the *ARD* case seems to show the Commission engaging in some attempt under Article 85(1) to assess the impact of the agreement in its market context. Closer examination belies the appearance. In the Commission's eyes, *Coditel II* did not apply because too many films were

---

162 *German Television Stations Film Purchases* OJ 1989 L284/36 under appeal T-157 & 168/89 OJ 1990 C14 and 23; see Warwick A. Rothnie, 'Commission Re-runs Same Old Bill (Film Purchasing by German Television Stations', [1990] EIPR 72.

licensed for too long. So, the exclusivity was disproportionate to the needs of the industry. The extra licensing windows did not relieve this because *third parties* were still denied *full* access to the films.[163] That is, intra-brand competition was restricted. The alarming aspect is the Commission's stated reason for its conclusion: it was not customary in the industry for television networks to enter into agreements for so many films for so long; ARD itself had never done so. It can hardly be right that competition policy, which in large part must be about the search for innovation and the encouragement of innovation through flexibility, condemns something just because it is novel.

The Commission dismissed the fact that ARD tied up only 4.5 per cent of the world's film stock by pointing out that the licence's selective nature gave it 'an importance which went beyond the purely numerical quantity involved'.[164] Moreover, the Commission did not even refer to two other important considerations. MGM and United Artists could hardly be held to ransom by ARD. In Germany, ARD was only one of four national networks with a fifth developing. Admittedly, in its statement of facts (not its reasons) the Commission suggested that ARD as a publicly-owned network had an advantage over its private competitors because it could resort to funding from licence fees as well as advertising revenues. The private networks had been broadcasting only since 1984 but the development of a fifth network hardly suggests the private sector was struggling to compete.

The second important omission is the shadowy presence of the licensing intermediary referred to in passing at points 28 to 29 of the factual record. This body tied up German-language broadcasting rights to 15,000 feature films (50 per cent of the world's stock) including 'the essential parts' of the American majors. It also had endless supplies of television product (50,000 hours compared to the 416 ARD bought with its film rights). It seems normal industry practice would be to license a few films from the majors for short periods and, more frequently, go cap in hand to the licensing intermediary for a sub-licence. Ordinarily, one would expect competition policy to encourage a reduction in such monolithic powers or at least explain why it was not a relevant consideration.

Doubts about these aspects are reinforced by the identity of the appellants from the Commission's decision: not ARD, but the apparent beneficiaries of the windfall, extra licensing windows, MGM/UA Co., one of the film library owners. Now that ARD had done the hard work for it by selecting the best prospects for German television broadcast (including many not previously thought suitable),[165] it presumably anticipated a stronger bargaining position if it could put the rights up for auction afresh.

The rejection of these inter-brand factors coupled with the reference to third parties being denied *full* access to the films shows the Commission engaging in a formalistic analysis which seems largely at odds with the

163   For these three points, see *ibid.* at ¶¶43 to 45.
164   *Ibid.* at ¶43.
165   The author is grateful to Professor Korah for this comment on the author's suppositions in [1990] EIPR 72.

broader inquiry recommended by the ECJ in *Coditel II*. Similarly, the Commission's analysis of the selection period and, to a lesser extent, the right of first negotiation. In neither case did the Commission explore why ARD might have required such rights although each was exempted without modification indicating their indispensability.

The question still remains how far the Commission's approach illustrated by *GEMA-Custom Pressing* is consistent with the ECJ's in *Coditel II*. In *Coditel II*, the ECJ was dealing with broadcast/performing rights which it reaffirmed had different implications to articles embodying copyright works. So, the answer depends on how broadly or narrowly the principles in *Coditel II* and *Maize Seed* extend. The sort of formalistic analysis underpinning *GEMA-Custom Pressing* with its emphasis on restrictions on conduct and *ex post* analysis, however, also underpins the Commission's approach in the *ARD* case, at least insofar as it treats open exclusivity as restrictive of competition *per se*. Accordingly, *GEMA-Custom Pressing* seems inconsistent with both *Maize Seed* and *Coditel II*.

7.3.2 Export bans

On the layered approach taken under EC competition policy, export bans represent a step up from promises of exclusive rights in the degree of seriousness. In the simplest case, of a direct ban on the exclusive concessionaire exporting out of its territory, parallel imports (and so, market integration) are directly interfered with. The impact of these may well be magnified by the 'network effect': similar promises by other members of the network in other territories. EC competition policy has also been astute to detect indirect disincentives operating like export bans such as differential pricing where a higher price must be paid for export.

Under its group exemptions, however, the Commission permits bans on actively seeking customers outside the conceded territory ('active sales') as a matter of course. In technology licensing, the group exemptions even permit bans on filling unsolicited orders from customers outside the seller's territory ('passive sales') for more limited periods. These 'automatic' exemptions do not apply if the members of the network conspire to obstruct parallel importing by third parties or if the contracting parties are rival producers where the risks of market sharing are higher.[166]

Arguably, once again, the underlying rationale of these exemptions is the need to encourage desirable investment; investment which increases the range of choice available to consumers by enhancing inter-brand competition. The same purpose motivates the ECJ's most far-reaching step since *Maize Seed*. In *Erauw Jacquery*, it refused to condemn export bans as automatically restrictive of competition,[167] thus confirming to some extent those who argue

166 Individual exemption may sometimes be possible by analogy: most recently *Fluke/Philips* OJ 1989 C188/2; [1990] 4 CMLR 166 (19(3) Notice); *Moosehead/Whitbread* OJ 1990 L100/32; [1991] 4 CMLR 391 but contrast *Siemens/Fanuc* OJ 1985 L376/29.
167 Section 7.2.4 above.

for a broad interpretation of *Maize Seed*. The Commission, however, appears to have other ideas.[168]

(a) *Direct export bans*

In distribution arrangements, *Consten & Grundig*, which included a network of reciprocal export bans as part of the scheme of absolute territorial protection, established EC policy. The ECJ has subsequently confirmed on a number of occasions that export bans in distribution arrangements are of their very nature restrictions on competition contrary to Article 85(1), permitted under EC competition policy, if at all, only on exemption by the Commission. Many of the cases include absolute territorial protection as well as export bans. But, the simple case seemed to have been at stake in *Miller International*. There, the German producer of a range of budget sound recordings bound its distributor for Alsace-Lorraine not to sell outside its territory and the ECJ rejected the producer's appeal from the Commission's condemnation.[169]

But, provided parallel imports were possible and the agreement was not between rival producers of any significance, the Commission would exempt a limitation on active sales by the dealer (that is, a partial export ban). The dealer, however, must still be permitted to sell to customers outside its territory if they approached it. The explanation offered for this exemption is the intensification of inter-brand competition and cheaper prices resulting from the elimination of transaction costs and the more effective establishment of the brand in the licensed territory by encouraging the dealer to concentrate its sales efforts there.[170]

Eventually, the Commission evolved a similar position for technology licensing although, initially, it had refused to countenance the grant of exclusive sales rights at all.[171] Now, under the patent regulation, the ban on 'active' sales may last as long as licensed patents are in force in both the licensed territory and the territory where the licensee is forbidden

---

168   See *Comasso* OJ 1990 C6/3; [1990] 4 CMLR 259 (19(3) Notice), see Note 181 below.

169   19/77 *Miller International Schallplatten GmbH v Commission* [1978] ECR 131. The appeal concentrated on the issue of whether the agreement would have an appreciable effect on trade between Member States. The defences that the trade was too insubstantial in volume and would not take place in view of the economic circumstances were rejected out of hand. See also 22/71 *Béguelin* [1971] ECR 949, at ¶12 see Chapter 6.2 Notes 66 to 67 above; 319/82 *Société de Vente de Ciments et Betons v Kerpen & Kerpen* [1983] ECR 4173, ¶¶6 to 7. The latter seems to have been a horizontal conspiracy, see the cases cited by the Commission at [1983] ECR 4177 to 4178, 8/72 *Cementhandeleran* [1972] ECR 977 and 43/73 *Suiker Unie* [1975] ECR 1662, adopted by Advocate-General Verloren van Themaat at 4188.

170   See for example Regulation 1983/83, Article 2(2)(c) and recitals 6 and 8.

171   *Davidson Rubber* [1972] CMLR D52, see section 7.3.1(b) above. This was apparently in part because the Commission viewed technology licences as horizontal rather than vertical arrangements, see *Campari* [1978] 2 CMLR 397 and Johannes, 'Technology Transfer Under EEC Law – Europe between the Divergent Opinions of the Past and the New Administration: A Comparative Law Approach', at 83 to 84.

actively to pursue sales.[172] The ban may last ten years from the date of the first licence in the EC or the duration of any patent protection, whichever is longer, under the know-how regulation.[173] The ramifications for parallel territories are complicated and not altogether clear.[174] If sufficiently substantial know-how ceases to remain secret in the licensed territory, however, the exemption under the know-how regulation is automatically lost.[175] Given the explanation for not extending the benefit of the patent regulation to parallel territories not covered by patents, it would seem that either a licensed patent or substantial, secret know-how must also exist in the parallel territory. But, the rationale of concentrating the licensee's efforts in its licensed territory contradicts this conclusion.

For technology licences, the Commission has now gone further than the distribution rules in two respects. First, for both patent and know-how agreements, in addition to the ban on active sales it will also permit a ban on satisfying unsolicited orders, passive sales, for a limited period of five years from the date the product is first marketed in the EC under the patent regulation or, under the know-how regulation, for five years from the first licence of the know-how in the EC.[176] The existence of parallel patents does not extend the potential term of the passive sales ban under the know-how regulation.

The second advance on the distribution rules in the Commission's treatment of export bans in technology licences lies in the justification for exemption. The Commission expressly acknowledges that bans on exports into parallel territories may be necessary to encourage transfer of the technology.[177] This illustrates the somewhat artificial nature of the Commission's acceptance of the need to encourage investment, particularly in its individual decisions. It may be possible to say the licensee's investment is encouraged by promises of manufacturing exclusivity and of no sales competition from the licensor. But, the licensee's need for protection from competition does not justify its own promise not to export into a parallel territory (although confining it may intensify its efforts there). Any encouragement to invest comes only from the licensee's understanding that the licensor will extract similar promises from the other licensees, thus

---

172 Regulation 2349/84, Article 1(1)(4) to 1(1)(5). The requirement of patents subsisting outside the licensee's territory follows from the regulation's wording: see *Boussois/Interpane* [1988] 4 CMLR 124 discussed Korah, *Know-how Licensing Agreements and the EEC Competition Rules*, at 41 to 43. The requirement for a subsisting patent in the licensee's territory is implicit in the regulation and see now *Bayo-n-ox* OJ 1990 L21/71; [1990] 4 CMLR 930.

173 Regulation 556/89, Article 1(1)(4) to 1(1)(5), 1(2) and 1(4). In theory, longer terms may be sought by individual decision.

174 On this point generally, see Korah, *Know-how Licensing Agreements and the EEC Competition Rules*, at 116 to 119.

175 Regulation 556/89, Article 1(6).

176 Regulation 2349/84, Article 1(1)(6); Regulation 556/89, Article 1(1)(6), 1(2). Under the patent regulation parallel patents are required as for active sales and substantial know-how remaining secret is necessary under the know-how regulation. In theory, longer terms may be sought by individual decision.

177 See for example Regulation 2349/84, recital 12; Regulation 556/89, recital 7.

preventing them from competing directly with the licensee in question. Indeed, the Commission's interpretation is also not true for the licensee's reciprocal promise not to compete for sales in the licensor's territory which, if necessary, be so for the licensor to license at all.[178]

Franchisees, and the licensees of trade marks, may be subjected to bans on pursuing active sales policies outside their licensed territories.[179] Although these started off by analogy to distribution systems, the Commission has expressly recognised that the restraint is necessary to encourage investment in the network as well as concentrate efforts within the concession.

Arguably in line with *Consten & Grundig*, *Maize Seed* and *Pronuptia*, the Commission's treatment of export bans has been by way of exemption under Article 85(3). But, more recently, in *Erauw Jacquery*, the ECJ went even further and *cleared* export bans; according the owner of plant breeders' rights the right to obtain protection against 'improper' handling of its varieties, although, it was unclear from the context precisely what 'improper' meant.[180] The Commission had argued that the right was necessary to guarantee the *existence* of the plant breeders' rights subject-matter and, subsequently, it appears unsurprisingly to be opting for a narrow interpretation.

Comasso concerned the arrangements between licensing and collecting agencies of plant breeders' rights and the commercial multipliers which produce the basic and certified seed[181] for sale to farmers for cereal crops. Among other things, the multipliers, licensed to produce and sell seed according to the licensed variety, were subjected to a number of bans on export. The multiplier itself was forbidden to export: (1) basic seed; (2) certified seed which had not been on the common catalogue for at least four years; (3) first generation certified seed to Member States (a) recognising two or more generations of certification or (b) which did not recognise plant breeders' rights. (However, the export ban on first generation certified seed was relaxed if the seeds were reclassified as being for non-regenerative purposes.) In addition, each multiplier was required to forbid its customers (that is, third parties) to export basic seed and first generation certified seed.

In its 19(3) Notice, the Commission announced its intention to treat all these bans 'favourably', subject to any submissions of third parties. That

---

178   Regulation 556/89, recital 7 refers to the need to encourage technology transfer and thus may be more positive. Recital 12 of Regulation 2349/84 refers to increasing patentees' willingness to license and yet the subsequent know-how decisions reverted to the licensee encouragement theory. On the reluctance of licensors to license when they perceive threats to their 'domestic' market, see Bleeke and Rahl, 'The Value of Territorial and Field of Use Restrictions in the International Licensing of Unpatented Know-How: An Empirical Survey', at 450 and Mansfield, Romero and Wagner, 'Foreign Trade and US Research and Development', at 54 to 56.

179   Regulation 4087/88, Article 2(c); *Campari* [1978] 2 CMLR 397; *Moosehead/Whitbread* OJ 1990 L100/32; [1991] 4 CMLR 391.

180   [1988] ECR 1919, at ¶10.

181   *Comasso* OJ 1990 C6/3; [1990] 4 CMLR 259, a 19(3) Notice. Where it is used for generation purposes, certified seed needs handling largely as if it were basic seed and is classified as 'first generation' certified seed; 'second generation' seed, generated from first generation certified seed, is used only for sowing.

is, on the information before it, the Commission considered that the clauses either do not restrict competition contrary to Article 85(1) or, if they do, merit exemption under Article 85(3). This is an important advance in a number of respects.

The Commission's intentions go further than the ECJ in *Maize Seed* in that the obligations to be imposed on customers not to export certainly appear to trespass into the area delimited by 'absolute territorial protection'. In addition, both *Maize Seed* and *Erauw Jacquery* applied only to basic seeds and Advocate-General Mischo in the latter considered the corresponding bans on certified seeds to be absolute territorial protection.

It is not clear, however, on what basis the Commission proposes its favourable treatment. It might be thought that the agreements insofar as they do not limit exports by purchasers should be cleared following *Erauw Jacquery*; the controls on first generation seed being analogous to those on basic seed. This may possibly be the outcome. Whether clearance or exemption ensue, it seems that the Commission will do so on the more limited interpretation of *Erauw Jacquery* suggested earlier. The 19(3) Notice devoted considerable space to the delicate nature of engineered plant varieties and the complicated legal regime evolved to maintain the commercial utility of hybrids. This could lead the Commission to approve the obligations on the ground that the breeder must be able to take steps to protect its investment in developing the licensed variety. However, the emphasis devoted to the legal regime affecting the marketing of varieties suggests that the Commission will base itself on the breeder's legal obligation to control quality.[182] The proposed favourable treatment even for bans on parallel imports, could be justifiable on either ground.[183] But, it goes much further than the ECJ or the Commission have previously permitted under the need to protect investment.

Informally, in a distribution case, the Commission has also *cleared* a ban on active sales, although the clearance was put on the grounds that the restriction was not appreciable rather than no restriction at all.[184] Finnish Paper Mills Association ('Finnpap') operated a joint sales organisation for newsprint. According to the Commission, about 60 per cent of the EC's needs were 'homegrown', the remaining 40 per cent coming from imports. Finnpap accounted for about 9 per cent of the EC's total newsprint needs (although in the United Kingdom and Denmark it was one of the five major suppliers, with market share between 8 and 15 per cent and 13 and 19 per cent, respectively). Two or three other non-EC suppliers also had similar market shares. Indeed, apart from Finnpap, EC newsprint users could turn to at least three large Swedish suppliers, one large Norwegian supplier and Finnpap's rival in Finland. In addition, supplies were available from Austria

---

182   See for example *Bayo-n-ox* OJ 1990 L21/71; [1990] 4 CMLR 930, at ¶¶40 to 42.
183   For the application of the investment incentive rationale to absolute territorial protection, see *Maize Seed* and *Erauw Jacquery*.
184   IP(89) 496, 27 June 1989. For the 19(3) Notice, see OJ 1989 C45/4.

and Canada, the latter not yet fully utilising its duty-free quota. These facts suggest that Finnpap was not really in a position to exercise market power.

However, Finnpap had registered its request for clearance as long ago as January 1980 and clearance was only granted *after* Finnpap agreed to permit passive sales: the organisation's rules were changed to permit EC purchasers to buy directly from individual members (although such sales would be taken into account in Finnpap's allocation of orders among its members).

According to the Commission's Press Release, by permitting passive sales the joint sales organisation was 'not now liable substantially to affect trade between Member States'.

This conclusion, rather than explaining the effect of relaxing exclusivity, seems to follow from the finding in the 19(3) Notice that newsprint was a product highly tailored to the individual customer's needs. Hence, it was rare for newsprint to be imported into one Member State and re-exported to another.[185] It would seem also that the characteristics of the market were such that buyers of newsprint were likely to seek out suppliers rather than *vice versa*. So, the ban on passive sales would take on increased importance. Despite this, the Commission allowed the association to take into account any passive sales made by an individual member when allocating shares under the orders it obtained.

Accordingly, while it could be argued that, on a broad view, the Commission was approaching recognition that exclusivity *per se* did not restrict competition, it seems more likely that *Finnpap* is explicable on the special nature of its facts. Its members were small concerns and the industry had a special nature, there was unlikely to be any trade between the Member States.

(b)   *Implied export bans*

Apart from express prohibitions on export, suppliers and licensors have resorted to a variety of measures which may indirectly limit a firm's ability to export.[186] One common method is differential pricing, charging a higher price (over costs incurred) for goods intended for export. Only slightly less blatant are restrictions on output or unilateral reductions in quantities supplied. As in other areas, the slightest suggestion of an intention to partition the common market will attract *per se* condemnation by the Commission under Article 85(1) and the prospects of exemption are slim.

The Commission's well-known decision in the *Distillers Red Label* case is a notable example.[187] The price at the wholesale level for Distillers' scotch, gin and Pimms were much higher on the continent than in the United Kingdom.

---

185   OJ 1989 C45/4 at point 8.
186   On the use of discriminatory terms in warranty protection and other discriminatory measures not considered here, see Whish, *Competition Law*, at 583 to 584.
187   [1978] 1 CMLR 400 appeal dismissed 30/78 [1980] ECR 2229. See Hawk, *United States, Common Market and International Antitrust: A Comparative Guide*, at 416 to 421.

To maintain this, Distillers adopted a uniform list price but offered its UK distributors generous discounts for agreement not to export the spirits to other Member States. Distillers sought to justify this by differences in market conditions between the United Kingdom and the continent which, it claimed meant its continental distributors had to incur considerably higher marketing costs than its UK distributors. Scotch, gin and Pimms were not as well established on the continent where they faced resistance from traditional, national preferences reinforced by discriminatory national taxes. In addition, Distillers' main competitors for scotch and gin sales on the continent were not the same as its main rivals in the United Kingdom and, were it to raise its prices in the United Kingdom, it would rapidly lose sales to rival brands while allowing imports from the United Kingdom would undermine the continental marketing scheme by free riding.[188]

The differential prices were condemned under Article 85(1) of their very nature. They were clearly designed to impede parallel imports from the United Kingdom to the rest of the EC and this isolation of the United Kingdom deprived consumers in the rest of the EC of the benefit of the lower UK prices.[189] The logic is inescapable, but it ignores Distillers' point: its products could not be in both markets without some discrimination.

In a decision heavily criticised by Advocate-General Warner,[190] the Commission addressed and bluntly rejected this point under Article 85(3). It ruled that price discrimination intended to hinder exports could not improve distribution or benefit consumers.[191] Even if it could, it was not indispensable since, contrary to Distillers' assertions, its spirits were not new products which required extraordinary promotional efforts to secure market share. (This seems to repeat the ECJ's approach in *Consten & Grundig*.) In any case, there were less restrictive ways of achieving the same result. For example, according to the Commission, Distillers could take on the promotional costs itself or (which amounts to the same thing) it could charge continental distributors lower prices instead of the same prices as its UK distributors. As in *Consten & Grundig*, without any apparent exploration of whether Distillers had sufficient resources to undertake promotion costs itself for the whole of the continental market or whether there were any other reasons why Distillers operated there through independent firms, the Commission proclaimed its assertions over Distillers' protests to the contrary.

---

188 On the economics of these effects, see C.W.F. Baden Fuller, 'Economic Issues Relating to Property Rights in Trademarks: Export Bans, Differential Pricing, Restrictions on Resale and Repackaging', (1981) 6 ELRev. 162, at 169.
189 [1978] 1 CMLR 400 at ¶¶91 to 92.
190 The decision is attacked even more scathingly by several commentators, see Ivo Van Bael, 'Heretical Reflections on the Basic Dogma of EEC Antitrust: Single Market Integration', 8 Swiss Rev. of Int'l Antitrust Law 39 (1980); Valentine Korah, 'Goodbye, Red Label: Condemnation of Dual Pricing by Distillers', (1980) 3 ELRev. 62 and J.S. Chard, 'The Economics of the Application of Article 85 to Selective Distribution Systems', (1982) 7 ELRev. 83; but for a defence not distinguishing between dominant brand owners and competitive markets, see Thomas Sharpe, 'The Distillers Decision', (1978) 15 CMLRev. 447.
191 [1978] 1 CMLR 400, at ¶111.

The ECJ did not reach the substantive questions, upholding the Commission's decision on the formal ground that Distillers had failed to notify its agreements properly.

Subsequently, Distillers withdrew Red Label Scotch from the UK market. Not only did continental customers fail to get the benefit of the low UK prices, but the UK customers were deprived of the opportunity to buy the product at all. It also raised the price of two other brands of its whisky in the United Kingdom and reduced the price of a third on the continent. Sales in the United Kingdom of the first two declined markedly and sales of the third on the continent also reduced to insignificance.[192] After further negotiations with Distillers, the Commission announced that it was considering exempting a dual pricing scheme to facilitate the re-introduction of Red Label Scotch into the United Kingdom. The announcement emphasised the exceptional circumstances of the case and stressed the very limited nature of the proposal under consideration: for one brand and for a very short period on a stepped, reducing basis.[193] In the event the Commission avoided formally setting the precedent when the notification was abandoned after it had been under consideration for some seven or eight years.[194] During this period, Distillers was presumably able to practise the price discrimination subject to the uncertain status of an arrangement meriting, but not granted, 'favourable treatment'.

In a rare case, *Sandoz*, the Commission has accepted that there could be justifications for what appear to be indirect export bans while at the same time condemning an express export ban: the invoices were endorsed 'Export Prohibited'.[195] During the investigation into the express export ban, the Commission's interest was also attracted by the Sandoz subsidiary's practice of unilaterally supplying its customers with quantities lower than they had ordered. According to the Commission reducing supplies to customers may be an attempt to obstruct parallel trade by limiting the customer's capacity to that thought sufficient to satisfy the demands of its local territory. However, the Sandoz subsidiary was able to provide the Commission with evidence supporting other, permissible motives. The reductions were part of its overriding need to plan production, its warehouse policy and distribution in Italy. Its evidence indicated customers often ordered unusually large quantities to take advantage of delayed payment periods resulting from holidays and warehouse shortages arising at the start and end of years or for short-term causes in local markets.[196]

---

192   For the results of the price changes, see Baden Fuller, 'Economic Issues Relating to Property Rights in Trademarks: Export Bans, Differential Pricing, Restrictions on Resale and Repackaging', at 175 to 176.

193   *Re Distillers Company plc* [1983] 3 CMLR 173, at ¶12. Distillers had initially claimed exemption for a wide range of its products.

194   For the announcement that the application had formally been abandoned, see *17th Competition Report*, EC Commission, 1988, at ¶65.

195   OJ 1987 L222/28, appeal dismissed 277/87 *Sandoz Prodotti Farmaceutici SpA v Commission*, unreported judgment 11 January 1990, the operative part is at [1990] ECR I-45 (6th Chamber).

196   *Ibid.* at ¶¶18 to 19, 30.

Bayo-n-ox shows the broad, teleological approach the Commission will use to reveal a conspiracy to partition the internal market by insulating national markets.[197] Like *Sandoz*, it raised the issue of how the EC should deal with disparities between national laws. According to the Commission, following the ECJ in *Merck* the issue should be ignored.

Bayer's patents in West Germany for a growth promoter used as an additive in feedingstuffs, bayo-n-ox, had expired. The price on the market consequently fell as it became subject to competition, but Bayer maintained the price in Belgium and France where patents were still in force. When West German customers started exporting to Belgium and France, Bayer sold bayo-n-ox to them at a discount on condition that they use it only for their own requirements. The Commission characterised this as a 'restriction on competition' caught by Article 85(1) because it prevented the customers from reselling the product and acted as an export ban. Moreover, compartmentalising a large proportion of an aggregate, cross-frontier market was *prima facie* incompatible with the Common Market for which, in this case, there would be no saving justifications. Bayer was fined ECU500,000 since, the agreement not having been notified, exemption was not forthcoming.

For those of Bayer's customers which did not accept the 'own requirements' commitment in writing, agreement was *imputed* because throughout the period Bayer also offered the product without the 'own requirements' commitment at a higher price and they bought at the lower price. (In some cases, this seems a bit hard on the customers since many apparently sold the product in disregard of the condition.[198] The customers were not, however, fined.)

To establish the 'object or effect' of restricting competition, the Commission did not seem to rely on what must be regarded as a series of largely damning factors. The 'own requirements' commitment was adopted at a time when the patents in West Germany expired and West German customers began engaging in parallel trade to Belgium and France where patents were still in force. Perhaps less than coincidentally, the discounted price for sale on the 'own requirements' commitment was the same as the West German market price in Germany once other producers could make and sell the product on the expiry of the patent. These events were linked by a 'smoking gun' memo found lurking in the records of Bayer's legal department. Moreover, Bayer had a history of trying to stop parallel flows of bayo-n-ox from 'low-priced' Member States to 'higher priced' Member States.[199]

Instead, according to the Commission, competition was restricted because

---

197 OJ 1990 L21/71; [1990] 4 CMLR 930, now on appeal T-12/90 OJ 1990 C91/3.
198 The published decision does not include the Annex, so it is unclear exactly which of Bayer's customers were considered by the Commission to participate in the agreement.
199 Before the agreements in question were adopted, prices in France were under pressure by parallel imports first from Belgium, then Spain and Italy. In Switzerland, parallel imports were dealt with by limiting the quantities sold to the parallel importing source.

the freedom of action of Bayer's customers was fettered and so was the range of suppliers for third-party purchasers.

Bayer had argued that the controls were necessary to stop customers mixing bayo-n-ox with inferior quality products and, in some cases, misusing the product from lack of skill. This, according to Bayer, was particularly important since the product was only provisionally authorised for use on the EC market and any adverse reports could prejudice that authorisation. Furthermore, Bayer claimed it was under a legal obligation to ensure that the product was not sold to unauthorised users.

The Commission accepted that a control imposed by law would not 'restrict competition'. Bayer's controls, however, went further than was necessary since they did not just prohibit sales to people lacking the necessary legal authorisations.[200]

The Commission did not deny that quality control may have formed some part of Bayer's intentions. But, it was relevant only to exemption under Article 85(3) and, even admitting such an intention, the object or effect was still to restrict competition.

Regardless of Bayer's subjective intentions, the Commission ruled that 'object' for the purposes of Article 85(1) required an *objective* meaning and so Bayer's actual intentions were irrelevant. The object of the agreement was assessed not by reference to the parties' actual intentions but from the very presence in the agreement of a clause obstructing the goal of integrating the internal market regardless of any justifications.[201] In any case, the proscribed *effect* on competition was also achieved because avenues for the supply of third parties were reduced. This reasoning must give serious pause for thought.

The distinction between 'object' and 'effect' adopted here is more than tortuous. The broad meaning attributed to 'object' seems to leave little scope for 'effect', as the Commission's artificial distinction between restricting the freedom of action of Bayer's customers (object) and their potential customers (effect) seems to indicate. In *Maize Seed, Coditel II* and *Erauw Jacquery*, the ECJ adopted a more flexible approach having regard to the nature and purpose of the 'restrictions' and the Commission's formalistic analysis of effect lies in stark contrast to the far more elaborate inquiry authorised by the ECJ.[202]

Without resorting to such devices, the background facts already indicated do not suggest that the conclusion reached by the Commission is wrong. But, they do not remove the need to deal with the justifications raised by Bayer. Although the purported legal obligation was dealt with in passing by Bayer's admission that it went further than was necessary, the Commission

---

200   OJ 1990 L21/71; [1990] 4 CMLR 930, ¶¶40 to 42.
201   In the Commission's words, 'the ban on trading was directly evident from the wording of the "agreement"': *ibid.* at ¶46. Contrast the reliance on objective factors to raise a rebuttable presumption of subjective knowledge adopted in *RCA Corporation v Custom Cleared Sales Pty Ltd* (1978) 19 ALR 123, see Chapter 4 Note 226.
202   See also 161/84 *Pronuptia v Schillgallis* [1986] ECR 353, [1986] 1 CMLR 414 and 42/84 *Remia and Nutricia v Commission* [1985] ECR 2547, [1987] 1 CMLR 1.

did not find the quality justifications unsupported. Certainly, on one view of the ECJ's case law, they were relevant.[203]

Bayer Dental is of interest because the Commission condemned clauses in standard form contracts based on the exceptions to the doctrine of Community exhaustion found in *Valium* and *AHPC*.[204]

Bayer Dental is a division of Bayer AG operating, as its name suggests, in the market for dental products. It seems that there were a number of suppliers on the market of varying size with Bayer being one of the larger ones although it was not dominant. Bayer Dental supplies the market directly in Germany and, it seems, in Denmark. In other Member States, the supply function was performed by 'associated companies', the manner of association being unspecified. The price list which Bayer Dental supplied its dealers included the following clause:

XIV.　Resale

1.　Original packages of the seller which carry a registered trade mark may be supplied to a third party only in unopened form.
2.　The seller's preparations are intended for distribution solely in the Federal Republic of Germany, including West Berlin. Their resale abroad may, in the country concerned, be prohibited because they contravene registration regulations, and may lead to claims for damages because they infringe industrial property rights.

Following the reasoning adopted by the ECJ in *Sandoz* at points 2 and 9, the price list was taken to be incorporated into the general terms and conditions of sale. After the Commission challenged the clause, the next price list included an amended clause which did not include a prohibition on repackaging and, further, made it clear that exports were permitted. Not having been notified, the earlier version was not eligible for an exemption, but the Commission would have refused one anyway because the clause's object was to prevent exports.[205] Fines were not, however, imposed; presumably because Bayer Dental had never actually enforced the clause, the legal point was, perhaps, unclear and Bayer acted promptly to remedy the situation once the Commission intervened.

For present purposes, Bayer ran two defences.[206] It claimed that the ban on repackaging was intended solely to prevent interference with the original state of its products. The warning against export was intended solely to exclude any contractual liability under the German Civil Code should any exporter become liable under product registration or industrial property laws in the country of destination. Once again, Bayer was condemned by the clear

---

203　Compare also *Comasso* [1990] 4 CMLR 259, above at Note 181.
204　OJ 1990 L351/46, 15 December 1990 [1992] 4 CMLR 61. See generally, Rothnie, 'EC Competition Policy, the Commission and Trade Marks'.
205　*Ibid*. at ¶18.
206　It also ran unsuccessfully two of the arguments rejected in *Miller International*; that it had never taken action to enforce the clause and, as its prices were almost the same throughout Europe, there was unlikely to be any parallel trade anyway: *ibid*. at ¶¶12 and 17.

intention of the clause objectively determined. At point 10 of the decision, the Commission found that the combination of the two prohibitions in the clause had the object of preventing any resale whatsoever outside Germany following repackaging.

The ban on repackaging was condemned because it went further than permitted in *Valium* since it did not allow for the possibility of repackaging which did not interfere with the original state of the product. Furthermore, the wording was: ' . . . apt to awaken in the minds of resellers so much doubt as to their actual rights that they will refrain from reselling repacked products'.[207]

A process of deduction found that the second part of the clause was an export ban. As such, the possibility of exemption could not even be considered. The Commission's chain of reasoning shows its determination to stamp out anything it perceives as a hindrance to trade within the internal market.

The statement in the clause that the goods were intended for sale in Germany *implied* the negative proposition that they were *not* intended for sale elsewhere. This implication was confirmed as a certainty by the fact that schedule numbers and packaging for products intended for sale on the German and foreign markets were '*sometimes* the same'.[208] The interpretation was further entrenched by the remainder of the clause which highlighted the considerable risks and penalties which an exporter might incur, leaving the nature of those risks quite vague. In particular, it was not clear whether the industrial property rights which the exporter might infringe were owned by third parties or Bayer itself. Further, Bayer, as a company trading in all Member States and so which ought to have a precise knowledge of the nature of any risks, was hardly able to identify any real danger of infringing third parties' rights, eventually finding two cases.[209]

The claim that the clause was intended merely to exclude Bayer's potential contractual liability for a reseller's actions was dealt with bluntly in point 15. The Commission doubted that Bayer was under an obligation to advise resellers of legal difficulties prospectively arising in export trade. In any case, the claimed object could be achieved more simply by direct exclusion of liability for defects in title. The failure to take this plain course was 'incomprehensible'.

Bayer Dental demonstrates the Commission's hostility to export bans, particularly in 'mere' distribution agreements, regardless of market circumstances. The Commission, however, did not completely deny Bayer's rights to take action to protect its trade mark rights as indicated by the ECJ in *Valium*. In fact, at point 12, the Commission expressly acknowledged Bayer's rights to do this. But, as this case shows, the burden on a party seeking to exploit those rights is a heavy one.

---

207   *Ibid*. at ¶11 for both points.
208   *Ibid*. at ¶13.
209   *Ibid*. at ¶¶14 and 15.

7.3.3   Absolute territorial protection

In *Maize Seed*, the ECJ gave short shrift to arguments that absolute territorial protection should be exempted. Shortly after, in *Coditel II*, the ECJ did not distinguish between open exclusive licences and absolute territorial protection in clearing the grant of exclusive broadcast rights in a film. The justification given was the same as for open exclusivity in *Maize Seed*, the need to encourage investment, but the ECJ also emphasised the specific needs of the film industry in Europe. The prospect of exemption for absolute territorial protection, or at least one form of it, was confirmed in *Pronuptia*.[210] One would expect reasoning acceptable for a well-known trade mark would also extend to technology licensing. But, in *Pronuptia*, the absolute territorial protection did not include restrictions on the franchisee selling to customers outside its territory. In *Erauw Jacquery*, the ECJ came much closer to, but did not address, the issue of bans on direct or indirect exports of certified seed and the wording of the export ban on basic seeds did not expressly require bans on customers' exporting.[211] Moreover, it is not clear from the judgment whether the ECJ relied on the need to encourage investment or the specific nature of the products in question or a combination of both. In contrast, the Advocate-General treated the bans on customers' exports of certified seeds as absolute territorial protection requiring exemption to be permissible.

Two separate strands are apparent in the Commission's approach to absolute territorial protection. On one hand, it seems to be working on a narrower definition of absolute territorial protection under Article 85(3) than the ECJ in *Maize Seed* under Article 85(1). More recently, in *Comasso*, it seems to have raised the prospect of treating products differently according to their specific nature.

Prior to *Comasso*, the Commission was virulently opposed to measures which obstructed parallel importing by third parties. Attempts to use intellectual property rights against parallel imports or otherwise make it difficult for intermediaries to engage in parallel trade automatically preclude the group exemptions applying.[212] That approach has been maintained in *Bayo-n-ox* and *Bayer Dental*.

But, while the ECJ in *Maize Seed* included parallel importers *and* other licensees in its definition of absolute territorial protection, the exclusive distribution, patent, know-how and franchise regulations *all* permit restriction on concessionaires actively seeking customers in the territories of other concessionaires and the patent and know-how regulations also permit bans on passive sales in other concessionaires' territories for limited periods. This is consistent with the later concession in *Pronuptia* that absolute territorial protection could be exempted. Moreover, in *Maize Seed*, the refusal to

---

210   [1986] ECR 353, at ¶24.
211   [1988] ECR 1919.
212   See especially Regulation 1983/83, Article 3(c) and (d); Regulation 2349/84, Article 3(11); Regulation 556/89, Article 3(12); and Regulation 4087/88, Articles 4(a) and 5(g).

exempt absolute territorial protection in point 77 only refers to obstructing parallel importers, not other licensees. So, there are grounds for considering that restraints on competition between licensees may not amount to absolute territorial protection for the purposes of Article 85(3), at least where the restriction affects active sales only.[213]

In *Comasso*, the Commission has announced its intention to 'treat favourably' a number of export bans including several on customers of the licensee, potentially among the most likely parallel importers. Hence, the Commission appears ready to approve some form of absolute territorial protection under the competition rules. (Such action would also suggest further qualification of the rules on the free movement of goods since a legal action to enforce the ban must take on the appearance of a national measure impeding exports or imports potentially contrary to Articles 30 and 34.)[214] The need for this qualification arises at least in part from the need to encourage investment which is a consideration that applies generally. However, it seems more likely that the Commission's reasoning will focus on the specific nature of the products in question.[215]

7.3.4   Summary

In fact, although it applies a similar approach under Article 85(3), the Commission seems to have a very narrow view of when, if ever, the circumstances identified by the ECJ in its judgments since *Maize Seed* will apply under Article 85(1). Since they interfere with market integration, the Commission has been particularly hostile under Article 85(1) to exclusive territories and obstructions of parallel imports. The Commission has only cleared open exclusivity or bans on active sales in trivial cases.[216] Generally, it has exempted such agreements, even going so far as to accord many such 'restrictions' automatic exemption under its various group exemptions.[217]

To achieve this result, the Commission treats 'competition' under Article 85(1) formalistically. An agreement 'restricts' competition because it fetters

---

213   But, in the distribution context, contrast *Consten & Grundig*, see Chapter 6.2.

214   See for example Giuliano Marenco and Karen Banks, 'Intellectual Property and the Community Rules on Free Movement: Discrimination Unearthed', (1990) 15 ELRev. 224, at 225; and René Joliet and David T. Keeling, 'Trade Mark Law and the Free Movement of Goods: the Overruling of the Judgment in Hag I', 22 IIC 303 (1991).

215   See Note 181 above.

216   See *Finnpap* IP(89) 496, 27 June 1989; for the 19(3) Notice see OJ 1989 C45/4; *Grosfillex* [1964] CMLR 237, *Burroughs/Delplanque and GEHA* [1972] CMLR D67 and 72, *Raymond/Nagoya* [1972] CMLR D45, but contrast *BBC Brown Boveri/NGK* [1989] 4 CMLR 610.

217   Certainly, in some cases involving joint ventures, the Commission has stated that grants of manufacturing exclusivity did not restrict competition where the parties were not potential competitors, but has then proceeded to find other obligations in the same agreement which did. See for example *Mitchell Cotts/Sofiltra* [1988] 4 CMLR 111 discussed in Korah, *Know-how Licensing Agreements and the EEC Competition Rules*, at 37, Note 4. That approach appears to have been shortlived, for example *Boussois/Interpane* [1988] 4 CMLR 124, *BBC Brown Boveri/NGK* [1989] 4 CMLR 610 and see Korah, *EEC Competition Law and Practice*, Chapters 12 and 14.

the parties' freedom of action.[218] In reaching this conclusion, the Commission does not engage in any economic analysis such as whether third parties are actually (or potentially) excluded from the market-place since, usually, it is the very existence of inter-brand alternatives which warrants exemption under Article 85(3) when coupled with the 'indispensable' nature of the restriction concerned. Instead, under Article 85(1), the Commission seems to focus almost exclusively on the intra-brand effects – rival traders are foreclosed from selling the brand itself.[219] The Commission has also tended largely to assess the competitive impact of agreements *ex post* and has often seemed to regard technology licensing as horizontal in nature.[220]

The Commission's approach is not without some justification in the ECJ's case law: see especially *Consten & Grundig*. However, that case, as the *STM* case shows, was conclusive only on the question of absolute territorial protection. Moreover, its emphasis on the importance of intra-brand competition is markedly at odds with *Maize Seed*'s emphasis on inter-brand competition and *ex ante* analysis which subsequent cases extend even into fields associated with absolute territorial protection.

Finally, as with the ECJ, movement can be seen in the Commission's position. It has for a long time been prepared to exempt grants of exclusivity and bans on active sales outside the conceded territory. So, in theory, territorial protection has been limited to search costs and the transport costs of getting the product from another territory. However, since *Maize Seed*, the Commission has relaxed its pursuit of the goal of integrating the internal market in two key ways. First, in technology licensing, it has been prepared to permit limited bans on passive sales outside its territory by the licensee. These were expressly conceded on the Commission's view of the need to encourage investment. Second, most recently, the Commission has foreshadowed willingness to treat favourably an agreement requiring export bans to be imposed on third parties and so creating some form of absolute territorial protection. While the need to encourage investment could explain this, the Commission seems likely to emphasise the specific needs of the products in question. Logically, if such bans are to be enforceable, some reconsideration will be necessary on the outright prohibition on parties agreeing to use separate national ownership of intellectual property rights to defeat parallel imports.

218 The further qualification that the restriction have a perceptible effect is rarely a problem since the Commission has on a number of occasions found market shares under 5 per cent to be perceptible, for example *Charles Jourdan* [1989] 4 CMLR 591.
219 See for example Schröter, 'Antitrust Analysis under Article 85(1) and (3)', at 686 to 687.
220 For the latter point, see Johannes, 'Technology Transfer under EEC Law – Europe between the Divergent Opinions of the Past and the New Administration: A Comparative Law Approach', at 83 to 84.

7.4   Abusing a Dominant Position

The ECJ has confirmed that using intellectual property rights in a way permitted by the free movement rules to block or impede parallel imports may give rise to an abuse of a dominant position contrary to Article 86.[221] Provided the right owner was in a dominant position, the same conclusion would seem to apply with even greater force to attempts to block parallel imports which were not supported by the free movement rules.[222]

Breach of Article 86 involves a two-step process. It is first necessary to show that the right owner possesses a dominant position in the relevant market. Then, it is necessary to show that the dominance has been abused.[223] The ECJ generally defines dominance in the following terms:

> a position of economic strength enjoyed by an undertaking which enables it to prevent effective competition being maintained on the relevant market by giving it the power to behave to an appreciable extent independently of its competitors, customers and ultimately of consumers.[224]

The ECJ has ruled on a number of occasions that mere ownership of an intellectual property right does not in itself necessarily create a dominant position.[225] So, it is necessary to investigate the market context to establish whether the required degree of economic strength is present. Although the thresholds applied in the EC may not be as high as the corresponding tests in the United States, this still requires an examination of substitutes on both the demand and supply sides. In doing so, the ECJ has often referred to the structure of the market and whether rivals would be foreclosed.[226]

Most of the ECJ's rulings on this issue have been by way of preliminary reference, so the question of whether or not there was actually a dominant position was a matter for the national court to decide. For parallel imports, the clearest example of a dominant position considered by the ECJ is the case of national, copyright collecting agencies as in *Tournier*.

More controversial are the cases of 'lock-in'. So far, these cases have arisen in the context of design rights over spare parts. In one case, the

---

221   395/87 *Ministère Public v Tournier* [1991] 4 CMLR 248, at ¶38; judgments in 110, 241 and 242/88 *SACEM v Lucazeau* [1991] 4 CMLR 248 in similar terms; see also Chapter 6 from Note 218 and Section 7.6.
222   The competition rules also being used as instruments of integrating the internal market, see 258/78 *Maize Seed* [1982] ECR 2015, at ¶¶62 to 64.
223   On Article 86, see generally, Korah, *EEC Competition Law and Practice*, Chapter 4; Whish, *Competition Law*, Chapter 8; Hawk, 2 *United States, Common Market and International Antitrust: A Comparative Guide*, Chapter 12.
224   27/76 *United Brands Corporation v Commission* [1978] ECR 207, at ¶65.
225   24/67 *Parke, Davis & Co. v Probel* [1968] ECR 55, at 72 (patent); 40/70 *Sirena Srl v Eda Srl* [1971] ECR 69, at ¶16 (trade mark); 78/70 *Deutsche Grammophon v Metro* [1971] ECR 487, at ¶16 (copyright); 238/87 *Volvo AB v Eric Veng (UK) Limited* [1989] 4 CMLR 122, at ¶8 and 53/87 *Consorzio Italiano della Componentistica di Recambio per Autoveicoli and Maxicar v Régie Nationale des Usines Renault* [1990] 4 CMLR 265, at ¶15 (industrial design).
226   *Ibid.*, apart from *Parke, Davis*; see also 51, 86 & 96 *EMI Records Ltd v CBS United Kingdom Ltd* [1976] ECR 811, at ¶36, Section 7.5 below. On market assessment, see also Chapters 2.3.4(a) and 10.2.1 below.

ECJ upheld the Commission's finding that a non-dominant producer of cash registers was dominant in the market for the supply of spare parts for its own products.[227] Later in *Volvo* and *Renault*, however, the ECJ did not refer to the issue, concentrating instead on the question of what would be an abuse if the right owner were found to be dominant. This has been taken as an indication that *Hugin* may no longer command a majority of support within the ECJ.[228] The Advocate-General, however, considered that each car manufacturer was likely to be dominant over the supply of its models' spare parts even in the absence of design protection. The Commission would seem to be proceeding on the ground that *Hugin* is still good law.[229]

Outside the field of spare parts, the issue could take on considerable importance in the field of software since a user of a particular brand of software may find itself subject to massive costs in rekeying data and retraining if it were to change to a rival program. It remains to be seen whether this potential difficulty will be obviated by the increasing commercial pressures for 'inter-operability'. It would, in any case, be necessary to take into account that many of the users likely to suffer from this problem may well be the sort of large, corporate customers which might be expected to make informed choices.

A further problem area in EC competition policy is the question of when a trade mark will create a dominant position. To some extent, the ECJ has tended to treat trade marks permissively and has recently confirmed the vital role they play in the proper functioning of a competitive market.[230] Anticipating *Hag II*, the Commission has also acknowledged that, for some purposes, a trade mark was likely to create a barrier to competition only where the ability to use it conferred an important advantage on new entrants or competitors. Precisely how important the advantage must be has yet to be defined and, indeed, in *Moosehead*, the Commission only applied the test to assess the validity of a promise not to challenge the validity of the trade mark's registration.[231]

227 22/78 *Hugin Kassaregister AB v Commission* [1979] ECR 1869.
228 See Valentine Korah, 'No Duty to License Independent Repairers to Make Spare Parts', [1988] EIPR 381, at 382 at Notes 7 to 8 referring also to 247/86 *Alsatel v Novasem* [1988] ECR 5928 as further contradiction of *Hugin*. But, see *Volvo v Veng* [1989] 4 CMLR 122; *Renault* [1990] 4 CMLR 265.
229 *Ford Body Panels*, Commission Press Release IP(90) at 4. See also T-30/89 *Hilti AG v Commission* [1992] 4 CMLR 16 in which Hilti's claimed justifications seem to have been severely handicapped by lack of factual credibility: compare *Queensland Wire Industries Pty Ltd v Broken Hill Proprietary Co. Limited* (1989) 167 CLR 177 discussed in Peter Alexiades, 'Refusal to Deal and 'Misuse of Market Power' under Australia's Competition Law,' [1989] ECLR 437. It is not immediately apparent, however, why Hilti's intellectual property rights were evidence of anything other than a superior product, the innovation and development of which competition policy should foster. Indeed, notwithstanding ¶93, the CFI at ¶¶89 to 92 seems to have found Hilti dominant independently of its intellectual property rights.
230 *Hag II* [1990] ECR I-3717 [1990] 3 CMLR 571 at ¶13 and see Chapter 6 from Note 220. But, note *United Brands* [1978] ECR 207.
231 *Moosehead/Whitbread* [1991] 4 CMLR 391 at ¶15.4(a), see Rothnie, 'EC Competition Policy, the Commission and Trade Marks', at Notes 23 to 27. On further possible limits to the test, see the Commission's finding of dominance in unspecified circumstances in *Coca Cola Italy*, Commission Press Release, IP(90) at 7.

Assuming a dominant position be established, it is also necessary to prove its abuse. There is no clear definition of precisely what constitutes an abuse and the categories of 'abuse' do not seem to be closed.

For quite some time, the ECJ usually ruled that merely using intellectual property rights as permitted under the free movement rules would not itself constitute an abuse. In *Basset*, however, it indicated that the imposition of unfair conditions by an undertaking in circumstances which were not condemned under the free movement rules could be an abuse. The abuse claimed there was the charging of excessive licence fees but, since the level of the royalty payments there had been regarded as reasonable by the national court, the point was not taken further.[232] Unfair prices were directly in issue and *Basset* was confirmed in *Tournier*, subject to the possibility of justification. Hence, it is now clear that exercising intellectual property rights against parallel imports in terms permitted under the free movement rules can breach Article 86 in some situations.

Under Article 85, the ECJ and the Commission have accepted some limitations on the ability of parties to a contract to compete in each other's territory, generally provided parallel imports are still possible. The question arises whether Article 86 permits similar latitude to a dominant undertaking. It seems more likely that dominant undertakings are subject to more stringent controls.

For example, in a decision upheld by the Court of First Instance ('CFI'), the Commission found that Article 86 would be breached by an already dominant undertaking acquiring an exclusive licence for rival, patented technology. The CFI confirmed that acquisition of an exclusive licence by a dominant undertaking was not necessarily an abuse. It was still necessary to examine all the surrounding circumstances, particularly the impact on market structure. The acquisition not only strengthened Tetra Pak's dominance over the market, but, since access to the technology was essential to enable a new entrant any possibility of competing effectively, would effectively foreclose the market to new entry.[233] As a corollary, the Commission indicated that an exclusive licence of the patented technology to the dominant undertaking in these circumstances could not take the benefit of a group exemption.[234]

While it may be possible to argue the question of dominance, the overall approach seems consistent with earlier decisions by the ECJ. In particular, in *United Brands*, the ECJ indicated that the reaction of a dominant undertaking to competitive threats had to be proportionate to the nature of those threats. Accordingly, the dominant undertaking could not bluntly refuse to supply

---

Contrast Baden Fuller, 'Economic Issues Relating to Property Rights in Trademarks: Export Bans, Differential Pricing, Restrictions on Resale and Repackaging', at 162 and Steiner, 'The Nature of Vertical Restraints', at 143.

232   402/85 *Basset v SACEM* [1987] ECR 1747 at ¶¶19 to 20. For the facts, see Chapter 6 from Note 174.

233   T-51/89 *Tetra Pak Raussig SA v Commission* [1991] 4 CMLR 334, especially at ¶¶23 to 24.

234   *Elopak v Tetra Pak* [1990] 4 CMLR 47; for the imposition of a fine of ECU 56,000,000, see [1992] 4 CMLR 551.

a dealer which was alleged to be engaging in activities detrimental to the brand reputation when the dealer became the main outlet for the leading rival brand. In *United Brands*, the ECJ also rejected justifications of measures to prevent parallel imports on grounds of preserving the quality of the goods, differing costs of distribution or other national factors causing price variations.[235]

In two cases which did not involve parallel imports, the ECJ has offered further guidance on when the use of intellectual property rights could constitute an abuse. Both *Renault* and *Volvo* arose out of the refusal to license independent suppliers to use designs relating to replacement body panels for cars. The ECJ considered that an abuse might occur in the following situation:

> Exercise of the exclusive right may be prohibited by Article 86 if it gives rise to *certain abusive conduct* on the part of an undertaking occupying a dominant position *such as* the arbitrary refusal to supply spare parts to independent repairers, the fixing of prices for spare parts at an unfair level or a decision no longer to produce spare parts for a particular model even though many cars of that model are still in circulation, provided that conduct is liable to affect trade between member-States[236] (*Emphasis added*).

Hence, an abuse might arise if the right owner refused to supply an existing demand for its products at all; if it refused to license a particular user for 'arbitrary' reasons; or if it charged prices at an unfair level.

In his opinion, Advocate-General Mischo considered that prices might be unfair if they allowed the right owner to recover more than its production costs, expenditure on R & D and a reasonable profit margin.[237] The ECJ did not expressly adopt the Advocate-General's opinion on this point and there is still some doubt whether it accepts that a 'reward' theory is the rationale of intellectual property rather than an 'incentive' theory.[238]

The mere fact that price levels between Member States vary, however, does not necessarily mean that there has been an abuse.[239] In the special circumstances of *Tournier*, the ECJ considered, however, that price differences between Member States might be used to show that there was unfairness. In points 38 and 46, the ECJ stressed that any price comparison must be 'consistent'. The Advocate-General's opinion referred to tentative evidence before the ECJ indicating that price levels in France and, perhaps, Italy, were far, far higher than elsewhere in the EC; this was supported by evidence that SACEM assessed royalties on a different basis,

---

235 [1978] ECR 207, at ¶¶182 to 196 (proportionality); for resale and pricing practices, see ¶¶130 to 159 and 204 to 265, respectively. Note also the rejection of similar 'national' considerations in *Tournier* [1991] 4 CMLR 248, at ¶¶39 to 42, especially the rejection of the argument based on different costs.

236 *Renault* [1990] 4 CMLR 265 at ¶16; *Volvo v Veng* [1989] 4 CMLR 122, at ¶9.

237 *Ibid.* at 278 to 279; and see the criticism in Korah, 'No Duty to License Independent Repairers to Make Spare Parts', at 382 to 383.

238 For a review, see Korah, *Know-how Licensing Agreements and the EEC Competition Rules*, at 28 to 30. Contrast the approach in *Studiengesellschaft Kohle* 670 F 2d 1122 in Chapter 3 from Note 230.

239 *Parke, Davis* [1968] ECR 55, at 72 and *Renault* [1990] 4 CMLR 265 at ¶17.

seemed to have much higher overheads and differences over the distribution of royalties.[240]

The Commission has also addressed the case of a right owner refusing to license rival suppliers of parts for cars. In a press release, it announced that it had closed proceedings after 'Ford' agreed to relax its refusals to license. In essence, Ford agreed to grant licences of its remaining design registrations to independent suppliers after a period of three years from when a 'market of some significance' in the products had developed.[241] The roughly five years of overall protection allowed Ford took into account its need to recover investment costs, its six year anti-corrosion warranty and the usual development of a demand for independents' products after about five or six years.

Finally, the Commission's approach on refusals to deal has also been taken up by the CFI in *Magill*.[242] It is tempting to dismiss *Magill* as being a mere curiosity, dealing with a very particular case and confined to its facts. That would be a mistake. First, while copyright protection in radio or television schedules may be a limited issue, it raises the broader question of encouraging investment in the creation of commercial databases. Second, within the EC context, *Magill* can be seen as raising a conflict of different cultures. Many of the Member States with Civil Code backgrounds do not recognise copyright protection in programme listings to the same extent as in the United Kingdom and Eire.[243] Also, of primary concern here, there is the relationship between competition policy and intellectual property.

Television viewers in Eire and Northern Ireland could view up to six channels broadcast by 'RTE', 'BBC' and 'ITP', apart from satellite and cable channels. RTE, BBC and IPT were, once again apart from the satellite and cable channels, the only licensed broadcasters for either Eire or Northern Ireland. As part of their activities, RTE, BBC and ITP necessarily prepared

---

240 [1991] 4 CMLR 248, at 273 to 279; note also at ¶42, the ECJ rejected SACEM's reliance on its different methods of collection.

241 *Ford Body Panels* IP(90) at 4, 10 January 1990. The market would be deemed 'of some significance' after either Ford had sold 250,000 units or two years from launch, whichever were the shorter. For an earlier ruling under the Competition Act 1980 (UK) by the Monopolies and Mergers Commission, see Conrad 9437 (1985) and note *British Leyland Motor Corporation plc v Armstrong Patents Ltd* [1986] AC 577 given effect in section 237 of the CDPA 1988.

242 T-69/89 *Radio Telefis Eireann v Commission* [1991] 4 CMLR 586; T-70/89 *BBC* [1991] 4 CMLR 669; T-76-89 *ITP* [1991] 4 CMR 745. For comments, contrast Ronald E. Myrick, 'Will Intellectual Property on Technology Still be Viable in a Unitary Market?' [1992] EIPR 298; James Flynn, 'Intellectual Property and Anti-trust: EC Attitudes', [1992] EIPR 49; Jonathan Smith, 'Television Guides: The European Court Doesn't Know 'There's So Much In It' ', [1992] ECLR 135 to Brenda Sufrin, 'Comment on the Magill Case', [1992] Ent. LR 67.

243 The UK Government subsequently introduced a form of compulsory licensing for programme listings: section 176 of the Broadcasting Act 1990 which, although not under the copyright legislation, would seem to alter the nature of the right fundamentally, see 434/85 *Allen & Hanburys* [1988] ECR 1245 ¶¶12 to 14 at Chapter 6 Note 194, above. For a survey of the legal treatment of listings, see Margot Watts and Robyn Durie, 'A Comparative Study of TV Listings with Reference to the United Kingdom, Australia, New Zealand and Europe', [1992] Ent. LR 133.

programme listings. They each supplied copies of these listings in advance to newspapers and weekly magazines. They each permitted daily publications to publish the next day's listings in advance for free. They each also permitted weekly publications to print in advance the forthcoming week's 'highlights' (it is not clear from the report how the 'highlights' were determined). With the exception of some magazines published in the Netherlands, however, they each refused to permit the publication in advance of the week's full listings as each published its own weekly guide of its own programmes. (In RTE's case, sales of its magazine, the RTE Guide, generated almost IR£14 million in 1985.) Therefore, to obtain in advance the full week's programmes for all six channels, a viewer would need to purchase three magazines. Alternatively, the viewer could rely on the published 'highlights' in other magazines and the daily listings published each day. Not more than 20 per cent of households with television in Eire and Northern Ireland apparently found it necessary or desirable to buy RTE's weekly guide.

Magill chose to publish a magazine incorporating the full, advance weekly listings for each of the RTE, BBC and ITP ('comprehensive listings'). The Irish High Court ruled that RTE held copyright in its programme listings which was being infringed by Magill. Anticipating this eventually, Magill had complained to the Commission that RTE, BBC and ITP were acting in breach of Articles 85 and 86 of the EEC Treaty by refusing to grant it licences to publish comprehensive listings. The Commission sustained Magill's complaint and ordered RTE, BBC and ITP to license their programme listings for inclusion in comprehensive listings on no more than reasonable royalties.[244] RTE, BBC and ITP appealed. A further appeal from the CFI's ruling to the ECJ is apparently on foot.[245]

The CFI held that the relevant market was the market for each 'applicant's weekly programme listings and the television guides in which those listings are published', not the market for information on television programmes in general.[246] Each applicant was dominant in 'the market represented by its weekly listings *and* on the market for the magazines in which they were published . . . .'[247] Finally, the refusal to license Magill to produce comprehensive listings was 'not related to the actual substance' of the copyright and so an abuse contrary to Article 86.[248]

Even Ms Sufrin, who otherwise commends the ruling, is moved to remark the very narrow definition of the market at work here.[249] On such a narrow definition, RTE (and each of BBC and ITP) could hardly be anything

---

244 1989 OJ L78/34 [1989] 4 CMLR 757. For the Commission's consistent treatment of databases, see Article 8.1 of the draft EC Database Directive COM(92)24 Final, cited in Watts and Durie, 'A Comparative Study of TV Listings', at 134.
245 Myrick, 'Will Intellectual Property on Technology Still be Viable in a Unitary Market?'
246 [1991] 4 CMLR 586 ¶61.
247 *Ibid.* ¶63 (*Emphasis added*).
248 *Ibid.* ¶74 and 75. The CFI also found against RTE on two other issues: whether the conduct affected a substantial part of the common market and would perceptibly affect trade between the Member States, see *Ibid.* ¶¶64, 76 and 77.
249 Sufrin, 'Comment on the Magill Case,' at 67.

but dominant. If right, however, it means that any undertaking which has captured barely 20 per cent (if that) of its potential market could find its actions heavily circumscribed by Article 86; perhaps without any showing that the undertaking has such economic strength as 'to behave to an appreciable extent independently of its competitors, customers and ultimately of consumers.'[250] The CFI relied on two factors to reach its conclusion. First, it considered that there was very limited substitutability between daily comprehensive lists and weekly comprehensive lists:

> 62.   Only weekly television guides containing comprehensive listings for the week ahead enable users to decide in advance which programmes they wish to follow and arrange any leisure activities for the week accordingly.

This was buttressed by the very demand for the individual guides of RTE, BBC and ITP and the success of comprehensive weekly listings elsewhere in the EC.

The factors leading to the CFI's finding of abuse are even more disturbing. The CFI considered that Article 36 of the EEC Treaty established that the exclusive right to reproduce the protected work established under national law could not be exercised contrary to the objectives of Article 86:

> 71.   . . . while it is plain that the exercise of the exclusive right to reproduce a protected work is not in itself an abuse, that does not apply when, in the light of the details of each individual case, it is apparent that that right is exercised in such ways and circumstances *as in fact to pursue an aim manifestly contrary to the objectives of Article 86*. In that event, *the copyright is no longer exercised in a manner which corresponds to its essential function*, within the meaning of Article 36 of the Treaty, *which is to protect the moral rights in the work and ensure a reward for the creative effort*, while respecting the aims of, in particular, Article 86. In that case, the primacy of Community law, particularly as regards principles as fundamental as those of the free movement of goods *and freedom of competition*, prevails over any use of a rule of national intellectual property law in a manner contrary t those principles. (*Emphasis added*)

The CFI's reference to the role of Article 36 in the application of Article 86 and its unique definition of the *essential function* of copyright are questionable, but, in light of *Basset, Tournier, Volvo* and *Renault*, it is difficult to challenge the CFI's conclusion that an exercise of copyright may *in appropriate circumstances* be challenged under Article 86.[251] Therefore,

---

250   27/76 *United Brands* [1978] ECR 207 at ¶65. The CFI's judgment does not specifically address this issue. Contrast *Broderbund Software v Computermate Products* [1991] 22 IPR 215 (Fed. C). Although outside the EC, the definition of market power from *United Brands* was adopted. Beaumont J rejected Computermate's assertion that the relevant market was the market for Broderbund's program 'Where in the World is Carmen Diego?' and held instead that the relevant markets were the markets for computer software for educational purposes and computer software for purposes of entertainment. As Broderbund's market share was between 10 and 17 per cent and there were competitors, it did not have a sufficient degree of market power. See also the US approach in patents, *Studiengesellschaft Kohie* 670 F. 2d 1122 (DC Cir. 1981) at Chapter 3 Note 230 above.

251   All parties before the CFI approached the case as turning on the specific subject matter of copyright. On the effect of Article 36 on the competition rules, contrast for example 56 & 58/64 *Consten & Grundig* [1966] ECR at 345. Arguably, the CFI's

the issue is what factors persuaded the CFI that RTE's use of its copyright to block Magill's competition was abusive – in the CFI's words, 'manifestly contrary to the objectives of Article 86'. According to the CFI, RTE was preventing the emergence of a new product in competition with its own listings guide.

> 73. . . . it must be noted that the applicant, by reserving the exclusive right to publish its weekly television programme listings, was preventing the emergence on the market of a new product, namely a general television magazine likely to compete with its own magazine, the RTE Guide. The applicant was thus using its copyright in the programme listings which it produced as part of its broadcasting activity in order to secure a monopoly in the derivative market of weekly television guides . . . .
> Conduct of that type – characterised by *preventing* the production and marketing of *a new product*, for which there is potential consumer demand, *on the ancillary market* of television magazines and thereby excluding all competition from that market *solely in order to secure the applicant's monopoly* – clearly goes beyond what is necessary to fulfil the essential function of the copyright as permitted in Community law. The applicant's refusal to authorise third parties to publish its weekly listings was, in this case, arbitrary in so far as it was not justified either by the specific needs of the broadcasting sector, with which the present case is not concerned, or by those peculiar to the activity of publishing television magazines. (*Emphasis added*)

Compared to the very narrow definition of the market adopted by the CFI, with respect, this reasoning is, if possible, even more alarming. In effect, the first sentence states that RTE abused its copyright by refusing to license it to a potential competitor. Yet, as the CFI had earlier acknowledged in point 70, copyright by conferring on the owner the right to reproduce the work to the exclusion of all others confers on the owner *exactly* that very power. In *Warner Brothers*, the ECJ had gone on to state *the rules of the Treaty* did not call in question that essential right of the copyright owner.[252] That ruling, of course, concerned only the application of the rules on the free movement of goods to intellectual property and subsequently *Basset, Volvo, Renault* and *Tournier* have confirmed that the reach of the competition rules goes further.

The CFI seems to advance possibly two reasons to explain why it was necessary to go further in this case. First, it was not permissible as a matter of EC law to use copyright derived from activities in a 'primary' market to block competition in a 'derivative' or 'ancillary' market. Such use of copyright 'clearly goes beyond what is necessary to fulfil the essential function of the copyright as permitted in [EC] law.' Therefore, or alternatively, RTE's refusal to license was arbitrary in that it was not justified by the specific

---

reference to 'moral rights' deceived it into undervaluing the significance of the copyright owner's economic rights, but earlier in ¶70 it did refer to the ECJ's ruling in 158/86 *Warner Bros* discussed in Chapter 6 at Note 184.

252   156/86 *Warner Brothers* [1988] ECR 2605 at ¶13, quoted in Chapter 6 at Note 186. See also, in the patent field, 35/87 *Thetford v Fiamma* [1988] ECR 3585 at ¶24 (Chapter 6 Notes 205 to 206).

needs of *either* the broadcasting sector *or* the activity of publishing television magazines.[253]

One might well wonder why a refusal to license a competitor in the publication of television magazines is an arbitrary exercise of the exclusive right granted by copyright; after all, it is hard to imagine any other use of copyright in programme listings and the choice of whether to license or not must go to the essence of that exclusive right. The CFI felt supported in its conclusion that RTE had behaved arbitrarily because it licensed its listings free of charge to daily publications, to weekly publications for 'highlights' and to weekly publishers in other Member States. Does this mean that the right owner must choose between licensing all or none?[254] On the CFI's own analysis, the daily publications should have been irrelevant as they were a separate market. In addition, in *Coditel II*, the ECJ had referred to the existence of national controls over broadcasting licences – *television avec frontieres* – as a factor potentially justifying licensing on a national basis.

It is difficult to resist the conclusion that the CFI considered RTE's conduct arbitrary because RTE used its copyright to stifle new competition in a 'derivative' or 'ancillary' market. This conclusion may show an extremely *dirigiste* and questionable conception of commercial activity: undertakings are thought to operate primarily at only one level of the chain of production and distribution of a 'product'. Moreover, the CFI's analogy to *Volvo* and *Renault* in support of its conclusion on this part of the case seems misplaced. In *Volvo* and *Renault*, the ECJ referred to an arbitrary refusal to supply independent repairers as a potential abuse. The independent repairers in that example are more accurately compared to the newsagents and other outlets for RTE's magazine. Magill, however, had engaged in the very activity which Veng and CICRA were denied by the ECJ.[255] The conclusion in *Magill* suggests that, if Marks & Spencer reached a threshold of 20 per cent market share, it would risk contravention of Article 86 by refusing to make its products under the St Michael brand available to wholesalers and retailers.[256]

There are, perhaps, two other grounds on which *Magill* could be rationalised. *Magill* could be explained in terms of the injunction in

---

253   Compare 262/81 *Coditel II* [1982] ECR 3361 at ¶19; Chapter 7.2.2, above.

254   Compare the policy choices discussed at Chapter 3 Notes 181 to 183.

255   See Myrick, 'Will Intellectual Property on Technology Still be Viable in a Unitary Market?' at 303 Note 49 and Flynn, 'Intellectual Property and Anti-trust: EC Attitudes', at 53 to 54. The analogy to 311/84 *Centre Belge d'Etudes de Marché Telemarketing SA v Compagnie Luxembourgeoise de Télédiffusions* [1985] ECR 3261 and *London European-Sabena* (88/589/EEC) [1989] 4 CMLR 662 both cited in Sufrin, 'Comment on the Magill Case', at 68–9 is similarly misapplied. Moreover, both are distinguishable precisely because they did *not* involve intellectual property rights. For a critique of the *dirigiste* analysis, see A.D. Neale, *The Antitrust Laws of the United States of America*, Cambridge University Press, 1970, (2 edn), 250 to 256.

256   The fact that this example involves a trade mark should not make any difference as it also confers an exclusive right. Moreover, on the CFI's analysis in T-30/89 *Hilti AG v Commission* [1992] 4 CMLR 16, Marks & Spencer would be all the more at risk if it claimed copyright or design rights in any of its products.

Coditel II at point 19 to investigate whether or not the exclusive right was being exercised to charge fees which exceed a fair return on investment. Apart from the slippery question of what is a 'fair return',[257] this raises the question of the relevant product. For present purposes, RTE held copyright in its magazines but, as already noted, the CFI did not expressly find that RTE was charging outrageous or even 'high' prices for those magazines. Some economists might argue, however, that copyright protection was not necessary to induce RTE, BBC or ITP to create the information embodied in the listings.[258] In that sense, it might be possible to argue that, by refusing to license, RTE and the other broadcasters were charging fees in excess of a fair return on their investments. If so, the relevant product for that purpose is the information. But, in that case, the CFI's finding of dominance is, was not, and could not be, sustained.

Alternatively, the CFI's theory could possibly be sustained if it were shown that RTE's copyright in its programme listings constituted a 'bottleneck monopoly' or an 'essential facility'.[259] This does not, however, seem to be the approach taken by the CFI. If the theory applies, it highlights once again the very narrow definition of the market adopted by the Commission and the CFI. Moreover, it raises directly the issue of what is a 'fair return' on the investment. Arguably, there is very little point in compelling the owner of the essential facility to grant access if the owner may charge market price for entry as the owner of the facility could still extract the monopoly profit.[260] In *Magill*, the Commission 'solved' this dilemma by ordering the copyright owners to license their rights for 'reasonable' royalties only. It is far from clear, however, how reasonableness could be assessed.[261] What will be reasonable from the view point of a potential licensee will not necessarily be reasonable from the view point of a licensor faced with a threat to a business worth several million pounds. If the Commission be the arbiter of 'reasonableness', how will it reconcile its view that copyright protection for listings was 'banal' with the Member State's different view? In the absence of harmonisation, why should the views of the makers of competition policy in the EC simply override the views of those whom the EEC Treaty nominates as responsible for intellectual property policy?

257 See Note 261 below.
258 See Chapters 4.1 and 10.2.3.
259 Korah, *EEC Competition Law and Practice*, 4 edn, §12.2.3 and Phillip Areeda, *Antitrust Law 1992 Supplement*, Little, Brown & Co. Boston (1992) ¶¶736.1 and 736.2.
260 Areeda, *Antitrust Law 1992 Supplement* at ¶736.2a. The argument may not apply in the case of programme listings as public welfare could be enhanced by the creation of comprehensive listings: for example *Aspen Skiing Co. v Aspen Highlands Skiing Corp.* 472 US 585 (1985). In the absence of further controls, however, the suppliers of the inputs could, presumably, capture this gain in their prices. Moreover, *Magill* would represent at least one major step from this situation in that it forces the creation of a *new* product rather than restoration of a previously existing one.
261 For the contrasting interpretation of 'reasonable' in the United Kingdom and New Zealand, see Watts and Durie, 'A Comparative Study of TV Listings', at 134–5. See generally, Friedrich-Karl Beier, 'Patent Protection and the Free Market Economy', 23 IIC 159 (1992) and the commentaries cited at Notes 237 and 238 above, noting also that it is not yet clear whether the ECJ has adopted a 'reward' or an 'incentive' theory for intellectual property.

At this stage, therefore, it is not very clear when the owner of an intellectual property right will engage in conduct proscribed by Article 86. The ECJ has adopted a cautious approach to the question so far; indicating that the application of Article 86 depends on very special circumstances. However, the Commission with the support of the CFI has circumvented that caution by adopting very narrow definitions of the relevant market.[262] The extremely vague definition of 'abuse' under Article 86 makes caution even more warranted as some types of conduct usually considered an 'abuse' are precisely the kinds of conduct which, as *Magill* shows, authorised by intellectual property laws.

7.5   Trade with Third Countries

As discussed in Chapter 6.3.2, the role of the free movement rules in promoting parallel imports is limited to trade in the internal market. The competition rules are not so limited. Hence, an attempt to repel parallel imports from a country outside the EC could potentially involve the right owner in a contravention of either Article 85 or Article 86.

The potential application of the competition rules was confirmed by the ECJ in *EMI v CBS*, where, as a result of a transfer of business interests dating from the 1920s and 1930s, the trade mark for sound recordings, *Columbia*, was owned by independent businesses: CBS in the United States and EMI in the EC.[263] Having rejected any application of the doctrines of Community exhaustion or common origin, the ECJ ruled in point 27 that EMI's use of its trade mark rights in the EC to block CBS' imports from the United States could be subject to Article 85(1) if that use 'were to manifest itself as the subject, the means, or the consequence of a restrictive practice'.

The thrust of the argument in *EMI v CBS* focused on whether EMI's conduct in blocking the imports was a restrictive practice. There seem to have been two aspects to CBS' claims on this point. One was the fact that EMI's rights to the trade mark only arose at all because of their assignment from CBS to EMI. The other was a history of repertory exchanges between the two businesses which EMI claimed had ended on a systematic basis by the time of the action.

After reiterating that a trade mark did not itself create the elements of concertation necessary to trigger Article 85 but that the exercise of the rights conferred by it *might* if that exercise was 'the subject, the means, or the consequence of a restrictive practice', at point 28 the ECJ considered that an agreement to use trade mark rights to isolate the EC from third countries

---

262   Contrast *Broderbund Software v Computermate Products* (1991) 22 IPR 215 (Fed. C) at Note 250 above and *Studiengesellschaft Kohle* 670 F. 2d 1122 (DC Cir. 1981) at Chapter 3 Note 230 above.
263   51, 86 & 96 *EMI Records Ltd v CBS United Kingdom Ltd* [1976] ECR 811, see also Chapter 6.3.2 and Section 7.6.

might therefore breach Article 85. It did not then simply enjoin the national court to investigate whether or not the EC was being isolated as part of an agreement or concerted practice. Instead, the ECJ ruled:

> 30. For Article 85 to apply to a case, such as the present one, of agreements which are no longer in force it is sufficient that such agreements continue to produce their effects after they have formally ceased to be in force.

However, the ECJ continued:

> 31. An agreement is only regarded as continuing to produce its effects if from the behaviour of the persons concerned there may be inferred the existence of elements of concerted practice and of coordination peculiar to the agreement and producing the same result as that envisaged by the agreement.
> 32. This is not so when the said effects do not exceed those flowing from the mere exercise of the national trade-mark rights.
> 33. Furthermore it is clear from the file that the foreign trader can obtain access to the common market without availing himself of the mark in dispute.

Although it is not entirely clear, it seems from this passage that the ECJ was not concerned with the argument that the assignment of the trade mark itself sufficed to supply the necessary 'agreement' since points 31 and 32, in particular, seem directed to the allegations about ongoing collusion. For CBS to succeed, it would be required to prove that EMI and it were still conducting themselves in concert as would be the case if they were carrying out an agreement. Furthermore, point 33 indicates that CBS was not foreclosed from the market by EMI's exercise of its trade mark rights.[264]

The ECJ also abruptly dismissed the possibility of Article 86 being invoked on the facts before it:

> 36. Although the trade-mark right confers upon its proprietor a special position within the protected territory this, however, does not imply the existence of a dominant position within the meaning of [Article 86], *in particular where, as in the present case,* several undertakings whose economic strength is comparable to that of the proprietor of the mark operate in the market for the products in question and are in a position to compete with the said proprietor.
> 37. Furthermore in so far as the exercise of a trade-mark right is intended to prevent the importation into the protected territory of products bearing an identical mark, it does not constitute an abuse of a dominant position within the meaning of Article 86 of the Treaty. (*Emphasis added*)

The emphasised part of the quotation from point 36 suggests the ECJ did not deny the possible application of Article 86 to the situation. On the facts, however, EMI's use of its trade mark did not result in foreclosing the market. But, point 37 seems to suggest that a mere use of trade mark rights to block imports of identical goods from third countries could never be an abuse. This

---

264 This is consistent with interpreting *Consten & Grundig* as not condemning the assignment of the trade mark *per se*, but rather its role in a continuing scheme to partition the internal market. See also Joliet and Keeling, 'Trade Mark Law and the Free Movement of Goods: the Overruling of the Judgment in Hag I'.

point should be immediately qualified by recalling from points 31 and 32 that the ECJ seems to have regarded EMI and CBS as completely independent businesses. So, it may be more questionable whether an attempt to block parallel imports proper could be regarded as a mere use of trade mark rights. The developments in *Basset, Renault, Volvo* and *Tournier* noted in section 7.4 above must also be borne in mind.

Of course, the possible application of Article 86 is predicated on the right owner holding a dominant position in the EC (or a substantial part of it). On this issue, the considerations explored in section 7.4 above arise again.

The next point must be even more tentative. Article 86 does not incorporate an exempting provision like Article 85(3). So, arguably, the Commission would not have as much flexibility to overlook economic justifications for different prices between the EC and the third country as it does under Article 85(1) for trade in the internal market. The history of the 'success' of such arguments before the Commission unless supported by perceived requirements of the specific subject-matter of the right does not augur well unless considerable force can be placed on an EC licensee's need for protection from particularly cheap import competition. In that case, however, anti-dumping procedures might be more relevant.

The Commission has actually refused to condemn agreements banning exports from the EC or imports into the EC. This has not been on the ground that the ban did not, or could not, restrict competition. Rather, the Commission has considered that, in the particular circumstances of the case, there was unlikely to be trade entering the EC anyway.[265]

7.6   Assignments, Oligopolies and Horizontal Problems

The focus of this chapter has been the extent to which both the ECJ and the Commission have accepted qualifications on the unity of the internal market resulting from the need to encourage desired investment. From the perspective of parallel imports, that has necessarily concentrated on the extent to which a particular territory may be protected against intra-brand competition. For the most part, the analysis has examined how far contractual restraints can be placed on a party binding it not to engage in competition with other authorised users of the intellectual property or to prevent third parties (parallel importers) from doing so. Before the parallel importer can engage in promoting the unity of the internal market, however,

---

265   For example, in distribution, customs duties and transport costs were thought likely to preclude imports or reimports in *Grosfillex* [1964] CMLR 237; *Kodak* [1970] CMLR D19; *Distillers Red Label* [1978] 1 CMLR 400, at ¶72 to 73. The issue is not discussed in *Fluke/Phillips* [1990] 4 CMLR 166, although there the exemption was being granted because of the parties' inability to penetrate the market. In technology licensing, see *Raymond/Nagoya* [1972] CMLR D45 at ¶9(i) where imports were unlikely in view of the custom nature of design and the difficulties of co-operation, but contrast *BBC Brown Boveri/NGK* [1989] 4 CMLR 610 where the restriction was exempted as necessary for recovery of the investment.

it must be able to obtain the goods from someone authorised to release them into the internal market. What happens if the parallel importer cannot get the product at a sufficiently low price to make parallel trade economic?

The problem might arise in either of two ways. The intellectual property rights for the Member State where the price is low might have been sold off to an independent business or the local distributor (or licensee) may simply refuse to sell to the parallel importer. The first situation raises in part whether or not an assignment of rights to, say, France, allows a right owner in Germany which operates an independent business to block imports sold by the French right owner; a point which may assume some importance following *Hag II*. The second raises the question of 'unilateral conduct'.

Taking the second issue first, unless perhaps the undertaking be dominant, there is generally no obligation on it to deal with anyone so it may refuse to sell directly to a prospective customer.[266] Where the customer refused is based in another concessionaire's territory or is suspected of wishing to engage in parallel importing, however, considerable caution must be exercised that the refusal is a truly unilateral act. Particularly in distribution cases, it will not take much to raise an inference of collusion. If the concessionaire refuses to deal as a result of pressure from a co-ordinating supplier (or licensor when bans on passive sales are not permitted) rather than from its own objective business reasons, it is very likely that collusion to block parallel imports will be found.[267]

The issue was a third set of questions in *Tournier*. The national copyright collecting agencies had entered into reciprocal agreements appointing each of the others its representative in their respective territories. The Commission had forced them to drop mutual obligations refusing to license their repertoire to users in other Member States. In practice, however, nothing had changed. They also refused to grant licences only for particular categories of their repertoire.

The ECJ first pointed out that the reciprocal contracts were not in themselves restrictions of competition since they served permissible ends.[268] This was particularly the case after the deletion of the obligations denying direct access. But, the continued failure of any agency to grant direct access could be taken to indicate the existence of a concerted practice of the sort condemned in *Dyestuffs*.[269] This would not be the case:

266   For a dominant undertaking, see *United Brands* [1978] ECR 207, at ¶¶182 to 190; *Renault* [1991] 4 CMLR 265, at ¶16 and Section 7.4 above.
267   10/82 *AEG Telefunken v Commission* [1983] ECR 3153; 279/87 *Tipp-Ex v Commission*, unreported judgment of 8 February 1990, for the Commission's decision, the operative part is at [1990] ECR I-261, see [1989] 4 CMLR 425; 277/87 *Sandoz* unreported judgment 11 January 1990, the operative part is at [1990] ECR I-45. See generally, Korah, *EEC Competition Law and Practice*, at 27 to 28; Whish, *Competition Law*, at 226 to 228.
268   [1991] 4 CMLR 248 at ¶20. The ends identified were: (1) enabling users to get access to all musical works regardless of origin on the same terms, as required by international convention; and (2) allowing the agencies to protect their repertoire in other countries without having to set up there: ¶19.
269   48/69 *ICI v Commission* [1972] ECR 619. See further Korah, *EEC Competition Law and Practice*, at 30 to 32 and Whish, *Competition Law*, at 221 to 226.

24. . . . where the parallel behaviour can be accounted for by reasons other than the existence of concerted action. Such a reason might be that the copyright-management societies of other member-States would be obliged, in the event of direct access to their repertoires, to organise their own management and monitoring system in another country.

Although the ECJ left determination of whether the parallel conduct was evidence of concertation or otherwise justifiable independent action to the national court, it seems from the Advocate-General's opinion that the small proportion of the repertoire administered by each agency originating in its own territory made it economically unlikely they would attempt to enter another national market.[270] On the question of the agencies' refusal to grant licences to a part only of their repertoire, the ECJ indicated that this was permissible to the extent that it was necessary to safeguard the interests of copyright owners. To the extent that the refusal went beyond that:

Those limits may be exceeded if direct access to a sub-division of a repertoire, as advocated by the discothèque operators, could fully safeguard the interests of authors, composers and publishers of music without thereby increasing the costs of managing contracts and monitoring the use of protected musical works.[271]

Hence, the national court was directed to engage in a process of balancing the competing interests of copyright users and owners. The copyright owners were able to work through a collecting agency as the only practicable way of administering the performing right. In deciding whether or not a refusal to grant anything other than a blanket licence over the whole repertoire was anti-competitive, it was also permissible to take into account the savings on transaction costs gained in the management of contracts and monitoring use. In point 32, however, the ECJ indicated that what was permissible in one Member State may not necessarily follow in another.

The first issue raised at the start of this section, the competitive effect of assignments, may receive greater importance with the apparent demise of the doctrine of common origin following *Hag II*.[272] It has long been settled that parties cannot by agreement, or concerted practice, use the national character of intellectual property rights to partition the Common Market. But, it is not entirely clear on what basis the trade mark assignment in *Consten & Grundig* was condemned. The assignment itself may have been the 'conspiracy' to divide the then fledgling Common Market. In which case there would be considerable scope to attack use of trade marks having a common origin divided by voluntary assignment. Alternatively, Consten and Grundig may have been taking part in an ongoing 'conspiracy' of which the assignment together with other circumstances such as the reciprocal export bans, the establishment of parallel networks in other Member States and action against parallel importers were merely evidence. Some support for this interpretation can be found in the references, in cases like *Maize Seed*

---

270   [1991] 4 CMLR 248, at 262 to 263 *per* Advocate-General Jacobs.
271   *Ibid*. at ¶31. For a similar US case, see *Broadcast Music Inc. v Columbia Broadcasting Systems Inc.* 441 US 1 (1979).
272   See Chapter 6 from Note 220.

and *Pronuptia*, to *Consten & Grundig* as condemning 'absolute territorial protection'.

If the latter be correct, then an assignment without more, the two owners thereafter operating their respective businesses completely independently, is arguably exhausted once the transfer is complete. Hence, there would be no agreement to condemn under Article 85 and the use of trade mark rights to block imports sourced from the other business would be justifiable to prevent end-user confusion.

Some support for that approach can be found in *EMI v CBS*. There the ECJ ruled that, for an agreement to have continuing effects, there must be evidence from which an ongoing relationship of concertation and co-ordination could be inferred. That required more than what would result from the mere exercise of national intellectual property rights.[273]

A number of difficulties lie in the path of regarding *EMI v CBS* as a definitive statement of principle. *EMI v CBS* involved assignment of rights for the whole of (what subsequently became) the EC. The imports being blocked came from outside the EC. There is little doubt that the Commission in the past has energetically encouraged business to treat the EC (and intellectual property rights held within it) as a single unit. That, after all, is largely the purpose of the internal market programme. Much of industry, and its advisers, have been forced to act accordingly. However, on its 'true' facts, the ECJ's ruling in *Sirena* is consistent with the application of the approach in *EMI v CBS* to assignments of rights in different Member States.

But, the argument that any partitioning of the market is only the natural consequence of the division of national intellectual property rights has not met with much success. Both the ECJ and the Commission have inferred ongoing concertation with little difficulty. In fact, where a trade mark has been assigned and the assignee continued to act as distributor of products made by the assignor one can almost say that a continuing agreement will be found.[274] Prior to *Hag II*, however, the ECJ seemed more willing to treat assignments of other intellectual property rights more liberally where the assignee was accorded considerable independence.

Then, both *Sirena* and *EMI v CBS* concerned assignments effected long before the EC had even been conceived, let alone created. It is questionable whether considerations applying to such long-standing assignments would necessarily apply to assignments effected now that the Common Market is reaching a considerable degree of integration notwithstanding the many obstacles still remaining.

---

273 See Section 7.5.
274 In 170/83 *Hydrotherm Gerätebau GmbH v Andreoli* [1984] ECR 2999, the agreement was saved because there was no evidence of it being used to partition the Common Market more than permitted by the relevant group exemption, Regulation 67/67.

7.7   Conclusion

Under the competition rules, both the ECJ and the Commission have relied on the need to encourage investment to qualify the goal of integrating the internal market. Each has done so across the range of intellectual property subject-matter considered by it. However, while the ECJ has shown great willingness to consider the need to encourage investment in the creation of intellectual property under Article 85(1), the Commission has almost invariably done so under Article 85(3).

The pivotal point is the ECJ's decision in *Maize Seed*. There the ECJ first clearly approved the importance of the need to encourage investment under Article 85(1). In doing so, it treated the technology licence as vertical in nature and analysed *ex ante*. All three aspects were contrary to the Commission's own previous practice under Article 85(1).[275]

But, the scope of the ECJ's approach in *Maize Seed* is unclear – does it apply just to plant breeders' rights, must the technology always be new and what is 'new', what was the specific nature of the products in question justifying the broad approach espoused by the ECJ, does the reasoning only apply to open exclusivity? Some commentators argue that much of the reasoning in *Maize Seed* applies generally and should be interpreted broadly.[276] In reaching this conclusion, they rely first on the similarities between the judgments in *Maize Seed*, *Coditel II* and, in Korah's case, *Erauw Jacquery* and secondly on the underlying purpose of intellectual property laws, the promotion of incentives to innovate. Both aspects, understood in a broad sense, can be seen in *Pronuptia* as well.

On the other hand, the Commission tends to favour a much narrower interpretation.[277] Prior to *Erauw Jacquery*, it appeared to have accepted that *Maize Seed* applied to technology licensing generally and was not confined solely to plant breeders' rights.[278] Following *Erauw Jacquery*'s extension of *Maize Seed* to export bans, the Commission appears to be reviving its interest in qualifications based on 'the specific nature of the products'.[279] Even before then, however, it had relied on other aspects of *Maize Seed* to

---

275   An intriguing parallel may be a perceived crisis in 'European competitiveness' suggested for the late 1970s and early 1980s. See for example Margaret Sharp, 'Technology and the Dynamics of Integration', in William Wallace, *The Dynamics of European Integration*, Pinter Publishers, 1990, Chapter 3. Of the range of institutional responses cited, Ms Sharp does not address competition policy although she highlights an increased emphasis on collaboration and, increasingly, mergers. See also Angus K. Maciver, 'EEC Competition Policy in High Technology Industries', [1986] *Fordham Corporate Law Institute* 521 (the author was then International Counsel, Corning Glass Works).

276   Korah, *Know-how Licensing Agreements and the EEC Competition Rules*, at 30 to 36; Siragusa, 'Technology Transfers Under EEC Law: A Private View', at 116 to 123, 137 to 142.

277   See also Schröter, 'Antitrust Analysis Under Article 85(1) and (3)', at 666 to 688 and the critique in Waelbroeck, 'Antitrust Analysis under Article 85(1) and (3)', at 693.

278   See for example Regulation 2349/84, recital 11; Regulation 556/89, recital 6.

279   See *Comasso* OJ 1990 C6/3; [1990] 4 CMLR 259 (19(3) Notice) at Note 181 above.

reduce its scope. In its first application, *Knoll/Hille-Form*, the Commission refused to apply *Maize Seed* in part because neither the 'newness' of the technology nor the size of the investment justified it.[280] The horizontal nature of the agreement suggests sound reasons for careful application of *Maize Seed*, but the detail of the report is not sufficient to form a view on the standard of novelty applied. Two later decisions concerning know-how do raise concern, however. In *Rich Products/Jus-rol*, the Commission concluded that the technology licensed for snap freezing dough was not 'new' because other methods of carrying out the process existed.[281] Then, in *Delta Chemie*, the Commission denied novelty because the licensee had been acting as a distributor of the product even though without the licence it never had the capacity to engage in production.[282] These cases seem inconsistent with the ECJ's ruling in *Maize Seed* where it rejected the Commission's interpretation of the licence as not involving new technology.

The hope has been expressed that the Commission's narrow interpretation of *Maize Seed* will not survive its need to gain experience prior to adopting a group exemption.[283] But, in the light of the way the Commission has historically interpreted Article 85(1) as forbidding any restraint on a party's freedom of action, it seems more realistic to consider that full acceptance of *Maize Seed* by the Commission will require a significant change in its thinking.[284]

The Commission's approach could potentially have unfortunate results, threatening to undermine dynamism in the market-place. On the one hand, its use of Article 85(3) increases legal uncertainty which may have a chilling effect on investment in innovation.[285] On the other, it promotes rigidity at the expense of flexibility by channeling licensing and distribution structures into forms approved in its group exemptions. Yet flexibility and diversity in the variety of means used to get goods to the market are highly important.[286]

---

280 *13th Report on Competition Policy*, EC Commission, 1984, at ¶144. It went on in ¶145 to deny exemption because the agreement was between two competitors and totally blocked intra-EC trade.

281 [1988] 4 CMLR 527, see further Korah, *Know-how Licensing Agreements and the EEC Competition Rules*, at 34, 43 to 45.

282 [1989] 4 CMLR 535, see further Korah, *Know-how Licensing Agreements and the EEC Competition Rules*, at 34, 45 to 47.

283 Korah, *Know-how Licensing Agreements and the EEC Competition Rules*, at 36 to 37.

284 See also Hawk, 2 *United States, Common Market and International Antitrust: A Comparative Guide*, at 644 to 645.

285 There is some evidence that US firms' licensing practice *within* the EC have not been affected provided they can rely on US patent barriers to block competition in their US markets, see Bleeke and Rahl, 'The Value of Territorial and Field of Use Restrictions in the International Licensing of Unpatented Know-How: An Empirical Survey', at 450 with some support from Mansfield, Romero and Wagner, 'Foreign Trade and US Research and Development', at 54 to 56.

286 See for example Eleanor M. Fox, 'The Modernization of Antitrust: A New Equilibrium', 66 Cornell LRev. 1140 (1981); F.M. Scherer, 'Antitrust, Efficiency and Progress', 62 NYULRev. 998 (1987).

It could be argued that the circumstances within the EC are different to those of, say, the United States. That would certainly be a valid consideration.[287] The main difficulty with the explanation is that it is not the reason the Commission gives for its decisions. Then, it raises the question of why the Commission is prepared to grant blanket exemptions for much of the same conduct under Article 85(3). It could also be argued that the Commission's approach is necessary to promote certainty. At least, clear lines are drawn. That is only true if the parties are willing and able to adopt the form prescribed by the Commission in a group exemption. Furthermore, it does not explain why it is necessary to find an array of practices formally to restrict competition, but then to accord many almost blanket exemption, particularly if there are potential costs through disincentives and loss of flexibility. The potential disincentives to investment if that is not the case may be magnified by the Commission's tendency to modify agreements after one or the other party's bargaining position may have changed.[288]

The argument that *Maize Seed* applies broadly emphasises the ECJ's references to the need to encourage investment and the strengthening of inter-brand competition.[289] However, its history in the ECJ's case law makes it impossible to overlook the reference to 'new technology'. Subsequent cases also include counterparts to the reference in *Maize Seed* to 'the specific nature of the products'. Notwithstanding these qualifications, the ECJ's case law shows a clear trend towards broad acceptance of the general proposition: if exclusivity and related 'restrictions' be necessary to encourage the desired investment, it will be necessary to qualify the goal of market integration. To do so, the ECJ has consistently used a dynamic analysis of the agreement's impact in the market-place by analysing *ex ante*.

287   For example, Waelbroeck, 'Vertical Agreements: Is the Commission Right not to Follow the Current US Policy?', at 45; Luc Gyselen, 'Vertical Restraints in the Distribution Process: Strength and Weakness of the Free Rider Rationale under EEC Competition Law', (1984) 21 CMLRev. 647.
288   The *ARD* case is a noticeable instance, see Note 162 above.
289   See especially Siragusa, 'Technology Transfers Under EEC Law: A Private View,' at 116 to 123, 137 to 142.

Chapter 8: Pharmaceuticals

8.1 Introduction

Thus far the author's examination has focused on the legal treatment of parallel imports. A key point emerging from that analysis is the failure of the law to look at why parallel imports occur. The consequences have not necessarily been happy. In the Anglo-Commonwealth jurisdictions, in the United States and in the EC, the legal rules governing parallel imports are becoming increasingly complicated and technical. As already discussed, even within jurisdictions and the same subject-matter, there are many apparent contradictions and inconsistencies. The pressure from intellectual property owners for protection against parallel imports continues. The search for standards goes on.

Of course, much of this state of flux is inherent in the nature of the legal process. As new facts, new knowledge and new situations arise, the courts adjust old solutions in the light of the new considerations. However, unless the courts and policy-makers address why parallel imports occur, it is unlikely that the resulting policies will be formulated correctly. Unless the considerations are open and explicit, they cannot be tested by debate, nor will it be possible for businesses to order their affairs soundly.

The pharmaceuticals industry is an obvious candidate for attempts to assess the impact of parallel imports. It is the industry where claims about the importance of patent protection arguably have the strongest force. In addition, within the EC, it is one of the industries most subject to the attentions of prospective parallel importers.

From the perspective of intellectual property law, the pharmaceuticals industry presents a striking paradox. It is difficult to imagine an industry whose products could be of more immediate importance to the human condition. Particularly since the Second World War, most of those products have only come into existence as a result of considerable investment in innovation. Yet, there can be few areas where governments of almost all persuasions intervene so much to limit the effects of the patent system. Indeed, many countries refuse even to grant patents to protect medical products and the processes for their manufacture.[1] If the theories justifying

1 For a list of some, see R.B. Saxena, 'Trade-Related Issues of Intellectual Property Rights and the Indian Patent Act – A Negotiating Strategy', 12 *World Competition* 81,

patent protection have validity, such conduct might be thought counter-productive! The inconsistencies and contradictions multiply when an attempt is made to assess the impact of parallel imports on the pharmaceuticals industry.

The cost of providing effective health care is a worldwide issue. Regardless of political hue, population, geographical location or state of industrial development, all governments are faced with a need to balance the demands of their people for good health care with increasing strains on their budgets.[2] However, although cost and care are the common central issues, the problems confronting each country are not necessarily the same. For example, in the so-called developing countries, there is a greater need to deal with basic issues related to sanitation, hygiene and infectious diseases as well as provide the latest drugs and other technology at the forefront of medical research in the developed world.[3] In addition, while average spending on drugs in the developed world had been estimated at 8 per cent of health spending, it is thought to be 40 per cent in developing countries.[4]

Health care, and its cost, also provokes strong emotions. When someone is ill, they, and their relatives and friends, demand a cure. If a remedy exists, quibbling about payment is hardly the issue. Nor are the circumstances conducive to refined arguments about the need to recoup risky investments particularly when the source readily appears to hold a monopolistic position. Tensions are even more exacerbated when the apparently exorbitant payments are demanded by, usually, large corporations which, in many countries, are also foreign. Nevertheless, the uncomfortable fact remains; someone must pay for the development and delivery of often expensive remedies.

Whether pharmaceuticals, if protected by patents at all, should also be shielded against intra-brand competition from parallel imports is an issue which has confronted policy-makers around the world.[5] However, this study

at 92 (1988). See also Daniel Chudnovsky, 'Patents and Trademarks in Pharmaceuticals', (1983) 11 *World Development* 187, at 189. In the late 19th Century, both Germany and Switzerland conferred protection on processes only. For Germany, see Saxena, 'Trade-Related Issues of Intellectual Property Rights and the Indian Patent Act', at 92 (1988) and for Switzerland, see F.M. Scherer, *The Economic Effects of Compulsory Patent Licensing*, New York University, 1977, at 35 to 37.

2   For example, as discussed below, France, Germany, Italy and the United Kingdom have wrestled with the problem; India has been grappling with the struggle since at least the 1960s, see *ibid.*; New Zealand introduced a bill to facilitate parallel imports following complaints about the price of drugs: Medicines Amendment Bill 1989, No. 59.

3   For some discussion of this issue, compare Anwar Fazal, 'The Right Pharmaceuticals at the Right Prices: Consumer Perspectives', (1983) 11 *World Development* 265 and S. Michael Peretz, 'Pharmaceuticals in the Third World: The Problem from the Suppliers' Point of View', (1983) 11 *World Development* 259.

4   Mahesh S. Patel, 'Drug Costs in Developing Countries and Policies to Reduce Them', (1983) 11 *World Development* 195, at 196. To put these percentages in perspective, developed countries' average spend on drugs of US$50 per person compared to US$6 per person in developing countries; but, developed countries spend, and are able to spend, even more on other aspects of health care: *ibid.* at 195.

5   For present purposes, the discussion is intended to relate to so-called 'ethical' drugs, those which can only be sold on a doctor's prescription. Such drugs should be contrasted to 'over the counter' drugs (or OTCs).

relates mainly to examining experience in the EC. The problems in other countries are mentioned only in comparison.

The EC presents a useful focus for two reasons; one of diversity, the other of similarity. The various Member States have opted for different policies towards the pharmaceuticals industry. Some have favoured relative degrees of pricing freedom with the aim of promoting a strong pharmaceutical industry. Others have been more concerned to satisfy consumers' demands at low prices without feeling the need to promote industry. Still others have sought to achieve both ends. To a considerable extent, particularly historically, there have also been major concerns about foreign domination. Second, compared to many parts of the world, the Member States of the EC discussed here, despite their many and obvious differences, present a reasonable degree of similarity in terms of income levels, life expectancy, disease incidence and economic circumstances – certainly to a greater extent than a comparison of them with a developing country. In this setting, it is possible to examine the impact of a vigorous exhaustion doctrine (promoted within the EC).

An attempt is made to assess the effect of the exhaustion rule: whether it can be counted a success in terms of the market integration goal and/or the goal of reducing costs or whether the feared injury has arisen (or is likely to arise). Unfortunately, the somewhat tentative findings are not as conclusive as could be desired. Rather, the study serves to demonstrate complexity. Simply announcing the adoption of an exhaustion doctrine does not fuse a single market. The further actions required and their costs may be the necessary price of the political objective of integrating an internal market in the EC. But, what of countries which are not involved in, and do not wish to embark on, such an enterprise? On the other hand, the survey reveals the considerable potential for (in particular) large transnational firms to engage in strategic behaviour, first, to exploit the disunities underlying the fallacy in the principle of universality and, second, to pressure national policy-makers who overlook commercial considerations. This leads into a third point – the failure of the 'low-price' strategy to reconcile the demands of health budgets and industry policy.

8.2 Parallel Imports Now

In the EC, parallel imports affecting the pharmaceuticals industry are largely a matter of trade between Member States. According to representatives of the UK industry, parallel imports of drugs from outside the EC are not a problem.[6] These claims seem to be supported by the legal treatment of

6 As with some of the larger companies active in the computer industry, individual pharmaceutical producers refused to be interviewed about parallel imports, referring the author to the trade association, the Association of British Pharmaceutical Industry (ABPI), for comment. In addition to interviews with ABPI officials, the state of the industry has been the subject of a number of reports and commentaries of varying degrees of independence over the last decade.

parallel imports in most Member States where patent laws allow imports from outside the EC to be blocked with relative ease.[7] Within the EC, then, the impact of parallel imports could be seen as a question largely of the effect of the doctrine of Community exhaustion.

Of the many features of the EC market for drugs, two are particularly notable for present purposes. Prices of drugs vary quite markedly from Member State to Member State. Even so, parallel importing, although increasing, does not yet seem to have reached the levels which might be expected from comparisons of simple price differences.

8.2.1 A fragmented market

Given the controversy aroused by cases like *Sterling Drug* and *Merck*,[8] with excitable claims heralding the establishment of a single market contesting alarms about the destruction of incentive, perhaps the most surprising thing about the EC market for drugs is that, by and large, it does not exist. For the most part, each Member State is a distinctly separate *national* market. The most obvious indicator of this fragmentation along national lines is the different price levels as illustrated by Table 8.1.

The body of Table 8.1 shows drug prices for individual Member States relative to prices in the United Kingdom. The comparisons are based on the prices charged by the manufacturer, not the retail price. The first column shows the prevailing prices claimed for the drug Moduretic by the defendants in *Merck*. The next four columns are various attempts to estimate average price levels in the Member States. These are at best only very rough guides. The divergence of the European Federation of Pharmaceutical Industry Associations' (EFPIA) figures from the trend common to the others could be explained by a number of factors. Of the main two, the different time period for the survey is discussed further below. The second factor is the composition of the 'bundle' of drugs from which the average is derived. As the remaining seven columns show, the price of any given drug may vary quite considerably from one country to another. So, any attempt to find an average value will vary depending on which drugs are included in the bundle. Further variation will be introduced depending on whether or not any attempt is made to weight values according to sales levels achieved.[9]

---

7 For example, the national exhaustion doctrines applied by Dutch and German law do not extend to sales outside their borders: for Dutch law, see 15/74 *Centrafarm v Sterling Drug* [1974] ECR 1147; for German law, see Chapter 1 Note 20. In the United Kingdom, sales abroad by the patentee require notice of the restriction to be effected, but this is in practice a minor qualification, see Chapter 3.2.3 above. For a brief survey of the position in most Member States, see AIPPI, *Annuaire 1990/V: Parallel Import of Patented Products*, AIPPI, 1990.

8 187/80 *Merck v Stephar* [1981] ECR 2063.

9 For example, lists of the top ten drugs for 1988 in each of France, Germany, Italy and the United Kingdom show only one, Bayer's Adalat(e), common to all (with estimated sales ranging from US$78 to 120 million in each country). Glaxo's Zantac was common to Germany, Italy and the United Kingdom with sales ranging from US$62 to 175 million and, in both Germany and Italy, it was in competition with another higher ranked

Table 8.1
Manufacturers' Pharmaceutical Prices Within the EC

	Merck[a]	EFPIA[b]	BEUC[c]	Burstall[d]	SLH[e]	Zantac[e]	Tenormin[e]	Voltarol[e]	Tagamet[e]	Adala[e]	Feldene[e]	Zovirax[e]
FRG	172	209	124	113	127	144	139	74	218	117	127	98
UK	100	100	100	100	100	100	100	100	100	100	100	100
It	97	109	58	74	81	112	85		110	81	66	66
Fr	88	101	56	58	79	79	39	46	112	52	93	80
B	176			74	73	100	52	56	104	78	78	67
Ire				112								
N	241			109								
Dk	131			103								
P				66								
S				62								
Gr				61								

Sources:
(a) 187/80 *Merck v Stephar* [1981] ECR 2063, at 2075 (author's conversion)
(b) Walton, Adkins and Smith, *A Controversial Vision of the Future*, at 7 (figures for 1985)
(c) Walton, Adkins and Smith, *A Controversial Vision of the Future*, at 7 (figures for 1987)
(d) Burstall, *1992 and the Regulation of the Pharmaceutical Industry*, at 9 (Table 2.1)
(e) Walton, Adkins and Smith, *A Controversial Vision of the Future*, at 7.

Additional complications are introduced by the need to engage in exchange rate conversions.[10]

The seven individual products listed in Table 8.1 are included only for illustrative purposes. Shearson Lehmann Hutton Securities' data, which they are based on, set out values for 19 products.[11] To the extent that the 19 are representative of manufacturers' pricing levels,[12] it would seem that roughly two of every three products sold in Germany could be priced at least 15 per cent higher than in the United Kingdom. However, just under one in four could be sold at a price at least 15 per cent lower. Correspondingly, at least two-thirds of products marketed in Italy could be priced at least 15 per cent lower than in the United Kingdom. In France, the proportion sold at prices at least 15 per cent lower than the United Kingdom could be half; with the figure in Belgium just under half.[13] None of the prices surveyed for Italy, France or Belgium exceeded UK prices by at least 15 per cent. In addition, although the German price was also lower than the Italian price in one case where it was lower than the corresponding UK price, French, Belgian and Italian prices tended to be much lower relative to UK prices.

Apart from the disparate price levels around the EC, the other important factor which Table 8.1 exposes to some extent is the shift in the United Kingdom's position. Ignoring the figures attributed to EFPIA as inconsistent with the trend shown in the other data,[14] UK drug prices appear to have become more expensive relative to other Member States. The gap between UK prices and those in France and Italy has widened. UK prices, which used to be cheaper than Belgian, now appear to be more expensive.[15]

product based on the same active substance. At the other extreme, 24 different branded drugs were ranked in the top ten in only one country. See Jo Walton, Stewart Adkins and Ian Smith, *A Controversial Vision of the Future: Challenges Posed by Pharmaceutical Deregulation*, Shearson Lehmann Hutton Securities, 1989, at 74 to 75, the figures for 1987 are similar: *ibid.* at 72 to 73.

10   All the estimates relate to periods before the United Kingdom entered the Exchange Rate Mechanism (ERM).

11   Walton, Adkins and Smith, *A Controversial Vision of the Future*, at 7.

12   The slender nature of the comparison can be illustrated by the fact that in 1987 some 1,200 physiologically active substances were on sale and appearing in some 3,500 different brands: M.L. Burstall, *1992 and the Regulation of the Pharmaceutical Industry*, IEA Health and Welfare Unit No. 9, 1990, at 7.

13   French and Belgian estimates are further complicated by the fact that SLH obtained no data for 5 of the 19 products in France and 7 of the 19 for Belgium: Walton, Adkins and Smith, *A Controversial Vision of the Future*, at 7. French estimates for 1986 indicated that French prices were about 30 per cent below the European average: *Les Informations Chimie*, special issue, June 1986 cited in Leigh Hancher, *Regulating for Competition*, Clarendon Press, 1990, at 252.

14   Apart from the problems of 'timing' and 'bundling', the reported results do not fit data in *Sterling Drug, Merck v Stephar* and those of *Les Informations Chimie*, Note 7, 8 and 13 above.

15   By 1985, the United Kingdom was described as having risen from near the bottom to a mid-position in EC prices: M.L. Burstall, *The Community's Pharmaceutical Industry*, EC Commission, 1985, at 42 Note 13. In 1988, when the price of drugs was compared to the price of other goods, UK drugs were thought to be the most expensive in the EC: Burstall, *1992 and the Regulation of the Pharmaceutical Industry*, at 29 (Table 3.3), and 31 to 32. This, apparently, despite the fact that the United Kingdom alone has a large market for pure generics, which account for about 39 per cent of NHS demand (the

So, despite 15 years of the workings of the 'pernicious' Community exhaustion rule, 'the market' is still fragmented, largely along national lines. In many cases this fragmentation results in quite substantial price differences.

8.2.2 The volume of parallel imports

Depending on the method of calculation used, the potential volume of parallel imports and savings in terms of lower prices paid could be quite substantial. For example, the independent stockbroking analysts, Shearson Lehmann Hutton Securities, calculate that prices would fall 20 per cent if they were reduced across the EC to Belgian levels.[16] Alternatively, if calculations are based on the cheapest EC price for a particular product, Shearson Lehmann Hutton suggest that savings in the United Kingdom could be 27 per cent; in Germany, 33 per cent; and in Italy, up to 20 per cent.[17] As Shearson Lehmann Hutton acknowledge, such calculations are theoretical maxima. What happens in practice is substantially different.

The Association of British Pharmaceutical Industry in the United Kingdom claim to have commissioned a market survey of the extent of parallel imports around the EC. Its results, however, are not available for public discussion.[18]

The sources considered below claim that parallel imports have penetrated the market in the United Kingdom to a greater extent than any other Member State. If so, that would appear to be a phenomenon of the 1980s as prices in the United Kingdom increased relative to other Member States and the government introduced a range of cost-saving devices.[19] In the first part of the decade, parallel imports were thought to account for 5 per cent of the Dutch market and 1 to 1½ per cent of the German and UK markets respectively.[20]

By 1989–90, parallel imports into the United Kingdom were thought to range anywhere from 3 to 10 per cent of the market. Hancher and an

corresponding figure for France being 2 per cent): Hancher, *Regulating for Competition*, at 59, also noting at 177 that the United Kingdom became a net importer of drugs for the first time in 1982.

16 Walton, Adkins and Smith, *A Controversial Vision of the Future*, at 8; they note savings would be even greater on BEUC's figures. Burstall quotes the same figure from interviews with representatives of US and Swiss pharmaceutical companies: Burstall, *1992 and the Regulation of the Pharmaceutical Industry*, at 69.

17 *Ibid.*

18 Interviews with ABPI officials, July 1990.

19 Hancher puts the threshold year at 1982: Hancher, *Regulating for Competition*, at 57 and 177 when, for the first time, the United Kingdom became a net importer of drugs. For the government measures, see section 8.3.3(b) below.

20 These figures are restated in Burstall, *1992 and the Regulation of the Pharmaceutical Industry*, at 69 as coming from 'most estimates' and relating to 'the early to mid-1980s'. The same figures are given in Burstall, *The Community's Pharmaceutical Industry*, at 100, where they are described as coming from 'commercial sources' and appear to relate to the year 1983. 'Commercial sources' seems to describe reports in *Scrip* cross-checked with industry (as a result of which a figure of 10 per cent for parallel imports into the Netherlands is described as 'inflated', see *ibid.*, at Note 10).

organisation called the Office of Health Economics both put the figure for 1989 at 10 per cent.[21] Burstall reported an estimate of from 5 to 10 per cent for 1987 which, if penetration continued to expand, would tend to support something in the order of 10 per cent by 1989–90.[22] The UK Government discounts repayments to pharmacists for prescription dispensing by an amount of about 12.5 per cent, but it is unclear whether this is the level it believes parallel imports to be running at or the level it is trying to encourage.[23] Shearson Lehmann Hutton discounted the figure of 10 per cent claimed by the Office of Health Economics as unlikely in the face of poor acceptance at the wholesale and retail level. Instead, they reported 'other sources' as estimating a total market share of between 3 and 7 per cent.[24]

Shearson Lehmann Hutton also reported all their sources as agreeing that penetration of the UK market by parallel imports was 'growing fast'. Against this, Hancher indicates that use of parallel imports in the United Kingdom began falling off in 1987 when a government-endorsed advertising campaign warned pharmacists they risked disqualification if they substituted parallel imports or generics for brands specifically named in prescriptions, a warning subsequently approved by the ECJ.[25] The question of the *potential* scope of parallel imports is discussed further below in section 8.3.3(c). For present purposes, the important point is that the highest estimate puts parallel imports into the United Kingdom at 10 per cent and there are reasons to believe that figure to be inflated.

In Germany, there is some evidence that the gap between potential and reality is even greater. Based on sales and estimated market share of its largest parallel importer, Eurim-Pharm, Shearson Lehmann Hutton thought parallel imports might have achieved only 1 per cent of the German market in aggregate.[26] That would indicate no growth at all from the start of the decade although German prices had consistently remained high. However, it seems that the bulk of this trade is concentrated on a few high-profile drugs.[27]

21   Hancher, *Regulating for Competition*, at 57 (source of estimate unspecified); the Office of Health Economics' estimate is reported in Walton, Adkins and Smith, *A Controversial Vision of the Future*, at 16.

22   Burstall, *1992 and the Regulation of the Pharmaceutical Industry*, at 69. The assumption of continued expansion is addressed further below.

23   In the United Kingdom, participating pharmacists are paid a fee by the government and the reimbursement amount allowed for the drug prescribed. There is a discount built into the reimbursement to take into account sales of parallel imports and larger discounts offered by wholesalers: interviews with ABPI officials, July 1990.

24   Walton, Adkins and Smith, *A Controversial Vision of the Future*, at 16. According to them, most of the major wholesalers and Boots, with 18 per cent of retail sales the main dispenser of prescriptions, were not at that stage prepared to stock parallel imports.

25   Hancher, *Regulating for Competition*, at 215. For the ECJ, see 266 to 267/87 *API* [1989] ECR 1295 below at Notes 105 and 107; see also Hancher, 'The European Pharmaceutical Market: Problems of Partial Harmonisation', (1990) 15 EL Rev. 9, at 27 to 30.

26   Walton, Adkins and Smith, *A Controversial Vision of the Future*, at 16.

27   For example, parallel imports were thought to account for between 5 and 10 per cent of sales of the second-best-selling drug on the German market: *ibid*. British evidence tends to support such concentration. By 1989, some 2,000 parallel import licences had

So, there seems to be considerable disparity between *potential (estimated)* savings and the *actual* extent of parallel importing. But, there is evidence to suggest that such parallel imports as occur are concentrated in particular products. Before turning to that issue, it is necessary to consider how the fragmentation of the market has come about and why it is not, apparently, breaking down as quickly as has been predicted.

8.3   Market Characteristics

To gain some understanding of why price differences around the EC persist and why parallel imports have such an apparently patchy record of penetration to date, an overview of how the industry works and is structured is necessary in conjunction with an examination of the forces acting on it. A further aspect is how the changing nature of the forces acting on the industry may act to influence the rate of parallel imports.

8.3.1   A drug market or markets?

Most drugs serve fairly specific purposes; attacking, at best, only a few ailments. Further, many drugs affect people in different ways. The side-effects a drug causes one person may be more, or less, exaggerated in another or even very different. Thus, there is sometimes scope for different types of drug or different formulations to be used against the same or similar ailments. Therefore, demand for even the best-selling drugs is quite small as a proportion of the overall demand for drugs. Some achieve market shares of about 5 per cent, but most successful drugs usually only approach 1 to 2 per cent.[28] So, it is more accurate to describe the 'drugs market' as a number of sub-markets, some of which are interrelated or overlapping, than as a composite whole. There is also evidence that the pharmaceuticals industry specialises in the sub-markets that firms operate in, particularly in the R & D sector.[29]

These factors mean there is often much scope for new products to improve cures for which treatment already exists or find new cures for completely different ailments. But, the exact scope varies considerably from drug to

been issued, but there were 36 active importers dealing in about 200 individual medicines in a market of 1,200 drugs appearing in 3,500 brands: Burstall, *1992 and the Regulation of the Pharmaceutical Industry*, at 70, and 7 for the overall size of the market in 1987.
28   The 1 to 2 per cent figure is Burstall's claim: Burstall, *1992 and the Regulation of the Pharmaceutical Industry*, at 7. For the higher estimates, see the figures quoted in Walton, Adkins and Smith, *A Controversial Vision of the Future*, at 35, 72 to 73.
29   Burstall, *The Community's Pharmaceutical Industry*, at 84 to 91; but contrast Henry G. Grabowski and John Vernon, 'The Determinants of Research and Development Expenditures in the Pharmaceutical Industry', in Robert B. Helms (ed.), *Drugs and Health*, American Enterprise Institute, 1981, at 14, 16 and Scherer's comments at 46 to 47.

drug and ailment to ailment depending on technological possibility and the effectiveness of patent barriers.[30]

8.3.2   A description of the industry

The pharmaceuticals industry also is not homogeneous. In very broad terms, it is characterised by a two-tiered nature – large, transnational firms engaging in research and development ('R & D firms') and, generally, smaller, national 'generics' – which in turn somewhat reflects a dichotomy in the product it is selling.

In the developed world, an important characteristic of drugs is whether they are 'off-patent' or patented.[31] In theory, once a drug loses patent protection, anyone can manufacture and sell it under its generic name or their own brand name. With time, the proportion of 'off-patent' drugs is steadily increasing and, moreover, it is becoming increasingly expensive to find and market new drugs. Hence, almost all the research and development of new drugs is concentrated in the hands of a relatively few large, transnational companies, the R & D firms.[32] On the other hand, competition to make and sell off-patent drugs involves a far greater number of companies. The large, transnationals are active in this part of the market too. But, there are also a very large number of often relatively small companies often operating almost on national lines.

As the object of this study is to attempt an assessment of the impact of parallel imports on incentives to innovate, the author's main concern is with the operations of the large transnationals since they carry out the bulk of the world's research and development into new drugs.[33] They are characterised by their relatively small number and the global scale of their operations.

Historically, these companies have operated on a global scale. To some extent, they have centralised in their 'home' country production of basic active substances and research and development functions, carrying out formulation, preparation and testing operations in national subsidiaries. However, the nature, range and scope of activities delegated to national subsidiaries has tended to increase with time.[34] Hence, for example, an

---

30   On the effectiveness of patent barriers in some sub-markets, see for example F.M. Scherer and David Ross, *Industrial Market Structure and Economic Performance*, Houghton Mifflin, 1990 (3rd ed.), at 76 and 624 to 626.

31   For every patented drug, there are roughly two off-patent: Hancher, *Regulating for Competition*, at 57; Burstall, *The Community's Pharmaceutical Industry*, at 67 to 68.

32   Burstall puts the worldwide figure at about 50 firms while, within the EC alone, there are about 1,500 other firms engaged in the industry: Burstall, *The Community's Pharmaceutical Industry*, at 50 to 59. Another estimate claims that 30 large firms account for over 50 per cent of production in market economies: Patel, 'Drug Costs in Developing Countries', (1983) 11 *World Development* 195, at 198.

33   Estimates put the share of new drugs introduced by drug companies since the Second World War as high as 90 to 95 per cent: E. Jucker, *Patents and Pharmaceuticals*, Buchdruckerei Gasser & Cie AG, 1980, at 46 to 47; Heinz Redwood, *The Price of Health*, Adam Smith Institute, 1989, at 31.

34   For example, Hancher, *Regulating for Competition*, at 35 to 46.

American transnational may well be carrying out R & D functions in several EC Member States at the same time as in the United States. This has been partly in response to national policies discussed below and partly a natural tendency.

A further feature of the pharmaceuticals industry is the nature of competition. Product differentiation plays a major role. The R & D firms, in particular, have fought for sales by introducing new products, de-emphasising the role of competition over price to some extent. New products, protected by patents, trade marks and promotional efforts are introduced at prices with large mark-ups over simple manufacturing cost and consumers, it is claimed, are denied the benefits of cheaper prices by the persisting effects of product differentiation.[35]

Patents can form an effective block on a particular sub-market, although this depends on the scope of the patent in question and the technological possibilities for inventing around it. Only something of the order of 5 to 10 per cent of the drugs that get patented are ever exploited on a commercial scale.[36] There have been claims that this evidences an attempt by large transnationals to use patenting strategically by raising barriers to competition; foreclosing areas of potential competition to new entrants. But, it also seems likely to derive in large part from the nature of drugs and the requirements of the patent system.

The patent system forces applications to be filed quite early in the life cycle of a drug's discovery and preparation for the market. At present, estimates suggest that most drugs take between 8 and 12 years from initial discovery until first commercial marketing.[37] Of this, about one-third is spent on discovery and the remainder on development (which includes attempting to produce the chemical entity on a commercial scale and the full range of clinical testing). The process is highly speculative. Most discoveries never survive the process and, of those that do, few achieve anything but a meagre return on the market. Rough estimates suggest that somewhere between one compound in 5,000 and one in 10,000 survive to the marketing stage. Of the 150 new chemical entities reaching the market between 1981 and 1984, 20 were thought to have achieved commercial success and seven had proved highly successful.[38]

---

35 *Ibid.* at 48 to 55; For the most extensive (and critical) review of the arguments on both sides, see William S. Comanor, 'The Political Economy of the Pharmaceutical Industry', 24 JEconLit. 1178 (1986).
36 Among others, see Saxena, 'Trade-Related Issues of Intellectual Property Rights and the Indian Patent Act', at 107.
37 Burstall, *1992 and the Regulation of the Pharmaceutical Industry*, at 14 to 15; Redwood, *The Price of Health*, at 36; Touche Ross, *An Examination of the Implications for the UK of the Proposal to Extend the Patent Term For Pharmaceutical Products in the European Community*, Touche Ross Management Consultancy, 1990, at 2.
38 *Ibid.* (it is not entirely clear whether the 7 are part of, or in addition to, the 20); Redwood, relying on similar sources, describes the cumulative chain of attrition thus: 1 in 400 new chemical entities (NCEs) survive the discovery phase, 1 in 2,600 NCEs passes the development stage to marketing, 1 in 21,000 NCEs is moderately successful on the market and 1 in 60,000 is highly successful: Redwood, *The Price of Health*, at 25.

Despite the apparently risky nature of the business, the large transnationals as a group seem to be more profitable than other industrial sectors, suggesting greater than normal market power. The UK Government, for example, permits R & D firms an average return on capital of slightly above 20 per cent, which is significantly higher than that permitted other industries supplying the government.[39] Profitability is thought to be higher than similar activities in the chemical sector.[40] Against this, the pharmaceuticals industry has raised two inter-linked claims: denying that its 'real' profitability is as high as its critics have estimated and claiming that the apparent rates of return are necessary to fund its investment in innovation.[41] More recently, there has been evidence of merger activity in the ranks of R & D firms, suggesting a squeeze on the profits of some firms.[42]

There is, however, some evidence (and many claims) that the role of innovation serves a more malign end. The argument is that innovation is used strategically to generate a stream of higher than normal profits, at least some of which persist beyond patent term.

In all EC markets, the best-selling and most profitable drugs are the branded products of the R & D firms.[43] Such evidence as there is tends to support the conclusion that such firms earn high profits on their newer products, but that over time returns decline to a 'normal' level.[44] Hence, the strong performance of R & D firms is related to their power to introduce on a repeated basis a few new products for which high premiums may be charged. If the higher profits just reflected improved products, they would arguably be readily justified. The evidence on this supports both positive and negative interpretations.

One of Hancher's constant, underlying themes is that the higher profitability of R & D firms does not reflect the nature of the improvements offered. She argues that much of the innovation is of a socially wasteful 'me-too' nature.[45] Second, she claims that the R & D firms have skilfully manoeuvred to defeat government moves to compare the therapeutic effectiveness of new products with existing ones.[46] Further, she cites evidence that

---

39   Hancher, *Regulating for Competition*, at 195, 197 to 198, 207 to 211. For more extensive discussion of the 'real' rate of return, see Comanor, 'The Political Economy of the Pharmaceutical Industry', at 1182 to 1186.

40   Burstall, *1992 and the Regulation of the Pharmaceutical Industry*, at 67 to 68.

41   See the discussion in Comanor, 'The Political Economy of the Pharmaceutical Industry', at 1182 to 1186.

42   For examples in the late 1980s, see Burstall, *1992 and the Regulation of the Pharmaceutical Industry*, at 68 (Beecham/Smith Kline Beckman, Squibb/Bristol Myers). For the successes and shortcomings of the Smith Kline Beecham merger, see Matthew Lynn, 'Hooked on the Growth Wonder Drug', The *Independent*, 21 July 1991, at 21 and 'Hedging Bets at SmithKline', The *Independent*, 1 August 1991, at 23.

43   Burstall, *The Community's Pharmaceutical Industry*, at 76 to 91.

44   Comanor, 'The Political Economy of the Pharmaceutical Industry', at 1187 to 1188, 1193 (surveys of US industry).

45   Where the advance is of such an insignificant nature as not to justify the resources wasted on it or the elevated prices charged: Hancher, *Regulating for Competition*, at 51.

46   *Ibid.* at 203 to 204, 211.

R & D firms in France have used their ability to introduce new products to extract higher prices under the French system of regulation.[47] Combined, these factors show that the R & D firms at least have the capacity to act, and have acted, strategically (whatever the justification for their action) in contrast to their protestations that simple, pro-competitive forces drive their every action.

There is, however, some evidence that the extent of 'me-too' competition is exaggerated.[48] Also, it may be wrong to condemn all 'me-too' competition out of hand. Arguably, a firm may be left with no option if a rival gets a patent on to the market first or to tide it over periods while more promising avenues of research are being brought to fruition.[49] Further, in an industry where lead times are so long and outcomes so uncertain, duplication must be expected if more than one firm is to be permitted to seek advances in any given area.

The second aspect of the malignant uses of innovation is evidence that monopoly profits persist long after patent protection expires. Part of the argument is that the period of patent exclusivity is used to build up unassailable brand loyalty. Another part is that overinvestment in promotion and marketing is in itself socially wasteful and also excludes smaller firms by requiring them to spend on a similar scale to gain 'market space'.[50] The evidence on persisting profits is complicated by a number of factors, however.

First, much of the same US evidence establishing the profit persistence lends support to the conclusion that the power to price above cost once the patent expires is related to the therapeutic effect of the drug in question. The bigger the breakthrough the drug represents, the better its innovator's ability to retain prices above manufacturing cost once patent protection is

47   See below at Notes 82 and 87. While this certainly demonstrates her thesis about the strategic nature of government/industry relations, it is questionable whether it proves the socially wasteful nature of their conduct. It may do so, but that depends on the assumption that the price fixed by the French Government accurately reflected what was necessary to call forth the desired level of investment in R & D.

48   Redwood, *The Price of Health*, at 28, relying on evidence of diminished effort in certain still profitable therapeutic areas. This would be consistent with a view of the pharmaceuticals industry as having reached a mature state of technology by the 1970s and beginning to embark on a phase of exploiting new technology in the 1980s. For tentative steps on the role of technological vigour, see Scherer and Ross, *Industrial Market Structure and Economic Performance*, at 644 to 660 and note Scherer's speculations in Helms (ed.), *Drugs and Health*, at 47 to 48.

49   *Ibid*. If, as is often claimed for so-called 'high technology' projects, the ability to compete in the next generation of technology depends on cumulative knowledge, a considerable degree of 'me-too' competition will be necessary. For a summary, see Giovanni Dosi, Keith Pavitt and Luc Soete, *The Economics of Technical Change and International Trade*, Harvester Wheatsheaf, 1990, Chapters 4 and 5.

50   Hancher, *Regulating for Competition*, at 53 to 55; Comanor, 'The Political Economy of the Pharmaceutical Industry', at 1187. Not all economists would accept that this is a barrier to competition. For critical reviews of the dissent, see for example Richard Schmalensee, 'Ease of Entry: Has the Concept Been Applied Too Readily?', 56 Antitrust LJ 41 (1987) and Jonathan B. Baker, 'Recent Developments in Economics That Challenge Chicago School Views', 58 Antitrust LJ 645, at 651 to 652 (1989).

gone. Correspondingly, where the advance is small or negligible, even where there is patent protection, price reflects greater competitive pressure.[51]

To deny firms which introduce substantial improvements the ability to charge higher prices by exploiting their reputation may seem questionable. It may have some negative impact on their incentives to invest in future innovation and, even if no further innovation were desired, ignores the positive role of product differentiation in promoting competition by providing an incentive to maintain quality. Of the three broad factors lending power to the role of image (or brand) in promoting discretionary power over price, two are particularly important in the pharmaceuticals industry.[52] Brand marking may help raise price over cost where the consumer cannot tell in advance whether one product is superior to another. It may have a similar effect where there are high costs of an unfavourable experience with the product after consumption. Drugs are an extreme case of the second factor: if the drug consumed is of poor quality or contaminated the consequences to the patient could be very severe; also, prescribers and dispensers could risk malpractice liability. Drugs also present a strong case of the first factor: the patient can rarely assess the therapeutic effects of alternative prescription choices, and doctors, even if they are known to them, often may not take the time to weigh the considerations.

These considerations suggest mixed results. A brand reputation which reduces the risks of poor quality is obviously a favourable factor.[53] Merely permitting a 'short cut' to save time simply because of the first factor seems more equivocal. Interestingly, some of the reforms adopted in Germany and the United Kingdom seem designed to force more careful consideration on doctors.[54] Moreover, many EC Member States seek to control outlays on advertising in the drug market.[55] But, it may well be questionable whether governmental administrations possess any greater ability and flexibility to determine when product differentiation passes what is reasonable and beneficial and becomes excessive than free market forces.[56]

---

51 See for example Scherer and Ross, *Industrial Market Structure and Economic Performance*, at 587 to 592; Comanor, 'The Political Economy of the Pharmaceutical Industry', at 1187 to 1188, 1197 to 1199 (but note the author's additional questions). On the controversial question of Hoffmann-La Roche's UK prices for Valium and Librium, compare Hancher, *Regulating for Competition*, at 329 to 332 and W.R. Cornish, *Intellectual Property*, Sweet & Maxwell, 1989 (2nd ed.), at ¶¶A1-012 to A1-013.

52 For the generalisations and the use of drugs as examples, see Scherer and Ross, *Industrial Market Structure and Economic Performance*, at 382 to 383. The third factor, not discussed here, is attributions of status.

53 Note the experiences of Pakistan reported in W.R. Cornish and Jennifer Phillips, 'The Economic Function of Trade Marks: An Analysis with Special Reference to Developing Countries', 13 IIC 41, at 59 Note 31 (1982); and Sri Lanka, in Peretz, 'Pharmaceuticals in the Third World: The Problem from the Suppliers' Point of View', (1983) 11 *World Development* 259, at 260 to 261.

54 See subsection 8.3.3(b) below.

55 See for example Hancher, *Regulating for Competition*, Chapter 8.

56 Compare Scherer and Ross, *Industrial Market Structure and Economic Performance*, at 610 to 611, earlier indicating that a more feasible alternative may be to provide independent, objective evidence of quality comparisons.

8.3.3 Fragmentation along national lines

There is little doubt that the pharmaceuticals industry sets prices at the level it thinks the market will bear *when* it gets the chance. But, ABPI's claim is that the wide price variations seen in Table 8.1 above are caused by government intervention to depress prices to artificially low levels. How these price differences came about and why they are not eroded by parallel trade are the two sides of this question. The further question, the potential effects of the differences, is considered in subsection 8.3.3(c) below. In theory, three main factors could be at work: differences in local consumption and demand; national government intervention; and the role of industry itself.

(a) *National consumption and demand patterns*

Demand for a particular drug varies quite substantially from Member State to Member State. As already mentioned, in 1988 only one drug, Bayer's Adalat(e), achieved ranking in the ten best-selling drugs in each of France, Germany, Italy and the United Kingdom; Glaxo's Zantac achieved the same status in three countries; four others did so in two countries; leaving 25 different branded drugs ranking in the top ten for one country alone.[57]

One explanation suggested for the differences in demand lies in the existence of different medical 'cultures'. These manifest themselves in two ways. The types of ailments which people demand cures for vary quite considerably from country to country. Apparently, in 1985 treatments for the liver made up 5 per cent by value of the Italian market, but only 0.5 and 0.1 per cent of the Danish and UK markets respectively; vitamins and tonics were big sellers in France and Germany, but not in the United Kingdom; while painkillers and tranquillisers were in high demand in the United Kingdom, but not in Italy.[58] Furthermore, it seems that consultations with a doctor are more likely to result in a prescription in Belgium, France and Italy than in Denmark, the Netherlands and the United Kingdom.[59] All in all, it seems that as a proportion of gross domestic product, the Belgians, French, Germans and Italians spend more per person than the Danes, the Dutch and the British.[60]

Apart from these two factors, two other matters could potentially affect the demand for particular drugs: their price and, possibly, the identity of the company producing them.

The evidence on price affecting demand is somewhat equivocal. With the exception of Germany, the volume consumed nationally is higher in the

---

57 Walton, Adkins and Smith, *A Controversial Vision of the Future*, at 74 to 75, for similar results (for different drugs); in 1987 see *ibid.* at 72 to 73.

58 Burstall, *1992 and the Regulation of the Pharmaceutical Industry*, at 79.

59 *Ibid.* at 10. For example, 93 per cent of consultations in Belgium end with a prescription while in the Netherlands the figure is 55 per cent.

60 *Ibid.* at 8 to 10. As a rough guide, Burstall notes that volume of consumption per person in France is roughly four times that of the Dutch, although incomes, age structures and causes of death are much the same.

'low-priced' countries. Further, there is some evidence that for some drugs removal of governmental subsidies can drastically affect demand.[61] However, just as it is misleading to talk of the 'EC drug market', it is also misleading to talk of 'the drug market' as if it were a uniform whole. For many potential purchasers of vitamins, there are other possible sources and, for many, the consequences may not be severely life-threatening. Hence, whether evidence of price sensitivity for some drugs can be extended to others is questionable. Table 8.2 shows a further aspect.

Table 8.2
Price and Sales for Two Drugs in the EC

| | ZANTAC | | FELDENE | |
	Price Index UK = 100	Sales (£ million)	Price Index UK = 100	Sales (£ million)
FRG	144	30	127	15
It	112	124	66	15
UK	100	80	100	6

Source: Walton, Adkins and Smith, *A Controversial Vision of the Future*, at 7.

Table 8.2 records the prices (relative to the United Kingdom) and the sales value in pounds sterling for two drugs, Zantac and Feldene, in three Member States.[62] These two were chosen because they represent, respectively, the highest- and lowest-priced drug in Italy for which data is given for all three countries by Shearson Lehmann Hutton Securities. The sales values should be treated with caution. They are the figures reported. But, since they are expressed in terms of pounds sterling, they are unlikely to be directly comparable in terms of quantities actually sold in each Member State. For example, the German price of Feldene is almost double the Italian price. Since the sales value is the same, it seems likely that more of the drug was sold in Italy than in Germany. However, the data reported do not suggest a similar relationship between price and quantity for Feldene in the United Kingdom. The absence of any relationship between price level and quantity is even greater with Zantac which, in Italy, is not only the most expensive drug of the 19 in the survey but also far and away the largest selling. Deviations from price/quantity relationships for at least two of the three Member States can also be found for the other drugs for which data are given. So, it would seem that price differences are unlikely to explain all or a major part of the different consumption patterns.

Another possible explanation might lie in the nationality of a drug's producer. For example, drugs made by French companies might sell better in France than, say, drugs made by American or UK producers. This could result because, say, a French company is more in tune with the demands and

61   *Ibid.* at 11, referring to vitamins and tonics in Italy.
62   Walton, Adkins and Smith, *A Controversial Vision of the Future*, at 7.

needs of French customers, or a producer is better placed to market and distribute its products in its national territory,[63] or simply because prescribers operate some nationalistic preference. The only suggestion the author has found that some nationalistic preference may be at work is estimates that for French, German and Italian companies, over 70 per cent of their sales through retail pharmacies in 1982 were achieved in their home countries.[64] Since, as will be discussed further below, the research and development companies are large firms operating transnationally and have been doing so now for many years, it seems unlikely that barriers in marketing and distribution would be major hurdles. So, the national origin of a firm may have some, relatively small, impact on demand patterns.

It seems that demand differences between Member States play some role in the prevailing pattern of different price levels. This would be consistent with drug companies charging what they thought the market would bear. However, it seems fairly clear that the most significant factor contributing to consistently low prices in some Member States must be sought elsewhere.

(b) *National regulatory intervention*

All Member States regulate all aspects of the pharmaceuticals industry to a considerable degree at all stages of production and distribution. Broadly speaking, there are three, not entirely consistent, aims. First, since drugs 'are poisons that heal', governments seek to ensure that the products released on to their markets are safe and effective.[65] Governments must take steps to prevent disasters like the Thalidomide tragedy. So, before a drug can be released on to the market, it must receive a national marketing authorisation. Producers, wholesalers and retailers are all also subject to licensing approvals and continuing inspection.[66]

Although it is claimed that such controls are a prime factor in the increasing cost of developing new drugs, they exist in all Member States.[67] There are divergences in the standards and systems applied to enforce the controls within this group. These could lead to pricing effects if there are substantial delays in obtaining marketing approval. For example, if there were serious erosion of the expected effective patent protection for a particular drug, there would be pressure to recoup investments quicker by

---

63 On the importance and expense of effective marketing, see for example Burstall, *1992 and the Regulation of the Pharmaceutical Industry*, at 17 to 19.

64 Burstall, *The Community's Pharmaceutical Industry*, at 94 (Table 8.1). For French firms, the figure rises to 82 per cent and for Italian firms, almost 97 per cent. For UK firms, the percentage was under 50. See also *ibid.* at 92 to 93 where proportions for total sales are discussed, but the conclusion of home advantage still stands.

65 The phrase is from Burstall, *1992 and the Regulation of the Pharmaceutical Industry*, at 37.

66 For a more detailed treatment of the various control regimes, see Burstall, *The Community's Pharmaceutical Industry*, at 36 to 39; Burstall, *1992 and the Regulation of the Pharmaceutical Industry*, at 23 to 25.

67 For example, Burstall, *1992 and the Regulation of the Pharmaceutical Industry*, at 45 to 48 with other factors acknowledged at 13 to 17.

charging a higher price. On the other hand, the drug may be introduced into a more competitive environment. Whether this factor has significant effects on price levels might be determined by systematically examining length of approval period, date of introduction and price at introduction to see if there were any correlation between length of approval/date of first marketing and countries having consistently high prices. It might also be necessary to explore the impact of any differences in product liability laws. Without such a survey, such evidence as there is is at best equivocal.[68]

Most claims to date about the price variation have centred on the varying emphasis of governmental intervention dictated by the other two, more directly antagonistic, goals. Governments intervene to control costs to restrain their expenditure on health. But, some also adopt policies designed to promote investment in a local industry. All governments intervene to some extent with the pricing decisions of producers. Some governments also regulate prices and profit margins at the wholesale and retail level. ABPI's claim is that the low prices in some Member States reflect a policy choice by those Member States to contain costs at the expense of industry policy. Accordingly, the doctrine of Community exhaustion decreed in *Sterling Drug* ought to be qualified to prevent the flow of drugs from such Member States into those where governments have opted for higher prices as a means of promoting the pharmaceuticals industry. Not only is the doctrine unfair, but, ABPI claims, it is also counter-productive and detrimental to vital EC interests, both in the discovery of new, better drugs (and so, potentially reducing health care costs) and in preserving a valuable industry.

The evidence for this is the almost universally acknowledged pattern that drugs tend to have higherr prices in those Member States where government intervention is indirect and relatively minimal. Such countries tend to accord greater value to promoting an R & D industry.[69] While where governments intervene directly to fix prices, the prices of drugs tend to be among the lowest in the EC. Further, in France, where intervention is among the strongest in the EC, there is evidence that prices for drugs not subject to control increased far more rapidly than those subject to control.[70]

---

68   The United Kingdom and France are thought to process marketing authorisations with less delay, while Germany, Italy and Spain are longer: *ibid.* at 27. Then, even before the adoption of the French Supplementary Protection Certificate, effective patent life in France was thought to be longer than in the United Kingdom: *ibid.* at 33. (It is unclear whether this includes allowance for the estimated average two-year delay between marketing approval and price approval in France: Walton, Adkins and Smith, *A Controversial Vision of the Future*, at 44.) Finally, 1985 estimates ranked French, German and Italian standards easier to comply with than UK and Dutch systems: Burstall, *The Community's Pharmaceutical Industry*, at 38.

69   See for example the dichotomy drawn even in Leigh Hancher, 'The European Pharmaceutical Market: Problems of Partial Harmonisation', at 11.

70   Hancher, *Regulating for Competition*, at 252 to 253. For an index of values set at 100 in 1970 for both reimbursable and non-reimbursable drugs, by 1987 the values had increased to 180.3 and 349.1 respectively. See also, Frederick T. Schut and Peter A. G. Van Bergeijk, 'International Price Discrimination: The Pharmaceutical Industry', (1986) 14 *World Development* 1141 for a 32 country survey arguing that a 10 per cent rise in per capita GDP is associated with an 8 per cent increase in drug prices while direct price control by governments depresses drug prices by, on average, 20 per cent.

There are two aspects of the drive to restrain costs. Within the EC, all governments bear the bulk of the costs in providing health care. These are always large. Hence, all governments are under pressure to control their spending. Almost all governments have sought to find savings in their drug budgets.[71] These pressures have, apparently, increased considerably over the last two decades and have been attributed to a drive to control inflation following the second oil shock of 1979, increasing demands on the health system as the population ages and more costly drugs and systems are employed, and the breakdown of previous regimes to control prices.[72] For example, if 1975 is taken as a base year in which drug costs were 100, by 1983, costs were found to have risen to 248.7 in the United Kingdom and, in France, to 161.1.[73]

Moreover, the debate over the focus on product differentiation as the main outlet for competition in the pharmaceuticals industry and humanitarian demands for cures to ailments reinforce the budgetary pressures. Economists and governments are certainly not unanimous that social welfare is necessarily increased by allowing what they see as an oligopoly to pursue its chosen high price-innovation policy.

Promoting investment locally is not something that all governments can readily dismiss. By 1985, the pharmaceuticals industry provided more than 60,000 jobs in each of France, Germany, Italy and the United Kingdom and its production in each country ranged from £4 billion in the United Kingdom to £5.8 billion in France.[74] What began as a measure to preserve foreign currency reserves after the Second World War, now provides considerable employment in an industry increasingly dependent on 'high-technology'.[75]

Three broad approaches to regulating drug prices have developed in the EC. Denmark, Germany, and the Netherlands, where intervention in the past has been minimal compared to other Member States, consistently have higher prices than other parts of the EC. The United Kingdom, which is now considered to have among the highest prices in the EC, has a system

---

71 For example, the recent French history documented by Hancher seems to consist of yearly crises over how to deal with ballooning social security costs: *ibid*. Chapter 7. This problem is, however, EC-wide; witness the German and the UK reforms discussed below.

72 *Ibid*. 191 to 192. The burden of ageing populations is a theme stressed in Redwood, *The Price of Health*, at 3, 9.

73 Hancher, *Regulating for Competition*, at 192 citing figures from Organisation for Economic Co-operation and Development, *Measuring Primary Health Care*, OECD, 1985, at 53. Whether these figures prove the ballooning nature of drug prices is returned to below.

74 For example, Burstall, *1992 and the Regulation of the Pharmaceutical Industry*, at 18 (Table 2.2).

75 Burstall, *1992 and the Regulation of the Pharmaceutical Industry*, at 39 to 40. For France, see Hancher, *Regulating for Competition*, Chapters 3 and 7. For Italy, note in particular the proposals for an extension of patent term discussed in Touche Ross, *An Examination of the Implications for the UK of the Proposal to Extend the Patent Term For Pharmaceutical Products* and see also the qualification on Italy as a member of the group not concerned to promote investment in Hancher, 'The European Pharmaceutical Market', at 11.

of profit rather than direct price control. The other Member States have systems based on direct price control.

Until relatively recently, Denmark, Germany, and the Netherlands limited intervention to the promulgation of 'negative lists' which excluded certain products, or classes of products, from reimbursement under state-run health insurance schemes.[76]

German prices were uncontrolled until the negative list was introduced in 1983. However, the list was felt to have failed to control expenditure and reforms were introduced from 1 January 1989 with the object of generating savings in the order of DM2.35 billion, about half of which were expected to come from drug producers. The reforms have four key elements. First, reimbursement funds would only repay 'reference prices' for products having more than one source. Such prices would be introduced two years after the patent for a branded drug expired. Second, the negative list was expanded to include all drugs which contained substances unnecessary for their therapeutic effect, which could not be sufficiently evaluated or for which no therapeutic benefit could be shown. Third, prescription forms would be introduced on which doctors could indicate, by ticking a box, that the pharmacist could substitute a generic product for a named branded product.[77] Fourth, doctors' prescription budgets would be monitored with the risk that their salaries could be exposed to subvention to recover any excess. Further extensions of the reference pricing system to all drugs of comparable pharmacologic and therapeutic effect have been foreshadowed.

It is too early yet to assess the effect of the changes to the German system. There have certainly been rumblings that the changes have acted as a disincentive to business investment. A comparison with generic substitution laws in the Canadian provinces suggests that generics may well start to capture an increasing share of the market. In Canada, two factors have been found to play a crucial role in the extent of generic penetration.[78] First, the extent to which dispensers bear the cost of higher prices for brand names over generic substitutes. Where the dispenser bears the bulk of that cost, rates of generic substitution rose substantially. Substitution rates were also markedly affected by whether or not the product was included in the provincial formulary which certified biological equivalence and usually exempted the dispenser from malpractice liability. Hence, the second factor emphasises the importance of quality control and information provision.

At the other end of the EC scale are the direct intervention countries. Belgium, France, Italy, Greece, Portugal and Spain all use a combination of devices to keep prices down. The systems of individual countries vary

---

76   See generally, Burstall, *The Community's Pharmaceutical Industry*, at 39 to 44, 131 to 134; Burstall, *1992 and the Regulation of the Pharmaceutical Industry*, Chapter 3. Germany is dealt with at greater length in Walton, Adkins and Smith, *A Controversial Vision of the Future*, at 34 to 36 which is the basis for the following discussion on Germany unless specifically indicated.

77   Contrast 266 to 267/87 *API* [1989] ECR 1295 at Notes 105 and 107 below.

78   This account is based on the summary in Scherer and Ross, *Industrial Market Structure and Economic Performance*, at 590 to 592.

somewhat, but they all rely heavily on two key elements: direct price controls and positive reimbursement lists.[79] In these countries, apart from the marketing authorisation dictated by safety considerations, the price of a drug must also be approved before it can be sold and qualify for participation in the reimbursement systems. That approval will also specify the level of reimbursement which the drug will qualify for; there being five levels: no reimbursement, 25, 40, 70 and 100 per cent reimbursement. Shifts between reimbursement levels can affect sales substantially.[80] In theory, price rises once a product is marketed are possible, but considerable discretion lies in the government's hands. For example, in France, general price rises for all drugs are supposed to be decreed half-yearly. In fact, between 1984 and April 1988, only two general rises were allowed; one of 2 per cent in July 1986 and the second in April 1988 of 1 per cent.[81] Companies may also seek individual price rises. However, it seems these are not readily granted.[82]

This bleak outlook, from the R & D firms' point of view, must be seen in context. Companies apparently have scope to manipulate the system in their favour short of using blackmail threats. One source suggests that drug price in France showed annual rises of 5 to 6 per cent each year. One explanation is that advantage of general price increases was taken to reprice drugs in the firm's portfolio so that, while the general average was reached, prices of successful drugs were raised by larger margins while margins on the less successful were reduced.[83] An alternative explanation posits that companies exploited the system by withdrawing products and reintroducing them in new guises or consistently adopted policies of introducing to France only their most successful and highest-priced drugs.[84] In addition, large, export-oriented companies were able to take advantage of the French Government's 'European prices' policy.[85]

Although this group of countries share the common factor of direct and persistent intervention to control drug prices, there are important differences in the ways they determine the price set reflecting different emphasis on the objects of cost restraint and industry promotion. All take into account what

---

79 The French and UK systems are studied exhaustively in Hancher, *Regulating for Competition*, Chapters 3, 6 (United Kingdom), and 7. Shorter reviews for France and Italy can be found in Walton, Adkins and Smith, *A Controversial Vision of the Future*, at 44 to 51, 38 to 43, respectively. Generally, see also Burstall, *1992 and the Regulation of the Pharmaceutical Industry*, at 27 to 32; Burstall, *The Community's Pharmaceutical Industry*, at 36 to 44.

80 Among other things, there is evidence that French doctors changed their prescribing habits in favour of drugs remaining in the 70 per cent category when drugs which they had been prescribing were reclassified into the 40 per cent category: Walton, Adkins and Smith, *A Controversial Vision of the Future*, at 48. See also Note 61 above.

81 *Ibid.* at 45.

82 They seem to have been granted in France in the face of credible blackmail threats, see for example Hancher, *Regulating for Competition*, at 245 to 246, 249.

83 Walton, Adkins and Smith, *A Controversial Vision of the Future*, at 45; the time frame specified is 'in recent years'.

84 Hancher, *Regulating for Competition*, at 250, 246.

85 See below, Note 87.

they think they can afford to pay.[86] Some attempt to set prices based on the cost of manufacturing plus some allowance for profit. Some take into account prices for the same drug on other markets. Some include reference to the price of competing products already approved for their market. France and Italy, of this group of countries, are also notable in taking into account the applicant's level of investment locally.[87]

Historically, the United Kingdom has taken a third approach. Instead of regulating prices directly, the main thrust of policy in the United Kingdom has been to control the profit levels of the pharmaceuticals industry.[88] The 1980s have also seen the introduction of other policy measures designed to increase and, in one case, directly control prices in a continuing effort to bring health spending 'under control'.

The government's efforts to promote research and development and, at the same time, to restrain spending have seen the emergence of a two-tiered structure to the pharmaceuticals industry in the United Kingdom. On one hand are ABPI's members; generally the transnational R & D firms competing on the basis of product differentiation. On the other are firms competing largely on the basis of price; either by parallel importing or by producing their own version of off-patent drugs. The profit control device seems mainly directed at the research and development companies and is intended to foster their research activities.[89] By this means, the government has sought to restrain the overall returns to capital within specified (relatively high) levels, leaving it to individual companies to fix prices for individual products at levels aimed to achieve the target average overall. Thus, higher profit margins on some products may be tolerated if prices on other drugs were closer to cost. The permitted rate of return is itself negotiated at two levels. A general average for the industry is fixed in negotiation with ABPI and individual firms then have some scope to negotiate even higher levels on the basis of performance and commitment. A further important element of flexibility is introduced by provision for a so-called 'grey area' of rather indefinite magnitude in which companies will be permitted to exceed their specified limit.

The UK Government's commitment to the research and development industry did not lead to reduced pressures on health spending and, together with amendments to the profit control scheme, further steps have been introduced. Most drastically, 1983–84/5 saw the imposition of a price cut

---

86   As the introduction of increasing controls in Germany and the United Kingdom indicate, this factor is increasingly not distinguishing.

87   The French Government, in particular, permits higher, so-called 'European prices' to companies which agree to invest in France, meet specified employment levels or accept export targets: Hancher, *Regulating for Competition*, at 244 to 247.

88   The present scheme is the *Seventh Pharmaceutical Prices Regulation Scheme*, DHSS, 1986. It and the UK history is discussed exhaustively in Hancher, *Regulating for Competition*, Chapters 3 and 6. See also Burstall, *1992 and the Regulation of the Pharmaceutical Industry*, at 30; and Walton, Adkins and Smith, *A Controversial Vision of the Future*, at 51 to 53.

89   *The Seventh Pharmaceutical Prices Regulation Scheme*, at ¶12.1 and see the discussion in Hancher, *Regulating for Competition*, at 207 to 208.

and freeze on NHS purchases.[90] Further measures were taken to promote price competition between drugs of similar therapeutic effect: in 1985, a list limiting the availability of NHS payments in certain classes of drug was introduced;[91] special, simplified procedures were introduced to permit easier authorisation of parallel importers and producers of copies and generics of off-patent drugs;[92] the government has also announced plans to introduce prescription budgets for general practitioners.

Therefore, in very broad terms, a picture emerges of high drug prices or low prices corresponding to whether the country in question attempts to regulate prices directly or indirectly. But, a number of qualifications must be drawn.

First, in efforts to reduce costs, Germany and the United Kingdom are introducing increasingly interventionist measures. On the other hand, France and Italy, in particular, do attempt some recognition of the need to encourage investment through pricing levels.[93] These steps lead to the second qualification. Price disparities between countries tend to be more extreme the older the drug in question. It is not always the case, but, the older the drug, the more likely there will be significant price differences. The third qualification stems from the rise of the United Kingdom to a 'high price' status. Before the cost-cutting strategies of the 1980s were introduced, the major direct change of policy was the removal of the power to grant licences of pharmaceutical products almost as of right.[94] Given the continuing existence of the government's Crown Use provisions and the virtual monopsony bargaining position of the NHS, the impact of this change may be debated. Here, the impact of macroeconomic policy through exchange rate fluctuations cannot be overlooked.[95]

Finally, it should be noted that this fragmentation does not come without its costs. There are claims that the multiplicity of regulatory authorities throughout the EC leads to annual losses of £500 million in costs directly attributable to multiple applications and lost sales from delays in marketing

90 Hancher, *Regulating for Competition*, at 197 to 198. Cuts were also imposed on the allowable rate of return on capital and on permissible levels of advertising expenditure.
91 *Ibid.* at 200 to 201; Burstall, *1992 and the Regulation of the Pharmaceutical Industry*, at 28, Note 1.
92 See the Product Licence (Parallel Import) scheme which is said to be implemented by Medicines Act (Licensing) Regulations 1984 SI 673: Hancher, *Regulating for Competition*, at 177 Note 116 and see *R v Secretary of State for Social Services; ex parte Wellcome Foundation Ltd* [1988] 3 CMLR 95 (HL); Denmark, Germany, Ireland and the Netherlands have similar schemes; for generics, EC Council Directive 87/21 at issue in *In re Smith Kline & French Laboratories Limited* [1990] 1 AC 64 (HL).
93 There is, after all, no necessary link between low prices and government controls. Japan reputedly has the highest drug prices in the world, but also operates a strong system of price control: for example Redwood, *The Price of Health*, at 38.
94 Patents Act 1949, section 41.
95 Burstall attributes at least *part* of the UK rise to exchange rate movements: Burstall, *The Community's Pharmaceutical Industry*, at 42 Note 13. Note also that currency movements accounted for at least half the price difference in *Sterling Drug*, see Chapter 6 at Note 93. A comparison of 'European' and Japanese prices between 1980 and 1981 in US dollars found a difference of 35 per cent caused by exchange rate movements: Schut and Van Bergeijk, 'International Price Discrimination: The Pharmaceutical Industry', at 1149, Note 16.

approvals from Member State to Member State. Even a 'realisable' recovery rate of £100 to £200 million each year from rationalisation would lead to savings corresponding to the *whole* yearly estimated value of parallel imports into the United Kingdom.[96] In addition, it is claimed that between half and two-thirds of the downstream production capacity in the EC is excess capacity. Estimated savings from rationalisation here are between two and four times the annual value of parallel imports into the United Kingdom.[97] Most importantly, the delays in regulatory approval can directly affect consumers in different Member States by denying them access to drugs approved for sale up to several years earlier in other Member States.

(c)   *Parallel imports: the potential*

Even in the United Kingdom, where parallel importers are reportedly most active, the level of parallel imports does not yet seem to have reached the levels predicted either by the potential theoretical savings or believed 'realistically' achievable.[98] A large part of the explanation for this lies in the existence of an array of barriers to parallel trade apart from simple patent rights. These have been exploited by the R & D firms to block parallel imports. However, there are indications that at least some of these barriers are, or will soon be, eroding, thus increasing the pressure of parallel imports on the R & D industry.

One constraint on the extent of parallel importing is the commercial parallel importer's need to turn a profit. As a rough rule of thumb, estimates suggest that average price differences of at least 15 to 20 per cent between the place of export and import are required to sustain commercial viability.[99] This, together with informational problems, indicates that there could always be some potential price variation which the threat of parallel importing is unlikely to discipline.

Serious obstacles still exist, however, even where the price differential is clearly large enough to support commercial enterprise; witness, in particular, the low penetration of Germany. These fall broadly into two types: governmental regulation and commercial pressure. A third factor, national or prescriber/dispenser's prejudice, is probably at work too, but is difficult to quantify.[100]

---

96   Burstall, *1992 and the Regulation of the Pharmaceutical Industry*, at 53 to 54.
97   *Ibid.* at 73.
98   Section 8.2.2 above.
99   Burstall, *1992 and the Regulation of the Pharmaceutical Industry*, at 69. Similar figures have been suggested to the present author by government officials and industry sources. The Commission has indicated toleration of price variations up to 12 per cent under Regulation 123/85, Article 10(3), see Commission Notice of 12 December 1984 concerning Regulation (EEC) 123/85 OJ 1985 C17/04, Part II.1 and (then) Commissioner Sutherland's reply to Written Parliamentary Question, OJ 1989 C57/17, 6 March 1989. Whether transport costs would be as big an obstacle to parallel trading of drugs as for cars may be questionable.
100   Although 77 per cent of UK pharmacists taking part in a survey are reported to have 'reservations' about parallel imports and their impact, 50 per cent of those surveyed still admitted to having dispensed parallel imports: *ibid.* at 70.

Governmental regulation falls into two categories. Some measures are directed to protecting intellectual property, others effect consumer protection. As already indicated, the system of marketing approvals for drugs is still mainly in the hands of national administrations. It seems generally agreed that Member States do not use their marketing approval systems to discriminate against foreign traders.[101] However, a prospective importer of drugs for sale requires authorisation. This requirement presents an obvious disincentive to parallel importing since the process requires preparation of a medicinal effects dossier and, once that has been prepared, delay while it passes through the regulatory mechanism.[102] Based on the ECJ's ruling in *de Peijper*, the Commission issued a non-binding notice designed to encourage Member States to adopt abbreviated approval procedures for parallel imports aimed at reducing the burdens of preparing a dossier and bringing down processing periods ideally to a recommended 45-day period.[103] The five higher-priced Member States have introduced schemes based on these guidelines although, as discussed in section 8.2 above, they have been of varying impact.[104]

In principle, all intellectual property rights are subject to the Community doctrine of exhaustion. In practice, some intellectual property rights have proved to offer plenty of scope to place obstacles in the way of parallel trade. Since the ruling in *Sterling Drug*, patents have proved singularly ineffective against parallel imports. However, other rights have been called into play.

The exhaustion doctrine also applies to trade marks. But, unlike the case of patents at least two qualifications have arisen. Quite often, a drug company uses a different trade mark in different parts of the EC for the same therapeutic substance.[105] Often these differences can be justified on the grounds that a mark adopted in one Member State may conflict with rights existing in another or because language or cultural differences make its use in a particular Member State inappropriate.[106] Hence, it is not illegal for a drug company to use its trade mark rights to stop a parallel importer substituting the trade mark used in the place of importation for that on the

---

101 For example, Burstall, *1992 and the Regulation of the Pharmaceutical Industry*, at 27.

102 The overall UK average for all product licences other than NCEs was reported as 14 months: *ibid*.

103 Commission Communication on Parallel Imports, OJ 1982 C15/5. For *de Peijper*, see 104/75 [1976] ECR 613 in Derrick Wyatt and Alan Dashwood, *The Substantive Law of the EEC*, Sweet & Maxwell, 1987 (2nd ed.), at 133, 140 to 141 and compare Hancher, 'The European Pharmaceutical Market: Problems of Partial Harmonisation', at 18 to 19.

104 Denmark, Germany, Ireland, Netherlands and the United Kingdom: Hancher, 'The European Pharmaceutical Market: Problems of Partial Harmonisation', at 23.

105 3/78 *AHPC* [1978] 1823. In 266 to 267/87 *R v Pharmaceutical Society; ex parte the Association of Parallel Importers* [1989] ECR 1295 ('*API*'), it was reported that some 50 of the 220 products for which Product Licence (Parallel Imports) (PL(PI)) licences had been granted were marketed under a different name in other Member States. For *AHPC* and *API*, see also Chapter 6 Notes 116 and 214 respectively.

106 For some discussion of the issue, see Jeremy Phillips, 'Do National Brands Have a Future in the European Market?', [1991] EIPR 191.

product in the place of export. To date, there do not appear to have been any reported instances where a parallel importer has successfully established that such trade mark differences were unreasonably discriminatory or otherwise arbitrary and unjustified. Moreover, pharmacists' practices of substituting parallel imports under different brands for drugs specified by brand has been sharply curtailed in the United Kingdom following warnings from the regulatory body that substitution could result in disqualification from practising.[107] A further qualification on trade mark exhaustion is the trade mark owner's power to prevent a parallel importer repackaging the drug and applying the *same* trade mark to the new packaging. This is particularly important because most Member States require pharmacists to dispense drugs in their original packaging and, for one reason or another, package sizes and quantities prescribed quite often vary considerably from Member State to Member State.[108] Even where trade mark rights have not been registered in the importing Member State, legal rights like passing off and unfair competition may be used to block perceived potential to mislead consumers about product quality or source.[109] Even if a Community trade mark right be achieved, these differences can be expected to persist since local rights and the potential for trade mark conflicts will continue long after. Furthermore, the cultural differences are likely to prove enduring.

In addition to packaging and labelling requirements, drugs sold in Member States must be accompanied with appropriate instruction sheets. Allen and Hanburys Ltd, having failed in their attempt to use patent law to block parallel imports of their drug Salbutamol, which had been endorsed with a licence of right, successfully sued the parallel importer for breach of copyright in the accompanying information leaflet.[110] The basis of the infringement is unclear. However, it seems that language differences could be used to exploit copyright entitlements. For example, the Salbutamol was brought into the United Kingdom from Italy. If the product had been marketed in Italy with a leaflet only written in Italian (or Italian and another low-priced country's language, say, French), its simple translation into English by the parallel importer would infringe copyright. Given the ECJ's qualifications on the use of trade marks to partition the market, it

---

107   *API* [1989] ECR 1295; Hancher, 'The European Pharmaceutical Market: Problems of Partial Harmonisation', at 27.

108   Eire, the Netherlands, the United Kingdom and, since January 1989, Germany permit, but do not require, original pack dispensing: Burstall, *1992 and the Regulation of the Pharmaceutical Industry*, at 34 to 35; Walton, Adkins and Smith, *A Controversial Vision of the Future*, at 14 (and 14 to 15 on the importance of pack size differences). In the first three, pharmacists commonly buy the drug in bulk and dispense dosages as required. For examples of differences between the United Kingdom and Germany, see 102/77 *Valium* [1978] ECR 1139 and 1/81 *Pfizer* [1981] ECR 2913 in Chapter 6 at Notes 110 and 113 respectively. *Pfizer* also illustrates a successful attempt to repackage within the EC rules.

109   Judicious use of unfair competition laws has been suggested as one reason for the low penetration of parallel imports into Denmark, in addition to the small size of its market: Burstall, *The Community's Pharmaceutical Industry*, at 100, Note 10.

110   *Glaxo v Europharm*, unreported, [1986] *Scrip* No. 1078, at 10 cited in Hancher, 'The European Pharmaceutical Market: Problems of Partial Harmonisation', at 25.

seems questionable whether it would regard a deliberate use of the copyright for this purpose as not being arbitrary and unjustified or discriminatory. Since the matter was not, however, referred, the question still remains open.[111]

Shearson Lehmann Hutton report that drug producers have taken advantage of these 'holes' in the exhaustion doctrine to segment the common market, particularly by changing product formulation and exploiting national preferences for different packet sizes.[112] In addition, they claim that producers have taken advantage of wholesalers', prescribers' and dispensers' distrust of parallel imports by using 'friendly persuasion' to block purchases from parallel importers.[113] The changing commercial environment, however, has considerable potential to undermine such informal pressures.

Once again, the most significant factor is governmental pressure to reduce expenditure. At the retail level, Germany and the United Kingdom have attempted to increase pressure on doctors and pharmacists to economise by steps such as tightened monitoring of prescribing budgets with the threat of 'clawbacks' and, in the United Kingdom, the automatic discounting of pharmacists' reimbursement claims to take into account savings from parallel imports. Also, in the United Kingdom, parallel importers are believed to offer greater trade discounts than regular wholesale channels, 20 per cent against 7 to 8 per cent. The German authorities responsible for reimbursement of drug fees are also negotiating to derive benefits from parallel imports.[114]

Wholesalers have typically been allowed only a narrow profit margin by governmental regulation. Particularly in France, Germany and the United Kingdom, these constraints have led to increasing concentration in the market to supply outlets other than hospitals with over 60 per cent in each market being captured by three or four groups. This consolidation has led to improved efficiency in warehouse operation, stock control and also created a better ability to engage in long distance transport. It has also left them with little further scope to expand in their own markets. In the last two years, some have responded by seeking cross-border mergers particularly in France. In such circumstances and faced with increasingly competitive demands from their buyers as well as continued pressure on prices by their governments, the larger wholesalers would seem increasingly likely to take advantage of persisting large price differences by parallel importing. Moreover, the ability of producers to practise 'friendly persuasion' on wholesalers is reduced as the wholesalers increase in size.

A further factor promoting an increase in parallel importing is the ever-widening impact of the EC. Although the influence of EC law has been

---

111 This may be affected by C-347/89 *Freistaat Bayern v Eurim-Pharm GmbH*, unreported, 16 April 1991, see McKenna & Co., *European Community Law Bulletin*, May/June 1991, at 5.
112 Walton, Adkins and Smith, *A Controversial Vision of the Future*, at 17.
113 *Ibid.* at 20. The following discussion of changing commercial climate is based largely on *ibid.* at 18 to 22.
114 For the German 'Sick Funds', see *ibid.* at 10.

referred to, the thrust of the account has concentrated on the differences between Member States which have created, or been exploited to create, obstacles to parallel trade. That emphasis reflects the gradual nature, apart from spectacular instances like *Sterling Drug* and *Merck*, of EC intervention in this area. In her extensive account, even Hancher is driven to recognise that the Commission's efforts to create an internal market in pharmaceuticals is fraught with difficulty:

> First, it must persuade member states to surrender complete sovereignty over safety regulation in a highly sensitive policy area. Secondly, if it attempts to intervene in controls over prices or national reimbursement rules, it risks trespassing into the general economic policies, as well as the health policies, of the member states. In the meantime . . . the existing competitive distortions within the Community have been exacerbated by the disparate progress on the harmonization of the former, but not the latter, set of national rules.[115]

The last sentence is, perhaps, overly optimistic since, as the first two sentences recognise, the disparate progress on harmonisation is inextricably tied up with Member States' economic and health policies.

Both the Commission's efforts to promote legislative measures removing the barriers to trade within the EC and the ECJ's supervision of Member States' legislation (perhaps, apart from the early cases on the doctrine of Community exhaustion) have concentrated on what Hancher calls 'administrative' or 'framework', rather than 'substantive', matters.[116]

The Commission's programme started in 1962, first culminating in Council Directive 65/65.[117] The main effect of this directive was to require all Member States to adopt the initial standard that proprietary medicinal products could not be sold without the necessary marketing authorisations and to provide for the suspension and withdrawal of authorisations. Some provision was also made for informational requirements and labelling. Subsequently, it proposed two draft directives aimed at fixing common evaluation criteria and automatic mutual recognition of marketing authorisations approved by other Member States.[118]

It was not, however, until 1975 that the Commission succeeded in persuading the Council to adopt further legislation; the price included abandoning implementation of automatic mutual recognition.[119] Some progress was made on setting standards and a requirement that compliance

---

115 Hancher, *Regulating for Competition*, at 152.
116 For a more detailed review from which this account is largely drawn, see *ibid.* Chapters 4 and 5, in particular, and see also Hancher, 'The European Pharmaceutical Market: Problems of Partial Harmonisation', at 9. Note the qualifications on uniformity in Burstall, *1992 and the Regulation of the Pharmaceutical Industry*, at 25 to 27.
117 JO 1965 L22/369, reprinted in 12 *Secondary Legislation of the European Communities Subject Edition*, (HMSO, London, 1972), 1.
118 JO 1968 C14/4 and C248/3, referred to in Hancher, *Regulating Competition*, at 129 Note 97. The key point of automatic mutual recognition is that, under the free movement rules, once a Member State granted a drug marketing authorisation it could then be sold freely in all other Member States. Under the present regime, a drug authorised for one Member State still may not be sold in another until the authorities there have also granted it their marketing (and any other) authorisations.
119 Directives 75/318 and 319 OJ 1975 L147/1, 13, respectively.

be assessed on the basis of reports prepared by experts after scientific, clinical testing. In place of automatic mutual recognition, a Committee on Proprietary Medical Products (CPMP) was set up. This was intended to advise on applications for authorisation in five or more Member States with the object of removing some of the costs and delays attendant on prosecuting applications through several national systems. However, in its first four years, it attracted only eight applications and each of these was subjected to national objections by at least one Member State.[120]

The next step was Directive 83/570 which involved further postponement of automatic mutual recognition but compensated by strengthening the CPMP procedure.[121] In essence, where marketing authorisation is sought for at least three Member States this allows an application for authorisation of a new chemical entity (NCE) to be dealt with fully by one Member State. Its report may then be used as the basis of applications in other Member States which must issue a response in 120 days. It is, however, only advisory. If a subsequent Member State raises objections contrary to the first Member State's examination, these may be subject to arbitration by the CPMP. Although the CPMP has not proved hostile to authorisations issued by the Member State where the first application was made, there is evidence that subsequent Member States are conducting full inquiries of their own.[122]

Further steps were taken in 1987.[123] These included the formation of a committee charged with adapting technical standards more speedily to progress, co-ordinating increasing convergence on technical standards and a more centralised procedure for resolving matters of principle affecting authorisation of biotechnology products. Directive 87/18 obliged Member States to ensure that non-clinical tests carried out on chemical products were performed in accordance with good laboratory practice.

EC regulation of product safety issues in the field of marketing authorisations for drugs has made considerable advances since 1962. However, as even Hancher acknowledges, it still has a considerable distance to go. In particular, there have been and remain substantial differences between scientific and medical traditions applied by the several Member States which the Commission's attempts to force co-ordination of evaluation techniques have consistently underestimated.[124]

Attempts to reconcile scientific and medical principles and the applicable methodology relate to only one aspect of the departure from the ideal of an internal market in drugs, the problem of product safety. Member States' governments are understandably reluctant to surrender their power

---

120 Hancher, *Regulating for Competition*, at 154.
121 OJ 1983 L332/1; for the original proposal, see OJ 1980 C355/1, 6.
122 Hancher, *Regulating for Competition*, at 156 to 157, reporting only 2 negative opinions on 12 references.
123 For a package of measures relating to medical and scientific issues, see Directives 87/18 to 22; OJ 1987 L15/29, 41. Directive 87/20 relates to veterinary products.
124 Hancher, *Regulating for Competition*, at 157. Her account also records repeated objections from consumer associations to full free movement on precisely this ground.

to control which drugs are released in their countries when, first, there remain wide differences between each Member State on the relevant criteria and, second, the political consequences of a disaster will fall on their own heads.[125]

Moves to reconcile measures giving rise to other obstacles are proceeding even more gradually. Proposals for directives on advertising and labelling requirements are being advanced. The proposal on advertising would require Member States to ban all advertising and the distribution of free samples to members of the general public relating to drugs available only on prescription or not suitable for self-prescription. Standards at a very general level are also prescribed for advertising that is permitted.[126] A further proposal will require Member States to classify a drug as for sale only by medical prescription or not before granting marketing authorisation.[127] Another proposal will identify the general categories of information for inclusion in labelling of packaging and informational leaflets.[128] Still another proposal begins to harmonise the requirements relating to approval of wholesalers by making their licensing mandatory and conditional on complying with quality standards and continuing obligations like purchase from and sale to only licensed persons.[129]

The EC has also made a tentative start on reforms affecting what is probably the most sensitive area of all in the so-called transparency directive.[130] In essence, it requires national decisions fixing price levels, positive or negative listing and reimbursement level classification subject to determination only for objectively justifiable reasons. Applicants are also entitled to a statement of reasons identifying why their application has been dealt with in a particular way. The regulation of profit controls is more limited, primarily requiring the publication in advance of definitions of profitability and returns on capital. The objective of these limited obligations is an attempt to start forcing publication of the underlying reasoning with the ultimate aim of exposing or restricting the scope of national authorities to base decisions on matters like commitments to invest in local industry. Significantly, the directive in the form adopted abandoned the Commission's plans to create centralised bodies co-ordinating principles and empowered to issue guidelines.[131]

This catalogue of regulation is recited not so much to indicate how an internal market must be achieved. The approach taken by the EC is dictated in large part by its own governmental and philosophical traditions. What

---

125 The alternative has its own political problems. The Commission has been reported as refraining from proposing a fully centralised authorisation body at least in part to avoid the wrangling over where its headquarters would be based, see *European Reporter*, No. 1600, 'Internal Market', at 2, June/July 1990.
126　OJ 1990 C163/10.
127　OJ 1990 C58/19.
128　OJ 1990 C58/21.
129　OJ 1990 C58/16.
130　89/105, OJ 1989 L40/8.
131　See Hancher, *Regulating for Competition*, at 170.

is important, however, is the recognition that all these problems must be addressed by some means if a truly internal market is to be created. Much greater effort is required than simply decreeing an exhaustion doctrine. Certainly, an exhaustion doctrine could have been developed which overrode some, if not all, of the obstacles which have been identified. But, that would have entailed ignoring genuine concerns at the policy level about product safety, health policy, industrial policy and, at bottom, economic policy. The inability of the Member States through the Council to resolve their disparate aims at the policy level seems like the major cause of the gradual progress of harmonisation at the EC level and the consequent persistence of distortions of the internal market despite the edict issued by the ECJ:

> It is part of the Community authorities' task to eliminate factors likely to distort competition between Member States, in particular by the harmonization of national measures for the control of prices and by the prohibition of aids which are incompatible with the Common Market, *in addition to* the exercise of their powers in the field of competition.[132] (*Emphasis added*)

Notwithstanding the gradual nature of progress at the EC level, in the United Kingdom, at least, the effect of the government's reforms have led to a considerable expansion in the market share captured by parallel imports. The pressures leading to that growth are likely to continue. Whether similar growth can also be expected in other high-priced Member States remains to be seen. Certainly, however, much the same factors are at work, particularly in Germany, and, unless there be some specific cultural bias against parallel imports, market share affected by parallel imports can be expected to increase there. In the absence of such a bias, growth of parallel imports leading to a decline in overall EC market value of 10 per cent does not seem unreasonable, over time. Those savings will be concentrated in the R & D firms' best-selling brands.

8.4   The Price – R & D Success Link

There are two points at the core of ABPI's argument. First, successful R & D is vital to a successful pharmaceuticals industry and, second, the level of R & D is linked directly to the high prices associated with a largely unfettered exercise of the exclusive right granted by a patent. According to ABPI, the link is 'proved' by the fact that the successful R & D companies are based in countries which, historically, have not controlled drug prices. On the other hand, in those countries where government intervenes directly to depress drug prices, the R & D industry is in crisis or decline. Accordingly, the continued viability of even the successful R & D firms within the EC is now, or in the near future, under threat from all governments' insistent pressure to cut costs and the export of artificially low-priced drugs from some Member States.

132   15/74 *Sterling Drug* [1974] ECR 1147, at ¶23.

There can be little doubt that drugs resulting from R & D have brought enormous benefits.[133] What may be more open to question is whether all drugs resulting from R & D have justified the social costs of considerable monopoly power in a fairly oligopolistic market.[134] The question then arises of how best to pick and reward the winners. As already discussed, there is evidence that the market acts as a filter. Critics argue that this filtering process takes place at a price level which is too high and argue for a greater role by government in assessing the therapeutic benefits of NCEs.[135]

High prices in ABPI's argument substitute for profits. The link between profits and R & D is expanded by Burstall.[136] The development costs of an NCE are roughly estimated at about £100 million spread over a ten-year period. In addition, most of the R & D firms spend between 10 and 15 per cent of annual sales revenue on R & D.[137] The suggestion is that developing an NCE requires spending at least £10 million on R & D and total company sales of about £100 million each year. Given the risks associated with the R & D process, in 1985 industry sources apparently felt that a firm's viability on a continuing basis required an annual R & D expenditure of four or five times the bare minimum suggested above.[138] A further aspect of this argument is the necessity of successful sales on a worldwide basis. Demand for a particular drug in any given country will be affected by that country's consumption preferences and, in addition, revenues could well be subject to government regulatory intervention. Hence, it is believed that a drug can be classified as successful if it achieves worldwide sales of at least £40 million.[139]

---

133   For example, see the 'rough and ready' estimate of a 55 per cent drop in the number of 'bed days' between 1957 and 1982 in the United Kingdom: Burstall, *1992 and the Regulation of the Pharmaceutical Industry*, at 50; note also the arguments in Redwood, *The Price of Health*, at 3 to 23.

134   Comanor, 'The Political Economy of the Pharmaceutical Industry', at 1211 to 1215.

135   For example, the R & D firms are claimed to have diverted the UK Government's reforms away from such assessments: Hancher, *Regulating for Competition*, at 203 to 204.

136   Burstall, *1992 and the Regulation of the Pharmaceutical Industry*, at 13 to 17; Burstall, *The Community's Pharmaceutical Industry*, at 50 to 57. On the importance of a firm's cash flow to its R & D budget and the poor substitutability of financing through borrowing, see Grabowski and Vernon, 'The Determinants of Research and Development Expenditures in the Pharmaceutical Industry', in Helms, *Drugs and Health*, Chapter 3-20 and the impact of foreign sales on R & D financing revealed in Edwin Mansfield, Anthony Romeo and Samuel Wagner, 'Foreign Trade and US Research and Development', 61 Rev. of Economics and Statistics 49 (1979).

137   A similar, if not larger, proportion of sales revenue is spent on advertising and promotion costs: the average rates for the United Kingdom and France have been estimated at 12.5 per cent and 16.9 per cent respectively, Hancher, *Regulating for Competition*, at 265; US estimates vary with at least one survey reporting that twice as much is spent on 'promotion' than R & D, see Comanor, 'The Political Economy of the Pharmaceutical Industry', at 1196.

138   Burstall, *The Community's Pharmaceutical Industry*, at 50. The 1985 figures are given in US dollars and seem, by 1990, to have been simply transferred into pounds sterling.

139   On the importance of international success, see also Redwood, *The Price of Health*, at 37 to 38.

The link between price and R & D requires closer examination. There is no necessary logical link between high prices (or profits) and the site where the R & D is carried out. Historically, it is argued, most firms concentrated their most sensitive R & D in their country of origin. Such a link might seem natural when an industry was starting up. But, the modern R & D firms operate on a global scale and have done so for many years. What might be expected to be important is the question of whether such a firm could expect to recover a sufficient return on its investment on the full global scale of its operations.

Even historically, there are many exceptions to the rule that R & D is carried out mainly in the home base.[140] Furthermore, the Swiss, regularly regarded as among the world's strongest pharmaceutical performers, have achieved success despite a home market featuring strong price controls.[141] In addition, the United Kingdom only emerged as a 'high-price' economy towards the end of the 1970s.

Another factor which weighs against complete acceptance of the high price–strong R & D link is that many low-price countries within the EC have significantly higher levels of drug consumption. Drug companies have been reported as confirming that the high sales volumes generate significant profit levels.[142]

Nevertheless, most commentators and even the French and Italian Governments seem agreed that their domestic industries are losing ground in international competitiveness.[143] The industry in both countries depends heavily on domestic sales and is subject to strong price control there. It is also interesting to note the shift in assessment of German industry's prospects between 1985 and 1990.[144] A less pronounced note of doubt has also been

140 Burstall, *The Community's Pharmaceutical Industry*, Tables 5.3 and 5.4, list an extensive array of R & D decentralisation around the EC. However, it appears likely that there are qualitative differences in the value of these plants as the United Kingdom is described in the text as 'the favoured location for satellite research centres': *ibid.* at 63; see also Redwood, *The Price of Health*, at 37 to 46. Note the reports of increasing globalisation of R & D functions: Hancher, *Regulating for Competition*, at 42.

141 Renée Galbraith-Kuehni, 'Practical Problems for the Free Movement of Medicines: A Perspective from within EFTA', *EEC Pharmaceutical Law Forum 1990*, Worldwide Information Conference, Brussels, 24–25 April 1990.

142 Walton, Adkins and Smith, *A Controversial Vision of the Future*, at 30.

143 The assessment here seems to be based more on a matter of degree than any clearcut failing particularly in France. Perhaps, the strongest factor is the degree a country's industry penetrates foreign markets. Even Hancher stresses the shortcomings of French industry overall: Hancher, *Regulating for Competition*, Chapter 7 which is consistent with the findings in Mansfield, Romeo and Wagner, 'Foreign Trade and US Research and Development', at 49. However, at least one French firm, Hoechst-Roussel, is at the forefront of the developing biotechnology field. For the French and Italian Governments, see Touche Ross, *An Examination of the Implications for the UK of the Proposal to Extend the Patent Term For Pharmaceutical Products*, for a discussion of those governments' proposals to extend effective patent protection as a stimulus to industry. Note also the moves to permit higher prices discussed above.

144 Compare the positive rating in Burstall, *The Community's Pharmaceutical Industry*, at 114 to 116 with the more equivocal review in Redwood, *The Price of Health*, at 38 to 40, 43 to 46 emphasising the international nature of UK success. No doubt, some part of this is due to the authors' different perspectives, but both rely on similar considerations to base their assessments.

introduced into assessments of the UK industry. The main characteristic distinguishing it from the German seems to be its greater international orientation although it is smaller in absolute size.

Critics of the high price–R & D success link argue that the crucial factor is the presence of scientific expertise.[145] On this argument, British-based expertise in the main areas of research until recently is now yielding to Japanese and American expertise in biotechnology.[146] Strong theoretical support for this claim can be found in claims by economists that the crucial 'value-added' in production is no longer actual manufacturing processes but the input of intellectual expertise.[147] The counter-argument does not deny the importance of a strong scientific base. Instead, it argues that such a base must be combined with an atmosphere conducive to long-term R & D investment and an international marketing orientation. This view makes much of the fact that strong R & D firms have not flourished in countries which have, of these three factors, only a strong scientific culture.[148]

Arguably, then, the case against parallel imports is not as straightforward as simple claims of a high price–strong R & D link would have it. However, a number of other considerations suggest that parallel imports are undermining, or have a clear potential to undermine, desirable investment in innovation by the European pharmaceuticals industry.

First, parallel imports affect the most successful drugs. These tend to be the ones with more improved therapeutic benefits, the drugs which it is most desirable to encourage.[149] Drug companies are also crucially dependent on them to sustain their levels of profitability.[150] Therefore,

145 This view was put to the author most forcefully by a representative of a UK firm active in generic production, but who had previously worked at a senior level for a major R & D firm.

146 Some confirmation of this comes in a report that German firms are shifting investment out of Germany to a climate more favourable to biotechnology in the United States: Redwood, *The Price of Health*, at 42.

147 Michael Porter, *The Competitive Advantage of Nations*, The MacMillan Press, 1990; Robert B. Reich, 'The Real Economy', 267(2) *The Atlantic* 35 (1991).

148 Redwood, *The Price of Health*, at 42 to 46. He relies, in particular, on the equivocal position of the French industry and the failure to develop a successful industry in Australia and Canada which he attributes to strong low-price drug policies in each country. He does not give much weight to the small size of their domestic economies and the difficulty for either to penetrate any large neighbouring markets.

149 Apart from the importance of innovation in sustaining mark-ups over cost, Mansfield's research characteristically opens up two intriguing considerations. First, in a survey of 30 firms, evidence was found that firms engaging in more intensive R & D tended to devote more of the R & D to longer term, basic R & D: Mansfield, Romeo and Wagner, 'Foreign Trade and US Research and Development', 61 Rev.Econ.Statis 49, at 54 (1979). Second, there was evidence in a survey of 17 inventions, that the social gains from more important innovations were on average twice as great as the private gains appropriated by the innovator *although* there were significant variations: Edwin Mansfield, John Rapoport, Anthony Romeo, Samuel Wagner and George Beardsley, 'Social and Private Rates of Return from Industrial Innovations', 91 QJEcon. 221, at 233 to 238 (1977).

150 Apart from the discussion above, Burstall notes that in extreme cases drug companies may depend for one-half or more of the revenues from such drugs: Burstall, *1992 and the Regulation of the Pharmaceutical Industry*, at 70. See also, Walton, Adkins and Smith, *A Controversial Vision of the Future*, at 11.

greater encouragement of parallel imports is likely to have an exaggerated effect on both ability and incentives to carry out desirable R & D.

The mergers of companies like Smith Kline Beckman with Beecham and Squibb with Bristol Myers are suggested as possible examples of situations where the returns from successful R & D have been reduced below a level required to continue with risky R & D. Certainly, it seems some of these companies were exposed by extreme reliance on the success of particular, ageing products. However, their demise could equally reflect a loss of competitive skill and so would instead show the market functioning efficiently. In the latter case, concerns about increasing concentration would not be met best by tolerating higher prices, but by examining any barriers to entry potentially blocking new competition.

The merger of Smith Kline Beecham provides an interesting example. The combined company has reported a significant improvement in profitability from rationalising costs and better penetration of the market through its more effective sales force. Its R & D programme is, however, still considered weak and it is reportedly looking to offset this by increasing its acquisitions of innovations from smaller enterprises with less effective marketing networks.[151] To the extent that that summary reflects the real state of affairs, it offers support for three possibly contradictory points. First, it supports those who claim the real strength of the R & D industry lies in its ability to exploit product differentiation and sales networks in an oligopolistic market. There is also support for the argument based on loss of competitive skills. But, perhaps in some contradiction of these negative factors, it also reveals a potential market opening opportunity, enabling smaller innovators a chance to penetrate the market more effectively. Their ability to do so profitably would depend in part on their power to bargain effectively which, in turn, depends in part on them having secure rights to bargain over.

A second factor is the inconsistent nature of the policies being adopted or under consideration by governments. On one hand, governments are taking steps to encourage increased price competition by promoting the use of parallel imports and generics. On the other, the EC has adopted a proposal which will have the effect of extending patent protection, thus delaying the entrance of generic competition.[152] The apparent conflict between these measures may be rationalised by viewing them as a choice to spread the returns to the investment over a longer period and so reduce the margin of price over cost. However, the theoretical grounds for the presumed stimulus

151 Lynn, 'Hooked on the Growth Wonder Drug', The *Independent*, 21 July 1991, at 21 and 'Hedging Bets at SmithKline', The *Independent*, 1 August 1991, at 23.

152 Council Regulation on Supplementary Protection Certificates for Medicinal Products 1992 L182/1, 2 July 1992, see Robin Whaite and Nigel Jones, 'Pharmaceutical Patent Term Restoration: The European Commission's Regulation', [1992] EIPR 324. France has already adopted such a certificate at the national level, Law of 25 June 1990, JO 27 June 1990: see Gérard Dassmann, 'A New Industrial Property Right for Pharmaceutical Products in France – The Complementary Protection Certificate', 21 IIC 615 (1990). For Italy's plans, see Touche Ross, *An Examination of the Implications for the UK of the Proposal to Extend the Patent Term for Pharmaceutical Products*.

to investment incentives are slender. Theorists have long argued that beyond a certain point extension of patent term provides diminishing returns and that a more effective stimulus is injected by shortening delays in bringing the product to market.[153]

A third factor is the global mobility of the R & D industry. It is necessary to take into account strategic interaction. The mixed motives of Member States' governments means that they are not completely independent of the R & D firms. Not all national governments simply demand drugs at the cheapest prices possible; many of them, the four or five largest in particular, have an interest in maintaining the jobs, revenues, foreign currency reserves and such like which depend on attracting strong R & D commitments within their territories. Firms can make credible threats to remove such facilities to more hospitable environments.[154]

A fourth factor is admittedly crude and arises in part out of the third – the short-comings of the 'low-price' strategy. As already mentioned, there has been a general consensus that the 'low-price' strategy pursued in France and Italy has proved inadequate to foster a strong 'domestic' industry. In an effort to encourage increased investment by the pharmaceuticals industry, the Canadian Government has amended its liberal compulsory licensing scheme to offer drug companies the prospect of higher prices in return in part for commitments to invest in Canada.[155]

In 1970, perceiving that transnational corporations were exploiting the patent system to hinder the emergence of domestic competition and to deny Indian access to essential needs at affordable prices, India amended its patent law to limit patent protection for drugs to their processes of manufacture.[156] In 1978, the government took its programme a step further and introduced price controls on some 400 essential drugs and made the use of generic names compulsory.[157] It also required foreign ownership of firms engaged solely in

---

153   Burstall offers a striking theoretical example in which a reduction of development time by half to five years leads to an increase of present value from £139 million to £321 million; with about two-thirds of the difference coming from the earlier marketing of the product and only one third due to extending effective patent life by five years: Burstall, *1992 and the Regulation of the Pharmaceutical Industry*, at 47 to 48. For an intriguing theoretical simulation, see Henry G. Grabowski and John M. Vernon, 'Pioneers, Imitators, and Generics – A Simulation Model of Schumpeterian Competition', 102 QJEcon. 491 (1987).

154   As apparently happened during the 1980s in both France and the United Kingdom, see Hancher, *Regulating for Competition*, at 245 to 246 (Sanofi's threat to relocate the 50 per cent of its activities remaining in France elsewhere if it was not awarded 'European prices'); at 205 (ABPI claiming that £138 million in capital investment cancelled or deferred and 2,000 jobs lost in response to UK crisis in 1985).

155   See John W. Rogers III, 'Revised Canadian Patent Act, the Free Trade Agreement and Pharmaceutical Patents: An Overview of Pharmaceutical Compulsory Licensing in Canada', [1990] EIPR 351.

156   See for example, Saxena, 'Trade-Related Issues of Intellectual Property Rights and the Indian Patent Act', at 90, 92 to 94, 104 to 105 (1988). For examples of price discrimination in other Asian countries, see 'A Pricing Policy That's Hard to Swallow', *Far Eastern Economic Review*, 11 April 1985, at 47.

157   Lincoln Kaye, 'India's Wrong Prescription: Liberalised Drug Controls Prove to be Weak Medicine', *Far Eastern Economic Review*, 17 December 1987, at 128 to 129.

formulation to be reduced to 40 per cent and, for firms manufacturing bulk drugs and formulation, 74 per cent.[158]

One aspect of these reforms is that India reportedly has among the lowest prices for many drugs in the world. It seems that new drugs are also now brought on to the Indian market within four to six years after marketing elsewhere in the world.[159] Two state owned firms were reported to be producing 26 per cent of India's domestic requirements of bulk drugs while in 1979–80 there were some 5,156 firms engaged in drug manufacture. Apart from the public sector firms, 130 of these accounted for 63 per cent of bulk drug output and 66 per cent of formulations. The remaining 5,000 firms would seem to have been competing for about 27 per cent of the formulation requirements.[160]

It would seem that much of the industry, both state and privately owned, was supported by favourable grants of bulk licensing orders for governmental use and credit concessions. It also seems that much of the industry suffered from chronic financial difficulties resulting from fragmentation, uneconomic plant sizes, obsolete technology, low labour productivity and the high costs of materials. Profitability had fallen from 16.5 per cent in 1965–66 to 12 per cent in 1979 and 5 to 6 per cent in 1985–86. After nine years, by 1987, only one-fifth of the investment anticipated for the industry to meet the government's programme of 'Health for All by 2000' had been achieved. Under the economic liberalisation programme of the then Gandhi Government, part of the government's response in 1987 was to reduce the number of price-controlled drugs by almost half and to increase the mark-ups permitted on those still price controlled.[161]

No doubt, in all this, there has been considerable scope for the transnational R & D drug companies to engage in strategic behaviour. It is, however, impossible to overlook the parlous financial state of much of the industry and the Indian Government's recognition of its inability to finance and run the industry in its present form to meet its desired goals.

A further factor to consider has been the ineffectiveness of moves to control drug prices in controlling overall health expenditure. One of the strongest impressions of French regulatory tactics during the 1980s is the

---

158 P.N. Agarwala, 'The Pragmatic Approach May Solve Problems', *Far Eastern Economic Review*, 11 April 1985, at 61.
159 Saxena, 'Trade-Related Issues of Intellectual Property Rights and the Indian Patent Act', at 93 to 94. He also provides evidence that patenting in India has not declined but nor had it increased and that, after a decline, foreign patenting had returned to former levels or slightly higher by 1985: *ibid.* 100 and some limited evidence of increasing foreign investment through joint ventures particularly with the passing of the 1980s: 103–4.
160 See Agarwala, 'The Pragmatic Approach May Solve Problems', at 61.
161 See Kaye, 'India's Wrong Prescription: Liberalised Drug Controls Prove to be Weak Medicine', at 128 to 129 and Agarwala, 'The Pragmatic Approach May Solve Problems', at 61. Saxena notes that transnationals had at times closed down production of bulk drugs 'on the pretext of lost income', in some cases going on to produce low-technology products like baby powder and chewing gum: Saxena, 'Trade-Related Issues of Intellectual Property Rights and the Indian Patent Act', at 105. See also Lincoln Kaye, 'Patent Pressure: US Urges India to Protect IPR', *Far Eastern Economic Review*, 29 December 1989, at 53.

failure of continual intervention to reduce drugs' expenditure to restrain ballooning overall health care budgets.[162] In the United States, increasing penetration of generics after patent expiry has led to rising real average drug prices as drug companies respond to quicker erosion of revenues after patent expiry with higher prices during patent term.[163]

It may be that attention is being directed to the wrong part of the health budget. Throughout the 1970s and 1980s, it has been claimed that the proportion spent on drug purchases has been remarkably constant at about 10 per cent.[164] To achieve even a modest fall of 1 per cent on the overall budget would require a cut of 10 per cent in drug spending while savings in other areas of the budget would be of a considerably smaller magnitude.[165] In addition, simply to class the costs of drugs in terms of what is spent on buying them fails to take into account the savings that they may generate elsewhere in terms of, say, reduced hospitalisation or improved patient comfort.

8.5   Conclusion

This survey has attempted to review the impact of parallel imports on the pharmaceuticals industry in the EC. A complicated process is at work; involving the interaction of governmental policies, corporate strategies and consumer preferences.

In the EC, parallel imports in this sector do not seem to arise mainly because of the pricing policies adopted by transnational corporate groups as part of a scheme of international price discrimination. Rather the price differences giving rise to the potential for parallel imports are born of conflicting governmental policies. In the past, some Member States have chosen to concentrate on ensuring that drugs are available cheaply. In these 'low-price' countries, governments intervene to fix prices closer to manufacturing cost with little, or reduced, allowance for returns on the use of intellectual property. On the other hand, other Member States have allowed drug companies greater freedom to set prices including allowance for use of intellectual property. To a considerable extent, countries which have adopted the second, 'higher-priced' policy are those which have and wish to foster an

---

162   See especially Hancher, *Regulating for Competition*, Chapter 7. See also Walton, Adkins and Smith, *A Controversial Vision of the Future*, at 48 for the successful control of drug consumption in 1987, despite a shift in prescribing patterns, at the same time as overall spending increased by 6.5 per cent.

163   Burstall, *1992 and the Regulation of the Pharmaceutical Industry*, at 78. A similar effect may be at work in the United Kingdom.

164   Redwood, *The Price of Health*, at 8 to 12. Burstall, *1992 and the Regulation of the Pharmaceutical Industry*, at 9 (Table 2.1). Figures quoted by Hancher for the United Kingdom in the early 1980s contradict Redwood: Hancher, *Regulating for Competition*, at 192.

165   *Ibid.* arguing that costs attributable to institutional care account for over 50 per cent of the overall budget. On the other hand, much of the other factors may be spent on more 'painful' areas: Burstall, *1992 and the Regulation of the Pharmaceutical Industry*, suggesting that labour costs account for 70 per cent of spending.

export-oriented, strong R & D sector in their pharmaceuticals industry. The 'low-price', interventionist countries usually do not have similar ambitions.

In theory, the Community exhaustion rule should lead to drugs from the 'low-priced' countries being transferred to the 'higher-priced' ones. This has so far only happened apparently in the United Kingdom where parallel importing grew markedly during the 1980s; partly as a result of the rise in UK prices relative to other Member States and partly due to government policy. The relatively small scale of parallel importing to date arises partly from differences between countries in consumers' demands. More important have been the existence of other governmental regulatory barriers and the large drug companies' skilful manipulation of these and other commercial options open to them to impede the flow. If parallel importing is to be promoted, attention must be increasingly directed to removing these obstacles.

The situation is not static, however. The regulatory position is changing and commercial pressures are fluid. Two of the interventionist states have accepted some high prices and taken other steps designed to promote more investment in their domestic industries. Two of the 'higher-priced' countries have also embarked on a number of cost-cutting initiatives. All are collectively considering other measures designed to encourage more investment in R & D.

The cost-cutting measures, in particular, are likely to intensify parallel importing. Best estimates suggest that EC-wide savings in the order of 10 per cent can be expected. Such an increase in parallel imports is likely to have a disproportionate effect in view of the nature of the market for drugs. It will be concentrated in the most popular, commercially successful drugs which the large R & D firms are heavily dependent on for the levels of profitability from which they fund further R & D. Furthermore, it is likely that such drugs represent more important medical advances which deserve encouragement.

Almost all companies which develop new drugs and successfully bring them to market are large transnationals. This reflects the profitability which successful R & D can bring. However, it also reflects the high costs of R & D increasing governmental regulation for reasons such as safety and the fragmented nature of demand for particular drugs. The global organisation of the firms engaging in R & D means that they are able to threaten to shift their mobile R & D resources to environments they perceive as accommodating long-term investment in R & D and away from countries seen as hostile.

Thus, the prospect of increasing parallel imports within the EC poses a dual threat. Potentially, it will reduce the ability of some firms to continue investing in increasingly expensive and risky R & D in new drugs. There are some contestable claims that this has already happened. The likelihood of it actually happening increases with the scale of parallel imports. Even more likely, those firms which continue to engage in R & D will relocate their activities to more favourable environments or use the threat of relocation to extract concessions from governments. Governments are not without bargaining threats of their own. But, if a stable environment conducive to long-term investment in innovation is to be created, both governments and industry will have to reach an accommodation.

The risk to the EC is that its exhaustion policy will scare away desirable sources of investment by 'exporting' the 'low-price' policies of some Member States to others which have not wholly accepted the objects of those policies. If, as it must, integration of the Common Market is to remain the EC's main aim and parallel imports are to be used as a tool in achieving this without threatening continuing EC investment in the sector, greater co-ordination at the centre is essential. The primary objective must be to reconcile the competing objects of 'cost cutting' and investment promotion in ways acceptable to all Member States. If the 'incentives' which international price discrimination within the EC effectively provides are to be eroded, as parallel imports will do, they must be replaced at other levels if the EC wishes to retain as much of the industry as possible. The most powerful incentives are those which come earlier in patent life such as reducing the costs of fragmented marketing authorisations around the EC. If prices are deemed too high, needless additions to producers' costs, such as overinvestment in reduplicating facilities in several Member States, should be eliminated. After all, one of the strongest motivations sought through the Common Market is the reduction of costs by rationalising production and seeking economies of scale.

If the pressure for an internal market in the EC were not so dominant, it might be appropriate to ask whether promoting parallel imports be the right way to control fears of anti-competitive behaviour by the large R & D firms. Parallel imports work by promoting intra-brand competition designed to ameliorate the effects of the perceived barrier to competition raised by patents. They pose the danger of reducing the incentives the patent system is intended to foster. There are, however, other potentially substantial barriers to competition. These impede the access of inter-brand competition even after patent protection has expired. If the main danger to competition is perceived to be the foreclosure of inter-brand competitors from the market-place after the patent expires for want of sufficiently large sales networks and enduring brand loyalty, more rational policies might be directed to improving access through more stringent application of abridged licensing procedures and more effective generic substitution schemes.[166] Provided it were recognised that these measures affect appropriability, and so, that interference during the patent term would need to be correspondingly relaxed, the dangers to incentives to invest in innovation and quality could be reduced while at the same time reducing the scope for strategic behaviour.

---

166   On the effectiveness of generic substitution schemes, see the summary of Canadian experience in Scherer and Ross, *Industrial Market Structure and Economic Performance*, at 589 to 592, above at Note 78.

Chapter 9: Computer Products in Europe

In May 1988 a magazine catering to the interests of computer enthusiasts featured what it called an 'Open Forum': the subject, pricing.[1] At the time, relations between customers and those involved in the production and sale of 'computer products'[2] were the subject of considerable acrimony. The writer of an article introducing the 'Open Forum' put the issue succinctly in a series of rhetorical questions:

> . . . how do you account for the fact that a Macintosh SE costs nearly £1,000 more in Switzerland than in America (£2459 as against £1571)? Or an ImageWriter II costs nearly twice the price in Germany than it does in the USA? Why do the Irish pay much more than us [customers in the UK] for a Macintosh II, and notably less for an SE? Why are LaserWriters so cheap in Switzerland and France; so expensive here?

Turning from 'hardware' to 'software', he continued:

> You frequently see *at least* a direct dollar-for-pound conversion which in effect sticks a straight 75% mark-up on to software prices in the UK without any effort. If you want examples there are plenty.[3]

For the three named software packages which he mentioned the apparent price disparity is even greater than a mere 'dollar-for-pound' conversion at a time when, at straight currency exchange rates, one pound sterling bought about 1.79 US dollars. Table 9.1 demonstrates the price difference. The columns headed 'UK Price' and 'US Price' show the prices Bywater quoted; the columns headed 'US Price (FX)' and 'US Price (PPP)' convert the US price to pounds sterling at the foreign exchange and purchasing power parity rates, respectively, then prevailing.[4]

---

1 Michael Bywater, 'Pricing! The MacUser OPEN FORUM', 23 *MacUser* 49, May 1988 ('Open Forum'). For an exploration of the issue in Australia, see Prices Surveillance Authority, Inquiry into Prices of Computer Software: Interim Report, PSA Report No. 44, 12 October 1992.

2 This term will be used to refer loosely to retail products made in large volume, what the trade seems to call 'box shifting'. Hence, the discussion concentrates on the market for personal or mini-computers and software developed commercially for use with these machines.

3 Both extracts and the following prices are taken from Bywater, 23 *MacUser* 49 to 50, May 1988.

4 The foreign exchange value used here is the nine-week average of the rates published in the *Economist* from the end of January 1988 to the end of March 1988, see (1988) 306

Table 9.1
Software Prices: The United States and the United Kingdom in Comparison, May 1988

	UK Price	US Price	US Price (FX)	US Price (PPP)
1.	£295.00	$159.95	£89.36	£96.36
2.	£395.00	$219.00	£122.35	£131.93
3.	£375.00	$289.00	£161.45	£174.10

Source: Bywater, 'Pricing! The MacUser OPEN FORUM', 23 *MacUser* 49, May 1988

These examples are not intended as a valid comparison on economic grounds. Rather, they *highlight* how the issue was *seen*. In the minds of European customers, there was a vast disparity between the prices they were being asked to pay and the prices available for (often) essentially similar products in the United States. However, as the first extract highlights, even within 'Europe' substantial differences could arise seemingly without reason.

By the northern summer in 1990, the exchange rate values for the pound sterling and the US dollar had reached levels similar to those prevailing in 1988 and UK copyright law had been amended, allowing exclusive licensees to block parallel imports sourced from foreign copyright owners. Yet, the same enthusiasts' magazine was now regularly carrying advertisements at least implying the potential for grey market imports[5] alongside those proclaiming that they sold only authorised products.[6] Nonetheless, the price gap does not appear to have been affected much.[7]

In an attempt to explore why such apparently large price differences come about; why they appear to persist; what, if any, impact parallel imports of computer products have; what, if anything, have those making and

the *Economist, passim*. The PPP rate used is US$1.66 = £1.00: F. Fishwick, *Comments on the Interim Report by the Australian Prices Surveillance Authority of its Inquiry into Book Prices*, UK Publishers' Association Paper, December 1989, Table 2.
5 For example, compare Application Research Technology Limited's changing advertising campaign. In 6(9) *MacUser* 40, 4 May 1990, an advertisement superimposed over a 'logo' simply exhorted readers to 'Call our competitors Then . . . call us'. By 6(10) *MacUser* 78, 18 May 1990, the advertisement headed 'If we printed our prices you'd have an ART attack' was superimposed over a depiction of the Statue of Liberty. Then, in 6(14) *MacUser* 38 to 39, 13 July 1990, the advertisement was still superimposed on a depiction of the Statue of Liberty but running under a banner headline 'One Europe One Price'. Advertisers now expressly acknowledge their 'grey market' import policies (although not necessarily at cheaper prices), see 'MacMegastores', 7(11) *MacUser* 44, 31 May 1991; 'MacCentral', 7(11) *MacUser* 71, 31 May 1991; 'Mailordermac', 7(11) *MacUser* 87, 31 May 1991; all with 'own' warranties and support.
6 See for example advertising by 'Applekart' in 6(10) *MacUser* 76, 18 May 1990; 6(16) *MacUser*, 20, 10 August 1990; 6(17) *MacUser* 98 to 99, 24 August 1990; Newtech Systems Ltd 6(10) *MacUser* 58, 18 May 1990; 'Mac Express' 6(9) *MacUser* 104, 4 May 1990; 'MacLine' 6(17) *MacUser* 68 to 69, 24 August 1990; 7(11) *MacUser* 72 to 74.
7 Steve Hannaford, 'Here and There', 6(11) *MacUser* 21, 1 June 1990.

selling computer products done or tried to block parallel imports, the author approached a number of people involved at different levels in the computer industry in an effort to clarify some of these issues. Apart from published sources, questionnaires were sent to some 23 firms and organisations involved with the computer industry. These ranged from large transnationals engaged in making and selling both hardware and software to smaller firms based in the EC which produced only a small number of products. They also included firms engaged solely in distribution throughout the EC or in national markets. Some eight of the 23 firms responded to the questionnaire and their representatives (usually the senior corporate lawyer, sometimes with the product or sales executive) were subsequently interviewed. The interviews on average lasted about one hour, although some were as short as half an hour. Two firms indicated by letter that they were not prepared to participate and the remaining 13 did not respond at all. The questionnaire and interviews were conducted between July and October 1990; further attempts to obtain responses were made in December 1990 and March 1991. In view of the small numbers involved and the difficulty in verifying claims, what follows is largely impressionistic and necessarily generalised.

There are, unfortunately, no clear answers. To some extent, the inconclusive nature of the investigation appears to reflect differences in perspective and experience. The view of the global product manufacturer is different to that of the local sales representative. Even at the same level of production, views may differ. For example, one producer's goods may not have achieved sufficient local recognition to interest a prospective parallel importer in hunting around for cheaper sources. Alternatively, another producer may have formulated a commercial plan which, as it goes into implementation, may be confidently hoped will forestall the incentive to engage in parallel trade. Another reason for the inconclusive results is that many computer companies regard information about the extent to which they suffer from parallel imports – and any plans to combat them – as vital, confidential commercial information. A third factor, of particular importance within the context of the EC, is the special role of parallel importers in integrating the Common Market and the legal sensitivity of attempts to block parallel imports.

Then, there are the characteristics of the industry itself. In the United Kingdom, the market for personal computers and associated products seems to be of fairly recent origin.[8] In many respects it may be regarded as highly competitive. While there are some quite large companies involved, particularly in the production of hardware, there are also many small concerns and, as yet, there do not appear to be great obstacles to new firms entering the market on some scale. Several correspondents stressed the vital importance of improving existing products and developing new

---

8 Some interview subjects suggested that it had really only developed in the last five to ten years, some years behind the United States.

ones just to survive in the market. A company which did not innovate and upgrade continuously would simply be overtaken and disappear. This continual competitive striving has had two obvious effects. Products are, first, much more sophisticated and efficient than their predecessors, capable of performing much more elaborate (even undreamt of) tasks much more quickly. Second, over time there has been a continuous downward pressure on prices; partly as demand increased and technology also became cheaper, but partly because the product itself was overtaken by more recent developments. Hence, at this stage, the computer industry seems to be characterised by an emphasis on innovation and development.

Another feature of the industry is that much of the initiative in the past has lain with the United States. Product development and much of its production took place largely in the United States in response to demand from US customers who made up the bulk of the market. In such a climate, some interview subjects suggested, sales in Europe were considered ancillary; additional revenue once demand in the United States had been met.[9] As a result of these factors, many producers in the computer industry focused their European operations on marketing and distribution rather than major product development. This is, of course, not true of all companies. Moreover, by 1990 there were signs of change. There have been 'European' hardware producers for some time and flourishing, if not giant, software houses are developing.[10] Further some interviewees reported increasing attention to the 'European' market as sales in the United States stagnated and demand in Europe grew at a faster rate for an increasing volume.

Hence, at least for the larger companies (and speaking very broadly), operations in Europe seem to have evolved into a three-tiered structure. Often, there is a European headquarters co-ordinating policy and operations throughout the EC and other European countries. Particularly for many foreign-owned companies, the role of European headquarters is largely concentrated on distribution and marketing rather than research and development of new products.[11] Under the European headquarters, these companies generally have a series of distributors organised along national lines; often subsidiaries, sometimes independently owned operators and sometimes a mixture of both. These are primarily responsible for building up, maintaining and expanding the national market and it is these with whom national and sometimes regional and local wholesalers and retailers and some institutional buyers would generally deal. Independent of the computer companies and software houses, there are now at least three distributorships operating on a EC- or Europe-wide basis. These pan-European distributors typically stock

9   One interviewee described US head office as having regarded 'European' sales as a 'bonus'.

10   For a survey of some of those developing programs for use on Apple computers, see David Tebbutt, 'EuroVisions', 6(15) *MacUser* 67, 27 July 1990.

11   As previously indicated, this is by no means true of *all* companies and, even for those companies of which it is largely true, does not preclude some role in product development.

products from a number of manufacturers and may deal directly with both the manufacturers' European headquarters and their national operations.[12]

At least in the United Kingdom, parallel imports seem to have two likely sources: first, and mainly, the United States; second, other Member States of the EC. The generally cheaper price explains the United States as a source. Products are often also released there earlier. As some of the examples already mentioned from the Open Forum show, cheaper market price is also the explanation for parallel imports between Member States of the EC. However, it seems that much of this trade often arises as a result of exchange rate fluctuations.[13]

It is not possible to provide an estimate of the size of the parallel import market affecting the computer industry in the United Kingdom. At least one company representative claimed that he was unaware of parallel imports occurring at all. If they did, he speculated, it would be impossible to estimate quantity given the ease with which computer products, especially software, could be sent across borders. Another hardware manufacturer claimed to have estimated volume but was 'not at liberty to disclose details'.[14] Other interview subjects indicated that the rate of parallel imports fluctuated considerably over time. This last view seems plausible and is consistent with the results of the general surveys discussed in Chapter 11 below. One distributor indicated that a decision to engage in parallel trade depended on constant monitoring of prices at national and local levels, exchange rates, the level of demand, availability of stock and expected impact on relations with suppliers.

Some manufacturers' representatives at the European headquarters level believed that prices in Europe were not significantly different: they claimed largely to adopt 'a European pricing policy'. To the extent that they acknowledged price disparity, this was largely between the United States and Europe (particularly the United Kingdom). However, the picture changes even within Europe when viewed from a perspective other than that of European headquarters. Then, differences in national and regional policy became important and exchange rate fluctuations even within Europe could prove significant.[15]

The first reason for higher prices of products in Europe are transport costs between the United States (or other foreign source) and Europe together with import duties. Of course, in themselves these can hardly explain why

---

12 The operations of one pan-European distributor have been the subject of an individual exemption under EEC Treaty Article 85(3): *Re Computerland Europe SA* [1989] 4 CMLR 259.
13 This will be discussed further at Note 24 below.
14 Letter from the Strategic Marketing Manager of the manufacturer's subsidiary concerned.
15 Prior to the United Kingdom's entry into the ERM, respondents suggested that problems were experienced particularly between Germany and the United Kingdom and, to a lesser degree, Benelux and the United Kingdom. An attempt to compile data on the extent of 'European pricing' failed through inability to obtain price lists or, when price lists were available, compare the specifications of the products being offered.

margins are sufficient to attract parallel importers. Nor could they be an explanation for product made in Europe itself.

Another factor generally acknowledged are different market sizes requiring overheads to be spread over a smaller volume of units sold.[16] The argument applies to Europe as a whole (although, as previously indicated, there are some signs that the 'European' market is growing at a faster rate than the United States, thus reducing the gap), but in the computer industry has special significance as a result of language and technical standards; the costs of a local language version in, say, Danish or even German must be spread over a much smaller market.[17] A further factor is that the standard warranty period in the United States is 90 days while one year is common throughout Europe.[18]

However, perhaps reflecting the historic prominence of the United States, much of the responsibility for price differences is laid at the door of different marketing and promotional costs. The larger companies would seem to have characterised 'Europe' as a 'new' market, requiring much greater effort to create, educate and sustain demand for their products. Thus, heavier advertising and promotion is required and more reliance on specialised retail outlets capable of providing extensive support and advice.[19] For smaller producers, which operate in Europe only through independent distributors, the distributors claim that their prices are higher because they bear all the expense of advertising and promotion while their counterparts in the United States are largely acting as 'warehouses', the producer bearing the marketing costs there.[20] This argument makes some sense if they are buying from US wholesalers rather than directly from the producer. But, one might also expect the rational European distributing agent to start dealing closer up the distribution chain to the actual producer and to negotiate some form of discount or allowance to take into account the fact that the producer's advertising costs were not incurred for Europe.[21]

Moreover, the manufacturers' claims of the need for extra servicing do not pass unchallenged. There are accusations that some producers use international frontiers (at least, the dichotomy: United States/Europe) to pitch their products at different market segments. Products are priced cheaply to catch the high volume market in the United States while in

---

16 These would include some contribution towards recouping R & D outlays.

17 This would also include costs of translating and preparing special language versions of manuals and other documentation. The author has not been able to obtain estimates of just how significant these costs are.

18 Apart from any legal obligation, purchasers who valued the longer period could always be given the option to purchase it.

19 To a considerable extent, this claim seems to underlie the rationale behind IBM's adoption of a selective distribution system and Apple's AppleCentre concept. For IBM, see *Re IBM Personal Computer* [1984] 2 CMLR 343. For some discussion of the AppleCentre concept intertwined with Apple as a 'value-added' product, see John Leftwich, 'What Price A Macintosh?', 23 *MacUser* 57, May 1988. See also *Re Computerland Europe SA* [1989] 4 CMLR 259.

20 See for example Jim Mangles, 'Fighting the Parasites', 23 *MacUser* 53, May 1988.

21 Of course, to the extent that there are differences in market size, the discount may not equal the expenditure of the European distributor exactly.

Europe an image is created to help pitch the same, or essentially the same, products at a higher-price, 'quality' market.[22] In turn, the producers reply that the different marketing systems for 'Europe' and the United States reflect different market needs with, as already mentioned, a greater perceived need for customer education in 'Europe'. The challenge also runs into the difficult question of how much the state should interfere with the businessman's choice of how he markets his products.

A Commission official, speaking in his personal capacity, has suggested that the state of consumer understanding in the EC may well be nearing levels where intensively provided pre-sales services are no longer necessary.[23] There has also been a large increase in the number and importance of mail order sellers.

The rosy view of 'one European price' seen from European headquarters, if really true, demands qualification further down the distribution chain. The organisation of marketing along largely national lines means that price differences do arise and these can be exacerbated considerably by currency fluctuations.[24] Each national distributor largely determines its own distribution policy; how much it will devote to advertising and promotion, how much to support services, what commissions it will allow, what discounts and when it will run special promotions. As a result considerable scope arises for variations from list price. A firm which is prepared to shop around can earn considerable margins given the daily interaction of all these factors and, particularly prior to 8 October 1990, currency fluctuations.

This can lead to considerable friction. Viewed from the perspective of the group as a whole, say, at European headquarters,[25] producers are prepared to claim that it really makes no difference to them whether their product is sold in, say, Luxembourg or the United Kingdom. (Although, obviously, they would be very happy if all consumers bought at the highest price possible!) The position of the national subsidiary or agent is different. It will usually be required by European headquarters to meet some budgetary

---

22 In the case of Apple, the view, often expressed by disgruntled end-users in the letters' section of magazines is pungently put by 'The Grey Importer', 'Alternative Remedy', 23 *MacUser* 56, May 1988. His challenge is somewhat undermined by subsequently shifting his justification to one declaring that users should only have to pay for service if they want it: *ibid.* at 57.

23 Michael Sücker speaking at a Worldwide Information Systems conference on computer software, London, November 1990 comparing *Re IBM Personal Computer* [1984] 2 CMLR 343, at ¶¶4 and 14 with *Re Computerland Europe SA* [1989] 4 CMLR 259, at ¶3. He went on to express the view that, once consumers reached the desired degree of sophistication, the use of selective distribution systems for computer products would no longer be justified.

24 Foreign exchange fluctuations were mentioned as particularly important between the United Kingdom and Germany and, to a lesser degree, the United Kingdom and Benelux. The United Kingdom's entry into the European Exchange Rate Mechanism (ERM) on 8 October 1990, albeit on a 6 per cent margin rather than 3 per cent, may alleviate this problem to some extent while the United Kingdom remained in the ERM.

25 Some producers have made these points also in the context of the global business, not just European operations.

target or remit some form of lump sum (perhaps characterised as a licence fee). Sales 'poached' from its territory by another member of the group will be regarded as undermining its ability to meet that target. Perhaps as important are the pressures of intra-group politics and prestige.[26] Moreover, the subsidiary faces the problem of sales force motivation. The feeling among most of the producers interviewed is that, following the Commission's ruling in *Re IBM Personal Computer*,[27] they must be seen to provide *active* sales support and customer information to all customers regardless of whether that customer is known to engage in parallel importing.[28] It is understandably difficult for a distributor or agent to maintain this level of service if it realises it will not reap the full rewards and is further exacerbated by the way in which the sales staff are rewarded, a wage or salary plus commission. Any incentive effect of commission payment here hardly seems calculated to promote the objects of the internal market.[29]

Another reason why parallel imports often occur in the computer industry is that new products, or the latest releases, are often available in the United States earlier, sometimes much earlier. There is considerable tension here between the public's desire to get access to the latest products as soon as possible and the producer's desire both to develop localised versions of appropriate quality and to ensure that when its products are released it is able to support them adequately.[30] To some extent, this problem should be alleviated as the European market continues to grow in both size and sophistication relative to the United States. However, as discussed below, it may well remain a problem particularly for the smaller producers and also for languages where demand will remain small. In these cases, provision for effective, secure licensing would seem vital.

Parallel imports have had an impact on the computer industry, although there are some surprising, apparent failures to cause obvious effects. First, strikingly, from the viewpoint of the consumer, there does not seem to have been any great fall in the price difference between the United States and Europe.[31] Nor, at least in the United Kingdom, has there been a rash of litigation against parallel imports. There are, however, claims of a fairly uniform move towards 'European' pricing (with the qualifications already described). Another largely uniform response has been a move by sellers of computer products to emphasise the importance of local

---

26   On these problems, see Oliver E. Williamson, *The Economic Institutions of Capitalism*, Free Press, 1986, Chapter 2; Jean Tirolé, *The Theory Of Industrial Organization*, MIT Press, 1988, Chapter 1; Oliver E. Williamson, *Markets and Hierarchies: Analysis and Antitrust Implications*, Free Press, 1975.

27   [1984] 2 CMLR 343.

28   As discussed below, the qualified nature of this statement is justified.

29   One estimate suggested that commission may represent as much as 70 per cent of the sales representative's income. As discussed below, at least one producer has adopted some form of 'profits transfer' to alleviate this problem.

30   The Commission accepted that releasing products without proper support could well have undesirable consequences in both *Re IBM Personal Computer* [1984] 2 CMLR 343 and *Re Computerland Europe SA* [1989] 4 CMLR 259.

31   See for example Hannaford, 'Here and There'.

customer support and services. There are also reports, discussed below, of a far more sophisticated use of informal pressure to dissuade prospective parallel importers and their customers from shopping around.

The successful maintenance of the price difference between the United States and 'Europe' probably goes some way to explaining the dearth of litigation against parallel imports in the computer industry. If customers in Europe are still paying the higher price, litigation would hardly seem urgent. There are other factors contributing, however.

Many of the interview subjects were prepared to admit that, at least during summer 1990, parallel imports had not yet reached the levels which precipitated the controversy of which the Open Forum was a symptom. One consideration suggested was that it may be 'early days yet'. If the pound sterling continued trading at a level of almost two US dollars for any length of time,[32] the incentive to parallel import might loom larger and the benefit of paying 'high' prices for local support and services might diminish somewhat.

Another consideration is the changes in the industry's level of development. There is a suggestion that the computer products industry in Europe was in its infant stages late 1987 – early 1988. It was not yet in a position to supply the sort of sophisticated customer services which are now being offered as a justification for the price differential. At least as important, extensive distribution networks of the sort now established had not been built up and, in any event, the European operation did not always have stocks available to fill orders even if it had found the customer. At the same time, US producers apparently weighed down their US outlets with large volumes of stock in what some interviewees claimed was then a depressed market. Hence, the US distributors had strong incentives to 'offload' product wherever the order came from. It was claimed that stockholding levels in the United States were no longer as onerous. Furthermore, US producers may have become more aware of the destination of products sold by their US distributors.

At the same time, however, there has been a large growth in the number of mail order distributors in the United Kingdom during 1990 and 1991. A number of these make a point of indicating that they stock parallel imports and offer their own warranties.[33]

Further, many of the interview subjects advanced two main reasons why parallel imports were unlikely to result in large numbers of legal cases: the nature of the industry and legal uncertainty. Put simply, people within the industry had (and have) considerable doubts about the legal standing of computer technology and the industry's licensing practices. These questions range over the whole spectrum of licensing and contractual issues, such as the validity of 'shrinkwrap' licensing or of clauses tying the use of a particular package to a designated central processing unit as well as, for much of the

---

32   The *Independent*, 15, 16 and 17 October 1990 gave rates of US$1.95, 1.94 and 1.95, respectively, for the UK£.
33   See Note 5 above.

industry's life, whether it could rely on intellectual property protection at all. The legal basis of protection will be clarified to a large degree with the adoption of the 'Computer program directive', but the application of the competition rules under the EEC Treaty to many practices in the industry is still far from clear.[34] Given these doubts, many interview subjects were considerably wary of 'upsetting the apple-cart' by setting an unwanted legal precedent. They claim to prefer the present air of uncertainty to clearly adverse rulings. All interviewees were alive to the potential for intervention by the European Commission.

Most interviewees were also concerned about the negative impact aggressive use of intellectual property rights might have on customer relations. In conjunction with this concern, it seems that corporate customers operating in more than one country are apparently prepared to tolerate at least some price differential as the price of having access to local customer support services.

Another factor explaining the limited amount of litigation is the particular nature of the industry. As already discussed, it seems to be characterised by a high degree of competition to develop new and improved products. Hence, the industry places a high premium on quick results. Except in the rarest case, many thought the time and cost involved in intellectual property litigation therefore hardly made it an attractive option. These views must be seen in context. Many interview subjects viewed the legal position as at best uncertain. Moreover, at the time the interviews were being carried out, most regarded parallel imports as less than a pressing problem. Apart from the apparently small and fluctuating volume of parallel imports at present, other matters, particularly piracy, were considered far more pressing; occurring on a far greater scale and requiring more immediate attention.

On the other hand, many interviewees claimed that parallel imports, or the threat of parallel imports, had forced some alteration in their policies. Interview subjects within the European headquarters claimed an increasing shift towards a 'European' pricing policy by which they meant a largely common price throughout 'Europe'. At this stage, however, this should probably be seen as a move to reduce price differentials between different European countries. The existence of differences in language and technical standards still presents some opportunity for discriminating between markets and, in addition, there is the potential for price variation arising from the use of national distributions systems and currency fluctuations already discussed.

At least one producer has sought to address the incentive problem of its distributors by adopting a form of profits transfer. While it apparently prefers customers to buy from the local subsidiary where the customer is based, in light of the potential application of the EEC Treaty's rules on free movement it will conclude sales if the customer persists. If the customer has already had dealings with the marketing subsidiary responsible for the territory in

34   OJ 1991 L122/42, 14 May 1991.

which the customer is based, the full profit is transferred from the selling subsidiary to the local subsidiary; in other cases, the profits from the sale are shared. One could imagine this procedure would be more difficult to implement if one of the distributors were an independent agent rather than a subsidiary.[35]

The second main impact of parallel imports is a move in a direction opposite to standardising prices: greater emphasis on customer service and support. In effect, customer service and support is being used as another form of 'localisation'. This highlights an interesting paradox. Vertical restraints, particularly in the field of distribution, are usually justified on the ground of forestalling free riding on such services. Yet, here, such services are being used to discourage free riding. The object (which by all accounts seems to be succeeding in large measure) is to build a justification for at least some premium by providing the customer with (desirable) services. It seems that many customers, particularly business and institutional buyers, are willing to accept higher local prices in return for an established distribution and service network. While this form of enhancing product differentiation might suggest the potential for anti-competitive market power, some interviewees acknowledged that the success of such a policy depended on the effectiveness of the services provided and the size of any price differences.

Notwithstanding all these factors, computer industry producers would also seem to have developed increasingly sophisticated means of informally pressurising dealers and customers not to engage in parallel importing. As already indicated, most producers' representatives considered that the policy of the European Commission prevented them from overt discrimination such as refusing to sell to someone engaging in intra-EC parallel importing. However, there was considerable scope for discretionary action of a less overt nature. Over time expressions of displeasure have become increasingly sophisticated. They range from the fairly trivial to those having more immediate commercial effect. Producers have considerable discretion over 'soft dollar support', matters such as whether to waive strict compliance with payment deadlines or what level of discount to permit for example. Similarly, not inviting a recalcitrant parallel importer to cocktail parties or perks of a similar 'social' nature, can give the parallel importer pause for thought at the same time as marking him out to the rest of the industry as a pariah (and signalling corresponding treatment to others who do not abide by the 'rules').

Most of the interview subjects did not consider that allowing parallel imports would affect their own company's decisions to invest in research and development ('R & D') of new products. Almost all of the factors already discussed led them to that consideration.

---

35 If one of the parties be an independent undertaking, questions may arise under EEC Treaty, Article 85(1) as a profits transfer arrangement may be seen as a disincentive to intra-brand competition. The Commission has exempted such a clause in *Transocean Marine Paint Association* [1967] CMLR D9, but refused to do so in the three subsequent renewals: see Valentine Korah, *EEC Competition Law and Practice*, ESC Publishing, 1990 (4th ed.), at 138.

Most, however, also considered that the nature of the industry itself was such that any failure to continue innovating would lead to the firm's certain extinction quite rapidly. They expected that most products on the market now would be outdated within two to three years. Some speculated that parallel imports may well undermine R & D incentives in the long term, say, over ten years. But, they agreed it would be extremely difficult to point to parallel imports as the sole (or even main) cause of a company's demise over that time frame. At the same time, most of the interviewees represented firms where the bulk of R & D took place outside 'Europe' and from their perspective the effect of parallel imports was to undermine their distribution systems. Some speculated that any impact of parallel imports on R & D incentives would have most significance by inhibiting the development of domestic industry. They did not, however, have any information that that was indeed the case.

Although 12 'European' producers of computer products were approached, only one provided any kind of detailed response, so it is not possible to generalise about the impact of parallel imports on the development of a 'domestic' industry. This respondent indicated that his firm earned up to ten times the revenue on domestic sales as it did on foreign sales. Unless it earned those revenues, he claimed that the firm would not be able to continue in the business of developing computer products.

The different level of revenue generated by selling essentially the same product in different markets was attributed to two factors. First, in the 'domestic' market, the firm acted as both designer/producer and distributor for its own products. In the United States in particular, however, the firm's size obliged it to operate through several layers of distributor. Consequently, the firm only received about 15 per cent of the US importer's margin. Second, the respondent believed that US margins for distributors were lower than those available in 'Europe'. He suspected that US sales were concentrated through mail order houses and some specialist resellers. As a result, the respondent indicated that the sale of one unit of the firm's product in the United States might earn the firm £6.00, while the same sale in its 'domestic' market would generate £60.00 in revenue. He stressed that the firm could not continue developing products without the revenues generated by its domestic sales.

The firm had apparently suffered some parallel importing. The respondent indicated that unless parallel imports were effectively forestalled, the firm would have to stop selling in the United States. A number of strategies, however, were being used before taking such drastic action. The product's box was clearly stamped to identify the market it was intended for sale in. Another strategy was 'localisation' – adapting the product so that the version sold in one market would not work (or was less attractive) in other markets. The demand for localisation was given as a reason why parallel imports were not a very significant problem within the EC. Localisation was not quite as effective between the United States and the United Kingdom (although the US market was described as 'very insular') and depended on taking advantage of any differences in the operating systems used in the two markets, language differences and the United States' units of measurement. Litigation was not considered an option against parallel imports, partly because of the expense and partly because it was not felt acceptable in the industry 'culture'.

Hence, it seems that for larger, established firms parallel imports are not likely to undermine incentives to invest in R & D while the pace of technical change remains high.[36] This may not be the case for smaller, 'start-up' firms. How long that will remain true is highly speculative. Once the pace of change slows as innovations become more complicated or otherwise require greater resources, a process of concentration could be expected which parallel imports may exacerbate.[37]

In conclusion, it would seem that the effects of parallel importing on the computer industry are complicated. With two notable exceptions, none of the industry representatives the author has surveyed considered that parallel imports were a major problem during the northern summer, 1990. The apparent lack of aggressive litigation or media campaigns tends to confirm this conclusion. But, by the same token, the threat of parallel imports does not seem to have substantially reduced the difference in prices between the United States and Europe. Hence, within certain limits, it seems fair to conclude that obstacles to parallel importing remain. Still, there is some evidence that company policies have changed in response to the threat of parallel imports.

To the extent that it occurs, parallel importing may have either or both of two main effects on the supply side. It may undermine incentives to invest in innovation or it may disrupt the producer's authorised distribution network. At the moment, the nature of the computer industry is such that parallel imports seem unlikely to undermine incentives to invest in R & D for most firms. However, there is a suggestion that a fledgling domestic industry would find it harder to get established in the face of parallel imports. The main effect of parallel imports observed has been on firms' distribution networks.

Companies are certainly more aware of the need to justify price differences within 'Europe'. There are moves towards standardising prices around 'Europe', albeit to a greater or lesser degree. There are also definite moves to enhance local 'value added' by developing customer support services. Whether this is desirable from a social welfare point of view will depend on two different considerations. If all customers uniformly desire such services, then presumably welfare is enhanced. There is evidence, however, that not all customers need or want all the extensive services which the industry seeks to entrench its position with. If such customers have access to a sufficient

---

36 This is consistent with economists' work on the importance of technological opportunity, see for example F.M. Scherer and David Ross, *Industrial Market Structure and Economic Performance*, Houghton Mifflin, 1990 (3rd ed.), at 630 to 660.

37 At that stage, leading brands may have become sufficiently well established that freeing up intra-brand restraints might promote inter-brand competition, see for example Robert L. Steiner, 'The Nature of Vertical Restraints', 30 *Antitrust Bulletin* 143 (1985).

range of choice and hence the option of satisfying their needs more cheaply from sellers competing on price rather than services, the justification for parallel imports would be lessened. In the absence of such choice, the role of parallel imports would be significantly more important. The fact that those interviewed at present see parallel imports as a fairly minor priority lends some support to the view that customers are willing to pay for the services provided or have access to a range of options. But, the demand for service at the expense of price has its limits. Moreover, the existence of some parallel importing indicates that there are customers who neither need nor want the 'localisation' advantages offered by the locally authorised distributor.

A third, perhaps less positive, response within the industry has been the development of more subtly sophisticated methods of deterring prospective parallel importers. Whether this is desirable depends on whether parallel importing is viewed as harmful or not. In the EC, this depends largely on whether the imports are from another Member State or a third, non-EC country. Moreover, it seems likely that the scope for discretionary action is greater the larger the producer and correspondingly less for smaller, fledgling firms. Accordingly, this 'informal' pressuring seems less than desirable but, since producers have fairly large scope for discretionary action, it seems unlikely that it would be possible to eliminate such pressure completely.

Chapter 10: Is It 'Broke'?
Let's Fix It . . . Books, 'Buying Around'
and Copyright in Australia

10.1 The Lucky Country

In the two decades from 1970, 'Australian' publishing had demonstrated 'massive growth'.[1] However measured, the publication of books in Australia, as opposed to their mere importation and sale by distributors, was a rapidly expanding business. For example, Table 10.1 shows one writer's claims that the percentage of the Australian retail sales market captured by 'Australian-originated' titles had changed dramatically. The number of new titles published each year had surged from 1,615 in 1974 to 4,219 in 1987.[3] Even admitting a 'boom' from euphoria generated by the Sydney bicentennial, growth appears to have been experienced in all sectors of the market. New fictional titles, for example, increased by 53 per cent (to 253 new titles in 1987) and children's books up 29.6 per cent (with 492 new titles).[4] The value of book exports from Australia was also growing at a rate of 11.6 per cent each year.[5]

Table 10.1
Books: Market Share in Australia by Place of Origin[2]

	Australian (%)	Imported (%)
early 1970s	10	90
early 1980s	44	56
1986	50	50

Sources: Judith Brett, *Publishing, Censorship and Writers' Incomes 1965–88*, 1988
Jan Paterson, *The Future of Australia as an Export Market*, 1989

1 Australian Book Publishers' Association (ABPA) submission to the Copyright Law Review Committee (CLRC) cited in CLRC, *The Importation Provisions of the Copyright Act 1968*, AGPS, 1988, at ¶65.
2 Jan Paterson, *The Future of Australia as an Export Market*, The Sir Stanley Unwin Foundation, 1989, at 8 citing Judith Brett, *Publishing, Censorship and Writers' Incomes 1965–1988*, 1988.
3 *Ibid.*
4 *Ibid.*
5 Australia Council, *Books – Who Reads Them?*, Australia Council, 1990, at 206, but note the qualifications.

Not only were more titles being published in Australia, but more of them were by Australian authors. More of these were achieving international success and increasingly relying on agents to exploit their commercial potential more fully.[6] Increasingly, publishing contracts involved splitting rights for Australia from the UK ownership.[7]

Some care must be taken with these figures. What is meant by 'published' and what by 'Australian' are hardly precise categories. In addition to definitional problems, the data from which the statistics are derived is not as precise as might be hoped.[8]

Hence, at best, the examples here can only be taken to indicate the broad contours of a developing trend. A trend, however, confirmed. The PSA's data showed Australian publishing capturing an additional 3 to 4 per cent of market share overall in the years from 1981 to 1987; the Australia Council's figures suggest at least 6 per cent between 1978 and 1989.[9] Australian demand for books was increasingly being met by publishing activities in Australia. Paterson, an insider of the UK publishing world, was convinced that this trend would continue.[10]

Despite this sunny picture of a competitive market, all, apparently, was not well. The most striking facts about Australia as a market for books are that it is predominantly an English language market and that it is quite distant from the two main centres where those books are produced, the United Kingdom and the United States. Its population is small compared to both. Moreover, although its population is largely urban, the main urban centres are quite distant from each other. The comparatively small size of the market together with its colonial past have meant that, historically, Australia is a net importer of copyright. That is, of the books on sale in Australia whether domestically published or imported, most have been written by foreign authors. As already discussed, the predominance of foreign authors and offshore publishing has been changing significantly since the 1970s. Still, in March 1986, of the over 257,000 titles held in stock by some 70 publishers, 216,840 were imported.[11]

---

6   Paterson, *The Future of Australia as an Export Market*, at 10 to 11.

7   *Ibid.* at 11, 35, 43 to 44. By no means had this developed to its full potential, however, see *ibid.* at 10, 35, 37, 38, 44.

8   There are inconsistencies in the figures in Paterson, *The Future of Australia as an Export Market*, at 7 to 8; the Prices Surveillance Authority (PSA) offered 18 alternative measurements of market value and share: PSA, *Inquiry into Book Prices: Interim Report*, PSA, Report No. 24, 1989 (*Interim Report*), at 90 to 91, Tables H1 and 2; see also the discussion in Australia Council, *Books – Who Reads Them?*, at 210 to 214, 57 to 64.

9   PSA, *Interim Report*, at 91, Table H2; Australia Council, *Books – Who Reads Them?*, at 60, 210 to 214. Within the period reported by the PSA, there is a quite substantial fluctuation in market share including a large dip in 1985 possibly explained by an appreciation in the Australian dollar's value against the pound sterling in 1984.

10   Paterson, *The Future of Australia as an Export Market*, at 14, 28, 35, 37. He was less clear about whether this would necessarily lead to indigenous publishers supplanting foreign-owned.

11   CLRC, *The Importation Provisions of the Copyright Act*, at ¶65. Another estimate claimed 500,000 English-language titles in print with 100,000 additions annually: Australia Council, *Books – Who Reads Them?*, at 201.

Further, it seems that during the 1980s there was little, if any, real growth in the Australian market's volume. The apparent growth in retail value was due to inflation and higher prices. The number of books actually bought did not increase. In real terms, their prices rose.[12]

On Saturday, 5 November 1988, the *Sydney Morning Herald* published 'Bound for Botany Bay', the first in a series of articles examining the book trade in Australia. As the celebrations of the Sydney bicentennial neared their end, with a strong appeal to national sentiment the report asked why British publishers were allowed to dictate what Australians read and when. Worse, it exposed that the failure to cast off the 'last colonial shackle' had cost Australians dearly. Simply compared to prices in a New York book shop, the price Australians paid for books was far too high and they had to wait far too long for new titles to appear in their bookstores.[13] A public furore erupted. Several months later, the Commonwealth Government directed the PSA to investigate.[14] Something must have been wrong. It was the third governmental inquiry into book prices in ten years.

A regulatory body in the State of New South Wales had started, but never completed, an investigation in 1979.[15] In an inquiry lasting almost five years, the CLRC concluded that repeal of the copyright provisions blocking parallel imports was not warranted by 'a supposed high level of prices', but did recommend relaxation of the provisions to permit parallel imports of books not readily available in Australia within a reasonable time.[16] Twelve months later, however, the PSA considered that the prices of books in Australia were excessively high. Moreover, the power to block parallel imports was being used to shield a considerably inefficient distribution sector. Accordingly, it recommended repeal, subject to a ten-year transition period of protection for 'Australian' publishers as an 'infant industry'.[17]

The root of the controversy lay in the importation provisions in the Copyright Act 1968 (Cth). As discussed in Chapter 4 above, these made it an infringing act to import into Australia and deal commercially with works protected by copyright unless the copyright owner has consented to the importation. This is so even if the imported copies were first marketed abroad under the authority of the same person owning the

---

12 Australia Council, *Books – Who Reads Them?*, at 214 to 217; inflation being 8.5 per cent per annum compound, average book prices rising at a compound rate of 12.8 per cent per annum. The Australia Council also documented a shift to borrowing between 1978 and 1989, although those claiming that they were borrowing because of higher book prices actually fell from 40 per cent to 28 per cent: *ibid.* at 76.
13 Robert Haupt, 'Bound for Botany Bay: Why Britain Still Decides What You Can Read', *Sydney Morning Herald*, Saturday, 5 November 1988, at 86 to 87.
14 Reference dated 19 June 1989 reproduced as Annex A in PSA, *Final Report*, at 41.
15 NSW Prices Commission, see CLRC, *The Importation Provisions of the Copyright Act*, at ¶81.
16 CLRC, *The Importation Provisions of the Copyright Act*, at ¶¶88 to 91. The CLRC did, however, acknowledge its limitations in determining any differences between price levels.
17 PSA, *Inquiry into Book Prices: Final Report*, PSA, Report No. 25, 1989 (*Final Report*), at 39 to 40; PSA, *Interim Report*, at 70 to 73.

Australian copyright.[18] In the book trade, this is apparently often called 'buying around'.

This sequence of circumstance and events reveals two sets of interests in conflict: copyright owners and consumers. Consumers demand access to books quickly and cheaply. Copyright owners claimed that the price differences arose from cost differences in supplying Australia and so were justified. It cost more to transport the books to the Australian market; it cost more to establish and maintain an effective marketing operation in Australia and these costs had to be spread over a smaller market. In a country like Australia, the problems of distance and size are exacerbated by cultural aspirations. Australians, increasingly, want to buy books about 'Australian' experience and by Australians. Some Australian experience prior to the Second World War suggests that it was difficult to satisfy both interests simultaneously.[19] Balancing the competing interests – short-term demands for cheap copies against longer-term claims of encouraging Australian writing – requires some trade-off.

10.2 'Lizard's Leg, and Howlet's Wing'

The conclusions reached by the PSA are informed by three underlying themes. First, the historic predominance of UK interests in Australian copyright ownership which resulted, in its view, in the Australian market being a barricaded oligopoly. Second, the PSA seems quite frustrated by the real world's failure to conform to the paradigm of perfect competition. Its analysis is driven by the goals of static allocative efficiency and an *ex post* view of the competitive process. Third, in view of Australia's small size compared to the main sources of copyright, it was a 'net importer' of copyright. Therefore, the harm (welfare losses) suffered by Australian copyright owners from changing the copyright law would be more than offset by the gains to Australian consumers from lower prices and increased allocative efficiency.

All three themes heighten the magnitude of the costs consumers must bear if a copyright system which blocks parallel imports is maintained. Correspondingly, all three themes downplay the gains to society from operating such a copyright system. Reliance on them can be challenged at two levels. Is the static, *ex post* view of allocative efficiency the right test to apply? The author will argue below that it is not. Before then, however, the author intends to examine the grounds for believing that the PSA's conclusions may have been wrong on their own terms. Was the market

---

18 *Interstate Parcel Express Co. Pty Ltd v Time-Life International (Nederlands) BV* (1977) 138 CLR 534.
19 UK publishers reportedly flooded the market from time to time with cheap 'colonial' editions at prices lower than Australian publishers could compete against, see Richard Nile, 'Cartels, Capitalism and the Australian Book Trade', (1990) 4(1) *Continuum* 71.

for books in Australia in the hands of an entrenched oligopoly unresponsive to competitive pressures?

Using the lens of price theory, the PSA developed a theoretical analysis demonstrating that copyright owners would use their powers in Australia to block imports and practise price discrimination against Australian consumers. The conclusion was confirmed by interpretation of the available empirical evidence. The PSA rejected copyright owners' claims that any differences between Australian and foreign prices were justifiable on grounds of different costs and, contrasting it to a model of pure, perfect competition, concluded that the distribution of books in Australia was riddled with inefficiency.

For effective price discrimination, three conditions are *necessary*: first, the suppliers (copyright owners) must have market power; second, there must be differences in the demand or supply conditions between the markets; and third, it must be possible to insulate the different markets from each other.[20] These conditions are cumulative. The absence of any single one would be sufficient to undermine any attempt to practise effective price discrimination between two markets.[21]

If there be no market power in the 'high price' market, price discrimination cannot be profitable. In a competitive market, the producer could sell all its output at the market price and so has no incentive to discount. On the other hand, if it attempted to charge above the market price, consumers would simply switch their purchases to other producers. Hence, in the absence of market power on the supply side, the supplier or suppliers cannot fix price.[22]

Price differences between markets may be caused by two factors. The potential for price differences between the markets arises if buyers in one market are less influenced by price changes than buyers in the other market (or markets). This could happen if one country's consumers valued books more than the other's; or if there were differences in income levels; or because one group had easier access to competing editions.[23] Alternatively, from the supplier's viewpoint, it may cost more to supply its product to one market. There could be extra transport costs or costs associated with shorter print runs.

Differences in demand conditions, however, cannot be exploited if the supplier cannot stop the goods in the 'cheap' market leaking into the more expensive market. To the extent that they were enforced, the copyright powers to block imports satisfied this condition.

---

20   PSA, *Interim Report*, at 33. See also F.M. Scherer and David Ross, *Industrial Market Structure and Economic Performance*, Houghton Mifflin, 1990 (3rd ed.), at 489 who define 'price discrimination' as selling the same good to different consumers at different prices where the difference is not based on different costs of supply.
21   As the PSA notes: PSA, *Final Report*, at 18.
22   See for example Scherer and Ross, *Industrial Market Structure and Economic Performance*, at 489.
23   For example, the PSA believed prices were cheaper in Canada because Canadians could quite easily buy cheaper US editions: PSA, *Interim Report*, at 33 to 34, PSA, *Final Report*, at 17 to 18.

Despite some evidence of 'buying around', the conclusion that the Australian market was, or could be, effectively insulated hardly seems controversial.[24] Satisfaction of the other two conditions does, however, require much closer scrutiny.

10.2.1 Market power

In essence, the PSA found the condition of market power satisfied because copyright owners exploited the copyright law to establish a monopoly over the distribution of individual titles. This was backed up by allegations of oligopolistic collusion or 'tacit price leadership'.[25]

The determination of market power requires the definition of the appropriate market. This, in turn, requires consideration from the point of view of consumers' options and alternative sources of supply.[26] It must be a rare case indeed where copyright in an individual title will satisfy the necessary tests.

The exclusive right conferred by an intellectual property right *does* confer a degree of market power in the sense of power to raise price over marginal cost. That is the whole point of patent and copyright systems. They grant the copyright owner an exclusive right to stop others simply copying the work without incurring the costs and risks of development and they confer some power to price above marginal cost so that investment in 'development' can be recouped together with some premium for risk. To find that every attempt to capitalise on the market power associated with an intellectual property right conflicted with competition policy would render the intellectual property right pointless.

Moreover, the degree of market power conferred by copyright, particularly in an individual title, is not usually considered hostile to the goals of competition policy properly defined. Copyright does not give its owner power to control the whole market for books.

To talk of 'the market for books' can convey a misleading impression. Rather, books comprise a number of interlocking and overlapping sub-markets. For example, in a market for, say, wheat, one bushel will readily serve in the place of another. However, it is not possible to say the same of books. Someone who needs a mathematics textbook is unlikely to be satisfied with a copy of an Agatha Christie novel.[27] Books serve a number of different purposes: leisure, sources of information, educational or professional use and

---

24 For 'buying around', see Paterson, *The Future of Australia as an Export Market*, at 37 to 38. Given the legal power to block parallel imports, it seems likely that major publishers would not hesitate to enforce legal sanctions if the level of parallel imports threatened revenues seriously.

25 PSA, *Final Report*, at 17. According to the PSA, the *existence* of copyright in *individual* titles gave copyright owners market power 'especially in terms of distribution'. A similar error is made in Stephen Corones, 'Parallel Importing Computer Software: Consumer Welfare Considerations', (1992) 3 AIPJ 188, 193.

26 Scherer and Ross, *Industrial Market Structure and Economic Performance*, at 75 to 76; *Re Queensland Co-operative Milling Association Ltd* (1976) 25 FLR 169, at 190.

27 This example is taken from PSA, *Interim Report*, at 11.

cultural enrichment. A particular book may serve one or several of these purposes, but it is unlikely that for the majority of prospective purchasers all books will be ready substitutes for each other. So, to assess the degree of market power which copyright confers over 'books', it is necessary to examine sub-markets rather than 'the market'.

In the same sub-market(s), the demand conditions affecting any particular books will depend on the availability of substitute titles, other ways of satisfying the purpose(s) the book is sought for and the characteristics of the prospective buyers. The prospective purchaser of a dictionary, for example, has quite a wide range of choice to select from according to need and means. If the purchaser were seeking a book as a gift, they might well be willing to consider a range of options across many different types of book.[28] Also, however, the book would be competing with many other potential types of gift such as, say, records, socks, ties, perfume. Reviewing survey evidence, the PSA concluded that reading newspapers and magazines and watching television were 'powerful competitors' against books for the use of leisure time and money. On the other hand, the PSA considered that, as income and educational levels increased, the attraction of books was more likely to increase.[29]

In most cases, there is nearly always a diversity of titles to choose from as well as a range of alternative ways to satisfy demands for leisure or information. Furthermore, as the PSA acknowledged, copyright at its most basic confers protection on the form of expression, not on the ideas embodied in the work. There is nothing to stop another author taking the ideas in one book and producing his or her own version on the same theme or subject. Hence, consumers usually have available a considerable range of choice as a counterweight to an author or publisher who attempts to charge too high a price. Even where the presently existing range of choice is limited, it seems unlikely that there are often significant obstacles to the publication of new, competing titles. So, while it is true to say that copyright confers a monopoly over an individual title, that is a narrow, static and, with respect, inadequate definition of the market.

Moreover, if the prices which the PSA felt foreign publishers were charging for imported books were higher, they would seem to have been acting as a magnet to attract new entry. Which is exactly what would be expected if the market is competitive.[30]

The PSA attempted to buttress its conclusion through the shadowy presence of oligopoly. With oligopoly, individual shortcomings in market

---

28 Dymocks, a bookseller and one of the main campaigners for repeal, reported to the PSA that up to 40 per cent of their main store's customers were gift shopping: *ibid.* at 12. Other evidence suggests that gift buying accounted for between 10 and 25 per cent of the market: Australia Council, *Books – Who Reads Them?*, at 76 to 78.
29 *Ibid.* at 15 to 17.
30 See for example Scherer and Ross, *Industrial Market Structure and Economic Performance*, Chapter 10; Richard A. Posner, *Antitrust Law: An Economic Analysis*, University of Chicago Press, 1976, Chapter 2 and note also Judge Oberdorfer's comments in *Studiengesellschaft Kohle* 670 F. 2d 1122 (DC Cir. 1981) in Chapter 3 from Note 230.

power may be replaced by collusion. The oligopolists may form a cartel or may effectively operate as one through tacit collusion. In either case, collusion is unlikely to persist unless the number of participants is small enough to facilitate co-ordination readily and there are high barriers to new entry.

But, if there were a cartel, then the most effective way of dealing with it would be under the competition laws. It is no answer in an inquiry such as the PSA's to say that the Trade Practices Act 1974 cannot reach the cartel because of the special protection afforded intellectual property by section 51(3). If necessary, amendment of the Act to remove that special, unwarranted protection would seem to be indicated.[30a] The PSA, after all, was prepared to recommend wholesale change to the Copyright Act.

In any case, on the published evidence, there would seem to be considerable doubts about whether a formal cartel or an oligopoly were in place. The evidence of a formal cartel is slender. A single witness claimed that UK publishers of books which formed close substitutes met to fix prices:

> The application of this market power is made more effective through either formal collusion on Australian prices or by tacit price leadership. Mr Ken Wilder alleged at the Inquiry that formal collusion by British publishers does in fact take place.[31]

The basis for Mr Wilder's knowledge of cartel meetings is unspecified. He was apparently a former managing director of Collins (Australia). But, he had retired in 1986. Here, any dynamic, changing nature of the market in Australia may become important.[32] Indeed, even if such slight evidence were satisfactory, the alleged cartel seems to have been built on shaky foundations, besieged by new entrants.

Historically, the copyright in Australia associated with books had been controlled by UK publishers. The PSA considered that the demise of the Traditional Markets Agreement, by which US and UK publishers shared the rights to English-language publishing, changed nothing.[33] However, the dynamics of the market-place during the 1970s and 1980s led to these arrangements unravelling more and more. The quotation from Paterson which the PSA relied on must be set in context: it relates mainly to the 'general' market and was increasingly threatened. As already noted, an increasing share of the market was captured by 'Australian' publications.

30a   It is by no means clear that section 51(3) of the Trade Practices Act 1974 would immunise a horizontal conspiracy.

31   PSA, *Final Report*, at 17; PSA, *Interim Report*, at 33.

32   Laurie Muller, 'Copyright as Defence Against Pagan Hordes', *Sydney Morning Herald*, Thursday 3 August 1989, at 9. Muller was then general manager of University of Queensland Press and President of ABPA. He highlighted the generation gap between Wilder and the present industry heads and claimed that Collins itself failed to grasp the changing nature of the market in Australia.

33   PSA, *Interim Report*, especially at 19. For the consent decree, see *US v Addison-Wesley Publishing Co.* (1976) CCH-Trade Cases at ¶61,225 in Chapter 4.2.4 above.

Apart from News Corporation's takeover activity, the penetration of US publishers was also increasing.[34]

Of course, not all publishers hold just one copyright and large, globally operating transnationals are certainly readily identifiable. To a considerable degree, publishers are either whales or minnows. It has been claimed that there are approximately 1,000 publishers operating commercially in Australia.[35] Of the ABPA's 149 members, 100 had an annual turnover under A$1 million, 28 between A$1 and 10 million, 17 between A$10 and 30 million and 4 over $A30 million. In all, 21 accounted for over 80 per cent of sales by ABPA's members.[36] The largest, News Corporation, owned interests variously estimated to control turnover between A$90 and 110 million out of a total market of about A$1,000 million; its nearest competitor around A$50 million.[37]

Whether these publishers were sufficiently strong to choke off supply is debatable. Co-ordination problems (and policing, if there be a formal cartel) are much greater the higher the number of participants. Admittedly, for publishers, there are considerable economies of scale and scope. Fixed costs per title, such as editing, typesetting and some marketing costs, can be quite substantial, while the costs of producing an extra copy are usually quite small in comparison. But, on the other hand, technology and the ready availability of sub-contracting for particularly capital intensive operations like printing mean that entry on a small scale is relatively easy.[38] Once again, the increasing penetration of the Australian market by both American and Australian publishers suggests that any barriers were largely ineffective and emphasises competitive behaviour.

Many of the smaller new entrants did, however, perceive access to distribution channels as something of a problem.[39] The larger publishers undertook both the traditional publishing functions and carried out distribution themselves. Those whose turnover did not support their own warehousing and distribution networks usually arranged for one of the other, larger publishers to act as its distribution agent for Australia. Thus, Penguin stocked and promoted not only its own titles but also those of other foreign and domestic publishers.

Again, there are considerations suggesting that smaller publishers were not being effectively foreclosed from the market. Some economic work indicates that minimum scales of efficiency need to exceed 10 per cent of market

---

34 For increasing US penetration, see Paterson, *The Future of Australia as an Export Market*, at 5, 15 and 42 as well as 17 to 28 *passim*. The PSA also recorded, but seems to have discounted, these developments; focusing instead on increasing concentration at the upper end and arguing that it was just as much in US publishers' interests to discriminate: PSA, *Interim Report*, at 17 to 26.
35 Australia Council, *Books – Who Reads Them?*, at 203, Note 93.
36 *Ibid.* at 203 to 204.
37 See Paterson, *The Future of Australia as an Export Market*, at 15.
38 For example, PSA, *Interim Report*, at 18.
39 Paterson, *The Future of Australia as an Export Market*, at 16 to 17.

capacity to act as effective barriers.[40] There is also evidence that independent wholesalers were developing at the state, if not yet the national, level.[41] In addition, the number of exclusive distributors active in the markets seems to have been large.[42] Moreover, many smaller publishers were producing 'Australian' books which retailers were under increasing pressure to supply from consumers who wanted 'Australian' books to an extent not satisfied by the foreign publishers. The prominence and size and so bargaining power of some retailers was increasing considerably. Hence, the indications seem to be that individual publishers were not in a position to exclude undesired rivals from the market.

10.2.2   Conditions of demand

The PSA was also satisfied that copyright owners were exploiting differences in demand conditions between Australia and overseas markets. This was a two-fold process. First, the price of books in Australia was higher than the corresponding price charged for them overseas. Second, those differences could not be attributed to effective costs of supply.

(a)   *Higher prices*

The crucial results were the PSA's own survey of the prices charged by three UK publishers. In this, the current catalogues of each were examined to find the (recommended) retail price for each title available in Australia, the United Kingdom and Canada, the prices being converted to Australian dollars at average exchange rates for 1988/89. For all titles, Australian prices were found to be on average 31.3 per cent *above* the UK price while the corresponding Canadian value was 2.58 per cent *below* the UK price.[43] Even without the knowledge that shipping costs were cheaper to Australia than Canada, the PSA considered that such large disparities in price could only

---

40   Richard Schmalensee, 'Ease of Entry: Has the Concept Been Applied Too Readily?', 56 Antitrust LJ 41, at 49 (1987) and Richard Schmalensee, 'Economies of Scale and Barriers to Entry', 89 JPolEcon. 1228 (1981). At least one Australian source claimed that a viable distribution operation required turnover in the order of A$10 million per year: Paterson, *The Future of Australia as an Export Market*, at 16. Schmalensee identified two qualifications where his analysis might not apply, see 89 JPolEcon. 1228, at 1236. One was where transport costs are high and markets regional. The sub-contracting of printing for Australian publishing 'offshore' and the PSA's treatment of freight absorption seem to suggest that this qualification does not apply. The second qualification was advertising where (1) there were significant scale economies in advertising *and* (2) it had relatively long-lasting effects on demand. The implications of this are not as clear since the PSA's suggestion that advertising in an oligopolistic market created a significant barrier to competition seems to depend on the effects of advertising being *short-lived* rather than long-lasting, see Scherer and Ross, *Industrial Market Structure and Economic Performance*, at 436 to 437.
41   Australia Council, *Books – Who Reads Them?*, at 205.
42   See the evidence of Mr J. Ruwolt, discussed in the text to Note 75 below.
43   PSA, *Interim Report*, at 51.

be explained by exploitation of differences in demand conditions – deriving particularly from Canadians' ready access to competing US editions.[44]

There has, apparently, been strong criticism of the PSA's survey evidence about Canadian prices.[45] However, four surveys, three of them available to the PSA, reinforce its conclusion that Australian prices were higher than UK prices. Three of them (two seen by the PSA) highlight the marked variation in price discrepancies depending on the sub-market in question.

Monash University Library surveyed nine foreign publishers to find that six applied markedly varying conversion rates depending on the book's classification.[46] Curtain University Library surveyed 512 titles in Perth covering all classes of the Dewey Decimal classification to compare local retail price against published overseas price and found a range of mark-ups from straight conversion at prevailing foreign exchange rates varying from 28 per cent (general geography/history) to 82.3 per cent (pure science).[47] From the body of the evidence before it, the PSA singled out two sub-markets for particular comment.[48] It considered tertiary textbooks to be a competitive market where imports were charged 'at reasonable prices' while the market for professional and technical books was rife with excess profiteering.

If anything, the evidence presented to the PSA by the ABPA and, subsequently in submissions to government by the Publishers' Association, tends to confirm rather than rebut the conclusion that Australian prices were higher than those in the United Kingdom. ABPA's survey of bestsellers showed a 15 per cent mark-up over UK prices. It was disparaged and dismissed.[49] For the PSA, 15 per cent was too high a mark-up just to cover freight and so demonstrated unreasonable price discrimination anyway. Less controversially perhaps, it also pointed out that a survey confined to bestsellers was not likely to include titles in the inelastic markets which were the priorities for concern. Figures provided by the Publishers' Association

---

44 PSA, *Final Report*, at 20 to 21 citing one source for transport cost.
45 Australia Council, *Books – Who Reads Them?*, at 216, referring to the fact but not the substance.
46 PSA, *Interim Report*, at 52 to 53. Three publishers did not disclose their rates. Categories included general, academic, graduate, professional. Significantly, with one US publisher's scientific publications excepted, UK publishers applied much higher mark-ups: see *ibid.* at 53, Table 4.
47 *Ibid.* at 54 to 55. An informal survey conducted by the CLRC in March 1988 revealed price differentials based on converting published recommended price at then current exchange rates of 11.16 per cent lower than Australia in the United Kingdom (213 titles); 11.87 per cent lower than Australia in the United States (54 titles) and 17.11 per cent lower than Australia in Canada (108 titles): CLRC, *The Importation Provisions of the Copyright Act*, at 388 to 389 but note the caution which the CLRC treated its findings at *ibid.* at ¶¶83, 88 to 90.
48 *Ibid.* at 52, 53 to 54. For tertiary books, there were also submissions from three other witnesses and acknowledgement of 'the availability of cheaper International Student Editions'.
49 *Ibid.* at 49. While acknowledging the shortcomings of its evidence, the CLRC had not considered that its evidence of price differences of about 12 per cent between Australia and both the United Kingdom and the United States and 17 per cent between Australia and Canada were excessive: above at Note 47.

to the Commonwealth Government in conjunction with submissions against adoption of the PSA's recommendations lend some support to the latter point. Although based on 'bestseller' lists for the period from 1979 to 1988 and using recommended list prices, the author concluded that:

> When prices are converted at purchasing power parity, there is generally little difference between UK and Australian prices of bestselling 'hardbacks' (these include some softback general books) – the overall average for Australia is 2.6 per cent greater than the UK figure. For mass-market paperbacks Australian prices are higher, usually by about 30 per cent.[50]

In the present context, perhaps the strongest point is that, even within the broad classification 'bestsellers', there exists a range of sub-markets which may be subject to different conditions of demand and/or supply.

The validity of the PSA's data was also challenged on the grounds that the short period over which prices were compared missed the significant impact of currency exchange rate fluctuation. The PSA dismissed the claim on purely theoretical grounds, arguing that any variation in price levels resulting from exchange rate fluctuations (even allowing for lags in adjustment) would be taken into account by using the appropriate exchange rates.[51]

Unfortunately, the PSA did not publish any exploration of whether this theory was borne out in fact. As Figure 10.1 shows, evidence submitted to the Commonwealth Government on behalf of the Publishers' Association indicates quite substantial variation in the pricing disparities over a longer term.[52] Once again, this evidence is consistent with the view that different conditions affect different sub-markets.

Figure 10.1(A) shows the Australian price as a ratio of the corresponding UK price from 1979 to 1988. The UK price has been converted to Australian dollars at actual exchange rates. Figure 10.1(B) shows the same comparison relying on conversion to Australian dollars at purchasing power parity (PPP) exchange rates. For comparison, Figure 10.2(A) shows exchange rate fluctuations of the Australian dollar against both the pound and the US dollar for the same period. It also shows US dollar movements against the pound. All three comparisons are shown in terms of both actual and PPP exchange rates. Finally, since the Publishers' Association materials do not explain how the exchange rates were selected, Figure 10.2(B) compares the exchange rates used in the Publishers' Association materials with figures published by the PSA.[53] Although there is considerable discrepancy between the two sources for the rates applying for the US and Australian dollars, those for the Australian dollar and the pound are quite close.

---

50   F. Fishwick, 'Comments on the Interim Report by the Australian Prices Surveillance Authority of its Inquiry into Book Prices', unpublished manuscript, Cranfield School of Management, December 1989, at 2 to 3.
51   PSA, *Final Report*, at 20. Its data related only to a period during 1988/89.
52   Fishwick, *Comments on the Interim Report*, Table 3 for the price comparisons and Table 2 for the exchange rates.
53   PSA, *Inquiry into Effects of Exchange Rate Appreciation on Prices of Consumer Goods*, PSA, 1989, Table F1 at 159. The PSA data sets out the exchange rate at the end of June for the years 1982 to 1988.

Figure 10.1(A)
Mean Price Ratios: A$ Price as a Ratio of UK Price
(UK Price in A$ at actual exchange rate conversion)

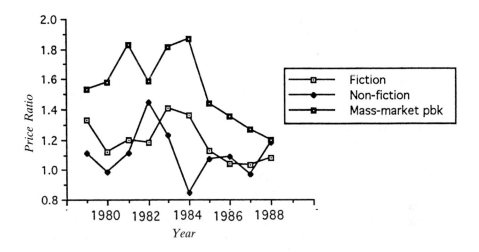

Source: Fishwick, *Comments on the Interim Report*
PSA, *Exchange Rate Appreciation Inquiry*

Figure 10.1(B)
Mean Price Ratios: A$ Price as a Ratio of UK Price
(UK Price in A$ at purchasing power parity conversion)

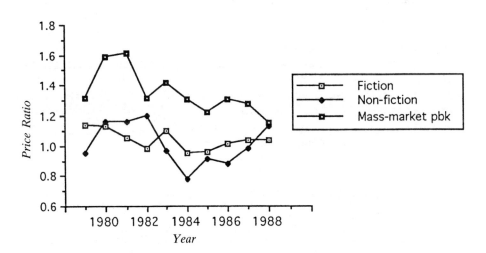

Source: Fishwick, *Comments on the Interim Report*
PSA, *Exchange Rate Appreciation Inquiry*

Figure 10.2(A)
Exchange Rate Movements

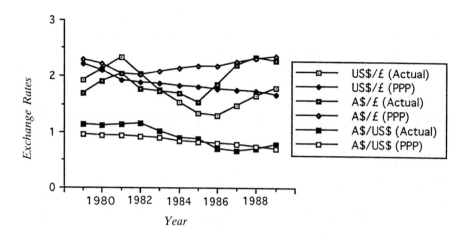

Source: Fishwick, *Comments on the Interim Report*
              PSA, *Exchange Rate Appreciation Inquiry*

Figure 10.2(B)
Exchange Rates: Fishwick Data and PSA Compared

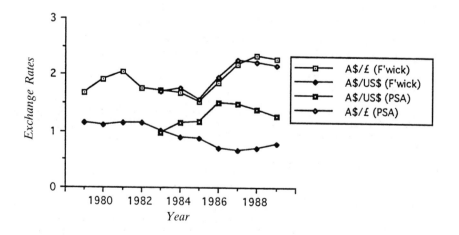

Source: Fishwick, *Comments on the Interim Report*
              PSA, *Exchange Rate Appreciation Inquiry*

Figure 10.1 does not refute the PSA's claim that prices in Australia were higher than those in the United Kingdom. However, it does show that the ratio of any price differences can vary quite substantially over time. At the very least, the issue should have been explored.

It also shows the extreme importance of particularising the sub-market being considered even though it is prepared from a limited number of observations for a broad category described as 'bestsellers'.[54]

A further aspect calls for comment. In broad terms, only the data for the fiction and non-fiction support the publishers' claim that price ratios could be attributed to currency movements. The mass-market paperback category seems to run counter to the argument. The falling trend in price ratio seems to require some other explanation.[55]

(b) *Unjustified higher prices*

Accepting that prices in Australia for some categories of books are certainly higher than in the United Kingdom does not necessarily prove the PSA's second condition: that copyright owners were exploiting demand differences between the Australian market and overseas. The PSA, however, also rejected claims that the higher prices reflected justifiable differences. In doing so, it relied on three sets of arguments; perhaps surprisingly not mentioning a fourth.[56] It is hard to resist the conclusion that the theoretical predilections underpinning the PSA's reasoning dictated its answer to this question.[57]

First, and most importantly, the PSA was clearly impressed by the contrast between Australia's position and Canada's particularly since, in the PSA's view, Canada was likely to resemble Australia as a market for UK books in terms of living standards, geographical distances and population size and density. In the PSA's view, this result could *only* be explained in terms of Canadians' much readier access to competing editions of cheaper priced books from the United States. If the United States had been closer to Australia than Canada, the position would have been reversed.[58] Strangely, given its earlier rejection of the impact of exchange rate movements, the PSA also attributed the decline of Canadian prices relative to the United Kingdom

---

54 In two cases, the number of observations per category was only 3 (1983, non-fiction). The highest number of observations for any category was 36 (1987, fiction). Also, there is no indication of how the exchange rate for any given year was determined (although, the correspondence with the PSA's data on the crucial pound conversion may limit this last concern).

55 Delays in 'pass through' into the second and third years might seem excessive. Cutting margins to preserve market share may be more likely. Increasing competition in the retail market could be another explanation.

56 The so-called 'double profits' mentioned in Paterson, *The Future of Australia as an Export Market*, at 33. Arguably, it is unlikely that profits can be increased or leveraged by spreading their extraction over several layers of distribution. However, the rebuttal of 'leveraging' only holds true if the market is not concentrated at both levels and the risk of foreclosure is low (both assumptions contrary to the PSA's reasoning): Scherer and Ross, *Industrial Market Structure and Economic Performance*, at 526.

57 See section 10.2.3 below.

58 PSA, *Final Report*, at 18.

since 1971 to the appreciation of the pound against both the Canadian and US dollars.[59]

A second influential indicator was the conversion rates from pounds sterling or US dollars to Australian dollars adopted by local subsidiaries. As already discussed, these varied substantially according to the book classification in question. Further, evidence to the PSA (supplied by the ABPA and a publisher) showed that the local subsidiary fixed the conversion rate or recommended retail price 'at what the market will bear' and then determined the transfer price accordingly. This method, however, was apparently used in both Australia and Canada.[60] It did not lead to harmful results in Canada because, presumably, on the PSA's view, Canada is an open, competitive market. Thus, the importance of the conclusion about market power is highlighted.

The final factor is the PSA's rejection of the claims that higher prices in Australia fairly reflected differences in costs and that removal of the power to block buying around would have disastrous consequences for the publication and sale of books in Australia. The PSA rejected the claims that distribution would be undermined by reference to copyright principle and by attacking the efficiency of the present distribution system. Once again, the significant factor was the presence of market power suffocating competition in the distribution sector.

Copyright, according to the PSA, is a 'monopoly' over reproduction, not distribution.[61] Therefore, it could be inferred that concern about undermining distribution is misplaced. The bald assertion ignores the very provision under investigation. Surely, the point of the inquiry was to consider whether the power to control importation into Australia was being exercised prejudicially to Australia's interests given the prices demanded of consumers and the goals copyright was intended to serve? If so, it seems misplaced to talk of copyright as a 'monopoly' over reproduction but not distribution when the law conferred a 'monopoly' over the particular form of distribution in question.

The claim that existing distribution arrangements would be undermined to the detriment of Australian consumers rested on a number of grounds affecting all levels of distribution. At the level of the publisher's subsidiary/exclusive distributor, it was argued that the ban on buying around was needed to maintain stockholding levels and support advertising and promotional efforts by the publisher. At the retail level, it was argued that repeal would destroy the viability of many small, particularly country, booksellers.

The arguments were rejected. The present system was riddled with inefficiencies which could only survive because competition had been

---

59   PSA, *Interim Report*, at 51; citing data from Economic Council of Canada, *Report on Intellectual and Industrial Property*, 1971 and Ake G. Blomqvist and Chin Lim, *Copyright, Competition and Canadian Culture*, Department of Consumer and Corporate Affairs Canada, 1981.

60   PSA, *Interim Report*, at 35, 49.

61   See for example PSA, *Interim Report*, at 27, 70; PSA, *Final Report*, at 3. Contrast also the view emerging in the United States in cases such as *BMG Music v Perez* 952 F. 2d 318 (9th Cir. 1991), see Chapter 4 from Note 431.

suppressed. Alternatively, once competition was reintroduced, there would still be strong incentives to maintain and extend some of the practices while others, less desirable, would be curbed in the search for cost efficiencies. The tenor of the PSA's approach is well illustrated by its views on retailing.

From its Reports, the PSA gives the impression that it found it hard to imagine a more inefficient system than the retailing of books in Australia. The sector was characterised by a large number of small outlets, with easy entry and exit, motivated by attraction to 'a lifestyle rather than a commercially profitable activity'.[62] These anachronisms were perpetuated in their cosy worlds by the disreputable practice of 'sale or return' of which it was 'difficult to see how such a wasteful system of distribution could be sustained under competitive market conditions'.[63] All in all, retailing of books was 'not particularly dependent on entrepreneurial flair or market knowledge to succeed'.[64]

But, contradicting part of its own condemnation, the PSA noted that other competitive sectors of the economy used 'sale or return' efficiently.[65] Nor does its conclusion seem borne out by experience in other book markets. Return rates are reportedly higher in Australia than the United Kingdom where resale price maintenance is enforced. Return rates are apparently at similar levels in the United States, which is usually held up as the most competitive of book markets, and Canada.[66] Hence, the practice of 'sale or return' seems to be a fairly neutral indicator; it may signal inefficiency, but it may also be used efficiently.

According to the PSA, a market consisting of complex sub-markets like books should feature three characteristics: specialisation, the development of mass-handling and 'marketing concepts'.[67] Since the abolition of retail price maintenance in 1971, that seems to have been precisely what was happening. The PSA noted that owner-operated, independent bookshops still dominated retailing in terms of numbers. But, it also reported significant developments reflecting an increasingly competitive commercial outlook with an emphasis on price competition and efficiency. Bookstore chains were 'becoming increasingly important'. The number of discount bookstores and of discount stores offering large discounts on bestsellers had grown since the abolition of retail price maintenance in 1971 and department stores

---

62 PSA, *Interim Report*, at 24.
63 *Ibid*. at 26, return rates of 20 per cent being 'not uncommon rising to 40%': *ibid*. at 25; the practice is also described as 'extremely wasteful': PSA, *Final Report*, at 28 where another effect of 'sale or return' noted is increasing barriers to competition at that level because the costs of the policy fall on the publisher.
64 PSA, *Final Report*, at 29.
65 PSA, *Interim Report*, at 60.
66 In Canada, return levels between 20 and 50 per cent have been claimed: Andrew Franklin, *Publishing in Canada*, Sir Stanley Unwin Foundation, 1986, at 7. For similar levels in the United States, see F. Fishwick, *Book Prices in Australia and the United States of America*, EC Commission, 1985, at 88. Earlier, US costs attributable to returns had been estimated at double Canadian costs: Blomqvist and Lim, *Copyright, Competition and Canadian Culture*, at 83; US average: 24.8 per cent, Canada: 12.69 per cent.
67 *Ibid*. at 41 to 43 and PSA, *Final Report*, at 29. But, contrast Table 10.2 and the accompanying text.

Table 10.2
Book Sales by Type of Retail Outlet

	1978 (market %)	*1988 (market %)*
Bookshops	37	40
Newsagents	33	20
Department stores	17	30
Book clubs	5	5
Mail order	7	5

Source: PSA, *Interim Report*, at 24.

had captured a larger share of the market.[68] The rise of department stores, in particular, and increasing specialisation is reflected in Table 10.2. But, for the PSA, specialisation had not advanced since 1971 and the other characteristics were not developing fast enough. Change would have been faster without copyright.

The stockholding argument, like retailing, relates to the most effective way of ensuring that the books Australians want are available to them when they are wanted. Imported books are, apparently, for the most part supplied to Australia by sea. Coming from the United Kingdom, there is usually at least a three-month delay between the order being placed and filled. Publishers, therefore, have established large warehouses in Australia intended to hold stocks sufficient to meet the demand expected until the next boatload.

The PSA argued that this tied up costly capital wastefully. The system also meant that first publication dates in Australia were delayed and, once published, books were often unavailable. But, between the Interim and Final Report, the PSA's argument underwent a subtle shift: from fact to theory and from delays in publication to stockholding levels.

In its Interim Report, the PSA reported that two-thirds of the titles listed in the UK and Canadian catalogues were not yet available in Australia or only available in hardback form when paperbacks were on the other markets.[69] In short:

> *Most books* are released in Australia later than they are published overseas. Backlist titles are *frequently unavailable* without lengthy delays. This is an issue of both cost and allocative efficiency. It is difficult to see how the late release of a title in Australia is more cost efficient than its simultaneous release with overseas countries. Whether or not the length of time taken to deliver many back-orders is cost-efficient can only be determined by the market.[70] (*Emphasis added*)

But, by the time of its Final Report, the emphasis fell on the theoretical absence of any correlation between stockholding and availability to customers: 'In a closed market, with no competition between distributors,

68   PSA, *Interim Report*, at 24 to 25.
69   PSA, *Interim Report*, at 52.
70   *Ibid.* at 43.

there is no guarantee that the *composition* of stockholdings will be in line with consumer demand. . . . (*Original emphasis*)'.[71] Then, in contrast to earlier bold assertions of 'most' and 'two thirds', the Final Report concluded with the relatively lame 'evidence to the Inquiry suggests that indeed they are quite out of line'.

Perhaps, the shift in emphasis lay in the absence of serious challenge to the PSA's conclusions. The UK Publishers' Association's later figures for 'bestsellers' show that about 15 per cent of titles are published in Australia before the United Kingdom with two-thirds finding their first Australian publication within six months of UK publication.[72]

Of course, not all new titles would be appropriate for simultaneous release. To take an extreme example, the efficiency of simultaneously releasing in Australia a gardening book timed to coincide with growing cycles in the northern hemisphere may be doubtful. Release of cookery books without first editing them to take into account differences of Australian terminology or measurement units is another common example.[73]

Whether publication of new titles is delayed (for which there may be some acceptable reasons) is a separate issue to that of stockholding. The fact that copyright has historically given the copyright owner the right to choose when and how the copyright is exploited within a given national territory has nothing to do with making sufficient numbers of copies available to meet demand once the work has been published. In its Final Report, the PSA concentrates on the latter, stockholding, issue.

With over 500,000 titles reportedly in print, it would be highly surprising if some were not available when customers wanted them. But, the published evidence for the assertion that stockholding levels were 'quite out of line' with demand seems flimsy. In the PSA's two reports it consists of the assertion that '[b]acklist titles are frequently unavailable without lengthy delays' derived from 'a major focus of many submissions (see, for example, those by the ABA, Dymocks, Hotline Books and Review Publications)'.[74] From this discussion, it is impossible to form any assessment about the strength of one of the inquiry's key findings.

The theoretical nature of the assertion exposes the conclusion further to question. On the PSA's own reasoning as quoted above, for there to be 'no guarantee' that stockholdings will be in line with demand, there must be 'no competition between distributors'. This raises the question of market power yet again. As before, scepticism seems warranted. The PSA gave prominence to testimony by a Mr J. Ruwolt from Hotline Books, one of the (non-existent) specialist booksellers which the closed market

71 PSA, *Final Report*, at 24.
72 Fishwick, *Comments on the Interim Report*, at 6. The split for delayed publication is roughly half in the first three months, half in the second three months. These figures are the basis for Fishwick's claim: 'In fact, most titles appear in Australia very soon after (or even before) they appear in the UK.': *ibid.* at 5.
73 Paterson, *The Future of Australia as an Export Market*, at 21 to 22.
74 PSA, *Interim Report*, at 43. Note also the earlier 'many inefficient publishers' at 40.

was doing so much to thwart: 'I would probably only need 10 or 20 accounts, whereas at the moment, I am running 94 accounts, and I am dealing with 25 warehouses that import American books, and each of them are exclusive lines. . . .'[75] This evidence was directed to the proposition that the system of distribution developed under the closed market was highly inefficient. But, it has relevance to the 'no competition' claim too. Twenty-five warehouses importing American books – and these were only the warehouses carrying lines relating to a particular specialty – is a large number for even a formal cartel, let alone an informal oligopoly, to maintain discipline effectively. Certainly, not all will always carry titles competing on a particular subject. But, equally, many other imports come from the United Kingdom, suggesting that the number of distributors could have been even larger.

The PSA also rejected claims that the closed market was necessary to stop free riding on advertising and promotional expenditure, largely carried out by publishers. First, copyright was simply a distortion of market conditions and so there was no guarantee that the level of advertising and promotion was 'appropriate'.[76] Further, there was no reason why publishers rather than wholesalers and retailers should pay for advertising and, anyway, publishers would continue to have an incentive to continue advertising 'as they currently advertise their more generic books, such as dictionaries and textbooks'.[77] Advertising could also create barriers to competition by creating brand loyalty and improving access to retail shelf space.[78]

There does not seem to be much dispute that books sell better when they are exposed on the retailer's shelf,[79] although there may be some doubt about whether it is true of those narrow, inelastic markets such as specialist professional and technical books which the PSA seemed primarily concerned about. It is also possible that advertising and promotional efforts could create barriers to competition.[80] The danger primarily arises where the market is monopolised or is barricaded and tightly oligopolistic (which is how the PSA characterised the Australian market). But, that is questionable and a small publisher seems to have had quite a number of larger publishers as well as developing wholesalers, retail chains and even department stores as potential avenues to the consumer.

---

75 *Ibid.* at 42.
76 PSA, *Final Report*, at 25.
77 *Ibid.* at 26. Although not suggesting that producer control of such operations is *never* a concern, it has, however, been argued that major improvements in the efficiency of distribution have been brought about in part by the shift of marketing and promotion functions from distributors to producers, see for example Robert L. Steiner, 'The Nature of Vertical Restraints', 30 *Antitrust Bulletin* 143, at 153 to 154, 195 Note 89 (1985) and Theodore Levitt, 'Marketing Myopia', *Harvard Business Review*, July-August 1960, at 45.
78 *Ibid.* at 25 to 26.
79 For the PSA's acknowledgement, *ibid.* at 26.
80 See Scherer and Ross, *Industrial Market Structure and Economic Performance* at 405 to 407, 436 to 438 and Chapter 16. Economists are not unanimous about this; for the contrary view, see Posner, *Antitrust Law: An Economic Perspective*, at 92 to 93.

The talk of brand loyalty seems misplaced. Do consumers buy books because they are published by Penguin or Picador or, rather, because they are written by a particular author or on a particular subject?

In any case, according to the PSA, experience with so-called 'generic books' showed that the incentive to advertise would survive the closed market's demise. With respect, this seems to miss the point. It is not entirely clear what the difference between so-called 'generics' and other books is. The supposition seems to be that dictionaries and, for some reason, textbooks are in competition with other publishers' offerings in the same field, but that novels and biographies and treatises on the esoterica of international copyright are not, no matter how many other publishers offer equivalent titles. If so, the concept seems questionable. Moreover, the 'generic' competition described by the PSA is a species of inter-brand competition; that is, between different copyright owners competing with separate titles on the same subject. Parallel importing, however, is a form of competition over the supply of an individual title. It is intra-brand competition. Assuming there be a category of so-called 'generics', any incentive to advertise them seems unlikely to carry over much to titles subject to competition from buying around because the free riding which may undermine incentives to advertise mainly affects intra-brand competition, not inter-brand competition.[81]

The long lead times for the transport of books by sea to Australia also troubled the PSA. In its view, opening up distribution to competition by removing the power to close the market would ameliorate stockholding and delay problems because unrestricted competition would lead to the introduction of air freight, the costs of which would be absorbed by the supplier.[82]

'Freight absorption' involves the producer in not charging the full cost of delivering its product to some customers. The PSA took the setting of uniform recommended retail prices together with the granting of uniform discounts to similar classes of bookseller throughout Australia as indicating a high degree of freight absorption *within* Australia. Customers remote from the main warehousing points, Melbourne or Sydney, were likely to be charged the same as customers in those two cities. This 'full freight-absorption' was consistent with profit maximisation *in a competitive market* according to the PSA when 'demand is more elastic in the distant market and/or marginal costs fall with economies of scale'.[83] From this, the PSA appears to conclude that repeal of the power to block parallel imports would lead publishers to absorb the costs of transport to Australia. The savings of up to 30 per cent achieved by Australian libraries buying directly from US wholesalers and being served by air freight confirmed its conclusion.[84]

---

81 The point is explained succinctly in Posner, *Antitrust Law: An Economic Perspective*, at 149 to 150.
82 PSA, *Final Report*, at 24.
83 PSA, *Interim Report*, at 31 and 62.
84 *Ibid.* at 62.

At this point, the PSA's analysis seems somewhat contradictory to its main argument. The thrust of the PSA's main argument is that the 'closed' market was operating inefficiently because it was not competitive and, not being competitive, the 'closed' market allowed copyright owners to exploit demand differences between Australia and, particularly, the United Kingdom. That is, a large part of the PSA's argument was that demand in Australia was less responsive to changes in price than elsewhere. Yet, it appears to predict considerable savings to Australian consumers from its proposed reforms on the ground that demand in Australia is *more* elastic than in other markets. That its conclusions do not just depend on falling marginal costs is indicated by an interesting shift in the reasoning between the Interim and Final Reports. In its Interim Report, the PSA contended that aggregate demand in Australia, not just in some sub-markets, is quite inelastic. But, by the Final Report, the PSA clearly based many of its conclusions on evidence that overall demand in Australia was *quite elastic* and so quite responsive to price changes.[85]

A further point about the analysis underlying the freight absorption argument is that it is based on the assumption that high, fixed production costs will need to be met by a subsidy to enable pricing at marginal cost. The PSA's argument is consistent with this since it does recommend increased governmental subsidies to Australian authors and publishers in place of copyright protection against parallel imports.[86]

(c)   *Summary*

The PSA set three conditions according to the tenets of price theory which must be satisfied for price discrimination to be practised unfairly against Australians. For any price discrimination to be effective, all the conditions must be satisfied. Only one seems to have been established conclusively.

Despite the evidence from other sources that some buying around took place, the import provisions in the Copyright Act 1968 would seem to allow effective isolation of the Australian market from other markets.

There must, however, be serious doubts about the PSA's conclusion that the necessary market power existed. Copyright in individual titles seems rarely likely to confer the market power sufficient to attract scrutiny under competition policy. The ease of substitution on both the demand and supply sides described by the PSA demonstrates the weakness of copyright in this respect. The reported evidence of collusion to establish a price-fixing cartel seems at best flimsy. The ineffectiveness of the presumed cartel or

---

85   Contrast PSA, *Final Report*, at 35 with PSA, *Interim Report*, at 16 to 17. The Australia Council's evidence, such as the shift from buying to borrowing, supports the conclusion in the *Final Report*: for example Australia Council, *Books – Who Reads Them?* 76.

86   See George Norman, 'Spatial Competition and Spatial Price Discrimination', (1981) 48 Rev.Econ.Studies 91, for example Note 6. The issue of subsidisation is considered from Note 95 below.

oligopolistic co-ordination is further demonstrated by the ease with which Australian and American publishers seemed to penetrate the market and gain market share. The merger activity affecting some of the established indigenous publishers does raise concern. But, others remained viable. The continuous attraction of new entrants and the continued success of many, rather than demonstrating a market imperfection, seems more like a case of a market functioning effectively.

The third condition required by the PSA are differences in conditions of demand and/or supply. The crucial factor here must be differences in demand conditions. The relatively small size of the Australian market and its distance from the two main sources of supply would seem to indicate some differences in supply conditions.

One tack used to establish differences in demand conditions was to identify whether prices were higher in Australia than in other markets supplied from the same source, principally the United Kingdom and Canada. A major difficulty with the approach taken by the PSA was its limitation to a short time period. Other evidence suggests that it is not accurate simply to extrapolate findings from one or two years. Furthermore, that evidence also suggests that price ratios fluctuate considerably according to the category of books under consideration. The fluctuation by categories may well show differences in demand conditions. But, since the areas where demand was most likely to be inelastic are small, specialist markets, the question is raised whether intervention on the broad scale like that proposed by the PSA would be justified.

Indeed, in the end, to support its proposed reforms, the PSA itself falls back on evidence that demand in Australia is quite elastic which seems to violate one of the necessary conditions for effective price discrimination.

The other tack taken was to demonstrate that the distribution system operated in Australia was riddled with inefficiency. Thus, even if any prices were higher because of the costs of distribution in Australia, the costs themselves were not justifiable. Once again, for one key finding – that stockholding levels were well out of line with domestic demand – the PSA does not seem to document a strong case. Most importantly, the whole analysis turns on the PSA's conclusion that distribution was not competitive. At the theoretical level, the PSA's view can be challenged as applying a very narrow view of competition – stressing intra-brand at the expense of inter-brand competition and looking *ex post*.[87] But, as discussed in section 10.2.2(b), there must be doubt about the conclusion; not just at the level of publishing, but also in distribution and retailing.

---

87   Restraints on intra-brand competition may not always be justified, if at all, by enhancement of inter-brand competition, but the main areas of concern are generally situations of tightly barricaded oligopolies and entrenched, leading 'brands': see for example Steiner, 'The Nature of Vertical Restraints', 30 *Antitrust Bulletin* 143 (1985).

10.2.3   Of cheese and chalk

So far, the PSA's investigation has been considered on its own terms. Whether or not the PSA showed demand and supply to be out of line is open to question although the issue certainly permits of matters of degree. Section 10.2.2 has suggested reasons for questioning the views advanced by the PSA. But, a more fundamental objection lies against the PSA's approach: it tested the supply of books in Australia against the wrong standard. This is seen most strikingly when the PSA dismissed one defence of the present system largely on the ground that copyright is a distortion of the market.[88] The PSA fails to give due consideration to the reasons why copyright introduces that market distortion.

In broad terms, three propositions inform the PSA's reports and are crucial to its conclusions. First, if more competition were introduced, book prices in Australia would be lower and resource allocation would be more in line with demand. Second, more competition would be introduced if Australian consumers were simply not denied choice between competing UK and US editions of the same title. Third, Australia is a 'net importer' of copyright, therefore, the gains to consumers from reducing copyright protection will outweigh the losses sustained by Australian publishers and authors.

Assuming that resource allocation be inefficient, the biggest problem with the first finding is its static *ex post* nature. It is based on a narrow, perhaps inappropriate conception of competition. For example, parallel imports were expected to increase booksellers' total turnover as lower prices expanded demand.[89] Even if this proves perfectly accurate for the existing stock of books, it says nothing about and is not directed to the problem of generating new titles which is the problem copyright is designed to address. Copyright is a trade-off, requiring some present sacrifice in the hope of future gain. Cheaper prices from forms of intra-brand competition may be forgone today in the hope of having a wider stock of titles to choose from tomorrow. The PSA itself admitted that, as a result of its proposed reforms, Australian writing would suffer.[90] This seems to be supported by Australian experience prior to the Second World War when, apparently, local publishers and even booksellers often found their businesses undermined by large quantities of cheaply priced, imported books.[91]

The PSA's second finding suffers from much the same *ex post* vice. Furthermore, it fails to examine properly why UK publishers have achieved their now waning predominance. Historically, colonial ties and then the cartel entrenched by the Traditional Markets Agreement left Australia to be treated as an appanage for the UK publishers. But, as in many areas of Australian economic life since the Second World War, a number of factors seem to have been eroding that position. The Traditional Markets

88   PSA, *Final Report*, at 25; dismissing free riding on advertising, see text at Notes 78 to 81 above.
89   *Ibid.* at 30.
90   PSA, *Interim Report*, at 68 to 69, 71 to 72.
91   See Nile, 'Cartels, Capitalism and the Australian Book Trade', at 71.

Agreement had been ended as a binding cartel, US publishers have been increasingly seeking entry into the Australian market, domestic demand patterns have been changing and Australian authors and publishers were also starting to do more to help themselves, a development of entrepreneurial flair which should be encouraged. So, there seem to have been strong forces suggesting that the historic UK pre-eminence was unravelling.[92]

The third and principal finding is the crux of the matter. The PSA considered that Australia's position as a net importer of copyright meant that overall welfare of the Australian community would be improved by sacrificing the writing and publishing interests to the demands for cheap copies:

> . . . while an 'open market' would impose costs on publishers and on some booksellers and authors, as a net importer of books this would be more than outweighed by the benefits to consumers of improved efficiency and lower prices.[93]

It is, of course, open to a country to decide as a matter of policy that it does not want to redirect resources in such a manner. But, that decision should be made consciously, rather than in some muddled hope of achieving two contradictory ends.

In the PSA's eyes, copyright was a blunt instrument. Transitional protection against parallel importing could be afforded Australian writing as an infant industry,[94] but the most effective means of securing the production of Australian writings would be through targeted subsidies.

The proposed solution is not new.[95] Like the economic justification for intellectual property it is based on the perception that there will be underinvestment in creating the desired product if market forces are left unrestrained. However, it attacks the problem from a different angle.

---

92 For suggestions of a 'generation gap' and the increasing speed of change, see Note 32 above. If the market were oligopolistic and characterised by high barriers to competition, mere replacement of UK ownership by US ownership, further assuming the US firms could break into the market, would not necessarily undermine any price discrimination, see PSA, *Final Report*, at 19.

93 PSA, *Final Report*, at 7.

94 The theory of protecting an 'infant industry' also attracts economic opprobrium, see R.R. Officer, *Parallel Imports: An Economic Perspective*, paper presented to the First National Conference of the Intellectual and Industrial Property Society, Canberra, 24 May 1987, who also considers that parallel imports create an empirical problem although he would seem only to support their exclusion where the price discrimination was necessary to make the product available at all.

95 The following account is based on Michael A. Spence, 'Cost Reduction, Competition and Industry Performance', (1984) 52 *Econometrica* 101; Brian D. Wright, 'The Economics of Invention Incentives', 73 *American Economic Review* 691 (1983); Robert M. Hurt and Robert M. Schuchman, 'The Economic Rationale of Copyright', 56 *American Economic Review* 421 (1966) and Arnold Plant, 'The Economic Aspects of Copyright in Books', (1934) 1 *Economica* (May) reproduced in Sir Arnold Plant, *Selected Economic Essays and Addresses*, Routledge & Kegan Paul, 1974, Chapter 4. See also Kenneth J. Arrow, 'Economic Welfare and the Allocation of Resources for Invention', in *The Rate and Direction of Inventive Activity: Economic and Social Factors*, Princeton University Press, 1962, at 609 to 625 reprinted in Kenneth J. Arrow, 5 *Collected Papers of Kenneth J. Arrow: Production and Capital*, Bellknap Press, 1985, Chapter 4.

Both systems recognise that creators of intellectual property will not invest sufficient resources in creation if others can copy the fruits of their investment without incurring the same costs. It would be more sensible to wait for someone else to make the initial investment and copy. Intellectual property regimes attack the problem by giving the creator/owner power to charge a price exceeding the marginal cost of producing units of the product; the prospect of the excess being offered to recoup the outlays on creation.

The subsidy solution proceeds from recognition that pricing above marginal cost is wasteful in economic terms because it leads to consumers paying more for the good than the value of the resources being used.[96] This solution acknowledges, however, that the desirable amount of investment may not be undertaken if the market were left to itself. Hence, it would enforce marginal cost pricing and provide some form of governmental payment to the creator by way of compensation for the benefits the act of creation would confer on society as a whole. In this way, consumers would only pay the true cost of producing each unit of the good (so avoiding any allocative efficiency) and the incentive to engage in the desirable creative activity would not be undermined.

In the field of copyright, Hurt and Schuchman (restating Plant) carry the argument even further, arguing that any disincentive to invest in creating new writings is very small. Hence, they consider that there is only a very limited need for incentives. In particular, among other things, this group of authors places particular importance on the fact that prior to 1891 US publishers frequently paid UK authors substantial sums for first publication rights in the United States although US law did not recognise copyright in foreign authors. The point has been criticised on the ground that for a considerable time prior to 1891 US publishers apparently operated a system of 'trade courtesy' in which the main publishers recognised the 'rights' of the first US publisher to the work. It was only as their numbers grew and competition became more intense that the custom broke down and the publishers soon joined with authors in persuading Congress to extend copyright protection to foreign authors.[97] A further point is that the US publishers would not bear quite the same level of risk as the first publisher in, say, the United Kingdom since the US publishers would be able to concentrate on publishing only those works which had already succeeded in the place of first publication.

The subsidy solution certainly has some advantages, but it is not without considerable disadvantages. Indeed, to a considerable extent, governments today have adopted it in various forms. For example, government has shouldered a large part of the burden of funding research into basic science and in areas like defence.[98] Australian government funding through the

---

96   The analysis has been challenged, see for example R.H. Coase, 'The Marginal Cost Controversy', (1946) 13 *Economica* (August) reprinted in R.H. Coase, *The Firm, the Market and the Law*, University of Chicago Press, 1988, Chapter 4.

97   See the comments on the Hurt and Schuchman paper by Robert W. Frase, 56 *American Economic Review* at 437, also addressing other criticisms.

98   On the advantages of funding research into 'basic' rather than applied research, see for example Arrow's paper cited at Note 95 above.

Australia Council has certainly played an important role in funding the rebirth of Australian writing. But, the proposals envisaged by the PSA would require a massive increase in funding at a time when budgetary constraints are increasingly pressing.

There are other problems of both a theoretical and a practical nature. One of the main reasons why market-based systems like copyright and patents have been preferred in the past is the sheer scale of administrative organisation which would be required for the government to take on the burdens of identifying all the possible projects to be undertaken and ordering them according to some social priority.[99]

Having successfully picked a 'winner', the bureaucracy would need to choose a sum which represented suitable remuneration for the author's efforts. There would be considerable temptation for undervaluing. Tax incentives and governmental subsidies are not without their own problems of moral hazard. Moreover, in an age when governments are increasingly exploiting copyright to censor views which they deem unfavourable, one must question the wisdom of placing authors under the purse strings of official patronage.

Then, something of a paradox. In the interests of promoting more free market competition, government is urged to intervene to promote national champions and attempt to pick winners. Subsidies, presumably funded from the general revenue, should be used to reduce prices for the wealthier and better educated part of society.

It may be possible that too many resources had been redirected away from the operation of the market. But, whether this had happened in Australia was questionable. One might have thought that a market having the characteristics of the Australian market could be regarded in many ways as a success tested against the goals of copyright. Entry on the supply side seems to have been relatively easy and, increasingly, being taken advantage of. More books were being published locally than ever before and more of them were by increasingly successful local authors. Customers had demonstrated considerable interest in and willingness to buy the new product. There was some evidence of an independent wholesale sector developing and the retail sector was showing increasing signs of rationalisation and the development of competitive strategies. Yet, in precisely such a market, the PSA felt compelled to recommend major policy reform using theoretical analysis unsympathetic and, arguably, unsuited to the occasion.

10.3 Canada

In reaching its conclusions, the PSA placed much emphasis on comparing the plight of consumers in Australia to those of Canada. Canadians were found

---

99 Paul Demaret, *Patents, Territorial Restrictions and EEC Law*, Verlag-Chemie, 1978, at 9 to 12. See also such luminaries of classical economies as Adam Smith and J.S. Mill quoted in Friedrich-Karl Beier, 'Patent Protection and the Free Market Economy', 23 IIC 159 at 162 (1992).

to have the benefit of much cheaper prices and faster, more comprehensive availability. Their advantageous position derived from the looming proximity of the United States and, among other things, their consequent ability to choose between competing US and UK editions of many titles.[100] Apart from the question of whether the PSA's price comparisons are supported, the shared border with the United States is certainly a significant factor in Canadian pricing, but there are also other important contributors. Moreover, the problems plaguing Canadian publishing, particularly in the past two decades, demonstrate that significant difficulties could attend on the PSA's programme. Once again, the clash between relatively short-term goals and longer-term policies is exposed. Cheaper prices and rapid availability can be achieved, but the price may entail a marked reduction in domestic writing and publishing.

Buying around has been the subject of much debate in Canada, particularly over the last decade. In 1981, anticipating the PSA, two economists recommended opening the market to import competition completely.[101] The recommendation has never been taken up. Consecutive Canadian Governments considered that copyright with the power to block parallel imports was an important tool of cultural policy.[102] But, the controversy over buying around has not abated. In the context of the broader debate about how best to reconcile consumers' demands for cheap copies with cultural aspirations, the Federal Government embarked on a round of consultations from the middle of 1990.[103] On 28 January 1992, the Canadian Government announced a new policy which included strengthening of copyright owner's powers to prevent buying around.[103a]

Books in Canada form a divided market. In addition to the sub-markets which make up any 'market', there are two additional fault lines, language and geography. Publishing is divided into English-language and French. Although there have been a number of court cases about parallel imports of French-language titles, the domestic publishers are much stronger.[104] Among other things, the small market, language and provincial policy have insulated domestic French-language publishers from the threat of foreign invasion.[105] The distances between Canadian markets creates regional centres which are

---

100 'If the USA bordered Australia rather than Canada, the reverse outcome in terms of prices could be expected.': PSA, *Final Report*, at 18.
101 Blomqvist and Lim, *Copyright, Competition and Canadian Culture*.
102 See for example Consumer and Corporate Affairs Canada, *From Gutenberg to Telidon: A White Paper on Copyright*, Consumer and Corporate Affairs Canada, 1984, at 24 to 25; Sub-Committee on the Revision of Copyright, *A Charter of Rights for Creators*, House of Commons Canada, 1987, Recommendation No. 20.
103 See for example Canadian Booksellers' Association, *News Release*, 8 July 1990.
103a See Notes 127–131, below.
104 The market is much smaller, but Canadian-controlled companies account for about 80 per cent of French-language sales in Canada: figures supplied by the Association of Canadian Publishers (ACP), 7 January 1991, see Table 10.4. Compare Hamish Cameron, 'StatsCan's Book-publishing Picture Gets Clearer', [November 1990] *Quill & Quire* 6.
105 The author will concentrate here on English-language publishing. French-language interests in Canada have not responded to his approaches. Some of the problems are raised briefly in Franklin, *Publishing in Canada*, at 10 to 11.

often closer to major US sources than to Canadian English-language centres based in Toronto.

With some important exceptions, English-language publishing in Canada has much in common with Australia. Canadian authors have captured increasing international prominence. Agents and domestically based publishers are increasingly persuading foreign rights owners of the benefits of local publishing contracts.[106] Based on figures compiled by Statistics Canada for 1988–89, some 198 (or 64 per cent) of firms had revenues of less than C$1 million.[107] These firms accounted for some 30 per cent of own titles in print or about 7 per cent of publishers' total revenues from own titles. Some 60 firms (or 19 per cent) had revenues of between C$1 and 5 million, accounting for 16 per cent of own titles in print which was also about 16 per cent of total revenues. A further 24 firms (or 8 per cent) had sales exceeding C$5 million. They held 53 per cent of own titles in print which was about 76 per cent of total revenues from own titles.

To put sales of 'own titles' in context, Table 10.3 shows a breakdown of the Canadian market in 1987–88. Out of an estimated market value of C$1,529.8 million, slightly less than one-third were 'own titles', slightly more than one-third were imports by either copyright owners or their exclusive agents and about one-third were 'direct imports'. The large size of the last category lies very much at the heart of the present controversy.

Table 10.3
Composition of the Canadian Market for Books 1987–88

	C$ millions	%
Publishers' own titles	475.5	31
Imports by exclusive agents	126.1	8
Imports by publishers	411.1	27
Imports by direct importers	517.1	34
Total Market	1,529.8	100

Source: Gilpin interview, 7 January 1991

Table 10.4 illustrates two other aspects of the Canadian industry. First, it breaks down sales by publishers and exclusive agents in terms of whether they are foreign or 'Canadian'. Second, it shows the difference between English-language and French-language publishing. The breakdown is not directly comparable to the Australian position since different definitions of 'foreign' ownership are used. The most striking point is the contrast between the extent of foreign penetration in the two Canadian sub-markets;

---

106 For both points, see Franklin, *Publishing in Canada*, at 9 to 10, 32 to 34, respectively. Note also about 40 per cent of Canadian-controlled publishers' total revenues are earned from exports: Cameron, 'StatsCan's Book-publishing Picture Gets Clearer', at 6.
107 Cameron, 'StatsCan's Book-publishing Picture Gets Clearer', at 6. The precise definition of 'own titles' is not clear, but it excludes sales as an agent or distributor.

Table 10.4
Sales by Publishers and Exclusive Agents in Canada 1987–88

Ownership	Sales	
	C$ millions	*%*
English-language		
Canadian controlled	309	37
Foreign controlled	509	63
Sub-total	818	100
French-language		
Canadian controlled	159	81
Foreign controlled	35	19
Sub-total	194	100
Total	1,012	100

Source: Gilpin Interview, 7 January 1991

comparatively quite small in French-language publishing, while controlling just under twice as much of the market in English-language publishing. A further point to note is that Table 10.4 does not include imports by direct importers which, as discussed below, do not primarily engage in resale. The value of their imports, however, is about half that of the market reached by Canadian publishers and exclusive agents.

One major difference to Australia is that foreign-controlled publishers operating in Canada are predominantly American rather than UK owned.[108] The areas in which Canadian-controlled publishers have been most successful is a second important difference. In both countries, the bulk of the distributorship and agency business is in the hands of the foreign-controlled publishers. But, in Canada, the foreign firms have the largest share of the educational market.[109] On the other hand, Canadian-controlled publishers account for 81 per cent of the professional and technical sub-market, the market in which the PSA considered that foreign price discrimination was rife in Australia.[110] A third area of difference, already indicated, is the scale of direct importing.

108   In a personal interview, Wayne Gilpin, executive director of the ACP, described the UK presence as 'trivial'. In 1985–86, 5 UK publishers' subsidiaries were members of the Canadian Book Publishers' Council while 20 US firms were members: Franklin, *Publishing in Canada*, at 6.
109   64 per cent of the schools market and 72 per cent of the post-secondary market: Franklin, *Publishing in Canada*, at 5; in Australia, market shares are almost reversed with 'Australian' publishers holding about 60 per cent, although the share of the tertiary sector was only around 40 per cent: Australia Council, *Books – Who Reads Them?*, at 210 to 213. (Figures are quoted only to illustrate the overall picture. It has not been possible to obtain data for precisely corresponding time periods and the definitions of 'Australian' are not as strict as those applied in Canada.)
110   The Canadian figures are for 1988–89: Cameron, 'StatsCan's Book-publishing Picture Gets Clearer', at 6. Notwithstanding the PSA's findings, the Australia Council reports that Australian publishers account for about 60 per cent of the 'professional' sector of the educational market: *Books – Who Reads Them?*, at 212. As with most of these terms, it is not exactly clear how this category is defined.

The legal regime affecting buying around is also potentially different. The Canadian legislation is not explicitly worded to block buying around. There are, however, court decisions interpreting Canadian law in line with the Australian law.[111] But, particularly over the last three or four years, copyright owners have become increasingly reluctant to press their claims.[112]

Promotion of Canadian writing and publishing has operated at several levels. The federal and provincial governments have granted direct subsidies to authors and publishers, targeted specifically to Canadians.[113] Provincial governments also have strong policies requiring textbooks to be authored by Canadians and made in Canada before schools may adopt them.[114] Although significantly raising the number of Canadian writers being published, neither policy is felt by Canadians to have seriously reduced the overall control of foreign-owned publishers. Canadian-owned publishers have, by and large, remained too small in size, many of them dependent on government subsidies to function at all.

Unlike the PSA, government and, it seems, the larger members of the domestic industry have long regarded cross-subsidisation as the solution to the problems of 'Canadian' publishing. This was a main object of the measures to increase penetration of the educational market by Canadian publishers. A second approach has been to secure increased access to what is seen as the lucrative foreign agency/distributorship business.[115]

To prosecute the second approach, the Canadian Government in 1985 adopted a divestment policy known as 'the Baie Comeau policy'.[116] The policy has two limbs. New entry into Canadian publishing or distribution by foreign-controlled firms was forbidden. If a foreign-controlled publisher already operating in Canada was acquired by a foreign investor, the new owners would also be required to sell at least 51 per cent of the firm within two years of the purchase. The rule extends to acquisitions through changing control over corporate groups, a member of which was a Canadian publishing subsidiary such as Bertelsman's acquisition of Doubleday & Co. which owned Doubleday Canada.

---

111 See Chapter 4.2.2(b) above. For the contrary view, see Duncan C. Card, 'Parallel Importation of Copyright Property: A Proposal to Amend the Canadian *Copyright Act*', (1990) 6 IPJ 97. For reform proposals, see Note 127–131.

112 Gilpin interview (see Note 108 above). Retailers apparently argue that the law only bans importing books by Canadian authors with Canadian publishers: Personal interview with Chris Keen, chairman of the Canadian Booksellers' Association task force on buying around, 8 January 1991; see also Sharon and Steve Budnarchuk, 'Buying Around', [October 1990] *Quill & Quire* 6.

113 Franklin, *Publishing in Canada*, at 14 to 16.

114 *Ibid*. at 16 to 17.

115 Keen interview (see Note 112 above); Roy MacSkimming, 'Sunset over Baie Comeau', [July 1990] *Quill & Quire* 10; Franklin, *Publishing in Canada*, especially at 4 to 6, the government estimating returns at 5 to 10 per cent, relatively free of risk because most of the overheads are borne by the foreign publisher, often on a fully returnable basis.

116 Named after Conservative Prime Minister Mulroney's home town where it was announced. Franklin, *Publishing in Canada*, at 17 to 27, 36; MacSkimming, 'Sunset over Baie Comeau', at 10.

While there have been successes, implementing Baie Comeau has met with a number of major difficulties. As part of the Free Trade Agreement negotiated with the United States in 1987, the Federal Government was obliged to become a buyer of last resort 'at fair open market value' for firms subject to divestiture. Foreign owners have apparently been astute to offer sales on terms unacceptable to private industry. As in the case of Gulf & Western (now Paramount), they have also employed heavy political lobbying. Even more significantly, there are no guarantees that a divested firm will continue to distribute the foreign titles on its lists under the previous ownership. A US firm, for example, with rights to both the United States and Canada could attempt to supply the Canadian market through its US wholesalers and book club operations, leaving its former subsidiary orphaned.

In short, the bold policy has demanded strong will to enforce, at the risk of considerable costs. Furthermore, as international takeover activity grew, the government has been threatened with an open-ended commitment to buy up firms subject to divestiture.

The large volume of direct imports potentially suggests that parallel importing, or the threat of it, has played a considerable role in the low prices which the PSA considered Canadian consumers paid compared to Australians. As in other markets affected by parallel imports, estimates of volume vary. Estimates in the Canadian book trade also need to be treated with some degree of caution since not everything falling under the rubric of 'buying around' is necessarily parallel importing. At least in Canada, buying around is used to refer to any of three categories: first, imports of titles for which there is an exclusive publisher or distributor appointed for Canada and which are in stock and on sale; second, imports of titles presently out of stock at the relevant exclusive distributor (or agent); or third, imports of titles for which no Canadian distributor has been appointed. The first two categories are the ones most likely to give rise to pro-competitive justifications for blocking parallel imports.

Publishers have claimed that buying around costs them anywhere between 20 to 30 per cent of their business.[117] Retail booksellers claim that buying around by retail booksellers never exceeds 15 per cent and averages between 3 and 7 per cent.[118] Further, they claim that about 80 per cent of retailers' buying around falls into the third category where, arguably, no damage is inflicted on local investment because the titles are unlikely ever to generate enough business to attract a publisher or agent.[119] The bulk of the buying around seems to be by public libraries and educational institutions with claims that as many as one-fifth of such bodies spend half or more of their

117 Holly Millinoff, 'Import Licensing Proposals Touch Off Industry Debate', [September 1990] *Quill & Quire* 6, at 10. The ACP estimated the overall level at around 33 per cent in line with the value of direct imports: Gilpin interview.

118 Keen interview. The ACP estimated retailers' buying around at 6 to 10 per cent: Gilpin interview.

119 Millinoff, 'Import Licensing Proposals Touch Off Industry Debate', at 6.

budgets on purchasing outside Canada.[120] To some extent, this expenditure may well be on titles falling in the third category. However, the proportion in the other two categories is much higher than for retailers. Cheaper prices, faster service, one-stop shopping and savings associated with rebates on import tariffs have all played important roles in why libraries and the like buy around.[121]

Booksellers readily acknowledge the pressures from customers both to justify prices compared to US list price and to provide a fast, efficient service.[122] However, they also compete for sales with book clubs, a form of authorised intra-brand competition much stronger than in Australia, which are usually American and operated from New York. It has also been suggested that the predominance of US ownership over foreign-controlled publishers active in Canada and a switch to US editions has contributed to a fall in Canadian price levels.[123]

Two other factors, however, are also indicated as highly important in any reduction of Canadian prices relative to the United Kingdom. Despite the PSA's dismissal of their importance, industry sources agreed that a major part in the fall was played by currency exchange rate movements since, over the last two decades the value of the pound was thought to have fallen against the Canadian dollar.[124]

The second factor has been a great rationalisation of the retail sector. The development of chains is further advanced than in Australia with two chains capturing 50 per cent of the retail mass market (about 25 per cent of the market overall). Both bargain strongly to negotiate higher discounts and, competing on volume and fast turnover of stock, discount bestsellers heavily.[125] A recent extension of this has seen growing entry of general merchandise retail chains.[126]

The price of all these downward pressures on book prices has been increasingly urgent pleas for help from publishers. After 18 months of consultations, the Federal Minister of Communications, Perrin Beatty, announced the new policy on 28 January 1992.[127] The policy involves a three-pronged attack, introduced in stages: increased funding for Canadian publishers, modification of the ownership policy and strengthening of copyright owners' powers to block parallel imports.

---

120 Letter from George Bryson, President, Canadian Book Publishers' Council to Hon. Marcel Masse, Minister of Communications, 14 January 1991.
121 Gilpin interview, Franklin, *Publishing in Canada*, at 29, 30 to 32; Millinoff, 'Import Licensing Proposals Touch Off Industry Debate', at 6.
122 Illustrated in Budnarchuk, 'Buying Around', at 6.
123 Gilpin interview, these were cited as factors. On the other hand, Keen did not think there had been any significant change in these trade patterns: Keen interview. Book clubs are themselves controversial, with allegations of poor support for Canadian authors.
124 For example, *ibid.* and the Keen interview.
125 Gilpin interview; Franklin, *Publishing in Canada*, at 7 to 8.
126 Bryson letter to Masse, 14 January 1991; Budnarchuk, 'Buying Around', at 6.
127 Unless specified otherwise, the following account is based on Ted Mumford, 'Proof's in Pudding', [March 1992] *Quill & Quire* 1.

First, the Federal Government has undertaken to increase grants to Canadian publishers from CDN$38 million to CDN$140 million over five years. The funding will be available only to firms with at least 75 per cent Canadian control. If honoured, this seems to represent a very substantial increase in the level of funding.[128]

The second aspect involved changes to the policy on ownership of Canadian publishing.[129] Under the new guidelines, it is proposed to limit new foreign investment to joint ventures in which Canadians hold at least 75 per cent of control. Direct foreign acquisition of Canadian-controlled businesses would not be permitted except, possibly, in 'extraordinary circumstances'. This would potentially involve showing that the business was in clear financial distress and Canadians had been offered a 'full and fair opportunity to purchase' it. If a business already operating in Canada were to be acquired indirectly as part of a larger acquisition, the acquisition would be conditional on a showing that it was 'of net benefit to Canada and to the Canadian-owned industry'. If a foreign owner wished to divest itself of an existing Canadian operation independently of any other transaction, the vendor would be required to allow Canadian interests the chance to buy it. Foreign purchasers would be required to provide commitments about fostering the local industry.[130]

The third prong is amendment of the Canadian Copyright Act to strengthen the rights of distributors and publishers of Canadian editions of foreign books to block buying around. However, publishers will be required to negotiate with booksellers and libraries industry standards on such matters as mark ups over foreign prices and turnaround times in meeting orders. Assertion of the right to block buying around would be contingent on the copyright owner proving compliance with this standard.[131]

The first part of the Canadian reforms may offer some suggestion of the scale of funding which would be required under the PSA's proposals in Australia to remove the 'blight' of copyright's distortion of the interplay of market forces. In addition, in contrast to the PSA's recommendations for Australia, it will also be accompanied with some 'strengthening' of copyright owner's powers to block parallel imports. The second part, addressing foreign ownership, highlights the significance of cultural concerns in this area.

---

128 The first payments under the new policy started in July 1992: Julia Rhodes, 'Federal Program Starts Rolling', [June 1992] *Quill & Quire* Digest.

129 The bill to amend the Investment Canada Act was introduced into the House of Commons on 18 June 1992: *ibid*. This account, however, is based on the Minister's earlier announcement reported in Mumford, 'Proof's in Pudding'.

130 The commitments might include undertakings about developing Canadian authors, supporting distribution infrastructure and education. At least one Canadian publisher has questioned the workability of the proposal for undertakings: Mumford, 'Proof's in Pudding', at 6.

131 At the time of writing, it was planned that the amendments would be introduced into Parliament in the autumn of 1992. However, it would appear that the booksellers are waging a guerrilla campaign to delay this programme: Julia Rhodes, 'CBA stands firm on distribution rights,' *Quill & Quire's Show Daily*, 2, 5 July 1992.

10.4 The Future

If nothing else, a brief comparison of Canadian and Australian experience highlights the tension between the two competing interests brought into conflict by parallel imports. The two countries almost represent polar cases: one where parallel imports have been blocked absolutely, the other, in practice over recent years, qualifying as a fairly open market. In neither, however, has a stable balance been achieved. In both, insistent demand from consumers for cheaper copies has kept up unremitting pressure. That has led to a strong campaign for change in the law to open the market in Australia. In Canada, however, where consumers have largely gained priority, the larger domestic publishing operations clamour increasingly about crisis.

With respect, the author agrees with the PSA's view that simply describing copyright as a property right does not answer the question of whether it should confer the power to block parallel imports. Copyright is a creation of the state and its incidents, if justifiable, must be justified on the ground that they serve some end desirable for the state. Assuming that a country is to have copyright law at all, each must, therefore, determine for itself whether including a power to block parallel imports is in its interests. Economists and proponents of natural rights theories may well speculate in terms of global welfare or universal principle. Few governments act except in the pursuit of perceived national interest.

The problem is particularly acute for countries which are 'net importers' of copyright. The international copyright system affecting books was founded and designed mostly by countries which had (and have) large literary outputs shielded by language differences. So, there could be a considerable degree of reciprocity in conferring recognition on another country's authors under the domestic copyright law. For a so-called 'net importer', however, the bulk of copyright is owned by and held in foreign hands. This means that royalty payments and higher prices associated with copyright result in cash transfers from domestic consumers to foreign copyright interests. Even if this does not lead to balance of payments problems, there could be considerable tension between the interests of domestic consumers and those of the foreign copyright interests. It seems unlikely that any government dependent on popular will is going to put foreign copyright interests ahead of its domestic constituency if the tension surfaces into a public clash.

Of course, the domestic consumers are not left empty handed in return for their royalty payments and higher prices. They do get access to the entertainment and enlightenment embodied in the works bought. Unfortunately, they could still get access to the benefits of at least some of the foreign work without incurring the higher costs if copyright did not exist. Furthermore, since most countries which fall into the 'net importer' category are likely to be relatively small, their individual refusal to pay the price of foreign copyright may not have much impact on the creation of foreign works. (This is a variant of the classic free rider problem applied on an international scale.)

If, therefore, recognition of foreign copyright is to be justified, it must be done on the grounds of benefit accruing to the national interest. A power to block parallel imports must be similarly justified. According copyright protection to foreign authors and publishers does not necessarily entail acceptance of power to block parallel imports.

It has been suggested that a country will grant recognition to foreign copyright owners when it considers that the costs are outweighed by the benefits from the prestige of belonging to the family of civilised nations.[132] There does not seem any reason why the prestige factor should necessarily justify protection against parallel imports. A somewhat similar idea emerges from the demands of international bargaining. One country can only act in ways which harm another's interests if the risks of the second country's retaliation are low.[133] As the dealings of the United States with South East Asian countries, Brazil and Japan show, the threat of retaliation need not be confined to copyright or even intellectual property. Proper consideration will require a full assessment of trading relations with all the likely trading partners.

From Australia's perspective, the issue has been further complicated by the United Kingdom's belated move to block parallel imports which undermine exclusive licensing arrangements. But, assuming a historical trend in Australia's trade away from Europe to Asia, the Pacific and the United States, the risks of retaliation would seem low for books. US publishers only stand to gain from increased orders for their backlists which presently go to UK publishers. Historically, US publishers have tended to emphasise price competition to a greater extent and so may be less likely to feel the need of a closed market. US law on the power to block parallel imports of books is also presently unclear.[134] Similar considerations may not apply for other copyright interests, such as records and computer software, where US producers already predominate and have demonstrated greater sensitivity to the issue.

National interest in fostering a domestic writing and publishing sector is commonly asserted as the main justification for blocking parallel imports. Even the PSA accepted this argument to a considerable extent with its recommendation of interim ten-year protection of Australian writers and publishers as an 'infant industry' and its call for increased (and redirected) government subsidies.

If promoting and publishing writing is a desirable goal in countries like Australia, both Australian and Canadian experience suggest that any governmental programme of subsidisation would need to be on a much larger scale than at present. The prospects for such funding increases may not be too favourable. More importantly, there are serious questions about whether government can or should replace the market system. These questions loom all the larger when, as was argued in Chapter 10.2, the conclusion reached by

---

132   Stephen M. Stewart, *International Copyright and Neighbouring Rights*, Butterworths, 1989 (2nd ed.), at ¶12.04.
133   See John Whalley, 'International Aspects of Copyright in Canada: Economic Analysis of Policy Options', 8 *Research in Law and Economics* 274 (1986).
134   See Chapter 4.3.4 above.

the PSA, and its reasoning, that the copyright system was being manipulated against the interests of Australian consumers seem quite questionable.

What would actually happen under the PSA's proposals will remain a matter for speculation. As discussed in more detail in Chapter 4.2.4, the Commonwealth Government has elected not to follow into the brave new world mapped out by the PSA. It has, however, modified copyright owners' powers to block imports of copies lawfully marketed outside Australia. For all new books published on or after the 23 December 1991, the power to block parallel imports will only extend to those first published in Australia. If a book is first published in another Convention country, it will still qualify for protection against parallel imports if it is also published in Australia within 30 days of that publication. Second, booksellers may import copies of any title if the copyright owner fails to supply their reasonable needs within a set time (presently 90 days) after receiving a written order for that title from the bookseller. Under this provision it seems to be intended that the bookseller may demand, say, copies of the US paperback edition even though the local copyright owner has not yet released a paperback edition. The third reform allows consumers to order individual copies for personal use from a local bookseller. The fourth reform permits booksellers to import on behalf of non-profit libraries. This reform, introduced at a late stage, may well turn out to be of considerable importance if Canadian experience be any guide.

The history of this whole (as yet unfinished) episode demonstrates the intractable, basic nature of the problem posed by parallel imports. Indeed, it is a problem even more fundamental, lying at the heart of intellectual property. Short-term interest clashes with perceived long-term interest. Australian and Canadian consumers have apparently demanded access to cheap copies now. According to the theory of intellectual property, satisfaction of that demand will lead to a reduction in the number of new (domestic) titles available in the future. There is some evidence from Australia's past and Canada's present to support the theory. In Australia, the basic conflict is complicated by two further tensions, the 'nationalist' and the 'cultural'. Australia is a net importer of copyright: the vast bulk of books on the Australian market spring from foreign copyright owners.[135] Hence, the transfer of wealth becomes quite sensitive especially if Australians are being asked to place a higher value on the copyright than its creators do.[136] On the other hand, even the more strident campaigners against the 'closed market' recognised some value in the desire to foster Australian culture through publishing Australian authors. How best, then, to forestall the perceived undesirable foreign exploitation while at the same time fostering a vigorous, domestic writing and publishing industry?

---

135 PSA, *Interim Report*, at 64; CLRC, *The Importation Provisions of the Copyright Act*, at ¶89, at 109.
136 Even if one accepts some economists' rubric that transfers from consumers to producers (or vice versa) are neutral, it would require an extraordinarily altruistic national government to put 'global' welfare ahead of national interest.

Chapter 11: The Aggregate Effects of Parallel Imports

11.1 Introduction

The preceding three chapters have been attempts to assess the causes and impact of parallel imports in particular sectors. In this chapter, the focus shifts from the specific to a broader level; reviewing what happens across the whole of a country's economy. To set the economic studies considered in Chapter 11.3 in context, Chapter 11.2 summarises the competing claims made on behalf of both intellectual property owners and those who would promote parallel imports.

11.2 Disputed Claims

The debate over how the price differences arise and their implications is contentious and ranges over a broad spectrum. In no small degree, the arguments represent two very different views of the world. Those seeking to ban parallel imports claim that the problem is large in magnitude and emphasise a 'dynamic' view of competition. On this approach, short-term advantages of cheaper prices are a mirage which, in the longer term, seriously prejudice incentives to make desirable investments locally in innovation and brand reputation. The contrary view of parallel importers, playing down the volume of parallel imports and the need for investment incentives, highlights the spur of price competition in promoting consumer choice and forcing firms to adapt to changing circumstances.

Intellectual property owners, and their authorised surrogates, rely on four sets of basic arguments to support their campaigns to bar parallel imports.[1] Largely a legal argument, they point to the separate and independent nature of national intellectual property rights. Second, they claim that the authorised product released on the domestic market is different to what the parallel importers are bringing in. Third, even if the product be the same, the intellectual property owners may claim it costs more to put it on the domestic

---

1 From the US perspective, the competing business claims are set forth extensively and discursively in Yvon O. Heckscher, 'Parallel Imports Furore: A Case of Smoke Exhalation?', 15 *International Business Lawyer* 32 (1987).

market than the foreign market. Finally, often the intellectual property owners claim that the risks of getting the authorised product on to the domestic market are higher and so justify a higher return than that reaped in the foreign market. To a considerable extent, these arguments overlap and interlink. Parallel importers' rebuttals are simpler to summarise: they deny the factual basis of many of the intellectual property owners' claims; they stress the fundamental role of price competition in meeting consumers' demands and, as in the dispute over book prices considered in Chapter 10, they emphasise their own role in undermining price discrimination.

11.2.1 Intellectual property owners

The courts have frequently considered the argument relying on the separate and independent nature of national intellectual property rights.[2] Broadly, the intellectual property owners claim that this independence gives them the right to control what is released into each national market and the terms on which it is released. Moreover, because each right is separate, they deny that they are 'double dipping' by exacting a price for the right to use each separate, national right and so they are not being paid twice for the same thing if they can extract a royalty for the domestic market as well as the foreign market. Although the courts have often accepted such arguments, they are particularly reluctant to do so in some situations.[3]

Another aspect of this claim is that the rights granted in each country may not be equivalent. An extreme case is where the foreign country does not accord protection at all. In such circumstances, it is argued that allowing parallel imports undermines the grant of rights in the domestic jurisdiction since the domestic right owner was never afforded the chance to reap the quasi-rent in the foreign market which the domestic right recognises.[4]

The second argument is that the domestic product may differ from the foreign product brought in by the parallel importer. This may mean that

---

2 For examples see: trade marks: the *Katzel* case 260 US 689 (1923) in Chapter 2.3.3, the *Colgate* case [1989] RPC 497 (CA), see Chapter 2.2.3(b); patents: *Boesch v Gräff* 133 US 697 (1890), *Tilghman's* case (1883) 25 Ch. D 1 (CA), *Griffin v Keystone Mushroom Farm Inc.* 453 F. Supp. 1243 (ED Pa. 1978), Chapter 3, Notes, 256, 81 and 277; copyright: the *Time-Life* case (1977) 138 CLR 534, Chapter 4 Note 178, the *Barson Computers* case [1985] FSR 489, Chapter 4 Note 149, *Polydor v Harlequin* [1980] FSR 362 (CA), Chapter 4 Note 125 and 200; passing off: *Imperial Tobacco Company of India Limited v Bonnan* [1924] AC 755 (P.C.), Chapter 2.2.2(b).

3 For example, where the same person owns and markets the product in both countries: *Betts v Willmott* (1871) LR 6 Ch. App. 239; *Champagne Heidsieck* [1930] 1 Ch. 333; the *Charmdale* case [1980] FSR 289; at Chapter 3 Note 76, Chapter 2 Note 35 and Chapter 4 Note 107 respectively; where the operators in each market are members of the same corporate group: trade marks: the *Revlon* case [1980] FSR 85 (CA), the *Guerlain* case 155 F. Supp. 77 (SDNY 1957) contrast *Colgate* [1989] RPC 497 (CA) at Chapter 2.2.3(a), 2.3.4(a) and 2.2.3(b) respectively; patents: *Sanofi v Med-Tech Veterinarian Products Inc.* 565 F. Supp. 931 (DNJ 1983) (contrast the action under the same name 222 USPQ 143 (DKan. 1983)), Chapter 3 Note 280; copyright: *Sebastian International v Consumer Contact* 847 F. 2d 1093 (3d Cir. 1988), Chapter 4 Note 408. Compare the broad approach based on legal and economic ties in the EC, see Chapters 6 and 7.

4 See for example 187/80 *Merck v Stephar* [1981] ECR 2063, see Chapter 6 Note 141.

different costs of production or potential consumer confusion or deception support a ban on parallel imports. Product differences may occur in the physical product itself or they may stem from other, intangible factors such as the level of customer support required by the product or associated with it by consumers.[5] If the product must be adapted for the domestic market, the adaptations will impose costs not incurred in the foreign market where the parallel importer buys and so intellectual property owners claim the right to charge more for the product in the domestic market.

Against this, it could be argued that those who value the different characteristics can pay for them while those that do not should be free to buy the product at the 'best' price they can.[6] However, the power of attraction, and so effectiveness, of many pre-sales services may deteriorate markedly if attempts are made to charge prospective customers for them in advance.[7] Moreover, this 'fee-for-service' argument may overlook market imperfections and the potential for consumer confusion or deception highlighted by the *Colgate* case. If the English consumer does not know that 'Brazilian' Colgate toothpaste exists, let alone has a different taste and quality to 'English' Colgate, the unexpected experience could cause quite a shock. Enough unpleasant shocks will substantially impair the intellectual property owner's ability to exploit its rights.

The market imperfection involved arises from the consumer's need for information and the costs of searching for it. As all consumers do not have all the necessary information, someone must supply it. The cost of this is part of the third argument considered below. The point here is that a product supported by a known quality, a certain level of pre-sales services to advise and instruct on the product's uses and characteristics, and after-sales services such as warranties, repair facilities and technical advice is a different product to the bare, physical article. As the evidence in *Colgate* brought out, consumer confusion, even resentment, is an issue which intellectual property owners must consider.

The third argument used by the intellectual property owners is the different (higher) costs of marketing the product on the domestic market. Different costs may arise whether or not the physical product is the same.

---

5 The Brazilian toothpaste in *Colgate-Palmolive* is an example of a different physical product. Physical product differences are also at issue in the discussion of the computer software industry considered in Chapter 9. The issue of 'intangible' differences lay at the heart of *Consumers Distributing Co. Ltd v Seiko Time Canada Ltd* (1984) 10 DLR (4th) 161 (Sup. Ct Can.); *Sony K.K. v Saray Electronics (London) Limited* [1983] FSR 302 (CA) in section 2.2.3(c), above; *CAL Circuit Abco* 810 F. 2d 1506 (9th Cir. 1987), Chapter 2 Note 289 and contrast *Artworks* 816 F. 2d 68 (2d 1987), Chapter 2 Note 300.

6 See for example the flexibility and range of choice of developing US practices for branded goods discussed in Note 23 below. The point is akin to the separate fee-for-service argument suggested as an alternative for the 'free rider' problem.

7 Richard A. Posner, *Antitrust Law: An Economic Perspective*, The University of Chicago Press, 1976, at 149 citing admission fees to car-dealer showrooms and for vehicle 'test-drives'. But, note the development of such fees, sometimes refundable on purchase: F.M. Scherer and David Ross, *Industrial Market Structure and Economic Performance*, Houghton Mifflin, 1990 (3rd ed.), 555.

Obviously, if the domestic market demands special features not present in the foreign product, the cost of incorporating those features into the domestic product may affect its price. Another set of cost differences, seen in the *Distillers Red Label* case, occurs where additional promotional and marketing efforts are needed in the domestic market. There, a more aggressive promotional campaign was needed to overcome lack of knowledge about new products and traditional prejudices reinforced by discriminatory taxes. More aggressive promotion meant that costs were higher.

Promotional and marketing efforts may also take the form of pre- and after-sales services. For complex products, such as cameras and computer products, pre-sales services may involve trained sales personnel able to provide detailed technical advice and instruction from an attractive sales premises with a full range of products as well as expensive advertising and presentations at trade fairs. Many of these arguments are also raised in Chapter 10's discussion of the book trade. After-sales services could include an effective warranty, other technical support such as skilled staff to deal with customer complaints and problems and adequate stock inventories to avoid customer frustration at repair delays.[8]

Intellectual property owners claim that parallel imports undermine the effective provision of these services. The parallel importer will rarely[9] incur these costs and so can sell more cheaply than the authorised outlets. If buyers can get the benefits of the services without paying for them and yet buy from the parallel importer, authorised distributors will rapidly lose their incentive to provide such services and will stop providing the service at effective levels. Then, consumers would be less well off.

Associated with the promotional and marketing efforts is the question of who bears their cost. Apple Computers has argued that one of the reasons for higher costs in the United Kingdom compared to the United States is that its distribution outlets carry out the bulk of the promotional and marketing activities in the United Kingdom while, in the United States, the distribution outlet largely performs a warehousing operation.[10] Unless there are significant economies of scale, this particular argument seems difficult to support in many situations. Promotional and marketing costs are part of the cost of distribution which must be reflected in the final price to the consumer whether the activities are carried out by the producer or the distributor. In theory, the producer would only use the distributor if the distributor could

---

8 But, question whether after-sales services can be effectively 'unbundled', thus avoiding the free rider problem: Scherer and Ross, *Industrial Market Structure and Economic Performance*, at 551.

9 Apparently, some of the larger 'gray marketers' in the United States now provide services such as their own warranties and so on: see *Bell & Howell Mamiya Co. v Masel Supply Co.* 719 F. 2d 42 (2d Cir. 1983) *revg* 548 F. Supp. 1063 (EDNY 1982); *Osawa* 589 F. Supp. 1163 (SDNY 1984); section 2.3.4(b), above; Heckscher, 'Parallel Imports Furore: A Case of Smoke Exhalation?', at 38.

10 Jim Mangles, 'Fighting the Parasites', 23 *MacUser* 53, May 1988 (Managing Director, The MacSerious Co., authorised distributor).

provide the desired activities in the domestic market more cheaply than the producer.[11]

The intellectual property owners also point to factors of international trade as causing higher costs in the domestic market. These factors include shipping costs, government taxation measures such as import duties and quotas and market lags in reflecting fluctuations in volatile currency exchange rates.[12] As these factors must also be borne by the parallel importers, it seems difficult to justify these claims except, perhaps, in two situations: first, where maintaining product quality requires a certain standard of shipping; and second, where lead times for ordering (and paying for) stock and sale of that stock are sufficiently long to preclude rapid, flexible adjustment to currency fluctuations. The latter consideration raises the issue of how best to determine efficient inventory levels.[13]

The last cost-related factor is the size of the domestic market. If the domestic market is smaller than the foreign market, the unit cost of each product sold on the domestic market may be higher than the equivalent unit cost for the foreign market where the two markets are supplied from separate, dedicated production plants. This would obviously be the case where the domestic product required adaptation, or additional services, and these costs needed to be spread over a much smaller sales volume. Accordingly, the price to the consumer could well be higher. Whether the two markets should be treated as separate markets rather than one unified whole may raise difficult questions of trade and macroeconomic policy and is the fundamental problem raised by parallel imports.

Finally, intellectual property owners often claim that the higher risks of operating in the domestic market justify a higher return than that claimed in the foreign market. To induce someone to take on the perils and additional efforts of breaking into a new market, or battling against established prejudices, may require the incentive of a higher rate of return to compensate for capital risk undertaken. Parallel importers may be attacked as 'free riders' appropriating the rewards without incurring the risks and burdens shouldered by the authorised outlet: 'reaping without sowing'.

11   Oliver E. Williamson, 'Assessing Vertical Market Restrictions: Antitrust Ramifications of the Transaction Cost Approach', 127 U. Penn. L. Rev. 953, at 958 to 959 (1979). On the assumption that the production and marketing efforts in the foreign market do not 'spill over' into the domestic market, the wholesale price to the authorised domestic distributor cannot legitimately include the producer's charges to foreign wholesalers for activities which the producer carries out in the foreign market. Accordingly, if distribution costs in the domestic market are higher than those in the foreign market, it must be for reasons other than the identity of the entity carrying out the activity.

12   See for example John Leftwich, 'What Price a Macintosh', 23 *MacUser* 57, May 1988; Mangles, 'Fighting the Parasites'. Although, perhaps interestingly, Mangles argues that shipping costs and import duties (levied on the 'landed' cost) should be higher for the parallel importer.

13   This is part of the unresolved battle between those who favour regulatory intervention exposing all aspects of business to the blowtorch of unbridled competition and those who believe that business will act rationally and so should be left free to determine its own conduct subject only to the sanction of market forces.

11.2.2   Parallel importers

In contradiction, parallel importers stress their role in breaking down price discrimination. They claim that intellectual property owners use their rights unfairly to insulate markets where higher prices can be charged from those where competition forces prices down. They infer some degree of support for this argument from an alleged reluctance on the part of intellectual property owners to sue parallel importers for infringement. If parallel imports were really a problem, there would be more litigation and public controversy. Instead, parallel importers claim that intellectual property owners often connive at many parallel importing activities as a means of disciplining authorised distributors in the domestic market since a degree of parallel importing forces the insulated domestic outlets to pass on to consumers at least some of the benefits of price changes in the international context.

Parallel importers further stress the fundamental role of the price mechanism in a market economy. Traditionally, the rigours of stringent price competition have ensured that consumers get the products they want at the cheapest possible prices. The continuous pressures of price competition also force producers to strive for more cost-effective ways of getting the product to the consumer. Not only are the products made and delivered more efficiently, but the market adapts more flexibly to changes in consumers' wants.[14]

They contend that effective working of the market demands that consumers be offered a choice. Consumers should be allowed to choose for themselves whether they want the additional factors the producer deems it necessary or advisable to sell with the basic product. If the consumer wants the product adaptations, or the additional services, the consumer should have the chance to pay for the differences. If the producer wants to avoid consumer confusion, it should clearly and properly label its product. The attractiveness of this argument needs to be seen in light of current theories about vertical restraints: if inter-brand competition be effective and entry barriers low, consumers should normally be provided with the desired level of choice.

A further attack on the additional services argument is the claim that most distributors do not provide the additional services, or do not do so effectively, anyway.[15]

11.3   Empirical Evidence: Aggregated Surveys

The issue of parallel imports does not appear to have inspired many empirical surveys. Attempts to assess the impact of parallel imports at a fairly broad

---

14   For example, 'free riders' have been described 'as the very heart of a free market competitive system' in Robert Pitofsky, ' "In Defense of Discounters": The No-Frills Case for a *Per Se* Rule Against Vertical Price Fixing', 71 Geo. LJ 1487, at 1491 (1983) (discussing domestic trade only).
15   See for example 'The Grey Importer', 'Alternative Remedy', 23 *MacUser* 56, at 57, May 1988. The number of complaints in the *MacUser* correspondence columns suggests some sympathy for the claim: for example Issue 24, June, at 18; Issue 25, July, at 22 to 23.

level have been made by economists in both the United States and the United Kingdom.[16] Although the tone and emphasis of the two articles is at odds, powerful common points do emerge.

Near its peak, estimates for the volume of parallel imports of trade-marked goods into the United States put them between US$7 and 10 billion in 1984 or about 0.2 per cent of GNP, 2.1 per cent of total imports and 6.0 per cent of the US trade deficit.[17] Furthermore, particular kinds of goods may be affected more heavily with, for example, Mercedes Benz cars and certain camera brands experiencing parallel import rates as high as one in every five.

Hilke drew on a number of sources to reach his conclusions: a 1985 survey carried out for the US Department of Commerce of some 60 firms operating in the US supplemented by news articles, Federal Trade Commission (FTC) investigations and other data available to the FTC.[18] The survey, like Hilke's article, dealt solely with the issue of parallel importing of trade-marked products. Its respondents included 'gray' market importers as well as authorised distributors. Hilke himself regarded the evidence on gray market imports as 'too fragmented and anecdotal' and so conducive only to forming general impressions.[19]

Drawing on this information, Hilke identified six common characteristics of products subject to gray marketing in the United States. First, gray market problems track movements of the relative value of the US dollar compared to other currencies; increasing as the value of the dollar appreciates and falling as the dollar depreciates. However, his evidence is that this relationship was not observed in the United States until the rapid appreciation of the US dollar against foreign currencies beginning in 1981.[20] Second, gray markets typically arose for premium brands highly differentiated from their rivals. Some of these were the subject of substantial advertising. Some were not distributed through discount houses or bulk outlets.[21] Third, there was evidence of price discrimination between countries at the wholesale level.

---

16   For the United States, see John C. Hilke, 'Free Trading or Free-Riding: An Examination of the Theories and Available Empirical Evidence on Gray Market Imports', 32 *World Competition* 75 (1988); for the United Kingdom, see J.S. Chard and C.J. Mellor, 'Intellectual Property Rights and Parallel Imports', (1989) 12(1) *The World Economy* 69. As considered in Chapter 10, Canada and Australia have conducted extensive inquiries into the more limited questions of the effect of parallel imports on the specific sectors of books and sound recordings.
17   Chard and Mellor, 'Intellectual Property Rights and Parallel Imports', at 71 citing Scott R. Baugh, 'The Seven Billion Dollar Gray Market: Trademark Infringement or Honest Competition?', 18 Pacific LJ (1986) and see also John A. Young Jr, 'The Gray Market Case: Trademark Rights v. Consumer Interests', 61 Notre Dame LRev. 838, at 838 Note 3 (1986).
18   The survey is Patent and Trademark Office, *Economic Effects of Parallel Imports: A Preliminary Analysis*, US Dept. of Commerce, 23 January 1985 'PTO, *Economic Effects of Parallel Imports*'. In drawing on this survey, it is necessary to bear in mind the survey compilers' caution that the data was largely unverifiable and incomplete: *ibid.* at 4.
19   Hilke, 'Free Trading or Free-Riding', especially at 83, 91 (1988).
20   *Ibid.* at 83 to 84, 88 to 89. (The author's numbering here does not track Hilke's precisely as he adopts slightly different ordering in sections V and VI of his paper.)
21   *Ibid.* at 84.

In some cases, this may have been attributable to delays in adjusting to currency fluctuations.[22] Fourth, most of the complaints about gray market goods related to products which required only limited dealer services, or services which could be sold separately.[23] Fifth, depending on the industry, producers did not always attack gray market goods systematically or vigorously.[24] Sixth, FTC investigations did not establish evidence of consumer deception sufficient to warrant intervention.[25]

In reaching his conclusions, Hilke first noted that no single reason suggesting why parallel imports might be cheaper in the foreign market satisfactorily explained all the observed characteristics of parallel imports. He did, however, draw two overall impressions from his observations. First, he concluded that, on the evidence available to him, free riding by parallel importers on services provided by authorised dealers in the domestic market was only a weak factor. It was not the main cause of parallel imports. Instead, lags in exchange rate adjustments were the most likely explanation for parallel importing in most industries. Notwithstanding the rejection of this explanation by the Prices Surveillance Authority discussed in Chapter 10.2.1 above, these results are supported by the perceptions found in Chapter 9's survey of the software industry. As a result, he further concluded that a general ban on, or government obstruction of, parallel imports was 'probably unjustified'. However, to the extent that parallel imports resulted from free rider problems, Hilke argued that the best mechanism for dealing with them was use of private contractual restraints regulated by the anti-trust laws.[26]

The link between parallel imports and exchange rate movements, but *only* since 1981, is intriguing. Hilke takes the absence of parallel imports before 1981 as excluding free rider or consumer deception arguments as the sole explanations of parallel importing since it seemed unlikely that there was a sudden expansion in provision of service potentially subject to free riding at that date. Therefore, parallel imports should have been observed before 1981 if free riding or consumer deception were powerful explanatory factors. It might also be added that similar arguments negate attributing parallel imports solely to exchange rate movements or international price

---

22 *Ibid.* at 84 to 85, 90.
23 *Ibid.* at 89 to 90. Note Notes 47 and 49 identify some changing merchandising practices. Gray marketers were increasingly providing their own warranties and back-up services or providing a choice of the authorised product with the official warranty and a gray market product without warranty. An advertising convention was also cited as emerging to identify the words 'US warranty included' with the producer's official warranty. See also Heckscher, 'Parallel Imports Furore: A Case of Smoke Exhalation?', at 32.
24 *Ibid.* at 85, 90. Hilke considered this factor indicates free riding is not as widespread as claimed, otherwise gray market goods would be attacked much more consistently and thoroughly. Additional factors not discussed by Hilke on this point could include the size of the producer or its authorised distributor, the identity of the gray marketer and the uncertain state of US law in this area, uncertainty which has largely developed since the 1970s.
25 *Ibid.* at 86, 90 to 91. This would seem to relate to claims about warranty practices.
26 *Ibid.* at 91.

discrimination. Accordingly, if the non-existence of parallel imports prior to 1981 is true, it seems that some other factors must have been at work also. Hilke is prepared to concede that a combination of currency movements and the free rider effect could be at work.[27] But, as he also acknowledges, parallel imports did in fact take place before that date in the United States, although seemingly not on the scale witnessed during the 1980s.[28] Perhaps, other factors which also need to be taken into account include developments in transport and communications, increasing awareness of international trading opportunities and, perhaps particularly, the increasing uncertainty of US trade mark law discussed in Chapter 2.3 above.

The impact of parallel imports on highly differentiated products is high-lighted by indications that parallel imports captured anywhere between 1 to 40 per cent of product sales for affected markets.[29] This prevalence is, however, also an ambiguous characteristic since the price difference could result from either the provision of special services vulnerable to free riding or attempts to practise international price discrimination.[30]

The third and fourth characteristics outlined above suggest that a significant factor in international price differences was price discrimination particularly because the services apparently most threatened were after-sales services, such as warranty provision, for which the free rider argument seems less tenable. The US Patent and Trademark Office's Survey does in fact report that most respondents agreed different production costs were *not* the cause of international price differences.[31] There is also evidence that warranty and after-sale repair work were areas of considerable concern for authorised distributors. To the extent that this evidence is the basis for downplaying the significance of the free rider justification, however, the US Patent and Trademark Office's Survey appears to include a number of important qualifications.

In answer to one survey question, most respondents are summarised as stating:

> *Investment in product development and market creation are particularly important* and are activities in which the parallel importer does not engage. Tied-in services include specially trained sales staff; newsletters and technical information; mailings and instructions to customers; warranties; service centers; inventory maintenance, including replacement parts and peripherals; local and national advertising support/ specially trained service technicians; launch campaigns; in-store promotional activities; external promotions; research and development; US market research; test marketing; US manufacturing, assembly, and packaging operations; warranty service departments and centers; and

27   *Ibid.* at 88.
28   Both Hilke and the US Patent and Trademark Office's survey recognise that parallel imports of photographic equipment took place in considerable volumes during the 1970s: *ibid.* at 84, Note 37.
29   PTO, *Economic Effects of Parallel Imports*, at 5.
30   For an extensive treatment of the issues raised by product differentiation, see Scherer and Ross, *Industrial Market Structure and Economic Performance*, at 571 to 611.
31   PTO, *Economic Effects of Parallel Imports*, at 7 and Appendix, at 11 (Replies to question A.7(c)).

customer relations. Not each respondent mentioned all of these; this is a composite list.[32] (*Emphasis added*)

Parallel importers, on the other hand, denied that tied-in services were the main reason for price differences and emphasised differences in wholesale price levels set at what each market would bear as well as exchange rate movements.[33] Authorised distributors did not dispute the latter two points. Counting somewhat against the parallel importers' denial, however, is their hostility to proposals to remove trade marks from parallel imports because 'brand names are an important factor in consumer decision-making'.[34]

Further, according to authorised outlets, spending on advertising, promotion, service network development and new product launch costs accounted for between 5 and 30 per cent of final price depending on the particular product and company while costs attributable to warranty services accounted for between 1.7 and 14 per cent of retail price.[35]

Interestingly, as reported in Chapter 9 above, many authorised outlets seemed to respond to the threat of parallel imports by *increasing* the differences to the parallel-imported product; for example, by extending warranty periods, increasing advertising and stressing the benefits of the warranty and adding in extra services.[36]

Accordingly, at least on the 'fragmented and anecdotal' evidence of the US Patent and Trademark Office's Survey, there may be grounds for thinking that the importance of free riding as a cause of parallel imports has been treated harshly. Even so, a large role for currency exchange rate movements is clear; as also for attempts to practise some form of price discrimination. Certainly, there are strong grounds for the conclusion that parallel imports may arise for any, or a combination, of several reasons.

In contrast, Chard and Mellor concluded that, on balance, parallel imports were likely to have a negative effect on the domestic economy. Parallel imports caused two certain and real detriments to the economy which might be partially compensated by less certain benefits in undermining price discrimination.[37] Chard and Mellor found that parallel imports 'often' resulted from free riding.[38] They also found considerable evidence that parallel imports undermine sales volume predictions and so cause production inefficiencies. Hence, they concluded that adopting a doctrine of international exhaustion was an 'unnecessarily blunt instrument' to secure the benefits parallel imports might bring and urged

32 *Ibid.* at Appendix, at 9 (question A.6(a)).
33 *Ibid.* at Appendix, at 9, 11 and 12 (questions A.6(a), (d) and (e)).
34 *Ibid.* at 12.
35 *Ibid.* at Appendix, at 24 to 25 (question B.3) and 35 (question B.9). One company alone reported that warranty costs exceed costs attributed to other causes.
36 *Ibid.* at Appendix, at 19 to 22 (question B.1). Note, however, these factors were in addition to other steps such as refusing to service parallel imports and increasing steps to track down sources of parallel imports.
37 Chard and Mellor, 'Intellectual Property Rights and Parallel Imports', at 78 to 79.
38 '. . . parallel imports often undermine attempts of rights owners to guarantee consistent qualities of products and to maintain pre-sales and after-sales services' and later '. . . the implication must be that innovation is likely to be reduced': *ibid.*

reliance on competition policy as 'the most appropriate policy for dealing with those relatively infrequent situations where the use of intellectual property rights to prevent parallel importation has detrimental economic effects'.[39]

Perhaps, the most striking point is the different importance attributed to the free rider effect by these two broad surveys.[40] The study by Chard and Mellor is not directly comparable to Hilke's because the former is not limited to trade marks and they do report welfare effects prejudicial to innovation, particularly in the field of pharmaceuticals. They also include in their theoretical assessment the more questionable impact on after-sales services. However, they do claim support from empirical evidence for both the United States and the United Kingdom.[41]

The US evidence is a report of a study by the Coalition to Preserve the Integrity of American Trademarks (COPIAT) which claimed that domestic marketing expenditures ranged from 8 to 25 per cent of the US distributor's sales price while shipping costs were only 1 per cent.[42] Although slightly different, this evidence is broadly consistent with the qualifications suggested by the US Patent and Trademark Office's Survey. However, two cautions should be noted. COPIAT is an organisation representing the interests of trade mark owners (the unsuccessful party in the *K Mart* case)[43] and, as in the US Patent and Trademark Office's Survey, it is not clear how the data were compiled. Furthermore, COPIAT's figures relate to selected markets which are '[s]ome of the most heavily publicized'.[44]

The UK evidence is unspecified. Before publishing their article, however, Chard and Mellor were part of a team which carried out a particularly comprehensive study of the effects of parallel imports on the UK economy.[45] The data for the study were collected between mid-July and September 1988. Some 636 questionnaires were sent out to industrial and commercial firms selected from *The Times 1000*, 1987–88. Of the replies, 194 returned completed questionnaires. There were 99 express refusals to participate.

Against US estimates that gray market goods had accounted for about 0.2 per cent of GNP in 1984, estimates put the total value of domestic sales lost to parallel imports in the United Kingdom for 1988 at about £350 million or 0.1 per cent of GDP.[46] These figures are not directly comparable however.

39   *Ibid*. at 80.
40   Hilke did not, it must be remembered, reject the free rider effect in all situations; he found the evidence inconsistent with the 'strong' form of the argument: Hilke, 'Free Trading or Free-Riding', at 91.
41   Chard and Mellor, 'Intellectual Property Rights and Parallel Imports', at 73 to 74 and 78.
42   Young, 'The Gray Market Case: Trademark Rights v. Consumer Interests', at 853 to 854 Note 108 citing an unpublished manuscript, Lexecon Inc., 'The Economics of Gray Market Imports', May 1985.
43   *K Mart Inc. v Cartier Inc*. 6 USPQ 2d 1897 (1988), see Chapter 2.3.5 above.
44   Young, 'The Gray Market Case: Trademark Rights v. Consumer Interests', at 853 to 854 Note 108; the markets being cameras, optics, home electronics products, watches, perfumes, batteries and tyres.
45   John Chard *et al.*, *International Exhaustion of Intellectual Property Rights*, unpublished, November 1988.
46   *Ibid*. at 78 to 79.

Those for the US deal only with parallel imports of trade marked goods, not all types of intellectual property; they are also expressed in terms of national, not domestic, product. But, as in the United States, it seems that parallel imports affect some products more than others.

Of the 194 respondents, 49 (25 per cent) were aware of parallel imports in their products.[47] It would seem that intellectual property rights play a more important role in the business of those aware of parallel imports than those not. Trade mark protection would seem to be the most likely involvement with some 85 per cent of those aware of parallel imports claiming trade mark protection for more than 80 per cent of their total UK turnover. By comparison, for those aware of parallel imports, about half of those relying on patents or copyright claimed it affected under 20 per cent of their total UK turnover. Interestingly, of those relying on copyright, only slightly less than half also indicated that its protection affected over 80 per cent of their total UK turnover, suggesting that firms depended on copyright either heavily or largely not at all.[48]

A first point of interest lies in the reasons respondents gave for why the prices of their products varied between markets. These are summarised in Table 11.1 which ranks the causes of price differences in three categories: for all firms, for those aware of parallel imports and those which did not experience parallel imports. Results are only shown for trade between different member states of the EC. The study reports findings for trade between member states of the EC and non-EC trade, but there is no significant difference. A much more important distinction lies between the firms aware of parallel imports and those not.[49]

The single most important factor, likely to occur in four out of every five cases, is perceptions about what the market will bear. In other words, at least some part of the price difference is likely to arise from producers' *attempts* to practise some form of price discrimination between markets. Thereafter, important differences begin to emerge.

For firms aware of parallel imports, shifts in currency exchange rates are claimed to operate in two out of every three cases compared to slightly more than half for firms not affected. Here, some difference between EC and non-EC trade arises for firms unaware of parallel imports. The percentage citing exchange rate movements rises from 54 (EC) to 61 (non-EC).[50] Some role for the EC's exchange rate mechanism might be envisaged, but a similar disparity for firms aware of parallel imports is not reported. Without more information about the types of goods involved and, perhaps, the markets in question, it is not immediately apparent why this happens. However, currency exchange rate movements are clearly an important factor.

---

47   *Ibid.* at 60.
48   *Ibid.* at 59 to 61. For firms unaware of parallel imports, only 38 per cent claimed trade mark protection for over 80 per cent of their total UK turnover; and slightly more than three-quarters said that patents or copyright affected under 20 per cent of their total UK turnover.
49   *Ibid.* at 68.
50   *Ibid.* Table 6(c).

Table 11.1

Causes of Price Differences between International Markets

(Trade Between EC Member States)

	All Companies			Aware of Parallel Imports			Unaware of Parallel Imports	
	Cause	%		Cause	%		Cause	%
1	What market will bear	82		What market will bear	80		What market will bear	82
2	Exchange rate shifts	58		Exchange rate shifts	65		Exchange rate shifts	54
3	Transport cost	48		Promotional strategies	46		Transport cost	54
4	Promotional strategies	34		Transport cost	37		Technical specification	34
5	Technical specification	31		National tax. levels	30		After-sales services	29
6	Manufacturing cost	24		Technical specification	26		Promotional strategies	27
7	After-sales services	24		Manufacturing cost	22		Manufacturing cost	26
8	National tax. levels	18		Other	17		National tax. levels	12
9	Other	10		After-sales services	13		Other	6
10	Pirate goods' sales	4		Pirate goods' sales	9		Pirate goods' sales	1
	Sample = 131			Sample = 46			Sample = 85	

Source: Chard *et al.*, *International Exhaustion of Intellectual Property Rights*, at 67 to 68, Table 6.

Notes 1. All percentages rounded to nearest whole number.
2. For firms unaware of parallel imports, percentages for transport costs and exchange rate shifts corrected in line with number of observations reported.
3. 'Other' includes local price policy, local competition, local price controls, market risk, import duties, differences in economic conditions.

Firms aware of parallel imports attribute much more importance to different promotional strategies. It is cited as a factor by just under half of the sample, falling to only 27 per cent for firms unaware of parallel imports. This emphasis, and difference, lends support to the free rider claim. But, almost as striking, firms aware of parallel imports report much less significance to the provision of after-sales services. Therefore, parallel imports may not arise from the provision of after-sales service (indeed, as suggested in Chapter 9, such provision may be a means of limiting free riding; but see Table 11.2, below).

Table 11.2
Effects of Parallel Imports

	Effect	%
1	Undermines geographical price discrimination	84
2	Free riding on promotional expenditures	65
3	Undermines sales volume predictions	59
4	Reputation damage from quality differences	39
5	Free riding on after-sales services	20
6	Undermines detection of 'pirate' copies	14
7	Undermines profitability of licensing	14
8	Other	8
	Sample = 49	

Source: Chard *et al, International Exhaustion of Intellectual Property Rights*, at 63, Table 4.
Notes   1.   Percentages rounded to nearest whole number
        2.   Respondents could identify one or more effect

Although transport costs are a sizeable factor for all categories, they appear markedly less important for firms aware of parallel imports than those unaware. Price differences caused by transport costs seem unlikely to be a large factor in causing parallel imports since the parallel importer should also need to incur them. However, the somewhat lesser importance attributed to transport costs by firms aware of parallel imports could be explained on the basis of higher product values compared to costs of transportation in which case increased susceptibility to parallel importing might be expected in conjunction with other factors. Once again, more detailed information would be necessary.

A further distinction between the two categories lies in the role claimed for national taxation levels which achieves a much higher ranking for firms aware of parallel imports than those unaware. A similar effect can be observed in the respective rankings for the category 'Other' which includes local price policies, local competition, local price controls, market risk, import duties and variations in economic conditions. Some of the latter factors may support claims of price discrimination. Most seem to suggest the argument that parallel importing would be 'unfair' competition. Unfair competition can also be seen in the enhanced importance of competition from unauthorised products (pirate goods' sales) for firms aware of parallel imports.

The US Patent and Trademark Office's Survey suggested little scope for price differences caused by differences in production costs.[51] Table 11.1, however, suggests some qualification of this since manufacturing cost is specified as a cause of price differences up to 25 per cent of the time. Differences attributed to technical specifications may be even more common. But, the higher ranking of technical differences by firms unaware of parallel imports suggests that they are also likely to be a barrier to parallel importing.

To a considerable degree, the data on the causes of price differences between markets are supported by the effects of parallel importing reported by respondents aware of parallel imports which are set out in Table 11.2. Once again, the importance of attempts to practise price discrimination is highlighted. However, in contrast to Hilke's qualified view, the free rider effect is highly significant with a very high score for free riding on promotional expenditure and a fairly high potential for consumer deception from quality differences with consequent harm to 'brand' reputation. Also particularly noteworthy is the factor ranked third. Uncertainty about sales volume is, of course, a factor which affects all producers whether they have intellectual property rights or not. This indicates that parallel imports are likely to induce inefficiencies in production. Although it scores a high ranking, there is no indication about the scale of the inefficiencies induced. Nor does this factor appear to reflect any of those listed as a cause of price differences between markets. Moreover, if parallel imports were a regular activity, some production efficiencies might be realised as producers were able to exploit scale economies in production.

The complexity of the relationships at work is borne out by a further factor. Respondents aware of parallel importing claimed that the volume of parallel imports fluctuated significantly over time.[52] When asked to identify the causes of this fluctuation, 69 per cent identified rapid exchange rate fluctuations; 28.6 per cent referred to the 'fly-by-night' nature of parallel importers; and only 4.8 per cent attributed importance to changes in national taxation regimes. Slightly more than half of the respondents also indicated that 'other' factors might be at work. These included price changes, legislation changes and state price controls.[53] This finding confirms the emphasis Hilke placed on exchange rate movements, leaving scope in any given case for other factors to be at work either alone or in combination. Where other factors are at work it would seem likely that exchange rate movements exacerbate differences.

Hilke commented on the apparent failure of intellectual property owners to

---

51 PTO, *Economic Effects of Parallel Imports*, at 7 and Appendix, at 11.
52 *Ibid.* at 61; about 86 per cent reporting this effect.
53 *Ibid.* at 61, Table 2. Forty-two of the 49 respondents replied and they were allowed to identify one or more causes.

respond vigorously to the supposed threat of parallel imports.[54] The evidence of the UK study suggests greater vigour. Only 7 of the 49 respondents aware of parallel importing in their products claimed that, in the previous five years, they had refused to supply a market where there was a risk of parallel imports flowing back to the United Kingdom. But, 32 claimed they had taken some action against the threat of parallel imports.[55] Only 18 of the 49 identified steps they had taken: 13 had threatened infringement actions, six had actually sued.[56] Of 147 respondents, a mere 20 claimed to have altered their supply strategies to other markets within the EC; 18 of these were firms affected by parallel imports. The most likely responses were to harmonise price policies or restrict sales to countries likely to be sources of parallel imports.[57] Whether firms were aware or unaware of parallel imports in their products, a large proportion of licensing arrangements were also likely to include terms offering protection against parallel imports.[58] Almost half always or sometimes offered protection against parallel imports to their licensees. There was, apparently, little difference between licensees based in the EC or outside. Correspondingly, where firms were themselves licensees of others, 80 per cent admitted protection at least some of the time. At least half promised contractually to bring infringement actions against parallel imports. At least half promised not to export into licensees' territories.[59] Correspondingly, three-quarters banned their licensees from exporting back to the home markets.

Neither Hilke nor Chard and Mellor accord much weight to claims that parallel imports undermine trade policy or adversely affect domestic employment. The US Patent and Trademark Office's Survey[60] gleaned only patchy claims, with some undetailed claims of manufacturing job losses and indications of employment transfers between authorised and gray outlets in

---

54 Hilke, 'Free Trading or Free-Riding', at 85, 90; the examples of failure given tend to be non-use of the Customs Service (which was itself the subject of much litigation: see Chapter 2.3.5) and use of private remedies like trade mark differentiation and labelling policies (Chapter 2, Notes 274 to 278). On increased efforts at tracing, compare PTO, *Economic Effects of Parallel Imports*, at Appendix, at 19 to 22.

55 Chard *et al.*, *International Exhaustion of Intellectual Property Rights*, at 61. Compare the findings for licensing practices involving US firms' know-how reported in Joel A. Bleeke and James A. Rahl, 'The Value of Territorial and Field of Use Restrictions in the International Licensing of Unpatented Know-How: An Empirical Survey', 1 *Northwestern Journal of International Law & Business* 450 (1979).

56 *Ibid.* at 62.

57 *Ibid.* at 65 to 66. The 18 firms represented 40 per cent of the sample affected by parallel imports.

58 *Ibid.* at 69 to 71.

59 The types of contractual protection offered licensees were specified by 45 respondents, 18 aware of parallel imports and 27 unaware. Interestingly, those unaware of parallel imports report the greater use of contractual clauses: *ibid.* at 70.

60 PTO, *Economic Effects of Parallel Imports*, at Appendix, at 9 to 10 (question A.9). Note also the FTC's hostility to 'short-sighted' protectionism, see Daniel Oliver, 'Federal Trade Commission Antitrust Policy in International Trade', [1986] *Fordham Corporate Law Institute* 1. See also R.R. Officer, *Parallel Imports: An Economic Perspective*, paper presented to the First National Conference of the Intellectual and Industrial Property Society, Canberra, 24 May 1987.

the distribution sector. Presumably for similar reasons, Chard and Mellor describe the impact on output and employment as 'relatively minor'.[61]

11.4   Overview

Perhaps, then, two broad points emerge from these studies. First, the price differences giving rise to opportunities for parallel importers may arise from a range of factors. Second, the volume of parallel imports is likely to fluctuate over time.

In any given case, there would seem to be considerable likelihood that at least part of the price difference between the two markets arises from some attempt to practise price discrimination. However, for those goods subject to parallel importing, there is also a high risk that some form of free riding is taking place. Furthermore, there is a smaller, but still sizeable, danger that consumer deception is likely.

Accordingly, there are grounds for believing that greater weight should be accorded to the risks of free riding and consumer deception than Hilke believed was likely. On the other hand, Chard and Mellor were not much impressed by the dangers of price discrimination. Three factors seem to have been at work here, two theoretical and one empirical.

Starting from the premise that transfers between producers and consumers are welfare neutral,[62] they point out that gains to consumers from lower prices resulting from the undermining of price discrimination will also lead to welfare losses for producers. Hence, they conclude that it is only where the producers (intellectual property owners) are foreign that there will be fairly certain gains in welfare for the UK economy.[63] Then, they consider that price discrimination can only be effective when the right owner possesses market power and there is minimal competition from other producers. In the absence of either, consumers cannot be harmed because they could simply switch to one of the rival brands.[64] Finally, there was evidence that prices in the United Kingdom were often lower than in other markets and that the United Kingdom was almost as likely to be the *source* of parallel imports as the destination.[65] Hence, the UK economy as a whole could well suffer if attempts to practise price discrimination were undermined.

---

61   Chard and Mellor, 'Intellectual Property Rights and Parallel Imports', at 78; confirmed by Chard *et al.*, *International Exhaustion of Intellectual Property Rights*, at 80 to 81.

62   That is, that policy considers a transfer of, say, £10 from consumers to producers exactly equivalent to a transfer of £10 from producers to consumers and so cannot prescribe one or the other result as 'better' on welfare grounds.

63   Chard and Mellor, 'Intellectual Property Rights and Parallel Imports', at 76 to 77, 79; similar arguments are made about undermining collusion: at 78. It has been claimed that, although market power is unlikely, in some cases its absence will be supplied by governmental policies such as voluntary export restraints and quotas, see Robert J. Staaf, 'International Price Discrimination and the Gray Market', (1989) 4 IPJ 301, at 305 to 312. Price discrimination forms a central part of the discussion in Chapter 10.

64   *Ibid.*

65   Chard *et al.*, *International Exhaustion of Intellectual Property Rights*, at 66 to 67.

The second broad point emerging from the two studies is the fluctuating nature of the volume of parallel imports. This is most likely to result from rapid movements in currency exchange rates. The implications of this are not necessarily clear. Hilke argued that consumers would generally gain from parallel imports which pass on the benefits of currency fluctuations more rapidly.[66]

On the other hand, intellectual property owners claim they need stable environments to plan properly and penetrate markets effectively. Allowing parallel imports in the interests of short-term price benefits may disrupt necessary investment in distribution networks and promotional strategies.

Where the products subject to competition from parallel imports are themselves imported, even the Australian Prices Surveillance Authority has acknowledged that it would be unreasonable to expect price changes caused by exchange rate fluctuations to be passed on to the consumer immediately.[67] For example, orders might be placed and finance arranged as much as 8 to 12 months in advance. Companies might hedge against exchange rate movements by taking out 'forward exchange cover', a type of insurance the costs of which would need to be included in prices.[68] Firms might respond to currency depreciation by sacrificing some price rises in an effort to retain market share and in the hope of restoring margins if the domestic currency subsequently appreciated.[69] More generally, considerable administrative costs might be incurred in changing wholesale and retail prices.[70] This could be particularly important for differentiated products based on carefully planned marketing strategies. For such goods, durable pricing strategies were adopted and the 'market prices for most consumer goods do not move up and down on a daily basis like the prices of fruit and vegetables'.[71]

Consideration of these points suggests that, once again, the greatest importance should attach to whether the domestic market for the goods in question is subject to effective competition. Hence, it does not seem possible to prescribe the consequences of this factor in advance.

---

66 Hilke, 'Free Trading or Free-Riding', especially at 86 and 91.
67 PSA, *Inquiry into Effects of Exchange Rate Appreciation on Prices of Consumer Goods*, PSA, Report 21, 1989, at 43 to 47. This report was not directly concerned with parallel imports, but rather was directed to the question of whether Australian prices were sufficiently responsive to currency exchange rate movements. See also Staaf, 'International Price Discrimination and the Gray Market', at 313. The latter's earlier paper would seem more consistent with Hilke's apparent view since it seems to be predicated on the ground that parallel imports always enhance welfare *unless* they lead to consumer deception, see Robert J. Staaf, 'The Law and Economics of the International Gray Market: Quality Assurance, Free-Riding and Passing Off', (1989) 4 IPJ 191. Perplexingly, the paper acknowledged that parallel imports will undermine the value of past investments and also affect future incentives (at 228), but seems to argue that the mere fact of currency exchange rate fluctuations will always reduce the need for 'domestic' investment in quality assurance and marketing by lowering the price of the good although also noting that the impact of parallel imports is an empirical question (at 216).
68 *Ibid.* at 52 to 59.
69 *Ibid.* at 19, 70 to 73, 146.
70 *Ibid.* at 60 to 61.
71 *Ibid.* at 149, 60 to 61.

Chapter 12: Conclusion

At this point, it is perhaps time to recall the illustrations raised in Chapter 1. When parallel imports can be sold sometimes as much as half the price (if not lower) than that offered by the authorised outlets, does it matter to the shopper in Sydney (or wherever) that the authorised outlet is the same person who sold the parallel imports abroad, or a member of the same corporate group or an independently owned business? Does it matter to that same shopper whether the goods embody copyright, a patent or a trade mark or, even, some other intellectual property right? Then, looking at the issue from the point of view of a business which needs to make special investments in trying to exploit the domestic market effectively, does it make any difference that the source of the foreign competition derives from an assignment or a licence or even its own foreign operations? Once again, is the impact, if any, any different depending on the type of intellectual property right which is being asserted?

There are two different answers to these questions, depending on whether the answer is made from a legal or (for want of a better word) 'economic' perspective. Our self-interested (and properly so) consumer in the High street or shopping mall is probably mainly concerned with the price to be handed over at the cash register in return for the purchase. It is probably fairly safe to assume that he or she is not interested in the web of contract and corporate ties which gets the product there or the refined intricacies of particular intellectual property rights.[1] Likewise for the business; the return on investments sunk into exploiting the domestic market (and therefore the incentives to commit capital in the future) *may* be undermined just as much by foreign competition whether the ultimate source be an independently owned business, associated by contract, a corporate affiliate or, perhaps, even its own foreign operations. Nor does the kind of intellectual property right being exploited necessarily change the quality of the 'economic' injury.[2]

---

1 That is, of course, in the happy situations where nothing has gone wrong – whether it be the product's failure to arrive or a defect arising after purchase. See W.R. Cornish and Jennifer Phillips, 'The Economic Function of Trade Marks: An Analysis with Special Reference to Developing Countries', 13 IIC 41, at 43 (1982).

2 Compare *Time-Life* (1977) 138 CLR 534; the *Harlequin* case [1980] FSR 297; *Fender v Bevk* (1989) 15 IPR 257; 30/78 *Distillers* [1980] ECR 2229.

But, in the common law world, on the decided cases, all these considerations are relevant.[3] In many cases, it makes a big difference whether
exploitation of the foreign and domestic markets has been split, whether by
assignment or licence. It may also depend on how particularly the assignment
or licence in question has been drawn. In the United States, particularly if
trade marks are involved, it is also more than likely to be significant that
the assignment or licence involves corporate affiliates; exceptionally so in the
Anglo-Commonwealth countries.

Further technicality is introduced by considerations about subject-matter.
In patents and trade marks, when the initiator of the foreign sale also has
authority to sell on the domestic market, it makes a difference whether
or not the importer had notice before purchasing the goods in question
that the rights to deal in the article were limited to the foreign market.[4]
In copyright, on the other hand, strict notice of a limitation may be
irrelevant. Even here, there is divergence. On one interpretation of US
law, stipulations against importation will not preclude the 'first sale' doctrine
even if brought home to the importer; so also under the interpretation of
the hypothetical manufacturing requirement in South Africa and the United
Kingdom under *Charmdale*. But, when the question goes to consent, notice
is irrelevant in copyright and a principle of territoriality seems to apply in
the Anglo-Commonwealth countries.[5]

Hence, the accidents of business structure and field of endeavour and the
hazards of legal advice play crucial roles in the treatment of parallel imports
in the common law world. In some situations, the principle of territoriality
will be found to apply; in others, an approach based on universality or
exhaustion. Yet, in none, do the explanations usually offered suggest that
the difference in treatment is warranted as a general rule.

The policy of commercial convenience underlying the so-called rule against
restraints on alienation – if appropriate in the modern world[6] – is no more
powerful in the case of a sale abroad by the domestic right owner than by
a limited licensee. If there be no business necessity to imply a licence to
import and sell when the purchase abroad is made, for example, from a
limited licensee it has not been adequately explained why there is any greater
necessity when the purchase is made from someone also having power to sell
in the domestic market.

Similarly, the courts have failed to explain why the exclusion of parallel
imports would lead in some situations to unsupportable 'double dipping'
but, in others, is merely the exercise of separate and independent legal

---

3 A comparison of the treatment of parallel imports across jurisdictions and subject-
matter is made at Chapter 5 above; individual rights are considered in Chapter 2 (trade
marks), Chapter 3 (patents) and Chapter 4 (copyright).

4 The position under Anglo-Commonwealth trade mark law must be regarded as
uncertain following *Colgate* [1989] RPC 497 (CA).

5 In the Anglo-Commonwealth countries, however, knowledge of facts suggesting the
prospect of copyright infringement is also an element of the wrong additional to
consent.

6 See *Continental TV Inc. v GTE Sylvania Inc.* 433 US 36 (1977). Contrast 56 & 58/64
Consten & Grundig v Commission [1966] ECR 299.

rights. The different legal treatment has certainly not resulted from any investigation of whether the right owner received a chance to reap the prospect of a quasi-rent by the foreign marketing. Nor can it be said to derive from any perceived difference in the functions of the various intellectual property rights. The same 'rules' are sometimes proposed across different subject-matters.[7] Indeed, when examined, the perceived differences in the function of the intellectual property right may seem rather speculative,[8] or suggest a result contrary to the conclusion reached by the court.[9] Nor can the differences be attributed to questions of statutory interpretation.[10] Within the international system, all intellectual property rights are separate and distinct in their territorial nature. Patents and copyright, where differences have been explicated, are also both *bundles* of divisible rights. Furthermore, the ambiguities in much of the legislation can hardly be said to have driven the courts unwillingly to contradictory results.

It might be argued that the common law's approach reflects a philosophy of encouraging intellectual property owners to assign or license their rights in foreign countries to *independent* firms, almost as a form of technology transfer. Such an approach may be perceived in, say, the *Sebastian* case, some of the US cases on trade marks and, perhaps, the protection from parallel imports conferred on exclusive licensees by the Copyright Designs and Patents Act 1988.[11] Certainly, there is little doubt that the international regimes of intellectual property have been intended to encourage the exploitation of intellectual property across international frontiers.[12] But, that is not necessarily the same as a commitment to 'technology transfer'. Moreover, one major difficulty with the proposition is that it does not reflect what the courts have often said in grappling with parallel imports. It assumes a hostility against efforts to block parallel imports which is not always easy to discover in the cases and, indeed, is contrary to the approach often taken.[13] If such a policy did underlie the law, a much stronger hostility to corporate

7   For implied consent favouring parallel imports, compare trade marks (*Revlon* [1980] FSR 85 (CA), *CAL Circuit Abco* 810 F 2d 1506 (9th Cir. 1987)); patents (*Betts v Willmott* (1871) LR 6 Ch. App. 239; *Holiday v Mattheson* 24 Fed. 185 (SDNY 1885)). For the separate and distinct territorial nature of intellectual property rights, compare copyright (*Barson Computers* [1985] FSR 489); trade marks (*Colgate* [1989] RPC 497 (CA)); patents (*Tilghman's* case (1883) 25 Ch. D 1 (CA) and *Griffin v Keystone Mushroom Farm Inc.* 453 F. Supp. 1243 (ED Penn. 1978)).
8   For example, the *Time-Life* case's purported distinction between copyright and patents.
9   For example, note the actual consumer confusion seemingly ignored by the courts in *CAL Circuit Abco* and *Weil Ceramics v Dash* 848 F. 2d 659 (3d Cir. 1989).
10   Exceptions to this conclusion would seem to be the copyright legislation in Singapore and Malaysia and the amendments affecting copyright in books in Australia.
11   *Sebastian International Inc. v Consumer Contact (PTY) Ltd* 847 F. 2d 1093 (3d Cir. 1988); Copyright, Designs and Patents Act 1988 (United Kingdom) section 27(3).
12   See for example the overview of the history of copyright in Chapter 4.2.2 above; Clive Bradley, 'Market Rights: When Does Importation Infringe?', (1991) 5 *Rights* 1.
13   See for example the *Tilghman's* case (1883) 25 Ch. D 1 (CA), *Griffin v Keystone Mushroom Farm* 453 F. Supp. 1243 (ED Pa. 1978), the *Beecham* cases, *Time-Life, Barson Computers, India Book Distributors* [1985] FSR 120; *Colgate, Bourjois v Katzel* 260 US 293 (1923); *Lever Bros v US* 877 F. 2d 101 (DC Cir. 1989).

affiliate relationships might also be expected.[14] Furthermore, such a policy might well lead to counter-productive results if it served to encourage greater vertical integration.[15]

Hence, within the 'common law world', there is an unresolved tension in treating parallel imports between an approach based on 'universality' and one based on 'territoriality'. That tension results in an uncertainty, a complexity and technicality which can hardly be in the interests of consumers or the various competing business interests affected by or engaging in parallel imports, the more so as it does not reflect any searching attention to the underlying economic issues.

Examination of the EC's treatment of parallel imports explores the potential consequences of one solution to the tensions found in the common law's jurisprudence – adopting a form of international exhaustion.[16] Where the approach applies, it has the logical merit of treating ties by contract or corporate affiliation the same.

The first point to be made about the EC's experience is that it is not a 'true' doctrine of international exhaustion. Insofar as the doctrine is applied in the EC, it does not apply to *all* international trade, but *only* to international trade between Member States of the EC.[17] This is in keeping with a conception of the EC as a *sui generis* entity having some of the attributes of an international organisation and some of the attributes of a federation, where the emphasis has historically lain on fusing the separate national markets into one, unified economic area – the internal market.[18]

The second point is that the interpretative approach applied by the European Court of Justice (ECJ) has undergone a considerable shift. For perhaps understandable reasons, the first stage exhibited a markedly doctrinaire drive to effect market integration. Hence, within the EC, a strict doctrine of exhaustion was applied. Once the right owner released the goods in one Member State, the intellectual property laws of another Member State could not be used to impede imports from the first Member State. Apart from goods entering trade from outside the EC, the only exception contemplated to this rule was where the right owners were completely independent of each other *and* each derived its ownership completely independently of any

---

14 See Chapter 5 Notes 23 to 24 and 34.
15 Examples of integration following efforts to encourage independent licensees include *US v Arnold, Schwinn & Co.* 388 US 365 (1967) cited in F.M. Scherer and David Ross, *Industrial Market Structure and Economic Performance*, Houghton Mifflin, 1990 (3rd edn), 563, Note 65; *Consten & Grundig* [1966] ECR 299 cited in Valentine Korah and Warwick A. Rothnie, *Exclusive Distribution and the EEC Competition Rules*, Sweet & Maxwell, 1992 (2nd edn), at 39; *Campari* cited in Valentine Korah, *Know-how Licensing Agreements and the EEC Competition Rules*, ESC Publishing, 1990, at 39 to 40.
16 Chapters 6 and 7 above.
17 Contrast the doctrine applied in German trade mark law, see for example Case 1ZR 85/71 *Francesco Cinzano & Cie GmbH v Java Kaffeegeschäfte GmbH & Co.* [1974] 2 CMLR 21.
18 On the legal nature of the EC, see Derrick Wyatt and Alan Dashwood, *The Substantive Law of the EEC*, Sweet & Maxwell, 1987 (2nd edn), especially Chapter 3; T. C. Hartley, *The Foundations of European Community Law*, Clarendon Press, 1988 (2nd edn), Part II.

association with the other.[19] Subsequently, however, the ECJ has adopted a much more discriminating approach, recognising the territorial limitations of intellectual property rights to individual Member States and permitting their use to repel parallel imports within intra-EC trade in *some* situations.[20]

Hence, it has been found, even within the EC, necessary to temper a strict application of the doctrine of exhaustion with recognition of limitations based on the principle of territoriality. This need, to the present author's mind, demonstrates a fundamental flaw in the principle of universality and the doctrine of exhaustion raised up on it – the fallacious assumption that the world is a single, uniform market. Even within the EC, there were, and are, quite considerable departures from the theoretical construct. Sometimes, the 'foreign' Member State has not even accorded an intellectual property right at all.[21] In others, where a right is recognised, it has not always entailed the same incidents.[22] Within the EC, divergences of this nature are gradually being whittled down by action at the Community level, but it is a long process.[23] But, as EC experience unremittingly shows, even where rights are *harmonised* or *unified*, there remain quite a large number of distortions which provoke outcries from business and *may* threaten to undermine the goals pursued by intellectual property laws. To mention just some: price controls imposed by a Member State's government are a frequent disruption;[24] compulsory licensing another;[25] divergent industrial or social policies a third.[26] Competition policy has also recognised, to varying degree, the difficulties of doing business in what is still another country.[27]

Although it is complicated by the political objective of market integration, the treatment of parallel imports in the EC, then, also shows the hallmarks of complexity and uncertainty which infect the attempts of the 'common law world' to grapple with the issue. Once again, particularly in the past, much of this has been due to a failure (or inability) to address the economic causes at the root of the matter.

---

19   Hence, an association by way of licence, corporate affiliation or even expropriation by act of state were held to trigger exhaustion: see for example 15/74 *Centrafarm BV v Sterling Drug Inc.* [1974] ECR 1147 at ¶11; 192/73 *Van Zuylen Frères v Hag AG* [1974] ECR 731; 119/75 *Terrapin (Overseas) Ltd v Terranova Industrie CA Kapferer & Co.* [1976] ECR 1039. But, on expropriation, see now C-10/89 *Hag II* [1990] ECR I-3717; [1990] 3 CMLR 571.
20   See for example 158/86 *Warner Bros Inc. v Christiansen* [1988] ECR 2605; 19/84 *Pharmon v Hoechst* [1985] ECR 2281.
21   187/80 *Merck & Co. Inc. v Stephar BV* [1981] ECR 2063.
22   *Warner Bros*, no rental right for videos in the United Kingdom at the time.
23   For example, considerable patent harmonisation has been achieved through the European Patent Convention, but Denmark only joined in 1990 and Eire with effect from 1 August 1992. The Community patent, finalised in 1975, is still not operating.
24   Significant particularly in pharmaceuticals, see Chapter 8; but sometimes a consideration in copyright, for example 78/70 *Deutsche Grammophon GmbH v Metro* [1978] ECR 487.
25   19/84 *Pharmon v Hoechst* [1985] ECR 2281; 55 & 57/80 *Musik-Vertrieb Membran GmbH v GEMA* [1981] ECR 147.
26   See, once again, pharmaceuticals in particular, in Chapter 8.
27   See for example 56/65 *Société Technique Minière v Maschinenbau Ulm GmbH* [1966] ECR 235; 258/78 *Nungesser (LG) KG and Eisele v Commission* [1982] ECR 2015 ('*Maize Seed*').

So then, in summary form, a review of what 'the law' is or, rather, what the laws are. The unresolved issue is how should 'the law' deal with parallel imports. Consideration of that issue requires a return to the question of whether the fact that the goods cross an international frontier introduces considerations different to those applying to trade limited to the domestic market. As has perhaps been foreshadowed, in the author's opinion it often does. The reasons lie in what causes parallel imports and the impact that they have in the domestic market when they arrive in any quantity.

Chapters 8 to 11 have attempted to explore both these issues from a number of different perspectives. Attempting to look, as it were, from on high at a broad level or, on the other hand, from within particular industries; testing different types of intellectual property subject-matter; and, to some extent, the points of view of economies with different positions in the world trade order. A number of points emerge.

Perhaps, the clearest point is the unending nature of the struggle. Consumers, or some branches of their governments, will keep up an unremitting demand for cheaper prices and faster availability. But, they also want new and better products and guarantees of quality. The businesses that meet these needs will continue to demand higher returns for their successful products and are astute to find ways of diverting pressures on profit margins from consumers. Balancing the trade-offs between these forces is far from easy.

The broad, empirical surveys reviewed in Chapter 11 raise three main considerations. They indicate quite strongly that a variety of factors cause the cheaper prices which parallel importers capitalise on. In addition, as casual observation and the case of the software industry confirm, the volume of parallel imports fluctuates over time. Third, the effects of parallel imports do not fall evenly. Parallel trade is likely to affect businesses which depend to a greater extent on intellectual property protection and even then is more likely to involve specific products for which there is particularly high demand. The success of firms responsible for these products may be particularly dependent on revenues from sale of these products.

In any given case, any one of the factors causing parallel imports may be at work either alone or in combination with others. In many, if not most, cases attempts to discriminate between the prices charged in different international markets – that is, charging what the market will bear – are very likely to be involved. While theory predicts that price discrimination is only a problem where markets are not open and competitive,[28] many businesses clearly seek, seemingly perversely, to pursue a counter-productive policy. This may reflect the fact that markets are not necessarily open and competitive but, rather, closed and oligopolistic. On the other hand, as may be the case with pharmaceuticals in the EC, it may also accord with rational economic action in a fairly competitive environment. As long as marginal costs are being covered, it makes sense to sell in a market if quasi-rents sufficient to

---

28　See for example Chapters 9, 10 and 11.

cover investment costs can be earned in other markets. Furthermore, where quasi-rents are earned in one market, they may act as a magnet attracting new, even local, investment which will compete away the rents. But, as the case of books in Australia seems to indicate, the success of such a policy may not be strong enough to withstand 'irrational', nationalistic sensitivities about exploitation by large, foreign-owned firms.

Attempted price discrimination is not the only factor which may be at work, however. There are also high probabilities that price differences will be linked to factors affecting incentives to invest in pro-competitive business activity. In these cases, parallel imports lead to free riding on desirable investments in innovation or market making.

The broad, empirical surveys indicate that different promotional strategies are often a strong factor causing price differences between markets and that parallel imports will often undermine such investment. As these surveys and the case of pharmaceuticals in particular show, parallel imports tend to be concentrated in products which have a high brand profile and reputation. Of lesser magnitude, but still sizeable, there are also risks of consumer deception and damage to brand reputation through parallel imports of differing quality.

Product differentiation is essential to competition.[29] Carried to extremes, however, there is a risk that it may become a tool to engineer undesirable market power. The case of pharmaceuticals shows firms exploiting product differentiation to interrupt efforts to break down barriers to intra-EC trade. Similarly, like some of the responses reported in the 1985 survey by the Patents and Trade Marks Office in the United States, many software houses have responded to the threat of parallel imports by enhancing product differentiation at the national level. No doubt, to the extent they admit this happens, these firms would claim that they have tried to find another means of appropriating the benefits of their investments out of necessity from the reduced utility of intellectual property rights. For books, the considerations may be slightly different in that it is argued that parallel imports would concentrate on 'best-selling' authors and titles rather than brand names. This may still prejudice the creative process which copyright is supposed to foster, however, since publishers may depend on reaping high rewards for their successes to cover the losses and risks associated with marginal publications and failures.[30] An extreme form of this type of free riding can be seen in the field of pharmaceuticals where price differences around the EC often stem from governmental policies such as price controls.

The volume of parallel imports fluctuates. This is confirmed by both of the broad, empirical studies and can be seen most strikingly in the contrasts of

---

29   See W.R. Cornish, *Intellectual Property*, Sweet & Maxwell, 1989 (2nd ed.), at ¶¶15.002, 15.013 to 15.017 and see Scherer and Ross, *Industrial Market Structure and Economic Performance*, Chapter 16 for the full complexity of the issue and some healthy scepticism about the role of government.

30   For a contrary view, see Arnold Plant, 'The Economic Aspects of Copyright in Books', (1934) 1 *Economica* 137 reproduced in Arnold Plant, *Selected Economic Essays and Addresses*, Routledge & Kegan Paul, 1974, Chapter 4.

the computer industry's approach over time. In the first half of 1988 parallel imports produced a response from producers and authorised distributors in the United Kingdom verging on the hysterical. Two years later, things were much more muted (although, as Chapter 9 reveals, strong, but more subtle, steps were still being taken against parallel importers).

The fluctuating nature of parallel imports highlights the key role of rapid movements in currency exchange rates. All aspects studied reveal this. Hilke considered that parallel imports caused by this factor were a pro-competitive benefit for consumers.[31] On the other hand, even the Prices Surveillance Authority (PSA) has acknowledged that sound and effective business operation will not result in immediate pass through of currency exchange movements.[32] Effective marketing may require strategic planning and commitment to orders many months in advance. Sound business practice will often warrant hedging against currency movements. In either case, price changes caused by currency movements will not be passed on to the consumer in the short term. The role of currency movements in causing sharp increases in the volumes of parallel imports may indicate that firms do make some effort, albeit apparently unsuccessful, to ensure that price differences between markets are kept within some bounds.

More than the other aspects of the study, the examination of the pharmaceuticals industry shows both the fallacy and the danger of a doctrine of international exhaustion. Fallacy because the simple adoption of an exhaustion rule did not, and has not, led to a single, internal market in pharmaceuticals within the EC. Intellectual property owners have proved tenacious in exploiting all possible means to insulate high-price markets from those of low prices. These have included exceptions to the exhaustion doctrine affecting trade marks; barriers raised by product safety laws and strategic bargaining power such as threats to shift increasingly mobile capital resources and delayed or non-release of some products. More needs to be taken into account, however, before their efforts to price above cost can be condemned or judged necessary to reap the returns required for desirable investment in innovation.

The second part of the fallacy is the assumption that, intellectual property owners' behaviour apart, the conditions in each market are the same. The 'market' for pharmaceuticals in the EC is not of a piece. One of the most powerful differences lies in the existence of different national regimes on pricing; some governments tolerating higher prices as a spur to innovation, others regulating prices to depressed levels. Attempts to harmonise these differences involve not just considerations of health and social policy, but ultimately the national budget, fiscal and taxation policies.

---

31 Presumably because they forced greater flexibility of response to consumers' wants and continued the drive for efficiencies in distribution, see John C. Hilke, 'Free Trade or Free-Riding: An Examination of the Theories and Available Empirical Evidence on Gray Market Imports', 32 *World Competition* 75 (1988).

32 PSA, *Inquiry into Effects of Exchange Rate Appreciation on Prices of Consumer Goods*.

Such considerations cannot simply be dismissed or ignored. The danger lies in the threat to investment in innovation and of increasing concentration. Increasingly, the industry perceives the pressure for lower prices as creating an environment hostile to investment. Increasingly also, firms based in low-price environments are seen as falling behind in the competitive struggle.

Experience outside the EC and also outside the field of pharmaceuticals lends support. In India, the large, innovative drug producer has tended to adopt strategies like those firms which it was set up to challenge. Where brand identification has been proscribed, quality problems have ensued. Small firms set up to gain expertise by producing generics have failed to flourish on narrow margins and have failed to develop strong R & D arms.

The software case shows an historical dichotomy between larger, foreign-owned firms which have primarily acted in the past as distributors throughout the EC and smaller, often domestic firms engaging in innovation. The market is, however, a rapidly changing and developing one. The threat of parallel imports has often forced them to react in similar ways; the drive for market integration reportedly being met by price harmonisation around the EC. Most suppliers also report steps to build in to 'the product' specifications based on national or regional lines such as language-specific versions or strong local support networks. An important difference arises, however, in the effects of parallel imports. For distributors, the main effect reported is some disruption of intra-group marketing arrangements. But, more serious prejudice to innovative activities is claimed by those whose R & D functions are mainly located within the EC.

It is too early yet to observe the effects of the Australian reforms in the field of copyright and books. To the extent that release dates are delayed, there may be an improvement. This seems particularly likely for the availability of paperbacks when US release dates are earlier than, say, at present in the United Kingdom or Australia. But, this may not be so for more marginal titles. Whether prices will fall is another matter since, provided the requirement of first publication simultaneously in Australia is met, the legislation leaves the Australian copyright owner with the option of remaining the exclusive importer. Hence, if the conditions for price discrimination perceived by the PSA exist, there will still remain no direct pressure from price competition and, potentially, higher costs associated with airfreight may be incurred (the prospect of further review by the PSA, scheduled for some 18 months after the legislation has been in effect, may act as a constraint). If the experience of domestic publishers and booksellers confronted by cheap imports in large quantities prior to the Second World War is any guide, there is a danger that the supply of titles which do not meet the first publication requirement may become markedly more haphazard. If the reforms have their intended effect of lowering prices, it remains to be seen whether a fall in the general price level of books will affect the scale or viability of local publishing operations. It will certainly be interesting to see whether the prospect of earlier availability of paperback editions from the United States will lead to any shift in the balance of copyright ownership retained in US hands and whether or not that leads to any change in the publishing culture in Australia. Perhaps, however, the largest question is whether the requirements of co-ordinating first publication dates and the release of paperback editions will not have the unintended effect of further increasing concentration. Canadian experience has not necessarily been as happy as the PSA depicted. Hence, in Canada, increased subsidies and strengthened protection against buying around are being introduced.

Proponents of exhaustion rules do not deny that parallel imports may threaten incentives to invest in innovation or risk confusion of domestic consumers *or* that the law should provide remedies for such dangers. The rule proposed by Professor Demaret includes express exceptions where parallel protection of commensurate effect did not operate in the foreign market or the domestic market imposes domestic manufacturing requirements.[33] He does not, however, attribute independent force to any need to provide licensees (or assignees) with incentives to invest by affording them protection from intra-brand competition.[34] Where the intellectual property concerned is a trade mark, Professor Beier appears to suggest that the necessary solutions are found in the German law of unfair competition or tort.[35] With respect, that view proceeds on an unduly narrow interpretation of the function of a trade mark which has not proved conclusively convincing in the 'common law world' and, further, overlooks the advantages to consumers and business alike of having clearly prescribed statutory rights, the consequences of which can be readily identified. In any case, the solution is not open in those Anglo-Commonwealth jurisdictions which have steadfastly rejected a broad prohibition on unfair competition.[36]

Thus, it seems to this author, the fact that parallel imports cross an international frontier can, and may well often, matter. There are likely to be large differences between countries in their laws, policies and economic environment. Trade between countries based on these differences may bring consumers short-term benefits in the form of lower prices. But, where intellectual property rights are concerned, there could also be trade-offs over the longer term. The studies considered here show that such trade-offs, in the form of free riding potentially undermining incentives in desirable investment, are a high likelihood. Conversely, policies favouring the longer-term view also involve social costs in the form of higher prices. There is, as already discussed, evidence that firms exploit their intellectual property powers to exacerbate those costs by practising some form of international price discrimination. Whether those attempts are actually harmful will depend on the particular market circumstances under consideration. Hence, given the potential for parallel imports to have different effects, some form of balancing is necessary.

---

33 Paul Demaret, *Patents, Territorial Restrictions and EEC Law*, Verlag-Chemie, 1978, Chapter 3(A). Contrast Friedrich-Karl Beier, 'Industrial Property and the Free Movement of Goods in the Internal European Market', 21 IIC 131, at 150 to 156 (1990).
34 Contrast 258/78 *Maize Seed* [1982] ECR 2015; the *Sylvania* case 433 US 36 (1977).
35 Beier, 'Territoriality of Trademark Law and International Trade', at 63 to 64.
36 See for example *Moorgate Tobacco Co. Ltd v Philip Morris Ltd* (1984) 156 CLR 414.

It could be argued, from the surveys suggesting that patents generally play only a minor role in inducing innovation, that the disincentive effects of parallel imports will be trivial. Such a sweeping proposition ignores those cases where patents are necessary and such contradictory evidence as there is. It also ignores those cases where protection from parallel imports is desirable in the interests of encouraging domestic investment. These surveys attempt to assess the role of patents only in large corporations listed on stock exchanges and, even within this range, point often to substantial variation between firms within a given industry. Furthermore, the relatively weak role found for patents in such surveys arises in part because these firms are able to use other means to appropriate the benefits of their investments in innovation. Parallel imports may well undermine the utility of those other means. Accordingly, once again, a blanket rule does not seem indicated.

As an economic phenomenon, the causes and effects of parallel imports depend on a complex interplay of many factors. In any one case, all or some of these may be at work. Some of them will involve the erosion of market power and price discrimination and may be seen to work in favour of consumers and, perhaps, welfare overall. Others, while apparently offering short-term advantages, may be illusory and instead mean that parallel imports undermine desirable, pro-competitive (and so welfare-enhancing) activities. In short, parallel imports may be desirable in some situations while not in others.

It is not clear on *a priori* grounds whether the balance favours falling on one side or the other. Certainly, all the evidence considered here indicates that attempts to discriminate between the prices charged in different markets are highly likely. But, how effective those attempts are in any given case depends on the factual circumstances. Moreover, the rationale of intellectual property rights is about conferring *some sort* of power to charge prices higher than marginal cost and so to encourage desirable activity which, it is speculated, may not otherwise take place in sufficient degree. Furthermore, the evidence indicates that the risk of parallel imports undermining incentives to invest in innovation or market making is also *very* high. The risk of consumer deception from parallel imports is not *as* high, but is still significant.

The dependence of the impact of parallel imports on the particular fact setting of any given case applies across the range of intellectual property rights. For example, the perceived need to encourage domestic investment by protection from foreign competition was the same in, say, *Fender* for trade marks, *Maize Seed* for plant breeders' rights and, in copyright, *Pitt Pitts*.[37]

Similarly, it cannot be said that the policies appropriate for one country are necessarily appropriate for another. The market circumstances may be

37 *Fender v Bevk* (1989) 15 IPR 257; 258/78 *Maize Seed* [1982] ECR 2015; *Pitt Pitts v George & Co.* [1896] 2 Ch. 886 (CA). The same, of course, can be said for attempts to practise international price discrimination, for example *Revlon* [1980] FSR 85 (on the view the Court of Appeal took); *Maize Seed* (on the view the Commission took); and *Time-Life* (on Murphy J's view).

completely different. It may, for example, be possible to describe the United States and the United Kingdom as competitive markets for book publishing. This would not necessarily mean that the Australian market was too. For example, the fact that the UK and US markets were competitive would be irrelevant to the Australian situation if, largely as the PSA alleged, all the large UK and US publishers had joined together in some cartel. Another situation which might require different treatment would be where the Australian market was of such a size that scale economies in book distribution were such that all authors and other publishers were dependent on only two or three publishers to act as their distributors and further entry into distribution were blocked. As discussed in Chapter 10, there might be considerable doubts about whether such circumstances prevailed in Australia.

The 'best' policy for a particular country may also depend on other, non-economic factors. Nationalist sentiments may 'cloud' the issue. Canadians, for example, have been aggrieved at their treatment as an outpost of US-based book clubs.

A country may also decide its national interest does not lie in establishing a strong patent or copyright regime. A small island-state such as Singapore or Hong Kong may consider that its resources and interests are better maximised by fierce competition on costs and a policy of free trade.[38] For many countries, this may not be a viable option and such a country may, however, find itself the subject of threats and sanctions from important international trading partners which consider its policies harm their interests.[39] Further-more, it has long been recognised that rising living standards, and a country's ability to enjoy them, depend crucially on innovation; static improvements in allocative efficiency have accounted for only a small proportion of progress.[40]

Significantly, if it is hoped to develop and maintain a domestic industry, it is fairly clear that that domestic industry is unlikely to prosper unless it can reap the benefits of its investments.[41] This does not necessarily

38 Such a policy did not, apparently, preclude Switzerland from developing a strong pharmaceuticals industry albeit one which took out patents in the much larger foreign markets it operated in, see F. M. Scherer, *The Economic Effects of Compulsory Patent Licensing*, New York University Graduate School of Management, 1977, at 39.

39 John Whalley, 'International Aspects of Copyright Legislation in Canada: Economic Analysis of Policy Options', 8 *Research in Law and Economics* 273 (1986). For reports of US pressure against counterfeiting in South East Asia, see 'Black Trademark: The Market for Fakes Flourishes', *Far Eastern Economic Review*, 23 July 1987, at 58; Lincoln Kaye, 'Copycats Unrepentant', *Far Eastern Economic Review*, 31 May 1984, at 82.

40 Scherer and Ross, *Industrial Market Structure and Economic Performance*, at 613 to 614; Michael E. Porter, *The Competitive Advantage of Nations*, Macmillan, 1990; Giovanni Dosi, Keith Pavitt and Luc Soete, *The Economics of Technical Change and International Trade*, Harvester Wheatsheaf, 1990.

41 See for example the claims of domestic software producers in the EC; the problems of domestic book publishing in Australia and Canada; the expansion of printing industries in Singapore and South Korea after the adoption of copyright laws; and the experience of the pharmaceutical industries in France, Italy, Canada and India. For a theoretical and empirical support for the claim, see Dosi *et al., The Economics of Technical Change and International Trade*.

mean that protection must be conferred on foreign producers, nor against parallel imports. However, the increasing expansion of the international system through the intellectual property conventions and, with increasing likelihood, GATT will make it much more difficult for an individual country to participate in the benefits of the international trading system without granting reciprocal treatment to foreigners. If parallel imports are not excluded, it will still be necessary to ensure that domestic price levels are sufficient to support a viable indigenous industry and to encourage any foreign investment desired, or necessary, for effective technology transfer.[42] Hence, it may be necessary to operate special forms of tax subsidy or other governmental payment or tolerate forms of strategic behaviour such as enhanced product differentiation or the use of vertical restraints in distribution. Such alternatives may not be possible and their desirability is at least as questionable as the case promoting parallel imports.

Given the dependence on the individual fact setting, precision would require a full-scale economic investigation every time the impact of parallel imports were to be investigated. On such an approach, it would be necessary to explore not only the circumstances of the foreign and domestic markets but also the extent the intellectual property right was necessary to call forth investment in the particular product in question and its preparation and marketing in the domestic market.[43] Even if workable tests could be found, such a system seems likely to prove too expensive and scarcely practical. The wide-ranging nature of the inquiry would prove costly in terms of time and money and generate uncertainty. The uncertainty, costs and delay would undermine the incentives for prospective parallel importers where parallel imports were desirable; equally, intellectual property owners could experience a corresponding, chilling effect.

What is needed is a solution which establishes an overall policy setting but which is also sufficiently flexible to deal with the demands of individual cases. This points to a role for both intellectual property laws and anti-trust (or competition) policy. Intellectual property laws *alone* are not suited to resolving the issue. A blanket rule banning parallel imports ignores those situations where parallel imports would have desirable effects. On the other hand, the situations where parallel imports would lead to consumer deception or undermine incentives to make pro-competitive investments are

---

42 Once again the pharmaceuticals industry is instructive. Note also the need for subsidies and the recommendations for much increased subsidies in the Canadian and Australian publishing sectors. As part of an unspecified 'economic liberalisation', it has been argued that foreign investment in India was not scared off by reforms to the patent system but transferred to joint ventures, see R. B. Saxena, 'Trade-Related Issues of Intellectual Property Rights and the Indian Patent Act – A New Negotiating Strategy', 12(2) *World Competition* 81, at 103 to 104 (1988).

43 For an example of the latter point, parallel imports could not harm the incentive role of domestic intellectual property rights if domestic manufacturing was chosen because the manufacturing costs were lower in the domestic market than the foreign market, see Demaret, *Patents, Territorial Restrictions and EEC Law*, at 68. Arguably, it would still be necessary to consider marketing costs and factors such as whether the foreign manufacture took place under, say, a compulsory licence.

denied by a rule of international exhaustion. Intellectual property laws set out broad policy norms towards encouraging desirable investments. Competition policy requires an inquiry into the competitive impact of the individual case. But, the use of presumptions and onuses of proof enables competition policy also to be oriented to establish a general approach capable of modification when particular circumstances dictate.

The remainder of this chapter seeks to outline a means of co-ordinating the use of the two legal regimes to achieve the desired objects. The vital point is that any application of competition policy must be sensitive to the goals of intellectual property. The relationship is complicated by the tendency to view competition or anti-trust as concerned with static, 'short-run' issues of lowering price while intellectual property is concerned with dynamic, longer-run questions. There is no point railing at intellectual property rights *because* they distort the operation of market forces; that is the point of adopting intellectual property laws. On the other hand, it is also necessary to recognise that not every use made of intellectual property rights should be accorded immunity.[44]

The first step is the role of intellectual property rights. They should all be interpreted in accordance with a principle of territoriality in the sense that mere sale abroad of a product embodying an intellectual property right protected in the domestic market should not *of itself* entail a licence to importation. Importation should be permitted where a licence has been expressly granted or can be clearly implied from the circumstances.[45] The proposed rule accords with the common law world's approach predominating in all subject-matters and is consistent with the rule in many Civil Code countries for rights other than trade marks. Furthermore, the rule is consistent with recognition of the fact that parallel imports may be injurious in some situations and not in others; but, alternative means of blocking parallel imports (where that is desirable) are likely to be neither as effective nor desirable in the public interest.[46]

That, however, is only a first step and, if the dangers of parallel imports are to be balanced against their potential benefits, a further step is necessary. The second step is the sensitive application of competition policy. A careful use of presumptions or rebuttable rules can be used to orient the general

---

44 Compare the approach taken in *Studiengesellschaft Kohle* 670 F. 2d 1122 (DC Cir. 1981) in the absence of horizontal cartels such as those found in *ICI* 100 F. Supp. 504 (SDNY 1951) and the *Addison-Wesley* case 1976–2 CCH Trade Cases at ¶61,225. For an Australian example, see *Broderbund Software Inc. v Computermate Products (Australia) Pty Ltd* (1991) 22 IPR 215 (Fed. C).

45 For example, implication might be appropriate in the case of the sale of a commercial quantity to a known reseller for delivery in the domestic market, see for example the *Time-Life* case (1977) 138 CLR 534, at 543 *per* Gibbs J.

46 Contract, dependent as it is on a relationship of privity, is plainly not adequate: the *Sebastian* case 847 F. 2d 1093 (3d Cir. 1988). Public notice of the potential risk is facilitated if the power to control imports forms part of the right, especially where interests in the right are required to be registered; contrast the uncertainties associated with laws like passing off and unfair competition (where available). See also Chapter 2 Notes 274 to 278 and Chapter 5 from Note 50.

approach to parallel imports under competition policy in accordance with the perceived characteristics of the national market.[47] For example, if the domestic market is generally perceived to be open and highly competitive, the onus could profitably be placed on the parallel importer to show that an intellectual property right owner was acting anti-competitively by using infringement proceedings to block the imports.[48] Conversely, where the market circumstances are tightly oligopolistic and entry is blocked, it would be more appropriate to presume an anti-competitive violation, placing the burden on the intellectual property owner to justify the need to block parallel imports.

On this approach, intellectual property rights would confer power to block parallel imports subject to the operation of competition policy. It would be open to a party to invoke competition policy in each case where intellectual property rights were sought to be raised against parallel imports. But, once the appropriate presumptions or rebuttable rules were in place, the likelihood of litigation could be markedly reduced. For example, parallel importers seeking to operate in an open and competitive market should come to realise that unsubstantiated allegations of market power and anti-competitive behaviour would not prove to be of much help.[49]

Reliance on competition policy has its dangers. These are particularly evidenced by the European Commission's approach under the EEC Treaty's competition rules when contrasted to the ECJ's analysis. Hence, the vital importance of viewing competition *ex ante* over the longer run as a dynamic process.[50]

Analysis of competition problems usually proceeds on either of two fronts. Where exploitation of the domestic market takes place by way of a licence of intellectual property rights or, perhaps, an assignment, it will be necessary to test for anti-competitive concertation.[51] Alternatively, the domestic right owner may be engaging in a unilateral misuse of market power which, apart

---

47   The suggestion is based on an interpretation of the distinction drawn in the United States between rules of *per se* illegality and the 'rule of reason' test, see for example *NCAA v University of Oklahoma* 468 US 85 (1984). For proposals to use filters or presumptions in the field of vertical restraints, see Oliver E. Williamson, 'Delimiting Antitrust', 76 Georgetown LJ 271, especially at 281 to 289 (1987).

48   This should not, of course, preclude the parallel importer from relying on any other defences or counter-claims which may be available such as proving consent to the importation or invalidity of the intellectual property right.

49   See for example *Model Rectifiers* 221 USPQ 502 (9th Cir. 1983), Chapter 2 Note 283.

50   Contrast the approaches of the ECJ and Commission in *Maize Seed*, above at Chapter 7.2.1, although arguably the ECJ's analysis did not take into account all the economic considerations, see 258/78 *Maize Seed* [1982] ECR 2015, and contrast the Advocate-General's opinion, the US approach in *Studiengesellschaft Kohle* 670 F. 2d 1122 (DC Cir. 1981) and the perceptive comments in Eleanor M. Fox, 'Maize Seed: A Comparative Comment', [1982] *Fordham Corporate Law Institute* 151.

51   That is, the type of conduct which would attract liability under EEC Treaty Article 85 or the Sherman Act, section 1. The possibility of a unilateral misuse of market power should not be ruled out.

from situations where it exploits the domestic rights itself, lies at the root of complaints about the activities of a corporate group.[52]

The crucial issue in both situations is an accurate definition of the relevant market in both its product and geographical dimensions.[53] Too wide a definition will lead to an underestimate of any anti-competitive potential; an overestimate will follow from a definition which is too narrow. The proper definition of the product market must take into account not just the intellectual property owner's products but *all* the possibilities of substitution from *both* the demand *and* supply sides. That is, the market includes the intellectual property owner's products, all other similar products which consumers might reasonably use in their place *and* the potential for suppliers of other products to switch into production of substitutable products. While it is certainly possible for intellectual property to create effective barriers to entry, the bulk of the empirical evidence suggests that these are rare cases.

When the concern is potential anti-competitive concertation, it is usual to distinguish between agreements between horizontal competitors and vertical competitors since the dangers of a horizontal cartel which restricts output and raises price may be greater.[54] Appropriate definition of the geographical market is also necessary on the issue of whether the parties to the licence (or assignment) are horizontal competitors, when anti-trust concerns will be more pronounced.[55] Even where the agreement is between horizontal competitors, US courts have tended towards a fairly permissive stance in the absence of a clear intention to cartelise; this, perhaps, follows from a too liberal allowance under the power to divide the domestic intellectual property right along territorial lines.[56]

How the law should deal with vertical restraints has provoked a voluminous literature.[57] As with the question of the impact of parallel imports, much

---

52   That is, the type of conduct attracting liability under EEC Treaty Article 86 or the Sherman Act, section 2, for example the allegation in *Guerlain* 155 F. Supp. 77 (SDNY 1958) *vacated and remanded* 357 US 924 (1958) *dismissed* 172 F. Supp. 107 (SDNY 1959).

53   See especially *Guerlain*, above at Chapter 2.3.4(a).

54   For other views, see Robert L. Steiner, 'The Nature of Vertical Restraints', 30 *Antitrust Bulletin* 143 (1985) and Thomas G. Krattenmaker and Steven C. Salop, 'Anticompetitive Exclusion: Raising Rivals' Costs to Achieve Power Over Price', 96 Yale LJ 209 (1986). Both place the emphasis on the presence or absence of market power.

55   Contrast *Davidson Rubber* [1972] CMLR D52 and Hartmut Johannes, 'Technology Transfer under EEC Law – Europe Between the Divergent Opinions of the Past and the New Administration: A Comparative Law Approach', [1982] *Fordham Corporate Law Institute* 65 to *Westinghouse* 648 F. 2d 642 (9th Cir. 1981) and 258/78 *Maize Seed* [1982] ECR 2015.

56   See for example Richard M. Buxbaum, 'Restrictions in the Patent Monopoly: A Comparative Critique', 113 UPenn.LRev. 633 (1965); but compare *Studiengesellschaft Kohle* 670 F. 2d 1122 (DC Cir. 1981), Chapter 3 from Note 230.

57   For a comprehensive review of the complexity, see Scherer and Ross, *Industrial Market Structure and Economic Performance*, Chapter 15. A clear summary from a lawyer's perspective is George A. Hay, 'The Free Rider Rationale and Vertical Restraints Analysis Reconsidered', 56 *Antitrust LJ* 27 (1987). For an EC perspective, with further references, see Barry E. Hawk, 'The American (Antitrust) Revolution: Lessons for the EEC?', (1988) 9 ECLR 53 and Valentine Korah, *Know-how Licensing Agreements and the EEC Competition Rules: Regulation 556/89*, ESC Publishing, 1989, Chapter 1.

of this literature indicates that the effects of vertical restraints vary very much with the facts of the particular case. However, a number of points have emerged which allow the formulation of some general presumptions.

The key point is, once again, the presence of market power. Generally speaking, if the right owner does not possess the necessary degree of market power, concern may well be less warranted. In addition, vertical restraints seem more likely to enhance inter-brand competition where they are imposed to facilitate the introduction of a new product or a product with a small market share which is battling to compete against entrenched market leaders.[58]

Where the intellectual property owner possesses significant power in a properly defined market, the (rebuttable) presumption should be against allowing parallel imports to be blocked. But, there may be situations where preventing parallel imports would be justified. In such cases, the onus of establishing that it is justified to block parallel imports should fall clearly on the intellectual property owner.

The crucial point is what constitutes market power. This is certainly a question of degree amenable to variation according to the particular circumstances. Steiner appears to suggest that a brand having 30 to 33 per cent of the market when its next four closest rivals together mustered a combined share of about 35 per cent constituted sufficient market power that a removal of intra-brand restrictions substantially *enhanced* inter-brand competition.[59] Perhaps more extreme, the Australian PSA seemed to consider the production and distribution of books in Australia to be a barricaded oligopoly although the largest supplier seemed to have only about 10 per cent of the market.[60] On the other hand, the market for dental X-ray machines in the United States was described as very competitive although two distributors each had 20 per cent market shares and seven producers account for 95 per cent of the market.[61]

Such economic work as there is tends to suggest that market shares under

---

58   Robert L. Steiner, 'The Nature of Vertical Restraints', 30 *Antitrust Bulletin* 143, at 187 (1985). *Maize Seed* is an example. On the appropriate meaning of 'new', see Korah, *Know-how Licensing Agreements and the EEC Competition Rules*, at §1.5.2.3.

59   *Ibid.* at 178 to 183, but see 196 to 197 citing *FTC v Levi Strauss & Co.* 92 FTC 171 (1978); but note the ambiguities reported by Scherer and Ross, *Industrial Market Structure and Economic Performance*, at 554. The efficiency purists would seem likely to challenge Steiner's view, see especially Frank H. Easterbrook, 'Vertical Arrangements and the Rule of Reason', 53 *Antitrust LJ* 135 (1984); 'The Limits of Antitrust', 63 Texas LR 1 (1984), but note the criticisms in Williamson, 'Delimiting Antitrust', at 271 and Eleanor M. Fox, 'The Modernization of Antitrust: A New Equilibrium', 66 Cornell LR 1140 (1981).

60   See further Chapter 10.2.1 above. Contrast *Broderbund Software v Computermalte* (1991) 22 IPR 215 (Fed. C) where Beaumont J found that a market share of between 10 and 17 per cent was insufficient to attract Australia's prohibition on misuse of market power.

61   *H. L. Hayden Co. of New York Inc. v Siemens Medical Systems Inc.* 879 F. 2d 1005 (2d Cir. 1989). For a similar characterisation in an EC case involving a joint venture to develop a new food packaging product, see *Odin* OJ 1990 L209/15, but contrast earlier rulings in patent licensing such as *Kabelmetal/Luchaire* [1975] 2 CMLR D40.

10 per cent are unlikely to cause concern.[62] Even here, however, there may be cause for concern if the market consisted of, say, eight or nine suppliers of roughly the same size which had all been in the industry for many years and new entry was precluded. In such circumstances there could be considerable risk of oligopolistic interdependence. Therefore, the most important consideration is probably whether or not the market structure is sufficiently diverse that rival suppliers have a range of options from which to choose the means of supplying consumers and consumers have access to equivalent products which are made available with varying levels of pre- and post-sales services allowing the consumer to choose.[63]

Given the wide range of causes and effects of parallel imports, it is perhaps not surprising that they have provoked such varied responses from commentators and the courts. Perhaps, some of the inconsistencies, complexities and uncertainties can be removed by addressing the economic issues at the root of parallel imports. This, the author has argued, requires a combination of both intellectual property law and competition policy to achieve the necessary mix of certainty and flexibility. One thing is certain: however the problem is resolved, contention will not go away. Businesses will often continue to strive to prevent parallel imports. In some cases, this will probably represent nothing more than the aggrandising tendencies which Adam Smith early warned against. But, there will certainly also be cases where their claims are justified. On the other hand, consumers will continue to demand faster, cheaper access to products which they know are already available in other parts of the world. Ensuring that pressure is transmitted to intellectual property owners while at the same time recognising the longer-term needs which intellectual property tries to serve remains the conundrum.

---

62 Richard Schmalensee, 'Ease of Entry: Has the Concept been Applied Too Readily?', 56 *Antitrust LJ* 41 (1987).
63 On the importance of diversity, see for example Fox, 'The Modernization of Antitrust: A New Equilibrium', at 1140, F. M. Scherer, 'Antitrust, Efficiency and Progress', 62 NYU LRev. 998 (1987).

Bibliography

Agarwala, P. N., Pragmatic Approach May Solve Problems, Far Eastern Economic Review, 11 April 1985, 61

Alchian, Armen A., Discussion, 56 Am.Econ.Rev. (Supp.) (1966)

Aldous, W. et al, Terrell on the Law of Patents, Sweet & Maxwell, 1982 (2nd edn)

Alexander, Daniel, Colgate-Palmolive v Markwell Finance – The Carving Knife Sharpened, [1989] EIPR 456

Alexander, Willy, Horizontal Effects of Licensing a Technology as Dealt with by the EEC Competition Law, [1987] Fordham Corporate Law Institute

Alexander, Willy, Industrial Property Rights and the Establishment of the European Common Market, (1972) 9 CMLRev. 35

Areeda, Phillip E., Antitrust Law: An Analysis of Antitrust Principles and Their Application, Little, Brown & Co., 1989

Armstrong, George M. Jr, From the Fetishism of Commodities to the Regulated Market: The Rise and Decline of Property, 83 Northwestern University LRev. 79 (1988)

Arnold, Richard, Can One Sue in England for Infringement of Foreign Intellectual Property Rights?, [1990] EIPR 254

Arrow, Kenneth J., Collected Papers of Kenneth J. Arrow: Production and Capital, Bellknap Press, 1985

Arrow, Kenneth J., Economic Welfare and the Allocation of Resources for Invention, in The Rate and Direction of Inventive Activity: Economic and Social Factors, Princeton University Press, 1962, 609

Australia Council, Books – Who Reads Them?, 1990, 206

Baden Fuller, C. W. F., Economic Issues Relating to Property Rights in Trademarks: Export Bans, Differential Pricing on Resale Pricing, Restrictions on Resale and Repackaging, (1981) 6 ELRev. 162

Baker, J. H., Introduction to British Legal History, Butterworths, 1986

Baker, J. H. and Milsom, S. F. C., Sources of English Legal History, Butterworths, 1986

Baker, Jonathan B., Recent Developments in Economics that Challenge Chicago School Views, 58 Antitrust LJ 645 (1989)

Ball, Horace G., Law of Copyright and Literary Property, 1944

Baugh, Scott R., Seven Billion Dollar Gray Market: Trademark Infringement or Honest Competition?, 18 Pacific LJ (1986)

Baxt, R. and Kewley G., Annual Survey of Australian Law 1986, The Law Book Company, 1987

Baxter, William F., Legal Restrictions on Exploitation of the Patent Monopoly: An Economic Analysis, 76 Yale LJ 267 (1966)

Baxter, William F., Vertical Practices – Half Slave, Half Free, 52 Antitrust LJ 743 (1983)

Beier, Friedrich-Karl, Industrial Property and the Free Movement of Goods in the Internal European Market, 21 IIC 131 (1990)

Beier, Friedrich-Karl, Territoriality of Trade Mark Law and International Trade, 1 IIC 48 (1970)

Beier, Friedrich-Karl, Trademark Conflicts in the Common Market: Can they be Solved by Means of Distinguishing Additions?, 9 IIC 221 (1978)

Bellamy, Christopher and Child, Graham D., Common Market Law of Competition, 1987 (3rd edn)

Benyami, A., Infringement of the Rights Conferred by a European Community Patent: Substantive Community Law, PH.D Thesis, University of London, 1990

Birrell, A., Lectures on the Law and History of Copyright in Books, Cassell and Company Ltd, 1899

Black Trademark: The Market for Fakes Flourishes, Far Eastern Economic Review, 23 July 1987

Blanco-White, T. A. and Jacob, Robin, Kerly's Law of Trade Marks and Trade Names, Sweet & Maxwell, 1986 (2nd edn)

Bleeke, Joel A. and Rahl, James A., Value of Territorial and Field of Use Restrictions in the International Licensing of Unpatented Know-How: An Empirical Study, 1 Northwestern Journal of Law and Business 450 (1979)

Blomqvist, Ake G. and Lim, Chin, Copyright. Competition and Canadian Culture, Department of Consumer and Corporate Affairs Canada, 1981

Board of Trade, Report of the Copyright Committee, Cmnd 8662, HMSO, 1952 (the Gregory Committee)

Board of Trade, Report of the Departmental Committee on the Law and Practice Relating to Trade Marks

Bork, Robert, Antitrust Paradox, Basic Books Inc., 1978

Bowen, Lionel, Deputy Prime Minister and Attorney General of Australia, Government Moves on Book Prices, News Release, 21 & 22 December 1989

Bowman, Ward S., Patent and Antitrust: A Legal and Economic Appraisal, University of Chicago Press, 1973

Bradley, Clive, Market Rights: When Does Importation Infringe?, (1991) 5 Rights 1

Brett, Judith, Publishing Censorship and Writers' Incomes 1965–1988, 1988 in The Future of Australia as an Export Market, The Sir Stanley Unwin Foundation, 1989

Bicks, Robert A., Antitrust and Trademark Protection Concepts in the Import Field, 49 TMR 1255 (1959)

Briggs, John de Q., Comment, 56 Antitrust LJ 37 (1987)

Brown, Andrew and Grant, Anthony, Law of Intellectual Property in New Zealand, Butterworths, 1989

Brown, Brendan, Parallel Importation: A New Zealand Perspective, [1989] EIPR 274 & 277

Budnarchuk, Sharon and Steve, Buying Around, [October 1990] Quill & Quire 6

Burrell, Timothy Donald, South African Patent Law and Practice, Butterworths, 1986 (2nd edn)

Burstall, M. C., 1992 and the Regulation of the Pharmaceutical Industry, IEA Health & Welfare Unit No. 9 (1990), 7

Burstall, M. C., The Community's Pharmaceutical Industry, EC Commission 1985

Buxbaum, Richard M., Restrictions in the Patent Monopoly: A Comparative Critique, 113 UPenn.LRev 633 (1965)

Bywater, Michael, Pricing: The MacUser OPEN Forum, 23 MacUser 49, May 1988

Card, Duncan C., Parallel Importation of Copyright Property: A Proposal to Amend the Canadian Copyright Act, (1990) 6 IPJ 97

Chafee, Zechariah Jr, Equitable Servitudes on Chattels, 41 Harv.LRev 945 (1928)

Chafee, Zechariah Jr, Reflections on the Law of Copyright, 45 Columbia LRev 503 (1945)

Chafee, Zechariah Jr, The Music Goes Round and Round: Equitable Servitudes and Chattels, 69 Harv.LRev 1250 (1956)

Chard, John et al, International Exhaustion of Intellectual Property Rights, Unpublished, November 1988

Chard, J. S., Economics of the Application of Article 85 to Selective Distribution Systems, (1982) 7 ELRev. 83

Chard, J. S. and Mellor, C. J., Intellectual Property Rights and Parallel Imports, (1989) 12 (1) The World Economy 69

Chisum, Donald S., Patents: A Treatise on the Law of Patentability, Validity and Infringement, Matthew Bender & Co. Inc., 1987, 1991

Chudnovsky, Daniel, Patents and Trademarks in Pharmaceuticals, (1983) 11 World Development 187

Coase, R. H., Nature of the Firm, (1937) 4 Economica, reprinted in 'The Firm, the Market and the Law', R. H. Coase, University of Chicago Press 1988, Ch 2

Coase, R. H., The Firm, The Market and the Law, University of Chicago Press, 1988

Coase, R. H., The Problem of Social Cost, 3 JL and Econ. 1 (1960)

Coggio, Brian D., Gordon, Jennifer and Coruzzi, Laura A., History and Present Status of Gray Goods, 75 TMR 433 (1985)

Colby, Richard, First Sale Doctrine – The Defence that Never Was?, 32 J Copr. Soc'y 77 (1984)

Coleman, Jules L., Markets, Morals and the Law, Cambridge University Press, 1988

Comanor, William S., Political Economy of the Pharmaceutical Industry, 24 JEcon.Lit. 1178 (1986)

Comanor, William S., Vertical Price Fixing, Vertical Market Restrictions and the New Antitrust Policy, 98 Harv.LRev 983 (1985)

Copyright Law Review Committee, Importation Provisions of the Copyright Act 1968, AGPS 1988, App.D. at 279–369

Cornish, W. R., Definitional Stop Aids the Flow of Patented Goods, [1975] JBL 50

Cornish, W. R., Intellectual Property: Patents, Copyright, Trade Marks and Allied Rights, Sweet & Maxwell, 1989 (2nd edn)

Cornish, W. R., Trade Marks, Customer Confusion and the Common Market, (1975) 38 MLR 329

Cornish, W. R. and McGonigal, Peter G., Copyright and Anti-trust Aspects of Parallel Imports under Australian Law, 11 IIC 731 (1980)

Cornish, W. R. and Phillips, Jennifer, Economic Function of Trade Marks: An Analysis with Special Reference to Developing Countries, 13 IIC 41 (1982)

Dassman, Gérard, New Industrial Property Right for Pharmaceutical Products in France – The Complementary Protection Certificate, 21 IIC (1990) 615

Davies, Gillian and von Rauscher auf Weeg, Hans Hugo, Challenges to Copyright and Related Rights in the European Community, ESC Publishing Limited, 1983

De Wolfe, Mark (ed.), Holmes-Pollock Letters, Cambridge University Press, 1942

Dean, O. and Puckrin, C., Case Comment: Infringement of Copyright by Parallel Importation, [1983] EIPR 190

Defalque, Lucette, Copyright – Free Movement of Goods and Territoriality: Recent Developments, [1989] EIPR 435

Demaret, Paul, Industrial Property Rights, Compulsory Licences and the Free Movement of Goods under Community Law, 18 IIC 161 (1987)

Demaret, Paul, Patents, Territorial Restrictions and EEC Law, Verlag-Chemie, 1978

Demaret, Paul, Selective Distribution and EEC Law After Ford, Pronuptia and Metro II, [1986] Fordham Corporate Law Institute 149

Department of Trade and Industry, Intellectual Property and Innovation, Cmnd 9712 HMSO, 1986

Department of Trade and Industry, Reform of Trade Marks Law, Cm 1203, HMSO, 1990

Derenberg, Walter J., Current Trademark Problems in Foreign Travel and the Import Trade, 49 TMR 674 (1959)

Dosi, Giovanni, Pavitt, Keith and Soete, Luc, Economics of Technical Change and International Trade, Harvester Wheatsheaf, 1990

Drone, Eaton S., Treatise on the Law of Property in Intellectual Productions, Little, Brown & Co., 1879

Drysdale, John, Castrol Ltd v Automotive Supplies Ltd: Parallel Imports – Revlon Revisited, [1983] EIPR 224

Dutch Publishers Association, 6th Report on Competition Policy, EC Commission 1976

Easterbrook, Frank H., Limits of Antitrust, 63 Texas LR 1 (1984)

Easterbrook, Frank H., Vertical Arrangements and The Rule of Reason, 53 Antitrust LJ 135 (1984)

Eccles, Richard, Patentees' Rights to Prevent Imports, [1989] EIPR 26

Economides, Nicolas, Economics of Trademarks, 78 TMR 523 (1988)

European Community Law Bulletin May/June 1991, 5, Freistaat Bayern v Eurim-Pharm GmbH (unreported) 6 April 1991, McKenna & Co.

Fazal, Anwar, The Right Pharmaceuticals at the Right Prices: Consumer Perspectives, (1983) 11 World Development 265

Feingold, Stephen W., Parallel Importing under the Copyright Act 1976, 32 J Copr.Soc'y 211 (1984)

Fejø, Jens, Monopoly Law and Market, Kluwer, 1990

Final Report of the National Commission on New Technological Uses of Copyrighted Works, 3 July 1978

Fishwick, F., Book Prices in Australia and the United States of America, EC Commission 1985, 88

Fishwick, F., Comments on the Interim Report by the Australian Prices Surveillance Authority of its Inquiry into Book Prices, U.K. Publishers' Association Paper, December 1989

Flynn, John J., The "Is" and "Ought" of Vertical Restraints After Monsanto Co. v Spray-Rite Service Corp., 71 Cornell LRev. 1095 (1986)

Flynn, John J. and Ponsoldt, James F., Legal Reasoning and the Jurisprudence of Vertical Restraints: The Limitations of Neoclassical Economic Analysis in the Resolution of Antitrust Disputes, 62 NYULRev. 1125 (1987)

Fox, Eleanor M., Maize Seed: A Comparative Comment, [1982] Fordham Corporate Law Institute 151

Fox, Eleanor, M., Modernization of Antitrust: A New Equilibrium, 66 Cornell LRev. 1140 (1981)

Fox, Eleanor M. and Sullivan, Laurence M., Antitrust – Retrospective and Prospective: Where Are We Coming From? Where Are We Going To?, 62 NYULRev. 936 (1987)

Fox, Harold G., Canadian Law and Practice Relating to Letters Patent for Inventions, Carswell Company Ltd, 1969 (4th edn)

Fox, Harold G., Canadian Law of Copyright and Industrial Designs, Carswell Co. Ltd, 1967 (2nd edn)

Franklin, Andrew, Publishing in Canada, Sir Stanley Unwin Foundation, 1986

Freeguard, Michael, Collective Administration of Rights, in International Copyright and Neighbouring Rights, Stephen M. Stewart, Butterworths, 1989 (2nd edn) Annex

Friden, Georges, Recent Developments in EEC Intellectual Property Law: The Distinction Between Existence and Exercise Revisited, (1989) 26 CMLRev., 193

Galbraith-Kuehni, Renée, Practical Problems for the Free Movement of Medicines: A Perspective from within EFTA, EEC Pharmaceutical Law Forum 1990 Worldwide Information Conference Brussels, 24–25 April 1990

Gellhorn, Ernest, Antitrust Law and Economics, West Publishing Co., 1986 (3rd cdn)

George, Keith E., Importation of Articles Produced by Patented Process: Unfair Trade Practices or Infringement?, 18 George Washington Journal of International Law and Economics 129 (1984)

Gibbons, Domestic Territorial Restrictions in Patent Transactions and the Antitrust Laws, 34 Geo. Washington LRev. 893 (1966)

Gladwell, David, Exhaustion of Intellectual Property Rights, [1986] EIPR 366

Goebel, R. J., Metro II's Continuation of the Selective Distribution Rules. Is This the End of the Road?, (1987) 24 CMLRev. 605

Gormley, Laurence, Current Survey: The Common Market, (1985) 10 ELRev. 447

Gormley, L. W., Prohibiting Restrictions on Trade within the EEC, I. M. C. Asser Instituut, 1985

Gotzen, Frank, Distribution and Exhaustion in the EC Proposal for a Council Directive of the Legal Protection of Computer Programs, [1990] EIPR 299

Gould, James Matthew, Protecting Owners of US Process Patents from the Importation of Pharmaceuticals Made Abroad by Use of the Patented Process: Current Options, Proposed Legislation and a GATT Solution, 42 Food and Drug Cosmetic Law Journal 346 (1987)

Goyder, D. G., EEC Competition Law, Clarendon Press, 1988

Grabowski, Henry G. and Vernon, John, Determinants of Research and Development Expenditures in the Pharmaceutical Industry, in Drugs and Health, Robert B. Helms (ed.), American Enterprise Institute 1981

Grabowski, Henry G. and Vernon, John M., Pioneers, Imitators and Generics: A Simulation Model of Schumpeterian Competition, 102 QJEcon. 491 (1987)

Green, Nicholas, Article 85 in Perspective: Stretching Jurisdiction. Narrowing the Concept of a Restriction and Plugging a Few Gaps, [1988] ECLR 190

Griliches, Zvi (ed.), R & D Patents and Productivity, NBER/Chicago University Press, 1984

Gyselen, Luc, Vertical Restraints in the Distribution Process: Strength and Weakness of the Free Rider Rationale under EEC Competition Law, (1984) 21 CMLRev. 647

Hancher, Leigh, European Pharmaceutical Market: Problems of Partial Harmonisation, (1990) 15 ELRev. 9

Hancher, Leigh, Regulating for Competition, Clarendon Press, 1990

Handler, Milton, Trademarks – Assets or Liabilities, 48 TMR 661 (1958)

Handoll, John, Pfizer Inc. v Eurim-Pharm: Repackaging of Drugs in Transparent Holders, [1982] EIPR 83

Hannaford, Steve, Here and There, 6 (II) MacUser 21, 1 June 1990

Hartley, T. C., Foundations of European Community Law, Clarendon Press 1988 (2nd edn)

Haupt, Robert, Bound for Botany Bay, Sydney Morning Herald, 5 November 1988

Hawk, Barry E., The American (Antitrust) Revolution, [1988] ECLR 53

Hawk, Barry E., US, Common Market and International Antitrust: A Comparative Guide, Prentice Hall Law & Business (1990 Supp.) (2nd edn)

Hay, George A., Free Rider Rationale and Vertical Restraints Analysis Reconsidered, 56 Antitrust LJ 27 (1987)

Hecksher, Yvon O., Parallel Imports Furore: A Case of Smoke Exhalation?, 15 International Business Lawyer 32 (1987)

Heilbroner, Robert, Worldly Philosophers, Pelican, 1983 (5th edn)

Helms, Robert B. (ed.), Drugs and Health, American Enterprise Institute 1981

Hicks, Michael, Harlequin, Who and Charmdale Cases: Parallel Imports – UK and EEC Law, [1980] EIPR 237

Hiebert, Timothy, Foundations of the Law of Parallel Importation: Duality and Universality in Nineteenth Century Trademark Law, 80 TMR 483

Hilke, John C., Free Trading or Free-Riding: An Examination of the Theories and Available Empirical Evidence on Gray Market Imports, 32 World Competition 75 (1988)

Hockley, John, Parallel Importation of Trade Marked Goods into Australia, 16 IIC 549 (1985)

Hurt, Robert M., and Schuchman, Robert M., Economic Rationale of Copyright, 56 Am.Econ.Rev. (Supp.) 421 (1966)

Jacobs, F. G., Industrial Property Rights and the EEC Treaty: A Reply, (1975) 24 ICLQ 643

James, Murray and James, Copinger & Skone James on Copyright, Sweet & Maxwell, 1980 (12th edn)

Joelson, Mark R., Parallel Imports into the United States: Copyright and Anti-Trust, [1980] EIPR 281

Joelson, Mark R., Lindsay, John C. and Griffin, Joe, US Omnibus Trade and Competitiveness Act of 1988, 16 International Business Lawyer 408 (1988)

Johannes, Hartmut, Industrial Property and Copyright Law in the European Community Law, Sijthoff, 1976, 67

Johannes, Hartmut, Technology Transfers Under EEC Law – Europe Between the Divergent Opinions of the Past and the New Administrations: A Comparative Law Approach, [1982] Fordham Corporate Law Institute 65

Joliet, René, Patented Articles and the Free Movement of Goods within the EEC, (1975) 2 Current Legal Problems 15 & Hag II [1990] CMLR 571

Joliet, René, Rule of Reason in Antitrust Law: American, German and Common Market Laws in Comparative Perspective, Martinus Nijhof, 1967

Joliet, René, Trademark Licensing Agreements under the EEC Law of Competition, 5 Northwestern Journal of International Law & Business 755 (1983) and 15 IIC 21 (1984)

Joliet, René, and Keeling, David T., Trade Mark Law and the Free Movement of Goods: The Overruling of the Judgment in Hag I, IIC, forthcoming

Jucker, E., Patents and Pharmaceuticals, Buchdruckerei Gasser & Cie AG, 1980, 46

Kaplow, Louis, The Patent-Antitrust Intersection: A Reappraisal, 97 Harv.LRev 1813 (1984)

Kaye, Lincoln, Copycats Unrepentant, Far Eastern Economic Review, 31 May 1984

Kaye, Lincoln, India's Wrong Prescription: Liberalised Drug Controls Prove to be Weak Medecine, Far Eastern Economic Review, 17 December 1987

Kaye, Lincoln, Patent Pressure: US Urges India to Protect, Far Eastern Economic Review, 29 December 1989

Kernochan, J. M., US' First Sale Doctrine, Association Littéraire et Artistique Internationale Study Session, 5–8 October 1988, Munich

Kertsen, Hans-Christian, EEC Anti-trust Policy on "Grey Market" Imports Within the Common Market, (1988) 16 IBL 134

Kingston, William, Innovation, Creativity and the Law, Kluwer Academic Publishers, 1990

Kitchin, David, Revlon Case: Trade Marks and Parallel Imports (UK), [1980] EIPR 86

Koch, Norbert, Article 30 and the Exercise of Industrial Property Rights to Block Imports, [1986] Fordham Corporate Law Institute 605

Korah, Valentine, Dividing the Common Market through National Industrial Property Rights, (1972) 35 MLR 634

Korah, Valentine, EEC Competition Law and Practice, ESC Publishing Limited, 1990 (4th edn)

Korah, Valentine, Exclusive Dealing Agreements in the EEC, European Law Centre, 1984

Korah, Valentine, Franchising and the EEC Competition Rules: Regulation 4087/88, ESC Publishing Limited, 1989

Korah, Valentine, Goodbye Red Label: Condemnation of Dual Pricing by Distillers, (1980) 3 ELRev. 62

Korah, Valentine, Know-how Licensing Agreements and the EEC Competition Rules: Regulation 556/89, ESC Publishing Limited, 1989

Korah, Valentine, National Patents and the Free Movement of Goods Within the Common Market, (1975) 38 MLR 333

Korah, Valentine, No Duty to License Independent Repairers to Make Spare Parts, [1988] EIPR 381

Korah, Valentine, Patent Licensing and the EEC Competition Rules: Regulation 2349/84, ESC Publishing Limited, 1985

Korah, Valentine, The Rise and Fall of Provisional Validity – The Need for a Rule of Reason in EEC Antitrust, 3 Northwestern Journal of International Law & Business 320

Korah, Valentine and Rothnie, Warwick A., Exclusive Distribution and the EEC Competition Rules, Sweet & Maxwell, 1992 (2nd edn)

Krattenmaker, Thomas G. and Salop, Steven C., Anticompetitive Exclusion: Raising Rivals' Costs to Achieve Power over Price, 96 Yale LJ 209 (1986)

Ladas, Stephen P., Exclusive Territorial Licences Under Parallel Patents, 3 IIC 335 (1972)

Laddie, Prescott & Vitoria, Modern Law of Copyright, Butterworths, 1980

Lahore et al, Intellectual Property in Australia: Patents, Designs and Trade Marks, Butterworths, 1981

Lahore, James, Intellectual Property Law in Australia: Copyright, Butterworths, 1988 (2nd edn)

Landes, William M. and Posner, Richard A., An Economic Analysis of Copyright Law, 18 JLS 325 (1989)

Landes, William M., and Posner, Richard A., Trademark Law: An Economic Perspective, 30 JLE 265 (1987)

Lane, Shelley, Status of Licensing Common Law Marks, forthcoming

Law on Copyright and Related Protection Rights Article 17 cited in Advocate-General Roemer's Opinion, [1971] ECR 504

Leftwich, John, What Price a Macintosh?, 23 MacUser 57, May 1988

Levin, Richard C., Klevorick, Alvin, K., Nelson, Richard R. and Winter, Sidney G., [1987] 3 Brookings Papers on Economic Activity 783

Levitt, Theodore, Marketing Myopia, Harvard Business Review, July/August 1960

Lipner, Seth E., Gray Market Goulash: The Problems of At-the-Border Restrictions on Importation of Genuine Trademarked Goods, 77 TMR 77 (1987)

Lipner, Seth E., Legality of Parallel Imports: Trademarks, Antitrust or Equity, 19 Texas International Law Journal 553 (1984)

Lipscomb, E. B. III, Lipscomb's Walker on Patents, The Lawyer's Co-operative Publishing Co., 1987 (3rd edn)

Lipsky, Abbot B. Jr, Current Antitrust Division Views on Patent Licensing Practices, 50 Antitrust LJ 515 (1981)

Lynn, Matthew, Hedging Bets at SmithKline, The Independent, 1 August 1991, 23

Lynn, Matthew, Hooked on the Growth Wonder Drug, The Independent, 21 July 1991, 21

Machlup, Fritz, Economic Review of the Patent System, Study of the Sub-Committee on Patents, Trademarks and Copyrights of the Committee on the Judiciary, US Senate, 85th Congress, Study 15, Washington, 958

MacSkimming, Roy, Sunset over Baie Comeau, [July 1990] Quill & Quire, 10

Mangles, Jim, Fighting the Parasites, 23 MacUser 53, May 1988

Mann, F. A., Industrial Property and the EEC Treaty, (1975) 24 ICLQ 31

Mansfield, Edwin, Rapoport, John, Romero, Anthony, Wagner, Samuel and Beardsley, George, Social and Private Rates of Return from Industrial Innovations, 91 QJEcon. 221

Mansfield, Edwin, Romero, Anthony and Wagner, Samuel, Foreign Trade and United States Research and Development, 6 Rev. Econ. & Stat. 49 (1979)

Marenco, Giuliano and Banks, Karen, Intellectual Property and the Community Rules on Free Movement: Discrimination Unearthed, (1990) 15 ELRev, 224

McFarlane, Gavin, Copyright: The Development and Exercise of the Performing Right, John Offord (Publications) Ltd, 1980

McKenna & Co, Cholay v Sacem C-270/86 (unpublished), European Community Law Bulletin January/February 1991

Millinoff, Holly, Import Licensing Proposals Touch Off Industry Debate, [September 1990] Quill & Quire 6

Monopolies and Mergers Commission, Supply of Beer, Cmnd 651 HMSO, 1989

Morison, W. L., Unfair Competition and "Passing-Off", (1956) 2 Syd.LRev. 50

Morris, Graig K., Manufacturing Clause: Death-Defying Provision of the US Copyright Law, [1982] ASCAP Studies in Copyright 185

Muller, Laurie, Copyright as Defence Against Pagan Hordes, Sydney Morning Herald, 3 August 1989

Muratore, Anthony and Robertson, Donald, Trade Marks Act 1955 and Parallel Imports, (1984) 7 UNSWLJ 117

Naresh, Suman, Passing-Off, Goodwill and False Advertising: New Wine in Old Bottles, [1986] CLJ 97

Nile, Richard, Cartels, Capitalism and the Australian Book Trade, (1990) 4(1) Continuum 71

Nimmer, Melville B. and Nimmer, David, 2 Nimmer on Copyright, Matthew Bender & Co. Inc., 1990

3 Nimmer on Copyright

4 Nimmer on Copyright

Norman, George, Spatial Competition and Spatial Price Discrimination, (1981) 48 Rev.Econ.Studies 91

Officer, R. R., Parallel Imports: An Economic Perspective, 24 May 1987, Canberra

Oliver, Daniel, Federal Trade Commission Antitrust Policy in International Trade, [1986] Fordham Corporate Law Institute I

Oliver, P., Free Movement of Goods in the EEC, London Law Centre Limited, 1988 (2nd edn)

Ordover, Janus A., Economic Foundations and Considerations in Protecting Industrial and Intellectual Property, 53 Antitrust LJ 503 (1984)

Orff, Edward, Television Without Frontiers – Myth or Reality?, [1990] EIPR 270

Organisation for Economic Co-operation and Development, Measuring Primary Health Care, OECD, 1985

Palmeter, N. David, Gray Market Imports: No Black and White Answer, 12(1) World Competition 49 (1988)

Patel, Mahesh S., Drug Costs in Developing Countries and Policies to Reduce Them, (1983) 11 World Development 195

Patent and Trade Mark Office, Economic Effects of Parallel Imports: A Preliminary Analysis, US Department of Commerce, 23 January 1985

Paterson, Jan, The Future of Australia as an Export Market, The Sir Stanley Unwin Foundation, 1989

Peretz, S. Michael, Pharmaceuticals in the Third World: The Problem from the Suppliers' Point of View, (1983) 11 World Development, 259

Pevtchin, Guy J. and Williams, Leslie, Pharmon v Hoechst – The Limits on the Community Exhaustion Principle in Respect of Compulsory Licences, [1986] Fordham Corporate Law Institute 287

Phillips, Jeremy, Do National Brands Have a Future in the European Market?, [1991] EIPR 191

Pitofsky, Robert, In Defense of Discounters: The No Frills Case for a Per Se Rule Against Vertical Price Fixing, 71 Geo.LJ 1487 (1983)

Plant, Arnold, Economic Aspects of Copyright in Books, (1934) 1 Economica 167

Plant, Arnold, Economic Theory Concerning Patents for Inventions, 1934 1 Economica

Plant, Arnold, Selected Economic Essays and Addresses, Routledge & Kegan Paul, 1974

Porter, Michael, The Competitive Advantage of Nations, The MacMillan Press, 1990

Posner, Richard A., Antitrust Law: An Economic Perspective, University of Chicago Press, 1976

Posner, Richard A., Next Step in the Antitrust Treatment of Restricted Distribution: *Per Se* Legality, 48 UChic.LRev. 6 (1981)

Powell, T. R., The Nature of a Patent Right, 17 Columbia LRev. 663 (1917)

Prices Surveillance Authority, Inquiry into Book Prices: Final Report, Report No. 25, 1989

Prices Surveillance Authority, Inquiry into Book Prices: Interim Report, Report No. 24, 1989

Prices Surveillance Authority, Inquiry into Effects of Exchange Rate Appreciation on Prices of Consumer Goods, 1989

Prices Surveillance Authority, Inquiry into the Prices of Sound Recordings, Report No. 35, 1990

Redwood, Heinz, The Price of Health, Adam Smith Institute, 1989

Reich, Robert B., The Real Economy, 267 (2) The Atlantic 35 (1991)

Reinbothe, Jörg and Howard, Anthony, State of Play in the Negotiations on Trips (GATT/Uruguay Round), [1991] EIPR 157

9th Report on Competition Policy, EC Commission 1979

11th Report on Competition Policy, EC Commission 1982

12th Report on Competition Policy, EC Commission 1983

13th Report on Competition Policy, EC Commission 1984

15th Report on Competition Policy, EC Commission 1986

17th Report on Competition Policy, EC Commission 1988

18th Report on Competition Policy, EC Commission 1989

Report of the Committee of the Attorney General of the Commonwealth to Consider What Alterations are Desirable in the Copyright Law of the Commonwealth – Commonwealth of Australia, 1959 (the Spicer Committee)

Report of the Departmental Committee on the Law and Practice Relating to Trade Marks, Cmd 4568, HMSO, 1934

Report of the Select Committee on the Copyright Bill 1986, A82–91, B34–37, 70–73, University of Singapore

Ricketson, Staniforth, Law of Intellectual Property, The Law Book Company, 1984

Rogers, John W. III, Demise of Section 337's GATT-Legality, [1990] EIPR 275

Rogers, John W. III, Revised Canadian Patent Act, the Free Trade Agreement and Pharmaceutical Patents: An Overview of Pharmaceutical Compulsory Licensing in Canada, [1990] EIPR 351

Rose, Michael, Passing Off, Unfair Competition and Community Law, [1990] EIPR 123

Rothnie, Warwick A., Commission Re-runs Same Old Bill (Film Purchasing by German Television Stations), [1990] EIPR 72,

Rothnie, Warwick A., EC Competition Policy, the Commission and Trade Marks, (1991) 19 International Business Lawyer

Rothnie, Warwick A., Gray Privateers Sink into Black Market: Parallel Imports and Trade Marks, (1990) 1 AIPJ 72

Rothnie, Warwick A., Hag II: Putting the Common Origin Doctrine to Sleep, [1991] EIPR 24

Röttger, Martin, Article 36 – More Subjective Views on Objectivity, [1982] EIPR 215

Röttger, Martin and Brett, Hugh, Hoffmann La Roche Ruling Repackaged by the National Court, [1979] EIPR 283

Satchell, R. D., Chemical Product Patent Practice in the United Kingdom, 1 IIC 179 (1970)

Saxena, R. B., Pricing Policy That's Hard to Swallow, Far Eastern Economic Review, 11 April 1985, 47

Saxena, R. B., Trade Related Issues of Intellectual Property Rights and the Indian Patent Act: A Negotiating Strategy, 12 World Competition 81 (1988)

Schatz, Ulrich, Exhaustion of Patent Rights in the Common Market, 2 IIC 1 (1971)

Scherer, F. M., Antitrust, Efficiency and Progress, 62 NYULRev. 998 (1987)

Scherer, F. M., Economic Effects of Compulsory Patent Licensing, New York University Monograph 1977

Scherer, F. M., Economics of Vertical Restraints, 52 Antitrust LJ 687 (1982)

Scherer, F. M., Innovation and Growth, MIT Press, 1984

Scherer, F. M. and Ross, David, Industrial Market Structure and Economic Performance, Houghton-Mifflin, 1990 (3rd edn)

Schmalensee, Richard, Ease of Entry: Has the Concept Been Applied Too Readily?, 56 Antitrust LJ 41 (1987)

Schmalensee, Richard, Economies of Scale and Barriers to Entry, 89 JPol.Econ. 228 (1981)

Schmied-Kowarzik, Volker, Chemical Inventions According to the New German Patent Act, 1 IIC 190, (1970)

Schröter, Helmut R. B., Antitrust Analysis under Article 85 (1) and (3), [1987] Fordham Corporate Law Institute 645

Schut, Frederick T. and Van Bergeijk, Peter A. G., International Price Discrimination: The Pharmaceutical Industry, (1986) 14 World Development 1141

Selinger, Jerry R., Patent Licensing in the Afterglow of Sylvania: Practicalities of Life Under the Rule of Reason, 63 JPat.Off.Soc. 353

Shanahan, D. R., Australian Trade Mark Law and Practice, The Law Book Company 1982

Sharpe, Thomas, The Distillers Decision, (1978) 15 CMLRev. 447

Siragusa, Mario, Technology Transfers Under EEC Law: A Private View, [1982] Fordham Corporate Law Institute 95

Spence, Michael A., Cost Reduction, Competition and Industry Performance, (1984) 52 Econometria 101

Spiro, Donald M., Patent Protection or Piracy: A CEO Views Japan, [September/October 1990] Harvard Business Review 58

Staaf, Robert J., International Price Discrimination and the Gray Market, (1989) 4 IPJ 301

Staaf, Robert J., Law and Economics of the International Gray Market: Quality Assurance, Free Riding and Passing Off, (1989) 4 IPJ 191

Steiner, Robert L., The Nature of Vertical Restraints, 30 Antitrust Bulletin 143 (1985)

Sterling, J. A. L., The Copyright Designs and Patents Act 1988: The New Issuing Right, (1989) EIPR 283

Sterling, J. A. L. and Carpenter, M. C. L., Copyright Law in the United Kingdom, Legal Books Pty. Ltd, 1986

Stern, Richard H., Case Comment: Nintendo of America Inc. v Elcon Industries Inc. & CBS Inc. v Scorpio Music Distributors Inc. Parallel Imports in the US – The Exercise of Copyright, [1984] EIPR 203

Stern, Richard H., US v Westinghouse Electric Corp.: Division of International Markets Permitted, [1983] EIPR 20

Stewart, Stephen M., International Copyright and Neighbouring Rights, Butterworths, 1989 (2nd edn)

Strivens, Robert, EMI Electrola GmbH v Firma Patricia, [1989] EIPR 297

Strobl, Killius and Vorbrugg, Business Law Guide to Germany, CCH Editions, 1988 (2nd edn)

Sullivan, Barbara, Trade Mark Infringement Decisions in Australia and New Zealand: Second-Hand Goods, (1991) 2 AIPJ 44

Taylor, Christopher T. and Silbertson, Z. A., Economic Impact of the Patent System: A Study of the British Experience, Cambridge University Press, 1973

Tebbutt, David, Eurovision, 6 (15) MacUser 67, 27 July 1990

Tee, Khaw Lake, 1990 Amendments to the Malaysian Copyright Act 1987, [1991] EIPR 32

Telser, Lester G., Why Should Manufacturers Want Fair Trade?, 3 JL&Econ. 86 (1960)

The Grey Importer: Alternative Remedy – Disgruntled End User, 23 MacUser 56, May 1988

Tirole, Jean, The Theory of Industrial Organization, MIT Press, 1988

Touche Ross Management Consultancy, Examination of the Implications for the United Kingdom of the Proposal to Extend the Patent Term for Pharmaceutical Products in the European Community, 1990

Turner, Donald F., Basic Principles in Formulating Antitrust and Misuse Constraints on the Exploitation of Intellectual Property Rights, 53 Antitrust LJ 485 (1984)

Ulrich, Hans, Impact of the Sirena Decision on National Trademark Rights, 3 IIC 193

Van Bael, Ivo, Heretical Reflections on the Basic Dogma of EEC Antitrust: Single Market Integration, 10 Swiss Review of International Competition Law 39 (1980)

Van Empel, Martijn, EEC Law and Intellectual Property: Free Movement and Positive Integration in the Internal European Market, (1991) Bar European News I

Vandenburgh, E. C., The Problem of Importation of Genuinely Marked Goods is not a Trademark Problem, 49 TMR 707 (1959)

Varcoe, F. P., QC, Report of the Royal Commission on Copyright 1957

Vitoria, Mary et al, Encyclopaedia of United Kingdom and European Patent Law, Sweet & Maxwell, 1977

Von Lewinksi, Silke, Rental Right, Lending Right and Certain Neighbouring Rights; The EC Commission's Proposal for a Council Directive, [1991] EIPR 117

Wade, E. C. S., Restrictions on User, (1928) 44 LQR 51

Waelbroeck, Michel, Antitrust Analysis under Article 85 (1) and (3), [1987] Fordham Corporate Law Institute 693

Waelbroeck, Michel, Effect of the Rome Treaty on the Exercise of National Industrial Property Rights, 21 Antitrust Bulletin 99 (1976)

Waelbroeck, Michel, Pronuptia Judgment – A Critical Appraisal, [1986] Fordham Corporate Law Institute, 211

Waelbroek, Michel, Vertical Agreements: Is the Commission Right not to Follow the Current US Policy?, 25 Swiss Review of International Competition Law 45 (1985)

Wallace, William, Dynamics of European Integration, Pinter Publishers, 1990

Walton, A. M. et al, Patent Laws of Europe and the United Kingdom, Butterworths, 1983

Walton, Jo, Adkins, Stewart and Smith, Ian, Controversial Vision of the Future: Challenges Posed by Pharmaceutical Deregulation, Shearson Lehmann Hutton Securities, 1989

Wei, George, Parallel Imports and Intellectual Property Rights in Singapore, as yet unpublished

Whalley, John, International Aspects of Copyright Legislation in Canada: Economic Analysis of Policy Options, 8 Research in Law & Economics 274 (1986)

Whish, Richard, Competition Law, Butterworths, 1989 (2nd edn)

Williamson, Oliver E., Assessing Vertical Market Restrictions: Antitrust Ramifications of the Transaction Cost Approach, 127 UPenn.LRev.

Williamson, Oliver, E., Delimiting Antitrust, 76 Georgetown LJ

Williamson, Oliver E., Economic Institutions of Capitalism, Free Press, 1986

Williamson, Oliver E., Markets and Hierarchies: Analysis and Antitrust Implications, Free Press, 1975

Wright, Brian D., The Economics of Invention Incentives, 73 Am.Econ.Rev. 691 (1983)

Wyatt, Derrick and Dashwood, A. S., Substantive Law of the EEC, Sweet & Maxwell (3rd edn), 1986

Young, John A. Jr, Gray Market Case: Trademark Rights v Consumer Interests, 61 Notre Dame LRev. 838

Index